THE CONTINENTAL
LEGAL HISTORY SERIES

VOLUME ONE

GENERAL SURVEY

The Continental Legal History Series

Published under the auspices of the

Association of American Law Schools

I. A GENERAL SURVEY OF EVENTS, SOURCES, PERSONS, AND MOVEMENTS IN CONTINENTAL LEGAL HISTORY. By VARIOUS AUTHORS Translated by RAPELJE HOWELL, F. S. PHILBRICK, JOHN WALGREN, and JOHN H. WIGMORE $6 00 *net.*

II GREAT JURISTS OF THE WORLD, FROM PAPINIAN TO VON IHERING By VARIOUS AUTHORS. Illustrated. (Extra volume. By arrangement with John Murray, London) $5 00 *net.*

III. HISTORY OF FRENCH PRIVATE LAW By J BRISSAUD, late of the University of Toulouse Translated by RAPELJE HOWELL, of the New York Bar $5 00 *net.*

IV. HISTORY OF GERMANIC PRIVATE LAW By RUDOLPH HUEBNER, of the University of Rostock. Translated by.DR. FRANCIS S. PHILBRICK, of New York, N. Y $4 50 *net.*

V HISTORY OF CONTINENTAL CRIMINAL PROCEDURE By A. ESMEIN, Professor in the University of Paris, with chapters by FRANÇOIS GARRAUD, of the University of Lyon, and C J A MITTER-MAIER, late of the University of Heidelberg Translated by JOHN SIMPSON, of the New York Bar $4 50 *net.*

VI. HISTORY OF CONTINENTAL CRIMINAL LAW. By LUDWIG VON BAR, of the University of Gottingen. Translated by THOMAS S. BELL, of the Tacoma Bar. $4.00 *net.*

VII. HISTORY OF CONTINENTAL CIVIL PROCEDURE. By ARTHUR ENGELMANN, Chief Justice of the Court of Appeals at Breslau, with a chapter by E GLASSON, late of the University of Paris Translated by ROBERT W MILLAR, of Northwestern University. $4 00 *net.*

VIII. HISTORY OF ITALIAN LAW. By CARLO CALISSE, of the Italian Council of State. Translated by JOHN LISLE, of the Philadelphia Bar. $5 00 *net.*

IX. HISTORY OF FRENCH PUBLIC LAW By J. BRISSAUD, late of the University of Toulouse Translated by JAMES W GARNER, of the University of Illinois. $4 50 *net*

X. HISTORY OF CONTINENTAL COMMERCIAL LAW By PAUL HUVELIN, of the University of Lyon Translated by ERNEST G. LORENZEN, of the University of Wisconsin $5 50 *net*

XI. THE EVOLUTION OF LAW IN EUROPE By GABRIEL TARDE, RAOUL DE LA GRASSERIE, and others. $5.00 *net.*

THE CONTINENTAL LEGAL HISTORY SERIES

Published under the auspices of the

ASSOCIATION OF AMERICAN LAW SCHOOLS

A GENERAL SURVEY

OF

EVENTS, SOURCES, PERSONS AND MOVEMENTS IN

CONTINENTAL LEGAL HISTORY

BY

VARIOUS EUROPEAN AUTHORS

BOSTON

LITTLE, BROWN, AND COMPANY

1912

Copyright, 1912,

By LITTLE, BROWN, AND COMPANY.

Norwood Press
Set up and electrotyped by J. S Cushing Co., Norwood, Mass., U.S.A.
Presswork by S J Parkhill & Co., Boston, U S.A.

LIST OF COLLABORATORS

EDITORIAL PREFACE . . . JOHN HENRY WIGMORE
INTRODUCTION. . . . . OLIVER WENDELL HOLMES
INTRODUCTION. . . . . . EDWARD JENKS

AUTHORS

PROLOGUE . . . . . . FREDERIC WILLIAM MAITLAND
PART I. FROM JUSTINIAN TO FEU-
    DALISM . . . CARLO CALISSE
PART II ITALY . . . . CARLO CALISSE
PART III FRANCE . . . JEAN BRISSAUD
            . . . HEINRICH BRUNNER
            . . RODERICH VON STINTZING
PART IV. GERMANY . . RICHARD SCHROEDER
            . . HEINRICH SIEGEL
            . . . OTTO STOBBE
            . . . HEINRICH ZOEPFL
PART V NETHERLANDS . . . JOOST ADRIAAN VAN HAMEL
PART VI SWITZERLAND . . . EUGEN HUBER
PART VII. SCANDINAVIA . . . EBBE HERTZBERG
PART VIII. SPAIN . . RAFAEL ALTAMIRA
PART IX CANON LAW . . . JEAN BRISSAUD

TRANSLATORS

PARTS I AND II . . . . JOHN HENRY WIGMORE
PARTS III AND IX. . . . RAPELJE HOWELL
PARTS IV, VI, AND VIII . . . FRANCIS S PHILBRICK
PART VII . . . . . . JOHN WALGREN

v

I might instance in other professions the obligation men lie under of applying themselves to certain parts of History, and I can hardly forbear doing it in that of the Law, — in its nature the noblest and most beneficial to mankind, in its abuse and debasement the most sordid and the most pernicious. A lawyer now is nothing more (I speak of ninety-nine in a hundred at least), to use some of Tully's words, "nisi leguleius quidem cautus, et acutus praeco actionum, cantor formularum, auceps syllabarum " But there have been lawyers that were orators, philosophers, historians there have been Bacons and Clarendons There will be none such any more, till in some better age true ambition, or the love of fame, prevails over avarice; and till men find leisure and encouragement to prepare themselves for the exercise of this profession, by climbing up to the vantage ground (so my Lord Bacon calls it) of Science, instead of grovelling all their lives below, in a mean but gainful application of all the little arts of chicane. Till this happen, the profession of the law will scarce deserve to be ranked among the learned professions And whenever it happens, one of the vantage grounds to which men must climb, is Metaphysical, and the other, Historical Knowledge. HENRY ST JOHN, VISCOUNT BOLINGBROKE, *Letters on the Study of History* (1739).

Whoever brings a fruitful idea to any branch of knowledge, or rends the veil that seems to sever one portion from another, his name is written in the Book among the builders of the Temple For an English lawyer it is hardly too much to say that the methods which Oxford invited Sir Henry Maine to demonstrate, in this chair of Historical and Comparative Jurisprudence, have revolutionised our legal history and largely transformed our current text-books — SIR FREDERICK POLLOCK, Bart , *The History of Comparative Jurisprudence* (Farewell Lecture at the University of Oxford, 1903)

No piece of History is true when set apart to itself, divorced and isolated. It is part of an intricately pieced whole, and must needs be put in its place in the netted scheme of events, to receive its true color and estimation We are all partners in a common undertaking, — the illumination of the thoughts and actions of men as associated in society, the life of the human spirit in this familiar theatre of coöperative effort in which we play, so changed from age to age, and yet so much the same throughout the hurrying centuries The day for synthesis has come No one of us can safely go forward without it. — WOODROW WILSON, *The Variety and Unity of History* (Address at the World's Congress of Arts and Science, St. Louis, 1904).

CONTINENTAL LEGAL HISTORY SERIES

GENERAL INTRODUCTION TO THE SERIES

"ALL history," said the lamented master Maitland, in a memorable epigram, "is but a seamless web; and he who endeavors to tell but a piece of it must feel that his first sentence tears the fabric."

This seamless web of our own legal history unites us inseparably to the history of Western and Southern Europe. Our main interest must naturally center on deciphering the pattern which lies directly before us, — that of the Anglo-American law. But in tracing the warp and woof of its structure we are brought inevitably into a larger field of vision. The story of Western Continental Law is made up, in the last analysis, of two great movements, racial and intellectual. One is the Germanic migrations, planting a solid growth of Germanic custom everywhere, from Danzig to Sicily, from London to Vienna. The other is the posthumous power of Roman law, forever resisting, struggling, and coalescing with the other. A thousand detailed combinations, of varied types, are developed, and a dozen distinct systems now survive in independence But the result is that no one of them can be fully understood without surveying and tracing the whole.

Even insular England cannot escape from the web. For, in the first place, all its racial threads — Saxons, Danes, Normans — were but extensions of the same Germanic warp and woof that was making the law in France, Germany, Scandinavia, Netherlands, Austria, Switzerland, Northern Italy, and Spain. And, in the next place, its legal culture was never without some of the same intellectual influence of Roman law which was so thoroughly overspreading the Continental peoples There is thus, on the one hand, scarcely a doctrine or rule in our own system which cannot be definitely and profitably traced back, in comparison, till we come to the point of divergence, where we once shared it in common with them. And, on the other hand, there is, during all the intervening centuries, a more or less constant juristic sociability (if it may be so called) between Anglo-American and Continental Law; and its reciprocal influences make the story one and inseparable. In short, there is a tangled common ancestry, racial or intellectual, for the law of all Western Europe and ourselves.

For the sake of legal science, this story should now become a familiar one to all who are studious to know the history of our own law. The time is ripe. During the last thirty years European scholars have placed the history of their law on the footing of modern critical and philosophical research And to-day, among ourselves, we find a marked widening of view and a vigorous interest in the comparison of other peoples' legal institutions. To the satisfying of that interest in the present field, the only obstacle is the lack of adequate materials in the English language.

That the spirit of the times encourages and demands the study of Continental Legal History and all useful aids to it was pointed out in a memorial presented at the annual meeting of the Association of American Law Schools in August, 1909:

"The recent spread of interest in Comparative Law in general is notable. The Comparative Law Bureau of the American Bar Association; the Pan-American Scientific Congress; the American Institute of Criminal Law and Criminology, the Civic Federation Conference on Uniform Legislation, the International Congress of History; the libraries' accessions in foreign law, — the work of these and other movements touches at various points the bodies of Continental law. Such activities serve to remind us constantly that we have in English no histories of Continental law To pay any attention at all to Continental law means that its history must be more or less considered. Each of these countries has its own legal system and its own legal history. Yet the law of the Continent was never so foreign to English as the English law was foreign to Continental jurisprudence. It is merely maintaining the best traditions of our own legal literature if we plead for a continued study of Continental legal history.

"We believe that a better acquaintance with the results of modern scholarship in that field will bring out new points of contact and throw new light upon the development of our own law. Moreover, the present-day movements for codification, and for the reconstruction of many departments of the law, make it highly desirable that our profession should be well informed as to the history of the nineteenth century on the Continent in its great measures of law reform and codification.

"For these reasons we believe that the thoughtful American lawyers and students should have at their disposal translations of some of the best works in Continental legal history."

And the following resolution was then adopted unanimously by the Association:

"That a committee of five be appointed, on Translations of Continental Legal History, with authority to arrange for the translation and publication of suitable works."

The Editorial Committee, then appointed, spent two years in studying the field, making selections, and arranging for translations. It resolved to treat the undertaking as a whole; and to co-ordinate the series as to (1) periods, (2) countries, and (3) topics, so as to give the most adequate survey within the space-limits available.

(1) As to *periods*, the Committee resolved to include modern times, as well as early and mediæval periods; for in usefulness and importance they were not less imperative in their claim upon our attention. Each volume, then, was not to be merely a valuable torso, lacking important epochs of development; but was to exhibit the history from early to modern times.

(2) As to *countries*, the Committee fixed upon France, Germany, and Italy as the central fields, leaving the history in other countries to be touched so far as might be incidentally possible. Spain would have been included as a fourth; but no suitable book was in existence; the unanimous opinion of competent scholars is that a suitable history of Spanish law has not yet been written.

(3) As to *topics*, the Committee accepted the usual Continental divisions of Civil (or Private), Commercial, Criminal, Procedural, and Public Law, and endeavored to include all five. But to represent these five fields under each principal country would not only exceed the inevitable space-limits, but would also duplicate much common ground. Hence, the grouping of the individual volumes was arranged partly by topics and partly by countries, as follows:

Commercial Law, Criminal Law, Civil Procedure, and Criminal Procedure, were allotted each a volume; in this volume the basis was to be the general European history of early and mediæval times, with special reference to one chief country (France or Germany) for the later periods, and with an excursus on another chief country. Then the Civil (or Private) Law of France and of Germany was given a volume each. To Italy was then given a volume covering all five parts of the field. For Public Law (the subject least related in history to our own), a volume was given to France, where the common starting point with England, and the later divergences, have unusual importance for the history of our courts and legal methods Finally, two volumes were allotted to general surveys indispensable for viewing the connection of parts. Of these, an introductory volume deals with Sources, Literature, and General Movements, — in short, the external history of the law, as the Continentals call it (corresponding to the aspects covered by Book I of Sir F. Pollock and Professor F. W Maitland's "History of the English Law before Edward I"), and a final volume analyzes the specific features, in the evolution of doctrine, common to all the modern systems

Needless to say, a Series thus co-ordinated, and precisely suited for our own needs, was not easy to construct out of materials written by Continental scholars for Continental needs   The Committee hopes that due allowance will be made for the difficulties here encountered. But it is convinced that the ideal of a co-ordinated Series, which should collate and fairly cover the various fields as a connected whole, is a correct one, and the endeavor to achieve it will sufficiently explain the choice of the particular materials that have been used

It remains to acknowledge the Committee's indebtedness to all those who have made this Series possible.

To numerous scholarly advisers in many European universities the Committee is indebted for valuable suggestions towards choice of the works to be translated. Fortified by this advice, the Committee is confident that the authors of these volumes represent the highest scholarship, the latest research, and the widest repute, among European legal historians.   And here the Committee desires also to express its indebtedness to Elbert H. Gary, Esq , of New York City, for his ample provision of materials for legal science in the Gary Library of Continental Law (in Northwestern University). In the researches of preparation for this Series, those materials were found indispensable

To the authors the Committee is grateful for their willing co-operation in allowing this use of their works. Without exception, their consent has been cheerfully accorded in the interest of legal science

To the publishers the Committee expresses its appreciation for the cordial interest shown in a class of literature so important to the higher interests of the profession.

To the translators, the Committee acknowledges a particular gratitude. The accomplishments, legal and linguistic, needed for a task of this sort are indeed exacting; and suitable translators are here no less needful and no more numerous than suitable authors. The Committee, on behalf of our profession, acknowledges to them a special debt for their cordial services on behalf of legal science, and commends them to the readers of these volumes with the reminder that without their labors this Series would have been a fruitless dream.

So the Committee, satisfied with the privilege of having introduced these authors and their translators to the public, retires from the scene, bespeaking for the Series the interest of lawyers and historians alike.

THE EDITORIAL COMMITTEE.

GENERAL SURVEY

CONTENTS

PAGE

GENERAL INTRODUCTION TO THE SERIES xi

LIST OF MAPS xxxii

EDITORIAL PREFACE, BY JOHN H. WIGMORE xxxiii

INTRODUCTION, BY OLIVER WENDELL HOLMES xlv

INTRODUCTION, BY EDWARD JENKS xlix

PART I. ROMAN AND GERMANIC LAW

FROM JUSTINIAN TO FEUDALISM (A.D. 475–1100)

§ 1 Preliminary Survey of Prior Events and Conditions in Europe   3

CHAPTER I   FIRST PERIOD: A.D 475–575

LAW UNDER THE GOTHIC KINGDOMS AND THE LATER ROMAN (BYZANTINE) EMPIRE

C

§ 2 The Gothic Kingdoms and the Roman Empire .   9

TOPIC 1. THE ROMAN LEGISLATION OF THE GERMANS

PAGE

§§ 3–5. The Edict of Theo-
    doric the Ostrogoth   10
§§ 6, 7. The Minor Ostrogothic
    Edicts   15

§ 8 The Roman Laws of the
    Visigoths (Alaric) . .   16
§ 9. The Roman Laws of the
    Burgundians (Papinia-
    nus)   18

TOPIC 2. THE ROMAN LAW OF ROME

§ 10. Roman Practice before
    Justinian   19
§ 11. Justinian's Legislation .   20

§§ 12, 13. Imperfect Diffusion
    of the "Corpus
    Juris" . . .   21

CHAPTER II.   SECOND PERIOD: A D 575–900

LAW UNDER THE LOMBARD KINGDOM AND THE FRANKISH EMPIRE

§ 14 Introduction The Mingling of Legal Systems   23

CONTENTS

TOPIC 1 THE LOMBARD KINGDOM

§§ 15, 16 The Lombards and their Civilization . 25
§§ 17-19. The Lombard Edict, its Formation and Enactment 26
§§ 20-22. The Edict of Rothar 29
§§ 23, 24 Supplements to the Edict . . . 31
§§ 25-27. Minor Sources of Lombard Law . . 34

TOPIC 2 THE FRANKISH EMPIRE

§ 28. Charlemagne's Dominion and its Significance . 36
§ 29 Charlemagne's Imperial Legislation 36
§§ 30, 31. The Capitularies . 38
§ 32 Collections of Capitularies . . . 41
§ 33. Italian Capitularies . . 43
§ 34. Effect of the Capitularies 44

TOPIC 3. THE GERMANIC POPULAR CODES

§ 35 The Codifying of the Germanic Tribal Customs 45
§§ 36, 37 Mode of Legislation . 46
§ 38. Relation of the Codes to Each Other . 48
§§ 39-41. The Gothic Group (Burgundian, Visigothic) 49
§§ 42, 43. The Saxon Group (Saxon, Frisian) . 52
§§ 44, 45. The Suabian Group (Alamannic, Bavarian) . . 54
§§ 46, 47 The Frankish Group (Thuringian, Chamavian, Ripuarian, Salic) 57

TOPIC 4 THE PERSONALITY OF LAWS

§§ 48, 49. Personality and Territoriality of Laws, contrasted . . . 60
§ 50. Personality under the Carolingian Empire . 62
§§ 51-53. "Professions" of Personal Law . . 63
§ 54. Conflict of Laws . . . 66
§§ 55, 56. Exceptions to the Rule of Personality 67
§ 57. Unifying Influence of the Capitularies 69

CHAPTER III THIRD PERIOD A D 900–1100

LAW UNDER THE FEUDAL SYSTEM

§ 58 Spirit of Feudalism 71

TOPIC 1. FEUDAL LEGISLATION

§§ 59, 60 Feudal Statutes . . 72
§§ 61-63. Compilations of Feudal Law . . 74

TOPIC 2. FEUDAL CUSTOMARY LAW

	PAGE		PAGE
§ 64. Growth of Customs . .	77	§§ 65. 66. Rules for the Validity of Customs . .	78

TOPIC 3. TERRITORIALITY OF LAWS

§ 67. Causes leading to Territoriality	80	§§ 68, 69. Dominance of the Territorial Principle	81

PART II. ITALY

CHAPTER I. FIRST PERIOD. A.D. 900–1100

ITALY DURING THE MIDDLE AGES

TOPIC 1. THE ROMAN LAW

§ 1. Persistence of Roman Law	87	§ 3 Influence of Roman Law	90
§ 2. Roman Law under the Carolingians and Feudalism.	89	§ 4. Relative Influence of Later and Earlier Roman Law	91
		§ 5. Progressive Stages of Influence	92

TOPIC 2. THE CHURCH'S LAW

§ 6 The Church's Influence on Secular Law . . .	92	§ 7 Effect of the Church's Influence	94

TOPIC 3. THE SCIENCE OF LAW

§ 8. Rise of Legal Learning .	95	§ 14. Legal Treatises . .	101
§ 9 The Schools of Law	96	§§ 15–17 Treatises on Lombard Law . .	101
§§ 10, 11 Schools of Lombard Law . . .	97	§§ 18, 19. Treatises on Roman Law	103
§§ 12, 13. Schools of Roman Law	99	§§ 20–22. Formularies and Documents . . .	104

CHAPTER II SECOND PERIOD· A D 1100–1700

ITALY DURING THE RENASCENCE

§ 23. Introductory	108

TOPIC 1. THE COMMON LAW

§ 24. The Diverse Elements .	109	§§ 27–29. The Canon Law .	113
§§ 25, 26 The Germanic Law	109	§§ 30–34 The Roman Law. .	117

CONTENTS

TOPIC 2. THE SCIENCE OF LAW

	PAGE		PAGE
§ 35 Beginnings of Legal Science	124	§§ 42–44 (a) The Glossators .	137
§§ 36, 37 The Schools of Law	125	§§ 45–48 (b) The Commentators. . . .	142
§§ 38, 39 The School at Bologna . . .	128	§§ 49–51 (c) The Humanists .	147
§ 40 Other Schools	131	§ 52 (d) The Practical Jurists	152
§ 41. The Jurists and their Methods.	132	§§ 53–55. (e) Jurists of France, Germany, and Holland . . .	154

TOPIC 3 THE LEGISLATION

1 THE COMMUNAL PERIOD

§ 56 Legislative Conditions in the 1200 s .	159	§§ 61–63 Compilation of the Statutes . . .	163
§ 57. Growth of the City Legislation . . .	160	§§ 64, 65. Industrial and Commercial Statutes .	165
§§ 58–60. Sources of the City Legislation . . .	160	§ 66 Commercial Institutions	168

2. THE MONARCHICAL PERIOD

§ 67. Imperial Legislation . .	169	§§ 68–75. Legislation of the Italian States . .	170

CHAPTER III. THIRD PERIOD A D 1700–1900

ITALY IN MODERN TIMES

§ 76. The Transition 176

TOPIC 1 SCHOOLS OF LEGAL THOUGHT

§§ 77–80 The School of Natural Law . .	178	§§ 81–83. The Historical School	183

TOPIC 2 THE CODIFICATION MOVEMENT

§§ 84, 85. The Italian Codes of the 1700s .	187	§§ 89–92. The Italian Codes of the 1800s . .	192
§§ 86–88. The French Codes in Italy . .	189		

TOPIC 3 RECENT TIMES

§§ 93, 94. Codification and the Historical School	195	§ 95. Other Schools of Thought	197
		§ 96 Conclusion . .	199

PART III. FRANCE

CHAPTER I. First Period a.d 1000–1500

THE ROMAN LAW AND THE REGIONAL CUSTOMS

Topic 1 The Territoriality of Law

§ 1. Origin of the Principle . 203

§ 2 Division of France into Country of Written Law and Country of Customs 204

§ 3. Some of the Differences between the Written Law and the Customs . . . 205

Topic 2. The Roman Law

§ 4. Authority of the Roman Law in the Regions of Written Law . . 206

§ 5. The Roman Law in the Regions of Customs during the 1200 s and 1300 s 207

§ 6. Same · In and After the 1500 s 207

§ 7 Teaching of Roman Law at the Universities . . 209

§ 8 Propagation of the Roman Law in Other Countries 213

Topic 3. The Customs

§ 9. Territoriality of Customs . 213

§ 10 General Features of Law under the Customs . . 216

§ 11. Municipal Charters of Privileges 222

§ 12. Books of Customs and Treatises on the Law . 224

Topic 4. Other Sources of Law

§ 13. Judicial Decisions . . . 231

§ 14 Deeds, Cartularies, Form-Books, and Land-Registers 239

§ 15. Commercial and Maritime Law . . 242

§ 16. Public Law and the Legal Philosophies 244

§ 17. Royal Legislation (1) Form of Enactment . 246

§ 18. Same (2) Character and Object 249

§ 19. Same (3) Principal Ordinances previous to the 1500 s 250

CHAPTER II. Second Period · a.d. 1500–1789

NATIONAL JURISTS AND ROYAL LEGISLATION

§ 20. Introductory 251

Topic 1. The Roman Law Jurists

§ 21 The Humanists 252

§ 22 The French School; Cujas, Baudouin, Doneau, Hotman . . 254

CONTENTS

TOPIC 2 THE OFFICIAL COMPILATION OF THE CUSTOMS

PAGE

§ 23. Reasons and Methods of the Redaction . . .   259 | § 24. Results of the Redaction   260

TOPIC 3. THE ROYAL LEGISLATION

§ 25 Introductory . .   263 | § 27 Ordinances of Louis XIV   264
§ 26 Ordinances of the 1500 s and Early 1600 s. .   264 | § 28 Ordinances of Louis XV   265

TOPIC 4. THE NATIONAL JURISTS

§ 29 The Courts and the Bar .   266 | § 31 National Jurists of the 1600 s and 1700 s   268
§ 30 National Jurists of the 1500 s   267

TOPIC 5 POLITICAL PHILOSOPHY

§ 32. Philosophies of the 1500 s and 1600 s . .   271 | § 33. Philosophies of the 1700 s   272

CHAPTER III. THIRD PERIOD: A D. 1789–1904

THE REVOLUTION AND THE CODES

TOPIC 1 THE RENOVATION AND UNIFICATION OF THE LAW

§ 34. The Intermediate Work of the Revolution . .   274 | § 36. Character and Contents of the Code Napoleon .   285
§ 35 The Preparation and Enactment of the Code Napoleon . . . .   279 | § 37. The Empire and the Other Codes   292

TOPIC 2. THE CIVIL LAW SINCE THE CODIFICATION

§ 38. Legislation since 1804 .   293 | § 40 Legal Science   300
§ 39. Judicial Decisions   299

TOPIC 3. THE CODE NAPOLEON IN OTHER COUNTRIES

§ 41 Prior Codifications. . .   302 | § 42 The Extension of the Code Napoleon . . .   303

PART IV. GERMANY

CHAPTER I FIRST PERIOD A D. 1000–1400

FEUDALISM AND THE PEOPLE'S LAW-BOOKS

§ 1 The Various Forms of the Law .   311 | § 4. Territorial and Local Law   322
  | § 5 Manorial Law   325
§ 2 Sources of Imperial Law   314 | § 6 Sources of Town Law .   327
§ 3. Compilations of Territorial and Feudal Law. .   317 | § 7. Charters, Deeds, and Formularies   331

CONTENTS

CHAPTER II. Second Period · a d. 1400–1600

THE RECEPTION OF ROMAN LAW

PAGE

§ 8   The Reception of Roman Law in General   334

Topic 1. The Rise of Learning in Roman Law

§ 9. Eike von Repkow and the
      "Sachsenspiegel" . .   342
§ 10. The Clergy and the Canon
      Law   344
§ 11. The Conception of the
      Imperial Law .   .   346
§ 12. The "Deutschenspiegel"
      and the "Schwaben-
      spiegel"   347

§ 13. Literature of the Canon
      and Roman Law down
      to 1500   . .   349
§ 14. "Summæ Confessorum"
      and Related Literature   350
§ 15 Canon and Roman Law
      in German Universities   352

Topic 2 The Victory of Roman Law

§ 16. Basic Conditions making
      possible the Authority
      of Roman Law   . .   356
§ 17. The Superior Technic of
      the Roman Law .   .   358
§ 18 The "Klagspiegel"   .   359
§ 19. Decay of the Popular
      Courts   361
§ 20. Transformations in the
      Administration of Jus-
      tice   .   .   368

§ 21. Political Significance of
      the Reception   . . .   367
§ 22. The Legal Profession ·
      University Professors
      and Practitioners . .   369
§ 23. Complaints against the
      Lawyers   373
§ 24. Legal Training, Smat-
      terers and Popular Lit-
      erature   375

Topic 3. Italian Humanism, and the Reformation

§ 25 Theology and Legal Sci-
      ence in the Middle Ages   378
§ 26 Early Humanism . . .   380

§ 27 Later Influence of Hu-
      manism   381
§ 28. The Reformation .   .   382

Topic 4 Methods of Jurists in the 1500 s

§ 29. General Character of Med-
      ieval Science   . . .   384
§ 30 Legal Science the "Mos
      Italicus"   386
§ 31. Effects of the "Mos
      Italicus"   388
§ 32. "Loci" and "Topica" .   390
§ 33. The Period of Unshaken
      Authority of the "Mos
      Italicus"   391

§ 34. Opposition, and the Be-
      ginning of Reform   .   393
§ 35. Unofficial   Academic
      Courses Seminars and
      Disputations   394
§ 36. Attitude of Humanism
      toward the "Mos Itali-
      cus"   and   the   New
      "Methodus"   . . .   396
§ 37. The Ramists and their
      Doctrines   397

TOPIC 5 LEGISLATION

§ 38. Imperial and Territorial Legislation of the 1500s . . . . . 400 (PAGE)

CHAPTER III THIRD PERIOD. A.D. 1600–1806

NATURAL LAW, LEGAL RATIONALISM, AND GERMAN NATIONALISM

TOPIC 1. NATURAL LAW AND LEGAL RATIONALISM

§ 39. Rise of the Natural Law Jurists . . . . . 407 (PAGE)

§ 40. Grotius, Bacon, Hobbes, Puffendorf, Leibnitz . 408

TOPIC 2 GERMAN NATIONALISM

§ 41 Rise of the German National Jurists 425

§ 42. Exponents of Nationalism

and Realism; Carpzov, Mevius, Conring, Thomasius, Beyer . . . 426

TOPIC 3 STATE-BUILDING AND LEGISLATION

§ 43 Decline and Fall of the Empire (to 1806) . . 432

§ 44. Territorial and State Legislation (to 1811) . . 434

CHAPTER IV. FOURTH PERIOD. A.D. 1806–1908

NATIONAL UNIFICATION AND CODIFICATION

§ 45. Influences in the Late 1700s favoring Native Law and Codification . 439

§ 46. Thibaut and Savigny; the Controversy over National Codification 441

§ 47 State Codes of the 1800s 445

§ 48 Progress of Political Unification, 1806–1871 . 445

§ 49. National Codification, 1848–1908 446

PART V. NETHERLANDS

§ 1 Introductory 455

§ 2 Primitive Period . . 456

§ 3 Evolution during the Middle Ages . . . 457

§ 4 Beginning of the Renascence 461

§ 5 Authority of the Roman Law . . 464

§ 6. Influence of the Canon Law 466

§ 7 The 1600s and 1700s; Formation of the Roman-Dutch Law . 467

§ 8. Same Specific Branches of Law (Criminal, Commercial, Constitutional, International) . . 471

§ 9 National Unification and Codification after 1795 475

§ 10 Legal Conditions in Modern Times 477

Huber

PART VI. SWITZERLAND

PAGE

§ 1. Introduction 484

Topic 1. The Pre-Confederation Period (to A.D. 1300)

§ 2. Primitive Germanic Local Law 484

Topic 2. The Old Confederation (A.D. 1300–1800)

A. CONFEDERATE RELATIONS

PAGE

§ 3 The Thirteen " Places " .	488	§ 7 Religious Relations . . .	497
§ 4. The Associated " Places " .	492	§ 8. Relations with the Empire	
§ 5 The Common Territories .	492	and Other Foreign States	498
§ 6. The Constitution	494		

B. THE CANTONS

§ 9. Development of the Can-		§ 11. The City Cantons . . .	502
tons, in General . . .	500	§ 12. The Rural Cantons . .	507
§ 10. The Reception of Alien		§ 13. The Associated " Places "	509
Law	501	§ 14. The Common Territories	513

C. LEGAL SOURCES

§ 15. General Traits 514

Topic 3 The New Confederation (A D. 1800–1912)

§ 16 Confederate Relations	516	§ 18. Legal Sources	520
§ 17. The Cantonal Constitu-			
tions	519		

Topic 4. The Jurists and the Movements of Legal Thought

§ 19. From the Period of Na-		§ 20. In the 1800 s	527
tional Independence to			
the 1700 s . . .	522		

PART VII. SCANDINAVIA

CHAPTER I. First Period to A D. 1200

THE LAW-MEN AND THE LAW-TEXTS

§ 1. Primitive Usages . . .	533	§ 4. The Swedish Law-Man .	535
§ 2. Early Modes of Preserving		§ 5. The Norwegian Law-Man	537
Traditional Law .	534	§ 6 The Danish Law-Man . .	537
§ 3. The Icelandic Law-man		§ 7. The Authority of the Law-	
and Law-saga Man . .	535	Men	538

CONTENTS

§ 8 Legal Terms "Law" and "Right" . 539

§ 9 The "Thing" in Sweden, Norway, Denmark, and Iceland . . . 539

§ 10 The Beginning of Central Legislation 541

§ 11 Early Law-Texts, the "Right-books" 542

§ 12. Law-Texts of Iceland . 543

§ 13 Law-Texts of Norway . 543

§ 14 Law-Texts of Denmark . 545

§ 15 Law-Texts of Sweden . 545

CHAPTER II SECOND PERIOD A D 1200-1700

THE MEDIEVAL CODES

§ 16. Denmark under the Jydske Code . . . 547

§ 17. Same the Courts . . . 548

§ 18. Norway under King Magnus Lagaboter's Statutes 549

§ 19. Iceland under King Magnus Lagaboter's Statutes 553

§ 20. Sweden under the Statutes of Kings Magnus Eriksson and Kristoffer 553

§ 21 Same Growth of the Courts 555

CHAPTER III. THIRD PERIOD A D 1700-1900

THE MODERN CODES

§ 22 The Danish Code of King Christian V 557

§ 23. The Norwegian Code of King Kristian V . . 559

§ 24. The Swedish Code of 1734 . . . 560

§ 25 Relation between the Codes and Auxiliary Law 562

§ 26 Later Legislation, Crimes, Procedure, Courts . 562

§ 27 Same Private Law . . 564

§ 28 Same Economic Legislation 565

§ 29. Recent Codes 567

§ 30. Law of Custom, Force of Judicial Decisions 568

§ 31. Philosophy of Law . 570

§ 32. Literature on Northern Legal History . . . 574

PART VIII. SPAIN

INTRODUCTION FACTORS AND PERIODS

§ 1. The Inadequacy of Existing Historical Accounts 580

§ 2 General Influences and Traditional Periods in Spanish Legal History 581

§ 3 Sketch of Legal Development by Periods from the Origins to the Present Day . . . 582

CHAPTER I. Pre-National Period: to a d 1252

SUCCESSIVE RACIAL LAYERS IN SPANISH LAW

Topic 1. Celtic-Iberian Foundations and Greek and Phœnician Colonies (to 200 b c)

	PAGE			PAGE
§ 4. Obscurity of the Celtic-Iberian Origins	587	§ 6. Institutions of Civil and Public Law		591
§ 5. Social Organization	588			

Topic 2. The Roman Rule (200 b c. to a.d. 400)

§ 7 The Roman Influence	592	§ 8 Institutional Results of the Roman Influence	593

Topic 3. The Germanic Invasions and Visigothic Dominion (a.d. 400-700)

§ 9 Contrast of the Roman and Visigothic Influences	594	§ 11. Legal Institutions of the Visigothic Period	598
§ 10 Sources of the Visigothic Law	596	§ 12 Hybrid Legal Institutions	599
		§ 13 The Legislation of Kindasvinth	601

Topic 4. Christian and Moorish Kingdoms (a d. 700-1300)

§ 14 The Influence of the Church	601	§ 15 Roman, Moorish, and Other Foreign Influences	603

Topic 5. The Indigenous Groundwork of the Law in the 1200 s

§ 16. Legal Sources in Castile	607	§ 18. General Results and Tendencies	613
§ 17. Legal Sources in Aragon, Catalonia, Navarre, and Valencia	610		

CHAPTER II. First Period: a d. 1252–1511

THE CHRISTIAN RECONQUEST AND POLITICAL UNIFICATION

Topic 1 Spread of the Justinian and Canon Laws in Castile and León

§ 19 History of the Legal Sources	617	§ 20 Roman Elements in the Statutory Law, and particularly in the Partidas	627

	PAGE			PAGE
§ 21 The Status of the Partidas after the Ordenamiento of Alcala (1348)	631		§ 23 Diffusion of the Canon Law	634
§ 22. The "Leyes de Toro"	632		§ 24. New Legal Institutions of the Period	636

TOPIC 2 SPREAD OF THE JUSTINIAN AND CANON LAWS IN THE OTHER KINGDOMS OF THE PENINSULA

	PAGE			PAGE
§ 25 History of the Legal Sources	641		vaire, Valeucia, the Balearic Islands, and the Basque Provinces	649
§ 26. Roman Elements in the Law of Catalonia	645		§ 28. Notable Jurists of the Period	654
§ 27. Roman Elements in the Law of Aragon, Na-				

CHAPTER III SECOND PERIOD A D 1511–1808

THE AGE OF ABSOLUTE MONARCHY

§ 29. Imperfection of Existing Historical Guides to these Centuries . 659

TOPIC 1. THE AUSTRIAN DYNASTY (1500 s AND 1600 s)

	PAGE			PAGE
§ 30 History of the Legal Sources	660		§ 32. Legal Science and Literature in the Habsburg Period	667
§ 31. Progress in the Unification of the Law	666			

TOPIC 2. THE BOURBON DYNASTY (1700–1808)

	PAGE			PAGE
§ 33. History of the Legal Sources	675		§ 34 Legal Science and Literature of the Bourbon Period	680

CHAPTER IV. THIRD PERIOD . SINCE A D 1808

MODERN LEGAL REFORMS

	PAGE			PAGE
§ 35 Reform of the Public Law	684		§ 39 General Character and Limitations of the Código Civil .	696
§ 36. Reform of the Private Law	688		§ 40. The Código Civil and the Customary Law .	699
§ 37. Partial Codifications of the Civil Law antecedent to the Código Civil	690		§ 41. Legal Science and Literature of the Period	700
§ 38. History of the Redaction of the Present Código Civil	694			

CONTENTS

PART IX. CANON LAW

Brissaud

PAGE

§ 1. Classification of the Sources of Church Law 705

§ 2. Early Canon Law . . 708

§ 3. Medieval Canon Law; Gratian's Decretum to the "Corpus Juris Canonici" 714

§ 4 Later Canon Law . . . 718

§ 5. Judicial Decisions . 719

§ 6 Treatises, the Canonists . 719

§ 7. Influence of Canon Law on Secular Law . . . 721

APPENDIX A COMPARATIVE CHRONOLOGICAL TABLE OF MEDIEVAL SOURCES . . 727

APPENDIX B COMPARATIVE CHRONOLOGICAL TABLE OF MODERN CODES . . 746

INDEX . . 747

LIST OF MAPS

FACING
PAGE

WESTERN EUROPE AS SETTLED BY THE GERMANIC IN-
VADING TRIBES ABOUT A D. 500 1

ITALY IN THE LATER 1400 s 85

MAP OF CUSTOMARY LAW IN OLD FRANCE 201

LEGAL MAP OF GERMANY IN THE 1500 s AND THE 1800 s 307

SPAIN ABOUT A D 1300 577

EDITORIAL PREFACE TO THIS VOLUME

By John H. Wigmore[1]

No other book of this scope and purpose exists (so it seems) either in the English language or in any other; nor has existed, for a hundred years past, or more. To state the reasons for this lack would take us too far afield. Suffice it to point out that both the demand and the supply (so to speak) are now, if never before, plain enough in the realm of legal learning

The demand is found in the spirit of the times,—the craving for larger generalizations in legal science. The outlook beyond local and national law has opened. We desire to understand the growth of our own law as a part of that legal life which nations have in common, and, therefore, to begin by understanding the integral growth of Continental law — that system which now broadly divides with Anglo-American law the spheres of influence in the western hemisphere. To satisfy this desire, the internal legal history of the chief countries must, of course, be studied individually But to get the perspective, to understand the relative part played by each country in the whole story, a General Survey of the events, sources, persons, periods, and movements in the common development is indispensable at the outset.

The supply for this demand is found in the solid historical achievements of the past generation, — a generation which is marked off broadly from its predecessors in spirit, in methods, and in results. Not until the rise of the Historical School, a century ago, could such a volume (in the modern spirit) have been conceived; and not until the present generation has the fruition of those labors been adequate for this purpose. Even now, no single European scholar has ventured to write such a book, out of his own studies. The task is too large. It is emphatically a case for synthesis (in the words of President Woodrow Wilson, prefixed to this Series), — a synthesis of the work of specialists

---

[1] Professor of Law in Northwestern University, Chairman of the Editorial Committee for this Series and Editor of this volume

The volume has therefore been constructed by fitting together chapters separately written, each by a specialist in his own field. The aim has been to weave them into a connected and inclusive story, giving to each country the proper proportions, tracing in each the principal elements of legal life common to all, and exhibiting their variances from the highway of development.

I **The Authors and the Translators.** — Some account will first be proper of the scholars whose work has thus been utilized.

One of the Introductions is written by OLIVER WENDELL HOLMES, now Associate Justice of the Supreme Court of the United States, and formerly Chief Justice of the Supreme Judicial Court of Massachusetts. His work on "The Common Law,"[1] was the lifting of the curtain for a wider view of the origins of Anglo-American law and its relations to early Continental law. Some of us can remember the thrill and the inspiration which its appearance in 1881 gave to the American legal profession. On the Continent its repeated citation by legal scholars bears witness to the homage there paid to its influence.

The other Introduction is from the pen of EDWARD JENKS, Principal and Director of Legal Studies of the Law Society of London, formerly Lecturer at Pembroke and Jesus Colleges, Cambridge, and at Balliol College, Oxford, and Dean of the Faculty of Law, Melbourne. His notable treatise on "Law and Politics in the Middle Ages"[2] made it eminently fitting that he should introduce to Anglo-American lawyers a volume so closely related to one of his special fields of learning.[3]

Part I, for the period from Justinian to Feudalism, is prologued by a brief passage from a masterpiece of the lamented FREDERIC WILLIAM MAITLAND, sketching the general events of European law prior to the epoch of Justinian.[4] Then follows the main text, by CARLO CALISSE; it forms the first third of the first volume of his "History of Italian Law."[5] Professor Calisse, member of the

---

[1] 1881, Boston, Little, Brown & Company
[2] 1898, New York, Henry Holt & Co From this work is taken the Synoptic Table of Sources, printed in the Appendix to the present volume.
[3] Other publications of his are · "Constitutional Experiments of the Commonwealth," 1891 ; "The Doctrine of Consideration in English Law," 1893 ; "History of the Australasian Colonies," 1896 ; "Modern Land Law," 1899 , "A Short History of Politics," 1902 , "Edward I," 1902 ; "Parliamentary England," 1903 : "Digest of English Civil Law," 7 vols already issued, 1902 + , "A Short History of English Law," 1912.
[4] "A Prologue to a History of English Law," pp 8–18, as reprinted in vol I of "Select Essays in Anglo-American Legal History."
[5] "Storia del diritto italiano di Carlo Calisse, prof ordinario nella R. Università di Pisa Volume Primo Le Fonti," 2d ed , 1902. Barbera, Firenze, revised to date, in March, 1912, by the author, in this translation.

Italian Council of State and Lecturer on Legal History in the University of Rome, was formerly Professor of Legal History at the University of Pisa. Among the several excellent histories of Italian law (notably the extended treatises of Pertile and Schupfer, and the one-volume works of Salvioli, Solmi, Nani, and Ciccaglione) this one commended itself as the most suitable, by reason of its compactness, breadth of view, lucidity of style, justness of proportions, consecutiveness of narrative, and philosophy of causes. The first part, here selected, is the only text in any European language which describes Continental legal history as a whole for the period ending with feudalism.

Part II, for Italy, represents the remainder of Professor Calisse's first volume. His other three volumes will form Vol. VIII of this Series, the "History of Italian Law."

Part III, for France, represents the first part of the "History of French Law,"[1] by J. BRISSAUD, late Professor of Legal History in the University of Toulouse. Professor Brissaud, who died in 1904, was one of Europe's two or three greatest legal historians of modern times. A further personal account of him is given in the Introduction to vol. III of this Series, which translates the third part ("Private Law") of his "History", a later volume of this Series translates the second part ("Public Law"). The last chapter of Part III is from the "Treatise on Civil Law," by MARCEL PLANIOL, Professor of Civil Law in the University of Paris.[2] Professor Planiol's book is esteemed throughout the Continent as the best modern treatise on French Civil Law.

Part IV, for Germany, is more composite. One main portion is taken from the "Elements of German Legal History,"[3] by HEINRICH BRUNNER, Professor of Legal History in the University of Berlin, and the acknowledged primate of modern scholarship in German legal history. His larger treatise, as yet unfinished, is the leading work of its kind.[4] His treatise on the "Origin of Trial by Jury,"[5] familiar to us through Professor Thayer's writings,

[1] "Manuel d'histoire du droit français (sources, droit public, droit privé) à l'usage des etudiants en licence et en doctorat Par J Brissaud, Professeur à la faculté de droit de l'université de Toulouse Paris, A. Fontemoing 1e Partie, Sources" 1898 (1st ed); 1900 (2d ed).

[2] "Traité elémentaire de droit civil, conforme au programme officiel des Facultés de droit Par Marcel Planiol, professeur de droit civil à la Faculté de droit de Paris Librairie Générale de droit et de jurisprudence." 5th ed , 3 vols , 1908 (1st ed , 1899).

[3] "Grundzüge der deutschen Rechtsgeschichte," 4th ed , 1910, Leipzig, Duncker & Humblot (1st ed , 1901).

[4] "Deutsche Rechtsgeschichte," 2 vols , 1887, 1892; 2d ed., vol. I, 1908.

[5] "Die Entstehung der Schwurgerichte," 1872.

and his essay on the "Sources of English Law," translated in the "Select Essays on Anglo-American Legal History," have made our profession peculiarly indebted to him as to no other European scholar.

A second main portion of Part IV is taken from the "History of Legal Science in Germany,"[1] by RODERICH STINTZING, Professor of Law in Basel, 1854, in Erlangen, 1857, and in Bonn, from 1870 to the time of his death in 1883[2] This "magnum opus" of Professor Stintzing is the most elaborate and best esteemed history of legal science in Germany, and is a rich mine for all students of the subject It was unfinished at the time of his death, but was completed by a colleague, ERNST LANDSBERG, Professor of Roman and Criminal Law at the University of Bonn, who edited the already collected materials as Part II of vol I and then himself wrote the remaining volumes, II and III, from these a brief passage has been taken

The remainder of Part IV consists of short connecting passages from the works of four eminent legal historians of Germany and Austria· (1) from the "History of German Legal Sources,"[3] by JOHANNES ERNST OTTO STOBBE, Professor of Law at the Universities of Königsberg (1856), of Breslau (1859), and of Leipzig (1872), who died in 1887; (2) from the "Handbook of German Legal History,"[4] by RICHARD SCHROEDER, Professor of Germanic Law at the University of Heidelberg (formerly at Bonn, Wurzburg, Strassbourg, and Gottingen, 1866–1888, whence he went to Heidelberg), one of Germany's greatest legal historians, devotedly

---

Other chief publications of his are "Das Anglo-Normannische Erbfolgesystem," 1869, "Zur Rechtsgeschichte der romischen und germanischen Urkunde," 1880, and essays collected in "Forschungen zur Geschichte," etc , 1894.

[1] "Geschichte der deutschen Rechtswissenschaft, 1ste Abtheilung, von R. Stintzing, 1880, R Oldenbourg, Munchen and Leipzig", 2te Abtheilung, 1884, by the same, edited after his death by *Ernst Landsberg*, professor in the University of Bonn, and published under the auspices of the Historical Committee of the Bavarian Royal Academy of Sciences at Munich; 3te and 4te Abtheilung, by Professor *Landsberg*, 1898, 1910. (The whole work forms Vol XVIII in a series entitled "Geschichte der Wissenschaften in Deutschland, Neuere Zeit," published under the auspices of the above Committee).

[2] Other chief publications of his are: Monograph on "Ulrich Zasius," 1857; "Geschichte der popularen Literatur des romisch-kanonischen Rechts in Deutschland," 1867

[3] 'Geschichte der deutschen Rechtsquellen, bearbeitet von O Stobbe," 2 vols., 1860, 1864, Braunschweig, C A Schwetschke & Sohn (M Bruhn). He wrote also a "Handbuch des deutschen Privatrechts," 2d ed , 1882–1885; 3d ed , by *Schulz and Lehmann*, 1896–1900.

[4] "Lehrbuch der deutschen Rechtsgeschichte, von Richard Schroeder," 5th ed , 1907, Leipzig, Veit & Co

admired by all foreign scholars who have worked under him; (3) from the " Manual of German Legal History," [1] by HEINRICH SIEGEL (1830–1899), professor at the University of Vienna from 1857 to the time of his death, at one time general secretary of the Vienna Academy of Sciences, and the only Austrian who has written a general history of Germanic law; and (4) from the " German Legal History " [2] of HEINRICH ZOEPFL (1807–1877), Professor of Law at Heidelberg from 1839 to the time of his death, one of the leading spirits in the revival of Germanistic legal ideas in the middle of the 1800s A passage by Professor ERNST FREUND, of the Editorial Committee, completes the Part.

Part V, for the Netherlands (including part of what is now Belgium), is a chapter specially written for this work by JOOST ADRIAAN VAN HAMEL, professor in the University of Amsterdam, and official delegate to the Eighth International Prison Congress at Washington (1910). Professor Van Hamel is one of the ablest of the younger Dutch scholars, — admitted to the Amsterdam Bar in 1902, appointed Professor of Criminal Law in 1910, and the author of many treatises and articles on the history and the present problems of constitutional and criminal law. In this chapter (the manuscript of which was prepared by him in English) he has skilfully presented, under hampering limitations of space, a clear and well-proportioned survey, such as does not elsewhere exist in print, of the external history of Netherlands law.

Part VI, for Switzerland, was also specially written for this work, by EUGEN HUBER, Professor of Legal History at Basel Professor Huber is the author of what is concededly the best general history of Swiss private law , [3] the relevant portion of that work being too long for the present purpose, he prepared this summary at the request of the Committee Professor Huber has also occupied chairs at Halle and Bern, and was principal draftsman of the Swiss Federal Civil Code of 1907. His varied scientific work shows

---

[1] "Lehrbuch der deutschen Rechtsgeschichte, von Heinrich Siegel," 2d ed 1895, Wien.
[2] "Deutsche Rechtsgeschichte, von Heinrich Zoepfl," 1871–1872, 4th ed , 3 vols Braunschweig, Friedrich Wreden.
[3] "System und Geschichte des schweizerischen Privatrechts. Von Eugen Huber, Professor zu Basel," 1886–1893, C. Detloff's Buchhandlung, 4 vols. This work, in a review by the late eminent Professor Saleilles of Paris, in the "Nouvelle revue historique du droit, etc ," XVIII, 764, is thus characterized "Professor Huber has now with his fourth volume crowned the important structure of his history of Swiss private law It is a work of the first rank. Histories of private law are rarely of the highest excellence. Having had the good fortune in this instance to meet one which seems to me worthy to be a model of its kind, a masterwork, I have taken much satisfaction in reviewing it "

an extraordinary versatility of scholarship;[1] and his honors include memberships in the Swiss National Council, the Hague International Peace Court and the Institute of International Law.

Part VII, for Scandinavia, is a condensation of the most authoritative modern work, entitled " Northern Legal Sources," by EBBE (Carsten Hornemann) HERTZBERG,[2] written with the partial collaboration of other eminent scholars in Denmark, Norway, and Sweden. Professor Hertzberg, graduating at Christiania in 1870, studied then at Munich under Konrad Maurer, became privat-docent at Christiania in 1873, attaché to the Norwegian-Swedish Legation at Paris in 1875, professor at Christiania in 1877, parliamentary director of the Norwegian Mortgage-Bank in 1903, and in 1906 chief of the National Archives. He is the author of numerous treatises and articles on legal history.[3] His treatise here used is marked by a completeness and sense of proportion rarely found combined with such learned scholarship.

Part VIII, for Spain, was specially prepared for this work by RAFAEL ALTAMIRA (y Crevea), until recently (1910) Professor of Legal History in the University of Oviedo Professor Altamira's versatile talents — as historian, educator, novelist, traveller — make him one of the most distinguished figures of young Spain.

---

[1] Other publications of his are: "Die schweizerischen Erbrechte in ihrer entwicklung seit der Ablosung des alten Bundes vom deutschen Reich," 1872, "Studien uber das eheliche Guterrecht der Schweiz," 1874, "Das kolnische Recht in den zahringischen Stadten," 1881; "Die historische Grundlage des ehelischen Guterrechtes der Berner Handfeste," 1884, "Das Friedensrichteramt u. die gewerblichen Schiedsgerichte im schweizerischen Recht," 1886, "Die Bedeutung der Gewere im deutschen Sachenrecht," 1894; "Betrachtung uber die Vereinheitlichung des schweizerischen Erbrechts," 1895; "Betrachtung uber die Vereinheitlichung u. Reform des schweizerischen Grundpfandrechts," 1898, "Erlauterungen zum Entwurf eines schweizerischen Zivilrechts," 1901–1903, "Die Eigentumerdienstbarkeit," 1903

[2] "Nordisk Retsencyclopaedi, samlet og udgivet af Dr Jur. T H. Aschehoug, Dr Jur K J Berg, og Dr. Jur A F. Krieger Kjøbenhavn, 1890, Gyldendalske Boghandels Forlag (F Hegel & Søn)   I De Nordiske Retskilder, ved Ebbe Hertzberg, fhv Professor ved Kristiania Universitet, under Medvirkning af Flere " There was cooperation in parts by Dr. S D R K Olivecrona, Dr V A. Secher, Dr L M B. Aubert, Professor J H. Deuntzer, and Dr V Finsen, all eminent names in Scandinavian legal literature Of this work Professor Teichmann says, in the "Zeitschrift fur vergleichende Rechtswissenschaft," X, 476: "Professor Hertzberg has rendered a great service in thus setting forth the sources of Scandinavian law in the light of the extensive literature and the most recent researches in this field "

[3] Among them may be named "Principles of Ancient Norwegian Procedure," 1874, "Glossary to Norwegian Ancient Law," Part V, 1895; contributions in the "Festskrifte" published for Professors Unger, Tars, and Daae, and many articles in the "Norsk Retstidende," "Historisk Tidskrift," "Tidskrift for Retsvidenskap," and in Salmonsen's "Konversationslexikon"

He is the author of what is concededly the best modern history of Spain;[1] he was official delegate to the International Congresses of History at Rome (1903), and at Berlin (1908); he ranks among the two or three foremost representatives of critical scholarship in Spanish legal history. As an educator, he has been secretary (1889) of the National Pedagogic Museum,[2] commissioner on methods of teaching history,[3] organizer of university extension in the Asturias; and in 1911 was made director-general of primary education.[4] The chapter here contributed is that of a master of the legal sources, and is admirably conceived to carry out the Committee's plan for the book.

Part IX, for Church law, is another passage from the same first part of Professor BRISSAUD's "History of French Law," from which Part III of this volume is taken.[5]

The translator of Parts I (Early Period) and II (Italy) is the editor of this volume.

The translator of Parts III (France) and IX (Church law) is RAPELJE HOWELL of New York. A native of New York City, he lived several years in France, attending the Lycée Carnot at Paris, obtained a B.A. at Trinity College, Cambridge, afterwards an LL.B. at Columbia University, and is a member of the New York Bar. He is the translator also of Professor Brissaud's "History of French Private Law," forming vol. III of the present Series.

The translator of Parts IV (Germany), VI (Switzerland), and VIII (Spain) is FRANCIS S. PHILBRICK, now of Washington, D.C. A native of Iowa City, Iowa, and a B.Sc. and M.A. of Nebraska State University, he pursued graduate studies at Berlin, Paris, and Madrid (including a special study of Spanish historical sources), and

---

[1] "Historia de España y de la civilisacion española" (4 vols, the last in 1910).

[2] The "Eco de Madrid," known to American students of Spanish, is a conversation manual prepared by him

[3] "La enseñanza de la Historia," 1890, 1895; "La reforma de los estudios históricos en España."

[4] Other publications are: "Historia de la propiedad comunal," 1889; "Psicología del pueblo español", "Psicología y literatura"; "España en America"; "Mi viaje á America"; "Cuestiones hispano-americanes", "Historia del derecho español", "Cuentos de Levante"; "Novelitas y cuentos"; "Fatalidad," a novel; "Cuadros levantinos"; "Nuevos cuentos de amor y de tristeza", "Cosas del día"; "Fantasías y recuerdos," etc. Professor Altamira took his university degrees in 1886–1888

[5] Here should be mentioned that liberties have been taken, with all these works, in omitting certain portions of the foot-notes and other bibliographical apparatus Lack of space imperatively required such omissions so far as feasible. Moreover, in a translation, the need for citations of foreign authorities was less apparent. The translators have indicated the extent of these omissions.

received the degree of Ph.D. at Harvard University in 1902. Appointed Instructor in Government and History at Harvard University, in 1904, he shortly afterwards resigned to become one of the editorial staff of the Eleventh Edition of the Encyclopedia Britannica (1904–8, 1910) After taking a part of the law course at Columbia University (1910), he removed to Washington, to complete his legal studies at George Washington University. He is also the translator of Professor Hubner's "History of Germanic Private Law," forming Vol. IV of the present Series.

The translator of Part VII (Scandinavia) is JOHN WALGREN of Chicago, a native of Danville, Illinois, graduate of the Oscarshaven high school (Sweden), LL B. of the University of Minnesota, and a member of the Chicago Bar. He has published volumes of Essays, entitled "The New Health Science," and "Camp-Smoke Tales " In 1903–1907 he officiated as Interpreter for the Federal Government, having received in the civil service examination in Scandinavian languages the highest average rating in the United States.

The Index to the volume was prepared by ERNST FREUND, of the Editorial Committee, professor of law in the University of Chicago.

II. **Scope of the Story.** — The story of the volume begins at the close of the Roman Empire of the West. At that time, the Germanic tribes, settling down everywhere west of what is now Russia and the Balkans, contribute a system of customary law in a relatively primitive stage; while the surviving Roman culture represents law in a more advanced stage

The ensuing period of political amalgamation, *From Justinian to Feudalism*, forms Part I of the narrative The modern national lines are nowhere yet to be seen. But by the period 1000–1200 the new lines are beginning to form , and so the story must be taken up separately for each region

Part II tells of *Italy* This must come first, because the revival of Roman law in the 1100s is the central fact of all later development "Italy," says Maitland, " was to be for a while the focus of the whole world's legal history." The later course of events in France and in Germany is understandable only in the light of the influences emanating from Italy. In those other countries the schools and their controversies were to be for a long time not much more than echoes of thoughts originating in Italian centres. Parts III and IV must be read as sequels to Part II.

Part III proceeds to *France*, for France was the first to develop the new influences independently. France succeeds Italy in the primacy of Europe's legal thinking. At the name of the French-man Cujas, law students in Germany rose and saluted. Later, in the era of the Revolution and of Napoleon, France becomes a new centre of development for more modern movements.

Part IV passes to *Germany*. Here the story must go back to follow the fate of the pure Germanic law in its second stage. Then arrives the wave of new legal science from Italy. For three centuries later, Germany is occupied in assimilating these diverse elements. By the 1800s it takes its turn in becoming a centre of international influence.

Parts V to VIII now turn aside to follow the story in four separate regions which as nations had less distinct influence in creating types and broad movements.

Part V takes up the *Netherlands* Here the history is, at first, the growth of local varieties of the Germanic stock, subject to the same general influences as in France and Germany Then, in the 1600s, with the arrival of national independence, individual thinkers vigorously give new impulses in certain fields to general European legal science.

Part VI, in *Switzerland*, finds the story here, also, at first and for a much longer time, a local one, with many separate units. There is no distinctive flavor. Ammerbach and the Godefrois, with the other jurists, belong really, in their spirit and methods, to the law either of Germany or of France. Towards the end, as in the Netherlands, individual jurists exercise an extra-national influence, and national legislation unifies the law.

Part VII deals with *Scandinavia*, where the Germanic stock of law was left to grow in undisturbed isolation. These peculiar conditions exhibit a unique instance of law almost solely self-developed.

Part VIII takes up *Spain*. Its mixture of racial elements makes its local legal history perhaps the most complex and interesting. As a source of movements of legal thought, it plays no extensive part. But as a colonizer, it carries its law over the western hemisphere, and thus acquires a world-importance.

Part IX traces the *Canon Law* sources. The story of the Church's law runs parallel, indeed, with that of all the nations from the beginning Its influence is constantly referred to in the narratives of the various other Parts, markedly in those of France, Germany, Italy, and Spain. How powerful and permeating, in every epoch, was this parallel stream of Church law, even for remote England, will be appreciated by all who have read Maitland's masterpiece, "English Law and the Renaissance," or his "Roman Canon Law in the Church of England," — or even by those who remember their Blackstone.

It remains here to note that this general story confines itself to western Europe, and thus omits to describe the three systems of eastern Europe, — the Slavic, the Byzantine, and the Hungarian. Slavic law branches mainly into Russian, Polish, Bohemian, and South-Slavic (interspersed with some alien stocks). Byzantine law represents the surviving effects of Justinian's Græco-Roman law within the old Byzantine dominions; scholars are still endeavoring to map out its historic sphere of influence. Hungarian law represents the system imported by those invaders a thousand years ago; it has suffered admixtures, and its records are largely in Latin, yet it is a non-European stock. But all these three stocks of law remained substantially beyond the pale, for the law of the Romanic-Germanic peoples. There was no reciprocal influence (except on the boundaries) There was no open market for the legal science of East and West, as there came to be between the peoples of the West After Justinian, says Maitland, the Græco-Roman Empire at Byzantium "lost forever the power of legislating for the West; and two halves of the world drifted apart." Hence the East and the West can be kept separate, in the history of Continental law. They are in substance two separate stories. This volume has, therefore, not attempted to go further afield into the history of the Eastern stocks of law.

III. **Some Comments** — To the lawyer of to-day, there is much more in this volume than a narrative of events, sources, persons, and movements, preliminary to a study of the several countries' law Here, casting his glance over the broad features of a thousand years' law in Europe, he may see in the long perspective that endless progression in which to-day's legal conditions appear merely as a stage from the past towards the future. He will see the present explained by the past; and he may therefrom deduce some lessons What are those lessons?

The one that seems here most worth noting may be called the Recurrence of Legal Cycles. Similar problems, methods, abuses, remedies, seem to recur, amidst diverse surroundings The thoughtful lawyer begins to discover (without waiting for the authoritative interpretation of some profound seer) that the legal life of mankind, variant as it is, deals with materials so simple and limited in type that the same situations, "mutatis mutandis," keep recurring, with startling persistence.

Take, for example, the dominance of technicalities in the days of the Bartolists, in the 1300s (Part II, §§ 45, 46). Read the passage describing their methods, their shortcomings, and their downfall; substitute a few terms more suited to describe our own legal sources, and behold — almost comical in its aptness — a picture of the state of American legal practice of to-day. It ought to reveal — to those who are not beyond enlightenment — that present methods are not inherently essential and fixed; that they are merely a passing stage; and that some new form will duly replace them, as it did those of six centuries ago

Look, again, at the rise of the new method of teaching law at Bologna, under Irnerius, in the 1100s (Part II, § 39). In its revival of the classic sources, in its revelation of a new spirit of research and instruction, in its rapid and universal spread, do we not see a striking parallel to the work of Christopher Columbus Langdell, at the Harvard Law School, now forty years ago? And if his method is as yet limited to Anglo-American law, and is even now not much used outside of America, may we not speculate that after a century's due season, the method may become (if other countries' conditions really need it) a world-method, like that of Irnerius?

Take, again, codification as a panacea for legal ills. How often has it recurred, in what varying conditions and forms, and with what similar results! On a large scale, it seems to have had three cycles, some six or eight centuries apart, — the compilation of Justinian and the coeval Germanic "leges", the gloss of Accursius; and the codes of the 1700s and 1800s. How far were the causes the same, how far were the methods necessary and efficient, and how far do they teach us anything? For History to-day as a teacher can do for us far more than it could ever do in past times.

Then, again, our problem of local law versus national law is seen to be no novel problem. The principle of existence, as old Heraclitus would have it, is found in a perpetual Flux and Reflux. Certain it is that in the history of peoples there come successive times of homogeneity and differentiation (in Spencerian phrase), when the law has to respond to these changes in popular national life. On a large scale, there seem to have been two great cycles in western Europe, in the 800s a period of localization, followed in 1100–1500 by a period of homogeneous tendency; then again an individualist period, 1600–1800, followed by an apparent promise (to-day) of a reaction to homogeneity. To-day's movement will take new forms; but it seems to be due in the order of time And, within to-day's larger field, each country (still recalling the Spencerian formula) will also have its similar problems and cycles of nationalization and localization. Witness notably France, Germany, Italy, and (in its later turn) the United States. Forgetting for the moment our narrow personal traditions for or against States' rights, or corporate regulation, or the like, may we not discover in history certain larger aspects of this problem ?

And, as a final instance, we perceive the recurrent problem of text versus commentary, which is perhaps but another aspect of the problem of statute versus court, *i.e.* of the just division of function between law as a formulated rule and law as a decision on concrete cases. Periods and nations emphasize now the one, and now the other Looking beyond Europe, we see five peoples markedly impelled to develop their system of law, in its native and formative stage, by building up from judicial precedents, — the Roman, the Jewish, the Chinese, the Japanese, and the Anglo-Norman, the others do not naturally choose this form And again, at different periods, we see each nation shifting the emphasis from its native method. The Romans shifted for a while from Papinian to Justinian; the Japanese, in the last generation, have shifted in like way; the English, of late, from Mansfield and Eldon to the Codes of Sales and Negotiable Instruments and the Companies' Acts. In the United States, David Dudley Field aspired in vain to produce a similar change France and Germany are to-day discussing whether they shall shift in the contrary direction. It is a question which method is at a given period most needed and best suited for a given people. But the conditions which govern the problem are as yet too complex and obscure for clear vision. We here need, for our point of view, an even larger platform than this thousand years of European law

These instances illustrate the rich possibilities of present-day suggestion latent in the history of Continental law. If law is a changing product of times and manners and needs, nevertheless human motives and methods are but limited. And so, for many problems, we may detect a Recurrence of Legal Cycles, and may learn from the past the meaning of the present and the trend of the future

In the concluding volume of the Series, the Committee will seek to gather some of the best modern attempts to discover those broad generalizations which the united materials of these volumes will enable us to test and appreciate

xliv

INTRODUCTION

By Oliver Wendell Holmes [1]

THE authors whose writings are offered in this volume and Series
do not need introduction. They introduce the man who has the
honor for a moment to associate his name with theirs. But a few
words from a veteran may catch the attention of those who still
are in the school of the soldier and have not seen their first fight.

The philosophers teach us that an idea is the first step toward
an act. Beliefs, so far as they bear upon the attainment of a wish
(as most beliefs do), lead in the first place to a social attitude, and
later to combined social action, that is, to law. Hence, ever since
it has existed, the law has expressed what men most strongly have
believed and desired. And, as the beliefs and desires of the Western world have changed and developed a good deal since the days
of the Twelve Tables and the Law of the Salian Franks, I thought it
dangerously near a platitude to say, a dozen years ago, that the
law might be regarded as a great anthropological document. But,
as a gentleman prominent at the bar of one of the States professed
difficulty in understanding what I meant, it is evident that the
rudiments need eternal repetition. Any man who is interested in
ideas needs only the suggestion that I have made to realize that
the history of the law is the embryology of a most important set
of ideas, and perhaps more than any other history tells the story of
a race.

The trouble with general or literary historical works is that they
deal with premises or conclusions that are both unquantified. We
readily admit their assumption that such and such a previous fact
tended to produce such and such a later one; but how much of the
first would be necessary to produce how much of the last, and
how much there actually was of either, we are not told. On the
other hand, in the history of philosophy and economics we can say
with more confidence that we trace cause and effect. The one
shows the inward bond between the successive stages of the thought

---

[1] Associate Justice of the Supreme Court of the United States.

of man; the other the sequence of outward events that have governed his action and (some believe) really have determined his thought   At all events the latter fits the former as the outside of a cathedral fits the inside, — although there are gargoyles and Mephistopheles without and angels and saints within.

There is no place for the history of law in this metaphor; but, in plain prose, it is midway between the other two.   As we follow it down from century to century, we see logic at work attempting to develop the concrete cases given in experience into universal rules, and the struggle for life between the attempted generalizations and other competing forms.   We watch the metamorphosis of the simple into the complex   We see changes of environment producing new institutions, and new taking the place of old beliefs and wants.   We observe the illustrations, as striking here as in poetry or music, of the universal change of emphasis that each century brings along.   An argument that would have prevailed in Plowden's time, and perhaps would have raised a difficulty to be got rid of in Lord Ellenborough's, now would be answered only with a smile.

The most obvious moral of what I have said is that the law will furnish philosophical food to philosophical minds.   The surgeon of my regiment in the War of Secession used to divide the world into external and internal men.   The distinction is as old as Plato. For I take it that what makes the Banquet immortal is not the divine gossip about Aristophanes and Alcibiades and Socrates, but that it and some of the Dialogues are the first articulate expression that has come down to us of what internal men believe, that ideas are more interesting than things.   To the internal men, I need say no more to recommend the theme of this and the following volumes.   But the profit is not confined to them.   When a man has a working knowledge of his business, he can spend his leisure better than in reading all the reported cases he has time for.   They are apt to be only the small change of legal thought. They represent the compromise of the moment between tradition and precedent on the one side and the free conception of the desirable on the other.   It is worth while, even with the most mundane ideals, to get as big a grasp of one's subject as one can.   And therefore it is worth while to do what we can to enlighten our notions of the desirable and to understand the precedents by which we are constrained   The history of the law stands alongside of sociology and economics as a necessary tool if one is to practise law in a large way.

If what I have said is granted, not much argument is needed to show that a survey of the general development of Continental law is necessary to understand our own. The relationship is too well established to need new proofs, — although I believe that there still are standard treatises that ascribe trusts to Rome and ignore the Salman. Indeed, I am not sure that the best way of proving the need of this Series would not be to present a series of Elegant Extracts from text-books and decisions.

I can but envy the felicity of the generation to whom it is made so easy to see their subject as a whole. When I began, the law presented itself as a ragbag of details. The best approach that I found to general views on the historical side was the first volume of Spence's Equitable Jurisdiction, and, on the practical, Walker's American Law. The only philosophy within reach was Austin's Jurisprudence It was not without anguish that one asked oneself whether the subject was worthy of the interest of an intelligent man One saw people whom one respected and admired leaving the study because they thought it narrowed the mind; for which they had the authority of Burke. It required blind faith — faith that could not yet find the formula of justification for itself. The works of foreign scholarship were then inaccessible. One had to spend long days of groping, with the inward fear that if one only knew where to look, one would find that one's difficulties and questions were fifty years behind the times. Now, a man can start with the knowledge that he starts fair — that the best results of Europe, as well as of this country and England, are before him. And those results are so illuminating that diligence alone is enough to give him an understanding of how the law came to be what it is, of its broadest generalizations, and (so far as any one yet can state them) of the reasons to be offered for continuing it in its present form or for desiring a change.

WASHINGTON, D.C., November 28, 1911.

INTRODUCTION

By Edward Jenks[1]

It is a great honour for an English student of law to be invited to take ever so humble a part in the work which this volume commences To stand at the laying of the foundation stone of a new palace of legal literature, by the side of the author of *The Common Law*, is itself sufficient glory for one who has learned so much from the teachings of that book. But to link hands, through him, with the great band of jurists who have made the name of Harvard, and, with Harvard, the roll of American Law Schools, famous throughout the civilized world, is, indeed, to be received among the immortals. Langdell, and Thayer, and Ames, Cooley, Wheaton, Bigelow, Gray — these are the names which rise to the memory, as one thinks of the years that are gone. And all the toil of the years when the work seemed hopeless, and the dint of the strife when the armies of the Philistines were strong, seem to die away as one looks forward to the building of this new palace, in a purer air, with a wider sweep of line, and loftier roofs and towers, than we in our youth have known. For it is good to feel upon one's face the rays of the sun ; even though for us they are the rays of setting.

Standing in the Tower of Euric, at Carcassonne, long the key of Spain, and looking over the rolling valley of the Aude, one sees the path by which the van of the Teutonic hosts swept southward and west from their seats beyond the Rhine, and broke the ancient power of Rome. Frank and Goth, Saxon and Angle, Suabian and Lombard, Bavarian and Aleman — well, for peoples who, as M. Fustel would have it, did not exist, they accomplished somewhat of a work.

[1] Principal and Director of Legal Studies of the Law Society of England.

For, as the writer has elsewhere urged, and, he would fain think, has brought some considerable facts to prove, it is a profound mistake to suppose, that the work of the Teutonic hosts was done when the Roman Empire, shattered by their onset, fell to its doom.

That was but their first task. The Teutonic invaders were no mere destroyers Barbarians they were; but not savages. They had long emerged from the crude superstitions and fear-begotten cruelties which mark the savage type. They had courage, loyalty, faith, discipline, respect for beauty and learning They had come already to govern themselves by ordered custom. In some things they were the superiors even of the civilization which they overthrew

Two other great tasks, of infinite importance for the future, awaited them, and both were duly performed.

First, it was their task to save Western Europe for Christianity. The Barbarians were heathens when they burst in upon the Roman Empire, but they rapidly embraced the teachings of that Faith which the colder civilization of Rome had rejected For their heathenism was not the subtle and proud indifference of philosophic reason; but the childlike worship of Nature, of bodily prowess, of the memory of dead ancestors. Faced by the pure and lofty teachings of Christ, they bowed before the nobler ideal, and became champions of the Cross.

But in the south, on the burning shores of Africa, Europe was faced by a deadlier heathenism than the simple mythology of Thor and Wodin. For, just as and when the Teutons were overrunning Western Europe, the followers of Mahomet were overrunning Northern Africa, and blending the fierce fanaticism of Allah-worship with the subtlety of Arab learning and skill. And just as and when Charles the Great, the greatest of the Teutons, was binding the scattered branches of his race into a Christian Empire, the Moslem Caliphs were overrunning Spain, and the Moslem invasion of Europe was surging up to the Pyrenees, which thus became the march between Christianity and Heathendom, with Carcassonne as the watch-tower of Christendom.

For long centuries the warfare raged, and this way and that the tide of victory ebbed and flowed. But — after the Christian agony at Roncesvalles (where Roland fell), after the Visigoths, the hidalgos of Castile, had built, as bulwarks against the foe, those castles from which their province takes its name, after the exploits of Cid Campéador and the triumphs of Henry of Portugal, after

1

the victories of Ferdinand of Aragon — the last of the Moslem
banners was captured or driven over sea, and

> ' Down from th' Alhambra's minarets,
> Were all the Crescents flung '

Thus, and on other borders of the south and east, the Teutonic
hosts accomplished the second of their three great tasks. Defence
had followed Destruction.

Their third and final task was to build a new, a Christian civilization, upon the ruins of the Roman world. This task they had
taken in hand even before they had joined issue with the Moslem.
The Frank in the north and west, the Lombard in Italy, were the
chief architects. United for a time under the brilliant sway of
Charles the Great, they fell apart again, but each continued the
task. A powerful ally, the purest and the fieriest of all the
Teutonic races — those Northmen, or Normans, who, going down
to the sea in ships, and making their paths in deep waters, carried
their resistless arms to Neustria in northern France, to England,
to Sicily in the south, to Russia in the east, and even, as Crusaders,
to the very home of Moslemism in Africa — infused a new and
splendid energy into the task

Doubtless, in the early days at least, the Barbarians used, for
the building of their new civilization, many of the fragments of
that they had destroyed. But the error is, surely, to assume that
the makers of the fragments were the builders of the new fabric.
If I use, as quarry for my house, the stones of a ruined castle, is the
builder of the castle the builder of my house? Is the springing roof
or the pointed window of the Gothic cathedral copied from a Roman
temple? Is the *Divina Commedia* of Dante a translation of the
Æneid of Vergil? Or the *Sachsenspiegel* of the Roman *Digest?*
After Destruction, and Defence, had come Construction.

The last example brings us to that aspect of Teutonic civilization
which is the special subject of the series of which this volume is
the opening. For, if the inspiration of Teutonic civilization was
the Christian Faith, its conscience was Teutonic Law. And it is
just in regard to this aspect, that the hasty observer is apt to err.
He knows, perhaps, and, if he does not, this volume will tell him,
that the Teutonic invaders were profoundly impressed by the
magnificent system which the great jurisconsults of Republican
and Imperial Rome had bequeathed to posterity, and which, shortly
after the invasions had begun, was cast into an eternal mould by

the genius of Justinian. He may be aware, also, that Justinian ruled from Byzantium, not from Rome; but, if so, he will believe, and rightly, that the *Corpus Juris Civilis* soon found its way into Western Europe, and became the object of arduous, even of passionate study in the schools of the West. This volume will tell him of the revival of Roman Law in Bologna, Paris, and Oxford, in the universities of the Middle Ages. He will read of the Glossators, who devoted their lives to the exposition of the Digest — of Irnerius, Azo, and Accursius, of Cujas who taught at Paris and Bourges and Valence, and of Vacarius who lectured at Oxford. Above all, He will learn of that greatest of all legal tragedies, the " reception " of Roman Law in medieval Germany.

But, if he studies this volume with care, he will learn the far deeper and more important truth, that, as with the stones and bricks of the Roman builder, the works of the Roman jurists were really but the quarry from which the Teutonic genius drew some of its materials — that the fabric of medieval law was the creation, not of the Roman, but of the Teuton. For, as the child cannot wear the clothes of the full-grown man, but must be clad from year to year in garments adapted to his growing stature, so a youthful civilization cannot adopt the law of an ancient polity, it must, if it be really alive, fashion its own law from age to age. If the colonists who founded the American Republic could, and did, take with them the common law of England, that was because it was their own law, the law, not of an older and alien civilization, but of a civilization of which they formed a vigorous and progressive part. History moves in cycles; the ' unity of history ' is a spiral, not a straight line.

Even Teutonic civilization itself is witness to this truth. The artificial unity of the Carolingian Empire was premature and short-lived; being based, as its name of ' Holy Roman Empire ' implied, too much on the past and too little on the future. Not until after the long night of feudalism came the dawn of the Reformation, and the appearance of vigorous national life — a life so vigorous and various, that at times the sense of Teutonic unity seemed almost lost. But here a thought arises which may have some interest for American readers.

For if, on our standpoint in the Tower of Euric, we turn our eyes from East to West, from the Mediterranean to the Atlantic, from the valleys of the Aude to the valleys of the Susquehanna and the Merrimac, what is it that we see? We see once more a land which has been invaded, for nigh three centuries, by successive bands of Teutonic immigrants, from all Teutonic lands, seeking, not now to plunder and destroy, but to prosper by labour and toil. Once more they set to work to build up the mighty fabric of a State, with all the experience of Europe behind them, with all the promise of a virgin soil before. Once more there is the diversity which comes of healthy energy and independence of thought ; but, over all, the unity of a common faith, a common speech, and common ideals of justice and right.

Nay, beyond the borders of the Great Republic — in Canada, in Australasia, in South Africa — we see still the countless progeny of that immortal race which, sixteen hundred years ago, burst upon the astonished Roman, and built the towers of Carcassonne Not, indeed, a World-Empire, but, in the truest sense, a World-City, ' with the sea for streets ' — this is the vision that one sees from the Tower of Euric.

CARCASSONNE, April, 1912.

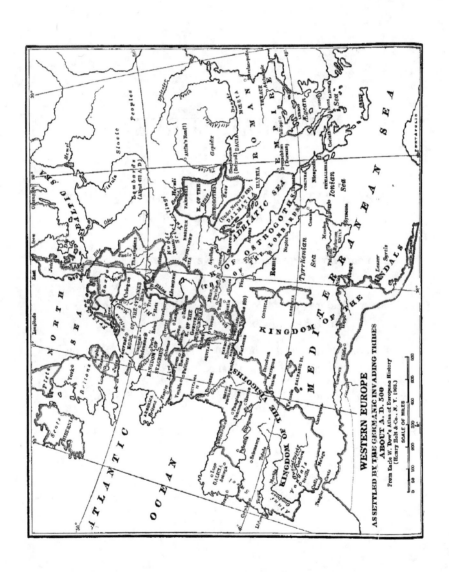

WESTERN EUROPE
AS SETTLED BY THE GERMANIC INVADING TRIBES
ABOUT A. D. 500
From Earle W. Dow's Atlas of European History
(Henry Holt & Co., N. Y. 1905.)

SCALE OF MILES

GENERAL SURVEY

PART I.

ROMAN AND GERMANIC LAW FROM JUSTINIAN TO FEUDALISM (A.D. 475–1100)

INTRODUCTION   PRELIMINARY SURVEY OF LEGAL EVENTS AND CONDITIONS BEFORE JUSTINIAN.

FIRST PERIOD (A.D. 475–575): THE GOTHIC KINGDOMS AND THE LATER ROMAN EMPIRE.

SECOND PERIOD (A.D. 575–900)   THE LOMBARD KINGDOM AND THE FRANKISH EMPIRE.

THIRD PERIOD (A.D. 900–1000): THE FEUDAL SYSTEM.

LIST OF TREATISES FREQUENTLY CITED

Brunner, Heinrich, "Grundzuge der deutschen Rechtsgeschichte," 5th ed 1910

Id , "Deutsche Rechtsgeschichte," 1st ed , vol I, 1887, vol II, 1892 , 2d ed , vol I, 1910

Canciani, "Barbarorum leges antiquæ," 5 vols , Venezia, 1781-1792

Muratori, L A , "Rerum italicarum scriptores," Milan, 1723-1751

Id , "Antiquitatos italicæ medii ævi," Milan, 1738-1742

Padelletti, G., "Fontes juris italici medii ævi," Turin, 1877

Pertile, A , "Storia del diritto italiano," 6 vols , 2d ed , 1903

Salvioli, G., "Manuale di storia del diritto italiano," 6th ed , 1907

Savigny, F. C von, "Storia del diritto romano nel medio evo," transl. Italian by Bollati , original edition in German

Id , "Geschichte des romischen Rechts im Mittelalter," 1st ed , Heidelberg, 1822, 2d ed , 1834

Schupfer, Francesco, "Manuale di storia del diritto italiano," 3d ed , 1904

Id , " Il diritto privato dei popoli germanici, con speciale riguardo all' Italia," 2 vols , Rome, 1907-1909

Walter, F , " Corpus juris germanici antiqui," 3 vols , Berlin, 1824

LIST OF ABBREVIATIONS USED FOR JOURNALS AND SERIAL WORKS CITED

A.G S = "Archivio Giuridico," founded by Serafini, Bologna

A.R = " Atti e memorie della Deputazione di storia patria per la provinza di Romagna "

A R A L = "Atti della Reale Academia dei Lincei, classi di scienze morali "

A R A T = "Atti e Memorie della Reale Accademia della Scienze di Torino "

A S I = "Archivio di storia italiana."

A S L = "Archivio di storia lombardia "

A S M P = "Atti e Memorie della Deputazione di storia patria per la provinzia Modena e Parma '

A V I = "Albori della vita italiana "

B A = "Sitzungsberichte der koniglichen Berliner Akademie der Wissenschaften "

B D R = "Bolettino dell' istituto di diritto romano "

F D G = "Forschungen zur Deutschen Geschichte "

J S = " Journal des Savants," Paris.

M G H = "Monumenta Germaniæ Historica," ed by the Societas aperiendis fontibus rerum ger-

manicarum medii ævi , folio edition, 1835-1891 ; quarto edition, 1888 + .

M H P = "Monumenta Historiæ Patriæ," Turin

M O G F = " Mittheilungen fur osterreichischen Geschichts-forschung "

N A = "Neues Archiv "

N R H = "Nouvelle revue historique du droit français et étranger "

P A = *Pertz,* "Archiv "

R A L = "Rendiconti dell' Accademia dei Lincei "

R I L = "Rendiconti del Istituto Lombarda "

R H D F E = "Revue historique de droit français et étranger "

R E = "Rivista europeana "

R I S G = "Rivista italiana delle scienze giuridiche "

R S I = "Rivista di storia italiana "

S S = "Studi senesi, Siena "

S W A. = "Sitzungsberichte der Wiener Akademie der Wissenschaften "

S D S D = "Studi e documenti di storia e diritto "

Z S S = "Zeitschrift der Savigny-Stiftung fur Rechtsgeschichte "

INTRODUCTION

PRELIMINARY SURVEY OF LEGAL EVENTS AND CONDI-
TIONS IN EUROPE BEFORE JUSTINIAN[1]

§ 1. We may, before we settle to our task, look around for a moment at the world in which our legal history has its beginnings. We may recall to memory a few main facts and dates which, though they are easily ascertained, are not often put together in one English book, and we may perchance arrange them in a useful order if we make milestones of the centuries.

A.D. 100–200 — By the year 200 Roman jurisprudence had reached its zenith. Papinian was slain in 212, Ulpian in 228. Ulpian's pupil Modestinus may be accounted the last of the great lawyers. All too soon they became classical; their successors were looking backwards, not forwards. Of the work that had been done it were folly here to speak, but the law of a little town had become ecumenical law, law alike for cultured Greece and for wild Britain. And yet, though it had assimilated new matter and new ideas, it had always preserved its tough identity In the year 200, six centuries and a half of definite legal history (if we measure only from the Twelve Tables) were consciously summed up in the living and growing body of the law.

A D. 200–300. — Dangers lay ahead. We notice one in a humbler quarter. Certain religious societies, congregations ("ecclesiæ") of non-conformists, have been developing law, internal law, with ominous rapidity. We have called it law, and law it was going to be; but as yet it was (if the phrase be tolerable), unlawful law, for these societies had an illegal, if not a criminal, purpose. Spasmodically the imperial law was enforced against them; at other times the utmost that they could hope for from the State was that in the guise of "benefit and burial societies" they would obtain some protection for their communal property. But internally they were developing what was to be a system of constitutional and governmental law, which would endow the overseer (episcopus) of every congregation with manifold powers. Also they were

[1] [This passage is taken from Professor FREDERIC WILLIAM MAITLAND'S "Prologue to a History of English Law," as reprinted in "Select Essays in Anglo-American Legal History," I, pp 8–18 —ED]

3

developing a system of punitive law; for the offender might be excluded from all participation in religious rites, if not from worldly intercourse with the faithful Moreover, these various communities were becoming united by bonds that were too close to be federal In particular, that one of them which had its seat in the capital city of the Empire was winning a preëminence for itself and its overseer. Long indeed would it be before this overseer of a nonconformist congregation would, in the person of his successor, place his heel upon the neck of the prostrate Augustus by virtue of God-made law. This was not to be foreseen; but already a merely human jurisprudence was losing its interest The intellectual force which some years earlier might have taken a side in the debate between Sabinians and Proculians now invented or refuted a Christological heresy. Ulpian's priesthood was not priestly enough.

The decline was rapid. Long before the year 300, jurisprudence, the one science of the Romans, was stricken with sterility, it was sharing the fate of art. Its eyes were turned backwards to the departed great The constitutions of the emperors now appeared as the only active source of law. They were a disordered mass, to be collected rather than digested Collections of them were being unofficially made: the Codex Gregorianus, the Codex Hermogenianus. These have perished, they were made, some say, in the Orient. The shifting eastward of the imperial centre and the tendency of the world to fall in two halves were not for the good of the West. Under one title and another, as coloni, læti, gentiles, large bodies of untamed Germans were taking up their abode within the limit of the Empire. The Roman armies were becoming barbarous hosts. Constantine owed his crown to an Alamannian king.

A.D 300-400 — It is on a changed world that we look in the year 400. After one last flare of persecution (303), Christianity became a lawful religion (313). In a few years it, or rather one species of it, had become the only lawful religion The " confessor " of yesterday was the persecutor of to-day. Heathenry, it is true, died hard in the West; but already about 350 a pagan sacrifice was by the letter of the law a capital crime. Before the end of the century cruel statutes were being made against heretics of all sorts and kinds No sooner was the new faith lawful, than the State was compelled to take part in the multifarious quarrels of the Christians. Hardly had Constantine issued the edict of tolerance, than he was summoning the bishops to Arles (314), even from remote Britain, that they might, if this were possible, make peace in the church of Africa. In the history of law, as well as

4

in the history of dogma, the fourth century is the century of ecclesiastical councils.   Into the debates of the spiritual parliaments
of the Empire go whatever juristic ability and whatever power of
organization was left among mankind.   The new supernatural
jurisprudence was finding another mode of utterance, the bishop
of Rome was becoming a legislator, perhaps a more important legislator, than the emperor   In 380 Theodosius himself commanded
that all the peoples which owned his sway should follow, not merely
the religion that Christ had delivered to the world, but the religion
that St. Peter had delivered to the Romans   For a disciplinary
jurisdiction over clergy and laity the State now left a large room
wherein the bishops ruled.   As arbitrators in purely secular disputes they were active; it is even probable that for a short while
under Constantine one litigant might force his adversary unwillingly
to see the episcopal tribunal   It was necessary for the State to
protest that criminal jurisdiction was still in its hands.   Soon the
Church was demanding, and in the West it might successfully
demand, independence of the State and even a dominance over the
State. the Church may command and the State must obey.   If
from one point of view we see this as a triumph of anarchy, from
another it appears as a triumph of law, of jurisprudence.   Theology
itself must become jurisprudence, albeit jurisprudence of a supernatural sort, in order that it may rule the world

  A.D 400–500. — Among the gigantic events of the fifth century
the issue of a statute-book seems small.   Nevertheless, through
the turmoil we see two statute-books, — that of Theodosius II,
and that of Euric the West Goth.

  The Theodosian code was an official collection of imperial statutes
beginning with those of Constantine I.   It was issued in 438, with
the consent of Valentinian III, who was reigning in the West.   No
perfect copy of it has reached us.   This by itself would tell a sad
tale; but we remember how rapidly the Empire was being torn to
shreds.   Already Britain was abandoned (407)   We may doubt
whether the statute-book of Theodosius ever reached our shores
until it had been edited by Jacques Godefroi.   Indeed we may say
that the fall of a loose stone in Britain brought the crumbling edifice to the ground.   Already, before this code was published, the
hordes of Alans, Vandals, and Sueves had swept across Gaul and
Spain; already the Vandals were in Africa.   Already Rome had
been sacked by the West Goths, they were founding a kingdom in
southern Gaul, and were soon to have a statute-book of their own.
Gaiseric was not far off, nor Attila   Also let us remember that this

Theodosian code was by no means well designed, if it was to perpetuate the memory of Roman civil science in a stormy age   It was no " code " in our modern sense of that term.   It was only a more or less methodic collection of modern statutes   Also it contained many things that the barbarians had better not have read, bloody laws against heretics, for example.

We turn from it to the first monument of Germanic law that has come down to us.   It consists of some fragments of what must have been a large law-book published by Euric for his West Goths, perhaps between 470 and 475   Euric was a conquering king, he ruled Spain and a large part of southern Gaul; he had cast off, so it is said, even the pretence of ruling in the emperor's name. Nevertheless, his laws are not nearly so barbarous as our curiosity might wish them to be.   These West Goths, who had wandered across Europe, were veneered by Roman civilization.   It did them little good.   Their later law-books, that of Reckessuinth (652–672), that of Erwig (682), that of Egica (687–701), are said to be verbose and futile imitations of Roman codes.   But Euric's laws are sufficient to remind us that the order of date among these Leges Barbarorum is very different from the order of barbarity.   Scandinavian laws that are not written until the thirteenth century will often give us what is more archaic than anything that comes from the Gaul of the fifth or the Britain of the seventh   And, on the other hand, the mention of Goths in Spain should remind us of those wondrous folk-wanderings and of their strange influence upon the legal map of Europe.   The Saxon of England has a close cousin in the Lombard of Italy; and modern critics profess that they can see a specially near kinship between Spanish and Icelandic law

A. D. 500–600. — In legal history the sixth century is the century of Justinian   But in the west of Europe this age appears as his, only if we take into account what was then a remote future   How powerless he was to legislate for many of the lands and races whence he drew his grandiose titles — Alamannicus, Gothicus, Francicus, and the rest — we shall see if we inquire who else had been publishing laws.   The barbarians had been writing down their customs The barbarian kings had been issuing law-books for their Roman subjects.   Books of ecclesiastical law, of conciliar and papal law, were being compiled

The discovery of fragments of the laws of Euric the West Goth has deprived the Lex Salica of its claim to be the oldest extant statement of Germanic custom   But if not the oldest, it is still

very old; also it is rude and primitive. It comes to us from the
march between the fifth and the sixth centuries, almost certainly
from the victorious reign of Chlodwig (486–511). An attempt to
fix its date more closely brings out one of its interesting traits
There is nothing distinctly heathen in it, but (and this makes it
unique) there is nothing distinctively Christian. If the Sicam-
brian has already bowed his neck to the catholic yoke, he is not yet
actively destroying by his laws what he had formerly adored   On
the other hand, his kingdom seems to stretch south of the Loire,
and he has looked for suggestions to the laws of the West Goths.
Let us remember that, by virtue of the Norman Conquest, the Lex
Salica is one of the ancestors of English law.

There seems little doubt that the core of the Lex Burgundionum
was issued by King Gundobad (474–516) in the last years of the
fifth century   Burgundians and West Goths were scattered among
Roman provincials. They were East Germans, they had long
been Christians, though addicted to the heresy of Arius. They
could say that they had Roman authority for their occupation of
Roman soil   Aquitania Secunda had been made over to the West
Goths, the Burgundians vanquished by Ætius had been deported
to Savoy. In their seizure of lands from the Roman possessors
they had followed, though with modifications that were profitable
to themselves, the Roman system of billeting barbarian soldiers
There were many Romani as well as many barbari for whom their
kings could legislate   Hence the Lex Romana Burgundionum
and the Lex Romana Visigothorum

The West Goths' power was declining. Hardly had Alaric
issued his statute-book when he was slain in battle by the Franks.
Soon the Visigothic became a Spanish kingdom. But it was not in
Spain that the Breviarium made its permanent mark. There it
was abrogated by Reckessuinth when he issued a code for all his
subjects of every race. On the other hand, it struck deep root in
Gaul. It became the principal, if not the only, representative of
Roman law in the expansive realm of the Franks. But even it was
too bulky for men's needs. They made epitomes of it and epitomes of epitomes.

Then again, we must remember that while Tribonian was busy
upon the Digest, the East Goths were still masters of Italy   We
recall the event of 476, one emperor, Zeno at Byzantium, was to be
enough. Odovacer had ruled as patrician and king. He had been
conquered by the East Goths. The great Theodoric had reigned
for more than thirty years (493–526), he had tried to fuse Italians

7

and Goths into one nation, he had issued a considerable body of law, the Edictum Theodorici, for the more part of a criminal kind.

In 528 Justinian began the work which gives him his fame in legal history; in 534 (though there were novel, *i.e.* later, constitutions to come from him) it was finished. Valuable as the code of imperial statutes might be, valuable as might be the modernized and imperial edition of an excellent but ancient school-book, the main work that he did for the coming centuries lies in the Digest. We are told nowadays that in the Orient the classical jurisprudence had taken a new lease of life, especially in the schools at Berytus. We are told that there is something of a renaissance, something even of an antiquarian revival, visible in the pages of the Digest, a desire to go back from vulgar practice to classical text, also a desire to display an erudition that is not always very deep. Great conqueror, great builder, great theologian, great lawgiver, Justinian would also be a great master of legal science and legal history. The narrow escape of his Digest from oblivion seems to tell us that but for his exertions, very little of the ancient treasure of wisdom would have reached modern times, and a world without the Digest would not have been the world that we know.

CHAPTER I. FIRST PERIOD: A.D. 475–575

LAW UNDER THE GOTHIC KINGDOMS AND THE LATER
ROMAN (BYZANTINE) EMPIRE [1]

§ 2   The Gothic Kingdoms and the Roman Empire

TOPIC 1. THE ROMAN LEGISLATION OF THE GERMANS

§§ 3–5. The Edict of Theodoric the Ostrogoth.

§§ 6, 7. The Minor Ostrogothic Edicts

§ 8   The Roman Laws of the Visigoths (Alaric)

§ 9.   The Roman Laws of the Burgundians (Papinianus).

TOPIC 2. THE ROMAN LAW OF ROME

§ 10. Roman Practice before Justinian

§ 11. Justinian's Legislation

§§ 12, 13. Imperfect Diffusion of the "Corpus Juris"

§ 2. **The Gothic Kingdoms and the Roman Empire.** — The Byzantine epoch extends from the fall of the Roman Empire of the West (476) to the invasion of Italy by the Lombards (568). In the legal sources of this period the Roman law dominates. It might even be said to be in sole possession of the field, except that in the same epoch belong the first legislative enactments of the Germanic peoples in Italy. But even in those enactments the Roman law is the principal and almost the only element.

In the brief and stormy period of the supremacy of Odoacer the Goth (476–493) we find no legislation, in the strict sense of the word   Nor was any need of it felt by the community. The conquering tribes had kept in force the Roman public and private law for the native inhabitants of the conquered land. It was merely not adopted for the conquerors themselves; they remained faithful to their own national customs   If we do find mentioned a few "laws" of Odoacer, the term signifies merely some measure taken by him to meet some particular need. It is called a "law," for example, when Odoacer, in 483, summoned a Roman council to check the corruption prevailing at the election of a pope.[2] There is, indeed, in the succeeding (Ostrogothic) dynasty (493–

[1] [This Part is a translation of Professor CALISSE's "History of Italian Law," vol I. For the title of that work, and an account of the author, see the Editorial Preface to this volume   Chapter I, §§ 1–13 = CALISSE, Part I, §§ 1–13, pp 1–19 — TRANS]

[2] M G H., "Auctores antiquissimi," 1894, xii, p. 414.

9

554) a real legislative activity, inspired by the Germanic kings.
But it was of short duration; for the Italian territory, so soon as
it was won back by the Empire of the East, reverted entirely to
the Roman law, as being the law common to all the subjects of
the Empire.

In this first period, then, which is nothing more than a continuation of the Roman epoch and a preparation for the Middle Ages,
the sources of law, all essentially Roman, may be divided into two
classes, according to their authors and scope. (I) The first includes
those which the invaders adapted to the conditions of their new
kingdom (II) The second comprises those which emanated
directly from the Roman Emperor of the East at Constantinople.
The former is represented by the Roman laws of the Germanic
tribes; the Ostrogothic edicts being the most important for
Italy. The latter consists in the Roman law properly so called,
as codified and restated in this period in the legislative labors of
Justinian.

Topic 1. The Roman Legislation of the Germans

§ 3. **The Edict of Theodoric the Ostrogoth.**[1] — The Edict of
Theodoric is the first, in point of time, among the legislative
memorials of this period. But the precise time of its compilation is not known, and has led to a divergence of opinions, each
more or less probable.

According to one opinion, the compilation could not have taken
place before 506, because (as is asserted) one of its sources must
have been the "Interpretatio," a commentary appended to the
Breviary of Alaric,[2] which was promulgated in that year for the
Roman subjects of the Spanish Goths (*post*, § 8) There is indeed
considerable affinity between the Edict and this commentary.
Yet that alone hardly suffices to show that the compilers of the
former had used the latter, for a legislator composing in Italy
could hardly have any occasion to resort for his knowledge of
Roman law to a compilation made in a foreign country. More-

---

[1] Texts   ed *Bluhme*, in M G H , "Leges," 1893 ; ed *Padelletti*,
"Fontes," 1877
Treatises and Articles   *Pertile*, "Storia," I, § 11 ; *Schupfer*, "Ma-
nuale," p 32 , *Salvioli*, "Manuale," p 45 ; *Savigny*, "Storia," I, 377 , *Brun-
ner*, "Rechtsgeschichte," I, § 52 , *Gaudenzi*, "Gli editti di Teodorico e di
Atalarico," 1884 ; *Id*, article in Z S S , VII, 29, "Die Entstehungszeit des
Edictums Theoderici" ; *Schupfer*, article in A R A L , ser IV, vol III,
"L' editto di Teodorico" , *Patetta*, article in A.R A T , 1893, "Sull' anno
della promulgazione dell' editto di Teodorico "
[2] *Pertile*, "Storia," I, § 11 , *Brunner*, "Grundzuge," 1901, p 48.

over, the similarity between the two works can be amply explained
on the hypothesis that the authors of the Spanish or Visigothic
commentary and those of the Italian or Ostrogothic Edict had equal
access to some common source, — probably to a compendium of
Roman law intended for court practice and widely used among
the lawyers of the 400s.[1] There being thus no need for conceding that the " Interpretatio " of the Breviary was drawn
upon for the Edict of Theodoric, the supposed reason fails for
attributing the Edict necessarily to a date not earlier than 506.

Others[2] seek to fix the date between 512 and 515. Their argument is this : The Edict could not have been composed between
506 and 511, nor after 515, because at both those periods Cassiodorus was questor, it was certainly not of his composition, for
it would have been extant in his records (like the edict of Atalaric),
since the questor's functions included that of inditing the decrees.
Thus (by this view) there remain two hypotheses for the date of
the Edict ; namely, prior to 506, and between 512 and 515. But
the former is negatived not only by the above-mentioned use of
the Edict by the " Interpretatio," but also and more decisively
by the fact that certain enactments found in the records of the
first questorship of Cassiodorus (506–511) were also incorporated
in the Edict ; the date of which could therefore not be prior to his
first questorship   The other hypothesis may be tested by the
circumstance that the Edict exhibits[3] traces of having been composed after a war fought in Gaul in 510. But this argument may
be answered by pointing out that, even conceding the Edict not
to be attributable to either period of Cassiodorus' questorship, it
is not demonstrated to be later than his first questorship (i.e. 506) ;
for the identity between certain provisions of the Edict and certain records of Cassiodorus can better be explained, not as a development of ministerial regulations into laws by insertion in the
text of the Edict, but as applications of the Edict made by the
minister for specific cases in which the Edict was invoked. And as
to the war referred to in the Edict, there is no reason to believe that
it was the Gallic war of 510, for it might have been any other of
Theodoric's numerous campaigns, and in any event the chapter
that refers to it, being one of the last in the Edict, might have been
subsequently appended

So that the most plausible opinion is still that which attributes
the Edict to the year 500.[4] This would make its promulgation

---

[1] *Haenel,* " Lex Rom. Vis.," p xci   [2] *Gaudenzi,* " Editti Teod ," *supra* n 1.
[3] Cap XLVIII.   [4] *Schupfer, Salvioli,* and others.

11

coincide with the date of Theodoric's formal entry into Rome.
On that occasion the king did make a "law," as the chroniclers
expressly tell us, and there are reasons for thinking that it was this
very Edict For it is recorded that Theodoric, on entering Rome,
inflicted the death penalty on certain corrupt judges who were not
rendering justice to litigants, and the opening chapter of the Edict
deals with this very offence and names for it the penalty of death.
It is also worth remembering that Theodoric, while celebrating at
Rome his "decennalia" (that is, the tenth anniversary of his reign
reckoning from his entry into Italy) was desirous of imitating the
ancient usages of the Roman emperors, and with that purpose he
provided popular games, distributed rations, made a public address,
and allotted a fund for the preservation of the civic monuments;
and, as a part of this usage, he also promulgated a law, — as Hadrian had done on his fifteenth anniversary with the "Edictum
Perpetuum," and as Theodosius had done on his thirtieth with his
Code.

§ 4. The *contents* of the Edict (which consists of one hundred and
fifty-four articles, not counting the prologue and the epilogue)
deal principally with criminal law and with procedure This was
natural, for its main object was to suppress the frequent disorders
complained of in his reign, and to provide assurance of the just
administration of the laws.

The subjects are allotted among the various articles without
any system; nor indeed were they all the product of a single
legislative act, for several were later added to the compilation
The precise author is unknown; but everything points to his being
a Roman holding some office under the king A German (to mention no other reason) could not have possessed the thorough
knowledge of Roman law which the Edict exhibits Its sources
are exclusively Roman, — the "Sententiæ" of Paulus, the earlier
Roman Codes (the Gregorian, the Hermogenian, and especially
the Theodosian), together with some of the compends or manuals
then in use in the schools or at the bar. Specific provisions can
even (for the most part) be identified with the corresponding
ones in the Roman sources[1] The legislator himself expressly
cites, here and there,[2] the "leges," that is, the imperial constitutions, which he wishes should be observed, and in the epilogue
he further declares that the Edict is the result of what he has

---

[1] Compare the references given for the respective chapters in Padelletti's edition.
[2] Compare Caps LIII, LXIX, LXXII, CXLIV, etc.

12

compiled from the law already in force either in constitutions or jurists' opinions: "quæ ex novellis legibus ac veteris juris sanctimonia pro aliqua parte collegimus."

An edict of such brevity could hardly concern itself expressly with more than the few legal topics which were brought into general importance at that epoch by the conditions prevailing in Italy. All remaining matters of law, that is, the system as a whole, were left to be regulated by the Roman law, — as expressly declared by the legislator in his preamble.[1]

But the Germanic settlers, in point of private law, were not to lose their own usages and rules. This result, indeed, was quite consonant with the Roman law itself; for the foreigners who were enlisted as soldiers for the Empire had always been, by Roman law, left subject to their native usages, and since that was technically the legal status of the Ostrogoths, they were not bound to be governed by Roman usages. There is a reference to this in the Edict itself.[2] But confirmation is further supplied by several circumstances. The conqueror-element in the population could hardly have been expected to submit itself, in matters of private law, to the customs of the conquered race, even in matters of governmental regulation, it submitted none too readily, notwithstanding the pressure exerted by Theodoric himself Moreover, the Ostrogoths in their own lawsuits had hitherto possessed their own magistrates, who were quite lacking in knowledge of Roman law, — so lacking that a Roman jurist sat with them, in controversies between persons of the two nationalities, where Roman law was to be applied And it was this double system, hitherto prevailing, that made necessary some legislation, which should be applicable in common to both races, and capable of obviating the conflicts of law in the relations of Romans and Ostrogoths, while not pretending to subject the latter entirely to the customs of the former.[3]

§ 5 Nevertheless, from the *political point of view*, even that extreme result would have been agreeable to Theodoric. He would have preferred to make thorough Romans out of his Ostrogoths. By combining the Germanic military prowess with the Roman civilization, he could hope to solidify his kingdom, for it could not exist otherwise than as Roman, planted as it was within the imperial confines and founded upon an imperial franchise.

[1] "Salva juris publici reverentia et legibus omnibus cunctorum devotione servandis."
[2] Cap. XXXII "Barbaris, quos certum est reipublicæ militare quomodo potuerint et voluerint, faciendi damus licentiam testamenti"
[3] Compare Justinian's Code, I, 38, 1.

13

The legislative work of Theodoric was framed in accord with this theory. Legislative authority he did not in his own right possess. That was a prerogative of the Roman emperor, whose authority the Ostrogoths on their entry into Italy had pledged themselves to respect But Theodoric was bound and entitled to promulgate such ordinances as he thought requisite for administering his territory. This would be the act, not of a legislator, but of a magistrate; in which office Theodoric exercised supreme powers for Italy Every Roman provincial magistrate had been accustomed to put forth edicts containing the regulations by means of which he would administer the law during his term of office Similarly, what Theodoric promulgated was not so much a law as a magisterial edict, it conformed to the law of the Empire not only in details but also in general purpose. In Theodoric's purpose his Edict (as already remarked) was to be a means of harmonizing the two races, — by Romanizing the Ostrogoths, however, and not contrariwise. In his own words,[1] he aimed by means of the Edict to remove the occasions of friction between Germans and Romans. Taken, as it was, chiefly from the Roman law, that law would come to be, at least in the more important litigation, a common possession

Undoubtedly the Edict was to be binding upon Goths and Romans alike. No exemption was conceded on any ground of official title or of status. Magistrates who did not strictly enforce it were to be punished with exile. In all subjects of law on which the Edict was silent (and these outnumbered the others), the law to be used was Roman law for Roman litigants, and Germanic law for Germanic litigants [2]

In the foregoing features the Edict is in marked contrast to the other enactments promulgated by Germanic rulers (*post*, §§ 8, 9) for their Roman subjects. Their source — the Roman law — was the same. But Theodoric's Edict was to serve as a law common to both peoples, while the other enactments of Roman law were to have force for the Roman population only, not for the Germanic population, and thus the two peoples, each left with its own law,

---

[1] In the preamble "Querelæ ad nos plurimæ pervenerunt, intra provincias nonnullos legum præcepta calcare   nos, cogitantes generalitatis quietem,   presentia jussimus edicta pendere   "
[2] In the preamble "Quæ Barbari Romanique sequi debeant super expressis articulis edictis præsentibus evidenter cognoscant " In the epilogue "Quæ omnium Barbarorum sive Romanorum debet servare devotio "
An occasional passage (see Cap. CXLV) dealt solely with the interests of the barbarians and therefore was of force for them only.

were without that powerful motive which could bind together the conquerors and the conquered. Theodoric's Edict, moreover, when its articles were silent, left each people to its own existing system, while the other Roman codes made by Germanic kings abolish the preëxisting system, substituting, by way of concession, the new codes.

The Edict was widely promulgated, not only in Italy proper, but also beyond its confines, in Provence and other regions adjoining the conquests of Theodoric. Its influence upon the civilization of the Germanic tribes was important; for it made them familiar with many principles of Roman law hitherto unknown to them. It modified, too, or extirpated, many of their own customs which were in conflict with the policies of the new State. Thus the legislative labors of Theodoric were not without beneficent consequences even though the main purpose — the amalgamation of the two races — was impossible of achievement in his day.

§ 6. **The Minor Ostrogothic Edicts.** — Theodoric was also the author of some lesser edicts. Among the records of his chancery, during the questorship of Cassiodorus, is one which was promulgated in the provinces of Campania and Sannio, and aimed to suppress the abuse (more common in those regions) of extrajudicial distraint.[1] Though Theodoric's edicts were all confirmed by his successor Atalaric,[2] the latter also promulgated edicts of his own, aided by his questor Cassiodorus. Of these, a notable one imposed regulations for electing the pope at Rome, it was published first by the prefect reading it to the Senate and then by nailing it to the portals of St. Peter's.[3] Another important one is known preëminently as the Edict of Atalaric. Its style reveals the hand of Cassiodorus; its contents (in twelve articles, besides a preamble) are exclusively penal, and are aimed at wrongful disseizins of estates, at concubinage, and at other abuses then rife.

The edicts of the ensuing kings were of varied and only temporary interest; they owed their motives to the untoward troubles brought on by the Byzantine war, which then threatened the existence of the Ostrogothic kingdom. Among these legislative records may be mentioned the Pragmatic Sanction of Justinian, which confirmed the edicts of the earlier Ostrogothic kings down to Theodatus (so far as consistent with the new Code) and annulled

[1] *Cassiodorus,* "Variarum," IV, 10
[2] "Edictum Athalarici regis," c. XXI (in *Padelletti,* "Fontes").
[3] "Var.," IX, 15

those of the later kings. The legal sources of this period include
also the chancery formulas preserved by Cassiodorus[1] These are
important chiefly for their enumeration of the titles and duties of
the public officers, though pompous in style and metaphorical in
verbiage (as customary in that decadent era of the Latin language),
they are valuable for the history of public law, and reveal still more
plainly that the Ostrogothic public law was essentially Roman

§ 7 Such were the principal features of the Ostrogothic legal
development in Italy. It followed the fortunes of that kingdom, —
reaching its prime under Theodoric, then declining, and finally
disappearing without a trace. Except for a few details, the sway
of Ostrogothic law ended with the kingdom, at the reconquest of
Italy by the Eastern Roman empire seated at Byzantium. It could
not be expected, after the extension of Justinian's Code to Italy,
that the Ostrogoths who remained there should be left in undisturbed adherence to their own customs and especially to the edicts
of their former kings There is, to be sure, a reference, in a Ravenna document of 551 (when Ravenna had been already eleven
years in Byzantine control), to the Ostrogothic edicts as still in
force But the Pragmatic Sanction, which made the laws of
Justinian binding on all, had not then been promulgated, and
probably up to the date of that Sanction the Ostrogoths (with
whom Justinian had made a preliminary treaty) still preserved their
own laws, as they did their churches and estates in Ravenna.
These (and presumably also their laws) they afterwards lost, when
upon the victory of the Roman general Narses all attempts at
reconciliation were given over But there are besides this several
direct proofs of the abolition of the Ostrogothic laws; first, the
capitulations made by them, on deciding not to evacuate Italy,
contain a clause pledging obedience to the imperial laws; furthermore, in certain documents Ostrogoths are found admitting their
subjection to the Roman law of Justinian; and finally, the above-
mentioned Pragmatic Sanction expressly declares that Justinian
intended it to apply to all inhabitants of the Empire of the West
("ad utilitatem omnium qui per occidentis partes habitare nos-
untur ").

§ 8. **The Roman Laws of the Visigoths (Alaric).**[2] — Of all the

---

[1] "Var.," VI, VII.
[2] TEXTS *Haenel,* "Lex Rom Vis ", *Bluhme,* "Lex Rom. Burg ," in
M G H , "Leges," III; *Salis,* "Lex Rom Burg ," in M G.H , "Leges," III.
    TREATISES AND ARTICLES *Brunner,* "D Rechtsgeschichte," §§ 49, 50;
Pertile, "Storia," § 11, *Salvioli,* "Manuale," p 54, *Savigny,* "Storia,"
I, 307, *Schupfer,* "Manuale," pp 38, 42

laws enacted by the invading Germanic tribes for their Roman subjects, the most important undoubtedly was that of the Visigoths It is known usually as the "Breviary of Alaric." But it went also by various other titles, — "Liber legum Romanarum," "Corpus legum," "Lex Theodosii," "Lex Romana," "Liber Theodosianus legis Romanæ," and especially "Lex Romana Visigothorum." This was the work of Alaric, the second Visigothic king (485–507) It was Alaric's object to remove the uncertainty and confusion prevailing in the use of the Roman law by reason of its multiple texts. He planned to epitomize the most important rules of practice. This task he intrusted to a commission of jurists, who executed it on a plan not unlike that of the later compilers of Justinian's law-books.[1] As sources they used not only the "jus" (as the Romans called it), but also the "lex" As "leges," they resorted to the Code of Theodosius (which thus for the greater part came to be preserved to us), and to the Novels of Theodosius, Valentinian III, Marcianus, Magiorianus, and Severus. As "jura," they employed the Institutes of Gaius (not in the original, but in a compendium known as "Liber Gai," designed for use in court practice and then much in vogue in Roman schools of the 300s and 400s), the "Sententiæ" of Paulus; some constitutions selected from the Gregorian and Hermogenian Codes (which, being private compilations, did not pass for "leges," though their material was "leges ") ; and a passage from the "Responsa " of Papinian The part taken from the "Liber Gai," having been originally adapted to practical use, needed no further treatment. But the remainder was furnished with an "interpretatio," that is, a commentary partly summarizing and partly paraphrasing the text, and serving to explain the obscurer rules. This commentary, however, was not (as often supposed) composed by the Gothic compilers of the Breviary, but by the Roman law teachers themselves, whose chief task in the later period of the Empire was to adapt the earlier texts to the new conditions.

At the close of their labors, the Breviary was laid by the king before the popular assembly for its approval, in the year 506, at Aire, in Gascony. The original was then deposited in the royal

---

[1] The compilers under Alaric, however (in contrast to those under Justinian), made no alterations in the text of the passages which they selected, nor did they mutilate them. In fact, whole books of the Theodosian Code were transferred into the Breviary. They merely cut out of the earlier text those parts which had ceased to be appropriate to existing social conditions, principally in the governmental organization.

archives; then a copy, prepared by Count Goiaric and authenticated by the Chancellor Anianus, was forwarded to each count in the kingdom, with a royal order, or "commonitorium," ordering that henceforth all other Roman laws be ignored and this Code alone be observed.

The Breviary remained officially in force until the change of policy on the part of the Visigothic kings

For later, upon setting to work to unify and strengthen their State, they resolved to eradicate all distinctions between their two subject races, and to this end, instead of placing the Germanic race under Roman law (as Theodoric had attempted to do in Italy), they sought to incorporate the Roman element with the invading conquerors Recesvind, therefore, towards the middle of the 600s, repealed the Breviary. Outside of his Franco-Spanish dominions, however, its vogue was not terminated, as we shall now see.

§ 9. **The Roman Laws of the Burgundians** — Gondebad, king of the Burgundians (467–516), when promulgating a written code for his own people (*post*, § 40), had promised to provide also a special law for his subjects of Roman race This Roman legislation of the Burgundians is found in the book later known under the name "Liber Responsorum " or "Responsum Papiani," or merely "Papianus." But this title is due to an error The name Papian (that is, Papinian, the classical jurist) was found inscribed, without any mark of separation, at the end of one of the manuscripts of Alaric's Breviary, a response of Papinian was in fact the last passage in the Breviary; but it was mistakenly supposed that this passage was the beginning of the Burgundian Law, which followed in the same parchment; hence the name of Papian was given to it Everything points, however, to Gondebad's having indeed fulfilled his promise, this law therefore antedates his death, which occurred in 516 This is indeed not known with certainty; for, besides the absence of any precise statement of the date, we find in one of the preambles a mention of Sigismund, the son of Gondebad, as if he were the author If, then, he is to be regarded as the author, not merely of a revision, but of the original, the earliest date for it would be 517.

The contents of this statute cover the civil law, the criminal law, and procedure A portion is taken up with provisions founded on the Burgundians' own Germanic law (of which an account is given *post*, § 40); this it follows in the order of topics and in the names of most of the forty-seven titles into which it is divided But the

Roman sources were also used, including, as was customary, the Theodosian Code, the Novels, the treatises of Gaius and Paulus, and the Codes of Gregorius and Hermogenianus   But it cannot be said with certainty whether these sources were used in their original texts or were merely followed as they appear in the Breviary of Alaric, unless, to be sure, one concedes that the Burgundian document is earlier than the Visigothic, that is, dates before 506, — an inference deducible from the circumstance that certain passages of Roman law appear in the Burgundian which are not found in the Visigothic statute.

The Visigothic Breviary, however, was in its value as a compilation of Roman law much more suited to the purpose at which both of these statutes were aiming.   And thus, when in 534 the Burgundian kingdom was overthrown by the Frankish conquest, the Breviary survived in influence the Burgundian statute, and diffused itself even among the Roman Italians who had been subject to the latter sway, as well as among those in other localities.   Throughout the Middle Ages the Breviary preserved a great authority.   In Italy, indeed, t never went out of vogue, — partly because of the intimate intercourse between Italy, Gascony, and Spain, partly because the Breviary contained a large part of the Theodosian Code already there accepted   The Frankish conquest must also have helped to spread its influence anew north of the Alps.   Charlemagne and Pepin both ordered it to be included in their legislation; and Pepin, who was the sole ruler in Italy, would not have done this if the Breviary had not in that country been authoritative.   Several manuscripts of it, indeed, have been discovered in Italy; legal documents there reveal traces of its Theodosian passages; the commentaries and the compendia of it are of Italian origin.[1]   All these circumstances go to confirm the conclusion that the Breviary, even after it had lost its legal authority in its original home of Gascony and Spain, continued in Italy to be known and used as the principal source preserving the ancient law of Rome and surviving alike in the traditional customs and in the practice of litigation.

TOPIC 2. THE ROMAN LAW OF ROME [2]

§ 10. **Roman Practice before Justinian.** — During the Byzantine epoch (476–578), though the sole seat of imperial power was

---

[1] *Patetta*, in A G S , 1891, "Il breviario alariciano in Italia "
[2] *Brandileone*, in A G.S , 1886, "Il diritto bizantino nell' Italia meridionale"; *Calisse*, "Il diritto di Teodosio in Italia," 1889 , *Ferrini*, in

at Constantinople, there persisted in Italy the conception of a
Roman State; and during that period the Roman law also dominated. No longer, however, was it Roman law in the classical
sense. On the contrary, it was far from being comparable to that
of any preceding period The Byzantine legislation of Justinian,
when promulgated in Italy towards the close of this period (554),
did indeed become the best known, and was finally to dominate
over the other bodies of law. But alongside of it (and quite apart
from any Germanic influences of the invaders' law) there survived
the older sources of Roman law. Other such sources, too, were
formed later, varying with the conditions of diverse parts of the
country. To these must be added the varieties of customary law
which developed among the inhabitants under pressure of so many
novel necessities. This multiplicity of sources gave to the Roman
law of this period certain new features. A process of transformation began, analogous to that which took place in the language
The outcome was what has since been termed Popular (or Vulgar)
Roman Law.

§ 11 Justinian's Legislation — In 554, Justinian promulgated
his Pragmatic Sanction. This general title was applied to a series
of enactments designed to restore that law and order which the
long wars had shattered. They put into force, for all regions and
persons, the Roman law, in its revised form, that is to say, as contained in Justinian's Pandects, Code, and Novels

This much, indeed, had already been done once before (as the
Pragmatic Sanction itself reveals) by Justinian, in an edict of
uncertain date — perhaps 540 or 541 — termed the "Edictale
Programma" At that time Ravenna had fallen, and the Ostrogothic king was a prisoner at Constantinople. The restoration of
imperial power in Italy seemed complete. No one could foresee
that Totila the Goth would again (though not for long) wrest
Italy from the Empire When we notice that by § 11 of the Pragmatic Sanction all the laws and acts of Totila are annulled, with
an anathema upon his name as a usurper, while those of his Ostrogothic predecessors are confirmed, we may infer, as the reason for
this distinction, that from and after the capture of Ravenna the
Italian territory was regarded as subject to the legislation of Justinian and the imperial jurisdiction, and that therefore any other
legislation was void and any rival legislator a usurper.

R I L , 1884, ser II, vol 17, "Glossa torinese' . *Fitting*, "Ueber die
sogenannte Turiner Institutionenglosse," etc, Halle, 1870, *Schupfer*, in
R A L , II, 1886, "Il diritto romano nell' Italia meridionale "

Nevertheless the period succeeding Justinian's edict of 540 had been a period of chaos in Italy. Consequently, when the victories of Narses, towards 555, regained control and brought about a final settlement, a new decree was practically called for, to readjust these conditions and to reaffirm the legislation of Justinian And thus the Pragmatic Sanction, as above stated, put it universally and actually into force.

How real was its force and how rapid its diffusion is recorded (if other evidence were needed) in various ways. For example, the legal documents of the early Middle Ages exhibit constantly the use of the Roman law [1] Expositors of the law, moreover, are found referring to it. An interesting work of this sort is the "Glossa" of Turin, composed probably (at least in its original portion) in the very period of Justinian, but certainly later than 543, as it cites a Novel of that date. Its author's care in giving definitions and etymologies shows that its purpose was to teach and make known, in the schools and at the bar, the then newly promulgated body of law. That this law is new to him is apparent from his unfamiliarity with it, while his comments on the superseded rules not only show him to be expert in them, but accord to them sometimes a greater validity than they could legitimately have after Justinian's legislation

§ 12 **Imperfect Diffusion of the "Corpus Juris."** — This continued reference to the preexisting law is not an isolated instance. Others of the sort show that Justinian did not succeed completely in supplanting in practice the Theodosian Code. Promulgated by the Emperor Theodosius in 438, at Byzantium, the Roman Senate had accepted it for Italy also. It was already ancient and familiar, national in its traditions, and entrenched in the rights and liabilities of the inhabitants. To supplant its observance by that of Justinian's laws, a long period of time would in any event have been needed, as well as a rigid exercise of State power. Neither of these things, however, could yet assist it. The rule of the Byzantine emperors was not willingly accepted Within a few years it was to be overthrown (in the greater part of Italy) by the Lombards' invasion. Furthermore, the Theodosian Code was still in acceptance among the Roman inhabitants of Gaul and of Spain, who did not acknowledge Justinian's empire and did maintain intimate relations with the people of Italy, especially in commerce. The Church, too, was interested in preserving the Theodosian

---

[1] See the collections of *Marini* and of *Fantuzzi*.

Code, for the foundations of its constitution and its liberties had been laid under the governments prior to Justinian In the schools and at the bar, moreover, the books which served to expound the law were founded on the Theodosian Code, and even when their authors attempted to set forth the new laws, they could not (as above noticed in the " Glossa " of Turin) easily detach themselves from the older learning.

If we weigh the united influence of all these circumstances, we may easily appreciate that the classic Roman law would still retain a vogue and authority even after the introduction of Justinian's books. It is at once a proof and a result of this continued vogue that we find, in the succeeding period, the Gothic domination producing numerous copies and summaries of Alaric's Breviary, which contained principally Theodosian law (as already noted in § 8), and the Lombard legislation succumbing to Roman influence and drawing many principles from the same Theodosian Code.

§ 13. Nevertheless, it must not be supposed that Justinian's legal system did not strike root in Italy. Though the northern regions fell shortly under the invading Lombards' rule, yet the central and especially the southern regions were governed from Byzantium for centuries thereafter. By this persistence of power the Byzantine law was certain to become a permanent system. And, in fact, not only did it remain long in use, but as a matter of course its later legislation also took effect there. This later law — the Græco-Roman law, properly so called — was elaborated particularly in the legislative reforms of the emperors Leo the Isaurian (739), Basilius the Macedonian (886), and Leo the Philosopher (911). This accounts for the making and using of numerous compends of Byzantine law in the southern Italian provinces, as well as for the numerous traces of it in local custom and in the subsequent legislation of the Norman and the Suabian dynasties. In Sicily, too, the Roman and the Byzantine law did not disappear, even under the dominion of the Arabs. The latter preserved for the conquered population its existing law and even its own courts. Nor was there (in some parts of Sicily), even under the Arabs, a cessation of intercourse with the Greek Empire; from which, indeed, the Sicilians hoped to obtain .that political deliverance which was afterwards bestowed on them by the Norman dynasty.

22

CHAPTER II. SECOND PERIOD: A.D. 575–900

LAW UNDER THE LOMBARD KINGDOM AND THE FRANKISH EMPIRE

§ 14. Introduction: The Mingling of Legal Systems

TOPIC 1. THE LOMBARD KINGDOM

§§ 15, 16. The Lombards and their Civilization
§§ 17–19. The Lombard Edict; its Formation and Enactment.
§§ 20–22 The Edict of Rothar.
§§ 23, 24. Supplements to the Edict
§§ 25–27. Minor Sources of Lombard Law.

TOPIC 2. THE FRANKISH EMPIRE

§ 28. Charlemagne's Dominion and its Significance.
§ 29 Charlemagne's Imperial Legislation
§§ 30, 31. The Capitularies
§ 32. Collections of Capitularies.
§ 33 Italian Capitularies
§ 34. Effect of the Capitularies.

TOPIC 3. THE GERMANIC POPULAR CODES

§ 35 The Codifying of the Germanic Tribal Customs
§§ 36, 37. Mode of Legislation.
§ 38. Relation of the Codes to Each Other
§§ 39–41. The Gothic Group (Burgundian, Visigothic)
§§ 42, 43 The Saxon Group (Saxon, Frisian)
§§ 44, 45 The Suabian Group (Alamannic, Bavarian)
§§ 46, 47 The Frankish Group (Thuringian, Chamavian, Ripuarian, Salic).

TOPIC 4. THE PERSONALITY OF LAWS

§§ 48, 49. Personality and Territoriality of Laws, contrasted.
§ 50 Personality under the Carolingian Empire
§§ 51–53. "Professions" of Personal Law
§ 54. Conflict of Laws
§§ 55, 56 Exceptions to the Rule of Personality
§ 57 Unifying Influence of the Capitularies.

§ 14. **Introduction: The Mingling of Legal Systems.** — In the Germanic period it is no longer the Roman law that dominates. That of the Germanic invaders prevails, coincidently with their supremacy in government. The conquering German tribes held the upper hand in the community. At the time of their coming into occupation of Italy, their law was as yet in the form of un-

23

written custom only   These customs were transmitted orally
from father to son   They were expounded by the older to the
younger, and were enforced in the tribunals composed of the whole
tribe   But through their associations with the Roman element of
Italy's population there came about changes, not only in their
customs, but in the degree of their civilization and in their needs
and interests   These changes soon created a demand for written
records of their ancient traditional rules. But none the less the
people themselves remained the source of authority, — no longer,
to be sure, in those miscellaneous forms of expression which contribute to customary law, but in the form of a free and formal
approval expressed in the public assemblies.

This was in entire accord with the Germanic conceptions of the
State   But these conceptions themselves came to show changes,
all in the direction of emphasizing the power of the State, concentrating authority constantly in the person of the ruler, its representative   The ruler's power, increasing in comparison with that of
the people, ended by becoming almost independent of it. This
in turn led to changes in the source of the law   Alongside of the
law made by the people there coexisted the personal ruler's law.
The rivalry thus inevitably arising was destined to issue in a system of royal law, for the king possessed means of prevailing which
the people lacked

Among these means must be reckoned the Roman law and the
Church's law. The Roman law had developed the principle that
the sovereign's will is law.   The Church's law had charged the Emperor with a mandate to watch over the welfare of the people, and
had thus tended to make him independent of them in the choice of
means to that end. Thus the Germanic law, in becoming royal,
tended to absorb into the system these same Roman and ecclesiastical principles   This powerful influence was an improving
one, but it stood in marked contrast to the primitive national elements, and tended gradually to overlay and supplant them.

Thus, on the whole, the social conditions of the time were
reflected in its law   There was the same mingling of diverse
elements, the same rivalry between them, the same reciprocal
merging and modification   When the epoch marked by these
conditions closed in its social aspect, it closed also in its legal
aspect. The law of each territory came to acquire a unity and
an independent character of its own. But by that time a new
stage had been reached both in society and in law — a period of
renascence to scientific dignity and national unity.

24

TOPIC 1. THE LOMBARD KINGDOM

§ 15. **The Lombards and their Civilization.** — Like the other tribes of Germanic invaders, the Lombards, when they came into contact with the Romans, reduced to written form their ancient customs. This took place in 643, seventy-five years after their entrance into Italy The work was not done at one stroke. The legislative process extended through the reigns of several kings; nor was it completed before the dynasty ended, for it found its fulfilment only in subsequent times. Like that of the other German tribes, the Lombard law was to experience many modifications, more, indeed, than any other. The close relations of the Roman law, which in daily intercourse with the conquered population served as a constant example, and the authority of the Church's law, which at the hands of its ministers increased steadily, effected this quite naturally. The infiltration of these more advanced elements served not only to make a real improvement in the Lombard law itself (relatively to the other Germanic laws), but to adapt it thereby to actual conditions in Italy By thus losing its character as a foreign body of law, forcibly introduced through conquest, it acquired a consistency which fitted it to endure. The other Germanic legal systems, except for slight traces preserved in subsequent laws, disappeared from Italy as soon as the influences which had imported them ceased. But the Lombard law lasted. It penetrated so deeply that it not only survived in the regions where it was planted, but it gave rise to schools of thought, received a scientific treatment, competed vigorously with the Roman law for domination, persisted in practical use until almost the modern era of codification, and remained throughout as one of the constituent elements (though a minor one) in the composite legal system of Italy.

§ 16. This period is therefore of the greatest importance in the legal as well as the political history of Italy. The Lombard conquest was both speedy and tenacious. Though it did not extend over all Italy, there was no part of the country (except the islands) which did not feel the consequences of the new masters' presence; for their possessions were scattered throughout the peninsula, and their policy was constantly an aggressive one.

Among the various invaders of Italy, none differed more from the Romans than these Lombards Entering there with hostile aims upon the Empire, they remained essentially hostile to it throughout. To the Church, too, they were hostile, — at first,

25

because they were not Christians, and later, when converted, because they were rivals of the popes in their aspirations for the control of all Italy   More than this, however, the circumstance which subtly but powerfully kept apart the two peoples was their difference in the degree of civilization and culture.   The Roman population had passed through all the stages of culture which were attainable at that era of the world's history.   Decadent though they were, the fruits of their past were certainly not lost   Their culture had a potency of revival, pending the disappearance of those external circumstances which had repressed it.   The Germanic population, on the other hand, were still in the rudimentary stages of culture, — a stage relatively far behind that of the Romans.   They succeeded, to be sure, despite this inferiority, in maintaining their national existence by sheer predominance of physical strength, and in preserving obstinately their national customs   But the result, nevertheless, was a superimposition of diverse elements; and this forms the characteristic of the epoch and supplies the explanation of its legal features.

In this place it is enough to note how this affected the form of their law.   That the Lombards were led to reduce their ancient customs to writing was due to a purpose to protect them from disuse and degeneration   They sought thereby to save their national law and their national existence itself.   Politically, indeed, their efforts proved vain, for their independence later succumbed in turn to the Frankish power   But while their predecessors, the Ostrogoths, disappeared as a national influence under the Byzantine Empire's reconquest, yet the Lombards survived the victories of the Franks   The Ostrogoths had been no more than military adventurers in Italy; and the dispersal of their forces eliminated their population   But the Lombards, without losing their military disposition, had attached themselves to the soil, tilling as well as owning it   This attachment fortified them against military and political reverses, and left them through it all a powerful element in the population of Italy.   With equal pertinacity they clung to their racial law   Throughout the history of Italy, that law maintained a foremost position and left indelible marks

§ 17. **The Lombard Edict, its Formation and Enactment** [1] — The body of the Lombard legislation was known, by its authors

---

[1] TEXTS   *Bluhme*, ed , in M G H , "Leges," IV; *Padelletti*, "Fontes' ; *Baudi di Vesme*, in M H P

TREATISES AND ESSAYS   *Pertile*, § 13; *Salvioli*, cap III, § 35, *Schupfer*, lib I, tit I, c. I, § 2 , *Savigny*, II, 14 , *Brunner*, "Rechtsgeschichte," § 53; *Merkel*, "Langobardenrecht," transl in vol III of Savigny, *supra*, *Calisse*,

themselves and in later allusion, under the name of "Edict,"[1] like that of the Ostrogoths, their predecessors (*ante*, § 4). But the reason for the Ostrogothic term, *i.e.* their vassalage to the Empire, no longer existed The Lombards were supreme, by right of conquest. Their enactments were "leges," or statutes in the strict Roman sense [2] If, then, they were nevertheless called Edicts, the use of this term was a result of the Roman conceptions still dominant in Italy. This at the outset distinguishes the Lombard laws, fo the other purely Germanic statutes, being voted by the people in the assembly, were known as "Pactus" (*post*, § 36) The Lombard assemblies also did indeed have legislative power But the royal influence upon their action increased rapidly; and finally the king's rôle so dominated that he appears sometimes as the sole author of laws. In this aspect the term Edict takes on a new significance.

§ 18. Another proof of the rapidity with which the indigenous population succeeded in impressing its superior culture upon the conquerors appears in the language of the laws. From the very first, the Lombards' native customs were reduced to writing in the language of the conquered people [3] Their own language was abandoned Lombard words (though not many) were preserved only where a corresponding Latin one was lacking. This was the case where the idea or the institution was unknown to Roman law and therefore lacked a suitable legal term in Latin. But it is noticeable that even these words rarely retained their pure Germanic forms. As the Germans knew these words well enough, they usually took pains to Latinize them or to add explanations. The explanation was given by expanding the meaning in Latin words [4] The Latinizing was done by giving to the German word

---

"Diritto ecclesiastico e diritto longobardo," Rome, 1889, *Del Giudice*, "Tracce di diritto romano nelle leggi longobarde," Milan, 1889; *Kieb*, "Edictus Rotari," 1898, *Nani*, "Le fonti del diritto longobardo," Turin, 1877, *Solmi*, "Diritto iongobardo e diritto nordico," Modena, 1898; *Tamassia*, "Le fonti dell' editto di Rotari," Pisa, 1889.

[1] "Edictum Rotari," 386 "Praesentem vero dispositionis nostræ edictum, quem Deo propitio, cum summo studio," etc, "Edictum Grimoaldi," preamble· "Superiore pagina huius edicti legitur," etc , "Edictum Liutprandi," preamble: "Rothari rex . in Langobardis edictum renovavit et instituit "

[2] This term "leges" also was used by the Lombard kings "Edictum Rotari," preamble· "Necessarium esse prospeximus præsentem corregere legem", "Edictum Liutprandi," preamble "Leges quas cristianus ac catholicus princeps," etc

[3] *Bruckner*, "Die Sprache der Langobarden," 1895

[4] *E.g* . "Edictum Rotari," 147, "ferquido, id est similem", 199, "faderfio, id est quantum pater aut frater dedit," 277, "haistan, id est irato animo"; 278, "hoberos, id est curtis ruptura ", etc.

a Latin form (and this led to its introduction into the spoken language, where indeed it sometimes became the natural and permanent expression), [1] or else, by translating the Germanic word literally by a Latin one newly formed [2] Furthermore, and alongside these various forms of words, there are presentiments of the development of an Italian language Everything heralds it. The declension endings are omitted or exchanged, prepositions are often used in connection with case endings, [3] the future is formed with " have " (whence the later Italian future ending) ; the sentence structure departs from that of classical Latin , and sometimes words are inserted which are identical with later Italian.[4] In short, the language of the Edict is that found in the documents of contemporary transactions , except that the latter vary more or less in correctness according to the individual scribe. It is the language spoken at that period by the Romans of Italy , and it illustrates the marked influence which they exercised from the very outset upon the development of the immigrant Germanic culture

§ 19 Whether Roman experts took a part in the compilation of the Edict cannot be told with certainty   Rothar mentions in the preamble the old men to whom he had resorted for ascertaining and collecting the national customs. These were undoubtedly Lombards. At the end he names Ansoald the notary, who was to authenticate with his signature the copies of the Edict ; he too was a German, as his name and his office indicate. So that the share of the Romans in the work was, if any, quite secondary. Nevertheless, the traces of Roman and of Canon law are abundant, especially in the supplements to the Edict , the texts of the imperial decrees, of the Bible, of the canons and the fathers of the Church, are continually apparent, either in identical words or in close resemblance. It is therefore quite possible that certain chosen persons among the Romans, most likely ecclesiastics, were

---

[1] E g   "Edictum Rotari," 14, "barone, ' free man ; 15, "gastaldo," bailiff , 198, " camphio," champion , "Edictum Liutprandi, " 43, " trevva," truce , "Edictum Rachimburgi," 14, "wifa " measuring level , etc

[2] E g   "arimannus, id est exercitalis " It is noteworthy that the same method was followed later in the German language, when a large number of Latin words were taken over and germanicized literally by writers and others

[3] E g   the genitive is oftener indicated by the preposition "de" than by the case ending , the Latin "ab" before an ablative changes into "ad," preparatory to its later Italian "da " , etc

[4] E g   "Edictum Rachimburgi," 8, "decernimus ut si quis cartola vinditionis alicui de aliqua res fecerit, et ad scrivane publico scripta, vel ad testibus rovorata fuerit," etc

given considerable authority and weight in the work. Such men there were, among the most learned in letters and sciences, who possessed authority at court and in the administration, especially after the conversion of the Lombards to Christianity. Their services were of value to the State in numerous modes. On the whole, they must have used their influence a good deal, to the end that the new legislation should be, not merely not hostile to the interests they represented, but a source of growing influence for the Church.

§ 20. **The Edict of Rothar.** — Rothar's Edict, then, was given a written form by the labors of his Germanic councillors, with perhaps the aid of some Romans; and was founded on the ancient customs of his nation, as gathered from its old men. It was promulgated in Pavia, in 643. This was the seventy-sixth year since the entry of Rothar's nation into Italy, the thirty-eighth year of his own age, the eighth of his reign, and he was the seventeenth king of the Lombards.

In his preamble, he tells us that his reason for reducing the laws to writing was a solicitude for the welfare of his subjects He aimed to prevent the rich from oppressing the poor, and to secure for all a tranquil life And this may indeed have been his own actual motive. But when we remember that Theodoric in his Gothic Edict (*ante*, § 4), and Justinian in his Roman Code,[1] had said much the same thing, the thought occurs that Rothar's preamble was merely an imitation of theirs. Moreover, his preamble proceeds to tell us that, for the foregoing purpose, he designed also, along with the present legislation, to amend all former laws. Now, as there was no Lombard preëxisting legislation for him to amend, this phrase could have had no meaning for him. We are therefore obliged to believe that the compilers of the Edict, without any definite meaning of their own, merely transcribed the similar expressions used in the Gothic and the Roman codes. The precise phrasing of Rothar appears indeed in one of the Novels of Justinian.[2] The true reason for Rothar's legislation must rather be sought broadly in the changes and advances of national conditions, which had rendered the ancient customs no longer suitable.

To give validity to the new laws, the king submitted them (pursuant to ancient form) to the approval of the assembly. This

---

[1] Constitutio "de novo codice facendo," § 3; Novella LXXVII and LXXXII

[2] Novella VII, preface.

was composed of the higher officers of State and the entire body of arms-bearing men (" cum primatos judices cunctosque felicissimum exercitum nostrum "). Thus the Lombards alone took part; while the Romans, politically a subject people, did not share in their conquerors' government   After the assembly's approval, the Edict was circulated throughout the kingdom, by means of copies authenticated officially by the royal notary Ansoald

§ 21   Thus it appears that a prime and marked distinction between the Edict of Rothar and the laws of his successors lay in the objects at which they aimed   Rothar aimed to bestow upon his people a written code; he therefore made a new work, demanded by the conditions of the times. His successors, on the other hand, purposed merely to improve and complete the laws already in writing, taking advantage of the experience acquired in using them and of the new principles which civic progress was developing among the Lombards.

In consequence, we observe, in the two groups of legislation, two other contrasts not less important. One difference is that the Edict of Rothar represents the pure Lombard law.   Its essentially Germanic character appears particularly in the portions that deal with paternal authority, succession, self-redress, and money fines; and herein may be noted the slight traces of other Germanic elements, infused long before, by contact with other Germanic tribes, especially the Scandinavians and the Saxons (*post*, § 42). In the later laws, on the other hand, a much larger part is played by the new elements acquired on Roman soil and leading to changes of the law.   The second difference is that the later laws, having a different object, were a series of diverse enactments, lacking in that systematic arrangement which marked the Edict of Rothar.   That Edict in fact embodied a system, as is easily perceived.   Laying aside a few miscellaneous provisions, its contents exhibit the following orderly division.   I, Penal Law (cap. 1–152), with special regard to crimes against the State and against personal security,   II, Family Law (cap. 153–266), together with the law of succession; subdivided thus. (a) inheritance (cap. 153–157); (b) marriage, and the maintenance of the family status, together with the repression of crimes relating thereto (cap. 178–223), (c) manumission (cap 224–226), III, Property Law (cap. 227–366), and its judicial protection; in particular, (a) ownership, contracts, crimes against the property of another (cap 227–358), (b) procedure (cap. 359–366), IV, Supplement, for sundry matters (cap. 367–388).

30

§ 22. The Edict of Rothar is rightly regarded as the best of the legislative works of the Germanic invaders. It rises above a mere compilation In form and in system it stands by itself, independent of any other. Unlike all the other Germanic laws, it is not merely a barren series of collected rules, but attempts to state reasons, to supply definitions, and even to develop principles of law, which are often of notable worth Here must be recognized the Roman influence, for in the other Germanic laws, which were not equally exposed to that influence, this is not apparent in such a degree. To this systematic arrangement, moreover, it may well be due that the general form of the Edict was never afterwards (as were the other Germanic laws substantially) recast by the later enactments, even when they altered (sometimes in important ways) its particular principles.

In view of the Edict's prefatory statement that it was intended for the welfare of all and especially for guaranteeing the humble against oppression, and in view of its concluding injunction to all subjects to observe it faithfully, it is plain that the Edict's legal force was universal, and included the Romans as well as the Lombards.[1] But we are not to conclude that for both alike the whole law was codified and unified. When the Edict had no express provision, or when no public policy forbade, or when no Lombard was a party, the Romans were left to be ruled by Roman law The Lombard conquerors, similarly, preserved their ancient customs where not altered by the Edict. Rothar's plan to provide rules in common for the two peoples did not extend beyond a portion of the legal field. The rest remained as it was He was careful also to define the relation of the new law both to the past and to the future. The Edict was not to be retroactive, except that pending disputes were to be governed by its rules;[2] nor was it to be conclusive against such future changes as his successors might deem needful[3]

§ 23. **Supplements to the Edict.** — The succeeding kings availed themselves of this power of amendment, and made express acknowledgment of it.[4] Grimoald, in 668, was the first to exercise it. Acting with the approval of the national Assembly, his purpose was to remove from the Edict those features which the progress of culture had rendered harsh and inequitable. In its nine chapters these new influences appear at many points, — in

---

[1] "Ed Rothari," cap 386 "hæc lex .　　firmiter et inviolabiliter ab omnibus nostris subiectis custodiatur "
[2] *Ibid.*, cap 388　　[3] *Ibid*, cap 386　　[4] Grimoald's "Edict," preface.

the greater effect conceded to a thirty years' possession, in the right of representation to nephews, in the inheritance rights of grandfathers as against uncles, in the stricter protection to the marriage relation.

Then followed Liutprand (713 to 735), who showed an extraordinary legislative activity. He added one hundred and fifty-three chapters, in fifteen groups called " Volumina," one each for the several assemblies at which he had presented his proposed laws for approval. Several causes led to this prolific legislation. One of these was the Church. Its influence grew greatly during his reign, and he was its chief instrument in moulding the law to its doctrines. This indeed he declares, in his preamble, to be his object, for he wished to employ the authority, reserved by Rothar, to modify the Edict, by making it conformable to the law of God in accordance with the inspiration of his heart, the spiritual needs of his subjects, and the peace and prosperity of his kingdom. To this purpose of his, Liutprand remained ever faithful. It was Liutprand's enactments (made, sometimes, at the direct request of the Church [1]) which introduced into Lombard law not a few of the principles advocated by the ecclesiastics, — for example, the doctrines as to bequests for masses for departed souls,[2] impediments to marriage,[3] manumission by religious ceremony,[4] the recognition of the pontifical primacy,[5] the privileges of ecclesiastics, penalties upon the surviving pagan practices,[6] and still other provisions affecting government, procedure, property, and family. The Roman law, on the other hand, made no inconsiderable impression on Liutprand's legislation. Traces of it may be seen (quite apart from the frequent imitation of terms and ideas) in the reforms introduced for woman's rights of succession, in the guardianship of minors, in prescription of rights, in wills, in mortgages, and in fact at almost every point. A third notable source of legislative changes of Liutprand is to be found in the increased power of the State, the improved organization of all public administration, and in the general development of the people both intellectually and economically. An evidence of this is seen in the judicial origin of many of his decrees. They owed their promulgation to the popular need for some new or changed rule. It frequently happened that the personal litigation brought to the assemblies called for the interpretation or the amendment of some prior statute, or even for the settlement of

[1] *Liutprand*, 33   [2] *Ibid*, 6   [3] *Ibid*, 33, 34
[4] *Ibid*, 9, 23   [5] *Ibid*, 33.   [6] *Ibid.*, 84, 85

some novel legal principle. After settling the litigation, its general principle was inserted among the statutes; and the book sometimes notes expressly that such was the statute's origin.[1]

The development of the Lombard Edict continued, after Liutprand, under two more kings, — Rachi, who in 746 added fourteen chapters, and Astolf, the last legislator of the Lombard dynasty, who from 750 to 754 added twenty-two new chapters. Astolf's chapters introduced some important reforms not hitherto provided for, notably in testamentary manumission, and in the widow's life estate. These latest laws form also an integral part of the Edict, as both of their authors are careful to repeat [2]

§ 24. At the fall of the Lombard dynasty in the second half of the 700's, it was in the duchy of Benevento (in the south) that Lombard interests centred; the immediate national aspirations, as well as the future development of the national law, were made possible in the hands of those rulers   Arechi promulgated seventeen chapters, shortly after the kingdom ended, and eight more were prepared by Adelchi in the second half of the next century. These chapters were intended by their authors to form part of the Edict. The duke Adelchi, in his preface, after recalling again Rothar's authority for this purpose, recites that Arechi had used this authority and, following the example of his nation's kings, had made amendments to the Edict by his chapters. Adelchi, doing likewise, states his wish that these other chapters, approved by the assembly, should be regarded as an integral part of Lombard legislation   The contents of the Beneventine chapters confirm this announcement of Adelchi's; for the ducal chapters fit into the laws of the Lombard kings, constantly referring to them, and even making amendments. The changes are sometimes very important, and in all instances illustrate the progress of popular opinion and necessities. For example, Arechi repeals, as impious, Rothar's statute proclaiming as a family enemy him who gave his share of the family estate to a stranger   Arechi, moreover, lays down more minute rules than ever before for reckoning the " wergild," i e. the money compensation payable for a homicide to the deceased's family   Again, he decrees that when a man is for crime condemned into servitude, the innocent wife shall remain a free woman, and that her husband's owner shall allow him such labor time as he requires for providing support for her. Among Adelchi's laws may be noted one which

---

[1] E g., ibid , 127, 135, 136, 137, 138, 141.
[2] Rachi, preamble; Astolf, preamble.

brought to an end the ancient usage of the king's treasury to make
serfs of free women marrying serfs; even their separation from
their husbands is forbidden.   Another law puts an end to the loose
and dangerous rule that a legal transaction requiring publicity
could be reduced to writing by any one whomsoever; hencefor-
ward, only notaries were to have power to do this.

In this manner did the Lombard Edict maintain itself in force
among the people, and became at the same time adapted to the
changing conditions.   Those changes of conditions were less in
the North (the native home of the Edict) than in the South.   And
thus in the North the Edict's contribution to the subsequent law
is a large and enduring one.

§ 25.   **Minor Sources of Lombard Law** — The Lombard royal
enactments, other than the statutes contained in the Edict, were
not submitted for the approval of the popular assembly, and were
thus in strictness not statutes ("leges")   Their efficacy lay only
in the power of the king who issued them.   They were known by
various names, — "capitula extra edicta vagantia," "in breve
statuta," "memoratoria," "brevia," "jussiones"   In substance,
they were merely ordinances upon matters coming within the
king's field of action, or proposed statutes preparatory to approval
by the assembly.   Astolf, for example, in a preamble [1] declares
that after examining the institutions of his predecessors he has
found some which had not been included in the Edict but ought
to be, and therefore presents them to the assembly of the people.

A few examples of these enactments survive   There is the
"Notitia de actoribus regis" (733), a series of rules for the officers
of the royal courts, in six chapters, probably by Liutprand   To
the same king (or to Grimoald) is attributed the "Memoratorium
de mercedibus magistri commacinorum," a schedule of fees for the
various services of the "magistri commacini", these were the
master builders, who went about in various parts of Italy, erecting
buildings, with a corps of affiliated workers   Since the time of
Rothar, the Edict had contained provisions about their responsibility for injuries done by them in the course of their work.[2]
Rachi also promulgated several chapters of ordinances.   One of
them makes rules for guarding the national boundaries, and for
licenses to travel to Rome on pilgrimage   Another concerns some
privileges of the royal "gasinds," i.e persons specially accredited at
the royal court   A third treats of the armor and horses required to
be furnished by the "arimans," i e the freemen composing the army.

[1] Preamble II.   [2] "Ed Rothari," 144, 145

§ 26. The dukes of Benevento also issued certain ordinances of public law, besides the above-mentioned statutes with which they continued the Edict. They include the "Pactiones de liburiis cum Neapolitanis factæ," the "Pactiones Gregorii ducis et Johannis consulis Neapolitani," and the "Pactum Sicardi." In these treaties the contracting parties give mutual assurances as to free passage through each other's territories, warranty of merchandise, safety of property, extradition, Saracenic raids, and the prohibition of slave-trading. Sicard's treaty contains an important provision for suppressing wreckers (whose practices were then in vogue throughout Europe) ; it declared that shipwrecked persons should be unmolested, and that all goods taken from them should be restored. The statute of Udino (*post*, Part II, § 19), contemporaneous with that of Sicard, contains an analogous provision.

There are also to be mentioned the twenty-eight chapters enacted by Radelgis and Siginolf for the division of the duchy of Beneventum, when a part was detached from it, in 851, to form the principality of Salernum.

§ 27. Among the subordinate sources of Lombard law should be noted also the *popular customs*. These (as already mentioned) had been only in such respects incorporated into the Edict as the legislators deemed to involve public policies. Those which had remained unchanged continued to be observed in popular practice and enforced in court, — as is indeed sometimes expressly stated in the Edict itself. For example, Liutprand tells us, in one place, that the various amounts of "wergild" (personal-injury tariff) had been settled by custom ; in another place, that the crown had always been entitled, by custom though without express statute, to the inheritance of serfs manumitted by royal act and dying without descendants. We learn from another statute that a gift is not binding unless accompanied by the "launegild," *i.e.* some sort of earnest-money or other symbolic equivalent handed over by the donee, because this rule of custom is always enforced in court, though not stated in the Edict. So, too, the judges, without statutory provision, enforced the custom for the tenant to leave behind on the land the property acquired by him during his tenancy, if the landlord reimburses their actual cost [1] It is apparent that judicial practice had its share in contributing to the preservation and development of the law. In fact, as already noted, the larger part of Liutprand's enactments had come into existence through judgments in deciding lawsuits. This relation between

---

[1] *Liutprand*, 62, 73, 77, 133.

judicial decision and statute, and its strong influence, is the more manifest, when we remember that both alike were the work of a single organ of the State, i e the popular assembly, which exercised the judicial power (at least in important cases) in addition to its legislative function.

TOPIC 2   THE FRANKISH EMPIRE

§ 28 **Charlemagne's Dominion and its Significance.** — The institutions of the Frankish period, and particularly of the Empire as re-proclaimed in the person of Charlemagne, in 800, had momentous consequences for the law of Europe. Many more peoples than ever before were united under a single sway. Many bodies of law came thus into close relation, with equal recognition and equal validity. Over these systems of tribal or popular law stood the Empire, which claimed also the lawmaking prerogative To this prerogative the Roman law contributed the principle that the Emperor was the source of law, by virtue of the people's surrender of its ancient right to him The Church also contributed the conception of an imperial authority divinely bestowed , this rendered him independent of the people and charged him with the exclusive mission of legislating for their welfare. A new fountain of law thus sprang up from the Emperor's authority. It gushed forth indeed copiously, while not exhausting but even increasing and improving the outflow of the people's own law.

But the foundation of the Emperor's authority was both Roman and Christian. Hence a new and vast potency added to the law of Rome and the law of the Church. This influence was seen in most of the new laws issued by the Emperor. The people's ancient tribal or national systems were made to slough off their antiquated parts. They were thus improved, each in its own way, and they lost those features in which they contrasted most sharply. The time was beginning for them to develop those elements which would finally weld together, to form a single new system of law for each of the nations to be

§ 29. **Charlemagne's Imperial Legislation** [1] — The legislation which emanated from the Emperor was not, of course, a " lex "

---

[1] TEXTS *Boretius-Krause,* in M G.H , "Leges," Sect II ; *Padelletti,* "Fontes."

TREATISES AND ARTICLES *Pertile,* "Storia," § 30, *Salvioli,* "Manuale," c 5, *Schupfer,* "Manuale," p 117, *Brunner,* "Rechtsgeschichte," § 54; *Boretius,* "Die Capitularien im Langobardenreich," Halle, 1864; *Idem,* "Beitrage zur Capitularienkritik," Leipzig, 1874; *Gaudenzi,* article "Capitolari," in "Digesto Italiano"; *Patetta,* "Sulla introduzione in Italia della collezione di Ansegiso," Turin, 1890.

or statute, in the strict sense of either the primitive Germans or the early Romans; for the people had not shared in its enactment. None the less, it was given practically the full force of a statute. The revived imperial dignity dominated over the ancient popular institutions. This is seen, for example, in the disappearance of leaders or officers of the people having powers and duties in their own right, such as the Lombard dukes All officials now, from lowest to highest, owed office to the Emperor-King. He appointed, directed, removed them. They were thus mere instruments of his commands and policies. Another reason was the decline of the popular assemblies. The greater part of the freemen no longer kept up their attendance They were scattered over too wide a region; local interests were more exacting; there were dangers and expenses in a long journey. Thus their interest waned in the affairs of the central government. The officeholders — the Emperor's nominees — were almost the only ones to attend Thus the national assembly transformed itself into a royal council; and the king took advantage of this to increase his own power. The popular courts of justice, it is true, survived But over them was the royal tribunal,—an " aula regis," — whose judgments prevailed and furnished new precedents for citation in the lower courts The entire ancient constitution thus bowed under the weight of the royal power.

Among the many ways of securing in the royal hands a virtual legislative power, it remains to notice his " ban," or sanction, by which he enforced the execution of laws. This was only a fine, — not however a fine imposed on a lawbreaker for violating that public peace of which the king was the protector, but a fine for the personal offence done to him, in violating his royal command. And this " ban " of the king came thus to signify no less than the " lex " of the people

Another and equally important cause of the increased power of royal enactments was the steady increase in the number of subjects who had personal relations of dependence with the king. These persons bound themselves, by an oath of personal fealty, to obey his commands; they were his vassals. He in his turn bestowed on them " beneficia," that is, lands in feud or fee, liable to be retaken from them in case of disloyalty, and thus calculated to produce obedience to his ordinances. Such was the feudal system in its beginnings.

There is here a striking analogy between this imperial Germanic law and the pretorian (" honorary ") law of Rome, in the methods

of development. Neither was a " lex "; yet both had in practice
the effect of a " lex," by reason of the magistrate's power and
methods   They corresponded closely in their purpose and their
results.   The pretorian system developed and improved the native
law of Rome by using the new elements that had arisen in Roman
national life , its ancient rigidity was modified; it became fitted
to apply to others than the citizens only. So, too, the imperial
Germanic law, making use of advanced principles, and applying
these to the crude material of the tribal laws, enabled them to
progress.   By using rules which all the inhabitants must recognize
in common, it tended to remove the native crudities, and to meet
the needs of social progress, and thus at last to round out a single
system of law

§ 30. **The Capitularies.** — The various sorts of royal legal documents had borne varying names, — " notitiæ," " brevia," " decreta," " auctoritates," " edicta " (*ante*, § 25).   But when they
came to be genuinely royal *laws* (in the sense that the king, without
the people, enacted them), they were then known by a specific
term, " Capituli," or Capitularies. This name, to be sure, was
ancient enough. It had been used by Liutprand and Astolf in
the Lombard Edict, " capitula " signified the separate articles
in the Edict, and " capitulare " the articles or Edict as a whole.
But in the sense of a royal legislative act, " capitulary " was not
used until such legislative efficiency was a political fact, — that
is to say, not until the development of the royal power in the
Frankish epoch, when the Carolingian dynasty had supplanted the
Merovingian.

Here the influence of the Church's phraseology had probably
some share   The Church gave the name " capituli " to the canons
of a church council and to the ecclesiastical ordinances.   The
transfer of the term is easily understood when we perceive that the
king's laws were often mere repetitions of the Church's rules, and
that the State maintained the directest sort of union with the
Church, in legislation as in all other public affairs.

The scope of the " capitularies," which thus became, both in
tenor and in efficacy, the formulation of the royal legislation, was
of the widest   Matters lay and clerical, public and private,
political and administrative, civil and military, commercial and
educational, domestic and foreign, were all brought within the
royal jurisdiction, and were subjected to restatement and reform.
The validity of the capitularies was that of a general law, applicable to all subjects of the Empire, without any of the ancient re-

38

strictions as to personal nationality or the like   The source of their authority being unlimited, they served as rules for the conduct of all

The capitularies were required to be proclaimed and placed on record   The *proclamation* could take place in several ways   If made at a national assembly, copies were given to the barons who attended; these took them back to their fiefs and there published them by a public reading in the churches or at other popular gatherings.   Again, the chief of the royal chancery sent out authenticated copies to the higher officials, lay and ecclesiastic, who did likewise to their subordinates, and so on until the contents were universally made known.   Or, finally, the royal itinerant deputies (" missi ") were charged to carry copies into their districts, on their periodic journeys of inspection.   The *recording* was done by depositing the original in the royal archives   There were indeed no registers, corresponding to the " commentarii " of the Roman imperial archives ; hence much inconvenience, an impossibility of ready reference, and a risk of disappearance.   And, in fact, there were very many capitularies which even the royal chancery itself was later unable to find or to remember , so that it was obliged to resort to collections of them made by other persons.

§ 31. The capitularies may be classified into several groups   A first division, made according to their subject, is that of ecclesiastical and secular.   The *ecclesiastical* concerned the persons, property, functions, and other interests of the Church   Often they were nothing more than the canons or the decrees of councils or popes, inserted into the civil legislation, by the Emperor as protector of the faith, to give them a State sanction.   The other capitularies, *i.e. secular* or lay, may be further subdivided in several ways. They were either general or special , *i e.* they applied either to the whole Empire or to a part only.   But a more important division was based on their purpose, *i.e.* either to add to some existing law, or to stand as independent

The former sort, " capitula legibus addenda," were issued to supplement or to amend existing laws, — either some specific " lex " of the people (such as the supplements to the " Leges Saxonum," " Salica," " Bavariorum," " Ripuaria," " Longobardorum"), — or the general body of all laws   If they were thus annexed to some specific law, they shared its features, and in particular that of being " personal," *i.e.* not binding upon any except the specific nationality " professing" that body of law (*post*, § 48). But if they were applicable to the general mass of laws or to that of

a particular country (as were the so-called "Italian capitularies,"
for example), their force extended to all the inhabitants of the
country named.   In the latter case, for greater validity, they were
ordinarily submitted to the national assembly, and thus became
"leges" in the strict sense.   But this procedure was not indispensable   Often their presentation to the assembly consisted
merely in a formal communication of them, or in a substitution of
the signatures of the higher officials on behalf of the assembly
This virtual independence was a mark of the royal power, which was
now free from any other interference wherever it saw need of legislation.[1]

The other group of capitularies, "capitula per se scribenda,"
consists of those which have no reference to a specific law, and are
made applicable to all subjects   Their validity was territorial,
not "personal," in extent.   These exhibit the really royal law,
which by them attained its purposes   They were independent of
any vote of the national assemblies.   They secured their effect
(as above stated) by means of the "ban" and the oath of fealty.
The assembly, to be sure, was sometimes consulted.   This was
because no fixed line then divided the royal and the popular prerogatives   One or the other is found prevailing, according to the
personality of the ruler and the conditions of the country.   At
times when the royal power preponderated, the royal enactments,
though lacking popular sanction, are found enforced in the popular
courts   At other times, the king volunteered (or the people
forced him) to request the assembly's assent to a decree which
intrinsically might have dispensed with it — It may be added that
the king, as the author of the capitularies, had the power to repeal
a capitulary, whether his own or a predecessor's.

Among those capitularies which did not serve to supplement
preexisting laws, the "capituli missorum" had a distinctive character.   The "missi" were the magistrates sent out by the Emperor
periodically into different regions, to inform themselves on the
conduct of his vassals, or on other matters of public interest.
These capitularies are made up, in part, of the ruler's instructions

---

[1] It is noticeable, however, that no capitularies supplementing the
Roman law are found, although the Roman law at this period ranked
also as a "personal" law (post, § 48)   The reason given by the legislators
themselves ("Edictum pistense," A D 864, c 20, etc , Boretius, I, 145) is
that no one could suppose the Roman law capable of improvement   Yet,
in view of the imperial theory that the Frankish emperor succeeded to the
Roman emperor's authority, his legislative power was complete, not being
bound by the constitutional checks upon his power over the Germanic
national laws

to the "missi" how to perform their duties, *e g* how to identify the various "personal" laws (*post*, § 48). They contain decisions or responses to requests or inquiries made by the "missi" concerning their office, *e.g.* a ruling that they should strictly apply the Roman law principles when applicable. They contain also warrants of authority, as when the "missi" were charged to try some cause falling within the king's jurisdiction, or to proclaim a military levy, or to do some other act ordinarily beyond their authority.

§ 32 **Collections of Capitularies** — The large number of the capitularies, and the manner of their preservation, soon made the need felt of some systematic collection, which should arrange them in order and preserve them from the risk of loss No official provision was made for this. As at Rome, in the Theodosian epoch, so now it fell to private persons to satisfy the demand. Among the several collections which ensued, two merit attention The first is that of Ansegisus of Fontanelle, in the diocese of Rouen, a man of noble family, intimate at the Carolingian court Moved (as he says) by affection for his royal masters, by the love of learning, and by a desire for the welfare of Church and people, he set his hand to the task, which was finished in 827. Arranging the entire body of capitularies in four books, he placed in the first and the third books the ecclesiastical and the secular capitularies, respectively, of Charlemagne, and in the second and the fourth books the same two kinds by Louis. Within each book, the order of dates was followed. In three appendices were the capitularies of the "missi," with others not before known to him The total numbered only twenty-nine, which shows what wide dispersion of copies must have taken place by the epoch of Ansegisus, for the number of capitularies which we now possess, dated during the period covered by his collection, is more than four times as great. This difficulty, then experienced, of obtaining the texts, explains how Ansegisus' work came to obtain a wide vogue. Numerous manuscripts of it have been found, some in Italy, which suggests that its use extended even to that country, and accounts for its having quickly received an official status. Louis himself, for example, when he had to refer to his own and his father Charlemagne's capitularies, cited them from Ansegisus, Charles the Bald had copies made for his "missi," to serve for a text of the older capitularies, which were no longer recoverable And this royal countenance was, after all, well deserved by Ansegisus; for his work is a faithful reproduction of the originals He made only trifling alterations, such as to divide a single capitulary into two when its topics, being both ecclesiastical and secular, fell into separate books by his plan.

The same praise cannot be given to the other collection, appearing in the middle of the 800s, in the name of Benedict Levita. It has two prefaces, one in prose and one in verse. They profess that the author was a deacon of the church at Mainz on the Rhine, and by order of Archbishop Aucarius had continued the work of Ansegisus, by adding (in three books and four appendices) all the capitularies which were unknown to Ansegisus but had been rescued by searching in various places, particularly in the archives of Mainz. All this was duly credited, in the author's own epoch, and the book became authoritative. But the compilation was in truth a mere forgery. It belongs in the same class of Frankish forgeries of the 800s as the so-called Capitularies of Angilramnus and the Decretals of Isidorus. Its lack of genuineness is apparent from the very tenor of the supposed capitularies, which are really a mosaic of various well-known sources, such as the Theodosian Code (*ante*, §§ 3, 8, 12), the Breviary of Alaric (*ante*, § 8), the Epitome of Julian, the Germanic " leges," the Bible, the Church canons, and patristic writings. Besides this, certain of its assertions betray their own falsity, — as, that the book was compiled in Mainz, by order of Archbishop Aucarius; whereas his successor Rabanus was unacquainted with it, while at the same period it was in common circulation in western France. There in fact it originated. The motive lay in the Church's disorganized condition in that region. Not being able to free itself by regular methods from the influence acquired by the lay members, it sought to do so by the authority of these supposed capitularies These, rescued from oblivion, and needing no further sanction of king or parliament, contained the provisions apt for reforming abuses and for strengthening the clergy's independence of the secular powers. The Church resorted for succor to this imaginary law. It was precisely the same kind of emergency that gave rise to the forgeries known as the Decretals of Isidorus; indeed, they share the same country of origin, the same period, style, and sources, and perhaps the same author.

The Levita collection did not remain unknown in Italy; for the Church conceded its authority, until the forgery was discovered. But Italy was then (like the other parts of the Empire) in its own peculiar political condition, and made little use of foreign collections of capitularies.

§ 33. **Local Italian Capitularies.** — Italy was now an autonomous kingdom within the Empire. Its civilization was relatively the most advanced one. Thus, though subject to the expanding imperial power of the Carolingians, its circumstances gave rise to a special Italian law.

The general capitularies, valid throughout the Empire, were valid also for Italy; either by sole imperial authority or by approval of the general assembly. In this assembly (as in those of the other Germanic peoples) the local population was represented, though by the higher officials, particularly the ecclesiastics. But the Italians, relying upon their own legal and political traditions, put forward the claim that these capitularies should receive the assent of the assembly before they could possess the force of law. This claim was disputed by Charlemagne, who wrote to King Pepin to pay no heed to it, and to exact obedience to all imperial capitularies.[1] Louis the Pious, following his father's example, refused also to yield. But when the time came that the monarchy, enfeebled and threatened, needed the help of the Italian magnates, who had then become feudal chiefs, the royal resistance was withdrawn. In 832 Lothar I was obliged to submit to the Assembly at Pavia a revision of the entire body of capitularies, beginning with those of Charlemagne. A selection was enacted, known as the "Constitutiones Papienses," [2] including many of the general capitularies unchanged; and thus they became a local law for Italy.

These capitularies — that is to say, those of Charlemagne, Pepin, Louis I, Lothar, and Louis II (for the later ones fall without the Frankish epoch), — were such as particularly concerned Italian interests. They were both "per se scribenda" and "legibus addenda" (*ante*, § 31) The former applied territorially throughout the several parts of the kingdom without distinction of "personality" (*post*, § 48). The latter were amendments of the separate "personal" law systems in Italy; but in fact they affected Lombard law only; for the Roman law had never been amended by the capitularies (*ante*, § 31), and the other Germanic tribal laws (Burgundian, Frankish, etc.) had been amended only by general capitularies not especially applicable to Italy.

Thus the capitularies "legibus addenda" for Italy were those "ad legem Langobardorum addita," *i.e.* affecting only the Lom-

---

[1] Cap. 141; ed. *Padelletti*.

[2] "Haec sunt capitula quae dominus Lotharius rex, una cum consensu fidelium suorum, excerpsit de capitulis Karoli avi sui ac Ludovici genitoris sui"

bard law, and serving to develop it The Frankish conquest
of 774 had not put an end to the Lombard kingdom, but merely
changed the ruling family and the political system. Charlemagne
himself had declared that he intended only to improve the Lombard Edict, by supplying its deficiencies and by removing its
obscurities, so as to leave no room for the variable notions of the
judges or the usurpation of powerful nobles And indeed (were
it here proper to examine details) we should discover that this
purpose was precisely carried out. The amendments were marked
by a greater protection and vigilance (as the spirit of the age
demanded) for the interests of the Church. The administration
of justice was reformed, both in the magistracy (by substituting
" scabini," or popular judges,[1] for the whole body of freemen),
and in the procedure, and in the method of criminal repression.
In the civil (private) law were introduced measures for the government of the family, for the elevation of the marriage relation, for
individual responsibility, for the settlement of property rights,
and in general for adapting the ancient Lombard law to the
changed social and political circumstances.

Thus there arose, to supplement the collections of general capitularies, collections appropriate for Italy The chief one bears
the name " Capitulare Italicum," and dates from the second half
of the 900s. It is the work of jurists of Pavia, and will be examined in its proper place (*post*, Part II, § 17)

§ 34 **Effect of the Capitularies** — In whatever aspect we regard
the capitularies, — whether as general, or special, or " personal,"
— we see that they affect the entire law, in its broadest sense.
For law, they were what the Empire was for politics They served
to unify society into that harmony of government and morals
typified by the union of State and Church, without, however,
destroying the autonomy of the various peoples united under the
Empire Thus they did not supplant the preëxisting systems of
Germanic law, but stood alongside of them, — aiding their development, amending them, supplying their defects, and giving a unity
of purpose It was natural that the capitularies should be the
most important legal sources in their own day, and that their effects
should be recognizable long afterwards in later epochs. They
were one of the most civilizing influences of the Middle Ages. Like
the constitutions of the Roman emperors, which with slow, incessant labor completed the edifice of Rome's law, they introduced the
elements of universality, of moral philosophy, and of Christianity

[1 " Schoffen " in Germany , a sort of juror or lay justice — TRANSL]

Topic 3.   The Germanic Popular Codes [1]

§ 35. **The Codifying of the Germanic Tribal Customs.** — The
Germanic tribal laws (sometimes termed " people's " laws, more
commonly " barbarian " laws — " leges barbarorum ") were those
made by the " people " or general assembly of freemen. This
feature, and the name " popular," marks them off from the capitularies. Each of the tribes united in the Empire kept up its
own system, coexisting with the common law of the capitularies.
In Italy, as the centre of the Empire and of the Church, was seen
the greatest mingling of the various tribes and races, — not only
of the numerous Frankish conquerors, but of all the others. Thus
the other tribal laws came to be applied in Italy, and some of them
to take firm root.

The original sources of the tribal laws were their ancient customs,
from time to time put into writing. This process was going on
from the middle of the 400s (the fall of the Western Roman
Empire) to the beginning of the 800s, as the Germanic tribes
settled down into permanent contact with the Roman civilization.
They felt its influence, and a complete social change ensued

On the fall of the Roman Empire, the right of legislation —
hitherto solely the Emperor's — passed to those who found themselves masters of the several provinces. The need for such legislation was serious. Peoples occupying the same territory would
be found differing in customs, in needs, and in ways of governing
The promises made to the conquered Roman race were to be kept,
the duties of the vanquished were to be exacted, and all mutual
relations regulated. The conqueror's law, if it were to continue
as mere unwritten custom, would suffer in competition with the
highly developed Roman law. And so it came to pass that the
laws of Lombards, Franks, and some others were voluntarily
committed to writing   Still other tribes, however — the farthest
north — did so by command of Charlemagne   It was that ruler's
ambition, in thus consolidating the imperial institutions, not
merely to define the imperial powers, but to protect his weaker

[1] Text *Canciani*, B L A , *Walter*, C I G.I; the editions in M G.H.
are given *post*, under the respective codes
   Treatises and Articles *Pertile*, "Storia," § 12; *Salvioli*, "Manuale,"
II, c. 4; *Schupfer*, "Manuale," p 45, *Brunner*, R.G., § 37, and Gr.
Z , § 13; *Davoud-Oghlou*, "Histoire de la législation des anciens Germains,"
Berlin, 1845; *Gaudenzi*, "La legge salica e gli altri diritti germanici,"
Bologna, 1884, *Gengler*, "Germanische Rechtsdenkmäler," 2 vols , Erlan-
gen, 1875, *Stobbe*, "Geschichte der deutschen Rechtsquellen," Braun-
schweig, 1860–1864

subjects from the oppression of the stronger This same motive
had already been recorded by Theodoric the Goth (*ante*, § 4) and
by Rothar the Lombard (*ante*, § 17) And now Charlemagne the
Frank, not content with having caused some of the tribal systems
to be codified, called an assembly at Aix-la-Chapelle (Aquisgrana),
in 802, and proposed a compilation of the laws of all the tribes. He
ordained that those already in writing should be revised, and the
others now be reduced to writing. Thus came into being the
various tribal codes which we now possess.

The importance of the new economic and religious conditions
must here not be forgotten. The industrial life of the Germanic
tribes, after they settled in the Romanized regions of France,
Spain, and Italy, was quite altered. The values of things changed,
and likewise the modes of determining values. New incentives
and standards grew up. The system of compensation or penalties
for wrongs (which had consisted merely in a graded schedule of
fixed amounts) was particularly one of the things bound to alter
under the new conditions, and to make the need of a code keenly
felt. There was also the fact of the Germanic tribes' conversion
to Christianity, for the new regulations were not a part of the
ancient traditions, and were sometimes even hostile to pagan
customs And finally, the spread of a new civilization — under
the influences of Roman culture and the Church — had forced
upon their laws a spirit of progress, and stimulated them to confirm that progress by recording it.

§ 36. **Mode of Legislation** — By Germanic tradition, in recording or in amending a tribal law, the popular assembly, being the
supreme lawmaking power, would have to be summoned. Hence
the name "pactus" given to such legislation (in earlier times,
"ewa"), to mark its foundation in the popular consent, — a
meaning precisely similar to that of "lex," in Roman history, for
laws voted at the ancient "comitia," or assemblies The term
"judicium" was also applied to the vote of a popular assembly,
but only when acting in its rôle as a popular tribunal for lawsuits.
The terms "edictum" and "decretum," which are also found, are
merely adaptations from Roman law, and exhibit the growing
tendency of the king to share in lawmaking

The older of these Codes were begun and completed by the people.
This was true of the "Lex Salica," made "by common accord"
(as the phrase went) of all the Franks and of their chiefs (*post*,
§ 47) So, too, the earlier Alamannic Code, which always kept
the name "pactus." So, too, the earlier laws of those tribes

which for a long time maintained themselves without mixture of race elements. But in other Codes — mainly those which had most undergone the Romanizing influence — the people had taken a much less share. Usually this consisted in approving the proposals made by the king, who was the real principal in this legislation. Such was the Lombard Edict's history. Its provisions are attributed to the king; the people are noted merely as assenting. So, also, with the Burgundians, whose king Gondebad was able to say that their " lex " arose from " the king's preparation and the common will of all " And Charles the Bald likewise declared that the " lex " was made " by decree of the king and assent of the people."

§ 37. Whatever the varying circumstances that led to putting the ancient customs into codes, the method of preparation was always to give to the elders of each nation (who would best know the traditions) the task of collecting the rules. This function was termed " dictare legem," — a phrase borrowed from the Roman questor's " leges dictandæ " The elders were to formulate the rules of the native law, and then the popular assembly (Lombard, Burgundian, and so on) was to approve them. The elders (" antiqui homines ") are expressly mentioned by Rothar as those whom he consulted for drafting his Lombard Edict Theodoric the Goth, for the Salic Code, " elegit viros sapientes, qui legibus antiquis eruditi erant." Charlemagne the Frank, for the Frisian Code, appointed the " sapientes " Vlemar and Sasmond (*post*, § 43), and referred to the Code as " a sapientibus composita."

In drafting the Codes, the Latin language was used, — not the classical, to be sure, but the " low " Latin out of which the Romance languages later developed. The text was interspersed with Germanic terms, either literally reproduced or crudely transmogrified by Latin terminations (*ante*, § 18) [1] The general practice of using Latin for the Codes testifies to the Roman influence in the Germanic law. With such Latin, naturally there was a poverty of expression for the legal ideas. The older and more primitive the law, the harder the work of expression. Often the Code contained little other than a minute specification of offenses, and a lengthy list of the punishments, especially the fines or damages. Nor, indeed, was it intended to include the whole of the native law, but only the part that most needed a recording The greater part remained in unwritten custom, and this went on

[1] The Anglo-Saxon Code was the only exception, it was entirely in the native language.

being inserted in the Code from time to time, whenever controversy arose, or the risk of desuetude was pressing   The Codes were thus always receiving additions. This feature (though it hindered them from providing a completed system), adapted them to develop and improve the law, and prevented them from losing touch with the rapid changes of culture peculiar to such a period

This general method of expansion, though common to all the Germanic peoples, varied in particulars. The Lombards, for example, made their amendments and additions by appending them to the original Code, in order of time, so that one may trace plainly the path of development   In the Burgundian Code, on the other hand, the additions were made by inserting them under the suitable topic, while the original section was sometimes left intact and sometimes struck out; so that the prior text cannot always be distinguished or restored, and the history of the system is now often obscure to us

§ 38 **Relation of the Codes to Each Other.** — All these Germanic Codes show certain resemblances and certain differences. The differences arise from the peculiarities of the various peoples. They embrace the form of the Code, the kinds of penalties, the assembly's share in the administration, the extent of foreign rules incorporated, the territorial scope, the date of compilation, the imperial or popular share in their origin. The resemblances arise from the community of that racial stock whence came all the Germanic peoples. As their dialects descended from one original language, so their legal systems flowed from one common body of customs. Certain elements reappear constantly in all, — the composition (or money-payment) for offenses, the popular assembly as a court of justice, the family ownership of estates, the agnates (relationship through males) as prevailing over the cognates (blood-relationship in general), the restrictions on individual ownership, the inalienability of property by will, and numerous other features.

In another aspect, too, some (but not all) of the Codes show an affinity, — the result of a reciprocal influence of one on the other. This came about in two ways. The contact of location was one of these   The Lombards, for example, embodied in their Code some of the Saxon rules, for these two had migrated together into Italy, and remained there for some time in company. The other way was by one people's deliberately using another of the Codes as model when they came to reducing their own customs to writing.

48

In this way are explainable the marked traces of Visigothic law which appear in the Bavarian Code (*post*, § 45).

Attempts have been made to classify the various Codes into groups based on these resemblances and differences. But such attempts must be treated with caution. We do not accurately know the history of the various compilations, — partly for lack of records, and partly because what little has been handed down to us contains much that is misleading. However, the usual classification is into four groups   the *Gothic* (including the Visigothic and the Burgundian Codes), the *Frankish* (including the Salic, Ripuarian, Chamavian, and Thuringian Codes), the *Saxon* (embracing the Saxon, the Anglo-Saxon, and the Frisian Codes, as well as the Lombard, — though this is practically a distinct one from all the others), and the *Suabian* (including the Alamannic, and its scion the Bavarian Code).

§ 39. **The Gothic Group (Burgundian, Visigothic)** — These two Codes — the Visgothic and the Burgundian — bear a strong resemblance to each other, which thus sets them apart from the rest. Instead of merely collecting their customs or reducing to writing a few most needed rules, these two peoples set themselves the task of formulating a complete system, adequate to cover all the realm of law, public and private. The strong impress of Roman law is here to be seen. Each of the peoples had already become deeply Latinized. Each of them, moreover, formed a kingdom under the Roman Empire in the days before its fall (*ante*, §§ 2–8), and thus was bound to be susceptible to the dominion of the Roman law. Both in substance and in form the effect was seen. Hence, in no little degree, a reason why the southern provinces of Gaul (lower France and upper Italy) remained for centuries distinct in their legal development from the northern regions where the Germanic race, independent and unmixed, continued to bear sway

§ 40. The history of the *Burgundian Code* is not easy to reconstruct.[1] The records are scanty, and the successive changes of the original text cannot be accurately traced. The first author was certainly King Gondebad (474-516). The text ascribes it to him;

---

[1] TEXTS   *Bluhme*, in M G H , "Leges," vol III; *De Salis, ibid*, Sectio I, Tomus II, 1892; *Valentin-Smith*, "Loi Gombette," Paris, 1889–1890
   TREATISES AND ARTICLES   *Dareste*, "La loi Gombette," in J S, 1891, July; *Hubé*, "Histoire de la formation de la loi Bourguignonne," in R.H.B F.E , 1867, vol. XIII; *Zeumer*, "Zur Textkritik und Geschichte der Lex Burgundionum," in N A , vol XXV, p 259 , *Bluhme*, preface to his edition of the Lex, in M G H , "Leges," vol. III.

it bore his name ("gondebada"), and those who acknowledged it as their "personal" law were called "gondebadi" It was built out of decrees made by Gondebad and his predecessors He promulgated it in his so-called "prima constitutio" It was made obligatory, not only on the (Germanic) Burgundians themselves, but on their Roman subjects in all transactions with Burgundians, thus leaving Roman law in force only as between Romans. The date (which is doubtful) must have been after 499; because up to that date Gondebad (who is given as the sole author) was sharing the throne with his brothers. We may sufficiently credit the Code's preface, which places the date as the second year of Gondebad's reign, i.e. 501 [1]

Gondebad's lawmaking activity did not end with this Code. Like the Roman emperors, he issued "novellae," i e additional decrees; which, however, were not appended chronologically, but were inserted at the proper points in lieu of the original text. The later kings — especially his immediate successor, Sigismund — continued this practice. Sigismund, indeed, was later thought to be the author of the Code; and if he was not its author in its final form, he did at least complete its adaptation to the needs of the times.

This obscurity as to its historic growth is partly due to the lack of order in its arrangement Its provisions fall into three parts. Titles 1 to 41, which seem the oldest, are perhaps the earlier decrees retained by Gondebad. Titles 42 to 88, which are later, are in better form; they note the dates, give reasons, refer to earlier laws which they sometimes amend, and represent perhaps Gondebad's own text Titles 89 to the end are a medley, and could not have been part of the original text, they probably represent Sigismund's additions

When the Burgundian kingdom fell (in 534) at the hands of the Franks, its Code, made by a heterodox (Arian) sect of Christians, met opposition from the Frankish clergy. But it succeeded in preserving its validity for the Burgundians as their "personal" law.

§ 41. The *Visigothic Code* had a greater importance.[2] Its history has two periods, corresponding to its two parts

---

[1] *Schupfer*, "Manuale," p 90, confirms this opinion on additional grounds

[2] TEXTS · *Zeumer*, "Leges Visigothorum antiquiores," Hannover, 1894

TREATISES AND ARTICLES *Bluhme*, "Zur Textkritik des Westgothenrechts," Halle, 1872, *Dahn*, "Westgothische Studien," Wurzburg, 1872;

The first is known as the *Antiqua* — the name by which it is referred to in the later one But the Antiqua itself was composed of compilations and additions to the work of earlier legislators. Of these, the first was King Euric (466–483). Isidorus, bishop of Seville, tells us that Euric was the first king to give written laws to the Visigoths, who before then had been governed by unwritten custom only This assertion is confirmed by the state of things immediately ensuing the fall of the Western Roman Empire (476). Euric would have then had a strong motive to declare laws for his people, in the desire both to increase the independence just attained by his kingdom and to regulate the new social conditions which prevailed.[1] This Code, moreover, the earliest Germanic instance, came to serve as a model for ensuing ones. Other Germanic peoples would naturally be inspired to follow in the same path. Distinct traces of the Visigothic Code appear in the Salic, the Burgundian, the Lombard, and particularly the Bavarian Code.

According to the same Isidorus of Seville, Euric's laws were revised and enlarged by Leovigild (569–586); and according to others, the latter's son, Reccared (586–601), did likewise, moved by his people's change from the Arian to the Roman religious faith But none of these revisions (more or less obscure as to their scope) made any essential change in Euric's original compilation. It remained the fundamental law of the kingdom, until the later social mutations affected a general change of law

The two important factors in this progress were, first, the constantly increasing power of the Church, and, next, the gradual and complete fusion of the Germanic and Roman populations. The continuance of two systems of law, Roman and Germanic, side by side, became an anachronism. And since it was out of the question to substitute either one entirely for the other, it came about in the reigns of Kindasvind (641–652) and Recesvind (649–672) that the two were fused into a single system, suited to the conditions of the times. Both these kings, especially Recesvind,

---

Gaudenzi, "Un' antica compilazione di diritto romano e visigoto con alcuni frammenti delle leggi di Eurico," Bologna, 1886, *Rinaudo*, "Legge dei Visigoti," Turin, 1886, *Tardif*, "Leges Visigothorum," in N R H D, 1891, vol. XV, *Waitz*, "Abhandlungen zur deutschen Verfassungs- und Rechtsgeschichte," 1896; *Zeumer*, "Geschichte der Westgothischen Gesetzgebung," in N A., vols XXIII, XXIV, XXVI

[1] To Euric were formerly attributed certain fragments of laws discovered by *Gaudenzi* ("New Fragments of the Edict of Euric," R I S G , 1888, vol VI) But this ascription has not been generally accepted The preferable view is that the Fragments belong to the Ostrogothic legislation in Italy, *Schupfer*, "Manuale," p 78; *Paletta*, in A.G S , 1898, vols. XXII, XXIII.

promulgated numerous decrees He declared the Breviary of
Alaric (*ante*, § 8), the code for Roman subjects, to be abolished.
Uniting with his own enactments some of Kindasvind and those
parts of the Antiqua which were worth preserving, he compiled
the second Visigothic Code, known ever since as *the* "Leges Visi-
gothorum " It appeared in 654, and was made binding alike upon
Visigoths and Romans within his kingdom (of Spain and lower
France)

The Antiqua had not been divided into topics, but merely arranged by numbered chapters The new "Leges," however, were
classified (like Justinian's Code) into twelve books, each divided
into titles, and the titles into chapters or "constitutions." Each
constitution bore its royal author's name (as in the Roman codes),
or noted that it had been based on the Antiqua or its amendments

But this was not the last of the Visigothic compilations An
enlarged and later one is attributed to King Ervig (680–687), and
is known as "Lex Visigothorum Ervigiana." To this Egica added
some words, and his son Vitica (701–710) followed his example.
The style of this work is bombastic and prolix. It abounds in moral
reflections and tedious explanations The enactments are couched
as commands. But both in its latinity and its tenor it is superior
to any of the other Germanic codes, — imitating, as it closely does,
the Roman law and the Church's canons. For this reason it was
taken as a model, and served as a source for several of the Codes
of the other Germanic peoples. It acquired such popular vogue
that it survived the fall of the Visigothic monarchy at the hands of
the Arabs, in the regions where they did not penetrate. And even
after their expulsion, it was restored in some places; for example,
in Cordoba, where Ferdinand III of Castile, in the 1100s, translated into Spanish its latest text, as the "Fuero " (or local code)
of Cordoba

§ 42. **The Saxon Group**. — Leaving out of present consideration the law of the Anglo-Saxons,[1] we find in this group the laws
of the Saxons and of the Frisians.

The *Saxon Code*[2] is one of those whose origins are wrapped in
obscurity. There is controversy whether it was originally composed as a whole, or is of diverse periods and workmanship. The

---

[1] [The full consideration of this branch of the Saxon law in English
legal histories makes unnecessary any treatment of it here. — TRANSL]
[2] TEXTS *Richtofen*, in M G H , "Leges," V.
　　TREATISES AND ARTICLES *Gaupp*, "Recht und Verfassung der alten
Sachsen," 1837, *Merkel*, "Lex Saxonum," 1853, *Richtofen*, "Zur lex
Saxonum," 1868, *Usinger*, "Forschungen zur lex Saxonum," 1867

latter view commends itself; because (apart from minor differences) the whole first part stands in contrast to the second. The first part — "Lex Saxonum" strictly so called — consists of twenty chapters, entirely penal in form; and represents pure Saxon law, with no Frankish traces. It must have been put into writing before Charlemagne's conquest of the Saxons. But the second part — known as "Lex Francorum" — smacks strongly of Frankish law. In its phrases and rules there appear affinities with the "Lex Ripuaria" (*post*, § 46). The latter is expressly referred to in the "Capitulatio de partibus Saxoniæ" (782) and the "Capitulare Saxonicum" (797), — decrees of Charlemagne made to regulate his newly conquered territories. Subsequent to this date, therefore, we must suppose this second part to have been compiled The entire compilation, indeed, we may well believe to have been made in pursuance to Charlemagne's decree of 802, at Aix-la-Chapelle, ordering all the Germanic customs to be put into writing (*ante*, § 35).

Two features may be specially noted. In the first place, the earlier half reveals to us the social structure of the Saxon people. It mentions only two classes of persons, nobles and "aldi," *i.e* half free; the class of ordinary freemen appears as not yet developed. The other feature is that the later Saxon law is the harshest of all; for the death penalty is prescribed without discrimination, even for the lightest offences. Contrasting this with the fact that in the earlier part the penalties are all money-fines, the explanation seems to be that the later harshness was due to the continual state of hostility between the conquered people and the Franks, so that the latter were seeking to strengthen their own control and the domination of Christianity, to which the heathen Saxons were long obstinately recusant. Charlemagne's Saxon capitularies, though no less harsh, recognize the frequent need of mitigation by sanctioning an ample exercise of the pardoning power.

§ 43. The *Frisian Code* [1] had its home in the region between the Scheldt and the Weser (the modern Netherlands); the Zuyder Zee ("Flevo Lacus") and the Ems divided it into three parts, of which the central one was dominant. This Code was likewise a composite one. The most ancient part, the "Lex Frisionum," in twenty-two titles, each divided into chapters, contains general rules applicable to the entire people Then, where the northern or the

---

[1] TEXTS: *Richtofen*, in M G.H , "Leges," III
    TREATISES AND ARTICLES · *Patetta*, "Lex Frisionum, studi sulla sua origine e sulla critica del testo," in A C T , XLIII, 1892.

southern district follows a variant rule of its own, this is noted alongside of the general rule After these titles come twelve more, the " Additiones Sapientum " , these were additions made by two Frisian elders, Vlemar and Sasmund. As to the date of this Code, the belief is that the general rules represent the earlier part, put in writing when the central district was conquered by the Franks, in 734 ; thus the variant rules for the north and south districts might have been inserted when Charlemagne acquired the entire region in 785 The "Additiones" would of course be the latest portion, and might well have been made at the time of Charlemagne's Aix decree of 802 (above mentioned) calling for a general codification.

Writings from a private hand, laws made by the king or by the assembly, and even some maxims of general learning, go to make up the text of the Code. And, as a whole, it was probably put together unofficially. Rules of divers epochs and on unconnected topics — sometimes actually contradictory of each other — are found side by side For example (and it is a peculiarity of this Code), there occur not only laws for enforcing the Christian religion, but also customs plainly pagan, such as human sacrifices for expiating the vengeance of the gods The mixture of such inconsistencies shows that the compilation could not have been an official one

§ 44. The Suabian Group (Alamannic, Bavarian). — Southern Germany, and particularly Suabia and the neighboring region, was the home of the *Alamannic Code* [1] A preface (which also is prefixed to the Ripuarian and Bavarian Codes) declares " Theodoricus, rex Francorum, cum esset Catalannis elegit viros sapientes . . . jussit conscribere legem Francorum et Alamannorum et Baioariorum " ; and adds that, though Theodoric's plan was not carried out, Ildebert did it, Clotaire perfected it, then Dagobert revised it, and he was the real author of the laws thus set forth. This preface, however, is not of much authority ; it is lacking in the oldest manuscripts, and its statements are not consistent with what we know from other sources. Though there is here some obscurity, it is certain, however, that the text had its origin in two different epochs.

The earlier part is the " Pactus Alamannorum," dating from the end of the 500s or beginning of the 600s. It was enacted by vote

[1] TEXTS *Lehmann*, in M G H., "Leges," Tom V, Sect. 1
TREATISES AND ARTICLES *Brunner*, "Über das Alter der Lex Alamannorum," in B A , 1885, *Lehmann*, "Zur Textkritik und Entstehungsgeschichte des Alamannischen Volksrechts," in N A , X, 469

of the people, — as may be told from the name "pactus" (*ante*, § 36), and from its opening phrase, "et sic convenit." Christianity is seen to have been already introduced, and the alliance with the Franks was still vigorous, — which could not have been the case later in the 600 s.

The later part is the "Lex Alamannorum," strictly so called. Its legal rules, their form, and the political conditions, all point to its later origin The principal if not the sole author (according to the more probable view, based on the manuscripts) was Duke Lanfred, who governed from 709 to 730, when he was defeated and slain by Charles Martel the Frank. The Alamannic duchy, which then met its end, had already acknowledged the Frankish suzerainty, but was in fact independent, under the then weak power of the Franks; and had thus been able to frame its own Code, on the basis of its ancient "Pactus" and the local Customs. Some of the manuscripts speak of the "Lex Alamannorum" as composed in the time of the Frankish king Clotaire. This (unless it is merely an error based on an allusion to a Clotaire in the above-mentioned Preface) is explainable as meaning Clotaire II, who reigned 613–622; he may have made the original text, and Duke Lanfred may merely have revised this. But this assumption of successive compilations is not tenable. The political and other facts of the period, and the obvious unity of form, prevent us from referring the "Lex" to the time of Clotaire II. The earlier "Pactus" may indeed have been composed under his orders, but this cannot be verified. If, in order to account for the Preface's mention of a Clotaire, we are to attribute the "Lex" to any Clotaire at all, it must be Clotaire IV, a contemporary of Duke Lanfred; and on this assumption the date could be made more precise, for Clotaire IV reigned 717–719.

The Alamannic Code, as to its contents, falls into three parts. The first, cc. 1–23, contains "causæ ecclesiasticæ," *i.e* the ecclesiastical law This was moulded to favor the Church's interests; although, since the time of the "Pactus," the Church had been influential. The ecclesiastical form for freeing slaves is here given, which in Italy was not recognized until Liutprand's time. The second part, cc. 24–44, covers public law, "causæ quæ ad ducem pertinent." In the last part, cc. 45–98, comes private law, "causæ quæ sæpe solent contingere in populo." The remaining chapters, cc. 99–104, were added to Lanfred's original text, in the manner usual in the Carolingian period, and were probably a consequence of Charlemagne's general decree of 802, already mentioned.

§ 45 The *Bavarian Code*,[1] in contents and in form, is closely related to the Alamannic, and it bears the same preface, — which is not trustworthy, as already noticed A peculiarity of the Bavarian Code is its mingling of parts of different Germanic systems, and its variances of form. This feature, while it does not go far to help us in fixing the precise periods of the Code's origin, enables us to realize the diversity of peoples represented in it. The contents reveal, in the first place, an element of Bavarian law, *i e* the native rules of sundry Bavarian tribes, this part gave rise to the name " Pactus," by which the Code was also known. Then there is a large element of foreign law. The Alamannic rules (from Lanfred's compilation) here predominate The Frankish rules are most used for the public law; for the Bavarians were then subject to the Merovingian crown The Visigothic rules are also represented, this is explainable by the relations of the Bavarians with the provinces of southern Gaul (which belonged to the Visigothic kingdom), the compilers could thus have obtained the text of the Visigothic Code, — not Recesvind's revision (*ante,* § 41), but the text in force before the separation of southern Gaul. The Lombard Edict also is found in analogous rules, and this is accounted for by the intimate relations of kinship and interest between the two dynasties and peoples. Finally, the influence of the Church's law is not without its marks, as seen in the adoption of the Church council's rules for the clergy; this is explainable by the reforms in the system of the Bavarian church which we know to have taken place about the time of the Code's compilation

However, though these various elements may have had their origin at periods by no means identical, it is certain that their compilation into this single text must have been made about the middle of the 700s. This period is fixed by the circumstances that the Merovingian dynasty was still on the throne (though the "mayors of the palace") were already wielding the power), that the Alamannic Code of Duke Lanfred must by that time have been compiled, and that Duke Tassilo (749) could not yet have been governing Bavaria, because he made additions to the original Code and his contemporaries attributed it to his predecessors. These additions of his were chiefly two decrees, made with the Assembly's approval in 772 and 774, and serving to com-

[1] TEXTS· *Merkel,* in M G H , "Leges," III
TREATISES AND ARTICLES *Gengler,* "Beitrage zur Rechtsgeschichte Bayerns," 1889; *Merkel,* "Das Bairische Volksrecht," in P E , XI, 1858. *Riezler,* "Ueber die Entstehungszeit der Lex Baiuvariorum," in F.D G , XVI.

plete the Bavarian Code. But the Code is also regarded as including two capitularies made by Charlemagne in the first years of the 800 s, introducing new provisions and giving instructions to the circuit justices sent into Bavaria by him.

§ 46 **The Frankish Group (Thuringian, Chamavian, Ripuarian, Salic).** — The Franks were the people who prevailed ultimately, and brought into subjection the greater part of all the Germanic population. Their rule covers the longest span in the period known as the "barbaric," *i e.* Germanic. Naturally their legal system would be the most important and most widely diffused. Nevertheless, their history is so far from being clear and free from controversy that on many points it can only be supplied by conjecture. This group of peoples has bequeathed to us, first and foremost, the Salic Code, to which must be added the Codes of the Ripuarians, the Chamavian Franks, and the Thuringians.

The *Thuringian Code* [1] was known also as that of the *Angli* and *Verini*, because originating in their part of Thuringia, around Unstrutt, on the Saal and the Elster. It has most affinity with that of the Ripuarian Franks, who dwelt in the neighboring region, halfway down the Rhine. It is the shortest of all the Germanic Codes. The first part, in twenty-five articles, is entirely of a penal nature. The second part, in six chapters, deals with heritable possessions ("de alodibus"), theft, burnings, killing of freemen, deeds of violence, and minor matters ("de minoribus causis"). The Code belongs, in its final form, to the Frankish period, probably 802, when Charlemagne ordered the general revision of the tribal laws.

On the north of the Ripuarians, in the region then called Hamaland, belonging to the *Chamavi*, a special Code was in force, known as the "Lex Francorum Chamavorum," or the "Ewa, quæ se ad Amorem habet." [2] It is a system arising out of the overlapping of the systems of the several peoples who were there contiguous, *i.e.* the Ripuarians on the south, the Frisians and the Saxons on the north This Code, in forty-eight articles, is merely a "notitia" or "memoratio," *i e.* a memorandum made by the royal justices sent there on circuit, in pursuance to the order of Charlemagne.

[1] TEXTS: *Richtofen*, in M G.H , "Leges," V
TREATISES AND ARTICLES *Gaupp*, "Das alte Recht der Thuringer," 1834.
[2] TEXTS· *Sohm*, in M.G H , "Leges," V
TREATISES AND ARTICLES *Froidevaux*, "Etudes sur la lex dicta Francorum Chamavorum," 1891, *Zoepfl*, "Die Ewa Chamavorum," 1856.

The *Ripuarian Code* [1] is a more important one ; but the history of its compilation is more obscure, and is still in controversy.   Two periods can be distinguished.   One part, from chapters 1 to 31 and 65 to 79, contains an original compilation, and is perhaps the older. The other, from chapters 32 to 64, borrows so much from the Salic Code that it is perhaps merely a reediting of it.   As to its period, it belongs certainly to that of the Merovingian kings.   The preface (which is the same as that of the Alamannic and the Bavarian Codes) may be correct in attributing its compilation to successive authors, from Theodoric (son of Clovis) to Dagobert, *i.e.* from the first half of the 500 s to that of the 600 s.   Later than this it cannot be, for some of its provisions show that, when it was written, the royal court of France had not yet experienced that internal revolution which gave to the " mayors of the palace " the actual royal power and afterwards placed them on the throne and supplanted the Merovingian dynasty.   At a later period it is possible that the original text received additions.   Some of these are of Carolingian origin; there is indeed a memorandum of a " capitulare legi Ribuariæ additum," which might well have originated at the Aix general assembly of 802, already mentioned (*ante*, § 35), where Charlemagne planned to introduce needed amendments into all the tribal Codes

§ 47.   The foundation Code for all of the Frankish ones is that of the *Salic* Franks, the " Lex Salica " [2]   It is the oldest written Germanic Code that survives.   Its only rival in antiquity is the first Visigothic Code, assuming that the author of the latter was Euric (*ante*, § 41)   From its prefaces and endings, and from the numerous texts, this much appears substantially certain (in spite

[1] TEXTS· *Sohm,* in M G H., "Leges," V
TREATISES AND ARTICLES   *Mayer,* "Zur Entstehung der lex Ribuariorum," Munich, 1886, *Rogge,* "Observationes de peculiari legis Ribuariæ cum Salica nexu," 1823, *Sohm,* "Ueber die Entstehung der lex Ribuaria," in Z S S, V, 380, *Ficker,* "Die Heimat der Lex Ribuaria," in M O.G F., V, 52

[2] TEXTS· *J F Behrend,* "Lex Salica," 2d ed , by *R Behrend,* 1897; *Geffcken,* "Lex Salica, zum akademischen Gebrauch," 1898, *Holder,* "Lex Salica, nach dem Codex Lescurianus," 1880, *Hubé,* "Lex Salica," 1867, *Hessels and Kern,* "Lex Salica," London 1880, *Merkel,* "Lex Salica," Berlin, 1850, *Pardessus,* "Loi salique," Paris, 1843
TREATISES AND ESSAYS   *Clement,* "Die Lex Salica und die Textglossen," 1843; *id* , "Forschungen uber das Recht der salischen Franken," Berlin, 1846; *Gaudenzi,* "La legge salica e gli altri diritti germanici," Bologna, 1884 , *id* , article on "Legge Salica," in the "Digesto Italiano", *Grimm,* "De historia legis Salicae," Bonn, 1848 , *Hartmann,* "Beitrage zur Entstehungsgeschichte des salischen Rechts," in F D G , XVI, p 609, *Thonissen,* "L'organization judiciaire, le droit pénal, et la procédure pénale, de la loi salique," Paris, 2d ed , 1882 , *Waitz,* "Das alte Recht der salischen Franken," 1846

of controversies), — that the Code was in the beginning a law made by the people (a " pactus " established by common accord in the popular assembly, according to Germanic tradition), that this first compilation collected the ancient customs, after inquiry by skilled persons charged by the assembly to ascertain and record them ("omnes causarum origines"); and that this first compilation was then many times revised, amended, and enlarged, from the time of the early Merovingians to Charlemagne, whenever the changes of social conditions made it seem expedient.

The period of this first reduction to writing cannot have been far from the second half of the 400s, that is, at the time of Clovis' conquests in Gaul, which may well have led to the making of the compilation. The Code alludes to the Loire as the boundary of the kingdom, and the Franks had not reached that boundary till after Clovis' victory, in 486, over Syagrius (the Roman general who had set up a kingdom in northern Gaul) Moreover, the Code must have been made before the conversion of Clovis and his people to Christianity in 496, for it preserves traces of paganism and shows no Christian influence. After the conversion, the clergy acquired a share in power; the monarchy was consolidated; the conquered Romanic-Celtic population and their conquerors were brought into closer intimacy. These causes, and the expansion of Frankish dominion (following the victories over the Visigoths of the south in the early 500s), forced Clovis to revise the national law to suit the new conditions. Numerous revisions ensued, continuing into the imperial epoch under Charlemagne in the early 800s. Sometimes the text itself was altered ("lex salica emendata"), sometimes separate capitularies were added (*ante*, § 31)

The Salic Code is accompanied by some "glosses" (marginal comments) known as the Malbergian Glosses, because of the rubric "mall" or "malb" which marks them The meaning of this term has been disputed. The better view is that it stands for "malloberg," i e the assembly or popular court, thus the glosses would be practical instructions for applying the laws to suits at law. They contain many Frankish words which in course of time ceased to be understood and have been handed down to us in corrupt form by the blunders of copyists.

The domination of the Frankish people, emphasized by their resurrection of the Roman Empire in western Europe, gave to the Salic Code a great authority and a wide influence. It became an element (sometimes a considerable one) in many other Germanic

compilations. In Italy, it was in force (for Franks) so long as
" personal " law prevailed, and only the Lombard law surpassed
it in vogue   The latter, indeed, was its superoir in abundance of
legal principles, in the scope of topics regulated, and in precision
of style and language.

TOPIC 4   THE PERSONALITY OF LAWS [1]

§ 48. Personality and Territoriality of Laws, contrasted. —
The Germanic codes were not confined to the locality of the original tribal home. They spread throughout the Empire, and were
in force side by side, in its various regions. In the Carolingian
period, their relations were determined (so far as practicable) by
the principle known as the " personality of law." This means that
the law of the territory in which a person is living yields priority to
his personal law, which follows him wherever he is   His personal
law is usually that of the nation or tribe to which he belongs,
though it may exceptionally be a law adopted by him for some particular reason. By the territorial principle, on the other hand, the
law of the place of domicile applies   Under the principle of personality, the origin and status of a man indicate the system of law
by which all his legal acts are to be regulated. The Frankish epoch
saw this principle at its greatest vogue. Not uncommonly (in
Bishop Agobard's words) one might find, in a group of five or six
persons, no two who lived under the same law.

It must not be supposed, of course, that nothing like this had
been seen or known in prior periods. Some have thought, indeed,
to trace its origin to Roman conditions; for in certain instances
the peoples whose territories had been subjected to Rome had preserved their own laws, and within Rome itself, aliens were governed by a body of law different from that of the Roman citizens
But such instances, as is easily seen, do not contain the essential
marks of the system of personality as it was conceived in the Middle
Ages. At Rome there was no equality of footing for the legal systems of the various peoples embraced in the Empire. Most of them

---

[1] TREATISES AND ARTICLES   Pertile. "Storia," § 6, Salvioli. "Ma-
nuale," pt II, c 2, Schupfer, "Manuale," b I, tit I, c 1; Savigny.
"Storia," vol I, p 79 Brunner, "D Rechtsgeschichte," § 34, Padelletti,
"Delle professione di legge nelle carte medievale italiane " in A S I , sect.
III, vol XX, p 431, Salvioli, "Nuovi studii sulla professione di legge," in
A S M P , 1883 ser III, vol 2, Schupfer, "Una professione di legge Gota
dell' anno 769," in R I S G , 1866, vol II, Stouff, "Etude sur la principe
de la personnalité des lois depuis les invasions barbares jusqu'au XIIme
siècle," Paris, 1894

were not recognized at all   The few so recognized were favored by special concession, and not at all for the reasons which left the medieval systems in force side by side.   Under Rome, the Roman law alone was universal and sovereign   The full enjoyment of its rights was a privilege of Roman citizens only.   This unwillingness to admit others to share in it was the real motive (rather than a regard for the feelings of foreign peoples) which permitted the survival (in some instances and with many restrictions) of certain foreign systems.   The status of such a foreigner was rather that of a person kept outside of the ordinary law than of a person entitled to invoke a law different from the ordinary one.   So, too, the alien residing at Rome was in the status of one who was not conceded all the advantages of citizenship.   It was the status of a legal inferior   The elevation of it never consisted in granting him a freer use of his own law, but rather in assimilating it to that of a citizen by removing gradually the restrictions imposed by Roman law

The personal system of the medieval law was a radically different conception.   All the systems of law were of equal dignity. Each existed, not by concession of some other and sovereign one, but by the authority inherent in itself.   Each was reciprocally recognized and sanctioned by the other.

§ 49   Nor, on the other hand, can the origin of the personal system be sought for in Germanic antiquity.   Some, indeed, have affirmed the contrary.   The Germanic peoples (they maintain), like all other primitive peoples, must have conceived of law as personal, because a community was composed of individuals associated personally, irrespective of the territory occupied by them, the place of habitation changed constantly in such nomadic eras, without affecting their relations based on personal union. All this is true enough   But it does not suffice to explain how the personality of laws came to be applied reciprocally between diverse peoples.   The preservation of his own law, when an alien enters another community, or when a native travels away from his home community, is a fact not to be accounted for on the above ground Moreover, there are other circumstances which refute it.   If the Germanic peoples had been early acquainted with the system of personality, the most natural occasion for applying it would have been the period of their first incursions into Roman territory They would not have refused to recognize the juristic independence of the various nationalities which took part in the emigrations and aided in the conquests   Yet they did refuse it.   The dominant people habitually imposed its own law upon the lesser tribes.   In

Italv, for example, the Saxons, for the very sake of avoiding the
sacrifice of their own law to that of the Lombard conquerors, preferred to return to their original home and thus to lose all the fruits
of the conquest And after their departure, the Gepidans, the
Bulgarians, the Sarmatians, the Suabians, the Noricans, and all
the other tribes who joined the Lombards, abandoned their own
law and accepted that of the dominant people

§ 50 **Personality under the Carolingian Empire.** — The truth
is that the system of personality did not begin to develop until
after the Germanic peoples had permanently settled down in the
territories of the Roman Empire Here they found the Roman law
in force , and its intrinsic resistance was such that they could not
have supplanted it, had they wished to repeat their practice already
followed with other subject peoples. The Roman law survived
(*post*, Part II, § 1) , and this was the germ of the system of personality On the one hand were the Germanic settlers, on the other,
the subject Romans , each having its own laws, and racial nationality being the distinctive mark. But this contrast of personality as
yet went no farther. It was confined to the Roman law and that
of the particular dominant people; the latter having suppressed
the systems of the other German tribes mingled with it. Autonomy for each of the Germanic systems was obtained only when the
principle of personality became universal. This did not occur
until the period (some two centuries later) when the Empire of
Charlemagne brought into union the greater part of Western
Europe. The circumstances of this union explain the extension of
the principle, originally so limited in scope. One instance, indeed — that of the Franks — occurred prior to the Empire's
formation , the law of the Ripuarian Franks had already recognized
the principle; for the Franks were then scattered over central
Europe, and this was perhaps a means of preserving their own
customs as well as of guaranteeing reciprocally those of their neighbors But by the time of Charlemagne's Empire, the universal
extension of the principle had become nothing less than a necessity.
Many different peoples had been politically united. They were
not mingled in a uniform mass, but were so located that each still
preserved its peculiar traits and customs. Their national autonomy had not disappeared ; more or less political independence
remained ; in Italy, for example, the Lombards preserved a kingdom. As a national consequence, a juristic autonomy also remained, — the exercise of their own traditional laws and customs.
Moreover, a sound political wisdom was behind this , for the im-

position of a single legal system upon diverse peoples not easily kept in subjection (like the Saxons, for example) would have led to the dissolution of the new Empire And finally, since the Roman law must in any event be left undisturbed, a failure to concede an equal status to the law of the various subject Germanic peoples, who were therein no different from the Romans, would have involved an intolerable inequality of treatment, — an inequality, moreover, full of danger, and inconsistent with the social and political spirit of the Empire, which aimed to unite the various elements of the population without doing injury to their individual welfare.

§ 51. " **Professions** " **of Personal Law** — Since a person's legal rights and duties were determined according to his personal law, it was necessary that every person's law should be ascertainable. From this arose the " professiones juris," or declarations of law, which every one was obliged to make, when called upon, according to prescribed conditions. Sometimes an official inquest took place. The royal " missi," or circuit justices, who were charged with all general inquisitions, would on arrival in their circuit assemble the people and inquire of each what law he lived by.[1] Of such sort was the inquest held at Rome, in 824, by order of the Emperor Lothar; the imperial justices there made inquiry as to the law professed by every subject.[2] But, much oftener, the declaration of a man's law was made, not by exaction at an official inquest, but by reason of his wishing to do some legal act, such as becoming a litigant or a witness, or swearing loyalty to the emperor, or contracting marriage or some other obligation In such cases the party's declaration of his law was a preliminary for determining how the act was to be done by him Hence the notaries' documents, reciting these declarations, became the chief repositories of them, and served to transmit them in abundance to posterity.

§ 52. Whether a person had an *option* to choose whatever law he pleased, or was restricted to one or another system, has been disputed by historians. The latter view must now be accepted. In the first place, had there been an absolute liberty of choice, the very purpose of the personality principle would have been defeated, — in part, at least It would have permitted the individual's whim to undermine the distinction between the rule of law itself and the legal status of the different peoples, and that status rested, for its policy, not on the preference of the individual, but

---

[1] "Capituli missorum," A.D 786 (*Boretius*, I, 67).
[2] *Boretius*, I, 323

on the interests of the State in general. But there are numerous
other corroborating facts. Full liberty of choice, when conceded,
was a special exception for illegitimate children (*post*, § 53), and
no exception would have been needed, had such a liberty applied
to all. When a man transferred himself from one system of law
to another, he must state his specific reason ; which also would have
been superfluous, had he been quite free to choose If a legal transaction was done according to the rules of a law not that of the party,
it was void, — a result hardly conceivable, if the party was at full
liberty to select his law.

There was in fact no such liberty. There is abundant evidence
that the law declared in one's " profession " had to be the law of
the declarant's nation The earliest mode of declaring was indeed
merely to state one's nationality (*e.g* "ex genere Francorum "), or
to refer to it as that of one's ancestors ; so that when the notaries
afterwards came to devise a regular formula for the " profession,"
the original mention of one's nationality was preserved alongside
of the reference to the law professed , thus serving to contrast the
original nationality with any other circumstance that might have
caused a change of law For example, " Ego Mathilda ex natione
mea lege vivere video Longobartorum, sed nunc pro viro meo lege
vivere videor Salica " Some other Codes themselves expressly
provide that a man's national origin shall determine his law, —
e g in the Lombard Code (where there was practically no need for
it),[1] repeatedly at great length in the Ripuarian Code (the earliest
to mention unmistakably the system of personality)[2] and in
Charlemagne's instructions for the inquests of his circuit justices
(" missi ").[3]

§ 53. But, though a man's law, as a rule, was to be that of his
native nation, yet there were *exceptions* enough to avoid practical
inconvenience. These exceptions were all reducible to two general
classes ; (1) cases where the person's nationality was in doubt,
(2) cases where some new status required a change

(1) In the first class came the cases of a bastard child and a
manumitted slave. A bastard had no father whose nationality
could determine his , if he was not able to identify his mother, he
could choose his own law. A freedman, too, was born into his
legal rights without any legal ancestors uniting him to a specific

---

[1] *Liutprand*, 127, 153 , "formulae," *id* , 91.
[2] *Lex Rip.*, XXX, 3.
[3] "Capitulari missorum," 786 ("per singulos inquirant qualem habeant
legem ex nomine"), and see "Capitula italica," 143.

law; but there were differing rules as to the settlement of his law Sometimes his old master's law was taken, sometimes that of the act of his manumission, sometimes that of his native nation or of his new home, according to his own choice.

(2) The second class of exceptions applied to women upon their marriage, and to all persons on their entrance into holy orders A wife abandoned her own law for the husband's; this had been the rule since the Lombard Edict,[1] and would naturally be preserved as the system of personality came into wider vogue. Even upon widowhood, the husband's law applied; at least until a decree of Lothair's, which restored a widow to her native law [2] For ecclesiastics, from the time of the Lombard Edict, it was settled that they came under the Roman law; for this governed the Church, whose members they were. This rule, however, was not compulsory There are numerous instances of clerics who lived under the Germanic law of their nativity,— not only in the Lombard period, but even up to the beginning of the Frankish period.[3] At that time, a capitulary of Louis the Pious changed the rule, and made the Roman law compulsory for all persons and things appertaining to the Church.

Besides the foregoing cases, there was another case of mutation of law, namely, when the transaction concerned an estate which had been subjected to a particular law. An estate might have a permanent law, independent of the persons who had interest in it This was the law of the first possessor, and it adhered to the estate in spite of the subsequent owner's having a different personal law. This was none the less a logical consequence of the system of personality, for amidst the variety of personal laws, each having different details as to the appurtenant rights, the methods of acquisition, and the remedies, an estate which had once reached a definite legal status ought not to have to change it at every successive transfer Hence all future transactions relating to that estate followed its original law, regardless of that of its owner. When, for example, a party sought redress for injury to his rights in the estate, and for this purpose called upon the original grantor to warrant him, or brought in the original grantor's deed, judgment was rendered according to the law of the original grantor, not that of the now owner, even though the two were different. Thus the law of the ancient proprietor, not that of the momentary owner, governed the land, though the original owner (especially after repeated transfers) might be a person totally forgotten; and his

[1] *Liutprand*, 127   [2] "Capitula italica," 14.   [3] *Charlemagne, ibid*, 142

law became virtually the law of the estate, inseparable from it as it passed from hand to hand.

§ 54. **Conflict of Laws.** — This prevalence of diverse laws at one and the same moment might find several persons entering into a single transaction under different laws, which would easily give rise to a diversity or even a conflict of rules, and required some mode of solving such problems.

Two principles here came into play. The first was that, so far as possible, all the competing laws should be given effect. For instance, if persons having different laws were entering into a contract, the age or other element affecting their legal capacity was determined by the respective laws of each. So, too, when persons were called upon to give testimony or make oath or execute a bond or deed property, each one testified, made oath, acknowledged the debt, released his right, or gave delivery, according to the mode prescribed by his own law.

But this was not always feasible. Then the other principle came into play, namely, that when one only of several laws must be followed, the preference was to be given to the law of the person whose interest was the dominant one. This gave rise to two subordinate rules ; *i e.* either the chosen law prevailed throughout the entire transaction, or different persons' law prevailed in turn at various stages. Guardianship and succession were examples of the first sort. In guardianship (which at this period had become a family right, losing its earlier features) the dominant interest was deemed to be the ward's, hence the guardian, whoever he might be, was governed by the ward's law [1] In a succession, the deceased's interest was deemed the dominant one, hence all transactions concerning the estate followed the law of the deceased, whether testate or intestate.[2] Contracts and lawsuits were also examples of the first rule, the law used was that of the obligor or grantor, or of the defendant The judgment followed the law of the defendant, especially for penalties ; but where the object was not so much to punish a fault as to compensate for an injury received, the penalty followed the law of the person entitled to satisfaction, as for example in reckoning the composition or " wergild " for personal injuries.

The other subordinate rule applied, for example, to marriage questions The husband's law was followed in what personally most concerned him, *e g.* the dowry, the security for it, the pay-

[1] *Charlemagne,* "Capitula italica," 143 ; *Pepin, ibid.,* 5, 6
[2] *Charlemagne, ibid ,* 14.

ment of the "mefio" (or price for the purchase of marital power). But the law of the wife's "mundoald" (or guardian) was followed for his transfer of his right ("mundium") to the husband, his delivery of the woman, his payment of the "faderfio" (something additional to the wife's paraphernalia, but not the same as "dos"). Finally, the law of the woman herself was taken in matters where she was specially interested and responsible, e g. as to her obligations to the relatives when she remarried after widowhood.

§ 55. **Exceptions to the Rule of Personality.** — The general rule that every person should be governed by his own law had indeed some exceptions. These were reducible to two heads: cases where a person's individual law could not be recognized, and cases where the public interest ran counter to his individual law.

In the first class belonged aliens and non-Christians. The medieval State looked upon both such sorts of persons in much the same way. The law of aliens was not recognized. Aliens were all those whose nations were not included under the Empire They were under public protection (without however having full rights of citizenship) ; and, in the absence of special treaties, they were governed by the law of their protector, who would ordinarily be the ruler of the place where they were (though sometimes the Church) Of the non-Christians, a special class was formed by the Jews. Under the Roman Empire, they had obtained (mainly because of their commercial interests) certain privileges, afterwards confirmed by the Germanic rulers ;[1] and one of these privileges was the right to select their judges from among their co-believers and to have their own law applied. Sometimes, indeed, it was not a privilege, but a necessity imposed to protect those who dealt with them, — as when they were obliged, in making oath, to follow their own ceremonies, so as to bind their conscience. Except in a few such cases. the Jews were subject to the law of their place of domicile [2] This, in prior time. had meant the Roman law ;[3] though later the rule vacillated ; where Germanic law prevailed, it seems that this applied to them [4] In any event, their status was not affected by the principle of personality; for their law was merely conceded to them by toleration in exceptional instances,

---

[1] *Theodoric*, "Edict." 143; *Charlemagne*, "Capitulus de judiciis," c 6 (ed *Boretius*, I, 259)

[2] "Codex Justinianeus," 8, "de judæis et cœlicobs" (lib I, tit 9)

[3] "Cod. Just " *ibid*

[4] *Brunner*, D R., § 35. But others maintain that the Roman law always applied.

and not as of right, and is not to be reckoned among the legally recognized systems

§ 56. The cases of a personal law subordinated to the public interest were of more importance. It must not be forgotten, to begin with, that all persons were understood to be subjected in common to that part of the law on which the State's interests were based, i e. public or constitutional law; otherwise, the State could not have stood for a moment. In the field of criminal law, too, the principle of personality was kept well within bounds. Offenders against civil and ecclesiatical institutions were punished without regard to personality. Some basic principles of punishment, such as that of the "composition," or money penalty, applied to all alike. This part of the law arrived early at the doctrine of "lex loci delicti commissi," i.e. that the penalty should be determined by the law of the place of the offence, not by the offender's personal law, — especially when the circumstance of place counted in aggravation. A capitulary, for instance, of Charles the Bald [1] punished counterfeiters according to the Roman or the Germanic law, whichever governed at the place of the crime, the Saxons punished their own people for theft, when committed out of their dominions, by the law of the place; [2] perjury, homicide, and robbery or violence to the person were punished by the law of the place, not by that of the offender; [3] and this was the general rule for the more serious offences.

The Church's practice also involved other limitations on the principle of personality. The Church's commands bound its members regardless of personality, for it had its own law, applicable to all transactions affecting the Church's affairs. It was all the more ready to oppose squarely the principle of personality, whenever its own doctrines or interests were affected. This happened, for example, in the case of marriage. A marriage not contracted according to the proper law would be per se void, on the principles of personality; but the Church opposed this (in its eyes) pernicious consequence, and ordained in several councils (particularly that of Treves, 895) that a marriage should be valid, by whatever law contracted.

The Empire, as well as the Church, issued commands which by the very nature of its authority were binding upon all persons

---

[1] "Edictum pistense," of a d 864, cc. 13, 16, 20.
[2] *Richtofen*, "Lex Saxonum," p. 2
[3] "Capitulum Haristall," of a d 779 (ed. *Boretius*, I, 49), *Marculfus*, "Formulary," II, 37

(*ante*, § 29), regardless of personality. The Imperial law made no discrimination of race or nation, but included all who were within its realm. It differed thus in essence from the personal law of the peoples who were enabled to live side by side by reason of the principle of personality. And so long as that principle continued in force, it made no confusion between the two great sources of law; the various Germanic tribes had their " popular " or racial laws, and the Imperial law went on in its own line of development, acting chiefly (as has been noted) by the capitularies, and amending the others from time to time.

§ 57. **Unifying Influence of the Capitularies.** — Nevertheless, this did not go on without differences developing themselves. The civilizing elements in the Imperial law were drawn chiefly from the ecclesiastical and the Roman law, and this was bound to bring it into opposition to the Germanic laws. Furthermore, the newly developed Imperial law stood for the domination of the ruling sovereign's authority, as opposed to the ancient democratic spirit of the Germanic tribes. Hence, naturally, a resistance to this innovation, exhibited in more than one aspect. We see it in the fact that the dominance of the Imperial law increased in exact proportion to the sovereign's acquisition of personal power supplanting popular government; the latter yielded, more or less tardily, as the former advanced. Moreover, we notice also that the royal acts of legislation had constantly to be repeated, and were always accompanied by threats of penalties, even of outlawry. And the claim was continually advanced against them that the popular assembly must approve before they were valid for all persons; the Italian nobles, for example, openly protested in behalf of this principle. Charlemagne resisted this claim, and bade his son Pepin, king of Italy, not to yield to the Italians' demands[1] Louis the Pious followed his father's example in this. But after the government had become weakened (especially by the family wars for the succession to Charlemagne's sceptre), and each ruler had need for his vassals' aid in the contest with his rivals, these claims were assented to. In 832 Lothair laid before the national assembly at Pavia his capitularies, including those of Charlemagne, and not only asked the assembly's approval for them, but conceded that the sanction should extend only to those selected as valid for his kingdom of Italy. The capitularies thus selected (known as the Pavian Constitutions) were formally entitled, " Capitula quæ Lotharius rex, una cum

[1] "Capitulare italic ," 141, *Boretius*, I, 211, 212

consensu fidelium suorum, excerpsit de capitulis Karoli avi sui ac
Ludovici genitoris sui ''

All this shows how popular sovereignty (represented indeed only
by the rich and powerful nobles) again obtained the upper hand,
and how the entire political system of the Holy Roman Empire,
instituted by Charlemagne with the Church's acquiescence, was
now entering on a period of decline, which if continued would bring
it into danger of dissolution.   This was very apparent when the
national assembly took the step of sitting in judgment on the
sovereign, and even (as in Charles the Fat's case) of condemning
him; and this last event, in 888, brought to an end, forever, the
unity of Charlemagne's majestic empire.   It had thus far failed
in its supreme purpose, i e. to subject the entire people to an absolute sway exercised in the name of a divine mandate.   Those
classes of the population who held the economic and political
power resented the Empire's claims, lopped off more and more
of its prerogative, impaired its status with the people, and thus
gave rise to a new order of things and a new historical epoch, —
that of Feudalism.

CHAPTER III. THIRD PERIOD: A.D. 900–1100

LAW UNDER THE FEUDAL SYSTEM

§ 58. Spirit of Feudalism.

TOPIC 1. FEUDAL LEGISLATION

§§ 59, 60. Feudal Statutes.   §§ 61–63   Compilations of Feudal
                                                    Law.

TOPIC 2. FEUDAL CUSTOMARY LAW

§ 64   Growth of Customs.   §§ 65, 66.   Rules for the Validity of
                                                     Customs.

TOPIC 3. THE TERRITORIALITY OF LAWS

§ 67   Causes leading to Terri-   §§ 68, 69   Dominance of the Ter-
        toriality.   ritorial Principle.

§ 58. **Spirit of Feudalism.** — Under the conditions just described, the state of the Empire, at the time of its collapse, was in marked contrast to its earlier days. Weakness had succeeded power; and the tendency to centralization had been followed by a dismemberment of authority and its localization in the hands of the feudal nobles. Thus the copious flow of imperial capitularies was followed by a dearth of legislation in the feudal period. Moreover, the chief motive had ceased, namely, the desire to regulate the relations between the diverse races and to unite them as members of the Empire. Hence the need of new laws ceased also. Each independent State was providing for its own conditions. For private law, in particular, the existing capitularies and popular codes sufficed, while their slow transformation by means of Customary law went on

Thus the remnant of imperial authority (valid more in name than in fact) had little to exercise itself upon, other than the conditions peculiar to the new feudalism. These conditions were of two sorts, on the one hand, the political relations between sovereign and vassal, and on the other hand, the general social conditions (which indeed needed measures to suppress disorder, violence, and the insubordination of the powerful, and to protect the weak from injustice). Around these two main purposes centre the scanty

71

enactments of the feudal period. The local customs, which supplemented them, and the statutes themselves, were compiled from time to time, and formed virtually codes of feudal law.

TOPIC 1. FEUDAL LEGISLATION

§ 59. **Feudal Statutes.**[1] — The successors of the Carolingians were authors of some laws of great importance, — constitutions, treaties, or other enactments, — made sometimes by their own authority, sometimes by consultation with the nobles attached to their court, and sometimes with assent of the popular assembly. Most of them emanated from those few rulers who by their personal energy infused new vigor into the imperial institutions, and sought to free the throne once more from the shackles which feudalism had imposed. A few were due to Guido, Lambert, and Henry II and III; but the most important and numerous are those of Otto. The subjects of these, as of the earlier capitularies, were varied enough, — revenue, procedure, the Church, crime, family, property, and so on. But for the most part they bear the mark of the times, that is (as already noted), they concern feudal relations, without any other definite feature in common.

In this class belongs the famous Capitulary of Kiersy, under Charles the Bald, made at the Parliament of Kiersy, in 877. The demands of his vassals, who threatened to refuse to follow him in the war then waging, were acceded to, and the fiefs of the greater vassals were made hereditary, thereafter, they could be revoked only for specific causes and upon due process of law. Among the subsequent laws belong Otto I's important laws of procedure. They took a backward step, to some extent, but the conditions of the time made this inevitable. What Otto did was to restore and extend the wager of battle, though prior laws had limited its use, forbidding it for important issues and declaring it impious and foolish to let life's best interests depend upon the judgment of the sword.[2] Liutprand the Lombard, indeed, while limiting it all he could, had declared that he would have forbidden it entirely, but for the strong popular custom in its favor.[3] Feudal manners

---

[1] TREATISES AND ARTICLES *Schupfer*, "Storia," pt I, tit 1, c 3; *Boehmer*, "Die Reichsgesetze von 900 bis 1400," Frankfurt, 1832; *Bourgeois*, "Le capitulaire de Kiersy-sur-Oise," Paris, 1855; *Fustel de Coulanges*, "Les articles de Kiersy," in "Nouvelles recherches sur quelques problèmes d'histoire,' 1891
    EDITIONS M G H , *Padelletti*
[2] *Rothar*, "Edictum," 164, 165, 166   [3] *Liutprand*, "Edictum," 118

restored it to esteem, and this showed itself in Otto's above-mentioned statute of 967. By this enactment, wager of battle was made the compulsory method, especially in litigation over the possession of land, when forgery of the title-deeds was alleged. This mode of trial was made to include even Romans and ecclesiastics; but they, as well as women, children, and the aged, could substitute a champion.[1] It was an epoch of bodily prowess, justice was with the strongest; and Otto sought to recognize this ineradicable sentiment, while throwing the authority of law over a practice which would otherwise have gone on in defiance of law

§ 60 Particular mention must also be made of Conrad II's Milan statute of 1037, which gave the lesser vassals the same status of relative independence towards the greater ones which the latter had already obtained towards the king. It provided that no one could be deprived of his fief except on the conditions named in the law and by the judgment of his peers. Just as the greater vassals could appeal to the imperial tribunal, so the lesser ones could now appeal to the imperial commissioners (or judges on circuit). The fief, on the incumbent's death, was to pass to his issue, as of right, and in default of issue, to his brother. The lord of whom the fief was held could not alienate it without the tenant's consent.

Other emperors also enacted a few laws more or less directly affecting feudal holdings Otto III, deploring the violence of the times, and seeking to restore public order, urged upon the courts greater activity, by dispensing justice at all times, except on the important holidays as fixed by him Henry II, in the Strasburg Parliament of 1019 (called by consent of the great vassals, including some Italian bishops), issued laws on succession between husband and wife, on the punishment of parricide, and on homicide by one who had sworn to keep the peace, in the last two cases, the accused must personally wage his battle, unless belonging to one of the excepted classes. Henry III, with the assembly's consent, in 1047 and 1054, issued laws against judicial oaths by ecclesiastics, against poisonings and other secret murders, against high treason, and against marriage with a blood-relative's widow. An important law of Lothar, in 1136, dealt with the alienation of fiefs[2]

The Suabian emperors sought to restore the pristine imperial authority, and thus legislated much on feudal law. Frederic I's statute "de regalibus," at the Parliament of Roncaglia in 1158, is well known, and sought to prevent the usurpation of political

---

[1] Cap. Ottonis, in "Cap italica," ed *Padelletti*
[2] Text in M G.H and *Padelletti*

power by nobles and by towns. The subsequent statutes of
Frederic II belong really in a later epoch, when feudalism had not
yet disappeared, but the royal authority was being regained, and
at the same time democratic institutions were vigorously arising,
and a new order of things was beginning.

§ 61. **Compilations of Feudal Law** [1] — The Books of the Fiefs, or
"libri feudorum" (also called "usus feudorum," "consuetudines
feudales") may be regarded as the greatest memorials of feudal
law in Italy. In spite of their authority and wide diffusion, both
their authors and the precise period of their first composition are
unknown This is due to the diversity of their materials, for
statutes, judgments, and customs of various epochs were heaped
together by successive hands, and all of this was done by private
zeal and initiative, without official sanction. But it is certain that
the native home of the "libri feudorum" (in part, at least) was
Milan, whose jurists were the earliest composers After successive
revisions these books came to have, in the hands of the Bologna
jurists, their final form and vogue.

It was once believed (but without sufficient reason) that the
author of them (or, at least, of the essay which begins Book I) was
Gerard ("the Black") Capagisti, consul of Milan in the reign of
Frederic I. At the opening of Book II is another essay, consisting
of two letters from Oberto dall' Orto (also in that reign) written to
his son Anselm, a lawyer of Bologna, at his request Both Books
contain also diverse materials, apparently centring mainly around
the feudal enactments of Conrad, Lothair, and Frederic I When or
by whom put together, is not known. But it is inferred that there
was also a division of the work into titles and rubrics, on the plan
of Justinian's Digest, and this probably was done at Bologna,
where the Feudal law was at this period being taught, with copious
and important "glosses" (*post*, Part II, § 42), and where thus a
single systematic text would naturally develop, as it had done for the
Roman and the Canon law. A second rearrangement of the book is
attributed to Ardizo, who founded on it his "Summa Feudorum";
and a third one (fixing finally the books, titles, and rubrics) is
ascribed to Accursius (*post*, Part II, § 44), who used it for his
"gloss." Other rearrangements were made, ending in that of

---

[1] TREATISES AND ARTICLES· *Pertile*, "Storia," § 6; *Schupfer*, "Man-
uale," pt. II, tit I, c 5, § 3, p 548; *Laspeyre*, "Ueber die Entstehung und
die älteste Bearbeitung der Libri feudorum," Berlin, 1830, *Lehmann*, "Die
Entstehung der Libri feudorum," Rostock, 1891; *Siciliano Villanueva*,
"Libri feudorum," in the "Digesto Italiano"
TEXTS *Lehmann*, "Consuetudines feudorum," 1896.

Cujas (*post*, Part II, § 54), who made five books of it, but did
not succeed in substituting this for the older form

The Books of the Fiefs, though not official, were so important and
serviceable, and so much used in the law schools and the courts,
that the volume obtained a great vogue, — not only in Italy, but
also in France, as well as in Germany (where it was translated
in the 1500s). Its authority, indeed, became semiofficial when
it was included in the " Corpus Juris Civilis " by Ugolino of
Bologna (*post*, Part II, § 44), in the second half of the 1200 s ; he is
said to have been the one who gave it the status which it so long
maintained, *i e.* following the Novels of Justinian ; forming, with
the Suabian emperors' enactments, part X of the "Collationes "
(*post*, Part II, § 67).

§ 62. Another compilation of feudal law is the Assizes of Jerusalem (known sometimes as Letters of the Holy Sepulchre, because
deposited near there). Godfrey of Bouillon, after the founding of the Latin kingdom in the Orient, at the end of the 1000s,
aimed to establish a system of law for the diverse Christian
population which had followed in the Crusades from all parts of
Europe and had remained in Palestine under the new kingdom ;
and he caused their customs to be compiled for this purpose. Skilled
persons were selected, questions as to their home customs were
submitted (in the manner already noticed under Charlemagne)
to the people's assemblies, and especially at their judicial sessions ;
whence the term "Assizes." On approval of the feudal chiefs,
royal sanction was then given. Naturally, the result was essentially a system of feudal law, the newly born kingdom being
founded on that basis. It was the law common to all Europe, and
therefore the best suited for their circumstances Particularly is
the feudal feature seen in the part entitled " the High Court ",
for in a feudal system the people divide into two classes, viz , those
who possess a fief, and those who do not, and hence these two
jurisdictions (or " courts "), known as the " high court " and the
" lower court," were represented in the book of Assizes by the corresponding division of materials.

When the Christians lost Jerusalem (in 1187), the text of the
original Assizes was lost. But their memory was preserved in
legal practice, and new compilations were made for the territories
remaining under the Crusaders' sway. The best was that of John
of Ghibelin, Count of Jaffa and Ascalon, in 1266. Thus, after
first being carried from Europe into Asia, this feudal law retreated
step by step, sharing with its adherents the changing fortunes of

war. From the centre to the coast of Palestine, then to the
islands, particularly Cyprus, and finally to Eubœa (Negropont),
it here came to an end, when the Turks acquired sway In Cyprus,
however, before the Turkish conquest, the Venetians had held control, and in 1338 they had recognized the Assizes as the law of the
land. A new arrangement of them was translated into Italian in
1531. And so, in the end, Italy's protection preserved the life of
that law which had originally set out from Italy itself.[1]

§ 63 The two compilations just described represented diverse
systems of feudal law. The Books of the Fiefs followed a system
which had departed somewhat from its original purity, in emphasizing property and family rights rather than political and military
relations. The later, or Lombard, form, had developed in Italy,
especially in Lombardy; the earlier, or Frankish, was followed
wherever Frank rule prevailed. Thus the earlier one was not only
embodied in the Assizes of Jerusalem, but also was carried by the
Normans to southern Italy and Sicily. There the feudal law was
first organized by Robert Guiscard, and afterwards confirmed by
Roger When William (the Bad) refused to follow it, the barons'
insurrection occurred; their ancient customs being denied them,
they rose against their oppressor. In the ensuing disorders, the
text of the Assizes (preserved in the royal palace) disappeared, and
no more is now known of it than that it was called "Defetari,"
a word (of Arabic origin) which signifies "manuscript" or "record," i e. in which the feudal usages were recorded [2]

Besides the foregoing special books, the varied legislative archives of this period usually contain much feudal law. Kings as
well as cities dealt with the feudal relations of the times. And
in the decisions of the courts much also is found. The courts not
only applied the statutes, but also recognized the customary law;
and this had already grown to such proportions that we must now
notice its special features.

[1] TEXTS *Beugnot,* "Assises de Jérusalem," Paris, 1841–43 For the
other version of the Assizes of Jerusalem, which (in the form of the Assizes
of Antioch) was carried into Armenia by the Constable Sempad, see the
following "Les Assises d'Antioch," (Venice, 1876), "Mittelarmenisches
Rechtsbuch, Sempadscher Codex," text and translation, ed *J Karst,* 2
parts (1905)

TREATISES AND ARTICLES *Schupfer* "Manuale," p 544, *Monnier,*
"Godefroi de Bouillon et les Assises de Jérusalem," Paris, 1874, *Zeich-
mann,* "Ueber die Assisen von Jerusalem," 1904

The Assizes as used in Eubœa were sanctioned as its law by the Doge
Foscari, in 1421, and were in force (until the Turkish Conquest) under the
name of "Assizes of Romania "

[2] *Amari,* "Storia dei Mussulmani in Sicilia," Florence, 1869, III, p 324,
Capasso, "Sul catalogo dei feudi e feudatari sotto la dominazione normanna," Naples, 1870.

Topic 2. Feudal Customary Law

§ 64. Growth of Customs. — Law must in the long run be the immediate product of social conditions. And the law had by this time in great part caught up with the new social conditions which had left the earlier law behind. But new legislation alone was not enough. Custom and practice, the only ultimate basis of law, had still to supply what was needed

The Germanic tribes had done this, in the prior epoch, by committing to writing the customs which they had brought with them into Italy. But there was a notable difference in the present situation. The Germanic customary law had then already reached a stage of complete development It corresponded to social conditions of a prior epoch. Indeed, it began to be supplanted, soon after the arrival in Italy, by the written law which was substituted. The customs of the feudal period, however, were of contemporary origin; they were a development from new and existing social conditions Thus they led to precisely the opposite result, i.e. they tended, not to disappear into written laws, but to prevail over them and partly to supplant them. The new conditions, giving rise to the customs, were mainly feudal. Hence plainly, the customary law was formed practically by the feudal classes, in protection of their interests; and it is in the feudal organization that we must look to find the methods and means by which custom gave life to new law.

Popular usage and daily practice furnished the material of the rules. To ascertain it, to frame and ratify it, was the task of public officials, — chiefly, of course, the judges. In two different ways, the judges helped to form the law In the first place, they might seek merely to verify the existence of an alleged custom; i e. they might ask witnesses, old inhabitants, and trustworthy persons expert in the law, or even the neighboring judges, or might even submit the case to a higher court; or, to solve a doubtful or disputed case, they might resort to the " judicium Dei." But, in the second place, where the case was of novel impression, so that no custom existed or applied to it, they might proceed according to their own conscience and intelligence. " Ubi usus defecerit, inveniunt sententiam, sine fraude, secundum Deum." Thus would be laid down a rule, which, by repetition in analogous cases, gained all the force of customary law, and was known as " usus curiæ," " laudamenta curiæ," i.e. a rule of judicial practice. Such rules may well be classed as part of the people's customary law, because the people were present at the trial and argument, and because the membership of the tribunal included representatives named by the local popular assembly (" scabini," " schoeffen," etc.).

§ 65 **Rules for the Validity of Customs.** — Other marked differences between this Customary law of feudal times and the earlier Germanic type may be seen in the rules for giving legal effect to a custom. It fulfilled, of course, the essential requirements (long before laid down by the Roman lawyers) that a usage must be regular, contemporary, and general, and to be general, the feudal custom must be " regni et loci," *i.e* applicable in the local region as well as in the kingdom. But two further and novel distinctions were recognized, at the period we now are considering:

(1) Customs might be " bona " or " mala "; hence, the rule that a custom, to be valid, must be " reasonable " An unreasonable custom, to be sure, is hardly conceivable, and was not sanctioned in Roman law. But in medieval usage, " reasonable " here had a special sense, viz. " in harmony with Divine reason " or " justice." [1] This might be estimated from a triple point of view; for Divine reason was conceived to imply a triple standard. The first is that of revelation, *i.e.* the law directly given from God. The second is that of the Church, *i e.* the canon law, which is needed for fulfilling the Church's mission and thus shares in the Divine nature. The third is termed " natural law," *i.e.* common to the natural sentiments of all men; it consists of certain principles of moral rectitude universally acknowledged, and, as man derives his nature from God, so this " natural law " is a manifestation and application of the supernatural law. This supposed conformity to natural law had been originally an attribute conceded only to the Church's law; but the Church's influence in the formation of the civil law had easily led to the extension of the idea.

(2) From the foregoing distinction as to customs " bona et mala," developed another, of great consequence, namely, that of customs approved or not approved (" probata et non probata "). This had been unknown in either the Roman law or the Germanic law. The people, in both of those, had held the supreme legislative power; but on the medieval theory that God in heaven had

---

[1] [" Ragione divina," in Italian, as derived from the medieval Latin use of "ratio," conveys a strong double meaning, not at all represented in our words "reason" and "reasonableness." For "ragio" also means "justice," *e g* "far ragione" is "to do justice"; "palazzo di ragione" is the old term for "courthouse" in many Italian towns Thus the notion of "divina ratio" is a combination of "reason *and* justice." — TRANSL.]

fixed a standard of justice, to which popular practice must conform, it followed inevitably that this conformity must be made to appear, before the custom could be held valid. And this could only be by means of the approval of either the Church or else the king (for the king's authority, on the Church's teaching, was itself delegated from God). Thus arose the general rule, — enforced in all countries and even after the feudal period, by the bulls of popes and the enactments of kings and emperors, — that a custom, to be valid, must be an approved one

Sometimes, indeed, a custom might even be explicitly disapproved Pope Calixtus, at Rome, in 1122, disapproved the custom that the city prefect in Lyons should take by escheat the estate of inhabitants dying intestate without children Eugenius IV, in 1228, condemned the custom at Ravenna for the commune to take title to the archbishop's personalty on his death. Otto I forbade what he called the "mos detestabilis in Italia improbusque non imitandus," viz the custom of authenticating a disputed document by a single oath, — a frequent occasion of perjury. Frederic II did likewise for the "jus naufragii," or custom that shipwrecked goods might be seized by the first-comer as his own.

This rule that a custom must be an approved one was beneficent, in that it helped in repressing abuses of power or mistakes of ignorance which in the prevailing social conditions would easily have spread and become fixed upon the law. Moreover, it subjected the local law to the constant supervision of the State or the Church ; whereas under feudalism the tendency had been to evade both, and to weaken social bonds as well as to break up the unity of law. It thus reopened the road (closed by feudalism) for the law to be influenced by the Roman (or imperial) and Canon law. Therein the law by its own principle prepared the means for its improved development.

§ 66. Custom, which thus had obtained a far stronger status than before in the law, served ordinarily to supplement the written law. A capitulary of Pepin affirms, " Ubi lex deëst, præcellat consuetudo, et nulla consuetudo superponatur legi." [1] The second part of this rule, that custom cannot prevail over written law, had suited well enough the conditions of the Carolingian Empire in the 800 s when the imperial authority was the supreme source of law. But in the feudal period the rule had ceased to correspond to the conditions of the times. Custom had

---

[1] "Capitula italica," 35.

overleaped its former restrictions, and had taken an independent place alongside of written law. Hence arose an important consequence in the law's development The ancient surviving legislation was modified , customary law, for a while lacking in definite rules, soon became consistent and definite in the places where it arose , and this customary law, formed among the various peoples out of the various elements of their local life, began to be itself the highest object of study and of legislation. It was arranged, defined, and amplified , and thus, after long labors, it became the basis of the legislative systems.

This enables us to see how the law of Europe now lost another of its marked earlier features, namely, the principle of personality (*ante*, § 48). The new bodies of law could not possibly be personal, as were the systems of the nomadic tribes of Germanic stock Custom, which is to vary the law, must rest on the demands made by new conditions, and must consist in habitual acts of the community ; and thus custom cannot be personal, but must apply to all who live in common under those conditions Distinctions of race were bound to disappear, and the law was bound to be reconstituted on a territorial basis.

This great consequence must now be further examined.   •

Topic 3. The Territoriality of Laws

§ 67. **Causes leading to Territoriality.** — Throughout the feudal period we can perceive coming to a head the various causes which led finally to this abandonment of the principle of personality for that of territoriality. There were several.

In the first place, under feudalism the main conditions which had given rise to the principle of personality had now ceased to exist. The races had been mingled regionally. New regional languages had formed. Customs were growing upon national lines The life of wandering conquest had given place to a fixed home life ; homes bred patriotism and a sympathy for fellow-countrymen. A single religious faith had replaced the struggle between Christianity and Paganism. How could the law remain diverse as to persons ? It was bound to become uniform for all who lived within the region, — in short, to become territorial.

This would of course take place by gradual growth. The first signs are seen in a certain vacillation and interchange of rules between different personal systems. Starting timidly, and increasing with the pressure of daily needs, this ends finally in the domination of one particular rule. This process of substitution of one rule instead of many was of course going on all through the feudal period. Yet it had already the germs of development under the system of personality, which had sometimes imposed a single rule when the public interest required (*ante*, § 55), or when the transaction admitted of nothing else (*ante*, § 54), or when an estate of land was involved (*ante*, § 54), or when imperial statutes applied (*ante*, § 30)

Other causes, too, conspired to solidify the law territorially. A better knowledge of the diverse legal systems had assisted. Many officials were obliged to be acquainted with them. Notaries were required, by a decree of Liutprand (*post*, Part II, § 1), to be able to draw legal documents by Roman or by Lombard law The lay judges ("scabini," "schoeffen") must be acquainted with the differing systems, and manuals had been compiled for their assistance, these, indeed, tended often to confuse and mingle conflicting rules whose original reason had been forgotten.

Moreover, the feudal political system tended to territoriality. In spite of the fact that feudalism rested on personal loyalty of vassal to lord, and that every castle (it might almost be said) had its law, nevertheless within each fief differences of race were lost sight of. Romans or Germans, — Lombards, Franks, or Saxons, — all were but vassals within the fief, with the same rights and duties to their lord. And beneath the entire network of fiefs lay a common feudal law. The legal principles of tenure, vassalage, immunity, royal power, homage, chivalry, military service, — all these, however variant in the several fiefs, rested on general principles, which were of vast extent and in no sense personal.

Add to this that the only classes of population not governed by these rules of feudal allegiance were being welded by equally strong group-interests, — the cultivators of the soil, whose customs were naturally territorial; the citizens of the towns, whose customs were also local, and in Italy most y Roman; and the ecclesiastics, who of course had the Church's law. For the cultivators of the soil, it is plain that the system of personality could not long endure. For the other two classes, it is enough to note that in each instance there was an element of universality which would gradually subordinate the personal to the territorial principle.

§ 68. **Dominance of the Territorial Principle** —And so it came to pass. Everywhere law became territorial and locally uniform In each region one or another of the systems of law dominated. Local conditions, particularly the proportions of the various races, determined which one it should be. This is seen most plainly in France; in the southern provinces the Romanesque system prevailed; in the northern, the Germanic system (which indeed had been the fact since the 800s). In Italy the movement was slower and less marked. The first to lose their status there were those Germanic systems which had been imported only by virtue of the principle of personality, and represented elements of population which were small in number and alien to the soil For the Lombard law, however, the opposite result took place. The Lombards had settled down in the northern regions and adapted themselves to the country (ante, § 16), and when the time came that one system of law must yield to the other, theirs was the one to prevail, — not only over the other Germanic ones, but also in many parts over the Roman law In the various parts of Italy, the issue of the struggle was a varied one. In Rome and the vicinity, where Roman law had always dominated, its territorial force was recognized by the beginning of the 1000s. Such also was the result at Venice and Ravenna, where the Germanic authority had always been less than elsewhere In northern Italy, the Lombard law generally prevailed, as also in some of the western-central regions (at Lucca, for example), and even more notably in those parts of the South where the Lombard rule survived (for example, in the duchy of Benevento, post, Part II, § 25). But in southern Italy the principle of personality lasted much longer than elsewhere; the Normans had accepted it, and neither the Suabian nor the Angevin dynasties could abolish it, so that personal law was there permitted, except where it conflicted with public interests.

It must not be supposed, however, that the territorial systems did not retain and incorporate much from the personal systems which were supplanted. A system of law which maintains all of its rules permanently unimpaired never existed. The Roman law itself had become popularized (ante, § 10), just as Roman Latin had become Italian; the Lombard law also suffered Romanizing changes (post, Part II, § 3) Legal practice tends always to adapt itself to current conditions not yet recognized by the written law. And, in general, laws of a prior epoch never survive precisely in their original form, except by force of scientific study and as general principles. So that the new principle of territoriality must be understood to have become absolute only in the sense that it replaced the principle of personality. The actual extent of the various specific rules was purely relative. Thus there were as many territorial systems as there were fiefs in Europe. In the ensuing period, when (in Italy) the cities became the unit of dominion, each small communal region had a territorial law of its own. It was only in still later periods, when large States were formed, that a territorial law expanded in authority, and finally could be termed a national law.

§ 69 All this movement of law from one type to another is faithfully reflected in the " professions " of law which had come into vogue under the principle of personality (*ante*, § 51). Gradually becoming scantier, they finally disappear entirely. For some time after the growth of territorial uniformity had rendered them unimportant and really needless, they persisted in the traditions of notarial practice, but only as the relics of a system destined to extinction. The last of them (except the mere forms surviving in notaries' books) are seen to be merely the final symptom of the resistance of the old order to the new, in those regions where the very vigor of the minor racial elements destined them to complete extirpation They represented merely exceptional cases, where the presumption would otherwise have enforced territorial law. They were no longer of varied tenor, but usually represented the particular system which had longest survived in the struggle against the dominant law now become territorial ; at Rome, for example, there might be found "professions" of Lombard law ; in the Lombard cities, " professions " of Roman law. Nor were these " professions " now, as they were originally (*ante*, § 52), merely a declaration of a man's own law which he was obliged to follow. In the old days, a man could not change his law ; he merely declared which of the various systems of law he belonged to. But now he was merely entitled by special circumstances (for example, if he was an ecclesiastic) to avail himself of a special law variant from the common law. Thus it came to be, in these last examples, rather a privilege of electing between a personal law and the common law. And indeed the very formula of the document came to read " eligere " instead of " profitere." The common law was now a territorial law.

ITALY

IN THE

LATER 1400 S

SCALE OF MILES

0   25   50   100   150

From Earle W. Dow's Atlas of European History,
(Henry Holt & Co., N. Y. 1908)

Part II

ITALY

First Period (A.D. 900–1100)· Italy during the Middle Ages

Second Period (A D 1100–1700) Italy during the Renascence

Third Period (A D. 1700–1900): Italy in Modern Times.

Chapter I.[1] First Period: a.d. 900-1100

ITALY DURING THE MIDDLE AGES

Topic 1. The Roman Law

§ 1. Persistence of Roman Law.
§ 2. Roman Law under the Carolingians and Feudalism.
§ 3. Influence of the Roman Law.

§ 4 Relative Influence of Later and Earlier Roman Law.
§ 5. Progressive Stages of Influence.

Topic 2. The Church's Law

§ 6. The Church's Influence on Secular Law.

§ 7. Effect of the Church's Influence.

Topic 3. The Science of Law

§ 8. Rise of Legal Learning
§ 9. The Schools of Law.
§§ 10, 11 Schools of Lombard Law
§§ 12, 13. Schools of Roman Law.
§ 14. Legal Treatises.

§§ 15-17 Treatises on Lombard Law
§§ 18, 19. Treatises on Roman Law.
§§ 20-22. Formularies and Documents.

Topic 1. The Roman Law[2]

§ 1. **Persistence of Roman Law.**[3] — There was at one time a belief, supported by some historians, that the Roman law, as a law effectively in vogue, had ceased to exist during the Germanic rule

[1] [This Part is a translation of Professor Calisse's "History of Italian Law," vol I, in part For the citation of that work, and an account of the author, see the Editorial Preface to this volume. — Transl]

[2] [§§ 1-5 = Calisse, part II, title IV, chapters I, II, §§ 70-76, pp 120-133 — Transl.]

[3] Bibliography to this Topic Salvioli, "Manuale," part II, c 16; Schupfer, "Manuale," sect I, tit 1, § 2, Savigny, "Geschichte," passim; H. Fitting, "Mélanges Fitting," 1909, and article in Z S S, VI, 94 (1885); Patetta, "Contributi alla storia del diritto romano nel medio evo," in B D.R, years III and IV, id, "Per la storia nel medio evo," in R I S G, XII, 1891; Conrat, "Geschichte der Quellen und Literatur des römischen Rechts im fruheren Mittelalter." Leipzig, 1889-1890, D'Asti, "Dell' uso e autorità della ragione civile nelle provincie dell' impero occidentale," Naples, 1841; Grandi, "Epistola de Pandectis," Florence, 1727; id, "Vindiciae pro sua epistola de Pandectis," Pisa, 1728, Tanucci, "Epistola de Pandectis pisanis," Florence, 1731, id, "Difesa seconda dell' uso antico delle Pandette," Florence. 1729, J. Flach, "Etudes sur l'histoire du droit romain au moyen âge," 1890

[The names of Fitting and Flach are inseparably associated with the modern achievements on this subject The "Mélanges Fitting" contains contributions by various scholars as a memorial to Professor Fitting — Transl.]

in the feudal period of the Middle Ages. But the incorrectness
of this belief was long ago demonstrated by the great Muratori,
and (in the 1700s particularly) by Donato D'Asti, and by the
mathematician Guido Grandi, who carried on a long polemic with
Tanucci Finally, in 1822, Savigny's masterly work (on the
" History of Roman Law in the Middle Ages ") put an end forever
to this error [1] It is no longer a living issue. But the reasons for
the fact as now accepted may be briefly stated.

In the first place, the degree of culture represented by the Roman
law (as compared with the Germanic law) points *a priori* to its
persistence The Roman population could not possibly have been
subjected to a system so crude, incomplete, and alien as that of their
conquerors The Visigoths in Spain and the Burgundians in
France had left to the Roman population its native law, by preparing special codes different from the Germanic ones (*ante*, Part I,
§§ 8, 9) and the Lombards' failure to make such a Roman code
indicates that they left the Roman law untouched: Although
the Lombard kings had declared the entire population to be subject
to the Lombard Edict (*ante*, Part I, § 22) , yet the Edict was not a
complete code, and the existing Roman law could have remained
in force, except where expressly altered by some rule in the Edict.
This was the case with the native Lombard (Germanic) law itself
And in fact the Edict itself shows that its provisions were meant to
apply in varying scope ; for some of its sections begin broadly, " Si
quis homo," while others begin " Si quis Langobardus," and others,
" Si quis Romanus " Even its section about " foreigners' law "
(though this signified other Germans, not Romans), which has
sometimes been cited to show the abolition of Roman law provided merely that foreigners should be under Roman law, but that
the king might by special permission sanction their own special law ,[2]
why therefore could not the natural demand for the recognition
of Roman law have been satisfied under this provision ?

In the second place, the Church's powerful influence went to
protect the use of the Roman law. This was a matter of self-
preservation. The Lombards were not Catholic Christians on
their arrival in Italy , and even after their conversion, they showed
no political favor to it. But they left unharmed the Church's
patrimony, privileges, and laws , and this was hardly possible, if
the Roman law had been abolished

[1] [See the further account, *post*, § 41, note 2, where Savigny's passage
is quoted. — Transl]
[2] *Rothar*, " Edictum," 367.

Other facts furnish concrete evidence of the continued life of Roman law. General legislative expressions, for example, from Rothar's time, show this, by their frequent reference to the "persons subject to Lombard law," which implies that other classes of persons were under another law. Particular provisions point the same way. In Liutprand's amendments, for example, when a Lombard took orders in the Church, his children were to remain under their native law,[1] — showing that he himself went under another, *i.e.* the Roman law of the Church (*ante*, Part I, § 53), and that the latter would have controlled the children but for this provision. Another statute provided that if a Lombard woman, widow of a Roman, married again without consent of her relatives or Lombard formalities, the usual Lombard penalties should not follow, because by the first marriage she was under Roman law.[2] Still another statute provided that notaries should not draw up documents in any forms but those of Lombard or of Roman law.[3]

All these circumstances, and many others to be gleaned from the notarial documents and judicial decisions of the times, make it unquestionable that the Roman law remained continuously in force among the Roman inhabitants, except in matters expressly controlled by Lombard law alone (*ante*, Part I, § 56).

§ 2. **Roman Law under the Carolingians and Feudalism.** — Under the succeeding rule of the Frankish Carolingians, Roman law not only fared no worse, but obtained greater influence. The Imperial theory now gave it a chance to affect public law. The Church's increased authority gave it official standing. Under the system of personality of law (*ante*, Part I, § 48), it ceased to be merely tolerated; it obtained equal rights, and thus its intrinsic merits had freer scope. The universal jurisdiction of emperor and pope gave its experts a judicial status. And the common interest of Empire and Church to maintain the Roman law is seen in Leo IV's message of 847 to Lothair · "Vestram flagitamus clementiam, ut sicut hactenus romana lex viguit absque universis procellis et pro nullius persona hominis reminiscitur esse corrupta, ita nunc suum robur propriumque vigorem obtineat."

It has been thought, by some, that the feudal epoch was not favorable to Roman law. But this is an error In the first place, Roman elements are to be seen both in the tenures and in the per-

---

[1] *Liutprand, ibid*, 153   [2] *Liutprand, ibid.,* 127.
[3] *Liutprand, ibid*, 91. Some see in this rule merely the initial recognition of Roman law Troya, "Delle condizioni dei Romani vinti dai Longobardi," § 141; *Pertile,* "Storia, § 6.

sonal allegiance of the feudal systems The holding of land for
a special purpose, the dependence of one person on another, the
connection between rights and economic conditions, the union of
public authority with property rights, — these all had precedents
in Roman law. In the second place, the Empire, while repeatedly
struggling on the one hand to renew its authority over the feudal
princes, and on the other to repel the Church's claim of supremacy,
was obliged to fall back on the Roman law for its support. The
Ottos, indeed, who were foremost in this effort, favored the Roman
system so far as even to plan the renewal of the seat of empire at
Rome. In the third place, it must be remembered that the cities
were mostly not under the feudal system; and these not only had
mainly Roman law, but sought to eliminate the Germanic elements, in their struggle for communal independence. Thus,
when the territoriality of law (*ante*, Part I, § 67) became established (and it came about first and most fully in the cities), it found
the Roman law there decidedly dominant.

And so, alike throughout the Lombard, the Carolingian, and
the Feudal epochs, in one way or another, but constantly, the
Roman law is found surviving among the people, and stimulating
tendencies of progress which the times developed.

§ 3. **Influence of the Roman Law.** — We have already noticed
(*ante*, Part I, §§ 28 ff) some of the ways in which an indirect influence was exerted by the Roman law upon the Germanic peoples.
Its influence helped to lead to the system of personality; to the reduction of the Germanic systems into writing; to the development
of the imperial power; and, later, on the revival of the system
of territoriality, it disputed with Lombard law for the supremacy in Italy. Some particulars of its direct influence remain to
be noticed.

The Lombard Edict (*ante*, Part I, § 17), is full of its textual
traces [1] In the preface to Rothar's Edict, one of the plainest evidences that he took for his model Justinian's seventh Novel
(which had as its legislative purpose to amend and unify former
laws), is seen in this passage, borrowed literally : " Ob hoc necessarium esse prospeximus presentem corregere legem, quae priores
omnes renovet et emendat, et quod deest adiciat, et quod super-
fluum est abscidet." Justinian's compilers could use this language with propriety; but not Rothar's, for there were no prior
laws of his to correct, renew, and amend. This literal copying

---

[1] *Del Giudice*, "Le tracce di diritto Romano nelle leggi Longobarde,"
Milan, 1889.

of the Roman text, without regard to its real appropriateness, shows that the Roman laws were not only known and used by the Germanic conquerors, but were given great authority, and an almost superstitious veneration. Even the title of the Lombard Edict, which, as already noted (*ante*, Part I, § 17), had for them no such applicability as it had for the Ostrogoths, is explainable only as a blind imitation of Roman terms.   And a plain indication of the fruitful possibilities in adopting Roman legal usages is seen in Rothar's institution of the royal notary, Ansoald (a German, as his name shows), whose certified copies should be the sole method of authenticating the edicts; for this was a direct adoption of a Roman institution.

More profound, and more notable for the history of the law, was the influence on the *tenor of Lombard legislation*. The capacity of the primitive Lombard law to satisfy the complex and expanding needs of Italy was due to the Roman law; and its pervasive influence on the Lombard legislators. Not only in public law, but also in the private law of daily life in all classes, was this seen. Testamentary succession, female inheritance, prescriptive title, transfer of ownership, marriage, mortgage, obligations, possession, usufruct, guardianship, — these and many lesser legal ideas and methods were introduced or modified through the Roman law. The commentators on the Edict cited continually the books of Justinian, which indeed became virtually one of the sources of Lombard law

§ 4 **Relative Influence of Later and Earlier Roman Law.**[1] — But this influence of Roman law was exercised, as already observed (*ante*, § 12), not solely by the texts of Justinian's books, but also by the earlier compilations, chiefly the Theodosian Code, which had already a European vogue before the arrival of the Germanic tribes Thus we find often that the Lombard legislation, in accepting Roman rules, follows the earlier one, and not that of Justinian For example, Astolf's statute [2] that a widow on re-marriage loses her life-estate followed a decree of Valentinian, Theodosius, and Arcadius; and not the later rule of Justinian,[3] which forfeited the life-estate only when the first husband had expressly so provided by will   Marriage between cousins had been permitted by Justinian; [4] but the Lombard Edict forbade it,[5] following the earlier Roman rule of Theodosius.[6] And besides other like instances, we

---

[1] [This section has been abbreviated from the original — TRANSL.]
[2] *Astolf*, "Edictum," 14   [3] "Novellae," XXII, c 32
[4] "Institutiones," I, 10, § 4   [5] *Liutprand*, "Edictum," 33.
[6] "Codex Theodosianus," III, 10, c. 1.

find the forms of documents, the technical clauses, and other features, recalling constantly the earlier Roman law, and showing how it had remained well known and in daily use in Italy, independently of the compilations made by Justinian's jurists at his headquarters in Constantinople.

§ 5. **Progressive Stages of Influence.** — The influence of the Roman law, thus penetrating as a social force, far stronger than the Germanic conquerors could have wished or expected, was of course for a long period limited and gradual in its effects. Public law did not feel it seriously, until the Germanic Empire arose. Criminal law was for a while exempt, for Romans were tried in the courts of their conquerors, until under the system of personality the Roman accused became triable by his own law. - Private law was at first the main field of influence; and here it was applicable only to Romans, or (under the system of personality) to others who elected to live by Roman law. This much of scope, however, sufficed to keep it alive and strong, in a period when all else of Roman culture had been submerged. And this much sufficed also as a basis for its latent and wide influence, until that later period when it invaded aggressively the field of the competing systems, and finally arrived anew at a complete domination.

Topic 2. The Church's Law [1]

§ 6. **The Church's Influence on Secular Law.**[2] — If the Roman law handed down from prior generations was thus influential on the Germanic legislation in Italy, much more so would be the contemporary law of the Church, whose power daily waxed and spread. The mere contact with the Roman population would have tended to this. The codes of Theodosius and of Justinian contained many principles of Church law. Most of all, the papal authority availed. As long as the Lombards adhered to the Arian schism, nothing of this was seen, — in Rothar's Edict, for example. But when they became Catholic (in the early 600s), their legislation became permeated with ecclesiastical ideas. And the Church, indeed, deliberately sought to impose its ideas on society and on the law

The means and modes of acquiring this influence were diverse.

---

[1] [§§ 6, 7 = Calisse, part II, title IV, §§ 77, 78, pp. 133–139 — Transl]
[2] *Calisse,* "Diritto ecclesiastico e diritto Longobardo," Roma, 1889; *Tamassia,* "Langobardi, Franchi, e chiesa romana," 1889.

In the first place, clerical personages were frequently compilers of the laws. They took part in the assemblies; represented superior culture; had a monopoly of Latin, which was alike the language of legal and of churchly records. Furthermore, these clerical compilers had directly at hand the texts of the Church's statutes. Sometimes they expressly refer to these canons for their reasons.[1] The Capitularies continually reveal such instances. Moreover, in collating the statutes annually passed by the popular assemblies, the compiler would note the current ordinances of the Church councils touching the same subjects Here again the period of the Carolingian Capitularies shows the most frequent examples, but even in Liutprand's time we find in one of his enactments, which aimed to suppress the popular superstitious customs, the very language of a Church ordinance recently passed.[2] Finally, we find the papal authority directly urging the adoption of some Church rule. Liutprand, for example, when enlarging the number of impediments to marriage, avows that the pope has exhorted him to it.[3] The revival of the Western Empire under Charlemagne increased this mode of influence. Otto I's well-known statutes against wager of battle, for example, were passed after consultation with Pope John XIII.[4]

Nor were the Lombards averse to this ecclesiastical influence. The Church was, of course, in any case a power in the community. But two special motives were added. In the first place, their religious sentiment impelled them. As a primitive Germanic people, they had a tendency to mysticism. As new converts, they had enthusiasm for the Church. In the second place, political interest drew them to the pope; for he was at war with their enemies the Byzantines, and he was powerful with their subjects the Romans. And though this policy failed ultimately, it seemed to promise success while they followed it To accede to the Church's desire for the legislative sanction of Church principles was a plain dictate of that policy. When the Frankish dominion followed, the same motives became even stronger. And thus, if their religious zeal was no longer so great, at least their political interest served to keep the way open for the papal influence on the secular law.

---

[1] *E.g.* when Liutprand is extending the prohibition against blood-relatives' marriage so as to include the wife's sister, as well as the brother's wife, he declares that the canons also make no distinction: "quia canones sic habent de duabus sororibus sicut et de duobus fratribus," No. 32)

[2] No 84. Council of A D 721

[3] No. 33 · "papa urbis Romanæ per suam epistolam nos adortavit, ut tale coniugium fieri nullatenus permitteremus "

[4] *Padelletti,* "Fontes," p 438

§ 7. **Effect of the Church's Influence** — The result of this influence was that a general spirit of ecclesiasticism came to dominate in legislative ideas and expressions   For example, Rothar's
Edict had declared its aim to be the maintenance of public order,
repressing the unruly and protecting the weak; but his successor
Rachi, while reaffirming this, expresses the purpose in quite another spirit:[1] "quia dum pravi homines ea quæ ad Dominum
pertinent non considerant, magis huius sæculi lucrum quam ani-
marum suarum remedium intendunt, et per humanam astutiam
debiles et egenos opprimere non desistunt." This churchly point
of view grows more and more noticeable.   Sin and wrongdoing are
merged   Liutprand aims to prevent man "in peccati onus deinceps nequaquam procidant."[2] The laws will reenforce the
divine precepts, so that men by obeying them may avoid sin.
Liutprand asserts that his Edict has adopted "ea quæ recta secundum Deum comparuerunt."[3] Rachi made new laws because
"Christi Jesu et Salvatoris nostri adsidue nos convenit præcepta
complere";[4] and Astolf repeats this sentiment.[5] But the divine
precepts thus embodied in the law are made known by Holy
Church; and thus the Church, as interpreter of the divine law,
comes to inspire and modify the secular law.

No part of the law remained untouched by this influence.   In
public law, it affected the theory of sovereignty, the purposes of the
State, the relations of rulers and subjects.   In criminal law and
procedure, the principles of personal responsibility, of corrective
punishment, of equity and good faith, came in from the Church and
profoundly changed the primitive notions.   In private law, the
moderation of the paternal power, the introduction of wills and
of slave-manumission, the alteration of the principles of marriage
(including the ceremony, the increased number of impediments,
and the importance of the parties' consent), — all these features,
and many others, can be credited to the Church's influence.   They
suffice to show how the Church's teaching affected the very essence
of the law.   Law came to be looked at from a Christian point of
view, as an application of the divine precepts to human affairs.
These divine precepts were revealed in threefold manner, — in
the Holy Scriptures, in the Church's ordinances, and in that natural
reason (*ante*, Part I, § 65), impressed in the heart of man, which in
its purity must be identical with the divine will of man's Maker
And thus the medieval legislator conceived his work as an ex-

[1] Preface to the laws of A.D 746   [2] Preface, A D 717
[3] Preface, A D 721.   [4] *Ibid.*   [5] Preface, A D 755.

pression of the divine law, under guidance of the Church, leading all men to their highest good in the fulfilment of their nature as social beings.

All this, to be sure, is not the whole story. The Church's influence was indeed pervasive. But there were other sources of legal principle. The inherited traditions of Roman law, especially its point of view of public policy, and the Germanic traditions emphasizing individual freedom, remained vigorous and fruitful. And this network of separate influences is a peculiarity of the Middle Ages. The diverse and competing elements had not yet fused into a placid social uniformity.

Topic 3. The Science of Law [1]

§ 8   **Rise of Legal Learning.** — In the early Middle Ages, legal learning (of modest scope, indeed, as yet) developed in stages parallel to the law itself During the primitive period of popular customs it consisted in the instruction of the younger men by the elder ones, for practical use in courts and for transmission to posterity. After the reduction of the Germanic codes to writing, a certain sort of practical legal science arose; for the compilers, termed " wise and learned " (*ante*, Part I, § 37), had not only to collate and arrange the customs, but had also to give them written form in Latin, taking note of the new elements of Roman and Christian civilization; and this was no slight task. For this laborious effort, the best intellects of the nation were no doubt employed. A new field of learning now opened. The law must not become entombed in its text, but must keep pace with the national life. And it must be applied in actual controversies This gave rise to the learning of notaries, judges, and lay judges or jurors (to all of whom were applied the terms " legum doctores " or " juris magistri), and even of the king himself, when called upon to act as supreme judge. As the Lombard legislation brought changes and new principles, there arose a body of legal learning, to interpret the effect and reconcile the inconsistencies. The Frankish Capitularies copiously increased the need for this function. And it is from the Frankish period, indeed, that a real science of law may be dated. Schools of instruction arose. Practical treatises were written. The reason and the history of the law were formally expounded.

[1] [§§ 8–22 = Calisse, part II, title V, §§ 79–93, pp. 139–171. — Transl]

§ 9. **The Schools of Law.**[1] — During the Lombard rule, schools
had not utterly perished. They took refuge in the monasteries and
cathedrals, and their teaching was chiefly limited to the clergy.
Education was one of the heaviest charges on ecclesiastical prop-
erties This was partly because of the conditions attached by
founders to their bequests, and partly because the Church's function was looked upon as including, not only charity to the sick and
hospitality to pilgrims, but also instruction to the people. The
State paid no attention to schools ; the public interests had not yet
been conceived as embracing that work Thus legal education,
too, was left in private hands. The practitioners of the law —
judges and notaries — became the teachers of law, instructing
their successors and preserving the traditions of the profession
Not that the State did not protect and esteem and profit by
these private institutions. The Lombard royal court showed
favor to the law teachers, and made use of them. Cunibert,
when negotiating with the pope to put an end to the schism of
Aquileia, sent as his representative Theobald (698), a legal expert
(probably a cleric) whose skill had been acquired in the Church's
schools

Education made rapid strides in the time of Charlemagne. He
looked upon it as a means of universal progress and bent every
effort to improve it. Among the learned men with whom he surrounded himself, his intimates were Alcuin and Paul (the Deacon).
He founded the Palace School, and even attended it in person.
The rudiments were to be taught to all his people , all monasteries
and cathedrals were required to maintain schools with a complete

[1] *Pertile,* "Storia," §§ 13, 44, 64; *Salvioli,* "Manuale," part II, cc 10, 16;
Schupfer, "Manuale," book I, tit. II ; *Savigny,* "Geschichte," I, 261 , *Conrat,*
"Geschichte der Quellen und Literatur des römischen Rechts im früheren
Mittelalter," 1889 ; *Ficker,* "Forschungen zur Reichs- und Rechtsgeschichte
Italiens," Innsbruck, 1870, III, 110 ; *Fitting,* "Zur Geschichte der Rechts-
wissenschaft am Anfange des Mittelalters," Halle, 1875 , *id.,* "Die Anfange
der Rechtsschule zu Bologna," Berlin, 1888 ; *Rivier,* "La science du droit
dans la première moitié du moyen âge," in N R H., 1887, vol. I ; *Salvioli,*
"L'istruzzione pubblica in Italia nei secoli viii, ix, x," in R.E., 1879, vol.
XIV ; *Tarlazzi,* "La scuola di diritto romano in Ravenna e Bologna," in A.R.,
1881–1882, *Ricci,* "Sulle origini dello studio ravennate," in A R., 1881–1882;
Rivolta, "Discorso sopra la scuola delle leggi romane in Ravenna ed il collegio
de' giureconsulti ravennati," Ravenna, 1888 ; *Schupfer,* "Le università e il
diritto," in A V I , 1891, vol. III , *id* , "La scuola di Roma e la questione Irneriana," in A R A L., 1897 ; *Patetta,* "Delle opere attribuite ad Irnerio della
scuola di Roma," in B D R , 1895, *Tamassia,* "Le opere di P. Damiano,"
1903 ; *Merkel,* "Geschichte des Langobardenrechts," 1850 (translated by
Bollati, in App. to Savigny, vol III) ; *Boretius,* "Preface to Liber Papiensem," in M G H , Leges, IV ; *Tahni,* "Di Lanfranco Pavese e della
cultura classica in Pavia nel medio evo," in A S.L., 1877 , *Venetian Historical Society,* "Atti delle nazioni scolastiche di Pavia," 1910–12.

curriculum, — thus turning the existing usage into law ; and every
parish church must have a primary school.

The curriculum (above the rudiments) was grouped into " Trivium " and "Quadrivium " The Trivium included three subjects,
— Grammar, Rhetoric, and Dialectic.   The Quadrivium included four subjects, — Arithmetic, Geometry, Music, and Astron-
omy.   The Trivium thus stood for the moral sciences, or Ethics,
and the Quadrivium for the natural sciences, or Physics.   All of
these terms were at that time used in a larger sense than nowadays.
And so it was that Law came in under Dialectic, at the end of the
Trivium ; for since the fall of the Roman Empire, no separate
schools of law existed.

Charlemagne's scholastic ordinances shared the fate of all his
institutions upon his death.   The political convulsions upset most
of his work   Instruction was again left to private effort, usually
that of the Church and its antiquated methods.   But signs of a new
period soon appeared.   Here and there a teacher in some school
made it famous by his learning and zeal in a special subject.   Students thronged to these schools.   The rulers' attention was attracted.   If official status was not conceded at once and to all, at
least privileges were granted   Beginning with the Ottos, and then
the Suabian line, the emperors lent their countenance, and the
popes likewise.   Such was the origin of those celebrated schools
(or universities) of law in Italy, which afterwards spread throughout Europe

The law thus studied was of course predominantly Lombard or
Roman, according to the locality.   Thus the schools fell into two
marked groups.

§ 10. **Schools of Lombard Law** — Traces of schools of Lombard law are found at Milan, Mantua, and Verona.   But Pavía,
the capital, had the finest, and copious records of it remain.

From early times Pavía had indeed had a Trivium school, where
law was therefore in the curriculum.   But the Palace Court (the
supreme tribunal) was there, and this of course gave special impetus to the study of law, especially as in those days skill in procedure and practice were the chief end and aim of the study.   The
judges were recruited from the practitioners, and the practitioners
were at the same time teachers ; the documents of the time show
us the " iudices," " causidici," " rhetores," as making up the teaching body.

The system of university teaching had thus emerged gradually
from a system of practical apprenticeship.   This is why it is so

hard to give (as also for the other early law schools) a precise date
to the founding of the Pavía school ; there are no recorded notices
until after the school has become famous. In an " Exposition of
Lombard Laws," written at Pavía (*post,* § 16), we get the best account of the school's history   The jurists are there referred to
under two designations, the " antiqui " (or " veteres ") and the
" moderni." The former came down into the early 1000 s, when
Leo, bishop of Vercelli, administered justice (999–1022)   But
some of them, called " antiquissimi," were the contemporaries of
Otto I, in the late 900 s, when the Pavía school rose into fame.
The " moderni " were the contemporaries of the author of the
" Expositio," in the second half of the 1000 s. These two classes
(in one or the other of which the most notable names are found)
signified also a difference in legal thought. The " antiqui " had
devoted themselves chiefly to the national or Lombard law and its
interpretation. The " moderni " were more interested and better
versed in the Roman law, as a means of practical improvement for
the national law.[2] Bonifilius, for example, is classed with the " antiqui," and was opposed to the Roman law, though his contemporary,
Guglielmus (Wilhelm), is classed with the " moderni."

§ 11 The " Expositio " gives us the names of most of these
Pavian jurists   The oldest, Valcausus (or Gualcosius), belongs to
the early 1000 s, and is reckoned as an " antiquus "[3] and a champion of the national law.[4] Bonifilius and Guglielmus, successors
of Valcausus, were equally renowned   The school (" Bonifilii
discipuli ") founded by the former (who was a royal judge) was
opposed to Guglielmus, a modernist leader   It was also in controversy with Lanfranc (born 1005), the most famous of the Pavian
jurists, as well as one of the greatest men of his time   Lanfranc
was the son of a judge who had universal esteem. The boy was
instructed " in scholis liberalium artium legum secularium ad
suæ morem patriæ," and while yet a youth was ranked among the
leading lawyers. He went later to Normandy, where he founded a
school at the abbey of Bec, and students flocked to hear him " de

---

[1] "Expositio," note on lex 1, § 1, of Otto I.
[2] "Expositio," note on lex 2, § 1, of Grimoald ; on lex 90, § 5, of Liutprand
[3] "Expositio, ' note on lex 197 of Rothar
[4] Valcausus, indeed was in ill repute among later scholars — at least,
the glossators of Bologna, such as Ugolino, Accursius, and Odofred (*post,*
§ 43) for having falsified the texts of Lombard law   Some of his annotations were made to read like the text of the law, and repealed statutes
were represented as still in force   But the jealousies and hostilities between the Romanists at Bologna and the Lombardists at Pavía may
account for this repute.

secularibus et divinis literis tractantem." As adviser to William the Conqueror, he crossed to England and became Archbishop of Canterbury, dying in 1089.[1]

The list of Pavian jurists includes Sigifred, Bagelard, Ugo, and many of lesser note.[2] In the second half of the 1000s, the school of Pavía sank into decadence, and the centre of legal studies was transferred to Bologna, the home of the greatest school of Roman law. The circumstances leading to this will now be briefly noticed

§ 12 **Schools of Roman Law** — The school of Pavía, at the capital of the Lombard kingdom, was of course devoted to Lombard law. But the influence of Roman law was making itself felt. Paul the Deacon (at the royal court) was thoroughly familiar with Justinian's books The direct effects of Roman principles on Lombard institutions have already been noted (*ante*, §§ 3–5). The schools of law also felt these effects. While the " antiqui " jurists stood by the native law (*ante*, § 10), the " moderni " yielded to the Roman influence They sought to use Roman law for developing and improving Lombard law. The author of the " Expositio " continually refers to the former as a " lex generalis," which he finds to be in conflict with the views of the " antiqui " Obviously there must have been at Pavía some teachers expert in that field. Nor was their acquaintance with Roman law based on mere practice books or on hearsay ; the exactness of the citations shows a direct knowledge of the sources. Moreover, in the lesser schools also, kept by the bishops and the monks, Roman law was known, though in more elementary fashion. Their duties, indeed, both ecclesiastical and notarial, must have made such knowledge needful to the clergy.

These schools, however (as already noticed), had a private status only, without State regulation. The quality of their instruction and the numbers of their students were their sole reliance This, to be sure, was merely carrying out the traditions handed down under Roman rule. There had never been, in the entire Western Empire, a State school of law, — other than the one at Rome, which taught pure Roman law, and lasted through the greater part of the Middle Ages.

§ 13 During the classic period of Roman law, all instruction was given by the great lawyers, and their teaching was a voluntary

---

[1] [For Lanfranc's share in forming Anglo-Norman institutions, see the illuminating comments in *Pollock and Maitland's* "History of the English Law," 1st ed , I, pp 54–56 Lanfranc is supposed to have supervised the compilation of Domesday Book, among other things — TRANSL]
[2] "Expositio," note on lex 153, § 1, of Rothar ; lex 3, § 14, of Otto I.

and private undertaking, not a State appointment. The time not given to active practice they divided between writing and teaching In both ways their fame was preserved. From all quarters students resorted to Rome. An official organization of the schools appears to have been first made by Theodosius.[1] At any rate, by the fall of the Empire, the teachers at Rome were on official salaries, and an ordinance of Atalaric, providing for salaries to teachers and including the " iuris expositores," [2] shows that under the Ostrogothic kingdom this status continued.   Justinian maintained this policy. His decree " Omnem " (533) assigns official schools to Rome and Constantinople; and his Pragmatic Sanction (ante, Part I, § 1), decrees the continuance of the salaries of law teachers, " so that the youth may not fail of good instruction." [3] But when the Church's authority succeeded the Empire's at Rome, a change took place. The Church authorities, to be sure, did not cease to maintain a thorough acquaintance with Justinian's law-books, nor to have the interest and the disposition to foster the traditions and the science of Roman law (ante, § 2) [4] But they impressed upon it a purely ecclesiastical flavor Its ancient spirit was lost. If its study was to continue independently in pristine vigor, some other headquarters must furnish the opportunity. The city of Rome, indeed, was by the end of the 1000's, in all respects in its lowest decadence. The war of the Emperor against Gregory VII and the Norman invasion of lower Italy had helped to produce this. And so we find the Bolognese jurist Odofred reporting that, in consequence of wars, legal studies had removed from Rome to Ravenna

Certain it is that the ebb of the Roman school's fortunes coincides with the rise of the school at Ravenna. The latter is already flourishing at the end of the 1000's, though its origin, no doubt, dates back to the time of the Exarchate (ante, Part I, § 7), when Ravenna was the sole seat of Roman power in Italy, had ambitions to become the capital, and doubtless showed special favor to the Roman law At any rate Ravenna, at the end of the 1000's, had a well-organized school.[5] And Odofred's well-known comparison

---

[1] "Codex Theodosianus," XIV, 9, 3, "Codex Justinianeus," XI, 18.
[2] Cassiodorus, "Variarum," IX, 21
[3] "Constitutio Omnem," § 7; "Pragmatica Sanctio," § 22
[4] Their documents often mention the "legum doctores" and "qui leges veteres noverunt."
[5] Peter Damianus, for example, here wrote his treatise on the degrees of relationship, and tells us that he came to do it by listening to the Ravennese jurists descanting on that subject and abandoning the Canon law rules to follow the Roman law To confute their theories, which were

asserts that Ravenna's school attained its success by carrying off Justinian's law-books from Rome, just as Bologna's later arose by taking them from Ravenna   But the story of the Bologna school belongs rather in the next epoch (*post*, § 38).

§ 14. **Legal Treatises.** — The general situation is plainly reflected in the legal treatises of the time. They are essentially books of practice. Moreover, as the chief need was for plain information on the state of the law, and the law consisted mainly in antiquated and voluminous texts not easily accessible, the treatise writers naturally turned their efforts to making collections, compendiums, and practical manuals. This indeed had been the tendency since later Roman times, for Justinian's great collections, and his policy of confining legal science to the study of their pages, had restricted the lawyers to practical court work and the preparation of summaries of the works of Justinian

Moreover, with Lombard and Roman law side by side in daily life, the adjustment of their divergences led to a sort of customary law, in which practice was the predominant feature. And here again the existing conditions affected the form of the treatises. There were virtually three sorts : (1) those which dealt with Lombard law, chiefly Pavian , (2) those which expounded Roman law, emanating chiefly from Rome and Ravenna , and (3) those which explained the incipient customary law as used in practice.

§ 15. **Treatises on Lombard Law.**[1] — The first attempts of legal learning were merely to arrange the copious sources of the law in collections. The Lombard Edict was thus edited (809–832) by order of Eberhard, marquis of Rezia and Friuli, under the title " Capitula legis regum Langobardorum, seu concordia de singulis causis." [2] But the great mass of subsequent statutes and capitularies, including the special Italian enactments, made some further compilations needful. The most important was that prepared at the School of Pavía, covering the period to Henry II at the end of the 1000 s, and known as the " Capitulare Italicum " But this, too, had its shortcomings. Moreover, practical forms were needed, and a systematic commentary, such as the early Bolognese jurists were then developing for Roman law. Thus arose the celebrated

---

scientifically worked out ("ratiocinando, assumendo, colligendo"), he composed his work, in which he exhorted them not to contemn the Church's doctrines.

[1] Citations *ante*, § 9 , *Pertile*, "Storia," §§ 13, 44, 64 , *Salvioli*, "Manuale," part II, c. 10 , *Schupfer*, "Manuale," b I, tit , 2, c 2, §§ 2, 3

[2] Edited by *Bluhme*, in M G H , "Leges," IV, 255   It distributed the statutes, from Rothar to Astolf, into six topical chapters, arranged chronologically within each.

"Liber legis Langobardorum," better known as the "Liber Papiensis." [1] It belongs in the first half of the 1000s, between Henry I and Conrad the Salic. Being a treatise for practice, the authors did not always preserve the original text, but omitted obsolete and duplicate provisions, and amended errors or loose phrases. The correct text, used for teaching, was known as the "Vulgata of Pavía." [2]

§ 16 The "Liber Papiensis" (or Book of Pavía), by its practical utility, rapidly obtained vogue in the other parts of Italy, and ceased to be a merely local book. It shows us, moreover, that the study of law had passed beyond the mere editing of texts, and was concerning itself with commentaries and applications to practice. The decisions of the royal court at Pavía (*ante*, § 10) were probably here a stimulus. Thus, by the combined influences of judicial decisions, forensic argument, and legal teaching, numerous principles developed which could well form the subject of a systematic commentary on the native law. Such was the "Expositio ad librum papiensem," — a work similar to that "Interpretatio" which was issued with the Breviary of Alaric the Visigoth (*ante*, Part I, § 8) Its author is unknown, and its date is uncertain, [3] but it belongs presumably towards the end of the 1000s, when the Pavian school was on the verge of decline, and the Roman law was beginning to be cited as the "lex generalis" The later Commentaries attributed to Aliprand and Albert (judges in the marquisate of Este), at the beginning of the 1100s, show still more the Roman law influence [4] They are closely related to the "Lombarda," the last collection of Lombard statues, which appeared at the end of the 1000s [5] It differs from the previous collections in its arrangement, which is no longer chronological, but strictly topical, in books and titles, and shows the dominance of scientific method.

§ 17. The remaining treatises of this period, which also concern

---

[1] Edited by *Boretius*, M G H , "Leges," IV, 289 , *Padelletti*, "Fontes "
[2] Another collection of Lombard law, resembling the "Liber Papiensis," is known as "Collectio Valcausiana glossata," because attributed to Valcausus (*ante*, § 10) Edited *Walter*, ' Corpus juris germanici," I, 683 , *Muratori*, I, 2
[Parts of this section are omitted — TRANSL]
[3] Edited *Boretius*, M G H , "Leges," IV , *Padelletti*, "Fontes "
[4] Edited by *Anschutz*, "Die Lombarda-Commentáre des Aliprand und Albertu.," Heidelberg, 1855 , *Siegel*, "Die Lombarda-Commentare," in S W A , 1862, XI
[5] Edited by *Bluhme*, M G H , "Leges," IV, 607   It seems to have had several authors Two texts obtained chief vogue, the "Lombarda cassinese," found in the celebrated monastery at Monte Cassino near Rome, where so many ancient texts have been preserved , and the "Lombarda vulgata," used principally in the school of Bologna.

themselves mainly with practice, include notably the "Quæstiones ac monita,"[1] — a series of discussions of practical rules of frequent application, such as succession, wager of battle, procedure, prescription, and the like   There appeared also, while the Lombard school still flourished, some brief essays on specific topics,[2] and some form-books, particularly the "Chartularium Langobardicum,"[3] in which are collected and compared the notarial forms under the different systems of law, the Lombard law being taken as the general rule and the others as the exceptions.

§ 18   **Treatises on Roman Law.**[4] — The works of the schools of Roman law had much the same general purpose and style as those of Lombard law.   The influence of Justinian's legislation tended to confine the jurists' labors to mere commentaries and summaries.   Just as the Byzantine period had produced (*ante*, Part I, §§ 8, 11) the "Liber Gai," the "Interpretatio" to Alaric's Breviary, and the Turin Gloss, so now under Germanic rule we find the Romanists writing Summaries (such as that of Perugia[5]), Glosses (such as the one from Pistoia[6]), and Compendiums or short systematic expositions.   Three or four of these are important and famous enough to deserve special mention.   The "Exceptiones Legum Romanarum"[7] are a series of condensations or extracts from Justinian's books, for practitioners   They were put together by various hands from time to time, and their authorship and dates, though much discussed, are unsettled; they were by many attributed to a jurist Peter (hence often cited as "Exceptiones Petri "), but Damian has also been credited with them.   A compend usually called "Brachylogus," but originally entitled "Summa Novellarum" or "Corpus Legum,"[8] is the most interest-

---

[1] Edited by *Muratori*, R.I S , I, 2, 163; *Bluhme*, M.G.H., "Leges," IV, 590 , *Padelletti* ; "Fontes," 463
[2] Edited by *Padelletti*, "Fontes," 492
[3] Edited by *Boretius*, M G H , "Leges," IV ; *Padelletti*, 471
[4] *Salvioli*, "Manuale," part II, c 15; *Schupfer*, "Manuale," book I, tit II, § 2
[5] *Paletta*, "Adnotationes codicum dom Justiniani, Summa Perusina," Rome, 1900
[6] 'Glossa Pistoiee," edited by *Chiappelli*, in A R A.T., ser III, vol 37, 1885 ; compare the same author's "Nuovo esame del MS. pistoiese," Rome, 1885, and *Fitting's* "Juristische Schriften," Halle, 1876
[7] Edited by *Savigny*, "Geschichte," II, 321, and by *Fitting*, "Juristische Schriften," 1876, p 151, discussions in *Schupfer*, "Manuale," p 233 , *Ficker*, "Ueber die Entstehungsverhaltnisse der Exceptiones Legum Romanorum," Innsbruck, 1886 ; *Fitting*, "Glosse zu den Exceptiones, etc ," Halle, 1874 , "Le form proc delle Exceptiones Petri," Rome, 1897 , *Conrat*, "Das ashburn Rechtsbuch Quelle der Exceptiones Petri," Leipzig, 1886
[8] Edited by *Bocking*, Berlin, 1829 , discussed by *Schupfer*, "Manuale," p 227; *Ficker*, "Ueber die Zeit und den Ort der Entstehung des

ing one of this period, because it not only uses intelligently the
classic Roman sources, but purports to give the current and
modified Roman law, it dates probably from Ravenna in the 1000 s.
Two other treatises, which have given rise to the widest discussion
as to their date, author, and home, are the "Summa Codicis"
and the "Questiones de Juris Subtilitatibus" [1] These used to be
attributed to Irnerius (post, § 42), the most famous of the early
Bologna jurists, but at present the results of criticism point to
Rome as the place of origin [2]

§ 19 Another treatise to which also has been accorded an abundance of the critics' researches in determining its origin is the "Lex
Romana Udinese," [3] so called from the discovery of its first manuscript at Udine, north of Venice   Other manuscripts have since
been found at St. Gall and at Favaria, in Rhetian Switzerland,
hence much controversy as to its nativity The better opinion
seems to place it in the 800 s, in Italy. Its principal source is
Alaric's Breviary of Roman law (ante, Part I, § 8), but its use of
the Theodosian Code and later Novels, as well as of Gaius and
Paulus, help in an important way to demonstrate that, in northern
Italy at least, the legislation of Justinian had never succeeded in
suppressing the practical use of the earlier sources of Roman law.[4]

§ 20. **Formularies and Documents** [5] — The Formularies are
collections of forms of legal documents for the use of scriveners,

Brachylogus," Wien, 1871; *Fitting*, "Ueber die Heimat und das Alter
des sogenannten Brachylogus," Berlin, 1880; *Nani*, "Brachylogus juris
civilis." in A G S, 1880, XXV; *Chiappelli*, "La glossa vaticana del
Brachylogus," in R S I, 1885, II

[1] Edited by *Fitting*, "Questiones, etc," Berlin, 1894, "Summa Codicis
Irneri," Berlin, 1894, discussed by *Schupfer*, "Manuale," p 214, and in
"La scuola di Roma e la questione Irneriana," in A R A L, 1897, *Patetta*,
"Delle opere attribuite ad Irnerio e della scuola di Roma," in B D R,
1895, and "La Summa Codicis," in S S, 1897, XIV; *Besta*, "L'opera
d'Irnerio," Turin, 1896

[2] [This section has been abbreviated — TRANSL]

[3] EDITIONS *Zeumer*, in M G H, "Leges," V

ESSAYS AND TREATISES *Schupfer*, "Manuale," p 194, *id*, "La legge
romana udinese,' in A L (1881), *id*, "Nuovi studi sulla legge romana
udinese," in A L (1882, 1887, and 1889); *Wagner*, "Zur Frage nach der
Entstehung und dem Geltungsgebiet der lex romana udinese," in Z S S, IV,
Von Salis, "Lex romana curiensis," *ibid*, VI, *Zeumer*, "Ueber Heimath und
Alter der Lex rhætica curiensis," *ibid*, IV; *Zanetti*, "La legge romana
retica-coirese o udinese," Milan, 1900, *Besta*, "Per la determinazione della
età e della patria della così detta Lex romana rhætica curiensis," in
R I S G, 1901

[4] [This section has been abbreviated — TRANSL]

[5] *Pertile*, "Storia," § 18, *Salvioli*, "Manuale," part II, cc 6, 7, *Schupfer*, "Manuale," book I, tit 1, c 1, § 3, *Brunner*, "Rechtsgeschichte,"
§§ 57, 58

The general history of documents in the Middle Ages may be found
in the treatises of *Bresslau*, *Giry*, and *Paoli*

either official or private. To prepare and compile them was a peculiarly practical service in the early Middle Ages. The law was not yet unified nor settled. No special class of persons (like the notaries, who were soon to arise) had exclusive authority to draw up documents of legal sanction. In Roman times any one was free to draft a deed or any other legal document; and an important occupation of the lawyers was to do this. Such was still the custom in the Middle Ages; though the clerics (" clerks ") were now the usual scriveners. But the accurate legal knowledge which the scriveners of classic times had possessed had been the reason and the justification for the liberty then accorded to all, and such knowledge was now lacking. Hence a need now arose for well-drafted forms based on ancient learning and contemporary experience   Some modicum of legal learning was of course essential; and such as it was, it enabled the forms to react in influence upon the law itself. In the first place, they served to reduce it to greater certainty and safety in practice   And, in the second place, they helped to diffuse the Roman law. The Germanic invaders did not use writings for their legal transactions; they were obliged to employ Romans as scriveners. Thus, the traditional Roman forms and even principles persisted, in spite of the infusion of some Germanic principles.   Furthermore, it is in the form-books that we discover the first attempts at legal science   The scriveners, in developing their art, employed a florid style, with allusions to allegories, the Bible, moral truths, and religious maxims, being usually clerics, and drafting often for the Church's property, they found this natural and proper enough. This helped them to dwell upon the general principles which underlay the various legal transactions. And so they came to develop, as a scientific task, the composition of treatises directed to explaining the principles of correct drafting for persons who wished to draw up their own documents

For the history of the law, these formularies are invaluable. They serve to compensate our lack of the books and oral traditions which are now forever lost; to exhibit the law in its practical application, and thus to supplement and interpret the statutes and treatises, to reveal sources which would have remained unknown; and, in short, to mirror the whole legal life of the times   And, though they emanate often from the jurists of the law schools, they are not committed to the law of either the Germanic or the Roman system; they exist for themselves, and illustrate faithfully the actual conditions and the diverse influences which were in process of amalgamation.

§ 21 There were several sorts of form-books. First there were those for public officials ("regales"), for example, for the charters of the Imperial chancery or for the papal bulls   Then there were those for lawsuits, instructing the parties how to proceed. And finally there were the private, or notarial, form-books ("pagenses"), meant for ordinary deeds and the like. There was thus a great mass of forms; and the varied contents of the form-books (of which indeed only a portion have survived to us) show how active was the legal life which called them into existence.

Most of the compilations come from Frankish territory   They bear various names. Sometimes it is that of their author, such as the famous ones of the monk Marculf, in the second half of the 600 s. Sometimes it is that of the place of their discovery or authorship, — such as those of Angers ("Andecavenses"), Bourges ("Bituricenses"), Auvergne ("Arvernenses"), or Sens ("Senonenses"); these belong to the period 850–920, and exhibit Frankish law with a strong Roman infusion. Sometimes, again, they are named from some modern discoverer or first editor of the manuscript, — such as Bignon, Merkel, Lindenbrog, Sirmond.[1]

In Italy there were fewer form-books, — perhaps partly because of the greater diffusion of culture in writing, partly because of the survival of the Roman traditions of the scriveners. But some very important form-books have come down to us. From the Ostrogothic period, we have the invaluable repository of Cassiodorus (ante, Part I, § 6).[2] From a later period comes the "Liber Diurnus" of the papal court.[3] There are also Lombard forms, of the 1000 s–1100 s, in more ambitious treatises which also give instructions for lawsuits; the "Liber Papiensis" and "Chartularium" have already been mentioned (ante, §§ 15, 17).[4]

§ 22. The very documents of the legal transactions themselves have also survived us   "Chartæ" was the term applied to the formal constitutive document, which served as a permanent record of the transactions, "notitia" was applied to a memorandum or preparatory draft[5]   But the great distinction was between . "public" and "private" documents. A "public" document

---

[1] Edited by *Rozière*, "Recueil général des formules usitées dans l'empire des Francs," 1859–1871; *Zeumer*, "Formulæ merovingiani et karolingiani ævi," in M G H , "Leges," V
[2] Books VI and VII of his "Variarum," ed. *Mommsen*, in M G.H., 1894, XII, "Auctores Antiquissimi "
[3] Edited by *Sickel*, Vienna, 1889
[4] Edited by *Padelletti*, "Fontes," Turin, 1877
[5] *Brunner*, "Charta et notitia," 1877 (reprinted in his "Forschungen," 1894)

involved three features: it concerned certain kinds of transactions; it must be drawn by a public official; and it had certain special legal validity. " Public " documents were more finished in style, — partly because the form was of the essence, and partly because skilled officials drew them. The form of a document revealed its entire structure. There were two parts. First came the "protocol" or caption, containing all which served to identify, promulgate, and authenticate the document, — date, reigning sovereign, names of witnesses and parties. Then came the "text" or terms of the transaction, — the recital of facts, the rights granted or liabilities assumed, the description of the property, the conditions annexed, etc

These documents are to be reckoned among our safest sources for the history of the law; for they represent actual transactions in the application of the law and give that color and background which only usage and local circumstances can supply. Based as they were upon the form-books, they reveal the continual silent influence of the Roman law, which owes to them in part its preservation and diffusion through the Middle Ages, while at the same time they demonstrate the coexistence of the Germanic law through the centuries. The great repositories of these documents throughout that period were almost exclusively the monasteries; for the monastic orders came to be the largest landowners, and the sanctity of their buildings was usually respected amidst the feudal wars. In their archives were preserved registers containing copies or abstracts of the documents, and in modern times many reprints of them (beginning with Muratori's, in the 1600s) have been published for the purposes of science.[1]

[1] Some of these are selections relating to a specific region or period: e g Muratori, "Antiquitates Italicae"; Fantuzzi, "Monumenti Ravennati", Porro, "Codex Langobardiae"; Troya, "Codice diplomatico Longobardo", Brunetti, "Codice diplomatico Toscano"

Others represent an entire collection from a particular archive; e g. the "Regesto Farfense," from the monastery at Montecassino, the "Codex Cavensis," from the monastery at Cava; the "Regesti pontificii," from Roma, and the "Regesti imperiali," in M G H Many documents, chiefly from church archives, have been edited for publication in the last few years, by Hartmann, Pivano, Fedele, and others.

CHAPTER II   SECOND PERIOD: A.D. 1100–1700 [1]

ITALY DURING THE RENASCENCE

§ 23   Introductory.

TOPIC 1. THE COMMON LAW

§ 24   The Diverse Elements   §§ 27–29   The Canon Law.
§§ 25, 26.   The Germanic Law   §§ 30–34   The Roman Law.

TOPIC 2. THE SCIENCE OF LAW

§ 35   Beginnings of Legal Science   §§ 45–48   (b) The Commentators
§ 36, 37.   The Schools of Law   §§ 49–51.   (c) The Humanists.
§§ 38, 39.   The School at Bologna   § 52.   (d) The Practical Jurists.
§ 40.   Other Schools.   §§ 53–55   (e) Jurists of France,
§ 41.   The Jurists   Germany,   a n d
§§ 42–44   (a) The Glossators.   Holland.

TOPIC 3. THE LEGISLATION

1 THE COMMUNAL PERIOD

§ 56.   Legislative Conditions in the   §§ 61–63   Compilation of the Stat-
1200 s.   utes
§ 57.   Growth of the City Legis-   §§ 64, 65.   Industrial and Commer-
lation   cial Statutes.
§§ 58–60   Sources of the Legisla-   § 66.   Commercial Institutions.
tion.

2. THE MONARCHICAL PERIOD

§ 67   Imperial Legislation.   §§ 68–75   Legislation of the Italian States.

§ 23. **Introductory.** — As it emerged from the feudal period, the law found itself no longer in the midst of a struggle between diverse and disunited elements   System and unity were gradually coming to pass.   The respective amounts and kinds of the contribution of each element were being settled.   And this signified that, as a part of the general social transformation, the law was beginning to become national, Italian   The Renascence, in its other aspects, — literary, religious, artistic, — was proceeding more slowly , and in general history the end of the Middle Ages is placed at a date considerably later   But in legal history the new epoch

[1] [§§ 23–74 = CALISSE, Part III, §§ 92–162, pp 172–331 — TRANSL.]

certainly dates as early as the 1100 s. The city statutes, which then begin, mark essential changes in public law. The schools of law revive the study and knowledge of the Roman law, and cause its dominion to flourish anew. The Germanic law gradually wanes in power, and the Church's law becomes a special system for particular persons and subjects only.

The new body of law could not yet become a unified one for all Italy Political conditions prevented this But the tendency towards such a unity could be detected, partly in the influence of the Roman law as a common basis, and partly in certain uniform features of legislation which lessened the local peculiarities and gave them a national impress.

Topic 1. The Common Law [1]

§ 24. **The Diverse Elements.** — In all the enactments promulgated in Italy after the fall of the Roman Empire, it was noticeable that the rulers confined themselves to some specific subject of law which needed new regulation. All subjects untouched by such legislation were understood to be left to some preëxisting body of law, known to all and binding upon all. This was the "common" law, in contrast to those "particular" or exceptional laws which affected only certain regions or classes of persons This force of "common" law, it is true, had never permanently been gained by any one of the several systems. It had shifted more than once. Nevertheless, throughout all, it seemed that the Roman law would be the one most adapted to regain and retain that status. And if, already in the time of the Pavian school of Lombard law (*ante*, § 10), the Roman law had come to be termed the "general" law, much more markedly was this to be the result in the Renascence period; for the principal significance of that period, in legal history, is the growing prevalence of the Roman law, alike in science and in practice.

By "prevalence," however, is not meant the driving out of the other systems. The others remained, both the Germanic and the Church law, and in certain fields had even the features of a "common" law Their relations to the Roman law in this period must now be examined

§ 25. **The Germanic Law.** —When the various Germanic tribes reduced their law into writing (*ante*, Part I, § 35), the customary

---

[1] [This Topic, §§ 24–34, is in the author's text Part III, Title III, §§ 130–141, pp. 247–277, and is here transposed before Titles I and II, as making the development clearer for our purposes. — Transl.]

law remained for each tribe as the common law, to govern matters
not covered by the Codes.   This field became gradually narrower,
with the increase of statutes and the disappearance of primitive
customs, as the Renascence approached.   The racial elements were
becoming fused   The Romanic element, by mere weight of numbers, preponderated , the changes in political conditions weakened
the support for Germanic institutions and traditions ; and the
demands of new economic interests found the primitive principles inadequate   Their mission had been fulfilled, and they
must disappear.

Nevertheless, as already noted (*ante*, Part I, § 16), here and
there a compact nucleus of population kept them in vigor and long
preserved their traces.   When the personal system of law gave way
to the territorial (*ante*, Part I, § 67), the dominant law, which imposed itself on all the inhabitants of such regions, was the Lombard law, — just as elsewhere it was the Romanic law.

This local survival of the Lombard law is proved in several ways
In the first place, the family and property law tended to keep its
place tenaciously, even when the public law had been superseded,
— precisely as had occurred for the Roman population under the
Lombard rule.[1]   Furthermore, there are express legislative recitals
that the Lombard law prevailed as against the Roman law.[2]   And,
finally, the vogue of the Lombard law is shown by the prolific
scientific labors devoted to it

The centre of Lombard studies came to be the school at Bologna
(*post*, § 38)   The systematic compilation known as the " Lombarda " (*ante*, § 16) must have been prepared for its needs, so that
the lecturers on Lombard law might have a textual apparatus as
adequate as that possessed by the lecturers on Roman law [3]   They
also used the gloss method of exposition ; and, just as the Romanist glosses were superseded by the gloss compends used in practice
(*post*, § 42), so also the Lombardists developed their system.   The
Accursius (*post*, § 44) of Lombard law was Carolus Tocco, a
professor at Bologna, who in the early 1200s prepared a critical

[1] *Andrea Bonellus* records how the professional experts in Roman law
could be vanquished in a lawsuit by opponents of mediocre skill, when
Lombard rules were in issue   "Commentarium super legibus Langobar-
dum," Venice, 1537, with notes by *Carlo di Tocco*   See the essay of *Volpicella*, "Della vita e delle opere di Andrea Bonello di Barletta," Naples,
1872

[2] *E g* in the statutes of Benevento, in 1230 , and the Sicilian constitution of Frederic II ("Constitutiones Regni Siciliæ," b I, c 52)

[3] The commentaries of Ariprand and Albert (*ante*, § 16) also came from
the Bologna school.

apparatus of the entire Lombard gloss which acquired an authority so weighty as to be considered in practice almost equivalent to the text itself.[1]   In the south of Italy, the commentators on Lombard law were almost as numerous; it had there the longest and most extensive duration, for the reasons already mentioned (ante, § 16).[2]   Baldus (post, § 48) recognizes it as late as the 1300s; "professions" of it (ante, Part I, § 51) are found at late periods in northern Italy; at Bergamo (near Lake, Como) it was not expressly abolished till the 1500s; and the laws of Naples (post, § 68) show that certain persons there continued to live under it. A treatise on the differences between Roman and Lombard law was written by Ferretti, a Ravenna jurist, as late as 1541; another, "De regulis juris Langobardorum," at Venice in 1599,[3] and in the early 1600s the judges of the Abruzzi region were required to know Lombard law[4]   Not until the introduction of the French Codes, in the legislative period of the early 1800s, can the Lombard law be said to have quite lost its independent life

§ 26   A rivalry between Lombard and Roman law was of course inevitable.[5]   The Romanists actively took the aggressive. Throughout their works, a supreme disdain for Lombard law is apparent.   Odofred calls it neither law nor justice, but merely a bundle of rules, put together by the Germanic kings to serve their own ends.   Lucas of Penna thinks them beneath consideration · as lacking in reason, fit for animals only, trash rather than law, and wishes they could be abolished.   Andrew of Isernia calls them "asses' laws"; and in later times De Luca and Gravina express a like opinion.   Hostility so marked must have been engendered, not simply by the Lombard law's inferiority, but also by the difficulty of eradicating it.   And in fact the hostility was strongest in the South, where the Lombard system was most extensive and tenacious and (in some respects) independent.

Naturally, too, there was a counter influence upon the Roman

---

[1] The first printed edition was that of Venice, in 1537   "Leges Langobardorum, cum argutissimis glossis domini Caroli de Tocco"

[2] The monastery of Monte Cassino, in 1267, guaranteed the use of the Lombard law to some of its tenants.   Andrea of Barletta and Andrea of Isernia (in Sicily) also recognized it

[3] See also Rendella, "In reliquias juris Langobardi proloquium," Naples, 1609   The work of B da Morcone, "De differentiis inter jus Romanorum et jus Longobardorum," was edited in 1912 by Prof Joh Abiguente (Naples)

[4] Other instances are found in documents of the Duchy of Benevento, and in the comments of Matteo degli Afflitti on Frederic II's Sicilian constitutions.

[5] Salvioli, "Dell' uso della Lombarda presso i glossatori e i giuristi del secolo XIV," Turin, 1898

law itself   The lawyer-authors were in those days writing chiefly
for practitioners, and they could not help devoting some attention to the inveterate customary law, which existed and could
not be extirpated   The result was a sort of compromise, or bal-
ancing of accounts   Out of the opposing elements, there arose new
and composite institutions, savoring of both elements   For example, the family council, as it exists to-day, has taken from
Roman law the feature of a sole guardian, and from Lombard
law that of the participation of all family members in the
guardianship

Most notable of all influences in thus securing for Lombard law
a permanent place in the later composite institutions was the
feudal tenure   Politically, the fiefs had ceased to be of importance
under royal and municipal government.   But they continued to
exist, and under another form they even regained influence, by
furnishing support and prestige to the throne and receiving in
return new privileges   The family and property feature was their
predominant one, and thus they gave to Lombard law a different
trend from the Frankish law, in which the fief was in essence a
political and military institution.   The Lombard feudal system,
in its features of family control and property rights, remained
vigorous among the noble classes, who were usually of Germanic
extraction and naturally kept up the ancient traditions of their
race.   When, therefore, questions of feudal law came before the
jurists for solution, they could get little help from Roman law,
and perforce fell back on Lombard law as more serviceable, —
not the early Lombard law of the Edict, but the law which
had been evolved by the daily needs which it was obliged to
satisfy.

It was at Bologna, the very centre of Romanist science, that
Lombard feudal law also found its scientific treatment.   The
Romanists' example, which had earlier led to the systematization
of the Lombard Edict and to the "Libri Feudorum" (ante, Part I,
§ 61), now was followed in the glosses to the later feudal customs.
Compends (like the "Summa" of Jacobus of Ardizo) and essays
(like those of Hugo and of Roffred of Beneventum on wager of
battle) now collected its glosses or developed its special topics.
Systematic treatises came later to be written, on the model of
Roman and of Canon law.   And here, too, the reciprocal influence
was seen on the followers of the rival system.   Their doctrine, for
example, of the distinction in feudal estates between the legal and
the beneficial ownership (or use) was unknown to Roman law,

and had its source in Lombard customs.[1] And thus new illustrations were furnished of the reasons and modes by which the feudal proprietary institutions helped to preserve in vigor the Lombard law amidst Romanic rivalry, long after the disappearance of the social conditions amidst which it first entered Italy.

§ 27. **The Canon Law.** — The power of the papacy reached its height during the Renascence ; and so the influence of the Church's law, already notable in the preceding period (*ante*, § 6), was not destined now to diminish. Though the vigorous new growth of Roman law, and the altered trend of general culture, resulted in restricting the field of Canon law and in giving rise to sharp rivalries, and later to a readjustment of its relative sphere, yet there was no loss of its vitality nor check in its development.

The sources of the Canon law had in early times been put together without attempt at orderly arrangement. Apart from the Holy Scripture (the Gospels being the most weighty sources), there was no discrimination as to the relative authority of those sources which consisted in the Church customs and traditions and the opinions of the fathers and teachers of the Church But the decrees of the Councils and the ordinances of the popes — the two principal sources of Canon law — gave rise gradually to a number of important and well-marked distinctions.

(1) The *decrees* of the General Councils (that is, of those which alone were valid for the Church everywhere) were mostly of early date. Eight Councils had been held in the Orient, two at Nicæa, four at Constantinople (the last in 869), one at Ephesus, and one at Chalcedonia. Thirteen have been held in the West (not counting that of 1870 at the Vatican), — five at the Lateran Palace in Rome, two at Lyon, and one each at Vienna, Pisa, Constance, Basel, Florence, and Trent. The local Councils, i e national, provincial, or diocesan, had authority only over the region represented by their scope.

(2) The *ordinances* of the Popes were analogous (in some features) to the constitutions of the Roman emperors. They furnish the largest and most important part of Canon law, between the end of the Germanic period and the council of Trent. They were of several sorts. As to their subjects, they might be either dogmatic, *i.e.* dealing with the duty of the faithful as to creed or pious works,

---

[1] {On this connection between the English "use" and the Lombard analogy, see Professor *Maitland's* master essay, "Trust and Corporation," printed in German, in Grunhut's "Zeitschrift fur Privat-und Oeffentliches Recht," 1904, XXIII, 1, first privately printed in English, but now reprinted in his Collected Works (1911) — TRANSL]

or disciplinary, *i e* dealing with the ceremonies, the jurisdiction, the property, or other affairs of the Church in its external governance. As to their form, there were numerous other distinctions. " Rescripts " were responses inscribed at the foot or on the back of an inquiry or request " Decrees " were decisions by way of judgment in a controversy. " Epistles " were the generic and usual name for all ordinances originating in the Pope's own will; but these were further divided into " encyclicals," or circulars to a specific group of bishops, " chirographs," or letters signed by the Pope's own hand, " bulls " and " writs " (" breve "), or documents made by his officers, with varying degrees of formality, according to the subject's importance or the addressee's personality or the like. The proceedings of the Curia (or papal chancery), of the Congregation, and of the other officers of the papal court gave rise also to other regulations, which in certain conditions would become part of the Canon law.

And, finally, the civil law itself, involved as in the relations of State and Church, might also contribute rules. But here the parties' relative positions of strength would determine which law was really prevailing. Where the Church's power was dominant, the State's law acceded to and confirmed the Canon law ; this was the case with some of the Roman emperors' constitutions, and still more with the Frankish capitularies, and with most of the so-called Concordats Where, on the other hand, the State was in the position of superior power, it imposed its own rules for the recognition and control of the Church , and of this sort are the statutes of modern times

§ 28.[1] From the multiplicity of these sources, the need was soon felt for some simplified and systematic *compilation* The earliest collections had merely arranged the canons in order of time. Among these were the " Prisca," in the 400 s; the " Dionisiana," between the 400 s and 500 s, the " Adriana," presented to Charlemagne by Pope Hadrian, the " Decretals of Isidore," a forgery of Western France, in the 800 s, related to the forged capitularies of Benedict of Levita (*ante*, Part I, § 32). But finally the field was occupied, to the exclusion of all others, by the great systematic compilation of Gratian. He was a Benedictine monk of Bologna (born at Chiusi), and flourished in the first half of the 1200 s The title given by himself to his work was " Concordantia dis-

---

[1] [This section has been abbreviated, as its description of the sources partly duplicates that given by Professor *Brissaud* in Part IX (Canon Law) of the present work. — TRANSL]

cordantium Canonum," but it was always known in practice as the "Decretum." Its fame was extraordinary. It was likened to the Roman Digest (of which it imitated the arrangement); it was publicly expounded at Bologna and at Paris; it was followed by the courts; and it gave rise in its turn (like the Roman texts) to a multitude of glosses, commentaries, and special treatises.

But the Church was now advancing to that period of the culmination of its power when it seemed destined verily to become a world-wide monarchy. And the Canon law shared in this growth. In the period between Alexander III and Boniface VIII, it reaches the acme of its authority and its productiveness. The collection of Gratian, then become inadequate, was superseded by other collections. To these new ones, however, an official status was henceforth given The first of these was the "Decretale" prepared at the order of Gregory IX by Raymond of Pennafort and completed in 1230. It was sent by the pope to the schools at Bologna and at Paris, for publication and for instruction; it was to be the sole authority in courts and schools, and no other compilation was to be made without the papal consent. Gregory, in short, was imitating Justinian; and in fact the Decretale's arrangement was modeled after the Code.

But his successor, Boniface VIII, was not willing to be ranked lower as a legislator than Gregory IX; and so under Boniface, in 1298, we have the "Sextus," i e. a sixth book added to the Decretale Then followed, in 1317, the "Clementina" collection of Clement V. The ordinances not included in the foregoing three collections had been known as "extravagantes," or wanderers; but these also were now collected, first, by John XXII, in 1325 (the "Extravagantes Johannis XXII"), and by later popes to Sixtus IV (the "Extravagantes communes").

These various collections, being regarded as parts of a single systematic legislation, became known as the "Corpus Juris Canonici," — just as Justinian's "Corpus Juris Civilis" signified the union of the various books of his legislation. Gregory XIII, by a commission known as the "Correctores Romani," gave a definitive official text to the whole Corpus, and this official edition appeared at Rome in 1582.[1]

---

[1] The latest critical edition of the text is that of *Friedberg*, "Corpus juris canonici, editio lipsiensis," etc., Leipzig, 1879–1881 The ordinances after the Roman edition were collected in chronological order in "Bullaria," and the general collection of a series of these is known as the "Bullarium Magnum"; the editions begin in 1727; then the "Continuatio," 1838, "Editio locupletior," 1857, and later ones.

§ 29. The *authority* of the Canon law, as a common law, varied
for different periods, regions, and subjects

As to its *period* of greatest authority, this was certainly the Middle
Ages Not even the Roman law could then compete with it , and
its influence over the Germanic law has already been described.
In the later periods, it still remained a power, even though kept
within limits and sometimes even treated with hostility. The
municipal statutes could not supplant it, they themselves were even
tested by the criterion of their harmony with Church law (*post*,
§ 60) , and they may be said to have taken their sanction from it,
in so far as their sources, the local customs, had to be approved
by the Church's authority (*post*, § 58) The royal and ducal
statutes, also, recognized the Canon law as a common law.[1]

As to the *places* of its greatest authority, these were naturally
those regions which came directly under the political governance of
the Church , here the Canon law prevailed even over the Roman
law on points where they might be in conflict (*post*, § 70). Elsewhere much depended on the local political conditions Hence a
good deal of variation ; what was accepted in one jurisdiction might
be rejected in another

As to the *subjects* in which its authority was recognized, this was
naturally the crucial point of the rivalry. In some subjects,
strictly concerning secular affairs only, the Canon law was never
recognized. In others, where the interests or policies of State and
Church had something in common, they united to support the
Church law ; this happened, for example, in the matters of Church
property, tithes, the " peace of God " (or prohibition of personal
violence), usury, clerical immunities, and many others And, in
still other matters essentially touching the dogmas of the Church,
the authority of Church law was exclusive, and the State merely
confirmed it , for example, in matters of marriage (impediments,
ceremonies, consent, and especially divorce), of the status of those
who entered holy orders, and of the exclusive jurisdiction of the
Church over certain persons (*e g.* ecclesiastics) and over certain
offences (*e.g* sins) Of the latter sort, the most notable example
was the inquisition of heresy, where the civic laws implicitly accepted the Church's commands, and the civic authorities acted
merely in execution of its judgments

All this changed, as modern legislation accepted the inspiration

---

[1] The constitutions of Amadeus VIII expressly state this (*post*, § 71);
and in documents of southern Italy a clause frequently occurs renouncing
"omni jure canonico "

of new principles, especially that of the separation of Church and State. The Church's law yielded, and the domination passed entirely to secular law. Where secular interests came to be regarded as the exclusive ones, — as with marriage, — the secular law now acted from its own point of view alone. Where the Church's interests were necessarily involved, — as with the status of the Pope, the religious orders, the Church's property, and the like, — the State controlled them by special rules representing its sovereign power; and this is now the status of what is termed "ecclesiastical law" in the secular sense.

§ 30. **The Roman Law.**[1] — Even under the system of the personality of law (*ante*, Part I, § 48), the Roman law had maintained a powerful position in Italian legal life (*ante*, § 1). When the system of territoriality (*ante*, Part I, § 67) became reëstablished, the Roman law gradually regained the predominance which it had lost under the Germanic invasions and the feudal system. The causes of this were partly the increase of influences already originating in the feudal period, and partly new ones

The two supreme social institutions, the Church and the Empire, had welcomed the Roman law. The Church was born under Roman law, and drew therefrom the guarantee of its privileges; except on specific points of conflict of rules, the Church had always recognized the Roman law as valid. The Empire had come to accept it, partly because it furnished that element of universality which the Empire regarded as its own mission, and partly because the Roman law supported the Empire in its justification of absolute supreme power; so that the imperial authority, wherever it extended, favored Roman law. The jurists, in determining the applicability of Roman law in a given region, took as their criterion the fact that the region was subject to the Empire. Wherever Christianity went, moreover, there also the Church took Roman law; so that the influences were reciprocal, and Christianity tended to be coextensive virtually with the imperial authority. Thus the Roman law took on the quality of an international common law, relegating the other systems to the status of local laws for a particular country

Other reasons went to influence Italy's particular leadership in the development of Roman law   There was of course the univer-

---

[1] *Pertile*, "Storia," § 63 , *Salvioli*, "Manuale," part II, c 19; *Schupfer*, "Manuale," sect II, tit. I, c 2; *Brugi*, "Le cause intrinsecho della universalità del diritto Romano," Palermo, 1886; *Vanni*, "La universalità del diritto Romano e le sue cause," Urbino, 1887.

sal substratum of Latin culture and traditions, absorbing and transforming all the invaders, reviving vigorously under the growth of the city-states and the progress of the Renascence, and easily adaptable to the new modes of life and thought.   But the principal cause was that Italy had become the centre for Europe's *study of the Roman law.*[1]   Italy's schools of law made its cities famous as resorts of learning   They grew in population and in splendor. They sent forth judges, legislators, and other officials, to play a part in the government of other communities and to extend the influence of the system of law in which they had been educated.   The rulers of other States resorted thither themselves, to secure their legal advisers or to learn how they might found similar schools in their own dominions.   Foreign students flocked from all parts of Europe to study the science of law and to carry back its principles and apply them to the legislation of their various native countries

As a result of all these influences (which lasted beyond the Renascence, and down into fairly modern times) the Roman law, with its renewed glory and its vast diffusion, gave a character to the entire epoch.   It acquired the status, not only of the dominant system in Italy's law, but of a common law inspiring a renascence of legal science throughout Europe   Thenceforward Roman influence prevailed in the entire development of law to modern times.

Amidst this universal movement, what part remained for the other legal systems, as to their validity in principle and their importance in practice?   This question deserves more particular examination.

§ 31.   And, first of all, what relation did the Roman law come to occupy towards the *Church's law?*   In the earlier period, as already seen (*ante*, § 27), the Church's favor had been one of the very causes of the Roman law's prosperity.   But now that the latter was independent and stood in no need of the Church's countenance, things were bound to change.   The protegé of the Canon law became its rival.

Sundry reasons rendered inevitable this competition.   In the first place there was the political situation   The Empire was now striving to free the State from Church control; and in this struggle

---

[1] ["Italy was for a while the focus of the world's legal history" (*F W. Maitland* "A Prologue to a History of English Law," Select Essays in Anglo-American Legal History, ed for Amer. Law School Ass'n, 1907, vol 1, p 11).   "During the rest of the Middle Ages, hardly a man acquires the highest fame as legist or as decretist who is not Italian, — if not by birth, at least by education" (*Pollock and Maitland's* "History," I, 100). — Transl.]

the Roman law was of course the Empire's support. Then there was the economic reason. The new interests and policies which were building up social progress were chiefly commercial, — the citizen class, — and these found no support in Canon law. It was chained to dogma, it was unfitted for rapid adaptation to commercial methods; its religious and unworldly standards could not make concessions to secular usages; its ecclesiastical privileges and immunities, obstinately maintained, were an obstruction to commerce, it had a rooted reluctance to condone that pursuit of moneyed gain which was a vital aim of mercantile life. These circumstances serve to show how little favor the Canon law could expect from the mercantile classes. The Roman law, on the other hand, had everything to expect from the new candidates. It had reached an advanced stage of development, especially in the field of contract; it was inherently adaptable to new problems, and it could satisfy all these new demands. Moreover, it was a period of looking forward to the new, and the Roman law now itself shared this spirit, while the Canon law had its face to the past. Dante (who was an expression of his time) exhibits this spirit in his reproaches to those who clung to the study of the Decretals. Even the clerics themselves did not escape its influence, they deserted their cloisters to study the civil law in the secular schools. Hence a general attitude of antagonism between the two systems. The Canon law saw itself losing a dominion hitherto undisputed; the Roman law, aided by a conspiracy of circumstances, hastened to reap the profit and to complete its emancipation.

One of the results of this rivalry was soon seen in the course of the Church's effort to maintain its old position. It placed a ban upon the study of Roman law.[1] At first, this ban was confined to the clerics themselves. The Councils declared that it was a study not suited for ecclesiastics [2] This prohibition the popes followed up, from time to time, notably Honorius III, by his bull " Super

---

[1] There are numerous essays on this subject, the following are among the principal ones E. Caillemer, "Le pape Honorius III et le droit civil, Lyon, 1881 ; Tardif, "A propos de la bulle Super Speculam," N R H., 1881, De Monléon, "L'église et le droit Romain," Paris, 1887, Fournier, "L'église et le droit Romain au XIIIe Siècle," cited in N R.H., 1890; Digard, "La papauté et l'étude du droit Romain au XIIIe siècle," Bibl. de l'école des chartes, 1898

[For England, see Pollock and Maitland, "History of English Law," I, 102 — TRANSL]

[2] E.g the Council of Tours, in 1163, aiming to prevent "sub occasione scientiæ, spirituales viri mundanis rursus actionibus involvantur," ordained that "nulli omnino, post votum religionis, ad leges mundanas legendas permittatur.exire": C. 3, X, "Ne Clerici" (III, 50).

Speculam," in 1219,[1] and Innocent IV, in 1254, by his bull " Do-
lentes " [2] But the continual renewal of these orders proves their
futility Roman law went on flourishing, and the aggressive
hostility of the Church merely reacted upon itself, and resulted
in the complete exclusion of Canon law from the legal field. The
bitter open opposition ceased (though some of the Romanists
continued to vent their sentiments of contempt for the other system), but the Church then resorted to more subtle methods. It
attempted to compete with its adversary in the open market, by
equipping itself with its rival's own elements of strength It
established the centre of Canon law instruction at the headquarters
of the Romanists. At Bologna, each system now had its own
professorial chairs, its own texts, and its own commentaries, in
full rivalry. And it was at Bologna that the Canon law, in fact,
reached its zenith; for there Gratian compiled his " Decretum,"
and there the official editions of Gregory, Bon face, and Clement
were published. The aim of the papacy was to demonstrate its
then unprecedented power, by placing the system of Canon law
on a level with the authority of Roman law, and its success in this
aim cannot be denied.

And, after some time, indeed, when the study of Roman law had
itself begun to show signs of decadence, it found that a union of
forces would serve its interest If the Canon law was no longer,
as of old, to be the Roman law's champion, it could at least be an
ally, and could support the Roman law in the latter's claims to be
the common law The Canon law, in fact, was now ready to concede the propriety of a common law for secular affairs, — just as
the Church itself, while maintaining its supreme authority in
religion, had now conceded political supremacy to the State in
temporal affairs And so the allies agreed on a division of the field.
The Church was not to permit any open contradiction of certain
fundamental principles — the dogmatic basis of its existence.
Nor was it to yield up jurisdiction over certain subjects intimately

---

[1] After lamenting that secular interests have led to a neglect of ecclesiastical duties, he proceeds to repeat the prohibition, and especially to
forbid the teaching of Roman law at Paris, which was then the centre of
theological studies and a stronghold of clerical influence

[2] This one (of which, to be sure, the authenticity has been much doubted)
laments the failure of prior orders to accomplish the purpose, and extends
the prohibition to many other places, requiring for any exception a papal dispensation and the local ruler's consent Nothing is said as to Italian schools,
but the glossator John of Andrea notes that at Perugia the Roman law
was not studied, while strangely enough it was free from the ban at Rome
There must have been some prohibition for Italy, but doubtless the local
conditions at Rome were thought not to need any express provision

related to its spiritual function, — such as marriage, oaths, vows of celibacy, the clerical status, and the like. For the Roman law to submit to these conditions, as it did, was to suffer serious limits of power. And its submission may be explained by the larger fact that the Roman law, after continuing for a time in the van of social progress, ended by retiring from the field, and came to be regarded as an antiquated system, no longer suited to the times.

§ 32 The relation of the Roman law to the *territorial* and *municipal* laws gave rise also to a number of questions, though not so extensive in their import.

For the municipal statutes, the question arose which law should prevail, in case of a conflict with the common or Roman law. Those jurists who conceived the local law as existing merely by consent or delegation from the Imperial authority (*post*, § 57) would naturally regard the Imperial, *i.e.* the Roman law, as controlling. Scientifically, the Roman law was to them the "ratio scripta," the embodiment of " right reason," and whatever contradicted it was void. Politically, the Roman law represented the dominion of the Empire as against the cities and the princes who were seeking to make themselves independent, the inferior's law could not prevail over the superior's, and local policies could not be deemed paramount to policies of universal validity Such was the theory of most of the jurists, from the 1200s onwards But there were others, who, in the Roman texts themselves, found support for the contrary view. Secular (or civil) law, they maintained, was that which each people established for itself. Just as at Rome it had been conceded that the civil or national law prevailed over the " jus gentium," so now, some argued,[1] the municipal codes should take precedence of the Roman law, which had only the status of a " jus gentium." Other jurists based their argument on the moral law of nature. By that law, each people, like each individual person, had an inalienable right to its own existence, each required, for its own social life, its own laws; to oblige these laws to satisfy some superior universal law was to nullify the very existence of the community.

All of this reasoning, to be sure, was more or less artificial. The Roman law, in theory, was not disposed to admit any rule derogating from its own, the secular law emanated, not from the cities, but from the State; the Roman theory of sovereignty could not sanction its dismemberment into fractions, with each city possessing its fraction of legislative independence And yet, on the other

[1] *E g* Albericus of Rosate.

hand, the simple fact was that the cities did possess it, and were able in one way or another (sometimes by victory of sheer force) to exercise and defend their power   It was only when the power of the cities waned, and out of their units a real political State was built up, that in practice their statutory laws yielded to the general law and retained only such limited jurisdiction as might be conceded to them.

But the Roman law, though not able to maintain itself practically at these points of direct conflict, had nevertheless an important influence. In the first place, it served to supply considerable material which the city statutes absorbed and enacted. Moreover, their application in practice lay in the hands of lawyers and judges trained in the Romanist schools of law, and thus many Roman principles came to be introduced into the statutes   And, finally, as a common law, the Roman law applied where the statutes were silent

In spite of all this, it must be remembered that the statutes were based chiefly on local custom, into which there entered constantly a Germanic element; and that the new needs and policies of the times (especially in commercial affairs) were unrepresented in Roman law, which with all the efforts of its adherents could not be completely adapted to the situation. And so it was that the statutes inevitably diverged at many points from the Roman law; and this divergence, founded as it was on the needs of the time, would find the local law prevailing over the other

§ 33. Such also would be the result for the *national* (ducal, royal) laws of the various Italian States which succeeded the cities as the political units.   But here other causes entered into the result. Public law was the chief field of this legislation; for it was an epoch of political reconstruction. Moreover, after the first stage of activity, there ensued one of legislative quiescence, during the decadent period when foreign dynasties and political absolutism prevailed.   And so it happened that these subordinate bodies of law, which might have been entirely assimilated and deprived of validity if the original vigor of legislation had persisted (and which were in fact ultimately absorbed at a much later period, in the 1800s), sprang again into vigor, and once more extended their scope.

Especially was this the case with Roman law.   Both in study and in practice, it now became, more than ever before, the basis of a universal legal science   The Lombard law also, in its bearing on the feudal tenures, appropriated a special and limited field.

The Canon law, while retaining its dogmatic principles and its particular subjects of jurisdiction, in all else left the leadership to Roman law and worked in mutual support.

Thus in the field of *private* law (with which legislation meddled little) the Roman system now reigned without a rival.   Machiavelli, describing the justice of his day, tells us that it is nothing more than the decisions of the ancient jurists.   And when, at a later period, the critics of the law called for that reform which (ultimately) was achieved in the 1800s, the burden of the complaint was that the law was nothing more than Roman law, out of date amid modern conditions

Public law (the chief topic of the Renascence legislation), though much less subservient than private law to Roman influences, had not remained unaffected.   Some of the notions of sovereignty, as applied by the new States, were essentially Roman. The absolute ruler of the Roman law was the model for the Renascence princes and the dukes.   The State harked back to the memories of Rome, Machiavelli, for example, can do no better, in his counsels for a State's prosperity, than point to Roman times for his examples.   In *criminal* law, too, the same imitation was seen.   The penalties were those of Roman law, the Egidian ordinances recall the " lex Cornelia de sicariis ", the jurists in their treatises and the practitioners in their trials cite always the Roman texts   And thus things continued until the violent reaction at the close of the 1700s, under the leadership of Beccaria, when the prime cause of the evils which the reformers then complained of was the law's servile adherence to the antiquated principles of Justinian.

§ 34 Nevertheless, it would be a mistake to suppose that this antiquated common law — which dominated to the end of the Renascence period, was the pure Roman law of Justinian's Corpus Juris.   Into the web of that system had been woven, during the centuries, many cross threads of diverse texture   The Germanic customs; the new social and commercial conditions, the feudal system; the Canon law, — all these had meanwhile had their influence on pure Roman law, by inserting many new principles and entirely ousting many old ones   The family council, the beneficial interest (trust) in property rights, marriage, the feudalized perpetual leases (emphyteusis), — these are merely a few of the novelties which Roman common law had accepted   In this aspect, it fulfilled a kind of cycle in development, corresponding to that of the preceding period.   In the early Middle Ages, the Roman law of classic times (250) had once before assimilated into itself

the local customs, and had become the so-called " Roman popular
law " (*ante*, Part I, § 10)   And so now also, adapting itself once
more to changed conditions, the law of Justinian had taken on new
features, and was enabled to preserve its force as current law.

And in this second cycle, it became transformed into a genuinely
Italian law, — an Italianized Roman law.

This second cycle of adaptation, however, was the work of the
scientific jurists (and not, like the first, an absorption of popular
local customs).   Under the Renascence, there had arisen a scientific study of law, in contrast with the merely practical aims of the
earlier jurists.   But that type of scientific method which sought
to base itself on the pure Roman sources never developed far in
Italy, its chief support was in other countries   In Italy, the
history of the science of law had therefore a special significance,
not only for the form of the law itself, but also for its political and
social results.   To that topic we must now turn

TOPIC 2.   THE SCIENCE OF LAW [1]

§ 35. **Beginnings of Legal Science.** — By the end of the 800 s,
Charlemagne's system of government had been completely broken
up   His successors were constantly at war among themselves.
Feudal rule supervened   National civilization was at its lowest
ebb   Legal learning suffered, with every other form of culture.
Not until about the year 1000 can we detect a slow renascence
of legal studies.   The Roman law shows itself in the lead in this
new life.   At Pavía, it was recognized as "general law" (*ante*,
§ 10), at Ravenna, its chief home, it was in high honor (*ante*,
§ 12); and elsewhere there were signs of that movement which
later culminated in its dominion.

To external causes accounting for this new animation, little or
nothing is to be attributed   The merit of it was not due to the
Church, for the Church (while generally disposed to support
Roman principles) was at this particular stage under strong motives
rather to impede its study.   Nor can we credit the Emperors with
having given the initial impulse   They did favor it, indeed,
especially the Suabian dynasty, to advance their own political
interests, but not until after the revival and spread of the study
had shown them its utility for those interests.   The Romanists

---

[1] [§§ 35–55 = CALISSE, part III, title IV, §§ 142–162, pp. 277–331.
This title of the author is here transposed, to precede his titles I and II,
but to follow his title III, to make the development clearer for our purposes — TRANSL]

with whom Frederic II surrounded himself were the successors, not the predecessors, of Irnerius (*post*, § 42). The most famous exponents of Roman law included quite as many anti-Imperialists as it did Imperialists.[1] The centre of Romanist studies, Bologna, was rather hostile than friendly to the Imperialist party. Frederic II ended by showing disfavor to Bologna, in spite of which it continued to prosper, and all his efforts to make the Naples school (which he founded) the equal rival of Bologna were futile. The earliest universities, moreover, were not State schools, and this alone would show that it was not through imperial favor that the study of law sprang into new life. Nor, finally, can the newly arising city governments be given the credit They did indeed favor the schools, but here, too, the favor was not marked until the throngs of students and the repute of the new learning had made the citizens appreciate the advantages which accrued therefrom to the cities in which the schools flourished.

It is, in truth, in what we may call intrinsic causes that we must seek for this wonderful renascence of the study of Roman law. The revival of culture was already permeating society at large; and Romanist rather than Germanic culture was alone adapted to respond to this demand In the legal field, the crudities of the existing practice created needs which the Roman learning alone could satisfy. In its capacity for practical service and wide application, it far surpassed either the Lombard or the Canon law It was, in short, the one most adapted to be a " common " law. These, the real causes of the revival, may be traced alike in the history of the schools themselves and in the scientific literature to which they gave birth.

§ 36. **The Schools of Law.**[2] — The Roman law came first to be taught by the instructors in the ancient " grammar " schools (*ante*, §§ 9, 10) and by the practitioners of law (" jurisperiti," " legum doctores," " causidici," " judices"). The teaching was oral; and, by reason of the scarcity of manuscript books, the hearers were numerous; for there was practically no other way of learning. A master's talent and fame was the sole cause and limit of the size of his classes, for he had neither office nor salary from the

---

[1] ["Guelfs" and "Ghibellines," in the original. — TRANSL.]

[2] *Pertile*, "Storia," § 60, *Salvioli*, "Manuale," part II, cc. 16–18, *Schupfer*, "Manuale," sect. II, tit. II, c. 1; *Coppi*, "Le Università italiane nel medioevo," 3d ed, 1886; *Denifle*, "Die Universitaten des Mittelalters bis 1400," Berlin, 1885, *Schupfer*, "Le Università e il diritto," Milan, 1891; *Fournier*, "Histoire de la science du droit en France," 1892 (only vol III published, dealing with the universities), *Rashdall*, "The Universities of Europe in the Middle Ages," 1895, vol I

State   These voluntary groups of teachers, united by a common purpose, and located in various parts of Italy, made the beginnings of what later became the organized and chartered Universities.

This name they did not bear at first.   They were simply "Schools"   The later term "Arts" ("Study")[1] indicated a school that had attained a certain permanence and fame   Some of the "arts" came to be known as "general", *i.e.* they accepted all kinds of students, including foreigners, and their diplomas received general recognition, as qualifying the holder to teach and hold academic office in any place.   A school might acquire the status of "general arts" in two ways.   The first and earlier was simply by common custom, *i e* its acknowledged excellence had gathered students from all quarters, and had thus gradually established everywhere a high repute   The other and later mode was by charter from Pope or Emperor, whose supreme authority had universal recognition and could by this single act give the status of "general arts" to a school which perhaps had not existed until that moment

The earlier schools were all of the former sort, growing gradually into fame and completeness.   They were voluntary associations, organized much like the ordinary trade gilds, whose mode of governance was also analogous to that of the cities themselves. Every "corporation" (as the various associations were called), and therefore every academic "art," had its own ordinances, or "statutes," made and revised by elected representatives.   It had a chief, or "rector," elected for a short term, and aided by councils, general or special, like the mayor of a city.   And just as the other corporations and the cities had within themselves various smaller groups (trades or "arts"), of which some were inferior and others superior in rank or power, so too both teachers and students were divided into further groups   The students were formed into "nations," that is, according to the country or region whence they came.   And just as the cities had in some cases a democratic, in others an aristocratic constitution, so too, in the universities, we

---

[1] [The Italian word "studio" means also "an art or science," *i e.* a branch of study, and thus its implication includes both the subject of study or pursuit, and the group of persons so studying or working together   Moreover, in classical Rome, "schola" meant a trade gild or craft gild, like the later Italian "arte" and English "art"   This now lost usage of "art" is kept alive in our modern phrase "Arts and Crafts," which signifies precisely the scope of "studio"   But that same scope is also the origin of "Arts" as to-day traditionally used for the college department of a university and for the title of a graduate as "bachelor of arts"   Hence, it seems quite in keeping with university tradition to translate "studio" as "art." — Transl.]

find that in some cases the students constituted the corporation, and even elected the rector and the masters ;[1] while in others only the latter shared in the government, and the students were merely permitted to enjoy the benefit of the instruction[2]

By the period when this organization of the schools had been perfected, the term " university " had come into use. This term did not in any way imply that all branches of science were there taught , no such institution then existed, nor for long afterwards. It signified merely the legal nature of the body , *i.e.* it was an application of the technical Roman law word " universitas," importing a union of many persons for a common purpose, — here, that of teaching and being taught.

§ 37. This voluntary and unofficial status of the schools of law did not long continue.   In the second period of their development — beginning, on the whole, with the 1300s — the schools now founded would usually be authorized by charter of the Pope or of the Emperor The emperors came to realize (as Justinian and Charlemagne had done in their day) that education, especially, as fitting for public office, might well be taken under their control The Church, too, which had even in the Middle Ages charged itself with the work of education, was less than ever disposed to renounce this prerogative; for it had need to take measures to diminish the widening breach between Science and Faith And so it came about that nearly all the universities, either at the time of founding or afterwards, were now in possession of a papal charter carrying with it valued privileges.

Thus began the tendency, which resulted later in a universal practice, to treat the universities as agencies of government — in short, State universities. The University of Naples, for example, was explicitly founded as such by Frederic II; and in one way or another, with varying results, the other universities were subjected to State control. The city governments, indeed, had already been trying something of the same sort; for the jurisdictional independence enjoyed by the universities had often brought with it loose practices and town-and-gown disorders. The cities went about their object in several ways They would offer to famous professors elsewhere an official salary, which attracted them to the local university; once there, they were under the control of the city, which had now the right to nominate, to supervise, and to punish the incumbents of those chairs. Another means of control

---

[1] As at Bologna ("universitas scholarium")
[2] As at Paris ("universitas magistrorum").

was the students' customary oath, given in exchange for the privilege of residence in the city; it bound them not to remove the university from that place, nor to stir up breaches of the public peace.

When the independent city governments declined, and were succeeded by the despotic ducal States, their free institutions were suppressed, and with these the universities also suffered. Many went out of existence; they had lost touch with the popular needs. Those that survived were kept under strict official regulation. The present distribution of the surviving universities — invariably at the capital of one of the former Italian States — shows how closely they were related to the government. Where we find more than one in a single State — as in Tuscany and the Papal Territories — it is only because in those regions political power was late or incomplete in its centralization. The universities could no longer sustain themselves, except in those few important or capital cities where the State gave them countenance And thus it is that in numerous cities, where once flourished universities, —Vercelli, Brescia, Lucca, Arezzo, Fermo, Ascoli, Vicenza, Reggio, and elsewhere, — there remains to-day little more than a memory.

§ 38 **The School at Bologna** [1] — Of those schools of law that survived amidst all such vicissitudes, the most illustrious was that of Bologna, — the cradle of the revived learning, and the greatest centre for its diffusion throughout the civilized world The origin of this University is wrapped in obscurity This much is known, that it began, like the other schools, as a development from the medieval " grammar " schools and the gild of court practitioners. Its earliest recorded teachers bear the titles " rhetor," " artibus peritus," " causidicus," " judex." There is also a tradition of some specially legal learning here, at a date before the school becomes known However, the source of almost all of the little that is certain about its early teachers (including Irnerius) is no more than their mention in the court records of the time

---

[1] *Schupfer*, "Manuale," p 487, has an extended bibliography of this subject   Among the more recent books and articles are the following: *Ricci*, "I primordi dello studio di Bologna," Bologna, 1888; *Chiappelli*, "Lo studio Bolognese nelle sue origini e nei suoi rapporti con la scienza pre-Irneriana," Pistoia, 1888, *Fitting*, "Die Anfänge der Rechtschule zu Bologna," Berlin, 1888, *Leonhard*, "Die Universität Bologna im Mittelalter," Leipzig, 1888, *Rivier*, "L'Université de Bologne et la première Renaissance juridique," N R H, 1888, XII; *Tamassia*, "Bologna e le scuole imperiali di diritto," A G S, 1888, XL; *Schupfer*, "Le origini della Università di Bologna," A R A L, 1889, VI, *id*, "Studi critici su recenti pubblicazioni intorno allo studio di Bologna," R S I, 1889

Bologna was then (as were other cities) the seat of an episcopal school and a royal court of justice   Its central and accessible location; its commercial importance; the hearty support shown to the school by both city and sovereign, and, above all, the personal genius of some of its early teachers, — each of these no doubt helped to make the school prosper. But its attainment of that extraordinary distinction as the first and for a while the only real centre of general legal studies was due to two special qualities which early came to mark its teaching

(1) The first was its *comprehensive and non-partisan attitude* towards the several rival tendencies in legal thought. It united and assimilated all the elements which went to make up Italy's inheritance from the past. In particular, it merged and represented within its walls the contributions of Ravenna (*ante*, § 13), of Pavía (*ante*, § 10), and of the Constantinople of Justinian. (*a*) Not distant in location from Ravenna, it had replaced that city as the metropolis of the Exarchate. With this transfer of temporal fortunes follow the patronage of the student world. The very origin of the school is by tradition [1] ascribed to the circumstance that the manuscripts of Justinian's law-books were deported from Ravenna to Bologna. The discussions and decisions of the Ravennese jurists were often adopted into the Bolognese glosses. The school regulations were the same. Irnerius is said to have lectured at Ravenna before his famous career at Bologna. They were both primarily schools of Roman law, though using different methods. (*b*) With Pavía, also, Bologna was in intimate relations The "Lombarda" (*ante*, § 16), which became the basis of public instruction in Lombard law, was compiled at Bologna. The Glossators gave recognition to the doctrines of the Pavian lecturers. Irnerius himself, at Bologna, is said (in tradition) to have had as a colleague in his early days Lanfranc, the brilliant Lombard jurist (*ante*, § 11)   The very method which gave fame to Bologna was in essence none other than the method already used for Lombard law at Pavía (*ante*, § 15), applied by means of glosses and of parallel passages, compends, and the like. The adjacent Tuscan region, too, with Pisa then its leading city, had an influence at Bologna. The Tuscan cities were a home for the rapid spread of the Renascence, a headquarters for the rising commercial prosperity, a political centre well equipoised between the rivalries of pope and emperor; signs of their cultivation of legal studies are not wanting,

---

[1] As related by the glossator Odofred.

notably Pisa's long possession of the best and most complete text
of the Pandects [1] These traces of that study point towards
Bologna; [2] the Pisan text was known there, Tuscan jurists taught
there, — Pepo (the earliest), Burgundio (a Greek scholar), and
Gratian (the founder of the new school of Canon law). The very
beginnings of Bolognese studies lead us back to Tuscany, for
Irnerius had been a judge in the court of the famous Countess
Matilda of Tuscany,[3] and her encouragement is said to have led
him to found his school. (c) Finally must be recognized the relation of Byzantine culture to Bologna Here, too, legend has it
that Irnerius, the founder of the school, had studied in Constantinople [4] But behind all legend the fact is certain that
Byzantine legal science must have formed a background for
the Bolognese school, situated as it was in the region of early
Byzantine rule, where the traditions of the law doubtless long
persisted.

(2) The second quality, which helped to raise Bologna to celebrity and at the same time to give it an individuality and to foster
its leadership in Roman law, was its peculiar *political opportunity*
as a city. Pavía was the home of Lombard traditions, but those
were out of date Rome was the headquarters of the Church's
control, but that control was now being thrown off. Tuscany was
being compelled, by the intensely Guelf policy of Countess Matilda,
to abandon its ancient attitude of sympathy for the imperial cause
and thus to lose all prospect of imperial favor. There remained
only Bologna; and there, naturally, the study of the Roman law
would best flourish anew under its traditional patron, the imperial
throne

§ 39. This revival of Roman law, moreover, signified new
methods of study. In the first place, law was now separated from
dialectic, rhetoric, and the other branches, and made a separate
school or faculty. Furthermore, it ceased to be a mere tool, controlled by the needs of practioners, it was expounded strictly as

---

[1] [The copy which was afterwards taken by the Florentines and is
now in the Laurentian Library, the same which tradition once declared
to have been captured by the Pisans at the sack of Amalfi (see the note
to § 42, *post*) — Transl]
[2] *Chiappelli*, "Recherches sur l'état des études du droit Romain en
Toscane an XI siècle" (N R H , 1896).
[3] [The most learned, rich, and brilliant woman of her time, whose
dominion included Pisa, Pavía, and Bologna — Transl]
[4] Equally legendary are the stories that the Roman Emperor Theodosius II had founded the Bologna school, and that the Pisan text of the
Pandects had come directly from Constantinople or from Amalfi its tributary city; see note 2, § 42, *post*

a science, after the manner of the jurists in classical Rome. Returning thus to the classic period of eight centuries before, it paid no heed to the " popular " Roman law of the intervening feudal period, nor yet to the hornbooks and practice manuals which had hitherto been the materials of study. It devoted itself solely to the texts of Justinian It acknowledged no other aim than to know that text perfectly and to expound it faithfully. A method so novel and bold, wielded by a talent as remarkable as that of the early Bolognese jurists, could not but produce results hitherto unimagined. No wonder there grew up a universal opinion that Roman law could be really learned nowhere else than at Bologna. And the now unlimited demand for Roman law soon sent crowds of students from all quarters of Europe.

The School was now so influential that pope and emperor alike were obliged to reckon with it. The emperor, whose claims it had favored, owed it a good turn. Its oldest and greatest privileges were contained in a charter of Frederic I (Barbarossa), the " Habita " of 1158 (post, § 67). This charter, reciting how the students had left the comfort of their homes to travel afar and devote themselves to the pursuit of learning, and how the teachers were enlightening the world by their instruction, granted them a special imperial protection Whoever injured them must pay fourfold; magistrates who failed to enforce this rule would lose office and become infamous ; a member of the university, when sued or prosecuted, was to be tried either by his university superior or by the bishop of the city. And the city itself conferred privileges, chiefly directed to guaranteeing the comfort and convenience of university life within its walls. The Church also (after the early period of rivalry with the Romanists) added its share of privileges. And so the School's prosperity was assured on all hands.

§ 40. **Other Schools.** — Taking example from Bologna, other schools of law multiplied throughout Italy during the 1200s and 1300s New ones were founded , and those which already existed took on new life

Sometimes this occurred by *migrations* of bodies of teachers and students from Bologna (induced by some local epidemic, some conflict with the city authorities, or like motives). They would settle in a city which was conveniently near or which made them some offer of a special advantage. These new ventures did not always endure (as, for example, at Vicenza, Arezzo, Florence). But others prospered permanently, such as the schools of Padua (founded in 1122), of Siena (in the next century), and of Pisa (founded in 1338, when Bologna was put under the ban by Pope Benedict XII) [1]

In other instances, some *ruler* founded or restored a school of law, taking Bologna as his example. This was the origin of the State universities (*ante*, § 37), and was naturally a later development. The Naples school, 'the first of this sort, was founded in 1224, by Frederic II, who was out of humor with Bologna and planned a system of State preparation for public office. With this in mind, he introduced the novelty of organizing in a single institution all branches of learning Hitherto each school had usually represented only a single branch, — generally law (at least, at the outset), and Roman law at that, later, other branches of legal science, especially the Canon law, had been added Schools of medicine followed (notably the one at Salerno, near Naples); and one by one the others had developed. The school at Rome was also a government foundation (in 1303). In the course of time, conditions so changed that the older schools, with narrower scope and less governmental favor, found themselves at a disadvantage. They aspired to an equality, and sought the direct support of emperor or pope. In the end, almost all the universities of Italy (as elsewhere in Europe) could show a papal bull as the foundation or renewal of their status. Imperial charters are not so numerous, — partly because the Church's interference was never wholly to be evaded, partly because the imperial authority was on the decline in Italy from the 1300s onwards

Thus, throughout the period 1200–1400, we find the Italian universities multiplying; and it was left for local conditions to determine which of them should succeed in the competition for survival

§ 41. **The Jurists and their Methods** — The new scientific methods, employed by the early jurists of Bologna, and exhibiting the fusion of all the causes which had led to the foundation of the new schools, were pervaded by a single principle · To attain a complete familiarity with the texts of Justinian's books. What were these texts ?

The Institutes, the Digest, the Code, and the Novels, — all

---

[1] *Rondoni*, "Ordinamento e vicende principali dell' antico studio Fiorentino," Florence, 1884, *Gloria*, "Documenti della reale Università di Padova, 1222-1318," Venice, 1884, *id*, "Documenti, etc, 1318-1405," Padua, 1888, *Zdekauer*, "Lo studio di Siena nel rinascimento," Milan, 1894, *Fabroni*, "Historia Academiæ Pisanæ," Pisa, 1791-1795, *Schupfer*, "Manuale," p. 468, n 61, has an extended bibliography on the various Italian schools. See also the "Annuario delle Università," for 1899-1900.

those they possessed at Bologna, yet in a form which was peculiar to that period and controlled their course of study.[1]

The *Digest* was in several readings or texts, known as " literæ " The " litera vetus " (or " litera communis," " litera antiqua ") signified the manuscripts earlier than the Pisan (or Florentine) manuscript, as well as some others which varied from it. The " litera Pisana " was the Pisan manuscript.[2] The "litera vulgata " (or " litera Bononiensis ") was a composite text, prepared at Bologna by a collation of all the others, for use in the School   The contents of the Digest were peculiarly divided into three parts, — a classification which long persisted in Europe. First came the " Digestum Vetus," which went from the beginning to Book xxiv, title 2. Then came the " Infortiatum," onwards through Book xxxviii. Finally came the " Digestum Novum," from Book xxxix to the end (Book l). The origin of this curious division has been much disputed   It is now generally believed (following the traditions of the glossators themselves, as reported by Odofred) that it happened in the following way. When the law-texts were brought from Ravenna to Bologna (*ante*, § 38), and Irnerius began to make them famous, he did not at first possess

---

[1] *Pertile*, "Storia," §§ 61, 62; *Salvioli*, "Manuale," part II, c. 15; *Schupfer*, "Manuale," sect, II, tit II, c 2; *Savigny*, books III–V, *Panciroli*, "De claris legum interpretibus, libri IV," Venice, 1637; *Tiraboschi*, "Storia della letteratura italiana," Modena, 1781–1786, *Brugi*, "Disegno di una storia letteraria del medio evo ai tempi nostri," Padua, 1888

[2] This was the manuscript about which grew up the legend that it had been found at and taken from Amalfi, when the Pisans captured that city in 1135   It was indeed guarded with almost superstitious care, and its authority was very high   In the early 1400s, the Florentines carried it off from Pisa to their city   The following books and articles deal with its history. Zdekauer, "Sull' origine del manoscritto Pisano delle pandette Giustinianee e la sua fortuna nel medio evo," Siena, 1890, *id.*, "Note sulle due sottoscrizioni nel MS Pisano delle pandette Giustinianee," Roma, 1891, *Buonamici*, "Sulla storia del MS Pisano delle pandette," Bologna, 1890, *id*, "Di una opinione del prof F P intorno alla storia del MS. Fiorentino," Bologna, 1898, *Patetta*, "Sull' introduzione del Digesto a Bologna e sulla divisione in quattro parti," R I S G , 1892, XIV, *A P*, note in Z S S, VI, 300 (1885)   [The famous Florentine parchment has now been reproduced, by photographic facsimile, under the direction of the eminent librarian of the Laurentian Library at Florence, Comm Biagi (who attended the World's Congress of Arts and Sciences at St Louis, in 1904, as delegate from Italy)   The facsimile was issued (1905–1912) in a serial set of 100 copies only , one copy is in the possession of the Elbert H Gary Library of Law in Northwestern University

The legend of the Amalfi origin of this manuscript was mentioned by Blackstone in his Commentaries, and thus obtained a fixed vogue in English legal literature , even yet it occasionally reappears in Anglo-American books   But it was forever disposed of, as an historical delusion, ninety years ago, in Savigny's epoch-making work   Its persistence in English literature therefore gives Savigny's passage a special interest for us   The

the entire text, it was only afterwards that the missing middle portion became known to him, this welcome addition to his sources

following passage is translated from Savigny's second edition of 1834 (vol. III, p. 92, § 35), omitting footnotes

"There is a widespread belief that the Roman law was throughout the Middle Ages quite lost and forgotten   The story goes that the sole surviving manuscript of the Pandects lay in obscurity at Amalfi, whence the Pisans took it as a part of their booty at their capture of Amalfi in 1135; the emperor Lothair II, whose allies they were, permitting them to keep it as a reward for their help; and that he thereupon enacted that the Roman law should be enforced by the courts instead of the Germanic law, and thus by his command public instruction in Roman law came to be given

"Thus runs the full account, though usually we hear only one or another part of it asserted, while the rest is ignored or denied   Its most important feature is the assertion that Roman law was before that date not used, and that Lothair enacted such a law   The first of these assertions has been sufficiently disproved, in earlier parts of this treatise, by evidence extending through every century.   The second has never had the slightest evidence adduced in its favor   With these two assertions gone, it remains to notice the supposed rescue of the manuscript.   This part of the story is sufficiently accounted for by the once widespread belief that all other extant manuscripts were copied from the Pisan.   But that belief is now generally abandoned   The question, therefore, whether the Pisan MS. came from Amalfi, or anywhere else, is of little importance   Nevertheless, the basis for that remaining fragment of the story must be examined.

"The plunder of Amalfi rests on two ancient pieces of testimony. A. A passage from an imprinted Chronicle in Italian, probably of the fourteenth century, as mentioned by Diplovataccius and Taurellus   But Bologninus had already earlier procured through a notary a certified copy of this passage, from a surviving manuscript, and Brenkmann found this manuscript in Bologna and had the passage printed, in his history of the Pandects, Grandi afterwards printed it, correcting the errors   It was undoubtedly the same passage used by Bologninus and Taurellus, preserved in the hands of a Pisan family; and reads, "in la quale città (Malfi) trovorno le pandette composte dalla Cesarea Majesta di Justiniano Imperatore" B   A passage from a historical poem of the fourteenth century, which also plainly tells of the plunder of Amalfi ("unde fuit liber Pisanis gestus ab illis juris, et est Pisis Pandecta Cæsaris alti")   So on these two testimonies the story rests that the famous Pandect manuscript was plundered from Amalfi

"Now both of them date some two centuries after the event which they relate; and their whole character is far from trustworthy   But none of the other and better chroniclers mention the event   Moreover, Odofredus, living in the thirteenth century, says explicitly that this manuscript had been brought to Pisa from Constantinople in the time of Justinian himself And Bartolus asserts that the manuscript had always been at Pisa.   Both of these men, as jurists, had had plentiful occasion to learn the history of this copy, already famous in their day; its capture at Amalfi, if a fact, could not have remained unknown to them   There is therefore no ground for giving credit to such an event

"Still less reason is there for believing the part about the Emperor's presenting the copy to the Pisans   Taurellus tells us that Plotius Gryphius had once owned the deed of gift; but that it had been burned with other documents in an effort to eliminate the plague   This is the only evidence at all for such a gift, and its legendary character is so plain that a demonstration of its gross intrinsic improbability would be superfluous

"And so, of this whole story of the revival of the Roman law through the Pisan manuscript, there remains nothing whatever worth crediting "

[After noting two more supposed items in favor of the tradition, items

he therefore named the "Infortiatum"[1] However, assuming the correctness of this tradition, it at least proves that the peculiar triple division must have been already made before Irnerius' time, at Ravenna, where the manuscripts themselves had been in earlier usage so prepared that the text of the middle portion had become physically separated from the two others. That the bulky Digest should have been subdivided for convenience in study, is natural enough. But why the division should have fallen at those particular books is the unexplainable feature; unless we regard it as a reminiscence of Justinian's own instructions (persisting into the Middle Ages), for the study of his law-books[2] The teacher (following this tradition) was to expound, in the first three of the five years of study, twenty-three of the fifty Books of the Digest (through the topic of Dowry), with these, the first two titles (Marital Conveyances, and Divorce) of Book xxiv came to be included, because of their topical connection; and so this formed the first Part ("Digestum Vetus"). This would explain the further facts that the surviving manuscripts of this portion are more numerous and accurate, and that this Part was included

which had been called to his attention since the first edition of his work in 1822, the learned author concludes] "Surveying without prejudice all the known facts, the net result is this · In the fourteenth century a legend had arisen in Pisa, which attributed the Pisans' possessions of this manuscript to a famous military event of the twelfth century But this legend has no adequate verification, and is in conflict with other evidence of the same or much earlier date. And even the chronicles which give it in some degree an historical status speak only of the capture of the manuscript, all the rest of the story's ornamentation, particularly its presentation by the Emperor, is without even the slightest plausibility So the whole affair is more than ever reduced to one of those numerous legends by which the patriotism of the Italians sought to exalt the repute of their native city, — like the supposed foundation of the University of Bologna by the emperor Theodosius, which even in the thirteenth century was romanced about as a documentary fact " — Transl.]

[1] [*I.e.* "fortification," or "fortifying addition." See *Du Cange*, "Glossarium," where numerous examples are given in the sense "fortify," "equip with munitions." — Transl]

[2] Constit. "Omnem," prefixed to the Digest [This ordinance, which is too long for insertion here, and is of course omitted by the author as being at hand in the Corpus Juris copies used by all Continental students, gave elaborate and complicated directions for the order of study of the various books of the Digest Its essential part, for understanding the above explanations of the author, is found in these passages · "Ex triginta sex librorum recitatione fiant iuvenes perfecti; . . duabus aliis partibus, quæ in quatuordecim libros compositæ sunt, eis depositis, ut possint postea eos legere" (§ 65); "ex libris autem quinquaginta nostrorum digestorum sex et triginta tantummodo sufficere ad vestram expositionem quam ad iuventutis eruditionem iudicamus" (pr), "sed ordinem eorum et tramites per quos ambulandum est manifestare tempestivum nobis esse videtur" (pr); and the detailed directions for omitting certain books and for the order of those selected are then stated in full. — Transl]

among the "regular" books ("ordinarii"), i.e. those covered in
the regular morning lectures by the principal professors. But
those twenty-three Books were not obliged to be the *first* twenty-
three of the Digest, they had merely to be some twenty-three
among the first thirty-six (the number prescribed by Justinian);
with these, however, the next two Books, xxxvii and xxxviii
(on "bonorum possessio" of heirs), came to be included, because
of their connection with Book xxxvi (legacies and trusts), so
that, in the medieval tradition, the compulsory part of the
Digest went as far as Book xxxviii, and these extra Books, up
to xxxviii, which had not been taken up before, were studied
in the fifth year. Thus, in the manuscripts which contained
these Books i-xxxviii (and not merely Books i-xxiii and Book
xxiv, titles 1 and 2), the extra part would naturally enough be
called the "Infortiatum," or fortifying addition The remaining
twelve books (xxxix to l), which were not required to be studied,
became the "Digestum Novum"

Justinian's *Code* was also reckoned among the "regular" books,
and came in the fifth year of the course. Both in omissions and
inclusions, it differed slightly from the original text The last
three of the twelve Books, which dealt with public law no longer
applicable, were not used in the school But it included certain
"Authentica," or extracts from Novels modifying the Code;
these were inserted at the proper places (*post*, § 67).

The *Novels* themselves were rearranged. The text most known
and used in the Middle Ages had been Julian's Epitome But the
Bologna jurists possessed also the official collection, with a Latin
translation of the Greek Novels, which they called the "Authen-
ticum." But for the purpose of study they omitted those of less
practical importance; and the remainder they divided into nine
parts, called "Collationes," to which were added two more parts
made up from the later constitutions of the western Emperors
(*post*, § 67)

What was then known as the *Corpus Juris, i.e.* the entire body
of "legalis sapientia" of the times, was composed of the foregoing
four groups of sources (Institutes, Digest, Code, and Novels), together with the "Lombarda" (*ante*, § 16), the Books of Fiefs (*ante*,
Part I, § 61), and the Canon law-books (*ante*, § 28) The Corpus
Juris itself was regarded as having five "volumina," or Parts, i.e.
the three parts of the Digest made three Parts; the Code, in nine
books only, made the fourth, and the fifth comprised all the rest
(i e the Code's remaining three books, the Institutes, the Novels,

and the feudal laws) , this fifth volume, with its incongruous contents, came to bear distinctively the name " Volumen "

§ 42. (a) **The Glossators.**[1] — The method by which the Bologna jurists worked on these texts was known as the Gloss, or textual interpretation. This method developed out of several causes A principal one was that the school of law had arisen as an offshoot of the school of grammar (*ante*, §§ 9, 35), and thus followed its spirit. Another reason was the surviving tradition of Justinian's prohibition against altering the tenor of his laws by means of liberal interpretation. Still another was the paramount necessity, in that particular stage of the revived study of the manuscripts, for fixing the correct text as accurately as possible. The earliest teachers of Roman law thus came to be known as the Glossators ; and the first epoch of the revived science took its entire character from them. It was not that the use of glosses was new, either in other literary fields, or in its application to medieval Roman law (*ante*, § 18) or to Lombard law (*ante*, § 15). But it was now for the first time employed on the classic Roman texts , and it was this application of it which led to such brilliant results.

The gloss ("γλόσση," synonymous with " verbum," " lingua," " vox ") was at first merely a short explanation of some difficult word made by means of some equivalent , here was seen the connection with the earlier grammar schools But the jurists soon went farther. The gloss became an exposition of a textual passage, or a principle, or an entire law. It was not a commentary because it confined itself (at least in the beginning) to expounding the main text adjacent. But it thus naturally fell into two sorts Either it was merely an explanation of a word, and was placed under that word, between the lines ; hence called " interlinear " Or it was longer, interpreting a passage, and written alongside of it on the margin , hence called " marginal " The different Glossators identified their respective glosses by suffixing their signs-manual, i e. 'their initials or some other conventional mark. But as the gloss developed, it was used for conveying the results of the master's researches or the substance of his oral lectures ; so that it lost its original simplicity of purpose and became an elaborate compendium of knowledge It included critical notes on the variant readings (" variantia ") of different manuscripts. It brought together " loci paralleli," which helped to elucidate the point When

---

[1] *Del Vecchio*, "Di Irnerio e la sua scuola," Pisa, 1869; *Tamassia*, "Odforedo," A R , 1893–1894; *Besta*, "L opera di Irnerio," Turin, 1896; and *Schupfer's* extended bibliography in his "Manuale," p 491, n 63.

these passages were in conflict (" antinomia "), it sought to reconcile them or to decide on the preferable one   Thus, finally,
we find the gloss developing into a genuine commentary, with all
its proper appurtenances, — the summary (" summa,") the putting
of illustrative cases (" casi "), the deduction of a general maxim
(" brocardus "), and the discussion of concrete legal problems
(" quæstiones ") [1]

A gloss thus systematically carried out over an entire topic of
law was known as an " apparatus " ; of this sort, for example, was
Bulgarus' work on the concluding title of the Digest, " De regulis
juris."

§ 43. The Glossators begin with the second half of the 1000s.
Pepo, the first who is recorded as teaching by the new method, was
living in 1176.   But Odofred tells us that Pepo was never famous
(" nullius nominis fuit ") and that the real founder of the school
of Glossators was IRNERIUS, — the luminary (" lucerna juris ") of
all who followed him.   The scanty notices of Irnerius' life all
identify him with the founding of the Glossators' school ; but the
legend varies (ante, § 38), — sometimes making him a colleague
of the Pavian jurists, sometimes an adviser of Countess Matilda,
sometimes a student at Ravenna, and again a teacher at Ravenna.
We know that he is mentioned in documents of 1113–1125 ; and
the sudden rise of legal science and the rapid accession of students
indicate that he must be regarded as the real founder of the Glossators.   His teaching united both theory and practice ; for he had
been at the bar and had held public office.   His scientific work in
glosses ranged over the entire text of the law , but few of them remain to us, and those only through their mention by his successors.

Among these successors come first the " four doctors," — so
called because all four are found together, as advisers of Frederic
I (Barbarossa) at the Parliament of Roncaglia (1158), where they
invoked the Roman law in support of the Emperor's claims over the
Italian cities   These four, BULGARUS, MARTINUS, JACOBUS, and
HUGO, undoubtedly represent the most brilliant period of the school.
Next come Johannes and Rogerus, both pupils of Bulgarus, and
teachers of Azo and Hugolinus.   Azo (who held intimate relations
with Henry VI) was celebrated as the author of a " Summa " of
the Code and the Institutes which surpassed all prior works of the
sort [2]   It was esteemed no less indispensable for study than the

---

[1] [For a further account of these methods, as later applied in Germany,
see Professor *Stintzing's* account, *post*, part IV, § 29. — TRANSL]
[2] [For Bracton's use of Azo's work, in his great foundation treatise,
"Tractatus de Legibus," see Professor *Maitland's* monograph, "Bracton

text itself of the " Corpus Juris" , without it one could never enter the gild of judges; and the proverb at the bar ran, " Chi non ha Azzo, non vada a palazzo." [1] Hugolinus, who was also famous, and held public office (notably as ambassador), died in 1233 (or at least is then last mentioned).   He was reputed the author of the tenth collection of Novels (*post*, § 67), and left also glosses on the Digest, the Code, and the " Volumen," summaries on Digest and Code, besides legal opinions and comments on controverted questions, appended to Azo's " Summa " and the feudal summaries. Placentinus and Vacarius were two Lombard jurists, whose fame is associated with the foreign schools which they founded.   Placentinus established in France the school at Montpellier, where he died in 1192. Vacarius went to England and founded the school at Oxford.[2] Burgundio, who died in 1194, had acquired Greek by several visits to Constantinople, and translated the Greek passages in the Digest. Anselmus of Orta is known for the letters from his father Humbert on feudal usages (*ante*, Part I, § 61). Among the southern jurists, notable ones were Carolus of Tocco, who made an " apparatus " for the " Lombarda" (*ante*, § 16), and Roffredus of Benevento, who took part in the migration from Bologna to Arezzo (*ante*, § 40), and was influential in the contest between Frederic II and the Pope.

But the most famous among the Glossators is ACCURSIUS. Whether by his merit or by his cleverness, his name came to embody all that the school stood for. Born near Florence (in 1182), he studied and then taught at Bologna, retiring after forty years of teaching, to finish his gloss, and dying about 1260. This gloss, distinguished from all others by the name " Accursiana " or " ordinaria," was a comprehensive collection of all preceding glosses, summaries, and other works. By this time the practitioners, overwhelmed under the confused accumulations of a century and a half, were struggling hopelessly with the problem how to find their way amidst the prodigious mass   To them this work of Accursius came as a godsend.   It supplanted all that had gone before   The extraordinary repute of Accursius went on increasing after his death. Bologna showed its gratitude for the glory reflected by

---

and Azo" (Selden Society Publications, vol. VIII, 1894), and *Pollock and Maitland's* "History of English Law," vol I, c VI. — TRANSL]

[1] ["Who has not Azo, goes not to court"; "palazzo" signifying "palace of justice." — TRANSL.]

[2] [For Vacarius, see *Pollock and Maitland's* "History," vol I, p 98 (1st ed); that Vacarius actually founded the school is not conceded by them. — TRANSL]

him on the University; for on the expulsion of the Ghibelline party (in 1304), Accursius' descendants were expressly excepted. Florence, in 1396, ordered a monument to his memory.[1] In the courts his gloss was as good as law, and the saying was in vogue " Quidquid non agnoscit glossa nec agnoscit curia." In the schools, his gloss was the only text studied, for the other jurists, and even the books of Justinian, were laid aside

This great work of Accursius was of course not without its defects. He had not in all instances preserved the best nor excluded the poorest of his predecessors' glosses He did not always abridge correctly. Nor did he give help enough for the practitioners by plainly offering a decided opinion on points much controverted And yet it is hardly right to attempt to pass judgment in these matters upon Accursius' work as we have it For one thing, it would require a complete acquaintance with the sources abridged by him, and most of them either are long perished or repose still in manuscript Moreover, in the course of repeated copyings, so many errors have occurred, in omitting or exchanging the signs-manual which serve to identify the passages of the other authors and of Accursius himself, that it is now unsafe to base conclusions upon the authorship of particular passages.

§ 44 The school of the Glossators virtually ended with Accursius Glosses, of course, continued for a while to be written; but, with few exceptions, they lacked in originality or other merit. Accursius' three sons (Francis, Cervot, and William) merely prepared illustrative cases for his text Odofred has come down to us with the most distinction; but it is due entirely to his useful records of the anecdotes and traditions (some of them now known to be pure legends) about the early jurists Andrew of Barletta wrote a commentary on the Lombarda. Rolandinus Passagerius (who died in 1300) was famous for his lectures and writings on the notary's practice; his " Summa artis notariæ " and " Rolandina " are the best known of his works Albertus of Gandino obtained repute as a criminalist; his great work is entitled " De maleficiis." In the field of procedure, a wide and European fame was accorded in its day to the " Speculum Judiciale," a vast and systematic treatise by William Durante, dubbed the " Speculator" (" Imager ").

Of this decadence, the great work of Accursius was not so much a cause as a symptom. When he wrote, the original vigor of

---

[1] But it was never erected.

this method and school of thought had already been lost, and his work merely accelerated the decline   The scientific merit of the early Glossators had been to concentrate study upon the original sources.   They had succeeded, notwithstanding the scantiness of their materials, in developing an almost perfect familiarity with the texts, and in thus elevating the practice of the law to the dignity of a science.   The successors of Accursius, however, substituted the gloss itself for the text as the basis of their study, — a sure sign of decadence.   This may be ascribed partly to the outward political circumstances of the times, which had diverted men's minds from the original aims of the science, and partly to the intrinsic limitations of the method, which had now exhausted its scientific possibilities   To continue with it was merely to multiply fruitlessly its inherent defects.   How low the method had now fallen may be seen from the rule of decision used when divergent opinions were found collated by Accursius on a given point. It was this.   The principle being that Accursius' own view should be decisive, that view (when not expressly stated) was to be ascertained by presumption, and the presumption was that the opinion last quoted by him was his, except when it was prefaced by "alii dicunt" or "quidam dicunt," and except when some opinion prior in order was more favorable to equity or to marriage or to the Church!

A method like this, barren of all possibility of independent reasoning, had plainly gone to seed, and was certain to be supplanted by some more worthy rival.   Such had been Rome's experience, in the period after the classic jurists, when the law settled controversies by choosing that view which contained among its adherents the name of Papinian or a majority of all other names.[1] In the course of time the same replacement of scientific reasoning by petty mechanical rules had now again come about.   And a main reason was not far to seek.   The Glossators had sought to revive the laws of Justinian, for study and for practice.   But those laws were not and could not be fully suited to the needs of the time. After a short but brilliant period of this revival, the texts of those laws had been superseded by the glosses, because the glosses applied them to the needs of contemporary practice.   This desertion of the text itself was, however, the abandonment of the fundamental

---

[1] See *post*, § 46.   Another instance, in the earlier days, was the rule (Codex, I, 14, 3) for determining whether an imperial decree had force as a general law for all countries ; it was held a general law if it had been introduced in the Senate, or bore the name Edict, or contained the phrase "ad omnes partinebant," or had other such arbitrary features.

basis of the Glossators' method. It had lost its right to exist. The times now needed a method which, while remaining faithful to the Roman law, should cease to base itself upon that law as it was a thousand years before, and should expound it as a body of living principles, — a contemporary law, suited to the needs of society in the fourteenth century after Christ.

§ 45. (b) **The Commentators.**[1] — The actual beginnings of the new method had dated from the second half of the 1200s, while Accursius was still supreme. Its followers were variously termed — "commentators," "dialecticians," "practicians," "Bartolists" — according to some one of the features which contrasted with the Glossators' method. In essence, it stood for a reaction against the gloss. In this situation, two paths were open to pursue (though the new school had indeed no opportunity of freely choosing between them). One of these paths was that pointed to by the literary Renascence of the 1300s, — the era of Dante, Petrarch, and Boccaccio. But to this great intellectual movement the jurists were yet strangers. They were chained by tradition and cramped by the demands of daily practice. The time was not ripe for such a revival of juristic culture as came two centuries later, under their successors, the Humanists. And so they had no choice, on abandoning the gloss method, but to turn once more into the ancient path of scholasticism. They gave new vigor, it is true, to legal studies, by introducing the dialectic method, — that of logical reasoning and discussion. But this was already antiquated, in spite of their attempts to cover its decadence artifically by the outward forms of reasoning. When their system, after a formative period, was finally developed, it stood forth as the apotheosis of a painstaking logic. The jurist's ideal now was to divide and subdivide, to state premises and then to draw the inferences; to test the conclusion by extreme cases, sometimes insoluble and always sophistical, to raise objections and then to make a parade of overthrowing them — in short, to solve all problems by a fine-spun logic. He who nearest reached this ideal was accorded the highest fame in his science.

The method, to be sure, tended in itself to cease to be science in the highest sense. For its homage to the conclusions of artificial logic drew it gradually away, not only from the legislative sources

---

[1] *Bruqi,* "Alcuni osservazioni sul periodo storico dei postglossatori in Italia," Bologna, 1881; *Chiappelli,* "La polemica contro i legisti dei secoli XIV–XVI," A G S, 1881; *Vidalin,* "Bartole et les hommes illustres de son siècle," Paris, 1856; *Schupfer,* "Manuale," p. 515, has bibliographies on the individual jurists.

themselves, but also from any sound criteria of legal truth   And
the outward signs of a decadence were not long in appearing.
Lectures and treatises alike became so prolix that only a small
topic could be treated in them   Seeking to avoid this dilemma,
they confined their discourses to the easier topics, omitting those
difficult ones which required too much time.   The judgment of
Cujas upon them, in after times, is full of truth · " Verbosi in re
facili, in difficili muti, in angusta diffusi."   They totally lacked
literary culture ; their style was commonplace, and their diction
crude and harsh   As the new system progressed, all this became
more marked.   There was no attempt at literary elegance, nor even
at correctness of historical facts or of etymologies or of syntax.
None of the other branches of learning were made use of.   And
the inherence of these traits in the very method itself is apparent
when we find Cino of Pistoia, an accomplished poet, using in his
law-books a style as crude as that of any other jurist ; or when we
hear Baldus, one of the foremost jurists, advising the students to
pay no attention to style or form of utterance.   Their ideal was
quite satisfied with a stale rehashing of well-known ideas, expounded in a series of logical dilemmas and syllogisms, and interspersed with illustrative cases, which were supposed to explain some
legal principle, but might (as often as not) do quite the contrary
and merely leave the doctrine as muddled and uncertain as ever.

§ 46   Amidst the copious mass of such commentaries (which
together would have made, it was said, " multorum camelorum
onus "), it would have been hopeless to find and useless to invoke
the original texts on which they based their lucubrations   Legal
science was now a victim to the fetish of authority-worship.
The lecture, the forensic argument, the judicial decision, now consisted in little more than citing somebody's name and treatise.

The later Glossators had indeed already entered, in their day,
on this downward path , they had developed the rule of taking
for law whatever some authority had once asserted, and of deciding
(when there were opposing opinions on record) by the number of
opinions on one side and the other.   This practice owed its origin
to the great authority of Accursius, whose opinion was treated as
law when there was no express statute or custom on the point.
There was some justification for this ; because his authority rested
on his having collated all the best of the prior labors (" maximi
scientiæ et auctoritatis viri ") ; and no one (at least, in a decadent age) could presume to dispute the united wisdom of his
predecessors.   But the practice degenerated, and extended itself,

without reason, to include the other jurists; for example, a statute enacted that Dinus' opinion should stand for law whenever on a given point Accursius had expressed two opposite opinions. And when Bartolus came to dominate in the new school (he of whom Jason said, " ut terrestre numen colui et cuius vestigia adoravi ") his name received an even greater homage of authority The phrase long current, " Nemo bonus jurista nisi Bartolista," illustrates for us the extent to which mere authority had superseded principle

Nor, unfortunately, did this stop with jurists so distinguished as Bartolus Dogma and authority-worship having superseded reason and science, it was now an easy step to the logical culmination of the system, — the doctrine of " communis opinio," or weight of opinion; i.e the rule that the recorded opinion which had the greater number of adherents was the sound one. To this rule the practitioners were ready enough to yield support; for it reduced their labor to that of ransacking from the books as many opinions as possible, regardless of their intrinsic value, and then marshalling them in court, like hostile battalions, for the judges' mechanical enumeration. And the schools of law, which still had their eyes entirely on the preparation of practitioners, followed suit; they contented themselves with the same dull round of repetitious citation of musty authorities, whose chief virtue was that their opinions were at least likely to be better than those of the lecturers of that day

The story of the classic Roman law had offered an interesting parallel to this stage of legal science. There, too, when the product of juristic thought had passed its prolific and brilliant stage, the solution of legal doubts was sought by the mere rule of thumb By the law of Citations [1] the judge was to decide, not by aid of his own reasoning, but by following that opinion which numbered a majority of accredited names, and when the number was equal, Papinian's name controlled. There, too, it was a period of decadence; and the same effects are seen, a thousand years apart, recurring from the same causes. And herein is contained a lesson, by no means flattering, for us of to-day, when the same tendency is once more visible, to subordinate the living, active reason of the law to the mechanical counting of precedents.

§ 47 But it must not be supposed that the Commentators, with all their faults, did not contribute something worth while towards the advancement of legal science.

[1] 426 A D , by Theodosius II and Valentinian III.

In their defence it must be remembered, in the first place, that
the disfavor into which they fell, in their own day, was emphasized
by their aloofness from the general movement of the Renascence.
While literature and culture in general were casting off all the
marks of the Middle Ages, and were taking on new life in every
feature, while politics were resenting the ancient dominance of
Church and Empire, the jurists were adhering obstinately to the
traditions, the logic, and the diction of the past centuries. They
were thus bound to bear the stigma of being reactionaries. Moreover, the legal profession, and the schools of law, no longer enjoyed
the dominant influence of their former days. The ducal despotisms
had taken the place of the free cities, and the State was meddling
more with education. Italy's leadership in commerce was passing
to other countries. The centre of political equilibrium was no
longer in Italy, for the Empire was now essentially a German
power, the Papacy was losing ground, and the monarchies of France,
Spain, Germany, and England were more extensive in domain
than the fragmentary Italian principalities. So that it was no
longer possible for the jurists of Italy to play a brilliant part as
leaders of public thought and as interpreters of national sentiment.
This ancient function of theirs was being sacrificed to the rising
spirit of regionalism; and the fact that they struggled to preserve
their traditions, as much as in them lay, must be reckoned to their
credit.

And though these are merely extenuating circumstances, which
serve to explain the shortcomings of the school, there remain, moreover, some positive merits in the work of these jurists of the 1200s
and 1300s. Their predecessors, the Glossators, had at the best
done no more than expound the Roman law of six centuries before,
— centuries whose lapse had for them no meaning whatever.
Justinian, to the Glossators, was still living and legislating, the
needs of their own generation did not interest them; and, with all
their zeal and learning, their labors therefore could never have
culminated in a really national law. But the Commentators,
doing far otherwise, never lost sight of the demands of legal practice
around them. Endowed with less genius for science, and hampered by a sophistical and prolix method, their very incapacity
for a higher point of view saved them from losing touch with the
needs of their times, and made their labors practical and useful
In their writings we find, for the first time, the ancient principles
of Roman law harmonized and adapted to the city statutes, to the
feudal and Germanic customs, and to the Canon law's principles.

The old science was made over into a new one; and Roman law was transformed into an Italian law It is this success in the field of practice which justifies the frequent remark by historians that even the Commentators had their moments of brilliancy. The task of adapting Roman law to the new social conditions called for a talent of its own. The originality with which they developed the new principles — many of which were destined to stay permanently in the law — gave to the Commentators, in spite of their inferior science, an authority which neither the Glossators nor any other later school ever enjoyed in the legal world. Their treatises obtained the force of law itself; and their method was followed, not merely in Italy, but throughout all Europe.

§ 48. This method of theirs, which was destined in later times (and not unjustly) to be so roundly disparaged, was known in the legal world as the "mos Italicus," or Italian method It had given up the gloss, i.e the marginal analysis of a text. It had begun by framing an "apparatus" and a "summary" (ante, § 42); and it proceeded by developing vast and systematic commentaries, — whence the name given to the school. These in turn gave rise to independent treatises, essays, or tracts; and the name "tractists" was also applied to this school of jurists. Of its more famous members, we may now notice a few.

Cino of Pistoia (1270–1336), who was one of the earliest leaders, was a man of great personal talent, and law was one of his lesser interests, perhaps for these reasons his works are marked by more originality and human interest. Albericus of Rosate (died in 1354) gave such attention to practice in his writings that he was known as "the great practitioner," and even to-day his historical notes on this subject are interesting. BARTOLUS of Alfani, however, was and remains the prince of the Commentators He was born at Sassoferrato in 1314, and died at his early prime in 1357. After studying under Cino at Perugia, and under Raniero of Forli, he became lecturer at Bologna, at the age of twenty, removing thence to Pisa and finally to Perugia He held several public appointments; and his embassy from the Perugian government to Charles IV brought him the post of councillor to the Emperor, together with numerous special privileges from his patron. It was in recognition of these that Bartolus inserted into the Corpus Juris an eleventh series of Novels, which comprised some ordinances of Henry VII of Luxemburg, grandfather of the Emperor (post, § 67). His works include lectures given at the school, commentaries on all titles of the Digest, legal opinions ("consilia"), and treatises or essays on almost every part of the law, whether public, private, penal, or procedural. His writings show certainly a quality superior to that of the other Commentators. His thoroughness led him to give unusual attention to the sources (witness his textual comparisons of the Florentine manuscript of the Pandects); and he demonstrated that originality of view and vivacity of style were compatible with a careful attention to the demands of the practitioners. More than any other jurist of his school, he contributed to its great work in transforming the law of the past into the law of his day; and it is upon this achievement that his fame worthily rests. His repute throughout Europe was indeed extraordinary. His opinions were law as far away as Spain and Portugal. The "mos Italicus" was adopted in the rising schools of France and Germany.[1] The lawyers of his school were termed simply "Bartolists." At Padua and other universities a chair was founded solely for lectures on his works; as late as 1616 this was repeated at Naples   And the professional domination of his name culminated in the maxim "Nemo jurista nisi sit Bartolista," — no one is a jurist who is not a Bartolist.

But it is the shortcomings and not the merits of his school that again become the more notable features in the works of his successors. The best known of these was BALDUS of the Ubaldi (born at Perugia, 1327, died 1400). He was a pupil of Bartolus, and taught successively at Bologna, Pisa, Florence, Padua, and Pavía. He was a Canonist as well as a Romanist, and in the public affairs of his day (especially in the Church schisms) he rendered important service. Among his successors (none of whom approached him in fame) were Luke of Penna (lecturer in 1345), Bartholomew Salicetus (1330–1412), Raphael Fulgosius (1367–1471), Paul of Castro (died 1441), Marian and Bartholomew Socinus of Siena, Philip Decius, Jason of Mainus.

§ 49. (c) **The Humanists.**[2] By the period when these last-named Commentators were leaving the scene, the rise of Humanism had already cast so brilliant a light throughout Italy that

---

[1] [For the "mos Italicus" in France and Germany, and its successor, the "mos Germanicus," see also the accounts by Professors *Brissaud* and *Stintzing* in Parts III and IV of the present volume   For the spirit of this period, consult also Professor *Courtney Kenny's* essay "Bonus jurista malus Christa" (Law Quart Rev, XIX, 326) — TRANSL]

[2] *Dal Re*, "I precursori Italiani di una nuova scuola di diritto Romano nel secolo XV," Rome, 1878; *Buonamici*, "Il Poliziano gureconsulto e della letteratura nel diritto," Pisa, 1863; *Hach*, "Cujas, les Glossateurs, et les Bartolistes," Paris, 1883   For a further list of monographs see *Schupfer*, "Manuale," p. 607, n 83.

the adherents of the old methods were already overshadowed.
They had played their part; and the season had now arrived when
for the third time a new school of thought was to rejuvenate the life
of the law   The name Humanism is given to that movement
which throughout Italy in the 1400s made for the reform of letters,
arts, thought, and manners.   In the strong light of comparison,
the jurists of the old school, holding apart as they did from this
general social movement, had already begun to seem uncouth and
crude   The stirring events of the next two centuries only emphasized this contrast   Italy's ancient liberties had been suppressed by despots and foreign dynasties; the new ocean highway
had transferred immense trade to other countries, and politics and
commerce, hitherto the principal fields of activity for the most
active minds of the nation, were perforce closed to them   This
activity, not yet enervated nor accustomed to sloth, naturally
turned itself with accumulated force into the field of learned and
intellectual endeavor.   And several circumstances combined to
aid this new direction of energy.   The free discussion induced by
the great religious controversies helped to emancipate from the
dogmas of received authority.   The fall of the Greek empire of
the Orient had driven to Italy many learned refugees, who
brought with them the treasures of their libraries and revived
the culture of the Greek language and literature.   The invention
of printing led to the wide diffusion of information in books, and
made it possible for the new learning to reach an audience vast in
comparison with the limits imposed by oral teaching and manuscript copies.   All these things, together with the final development of the Italian language as a vehicle for learned thought, gave
a new impulse to university pursuits; and legal science could not
fail to share in the effects.

Not that the jurists themselves experienced an immediate conversion of heart.   It was rather the new sciences which made the
first approaches, and went to meet the law   By their researches in
philosophy and in history, they demonstrated that law was a part
of general science and needed to be so treated; and they thus
ultimately drew the profession of the law into the general train of
the movement   For some time there had been signs that things
were taking this trend.   At the very beginning of the movement
for the new culture, some of the best intellects had turned their
criticisms upon the jurists.   Dante, for example,[1] chides them
with holding aloof from the new philosophies of truth, and ad-

[1] "De monarchia," b II, c. 11.

hering in their decisions to the literal and self-centred interpretation of the law.   Petrarch, not mincing his words,[1] accused them of venality, of ignorance in rejecting the aid of the other sciences, and of wasting their lives in vain quibbles created by their own imagination.   Boccaccio[2] asserted that law had ceased to be a science at all   The later scholars, who were the real founders of Humanism, took up the attack with even greater vehemence. Ambrose Traversari (known as the Camaldolese, 1386–1439), when consulted by a friend who planned to study law, applauded his intention, but only on condition that he should ignore the Commentators, whose contemptible ignorance made their writings in great part unintelligible, and that he should give himself solely to the ancient jurists; otherwise his friend would merely waste the time which he might have spent on more profitable studies. Maffeus Vigeus, in giving like counsel, recommended the study of the Roman law, not in the commentaries, which merely obscured it, but in the original sources, where he could enjoy the elegant diction and the ripe wisdom of the ancients.   Tribonian was anathematized, for having sacrificed on the altar of immediate utility the masterpieces of the classic Roman jurists, the achievement of Tribonian's compilation (said Maffeus), instead of making the law clear and simple, was a crime, which had brought its own retribution; for the collected fragments of the classic jurists were now buried under the futile crudities of the Commentators

This outburst is notable as the first recorded protest against the Corpus Juris itself.   Hitherto venerated for centuries as the perfection of legal wisdom and the final goal of legal research, it was now condemned as a mere secondary compilation   This complaint was uttered, to be sure, from the standpoint of literary taste and reverence for the classics   But the path was now once for all opened to unrestricted criticism, and legal thought was thus invited to assume an independence of judgment to which it had hitherto been a complete stranger

§ 50. Signs of the times soon multiplied, showing the trend of the new methods.   Hitherto, the best minds had been turning in disgust from the study of the law, literary history was full of the names of those who (like Balzac in our own times) had abandoned its apprenticeship for the fields of polite learning   But now it was the scholars of classic training, even poets, who devoted themselves, enthusiastically and fruitfully, to legal research

[1] "Epistolæ familiares," IV, 20.
[2] "De genealogia deorum," XIV, 4.

Among this numerous throng may be mentioned Lorenzo Valla
(died in 1457), who combined an antipathy for the Commentators
with a pioneer's zeal for the history and philosophy of classic
Roman law, and Pomponius Leto (1428-1498), a pupil of Valla,
who enthusiastically followed in his footsteps, and was the first to
attempt the reconstruction of Roman legal history. Angelo
Politian (1454-1496), that prodigy and leader of learning and
literature, was drawn into the literary study of the legal sources,
and maintained that they embodied all the treasures of the Latin
tongue. Politian's great design, however, of compiling a vari-
orum edition of the Roman texts, was defeated by the untimely
end which cut short his brilliant career.

The textual studies of these men, nevertheless, were so far
superior, in method and resources, to those of the Glossators' days,
that a new horizon was opened. Moreover, the new classical
fervor was not content with Justinian's texts alone, but sought
to include the available fragments of the earlier jurists. The
Paraphrases of Theophilus' Institutes were resuscitated by
Politian himself and Paulus' Sentences by Valla; Gaius' fragments were identified in the Breviary of Alaric (ante, Part I, § 8);
the Theodosian Code was compared with Justinian's. These and
the other sources were edited during the 1500s.

And not only in textual criticism, but also in topics and methods,
legal research was broadened and advanced. Public law was now
included, not merely private law. To textual interpretation was
added synthetic reconstruction and general treatises. Practice
ceased to be the sole objective, a legal science in the true sense was
the inspired aim, and history and philology were pressed into
service The Glossators, to be sure, had in their day shared in
this general aim of a scientific interpretation of the text, and the
Humanists, with all their contempt for the Commentators, never
failed to give credit to the sound methods of the earlier school
But the Humanists' work was vastly superior to that of the Glossators, not merely in their auxiliary use of history and literature,
but in their determination to treat Justinian's texts historically, and to restore the classic Roman law itself, as the true
original from which Justinian's books were merely a compiled
mosaic

§ 51. The distinctive features of the new school of jurists are
seen in the works of ALCIAT, whose appearance marks the new
legal era Andrew Alciat was born in 1492, at Alzate, near Milan,
and his early training in history and literature equipped him well

for his great career in the law. He took up the warfare against all the shortcomings of the Commentators, — the doctrine of "communis opinio" (*ante*, § 46), the prolixity and crudity of expression, the petty analysis of detached rules and texts. He championed conciseness and purity of style, freedom of reasoning on principles, a systematic view of the law, and an adjustment of its parts as a whole. His works were few in number and scope; but in merit they placed him in the leadership of the new school. He was soon lost to Italy; for in 1518 he accepted a call to Avignon, where he transplanted the new method in French soil, and there achieved a brilliant career of European fame and influence. He afterwards moved to Milan, Bourges, Pavía, Bologna, and Ferrara, and died at Pavía in 1552   The works he has left include a dissertation on the Greek words in the Digest (written at the age of twenty-one, and serving to launch him into fame), a commentary on the Digest; and other works entitled "Paradoxa," "Parerga," "Emblemata," etc

But his early departure was a serious loss to Italy   He had some successors, to be sure, — Scipio Gentili (1563–1616), Lelius Torelli (who edited the Florentine text of the Pandects in 1553), Emilius Ferretti, Hippolytus of Colle, Turamini of Siena, Julius Pacius, and others   But for the most part the jurists clung to the old methods and opposed the new. The principal cause of this obstinacy was the support which they received from the practitioners. The solid traditions of the courts and the bar could not be upset in a moment   Moreover, the new school had excited strong antagonism by its own expressed contempt for the old school. And besides this, its novelties had to contend with the suspicion that they were in some way allied to that other and most radical novelty of the times, — the Protestant movement in religion, and this was enough to insure a coolness on the part of the Church and its supporters. Finally, we must remember that the old method, with its highly technical learning, had at this period given the legal profession a social supremacy and a firm monopoly of the avenues of justice, and was enabling them to gain a livelihood by this science of theirs, such as it was; how could they be expected to look favorably on new ideas which would rob them of these advantages? [1]

[1] [This recalls Lord Ellenborough's naïve remark, rebuking an objection to an old technicality, "If I did not adhere to this rule, a lawyer who was well stored with these rules would be no better than any other that is without them " — TRANSL]

§ 52. (d) **The Practical Jurists** [1] — And so the lawyers went on
turning the old treadmill of " comunis opinio " and casuistic logic
— the famous " mos Italicus " The science of law was left to
starve. But the courts were crowded, the lawyers prospered, and
the tomes of law continued to pile up No one, to be sure, could
master them all ; but the practitioners sought to pick out the most
necessary parts, to reduce them to rules of thumb, to learn them by
mnemonic devices, — in short, to make a mechanical trade of the
rules of practice, so that one could acquire it by mere plodding
industry. There was no attempt at science and no provision for
progress

And so the marked feature of this decadent stage of the law —
taking the place, in the 1500s and 1600s of the earlier Glosses
and Commentaries — is its elaborate system of *practical formulas*.
The apparatus of this system had a variety of technical details,
famous enough in their day [2] There were the " loci," or hornbook
rules, which were supposed to condense all the wisdom of the
Corpus Juris and the later writers. Then there were the " consilia,"
or opinions and decisions on cases, wherein judges and lawyers
alike delved for authority in arguing and deciding. There were
also the " comunes opiniones," or collated views of learned writers ,
the " observationes practicæ," the " formularia " and the " specula "
or practical treatises , the " cautelæ " for notaries' use ; the
" decisiones," the " aphorismi," the " concordantia," the " solu-
tiones ", and sundry other aids

Amidst the tedious bulk of literature chargeable to the jurists
of that period, we find, to be sure, some authors whose work
has merited to be remembered   Albericus Gentilis (1550–1611)
wrote " Dialogi sex de veteribus juris interpretibus," in which
he defended the ancient methods and disparaged the new ones.[3]
Menochius of Pavía (1532–1607) was famous in his day for a
practical compilation of the law as it then was   Antonius Faber
of Savoy (1557–1624) broke away from formalism in his " De

---

[1] [On this and the preceding period, especially on Alciat, the Italian
Humanists, and the more influential French representatives, see Professor
Maitland's masterpiece, " English Law and the Renaissance," reprinted in
" Select Essays in Anglo-American Legal History," vol I, p 168, particularly pp 172–198   No Anglo-American student can neglect his illuminating story of the influence which this great European movement was exhibiting in England in the 1500s — TRANSL]

[2] [On this "apparatus," see further Professor *Stintzing's* account, in
part IV, *post* — TRANSL]

[3] [Gentilis was afterwards professor at Oxford   His life is told by Professor *Holland*, in his essay on " Alberico Gentili " (Inaugural Lecture, 1874).
— TRANSL.]

erroribus pragmaticorum," "De conjecturis," and "Codex Fabrianus."[1] Cardinal Gian Battista de Luca (1614–1687) gained a long lease of fame by his learned and encyclopedic works, "Theatrum veritatis" and "Doctor vulgaris" Among the specialists in particular branches are notable the commercial jurists Straccha (1578) and Casaregis (1737), and the criminalists Clarus (1525–1575) and Farinacius (1554–1616).

The excellences which marked these jurists showed that the Humanist school had not been without influence. The style of writing had improved, mere authority was no longer worshipped; the tedious discussion of isolated passages and cases was discredited, and constructive work was not uncommon. Even the revival of legal history, which had been aided, in the meanwhile, in related fields, by such men as Panvinius, Sigonius, Ugellus, Tiraboschi, and Muratori, found an occasional champion in the law. The most notable was G. Vincenzo Gravina (1664–1718), who devoted his vast learning to tracing the derivation of Italian from Roman law, in his celebrated work, "Origines juris civilis"[2] He first showed the way to the philosophic study of the Roman law as means of improving the national law and not as an end in itself. The legal works of G. B. Vico took the same stand — though he devoted most of his efforts to the general philosophy of law.[3] This branch of science was now enabled, on the one hand, to cultivate free philosophic speculation, and on the other, to give systematic treatment to the national law as a product of national needs. And yet, in justice to the technical jurists, it was their great merit to have made this possible, without intending or perhaps being aware of it. Their sole concern was to adapt the vast stores of Roman law to daily practice. But the net result was a commendable fusion of theory and practice. Practice was moded and elevated by science. Theory ceased to be abstract, became useful and practical, and adapted itself to a contemporary and genuinely Italian law.

Henceforth, legal science takes a thoroughly different point of view. Roman law is no longer blindly worshipped as Written Reason ("ratio scripta"). Justinian's texts are not sacrosanct. Roman law is to be merely the supplementary or "common" law,

[1] [His fame survived chiefly through his treatise "De presumptionibus" — Transl.]

[2] [As late as Hallam's day, this author served as a leading authority on the history of the law. — Transl.]

[3] [Vico's philosophy is fully expounded in Miraglia's "Comparative Legal Philosophy" (1912), being vol. III of the "Modern Legal Philosophy Series" — Transl.]

while the national law comes into the foreground, discarding the ancient principles when antiquated and inapplicable, and adding such new ones as the present day conditions had developed The Bartolist practitioners still held their own; but the signs of the times were against them. No clearer proof of this is needed than Muratori's celebrated essay on "The Shortcomings of our Legal Practice," in which he openly combats the anachronistic reign of Roman law in the practice of the day. And its spirit was that of the Italian jurists of the 1700s; among whom the most notable are Averanius (1662–1738), a follower of the Frenchman Cujas, and author of the "Interpretationes Juris," and Richerus, author of the "Universa civilis et criminalis Jurisprudentia," published in 1774.

This growth of law on national lines was of course a part of the general movement of the times throughout Europe. On the successive ruins of Empire, Cities, and Principalities, there were now building the States of modern Europe. And this brought with it another marked change Hitherto, the universality of Roman common*law had signified a common science of law, the home and central influence of which had been Italy But with the break-up of the dominion of pure Roman law, and the systematization of local national law, so, too, legal science ceased to be a possession in common It took on an independent life in the various countries National character gave it national features And as Italy, now under foreign dynasties, had ceased to be politically independent, and (like all organic beings) was in a state of decadent reaction after a period of exuberant activity, so in legal science also it bowed to foreign authority. The rising schools of thought in France, Holland, and Germany, which from the time of Alciat and Zasius had been zealous rivals of their parent influence, had now finally won from Italy the primacy in legal science.

§ 53. (e) **Jurists of France, Germany, and Holland** At the period of the Germanic invasions and settlements of Western Europe, the Roman law still played a very small part in forming the law of those regions (*ante*, Part I, §§ 28–47). It had indeed already influenced the law of the southwest regions, under Roman rule, through the Canon law, other principles entered, and as a "common" law, for solving problems of conflict of laws, Roman law had been resorted to. But the native sources had thoroughly kept the upper hand, the pure Roman sources were seldom used, and in some regions were even expressly disowned.

By the time of the Renascence of Roman law in Italy, however, conditions in the other countries were radically changed. Charlemagne's Empire of the West had opened the way. It brought political unity to widely diverse peoples, its support of Roman law imparted a certain universal validity to that system. The revival of the study in Italy in the 1100s, and the fame of the Italian schools of law, gave the needed impetus. Roman law was transplanted into all parts of Europe.

But this took place in different ways in different countries. In some instances (*ante*, § 43), the opening of a university, and the appointment of Italian teachers (for example, Placentinus at Montpellier, and Vacarius at Oxford), introduced the law of Justinian, with the same methods, texts, and glosses as at Bologna, and sometimes with the same teachers. In some instances, the mere prestige of the Roman law, emanating from Italy, and supported by imperial favor, sufficed to secure its restoration by the ruler's mandate. This was the case in Spain, in the 1200s, under Alfonso of Castile, and in other countries under the Empire But the principal means was the constant stream of students of law, who sought the Italian schools from every quarter of Europe, and returned home full of the new learning And their legal learning had its effects in practice. These university doctors of law were soon (though gradually) substituted for the popular judges in the local courts ("scabini," "échevins," "schoffen"); and were also appointed to the royal councils which (like the English Chancery and Privy Council) were everywhere assuming a larger share in the administration of justice. In Germany, the ordinance of 1495, that the "Camera Imperii" ("Kammergericht") should apply the Imperial common law, and that one half of its members must be doctors of law, marks the triumphant arrival of Roman law in that country.[1]

And now was seen a repetition, in reverse order, of that course of events which had marked the Germanic settlement in Italy nearly a thousand years before. Then it was the Germanic law,

---

[1] The "reception" of Roman law in Germany has been treated in numerous works, of which the following may be here noted. *Schmidt*, "Die Reception des römischen Rechts in Deutschland," Rostock, 1868, *Moddermann*, "Die Reception des römischen Rechts," Jena, 1875, *Karlowa*, "Ueber die Reception des römischen Rechts in Deutschland," 1878, *Franklin*, "Beiträge zur Geschichte der Reception des römischen Rechts in Deutschland," Hannover, 1883, *Wilmans*, "Die Reception des römischen Rechts und die socialen Frage der Gegenwart," Berlin, 1890

[See also the works cited by Professors *Brunner* and *Stintzing*, in part IV, *post*. — TRANSL.]

which had entered Italy to compete with the Roman law already
flourishing there. Now it was the Roman law, which in turn
invaded the north and the west, there to compete with the native
law. Now, as then, the resultant was to be a new law of composite features. But it is worth noting that the Roman law now
imported was a law formed and developed by Italian science and
practice. The universities of France followed the traditions and
methods of Italy. The opinions of Bartolus were made the law
of Spain and Portugal And in Germany, the " mos Italicus,"
expounded by professors brought from Italy, became the universal
fashion.

§ 54 But the day came at last when this Italian primacy ended.
It dates from Alciat's departure from Italy into France, at the
invitation of Francis I (*ante*, § 51) Alciat made Bourges the
centre of influence for the new methods of the Humanists. And
a new term became current, the " mos Gallicus," to contrast the
new methods with the " mos Italicus," or old-fashioned methods
of the Commentators or Bartolists. In the struggle which then
ensued between the two systems, all Europe was involved. And
everywhere the new ultimately triumphed over the old.

In the French school thus founded by Alciat, the leading name
was that of JACQUES CUJAS (Jacobus Cujacius) ; born at Toulouse
1522, died at Bourges 1590 In 1566 he had taught awhile at
Turin; and he always enjoyed a high authority among the Italian
followers of the Humanist school, whence indeed had come the
inspiration for the powerful French thinkers who now took up the
work Cujas' chief work is his twenty-eight books of " Observationes et emendationes " His zeal and ingenuity in history and
philology carried research so far that it now became possible to
restore the works of many classical Roman jurists, in spite of Justinian's mutilations For Cujas' guiding purpose was the reconstruction of what Justinian's commissioners had destroyed By
his untiring labors, Papinian, Ulpian, Paul, and others of the golden
age before Constantine, were now restored to the hands of scholars.
The Glossators, indeed, had been likewise restorers of the text
But they in their primitive scholarship had stopped short at Justinian's compilation. The new standpoint and the new methods
were not content until they could dissect this artificial structure
and lay bare the elements from which it had been put together.
No doubt this concentration on one purpose caused other aspects
of legal science to lose something. But the diligent cultivation
of the historical method brought forth invaluable fruits , and the

period of Cujas is recognized as one of extraordinary brilliancy. It used to be said that if all the rest of the world's labors on Roman law were to disappear, those of the French school would suffice to preserve its treasures for our use.

But even the school of Cujas had its opponents And naturally enough; for it showed no mercy to the traditions of its predecessors, and it furnished no direct service to the needs of the practitioners. Its useless idealism became the target for the attacks of the practitioners. The Bartolists still held their own in Italy; and their counterpart faction in France was led by DONEAU (Donellus; 1527–1591), and by HOTMAN (Hotomanus; 1525–1590).[1] Both of these opposed the merely theoretic and historical methods of Cujas; they maintained that law must be studied in its relations to present-day needs. But they differed between themselves in their ideas of the proper method of doing this Doneau was willing to use the adapted Roman law, as the Bartolists did in Italy; while Hotman proposed to break loose entirely from Roman law as the basis, and to build up a national French law out of all the existing elements by combining the results of custom and experience into a philosophic system. Such, indeed, was the principle which triumphed ultimately. But, for the time, victory remained with Cujas The list of the brilliant jurists who espoused his cause includes the names of Dumoulin (Molinæus), Brisson (Brissonius), Douaren (Duarenus), the two Godefrois (Gothofredus), Denis, and Jacques, father and son (1587–1652).[2]

It was the 1600s which saw the decline of the school of Cujas. This came to pass partly by reason of France's political and religious convulsions, but chiefly because of the consolidation of national sentiment. The Latin tongue and the Latin law were to be discarded; and a national law was to be the outcome. Two great names stand for this final phase. DOMAT (1625–1696) wrote in French his great work on " Les lois civiles dans leur ordre naturel," combining into one system the materials of Roman law and French legislation and decisions. POTHIER (1699–1772), though in his rearrangement of Justinian's Pandects he showed an alliance with the Cujacian tradition, became the founder of modern French

---

[1] ["It is reported that Elizabeth invited Francis Hotman to Oxford .   He is best known to English law students as the man who spoke light words of Littleton, and thus attracted Coke's thunderbolt " (*Maitland*, essay cited *ante*, n 1, § 52) — TRANSL]

[2] [On this preceding section, see particularly pp 180–182 of *Maitland's* essay above cited, and the further account in part III (France) of this volume — TRANSL.]

law by his comprehensive series of treatises on all its subjects. The influence of Pothier in the labors of Napoleon's codifiers is well known, and that Code was the final event in the great contest against the Cujacian principle

§ 55 But the Romanist school, before the day for its exile from France arrived, had already established itself in Holland, where it took on new lustre. The independence of the Netherlands (then recently gained) found that country, at the middle of the 1600s, intellectually in the full flower of its strength   Scholarship was zealously encouraged, and some of Holland's names were already numbered among the world's jurists   A clearness of style and an originality of thought marked their works, and theory and practice were felicitously combined   They were known as the "jurisconsulti elegantiores"[1]   The Netherlands school is best known from the fame of HUGO GROTIUS, whose genius turned equally to the history of Dutch law and the exposition of international law. But in the field of Roman law also it had famous leaders, — Vinnius (1588–1657), whose Commentaries were long used in the law schools of Italy; and his successors Noodt (1647–1725) and Voet (1647–1714), whose works were once perhaps more widely read than any others and are even still worth perusal.[2]

The next turn, for the primacy in legal science, fell to Germany. There, too, Humanism had taken root   The soil was as unfavorable to it as in Italy, but its inherent power for reform gave it a vogue. The casuistry of the practitioners, the slavery to authority, the reverence for the "mos Italicus," — all yielded before the new scientific methods   Roman law ceased to be foreign law. Simplified and clarified, it adapted itself to the local needs. The composite result tended to become a national law, as it had done in Italy, in France, and in Spain   The main supporters of this movement were Carpzov and Conring; the former devoted himself to the exposition of the law of his own day; and the latter (in his "De origine juris Germanici") demonstrated that the reception of Roman law had not prevented Germany from developing a solid fabric of national law   But the great and brilliant contributions of Germany to legal science were to be reserved until the 1800s, when its Historical School, led by Savigny, and fostered by the revival of national sentiment after

---

[1] [On the "elegant" French jurists, compare *Maitland's* remarks, pp. 181, 182, in the essay above cited — TRANSL]

[2] A particular contribution of the Netherlands school was its development of the "thesaurus," — an encyclopedic treatise setting forth the whole of the legal learning of the day

the Napoleonic wars, was destined to influence all Europe, and to succeed to that leadership of inspiration which had been successively held by the Glossators, the Commentators, and the Humanists.

Topic 3. The Legislation of the Renascence [1]

1. COMMUNAL PERIOD

§ 56 **Legislative Conditions in the 1200 s** — We must now turn back, for a brief space, to the period beginning with the 1200 s, and review the accumulations of its legislative activity These formed an important source for the labors of the jurists whose history we have just examined, and were the outward evidence of that multifarious local life and political independence which after long vicissitudes was later welded into the modern Italian nation The legislation of the Renascance is markedly local and particularistic. In its first stage, it consists mainly of the ordinances of the independent cities or communes ; to these the term "statutes " is commonly restricted in Italian history [2] In its second stage, it emanates from the principalities and dukedoms, later the several kingdoms, which coexisted on Italian soil

The political independence which the Italian cities gained for themselves, as the feudal period and the Germanic empire ended in Italy, brought naturally with it the right to make their own laws for their own affairs This liberty of legislation, moreover, found them disposed and indeed driven to exercise it; for the authority of the ancient laws and customs had been weakened by the radical changes in local life. The personality had given way to the territoriality of law (*ante*, Part I, §§ 48, 67), and the city life, with its tendency to merge personal distinctions, had been an especial factor in this change Moreover, this community of customs varied from city to city, so that each ruled its own life in its own way. And, finally, this intense individuality of the cities, being the very lifespring of their political independence and power, was bound to find expression in its law, which, when it came to be

---

[1] [§§ 56–74 = Calisse, part III, titles I, II, §§ 94–129, pp 173–247 This portion of the text has been transposed to follow the author's titles III and IV, so as to make the development clearer for our purposes In omitting many details of the local legislation, abundant freedom has been used. — Transl]

[2] [But "Statuto," in modern Italian, is also used distinctively of the national Constitution. — Transl]

reduced to writing, was the most characteristic element in their legal life.

The development of this city law may be examined, first in its general conditions, and next in its particular codes

§ 57. Growth of the City Legislation.[1] — The characteristic form of the city legislation was the Statutes They were analogous to the regulations adopted for self-government by the various trades and crafts, or "corporations"; and the commune, or city, was in its origins merely a variety of corporation in this sense. Hence this form of regulation was natural enough But in the growth of independent city self-government, the Empire first fully recognized the cities' legislative power in 1183, in the treaty of Constance. This recognition went so far as to command the Imperial viceroys, residing in the cities for the conservation of imperial rights, to apply the cities' customary law in the appeals brought before the viceroys.

The constitutional status of these city statutes was, to be sure, much controverted. Some jurists (including Bartolus himself) held that the statutes were an exercise of power delegated by the Emperor. But others founded them upon some principle of popular sovereignty. Albericus, for example, invoked the Roman maxim "jus proprium quod quilibet sibi populus constituit" Baldus invoked the doctrine of natural law (*ante*, Part I, § 65), "ex propria naturali justitia," that a community without law is inconceivable, and that therefore the very existence of the community requires it to possess a law of its own, that "sicut omne animal regitur a suo spiritu proprio et anima," so also a community of human beings "non indigent alio directore" These theories, however faulty in juristic analysis, at least indicate the political restlessness of the times against any interference from imperial power, as well as a boldness and novelty of reasoning upon the nature and basis of a political State Both the statutes and the theory of their validity were alike the product of the economic and political forces of the times, making for a self-consciousness of independent strength. As the latter waxed and waned, so did the former also.

§ 58. Sources of the City Legislation. — Local custom was the prime source of the legislation The earliest instances of this re-

---

[1] *Pertile*, "Storia," § 67, *Salvioli*, "Manuale," part II, c 12, *Schupfer*, "Manuale," sect II, tit. I, c 4, *Orlando*, "La legislazione statutaria e i giureconsulti del secoli XIV," Turin, 1884 For the numerous works dealing with statutes of particular cities, see *Schupfer, supra*, pp. 320, 323, 327.

cording of the customs in a code of statutes are those of Genoa (in the second half of the 900s), of Pisa, with its " Constitutum usus Pisanæ civitatis " (1160), and of Milan, with its " Consuetudines -Mediolanenses " (1216) But in these earlier instances the written statute was intended merely to prove the customs, not to supplant or to change them, in Baldus' words, " potius ad roborationem, quam ad novi juris introductionem." The statutes, however, as they became more common, took on the feature of legislation in the strict sense, changing the old customs and providing for the new needs.

There were two kinds, depending on the organ of power which issued them. In the strictest sense, a " law " was an enactment of the popular assembly or the council or other supreme body But these laws were confined to matters of highly public importance or controversy The other sort, ordinances (we may call them), " brevia," or " promissiones," were issued by the magistrates in the ordinary exercise of their authority. These were renewed year by year, when the chief official (" consul " or "podestà ") assumed office, in the earliest, he makes oath to observe them, and they begin with " juro "; later the word "statuimus " took its place. His oath being personal only, each new official must renew the pledge. And as experience introduced new measures from time to time, the consolidated ordinances grew as an integral body of law, — much as the prætor's annual edict at Rome grew into an independent system. And as there were various officials having separate powers and duties, and as the people itself had also duties guaranteed by its own oath, so there existed, in the same city, several " brevia," — the " breve " of the people, the consul, the mayor (" podestà "), the council, the judges, and so on.

These various sources — customs, laws, " brevia " — were originally distinct But in the course of time they came to form a single body of law for the city; and this code is what became commonly termed the " statutes."

§ 59. Local and unwritten custom, to be sure, remained a part of the law. But in those cities (mostly northern) where independence of other lordship had reached its height, it obtained chiefly in matters of private law only; so that the " statuti " of those cities were largely occupied with public law, and " consuetudines," " mores," " usus," signified distinctively private law In the south, on the other hand, where royal authority had always continued dominant, the city legislation had concerned itself with the private law arising from the mixture of Roman, Byzantine, Frankish, and Lombard customary law, so that the city codes there bore commonly the name " consuetudines "

This distinction in city law between " consuetudines " and " statuti," in the usage of the northern cities, was well recognized. " Est duplex jus municipale," says Albericus of Rosate, " scriptum et non scriptum " It signified several contrasts In the first place, the " consuetudines " contained more survivals of Germanic law than the " statuti," which had more often followed Roman traditions. In the next place, the " consuetudines " were subject to the general principles (*ante*, Part I, § 65) that they must be " rationabilis, bona, approbata," while the " statuti " were limited only by the legislative discretion. And, finally, the " consuetudines " were merely a part of the general private law, varying those special rules in which custom had been peculiar; while the " statuti " formed practically the entire body of public law, covering all aspects of political and administrative life.

§ 60 But the Church's law was also not without recognition in the statutes. The limitation (*ante*, Part I, § 65) that a custom must be " bona et probata " opened the way for the Church to interpose its authority. It was a settled maxim that the statutes could not derogate from Church law, and they even expressly recognized many of its rules. The offenses of labor on holy days, and of blasphemy, the exemptions of the clergy from civic duties and secular jurisdiction; the authority of the pope, the licensing of usurious loans; and the establishment of the inquisition against heretics, — these all testify to the Church's influence in city law.

But the cities herein merely recognized that which they themselves were willing to indorse They by no means yielded their independence, or became merely a subservient instrument of the Church's pretensions. When Gregory IX, for example, ordained that the city statutes should be submitted for approval to the ecclesiastical authorities, he found himself powerless to exact an obedience.

The city statutes, indeed, were no one's law but their own. The three ancient elements — Germanic, Roman, and Church law — were there merged and transfused to serve the purpose and express the whole life of the people themselves. All three elements contributed their special emphasis, — the Germanic to the private law, the Roman to the public law, and the Church to both. The statutes, in short, are typical of a period when the transformation from several systems into a single system was taking place by means of the city life intensely localized at many centres; and this was preparing the way for a truly national law.

§ 61. **Compilation of the Statutes** — The cities which had statutes were not numerous until the 1200 s, although in the preceding century (even before the peace of Constance in 1183) some were already to be found, notably at Pistoia, Pisa, Alessandria, and Genoa.

In those cities which were entirely independent, the statutes were compiled by commissioners (" statutari ") appointed by the council or its authorized representatives; and the council or popular assembly afterwards approved them.   There were usually several commissioners, but sometimes one only, — perhaps an eminent jurist of the place.   Sometimes the commission came to an end on the completion of the specific compilation, sometimes it was permanent, and made amendments or insertions from time to time, — in this instance being known as " revisers " (" riformatori "). The commission, in making the compilation, would, among other sources, resort to the citizens themselves to learn accurately the local customs to be recorded   Sometimes it would adopt as a model the text of some other city's statutes which were held in esteem; and thus a close resemblance in provisions may often be traced.   For example, in the Sicilian statutes, Palermo, Catania, and Messina served as models, Bologna furnished some provisions to Florence and Pistoia, Milan was a model for Lombard cities; and Genoa for Corsica

In cities under the rule or suzerainty of some prince or of another city, the method of enactment was sometimes to draft the statutes as usual and then submit them for the overlord's approval, and sometimes for the overlord to have them drafted and to recognize the right of the people (more or less limited) to ratify them. Sometimes there were several cities under the same overlord, and here too a common type for their statutes would be found.

§ 62. The earliest statutes were *written in Latin*, interspersed with terms in the local vernacular, sometimes latinized.   But the statutes of the 1200 s begin to be written in Italian, and the earlier Latin versions were thereafter put into Italian in the later revisions. The earlier styles of expression are crude and unskilful, but the later ones develop into a facility which sometimes becomes prolix and even obscure in its subtilties of affectation.   The juristic method, too, develops.   The earliest type is a mere series of rules, arranged usually in the order of enactment   But as the bulk increased, and amendments multiplied, necessity produced attempts

at system. Usually, there was a division into four or five books.
The first contained public law, in the strict sense. The second
dealt with penal law The third contained procedure, which, in
that day, included much that we now regard as private law, for
a right was then constantly recognized by granting an " action ",
and, of course, this would not contain a complete treatment of
private law, but only such topics as had been changed by statute.
Another book, usually the fourth, included miscellaneous matters.
The fifth, when there was one, treated the varied subjects of city
regulation in industry, commerce, agriculture, and the like.

Once approved, the book of statutes was promulgated. It was
publicly read aloud and expounded to the people from time to
time, a copy was kept constantly accessible at the city hall for
public perusal; and here and there — at a church, for example —
other copies were deposited for consultation

§ 63. The book of statutes was a mirror of the constant advances in *popular life and law*. The changes and additions were
incorporated into it by the commission, sometimes within a few
days of the enactment, sometimes at the annual revision which
in certain places took place as a survival of the ancient inaugural
oath of the magistrates This mobility of the laws led often to
uncertainty and confusion, and was a symptom of that inconstancy
of popular opinion which later proved a powerful element in the
downfall of city independence. But it also served so faithfully
to adapt the city laws to the city habits and needs that it kept the
statutes solidly in touch with the facts, and the statute-book was
one of the most permanent institutions of city life, long after
political despotism had engulfed them.

For the same reason, the statute-books represent an extensive
segment of Italian law, and are vital to its understanding From
the 1100s to the codifications of the 1700s they are the embodiment of the bulk of the *local law*. It is unfortunate that a complete study of them is as yet impossible, for the greater part
remain unpublished. But any intelligent research in their texts,
to be of real utility, must distinguish their varieties of significance.
In the first place, with reference to public law, those of the independent cities occupy themselves mainly with their free institutions
and the guarantees of popular rights; while those of the vassal
cities are concerned mainly with protecting the interests of the
suzerain. In the next place, the cities themselves may be distinguished according as their economic interests were mainly rural
or mainly commercial In the former, the statutes regulate the

164

ownership of land, and the cultivation of the fields ; and the traditions of Germanic times, here found longest prevailing, stand for vested rights as against personal freedom. In the latter, the statutes concern themselves with the various sorts of merchandise, the instruments of credit, and transportation ; and here is seen at its best the spirit of personal freedom and social progress. In the third place, the statutes must be distinguished according as they are original types, of local growth, or are more or less imitations (as most are) of some other accepted model   Carried on in the light of these and other such discriminations, the study of the city statutes will be fertile for the history of Italian law.[1]

§ 64. **Industrial and Commercial Statutes** — The " statute " had become the typical form of that period for all kinds of communal rules established by general agreement   The " statutes " of a particular region, therefore, included several bodies of rules, enacted quite separately from each other.

In the first place, there was the *city statute* proper, — the laws made by the supreme council of the entire city.

In the next place, there was the statute of the common *people*, promulgated by the people's captain.   When the plebs of the cities, failing to obtain the upper hand in the struggles with the aristocrats, came to form a separate group within the city, they drew up rules for their own affairs.   The history of early Rome was repeated ; and in fact the term " plebiscita " was used for these rules

Again, the various departments of *city administration* had each its set of statutes, from the supreme judges down to the beadles. Sometimes these were all collected in a single volume, like the " Breve officialium communis " of Siena, in 1250 ; sometimes an important department had a book to itself, like the " Statutum judicis daciorum," or revenue department, of Mantua.

The *arts, trades, and crafts*, too, had each its statutes, — the oldest of all, indeed , older than the city government itself   Each " corporation," or gild, had a consul, who made oath to observe its statutes.[2]

Among these gilds, those of the *merchants* had attained the

---

[1] For bibliographies of the statutes in specific localities, see *Schupfer*, "Manuale," p 328
General lists are as follows   *Bonaini*, "Alcuni appunti per servire ad una bibliografia degli statuti Italiani" (Annuario delle Università Toscane, II, 1851) ; *Berlan*, "Saggio bibliografico degli statuti Italiani," Venezia, 1858 ; *Manzoni*, "Bibliografia statutaria," Bologna, 1876-1879 , *La Manna*, "Edizioni e studi di statuti Italiani nel secolo XIX," Torino, 1888.
[2] For a copious bibliography of the arts statutes, as well as the rural statutes, see *Schupfer*, "Manuale," sect. II, tit I, c 4, § 2 , c 5, § 1

greatest position and power [1] Their strength went back for beginnings to Roman days. The invading Germans had esteemed no
career save those of arms and the king's service, and merchandising had thus continued to remain in the hands of the conquered
Roman population Already in the Frankish period the Emperor's court was supplied from the oriental markets by great
traffic routes through Venice and the other northern cities.   The
Crusades showered a mercantile prosperity on Italy, and it was
this very prosperity which helped the cities to establish their
political independence. We find commercial interests enjoying
the highest honors and the most extensive privileges.   Thus the
statutes of the merchant gilds came to exceed all others in importance. They were something more than mere rules of the
gild, they had the status of a special law for all, forming an exception from the common law in matters of commerce. The
number and scope of these bodies of mercantile statutes in the
various cities gave them a wide influence in forming the commercial law of Italy; and this influence was seen in that universal
commercial law which Italy helped so much to form, even in times
long after the period of city independence

§ 65. But it was in *maritime commercial law* that the deepest
impress was left by the city statutes.   The carrying trade on the
Mediterranean was the basis of the commercial prosperity of the
great cities, and the maritime ports of Amalfi, Pisa, Genoa, Trani,
Ancona, and Venice developed codes of maritime law which have
always been recognized as prime historic elements in later maritime
law.   These statutes of the maritime cities owed more or less to
the continuous traditions of Roman commerce and law, the titles
" de nautico fœnore," " de exercitoria actione," and others in the
Digest, particularly the famous one on the Rhodian law, served
as a nucleus for the vast process of development which now ensued among the varied populations merchandising on the Mediterranean and its coasts.

Amalfi, on the southwest coast of Italy, near Naples, had maintained its independence, through a variety of circumstances; and
by means of close commercial relations with Constantinople it had
reached a maritime importance which, at an early date, gave its

---

[1] *Pertile,* "Storia," §§ 66–68· *Salvioli,* "Manuale," part II, c 13:
Schupfer, "Manuale," sect II, tit 1, c 5, *Wagner,* "Handbuch des See-
rechts," I, 1884; *Goldschmidt,* "Universalgeschichte des Handelsrechts,"
I, 1891, *Lattes,* "Il diritto commerciale nella legislazione statutaria Italiana," 1884; *Gonetta,* "Bibliografia statutaria delle corporazione di arte
e mestieri in Italia," 1891.

statutes an especial influence   The " Capitula et ordinationes curiæ maritimæ nobilis civitatis Amalphæ," usually known as the " Tabula Amalfitana," was a famous code, which figured as valid in the sea law of that region as late as the 1600s , its original compilation is variously dated (by modern research) between the 1100s and 1300s [1]   The city of Trani, on the Adriatic, had also a code of sea ordinances, the " Ordinamento et consuetudo maris," dating somewhere between 1063 and 1453, and probably from the earlier period.[2]   But Venice dominated on the Adriatic, in maritime custom as well as in politics.   Its earliest code, the " Capitulare nauticum," dates from 1255, and was revised from time to time under the title " Statuta et ordinamenta super navibus et aliis lignis." [3]   Ancona had a maritime code in the 1300s and carried on a famous controversy with Venice as to the liberty of the high seas   Pisa and Genoa had long had maritime rules, but they were not reduced to writing till the 1100s and later.   The codes of Pisa (" Constitutum usus Pisani " and others) extended their influence to Sardinia and Corsica and along the coast to Marseilles; while Genoa's influence, resting on its colonial possessions in the Levant, was dominant along the eastern shores of the Mediterranean.

But the codes of maritime commerce, unlike the ordinary city ordinances, represented the customs of trade among diverse peoples. Various elements, national and international, were thus fused into these codes, and the tendency was to develop a single uniform body of maritime customary law for all the Mediterranean peoples. Such a code was the " Consolato del Mare," or Sea Consular Rules, which was first reduced to writing (in the Romance language) prob-

---

[1] ESSAYS AND TREATISES: *Laband,* "Das Seerecht von Amalfi," 1864 ; *Alianelli,* "La tavola di Amalfi," Naples, 1871; *Racioppi,* "La tabula e le consuetudini marittime d' Amalfi," 1879 , *Schupfer,* "Trani ed Amalfi," 1892 , *Laudati,* "La tabula de Amalfi," Bari, 1894
   TEXTS   *Alianelli,* "Antiche consuetudini e legge marittimi delle provinze Napoletani," Naples, 1871 , *Pardessus,* "Collection des lois maritimes," 1828–1845, vol V
   The manuscript of the Tabula was first discovered at Vienna, in 1843, by E Gar, who published it in the R S I , Append II, 8, p. 253   There are other reprints, notably by *Camera,* in "Memorie storiche politiche d' Amalfi," 1876, vol I
[2] ESSAYS AND TREATISES · *Volpicella,* "Degli antichi ordinamenti marittimi di Trani," Naples, 1871 , *Alianelli,* "Su la data degli ordinamenti marittimi di Trani," Naples, 1866 , *Beltrami,* "Sugli ordinamenti marittimi della città di Trani," Barletta, 1873 , *Racioppi,* "Ordinamenti et consuetudini marittimi di Trani," Naples, 1879
   TEXTS   *Pardessus and Alianelli, ubi supra*
[3] *Predelli and Sacerdoti,* "Statuti marittimi Veneziani fino al 1255,"/ in "Nuovo Archivio Veneto," 1902, new ser., 1.

ably in the 1300s, at Barcelona, in Spain It became almost the
common law of the Mediterranean by the 1500s, and was translated
into Italian and other languages.[1]

§ 66 **Commercial Institutions** — The *consuls* of commerce,
whose name gave the title to the Consolato del Mare, were one of
the many commercial institutions whose origin can be traced
mainly to the practices of the Italian mercantile cities. The
trade among nations brought their peoples into constantly more
intimate contact, not only by the journeyings of ships, but by the
settlement of colonies of foreign merchants in the important sea-
ports. These colonies lived in a compound or quarter of the town
set apart for them, and enjoyed an exemption from the local jurisdiction, being governed by their own laws and magistrates or
" consuls." The Italian cities, with their leadership in foreign
trade, were the first to establish these consulates for their colonies
abroad (usually by treaty between the two peoples), and the
modern consul of international law derives his origin from this
commercial custom

So, too, may be traced back to Italian origin or influence various
other institutions of modern *commercial law* and custom The bill
of exchange is found in its earliest form in Italian documents. The
insurance policy appears first in Genoese records. The mercantile
corporation was typified in the famous company of the Lombards,
which was organized in Italy, but trafficked all over Europe and had
branches in every chief city [2] Banks arose first in Italy; the
Bank of Venice appears in the 1100s, the Bank of St George, in
Genoa, controlled the city's finances and politics, and was in its
day the most powerful institution of its kind, and the bankers of
Florence had as their debtors the crowned heads of Europe

Thus the intense and independent city life, which had given rise
to a vast body of local law, had served also to contribute far and
wide a national influence, and to form institutions of international
importance and permanence As popular independence ebbed,
the formation of popular custom and law declined Political con-

---

[1] *Schaube*, "Das Consulat des Meeres in Genua," in *Goldschmidt's*
"Zeitschrift fur Handelsrecht," XXXII, *id*, "Das Consulat des Meeres
in Pisa," Leipzig, 1888; *id*, "Neue Aufschusse uber die Anfange des
Consulats des Meeres," 1893, *Salvioli*, "Consolato di mare," in "Digesto
Italiano", *Desjardins*, "Introduction historique à l'étude du droit com-
mercial maritime," 1890, p 60, *Goldschmidt*, "Universalgeschichte des
Handelsrechts," p 208, *Zeller*, in his "Sammlung alterer Seerechts-
quellen," Mainz, begun in 1906, has not yet reached the Consolato

[2] [Its quarters in London have left the name of Lombard Street, see
Martin's "History of Marine Insurance" (1876) — TRANSL]

ditions had again changed, and a period of monarchical government and legislation was gradually taking its place.

2. THE MONARCHICAL PERIOD

§ 67. **Imperial Legislation.** — The cities, of course, had always been parts of some greater political entity, — of the Empire, if of no other. In the city period, strictly so called, there were a few lesser States to which some of the cities were tributary, — the Sicilian kingdom, for example, and the Papacy. Later there arose various principalities and foreign dynasties. Thus there were always some other sources of legislation than the cities themselves, during the Renascence and down to the general codification movement which began with the 1700s These sources were the Empire, on the one hand, and the various semi-sovereign principalities on the other. The legislation of the former lessened constantly, in scope and authority, that of the latter increased in proportion. After the time of Frederic II, the imperial authority waned rapidly. The efforts of Henry VII to restore it were futile; some of his decrees of the 1300s were not even inserted in the Novels of the Code until after his death, when Bartolus used his prestige to do so, in the 11th Appendix published by him (*ante*, § 48). From that time onwards, no imperial legislation affected Italy, except in a few rare instances, such as the Golden Bull of Charles IV in 1356 (which gave to seven German princes the election of the Emperor) and the "Constitutio Carolina" of Charles V (which as a code of criminal procedure had force in the regions of northern Italy).[1]

And it is interesting to note that this practical termination, in the 1300s, of the imperial law-giving for Italy, marks also the *closing of the text of the Corpus Juris* as it has come down to us Up to that time, the legislation of the later medieval empire had used a method of promulgation radically different from Charlemagne's earlier method, *i e* of sending copies of the Capitularies throughout the Empire to be read to the people in the assemblies and churches (*ante*, Part I, § 30) After the rise of the schools of law and of the authority of the jurists, an imperial decree was promulgated by sending it to the faculties of law, to be taught from the chair and included in the manuscript texts of the Corpus And, following the analogy of Justinian's Novels (or New Laws

---

[1] *Schupfer*, "Manuale," sect II, tit I, c. 2, § 3 , *Brunner*, "Grundzuge," §§ 27, 62 ; *Weiland*, "Constitutiones et acta publica imperatorum et regum," 1893, 1896.

since the Code), which already formed nine books, these later Novels were collected in two more books, — a tenth, by Ugolino (*ante*, § 43), and an eleventh, by Bartolus (*ante*, § 48). Some of them, however, were inserted in the Code itself, at the place where they modified it, not literally, but in a summary note, after the fashion of the Glossators (*ante*, § 40), the note was then termed "Authentica"[1] After Henry VII (in the early 1300s), no further insertions or collections were made. The era of the Commentators had arrived (*ante*, § 45), and the growth of the text of the Roman law was forever ended[2]

§ 68. **Legislation of the Italian States**[3] — The legislation of the various Italian States differed widely in different regions, just as the political conditions varied also. Sometimes its source of authority was an imperial grant, sometimes it was a power extorted or absorbed from the cities or feudal lords The process of acquiring it was a gradual one But parliaments, assemblies, councils, and other forms of popular participation ultimately gave way to absolutism; and the powers of legislation were deeemd to be exclusively in the sovereign ruler

Much of this law was naturally directed to fixing the new political conditions But much of it also was concerned with coordinating and restating the mass of law which had originated in so many diverse sources. To substitute general laws for local customs and special privileges; to eliminate ancient and contradictory provisions; to give orderly arrangement and certainty of rule, — this process, it will be seen, was in one sense a forecast and prelude of the codifying movement of the 1700s. But in its day it went on only slowly and incompletely. The State legislation did not supplant or absorb the city statutes, the feudal customs, the jurists' Roman law, and the Canon law; it merely cleared the ground, established its own domination, and fixed the mutual relations of the various bodies of law.

§ 69. In the kingdoms of *Naples* and *Sicily*, an historical kaleidoscope shows us a rapid succession of political dynasties of different races; and this variety of rule is reflected in its legislation.[4] The Lombards had had their day there (*ante*, Part I, § 26).

---

[1] The novel itself, in the earlier Latin, would be an "authentica."
[2] [This section has been in part condensed — TRANSL]
[3] [These §§ 68–74 are much abbreviated — TRANSL.]
[4] *Pertile*, "Storia," § 65, *Salvioli*, "Manuale," part II, sect II, c. 12; *Schupfer*, "Manuale," sect II, tit I, c 3, § 1, *Grimaldi*, "Istoria delle leggi e magistrati dello regno di Napoli," 1749–1752, *Giannone*, "Istoria civile del regno di Napoli," 1823, *Pecchia*, "Storia civile e politica del

The Normans, who succeeded them, enacted the "Assisiæ regum
regni Siciliæ," towards the end of the 1100s [1]   The ensuing rule
of the Swabian emperors is represented by Frederic II's "Constitutiones regni Sicilæ," in 1231 ; and their merits and duration gave
rise to commentaries by celebrated jurists like Andrew Bonellus
and others [2]   On Sicily's separation from Naples, in 1282, the
Angevin dynasty at Naples introduced its "Capitula " for its
French subjects there, [3] other Neapolitan codes of that period,
covering procedure, were the "Rites of the Great Vicarial Court," [4]
and the "Rites of the Masters of Justice " [5]   By this time the
dynasty of Aragon governed in Sicily, [6] its "Pragmatica" were the
laws of royal initiative, [7] and its "Capituli " represented the rem-

regno di Napoli," 1777–1796 ; *Capone*, "Discorso sopra la storia delle
leggi patrie," 1854 ; *La Mantia*, "Storia della legislazione civile e crim-
nale di Sicilia," 1866–1874 , *Busacca*, "Storia della legislazione di Sicilia
dai primi tempi fino all' epoca nostra," 1876
   [1] *Orlando*, "Il potere legislativo al tempo dei Normanni," 1844 , *Merkel*, "Commentatio qua juris Siouli sive Assisarum regum regni Siciliæ
fragmenta proponuntur," 1856 ; *Capasso*, "Le leggi promulgate dai re
Normanni nell' Italia meridionale," 1862 , *Perla*, "Le Assise dei re di
Sicilia," 1881 , *Crotto-Grasso*, "Del diritto pubblico Siculo al tempo dei
Normanni," 1883 ; *Brandileone*, "Il diritto Romano nelle leggi Normanne
e Sveve del regno di Sicilia," 1884 , *id*, "Frammenta di legislazione
Normanna e di giurisprudenza Bizantina nell' Italia meridionale,"
1886
   TEXTS   *Merkel, ubi supra, Brandileone, ubi supra; Carcani*, "Constitutiones regum regni utriusque Siciliæ," 1786.
   [2] *Raumer*, "Die Gesetzgebung Friedrichs II in Neapel," 1857 ; *Winckel-
mann*, "De regni Siculi administratione qualis fuit regnante Frid II,"
1859 ; *Capasso*, "Sulla storia esterna delle costituzioni del regno di Sicilia,"
1869 ; *Del Vecchio*, "La legislazione di Fed II imperatore," 1874 ; *Ciccaglione*, "Le chiose di Andrea Bonello da Barletta alle costituzioni
Sicule," 1888
   TEXTS : *Carcani, ubi supra*, note 2 ; *Huillard-Bréholles*, "Historia diplo-
matica Frid II," vol IV
   [3] "Capitula regni utriusque Siciliæ, ritus magnæ curiæ vicariæ et pragmaticæ, commentariis illustrata," Naples, 1773
   [4] *P Caravita*, "Commentaria super ritibus magnæ curiæ vicariæ regni
Neapolis," Venice, 1601
   [5] Later called "summary chamber "   "Ritus regiæ cameræ summariæ
regni Neapolis, nunc primum in lucem editi," Naples, 1689
   [6] *Gregorio*, "Introduzione allo studio del diritto pubblico Siciliano,"
Palermo, 1830 , *Clarenza*, "Storia del diritto Siculo," Catania, 1840 , *Orlando*, "I capitoli del regno di Sicilia," Palermo, 1866.
   TEXTS · *Muta*, "Capitula regum regni Siciliæ," Palermo, 1608–1618 ,
Testa, "Capitula regni Siciliæ," Palermo, 1741.
   [7] For Naples   *De Jorio*, "Introduzione allo studio delle prammatiche
del regno di Napoli," 1777 , *Vario*, "Pragmaticæ, edicta, etc ," Naples,
1777.
   TEXTS · *P. Caravita*, "**Pragmaticæ**, etc , in unum congestæ," 1575 ;
Giustiniani, Naples, 1803–1806, XV vols
   For Sicily · *Scibecca*, "Costituzioni prammatichi del regno di Sicilia
fatte sotto, etc , Colonna," 1583, continued to 1800 by *Nicastro*, 5 vols. ;
De Blasi, "Pragmaticæ sanctiones regni Siciliæ, etc ," Palermo, 1791–1793
(includes them to 1579).

nant of popular government.[1] Sicily and Naples were finally
united under the Bourbon dynasty in 1503, and as absolutism
reached its height, the " pragmatica " became the more numerous,
and other forms of unlimited monarchical legislation (" dispacci,"
" sanctiones ") were developed [2] But these multiple layers of
superimposed law formed a confused mass, almost incapable of
intelligent application or amendment The Lombard law had
never been formally abolished; Roman and Canon law were "common law ", Norman, Swabian, Angevin, and Aragonese statutes
were interspersed with Spanish, Austrian, and Bourbon decrees,
and legislation of a dozen varieties competed with judicial
decisions, treatises, and local customs Though Charles III, in
the first half of the 1700 s, sought to reform this unendurable state
of the law, it was not until the dawn of modern times that any real
success was attained.

§ 70. In the *Papal States*,[3] the Roman law and the Canon law
were naturally the chief sources For a long period the local
autonomy of the cities and the baronies was left without interference from the suzerain, though it was expected not to violate
the Church's principles But after the cities' independence declined, the papacy legislated directly for each locality The
Roman State was also divided into provinces, with a governor and
parliament, — Romagna, the Marches, etc, — and the provincial
legislation was an important body of law. Under Cardinal Albornoz, a leader in the restoration of the papacy from its exile at
Avignon, a commission of jurists made a notable revision of the
law of the Marches, published in 1357, with the title " Liber constitutionum sancti matris ecclesiæ," — more commonly known as
" Constitutiones Marchiæ Anconitæ," or " Collectio Aegidiana "
(after the Cardinal's name), and this continued for two centuries
as the basis of the law of the Marches.[4] The only other local law
of note was that of the duchy of Urbino (the scene of Castiglione's

---

[1] For Naples   *A. de Bottis*, "Capitula, etc ," 1588, and another edition, "Capitula, etc ," Naples, 1773
   For Sicily   *Raimondetta*, "Regni capitula, etc ," Venice, 1573; *Testa*,
"Capitula regni Siciliæ, etc ," Palermo, 1741
[2] *D Gatta*, "Regali dispacci, etc ," Naples, 1773–1777, XI vols , *Ger-
vasi*, "Siculæ sanctiones," Palermo, 1750–1755, VI vols.
[3] *Pertile*, "Storia," § 65, *Salvioli*, "Manuale," part II, sect. II, c 28;
Schupfer, "Manuale," sect II, tit I, c 3, § 4, *La Mantia*, "Storia della
legislazione Italiana, I, Roma e stato Romano," Turin, 1884
[4] *Brandi*, "Le Constitutiones, etc , del card E Albornoz," 1888, *Wurm*,
"Card Albornoz der zweite Begrunder des Kirchenstaates," Paderborn,
1892 , *Ermini*, "Gli ordinamenti politici ed amministrativi nelle Constitutiones Ægidianæ," 1893
   TEXT   "Ægidianæ Constitutiones recognitæ, etc ," Rome, 1543.

famous book, " The Perfect Courtier ") [1]   The central legislation
of the Church, for the governance of its own regions, formed, of
course, an immense and heterogeneous mass , the collections known
as " bullaria " are arranged merely in chronological order.

§ 71 The later monarchy of the house of Savoy [2] was formed
from a number of ·smaller principalities gradually united, —
Piedmont, Savoy, Montferrat, Saluzzo, Sardinia, and others.
Amadeus VIII was here the great legislator who first succeeded
in bringing order out of chaos. His " Decreti," a revision compiled by a commission of lay jurists and churchmen, was published
at Chambéry, in 1430.[3] His successors labored in the same direction [4] But the crowning work was accomplished by Victor
Amadeus II, who, after erecting into a monarchy the State which
had been so enlarged by his long wars, caused to be prepared by
a commission a most radical and comprehensive code, the " Constitutiones," published in 1723. This legislation was still in force
when the great epoch of reform arrived at the end of that century.

Sardinia, however, though then under the house of Savoy, was
not included in this legislation The peculiar legal status of that
island kept its individuality even down to the time of the modern
codes of united Italy. Local chieftains, known as " judices," had
there maintained themselves, as the arbiters of justice, throughout
all the Pisan and Genoan rule ; and a code of law in 198 articles,
known as the " Carta de logu," was published in 1395, by the
" judex " Eleanora (who was herein carrying out the uncompleted
work of her father Mariano IV) [5] This " Carta de logu " was of
such merit that it continued long in force under the succeeding

---

[1] *S de Campello*, "Constitutiones ducatus Urbini," etc , Rome, 1709
See *Schupfer*, "Manuale," sect II, p 545, n 72.
[2] *Pertile*, "Storia," § 65 , *Salvioli*, "Manuale," part II, sect II, c 26 ;
Schupfer, "Manuale," sect II, tit II, c 3, § 2 , *Sclopis*, "Storia dell' antica
legislazione del Piemonte," Turin, 1833.
[3] *Nani*, "Gli statuti di Pietro II, conte di Savoia," Turin, 1880 , id.,
"Statuto dell' anno 1379 di Amedeo IV," Turin, 1881 , *Cibrario*, "Degli
statuti di Amedeo VIII," Florence, 1856
[4] *Borelli*, "Editti antiche e nuovi dei sovrani principi della reale casa
di Savoia, etc ," Turin, 1680 , later editions by *Bailly* and by *Jolly* , then
by *Duboin*, "Raccolta per ordine di materie delle leggi, editti, etc.," Turin,
1818–1873, with continuations by *Muzio* and by *Cottin Sola*, "Commentaria ad, etc., decreta," Turin, 1625.
For Montferrat : "Decreta civilia et criminalia antiqua et nova marchiæ Montisferrati," Turin, 1571 ; *Saletta*, "Decreti antiche nuovi civili
e misti del Monferrato," 1675
For Saluzzo : "Stylus marchionalis, seu leges in tribunalibus marchiæ
Saluciarum observandæ, etc ," Turin, 1598.
[5] *G. E Del Vecchio*, "Eleanora d' Arborea e la sua legislazione," Milan,
1872 ; *Mameli de' Mannelli*, "Le costituzioni di Eleonora giudicessa d'
Arborea intitolate Carta de' Logu," Rome, 1805

foreign dominations of Aragon and of Savoy, and the "pragmatica," "capitula," and "ordinamenta" of these later rulers were only supplementary [1]

§ 72 In *Lombardy*,[2] the flourishing life of its important cities made the local "statuto" a source of continued importance, even under the despotic rule of the Visconti and the Sforza. The "decreti" or "constitutiones" of the rulers were first compiled, under Charles V, in 1541, as "Constitutiones domini Mediolanensis" These, with the new legislation of the Spanish and Austrian dynasties, including the ordinances of the Senate, continued in force until the French Revolution.

§ 73 In *Venice*, the individuality of its local law set it apart from the rest of Italy, and had never been lost amidst all the mutations of government and vicissitudes of Italian fate The fugitives, who, in the Germanic period, first entrenched themselves on the islands of the lagoon, brought with them a Roman-Byzantine law The first attempt to compile in writing the mixture of customs. Roman law, and ordinances which had gradually accumulated, was the criminal ordinance of 1181 [3] — called "promissione dei maleficii," because sworn to by the magistrate on taking office (*ante*, § 58); revised in 1195 by the doge Eurico Dandolo.[4]

§ 74. The doge Iacopo Tiepolo was the great legislator of Venice, in 1232 he revised the criminal code; in 1242 he compiled the civil statutes, and in 1244 a code of procedure ("statuti dei giudici delle petizioni"). Tiepolo's work remained as the foundation of all subsequent legislation. Of the numerous revisions, the last general one was in 1729, [5] after 1751 the criminal code was pub-

---

[1] *Dexart*, "Capitula sive acta curiarum regni Sardiniæ," Cagliari, 1645; *Vico*, "Leyes y Pragmaticas reales del Reyno de Sardeña, etc.," Cagliari, 1680, *Sanna*, "Editti, pregoni, etc ," Cagliari, 1775
[2] *Pertile*, "Storia," § 68, *Salvioli*, "Manuale," part II, sect II, cc 27, 28; *Schupfer*, "Manuale," sect II, tit II, c 3, pp 363 541; *Sclopis*, "Storia dell' antica legislazione del Piemonte," II, part 2 *a*, c 6, *Verri*, "De ortu et progressu juris Mediolanensis,' Milan, 1747, *Bonetto and Bracherio*, "In regio palatio apud fratres Malatesta;" *Marbio*, "Codice visconteo sforzesco," Milan, 1846, "Compendio di tutte le gride ed ordini, etc ," Milan, 1609, "Gridario generale delle gride, etc ," Milan, 1648
[3] Edited by *E Teza*, "Promissione dei maleficii," Bologna, 1863
[4] Texts edited by *Lazzari*, in A S I, IX, 1853; *Foucard*, Venice, 1853; *Romanin*, "Storia di Venezia," II, 430
Essays *Musatti*, "Storia della promissione ducale," Venice, 1888 The last "promissione" was that of *L Manin* in 1789
[5] "Novissimum statutorum et venetarum legum nolumen," Venice, 1729, *Besta and Predelli*, "Statuti civili di Venezia anteriori al 1242," Venice, 1901; *Griffii*, "Volumen statutorum, legum, et jurium d d Venetorum," Venice, 1678 and 1709, *Valsecchi*, "Bibliografia analitica della legislazione della repubblica di Venezia," 1871–1877, *Roberti*, "Le magis-

lished separately.   One peculiarity of Venetian law was that cases not expressly covered by its own enactments were solved by resorting, not (as elsewhere) to the Roman law, but to natural equity; so that the magistrate's discretion was an important feature, and Venetian justice (as Bartolus remarked) was administered " manu regia et arbitrio suo."   And a consequence was that they never yielded to the dominant worship of precedent, in the days of the Bartolists, and glosses and commentaries were forbidden.   Another marked feature was the absence of any Germanic principles, for their territory had remained unconquered.   And their intensely individual history developed numerous other peculiar principles, especially in public law; among which may be noted the rigor of their suppression of ecclesiastical power and their refusal to recognize the " dead hand " in church property.

§ 75.   In the remaining north-central regions — *Tuscany* (including Florence), *Modena, Parma, Piacenza,* and *Liguria* (including Genoa), the city statutes continued to form the basis of the law, with a mixture of " decreta," " capitula," " bandi," " gride," " ordinanze," mingled and superimposed by the various ducal rulers and foreign dynasties which succeeded from period to period.[1]   In spite of occasional compilations and revisions, the mass of law remained confused and complicated, awaiting the arrival of an era of genuine codification.

trature giudiziarie Veneziane e i loro capitolari fino al 1300," 3 vols., 1906–1910, Venice (Deputazione di Storia Patria)

[1] FLORENCE: "Legislazione Toscana raccolta e illustrata," Florence, 1800–1808; "Codice della Toscana legislazione, etc ," 1736 to 1786, Siena, 1788 , "Leggi e bandi della Toscana," Florence, 1765–1860

GENOA·   "Leges novæ reipublicæ Genuæ, etc ," 1617, "Statutorum civilium reip Genuensis nuper reformatorum libri VI," 1633; "Criminalium jurium reip G. libri duo," 1669 , *Traverso,* "Magistrature ed officiali della republica di Genova, studio storico-giuridico," Genoa, 1910.

Chapter III.   Third Period: a d. 1700–1900

ITALY IN MODERN TIMES[1]

§ 76.   The Transition

Topic 1. Schools of Legal Thought

§§ 77–80. , The Natural Law School | §§ 81–83.   The Historical School.

Topic 2. The Codification Movement

<table>
<tr><td>§§ 84, 85</td><td>The Italian Codes of the 1700 s.</td><td rowspan="2">§§ 89–92.</td><td rowspan="2">The Italian Codification of the 1800 s.</td></tr>
<tr><td>§§ 86–88</td><td>The French Codes in Italy</td></tr>
</table>

Topic 3. Recent Times

<table>
<tr><td>§§ 93, 94.</td><td>Codification and the Historical School</td><td>§ 95</td><td>Other Schools of Thought</td></tr>
<tr><td></td><td></td><td>§ 96</td><td>Conclusions.</td></tr>
</table>

§ 76   **The Transition.** — The transition stage between the decline of the Renascence Period and the opening of the Modern Period is represented by the last half of the 1700 s, when the European Revolution was preparing.   In its relation to legal sources, it has much similarity to the period in ancient Rome when the exuberance of production had ceased and the need for revision, coordination, and simplification had begun to be felt.   The intricate mass of edicts, decrees, opinions, statutes, and customs which encumbered the Roman law found its counterpart in the commentaries, city statutes, royal ordinances, judicial decisions, and local customs, which burdened Italy   Practice was embarrassed, judges were in doubt, rights were uncertain, legal science had lost all originality.

And the same remedies, now as then, were sought.   A prime evil was the doctrine of " communis opinio," or weight of authority by numbers (*ante*, § 46) ; and just as at Rome the law of Citations had tried to solve this by giving to the works of five selected jurists an

---

[1] [§§ 76–96 = *Calisse*, part IV, §§ 163–188, pp. 332–379. — Transl.]

exclusive authority, so now it was sought in some of the Italian States [1] to forbid the judges and the lawyers to cite any work of the jurists   Another remedy was sought by the compilation of systematic digests of all the law, and this expedient, begun by private hands and continued officially, prepared the way for a genuine movement of codification.

Three periods may here be distinguished.   The first is the period of private compilations, which alleviated the evils, but did not prevent their gradual renewal.   The second was the period of official compilation, — not a genuine codification, because it still left the " common law " and the local statutes in force, codes of this sort are typified in the Piedmont Constitutions of 1723 (ante, § 71) The third period, one of codification in the fullest sense, sees the law reduced to a single systematic form, exclusive in its dominion, and totally supplanting all special diversities of locality, status, jurisdiction, or privilege.

Justinian, too, had indeed codified in the same manner, and had hoped (but in vain) that his work would " in æternum valiturum." But there was a vital difference between his method and that of the Italian legislators.   The former had merely rescued and collated the results of the past, and had expected with those materials alone to build a permanent monument for all future times.   But the modern codifiers looked on the past merely as providing instruction for the future, they deliberately cut loose from the old, so far as it served no useful purpose in building for a new era.

This spirit (next to that which inspired the Declaration of the Rights of Man) is the greatest feature in the modern period of social reconstruction   The lack of it was the cause of the failure of all prior attempts at codification.   The community had not been adequately prepared.   It had lacked the consciousness of aim to realize its own needs; and it had been shackled by the bonds which thwarted such a purpose.   The first was supplied by the labors of the great philosophers of the 1700s, the moral authors of the Revolution.   The second was removed by the Revolution itself, which vindicated the rights of man against the abuses of absolutism and privilege, and secured freedom to legislate in harmony with social needs.   Legal Philosophy and Revision of the Law thus become the two topics for consideration in this period.

---

[1] E g. by Victor Amadeus of Savoy and by Ferdinand Bourbon (Stat. 1774, Costituzioni Piemontesi, book III, tit. 22, § 9).

TOPIC 1. SCHOOLS OF LEGAL THOUGHT [1]

§ 77   **The Natural Law School.** — The conception of a Natural Law is an old one, — a law, that is, founded in the very nature of man, common to all men, and alike for all times and places.   The Romans, alongside of their municipal law (" jus civile ") recognized another, " quod naturalis ratio inter omnes homines constituit." They sometimes based directly on it a rule of positive law, — occupation, for example, was " naturali ratione " a mode of acquisition of ownership   Sometimes they contrasted it with positive law; slavery, they said, was " contra naturam," for by nature all men are equal.   And sometimes the natural law was invoked to amend and give ethical value to the positive law; it was not lawful, for example, to infringe upon a good custom   But their conception of natural law never went so far as to see in it an entire system of principles independent of and superior to the various positive or national laws   Positive law, based on State policies, was the essential means of a State's preservation and development; natural law was merely a principle of the philosophers, of which occasional use was made.   And the influence of philosophy grew less and less as the State became decadent, despotism increased, and individual liberty and energy faded

The Middle Ages, too, had known a Law of Nature.   Under the influence of the Church, natural law underwent a profound transformation.   No longer philosophy, but Christian theology and morals, supplied its basis.   It now came to serve as the support and justification of all positive law   " Rex a recte agendo vocatur," says Isidore of Seville (*ante*, Part I, § 32), otherwise he is merely a tyrant and may be deposed or even killed.   Every rule of human law, says Thomas Aquinas, in order to be just, must coincide with the law of nature; a custom, to be valid, must be " bona "; and these laws of nature take form and are revealed in the laws of God and the Church (*ante*, Part I, § 65); for human reason alone cannot supply them   Thus the subordination of positive law to natural law is a logical consequence of the latter's origin in Divine authority superior to all human society.   In Dante's " Monarchia " it is laid down that law is only a manifestation of the Divine will; when it varies from that, it is but injustice and tyranny.

---

[1] *Salvioli*, "Manuale," part II, c 23, *Schupfer*, "Manuale," book II, tit. II, c 2; *Lerminier*, "De l'influence de la philosophie du XVIIIᵉ siècle sur la législation et la sociabilité du XIXᵉ," Paris, 1833, *Joyau*, "La philosophie en France pendant la révolution, son influence sur les institutions politiques et juridiques," Paris, 1892; *Rivalta*, "Diritto naturale e positivo," Bologna, 1898

This conception, which dominated through the Middle Ages, did indeed later serve in its turn to fortify the authority of despotism; for, on the postulate that sovereignty was delegated from God and that its exercise was to be judged by Divine standards, the logical consequence was built that the sovereign person was responsible for his acts to God alone and not to man or any set of men. In Vico's maxim, "Respublica uni Deo, præterea reddit rationem nemini," Absolutism found its strongest expression and support But in due season came a reaction. Law was given a new philosophic basis, and this was the work of the school of thought characteristically known as the school of Natural Law.

§ 78. The period of preparation was a lengthy one, and goes back as far as the Renascence; but the later thinkers, by new inferences and gradual additions of principle, ended in reaching results radically opposed to the earlier ones.

Among the earlier ones, Gian Battista Vico (1670–1740) stands out as an original and independent intellect; though he was not in touch with his own time and country, nor was he then appreciated [1] In his "De universi juris uno principio et fine," and his "Principii di scienza nuova intorno alla comune natura delle nazioni," he develops the idea of an eternal and ideal law, superior to human vicissitudes, and persisting through the recurring cycles of history, by virtue of a power which rules all human things. Thus in Vico's work we find the germ idea of a natural law which could serve as a universal justice When that school came to develop its position, it turned enthusiastically to the works of Vico for support, and bestowed upon him a posthumous fame which had been denied him in his lifetime. But Vico was in general attitude far removed from the genuine idea of natural law. His thought was still fettered by the Middle Ages' view of a Divine Providence which established the starting-point and the recurrent goal of the human mind; which coincides with human reason, when the latter does not stray from the Divine dictates; and which unites in itself all men and all nations in their entire life from the origin of the world down through the immutable paths of history until the final judgment day

It was in the realm of public law, and particularly international law, that the ultimate doctrines of the new school received clear and definite statement The aim of these writers was to lead the

---

[1] [Vico's philosophy is fully expounded by *Miraglia*, in his "Comparative Legal Philosophy" (1912), vol III, of the "Modern Legal Philosophy Series." — Transl.]

public conscience and the law to disfavor the bloody wars into
which Europe was then constantly plunged as a consequence of
religious and dynastic quarrels. The principle was advanced that
war was unjust unless undertaken as a lawful means of defending
a right or redressing a wrong, and this standard of lawfulness was
sought in natural justice, *i.e.* those rules which had their basis in
the nature of mankind and must therefore inherently furnish for
all men the supreme rule of conduct.

Foremost among these writers was ALBERICUS GENTILIS, of San
Ginnesio (1550–1608) The religious dissensions in Italy drove
him to seek liberty of thought in foreign lands, and he became a
professor at Oxford University.[1] In his " De Jure Belli," he treats
of the causes which justify a war and the permissible means of con-
ducting it. This work paved the way for a more famous book, the
" De Jure Belli et Pacis," of HUGO GROTIUS, of Holland (1583–
1645) Grotius is regarded as the real founder of the new school of
Natural Law With the object of lessening the frequency of unjust wars, he seeks to determine the principles of natural law.
These he finds in the dictates of right reason, which tells whether
men's actions conform to justice; God, being the author of our
nature, sanctions the principles of right reason, which controls our
nature. Positive (or civil law) derives its validity from natural
law, *i.e.* from that principle of natural law which binds us to observe the obligation of a contract; human beings living in organized
society have entered into a contract, expressly or impliedly, to
obey such officers and such laws as may be recognized to be necessary to preserve the existence of society This theory marks the
transition from the medieval to the modern point of view The
medieval view is seen in the postulate that God is the source of
natural law; the new view is seen in the interposition of human
reason as the basis of the laws and institutions of human society.
The significance of the new view is seen in Grotius' own admission
that his theory would have been equally valid even if the existence
of God were not conceded.

From Grotius' principles (whether or not he was aware of the
consequences), it was merely a matter of logic to deduce that
human reason must take the place of divine revelation in the field
of law; that human reason must supply the specific rules of natural
law, which being founded on the essential nature of man, would
be universal and immutable in their validity; that no institution
of society ought to be conserved except so far as it was in accord

---

[1] [See note 3, § 52, *ante* — TRANSL]

with that law , and that any institution, when not in such accord,
ought to be extirpated, even by revolution if necessary Such
were the consequences which Grotius' successors set themselves to
draw, especially the philsophers of the 1700 s.

§ 79 Philosophy, having thus established its dominion in the
field of law, proceeded to reconstruct the law (as it was aiming to
reconstruct all human society) on the basis of a universal Nature,
— that is, taking as its type the primitive man (reconstructed
in imagination), free from all the artificial trappings of human
society, and seeking to analyze his sentiments and needs For
this process, a criterion was sought in the observation of facts
Man as he appears in all times, places, and conditions was studied.
The abnormal or accidental traits of the individual man or society
were discarded; the object was to detach, collate, and compare
only that which was permanent and common to all, and thus to
ascertain the essential nature of man. Corresponding to this
nature there would be found certain laws of conduct necessary for
its conservation and development , and these laws, united into a
system, would be that natural law, to which all other laws must
yield.

The novelty of this conception lay here Preceding systems had
based the notion of man's nature solely on the operations of his
reason or conscience, as contrasted with the divine reason interpreted by the Church , but now his nature was studied in itself
alone, without regard to its supernatural relations, and solely with
the aid of logical reasoning and scientific observation. The Middle
Ages viewed man from the standpoint of his destiny beyond the
grave ; the new school observed him solely as a member of human
society. Theology had treated him as part of the scheme of salva-
tion , human science was now to treat him as a phenomenon of
nature, of a piece with all the other facts of nature.

These new views diffused themselves rapidly. They reached the
people, and penetrated popular thought. The treatises were
published in popular forms, and the themes were universally discussed. Of all this, France was the chief centre , but Italy was
also active in the work. The advocates of the new philosophy
welcomed this progress of its ideas , for it gave them the dominant
influence at the crucial period when radical changes were impending and the ancient order of things was already tottering

§ 80 The consequences of this new thought in the field of law
may be summed up under three heads:

(1) In the first place, revelation being abandoned as a basis of

right, human reason took its place, and the system of thought
known as *Rationalism* came into control Its principal champion
was IMMANUEL KANT. In Kant's system, the universal and immutable rules of reason protect against every violation of those rights
with which nature has vested man; law is merely the sum of those
conditions which insure that the liberty of one man shall not interfere with the exercise of corresponding liberty by another man.
This principle belongs, as effect to cause, with the principle of the
social contract, — the characteristic of this school. Men have
organized society by consent, with the object of attaining ends
not attainable by individual powers alone; but they have not and
could not have surrendered those individual rights which essentially
inhere in man's nature, and which must therefore be respected
and guaranteed by society. The final result of this principle, in
practice, was the proclamation of the Rights of Man.

(2) In the *political* field, the new thought led naturally to the
abolition of almost all the institutions inherited from the Middle
Ages. Feudalism, privilege, primogeniture and entailed estates,[1]
absolutism, and Church interference in the State, — on all these
things a ruthless war was now waged Whether founded on divine
authority, or on conquest, or on class domination, they were declared to violate the law of nature, and therefore to be doomed to
extinction. The State was founded by men, therefore it had no
superior right, but existed solely for the good of its members Its
aim must be to remove all obstacles to men's pursuit of their natural
happiness and the development of their natural powers. And
since, in the removal of these obstacles, there must be a discarding
of existing institutions and a transformation of the State, the resistance offered by all opposing interests must be overcome. In
short, by sheer logic, these theories led to Revolution.

(3) Finally, in respect to the *laws themselves* they must be made
to conform to the law of nature, and this meant that they must be
adapted to attain the social ends of man's existence. Here, first,
was challenged the domination of the Roman law as the " common"
law of the various countries Outside of Italy, it had the status of
an imported law, — a law imposed by conquest and foreign authority; a law suppressing the people's own natural law; an antiquated law, handed down through twelve centuries of bookish
learning, and constantly deviating more and more, in its subtilties,

---

[1] ["' Fideicommissum' is not exactly an entail, but it is a species of trust
estate, which, as used for family settlements, represented the corresponding thing in modern Europe — TRANSL.]

from the principles of nature. The Canon law was likewise attacked, as representing the influences most alien to the new thought; for the Church sought its inspiration in the supernatural, not in the needs of society as it existed. And, finally, the laws must be purified of all that rested on the false and discarded theories of government; they must be adapted to a society founded on equality, not on privilege.

The entire law, in short, must be *reformed*, — must be conformed, that is, to the precepts of nature. And since these precepts are immutable, the law, when thus recast in a system, could be and should be framed into a single permanent body of rules, known and accessible to all And so the demand arose for the Codification of the Law, — a codification, that is, in the most rigid sense, as then conceived and believed in.

§ 81. **The Historical School.**[1] — All these practical principles, which formed the logical outcome of the school of Natural Law, called forth opposition In time, a reaction set in, though not a permanent one at all points. In spite of the proclamation of the intrinsic rights of man, social inequalities persisted. In spite of the political changes made by the Revolution, the old European States and governmental systems were once more restored And over against the theory of law and the movement of codification, there arose a new school of thought, which denied the former and gave a new turn to the latter. The activities of the Historical School, after the fall of the Napoleonic empire, in 1814, raised in Germany a vigorous debate as to the propriety and feasibility of a national codification. The opposing sides in this debate were led by two celebrated champions, — Savigny, opposing the code, and Thibaut favoring it.

THIBAUT made use of the patriotic sentiment of Germany, in support of his natural law principles, to advocate the final liberation of that nation from foreign oppression and foreign law In the name of both causes, he called for the compilation of a single code for all the Germanic communities. His views were put forth in a pamphlet entitled " The Necessity for a Common Civil Law for Germany," published at Heidelberg in 1814. His plan was to construct this code on the general principles of justice and right reason, adapting them to Germanic custom, and eliminating all foreign law, and therefore rejecting the Roman law, which he

[1] *Vanni*, " I giuristi della scuola storica," in *Rivista di filosofia scientifica*, 1885; *Brugi*, "I romanisti della scuola storica," in *Circolo Giuridico*, 1883.

declared was uncongenial to the character and sentiments of German people.

To this slogan SAVIGNY replied, with his famous pamphlet, " The Vocation of our Times for Legislation and Jurisprudence," published also at Heidelberg in 1814   In this pamphlet was set forth the programme of the Historical School   Its fundamental principle was that law is not abstract nor absolute in its nature, nor a product of immutable principles superior to the changing vicissitudes of human society, but that it is intimately related — as effect to cause — with the definite character of each individual people, and that it is a product of the various conditions which from time to time arise. Each people, inevitably and almost unconsciously, develops its own language and its own customs, suited to its own beliefs and interests; so, too, it develops its own law.   There are indeed three distinguishable elements in that law. The *natural* element, arising out of the popular conscience, is found in the customs based on their conditions of life, and the *formal* (or political) element, the work of the legislator, is that which gives positive form and efficacy to the law, after the jurists have prepared the way.   The *technical* element is the work of the jurists, which rescues the law from the disorder of merely popular custom and gives it a scientific basis, — just as the philologists and grammarians do for the language. Hence, according to the Historical School, a people's law is first to be sought in its history, because it is in that history that we discover the reasons for its particular details and the conditions which have caused it to change and develop as it has

These three elements are inherently and closely related.   The first reveals to us the needs to be provided for, and also furnishes the materials to be employed in systematizing the positive law The second and the third, complementing each other by turns, are always to be kept in close touch with the first, i e with the beliefs and interests of the community, whence alone arise the efficacy and the justice of the law. The proportion, to be sure, in which these three elements contribute to the whole varies much at different times and places. Sometimes custom predominates, — as in the primitive Germanic epoch Sometimes the function of the jurist and the judge rises to greatest importance, — as at the beginnings of the Renascence And sometimes legislation, the direct work of the political authorities, occupies the foremost place, — as in the period after the reconstruction of the European States. But, throughout all, the law is essentially an historic fact, not only in

its earliest stage, but also in all the variety of its later manifestations.

§ 82 With such opposite views of the nature of law, there could
be no conciliation between the two schools of thought On every
point they were bound to arrive at opposite results. The one
viewed law as something universal, abstract, and immutable.
The other made it out to be different for every people, dependent
on external conditions, ceaseless in its changes as each new cause
produced a new effect. The one assumed law to arise from a condition preceding all human society, the other made each human
society the cause of its own law and the guarantee of its efficacy.
The one assumed that law could be molded into a single rational
system, common to all peoples, and therefore advocated codification. The other could not conceive this as possible, and therefore
opposed codification

Savigny, on this practical problem, took issue radically with
Thibaut If a people's law (he maintained) is always in the process of historical development, to codify it is merely to arrest its
life, to impede its natural modification in the course of events. A
codified law could never correspond to the reality of things, for,
as law inevitably continues to progress, the code never represents anything more than the law of a particular moment, which
has already become the past. Nor does it attain any purpose of
justice; because every code-rule remains to be applied by the
judges to new cases, and thus the new cases (created by new
conditions) are made to be governed by a rule representing only
the past of the community, — and a past which is more and more
rapidly retreating Moreover (and apart from these objections),
Savigny contended that in any event the time for codification
was then 'premature, the necessary historical knowledge and
scientific studies were totally lacking; any code that could then
be made was bound to be erroneous and imperfect (and he cited as
examples the Code Napoleon and those founded on it); so that
nothing but harm could come thereby to legal science. And, as
his final argument against Thibaut's proposal, he pointed out that,
if a code should be made at all, it would have to be based mostly
on the Roman law, inasmuch as that law (though once foreign)
had by centuries of use become nationalized in Germany.

§ 83. The Historical school had a brilliant vogue, not at all
limited to German scholars. But its views have not remained
unchallenged by modern criticism It exaggerates, and to some
extent, mistakes, the part played by custom. Historically, it is not

correct to say that law is always formed by a process originating in custom Nor can legislation be regarded as merely the law's form, giving completion and efficacy to custom or to the dictates of legal science , sometimes it is , but sometimes, and perhaps commonly, it is not.   History shows that law has often been imposed upon a people, even in conflict with the popular wish and customs, — either by a conqueror, or by a dominant class, or by a despotic ruler. Such facts do not disturb the adherents of the Natural Law theory , for that school treated all human circumstances merely as elements disturbing the original purity of the law.   But they cannot be consistently accounted for by the theory of the*Historical school, which regarded human conditions as the efficient cause of all law, and is thus inadequate to explain such contradictions.   Furthermore, its fundamental notion of a common or popular conscience or consciousness, producing the rules of custom and law, is but vaguely formulated.   It was in fact merely an abstraction serving as a link of development between the Historical school and its predecessor, the school of Natural Law.   The latter, in developing from the still earlier modes of thought, and though seeking to cut loose from every assumption incapable of positive demonstration, had come to conceive of human nature as a complete abstraction, and had laid down the famous postulate of the social contract, — undemonstrated and quite undemonstrable. So, too, its successor, the Historical school, though starting from the opposite direction, ended also by positing, as the source of law, its dogma of the common consciousness, — which was in essence nothing more than that same abstraction of a human nature, differing only in that it was supposed to take different forms according to time and place, instead of being a general nature independent of the varied facts of human society.   Besides these shortcomings of theory, the Historical school felt also the handicap of political conditions, which were far from permitting (even in Italy) a repudiation of all the legislative results of the Revolution.   And the codification of the law had been one of those results which was more and more demonstrating its value

And so the opposing voices of the Historical school were not listened to. On this issue they were defeated. The Codification movement spread more or less rapidly into every country. A new epoch was marked off in the external history of the law, — the epoch of modern times, which gave to the law in almost every country its latest systematization in the form of codes. And here France's example was followed with alacrity by Italy, where the

need was perhaps even greater than in the other countries which
had taken the same step.

Topic 2. The Codification Movement

§ 84. **The Italian Codes of the 1700 s.** — Italy, though it had
not been the centre of expansion for the new philosophical movements already described, had not failed to share in the results.
The new principles overcame all those obstacles interposed by the
political conditions of the country and by reactionary influences.
Not a few famous names are recorded among its champions of
universal reform   Cesare Beccaria (1735–1793), in his work entitled " Crimes and Punishments " (1764), sought to turn the criminal law into the paths of the new principles.   His aim was to
divest it of its prejudices, its cruelties, its judicial arbitrariness, its
inequalities of rule, — evils which had grown out of a blind adherence to the tradition of Roman law, the despotism of sovereigns,
the ignorance of the common people, and the meddlesome regulation of personal conduct by the judiciary   Filangieri (1752–1788),
in his " Science of Legislation," set for himself the task of recon-
structing that science throughout.   Starting from the principle
that there should be in legislation, as its objective, an absolute
good, constant and immutable, over and above the relatively good
(i.e. relative to time and place), he built up a complete and ra-
tionalized system of legislation, directed to procure for the people
a happiness based on political equality, economic reform, universal
education, family governance, and legal supervision   Spedalieri,
who wrote his " Rights of Man " at the behest of Pius VI, accepted
and defended the philosophical beliefs of his times as to a state of
nature and the social contract.   On the one hand, he maintained
that men had the right to regulate society to their own best advantage, and that therefore any power which obstructed this would
be tyrannous, and might be resisted even by rebellion.   On the
other hand, he sought to harmonize these doctrines with the principles of religion and the traditions of the Church.   Romagnosi
(1761–1835), a follower of the French Encyclopædists, and endowed
with a mind of vast scope, undertook to epitomize and coördinate
the entire body of the social sciences regarded as the common
principles of man's nature.

The people at large did not remain unaffected by the new influences.   They were called upon for participation, not only by
the social reformers, but by those of the rulers who were more or

less disposed to experiment with the new ideas. In fact, the latter
half of the 1700s witnessed a widespread tendency in governments
to reform statecraft on the principles of the legal and social thinkers.
In some regions these reforms were bold enough, — more radical
in fact than the times were then capable of receiving, and destined
therefore to be neither practical nor enduring.

One of the principal objects of reform throughout this new movement was the condition of the complex mass of legislation The
ideal aimed at was a clear and complete compilation of the laws,
which would then be equally enjoyed and equally obeyed by all
classes of people Accordingly, the latter half of the 1700s in
Italy is marked by numerous tentative measures of codification.

§ 85. In *Southern Italy*, where the Bourbons then held sway, and
the mass of legal sources was especially complicated (*ante*, § 68),
the drafts of Carlo Tapia (known as "Jus regni," or "Codice
Filippino," after Philip III), and of Charles III's commission (1751–
1789) were abortive, and the Revolution overtook this kingdom
while it was still planning and drafting In the *Papal States*, no
general compilation had been seriously thought of In *Tuscany*,
however, the work was undertaken with ardor, — though here too
with little result. Duke Francis of Lorraine began in 1745 to carry
out large plans, but their only fruit was a penal code in 1786
In the duchy of *Modena*, under Francis III of Este, a code of five
books was enacted in 1771, which accomplished much for simplicity.
In *Lombardy* (under the Austrian Maria Teresa and Joseph II)
the sole result was a code of practice in 1786. In *Venice*, the
mass of materials was in special confusion, and during the half
century a partial codification emerged, — a criminal code (1751),
a feudal code (1770), and a maritime code (1786) In *Piedmont*
the early compilations of 1723 (*ante*, § 71) lasted, with revisions,
throughout the century, and were so highly esteemed that they
served as models for the usually fruitless undertakings of the 1700s
in the other Italian States

With the extraordinary convulsion of the French Revolution,
all the bonds of past traditions were broken and a new era began.
First the army, later the ideas of the Revolution, overran Italy.
Its mistakes and its excesses, no less here than elsewhere, did harm
by interrupting that process of progress which had been steadily,
though slowly, maturing. But the Revolution's benefits also were
felt; for the fruitless attempts of the later 1700s showed that
nothing short of a revolution could have availed to eradicate the
inveterate evils of Italy's legal system.

§ 86. **The French Codes in Italy.** — For the full achievement of the task of codification, two great principles had first to be accepted.

One was the abandonment of an idea which would make fruitless any reforms, however intrinsically good (and there were not a few of these, under the benevolent rulers of the late 1700s), — the idea, namely, that they were a *concession* from the ruler, for this implied that their continuance rested entirely in the ruler's discretion. What a man is entitled to get, as of right, will never be accepted by him as a gift, even from the sovereign. The sovereign must give positive guarantees that the new rights would be respected But this proposition obviously could never have been recognized under the old political conditions, where divine right was the foundation-theory of the rulers' status. This theory, however, had been totally cast out by the Revolution. That the rights of the people were sacred and indestructible could now be fully recognized, and so the first great step had been taken.

The other principle, for the lack of which no general codification had been possible, was that of *civic equality* before the law. As long as the population remained separated into castes or classes unequal in their rights and privileges, — ecclesiastics, nobles, townspeople, etc, — it was useless to talk of unifying the law The Revolution brought to all an equality before the law, and thus supplied the second prerequisite for a real codification

And yet the Revolution, apt as it was for the task of destruction, did not prove itself equally so for that of reconstruction And the task of codification was indeed no less difficult than important. Centuries of legal materials were to be compassed and collated, purging them of the antiquated rubbish, and fitting them to the new social conditions. The first code was the work, not of the Revolution, but of that man who arose amidst the universal destruction and appeared on the scene as Destiny's instrument for restoring law and order and rebuilding the social edifice. Napoleon went about his task, not in any blind adherence to the new social theories, but with an eye always on the actual needs of the community Adjusting theories to actualities, and thus giving new life to each, he produced a work of permanent and world-wide usefulness; for his Civil Code has been taken as the basis in almost all modern legislations.

§ 87. When the Revolution broke out, French law still contained plentiful traces of the early Germanic invasions. In the north, where the first settlements were made, these settlements had been more dense and more destructive of the original popu-

lation than in the south, where the Romanic element predominated   Thus it came about under the medieval system of personal law (ante, Part I, § 48) that Roman law prevailed in the
south, while Germanic law was most copious in the north   When,
therefore, in the course of time, the territorial system of law (ante,
Part I, § 67) replaced the personal, Germanic law was the type
represented in the northern territories, and Roman law in the
southern   The Roman law, earlier developed, had been and remained a written law, with little or no change or local variety
The Germanic law, however, being an unwritten law, lost its unity
in the course of social changes, and was broken up into bodies of
local custom   These so-called " Coutumes " prevailed for centuries in a large part of France.   Neither the harmonizing influence
of the jurists, using the Roman doctrines as a common law, nor the
multiplicity of royal ordinances, valid in all regions, had ever succeeded in producing unity for French law.   And so, amidst the
varieties of sources there ran this broad line, dividing the country
into two general systems, the region of the " Coutumes " and the
region of the Written Law (" pays du droit écrit ").

Not until Napoleon's time was this distinction effaced. He
alone wielded the absolute power requisite for imposing unity upon
these conflicting elements. Like Justinian who, in compiling his
Digest, settled summarily, with sovereign decisiveness, all the disputed questions of the classic jurists, so Napoleon set himself, with
vigorous directness, to bring order out of this chaos of French law.
Much of the old he retained.   The " Coutumes " furnished several
institutions of Germanic type, — marital authority, marital com-
munity-property, testamentary executors, and others.   Roman
law (which now lost its status as a common law) supplied numerous
rules of property, easements, mortgage, obligations, and contracts.
In the royal ordinances he found the regulations for transactions
affecting civic status and other special matters   From the jurists
he also drew much in the way of general principles, especially from
Pothier , indeed, Pothier's great treatises were virtually one of
the principal sources for the Code, and hence rose, even in Italy, to
great authority, which had not disappeared even by our own times.

Moreover, Napoleon was skilful in grafting upon this traditional stock the new ideas, — those which had been proclaimed by
the Revolution as fundamental, and especially the principle of
equality for all before the law   Since equality is opposed to religious privilege, the State became a temporal power only , Church
and State were separated ; and marriage was now for the first time

190

put on the footing of a civil contract. Caste was abolished, as well as hereditary rights in public offices and other occupations Special privilege was destroyed in all its forms, — whether of primogeniture, or male relationship, or of judicial jurisdiction. Property was released from the chains of family and other hindrances. Every man, within the limits of the law, could freely follow his own career, and enjoyed his rights, under the guarantee of the State.[1]

The Code Napoleon was published in France in 1804. Thence it was extended to all the Italian States in succession, as they came under the French domination. It went into force in Piedmont in 1804, in Parma and Liguria, in 1805, in 1806, in Lucca and the newly formed Kingdom of Italy; in 1808, in Tuscany (which had become the Kingdom of Etruria); and in 1809 it arrived at Rome and the Kingdom of Naples. Imported product though it was, the people received it with acclamation; for it fulfilled their long pent-up aspirations, and they saw in it a relief from the confusion and uncertainty which had hitherto reigned in their law.

§ 88. But Italy did not on this account lose either its desire or its capacity to construct a legislative system of its own. In criminal law especially (where indeed Italy had been the home of the reform ideas) this tendency was marked. In the new kingdom of Italy, a commission prepared a new code of crimes and criminal procedure, on the advanced lines of Beccaria's principles, and it was to have been promulgated in 1807, when suddenly the illusion of legislative independence was shattered, and a decree from Paris (Dec. 8, 1810) introduced the French criminal law into the kingdom. At Naples (which from 1808 to 1812 had its own criminal laws) the same measure followed. Similarly, codes of civil procedure and of commercial law, merely translations of the French codes, were now enacted for Italy, — at Naples in 1809, in the Kingdom of Italy in 1808 and 1810, and in the Roman States in 1811.

Thus the Napoleonic Empire had extended its law over all Italy. And its law met with a better and more lasting fortune than its sovereignty, for when Napoleon was overthrown and the old dynasties were restored, his legislation survived, — as the law of Rome outlived the Roman empire. And as Roman law remained the

---

[1] [For this subject of the materials used by Napoleon, and the legal changes made by the Code, see the detailed studies in the master work entitled "Le Centenaire du Code Civil," by M. *Saleilles* and others (Paris, 1904), and the chapter from M. *Planiol* in part III of the present volume. — Transl.]

guide and inspiration of all succeeding legislators, so the Code of
Napoleon, triumphant over political change and national jealousies,
even where it had ceased itself to be law, remained a model for
other codes, which indeed owed to it their very existence. It was
the notable example and brilliant success of the Code Napoleon
which brought about a universal demand for codification, — a
demand which even the most reactionary governments were fain
to satisfy.

§ 89. **The Italian Codification of the 1800 s.**[1] — The dynasties
restored to thrones by the Congress of Vienna were powerless (however strong their desire) to repudiate the reforms instituted during
the French rule   Some of these, and especially the codifications,
had filled real needs, and were thoroughly popular, in spite of their
foreign origin. In Italy the restored governments made the cause
of codification one of their first cares. No longer, of course, was
legislative unity feasible, for there were several petty States.
But the same model served for all their codes ; and some at least of
the general principles of the Revolution were embodied in them.
Their enactment only increased the popular aspiration for a national
law, and prepared the way for that real and durable political unity
which was now not far off.

§ 90. In *Sicily* and *Naples* (now known as the Kingdom of the
Two Sicilies) a royal commission was set to work in 1815, and in
1819 was enacted its Code — divided into five books (civil, criminal,
civil procedure, criminal procedure, and commercial), after the
traditional fashion. This Code was modeled on the French Code.
But the spirit of the restored reactionaries was visible enough in
many details. The purely civic status of marriage was abandoned,
and its chief rules were once more supplied by the Canon law.
The old family-inheritance system was restored ; the only French
innovations retained were the children's inalienable share ("légi-
time ") and the surviving spouse's life estate. Copyhold tenure
(emphyteusis) was restored, in spite of the feudal abuses which had
led to its abolition. To the Church was given once more the power
to own land in perpetuity. In criminal law the same features of
partial reaction were met. Treason to king and Church took a
large place once more in the list of crimes. The death penalty was
more lavishly imposed, and was made to vary in degrees of cruelty.
Yet, by way of reforms retained, the code recognized the abolition
of attaints, the liberal theory of accessories, the oral delivery of

[1] [The account of the local legislation has been abridged at some points.
— TRANSL]

testimony, and the publicity of trials   Thus, in spite of some backward steps, the Neapolitan Code on the whole was a progressive one, compared to the others in Italy and even in the rest of Europe   And the country might have benefited much from it, had it not been for obstructive conditions — the confused mass of other reactionary laws, the lack of competent persons to administer the Code, the people's reluctance to abandon fixed traditions, and, above all, the constant agitation of political changes.

§ 91. In the *Papal States*, Pius VII undertook a policy of moderate reform.   But codes of civil procedure (1817) and of commerce (1821 ; a reënactment of the French code) were the only ones actually carried into effect   Under Leo XII and Gregory XVI, sympathizers of reaction, there followed codes of crimes (1832) and of criminal procedure (1831)   But Pius VII's code of civil procedure, in its various revisions, was the only important progressive legislation of the papal government, until the time of Pius IX, who did much to modernize the civil law.

In the Grand Duchy of *Tuscany*, Ferdinand III's first task was to restore all the former laws, including the Roman and the Canon law and the Tuscan legislation.   The only fruits of the Revolution retained by Ferdinand's code commission were the French code of commerce, the mortgage statute, and the law of evidence   None of the later rulers accomplished anything substantial, except a progressive criminal code in 1853.

In the Duchy of *Modena*, also, the ancient laws were immediately restored by Francis IV   Forty years later, the slow labors of the code commissions produced a civil code (1852), a civil procedure code (1852), and a fairly progressive criminal code (1855).

In the Duchy of *Parma*, the French Civil Code was temporarily preserved, and the Austrian emperor Francis I (regent for his daughter Maria Louisa) appointed a code commission.   The civil code thus produced in 1820 (after revision of the draft by three successive commissions) proved to be the best of all the codes so far framed in Italy.   It was founded in part on Roman law ; but took also due account of the French code and of all the improvements which an enlightened view of existing local conditions could be expected to recommend.   In the same year a code of civil procedure was put in force, and in 1821 codes of criminal law and procedure

All *Lombardy* and *Venice* were under Austrian rule ; and in 1816 the Austrian Code of 1811 was here put into force.   This code differed from the other Italian codes not only in substance (*i e*

in repudiating the French code as a basis), but also in those matters
of form which were peculiarly Germanic. It lacked the severe
conciseness, inherited by the Latin nations from Roman traditions. It followed German tradition in coupling to each rule
a statement of its purpose and " motives," and added definitions
and various auxiliary regulations. On the whole, it represented
moderate reform, — equality before the law, guarantees of personal liberty, the rights of illegitimate children, religious equality,
and the rights of resident aliens. The Austrian criminal code of
1804, however, which was put into effect in Lombardy-Venice
in 1815, was reactionary, and adhered to the practice of secret trials
and harsh penalties Unlike the civil code, it never found popular
support , and by 1852 it was displaced by a new one, which abandoned the illiberal features of criminal procedure. The French
Code of Commerce had been retained from the beginning, with
some modifications of Germanic origin.

In the Kingdom of *Sardinia* (including Genoa and Piedmont)
the reaction under Victor Emanuel I was at first a radical one.
The entire body of the old law was restored.[1] But later, under
Charles Albert, a comprehensive system of four codes was planned,
on liberal principles , and, after six years of labor by the commissions, a civil code was promulgated in 1837 , then a criminal
code in 1839, a commercial code in 1842, and codes of criminal and
civil procedure in 1848 and 1854 All of these were modeled more
or less after the French codes.

§ 92 Thus, as the time arrived for the complete political unity
of the Italian people, the various States had already succeeded in
reducing their local law to something like system. In law, as in
government, separatism was bound to disappear in Italy ; and the
country now girded itself up for this task, as soon as its political
reconstruction (beginning with 1861) had been achieved. The
first steps were of course provisional only. In some provinces the
old civil law was left for a while untouched, — notably in Tuscany,
in Lombardy, and in Naples and Sicily. In others — Emilia,
Romagna, and the Marches (including Parma, Modena, etc.) —
the government immediately introduced Charles Albert's Sardinian
civil code and the commercial code of 1842. The criminal law,
too, could hardly be made entirely uniform at the outset , and so
the Sardinian code was introduced in Upper Italy and the Roman

[1] Except in Liguria (Genoa), which had, until now, been independent of
the Savoyan dynasty, and therefore was left in possession of the French
Code, and except in Liguria, for the opposite reason, *i.e.* that here the
ancient government had persisted and the laws had never been changed

States, but only partly in the southern provinces, and not at all in Tuscany.

But the preparations for ultimate unity were undertaken without delay. The commissions began their labors in 1860, and by 1865 the greater part of their enterprise was completed. In that year were promulgated, for all Italy, a Civil Code, a Code of Civil Procedure, a Code of Criminal Procedure, and a Code of Commerce (replaced in 1882 by a new one) In criminal law alone, unity was not finally reached until the Code of 1890.

TOPIC 3. RECENT TIMES

§ 93. **Codification and the Historical School** — If the codification movement, now become universal on the Continent, signalized the defeat of the Historical School, which had had its origin in the opposition to that movement, still the doctrines of that School had in one respect triumphed ; for it left the indelible impress of its ideas on legal science The doctrine that law was subject, like all human life, to the process of evolution, was no new discovery, to be sure, of the Historical School. It had often been anticipated by earlier jurists, — by Vico, for example, who embodied it in his system. But the legal philosophy of the 1700s had quite repudiated it And the merit of the Historical School lay not merely in recalling it to life, but in verifying it in the realm of positive fact and in applying it to practical results. In the phenomenon of history two ideas stand out prominently. One is that of the continual transformations of law, modified by conditions of time and place, the other is the unbroken growth of law, each form growing directly out of the prior one, and at the same time preparing for the next to come. These principles gave a powerful impulse — which has continued even till our own day — to the scientific study of legal history. The methods of comparative law were enriched and inspired ; and these led in their turn to the sociologic methods, which studied the law amidst the facts of surrounding life and established ultimately the modern conception that law is merely a branch or aspect of general social science.

To these results the Historical School contributed, not only by its principle of the evolution of law, but also by its doctrine of the social conscience or consciousness as a generating force of law (*ante*, § 82). That this social conscience is something real, not imaginary, may be seen in the fact that law can never depend entirely on the physical power of the lawgiver who formulates it.

Force is necessary, to coerce those who might resist; but if law is to be really law, the rebelliously inclined must be only a minority, and the majority, including the strongest and the wisest, must be willing to support the law for some other reason than mere fear of penalties This much at any rate is true, that some parts of the law would be completely denatured if their sole sanction was a punishment Since, therefore, force is needed only exceptionally, and the community for the most part observes the law from its own choice, the law's main support must consist in some other element, *i.e.* the consent of the majority, and this consent is a manifestation of the so-called popular conscience (or, public opinion)

§ 94 Precisely where this is to be found, the Historical School did not tell us. But it offered a criterion for ascertaining it, — namely, that it was not to be sought in abstract speculations, but in the facts of social life in different periods and communities. This criterion is confirmed by historical science

In the first place, this public opinion or conscience is dominated by a sentiment observable from time to time in religion. The primitive Germans obeyed their customs as an inherited duty, in the rule of law they heard the voice of the ancestor, now in the lapse of time become a divine command, and thus the worship of the dead and the bonds of family relationship supplied the sanction for the law. The medieval peoples conceived of law as a reflection (in some sense) of the law of God; in obeying human authority, they obeyed God, and when afterwards rulers had attained absolute power, the power is regarded as delegated to them by the hand of God, and therefore as requiring the subjects' submission. In all these instances, the legal conscience of the people is merged in their religious conscience; and to disobey the law is to commit sin.

At another period of history, of which the 1700s are typical, the religious principle gives place to a philosophical notion, instilled into the masses by numerous able thinkers; the legislator is conceived of as the agent of the people, carrying out the mandate vested in him The people should obey his law, because they have authorized him to make it, and because otherwise they would fail in the very end for which they have joined together, and human society could not exist The social conscience here rests on a supposed voluntary contract, which implies a consent to the law. If this social contract was merely a utopianism of philosophy, still there was reality enough in its products, — the dogma of popular sovereignty and the principle that the State could not abolish the rights of man

That principle of delegated authority is now, in its turn, being abandoned. As times change, the popular conscience, too, alters its standpoint. The content of the law, and not its origin, now supplies the standard. Respect for law is rested on the degree in which that law is felt to be adapted to satisfy the community's needs and interests, public and private. The dictum of the Historical School was that social conditions caused those changes which form the life and growth of the law. This necessity for the law to satisfy the changing needs of social welfare serves to induce and inspire men to submit to the law; and in the perception of the welfare thus achievable is formed and strengthened the popular conscience.

§ 95. **Other Schools of Thought.** — The Historical School did not progress beyond these general principles   Their detailed development has fallen to the task of modern times, proceeding with the methods of objective research. Under these methods, two aspects of law have come to be emphasized and contrasted. The one regards man as an individual , the other, as a member of society. There is no necessary conflict; for society is made by men, and each man finds in social life the means of improving his own. Nevertheless, the two sets of facts may be considered separately. Hence, according to the relative importance of one or the other, we are led to different conceptions of the nature of law and its adaptation to man's nature   Out of this difference arise the two schools of thought which divide the field in modern times, — the Positivist (or Biological) and the Economic.

The Positivist School (taking a biologic standpoint) looks upon man as subject (because a living being) to the common principle governing all life , this principle containing three forces or elements, — evolution, adaptation to the environment, and the survival of those who are fittest to evolve or adapt themselves. The same principle governs social phenomena also, including the law. Hence the law will be right and just, and will have the support of the popular conscience or opinion, just in the degree that it shows itself capable, by evolution and adaptation, of supplying the needs and vital forces both of the individual and of society.

It would be easy to criticise a doctrine propounded so unconditionally. The laws of biology are not adequate, merely because they are common to all living beings, to explain and control all social facts whatsoever, for those facts themselves are not common to all living beings, but are peculiar to man. There must therefore be some special principle (not necessarily in conflict with

general biological ones) which explains the special characteristics
manifested by man in social life.

From this point of view, the Economic School looks upon the
fact of economic activity as the exclusive attribute of man. This
consists in the appropriation which he makes, by his labor, of the
forces and products of nature, towards serving his various needs.
The first command which man traditionally received was to work
in order to live Without labor there is no production; without
production there is no means of human progress; and without human progress, there is no society, or none that is worth while.
Hence, the principle which controls economic facts is adapted to
govern social life; social facts are its manifestations or consequences; and since law is one of those facts, law also must be
regarded as a product of that social substratum which consists in
economic interests and needs. These it is which have been the
cause and therefore the true explanation of those historical changes
which include changes of law. In its adaptation to those interests
and needs, law finds its justification, — harmonizing them with
popular opinion and securing its obedience; for the popular conscience is nothing else but the sense general of approval for that
which has been founded to be useful towards attaining man's ends
in society.

These doctrines, also. in their extreme form, offer an easy target
for criticism. In the first place, if history shows us continually
rules of law evolving from economic causes, still, it affords also
plenty of instances where this has not been the case. Slavery, for
example, in early society, was a legal institution plainly growing
out of economic interests and upheld by them, yet the popular
conscience by no means acquiesced entirely in it, and that protest
itself ultimately became law, in the name of human nature and
its equal rights for all Furthermore, economic interests (regarded
as the sole generative force for law) tend to resolve themselves
into the notion of utility as a standard; now utility is a purely
relative term (differing for different persons), and social utility
signifies little more than the welfare of the dominant class for the
time being. The struggle between classes, and the success of the
class having most numbers or wealth or other power, is after all a
mere manifestation of force; this force hardly represents the general
popular conscience, but at most that of the class that profited by it.
This is amply illustrated in the law of feudal times, in the medieval city laws at some periods, and in the laws of the absolute
monarchies.

These two objections (chosen from several) show that the Economic School is no better able than the Biologic School to explain the law as emanating from the conscience or nature of man. The theory has still to be revised and improved upon.

§ 96 **Conclusion.** — But, for us, the history of these doctrines here ends; for they are still struggling for supremacy in the field of social science. It remains to note only that the effect of these new ideas is bound to be felt in positive legislation; for the codes are merely the latest, not the last, form of law. In these days of rapid change and progress, the truth of the Historical School's assertion, that fixed codes cannot keep up with social progress, is plain to be seen. A mass of special legislation supplements and encircles the codes, and the jurists, whose labors inevitably precede in the process of adapting the law to social needs, are now preparing for an entire recasting of the codified law. History (as we may profitably remind ourselves) shows that no real opposition exists between law and public opinion. The two are always in a process of adjustment, through the combined action of legislative authority and the community's requirements, — the former giving shape and the latter giving support. It may be affirmed that, after all, law and public opinion are merely two aspects of the same general fact; the successive shapes and attitudes of public opinion are reflected in legal ideas; and the latter serve as indices of the changes of the former. History shows us this in times past, and predicts it for time to come. Law is the companion of man's progress, not merely in that it follows the changes in his material conditions, but also in that it follows and marks the development of his thought and of his continual aspiration towards the true and the good.

PART III

FRANCE

FIRST PERIOD (A.D. 1000–1500). THE ROMAN LAW AND THE
    REGIONAL CUSTOMS

SECOND PERIOD (A D. 1500–1789): NATIONAL JURISTS AND
    ROYAL LEGISLATION

THIRD PERIOD (SINCE A.D. 1789) THE REVOLUTION AND THE
    CODES

Chapter I. First Period: a.d. 1100-1500

THE ROMAN LAW AND THE REGIONAL CUSTOMS[1]

Topic 1. The Territoriality of Law

§ 1. Origin of the Principle.

§ 2. Division of France into Country of Written Law and Country of Customs.

§ 3. Some of the Differences between the Written Law and the Customary Law.

Topic 2. The Roman Law

§ 4. Authority of the Roman Law in the Regions of Written Law.

§ 5. The Roman Law in the Regions of Customs during the 1200s and 1300s.

§ 6. Same; In and After the 1500s.

§ 7. Teaching of Roman Law at the Universities.

§ 8. Propagation of the Roman Law in other Countries.

Topic 3. The Customs

§ 9 Territoriality of Customs.

§ 10 General Features of Law under the Customs.

§ 11. Municipal Charters of Privileges.

§ 12. Books of Customs, and Treatises on the Law.

Topic 4. Other Sources of Law

§ 13. Judicial Decisions.

§ 14. Deeds, Cartularies, Form-Books, and Land-Registers

§ 15 Commercial and Maritime Law.

§ 16. Public Law, and the Legal Philosophies.

§§ 17-19 Royal Legislation before the 1500s.

Topic 1. The Territoriality of Law *

§ 1. Origin of the Principle. — With feudalism, the new principle of the territoriality of law makes its appearance In each lord's domain, within the jurisdiction of each justice, the local Custom, and only the local Custom is applied. Everybody, without distinction of race, whether domiciled therein or not, permanent

---

[1] §§ 1-16 = Brissaud, section I, chaps II-XIV, pp. 150-345, extracted and condensed. For the citation of this work, and an account of the author, see the Editorial Preface
This chapter takes up the story for France where part I of this volume breaks off — Transl.]

resident or transient, is absolutely subject to it. It was about
the 900s that this system came to supplant that of the personality
law The first traces of it are to be found in the Edict of Pistoia,
867, in the 1000s it seems to be recognized in the "Petrus"
("Exceptiones"). It can therefore be dated from about the time
of the accession of the third French dynasty It coincides with
the establishment of the feudal system. Nor is this a pure acci-
dent; for the feudal system is a parcelling of the sovereignty and
the territoriality of the law, i e a parcelling of the law. Seigniorial
jurisdiction is dependent upon the local ruler, both judges and
parties know nothing of any law save the local law. The feudal
form of government thus led, through a natural inclination, to
legislative particularism.

But other causes had already brought about a tendency of this
same nature. The "consuetudo loci" rounded out the laws of the
barbarian period. In the criminal law there was a tendency towards territoriality, even during the period when the laws were
personal Distinctions of race were being blotted out; one no
longer knew whether he was of Frankish or of Roman origin, there
were no longer any Salians, Ripuarians, Burgundians, or Visigoths;
instead there were Bretons and Provençals, Poitevins and Gascons,
— pending the arrival of that final epoch when there should be
none but Frenchmen.

The territoriality of the laws led to 1st, The division of France
into two parts, countries (or regions) of Written Law, and countries
(or regions) of Customs, a division which lasted until the publication of the Civil Code, 2d, the feudal rule that "all customs
are real."

§ 2. Division of France into Country of Written Law and
Country of Customs — In the South the Roman population greatly
outnumbered the Germanic population, therefore the Roman law,
which was the law of the majority, was applied to everybody,
as the Custom of the region In the North, on the other hand,
the mixed remnants of Germanic and Roman law, the Capitularies
which had not yet fallen into disuse, the Canon law, and the local
usages, went to make up the Customary law. These Customs
varied as to details, but had a certain amount of unity in principles
and along general lines.

The *Line of Demarcation* between the regions of Written Law
and the regions of Customs coincides approximately with that
which to-day still separates the language of Oc (Southern France)
from the language of Oïl (Northern France) It is far from being

marked exactly by the course of the Loire, as sometimes said. In reality, the regions of Customs extend to the basin of the Garonne, and include two-thirds of France   They unite Angoumois, Marche, Auvergne, Bourbonnais, Burgundy, and Franche-Comté; to the regions of Written Law belong Saintonge, Périgord, Limousin, lower Auvergne, Gevaudan, Velay, Forez, Lyons, Bresse, and the region of Gex. Thus the actual boundary between the systems is an irregular line running from the island of Oléron to the lake of Geneva, more often above than below the central mountain mass   Moreover, parts of Auvergne were under Written Law, and the northern part of Saintonge and Saint-Jean-d'Angély were under Customs.

In another way the distinction is less absolute than one would think.   There are a great number of local Customs in the regions of Written Law, and the Roman law is not stripped of all authority in the regions of Customs.

§ 3. **Some of the Differences between the Written Law and the Customs.** — In regions of Customs, the *paternal power* is not found in its strict sense (that is, that it lasts only until the children attain their majority) ; in the South, the father's authority ceases only at his death (or when they are emancipated) — The power of the *husband* over his wife is very strongly developed in the North, where the spouses are the joint owners of their possessions , but it is on the other hand very much weakened in the South, where the marriage-portion system, with separate maintenance and inalienability of the wife's land, allows the wife a great deal of independence — Custody and Lease in the North take the place of the Roman *guardianship* (" tutor ") ; and wherever the latter is found, the rule applies that : " All guardianships are dative " (*i e.* arise by grant, not by right of relationship).   In the South there was, furthermore, a guardianship by will and a guardianship by right of law. — On the subject of *successions,* the principle of the Customs, " the dead seises the living," under which the heir was invested, by operation of law, from the mere fact of the death, with the ownership and even with the possession of the inherited property, is contrary to the Roman law. — The *reserve* of four-fifths, or Customary reserve, which affected the personal belongings (that is, the immovables which the deceased had acquired by inheritance from his relatives), differs on principle from the Roman legal share.   The latter is based on the affection which relatives owe one another, the " officium pietatis " which forbids them to enrich strangers while leaving the kindred in poverty , the former is due to the old ideas of the joint-ownership of immovables or inheritances by the family, every relative, even collaterals, has a right to it. In the North, there is no *appointment of an heir;* "solus Deus heredem facere potest, non homo" (Loysel, "Inst. cout." 2, 4, 5); this is another application of the idea of family joint ownership There is no heir in the absolute sense of the word, that is, one who carries on the personality of the deceased, having the same rights and obligations as the latter, and bound to pay the latter's debts out of his own possessions. By will one can only make legatees, successors to one's possessions; they take the possessions which one leaves, but only pay one's debts up to the amount of their emolument. The Roman law, on the other hand, places the testamentary heir upon the same footing as the heir at law.

Topic 2. The Roman Law

§ 4. **Authority of the Roman Law in the Regions of Written Law.** — In regions of Written Law, there is no village, however small, which does not possess *Municipal Statutes.* But these differ from the great Customs of the North in that they are not in derogation of the Roman law, except to a slight extent and upon special points, they are generally administrative and police regulations. The Roman law is none the less the Custom of the South. I say "Custom," and I do so intentionally, for it is under this designation that the Roman law is applied. It derives its authority, not from some forgotten promulgation of the Roman or Germanic period, but from its character as a local usage, a secular custom. It is on this footing that it is recognized by the rulers of the regions over which their sovereignty extends.

So true is this that Justinian's compilations are easily substituted for the Breviary of Alaric and the Papian, the Theodosian law is abandoned after the 1100s So true is this that, like usage and custom (though less than they), it varies from province to province and century to century. The legal decisions of the four great Parliaments of the South, those of Toulouse, Aix, Grenoble, and Bordeaux, are far from being uniform. At Toulouse they accept the "lex Assiduis," by which Justinian gives the wife a lien prior to that of creditors of her husband, even though the rights of these creditors existed previous to the date of marriage, the other Parliaments reject it.

The local statutes in their turn modify the Roman law; there is none, until the great Ordinances, which does not contain its element of diversity   The Edict of 1606, not to cite many others, abolishes the Velleianum Decree of the Senate (that women could not bind themselves on behalf of another person); a Declaration of 1664 to the same effect was published, these laws were only applied in the provinces of Written Law within the jurisdiction of the Parliament of Paris, such as Lyons and Beaujolais.

§ 5. **The Roman Law in the Regions of Customs During the 1200s and 1300s.** — The Roman law (which was the common law of all Christian peoples) always had a very great authority from the juristic or theoretical point of view, even in regions of Customs. At an early period the texts of the Digest were translated into French (e g. by P. de Fontaines and the author of the " Livre de Jostice "), as also the writings of the jurists of Bologna (for example the " Summa " of Azo). Legal authors as well as courts employ the Roman law in the interpretation and the application of the Customs; it is (in the phrase of Klimrath) a sort of universal logic applied to the law; it furnishes fruitful analogies, supplementary rules, and interpretative principles   With the Canon law it forms the only law taught in the Universities, and it is from these Universities that the lawyers come   Apart from the Decretal " Super specula " and the Ordinance of 1312 (infra, § 7) the question of the authority of the Written Law in the regions of Customs is scarcely raised before the 1500s.   No one asks whether or not in general it has the force of law; the place accorded it is more or less extensive, according to individual tendencies, but it is always a more or less important one.

§ 6. **The Roman Law in the Regions of Customs in and after the 1500s.** — During the 1500s, the Roman law is so brilliantly taught, it has become so firmly established in the courts and in practice, it is cited so lavishly by every author, that one begins to ask whether it is not the common law even of the regions of Customs.   Is it applied as the law in cases not provided for by the Customs? Are the Customs exceptional rules, which the person using them should take care to restrict, while allotting an ever increasing place to the " common law "?   At the time of the compilation of the Customs (post, § 23) was it necessary to conform local usage as far as possible in the direction of the Roman system?   Or, on the other hand, ought one to draw upon the common elements of the Customs, in order to fill in the gaps in each one when applying them, or reducing them to writing?   Had the Roman law no other authority than that which was derived from its merits, its own intrinsic value, or its status as written reason?

The question was an important one; for, if one made the Roman law the common law in the regions of Customs, as it was already for the regions of Written Law, the radical difference which separated the South from the North was effaced, or at least became greatly lessened   This problem was disputed until the very end, without coming to any accord.

There were two tendencies, neither one of which triumphed entirely. As a matter of fact, the Roman law was used extensively It was referred to at every turn, even when irrelevant. From its principles, combined with the Customary law, came a mixture, — our civil law of to-day   But it is an exaggeration to say that it was the "common law" of France   In regions of Customs it was not applied as law; it only had a juristic or theoretical authority, — a very great authority, it is true. But, in the compilation of the Customs, equal account was taken of the general principles of the Customary law, and, in their application, the Customs of Paris, rather than the Roman law, as the source whence enlightenment is sought. "The Roman Civil Law," says Guy Coquille, "is not our common law, and has not the force of law in France, but should merely be regarded as Reason. The laws made by the Romans we should call upon to help us when the constitutions and the Ordinances of our Kings or the unwritten *general law of France* or our Customs fail us   'To help us,' I say, for convenience and for its Reason, and not because of necessity. In this respect two great personages of our time, who have been successively First President of the Parliament of Paris, Maître Pierre Lizet and Maître Christophe de Thou, were of different opinions. The aforesaid Lizet held that the Roman law was our common law and as far as possible conformed our French law to it, and was reputed to be narrow in his interpretation of the law and to restrain that which is contrary to the Roman law. And the aforesaid de Thou was of the opinion that the Customs and the law of France were our common law, and called the Roman law only written reason." [1]

In the 1700s, President Bouhier said the same thing. Bretonnier, in his preface to the works of Henrys, 1708, champions the theory of Lizet, while making certain distinctions. In Burgundy and in Franche-Comté, in Flanders, and in the Netherlands, at Metz, Toul, Cerdun, and Thionville, the Roman law, he says, is recognized as the common law by the official texts. There are

[1] The general French law which Guy Coquille speaks of is similar to the English "common law" and the "gemeine deutsche Gewohnheitsrecht."

even Customs within the jurisdiction of the Parliament of Paris to which this rule can equally well be applied · Auvergne, Marche, Bourbonnais, Berry, and Nivernais   No difficulty really exists except for the others   And some of them, in certain of their articles, refer to the civil law (Orléans, Tours, Anjou, Reims, Vermandois, etc)   The conflict thus reduces itself to a rivalry for influence between the Custom of Paris and the Roman law, in cases where these other Customs are silent.   In certain very important topics, such as the theory of obligations, the Roman law prevailed without dispute.

§ 7. **Teaching of Roman Law at the Universities** [1] — The Universities of the Middle Ages had an importance entirely different from that of the Universities of our day.   The latter have rivals .   (a) the other establishments for teaching, from the public schools ("Lycée") to the great special schools, such as our School of Political Science , (b) above all, books in general, and the scientific press, which place the works of learned men within the reach of everybody.   During the Middle Ages there was neither higher education nor science, outside of the Universities.   This twofold monopoly made them veritable powers with which the State and the Church had to reckon , the University of Paris, "the eldest daughter of the Kings of France," played an important part in politics.

(1) *Education was either Public or Private*.   The latter sort was rare except in the colleges; for the Universities, having the monopoly of teaching, were opposed to the giving of free lectures independently of themselves   The University itself arranged its curriculum.   The academic course consisted of lectures ("*lecturæ*"), "repetitiones," and "disputationes."   A distinction was made between *Ordinary* lectures, given during the morning, by the regent doctors, and the *Extraordinary* lessons of the afternoon, mostly

---

[1] REFERENCES   *Savigny*, "Droit romain au moyen âge," III ; *Denifle*, "Die Universitaten des Mittelalters bis 1400," 1885 (vol. I, the preface contains a bibliography of the subject) , *G. Kaufmann*, "Die Geschichte der deutschen Universitaten," I (1888), and II (1896) ; *M Fournier*, "Hist de la science du droit en France," III, 1892, *id* , "Les statuts et privilèges des Universités françaises depuis leur fondation jusqu'en 1789," 1890–1892 , various works by the same author enumerated in the "Hist de la science du droit" , *Denifle*, "Les Universités françaises au moyen âge," 1892 ; *Denifle and Châtelain*, "Chartularium Universitatis Parisiensis," vols. I to IV, 1889–1897 , *Tardif, op cit* , p. 280 *et seq* , *G Peries*, "La Faculté de droit dans l'ancienne Université de Paris," 1890 ; *L v Savigny*, "Die franzosischen Rechtsfakultaten," 1891 , *Luchaire*, "Manuel des Institutions françaises" (direct Capetians), 1892, p. 126 ; *Hinschius*, "Kirchenrecht," IV, 640, 1888.   *Rashdall*, "The Universities of Europe in the Middle Ages," 1895.

given by mere doctors or bachelors. The morning lectures in law were called " ordinary " because they took up the ordinary books, *i.e* " Digestum Vetus," Codex, Decretum, and Decretales. The *"Repetitiones"* consisted of detailed explanations of a text already dealt with in a lecture, they were the complement of the latter. Each professor, at least if he read " ordinariæ," had to observe the " puncta taxata," *i.e* points required to be taken up, pursuant to an annual regulation made by the rector, who was assisted by a commission, the course must continue for a certain period of time, generally a fortnight. A ringing of bells announced the beginning and the end of the lectures; the professor had to stop at once under penalty of a fine. The *"Disputationes,"* or public discussions of a text selected beforehand, were given by a student (in Paris, only at the time of taking the doctor's degree), and consisted in maintaining some "thesis" against those present who might wish to attack his propositions. The Statutes of Padua required two masters who were called " concurrentes " to come each day to dispute for one hour before the Faculty.

The *Vacation* originally lasted only a month; later there were added leaves of absence, supplementary holidays, days following holidays or " crastines " (" dies legibiles " and " dies non legibiles "); the cessation of university work, caused by these holidays, was an abuse which later called for reforms.

(2) *Conferring of Degrees.* — University degrees were conferred in Paris by the Chancellor (at Bologna, by the doctors, under the control of the Archdeacon) The three University degrees were, as in our own day, the bachelor's, the licentiate's, and the doctor's. But originally there were (properly speaking) no degrees; the doctor's degree, or right to teach, gave rise to the two other degrees (while in turn distinguished from the office of professor). The licentiate's degree was at first only an incomplete doctor's degree; the bachelor's degree was only the right to pursue the studies necessary for the doctor's degree.

1st The *Bachelor's Degree* was conferred by the Chancellor upon the simple presentation of the candidate by a doctor, without any examination, provided that he could show that he had completed the required number of years of residence in study (sometimes as high as seven), that he possessed the books ordinarily required, and that he took an oath. 2d. The *Licentiate's Degree* (" licentia docendi," license to teach) also assumed a presentation, a residence, and an oath, but besides this it was necessary that the candidate should have pursued his studies as a bachelor (by the end of the

1300 s these no longer were required), and that he should have passed two tests, one " privatim " before the doctors (" examen "), the other public before the Chancellor (" conventus "). This last test was usually reserved for the doctor's degree, to which the licentiate's degree gave one a right (" licentia doctoratus "), and which was now reduced to a ceremony of investiture, especially sought for by those who intended to devote themselves to teaching. 3d. The candidate for the *Doctor's Degree* made a recitation and upheld an argument before the doctors, assembled together under the presidency of the Bishop. His patron presented him with the insignia of the doctor's degree. cap, book, and ring, installed him in his chair, and the new doctor gave a short lecture in the presence of those who had conferred his title.

At first, all the doctors taught, the words "doctor" and "master" being synonymous. But towards the middle of the 1100 s the doctor's degree became a degree merely There are doctors who teach, and these are termed (at least from the beginning of the 1300 s) *Regent Doctors*, " actu regentes." There are others who do not teach, but merely have the title, with the right to vote at promotions, and (after passing more tests) the right to become a member of the body of teachers The name of " master " was given only to those who taught the liberal arts; the teachers of Roman law (" legists," called " legum doctores " from the earliest times, or " domini "), the canonists (at least after 1213), and the professors of medicine (in course of time), reserved for themselves the title of " doctors."

(3) The *Teaching of Roman Law at the Universities* went on everywhere and in all periods, from their very beginning. The only break of continuity was that which occurred at Paris in the 1200 s. The papal Decretal of Honorius III, " Super Specula " (lib. X, 3, 50, 10, and 5, 33, 28), in 1219, which forbade monks and priests (not ordinary clerics) to study law and medicine, also forbade expressly the teaching of Roman law at Paris. Philip the Handsome, a century later, in 1312, confirmed the Decretal of Honorius in a royal ordinance. It is easy to see how much interest the Church had in preventing a competition which might weaken the following of theology and Canon law in Paris Paris was in the Middle Ages the centre of Europe's theological studies, as Bologna was of legal studies. Moreover, the Isle of France (of which Paris was the capital) was a district of Custom, and there was little real need for Roman law learning; Philip, indeed, in the above-named ordinance, speaks of " our kingdom " as " gov-

erned chiefly by custom and usage, and not by the written law."
But it is not so easy to perceive, at first sight, why the king of
France should have sanctioned the prohibition of Roman law
instruction at Paris The explanation doubtless lies in a jealous
fear of the political influence of that rising system. The doctors
at Bologna were teaching their pupils that the king of France was
a subject of the Holy Roman Emperor, a German. Philip Augustus could hardly be well affected towards the teachers of such a
system His own interest thus coincided with the canonists'
fear of competition; and the prohibition became natural enough [1]

In the other Universities, the Church, far from disapproving of
the teaching of the Roman law, was the first to encourage it. It
could not forget the fact that the Roman law had played a very
important part in the formation of the Canon law, the time was
not so long ago when it was said that the Church lived by the
Roman law The writers on the Civil law, it is true, seem to us
to-day, at this distance, rather adversaries than friends of the
Church Their enthusiasm for a profane learning, their desire
to resuscitate the Roman Empire for the benefit of the German
Cæsars, their religion of State, would naturally make them suspicious characters to the Church But it was not in their ranks
alone that defenders of the imperial Ghibelline theories were found;
the theologians themselves placed their sacred learning at the disposal of the Emperors, conversely, many legists, who might be
canonists at the same time that they were Romanists, upheld the
ultramontane doctrines of the papacy

From the 1200s, then, the Roman law could not be taught in
Paris except " privatim "; it was excluded from the official instruction. In the 1500s, the Ordinance of Blois (1579, Art. 69)
renewed the prohibition, three years before, it had been necessary
for the greatest Romanist of the 1500s, Cujas, to receive an express
authorization from the Parliament in order that he might teach it
in Paris. After another century, the Edict of April, 1679, repealing this article of the Ordinance of Blois, brought once more the
Roman law into the curriculum officially prescribed in Paris

At the same time the Edict instituted the teaching of *French*

---

[1] *Digard*, "La papauté et l'étude du droit romain" (Bibl. Ch , vol 50,
1890, p. 381), has shown that the false bull (Potthast No 15570) was an
English fabrication In it Innocent IV purported to exclude from church
benefices all professors of the civil (Roman) law, and to forbid the teaching
of Roman law, except by special license, in France, in England, and the
regions of Custom In fact, England was the only country in which the
Roman law encountered systematic hostility [See *Pollock and Maitland*,
"Hist of English Law," I, 103, where this question is examined —TRANSL]

Law. Before then, the student, after finishing his course in Roman law, became familiar with practice in the best way he could; for example, by going to work in the office of an attorney   This change led to another. Latin had up to that time been the language of the schools   But now the first professor of French law in Paris, de Launay, gave his lectures in the French language.

From the 1600 s until the Revolution, the Universities were in France State institutions, national establishments. This was for them a period of decadence, which closed with the Decree of Sept. 15, 1793, pronouncing the suppression of all the French Faculties and schools of lectures

§ 8. **Propagation of the Roman Law in other Countries.** — Europe, like France, has its countries of Customs and countries of Written Law. Italy and Spain, like the south of France, are governed by the Roman law; England and the Scandinavian countries have mainly Customs, and in them the authority of the Roman law is very small. In Germany, up to the 1300 s, the Roman influence was not much felt, from that time on it preponderated, then, by another reaction, the Roman law began to lose ground.

Among the people of the North, therefore, — the Germanic races, — the Roman law had more difficulty in making its way. The Latin races, on the other hand, received everything from Rome, — religion, language, and laws. In Italy the Greek conquest led to the compilations of Justinian   In Portugal the Codes of Emmanuel and of Philip II are half Roman. The same is true of Spain with regard to the "Fuero Juzgo" and the "Siete Partidas", the many local "fueros" (like the statutes of the Italian towns) did not prevent the basis of the law as a whole from being Roman   It was from Constantinople and from the Greeks that the Slavs of the South, even the Russians themselves (though not to a great extent), derived a portion of their old law. But in Dalmatia and in Croatia the influence of the Italian cities is once more to be found; the Universities of Warsaw and of Prague carried Justinian's law into Poland, Bohemia, and Moravia, and made of it that general law which is subsidiary to the local law.

Topic 3. The Customs

§ 9. **Territoriality of Customs.** — (1) "*All Customs are Real,*" said Loysel in the 1500 s. At the time when Loysel wrote, this meant that each Custom applied within its territorial limits to all lands without distinction, whether or not the owner were domiciled within its limits. But, during the early part of the feudal period, the maxim had a wider meaning. It meant that within a given territory there could be but one Custom, not only property, of whatever nature, whether movables or immovables, but persons themselves, whether domiciled therein or not, were subject to it. And, conversely, the Custom never applied outside of its own territorial limits (" Unaquæque consuetudo suo loco clauditur "). The result was that, in passing from one territory to another, a legitimate son might become illegitimate; a person who had reached majority might become a minor; and a married woman might escape from the power of her husband. " Intrasti urbem, ambula juxta ritum ejus " That the chances of a journey should decide the status and the capacity of a person was a fact calculated to be detrimental to some persons, by imposing upon them a law not made for them, and to be serviceable to others, who might seek to escape from rules which interfered with them. But such inequities were hardly felt, for a removal from place to place was a rare thing and a difficult one during this period

This rule as to the " reality " of customs had the advantage of cutting short all uncertainties; for the judge had but one law to apply, the only one which he knew anything about (ordinarily), that is, the local usage   The rule was a natural result both of the customary nature of law and of the feudal grouping together of persons. (a) The Custom, being formed by the indefinite repetition of the same practice, affected all the inhabitants of a particular locality, and affected only them, just as a local dialect is only comprehensible where it has grown up   (b) According to pure feudal principles, the lord, who was at once sovereign and owner, would have looked upon the application, within his domain, of a usage obtaining outside of his domain as an attempt to infringe upon his rights   Each barony is a little State, the lord is the sovereign therein; outside of it he has absolutely no power   The Customs, which were an expression of this local sovereignty, could not be valid outside of the territory which had given them birth.

(2) *Italian Doctrine.* — This principle of the territoriality of laws has in England been preserved until our own time, together with many other rules of feudal origin   On the Continent, it was bound to be abandoned at an early period. It is already disparaged in an early gloss, of unknown authorship, but reported by Accursius and dating from at least the 1200 s (because Accursius lived at that time), — the gloss upon the law " Cunctos populos," under the

title of " Summa Trinitate " in the Code of Justinian :   "Quod si
Bononiensis conveniatur Mutinæ, non debet judicari secundum
statuta Mutinæ, quibus non subest "

Theory of Bartolus. — Conflicts between the statutes of the
various Italian towns early brought about the formation of an
intermunicipal law. The theory of it was developed by Bartolus
and his disciples during the 1300s and 1400s   These are the
broad principles of this theory as well as they can be detected amid
much obscurity and controversy · (*a*) In real matters (that is,
immovables), the law of the place where the immovable is situated
is always applied, whatever may be the domicile of the parties
litigant (*Real Statute*). The rule of the reality of the Customs
reduces itself to this.   (*b*) In personal matters (that is, in whatever
concerns the status and capacity of persons), in each person's case
the law of his town, his fatherland, or his domicile is followed, if
the same city has several laws valid in its territory (*Personal
Statute*)   (*c*) In matters which affect the form of a document the
law of the place where the document is executed is followed
("locus regit actum ").   In many cases one could not do otherwise,
even if desired ; for example, how can one apply to a notary in a
place where there is none?   (Loysel, " Inst. Cout.," 302)   (*d*) On
the subject of offenses, the law of the place where the offense was
committed is applied, as local good order requires   Other laws
may either not punish this particular act or else only inflict a
lesser penalty.

This theory (known as the theory of the "Statutes," because
the conflicts which it solved arose between different municipal
laws or statutes) accorded in many of its solutions with the early
system of the reality of the Customs   But even in cases where
the solutions resembled one another, the reasons supporting them
were not the same. Neither feudal ideas nor the nature of the
Custom was the starting-point. It rested rather on the needs of
commerce, and of the community of interests existing between the
Italian cities, which, though independent in fact, were looked upon
by the law as parts of the Empire.

(3) *French School of the 1500s.* — The French jurisconsults of the
1500s, who were pupils of the Italians (such men as Dumoulin
and Argentré), limited themselves to giving orthodox standing to
the theory of the statutes, and to making certain alterations in it,
— sometimes not very happy ones, such as the recognition by
Argentré of a class of mixed statutes, which were real and personal
at one and the same time. Froland, Bouhier, and Boullenois in

the 1700s added little to the work of their predecessors. By this
theory all conflicts between the various French Customs were
regulated.   Persons domiciled in one province and litigating in
another were conceded their personal local "statute", nor did
the sovereign common to all the provinces see in this application
of different laws an attempt to curtail his rights.   To-day Article 3
of the Civil Code applies this same theory to conflicts between
French and foreign laws   Under the Old Régime that sort of conflict was rare, for the foreigner was under serious disabilities,
having no rights at all, and would have scant opportunity to invoke the law of his own nation.

(4) *Modern Private International Law.* — It has been left for our
own century to found a true international private law, that is,
to found upon ideas of justice the solution of conflicts between the
laws of the various nations.   Civilized States now treat one another as the Italian republics of the Middle Ages were wont to do ;
their laws are like the Customs of the provinces of France as they
formerly existed, they form a great Republic, as Boullenois used
to say, in which peace and common sense must be upheld.   Hence,
1st. Foreigners are no longer under the disabilities which formerly
burdened them, they are given (or there is a tendency to give
them) the same civil rights as natives.   2d. They are allowed,
so far as public order allows or justice requires, the benefit of their
own native law ; each time they invoke the latter, outside of their
own country, it is sought to ascertain what a prudent legislator
would do in deciding some litigation of an international character,
while at the same time taking into account the various interests
brought into play.

This was the very just and lofty point of view taken by Savigny.
Mancini and the Italian school which follows him exaggerate its
tendencies to such an extent as to distort them ; they go so far as
to hold that the foreigner has a right, on principle, to invoke the
law of his own nation.   They have thus taken a point of view
exactly the opposite of the old rule that " all customs are real."

§ 10   **General Features of Law under the Customs.** — (1) *Various Sorts of Customs.* — In society during feudal times each
class of persons had its own law and its own judges, — clergy,
nobles, peasants, townspeople, merchants, and artisans.   In each
one of these classes, usage becomes diversified ; it suits itself to
their manner of life   The Church is under its Canon law, and is
judged by its ecclesiastical judges   The nobles have their feudal
courts and their feudal law, — much the same throughout Europe

(" Lehnrecht "), sufficiently complex to have its own special jurisconsults, the "feudists." The citizens of the towns have their
"Stadtrecht," their statutes, and their municipal judges. Among
these citizens, the merchants later develop enough Customs of
their own to constitute a "jus mercatorum," a commercial law
and a maritime law, special courts (like the judge-consuls) administer this The artisans, grouped in corporations, have also
their own special statutes and judges. The peasants, in their turn,
in their colonists' courts, apply the "Hofrecht," the "jus curtis,"
that is, the usage of the lord's domain, which fixes the quit-rents
and services (customs, "consuetudines," as they are often called)
that they owe the lord. In England, the copyholders hold their
lands in accordance with the custom of the manor ("custom is
the life of copyholders ").

(2) *Racial Character of the French Customary Law* — The Customary law is a combination (in very varied proportions, depending on regions and periods) of Germanic rules, Roman law, Canon
law, and local usage Contemplating it as a whole, in France, it
has a rather pronounced Germanic character Zoepfl was able
to say that the Code Napoleon is more German than many of the
German laws This is even more true of our old Customs The
Code Napoleon has borrowed a great deal from them, no doubt;
but it has not reproduced the rules in their entirety and in the
complexity of their details.

(3) *When has Custom the Force of Law?* — The Custom should be
based upon facts of a public nature, multiple, and ancient. 1st.
Public, for, if they are not, nothing proves that the Custom has
the force of law in general opinion ("opinio necessitatis "), if
they are clandestine, their whole effect is lost. 2d *Multiple*,
that is, repeated "Once is not a custom," says Loysel. Neither
does the force of law exist in a single isolated fact 3d. *Ancient*
("longa," "inveterata consuetudo "). Recent facts may be the
starting-point of a Custom, but they do not prove that there is any
thought in them of a rule of law. They do not bear witness to a
sufficient consciousness in the community of the binding character
of the Custom.

Notoriety, multiplicity, and antiquity are susceptible of a greater
or a lesser degree. It was for the judge to decide whether the
facts from which the Custom is inferred are sufficiently notorious,
numerous, and ancient Upon these last two points, however,
exactness was attempted. Thus, two precedents, at least, were
required in order that the Custom should be taken as proved.

217

The Canon law required the Custom to be "legitime præscripta", that is, it must have been in existence, without interruption, during the period required for prescription — ten years if it supplemented the previously existing law, forty if it were "contra jus" Forty years was the period of prescription against the Church in the law of the Lower-Empire The "Grand Coutumier de France" also required a period of forty years before the Custom could become binding There is sometimes a mention even of an immemorial usage ("cujus memoria non extat"), which applies especially in matters of public law.

Needless to observe, the Custom may be abrogated by another and contrary Custom or by a law.

(4) *Restrictions upon the Authority of the Custom.* — Custom has many foes, — the Roman law, the Canon law, natural law, and positive law. From day to day its domain shrinks. The canonist required it to be praiseworthy, reasonable, and in accord with good morals, natural law, divine law, and even the positive law, at least the abrogation of the latter by non-user was conceded only on condition of the reasonable character and a forty years' or immemorial duration of the Custom.

In the Roman law was found the doctrine by which a law derives its authority from the "judicium populi" In the Middle Ages the people were no longer sovereign, as they had been in republican Rome; they had transferred their powers to the king From this it was concluded that Custom derived its authority from the tacit approval of the sovereign; next they proceeded to require that it should expressly approve of it. Thus a valid Custom came to be almost identical with a law. The sovereign was, if not its author, at least the person responsible for its publication; he had the right and the duty to cause the Customs of the kingdom to be respected, even upon the lands of the feudal lords when the latter violated them or allowed them to be violated

According to the extent of the territory where they apply, Customs are either *General* or *Special,* the Custom of a province is general, that of a town is special In case the local Custom is silent, the general Custom resumes its force; thus the question whether or not to have recourse to the Roman law will come up only if the general Custom itself is silent. In Spain the *General* "*Fueros,*" such as the General "Fuero" of Navarre, were contrasted with the special "Fueros" (for example the "Fuero" of La Guardia or that of Viana). The "*Landrechte,*" or German provincial laws, were ordinarily nothing more than general Customs. In

England, the general Customs of the kingdom formed the *Common Law*, this was an instance of immemorial usage A few special Customs were in derogation of this common law, — such as that of Gavelkind in the county of Kent, or the Custom of Borough English, by virtue of which the younger son succeeds to the inheritance in preference to his elder brothers. Not only do such special Customs have to be proved (whereas the common law is known by the judges), but in order to be invoked they must be " good," that is, reasonable, immemorial, uninterrupted, and binding

(5) *Proof of the Custom.* — The French Books of Customs of the 1200s and 1300s distinguish (as do the Canonists and the Civilians) between the following varieties of proof : 1st. *Notorious Customs*, practised from time immemorial (Beaumanoir) or for forty years (" Grand Coutumier de France "). The parties had neither to allege nor to prove these, especially when they were general ; their very notoriety established their existence Blackstone says of the English law that it is a general and immemorial custom, confirmed from time to time by the decisions of the courts of justice , the judges, who know it as a part of their profession, will apply a notorious custom " ex officio " 2d *Customs acknowledged in Court* in the course of a lawsuit (Beaumanoir). Judicial precedent is of itself a sufficient proof of the Custom. In England this became an essential feature in the formation of the Common Law The immemorial usage which forms the latter is augmented by means of judgments which prove it, interpret it, and modify it under pretext of stating it. The decisions of the courts were there kept in public registers (" Records "), set forth in books of reports, and discussed in the writings of the jurists 3d. *Customs Approved* by the king or the lords (" Grand Coutumier de France," " Constitutions du Châtelet," Boutillier). The proof then results from the act of approval. 4th *Private Customs*, parties who alleged them had to demonstrate their existence, like any ordinary fact. The Italian doctrine (and, following it, German practice) authorized in this case all the methods of proof , the French law and the English law had a special system (*infra*). 5th. *Style* signified the judicial usage, the procedure followed by each tribunal in its administration of justice (" style " of the Parliament, " style " of the Châtelet) ; it was sometimes applied to the usage of notaries

(6) *Anglo-French System of Proof ; Examination by a " Turba."* — According to the Gloss and the Italian theory, Custom was proved by witnesses, like any ordinary fact ; two witnesses sufficed to

219

establish its existence. All other methods of proof, however, were
admissible: judicial precedents, notarial deeds, and writings of
jurisconsults But in France the procedure was different It
consisted in an inquest by a " turba " (troop, company). This
was derived (like the English Jury), from an institution of the
Carolingian period, the " *inquisitio* " by " *pagenses*," — an examination of the inhabitants of the locality required by law in certain
cases, such as suits concerning the immovables of the Treasury.
The right to have recourse to this exceptional method of proof was
a privilege belonging to the king, or to those to whom he granted it.
In England, the proof of a special Custom was made (says Blackstone) to the twelve jurors, and not to the judges, except that
proof of the Customs of London was made by the Lord Mayor and
Aldermen certifying by the hand of their clerk

The Anglo-French system was a system of " legal proof " (*i e.*
requiring credit, under fixed rules) in the following sense, that the
judge was not at liberty to admit or reject the proof furnished by
the jury or the " turba." According to the Italian jurists, on the
other hand, it was a matter of convincing the mind of the judge ;
the witnesses deposed to the facts ; the judge remained free to
weigh them as he saw fit, and to deduce the existence or non-exist-
ence of the Custom

The " *Turba* " was a sort of jury. One of the witnesses (or experts in Customs) who compose it, was elected, like our foreman
of the jury, as the *chairman (Reporter) of the " Turba*," and he answered in the name of all They were not questioned one by one,
but as a group. Their answer (which might have been called a
" verdict " in the etymological meaning of the word, " vere-
dictum ") is collective ; whereas in the ordinary examination of
witnesses it is individual. As the " turba " constitutes but a
unit, it has but one voice, the witnesses must " accord upon the
same utterance " So also the English jury must be unanimous ;
their decision is not given (as in France) by the majority. Thus,
in case of a disagreement between the members of a " turba," the
proof of the Custom was not made ; for the chairman of the
" turba " cannot speak for all. But, as the " turba " only gives
one answer, in later times it came to be counted as only one witness
(Ordinance of March, 1489, Article 13) ; thus, under the rule
" testis unus testis nullus," it was held that the Custom had to
be established by at least two " turba," that is, by twenty persons.

The number of witnesses of which the " turba " was composed,
or " turbiers," was at first unsettled (twelve, fourteen, rarely less,

sometimes more, thirty at the most, according to Rebuffe). It finally came to be fixed at a minimum of ten; whereas the ordinary jury of the Norman law had twelve members (" jurea duodecim legalium hominium in visineto "). Was this due to the influence of the Roman law, according to which " decem aut quindecim turba dicuntur," and of the Canon law, which held that a " peuple " is composed of ten persons? This is what our old pleaders say The pleaders were in the habit of bringing more than ten witnesses to the examination, for fear that challenges might reduce the " turba " below the legal minimum.

Defects of this System. — Like ordinary witnesses, and for the same reasons, the members of a " turba " were looked upon with suspicion. They were reproached with not daring, or not being willing, to tell the truth . " He is foolish who puts himself upon an inquest; for he who best supplies drink best proves." Apart from the defects common to all inquests by jury, the inquests by " turba " had their own special disadvantages. They caused a great deal of expense, because of the large number of witnesses who had to be summoned ; they were often useless, for the witnesses of each " turba " might not come to any agreement, or one " turba " might bring in a finding contrary to that of another.

The official compilation of the Customs during the 1500s (*post*, § 23) rendered the inquest by " turba " useless, and thereafter it survived only in exceptional cases   Finally, the *Ordinance of April*, 1667 (Title XIII, Article 1), abolished inquests by the " turba," and substituted for them *Certificates of Notoriety*, given out by the judges of a locality, on order of a superior judge. These were official certificates based upon the report of the officers of the Attorney-General, after consultation with the advocates and attorneys of the district, or with other practitioners if there were no lawful advocates and attorneys therein.

(7) The "*Weistumer*" of the German Law. The German Customs, and especially the rural Customs, were proved, during the whole of the Middle Ages, by declarations made each year, at fixed times, by the elders or aldermen in the village assemblies. These declarations are termed "Weistumer," "Offnungen"; when put in writing, they are called "rolls" ("Rotel" or "Rotuli"). These declarations have no feature of a judicial finding ; they are no more than official statements of usages which the aldermen have observed to be practised.

(8) *Sources of the Customary Law.* — We cannot here attempt either a complete enumeration or a methodical classification of the

sources of Customary law. But we can study the principal
memorials of that law, by grouping them according to their natural
affinities, in the following order. 1st *Charters of Privileges* or
Municipal Statutes. Alongside of legislative provisions there are
ordinarily to be found many old usages   2d Collections of Customs, compiled by jurisconsults upon their own authority, sometimes in the form of treatises, in France, some call these *Custumals* (although this word "coutumiers" was not accepted in that
technical meaning in the Middle Ages), to contrast them with the
Customs ("coutumes") which were officially drawn up in the
1500s   In Germany they are called " Rechtsbucher." 3d.
Judicial Decisions. The compilations of decisions, judicial registers, form a class by themselves, although there are to be found
in the Customals many judicial decisions   4th *Deeds, Formulas,
Cartularies*, and private registers supplement all the foregoing
sources   5th. Commercial Law.

' § 11. **Municipal Charters of Privileges.** — *Origin of Municipal
Charters.* — Municipal statutes existed under the Roman State;
such were the laws of Salpensa and of Malaga (A D. 81–84), and
the law of the colony of Genitiva Julia (Roman year 710). But
there is no connecting link between these ancient "leges munici-
pales " and the charters of the 1100s. It is true that both of them
assume a certain amount of communal autonomy; but there the
resemblance ceases   The charters of the Middle Ages are due to
the same causes that led to the emancipation of the communes.
The institutions of peaceful life contributed to bring them into
existence. The cities increased in size and became once more
populous, their inhabitants, enriched by commerce, grouped
themselves into corporations, and became a force which the feudal
lord himself must often respect. At the same time new centres
of population were being formed; the abbeys founded asylums
and refuges, kings and lords created new towns endowed with
such privileges that their growth was assured. Among these old
and new towns, certain ones succeeded in freeing themselves from
the authority of their overlord, these were the communes in the
North and the consular towns in the South. Others acquired a
semi-liberty, they continued to be governed by a provost, but
the latter found his powers limited by charters of privileges which
the lord granted to his subjects

Date — Before the 1000s, charters are rarely found in France
or elsewhere. The Customs of La Réole (Gironde), which have
been supposed to date from 997, seem not to have been in existence

until the end of the 1100s (1187 or 1188).   The Customs of Strasbourg, instead of dating from 980 as has been claimed, date only
from the 1100s.

Object. — These municipal charters, drafted without any system,
a pellmell of rules of diverse origins and dates, are both very incomplete and very extensive   They deal with the respective rights
of the lord and the inhabitants, the attributes of the local authorities, the criminal law and police, and to some extent with the civil
and feudal law and with procedure.   They are at one and the
same time compilations of constitutional laws and brief criminal
and civil codes.

Contents. — Their contents include old local usages, far earlier
in date than the time of their reduction to writing, privileges
granted by the lord; rights arising out of contracts or transactions
between towns and lords; statutes; and regulations or laws
enacted by the town itself   The reduction to writing has ordinarily
an official character.   It was done after some important event,
such as a change of the lordship, a dispute, a revolt, or a lawsuit
between the lord and the inhabitants.   The latter, feeling their
rights endangered, sought to create a formal title for them.

Charters of Franchise granted by the King or the Lords. — As early
as the 1000s the lords were wont to grant privileges to their towns
as safeguards of the freedom of the individual; free ownership;
abolition of arbitrary or onerous taxes, fixing of rents and labor
services, exemptions in the interests of commerce, impartial
justice; abolition of confiscation and of the wager of battle.
Sometimes they went further, and allowed the towns to govern
themselves.   Lorris had only civil liberties; Beaumont had a free
government.

Charters of Communes are to be distinguished from the charters mentioned above, inasmuch as they recognize in towns the
right of self-government, the rights of having a budget, troops,
statutes and judges.   They make independent domains of these
towns   Moreover, whereas mere charters of privilege are often uni-
lateral deeds, communal charters have rather the character of
contracts between the lord and the citizens, — contracts upon
which royalty sets its seal of approval.   Usually the town buys
its freedom.   Sometimes an insurrection is needed, in order that
this freedom may be recognized and respected.

Statutes of Trade Bodies, of Guilds, Hanses, Charitable Societies,
and Brotherhoods, reveal to us the organization of the working
classes and of the merchants.   The supervision of associations of

223

merchants and of trades, the approval and the revision of their statutes, belonged to the municipal authorities in the free towns, communes, and consular towns, elsewhere, to the provost of the king or of the lord. It was in his capacity of Provost of Paris that Etienne Boileau caused to be reduced to writing, in the 1200s, the old regulations of the arts and crafts of Paris ("li establissements des mestiers de Paris") (1252 to 1271). He was not, as has been said by some, the legislator of the industries of Paris. He was satisfied with having the usages of the trades registered and ratified, after eliminating what was contrary to good laws. The corporations of artizans, represented by their sworn masters, appeared before him at the Châtelet, stated what their Customs were, and a clerk took them down before the Provost. These statutes, known as the "*Livre des Métiers*" of Etienne Boileau, give one some idea of the manner in which the working classes were organized in France, and countries other than France (such as England, Germany, and Italy) have statutes analogous to these.

§ 12 **Books of Customs, and Treatises on the Law** — It is not difficult to explain why private editions of the Customs and treatises on the law were made. Naturally enough, it was done in imitation of the compilations of the Roman law. But it was due especially to the necessity of making known the local usages, of giving them some degree of fixity, and by this means of limiting the despotism of the judges. These reasons led the jurisconsults to take the initiative; for public authority showed no interest. The embarrassments of the judges, forced as they were to deal with a mass of inconsistent customs, about this same period were being emphasized throughout western Europe. In the 1200s there grew up in England, in France, and in Germany, a legal customal literature, whose chief works are sufficiently analogous to serve to interpret and explain one another. Two tendencies come to light: in some of these works the Roman law predominates, in others it plays scarcely any part at all and the Customary law is set forth in all its purity. The Romanist tendency is found (in France) in Pierre de Fontaines, in the "Livre de Jostice," in Boutillier, and (in Germany) in the "Schwabenspiegel"; the Customary tendency, on the other hand, is more pronounced in Beaumanoir, the Norman Books of Customs, Glanvill (in England), and the "Sachsenspiegel" (in Germany).

(1) *Anglo-Norman Texts. Normandy.*[1] — 1st. The "*Très*

---

[1] *Cf.* as to the connection with Scandinavian law, V *Amira*, "Sybel's Hist Geitschr," N F, III 241

Ancien Coutumier de Normandie " [1] is not an official redaction of
the Norman law made under the orders of Philip Augustus a short
while after the conquest of Normandy ; it is a private work written
in two distinct treatises, one drawn up about 1200, the other
about 1220.[2] The French text is only a translation of the Latin
text, which must be regarded as the original.

2d. The *"Grand Coutumier de Normandie"* has come down to us
in three forms, — in Latin, in French prose, and in French verse. —
(*a*) In Latin ; "Summa de legibus Normanniæ," this is the early
form.[3]   (*b*) The translation into French prose, the " Grand Coutumier de Normandie," is but little later in date.[4] (*c*) The translation in verse by Richard Dourbault was made in 1280.[5] The
original itself is thus earlier than 1280 ; it is earlier than the Ordinance of 1275 dealing with amortizations, to which it makes no
allusion (Chap. XXX), it belongs between 1254 and 1258 or 1260,
and perhaps is even older than this.[6] It is one of the most re-

[1] EDITIONS : *Warnkœnig*, "Franz Staats- u Rechtsg," II ("Statuta
et Consuet. Normanniæ") ; *E-J Tardif*, 1881 ("Coutumiers de Normandie, textes critiques," 1st part, the "Très ancien Coutumier de Normandie," Latin text, 1881), French text, which is almost contemporary
with the Latin text, in *Marnier*, "Etabliss et Coutumes, assises et arrêts
de l' Echiquier de Normandie," 1839.
BIBLIOGRAPHY   Introduction by *Tardif*, *Brunner*, "Das anglonorm
Erbfolgsyst ," 1869, "Schwurgericht," 1871, and *Holtzendorff*, "Ency-
clopæd ," p 300
[2] The first treatise (up to "Jurea regalis," c 66) is concerned with private law, procedure, the penal law, and the competence of the seigniorial
courts   *cf Glanvill*   The second one describes the progress of a suit
involving title to property   *cf Bracton*, part 2 (procedure)
[3] Gothic editions of the sixteenth century , *Ludewig*, "Reliquiæ mss.,"
1720–1740, VII, 149 , *E.-J. Tardif*, "Coutumiers de Normandie, textes
critiques," vol II ; "La Summa de legibus Normanniæ in curia laicali,"
1896 (bibl , p vi) (chapters 113–124, § 8 were added before 1275 , chapters 124, § 9, and 125, before 1278 , other amendments took place before
1293)
[4] Gothic editions · Text brought up to date by *Bourdot de Richebourg*,
"Nouv Coutumier général," vol IV — *W Laurence de Gruchy*, "L'ancienne coutume de Normandie" (French and Latin text).
[5] *Houard*, "Dict de la cout de Norm ," IV, 1782
[6] According to *J. Tardif*, the "Summa" does not make any mention
of the Ordinance of 1258 or that of 1260 which abolished the duel, nor does
it refer to the restrictions brought to bear upon the right of tavernage in
Normandy in 1258   Chapter VI, 7, assumes St Louis to be still alive
Chapter IV and chapter VI seem to have been inspired by the Ordinance
of December, 1254, dealing with the reform of morals in Languedoc (*Tardif*,
p clxxxvii)   *Esmein*, "Cours d'hist du dr fr ," 3d ed , p 728, n 2, disputes this last point ; he regards the "Summa" as being a little later in
date than 1234, a time when Gregory IX published his compilation of
Decretals , for the second prologue of the "Summa" contains a few lines
borrowed from the bull of publication "Rex pacificus"   "Chapter cxi,
13, recalls the crude process by which the prescription of thirty years used
to be reckoned   Some event known to everybody, and dating back about
thirty years, was selected, and all deeds previous to that date were declared to be covered by the prescription   When the date selected had

markable legal works of the Middle Ages. "The author is not satisfied with setting forth the Customs of his country, he codifies them The method employed by him gives his work a scientific character which distinguishes it from other treatises composed in France at about the same time. The influence of the Roman and Canon law is not noticeable. The Norman law is so faith-fully portrayed that, though it was but the work of a private person, it acquired before long the authority of a regular Code, Philip the Handsome cited it and ratified it in 1302. It did not cease to be applied until 1583, the date of the official redaction of the 'Coutume de Normandie,' — and even at the present time, it forms the common law in Jersey [1] and the Channel Islands." [2]

England. — The "Tractatus de Legibus et Consuetudinibus Regni Angliæ," compiled between 1187 and 1189, and attributed to Ranulphe of GLANVILL, chief justice of England under Henry II, who died at St. John of Acre in 1190, sets forth the procedure fol-lowed in the King's Court, and at the same time describes the matters coming within that jurisdiction. This work, by reason of its date, its merits, and its subjects, is of great importance. This was so generally recognized that an edition of it was made for use in Scotland, under the title "Regiam majestatem" (the words with which the prologue begins).

About seventy years after Glanvill's time, BRACTON's great treatise was written, "De legibus et consuetudinibus Angliæ"

become too remote, another was fixed by a decision of the Exchequer. The last event so chosen, according to the 'Summa,' was the crowning of Richard Cœur de Lion in 1189; 'but the King,' it went on to say, 'ought to fix another, for more time has expired since then than is neces-sary for prescription' This manner of speaking is readily understood if the author of the 'Summa' wrote about 1234 Forty-five years had passed since 1189. It is hard to conceive that a prescription which nor-mally was of thirty years, should be allowed to extend to a period exceeding eighty years, which one would have to admit if this passage were written after the death of St Louis "

[1] W Laurence de Gruchy, "L'ancienne coutume de Normandie," 1881; cf J Havet, "Les cours royales des Iles normandes," BCh, 1870–1878

[2] Other texts of Norman law (A) Judgments of the Exchequer: "Recueil de   au XIII siècle," by L Delisle, 1864, Léchandé d'Anisy, "Méms de la Soc de Antiq de Norm," XV, 150; Warnkœnig, "Franz. Staats- u Rechtsg Urk," II, 120 After the 1300s they are not published — (B) Compilation of the Assizes, decisions rendered at Caen, Bayeaux, etc, from 1234 to 1237 (a) Latin · L d'Anisy, op cit, p. 144, Warnkoenig, p 46. (b) French· Marnier, "Etabl et Cout," 1839, p 89 — (C) Styles (a) Valroger, "Mém, de la Soc des Antiq. de Normandie"; XVIII ("Coustume, stille et usage au temps des Echiquiers de Normandie," first half of the fifteenth century) (b) "Le stille de procèder en pays de Normandie," a little later, in the style of the "grand Coutumier" in the Gothic editions — (D) "Coutumier de la vicomté de l'eau de Rouen," a compilation of maritime and commercial law, 1200 s: Ch de Beaurepaire, "De la vicomté de l'eau de Rouen," 1856.

(1250–1258), — Roman in appearance, but at bottom essentially English. It was compiled especially with the aid of the rolls of the cases before the judges of the King's Courts. Its borrowings from the " Summa " of the Italian legist Azo and from the canonist Tancred are entirely superficial and play but an unimportant part in it, without altering the character of the work ; it is an exposition of the procedure and the law followed in the royal courts Bracton was hostile to the feudal lords and the Church, and a partisan of the authority of the king, yet did not go so far as to support absolutism. His correct name was Henry de Bratton. He was an itinerant justice from 1245 on, and from 1248 until his death in 1268 he held assizes in the southwest. From 1248 until 1257, he was a judge in the Court of King's Bench. He received various benefices ; and in 1264 he was appointed Chancellor of the Cathedral of Exeter. Bracton's book became the basis of the legal literature of England in the time of Edward I. Gilbert Thornton, presiding justice of the King's Bench, made an abridgment of it Two treatises written about 1290 are little more than reproductions of it, — *Fleta* (from " Fleet," or " flotte," a prison in London where the author was imprisoned (?) and which appeared to be afloat because it was on the river Thames) and *Britton*, a French book which puts all the rules of law into the King's mouth (" we will," " we grant ")   Let us add to these important works a little treatise on procedure, the " Summa " of Ralph Hengham, Chief Justice under Edward I, and the worthless essay of Andrew Horne, the " Mirror of Justices "

Although the English law was far from remaining unchanged, yet the Customs of the 1200s reappear in the writings of later times, the most noteworthy of which it would be well to mention here. The " Tenures " of LITTLETON (1482) had almost the force of law until the time of Blackstone (1723–1780) , and the first book of the " Institutes of the Laws of England " by Sir EDWARD COKE (1628) is no more than a commentary upon them   Fortescue's treatise, " De laudibus legum Angliæ " (1463–1471) drew a parallel between English and Roman law, to demonstrate the superiority of the former. The classic " Commentaries on the Laws of England," by Sir WILLIAM BLACKSTONE (1765), afterwards superseded these old treatises. It was through Blackstone that Europe made its acquaintance with English law.

(2) *France (1200s)*. — " *The Advice of Pierre de Fontaines* " or " *Advice to a Friend* " (1253–1258). This title is a conventional literary phrase (like that of the book of Philip of Navarre) given

to a compilation of usages and Customs of Vermandois, written
by one of the best known Councillors of King St Louis, Pierre de
Fontaines His knowledge of the Customary law seems to run
short, so he ends by substituting an almost literal translation of
passages from Justinian's Digest and the Code. The " Advice "
contains chiefly rules of procedure, occasionally some rules of
private law

The " *Anciens Usages D'Artois* " or " *Coutumier D'Artois* "
(1283 to 1302) has extensive borrowings from P de Fontaines, and
perhaps even from the " Etablissements de Saint Louis," as well
as citations from the Roman and Canon law. Nevertheless, it is
the personal work of an author (a lawyer of Arras ? a sheriff ?) who
has used to good advantage his own experiences

The " *Livre de Justice et de Plet*," like the book of Pierre de
Fontaines, is for the most part a translation of the Roman texts,
except that the " Advice " is concerned with the usages of Vermandois, the " Justice " with those of Orléans. Neither date nor
author are known; it probably belongs shortly after 1259 Some
have thought that it represents a student's notes of lectures at
the University of Orléans, the teaching was there in French, as
early as the beginning of the 1300s, contrary to the general usage;
and the professors there used great liberty with the Roman texts.
But however this may have been, no lectures on Customary law
were then given at Orléans or anywhere else, and the " Justice "
must be the work of an experienced practitioner.

"*Etablissements de Saint Louis.*" — The word "stabilimentum,"
establishments, in the 1200s meant the Royal Ordinances. It
was in fact for a long time (and naturally) thought that the Book
of Customs which bears the name of " Etablissements de Saint
Louis " was an official compilation of the Ordinances of this King
Du Cange, Laurière, and Beugnot thought so. But Viollet has
demonstrated the fallacy of this view. It is scarcely possible that
Saint Louis had any thought of giving a uniform civil legislation
to his whole kingdom; the historians of his doings make no mention of a plan of this nature, and he was too much opposed to the
constitution of feudal society to have conformed to its point of
view as accepted in this book Nevertheless, the influence of the
" Etablissements " was great, it was felt even in distant provinces,
such as Brittany, Poitou, and Champagne, where an abridgment of
it was made, Beauvaisis, Artois, and even Hainaut.

Customs of Beauvaisis. — Philip de Remy, lord of Beaumanoir
(1246 or 1247–1296), spent a part of his youth in England. After

his return to France he became sheriff of Clermont in Beauvaisis (or Beauvoisis) ; it was during his tenure of this office that he wrote the Customs of Beauvaisis (" li livres des Coustumes et des Usages de Biauvoizins "). This book of Beaumanoir's is at once a compilation of the Customs and a treatise on Customary law   The author himself points out in his Prologue the sources from which he has drawn ; they are judgments rendered in his own day in the County of Clermont, settled usages shown by the judgments of neighboring baronies, and, finally, " the law which is common to the whole kingdom of France," that is, the Roman law   It is, as a legal work, much superior to most treatises of the Middle Ages. In spite of its great worth, — or perhaps because of its very qualities, because it had too much of its author's personality, — his book passed unnoticed.   No one imitated it ; no one made use of it.   In the 1600 s, Du Cange and La Thaumassière resuscitated it to some extent.

(3) *France* (continued), *1300 s and 1400 s; West* — In *Brittany* we have certain fragmentary Assizes of 1185 and 1301 ; and then the " Very Old Custom of Brittany," dating 1312–1325.   In *Anjou, Maine, Poitou,* and *Berry* there are compilations of Customs starting as early as the 1200 s

North of France and Belgium. — For this region, besides various Books of Customs, there is a learned treatise, giving a statement of the whole of the French law at the end of the 1300 s, — a sort of encyclopedia, in which the Roman and the Canon law mingle in a disordered and confused stream with the Customary law, — the " *Somme Rural*" of JEHAN BOUTILLIER, lieutenant of the sheriff of Tournay (died about 1395).   The sources from which Boutillier has drawn, outside of the decisions of the tribunals in which he attended, are Customs of the North of France, of Flanders, of Artois, of Vermandois, of Normandy, the " Etablissements de Saint Louis," and the "Styles" (noticed below).   Although it leaves much to be desired in method and in compilation, the " Somme Rural " met with great success among the practitioners of the time.   Charondas le Caron, as late as the 1600 s, reèdited it (1602–1611), and the following distich, in spite of its exaggeration, was not far from being regarded a simple statement of the truth :

" Quæ tibi dat Codex, quæ dant Digesta, quod usus,
　　Ruralis paucis haec tibi Summa dabit."   (Godefroy)

In our own day, it possesses this great interest, that it gives us an outline of the evolution which the Customary law was undergoing

at the end of the 1300s   Perhaps the changes in it are too much
accentuated, and are more in conformity with the Romanist tendencies of the author than with the truth   ✻

Central Region. — The "*Stylus Curiæ Parliamenti,*" or "*Style
du Parlement,*" is the work of an advocate of the Parliament of
Paris, WILLIAM DU BREUIL, a native of Figeac.   It was written
about 1329 or 1330, and is a treatise on civil procedure, — the
first to be produced in France.   The author was a skilled practitioner, of doubtful morality, but of very accurate knowledge
His work is methodical, precise, and modern in style; and reproduces the practice of the Parliament of Paris at the beginning of
. the 1300s, at a time when the influence of the Roman and the
Canon law had already made itself felt to a great extent.

The "*Grand Coutumier de France*" (or "*Coutumier de
Charles VI*").   This misleading title is given to a private compilation made at the end of the 1300s (between 1385 and 1388),
whose author, JACQUES D'ABLEIGES, was successively sheriff of
Châtres and of Evreux.   "That which is in it," he himself says,
speaking of his work, "I have found and received from others and
acquired in other ways"   He here brings together ordinances,
rules of practice, and rules from the "Coutume de Paris."   In this
composite work, which has no originality, procedure (especially
the practice of the Châtelet of Paris) and forms occupy much
space   The feudal law of the Ile-de-France is set forth in some
detail   The "Grand Coutumier" was extensively used by our
old practitioners, and was still being studied in the 1500s

(4) *Books of Practice.* — The "Practica forensis" of JEAN
MASUER (a student at Orleans and an advocate at Riom, died 1450)
is one of a sort of writings which had begun to appear as early as
the 1100s, and did not cease to have great vogue until the period
when our old law was superseded.   A Practice-Book is primarily
a book of procedure, an "Ordo Judiciarius"; it is contrasted with
the books of theory, the "doctrine."   Masuer's Practice-Book deals
with the districts of Auvergne and Bourbonnais, where the fusion
between Roman and Customary law was then going on.

The last notable Practice-Books were those of IMBERT (1552)
and Lange (prior to 1667)   The Netherlander Damhouder (died
1581) wrote a "Practica rerum criminalium" which had an extensive vogue.[1]

---

[1] [The foregoing account of the sources of Customary law has been
much abbreviated from the original — TRANSL.]

Topic 4. Other Sources of Law

§ 13. **Judicial Decisions.** — (1) *The Court Record.* — From what period do the official records of the courts date? They did not exist at the opening of feudalism, when procedure was public and oral. Were the fact or the tenor of a judgment contested, resort was had to the memory of the judges (*memory, " record," of the Court*). This method would have been of some value if the judges could actually have retained an exact memory of all their judgments, — and if they did not die in the meantime! In the kingdom of the Orient, they were often reduced to having the advocates plead all over again The "Abrégé de la Cour des bourgeois" (Assizes of Jerusalem) tells us that, at a combined session of the two courts, in 1250, it was decided that each branch should have a scribe, charged with keeping a book wherein he should set forth the " claims and replies, allegations, reasons, and statements;" that is, the complaints and answers and all the proofs of the parties. In the Occident, the Court's " memory-record " system was not abolished; but reforms were introduced, and little by little it fell into disuse. According to Beaumanoir (in the 1200s), in the lay courts, they still " remembered " whenever the parties came before the court a second time, but the judge was bound to keep a brief written finding of the facts and the parties' proofs so as to make up for the lapses in his memory. From these summary notes, made at the trial, there developed the system of embodying the entire pleadings and judgments in rolls or scrolls of parchment.[1]

(2) *Normandy.* — As early as the end of the 1100s[2] the services of the clerk of the court were regularly used in the highest Norman court, that of the Exchequer.[3] The judges had their judgments

---

[1] *Stouff,* "Rôle de la ville de Saint-Ursanne" (N R H , 1890, p 121), states that minutes or rolls of the pleas ("dingrœdel") were kept, from the beginning of the 1200s, in the Jura region; *Trouillat,* "Monum. de l'hist de l'ancien évêché de Bâle," I, 296.

[2] *L. Delisle, op. cit ,* p 353

[3] The Exchequer had two sorts of members, — the barons, and the "justitiarii," lawyers chosen by the king, who soon took precedence over the former Since the time of Henry II, this Court had held two sessions annually, one at the feast of St. Michael, the other at Easter, in the town of Caen Afterwards Rouen became the place where the Exchequer ordinarily sat, there were still, however, sessions at Caen and Falaise. The conquest of Normandy by Philip Augustus, in 1204, did not do away with the Exchequer, but it was the commissioners of the king who came to hold the sessions. The prelates and the barons continued to take part in them, and, with them, all the followers of the king; these came there to uphold the judgments which had been rendered by them and had been appealed from, to hear the reading of the Ordinances, and to render their accounts. All other jurisdiction was suspended while the Exchequer

inscribed "in rotulis scaccarii." Before long, the practice developed of taking important judgments from the rolls or scrolls and
copying them into registers, more convenient for reference.[1] The
Exchequer had such a register at least as early as 1225 [2] Under
the name of "Assises de Normandie" ("Assisiæ Normanniæ")
we possess a collection of decisions rendered by the judges of the
King at the assizes held in various towns, — Caen, Bayeux, Falaise,
etc. (1234–1237) [3]

(3) *England* [4] — The English judicial documents are even older
than those of Normandy. They are of three kinds.

1st. *Writs* ("brevia") issued by the King in each case, permitting
an exceptional procedure, the result of which was to do away with
the wager of battle and the wager of law (or trial by oath). After
the time of Henry II, the Chancery would give these writs to the
parties according to certain common forms and on conditions fixed
by custom; so that they ceased to be exceptional and dependent
on special favor, and became one of the regular forms of procedure.
These writs were used for varied purposes. The Writ of "præcipe"
(derived from the Frankish "indiculus commonitorius") gave
authority to bring the parties before the King's Court; an order
was issued to the Viscount (sheriff) to command the defendant
to restore the subject of the suit, under penalty of being brought

was in session   The Exchequer, thus organized, was, as it were, an am-
bulatory branch of the Parliament of Paris , the king's commissioners were
ordinarily chosen from the members of the court of Parliament   In 1499,
a permanent Parliament was substituted for it — The name "Exchequer"
given this Court is said to be derived from the fact that the table around
which its members met was covered with a cloth having black and white
squares, just as, in France, later on, the name of "Marble Table"
was given to certain tribunals — The English Exchequer is found under
Henry I, but the Norman Exchequer only made its appearance under
Henry II   *Langlois*, "De monum ," 9 , T A C , Norm , ed *J Tardif*,
p 35; *Stapleton*, "Magni rotuli scaccarii Normanniæ," 1840 (rolls of
the finances), "Rotuli Normanniæ," ed *Th Duffus Hardy*.

[1] Three jurisconsults were charged with this duty

[2] *L Delisle*, "Recueil des jugements de l'Echiquier de Normandie
au xiii siècle," 1200–1270 (printed from copies of the lost original compilation), 1864 , "Notices et Extraits des mss ," 1862, XX, 2d part, p
138 , "Mém Acad. Inscr ," 1864, XXIV, 2d part, p 343 ,   *Auvray*,
B Ch , 1888, p 635   From the death of Saint Louis until the 1300 s
Lechaudé d'Anisy, "Mém Antiq Norm ," XV, 150 , *Warnkoenig*, "Franz
Rechtsg ," II, V, 120 — Beginning with the 1300 s these judgments are
still unpublished

[3] This is a private work.   The Latin text was published by *Lechaudé
d'Anisy*, *op cit* , p 144, and by *Warnkoenig*, *op* and *loc cit* , the French
text by *Marnier*, "Etablissements et Coutumes, assises et arrêts de l'
Echiquier de Normandie," 1839   *L. Delisle* states that there were rolls or
registers in each jurisdiction in 1248 and 1253 ("Mém Ac Inscr ," XXIV,
357, 359, 362)

[4] "Encyclop d Rechtswiss " by *Holtzendorff*, p. 308; *Glasson*,
"Inst de l'Anglet "

before the King The " Breve recognitionis " commanded the Viscount to summon a jury, which was to decide the question of proof raised by the pleadings The " Breve de recto " was indispensable in any litigation affecting immovable property, even before the seigniorial courts, it was derived from the " indiculus de justitia " of the Frankish period The forms of these writs show a striking analogy to the forms of action of the Roman law. Their effect was to give each action a distinct individuality · " tot formulæ brevium, quot genera actionum." A distinction was made between the " brevia originalia," by which an action was begun, and the " brevia judicialia," used during the course of an action. "Brevia formata" were distinguished from "brevia magistralia";[1] the former corresponding to the direct actions of the Roman law, and the latter to the " utiles " (or equitable) actions, for they were issued by the Chancery " in consimili casu," *i.e.* for a case similar to one for which some other writ had been created.[2]

2d. *Records*, or official minutes of the decision of the court and of the trial which precedes it[3] They were entered upon rolls and registers, like the decisions of the Exchequer of Normandy. The Exchequer of England (the equivalent of our Court of Accounts, but forming at the same time a court of Justice), had its " Pipe Rolls " (rolls in the form of a tube or pipe) since the reign of Henry I (1100–1135)[4] One can still see in London judgment rolls of the time of Richard Cœur de Lion (1189–1199).

3d. *Reports*, kept officially[5] since the end of the reign of Ed-

---

[1] Statute of Westminster, 13 Ed I, c 24

[2] See forms of writs in *Glanvill*, and in the "Statutum Walliæ," 1284, which introduced English procedure into Wales Collections of writs: "Old 'Natura brevium'" under Edward I ; "Registrum brevium omnium" (official collection), 1531 , "New 'Natura brevium'" of *Fitzherbert*, 1534 (ed of 1794 with commentary). *Cf* T A C , Norm ; *Brunner*, "Entstehung der Schwurg ," 404

[3] *Bigelow*, "Placita Anglo-Normannica," 1879 (from William I to Richard I), *Palgrave*, "Rotuli curiæ regis," 1835 (from Richard I to John) , "Placitorum in domo capit. Westmonast ass abbreviatio" (Richard I to Edward II), compiled under Elizabeth and published by the State in 1811. The Record Commission has published a great number of them : *Pollock and Maitland*, I, xvii. — French was the law language of England until 1362 · *Pollock*, "First Book of Jurisp ," 299

[4] *Cf* "Dialogus de Scaccario" in the "Select Charters" of *Stubbs*, 1884 The minutes and records of the Court of Chancery each day increased in importance A special officer, the Master of the Rolls, "clericus et custos rotulorum," was appointed to have this custody in the twentieth year of the reign of Edward II. Like the Chancellor, he was chosen among the clergy, and had to take the former's place when he was prevented from appearing.

[5] [At the time of the learned author's death, he could hardly have known of the now accepted opinion of English scholars that the Year-Books were not "official " — TRANSL]

ward I   The reports contain chiefly the arguments of the parties
and the reasons for the judgment; the detailed facts of each case
are not found in them, as they are in the records, — the latter
being mainly intended to preserve the judicial decisions in order
that they may be applied, if need be, "inter partes."

(4) "*Le Parlement de Paris*"[1]—As early as the twelfth century
the proceedings in the King's Court were not entirely oral   There
was need of various written documents,[2] written proofs, inquests;
clerks made a note of the judgments, in order to furnish copies,
etc.   Once a lawsuit was ended, these documents were no doubt
preserved in some secure place,[3] and we know that under Philip III
and Philip the Handsome this was the "Palais de Justice."[4]

---

[1] EDITIONS: *Beugnot*, "Les Olim," 1839–1848 (collection of unpublished documents dealing with the history of France), restoration of the
"Liber Inquestarum" of *Nicolas de Chartres* which had been lost since
the 1500s, *L. Delisle* in the "Actes du Parlement de Paris," I, 315–464,
and in the "Notices et Extraits des mss de la Bibl Nat," XXIII, 2d
part; *Ch.-V. Langlois* in the B Ch, 1885, pp 440–447, extracts from
the Memorial of the court clerk attached to the third "Olim", *Klimrath*,
"Travaux," I, 73, *Beugnot*, "Olim," II, 880, *Grun*, "Notice sur les
Archives du Parl. de Paris," p lxxviii ("Actes du Parlement"); inven-
tory of the Orders of the Parliament by *Boutaric*, very useful for Orders
after the unpublished "Olim" (II, 294), but it ceased in 1328, in the
"Actes du Parl de Paris" ("Coll. des Archives nationales"), *Ch -V.
Langlois*, B.Ch, 1887, 177 and 535 (rolls containing Orders of the
King's Court in the thirteenth century) — The registers and the minutes
of the 1300s and the 1400s have been published in part only.   *Cf. Tuetey*,
"Journal de Nicolas de Baye" (court clerk, 1400–1410), 1885, and "Testaments enreg au Parl. de Paris sous Charles VI," 1880. — Prior to the
1200s, see *Luchaire*, "Hist. des instit. de la France sous les premiers
capétiens," II, 308, app. no 12 (cases from 1137 to 1180); *Boutaric*,
"Actes du Parl," I, p ccxcii (Orders of the King's Court from the accession of Philip Augustus until 1254, which is the date of the oldest register of the Parliament); *Ch -V Langlois*, "Textes relatifs à l'hist. du
Parl. depuis les origines jusqu'en 1314," 1888, *Guilhiermoz*, "Enquêtes,"
p 378 (Orders from 1313 to 1370).
    BIBLIOGRAPHY. *Beugnot*, "Olim," preface and notes; *Klimrath*,
"Travaux," 1842; *H Lot*, "Essai sur l'authenticité et le caractère
officiel des Olim," 1863, *Ch -V Langlois*, "De monumentis ad priorem
curiæ regis judiciariæ historiam pertinentibus," 1887. *Viollet*, 161, *Glasson*, IV, 172; *A Tardif*, "La procédure aux xiii et xiv s," 1885, p 122,
P Fournier, "Les Officialités," 1880; *Aubert*, "Le Parl de Paris"
(N.R.H, 1884, p 452 on the court clerk), "Hist du Parl. de Paris de
l'origine à François I," 1894, I, 229
    [2] *Luchaire*, "Inst mon sous les premiers capétiens," I, 319, *Lang-
lois*, "De monum," 8   The national archives contain some dating for
the beginning of the 1200s   *Langlois*, "Textes," VII
    [3] At the Treasury of Charters (the Sainte-Chapelle under Saint
Louis), for there are legal documents in the Supplementary Treasury
where they must have been forgotten, when the court clerk of the Parliament, on its separation from the royal Archives, was transferred to the
Palais de la Cité   *Langlois*, "Textes," *ibid*.
    [4] In two documents called "camera" or "gardaroba," perhaps the
session room ("camera placitorum") and the cloak-room of the Court
("gardaroba"); *Langlois*, *ibid*, VIII, ix.

The Session Rolls and the Sacks. — The judgments of each session were inscribed upon a roll (after 1254 at the latest), as had for a long time been customary in the Exchequer of Normandy.[1]   Each session had not only its " roll," but its " sack," in which the clerks of the courts classified the documents of the proceeding.[2]   These included 1st, " petitiones," or initial documents of claim (the " libelli " of the Canon law); 2d, " articuli " (or " rubricæ "),[3] summary and detailed statements of the facts which the parties were required to prove (another thing borrowed from the Canon law); 3d, inquests, extrajudicial information, views of lands, and " processus " (in case of an appeal, documents of the proceeding before the inferior court); 4th, " protestationes " or matters reserved; 5th, " decreta," or adjudications of property on which a distraint and its public announcement had been executed; 6th, " concordiae," or transactions ratified by the Parliament.[4]

The Registers. — Up to 1263, the decisions of the Parliament of Paris were only entered on the rolls. In that year, the court clerk, John de Montluçon or de Montluc (" Johannes de Montelucio ") copied into pamphlets (" cahiers ")[5] (whether of his own initiative or obeying an order of the Parliament is not known) the most important of the judgments. He filled out these " pamphlets " by the use of extracts from the rolls previously made up by him from 1254 to 1257. His successor, Nicolas de Chartres, 1273, finished the task by making a very brief summary of the judgments from 1257 to 1263,[6] of course while continuing to copy out the new judgments. After 1298 his place was taken by Peter de Bourges. The pamphlets or books made by these men make up what are called the *"Olim,"* or " Olim " registers. This name was

---

[1] As to the note "Inferius" which is found in the "Olim," the interpretation of which is difficult, *cf. Grün,* p. lxxi, and *Langlois,* "De monum.," 13.   It is probable that after 1263 Jean de Montluçon left to clerks of inferior rank the care of keeping the session rolls   As soon as the Auditorium of Written Law had been created, he played a special part, "rotulus auditorii"   "Olim," IV, *passim, Langlois,* "De monum.,' 21, "Olim," II, 46, *cf* Index, see "Rotulus"   These rolls were destroyed at the time of the burning of the Palais de Justice in 1618.   *Grün,* p ccxlix

[2] In the end, they were regrouped into bundles, each one of which sometimes contained more than one hundred rolls   In the 1700 s, the Archives of the Parliament consisted of not less than 7000 to 8000 bundles.   About one quarter of them still remain in existence. *Beugnot,* "Olim," I, 995

[3] *Beaumanoir,* I, 108; II, 129.

[4] These were not copied into the registers

[5] At this time registers were not a novelty.   The Exchequer of Normandy had them, and the Treasury as well.

[6] *Beugnot,* "Olim," I, 440

at first given to the second register,[1] which begins with the words
" Olim homines de Baiona," [2] and it was extended about the 1500s
to include four older registers of the Parliament. The "Olim" include 1st, " *Inquestæ*," which means, not the minutes of hearing,[3]
but judgments rendered after hearing, and called " *Jugés*," " judicia," " judicata " ;[4] 2d, " *Ariesta*," " arrestaciones," decisions rendered upon the pleadings, following an argument and trial by both
sides, 3d, "*Consilia*," preliminary decisions, interlocutory judgments, not final in character (for example those by which further
time was granted the parties, " dies consilii assignata est tali").[5]
Beugnot, the editor of the " Olim," considered them as a private
work, mere notes taken down by the clerks of the court for their
own personal use. But to this view we cannot accede After
1286 at least, the " Olim " are always cited as official documents.
Moreover it would have been surprising had the highest Court in
the realm not had official registers, when, for a half century at
least, the lowest ecclesiastical tribunal had had its own [6]

The Certification of Copies of Parliament's Judgments was done
in 1200s . 1st, by means of " cedules " (memoranda), or mere
extracts from the session rolls; they had the effect of a formal

---

[1] "In libro qui incipit Olim," said *Nicolas de Baye* in 1400
[2] The document which begins with these words deals with certain
acts of violence committed by the people of Bayonne against the Norman merchants, with the assistance of the English This document and
the few others which are placed at the beginning of this book differ greatly
from those which are to be found in the other registers , these are letters
or Ordinances relating to very high personages, the King of England, the
Count of Flanders, etc From this, perhaps, is derived the exceptional
value which has been given to this second register. — It has also been
said that the word "olim" was merely an allusion to the antiquity of
these registers The first criminal register of the Parliament is of the
year 1312: *Grun*, ccxxii
[3] Some are to be found in the Treasury of Charters Example in
"Olim," I, 959
[4] The "processus' mentioned with the inquests are written instruments
upon which a lawsuit was decided, and especially the instruments appertaining to cases which had been appealed (visis processibus et inquestis");
and, by extension, judgments pronounced upon written pleadings *See,*
' De judiciariis inquestis xiii sæculo agente," 1890, *Guilhiermoz*, "Enquêtes et procès," p 293
[5] The first "Olim," book by *Jean de Montluçon*, Examinations and
Orders, 1254 to 1273 (ed *Beugnot*, vol I), the second ' Olim," book by
Nicolas de Chartres, Orders, 1274 to 1298 (vol. II), the third "Olim,"
book by *Pierre de Bourges*, Orders, 1299 to 1318 (vol II); the fourth
"Olim," *P de Bourges*, Examinations, 1299 to 1318 (vol III, 1st and 2d
part)
[6] During the last centuries of the monarchy the Parliament looked
upon the "Olim" as the charter of its liberties and refused access to their
contents, excepting to a few learned men such as Du Cange and Lenain de
Tillemont The historical writer Moreau had to bribe the court clerk of
the Parliament in order to obtain a copy (1777).

judgment; 2d, by "diplomes," or letters patent, sealed in the Chancery and drawn up by the notaries of the clerk of the Court, — sometimes according to the accounts of them in the "Olim" registers, and sometimes before the court clerk had entered anything on his register, in the latter case it included only a summary, 3d, by "mandates," sent to the sheriffs or seneschals, 4th, by "rolls," delivered especially to sheriffs and seneschals, and containing the decisions upon the matters coming from their jurisdiction

Development of the Archives of the Parliament. — The session rolls disappeared in 1319. The text, or the summary of the judgments entered upon the rolls, were to be found in the "Olim," and in the so-called "Jugés," registers which follow the "Olim" after 1319 [1] The rolls thus served no further purpose except for interlocutory decisions not entered in the registers; in 1319 the "Registres du greffe" (clerk) were established, in which these were placed.[2] This provision removed all reason for the existence of the rolls. As the Parliament became divided into several Chambers, so the records of Parliament, which at first consisted only in a series of rolls, came to be split up into a series of registers; and these grew more and more numerous, — "Registers of the Letters," "Registers of the Council" (1364–1790), "Memorials" (inventories or tables, 1372), "Registers of the Ordinances" (1337–1790), of "Real Distraints" (1375–1790), etc.[3]

(5) *The "Châtelet" of Paris.*[4] — The Provost of Paris administered justice for the commoners; he held his court in a "châtelet," or little castle, upon the right bank of the Seine, at the end of the Pont-au-Change His court was, next to the Parliament, the most important one in the kingdom;[5] the law which he applied there consisted in a great measure of the "Ancienne Coutume de Paris."[6]

---

[1] This series of registers really includes three sorts of document, — the "Jugés," or decisions of the Chamber of Inquests, which are the most numerous and have given it its name; "Letters" (of the king, letters of pardon. mandates of execution, etc); "Arrêts," or decisions of the Great Chamber (and very rarely of the Chamber of Inquests).

[2] These registers also contain "statutes," so called because of the State Letters, a great number of which are connected with them, and "roles de bailliages," appointing days upon which the cases in each sheriff's court should be pleaded before the Parliament, and upon which, therefore, the sheriff had to attend the hearings

[3] *Langlois,* "Textes," XIII, "De monum," II, p 22.

[4] *Batiffol,* "Le Châtelet de Paris vers 1400" ("R. hist," 1896, LXI, p. 225).

[5] At the time of the Revolution there were no less than sixty-four councillors.

[6] *Tanon,* "L'ordre du procès civil au xiv siècle au Châtelet de Paris,"

It is known to us through various sources already mentioned, — the Registers of Parliament (the court of appeal for the " Châtelet "), the " Grand Coutumier " of Jacques d'Albeiges (3d book), the " Decisions " of Jean des Mares, and other special works which remain to be noticed   The "*Anciennes Constitutions du Châtelet,*"[1] at once a manual and a book of forms, containing eighty-six very short articles, arranged in no sort of order, are the work of a practitioner.   He gives us not only the rules of decision for the " Châtelet," but also the principal rules of the Customary law and of procedure followed at the end of the 1200s in the " pays (district) de France," before the seigniorial as well as the Royal Courts (about 1282)   The "*Coutumes Notoires du Châtelet,*" consis ing of one hundred and eighty-six articles, give summary of the decisions rendered by the " Châtelet," from 1300 to 1387, upon the doubtful points of the "Coutume de Paris."   Sometimes the Provost of Paris gives an opinion after having consulted the Committee of Burgesses ("Parloir aux bourgeois "), a body which gave its opinion only after consultation with the chief citizens.   Sometimes he holds an inquest by " turba " (*ante*, § 10), or applies to the magistrates of his court (lieutenant and councillors), to the advocates, examining magistrates, and attorneys connected with it, or to gentlemen, burgesses, and artisans of Paris   In one or another of these ways he finally proves and settles the usage as followed in Paris ; the decision by which he judicially settles the notoriety of the Custom becomes the law of his court , parties who afterwards rely upon this usage need not prove its existence   To these sources we may add the manuscript "*Styles*" (*ante*, par. 3) of the " Châtelet," and the *Criminal Register of the "Châtelet" of Paris* from September 6, 1389, to May 18, 1892.

(6) The "*Parloir aux Bourgeois*" (Committee of Burgesses) was the place where the water merchants met, — a brotherhood which recalls the old " nautæ parisienses " of the early times of the Roman Empire.   It had, at least in the 1200s, a Provost and Aldermen   In the 1300s it was the civic body.   This powerful brotherhood constituted a legal person, a sort of barony, and, as such, possessed a very extensive jurisdiction, — right of administering justice over certain streets, a commercial jurisdiction over

---

1886, p 80   "The Châtelet was the tribunal of the kingdom in which the surest, the least dilatory, and the simplest procedure was followed "
[1] *Ed Lauriere,* following the "Coutumes de Paris," 1696, and his Commentary upon these Customs, ed 1777, 205 , *Ch. Mortet,* "Le livre des Constitucions demenées el Chastelet de Paris," 1883 (with a learned introduction).

the other corporations, a non-contentious jurisdiction over the deeds which individuals presented for its seal of authentication.

§ 14   **Deeds, Cartularies, Form-Books, Ecclesiastical and Feudal Land-Registers.** — *Individual Deeds,* and collections or *Cartularies,* become so numerous that we must give up any attempt even to indicate the chief sources where they are to be found. There is no local history which does not contain a large number of them.   In making use of them, we must not lose sight of the fact that they were drawn up to regulate the relations of individuals, and that they deal with matters entirely local in their character To come to conclusions which can apply over an extensive region, one must compare a sufficiently large number of local documents They must be studied almost domain by domain, at any rate cartulary by cartulary, after which one must pass on to the provincial compilations, documents accompanying the history of provinces and towns. and compilations of documents made with a view to these histories (especially by the Benedictine monks) and preserved in manuscript form at the National Library, and finally the texts of the " Gallia christiana."   Then will come the compilations covering vast regions, such as those of Dom Housseau for Anjou, Touraine and Maine, of Dom Fonteneau for Aquitaine, and the collections of charters for frontier regions such as those of Miræus, Trouillat, and Lacomblet.   The whole will be completed by general collections of charters and diplomas, such as those of Dom Bouquet, the " Spicilegium " of D'Achery, the " Miscellanea " of Baluze, and the manuscript collections of Duchesne, Baluze, Dupuy, etc , documents taken from departmental archives and especially from the collection by Moreau.   These charters should be interpreted by means of chronicles, histories, the lives of saints, miracles, and collections of letters (Gerbert, Yves de Chartres, etc.).

(1) *Public and Private Deeds* — The deeds of the feudal period which have come down to us individually, and not as a part of a cartulary, are, for the most part, judicial deeds, notarial deeds, or deeds of some public officer   Further on we will deal with the last of these when speaking of the Royal Ordinances   We have already dealt with judicial deeds in speaking of the memorials of decisions. As to notarial deeds (the main rules for their execution have been already noticed) it remains to mention some variant practices.

(2) In the south of France, in imitation of the Italian practice, "tabellions," or *Notaries Public,* gave authenticity to the deeds drawn up by them   They sat in the public square in booths which must have very much resembled the stalls of the public scribes

of our day. There, in the presence of the parties and the witnesses, they took down the transaction — first writing notes in a register, and then in another register the draft as finally developed. The oldest of these registers now preserved date from the 1200 s They were called *Cartularies* or *Protocols* The parties received a copy of this, the " instrumentum publicum " or " carta in forma publica," delivered to them by the notary; this was the " grosse " (engrossed copy). In order to confer upon it " authenticity " (*i e.* an official form and consequently self-executory and probative force), the notary had to add his subscription, that is, his name, a mention of the authority (king, lord, etc) from whom he held his title, a mention that he was acting at the request of the parties, recital of the affixing of his sign manual (or distinctive personal scroll), and this sign manual itself. Towards the end of the 1300 s there appeared at the foot of the deed only the recital of the sign manual, the other recitals had been placed at the beginning, where the notary set forth his names and qualifications.

In the South, the subscription and the notary's sign manual gave the deed the effect of an official document. But in the North the notarial deed was not " authentic " until the seal of a court had been placed upon it, the notary had no authority of his own, he was only an assistant of the lay or ecclesiastical court After the time of Philip the Handsome, he no longer entered anything except the minute of the transaction upon his register or protocol; the royal " tabellion " (there was one at the seat of every royal court) delivered engrossed copies taken from this draft, another officer, the Keeper of the Seal, affixed the royal Seal to them. In Paris, there was only a Keeper of the Seal; there was no " tabellion "; the corporation of notaries of the " Châtelet " made both drafts and engrossed copies Charles VI placed them under the franchise of the King; thenceforth they were authorized to place the royal escutcheon upon their houses, and this is the origin of the escutcheons which still serve to indicate the offices of notaries. After the time of Philip the Handsome, the sovereign sought to restrict the discretionary jurisdiction of the lords, and to reserve the appointments of " tabellion " and notary for the royal prerogative It succeeded to the extent of giving to deeds of seigniorial notaries a rank far inferior to deeds of the royal notaries. The royal " tabellions " and notaries could draw deeds only within the limits of the jurisdiction of that royal court from which they held their authority (excepting those of the " Châtelet," who could draw deeds anywhere within the entire kingdom), but their deeds had executory force throughout the realm, and were accepted in every court. Deeds acknowledged before seignorial notaries were "authentic" only if made between persons domiciled within the lord's domain and amenable to the justice of the lord. Even when authentic, they had executory force only within the lord's domain, for outside of its limits the lord's seal was not recognized.

Deeds under private seal, or private deeds "sensu stricto," had to be acknowledged before a court, in order to be given credit as genuine and to have executory force. They are especially frequent during the monarchic period, when the use of writing was becoming widespread.[1]

(3) *Formularies* — We cannot here enumerate the collections of forms; they are too numerous   Treatises upon the office of notary and upon procedure for the most part contain forms; they occur in the Books of Customs, almost everywhere.   Notaries, court clerks, and scribes make current use of them, as in the monarchic period or in our own day.[2]

(4) *Feudal Registers.* — "Polyptyques" (a term inherited from the Theodosian Code), or registers of lands and feudal duties, continued to be drawn up during the feudal period, but those which are entirely ecclesiastic take the name of "*Pouillés*," in the common tongue; the others are seigniorial "*Terriers*"

"*Pouillés*" are registers containing the list of the ecclesiastical benefices of a province, a diocese, or an abbey.   The clergy themselves entered in them a summary of their title-deeds, they were not looked upon as proofs in case of litigation, but they furnished information often deemed sufficient when title-deeds were lacking.

"*Terriers*"   "Acknowledgments," "enumerations," "feudal recognizances" (documents in which vassals furnished proof of their obligations to their lords), were recorded in writing at an early period.   They are often found in the feudal cartularies of the 1200s.   The lords were not satisfied with making collections

---

[1] On the foregoing subject, see *Bauby*, "Responsabilité civile des notaires," 1894, *Pappafava*, "Geschichte des Notariats," 1895, *Giry*, "Diplomatique", *Bresslau*, "Urkundenlehre"

[2] The bibliography of these formularies has not been made.   There are a great many forms in the "Formul. Tabellionum" of *Tenerius* and the "Ars notaria" of *Rainerius of Pérouse*, "Bibl jurid med. ævi," published by *Gaudenzi*, *Giry*, "Diplom," p 764 (note).   *Cf* for the monarchic period, "Le nouveau et parfait notaire," by *De Visme*, 1749; "La science parfaite des notaires ou le Parfait notaire," by *Cl -J de Ferrière* 1741 (new edition)   In the 1400s, Metz had forms to be used by the municipal magistrates, the "Style du Palais," and, for the notaries, the "Style de l'Amandellerie" (1408 to 1431): *Bonvalot*, "Hist du dr de la Lorraine," p. 213.

of individual deeds, they proceeded to compile a census or general
enumeration of their fiefs   In 1171, the King of England, Henry
II, caused one of the great " recognitiones feudorum " to be made
in Normandy, and its result was to double his revenues; for not
only were previously existing rights settled thereby, but the lord
took advantage of the opportunity to annex all lands the status
of which was not settled, fiefs whose tenure was uncertain, and
freeholds which their timorous owners converted into fiefs.   Under
pretext of settling their rights the powerful lords extended them.
The census of Aquitaine, in 1272, was made by issuing letters
of convocation addressed to the residents of the Duchy, even to
those who owed nothing to the King of England and held nothing
from him, they were questioned by commissioners in the presence
of witnesses; they made their declarations under oath, stating
that they held such a piece of land from the King charged with
the rendering of homage or rents, and the notary drew up a deed
to that effect   The registers which contained these censuses or
recognizances were given the name of " *Terriers* " or " papiers
terriers." They are seignorial cadastral surveys   Their compilation was regulated during the monarchic period, in which they
were defined to be registers containing the declarations of the
individuals who held of a lord's domain (vassals or copyholders),
with the details of the dues, quit-rents, and rent-charges.

   § 15   **Commercial and Maritime Law** [1] — The uniformity of
commercial and maritime Customs is in contrast with the extreme
variety of civil Customs   The maritime law especially had, in
the Middle Ages, become international, whereas the land usages
varied from one parish to the next.   In the 1200s the " *Consulat
de la Mer* " on the Mediterranean, and the " *Rôles d'Oléron* " on
the Atlantic Ocean, form the common law of maritime commerce.
This was due to the fact that the conditions of this commerce were
everywhere uniform, whereas local customs and the political and
economic status which is the basis of civil law varied from country
to country and from one lord's domain to another   Commercial
law on land is found especially in municipal charters, the by-laws of

[1] EDITIONS· *Pardessus,* "Collection des lois maritimes antérieures au
xviii siècle," 1828-1845 ; *Travers Twiss,* "The Black Book of the Admiralty,"
1871-1876 BIBLIOGRAPHY *Goldschmidt,* "Handbook des Handelsrechts,"
vol I, "Universalgeschichte des Handelsrechts," 1891 (3d ed), gives a
detailed bibliography upon the subject, *Lyon-Caen and Renault,* "Cours
de droit commercial," 1889, *Pigeonneau,* "Hist du commerce de la
France," 1885-89, *Brunner,* "Encyclop " of *Holtzendorff,* 5th ed., 1889,
p 305, *Arthur Desjardins,* "Introduction historique à l'étude du droit
commercial maritime," 1890, *Schupfer,* p 301.

associations, and the regular Books of Customs.   But there are special documents about fairs, where the merchants of all countries met together and had their own special judges; for example, the " Privilèges et Coustumes des foires " (1200s) and the " Coustumes stille et usaige de la court et chancellerye des foires de Champaigne et Brye " (1400s).[1]

The maritime legislation of the inhabitants of Rhodes[2] was so celebrated among the ancients, that its name has been given to a private compilation of nautical usages, made in the 1000s (" Droit maritime des Rhodiens ").[3]   Book 53 of the Græco-Roman " Basilica " was a true maritime Code; but it has not come down to us.   As it was in Italy that commerce flourished especially, so it was in that country that during the Middle Ages the first collections of commercial law were compiled   The Statute of Trani (" Ordinamenta et consuetudo maris edita per consules civitatis Trani ") is the oldest of them, if it dates, as is stated at the beginning of it, from the year 1063.[4]   The Table of Amalfi ("Capitula et ordinationes curiæ maritime nobilis civitatis Amalfæ"), a manuscript of which was discovered in 1844, seems also to date back to the 1000s[5]   Venice had her statutes (1205–29–55, 1302 –46), the influence of which was felt in the usages of Dalmatia. Pisa had her " Constitutum usus," 1160, her " Breve curiæ maris," 1289 and 1305, which had an influence over the laws of her tributary cities (" Breve portus kalaretani," 1318), and Genoa likewise (statutes of Bonifacio, of Savona, etc.).   But it was not very long before these local laws were, if not supplanted, at least strongly affected by a very great work which eclipsed them, the " Consulat de la Mer."   The " Consulat de la Mer,"[6] containing

---

[1] *Bourquelot,* "Etudes sur les foires de Champagne," 1865 (Memorial presented to the Academy of Inscriptions, series II, vol 5). *Cf* details and bibl in *Goldschmidt,* p 224

[2] Digest, "De lege Rhodia de jactu," 14, 2

[3] *Pardessus,* "Coll des lois maritimes," I, 208

[4] *Pardessus,* "Coll," vol. V, *De Rozière,* "R. h. de dr ," 1855, p. 189, *Travers Twiss,* "Black Book," IV, 521. — Detailed bibl in *Schupfer,* p. 309 (with discussion as to the date)

[5] *Ed Volpicella,* "Consuet d Napoli," 1844, *De la Primaudaie,* "Et sur le commerce au moyen âge," 1848; *Ahanelli,* "Antiche consuet e leggi maritime delle provincie napoletane," 1871 ; *Travers Twiss,* "Black Book," IV, bibl in *Schupfer,* p 318; *Pardessus,* "Coll," I, 142; V, 223; *Laband,* "Z f. Handelsr ," 1864. — In the 1400s it is called "Tabula prothontina "

[6] EDITIONS *Pardessus,* "Coll des lois maritimes ' (after the edition of 1494) ; *Capmany,* "Código de las costumbres maritimas de Barcelona," 1791 (after the edition of 1502), *Travers Twiss,* "Black Book," III (on the edition of 1694 and the Mss. of Paris, which, however, were not sufficiently studied) — A critical edition is needed

the rules which were to be followed by the commercial judges or judge-consuls, was the Book of Customs of the entire Mediterranean. In its existing form it does not date back farther than 1370, but there were earlier editions, probably the original edition dates from the end of the 1000s or the beginning of the 1100s. It was at that time that the progress made by commerce led to the codification of the customs and traditions which flourished along the shores of the Mediterranean It is also very probable that the original text (which was in the Catalonian language) saw the light at Barcelona. It is not a legislative work, emanating from the kings of Aragon, it is a Book of Customs (far more extensive than the "Rôles d'Oléron"), a treatise with explanations of the text, rather than a Code It maintained its authority almost up to modern times; in the 1700s the Italian jurisconsult Casaregis was still taking it as the basis of his "Discursus legales de commercio" (1718), and adding thereto the decisions of the Rota of Genoa, a tribunal very renowned in maritime matters during the 1500s and 1600s.

The "Rôles d'Oléron," a compilation of decisions rendered (it is said) by the sea-judges of the island of Oléron, date, in their oldest form, from the 1000s or 1100s. Before long they became the common law of the Western Ocean, as the "Consulat de la mer" was the Code of the Levant To so great an extent did they become the common law that their French origin was and still is disputed. In the Netherlands they are called "Jugements de Damme" or "Lois de Westcapelle"; they form a part of the "Black Book of the English Admiralty," and they are found once again in the "Ordinantie" of Holland (1400s). in the maritime law of "Wisby," an island of Gothland (1400s), in the "Recessa" of the Hanseatic league, and in the "Siete Partidas" of Castile.

In the 1500s, the "Guidon de la Mer," drawn up at Rouen by an unknown author, is primarily a treatise upon maritime insurance; it was regarded as a good guide upon this subject for the framers of the Ordinance of 1681

§ 16. Public Law, and the Legal Philosophies — Public law belongs rather to the domain of theology than to that of private justice It is in the works of the theologians especially that we must seek to find the theocratic and ultramontane theories, the imperialist or monarchic systems of the divine law, and the heterodox doctrines of the social contract and national sovereignty.

(1) The Scholastic Philosophy — In the 1100s, Saint Bernard

244

(1153), and Peter Lombard, the "Maître de sentences" (1160), do not concern themselves in general with the political problems. But this ceases to be so with the scholastics of the following period Under the influence of Aristotle, they gave up the theological conception of the State, and substituted for it a purely rational conception, according to which the State is not the direct work of God, but that of human reason, — a secondary cause through which as an intermediary the first cause acts   With this conception as a basis, theology maintained its position in the quarrel between the priesthood and the Empire   Apparently it could defend it even better; for obviously the Church, the image of the city of God, is above the city of men, which is all too often erected in sin and iniquity.   But it also follows that the system of the latter is found to be open to discussion, as everything is which comes within the domain of reason, it may depart, and does in fact depart, from the early theocratic type in order that it may give way to political theories of a more modern character   This is noticeable especially in the works of the "Angel of the School," SAINT THOMAS AQUINAS (1225–1274), in his "Summa theologica," the "Commentary on the Sentences " and the " De Regimine principium "; his political system is a combination of the liberal theories of Aristotle and the theocratic principles of the Middle Ages.

(2) *The Empire and the Legists.* — The rights of the Empire were defended by Henry IV and his partisans against Gregory VII, in letters, and even in a great treatise, " De unitate Ecclesiæ conservandæ," written a short time after the death of Gregory VII. But the special partisans of the Empire are the *Legists* (or civil jurists), with their idea of a universal monarchy which should be a continuation of the Roman Empire. The independence of the Emperor with regard to the Church, in matters concerning the temporal power, is one of their essential dogmas. Dante and Occam are in these ranks. MARSILIUS OF PADUA (1270–1342 or 1343), another partisan of Louis of Bavaria, was a dangerous ally for the Empire, he comments upon Aristotle in his " Defensor pacis " (finished before July 11th, 1324), and, starting with the principle of the sovereignty of the people, he gives the people the right of appointing, of judging, and of deposing kings. This democrat is at the same time a decided champion of the liberty of conscience, — something never before seen at that period. He had as his collaborator a Frenchman, Jean de Jandun

(3) *The Gallican Doctrines* were formulated and defined in the documents bearing upon the quarrel between Boniface VIII and

Philip the Handsome. They were upheld at the Conference of
Vincennes, in 1329. The Virgin's Dream ("Somnium viridarii "),
a treatise of 1376, has been termed the "Grand Coutumier" of the
liberties of the Gallican church. With the schism in the West
(1378–1431), the Holy See found that it had an opponent even
upon spiritual grounds. The most eminent personages of the
Church, GERSON, Chancellor of the University of Paris (1429),
P. d'Ailly (1420), and Nicholas of Clemangis, were seen up-
holding the superiority of the Council over the Pope, and at
the same time the independence of the State against the
Church

(4) *England.* — Liberal ideas had already made their appearance
in the writings of BRACTON The famous maxim "Quidquid
principi placuit legis habet vigorem," so often invoked by the
partisans of absolute power, is interpreted by him to mean that the
force of law must be given, not to everything that the king may
will in his own pleasure, but to what he does upon the advice of
his magistrates who deliberate and decide The "Compendium
morale" (a commentary of the 1300 s), by Roger of Waltham,
Canon of St. Paul's, a treatise dealing with the virtues and duties
of the sovereign, has a tendency to exaggerate the ecclesiastical
power. Wycliffe, as early as 1368, maintained his bold theses
calculated to overthrow all authority. The great political theorist
of England was Sir JOHN FORTESCUE (about 1476), author of
"De laudibus legum Angliæ" (1468–1470), in this he shows the
advantages of limited monarchy over despotic monarchy In "The
Governance of England," he contrasts the "dominium regale,"
or absolute monarchy, of France with the constitutional system
of England, which he calls "dominium politicum et reale," a
monarchy with a certain amount of republican government thrown
in The power of the king is there derived from the people, he
cannot make any laws nor levy any taxes without the consent of
the nation through its representatives in Parliament. In France
the representative system had been abandoned, ownership on a
large scale prevailed, whereas England was covered with small
holdings, the peasant in France was wretched, while in England
he enjoyed a comparative well-being; the French were lacking
in courage, which prevented them from rebelling, France had
none of those bold bandits to be found in England, where there
were more men hanged for robbery and murder in one year than
in France in seven years.

§ 17. **Royal Legislation.** — (1) *Form.* — The main legal materials

of the feudal period in Europe consisted in the Customs and the
Roman law.   Nevertheless, the royal ordinances, both in France
and in other countries, were one of its important elements, especially in matters which concerned public law.

How have the Royal Enactments come down to us? — For brevity's
sake we shall treat together the royal enactments of the monarchic
period as well as those of the feudal period   They have come down
to us sometimes in the originals, sometimes in the form of copies,
and especially in the form of copies made in registers.   (A) *Registers of the Royal Chancery.*   "The Treasury of Charters
(about 1194) was divided into two parts· the '*Layettes*' (boxes,
coffers), which contained the political and domanial documents,
and the *Registers*, into which were copied enactments emanating
from the King."   These registers were kept up from 1302 until
1568,[1] though not all the royal enactments were transcribed
(B) *Registration by the Parliament*, etc.   Enactments of general
interest, such as the Ordinances, were sent to the royal Courts,
such as the Parliament, the Chamber of Accounts, the Court of
Finance, the Court of Aids, to the sheriffs, and the various bodies
who were to enforce them.[2]   Here they were copied upon their
registers   As is well known, this usage, introduced for the sake of
form, afterwards permitted the court of Parliament to play an
obstructive part in politics.[3]

(1) *Form of the Royal Enactments*[4] — From the point of view
of form, the enactments of the Kings of the third dynasty may be
divided into diplomas, letters patent, and sealed letters[5]   The
Diploma ("carta") was the most formal enactment which could
issue out of the Royal Chancery, and was used for proving ordi-

[1] Registration in the Courts of Justice caused the registers of the
Chancery to fall into disuse   In England the Chancery transcribed royal
enactments upon long rolls, there were "rotuli Normanniæ" or "Vas-
coniæ," or "Franciæ," containing a copy of enactments relating to Normandy, Aquitaine, or France   *F Michel*, "Rôles gascons" (1242–1254), 1885
(unpublished documents)

[2] Ordinance, VII, 112   The text of the Ordinance was "written in
big letters and posted up" in the bailiwicks and seneschals' jurisdiction in
order that it might be brought to the knowledge of everybody (1396)   *Cf
ibid*, I, 105, 484

[3] The clerk mentioned this formality in the original   "lecta et publicata"
(publicly read in audience) "requirente procuratore generali regis, Pari-
sius in Parlamento" (with the date and the signature).   They added "de
expresso mandato regis," when the Parliament had refused to register and
had only been compelled to do so by a "lit de justice" or letter of command

[4] See especially *Giry*, "Diplomat," p 705

[5] The documents of the English kings are divided into "charters" (less
complicated than diplomas, which ceased to be used after the time of
Henry III), "letters patent," and "sealed letters"; *Giry*, p 797

nances, important judgments, etc. Already becoming rare under
Saint Louis, diplomas ceased to be used under his successors,
mere letters being deemed sufficient. *Royal Letters* were in more
simple form than diplomas, once the latter had been abandoned,
by Royal Letters were understood all enactments of the King,
whether they emanated from the Chancery (Letters Patent) or
from the sovereign himself (Sealed Letters)   *Letters Patent* had
a seal as the only indication of their validity. Afterwards certain
forms of Letters Patent came to resemble Diplomas and to be reserved for the more important enactments

Letters with Stamped Seal were open, bore at the beginning the
statement " De par le Roy" (on behalf of the King), and at the
end the date and the year, the signature of the King, and the stamp
of the Privy Seal. *Sealed Letters*, closed and sealed with the Privy
Seal or the King's signet (" cachet "), formed his private correspondence, and served at the same time to transmit his secret
orders, and to deal with affairs of a confidential nature   The
customary *Final Clause* (at least after the 1400s) was. " Quoniam
sic fieri volumus," " for so do we will," " for this pleases us and
we will it to be done," " for such is our pleasure " This last
formula prevailed under Louis XIV, and is a translation of the
Roman principle " Quidquid principi placuit legis habet vigorem " [1]
After the time of Francis I the King's signature was a guarantee
of *authenticity*, as well as the seal   It was not always an autograph
signature, but it had the appearance of one; for the secretaries
who were authorized to reproduce it had to imitate the royal
signature, thus they were called "secretaries of the hand." During the 1300s, the signature of the notaries of the Royal Chancery
(clerks of the Privy Seal, notaries and secretaries of the King)
served to prove the authenticity of royal enactments, as the signature of ordinary notaries did for the deeds of individuals. Some
of these clerks acquired a prominent position, and in the middle
of the 1500s became Secretaries of State. No Letters Patent could
be delivered thenceforth without having been signed by the King
and countersigned by the Secretary of State for the department.
Such is the origin of the ministerial *Counter-signing*, — a mere

---

[1] The usual formula was not "car tel est notre bon plaisir," but as early as
the 1400 s, the expression "le bon plaisir du roi" was used in current speech,
and the Old Régime has often been called the régime of "bon plaisir."
"Plaisir " and "bon plaisir," moreover, both mean the will of the king.
J Papon, "Les secrets du troisième notaire," p 334: *De Mas Latrie*
B Ch, XLII, 1881, 560, G *Demante, ibid.,* LIV, 1893, 86; *Giry,*
"Diplom ," p. 769, Cl *Joly,* "Maximes p. l'instit du roy," 1652, p 401

official form at first, later a certificate attesting that the deed was indeed an expression of the wishes of the King, and to-day in our modern constitutions an important restriction upon the royal authority

§ 18 **Royal Legislation** — (2) *Character and Object of the Royal Enactments.* — The royal enactments applicable to the whole kingdom (still exceptional under Saint Louis) only became fairly frequent after the time of Philip the Handsome. This sort of enactment is called " præceptum," " auctoritas," " constitutio," "decretum," "edictum," and " pragmatica sanctio," and especially " stabilimentum," " ordinatio " ("establishments," "ordinances"). Enactments which deal with private interests are merely called " Letters."

For a long time, however, the terminology was uncertain. (*a*) *Ordinances* signified general legislative enactments affecting the whole kingdom or at least the royal domain, — at least since the time of Philip the Handsome. (*b*) *Edicts* were only Ordinances restricted to one subject or applicable to a part of the kingdom (*e g.* the "Edict of Second Marriages," 1560)   (*c*) *Declarations* were enactments interpreting the Ordinances or Edicts, but often altering while extending or restricting them. They may be compared with our Regulations of Public Administration. (*d*) *Letters Patent* (" sensu stricto") were divided into "Letters of the Great Seal " (sealed in the Great Chancery) and "Letters of the Small Seal " (sealed in the local Chanceries). There was also a distinction between " Letters of Grace," granted as a mere favor, and " Letters of Justice," granted less as a favor than by reason of some equity. (*e*) *Personal Orders of the King* were, at first, given by means of commands in the form of Letters Patent, later by letters called "Letters of Stamped Seal," and still later, by means of " Sealed Letters." (*f*) *Lettres de Cachet* (letters under the King's Privy Seal) were but a variety of these personal orders. The Ordinance of January, 1560, used the expression for the first time. Complaint was already being made of the abuses to which they gave rise. The employment of "Letters de cachet" became general only in the time of Richelieu, and rose by that period to the rank of a regular institution   They were the means of executing some " reason of State." They were used to summon the political and judicial bodies ; to order them to debate certain questions , to regulate public ceremonies; and to exile or to incarcerate, as an administrative measure, persons who were looked upon with suspicion by those in power, or who had been guilty of disgraceful conduct, thus allowing their families to avoid the disgrace of a public condemnation [1]

§ 19 **Royal Legislation** — (3) — *Principal Ordinances Previous to the 1500 s.*[2] — Neither the last Carolingians nor the first Capetians enacted any laws Their Charters contain grants of privileges to religious establishments, to towns, and to corporations Under St Louis the progress of the royal authority was evidenced by Ordinances upon the reform of morals (*e g* Ordinance of 1254) which dealt with everything, — administration, justice, finances, and general policing of the kingdom The famous Ordinance which abolished the wager of battle within the royal domain, and substituted for it the inquest, revolutionized procedure; it is generally dated in the year 1260, but probably it really dated back to 1258. On the whole, the striking feature of this period is that the legislation contained in the Ordinances has practically never dealt with private law, it formed essentially a political and administrative body of laws.

---

[1] The name was also given to orders of arrest lacking the king's signet. and bearing only the signature and counter-signature of a secretary of State. See *Mirabeau*, "Lettres de cachet et prisons d'Etat," 1782.

[2] EDITIONS No complete compilation and no good edition of the Ordinances exist Consult the following 1st, the "Ordonnances des rois de France de la troisième race," 1723-1847 (called "Collection du Louvre," the first volumes having come from the royal printing establishment of the Louvre) , this compilation was begun by *Eusèbe de Laurière*, and carried on by *Secousse, Villevault, Brequigny, Camus*, and *Pastoret*, and finished by *Pardessus*, to whom the Academy of Inscriptions confided this task. The Academy of Inscriptions is at the present time engaged in completing the "Collection du Louvre." With this object in view it has had drawn up the "Catalogue des Actes de François I," 1887-1898, 7 vols 2d, "Recueil général des anciennes lois françaises de 420 à 1789," published by *Jourdan, Decrusy, and Isambert*, 1823-1830 (cited by the name of the latter) 3d, *Fontanon*, "Edits et Ord des rois de France," 1580 4th, *Neron and Girard*, "Recueil d'Edits et Ordonnances royaux," 1720 5th, "Conférence des Ordonnances" by *Guénois*, 1660 These various compilations are very inadequate, *cf*. *Laboulaye*, "Note de quelques ordonnances" ("Acad Inscr.," 1853), *Aucoc*, "Mém sur les collections des lois ant à 1789" ("Acad sc morales," 1882, vol 120, p 43) and the "Institut de France," p iv — *Cf* bibl. in *Camus* p 204, *Viollet*, p 152, *Ginoulhiac*, p 603 For Belgium · "Collection des anciennes Coutumes et Ordonnances de la Belgique," 1860 *et seq*.

Chapter II. Second Period: a.d. 1500–1789

NATIONAL JURISTS AND ROYAL LEGISLATION

§ 20. Introductory.

Topic 1. The Roman Law Jurists

§ 21. The Humanists.   Baudouin, Doneau, Hot-
§ 22   The French School; Cujas,   man

Topic 2. The Official Compilation of the Customs

§ 23. Reasons and Methods of the | § 24. Results of the Redaction.
       Redaction

Topic 3. The Royal Legislation

§ 25. Introductory | § 27 Ordinances of Louis XIV.
§ 26. Ordinances of the 1500s and | § 28 Ordinances of Louis XV
       early 1600s.

Topic 4. The National Jurists

§ 29. The Courts and the Bar. | § 31 National Jurists of the 1600s
§ 30   National Jurists of the 1500s.| and 1700s.

Topic 5. Political Philosophy

§ 32. Philosophies of the 1500s | § 33. Philosophies of the 1700s.
       and 1600s

§ 20. **Introductory.**[1] — In this period the *Roman Law* kept its
position in the south, and reacted upon the interpretation of the
Customs in the north. The *Customary Law* underwent an official
compilation. But what distinguishes this period, more than anything
else, from those which precede it, is the expansion of legislation,
in the form of *Ordinances*. This is an entirely natural consequence
of the expansion of the power of the crown, and of the progress made
by the scientific elaboration of the law in the decisions of the courts

---

[1] [§§ 20–33 = Brissaud, section III, pp 346–414, extracted and condensed. — Transl.]

and the writings of the jurisconsults The Ordinances brought
about a legislative unity (except that in the field of civil law they
left it to the Revolution and the Consulate to complete the work, by
wiping out the distinction between regions of Customs and regions
of Written Law). These Ordinances were in their day true Codes;
they entered the domain which up to that time had been reserved
for Custom or the Roman law. They were supplemented by a
body of *Judicial Decisions,* emanating from the Courts of the Parliaments and the King's Council, which served to interpret these
various sources It was aided by *Juristic Treatises,* which become
more and more profuse and learned. *Historical Writings* and
treatises on public law lead the story quite naturally up to the
Revolutionary period.

Topic 1. The Roman Law Jurists

§ 21 **The Humanists.** — The century following the year 1500
(says Pasquier, in his " Recherches de la France ") brought us a new
method of studying the law which consisted in wedding the study
of law to the humanities, with the aid of a precise and polished Latin.
He names as the three earliest " patres familias " of this novel
marriage: WILLIAM BUDÉ, a Frenchman, a child of Paris, ANDREAS
ALCIAT, a Milanese Italian; and UDARIC ZASIUS, a German, born
in the city of Constance. This scientific and literary revival, the
great movement which led to a reformation even of religion, was
felt in the study of the law The Universities were at one time
divided between the Bartolists and the innovators Pasquier
also says "There are to be seen two sorts of legists, of which
some are called ' chaffourreurs,' bartholists, and barbarians,
and the others pure humanists and grammarians " In France,
at least, it was not long before the latter of these prevailed, by
the middle of the 1500s the triumph of the School was absolute.
It justified itself both by the excellence of the new method and by
the superiority of the men who directed it.

Their Method — The revived worship of the classic era had led
to a direct study of sources Texts which men already possessed
were criticised, new ones were discovered, old texts long since
forgotten were rediscovered: the " lex Dei," the Theodosian Code,
the Basilica, and the commentaries upon them The number of
editions of the Roman laws increased, and became more and more
accurate. Until the work of the modern German school, the texts
established by the jurisconsults of the 1500s continued to be almost

exclusively used. Douaren, who was one of the new men, reproached the Bartolists for their barbarous language, their lack of method, and their barren scholasticism ; instead of seeking for the truth, they quibbled, and applied themselves merely to combating the opinions of others Of those who studied under the old school, he maintained, " One can say that they are doctors the first year, licentiates the second, and bachelors the third, by the time they have reached their fourth year they are no longer good for anything. As for me, if I am told to teach a young man law, I begin by making sure that he has that literary tincture without which there can be neither jurisconsults nor statesmen, but only charlatans." This return to the sources, the literary renascence, led to the abandonment of the manner and the style of the Bartolists. The new school was an " elegant " or *Humanist* school. The finished expositions of its most illustrious representatives are in contrast with the prolixity, the dulness, the pettiness, and the interminable digressions of the writers of the 1400 s.

The new works differ still more by reason of their use of the *Historical Method*. The true successors of Bartolus were Dumoulin and the practitioners. A marked divorce took place between practice, as represented by the latter, and the historical science of the Roman law, as cultivated by such men as Cujas and Doneau Hotman was well aware of this, in his " Antitribonianus" he shows that the new direction taken by the study of the Roman law was bound to result in a revision of the civil law of France; he asks for a Code; he proposes to amalgamate the Roman law, the Customary law, and the decisions, reduced to one or two good-sized volumes, in ordinary and intelligible language; it would cut short chicanery (he asserts) and save a great deal of time for the young men in the Universities " The Roman laws " (said he) " are inapplicable on innumerable points. And even where they could be applied practically, their text, once confidently accepted, is to-day the subject of a critical revision. The Roman law of such men as Gaius, Julian, and Papinian, is not included in the compilation of Justinian, unless it be in fragments, in morsels cut out haphazard and placed end to end, without any regard for order and full of interpolations Under such conditions the Roman law, as studied in the new School, loses all practical importance " And it was not so absurd to find pleaders resorting to the books of Socin (it is Pasquier who speaks thus of an Italian doctor, Marian Socin the younger) for this reason alone, that he had not lost time in the study of humane literature as Alciat had.

What can in fact be less practical than the erudite researches of such men as Hotman and Cujas? They and the other adepts of the new School discriminated the strata of various ages in the enormous mass of the Roman law, they discovered, as our geologists did, by digging in the earth, a primary level, median strata, and others of more recent date. They perceived that here was a legal world to be reconstructed, — a world whose formation had required no less than ten centuries They set to work, using an extraordinary energy, by attacking the law from without, using the aid of philology, literature, and history. Their aim was to unearth, from beneath its Byzantine covering, the classic law in all its pureness For the first time the importance of these auxiliary sciences, hitherto so neglected by jurists, began to be understood. "Sine historia cæcam esse jurisprudentiam," Baudouin was wont to say Here we have the password of the new school Rabelais does no more than paraphrase it in his "Pantagruel," II, 10: "Inasmuch as the laws are weeded out from the midst of moral and natural philosophy, how can those fools understand them who (God knows) have made less study of philosophy than my mule? As to the humanities and the knowledge of antiquities and history, they were about as much burdened with them as a toad is with feathers, although the law is full of them and without them cannot be understood."

§ 22 **The French School, Cujas, Baudouin, Doneau, Hotman** — The initiator of the new method was, first and foremost, the Milanese ALCIAT, who taught at Bourges from 1527 to 1532 But after him the greatest names belong to France " Jurisprudentia romana, si apud alias gentes extincta esset, apud solos Gallos reperiri posset," said the Englishman, Arthur Duck Muret also assures us that one can only learn the civil law in France, and he adds (which is an exaggeration) only with CUJAS. If Cujas does indeed come first, he is closely followed by DONEAU, DOUAREN, BAUDOUIN, and HOTMAN With them we should include the learned Archbishop of Taragon, ANTOINE AUGUSTIN, and the German Van Giffen (" GIPHANIUS ") In the 1600 s, such men as GODEFROY, Denys (died 1622), the editor of the " Corpus juris civilis," and his son Jacques (died 1652), who worked twenty years upon the reconstruction of the text and on a Commentary on the Theodosian Code, ANTOINE FAVRE, president of the Senate of Chambéry (died 1624), author of the " Rationalia ad Pandectas," and of the " Codex Fabrianus," FABROT of Aix (died 1659), editor of " Théophileus " and the " Basilica," carried on with brilliancy the work begun by Cujas and the Doneaus. In the 1700 s, POTHIER sums up the labors of the School (and especially of Cujas) in his "Pandectæ Justinianeæ in novum ordinem redactæ" (1748), in it he kept the general division of the "Pandects" into books and titles, but in each of these the subdivisions, instead of following one another without any order, are methodically arranged and connected

A sketch of the life and the work of Cujas will give one an idea of this school, which was one of the glories of our old France.

JACQUES CUJAS (Cujacius), the son of a fuller, was born at Toulouse in 1522, and died at Bourges on October 4, 1590 A pupil of Arnaud Ferrier, one of the teachers won over to the method of Alciat, he opened at Toulouse, as early as 1547, a free course of lectures on the Institutes. In 1554 he left this town, and, if we may believe a tradition which has been much disputed, it was because of a defeat sustained by him in an open competition for the attainment of a chair in Roman law. It is said that Etienne Forcadel (of Beziers) was preferred to him, — which amounted to the same thing (according to Gravina) as preferring a monkey to a man. The reason why Forcadel succeeded (assuming him to have beaten Cujas) is twofold. The University of Toulouse was at this time still very much attached to the Bartolist school, and Forcadel belonged to this school (as witness the following utterance of his, "Patricios appello eos qui sunt de Bartoli familia, reliquos plebios ') , this was a prime reason for conferring upon him the chair to which he aspired Besides this, Forcadel had some claim to this chair, for he had had a long career as a teacher and was a man of gifted appearance, facility of speech, a skilful rhetoric (a bad style, to be sure, but one very highly esteemed at that time), many traces of which are disclosed in his books. Dumoulin seems to have professed to have some esteem for this jurisconsult, whose rivalry with Cujas has immortalized him

In November, 1554, Cujas, attracted perhaps by the offer of better treatment, replaced at Cahors the Portuguese Antony of Govea In July, 1555, we find him at Bourges, succeeding Baudouin. Douaren and Baudouin, followers of the same method, seeing in Cujas a dangerous rival, aroused so many enemies against him, both among the students and in the municipality of Bourges, that before long he left the town. In 1557 he withdrew himself to Paris, until Valence offered him a stipend of 600 livres to occupy a chair at that University, which he accepted. So great was his reputation already that the professors of Valence gave him their highest appointment, though some of them had had as much as forty

years' experience. The death of Douaren, which took place in
1559, allowed him to return to Bourges, his patroness the Duchess
of Berry at once recalling him. He was sufficiently generous to
avenge himself upon Douaren by delivering a eulogy upon him to
his patroness. When the latter became Duchess of Savoy, she
offered him Govea's chair at Turin; whether to show his gratitude,
or to study the manuscripts in the Italian libraries, or to escape
from the troubles which threatened France, Cujas accepted it
(1566). But his stay in Italy was not long Italian life was uncongenial As early as 1567 he had determined to return to France.
But he could not go back to Bourges, where his chair was filled by
François Hotman. So once more to Valence he went, yielding to
the entreaties of its inhabitants and of the Bishop John de Montluc,
his friend. But again he left Valence, this time for good and all,
in 1575, and now returned to Bourges. Here he was no happier
than he had been at Valence, for within a year he left and settled
at Paris. The Parliament of Paris, by Order of April 2, 1567,
gave him authority to teach Roman law publicly, thus making in
his favor a notable exception to the rule (*ante*, § 7) which forbade
this teaching at the University of Paris. In 1577 he once more
took up his abode at Bourges, nor again left it until his death in
1590

As a Man — This nomadic life of Cujas was no less that of such
men as Baudouin, Doneau, Hotman, and Dumoulin. In this respect
Cujas was quite in keeping with the times. So also his violent
criticisms of his adversaries, they too treated him badly. To-day
such amenities are exchanged only between intimates; in those
days they were printed in great works, to lend more spice to the
argument In the furious conflict of minds of that time, many
jurisconsults were noted for their harshness and extreme language.
Hotman and Doneau risked their lives in the cause of reform,
President Favre was an ardent Catholic; Dumoulin a most im-
placable Gallican

As a Teacher — It has been asserted that Cujas had not all the
gifts of the teacher, " his delivery was hasty, his voice uneven,
his pronunciation indistinct. But these defects were compensated
for by an authoritativeness, a methodical treatment, an immense
amount of learning, an abundance of ideas, and the animation conferred by keen thought " He prepared his lessons with a conscientiousness rarely seen. He also had the first of all good qualities
which should be possessed by one who teaches, — he endeared himself to his scholars. " He lived upon terms of intimacy with them,

often invited them to come to see him, received them at his table, had excursions for them in the country, took some of them to board in his house, placed his library at their disposal, lent them books, and even advanced them money "[1]

As a Jurisconsult. — The most famous of his writings are his " Commentaries upon Papinian " (published after his death), and his " Observationum et emendationum libri XXVIII " (published from 1566 until his death, except the last four books, which were edited by Pithou after his death).   His style of work was analytical, whereas his rival for fame, Hugues Doneau, adopted the synthetic method in his " Commentarii de jure civili," termed " on the whole about the best systematic exposition of the Roman law " until our own century   The German jurisconsults followed his model; the French on the other hand have preferred to adhere, with Cujas, to the exegetic method.

Bourges, in those days, was famous for other professors than Cujas.   FRANÇOIS BAUDOUIN (Balduinus), born at Arras in 1520 (died 1573), after having been secretary to Dumoulin, opened a course of free lectures in Paris in 1546.   He afterwards taught at Bourges, Strasbourg, Heidelberg, Paris, and Angers.   His fluctuating religious opinions and more than suspicious orthodoxy led him to leave France, to go and teach in Germany.   He had been summoned to the University of Bourges, then the most celebrated of French schools ("the great market for science," in the phrase of Hotman), by the Duchess of Berry, Marguerite of France, daughter of Francis 1, in her capacity of protector of science and literature, upon the advice of her Chancellor Michel de L'Hospital. He has been reproached for his versatile character, he changed his religion seven times, Bèze tells us.   This is not accurate; his religion was tolerance and freedom of conscience, upon this point he never varied, but it was enough to draw down upon him the general hatred.   He must be ranked with liberals like L'Hospital and de Thou, who desired reform (for they could not conceal from themselves the abuses under which the Church was suffering), but reform

---

[1] [" The learned Cujas had, in spite of his sedentary pursuits, led a very wandering life, he died at Bourges in the year 1590 'Sedentary' pursuits is perhaps not exactly what I should call them, having read in the 'Biographie Universelle' (sole source of my knowledge of the renowned Cujacius) that his usual manner of study was to spread himself on his belly on the floor   He did not sit down, he lay down, and the 'Biographie Universelle' has (for so grave a work) an amusing picture of the short, fat, untidy scholar dragging himself 'à plat ventre' across his room, from one pile of books to another " _ (*Henry James*, "A Little Tour in France," XII, "Bourges ") — ED]

without violence and without schism　Would an apostate have
hesitated about justifying the massacre of Saint Bartholomew upon
the demand of the Court?　Baudouin had sufficient courage to
refuse　As a jurisconsult he is one who did most towards introducing the historical method into the study of the Roman law.
DOUAREN (Duarenus), born at Moncontour, Côtes-du-Nord, 1509,
died at Bourges, 1559.　He gave up teaching in 1548 for the bar,
but he was offered such appointments that before long he came
back to teach at Bourges, and there brilliantly expounded the
doctrines of his master Alciat　HUGUES DONEAU (Donellus),
born in 1527 at Châlons-sur-Saône, a pupil of Coras and of Arnaud
Ferrier at Toulouse, of Baron and of Douaren at Bourges, left
France in 1572, and died at Altdorf in 1591.　He was one of the
most bitter adversaries of Cujas　He is the only Romanist of the
1500 s one can think of comparing with Cujas.　Though some have
erroneously attempted to classify him as a Bartolist, he belongs
clearly to the Humanist school.　Doneau was compelled to leave
France, because of his connection with the reformed religion, and
taught afterwards at Heidelberg, at Leyden, and at Altdorf (near
Nuremberg).

FRANÇOIS HOTMAN, born in Paris, August 23, 1524, belonged
to a family which had originally lived in Silesia.　His father
was a Councillor of the Parliament　He studied law at the
University of Orléans, "where still resounded the glory of P de
l'Estoile, the keenest jurisconsult of all the doctors of France."
After practising at the bar for a time, he came back to pure science,
and in 1546 opened a course in Roman law at the Faculty of Paris
The Reformed religion, which was rapidly spreading, especially
in circles of culture, made a convert of Hotman, and he became
one of the most notable Huguenot adherents.　But this change
of religion cost him dear, he broke with his family, and forfeited
his property and at last his native country　In 1555 he settled at
Strasbourg, where his fame soon became international　Prussia,
Saxony, and England made him offers　Finally, enabled to
return to France, he went to the University of Valence, and in 1566,
to that of Bourges　The massacre of Saint Bartholomew drove
him thence, as it did Doneau, thereafter he taught in Switzerland,
at Geneva, and at Bâle.　He died in 1590 in the latter town, broken
down with illness and poverty, but preserving to the end and
through a thousand trials the enthusiasm of his younger years
His " Franco-Gallia " (1573), one of the manifestoes of the Protestant cause, is a screed in favor of political freedom; for he was

ever a champion of free thought and action in both political and
religious matters.   In his "Antitribonianus" (1567), he pleads the
cause of unity of civil legislation.   Politics, theology, feudal law,
Roman law, were all in his mastery, and throughout he reaches
those heights which are attained only by the greatest minds.   No
doubt, if he had been content to be only a Romanist, he would have
equalled Cujas and Doneau.   But he was too much a man of action
also.   His career was so interrupted by political turmoil that we
stand amazed at the vast learning to which his writings testify [1]

TOPIC 2. THE OFFICIAL COMPILATION OF THE CUSTOMS

§ 23   **Reasons and Methods of the Redaction** — Towards the
middle of the 1400s many of the Customs had been put into writing
But official compilations were rare; their need could not be filled
by the private Books of Customs; these were inadequate, and were
too much encumbered by Roman doctrines and their authors'
personal opinions.   The tenor of the Customs was uncertain;
and the limits of their several jurisdictions were not well defined
Judges were forced to resort to the expensive, dilatory, and crude
inquest by " turba " (*ante*, § 10)   There was urgent demand to
remedy these two great evils, the uncertainty of the law, and the
slowness of justice   Charles VII proposed to attain this twofold
object by ordering the official compilation of the Customs of the
kingdom (Art 125 of the Ordinance of Montils-les-Tours, April,
1453).

When did this Compilation take place? — The Ordinance of 1453
was not put into effect immediately, Charles' successors had to
repeat his orders.   It was not until towards the end of the 1400s
that the work was begun (Custom of Ponthieu, 1494, etc.).   The
compilation and the publication took place almost entirely during
the 1500s   Many important *Revisions of the Customs* were likewise made during the 1500s   The Custom of Paris, compiled in
1510, was revised in 1580, that of Orléans, compiled in 1509, was
revised in 1583; that of Brittany, published in 1539, was revised
in 1580.   That such revisions became necessary so very shortly
after the first compilation was due largely to the study of the new
texts by jurists and judges, and the defects and anachronisms
thus disclosed.

---

[1] [On these great French jurists, compare the comments of Professor
Maitland, in his "English Law and the Renaissance" (reprinted in "Select
Essays in Anglo-American Legal History," vol. I) — TRANSL.]

How were the Compilations and the Revisions Made ?— The method used was intended to settle beyond a doubt the usages in force and to give them the double sanction of the Provincial Estates and the royal authority Thus the Custom, even after being codified, preserved its popular character, while receiving the authority of a perpetual and irrevocable law The five steps in the process were as follows 1st. Under Letters Patent of the King, ordering the compilation of the Customs of a certain province, the sheriff commanded the various officers, court clerks, mayors, and aldermen, to draft memorials upon the local usages, these formed the preliminary materials for the future Code. 2d At the same time the Provincial Estates assembled at the capital of the jurisdiction The memorials of the experts were turned over to a commission of members of the Estates, who were to compile therefrom a single draft. 3d The formal draft, thus being recommended, was read in the assembly of the Estates, presided over by members of the Court of Parliament delegated by the King as commissioners for the purpose. The draft articles of the Custom were voted upon by the Estates, if no agreement could be reached, if the majority or the weightier party did not accept them, the disagreement was settled by the Court of Parliament The part played by the royal commissioners was more subordinate than one would have supposed ; the text of the Customs was primarily the work of the practical men of each locality One could not expect from them either polish or method (says Fleury), and so there is little order in their work, and the language is by no means precise. 4th. The final text of the Custom was then read in the formal assembly of the Estates. This was the official *Publication*, and was accompanied by a royal decree by which the King's commissioners enjoined that the Custom should be observed as an inviolable law. *Minutes* of the whole proceedings were drawn up and were *registered*, with the official report of the Customs, at the clerk's office of the county or barony 5th. Finally the text of the Custom was certified by the royal commissioners and deposited with the clerk of the Parliament, but it was neither verified nor ratified by that Court, excepting those articles upon which the Provincial Estates had not been able to agree.

§ 24 **Results of the Redaction** — (A) *Proof.* — Each province had thenceforth its local Code, Customs which had been officially settled no longer had to be proved in court. Inquests by " turba " (*ante*, § 10) became useless and were prohibited (upon subjects provided for in the Custom).

(B) *Reforms.* — The chief aim was to settle the existing usage " ne varietur "; we must be careful not to regard the compilation of the Customs as a recasting of private law Nevertheless, the opportunity of making alterations and corrections was naturally taken advantage of; the Letters Patent of March 15, 1497, invited the officers, practitioners, and members of the three Estates to give their opinion as to what ought to be corrected, added, diminished, or interpreted. The idea of revision came to light especially at the time of the reformation of the great Customs. Here a double tendency was felt, sometimes in moulding the local usage towards the Roman law, and sometimes in adhering to the fundamental principles of the Customary law. The principal representative of the Romanist tendency was President Lizet (of Berry), and of the opposite tendency President Christophe de Thou, father of the historian. " Lizet," said Guy Coquille, " held that the Roman law was our common law, and conformed our French law to it as much as possible by putting narrow limits on all that was contrary to Roman law Master de Thou was of the opinion that the Customs and the French law were our common law, and called the Roman law merely written reason."

(C) *The Authority* of the Custom was no longer the same as of old. Because of its origin and its subject, it preserved its character of a usage, but at the same time the sanction of the King, now added, gave it the form and the force of a Written Law It must be observed as a statute, a perpetual and irrevocable edict. Hence, (*a*) to allege and prove any other Custom in opposition to the official Custom was forbidden, (*b*) it could only be modified by taking the same steps as in the original compilation.

(D) *Progress toward Uniformity of the Civil Law.* — (a) *Reduction of the Number of Customs.* Not as many Customs were compiled as there were lords' domains. Many bodies of local usages were absorbed in the general Customs of the barony, or county, or the province, simply because the interested parties did not make them known, in default of which the usage became void Although France was not yet to have a single Civil Code, still, at least, by these official Customs Provincial Codes were created; of which the minor local Customs were merely the complement It is generally said that there were at this period in old France sixty General Customs and three hundred Special Customs. This of course was far from being unity of law, but it was a great step in advance, as compared with the earlier days when each petty barony had its own Custom. For the achievement of a uniform

261

Civil Code, destiny was still to need two centuries of centralization, numerous general ordinances, and a body of decisions and law-books which should accentuate analogies and eliminate diver-gencies between the Customs. At this period of the 1500s, no doubt, a single Code would have remained a dead letter; ingrained tradition would have been stronger than the law In Germany, the "Landrechte," or provincial laws, corresponded to our General Customs, with this difference, that they were exclusively the work of the ruler, and that they did not exclude the application of the Roman law as a subsidiary rule. It was only towards the end of the 1700s that powerful States such as Prussia and Austria ob-tained true Codes, in the modern sense of the word, dispensing with any need for amplication from the Roman or Canon law.

(b) *Legal Science.* The official compilation of the Customs was the beginning of a great scientific movement. The text, being published, was easy to obtain and study. Comparisons were made between the various Customs, lectures were given upon their various articles. By this means, out of the extreme detailed di-versity of rules, there arose general principles, an identical basis, the *Common Customary Law* of France. These principles now became the special subject of study. Thus unity of legislation was first of all realized in legal treatises. The most noteworthy of these books were, in the 1500s, the "Institution au droit français," by GUY COQUILLE, and the "Institutes Coutumières " of LOYSEL, in which the essential rules of the Customary law are laid down in the form of proverbs In the 1600s we have the "Institution au droit français " by ARGOU (1692). a simple and concise exposition of the Customary legislation. The numerous treatises on civil law by POTHIER, in the 1700s, were written from the same point of view, Pothier seems to have worked upon a Code, of which there are several editions, representing preferred and variant texts. The Civil Code of 1804 is itself nothing more than the general law or common law of the Customs, rounded out and modified by the aid of the revolutionary law and cleared of its feudal elements.

(c) *Judicial Decisions,* in their turn, followed the impulse given by the treatise writers The Courts simplified and unified the Cus-tomary law, — giving the Custom of Paris a preponderance, which would have been still more marked had not this Custom had a formidable competitor in the Roman law This preponderance of the "Coutume de Paris" over the other Customs was due to various causes. 1st. The attraction which the capital already

exercised over the rest of the kingdom.   2d   The tendency of the
Court of Parliament to give it preference, a natural tendency because Parliament sat in Paris.   3d. The excellence of its compilation (at least in the revision of 1580), and the fact that it represented
a well-balanced middle course between Customs which were most
opposed to one another   But this Custom was far from covering
private law in its entirety, as one may see from a list of its titles :
fiefs, copyholds, seigniorial dues, kinds of property, possession,
mortgages, rent-charges, prescription, repurchase by the same
lineage, judgments, distraint and seizure, servitudes, marital community, dower, guardianship, gifts, wills, succession, public sale
These same subjects are to be found again in most of the other
Customs.   But certificates of civil status, marriage, paternity,
and filiation, as well as obligations and contracts, are not dealt with,
these matters being regulated by the Ordinances, the Canon law,
and the Roman law.

Topic 3. The Royal Legislation

§ 25. **Introductory** — *The Monarchic Period* is naturally the
one during which royal *Ordinances* and enactments predominate
in the sources of the law.   They increase, expand, and become
transformed into Codes, whereas the other sources of the law become less abundant.   They are rounded out by means of the
Regulating Judgments issued by the Parliament and the other
supreme Courts, and especially by the *Judgments of the Council*
which, particularly during the 1700 s become a more and more
important part of the law.

The *Regulating Judgments* of the sovereign Courts were decisions
of these Courts to be observed as laws within the limits of their
jurisdiction, they are on the boundary line between statutes
and judicial decisions.

Our archives contain almost eight hundred thousand *Judgments
of the Council*, covering the last two centuries of the monarchy.
This shows us what an important place these enactments had
taken in our old legislation.   The King's Council was the great
political organ of the monarchy, it played a part which may in
some respects be compared with that of the English Parliament.
Political development had been just the opposite in France to what
it had been in England, in England the King's Privy Council, in
France the States-General (that is, the body which corresponded
to the English Parliament), had become atrophied.   Not only did

the King's Council issue Judgments, but Ordinances and Edicts were submitted to it.

§ 26   **Ordinances of the 1500s and early 1600s.** — The great Ordinances of the 1300s and 1400s reforming the State had often been enacted in sequence to a session of the States-General or similar assemblies   They were often nothing more than the incorporation of the grievances of the deputies of the States-General into a single document; they affected most of the branches of administration, and were a pellmell of the most varied provisions   The Ordinances of the 1500s retain the same characteristics.   Of this sort was the celebrated *Ordinance of Villers-Cotterets* (August, 1539), under Francis I, dealing with the administration of justice.   It restricted the jurisdiction of the Ecclesiastical Courts, required the regis-tration of gifts, on the example of the Roman law, regulated the functions of notaries, and provided for registration of civil status. But its principal reform was in criminal procedure.   It substituted the inquisitorial system of the Courts of the Church for the old feudal procedure.   Complaint by the injured person and publicity of trial were now supplanted by *ex officio* prosecution and secrecy of trial   The *Ordinance of Moulins* (1566) substituted written proof for oral witnesses in civil procedure.   The *Ordinance of Blois* (1579) regulated the form of marriage.   A dozen other important Ordi-nances covered between them a large field of private law.   About 1580, a celebrated jurisconsult, BARNABY BRISSON (Brissonius), Advocate-General of the Parliament of Paris, and author of a widely used dictionary of law ("De verborum significatione"), compiled a systematic collection of the principal provisions con-tained in the Ordinances in force under Henry III   This prince, ambitious, it was said, to rival the glory of such men as Theodosius and Justinian, was about to give it royal sanction; but his death in 1589 prevented this.   Brisson's work was published after his death under the title of "Code Henri III, Basilica"

§ 27.   **Ordinances of Louis XIV** — The reign of Louis XIV was marked by the codification of numerous branches of law To Colbert's initiative we owe these great Ordinances, of which the Codes of to-day are scarcely more than revised editions.

Like most of the royal enactments, these Ordinances were pr-pared by councillors of State; but associated with them were legal and commercial experts, and (contrary to the usual practice) the Court of Parliament took part in drafting two of the most important, on civil procedure and crimes.   The *Civil Procedure Ordi-nance* of April, 1667, sought to reduce delays and expense and to give precision of rules, and at the same time to limit the discretion of judges.   The two most prominent in its drafting were Pussort, a Privy Councillor, and GUILLAUME DE LAMOIGNON, Chief President of the Court of Parliament, a liberal, of noble mind, who stood for the authority of Parliament against the enlightened despotism championed by Pussort   The *Criminal Ordinance of 1670* had much merit, but it was marred by numerous features, — the torture, the "monitories," or warnings (to be given by the clergy to the faithful, inculcating the disclosure of their knowledge under penalty of excommunication, and, in reality, says Voltaire, an inducement to the dregs of the people to accuse from mere jealousy the rich and the nobles); the system of numerical proofs obligatory on the judge; lawsuits against corpses, compulsory self-incrimination, and the like.   Lamoignon in vain championed the cause of liberalism.   It remained for the philosophers of the 1700s and their disciple Beccaria to revolutionize the penal law by insisting that repression of crime should not ignore the dictates of humanity and the rights of the defence.   The Ordinance of 1670 is in fact nothing more than a Code of Criminal Practice; it is not a Penal Code. The Old Régime never had one, and that was not among the least of its shortcomings.   The *Ordinance of Commerce*, March, 1673 ("Code Marchand," "Code Savary"), codified the commercial law (on land)   Its chief draftsman was a Parisian merchant, Jacques Savary, author of the "Parfait négociant," a book of European fame in its day   The *Ordinance of the Marine*, August, 1681, codified the maritime law.   That law had at an early period acquired an international character; and this Ordinance, founded on a careful study of international usage, preserved that character

§ 28   **Ordinances of Louis XV** — Colbert's work of codification was continued under Louis XV by the efforts of D'Aguesseau (*post*, § 31) in various branches   Even the civil law was now undertaken.   The illustrious Chancellor at one time contemplated unifying the entire civil law of the kingdom.   But he recoiled before the difficulties of such an undertaking, and was content with a partial codification upon certain topics, such as gifts, wills, entails, and mortmain.

Topic 4. The National Jurists [1]

§ 29. **The Courts and the Bar** —The lofty figure of MICHEL DE L'HOSPITAL (died 1573) dominates the pleiad of the jurisconsults of the 1500 s who devoted themselves to the Customs. Brantôme calls him "another Cato, sent to rebuke a corrupt world." As a legislator, he put on the statute-book many progressive rules; as a magistrate, he was one of the first of a long line of illustrious names whose integrity, strictness of morals, learning, and civic courage have placed so high the fame of our judicial body in the Old Régime. Among the chancellors and keepers of the seal, the best known of his successors are P. SÉGUIER (in 1635) and D'AGUESSEAU (in 1717). Among the chief presidents of the Court of Parliament at Paris may be mentioned CHRISTOPHE DE THOU (died 1582), ACHILLE DE HARLAY (died 1616), MATHIEU MOLÉ (died 1636), and GUILLAUME DE LAMOIGNON (died 1677). Among the advocates-general of the Parliament the best known are BARNABY BRISSON (1570), JÉRÔME BIGNON (1626), OMER TALON (1632) and DENIS TALON (1698), JOLY DE FLEURY (four of this name held office in the 1700 s), and GILBERT DES VOISINS (1718–1739).

At the *Bar* the most famous names in the 1500 s are those of ETIENNE PASQUIER (mentioned later); SIMON MARION (died 1605), whose daughter married Antoine Arnauld and "was the mother of twenty celebrated children ", MICHEL SERVIN (died 1626), of whom it was said· "Servinum una dies pro libertate loquentem vidit et oppressa pro libertate cadentem." [2] In the 1600 s we note OLIVIER PATRU (died 1681), the Boileau of the bar, who gave to forensic eloquence a classic tone and raised the standards of oratorical taste, though his speeches seem to us very cold, ANTOINE LEMAISTRE, who, in the midst of a most brilliant career, retired to

---

[1] BIBLIOGRAPHY *Camus and Dupin*, "Profession d'avocat," 5th ed., 1832 An alphabetical list of the old jurisconsults is to be found in the "Instit de Loysel," ed. *Dupin and Laboulaye*, 1846, vol. I, p xxxi — *Papire Masson*, "Eloges des jurisc," 1638, *Mornac*, "Feriæ Forenses," 1619, *Tisand*, "Vies des plus célébres jurisc," ed 1737; *Terrasson*, "Vies des jurisc. franc qui ont écrit sur le dr rom," 1750, *Blanchard*, "Eloges des premiers présid au Parl de Paris," *Bretonnier*, "Vie des jurisc les plus cé lèbres de France" (excepting those of Paris); *P. Nicéron*, "Mém p servir à la vie des hommes illustres," 1786; *Holtzendorff*, "Encyclop d Rechtsw," 1886; Dictionaries and biographies, for example, *Hœfer*; *Bardoux*, "Les Légistes," 1877, *Rodière*, "Les grands jurisconsultes," 1874

[2] As he was presenting to Louis XIII a remonstrance, at a "bed of justice," the king interrupted him with threats. Servin (the story goes) fell dead at the feet of the king

Port-Royal, where he died in 1658. In the 1700s eminent names are Cochin (died 1747), Loyseau de Mauléon (died 1771), Gerbier (died 1788), and Servan (died 1807)

§ 30. **National Jurists of the 1500s** — Though this was the century of the great Romanists (Cujas, Baudouin, Doneau, Hotman), yet the jurisconsults who labored upon the Customary law were not inferior   Foremost among them (in his own opinion, as well as in that of his contemporaries) was Charles Dumoulin ("Molinæus"), born in Paris in 1500, died in 1566, December 27. As a barrister he met with but little success   President De Thou, tired of listening to him, treated him as he would an ignorant lawyer and ordered him to be silent. This drew down upon the President's head a protest from the dean of the bar and association of barristers such as would not be tolerated to-day, even in favor of a Dumoulin. "You have insulted," he was told, "a man more learned than you yourself could ever hope to be;" and De Thou acknowledged his error. This anecdote (obviously open to doubt) at least explains how it was that Dumoulin came to abandon the bar and to confine himself to composition and consultations. Dumoulin did not limit himself, as did Cujas, to the law alone; his emotional character here felt itself confined within too narrow a sphere. He plunged with ardor into the religious disputes of his time   It was said that he could not with composure hear the words "right," "usurpation," and "abuse"; he was bound to express his feelings. It was easy enough to raise up enemies, in that epoch, and Dumoulin had plenty   Using little diplomacy, employing violent invective in his arguments, his life was threatened, his house plundered, and he was compelled to flee to Germany. He taught for some time at Tübingen, was driven out by a rival, gave lessons at Strasbourg, Dôle, and Besançon, attracting numerous listeners by his reputation. At last he returned to France   When the Count of Montbéliard, on asking an opinion, was refused, because Dumoulin found his cause an unjust one, the Count threw him into prison. But Dumoulin, none the less, refused to give the opinion. In Italy, his books were placed on the Church's Index of prohibited works.

Dumoulin's fame was only equalled by his self-conceit. At the caption of his opinions, he wrote· "Ego, qui nemini cedo et a nemine doceri possum." Did his abilities justify his own opinion? He had indeed great talents. His ideas were broad. He dreamed of amalgamating the Customs into a single Code ("Oratio de concordia et unione consuetudinum Franciæ").

He annotated them, on the basis of the Custom of Paris, "caput omnium hujus regni et totius etiam Galliæ Belgicæ consuetudinum " He upheld| the lawfulness of lending at interest, then contrary to the teachings of the Church. He took a stand against the theory by which the King was not only the sovereign but also the proprietor of the kingdom. Feudal charges were odious to him, and whenever he encountered an iniquitous custom, he attacked it with violence until he overthrew it. He fought against the narrow-minded feudists with a disdainful roughness and rigor. He was the champion of the new ideas and of the germinating thoughts of the Third Estate. With his modern conception of the rights of the State, and with the theory of natural law, he took up arms against the two great powers of the Middle Ages, the Church and Feudalism His writings gave direction to French judicial practice, and mapped out its future course

With Guy Coquille, Loysel, Pasquier, and Pithou, we reach a more peaceful region They were all men of amiable disposition, " elegant " jurists, humanists while also practitioners, collaborating with Passerat in the " Satire Ménippée," diplomatic, moderate, Gallicans They had all the good qualities, save one,—that powerful and rough-shod genius of a Dumoulin, by which a man stirs his century. GUY COQUILLE (1523–1603) was in the States-General three times, but is best known by his "Institution au droit français " and similar works ANTOINE LOYSEL (1536–1617), who had studied under Cujas, became famous in his "Institutions coutumières," a sort of code in the form of maxims, and his " Pasquier, or Dialogue des Avocats " ETIENNE PASQUIER (1529–1615) was eminent chiefly as an advocate. He stood out against Henry III's claims of legislative power. When in a celebrated lawsuit by the University of Paris against the Jesuits it was sought to exclude the latter from chairs of secular instruction, Pasquier espoused the cause of the University, which finally triumphed.

§ 31 **National Jurists of the 1600s and 1700s** — The century of Louis XIV is not the great century of French legal science. Nor is it a period of decadence, excepting for the Roman law. But with the exception of Domat and Lamoignon, there are no prominent names, at the most one can but mention the civilians Duplessis, Lebrun, Ricard, the erudite La Thaumassière, and Clement Fleury (1640–1723), author of a " Histoire du droit francais," and under-tutor of the children of France.

The classical spirit of the 1600s in law had a brilliant exponent in DOMAT (of Clermont-Ferrand, 1625–1696), a fellow-country-

man and friend of Pascal, like him a Jansenist (though brought up
by a Jesuit, his great-uncle Sirmond), and a magistrate vigilant,
upright, and absolutely disinterested.   His great work, "Les lois
civiles dans leur ordre naturel" was written at Paris, whither he
came in 1681, on a royal pension   It is distinguished by its lofti-
ness of thought and philosophic spirit.   "Domat," said Portalis, "is
the first man to deal in generalities."   His work has been called
the preface to the Civil Code, but (we must add) it was a preface not very well known, it was confidently admired, but very
little read   GUILLAUME DE LAMOIGNON (1617–1677) had no
rival as a jurisconsult   Besides his participation in the draft of
the Ordinances of 1667 and 1670, his great work is the "Arrêtes, ou
Lois projetées," in which, carrying out the plans of such men as
Dumoulin and Loysel, he laid down the principles of the Customary
law in the form of a Code   Louis XIV, when appointing him
Chief President of the Court of Parliament, said   "If I had known
a worthier man, I should have given him your place"

In the 1700 s we find the learned historian Eusebius de Laurière,
(died 1728), preparing the compilation of the Ordinances, the
Chancellor D'Aguesseau and Pothier, bringing the spirit of Lamoignon and Domat into the law, and Montesquieu, standing as the
representative of the philosophic spirit

H Fr. D'AGUESSEAU (of Limoges, 1668–1751), the great Chancellor, was a legislator like L'Hospital, and a magistrate like Lamoignon.   He was highly esteemed at Court for his learning and his
uprightness; his stubbornness hurt his career all the more in that
it did not prevent his sometimes changing his mind, for example,
with regard to the Bull "Unigenitus"   He began by opposing
with the utmost energy the ratification of this Bull; neither
entreaties nor threats from Louis XIV could make him yield.
Despite his failings, D'Aguesseau remains a great man.   He gives
an exalted idea of the magistracy of the 1700 s.   In his "Ordinances" he takes up in detail, but with less boldness in its execution,
the splendid draft of Lamoignon.   Upon the topics which they
covered — wills, gifts, and entails — he virtually wrote in advance
entire chapters of the future Civil Code of Napoleon.   His Memoirs
reveal his fine talents as a practitioner, and can still be consulted
with profit.

R J. POTHIER (1690–1772), professor at the University of Orléans
and counsellor to the Inferior Court of that town, was a true sage,
a lay saint.   His biographers show him to us as modest, disinterested, obliging, and charitable, fulfilling his double duties with

a conscientiousness rarely seen, at work from four o'clock in the morning to nine at night, without any sort of recreation or social diversions   His life is summed up in his works.   These extensive writings consisted mainly of two series· 1st, the " Pandectæ in novum ordinem digestæ " (1748), a systematic treatise upon each title of the Digest, the texts being rearranged so as to bring together those which were related, and the whole rounded out with definitions, distinctions, rules, and exceptions; 2d, numerous treatises on the civil law (notably the " Traité des Obligations "), which are models of clarity, of exactness, and of method   They extraordinarily simplified the work to be done by the framers of the Civil Code; it has been said of them that they were an advance Commentary upon the Code. Still, Pothier had neither the originality nor the genius of Cujas and Dumoulin, it is as a popularizer that he has no equal.

To read the treatises of the civilians (the works of Pothier, for example), one would never suspect that they were of the 1700s. Nothing therein betrays the great movement of ideas then stirring.   No breeze of the new spirit can be felt within their realm. But around the old cloistered edifice of the law, MONTESQUIEU was already building his boldest of new scaffoldings   He is the first to conceive of the law as a true science, to identify its method with that of the natural sciences, to discover the laws of the growth of law, and to subsume all its facts within the boundaries of general formulæ. His scheme may have since been perfected as to detail; but the conception has remained the same, it has never been improved upon. And besides propounding this broad truth, in his " Esprit des lois " (1748) he touched upon the essential points, and suggested the concrete solutions of the future. No more entails (for they hamper economic progress); no more mortmains (for the clergy is a family which should not multiply), fewer rent-charges and more money-loans, — such was his program for property-law. For the law of persons, no more serfdom (for agriculture depends less on fertility of soil than on liberty of its occupants). For family law, no more indissoluble marriages. The law of successions should be preserved, on grounds of political welfare. For procedure, he advocates less of formality, more of conciseness and simplicity. Such was his enlightened forecast.

Topic 5. Political Philosophy

§ 32. **Philosophies of the 1500s and 1600s.** — (1) *The 1400s.*
The Renascence was a return to paganism, a reaction against
asceticism and scholasticism. MACCHIAVELLI (1469–1527) was
a good exponent of it, with his realistic and positivist policy, having
no standard other than the reasons of State, and no principles save
that the end justifies the means. His work, "The Prince," had so
enduring an influence that Frederick the Great (before he was king)
wrote a book against it. Its merit was to have broken completely
with the theologic principles of the Middle Ages. He freed public
law from the yoke of scholasticism, and introduced the spirit of
utilitarianism.

(2) *The 1500s* The *Reformation,* like the Renascence, had its
policy; but a very different one, and in the beginning one very far
from being as liberal. The death of Michel Servet divided the
Calvinist faction; Sebastien Castellion was the first to write in
favor of the freedom of conscience. The wiser among the politicians
— L'Hospital, Pithou, Pasquier — were also won over to this principle. Thus arose one of the most essential of public liberties.
At the same time the vicissitudes of the struggle between Catholics
and Protestants gave rise to a school hostile to the theocratic
theories, or theories of the divine law which predominated in the
Middle Ages. The ideas of the social contract and of popular
sovereignty passed from the school and from books into the full
light of public life. The monarchic system of the Church, which
had served as a model for the State, was abandoned; instead of the
Catholic Church as a balance for the Empire, there arose National
Churches with an episcopal system, — sometimes with an aristocratic constitution (England, Germany), sometimes with a democratic constitution, laymen participating in the government of the
Church (Calvinists, Presbyterians) These changes had their
effect upon the political organization. One of the movements
was represented in the *Monarchomaques.* The Protestants, who in
France suffered under the absolute authority of the monarch,
aimed to limit this authority Such was the purpose of the
"Franco-Gallia" (1573) of the jurisconsult FREDERIC HOTMAN,
an apology for the limited monarchy tempered by the historical
point of view. The Scotchman Buchanan was among the most
radical of this School.

But absolutist and liberal tendencies were mingled in varying
degrees in the authors of the 1500s. PIERRE PITHOU's little book,

271

" Libertés de l'église gallicane," was like a Code for the Church
and State up to the end of the Old Régime   Among the political
writers the most illustrious is JEAN BODIN (1530–1596), with his
six books, "De la République."   The monarchic centralization in
France, the omnipotence of the Pope in the Catholic Church, and
the writings of the legists on the Empire furnished Bodin the elements of his system, which was at once monastic and juridical.
Hobbes was to draw from it the absolutist system of his " Leviathan." To Montesquieu, Bodin was to furnish the theory of
climates (which to be sure can be found in its germ among the
ancients).

(3) *The 1600s.* — England was the chief battle-ground, during
the 1600s, between liberal and absolutist ideas.   The former had
their roots as far back as Bracton in the 1200s and Fortescue in
the 1400s. The cause of absolute monarchy, no less old, was
defended not only by Hobbes, in his " De Cive " (1642) and
" Leviathan " (1651), but by King James I and by Filmer.   The
opposite array was led by Milton, Harrington, Sidney, and, chief
among all, by LOCKE (1632–1704).

Natural law had had a place in the writings of the theologians
of the Middle Ages, in those of Suarez in the 1500s, and (for international relations) in those of Victoria, Ayala, and Albericus
Gentilis   But it becomes far more extensive and far more important from the 1600s onwards, with the German Althusius (1557–
1638), and especially with the Dutchman GROTIUS (1583–1645),
founder of the modern law of nations

§ 33   **Philosophies of the 1700s.** — The jurists of this period
attach themselves, some to MONTESQUIEU, and some to JEAN–
JACQUES ROUSSEAU   Montesquieu's great work, " L'Esprit des
Lois " (1748), suggested as a model for the States of the Continent the English Constitution, with its representative system, its
separation of powers (in which he saw a valuable safeguard of the
freedom of the individual), and its bodies intervening between the
sovereign and the people — Nobility, Clergy, and Parliament, —
to deaden as it were the impact between them, and to prevent
abuse of power on the one hand and rebellion on the other.   He
realized that our complex societies, far more than the simple city-
state of olden times, had need of a complex constitution   The
simple terms to which the forms of government were commonly
reduced — monarchy, aristocracy, democracy, — were no longer
consistent (according to him) with our times. His merit lay, not
only in possessing a superior political sense, but in subjecting public

law and the legal system in general to the experimental method, — the only one which is capable of bringing some certainty into it. Auguste Comte rightly considers him as the creator of social science.

JEAN-JACQUES ROUSSEAU (1712–1778) was more a man of books, a theorist. He owed a great deal to the school of natural law, and much to Locke; personal observation furnished him with but little, excepting in those parts of his political system which are the counterpart of the Old Régime He strives in his " Contrat Social " (1764) to portray the rational organization of society His ideas upon the state of nature, upon the social contract (by which men agree to form a society), upon popular sovereignty, and upon the relation of the delegated executive power to the nation which creates it, have in themselves nothing new, save the eloquent and animated form and the radical logic with which he places them before us. Rousseau has little sympathy for the English Constitution, upon this point he reacts against the school of Montesquieu, through his disposition to equality and democracy; thus, he admits neither the separation of powers nor representative government. But he agrees with Montesquieu and Voltaire (and with most of the writers of his century) in his protests against the abuses of the Old Régime. Almost all of them champion what the Revolution was to call " the Rights of Man and of the Citizen " Rousseau is perhaps the least liberal of them, although a great individualist by temperament, he did not declare for tolerance in religious matters; we know how little he favored private ownership; in his view this right is the creature of the State. He is at one and the same time individualist and collectivist. And this twofold tendency he stamps upon the Revolution, so soon impending.

•

CHAPTER III. THIRD PERIOD · A.D 1789–1904

THE REVOLUTION AND THE CODES[1]

TOPIC 1. THE RENOVATION AND UNIFICATION OF THE LAW

§ 34   The Intermediate Work of | § 36   Character and Contents of
         the Revolution. | the Code Napoleon.
§ 35. The Preparation and Enact-| § 37. The Empire and the Other
         ment of the Code Napoleon. | Codes

TOPIC 2 THE CIVIL LAW SINCE THE CODIFICATION

§ 38. Legislation.   § 40. Legal Science.
§ 39   Judicial Decisions.

TOPIC 3. THE CODE NAPOLEON IN OTHER COUNTRIES

§ 41. Prior Codifications. | § 42. The Extension of the Code
                                 | Napoleon.

TOPIC 1. THE RENOVATION AND UNIFICATION OF THE LAW

§ 34. **The Work of the Revolution.** — (1) In general, the legislative work of the Revolution, which was considerable, formed a transitional stage between the old and the new law, and is usually termed "intermediate law" or "intermediate period"

As a general thing but little studied, authors are apt either to admire it too implicitly, or to disparage it too vehemently   It has been studied in its entirety by M Sagnac, in his "Législation Civile de la Révolution Française"[2]

This period can be given exact limits: it began with the 17th of June, 1789, the day on which the States-General were changed into a National Assembly and assumed the sovereign power; it ended on 30 Ventôse, year XII (March 21, 1804), the day of the publication of the Civil Code, which opens the modern period.

The Dominant Characteristic of the Revolution was a hatred

---

[1] [§§ 34–42 = PLANIOL, §§ 59–141, pp 23–52, with omissions. For the citation of this work, and an account of the author, see the Editorial Preface — TRANSL.]   [2] Paris, 1898.

of feudalism, — not of political feudalism (which had been destroyed by the King long before), but of civil feudalism   This signifies the mass of rights and usages, arising out of feudalism and affecting individual relations, which had survived the political system out of which they had sprung.   Of the feudal organization itself, there no longer remained anything excepting *special privileges* benefiting certain lands and certain persons.   There were only a few of these in the nation, there was no longer any reason for the recognition of these privileges; consequently they offended that sentiment of equality which is so strongly developed among the French.[1]   *The abolition of Feudal dues* was thus the first undertaking of the Revolution; this was enacted on the night of August 4.   Enough laws were afterwards passed to insure the effect of the fundamental principle enacted on this celebrated night.   It is worth while here to point out the blindness of those French statesmen who, a few years before the Revolution, instigated the Parliament of Paris to condemn to the pyre Boncerf's brochure on the " Inconveniences of the Feudal Privileges " (1776), at that very moment a neighboring monarch, the King of Sardinia, was peacefully instituting reforms which, had they been systematically undertaken in France, could have saved royalty.

The Results of the Revolution were mainly changes in public and political law.   In private law, the chief progress realized by the intermediate law was the *freedom of the individual* and a regard for *individual ownership*, both of which were made more secure than they had been under the Old Régime; yet it is only fair to add that the occasions upon which these rights used formerly to be violated were more sensational than numerous, and that the safeguards which are to-day provided are more apparent than real   Another principle gained by the Revolution was the *equality of persons*, and therefore the *equality of lands*.   Every trace of special privilege disappeared; since 1789 all Frenchmen are merged in a single class under the name of citizens.

(2) The successive labors of the various Assembles may now be noticed more in detail.

---

[1] It is most remarkable that the hatred of medieval institutions should have resulted in an outburst in France of all places   France was a country in which feudalism had already been three-quarters destroyed ; there were other countries (Germany and England) where these institutions, better preserved, still made their severity felt by the people. *Tocqueville* had noticed this fact ("L'ancien régime et la Revolution," 2d ed , p 57) For an explanation of so singular a fact, see *Robert Beudant*, "La transformation de la propriété foncière dans le droit intermédiaire," p. 125 *et seq.*

1st *The Constituent Assembly* (June 17, 1789–Sept. 30, 1791). This Assembly was actively occupied with the new administrative system to be put into effect. In public law, the reform which served as a basis for the others was the suppression of the old territorial divisions, made for administrative, judiciary, or financial purposes. The "provinces," "bailliages," and "généralités" were replaced by the division into *departments* (Law of Dec 22, 1789, Feb 26–March 4, 1790)

The *judiciary reforms* were radical. The old magistracy was destroyed The Parliaments were "sent on a vacation"; but these vacations were "indefinite," and they have never come back from them In their stead, "district tribunals" were created, these have since become our civil tribunals of the wards (" arrondissement ") The institution of the criminal jury was decreed on April 30, 1790. The formation of the Court of Cassation (review) was voted Aug. 12, 1790, its organization dates from Nov. 27–Dec 1, 1790. At this time the office of magistrate was still elective (Decree of May 5, 1790). The reorganization of the judiciary then became the subject of the great law of Aug 16–24, 1790, based on the principle of the *separation of powers*. This principle, upon which are founded the constitutions of every free people, was formulated in the 1700 s by Montesquieu · "In order that there may be no possibility of an abuse of power, it is necessary, in the very nature of things, that power should check power" ("Esprit des Lois," book XI, Chap IV) Here are the words of the law of Aug. 24, 1790: "The functions of the judiciary are distinct and shall always remain separate from the administrative functions. The judges shall not, under penalty of forfeiture, interfere, in any manner whatsoever, with the acts of the administrative staff, nor cite before them any administrator for any exercise of his office" (Tit II, art 13) Thus understood, the separation of powers amounts to freeing the executive from the control of the authority of the judiciary, — a result, however, which is the best protection for the rights of the citizens.

The Constituent Assembly enacted the first written *constitution* of France, that of Sept. 3–14, 1791, preceded by the Declaration of the Rights of Man and of the Citizen Let us also recall, merely to note it, the *civil constitution of the clergy*, which came to nothing (Law of July 12–Aug. 24, 1790) Besides these, the Assembly passed a great number of acts bearing on public law, dealing with the greatest variety of subjects.

In the field of *private law*, the Assembly legislated only on particular topics, almost all of which can be connected with two principal reforms. The first is the *enfranchisement of the soil* and the *reorganization of property-rights.* Feudalism had overburdened the land with all sorts of dues, rent-charges, quit-rents, tithes, etc ; the right of ownership, originally simple and undivided, had been separated into the beneficial ownership and the direct or superior ownership; rights inalienable and irredeemable were everywhere met with; powers of repurchase by relatives hindered the transmission of property. All this mass of confused rights the Constituent Assembly entirely wiped out, ownership, now emancipated and disencumbered, became once more absolute and complete, like the Roman " dominium ", and this simple idea has so firmly entered our minds that to-day we have some difficulty in conceiving the state of affairs prior to 1789 The second reform was the introduction of the *principle of equality in the regulation of inheritances.* The manner in which the inheritance of individuals is regulated has a direct influence upon the political condition of a people. The spirit of nobility and aristocracy in old France rested fundamentally on the law of succession. The noble houses, supported neither by trade nor by industry, preserved their fortune only by means of the privileges of the male line and of primogeniture, which compelled the younger sons to enter holy orders or to embark upon a military career The Constituent Assembly, to effect the parcelling of the great estates, did away with the right of primogeniture and all other privileges of succession, and proclaimed the principle of equal partition among children (Decree of April 8, 1791). Among the other reforms effected by the Constitutent Assembly may be noted the liberty of lending at interest (Oct. 3–12, 1789), liberty of the right of hunting, now given to owners over their own lands (April 28–30, 1790), abolition of the State's right to the property of a deceased alien (Aug 6–18, 1790); letters patent for industrial inventions (Dec. 31, 1790–Jan. 7, 1791), and finally the Rural Code (Sept 28–Oct 6, 1791).

2d *The Legislative Assembly* (Sept. 30, 1791–Sept. 21, 1792) When the Assembly was dissolved (Sept. 21, 1792), it had not sat quite a year, but had passed some noteworthy laws · the institution of adoption (Jan. 18, 1792); the abolition of entails (Aug. 25, 1792); the fixing of majority at the age of twenty-one years, and the suppression of the paternal power over children who had come of age (Sept. 20, 1792), the creation of " civil status " for all persons, — a reform which " secularized " marriage and made it thenceforth a mere contract under the civil law, the institution of divorce (Sept. 20, 1792).

3d *The Convention* (Sept. 21, 1792–Oct. 26, 1795). Amidst the storms which encompassed it and in spite of its disorder and violence, the Convention found time to pass a number of measures dealing with private law. We may mention among the most important. *a* A law of 17 Nivôse, year II (Jan. 6, 1794), upon successions. By this celebrated law the members of the Convention sought primarily to attach future generations to the order of things created by the Revolution This they accomplished by enacting that the family property should descend by preference to the youngest members of those families The law of succession was also affected by the Decree of 5 Brumaire, year II (Oct. 26, 1793), dealing with the illegal clauses inserted in gifts and legacies, and the Decree of 12 Brumaire, year II (Nov 2, 1793), dealing with the succession of illegitimate children, who were placed upon the same footing as legitimate children *b* A law dealing with mortgages, 9 Messidor, year III (June 27, 1795), called "Code hypothécaire" Though poorly planned as to details and defective in its system, which paralyzed legal distraint and execution, this law is a very remarkable one, it contained some excellent ideas on the system of mortgages, and its boldest innovation, the acknowledgments of mortgages, has been taken up again and imitated in our own time in various countries. *c.* The law of 3 Brumaire, year IV, called "Code of Offences and Punishments," a long text of over six hundred articles, took the place of the two Codes on the same subject passed by the Constituent Assembly in 1791.

4th *The Directory* (Oct 27, 1796–Nov. 9, 1799). In spite of its corruptness and its impotence, the Directory exercised a fortunate influence upon civil legislation It amended several of the extreme or vexatious provisions of the Legislative Assembly and the Convention. Thus, divorce, which the Legislative Assembly had permitted with too great ease, was more strictly regulated (Law of the 1st complementary day, year V, Sept. 17, 1797), arrest was restored as a measure to compel the payment of debts (24 Ventôse, year IV, 4 Germinal and 4 Floréal, year IV), the rights of succession of illegitimate children were restricted, and retroactive effect was taken from the law which had conferred these rights upon them (15 Thermidor, year V; Aug 5, 1796), the complications which had been caused by the Convention's laws on succession were settled and lessened (18 Pluviôse, year V; Feb. 6, 1797). The Directory also undertook several original reforms. The two principal ones are: 1. The law of 11 Brumaire, which provided for publicly recording transfers of immovables, — an excellent provision, which was misguidedly abandoned in the Civil Code and had to be restored in our own day (Law of March 23, 1855). 2d The law of 22 Frimaire, year VII, on registration and the tax on transfer of rights, which is still in force.

§ 35 **The Preparation and Enactment of the Code Napoleon.** — The Code Napoleon was the final realization of a dream which had many times inspired the jurists of the prior centuries.

(1) *Prior Plans for the Unification of the Law.* — Louis XI is said to have planned a uniform code for all France; Charles Dumoulin had advocated one. The States-General of 1560 had voted, and the king then promised, to compile one; but nothing came of it. Brisson's work, published in 1603 (*ante*, § 30) never received official sanction. The States-General had again twice recommended a code, in 1576, and in 1614, but to no purpose Under Louis XIV, Colbert had large plans; but the Ordinances of Civil Procedure, Criminal Procedure, Waters and Forests, Commerce, and Maritime Law (1667–1681) were the extent of his achievements. Chief President Lamoignon, in 1672, compiled an incomplete and unofficial work. Chancellor D'Aguesseau drafted three Ordinances (*ante*, § 31) in 1731–1747, which were thorough codifications, on the topics covered, and were in large part adopted by the drafts of the Code Napoleon; but D'Aguesseau's larger dream of a complete code never matured. Except for the Ordinances above named, the private law of France was still in the 1700 s what it had been in the 1400 s, — a bundle of small parcels of law independent of each other. In Voltaire's phrase, the traveler changed his law as often as he changed horses. No vigorous effort had ever been made, under the Old Régime, to unify the law. Royalty had little interest in the subject; chancellors and ministers had not time or energy to spare, adequate for success in such an undertaking. The great obstruction was the tradition of local independence and the spirit of opposition in the provinces Laurent has pointed out, with truth, that their very lack of political independence and liberty made the provinces cling to their Customs as precious privileges Every attempt at innovation was repulsed by the provincial Parliaments, the natural guardians of local law; in certain districts (Brittany, for example) the least proposal of reform was treated as a violation of the original compact by which they had become united to the crown of France. Nothing could avail, short of violence to the Parliaments themselves. When the

Revolution swept them away, with all the other institutions of the monarchy, the path to unification was clear, and for the first time.

The first national political assembly under the Revolution, the Constituent Assembly, planned a codification of all the law of France. On Oct. 5, 1790, it voted that a general code should be made, and in the Constitution of 1791 the promise was renewed. But the Assembly never had the time to undertake the task. The next body, the Legislative Assembly (1791), took some inchoate steps; but its brief and troubled career permitted nothing further. Then came the Convention (1792–1795) with a plan for a Civil Code. It gave to its committee on legislation the remarkable order to present a draft within one month, and (still more remarkable) this order was obeyed. In August, 1793, CAMBACÉRÈS, in the name of the committee, presented the convention with a plan for a Civil Code This plan was remarkable for its excessive brevity, there was only one article for certificates of civil status, only one for domicile, and the rest in proportion; the whole consisted of six hundred and ninety-five articles. Such a Code would have been very dangerous, for many important points were not touched upon, and judges would have found themselves without guidance and without control This feature of it, however, was deliberately adopted by its drafters The Convention professed a profound contempt for the Roman law and the Customary law, which they looked upon as barbarian and degenerate systems. They aimed (says Barrère) to realize the dream of philosophers — to make the laws simple, democratic, and accessible to every citizen. Besides this defect in form, Cambacérès' draft was too much inspired by the revolutionary ideas of the day. However, the Convention did not find it revolutionary enough to suit its taste; it rejected the draft and voted to appoint a commission of philosophers, charged with drawing up a new draft, more in conformity with its own spirit (Decree of Nov. 3, 1793). Fortunately other events distracted its attention, and nothing further was heard of this project. During the second period of the Convention, after the downfall of Robespierre, Cambacérès brought in a second draft (23 Fructidor, year II), which came up for debate; a few articles were passed, but it got no farther This second draft was even shorter than the first one, it had only two hundred and ninety-seven articles, all worded very briefly Finally the Directory, in its turn, set its hand to a Civil Code A draft was reported by Cambacérès to the Council of Five Hundred (24 Prairial, year VI;

1798); but it never came up for discussion, because of the partisan dissensions in the two Assemblies.

(2) *The Drafting of the Civil Code, under the Consulate* — What neither the Old Monarchy nor the Revolution had been able to do the ambition of a single man achieved. Bonaparte, now First Consul and the all-powerful ruler of the State, formed the plan of giving to France that Civil Code which had so long and so fruitlessly been promised. And he was a man who knew how to succeed As early as 24 Thermidor, year VIII (Aug 13, 1800), he appointed a commission of four members to prepare a draft. These four members were: TRONCHET, president of the Court of Cassation; BIGOT DU PRÉAMENEUX, government commissioner in that court; PORTALIS, government commissioner in the Prize Court; MALLEVILLE, a judge of the Court of Cassation. The commission met at the house of President Tronchet; it divided up the various subjects among its members, each one to draft a portion; at the end of four months the draft was finished. This is the draft known as the "Draft of Year VIII," and was printed by Fenet It differs considerably from the final plan which was submitted to the Tribunate of 1801. This draft was submitted to the Court of Cassation and the Court of Appeal, whose comments were often noteworthy (especially those of the Court of Cassation), and were a useful contribution towards the preparation of the text. The courts quickly sent in their comments; it was well known that Bonaparte wished despatch; to please him they made haste, so much so that the debates on the Code in the public bodies began that same year.

In order to understand what then took place a few details are here necessary. The Constitution then in force was that of 22 Frimaire, year VIII (Dec. 13, 1799), enacted by the Consulate and continued (except for a few modifications) during the whole time of the Empire. By it, the legislative power was distributed among four different bodies · the Council of State, the Tribunate, the Legislative Body, and the Conservatory Senate. 1st. The *Council of State*, consisting of eighty members appointed by the First Consul, and divided into five sections, legislation, interior, finance, war, and navy, was charged with the discussion of all legislative bills. These were first drafted by the appropriate section (ordinarily the section on legislation), and were then studied in the general session of the Council, which could be convoked only by the First Consul and was usually presided over by him The Council of State did not enact a law; its draft was sent to the

281

First Consul, who could either introduce it for legislation or
else abandon it; *i e* he alone had the initiative in laws   When
he wished thus to have a bill introduced, the First Consul appointed
three councillors of State, as commissioners to support it in the
Legislative body, the commissioner first appointed drew up a
" Statement of Reasons "   2d The *Tribunate* was composed of one
hundred members, appointed by the Senate   It debated the bills
prepared by the Council of State and introduced by the government, but it could neither enact them nor even amend them; it
was limited to passing a resolution on the whole bill, either for or
against, and the Tribunate then appointed three commissioners
to uphold its opinion before the Legislative Body   3d The
Legislative Body had three hundred members, chosen by the Senate
from lists proposed by a special and separate electoral body.   It
was this Legislative Body which enacted the laws; yet it did not
debate them   They were debated in its presence by the three
government commissioners (Councillors of State) and the three
Tribunate delegates   This peculiar part played by this body led
to a nickname, the " Body of Mutes."   Moreover, it had no right
whatever of amendment; it could only adopt or reject as a whole
the bill presented to it.   4th. The *Conservatory Senate* was composed
of irremovable members elected by their own number   It took no
part in the making of a law, it was merely to see that the Constitution was observed, by annulling any unconstitutional acts
which might be submitted to it by the Tribunate

Such was the complicated machinery by which the Civil Code
was enacted   But not without struggle, for serious difficulties
arose which nearly put an end to the whole project   The Tribunate numbered in its ranks many partisans of the Revolution,
who made parliamentary war on all the plans of the First Consul.
Naturally, when the draft of the Code was submitted to this body,
there arose a chorus of criticism.   It was argued that this draft
was merely a servile imitation of the Roman and Customary law;
that it was a vapid compilation, devoid of originality and fatu-
ously decorated with the title " Civil Code of the French "   Portalis very soundly retorted that this was a matter not requiring
originality, but rather clearness, for the contemplated legislation
did not apply to a new people, but to a society more than ten centuries old and still preserving, in spite of the Revolution, many of
its habits and much of its old character   The republicans in the
Tribunate opposed the Civil Code with the view of being as dis-
agreeable as possible to the First Consul   The Legislative Body

had already rejected the first title, and, at the request of the Tribunate, was about to reject the second also, when after a stormy debate there arrived a message from the First Consul, couched in the following terms: "Legislators, the government has decided to withdraw the legal drafts of the Civil Code   It regretfully finds itself compelled to defer until another time the laws which the nation awaits with interest, but is convinced that the time has not yet arrived when that calmness and unity of purpose which they require can be employed in these important discussions" (13 Nivôse, year X, Jan. 3, 1802)   In withdrawing its draft the government aim was, as Portalis said, "to put the Tribunate on a diet"   The debate was suspended   This was what the Tribunate desired, but it did not satisfy Bonaparte.   To gain his end and to renew the debate with the certainty of success, he resorted to a sort of "coup d'état."   He made the Tribunate impotent to harm his projects by eliminating those of its members who were hostile to himself; a Senate Decree of 16 Thermidor, year X, reduced the Tribunate to fifty members, and naturally those who were thus left out were not his friends.   Further to weaken this body, it was divided into three sections   legislation, internal affairs, and finances.   In this way it became an easy matter to obtain a favorable vote   As a further precaution, measures were taken to ascertain the opinion of the Tribunate before the public debate took place; the Council of State communicated to the Tribunate "semiofficially and confidentially" the draft elaborated by itself; the Tribunate studied it, gave its opinion, and then the draft went back to the Council of State to consider the criticisms of the Tribunate.   If necessary, the legislative section of the Council conferred directly with the Tribunate's committee until an agreement should be reached.   This was called the "semiofficial communication."   When the Council of State and the Tribunate had come to an understanding, the draft was sent by the Council of State to the Legislative Body, who transmitted it to the Tribunate, in conformity with the Constitution   this was the "official communication."   Under these conditions the public debate before the Legislative Body, by the speakers of the Council of State and of the Tribunate, was no longer a test to be feared; it was nothing but a formality.

(3) *The Enactment of the Code.* — The Civil Code draft consisted of thirty-six laws, these were voted and put into force, one after another, from March, 1803, to March, 1804   They were then united into a single Code of twenty-two hundred and eighty-one

Articles, under the name of "Civil Code of the French," by the
law of 30 Ventôse, year XII (Mar 21, 1804), the definitive date
of the final enactment of the Code.

(4) *Repeal of the Old Law* — The law of 30 Ventôse, year XII,
which united the thirty-six laws of the Civil Code into a single
text, contains in Article 7 this provision: "From the day when
these laws go into effect, the Roman laws, the Ordinances, the
local or general Customs, the Statutes, and the Regulations shall
cease to have the force of either general or special laws, on the
matters dealt with in the aforesaid laws composing the Civil Code."
What was the meaning of this provision? Without this Article,
the old law would be by implication repealed, but only in those
cases where the text of the Code disagreed with it, it would continue on all the points upon which the old rules should be reconcilable with the new law. These points might perhaps be many,
and consequently we should still find, partly preserved until our
own period, the diversity which existed in the old provinces. Now
it was this very diversity which they were anxious to do away with,
that unity of law might be established Hence this Article 7 decreed *expressly* the repeal of the old law as a whole.

We must not, however, exaggerate its effect. Two limitations
must be pointed out 1st Article 7 only applies to the *old law*,
not to the *intermediate law* which had been in force since June, 1789
The latter continued to exist on principle, except naturally where
specific provisions were inconsistent with those of the Code.
Thus a large number of the rules of the intermediate law disappeared, more especially the system of succession and that of mortgages On the other hand, to make up for this, certain provisions
of the Rural Code of 1791 were embodied in the Civil Code 2d.
The old law itself was repealed only for *subjects with which the
Civil Code dealt* Hence, on any subject in private law not dealt
with in the Civil Code, one might still resort to the old law (unless
there were in the intermediate law some rule on that subject);
while the old rules not reconcilable with the general provisions of
the Code would be impliedly repealed.[1]

---

[1] BIBLIOGRAPHY OF THE DRAFT WORK The two collections ordinarily
used are that of *Fenet*, "Recueil complet des travaux préparatoires" (1827–
1828, 15 vols), and *Locre*, "Législation civile, commerciale, et criminelle
de la France" (1827–1832, 31 vols) In the latter collection the first
sixteen volumes deal with the Code Napoleon, Locré has omitted the
comments by the Courts, which are included by Fenet One may also
consult *Malleville*, "Analyse raisoneé de la discussion du droit civil"
(4 vols 1804–1805, 3d ed 1822), and *Portalis*, "Discours, rapports, et
travaux inédits sur le Code civil," published by his grandson in 1845

(5) *Various Names borne by the Code.* — The Civil Code has had its name changed several times. It was first published under the name " Code civil des Français." The law of Sept. 3, 1807 gave it the title " Code Napoléon." The Charters of 1814 and 1830 restored its original name   A Decree of March 27, 1852, re-established the title of " Code Napoléon," " in order to defer to the historic truth," said the framer of the Decree. However, since the year 1870, universal usage (following that of the government) terms it merely " Code civil " To-day the term " Code Napoléon " is more suitably used to designate the original form of the Code, in contrast with its existing form, which is appreciably different.

§ 36. **Character and Contents of the Code Napoleon** — (1) *Its Plan.* Following an old custom which dates back to the Roman Codes, modern Codes are divided into " books," and the books are subdivided into " titles ", each title deals with a special subject, marriage, paternal power, successions, sale, etc   The French Code consists of a preliminary title and three books. The preliminary title has only six articles   They are general provisions as to the time of taking effect and the application of laws   These six articles are the remains of a much greater number which Portalis had placed there, — an entire book consisting of six titles. This preliminary title was almost entirely cut out, only six out of its thirty-nine articles being preserved; most of them embodied doctrinal opinions or philosophical assertions rather than enactments of a legislative nature. Book I is entitled " Persons," and contains Articles 7 to 515   It deals with the distinction between Frenchmen and foreigners, the status of foreigners residing in France; with certificates of civil status, and domicile. There follow marriage, divorce and separation, filiation, the paternal power, guardianship, emancipation, incapacities, and the family council   Book II, Articles 516 to 710, concerns " Property," with its various sorts, ownership, usufruct, and servitudes. Book III is more than twice as long as the others put together (Articles 711 to 2281). Its title is somewhat vague. " Of the Various Methods of acquiring Ownership " In reality, it covers seven broad subjects: successions, gifts and wills, general theory of obligations, rules for particular kinds of contracts, matrimonial property-sys-

The "Procès-verbaux du Conseil d'Etat " had been published officially but incompletely (Paris, year X–XII, 5 vols). Another publication, less complete than those of Fenet and Locré, had been made under the Empire by *Favard de Langlade* (10 vols. 1804–1820, 4th ed, 1838).

tems, hens and mortgages, and prescription. The massing of all these diverse subjects in a single book is scarcely logical. Moreover, the division into books is itself inapt, a single series of titles would have been more simple and would have allowed of making any addition which might become necessary.

(2) *Its Sources.* The sources made use of in the compilation of the Civil Code were very diverse The principal ones were the Customs (especially the " Coutume de Paris "), the Roman law, the Royal Ordinances, and the Revolutionary Laws

The *Customary law* furnished most of the provisions dealing with the disabilities of married women, the community of possessions between spouses, and a number of the rules as to succession. The *Roman law* served especially for the system of ownership, the general rules for obligations, the rules for particular kinds of contracts, and the marriage-portion system. The *Royal Ordinances* were preserved especially in the articles concerning certificates of civil status (Ord. of April, 1667), gifts, wills, and entails (Ord of D'Aguesseau, 1731, 1735, and 1747), evidence (Ord. of Moulins, of 1566, and Ord of April, 1667), and redemption of mortgages (Edict of 1771). The *Revolutionary Laws* were preserved chiefly for the time of majority, marriage, and the system of mortgages.

To these four sources, the most abundant, we must add two other secondary ones   The *decisions of the old Parliaments* furnished the entire parts dealing with absence, this affected materially certain parts based on the Roman law, for example, the marriage-portion system, modified by the addition of a partnership in acquests   The *Canon law* supplied several of the rules upon marriage and legitimation [1]

Predominance of the Customary Sources. — There were two general currents of law at the time of the unification of the French law. the Roman spirit and the Customary traditions.   It was the latter that prevailed   The Code was drafted in Paris, in the very centre of the countries of Customs; most of the Councillors of State came from the provinces of the North, the Parliament of Paris had played a preponderating part in the old law   There is therefore nothing astonishing in the predominance of the spirit of the Customs, the opposite would have been an historical anomaly. Yet the Customary character of the Code is materially weakened by the Roman law, on the one hand, and by the Revolutionary

[1] For further details, see   *Dard,* "Conférence du Code civil avec les lois anciennes." 4th ed. 1827,   *Dufour,* "Code civil avec les sources ou toutes ses dispositions ont été puisées," Paris, 1806, 4 vols. in 8vo.

ideas, on the other.   On only one important point did the Roman
law prevail, and even here not without difficulty; this was the
marriage-portion system, which was not only preserved, but extended to include the whole of France.

(3) *The Authors of the Code* — The two principal authors were
PORTALIS and TRONCHET.   Portalis was the philosopher of the
commission   He it was who inspired the principal doctrines of
the Civil Code, and was chosen to draw up the "Preliminary
Discourse"; his comments may be considered as the best   Possibly he has been too highly praised.   As a philosopher, he certainly did not possess an original mind; he attained only the heights
of mediocrity, and his style, filled with the phraseology of the
period, was soon antiquated.   But he was not a mere jurist; he
was an enlightened man, with an open mind, and a marked moderation; and it is for this that we should especially thank him.   He
and Malleville championed the Roman ideas, but without success,
against the traditions of the Customs, represented by Tronchet
and Bigot du Préameneu   Tronchet was a man of an entirely
different kind   He was twenty years older than Portalis (born
in Paris in 1726).   He was first and foremost a lawyer; he had
long practised before the Parliamentary Court of Paris, and was
experienced in practical affairs; he had been one of the counsel
defending Louis XVI.   His influence in the draft, though less
traceable and less brilliant than that of Portalis, was none the less
profound.   The First Consul used to say of him that he had been
the soul of the debates in the Council of State.

Alongside of these two men, one or two other names must be
mentioned· CAMBACÉRÈS, who had made a specialty of the preparation of drafts under the Convention and the Directory; his
rank of Second Consul alone prevented him from being a member
of Napoleon's Drafting Commission; TREILHARD, Councillor of
State, who played an exceptional part in the debates, and, finally,
BONAPARTE himself, whose personal share is deserving of more
particular mention [1]

The Part played by Bonaparte. — The First Consul was now only
thirty-two years old, much the youngest of the collaborators,
furthermore, he was a soldier and not a lawyer.   But he wished to
show himself the master, in this as in everything else.   He had

---

[1] For further details as to the personnel of the Legislature during this
period, see   *Gustave Bressolles*, "Étude sur les rédacteurs du Code civil"
("Revue Wolowski," 1852, XLIII, 357);   *Edmond de Beauverger*, "Étude
historique comparative sur la législation civile de la France" ("Acad.
des sciences morales," "Comptes rendus," 1861, LXI and LXII)

books lent him which he hastily ran through; he made speeches, which Tronchet and others helped him to prepare. His rôle as a jurist was naturally a minor one, but he reëstablished his primacy when it came to the debates, which he directed and led vigorously He excelled in the ability to settle with a single word a discussion which was going astray or becoming obscure. His phrases, his jokes, were often keen, always those of a soldier. The official minutes have eliminated all these eccentricities of speech, and give him a colorless style, almost academic, but his actual language has been preserved to us (in fragments) in certain contemporary memoirs of the Councillor of State Thibaudeau [1]

The personal influence of Bonaparte is found in several parts of the Code. 1st He introduced into it a set of detailed regulations on the *civil status of soldiers* (Arts. 93–98), certainly out of place in a Civil Code But he had noticed during his campaigns the deficiencies of the law on that subject, and he seized the first chance to remedy them 2d. He showed himself *hostile to foreigners*, whom he disliked, as a soldier, he saw in them only enemies Under his influence, the Civil Code in its final form showed them extreme harshness, — refusing them in general the enjoyment of civil rights (Art. 11), declaring them incapable of inheriting (Art. 726) and of receiving gifts or legacies (Art 912) The extremeness of these provisions served the purposes of the hostile faction in the Tribunate, and it was Article 11 which caused the failure of the first title before the Legislative Body. Though Bonaparte succeeded in having it adopted (at what cost and by what means has been seen above), we have since then had to revoke our course, and to return approximately to the original "Draft of the Year VIII" 3d And finally, to Bonaparte was due the insertion of the two institutions of *adoption* and *divorce by mutual consent*. He did this on grounds of policy, without children by Josephine Beauharnais, yet already contemplating a dynasty, he placed in our laws (as it were, in reserve) this double means of obtaining an heir, by either another marriage, or an adoption His own divorce, followed by his marriage to Marie-Louise and the birth of the King of Rome, relieved him from resorting to the second means. It is said that he even suppressed the minutes of debate on adoption, that no one

[1] "Mémoires sur le Consulat," 1826, a work now scarce Compare also in the "Archives," by *Goenner*, a dissertation upon the personal part played by Napoleon in the preparation of the Code See also *Thiers*, "Histoire du Consulat et de l'Empire," vol III , *E Jac.* "Bonaparte et le Code civil," 1898.

might ever learn what he had there uttered. On some points his influence may seem to have been unfortunate. But how small a price for the rest? His all-powerful will was the lever removing all obstacles His energy and (why ignore it?) his ambition were the instruments to which we owe the achievement of the great task, — a task which had been unfulfilled for centuries, and, but for him, might still in our own day have remained undone. And he greatly valued his title of legislator. At St. Helena, he wrote " My true glory is not in having won forty battles; Waterloo will blot out the memory of those victories But nothing can blot out my Civil Code That will live eternally " (*De Montholon*, " Récit de la captivité de l'empéreur Napoleon," I, 401).

(4) *General Character of the Civil Code.* — The Code Napoleon had the good fortune to be enacted at just the right moment. Had it been made sooner, during the Revolution, it would have yielded too much to revolutionary passions, to political vagaries Had it been made later, no doubt it would have felt the rigors of the military rule and of the increasing reactionary spirit. The period of its legislators' labors happened to be one of calm and quiet, after so many excesses and crises of every kind, men's minds were in a state of relaxation. Those few years of the Consulate were thus an exceptionally favorable time for a temperate consideration of the civil law The Revolution had thrown France into a state of inconceivable unrest and confusion, and this was due quite as much to the weakness of the Directory as to the violence of the Convention. Uncertainty was everywhere; security of the person and of property were gone, commerce had almost come to a stand-still; legal transactions were reduced to a minimum. A civic lassitude was universal When the First Consul took the power into his own hands, he said (and everybody else believed with him) that the Revolution was "finished" (Proclamation of 24 Frimaire, year VIII); and later he expressed the belief that, after Marengo and the peace of Amiens, war had ended and peace was assured Nothing remained, therefore, but to gather the long wished-for fruits of the Revolution, — better laws for a society now rejuvenated in a sort of springtide (such as Germany experienced after 1871).

It is this happy concurrence of circumstances which gave to the Civil Code its dominant merit — that *spirit of moderation and of wisdom* which has secured its permanence for a century. The most varied political systems have been able to accommodate themselves to it, no one has dared to destroy it, — no one has even thought of such a thing. The Code Napoleon is in fact a settlement

by way of compromise It arose out of the Revolution, it kept the
spirit of equality, and did not seek to restore the principles of
the Old Régime; and this has endeared it to the great body of the
French people At the same time, it abandoned all the chimerical
ideas, all the violent measures, of the Revolutionary Assemblies.
It is thus neither reactionary nor revolutionary. For all these
reasons, it must not be lightly tampered with A sort of tacit
understanding now prevails, in enlightened public opinion, to
maintain it, and to make the fewest possible alterations No doubt
it should not be made a fetich Nor need we refer to it in tones
of dithyrambic rhapsody as was the fashion under the second
Empire, — an admiration simulated for political motives. But it
is to be feared that in a general revision of the Code the same
moderation and the spirit of wisdom which prevailed under the
Consulate might not again be manifested [1]

(5) *Merits of the Code* Besides the merits due to its general
spirit, the Code possesses certain technical qualities, due to excellent draftsmanship These qualities are *unity, system, precision,*
and *clearness* Its *unity* is due to its being framed by a few men,
dominated by one preponderating will. The *system* adopted by
the authors of the Code, sometimes criticised as not scientific, is
nevertheless sound A scientific arrangement of topics, appropriate for lectures or books, is not necessary or even practicable in
a code. Legal instruction is an initiation, and calls for a special
method, a code is for practitioners who have already a knowledge
of the law Hence it suffices if the distribution of topics be clear
and convenient The *precision* and the *clearness* of detail, in the
phraseology of the articles, reached a grade which has never been
surpassed and very rarely equalled. Certainly the laws passed
in France since 1804 cannot bear comparison with the Code from
this point of view, in contrast, the limpidity of the Code Napoleon
becomes striking. — For all these exceptional merits, however,
our applause is due, not only to the men who drafted it, but just
as much, and perhaps more, to their predecessors who furnished
models for them, especially to Domat, a man of systematic and
truly logical mind; to D'Aguesseau, a conscientious worker, and
finally to Pothier, good, worthy Pothier, a mind of no pretensions
to brilliancy, but one ever sincere and a lover of clearness.

(6) *Defects of the Code.* — With all its good qualities, the Code
Napoleon is not without defects.[2] The imperfections of draft-

---

[1] [Passage here omitted — TRANSL]
[2] I am here speaking only of real defects The Code Napoleon was

ing, to be sure, — the articles useless, obscure, or inconsistent, — are so few as to be a negligible quantity in a total of almost twenty-three hundred articles; not a single other text, French or foreign, has fewer such faults than the Code. But certain topics were faultily dealt with in their substance. 1st, the *status of foreigners*, who were treated with excessive severity (*ante*, par. 3). This had to be amended, as early as 1819. 2d, the *marriage-portion system*. The spouses could adopt this without public notice, — a rule unfair to third parties, because of the inalienability of the wife's possessions. This defect was remedied in 1850. 3d, the *transfer of immovables*. The Revolution had initiated a system of publicity by registration. This the Code mistakenly abandoned, a few years later it was partly restored, by articles 834–835 of the Code of Civil Procedure. But only in 1855 did registration become once more compulsory. 4th, the *mortgage system*. This was the weakest spot in the Code; and the shortcomings of its framers were the less excusable as they had before their eyes (as also for land registration) superior models in the laws of the Revolution The mortgage system of the Civil Code has been amended several times, but is still far from being beyond criticism. It should be thoroughly brought up to date, for it is in this branch of civil law that the greatest progress has been made during the 1800 s. 5th, furthermore, the *lack of protection for the ownership of movables* is one of the defects of the Code. Upon this point, however, its framers are to be excused, wealth in movables was still in its infancy, and none could foresee the growth which it would attain under the form of corporate securities and other commercial instruments.

There were, besides this, certain topics, modern for the most part, and needing a place in civil laws, but omitted from the Code , and yet these gaps can hardly be charged to its framers' discredit, because of the modern origin of most of these principles. These include the *names of persons*, which give rise to numerous diffi-

---

attacked with fury, even in France, by certain political parties blinded by hatred of the Empire. Those whose ideals were the Decrees of the Convention could not help looking upon this Code with disdain , they felt it their duty to restore its original name of Code Napoleon and affect to call it "the Napoleonic compilation." This is a matter of taste and of partisan feeling. Abroad, also, the French Code was at one time much disparaged The German jurist *Savigny*, in his brochure, "Sur la vocation de notre temps," etc., took satisfaction in emphasizing the historical errors in certain of the debates by the Council of State; the framers of the Code, he said, talked and wrote like "dilettanti" (see the "Revue critique," 1886, vol. IX, p 349, n 1) His patriotism carried him too far. What if the framers of our laws were not learned historians like him ? They were statesmen wise and enlightened, jurists and practitioners well versed in affairs, and it was fortunate for France that they were.

culties; *artificial* or *legal persons*, a sort of fictitious entity, whose existence the Code assumes, but whose nature and attributes are nowhere settled, except for a few isolated and fragmentary provisions, hard to reconcile, the *long-term lease* (emphyteusis), which the Code had passed over in silence, — perhaps intending to abolish it, the Courts had preserved it, and a special law of 1902 regulated it, *literary and artistic property*, etc , now covered by special laws, the *bankruptcy of persons not traders,* which was entirely left out, except for some inadequate provisions for the death of the insolvent, *ministerial offices*, a sort of special property, established in 1816, *bills to bearer,* a form of paper often used for non-commercial claims; the *insurance contract, syndicates,* though mentioned for purposes of administrative supervision, were left unregulated as to the exercise of their powers, their relations with their members and with third parties, their responsibility, etc

§ 37 **The Empire and the Other Codes.** — The great effort for codification, culminating under the Consulate in its most important work, the Civil Code, was continued under the Empire   Napoleon gave us four other codes in all   The *Code of Civil Procedure* was put into force Jan. 1, 1807 (Art 1047). The *Commercial Code* was finished Aug. 29, 1807, and went into effect Jan. 1, 1808 The *Code of Criminal Procedure* was passed in 1808, and the *Penal Code* in 1810, both going into effect Jan. 1, 1811, after the reorganization of the magistracy by the law of April 20, 1810 [1]

Their Relative Inferiority — These four Codes are very inferior to the Civil Code   Of the two Criminal Codes, one is as faulty as the other.   Our criminal trial system, much out of date, is open to many criticisms, and there is some question of recasting it from top to bottom   Pending this vast undertaking, it has already been amended in important respects.   The system of penalties established under the Empire was far too severe and inflexible, and has been improved on several occasions, especially in 1832 and 1863 The Code of Civil Procedure also calls for numerous reforms, the practice is too costly, the delays are too long, the forms are out of date, only the lawyers are satisfied with it   As to the Commercial Code, it was entirely inadequate   On most points the legislators had limited themselves to a reproduction of the Ordinance of 1673 (on commerce) and that of 1681 (on maritime commerce).   Only

---

[1] As to these Codes, see   *Séruzier,* "Précis historique de la législation française," 1845   As to the Code of Procedure in particular   *Albert Tissier,* "Le centenaire du Code de procédure et des projets de réforme" ("Revue trimestrielle," 1906)

its provisions upon bankruptcy were new, but these were poorly drafted, and had to be recast in 1838. Many important laws have since been enacted on commerce, independently of the Code, on topics such as commercial partnerships, checks, warehouses, maritime mortgage, collisions, etc. In spite of these, our commercial law is very much behind the times Colbert's laws, more than two centuries old, still form its basis, and yet since then commercial methods have made rapid strides and have altered to an extent as complete as it was unforeseen.

Causes of this Inferiority. — Thus, between the Civil Code and the other Napoleonic Codes, we find a great difference of value. How is this to be accounted for ? The truth is that the drafting of the Civil Code was done in advance. Tronchet, Portalis, and the other drafting commissioners and councillors were not its only authors, long before them, our best jurists formed a host of illustrious collaborators who had already facilitated the task in an extraordinary degree. The drafting of a good code, like the Code Napoleon, is indeed only the result of the accumulated labors of several generations. On the other hand, for the other Imperial Codes there were few models to follow, or none at all; and the few were either incomplete or antiquated — quite unsuited to the needs of the new era Furthermore, critical legal science had given no help, for there were no texts to work upon Finally, the other codes were not drafted by competent persons, as was the Civil Code, nor were they prepared with the same care, the Commercial Code especially was a hasty piece of work. These circumstances should inspire hesitation in reformers who would improvise laws in a few hours Good legislation is the work of time

TOPIC 2. THE CIVIL LAW SINCE THE CODIFICATION

Formation of a New Body of Law — The life of the law never ceases All legislators mistakenly believe that their codifications will arrest its changes; perhaps this delusion was Napoleon's as well as Justinian's. Nevertheless, year by year, and almost day by day, the law changes , the Code Napoleon has in the course of time been covered by a fresh vegetation (so to speak), which is little by little transforming its nature. In reviewing the effects of this incessant process of modification, we must take up separately the work of the legislature, of the courts, and of the jurists.

§ 38. **Legislation since 1804.** — *The Influence of Political Changes.*

— The trend of legislation keeps pace, naturally and directly, with the changes occurring in the State's organization and its political orientation. Our civil legislation, studied in its development since 1804, would enable us to reconstruct the political history of France from a special and interesting point of view. We may now examine the influence of each of the successive political systems upon our civil law.

(A) *The Empire.* — The great effort at codification, producing five codes in less than six years, seems to have exhausted the legislative fertility of the Imperial system. Of the few special laws on civil topics we note only the important Concordat of 26 Messidor, year IX (July 15, 1801), concluded between Bonaparte and Pope Pius VII, followed by a law of 18 Germinal, year X (April 8, 1802), on *religious sects;* and the law on the organization of the *judiciary* (April 20, 1810).

(B) *The Restoration.* — This was for France, exhausted by so many wars and defeats, a period of rest and calm, almost sterile in legislation. Among the few reactionary statutes, the two most noteworthy were the *Sunday observance* law (Nov. 18, 1814), due to the new status, under the Charter of 1814, of Roman Catholicism as the State religion, and the law (May 8, 1819), abolishing *divorce* as contrary to the precepts of the Catholic religion. During the final years of this period, the aristocratic spirit which led the monarchy to its ultimate downfall produced the law (May 17, 1826) for entails, intended to preserve the wealth of the great families, and the bill (which came to nothing) for the *reestablishment of the right of primogeniture.*

(C) *Louis-Philippe.* — The Revolution of 1830 led to a great change in the world of politics. To the aristocracy of family, which had dominated under the "legitimist" Monarchy, there now succeeded a rich bourgeoisie; the great landowners, living upon incomes derived from agriculture, were replaced by great capitalists belonging to the world of commerce and industry. As a consequence, industrial interests took first place and supplanted agrarian interests. Their triumph was assured by the development of industrial enterprises organized on a large scale, dating from this period especially, and leaving its legal traces in the remarkable development of commercial corporations. The Monarchy of July was thus a reign of manufacturers, a little industrial oligarchy, serving as a transition from the absolute monarchy, in which the aristocracy had preponderated, to the Revolution of 1848, which handed power to the mass of small farmers and workingmen.

Nothing better reveals this characteristic of Louis-Philippe's reign than its legislation. The laws become much more numerous, — an increase due especially to two causes. The first was a greater *political freedom* for the press and the Legislative Chambers. Questions of every sort were discussed, the attention of the general public began to be aroused by the newspapers upon topics which formerly were indifferent to them. The second cause was an entirely new development of *economic activity* The Revolution and the Empire had almost ruined France. Commerce and industry, flourishing under Louis XVI, had seriously fallen off. From 1789 to 1815, riots, disorders, and wars had brought everything to a standstill. At sea, we no longer existed, so to speak; the continental blockade, the loss of our colonies, the battle of Trafalgar, had wiped out our navy On land the men were all away with the army, and this accounts for the apparent economic contradiction that under the Empire, in spite of the industrial and commercial downfall of France, wages remained at a very high rate, the reason for this was simple. not enough workmen could be found to do even the necessary work; the war had emptied every occupation. Under the Restoration, work was revived, but slowly; France was too weakened to recover quickly. Its recuperation finally arrived under Louis-Philippe; and steam machinery and railroads transformed and developed commerce and industry in an altogether unforeseen manner — These great causes thus contributed to increase the activity of the legislative power, — the *liberal movement in politics* and the *economic progress*.

(D) *The Second Republic.* — This short period (Feb 24, 1848, to Dec. 2, 1851) marks a decisive epoch in our history, with the introduction of universal suffrage, which has entirely shifted political power and changed the objects of legislation. The consequences of this great event are still unfolding before our eyes, and we cannot yet foresee where they will end. The Revolution had been achieved by the workingmen of Paris; overnight they found themselves masters of the situation. For the first year or two, questions bearing on industrial labor chiefly occupied the legislator

Then came the reactionary Assembly of 1849–1851, followed by the Prince President's "coup d'état" of December, and

(E) *The Second Empire.* — Nothing is more curious than the political evolution of the Second Empire. It was a system at once autocratic and democratic; it depended for its support upon the army, because it owed its power to a military "coup d'état";

and it rested also upon universal suffrage, for the imperial system found a firm support in the rural districts. Various economic conditions favored it. Some were accidental, such as the abundance of gold coming from California, and the completion of the great network of railways. Others were the work of the government, such as the letting down of tariff barriers by commercial treaties Grain and cattle could find a ready market, small agricultural products (fruits, vegetables, poultry, and eggs), which formerly had no outlet, were distributed by the railroads to the large cities, and gave prosperity to the country. But this relief did not reach the workingmen.   At a very early period, the Imperial government sought to reconcile to itself the sentiments of the working classes by all sorts of small favors, in this effort it failed, that portion of the population remained " irreconcilable," a word which became the fashion. Towards the end, a series of legislative measures changed the political system, originally entirely military, into one of semi-liberty

This political change in the Empire is clearly marked in its legislation; for everything depends upon the general trend of ideas, and the law, even in its most abstract parts, shares in the general life of the country. During its first years, the imperial government pursued a course of radical hostility to the workingmen (Laws of June 1, 1853, June 22, 1854) But after 1855, a great change in opinion took place. Numerous writers devoted themselves to the labor question, — notably Le Play (1854) and Jules Simon (1859–1866); and the penny newspapers, an innovation of the times, carried their ideas to the masses The Empire was compelled to follow this movement, and to relax its severity Markedly after 1868, it became a *Liberal Empire* (Law of May 11, 1868, on the press, Law of June 6, 1868, on the right of meetings), and it now began to tolerate workingmen's associations in every form

The general civil legislation is represented by a small number of important laws, — principally the law (March 23, 1855) for land-transfer registration, the final result of a thorough investigation undertaken in 1841 but a far more restricted reform than the one originally hoped for.

(F) *The Third Republic*   (1) *General Tendencies.* — Proclaimed at Paris, September 4, 1870, the day after the disaster of Sedan, the Republic was resisted until 1875; for the monarchic party hoped to restore royalty, especially after the "fusion," or reconciliation, between the Orléans family and the Comte de Chambord; but the check given to their attempt led to the Constitution of

February, 1875   Under the Republic two periods may be distinguished. The first lasted about ten years, from 1871 to 1880. The majority in the Legislatures belonged still to the different monarchic and conservative parties, united against the Republican party. Not until after the senatorial elections of 1879 did the Republican party obtain a majority in both Senate and Chamber of Deputies. This event reacted directly upon legislation From 1870 to 1880 the new laws were not very numerous, the reforms were moderate, almost timid In 1880 things changed in aspect, the legislative power entered upon an era of almost excessive production, such as it had never known since the period from 1789 to 1793; the year 1898 was especially fertile.

But in the laws passed since 1880 what is especially noticeable is less their number than their spirit. The tendency of a legislative power based on universal suffrage is necessarily to favor the masses at the expense of the old governing classes. This tendency (much more marked since 1889, and especially in 1899, when Waldeck-Rousseau for the first time placed the Socialistic party in power through Millerand) is especially apparent in *labor questions* (syndicates, insurance, pensions, passbooks, cheap dwellings) and in *fiscal questions* (for certain political parties look upon taxation as an instrument of spoliation), but it makes itself felt even in matters of pure civil law, where so-called " labor laws " frequently derogate from the traditional rules. Principles which legal science may deem to rest upon the most solid foundations cannot resist these proposals of reform, and the new statutes modify the law in its lowest depths.

One more thing remains to be pointed out. Dominant opinion in France believes that it is carrying out the tradition of the Revolution and drawing its inspiration from the Constituent Assembly. Yet, in reality, our modern legislation departs day by day from the most essential one of these ideas. The Constituent Assembly destroyed a social organization arising from the most remote depths of our national history, and based chiefly upon the ideas of local independence and the coexistence of separate powers. In place of this system, the Constituent Assembly established a purely individualist system; it sought to assure men's liberties by their isolation. Its principal work was the destruction of all the old Bodies, communities, and associations of every kind, under whose protection flourished so many abuses. It was for this reason that the most liberal Assembly which France has ever had refused to give her what nowadays is regarded as the principal

liberty the *liberty of association.* Now, since 1848, we have seen
going on in France one of the most remarkable movements. The
local collective forces, which the Revolution had proscribed, are
being reconstructed on every hand. Some are due to individual
initiative, occupational syndicates, partnerships of every kind,
which the State not only tolerates but encourages. Others are
created by the government itself The modern State, overburdened with powers and duties, weighed down by its financial
burdens, gets rid of them, as far as it can, by imposing them upon
local groups; it leaves to themselves the departments, towns,
universities, chambers of commerce, etc.; there is even talk of
reestablishing (under the name of "regions") districts larger than
our departments, to be the equivalents of our old provinces, done
away with by the Constituent Assembly. Thus (unless to reconstruct old France is to attempt the impossible) the abandonment
of the guiding principles of the Revolution could not be more
absolute by those who profess to be the continuers of them. The
new conception of the State is no longer the omnipotence of a
central power (as the Constituent Assembly intended it), standing
alone in contrast with the individual citizens, — at once disarming
and protecting them, but sharing its powers with no rival. —
Naturally this great change is affecting mostly administrative and
economic matters, but the civil law itself is feeling the effects; the
spirit of collectivity, of mutuality, and of association, which is
awakening and sweeping everything before it, is penetrating deep
into the law and custom of contracts, of ownership, and of succession

(2) *Plans for revising the Civil Code.* — In spite of the numerous
statutes since 1804, the Code Napoleon still represents the greater
portion of our civil law Its entire revision was demanded at an
early period; but this movement found little response until, in
1904, at the celebration of the centennial of the Civil Code, the
Minister of Justice appointed a special commission to prepare a
first draft of a revision. Up to the present time the idea of a
general revision seems to find but a cool reception in the world of
business [1] We must hope that the method of partial amendments

---

[1] See *Planiol,* "Livre du centenaire," II, 953, and *Thaller,* "Rapport
sur la revision du Code civil" ("Bulletin de la Société d'études législatives,"
1904, p 472; *ibid*, 1905, p 24) The second volume of the "Livre du
centenaire" contains various studies on the desirability of a revision of the
Code As to the celebration in Paris, see the various Law Reviews, and
especially the "Bulletins" of the two Societies "d'études législatives" and
"de législation comparée" for 1904

will suffice for a long time to come   In truth, the modern method of drafting laws in large legislatures has an irremediable defect (as every one admits), namely, that the cross-currents of factional majorities destroy the consistency of the texts; and (more often than not) the legislative draftsmen lack in technical competency.[1] The Revision of the Codes is to be welcomed only if a legislative procedure is adopted which insures an adequate method of achievement — a method such as Spain and Germany employ.

§ 39. **Judicial Decisions.** — What we call " jurisprudence " is the interpretation and application of the law by the Courts. As compared with the legislator, the judge's part is in appearance a modest one, in reality, it is almost an equal one. Practically, no law has any value unless it is applied and then only to the extent that it is applied   One fact is universally recognized and inevitable, namely, that the application of the law by the judiciary furnishes a thousand opportunities to modify the rule of law, and that sometimes the judge even succeeds in paralyzing the will of the legislator.

Judicial law has characteristics peculiar to itself. It does not work like writers or teachers, who set forth their ideas in synthetic and coordinated form, constructing systems out of collections of topics. The Courts pass, from day to day, on sundry points submitted to them, — always matters of detail, or at least distinct from one another. Moreover, one of the chief rules of our judiciary requires that a court shall never be bound by the decisions it has previously handed down, it may always change its mind. All the more is it not bound by the decisions of other courts, even of higher courts (except that in certain cases the decisions of the Court of Cassation are binding). The result of all this is that there are great variances; judicial decisions are often contradictory to one another.

Nevertheless, in the end, judicial law always arrives at certain fixed rules, and this for two reasons. 1st. In case of a conflict between two courts, the Supreme Court (" Cour de Cassation ") has the last word. When a question of new and doubtful law arises upon which there are divergent opinions, the case can always be taken to the Supreme Court, and the latter may impose its view upon the other tribunals   2d. The judicial bodies, whatever they may be, have a tendency to create a tradition for themselves, to

---

[1] See *Varagnac*, "Le Conseil d'Etat et les projets de réforme," "Revue des Deux-Mondes," Sept 15, 1892, *Em Tarboureich*, "Du Conseil d'Etat comme organe législatif," "Revue de droit public," Sept –Oct, 1894, *Louis Michon*, "L'initiative parlementaire et la réforme du travail législatif," Paris, 1898

decide always in the same may, when they have once adopted an opinion Under these two influences (the one of fact, the other of law), we see veritable streams of judicial law, which can be neither resisted nor turned aside. The judicial rule is then said to be " fixed," or " made " This general phenomenon, well known to men of the law, leads the advocates at the " Palais de Justice " always carefully to search for prior decisions in their favor; the more they find, the more sure are they of winning And so (it is said) at the " Palais de Justice " the decisions are *counted*, whereas at the Law School they are *weighed*.

As to the general results of modern judicial law, we can here only offer an estimate of its work as a whole. And in general it may be said that judicial law has held a very uneven course in its interpretation of the texts. It has shown itself, by turns, very bold and very timid. It has sometimes believed itself so rigidly bound that it has ignored its powers for more useful or equitable decisions At other times, it has succeeded, by roundabout means, in paralyzing legislative rules which it regarded bad; some have even maintained that in boldness it has not yielded the palm to the vaunted reforms of the Roman Pretor.[1]

Another part of its task has been to regulate various matters which legislation had not expressly provided for, — the insurance of land, the relations between employers and workmen, the long-term lease, the publisher's contract, and the like

§ 40 **Legal Science** — Legal treatises and essays (" doctrine ") in the science of law play approximately the same part as public opinion in politics, and an important one. Legal science gives direction to the law; its teachings prepare the way for changes in legislation and decisions But even when it reaches settled views, legal science is not (like judicial decisions) a source of the law, for the commentators possess no means of constraint Nevertheless, their books and their oral teaching formulate scientific principles which dominate judges and legislators, this body of principles is known as " tradition "

In the course of the 1800s, legal science has undergone many

---

[1] *Tarboureich*, "Du Conseil d'Etat comme organe législatif," p. 3 *Cf Celice*, "Du pouvoir législatif de la Cour de cassation ou de la permanence du droit honoraire," speech on entering, Aix, 1888. One of the most striking examples has been its gradual evolution of the rule that State securities may be distrained upon, in spite of the laws of the year VI and the year VII which declared that they could not be ("Cass ," July 2 and 16, 1894, note by M *Glasson*, "Dalloz," 94, 1 497). One may also cite its progress on the subject of trust-entails as ably set forth by M. Lambert ("De l'exhérédation," p 593, *et seq.*).

changes both of tendency and of method.   During the 1600s and 1700s, the treatise writers, whether professors or magistrates, had not (as a general rule) elaborate texts to comment upon.   The Customs were for the most part very short; the principal one, the " Coutume de Paris," contained but three hundred and sixty-two articles   Furthermore, they dealt with only a few subjects; the longest Title in the " Coutume de Paris " treated of fiefs, succession was given forty-six articles, gifts seventeen, wills ten; while on these last three the Civil Code alone numbers almost four hundred articles.   Many articles in the Customs dealt with details of secondary importance, questions of form or of procedure. Hence arose a special method for the study of legal principles. A writer who aimed at something more than a mere summary of the decisions, and aspired to expound a system of principles, sought for these principles in the Roman law, for the Roman law alone possessed a scientific method and value.   This necessary method of the old treatises becomes more apparent as one passes from the mere compilations to the great works of the Dumoulins, the Argentrés, and the Domats, — all of them Romanists.

After the Civil Code appeared, things changed.   Thenceforth jurists possessed a text uniting within itself every quality which had up to that time belonged exclusively to the Roman legal system. It was complete and self-sufficient; it was clear and well drafted in true legislative style, — exact, concise, imperious, in contrast to the loose style of the old French in the Customs.   And, finally, it contained a legal system, new principles; it had its own peculiar spirit, its own particular tendencies.   Moreover, the materials prior to it could no longer be made use of, the decisions of the old courts had lost their authority.   Hence arose an entirely new method, for commentators upon the Civil Code; and their books have no resemblance to their predecessors'.   They set themselves to a study of the specific terms of the Civil Code.   The text took on an enormous importance, — one which that of the Ordinances and the Customs had never had.   As its articles were numerous, various correlations of them began to be made; by interpretation they were sometimes restricted, sometimes extended.   A whole system of close, clever, and ingenious reasoning arose, around the Code was constructed a scaffolding of complicated and unforeseen theories.   This state of legal science had never been known, apart from the texts of the Digest and Code of Justinian. — Besides all this, the first generation of commentators, men who had witnessed the downfall of the Old Régime and the renascence which followed, were the victims of a perfectly natural delusion. They looked upon the Code as something entirely new, having no connection with the past, they commented upon it by isolating it from everything else, as though it had fallen from the sky. Thus the new legal science, absorbed in the Code alone, and obsessed by a sort of superstitious belief in its text, came to apply in the study of the law a process entirely artificial and a method purely dogmatic.

This school of jurists, nevertheless, produced some remarkable works, it succeeded in drawing from the Code everything it could possibly give. Napoleon, indeed, jealous for his own work, would gladly have seen the commentators refrain from meddling with his Code. When he saw the first commentary (that of Malleville), he exclaimed: " My Code is lost! " But commentaries soon became numerous. Among them may be noted that of TOULLIER, Professor at Rennes, the first commentator upon the Civil Code (1811–1848), of DURANTON, Professor at Paris (1825–1844), a great success, the first long and complete work upon the Code Napoleon; of TROPLONG, undertaken in 1833 to continue that of Toullier, a performance more brilliant than solid, and once termed "the law's romance", and of MARCADÉ and PAUL PONT (1842+), a remarkable work, but marred by its polemic spirit. Among the general treatises of later vogue (not including recent works) were those of AUBRY and RAU, of DEMOLOMBE, of DEMANTE and COLMET DE SANTERRE, and of LAURENT.

TOPIC 3. THE CODE NAPOLEON IN OTHER COUNTRIES

§ 41. **Prior Codifications.** — Most other European States, until the 1800 s, had remained in about the same condition as France; they lived under national customs, of obscure and early origin, for the most part antiquated and complicated, and possessing on the whole no scientific principles save those of the Roman law. The first principal codifications took place in *Germany*. The Prussian Code was undertaken by Frederick II in 1749. Its draft was prepared, in 1749–1751, by the High Chancellor Samuel Von Cocceij, and published in three volumes. But Cocceij died in 1755, and the Seven Years' War put a stop to the work, which was not resumed till 1780, and was completed in 1793. The Code was published Feb 5, 1794 and went into effect June 1, in the reign of Frederick William, with the title: "Allgemeines Landrecht fur die preussischen Staaten." The French government had an official translation made in 1801 by the bureau of foreign legislation. Then came the *Bavarian* Code (" Codex Maximilianeus bavaricus civilis "), published in 1756, and drafted by Baron Kreitmeyer. In *Austria*, the preparation for a Code had covered a still longer period than in Prussia. Maria Theresa had commanded it, following the example of her neighbor Frederick. But the first draft, prepared by Professor Azzoni, was laid aside in 1767; and the next one could not be completed until 1810, going into effect Jan. 1, 1812. Its authors were Kees (1786), Martini, and (at the end) Zeiller We may also here note the Victorian Code, published in the Sardinian States in 1723 and revised in 1770.

The Code Napoleon was thus not the first one undertaken in Europe. But not one of its predecessors could be compared with it, even remotely. Not one of them has been, as that was, a great enterprise of reform and unification; not one of them possesses the merits of thoroughness and form by which it is distinguished. The Bavarian Code was no more than a summary of the decisions, a sort of table of contents to the Roman law as then practised. The Prussian Code was too long, its topics poorly distributed, and its text overburdened with details, the principles in it are smothered under rules for concrete cases. Furthermore, none of these Codes became the general law of the country, they all left in force the local Regulations and the provincial Customs; and thus they had scarcely more status than that of a subsidiary law. As to the Austrian Code, its consummation postdated the Code Napoleon; and as it markedly showed the influence of the latter, it should be considered less a predecessor than a derivative.

§ 42. **The Extension of the Code Napoleon.** — The countries which received the French Code form three groups. (1) The territories which were united with the French Republic before the Peace of Amiens (1802) received the Code at the time of its publication in the same way as France proper. This first category includes *Belgium, Luxemburg,* the *Palatinate,* and all that portion of *Rhenish Prussia* and of *Hesse-Darmstadt* lying on the right bank of the Rhine, together with *Geneva, Savoy, Piedmont,* and the Duchies of *Parma* and *Plaisance* in the South. (2) Later, as Napoleon's conquests become more extensive, he introduced his Code in certain other countries: in *Italy* (March 30, 1806), in *Holland* (Oct. 18, 1810), in the *Hanseatic Departments* (Dec 13, 1810), and in the *Grand Duchy of Berg* (Dec. 17, 1811). (3) Certain countries voluntarily adopted the French Code. Such were the kingdom of *Westphalia* (Jan. 1, 1808), *Hanover,* united to Westphalia in 1810, the Grand Duchies of *Baden, Frankfort,* and *Nassau,* several of the *Swiss Cantons,* the free city of *Dantzig,* the Grand Duchy of *Warsaw,* the *Illyrian Provinces,* which became the kingdom of Illyria in 1819, the kingdom of *Naples* (Jan. 1, 1808).

Reaction against French Influence — The Code Napoleon thus enjoyed an authority and an expansion which only the Roman Codes have known Translated into almost every language, supported by the power of a mighty army, and endowed with an indisputable superiority, it seemed destined to give to Germany a uniform legal system But the reverses of Napoleon in 1812 and 1813 checked its fortunes Then Germany, led by Savigny, began an intellectual onslaught upon it. From that time on, its power waned Some of the States repudiated it, others made changes in it. In the *Netherlands,* the revision of the imported laws, though undertaken immediately upon the fall of the Empire, was not accomplished until 1837 In *Switzerland,* on the other hand, the French legislation was deliberately preserved, and was even imitated. And the same course was taken (surprising as it seems) in the *German countries,* which had so eagerly given the signal for the supreme struggle against the rule of Napoleon. It was notably in *Italy* that the reaction burst out with violence. The Bourbons, who succeeded Murat in the kingdom of Naples, were almost the only ones willing to preserve the French law, and under their orders was enacted a fairly faithful copy of it. But in other parts of Italy it was so promptly attacked that its very opponents came to regret their haste, and were compelled, after restoring the original laws, to return to a legislation based on ours. Such was the result in the Duchies of *Parma, Plaisance,* and *Guastalla,* where a Civil Code was published as early as 1820, in the reign of the ex-Empress Marie-Louise. In the kingdom of *Sardinia,* a Civil Code, called the "Code of Albertin," published in 1837, was put into effect Jan 1, 1838. This Code greatly resembled the Code Napoleon in its external form and the distribution of its topics, though in reality it restored upon many points the Roman traditions which the Code Napoleon had abandoned. In *Tuscany* only the title on Liens and Mortgages was preserved.

Return to Favor. — This reactionary movement soon subsided, and the Code Napoleon once more came into favor This was seen first in America, where our former possessions of *Louisiana* and *Haïti* in 1825 and 1826 imitated the French laws in their Codes. Next, in 1827, *Greece,* just freed from the yoke of the Turks, attempted to provide itself with a Code similar to ours. The South

American republics, especially *Bolivia, Uruguay,* and *Argentina,* copied it; later on, *Spain, Roumania,* and even *Italy* herself, one by one, came to feel the ascendency of its influence.

The Final Results. — To-day the final judgment of history may be passed upon our Code.   It gave the signal for an enormous movement towards codification, which filled the entire nineteenth century and has extended over the whole world.   Nothing in prior times can be compared to its propagation   It acted directly in a great number of countries, scattered over the four quarters of the globe, even upon the precise mode of codification as well as upon the spirit of the work.   In others, it has at least served as the example and the stimulus to bring about the result.[1]   Only the Anglo-Saxon countries have preserved their law in the condition of a body of customs and a series of scattered statutes.

---

[1] Volume II of the "Livre du centenaire" contains interesting studies upon the influence of the French Code abroad (Germany, Messrs *Crome-Kohler* and *Muller*, Belgium, *Van Biervliet* and *Hanssens*, Canada, *Mignault*, Egypt, *Armijon*, Italy, *Chironi*, Japan, *Gobai*, Luxemburg, *Ruppert*, Monaco, *De Rolland*, Netherlands, *Lasser*, Roumania, *Disses-cou*, Romanic Switzerland, *A. Martin*).

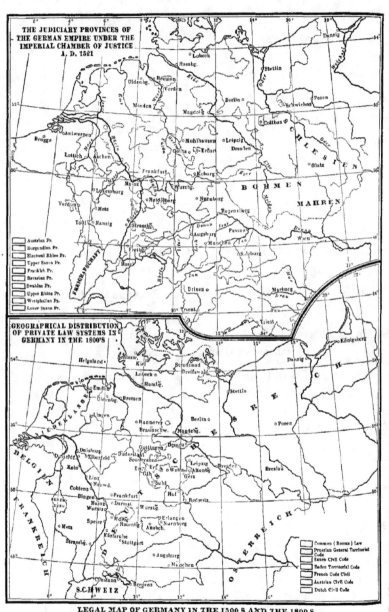

LEGAL MAP OF GERMANY IN THE 1500 S AND THE 1800 S.
[From R. Schröder's "German Legal History", Veit & Co., Leipzig.]

PART IV

GERMANY

FIRST PERIOD (A.D. 1000–1400) · FEUDALISM AND THE PEOPLE'S LAW-BOOKS

SECOND PERIOD (A.D. 1400–1600). THE RECEPTION OF ROMAN LAW.

THIRD PERIOD (A.D. 1600–1806): NATURAL LAW, LEGAL RATIONALISM AND GERMAN NATIONALISM

FOURTH PERIOD (A.D. 1806–1908): NATIONAL UNIFICATION AND CODIFICATION.

LIST OF ABBREVIATIONS OF CITATIONS IN PART IV

PERIODICALS AND CURRENT SERIES

A B.A = Abhandlungen der Berliner Akademie

Allg d Biog. = Allegemeine deutsche Biographie

A K O G Q = Archiv fur Kunde Osterreichischer Geschichtsquellen.

O Gierke (editor), " Untersuchungen " = Untersuchungen zur deutschen
Staats- und Rechtsgeschichte (since 1878).

Hans G B = Hansische Geschichtsblatter

Hildebrand's J N O = Jahrbuch fur Nationalokonomie.

H Vj S = Historische Vierteljahrschrift fur Gesetzgebung und Rechtswissenschaft (since 1859).

K Vj.S = Kritische Vierteljahrschrift (since 1898, continuing the D Z
G W = Deutsche Zeitschrift fur Geschichtswissenschaft, 1889–1898)

H Z = (von Sybel's) Historische Zeitschrift (since 1859).

K Z. = Kritische Zeitschrift

M O G F = Mitteilungen des Instituts fur osterreichische Geschichts-
forschung (since 1880)

N B Rg W = Nieuwe Bijdragen voor Regtsgeleerdheid en Wetgeving.

Preuss J B = (Treitschke's) Preussiche Jahrbucher

Wiener S B = Sitzungsberichte der kaiserlichen Akademie der Wissenschaften zu Wien, philosophisch-historische Klasse

Z D R = Zeitschrift fur deutsches Recht (1839–1861)

Z G R W = Zeitschrift fur geschichtliche Rechtswissenschaft (1815–1850).

Z.H V N S = Zeitschrift des historischen Vereins Nieder Sachsens

Z. Preus G L K = Zeitschrift fur preussische Geschichte und Landes-
kunde

Z Pr Off R = Zeitschrift fur deutsches Privat- und Offentliches Recht

Z ¹R G = (Rudorff Bohlau et al) Zeitschrift fur Rechtsgeschichte

Z² R G = Zeitschrift der Savigny-Stiftung fur Rechtsgeschichte, ger-
manistische Abteilung (unless "roman Abt " = romanische Abteilung, be added , 1880 fg)

Z R.W = Zeitschrift fur Rechtswissenschaft (1859 fg)

ABBREVIATED TITLES USED IN THE FOOTNOTES OF PART IV

H Brunner, " Grundzuge " = " Gr der deutschen Rechtsgeschichte " (4th
ed , Leipzig, 1910)

Bluntschli, " Geschichte " = " G des allgemeinen Staatsrecht und der
Politik " (Munich and Leipzig, 1864)

Bethmann-Hollweg, " Civil-process " = " Der germanisch-romanische Civil-
process im Mittelalter " (6 vols , 1868 fg) ; also entitled " Der Civil-
process des gemeinen Rechts in geschichtlicher Entwicklung "

Below, "Ursachen" = "Ursachen der Rezeption des romischen Rechts in Deutschland" (1905)

Daniels, "Handbuch" = "Handbuch der deutschen Reichs- und Staatengeschichte" (4 vols, 1859–1863).

Eichhorn, "Rechtsgeschichte" = "Deutsche Staats- und Rechtsgeschichte" (5th ed, 4 vols, 1843–1844)

Franklin, "Beitrage" = "B zur Geschichte der Rezeption des romischen Rechts" (1863)

O. Gierke, "Genossenschaftsrecht" = "Rechtsgeschichte der deutschen Genossenschaft" (3 vols, 1868+)

Lehmann, "Quellen" = "Q zur deutschen Reichs- und Rechtsgeschichte" (1891)

Muther, "Rom -kanon Prozess" = "Zur Geschichte des romisch-kanonischen Prozesses in Deutschland" (Rostock, 1872)

Muther, "Universitatsleben" = "Aus dem Universitäts- und Gelehrtenleben im Zeitalter der Reformation" (1866)

Muther, "Rechtswissenschaft" = "Zur Geschichte der Rechtswissenschaft und der Universitaten in Deutschland," in his "Gesammelte Aufsatze" (1876)

Muther, "Neue Sammlung = "Neue und vollstandige Sammlung der Reichsabschiede" (1747 fg, — Senckenberg, Schmauss, Olenschlager, editors)

Ott, "Beitrage" = "B zur Receptionsgeschichte des romischen Rechts in den bohmischen Landern" (1879)

Roscher, "Geschichte" = "G. der Nationalokonomie in Deutschland"

Savigny, "Geschichte" = "G des romischen Rechts im Mittelalter" (2d ed, 7 vols, 1834–1851)

R. Schroder, "Lehrbuch" = "L der deutschen Rechtsgeschichte" (5th ed, Leipzig, 1907)

Schulte, "Quellen" = "Geschichte der Quellen und Literatur des kanonischen Rechts" (vol. I, 1875).

O Stobbe, "Rechtsquellen" = "Geschichte der deutschen Rechtsquellen" (2 vols, Leipzig, 1860–1864)

Stolzel, "Richterthum" = "Entwicklung des gelehrten Richterthums in den deutschen Territorien" (2 vols, 1872)

Stintzing, "Pop Lit" = "Geschichte der populären Literatur des romischen und kanonischen Rechts in Deutschland" (1867)

Stintzing, "Geschichte" = "G der deutschen Rechtswissenschaft" (2 vols, Munich and Leipzig, 1880–1884)

Stintzing-Landsberg, "Geschichte" = vol 3 of the same work, by E. Landsberg (1898), with an accompanying volume of notes

Wegele, "Geschichte" = "G der deutschen Historiographie" (Munich and Leipzig, 1885).

Zeumer, "Quellensammlung" = "Q zur Geschichte der deutschen Reichsverfassung im Mittelalter, und Neuzeit" (1904)

H Zöpfl, "Rechtsgeschichte" = "Deutsche Rechtsgeschichte" (4th ed., 3 vols, Braunschweig, 1871–1872)

Part IV. GERMANY[1]

Chapter I. First Period: A.D. 1000–1400

FEUDALISM AND THE PEOPLE'S LAW-BOOKS[2]

§ 1. The Various Forms of the Law.
§ 2. Imperial Law.
§ 3. Compilations of Territorial and Feudal Law.
§ 4. Territorial and Local Law.
§ 5. Manorial Law.
§ 6 Town Law.
§ 7. Documents and Formularies.

§ 1. **The Various Forms of the Law**[3] — [At the period in which we now take up the thread of Germanic history] the written law of

---

[1] [The general object of the translator has been to give rather a metaphrase than a paraphrase. The original texts have been much condensed. Such condensation has consisted almost exclusively in the omission of entire sentences or larger units of the original   At the beginning of each chapter the sources of its several sections are indicated, and also what parts of the sources have been reproduced in full (footnotes aside) or only in part   Brackets are used in places where other words than those of the original were necessary in order to make a transition ; also in a few cases where the insertion of an explanatory word or two seemed imperative, and, finally, in a very few cases where the original was preserved in abbreviated form, because essential to the argument, but seemed more effective in the text than in a footnote   In the exceedingly few cases where omissions and joinders could involve by any possibility the ethics of quotation marks, dots appear in the text (   )   Lastly, in rearranging the material slight liberties have occasionally been taken, — such as those necessary in order to secure consistent cross-references, and like matters, — which are not indicated in the text.

The authors' notes, aside from mere references to authorities, have been for the most part omitted   Nor has there been exact adhesion to their form, so far as used, when mere notes of citation   Explanatory notes have been treated, when used, with the same respect as the text itself. The editions to which the references are made can be identified (when necessary) by the reference to the date of the works here translated   A list of abbreviations of the titles of journals, and of books often cited, is given at the beginning of this Part , the latter are then cited by an abbreviated title in the footnotes , " *op cit* " (or an equivalent term) is used sometimes, but in this case the title appears always in the same section — Transl]

[2] [§§ 1–7 = §§ 26–32, of Heinrich Brunner's " Grundzuge der deutschen Rechtsgeschichte " (4th ed , Leipzig, 1910)   For this author, see the Editorial Preface. The notes are generally omitted ; the bibliographies are only partially reproduced , and a few words are omitted in a few sections — Transl]

[3] References   *O Stobbe*, "Geschichte der deutschen Rechtsquellen," I, p 266 *et seq*, *Schröder*, " Ein Worterbuch der alteren deutschen Rechtssprache " (Festschrift of the 26th Deutscher Juristentag, 1902), p 118 *et seq* , *Roeppell*, "Uber die Verbreitung des Magdeburger Stadtrechts im Gebiete des alten polnischen Rechts ostwarts der Weichsel" (1857); *Halban*, "Zur Geschichte des deutschen Rechtes in Podolien, Wolhynien, und der Ukraine" (1886), *Frensdorf*, "Das Alter niederdeutscher Rechtsaufzeichnungen" (Hans G B VI, p 97 *et seq*)

311

the earlier period had gradually fallen into disuse in German lands.
The Leges [of Saxons, Franks, etc] and the Capitularies of Charlemagne and his successors were forgotten; for here they had not
been, as in Italy, the object of constant legal instruction and of
a legal literature. Their principles, even when these had taken
firm root in customary law, were gradually invalidated by fundamental changes in the constitutional bases of the Empire, by new
distinctions of class, and by the changes in legal conceptions induced by changing cultural conditions The contrast between
popular tribal law and that of royal officials disappeared after the
dissolution of the Frankish empire The principle of the personality of law was so far weakened in favor of the territorial principle that tribal law was transformed, practically, into a territorial law binding upon every inhabitant. Until into the 1200s
the law is still normally an unwritten law· it is developed by
the findings of lay-judges ("Schoffen "), in doubtful cases it is
settled by the adoption of a doom, *i e* by a declaration of what
is law in virtue of custom, such declaration being pronounced by
local worthies, learned in the law, upon official inquiry.

Legal development, like political development, followed the
course of dismemberment and particularism; a phenomenon that
is explainable, for the most part, by the absence of a coherent
judicial organization and by the upgrowth of numerous special
courts In addition to the peculiarity, which had come down
from the earlier time, of laws of different racial branches, new
jurisdictions now split off for certain classes of the population, for
certain territories, and for one and another legal status, these
jurisdictions being connected with the formation of the special
courts

Litigation over *feudal relations*, as well between lord and vassal
as between the vassals themselves, went to the feudal court, in
which the lord presided and the feudatories acted as the judgment-finders The law thus developed was feudal law, and was
complementary to the territorial law enforced in the folkmoots of
the county and the hundred Certain disputes between villein-
tenants were settled in the manorial court of the lord. The
manorial official — steward, bailiff, or the reeve of the vill —
held the court; the members of the manorial community found
the judgment according to manorial law, which took forms exceedingly diverse in different manors The *household servants* of
the manor were subject (in a court which was also called manorial)
to the jurisdiction of the lord they served With the increasing

importance of the manor's administrative service this class threw off the restraint of a special law (" Dienstrecht "), becoming subject in their tenures to the general feudal law and in other matters to the territorial law.

The *city* was not originally the district of a separate court or law ; the different classes of its population lacked a common court and a common law   The freemen lived under territorial law, the " servientes " under servitary law, the serfs under manorial law. With the development of the town economy, however, there arose a special city court for all the citizens in commercial matters. based upon the immunity enjoyed by or specially conceded to the city's lord, and there thus arose a law peculiar to the cities   In northern and middle Germany this city law has been known since the second half of the 1100 s as "Weichbild."   Only in a few cities was there an independent development of a town law . such possessed primitive laws.   On the other hand, many cities received their law by adoption, *i.e.* secured the conferment upon themselves of the town law worked out in another city   Through such adoption there arose extensive groups of town law, among which the Magdeburg and Lubeck groups were the most notable   The city of the mother law ordinarily remained in permanent connection, as an appellate court, with that of the filial law   Whenever the lay-judges of the latter were uncertain of the law, they sought instruction from those of the other as a higher tribunal, or else laid the case directly before these for decision   Lubeck, Magdeburg, Eisenach, and Frankfort o/M were the most celebrated of such higher courts   German town law penetrated also beyond the borders of the Empire into the neighboring Slavic and Hungarian lands   The numerous colonies which were there founded by Germans retained for themselves the German law.   In Poland, Magdeburg law became an essential characteristic of a city, and spread as a general city law into regions of wholly un-Germanic population

When, with the development of national sovereignty, independent territories had taken form within the regions occupied by the different Germanic racial branches, there was developed in some of them a territorial law, distinct from the general racial law, which the court of the territorial sovereign served to precipitate and constitute   Thus, for example, in Bavaria, where the disintegration of the racial law went farthest, separate systems of territorial law were developed for Austria, Salzburg, Upper Bavaria, and Styria.   And many a smaller district besides, many an

313

isolated hundred, shire, or earldom, produced its individual law

The German royal court, which was the sole organ of centralized legal growth, could only imperfectly combat the various forces working for legal differentiation. It did not enjoy, as the Frankish court had enjoyed, a dominating position   While the declaration of the law at the traditional seats of popular courts was left generally (in the courts for minor causes) to permanent lay-judges, whose lifelong office was often heritable, the judgments rendered at any temporary royal camp and residence were not found by such permanent law-finders, but by the nobles and the officers of the royal household who happened to be present.   In the struggle between the forces working for legal unity and legal diversity the organs of local legal growth had in their favor, therefore, from the beginning, the advantage of a firmer organization.

Among the bodies of racial law, the Saxon, as depicted in the extant legal literature devoted to it, shows the greatest consistency and most coherent development   The laws of the Swabians, Bavarians, and Thuringians reflect the dominant influence of the Frankish law, whose institutions, in consequence of a heavy Frankish colonization, took root also, in part, within the domain of the Saxon law   The law of the Bavarians disintegrated into a number of independent territorial laws   No attempt at a systematic presentation of this law like that of Saxon, Swabian, and Frankish law was ever made   The development of the Frisian law went on in relative isolation within a small domain of influence, its legal sources are distinguished by the extreme archaism of their provisions.

From the 1200s onward, written law appears in Germany in quantities.   According to its origin, it takes the form of either statutes, or simple memorandum-books, or books of legal exposition (law-books).   In the 1200s German takes place with Latin as the language of the legal sources, and from the middle of the century onward it predominates.   Side by side with the written law, unwritten customary law retained ascendency throughout an extensive domain

§ 2   Sources of Imperial Law.[1] — For imperial law down to the

---

[1] The statutes and other sources of imperial law down to 1313 are available in *Pertz*, "Mon Germ hist , Leges," vol II   A better and fuller collection is afforded by the quarto edition of the " Leges " under the title, " Constitutiones et acta publica imperatorum et regum," edited by *Weiland* (vol I, 1893, covering 911–1197), *Weiland* (II, 1896; 1198–1272), *Schwalm* (III, 1904–1906, 1273–1298), *Schwalm* (IV, pts. 1 and 2, 1906–

middle of the 1100s there are only scanty sources. Royal legislation became more active under the Hohenstaufen, who interpolated in the " Corpus Juris Civilis " a number of their own laws,
in order to procure for them a wider currency and higher credit.
Imperial statutes were enacted by the Emperor with the concurrence of the great nobles, which he secured in the imperial diets.
Among such statutes we must particularly distinguish, by their
content, two groups:

1st. *Public peaces,* "constitutiones pacis." With the ascendency
of chivalry private war had become so common among the knights,
and the abuses of self-help had so increased the insecurity of the
laws, that the State was no longer capable of repressing the frequent disturbances of the peace in a normal way, by the ordinary
administration of justice, and on the penal principles of the customary law. Thus the king found himself compelled to establish
from time to time by statute a king's peace, subjecting those who
broke it (usually) to the severer penalties appointed for the punishment of crimes. The establishment of such a peace of the king
generally took the form of a covenant, it was sworn first between
the king and the great lords with whom he joined, and these then
caused it to be sworn locally throughout the land. These statutes
of public peace either prohibited the feud outright or subjected
its use to certain legal preconditions and limitations They were
either promulgated as permanent law or proclaimed a peace for
only a definite number of years, establishing for this period a sort
of summary and covenanted justice. The provisions respecting
breaches of the peace constituted only the nucleus of the laws,
which contained various other criminal, procedural, and police
provisions Numerous peace covenants limited to particular
provinces preceded or accompanied the imperial peaces.

Public peaces proclaimed for the whole Empire go back as far
as the time of Henry IV In 1103 a peace of four years was sworn
at Mainz. Frederick I issued in 1152 a peace statute which, among
other things, regulated the price of grain and prescribed a summary

1908; 1298–1313), *Schwalm* (V, pt 1, 1909; 1313–1320) More modern
statutes are found in the collection of "recesses" (Reichsabschiede) of
the Diets (in the later and more complete edition of *Senckenberg* and
Koch, 1747) Better texts of the more important documents in *Zeumer*,
"Quellensammlung." Further, the "Deutsche Reichstagsakten" published
by the Munchener Historische Kommission, ed *Weizsacker, Kerler*, and
others, covering (up to the end of 1909) the period 1376–1437 in 12 volumes
— *Wyneken*, "Die Landfrieden in Deutschland von Rudolf I bis Heinrich
VII (1886) *Schwalm*, " Landfrieden in Deutschland unter Ludwig dem
Baiern" (1889), *von Zallinger*, "Kampf um den Landfrieden" (M O.G.F,
suppl. vol IV, 443 *et seq.*).

process for trying law cases involving issues of feudal tenure
From the same ruler we have also the Roncaglia "constitutio
pacis" of November 1158, and the Nuremberg peace of December
29, 1186, directed against incendiaries ("constitutio pacis contra
incendiarios") Of Henry VII, the son of Frederick II, we have
the renewal, voted at Frankfort o/M in 1223 (or 1221), of an older
Saxon peace; also the "Treuga Henrici," which probably originated
in 1224 at Wurzburg; and the Frankfort peace of 1234. The
most important and celebrated of these statutes is Frederick II's
"Constitutio Moguntina" (Mainz) of August 15, 1235, which, in
addition to feuds and breaches of the peace, regulated many other
matters, such as customs duties, coinage, safe-conduct, ecclesiastical stewardships, and the organization of the manorial court.
Drafted in German, it was promulgated in an official German
version in a diet at Mainz, and also recorded by the chancery in
a Latin text. About 1400 the jurist Nikolaus Wurm wrote a gloss
upon it. Upon this peace statute rest, in the main, the public
peaces declared after the interregnum by Rudolf I and his immediate
successors An attempt to take a new and independent course is
seen in the statute of 1438 drafted by Albert II, which undertook
to abolish the right of private war completely, and proposed, for
the administration of its provisions, a division of the Empire into
four (according to an earlier draft, six) circles On the other
hand, a limited right of feud is still recognized in the Frankfort
revision of Frederick III, of 1442, which treats also of the law of
pledge, of safe-conducts, coinage, and Vehmic courts. A public
peace of five years was proclaimed by Frederick III in 1467, and
one of ten years in 1474. Finally, in 1495 a permanent peace was
realized. In later Diets this was several times republished,
revised, and provided with supplements.

2d. *Constitutional Statutes.* As such are to be named, including
the Concordats, the following eight· (1) the Worms Concordat of
September 23, 1122, which ended the struggle over investitures;
(2) the "Sententia de regalibus" of Frederick I, of 1158, relative
to the imperial regalia in Italy, but later adopted for Germany
also on the strength of their embodiment in the "Libri Feudorum",
further, two laws important in the growth of national sovereignties,
— (3) the "Privilegium" of 1220 that granted immunities to
ecclesiastical princes, and (4) the "Statutum in favorem principium," resolved upon by King Henry in 1231 in a diet at Worms,
and confirmed, with some modifications, by King Frederick II in
1232 at Cividale; (5) the law of Ludwig of Bavaria of August 6,

1338, beginning "Licet iuris," passed in a Frankfort diet, (6) Charles IV's Golden Bull, the fundamental law of the Empire for the imperial election and the constitutional status of the electoral princes, and containing also provisions regarding the national peace, grants of municipal citizenship to rural residents, and other matters, — the first part (ch. 1–23) published at Nuremberg, January 20, 1356, the second (ch. 24–31) at Metz, December 25, 1356, [1] (7) the Concordat of Constance of 1418; and (8) the so-called Vienna Concordat (between Frederick III and Nicholas V) of February 17, 1448.

The edicts issued and the immunities granted by the Kings must be counted, as well as the statutes, among the sources of imperial law; and likewise the decisions of the royal court, particularly because, in doubtful questions, they stood as rules for like cases in the future To the activity of the royal court was also due the origin of the "maxims" of imperial law declared by the princes as dooms, which embody general pronouncements upon legal questions.

§ 3. Compilations of Territorial and Feudal Law [2] — In the

[1] The Golden Bull (so called only since the late 1300s) utilizes in some passages the so-called "Schwabenspiegel"

[2] REFERENCES · *Homeyer*, "Die deutschen Rechtsbucher des Mittelalters und ihre Handschriften" (1856); supplements available in the Z R G ; a new edition of the work is in prospect — *Steffenhagen*, "Deutsche Rechtsquellen in Preussen vom 13 ten bis zum 16 ten Jahrhundert" (1875)

"SACHSENSPIEGEL" *Homeyer*, editor, "Des Sachsenspiegels erster Theil Landrecht" (3d ed., 1861), "Des Sachsenspiegels zweiter Theil nebst den verwandten Rechtsbuchern" (I, 1842, II, 1844), *Weiske*, editor, "Sachsenspiegel Landrecht" (8th ed., 1905) — Of the abundant literature see *Homeyer*, "Die Stellung des Sachsenspiegels zum Schwabenspiegel" (1853), *Ficker*, "Uber die Entstehungszeit des Sachsenspiegels und die Ableitung des Schwabenspiegels aus dem Deutschenspiegel" (1859); *Frensdorff*, "Uber das Alter niederdeutscher Rechtsaufzeichnungen" (Hans G B , VI 97 *et seq*) — The basis for critical edition of the glosses, which we still lack, was prepared by *Steffenhagen*, "Die Entwicklung der Landrechtsglosse des Sachsenspiegels" (Wiener S B , vols 98–129).

"SPIEGEL DER DEUTSCHEN LEUTE" · *Ficker*, "Uber einen Spiegel deutscher Leute und dessen Stellung zum Sachsenspiegel und Schwabenspiegel" (1857); "Der Spiegel der deutschen Leute" (text, 1859) — *E. von Muller*, "Der Deutschenspiegel in seinem sprachlich-stilistischen Verhaltnis zum Ssp und zum Swsp" (1908) — Editions of the so-called "Schwabenspiegel" by *Freiherr von Lassberg* (1840), *von Wackernagel* (the Landrecht alone, 1840), *von Gengler* (Landrecht alone, 2d ed , 1875), and *von Daniels* (in the "Rechtsdenkmaler des deutschen Mittelalters"), this last synoptically with the "Ssp" and the French "Swsp."; *Matile*, "Le Miroir de Souabe" (1843) A critical edition of the "Swsp " is lacking, but is in preparation by *von Rockinger* upon the basis of an exhaustive study of the MSS. (See his reports in the Wiener S B , vols 73–122).

The "GORLITZ RECHTSBUCH" in *Homeyer*, "Sachsenspiegel," II, 2 — *J J Smits*, editor, "De Spiegel von Sassen of zoogenaamde HOLLANDSCHE SACHSENSPIEGEL" (N.B.Rg.W., pt XXII, 1872, based upon the single

"*Sachsenspiegel*" ("Speculum Saxonum," "Miroir de Saxe") we possess an epoch-making record of Saxon law, which marks the beginning of the working over of the law into a legal literature. It was probably composed in the third decade of the 1200s, certainly between 1198 and 1235, by a Saxon knight and lay-judge, EIKE VON REPKOW. His name appears in documents of 1209, 1215, 1218, 1219, 1224, and 1233. He was a member of the class from which the lay-judges of the manorial minor courts were exclusively recruited, and entered that other class of personal servants and administrative officers who managed the court and manor of a medieval lord. He wrote his work first in Latin, afterward working it over into German, probably of the low-Saxon dialect, at the instance of Court Hoyer von Falkenstein, steward of the abbey of Quedlinburg. Four prefaces precede the text of the law-book. Of the first, the so-called "prefatio rhythmica," the second part was written by Eike himself, who gives us in it information regarding the origin of his work. Of the dated manuscripts of the "Sachsenspiegel," the oldest is of the year 1295.

The "Sachsenspiegel" includes a law-book of territorial and one of feudal law. The presentation of servitary, manorial, and town law is wholly excluded by the author from his task. We lack the Latin original.[1] Though Eike von Repkow undertakes, it is true, a general presentation of Saxon law, the applicability of the legal principles of the "Sachsenspiegel" is often limited to the Ostphalian portion of the territory occupied by the Saxons. Special attention is given to conditions in the Saxon marches, and to the special law of the North Swabians. Legal practice in the bishoprics of Magdeburg and Halberstadt was the chief source of Eike's legal knowledge. He probably made use of the Frankfort peace statute for Saxony of Henry VII, or else of some unknown

MS known) — *Fidicin*, editor, "BERLINER STADTBUCH" ("Historisch-diplomatische Beiträge zur Geschichte der Stadt Berlin," pt I, with index and glossary in pt III, 1837, — reprint by *P Clausewitz*, 1883) — "Der LIVLÄNDISCHE SPIEGEL" in *Bunge*, "Altlivlands Rechtsbücher" (1879) —*L von Maurer*, editor, "Das Stadt- und das Landrechtsbuch RUPRECHTS VON FREYSING" (1839) — *Endemann*, editor, "DAS KAISERRECHT nach der Handschrift von 1372" — *C G Homeyer*, editor, "Der RICHTSTEIG LANDRECHTS nebst Cautela und Premis" (1857), the "RICHTSTEIG LEHNRECHTS" in *Homeyer*, "Sachsenspiegel," II, 1 — On the "VEHM-RECHTSBÜCHER," see *von Wächter*, "Beiträge zur deutschen Geschichte, insbesondere zur Geschichte des deutschen Strafrechts" (1845); *Lindner*, "Die Veme" (1888), pp 264 *et seq* — *Homeyer*, "Über die INFORMATIO EO SPECULO SAXONUM" (1856) — Bohlau, "Theodorich von BOCKDORFFS GERICHTSFORMELN, (Z ¹R G, II, 415).
  [1] The relation of the "Vetus Auctor de Beneficiis" to the "Sachsenspiegel" still demands an exhaustive study, it can hardly be an original text, *cf Ernst* in "Neues Archiv," XXVI, 207.

peace statute nearly related to it   The treatment of the truce
of God (II, 66, § 2) rests directly or indirectly upon the "Summa
Decretalium" of Bernardus of Pavia, written toward the end of the
1100s.   The legal doctrine laid down regarding the election and
coronation of the German king reflects the opinions which men
had been led to form, in Saxony, by the disputes between Otto IV and
Philip of Swabia with Frederick II over the succession.   With the
conservative spirit of a low-Saxon, Eike (as he tell us in his rhymed
preface) pursues the end of presenting the law handed down from
his forefathers.   In a few places, however, a certain fondness for
arithmancy dims the clearness of his vision.   On the other hand,
in his strongly marked legal sense and juristic logic he appears as
an epoch-making reformer, formulating with bold originality legal
principles which only subsequently, and on the strength of his
authority, became an actual part of the law.

The "Sachsenspiegel" quickly acquired great prestige.   Although the work of a layman, it was given the authority of a
statute-book in the Saxon courts.   In the 1300s it was already
believed to be in fact a statement of imperial legislation, the book
of territorial law being ascribed, in its greater part, to Charlemagne,
and the book of feudal law to Frederick I.   It was translated not
only into various Germanic dialects, notably into high German
and Dutch, but several times into Latin and also into Polish.
The medieval art of illustration lent itself also to the service of
the law-book, providing the text with a continuous series of illumi-
nated pen drawings in pictorial representation of its content.   Of
such illustrated manuscripts there have been preserved to us,
from the 1300s, those of Heidelberg (1300–1315), Oldenburg (1336),
Dresden (circa 1530), and Wolfenbuttel.   All rest, directly or indirectly, upon a lost manuscript of Meissen of the late 1200s

In the 1300s the "Sachsenspiegel" was furnished with a gloss
The oldest gloss on the territorial law we owe to JOHANN VON
BUCH, a knight of the march, who had studied in 1305 at Bologna;
it was written after 1325 and probably before 1335   It was later
worked over and enlarged by Nikolaus Wurm, still in the 1300s,
and by Brand von Tzerstede and also by the brothers Bocksdorf
in the 1400s   About the middle of the 1300s the "Sachsenspiegel"
feudal law was provided, after the pattern of the Buch gloss, first
with a short and then, in amplification of this, with a longer commentary, the latter being revised in 1386 by Nikolaus Wurm
About half a century later than the Buch gloss there originated
at Stendal an independent commentary glossing both the territorial

and the feudal law. The author shows acquaintance, not only with the Saxon law-books and the Buch gloss, but also with practice in the minor popular courts of Magdeburg and Stendal, the "Lombarda," and legal systems wholly foreign, and with their literature; but he is less free than Buch from the influence of the foreign law, making of its principles and those of the native law a motley mixture. — Several articles of the "Sachsenspiegel" were attacked as unchristian and heretical by a Saxon Augustine monk, Johannes Klenkok. A polemic tractate against it which he transmitted to the Pope in 1372 resulted in the bull "Salvator generis humani," by which Gregory XI, in 1374, reprobated fourteen articles of the law-book and forbade their enforcement.

The "*Spiegel der deutschen Leute*" (or "Deutschenspiegel") originated about the middle of the 1200s in South Germany, presumably in Augsburg. It is based upon the "Sachsenspiegel"; but, instead of confining itself to the law of a single Germanic racial branch, undertakes to present Germanic "common" law. In this work the territorial law of the "Sachsenspiegel" as far as II, 12, § 13 is so revised, with the aid of various German and foreign legal sources, as to represent South-German conditions From II, 12, § 13 onward it is translated with few changes into a South-German dialect The last is true also of the feudal law.

For the rest, this "Deutschenspiegel" was soon displaced by the "Kaiserliches Land-und Lehnrecht," — wrongly known since in the 1600s as the "*Schwabenspiegel*," — whose unknown author, a churchman, carried to completion the work left unfinished in the "Deutschenspiegel," working over the entire "Sachsenspiegel" (as known to him in a version of the former work) into a presentation of all Germanic law. In addition to a motley lot of diverse sources he used especially a German version of the sermons of Berthold von Regensburg. In the territorial law of this so-called "Schwabenspiegel" three parts must be distinguished a first, which is based directly upon the revision already completed in the "Deutschenspiegel"; a second, which works over and amplifies the translation given in that work of the "Sachsenspiegel", and, finally, as the third part, a collection (not quite critically made) of legal materials, — among others, passages from the "Lex Alemannorum," the "Lex Baiuwariorum," and the Epitome "Aegidii" The time and the place of origin of the law-book are disputed. According to an older view (maintained by Julius Fischer, and justly predominant), it dates from 1274-1275, and probably had its origin in Augsburg. On the other hand, Rockinger (who has for many years been preparing a critical edition of the "Kaiserliches Land-und Lehnrecht") has sought to prove that it was written first in preliminary form at Bamberg in East Francia, in 1259, and then revised the same year in Wurzburg While the history of the "Sachsenspiegel" manuscript was such as to compel an enlargement of the original text, that of the so-called "Schwabenspiegel" led to its abridgment. Like the "Sachsenspiegel" the "Kaiserliches Land-und Lehnrecht" attained a wide dissemination in manuscript, and an enduring reputation It was translated into Latin, French, and Czech.

Both law-books were revised to meet the needs of particular districts Such revisions of the "Sachsenspiegel" are. (1) the "Gorlitz Lawbook" (of territorial and feudal law) of the beginning of the 1300s; (2) the "Breslau Territorial Law," to be further referred to below, (3) the so-called "Dutch Sachsenspiegel," a law-book written by a churchman in the Netherlands, perhaps within the bishopric of Utrecht, which makes use (in rather an independent way) of the "Sachsenspiegel" and its glosses, containing also Mosaic law and the customary law of northern France, (4) the law of the minor popular courts included in the "Townbook" of Berlin of 1397 (Book III), which is a revision, with regard to Brandenburg law, of the "Sachsenspiegel," the Buch gloss, and the "Pathway through the Territorial Law" (§ 12, below); (5) the "Livonian Mirror," written probably in the 1300s, a selection from the "Sachsenspiegel" which ignores such of its principles as are impracticable for Livonia. A union of the Livonian Mirror with a book of Livonian feudal law (the so-called "Oldest Livonian Feudal Law") produced the "Feudal Law of Middle Livonia." A union of the Livonian Mirror with a peasant law intended for Oesel and with the Oldest Livonian feudal Law produced the so-called "Wiek-Oesel Feudal Law." A book of feudal law adapted to the bishopric of Freiburg rests upon a revision of the "Schwabenspiegel", its author was presumably Ruprecht von Freising, who in 1328 also worked out, with the aid of that work, a book of city law for Freiburg. Both works were united in the 1400s into one law-book for the town and territory of Freiburg.

In the last years of the 1200s or in the first half of the 1300s an author to us unknown, but probably of Franconian Hesse, wrote a law-book known as the "Kleines Kaiserrecht." It aims to present common law as fixed by Charlemagne for the whole of Christendom, and as the source for its different principles usually adduces the command of the Emperor. In the majority of the

manuscripts the work is divided into four books, which treat of
judicature, of private and criminal law, of the empire's administrative service, and of town law Special attention is given to the
imperial administrative under officers and to the free (imperial)
villages

The "Pathway through the Territorial Law," written by the
Johann von Buch already named, presumably in 1335, affords a
supplement to the "Sachsenspiegel," namely, a record of the
procedure of the Saxon territorial courts. A complement to this
law-book, the "Pathway through the Feudal Law," was prepared
before the end of the 1300s by an unknown author For Saxon
legal procedure one must take note, further, of two smaller works
of the middle of the 1300s, the "Cautela" and the "Premis"
of Hermann von Osfeld, which contain precautionary rules of conduct for one's guidance in court. Also of the "True Custumal
of feudal Law," a little book on feudal procedure, the books of the
Vehmic courts of Westphalia (of origin since 1437); and the
"Informatio ex Speculo Saxonum," a work which probably originated in the second half of the 1400s in Westphalia, and which
criticises the deviations from the "Sachsenspiegel" in the practice
of the courts of its time And, finally, a collection of practice rules
by Dietrich von Bocksdorf of the middle of the 1400s. In the
field of Frankish law mention must be made of a "Formulary of
Procedure against Pernicious People" ("wie man richtet vber
ainen mentschen"), which originated in Nuremberg in the late
1200s or the early 1300s, also of a Frankfort book of legal procedure of the 1300s the "Baculus Judicii," which was utilized
by Fichard in preparing the Frankfort "Reformation";[1] and
finally, a collection of practice rules for the courts of Mainz of the
1400s

§ 4 **Territorial and Local Law.**[2] — Of enactments affecting the

---

[1] [That is, the revision of municipal law — such as many cities undertook — after the Reception, for the purpose of harmonizing the old town
law with the new Romanistic elements The Frankfort revisions were
of 1509, 1578 — TRANSL]

[2] REFERENCES : *Merkel,* editor, "Constitutiones Henrici ducis Rans-
hofenses" (in "Mon Germ hist , Leges," III, 484), *K von Richthofen,*
editor, "Friesische Rechtsquellen" (1840), also an old-Frisian dictionary
(1840) , *De Haan Hettema,* editor, "Oude friesche Wetten" (1846–1847)
The "Uberkuren" and the Latin text of the "Vetus Jus Frisicum," also
the "Leges Upstalsbomicæ" are found in better form in *von Richthofen,*
"Untersuchungen uber friesische Rechtsgeschichte" (I. 1880) The low-
German legal sources of East Friesland edited by *von Borchling,* "I Die
Rechte der Einzellandschaften" (1908) The north-Frisian sources are in
von Richthofen, "Friesische Rechtsquellen," p 561 The Dietmarsch
territorial law is in *Michelsen,* "Sammlung altdithmarscher Rechtsquellen"

entire territory of a racial branch but few examples have come down to us.   An example of a ducal ordinance, from the end of the 900 s, is afforded by the Ranshof " Constitutions " of the Bavarian duke Henry II.

The effect of such a racial statute law is approached in importance by the Frisian " Elections " ("kuren," " keuren "), which belong to the oldest and most archaic sources of this period.   The Frisian districts (" gau ") between the Zuyder Zee and the Weser, which were parceled out among different earldoms, concluded an alliance for the maintenance of peace among themselves and with outside powers; thus supplementing rather than repudiating the authority of their earls, whose inability to meet the task had been proved, while no superior ducal authority that could have done it justice existed in Friesland.   The allied districts held meetings of their sworn plenipotentiaries (" iurati," " deputati ") at Upstalsbom, in Asterga, not far from Aurich.   Among the purposes of these assemblies was that of consultation regarding the law that the Frisians should observe   The activities of these assemblies at Upstalsbom, in fixing and improving the Frisian Law, have furnished us some of the older sources of the Frisian " common " law.   To such belong: (1) the Seventeen Elections (" kesta," " petitiones," " electiones "), a compilation of legal principles due to the pen of a scholar, presumably some ecclesiastic, which Charlemagne is represented as having guaranteed the Frisians upon their petition; (2) the Twenty-four Territorial Laws (" londriuchta," " constitutiones "), dooms of the contemporary Frisian law, in part textually identical with the Seventeen Elections; (3) the Seven Greater-Elections, of which the first three relate to the constitution of the confederation; (4) the general " Bót-tariff," which was primarily a catalogue of compositions paid for wounds.

(1842)   Bavarian territorial law in *Freyberg*, "Sammlung historischer Schriften und Urkunden" (1827–1836), IV, 381, *J. Fischer*, "Das ältere Rechtsbuch Ludwigs des Bayern" (1908)   The Drent territorial law in *von Richthofen*, "Friesische Rechtsquellen", in better form in *Magnin*, "Overzigt van de Besturen in Drenthe," II, 2, pp. 229 *et seq* (1842).   The so-called "Rheingauer Landrecht" in *Bodmann*, "Rheingauische Alterthumer," p. 624 (1819); followed by *Grimm*, "Weisthumer," I, 539 *et seq* ; *cf.* Z.²R.G , III, 87 (*Brunner*), XXIV, 309 (*H. Meyer*)   Austrian territorial law in A K Ö G.Q., vol. X, ed. by *Meiller*, *Victor Hasenöhrl*, "Österreichisches Landesrecht im 13. und 14. Jahrhundert" (1867), and *von Schwind and Dopsch*, "Ausgewählte Urkunden zur Verfassungsgeschichte der deutsch-österreichischen Erblande," pp. 55 *et seq* , 101 *et seq.* (1895).   Of the abundant literature, see *Hasenöhrl*, "Beitrage zur Geschichte der Rechtsbildung und der Rechtsquellen in den österreichischen Alpenlandern" (1905); *F. Bischoff*, editor, "Steirmarkisches Landrecht des Mittelalters" (1875).   On the Berg "Landesrecht," *Lacomblet*, in A.G.N.R., I, 79 (1832).

The legal sources just enumerated have all been preserved to us in the Frisian language and also (save the Greater-Elections) in a Latin text, and further (excepting the Bôt-tariff) in later texts of a low-German dialect. The time of origin of these older sources of Frisian common law is disputable and uncertain. The Elections, Provincial Laws, and Greater-Elections contain legal principles whose origin implies a time when the Frisian courts were frequented by heathen Northmen, this would indicate the 1000s as the time of their composition   At all events they were recorded before the beginning of the 1200s.

The Assembly of Upstalsbom broke up after 1231, but was renewed in 1323 in a somewhat altered character   While the older peace confederation did not affect the relation of the individual districts to their earls, the alliance of 1323, whose compact bears the name of the " Leges Upstalsbomicæ," was directed against the Count of Holland, the lord of the Westergoo, whose conduct had furnished the motive for the renewal of the Confederation.   The new confederation itself was dissolved after four years   A compact drafted at Groningen in 1361 owed its origin to an attempt by that city (which, with the aid of Frisian country districts, was trying to throw off the sovereignty of the bishops of Utrecht) to renew under its headship the confederation of the Frisian gau-s.

Besides the sources of Frisian " common " law, we possess special statutes and unofficial records of the law of individual " gau-s " and districts, — such as the taxation law of Westerloo, the Hunsing elections of 1252, the Rustring statutes (of the 1100s and 1200s) — " true pearls of ancient Frisian legal poetry," — and the comprehensive Brokmannen law, rich in materials, of the period 1276–1345

The " voluntary agreements " (" Beliebungen ") of the north Frisians, of the 1400s, the Ditmarsch territorial law, — which was first recorded in consequence of a resolve of the territorial Diet in 1448, with supplements down to 1467, — and the statutes or public books of some districts of Switzerland, were products of independent legal development.

Within those territories in which the ruler's power attained any considerable development toward sovereignty, the princes exercised the right of granting privileges and franchises, of establishing public peaces, and of issuing, with the assent of the great nobles of the land, general and binding rules of law.   Examples of such territorial ordinances originating as enactments are the Kulm Guarantees (" Handfeste ") of the Grandmaster Hermann von

Salza, of 1233, for the territory of the Teutonic Order; the Salzburg Ordinance of 1328 of the Archbishop Frederick III, the
Territorial Law of the Emperor Ludwig for Upper Bavaria, of
1336, revised and enlarged in 1346, and the Territorial Law of
1356 prepared for the principality of Breslau, an official recast of
the "Sachsenspiegel"   Mention must be made also of the Territorial Law of Drent of 1412, a canon of the Bishop of Utrecht,
Friederich von Blankenheim, not very comprehensive, which confirms the customary law of the district of Drent.   This appears also
in a pretended legal monument which was published as the territorial
law of the Rheingau, and whose first part is in fact a translation
or an abstract, in a south-German dialect, of the Drent law, while
the second part of the compilation consists of legal principles borrowed from various Dutch legal sources.

The older formulation of Austrian territorial law appears to
be a mere record of current unwritten law, composed in the winter
of 1236–1237, in the endeavor to perpetuate the legal conditions
of the time of Duke Leopold VI and secure a confirmation of the
same by the Emperor Frederick II, whereas the law in its later
version is presumably a statute of King Ottokar of Bohemia, then
the suzerain of Austria, worked out in 1266 upon the basis of the
older version.   Other records of territorial law are the feudal and
territorial law of the earldom of Berg, of the years 1355–1397;
and a Styrian territorial law of the middle of the 1300 s, which
was also adopted in Carinthia.

§ 5.   **Manorial and Servitary Law** [1] — Servitary law took shape
on the manors of different lords in great variety, because for the
manorial administrative service there lacked such a single head
as the feudal system possessed in the kingship   The necessity of
recording the rights and duties of the administrative class was first
felt in the chapter-houses, where the class first attained a conspicuous position   The oldest bodies of servitary law still treat

---

[1] REFERENCES · DIENSTRECHT · *Ficker*, "Über die Entstehungsverhaltnisse der Constitutio de expeditione Romana" (Wiener S B, vol
LXXIII, p. 173)   For the other forms of servitary law mentioned · *von
Furth*, "Ministerialen" (1836) — "WEISTUMER" see the collection of
J Grimm, continued after his death by *Schroder* (6 vols, 1840–1869, and
an index vol by *Schroder*, 1878), *Hardt*, editor, "Luxemburger Weisthumer als Nachlese zu J Grimm's Weisthumern" (1870), *Rochholz*,
editor, "Aargauer Weisthumer" (1876); *Habets*, "Limburgsche Wijs-
dommen, Dorpscostumen en Gewoonten" (1891), *Loersch*, "Die Weistumer der Rheinprovinz (I, 1, 1900)   An exhaustive collection of Austrian
dooms (in progress since 1870) has been arranged for by the Vienna
Akademie der Wissenschaften, including *Gmur*. "Die Rechtsquellen des
Kantons St. Gallen, Erster Teil   Offnungen und Hofrechte" (I, II,
1903–1906)

these administrative servants as a special group of the landholding community, or of the "family" of the church, whereas the later ones treat them as a wholly distinct class in society.

Of the records of servitary law, many assume the form of ordinances. The reason is that in the course of the 1100s the attempt was made in ecclesiastical establishments, especially in imperial abbeys, to settle (with the aid of forged documents) the rights and duties of the officials, who threatened to grow beyond the control of the church. In Reichenau there originated about 1150 the so-called "Constitutio de Expeditione Romana," a body of servitary law forged in the name of Charlemagne. A manorial and servitary law for three manors of the Strassbourg cathedral goes under the name of Dagobert II, a law of the cloister of Ebersheim, in Alsace, in the name of Lewis the Pious. The servitary law of Erstein, in Alsace, is forged in the name of the Empress Irmgard (853), that of St Maximin (in Trier) in the name of Henry III (1056) Records of servitary law which remained wholly free of forgeries are those of Bamberg (of the 1000s) Cologne (1154–1176), Basel (in German, of the second half of the 1200s), Magdeburg, and Hildesheim (both the last of the 1200s). The so-called "Leges Feudales Teklenburgicæ," an ordinance of Count Otto von Teklenburg of the end of the 1200s, are servitary law of secular lords

The manorial laws, in by far their greatest part, originated and developed as customary law Enactments of manorial law are rare One of the oldest and most important is the "Lex Familiæ Wormatiensis Ecclesiæ," an enactment of Bishop Burchard von Worms of the years 1023–1025, inspired by an endeavor to protect the serfs of the church against oppression by the stewards, the bailiffs, and other administrative officers. The majority of the manorial laws which we possess in written form can be traced back to dooms The reason lies in the practice of manorial communities to settle the current law every year on definite days, upon the basis of an official "inquisitio." The manorial official (steward or bailiff) asked in the assembly ("halimot") what might be the law in a given case the members of the manorial community, under oath, gave the answer By exchange of question and answer, the topics of the customary law were more or less completely exhausted Communities of the mark, of free villages, and of rural peasantry imitated this custom of fixed inquests upon the law. In course of time, owing either to particular causes or to the general consideration that writing is after all more durable

326

than human memory, these dooms were written down. The records, like that which they preserve, are known variously as "wisdoms" or dooms, "disclosures," "taidinge," "Bantaidinge," or "Ehehafttaidinge."[1]

§ 6. **Sources of Town Law**[2] — Written town law presents as its oldest source privileges ("Handfesten") conferred by the king or the town lord, particularly with a view to the town's foundation   From the 1200s onward the cities acquired, either by actual prescription or express grant, the right of independent enactment, — the so-called "elective right."   From this time on, the "self-governing rules" ("Willkuren," "Schraén") of the cities — ordinances of councils or declarations of law by the lay-judges — became a part of the sources of town law.   Not infrequently a

---

[1] ["Weistumer", "Offnungen" — i e that which is "eroffnet" (discovered, found) in the popular court; "Taiding" — "Ding" being the old name for the popular court, and "Tai-ding" an uncommon variant, "Bantaiding," the "ungebotenes (or, echtes) Ding" to which the suitors came without summons to try "causæ maiores," and which were held under bann, "Ehehafttaidinge," — i e. "Eh(e)haft," legitimate or "echte Dinge." — TRANSL]

[2] REFERENCES   A succinct review of the most important sources of town law is given in *Kraut-Frensdorff*, "Grundriss zu Vorlesungen uber das deutsche Privatrecht ' (6th ed), § 8, pp 25 *et seq* , *Gengler*, "Deutsche Stadtrechte des Mittelalters, teils vollstandig oder in Probeauszugen" (1852); *Gaupp*, "Deutsche Stadtrechte des Mittelalters mit rechtsgeschichtlichen Erlauterungen" (1851) — "Oberrheinische Stadtrechte" I, "Frankische Rechte ' (in progress; 8 parts, 1895–1909), II, "Schwabische Rechte" (in progress, 2 parts for Villingen and Überlingen, 1905–1908), III, "Elsassische Rechte" (in progress since 1902) — *Telting*, "De friesche Stadrechten' (1883) — "Westfalische Stadtrechte " I 1, Lippstadt (*Overmann*, editor, 1901), — *Keutgen*, "Urkunden zur stadtischen Verfassungsgeschichte" (1901), *Gaupp*, "Das alte magdeburgische und hallische Recht" (1826), *Laband*, editor, "Magdeburger Rechtsquellen zum akademischen Gebrauch" (1869), *Theodor Neumann*, "Magdeburger Weisthumer aus den Originalen des Gorlitzer Rathsarchivs" (1852). — Schoffen-judgments in *Wasserschleben*, "Sammlung deutscher Rechtsquellen" (1860), "Deutsche Rechtsquellen des Mittelalters" (1892), *Stobbe*, "Beitrage zur Geschichte des deutschen Rechts" (1865); *Friese and Laesegang*, editors, "Magdeburger Schoffensprüche" (I, 1901) — For town law-books *Thungen*, editor, "Das sächsische Weichbild ' (1837); *Walther*, editor, the same after a MS of 1381, with glossary (1871), *Ortloff*, editor, "Das Rechtsbuch nach Distinctionen nebst einem Eisenachischen Rechtsbuch" (1836); *Boehlau*, editor, "Die Blume von Magdeburg" (1868); *Behrend*, editor, "Die Magdeburger Fragen" (1865); cf *von Martitz*, "Die Magdeburger Fragen kritisch untersucht" (Z ¹R G., XI, 401), alphabetical collection of Magdeburg Schoffen-judgments in *Wasserschleben*, "Deutsche Rechtsquellen des Mittelalters," p. 1 (1892) — The "Neun Bucher Magdeburger Rechts" are available only in old prints; the oldest edition is of 1574, cf *Steffenhagen*, "Die Neun Bucher Magdeburger Rechts" (1865), *Toppen*, editor, "Das Danziger Schoffenbuch" (1878), *H Ermisch*, editor, "Das Freiberger Stadtrecht" (1889), *Schuster*, editor, "Das Wiener Stadtrechts- oder Weichbildbuch" (1873), *J A Fruin en Pols*, "Het rechtsboek van den Briel" (1880)

solicitation of the grant of one city's law to another gave direct
incitement for the recording of its customary law   Thus our
knowledge of Magdeburg law is derived in large part from the
legal notices that were forwarded from Magdeburg to Duke Henry
I of Silesia at the beginning of the 1200s (the so-called Magde-
burg-Goldberg law) , from the city of Halle (endowed with Magdeburg law) to Neumarkt in 1235; from Magdeburg in 1261 and
1295 to Breslau, in 1304 to Gorlitz, in 1338 to Kulm, in 1363 to
Schweidnitz, in 1364 to Halle   Similarly the law of Lubeck is
preserved for us in notices of its law forwarded to Tondern (1243),
Reval (1257, 1282), Danzig (1263), Elbing (1270), and Kolberg
(1297)   In some cities, to meet the need of the local administration
of justice, the council ordered the recording of the existing customary law   To such an order, for example, we owe the origin
of the detailed ordinances of Goslar, at the end of the 1200s or
beginning of the 1300s   Here and there "judgment books"
were opened; elsewhere "town books," whose purpose might be
various   either they were designed to compile the law peculiar to
the city (like the town book of Augsburg opened with the approval
of Rudolf I in 1276, and the " magnus civitatis liber " of Dort-
mund), or to be records of different branches of the city's administration (as the town book of Quedlinburg); or to be registers
of penalties decreed (" Wettebucher," wager books); or of sentences of imprisonment (as the prison book of Stralsund, 1310–
1472), or, finally, they were instituted — as, the so-called " ground
books," " cabinet books," " surety books," " court books," or
" Schoffen-books " — and with a continually increasing specializa-
tion of record, to give official authentication to the legal transactions of the citizens.

Among unofficial contributions to city law there must be named
(in addition to mere memorandum records) treatises on city law,
as well as private compilations and editions of the judgments of the
lay-judges in the town courts   The legal literature of city law
(like that of territorial and feudal law) had its beginning in Saxony.
The oldest are editions of Magdeburg law   Of these the following
are the most important   (1) The "Sachsische Weichbild," (" Town
Law "). At the end of the 1200s or beginning of the 1300s the
so-called " Schoffen-law " (by the lay-judges) of Magdeburg was
worked out on the basis of Magdeburg dooms that had been sent
from Magdeburg to Breslau.   Before 1269 an unknown author
wrote an instructive work upon the organization of the courts,
which was subsequently provided with a few additions.   The two

328

works were united without any effort to reconcile their content, and the result of this union was the much-used Saxon Town Law; it was translated into Latin, Polish, and Czech, and was glossed with reference to the Roman and the Canon law.   (2) The "Law book of Meissen" or the "*Rechtsbuch nach Distinktionen*," a book of Silesian territorial law and an amplified "Sachsenspiegel," so called because of its division into "distinctions"   The author undertakes to present the town law of Saxony generally, and strives to make clear the differences between territorial law, city customary law, and city law based upon imperial immunities   For the first, he utilizes the "Sachsenspiegel"; for the second, the Magdeburg law, for the third, the city law of Goslar.   This comprehensive law-book originated after the middle of the 1300s within the "mark" of Meissen   In the first half of the 1400s it was recast by Johannes Roth (died 1434), town clerk of Eisenach, with the assistance of other sources to fit the conditions of Eisenach, into a "Law-book of Eisenach."   This same Johannes Roth also composed for Eisenach the so-called "Law-book of Johann Purgoldt." (3) The "*Blume* (Flower) *von Magdeburg*." About 1386 *Nikolaus* Wurm of Neu-Ruppin, a jurist of the Romanist school and an author alike productive and tasteless, wrote a law-book under the above title, which purports to be a product of the bench of "Schöffen" of Magdeburg.   Wurm himself rehashed it later into a new work which he called the "Blume des Sachsenspiegels."   (4) The "*Systematisches Schoffenrecht*," of the middle of the 1300s, resting upon charters of the town law of Magdeburg and Breslau and the judgments of the lay-judges of Breslau   Its systematic arrangement is of interest because made in complete independence of the Roman and Canon law   (5) The "*Glogau Law-book*" of 1386, which utilizes very freely the "Systematic Schöffen-law,"   (6) The "*Alter Kulm*," the old lawbook of Kulm, a recast of the "Systematic Schoffen-law" (brought to Kulm toward the end of the 1300s), was adopted in the Prussian courts, and amplified with supplements from the "Schwabenspiegel."   The work was fitted out with a gloss that cites parallel passages from the "Sachsenspiegel" and various books of Saxon city law   (7) The "*Magdeburger Fragen*," a compilation and discussion of inquiries directed to Magdeburg as an appellate court, with the decisions given upon them.   The work exists in three versions, an unsystematic, a systematic, and an alphabetic.   The first is the oldest; it draws upon a judgment book compiled in Krakau from Magdeburg decisions, upon Magdeburg judgments forwarded to Thorn, and upon the Alter Kulm, it originated in Prussia, presumably in Thorn, between 1386 and 1400. The author of the systematic compilation was probably the same as that of the unsystematic, from which it is distinguished by its arrangement and also by a considerable addition of matter; it originated before 1400, likewise in Prussia. The alphabetic version, which adds, among other things, Pomeranian law findings, was written in Pomerania, presumably in Stettin, in the 1400s, on the basis of the unsystematic version   (8) The " Neun Bucher Magdeburger Rechts," or the " Distinctions of Walther," were begun in 1400 and completed in 1402 by Walther Ekhardi, town clerk of Thorn, who worked into them the " Sachsenspiegel " and its glosses, the " Lawbook of Meissen," the " Magdeburg Questions," the " Saxon Weichbild," and the " Alter Kulm " An abbreviated recast, probably executed by Walther himself before 1409, was first published by a notary of Konigsberg, Albert Polman, and is named after him as the " Polman Distinctions "   (9) The " Danziger Schoffenbuch " About the middle of the 1400s there originated at Danzig (without any provable utilization of other legal sources), an independent law-book, which bears the title, " The Customary Law of Kulm " It embodies a record of legal principles which were in current practice in Prussia under the influence of Kulm as an appellate court.   This law-book, together with ordinances of the lay-judges of Danzig, Danzig self-governing ordinances, and a few passages from the " Pollman Distinctions " and the " Law-book of Meissen," were united before the close of the 1400s in a compilation published as the " Danzig Schoffen-book." Independent of the Magdeburg law was the town law-book of the city of Freiberg in the mark of Meissen.   It is a private work, notable for its detailed consideration of legal procedure, which originated between 1296 and 1307, and acquired official authority.

Of the city law-books of southern Germany, in addition to that of Ruprecht von Freising, already named, there should be mentioned the " Vienna Lawbook," of the middle of the 1300s (subsequently enlarged by interpolations from the " Sachsenspiegel "), and the " Schoffen-Book of Brunn," one of the better legal works of the Middle Ages, compiled in Latin about the middle of the 1300s out of immunity grants, town ordinances, and " Schoffen-judgments " of Brunn, together with original commentaries of the compiler, all arranged alphabetically under rubrics by one Johannes (von Gelnhausen?), a town clerk of Brunn who was well versed in Roman and Canon law. The town law of Wiener-Neustadt, of the second half of the 1300s, is a private work which assumes the guise of an ordinance of one Duke Leopold of Austria.

Among the sources of the town law of middle Germany, the law-book of the Thuringian city of Muhlhausen, which originated about the middle 1200s, is conspicuous for its suggestiveness for legal history; and among those of the Netherlands the law-book of the city of Briel, written early in the 1400 s by the clerk Johannes Mathiæ (Jan Matthijssen).

§ 7   Documents and Formularies [1] — The documents of the royal chancery (of which only the more important charters were still made out in the elaborate form of diplomata) followed for two centuries their Carolingian models.   An essential innovation, which brought about a complete change in the personnel of the chancery, began under Henry IV, and became under Lothar III the rule: a document of the royal chancery lost its original and peculiar character in contrast with private deeds, as an indisputable and self-authenticating document.   The transition was facilitated by the custom (which began to appear under Henry IV) of naming as witnesses of the royal act the persons whose advice or presence was, in the former practice, mentioned in the text of the document. In the end, the witnesses came to be regarded as a means of attesting the formal genuineness of the royal document, equally with the signature and the seal.   Until in the 1100s the seal was pressed upon the document.   After Konrad III attached seals make their appearance, becoming the rule for franchises.   In the 1200s the practice begins of causing royal documents to be jointly sealed by the princes, as proof of their concurrence.   In more important cases it becomes customary to express that concurrence, not by such joint sealing, but in a supplementary document (a " Willebrief "). From the 1300s onward chancery usage distinguishes letters as " litteræ patentes " (patents), upon which the seal is stamped or hung, and " litteræ clausæ," which are locked with the seal.

As regards private documents, a retrogression began after the dissolution of the Frankish monarchy.   The formal " carta " disappeared, where it had come into use, and is replaced by the informal " notitia," or by wholly unauthenticated documents.   The

[1] REFERENCES: Jul. Ficker, "Beitrage zur Urkundenlehre" (1877–1878), Bresslau, "Handbuch der Urkundenlehre" (I. 1889); Posse, "Lehre von den Privaturkunden" (1887); Rockinger, "Uber die Formelbucher vom 13 ten bis zum 16 ten Jahrhundert als rechtshistorische Quellen" (1855), and "Briefsteller und Formelbucher des 11 ten bis 14 ten Jahrhundert, in "Quellen und Erorterungen zur bayrischen und deutschen Geschichte," IX (1863)

explanation of this deterioration in the usage for private documents is to be found in the [Germanic traditional preference for proof by witnesses and the] disregard for the self-authenticating effect of a document   But the rise and extension of the use of the seal [from the 1000s to the 1200s] led to a new stage in the usages for private documents   The seal had originally [in Roman and post-Roman times] served merely to fasten or identify the documents   But it now became, first for royal documents, then for those of clerical and secular magnates, one means of authenticating the document, and eventually the exclusive means.   The legal probative value of signature and seal gained complete acceptance almost everywhere in the course of the 1200s.   The party executing the document might append to the document his own seal, if he possessed one   Persons in authority — the king, princes, lords, dignitaries of the church, city officers, and courts — enjoyed also the right to authenticate with their seals the deeds of others.   In Italy, where a professional class of notaries existed, notarial documents attained the status of public [self-proving and indisputable] documents   From the 1100s onward, it became a general custom that the notary should enter in a register the substance of a document executed by him   These entries were known as "imbreviaturæ"   The system spread into the German part of South Tyrol   Legally chartered notaries are here found first in Bozen (half-way over the Alps from Italy), where Bavarian law was current.   From a notary of Bozen, Jakob Haas, has come down a book of "imbreviaturæ" of 1237, the oldest preserved to us on true German soil.

With the decline of conveyancing and drafting methods, the preparation of formularies (books of document forms) had also been discontinued in the post-Frankish period   Not until the 1100s and 1200s did this species of literature revive in Germany. Alongside of mere collections of document forms, there now appeared formularies adding to their forms some theoretical comments on documents generally or particular classes of such, — as, for example, the Baumbartenberg "Formularius de Modo Prosandi," of the early 1300s; or else offering exclusively such theoretical expositions of conveyancing methods, e.g the "Summa de Arte Prosand" of Konrad von Mure, of Zurich, of the years 1275–1276.

Chapter II. Second Period: a.d. 1400-1600

THE RECEPTION OF ROMAN LAW[1]

§ 8. The Reception of Roman Law in General.

Topic 1. The Rise of Learning in Roman Law

§ 9   Eike von Repkow and the "Sachsenspiegel."

§ 10 The Clergy and the Canon Law

§ 11 The Conception of an Imperial Law.

§ 12. The "Deutschenspiegel" and the "Schwabenspiegel."

§ 13 Literature of the Canon and Roman Law down to 1500.

§ 14 "Summæ Confessorum" and Related Literature

§ 15 Canon and Roman Law in German Universities.

Topic 2. The Victory of Roman Law

§ 16. Basic Conditions that made possible the Authority of Roman Law

§ 17. The Superior Technic of the Roman Law

§ 18 The "Klagspiegel."

§ 19. Decay of the Popular Courts.

§ 20. Transformations in the Administration of Justice.

§ 21 Political Importance of the Reception

§ 22 The Legal Profession University Professors and Practitioners

§ 23 Complaints against the Lawyers

§ 24 Legal Training; Smatterers and Popular Literature

Topic 3. Italian Humanism and the Reformation

§ 25 Theology and Legal Science in the Middle Ages.

§ 26. Early Humanism

§ 27. Later Influence of Humanism.

§ 28. The Reformation.

[1] [This chapter is translated from the following three works · H. Brunner, "Grundzuge der deutschen Rechtsgeschichte" (4th ed., Leipzig, 1910), vol. I of R. Stintzing, "Geschichte der deutschen Rechtswissenschaft" (2 vols., Munich and Leipzig, 1880-1884), R. Schröder, "Lehrbuch der deutschen Rechtsgeschichte" (5th ed, Leipzig, 1907) For these authors, see the Editorial Preface. The source of the thirty sections of the present chapter is as follows · § 8 is a mosaic, as detailed below, of § 61 of *Brunner* and § 1, ch. 2 of *Stintzing*; §§ 9–12 = *Stintzing*, ch 1, §§ 1–4; §§ 13–15 = *Ibid*, ch. 1, §§ 6–8, §§ 16–24 = *Ibid*, ch 2, §§ 2–10, §§ 25–28 = *Ibid*, ch. 3, §§ 1, 2–3, 4, 5, §§ 29–37 = *Ibid*, ch 4, 1–9, § 38 = *Schröder*, §§ 83–84   Of these materials, §§ 1–4 of ch 1, §§ 1–3 and 5 of ch 2, and § 1 of ch 3 of *Stintzing*, and §§ 83–84 of *Schröder* (part of the last being utilized in § 44 of this chapter) are the only portions of the originals translated without omissions. — Transl.]

333

TOPIC 4 METHODS OF JURISTS IN THE 1500s

§ 29   General Character of Medieval Science

§ 30   Legal Science · the "Mos Italicus"

§ 31   Effects of the "Mos Italicus"

§ 32   "Loci" and "Topica"

§ 33   The Period of Unshaken Authority of the "Mos Italicus"

§ 34   Opposition, and the Beginning of Reform.

§ 35.   Unofficial Academic Courses: Seminars and Disputations.

§ 36   Attitude of humanism toward the "Mos Italicus ' and the New "Methodus."

§ 37   The Ramists and their Doctrines

TOPIC 5. LEGISLATION

§ 38   Imperial and Territorial Legislation of the 1500s

§ 8   The Reception of Roman Law,[1] in General.[2] — When we speak of the Reception, in Germany, of the foreign laws, what

---

[1] [*Schroder's* references upon the Reception are (omitting a very few) as follows ("Lehrbuch," § 66) *Arnold,* "Studien zur deutschen Kulturgeschichte" (1882), pp 301 *et seq ; Below,* "Ursachen" (*cf. Schroder* in Z ²R G , XL, 462 *et seq* , and *Stolzel* in K V] S , XLVII, 1 *et seq*), *Bohlau* in K V] S , XXIII, 525 *et seq* , XXVI, 1 *et seq* and his "Mecklenburgisches Landrecht," 1, 80 *et seq , Brie,* "Stellung der deutschen Rechtsgelehrten der Rezeptions-Zeit zum Gewohnheitsrecht" (Breslauer Festgabe for Dahn, 1905, vol. I); *Brunner,* "Der Anteil des deutschen Rechts an der Entwicklung der Universitaten" (rectoral address, Berlin, 1896), *Carlebach,* "Badische Rechtsgeschichte," I (1906), 43 *et seq , Dahn,* "Deutschrechtliche Arbeiten" (1877), 57 *et seq , Eichhorn,* "Rechtsgeschichte," vol III, §§ 440–444, *Franklin,* "Beitrage," *Frensdorff* in Z ²R G , XXXIX, 237 *et seq , Gierke,* "Genossenschaftsrecht," II, 21 *et seq* , III, 645 *et seq* , and "Deutsches Privatrecht," I, 8 *et seq , Karlowa,* "Reception des romischen Rechts mit besonderer Rucksicht auf Kurpfalz" (rectoral address, Heidelberg, 1878), *Kaufmann,* "Geschichte der deutschen Universitaten " I, 75 *et seq* , II, 478 , *Kohler and Liesegang,* "Beitrage zur Geschichte des romischen Rechts in Deutschland" (2 vols , 1896–1898), *Krusch,* "Eintritt gelehrter Rate in der braunschweig Staatsverwaltung," in Z H V N S , XCI, 60 *et seq Kuhlmann,* "Romanisierung der Zivil-Prozess in Bremen" (*Gierke's* "Untersuchungen," no 36); "Statuta Reformata und der Codex Glossatus," p 97 *et seq , Laband,* "Bedeutung der Rezeption des romischen Rechts fur das deutsche Staatsrecht" (Strassburg, 1880), *Merkel,* "Der Kampf des Fremdrechts mit dem einheimischen in Braunschweig-Luneburg" (1904) and in "Quellen und Darstellungen zur Geschichte Niedersachsen," vol XIX (of. *Moller* in Z ²R G , XXXIX, 310), *Moddermann* (and *K Schulz),* "Rezeption des romischen Rechts" (1875) , *Muther,* "Rom -kanon Prozess " (Rostock, 1872), "Romisches und kanonisches Recht im deutschen Mittelalter " (1871), "Zur Quellengeschichte des deutschen Rechts" in Z ¹R G , IV, 380 *et seq* , IX, 50 *et seq* , "Rechtswissenschaft" (1876), *Rosenthal,* "Geschichte des Gerichtswesens und der Verwaltungsorganisation Baierns," I, 139, 422 *et seq W Roth* in Z ²R G , XXXV, 359 *et seq , Sartori-Montecroce,* "Beitrage zur osterreichischen Reichs-und Rechtsgeschichte," I (1895), *Schaffner,* "Das romische Recht in Deutschland wahrend des 12 und 13 Jahrhundert " (1859) , *C A Schmidt,* "Rezeption des romischen Rechts" (1868), *Schum* in Z ²R G., roman Abt , XXIV, 304 *et seq., J C Schwartz,* "Vierhundert Jahre deutscher Zivil-prozess Gesetzgebung" (1898), *Seckel,* "Beitrage zur Geschichte beider Rechte im Mittelalter," I (1898), *Sohm,* "Frankisches Recht und romisches Recht",

is meant thereby is the Roman law, the Canon law, and the Lombard feudal law.   The historical fact which we call the " Reception " [1] of the Roman law was a slow process, extending through several centuries.   Its course and eventual completion were influenced not only by the relations of Germany to the Latin nations, but also by causes grounded most diversely in the social conditions of Germany itself.   It is usual to regard this development in connection with the invasion of the Canon law, and, in truth, the reception of the two bodies of law not only took place (in a certain sense) synchronously, but the Canon law, as will be shown below (§ 10), though such result was not contemplated in its adoption, prepared the way for the Roman and drew this after it.   Nevertheless, the two movements must be described independently, because they were wholly different in their causes and in their course.   One cannot speak of a " reception " of the Canon law in at all the same sense as that of the Roman; because, so long as there had existed any Canon law, there was accorded to it, in Germany, from the beginning, an undisputed, definite sphere of authority and application.   For the entire field of the church's dominance it was always a practical, authoritative, statutory law; and only the enlargement of this domain — not, as in the case of the Roman law, the original establishment of its statutory force

in Z ²R G., XIV, 70 *et seq*, "Deutsche Rechtsgeschichte und die Kodificationsfrage" in Z Pr Öff R, I, 245 *et seq*, *Stammler*, "Recht des Breidenbacher Grundes" (*Gierke's* "Untersuchungen," no. 12), *Stintzing*, "Geschichte," vol 1, *passim*, "Pop Lit" (1867), "Zur Geschichte des römischen Rechts in Deutschland" in H Z, XXIX, 408 *et seq*, and in K Vj S, VI, 557 *et seq*, *Stobbe*, "Rechtsquellen," I, 609-655, II, 1-142, *Stolzel*, "Richterthum "(*cf Franklin* in Z Pr Öff R, I, 236 *et seq*), "Entwicklung der gelehrten Rechtsprechung des Brandenburger Schoppenstuhls," I (1891), "Brandenburg-Preussens Rechtsverwaltung," I, 30 *et seq*, "Urkundliches Material aus den Brandenburger Schoppenstuhlsakten" (4 vols 1901, *cf. Amira* in Z ²R G, XXXVI, 288-294, XXXVIII, 427 *et seq*, *Rietschel* in H Vj S, VI, 405 *et seq*, *Zeumer* in ' Forschungen zur brandenburgischen und preussischen Geschichte," XVI, 255 *et seq*) and in last named journal XVI, 345 *et seq.*, also in K Vj S, XLVII, 1 *et seq*; *Hassenpflug*, "Die erste Kammergerichtsordnung Kurbrandenburgs" (1895), *Laspeyres* in Z D R, VI, 1 *et seq*, *Maitland*, "English law and the Renaissance" (Cambridge, 1901), *Ott*, "Beitrage", *Reyscher* in Z D R., IX, 337 *et seq*.]

[2] [The first sentence is from *Brunner*, the rest of the first two paragraphs and also the last one from *Stintzing*, and all the rest from *Brunner*. In a portion of the latter's text which is omitted he differs from *Stintzing* (§ 10 below) in regarding the Reception of the canon law as a *consequence* of that of the Roman — TRANSL]

[1] *Stintzing*, ' U Zasius" (1857), p 30 *et seq*, *Franklin*, "Beiträge" (1863); *Stobbe*, "Rechtsquellen," I, 609 *et seq*, II, 9-110; *Schmidt*, "Die Reception des römischen Rechts in Deutschland" (1868), *Stolzel*, "Richterthum"; *Moddermann*, "Die Reception des römischen Rechts" (1875), *Ott*, "Beitrage."

and practical enforcement — was the object of a historical evolution

The authority of the Canon law will be discussed below (§ 15). We shall also see how Roman legal learning was carried into Germany as early as the 1200s We see the increasing attention given it in legal literature and practice The idea that the authority of the Justinian law-books is one current for the entire Empire becomes a historical force, the conception of an imperial common law takes form and hold Progressing slowly from this beginning, the actual naturalization of the alien law is realized under difficulties and amid contradictions, — unequally in different places, among different classes, and for different social relations, unequally also as between different branches and institutes of the law Here, progress is due to study and spontaneous assimilation, there, to the unreflecting pressure of those whose profession is bound up with the foreign law. And if the advance is unequal and wavering, the goal also is unclear toward which the movement is tending. So that, although we can regard the Reception as consummated by the first half of the 1500s, in so far as the predominance of the new law is thenceforth decisive in the practice of the courts, nevertheless one could not earlier nor could one then have exactly determined the extent of its validity, the measure of authority of its written sources, or its relation to the native law. The absolute, unlimited, and exclusive enforcement of all principles contained in the " Corpus Juris " was never seriously asserted; but neither the reasons for nor the limits of its authority were critically investigated, nor distinction made between the formal force of its laws " qua " laws and the rational authority of its content.

[In the process of the Reception] we can distinguish the stage of the theoretical from that of the practical Reception The theoretical Reception consists in the growth of the conviction that Roman law possessed a claim to validity in Germany; the practical consists in the penetration of Roman law into the German judicial law The former goes back into the 1100s, and has its root in the idea that the Roman Empire of the German Nation constituted a continuation of the ancient Roman Empire, so that the laws of the Roman emperors were laws of the forbears of the German kings, and as such had subsidiary force. The relation in which the kings of the house of Hohenstaufen stood to the teachers of the Roman law in Italy afforded abundant support for the spread and firmer rooting of this idea It gained vitality

and strength the more pronounced grew the particularism of the
Middle Ages, and the more widespread the local frittering of the
native law. It is, indeed, an oft-recurring trait in the history of
the German people that the most flagrant particularism has sought
and found its cure in the complement of an unrestricted universalism.   The Hohenstaufen kings Frederick I and Frederick II
had had certain of their own laws interpolated into the "Corpus
Juris Civilis."   Henry VII gave an order for the interpolation
of a law of 1312 against heretics (which, however, remained un-
executed).   A lively Romanistic activity was developed by the
kings of the house of Luxemburg, — particularly Charles IV,
who, among other things, extended to the electoral princes the
provisions of the Roman law relative to the "crimen læsæ maie-
statis"   A knowledge of the foreign law was spread among the
people by the law schools of Italy, whose world-repute drew many
students from Germany, — if only for the reason that the Canon
law, then grasping jurisdiction over so many questions of practical
life, rested in many parts upon the Roman law.   The influence
of the alien law manifested itself first in German legal literature.
The "Schwabenspiegel" itself adopted a few Roman legal principles. In the glosses on the "Sachsenspiegel" the attempt
was made to prepare a concordance between the Saxon law on one
hand and the "leges" and "canones" on the other   The knowledge of the foreign law had a still greater influence upon the works
of Nikolaus Wurms and the town clerk Johannes Von Brunn.

The practical Reception had its root in the appearance of judges
learned in the law.   Jurists schooled in the foreign law — to
whom this was only too often *the* law — came to be employed in
Germany, though at first only in administrative affairs.   They
first gained the opportunity of determining the law at the court
of the king, who referred to them cases which he personally decided, particularly arbitration cases.   Afterwards the king came
to choose in part from the class of jurisprudents the councillors
he appointed to his Chamber of Justice ("Kammergericht").
When the Imperial Chamber of Justice ("Reichskammergericht")
was established in 1495, its members, half of whom were required
to be men learned in the law, had to swear to judge according to
the "common laws of the Empire," — a formula within which
the Roman law was included   After the highest court of the
Empire had thus led the way, the territorial and the city courts
were bound, as courts of lower instance, to follow.   In Switzerland
and in Schleswig, where the "Reichskammergericht" did not

have jurisdiction, a reception of Roman law took place only to a very limited extent. In most of the Territories, however, a development similar to that which took place at the royal court had preceded this, for it often happened that litigants, at the instance of counsel trained in the new law, withdrew their controversies from the moribund " Schoffen "-courts and carried them for settlement to the administrative officers of the territorial sovereign, men likewise learned in the alien law. The law enforced in the village courts kept itself longest free from any intermixture of alien elements, its sources, the dooms, still affording for a long time a rich mine of popular legal ideas

In the struggle between the native and alien laws the latter found powerful support in the universities that had arisen in Germany since the middle of the 1300s University instruction in law was devoted to the foreign law alone, — at first to the Canon law, after the beginning of the 1400s to the Roman also. Upon the foreign law, again, was based the arbitration practice (§ 22) of the university faculties of law, by which these partially took the place of the old, popular appellate courts (§ 20). In favor of the foreign law, finally, there was the influence of a popular legal literature, immense in extent, written for the purpose of making accessible to the unlearned the doctrines of the Roman and the canon books This literature consisted in part of alphabetic compends; they began in the 1300s and ended with the often-printed " Vocabularius Iuris Utriusque " of Joducus of 1452 There were also systematic presentations, among which should be mentioned, as the oldest, the " Summa Legum " of RAYMUND VON WIENER-NEUSTADT, a text-book of private and criminal law, composed for the benefit of the author's sons in the 1300s (probably 1340–1348) upon the basis of Italian-Romanist literature, but taking account of Germanic legal institutions.[1] Among the works of this popular literature, composed in German dialects, two in particular attained the greatest influence upon legal practice (1) the " Clag, antwort und ausgesprochene urteyl gezogen aus geystlichen und weltlichen rechten " (Plaints, Answers and Judgments drawn from Ecclesiastical and Secular Law), which was written about 1425 by a city scribe in Hall (Swabia), and published in 1516 by SEBASTIAN BRANT under the title " Klagspiegel " (Mirror of Plaints); and (2) the " Laienspiegel " (Laymen's Mirror), written by ULRICH TENGLER (1509), an encyclopædic presentation of private, criminal,

---

[1] This work exercised a decisive influence upon legal development in Austria, Hungary, and Poland

338

and procedural law, which, in addition to foreign legal literature, made use of German legal sources.

There were, then, " received " in Germany: (1) the Roman law, in the sense indicated below; (2) the " Corpus Iuris Canonici Clausum," *i.e.* its content, so far as this had always been binding in the ecclesiastical courts, became henceforth a norm governing decisions in the secular courts; (3) the Lombard feudal law, embodied in the customaries or " Libri Feudorum," a compilation of pieces of different dates, which originated in part at Pavia, in part at Milan, upon the basis of the feudal statutes of Konrad II, Lothar III, and Frederick I, and of the Milanese feudal practice The most modern version of this collection was incorporated by the jurist HUGOLINUS DE PRESBYTERO, as the " decima collatio novellarum," into the " Corpus Juris Civilis," and was received with this into Germany.

As for the most important of the foreign laws, namely the Roman, the theoretical and the practical Receptions are distinguishable with regard to their respective materials, extent, and effects. The theoretical reception had as its materials the pure Roman law of Justinian's law-books: the Institutes, Pandects, Code, and Novels It was not a reception of individual legal principles and institutes, but comprised the " Corpus Juris Civilis " " in complexu "; this was received, however, only as subsidiary law. On the other hand, the practical Reception rested upon the judicial law that had been elaborated in Italy, based upon the " Corpus Juris Civilis," but with manifold modernizations and transformations of its doctrines Moreover, while its materials were the Roman laws as transmitted through Italian judicial practice, it extended also to the pure Roman law, — not, however, " in complexu," but only to individual principles and institutes thereof, albeit numerous and fundamental, moreover, it attributed to these an absolute validity, instead of limiting them, as alien law, to a subsidiary character

This contrast between the theoretical and the practical Receptions remained in part undefined , and, indeed, men were hardly conscious of it. This is shown, for example, by the fact that the advocates of Romanistic theory and practice, down to the most recent times, could not realize the indubitably correct idea that the result of the practical Reception, even though this rested upon a misunderstanding of Roman legal sources, made impossible the application of *pure* Roman law. For the rest, it is true that the sharpest contrasts between the two forms of the Reception

disappeared even during its progress   For this there were three
reasons. Firstly, the authority of the "Corpus Juris Civilis"
was restricted to those passages which the Italian jurists had
adopted and glossed, — this in order to explain the fact that the
"Corpus Juris Civilis" contained legal principles which were un-
applied   Secondly, resort was had to the conception of a modern
Roman practice" ("usus hodiernus pandectarum"), in order to
get around the fact that principles were applied which the "Corpus
Juris Civilis" did not contain.   Thirdly, the absolute authority of
the alien law, as against the native law, was cloaked by attributing
to the former a fictitious "fundatum intentionem," whereas the
rules of the native law were subjected as facts to the requirements
of judicial proof, and further by establishing as a condition for the
validity of the customary law a necessary period of usage.   Thus
it came about that Germanic law was shoved aside and disdain-
fully neglected by the learned jurists and the smatterers who filled
the courts.   Only in the lands of the Saxon law, where the traditional legal ideas were more firmly clung to, were the conditions
more favorable to the native element   In these, a knowledge of
the common Saxon law, as it had been developed upon the basis
of the "Sachsenspiegel" and its commentaries, was regarded as
the duty of a judge, so that (after the territorial and the local
ordinances) enforcement was given in the first place to the Saxon
common law; and only then did the Romanesque common law
receive a subsidiary application

The Reception cannot, in itself, be impugned.   It requires no
defence, if one grants at the outset that all progress in human
culture has as its precondition the adoption and assimilation of
culture gone before   Its explanation is found in the then state
of German law.   The increasing development of trade demanded
a coherent law   The need of this is reflected in the appearance of works like the "Deutschenspiegel," the "Schwabenspiegel," and the "Kaiserrecht," which were endeavors to constitute such a coherent law, although they did not even distantly
approach its realization   It is seen also in the effort to widen the
vogue of one or another body of law, — for example, in the grouping of extensive families of city law.   The consciousness of the same
need led (so late as in the 1400s, not long before the practical
Reception) to deliberate proposals for a reform, in a unitary sense,
of the native law.   Thus, in the year 1433, Nikolaus Cusanus
presented to the Council of Basel a memorial in which he demanded
an official inquest and digest of territorial customs, with the con-

currence of the provincial judges. This proposal, not being directed
to authorities friendly to such ideas, unfortunately remained without results. Its realization would have essentially strengthened
Germanic customary law in the struggle against its Roman rival,
it would have given the measure a significance (for Germany at
least) equal to that occupied, in the history of French law, by the
official redaction of the " coutumes " that had then recently been
undertaken in various districts of France, and was soon afterward
ordained for the whole country by Charles VII, in an ordinance
of Montilz-les-Tours (1454).

Since, thus, the native legal development did not rise above
provincialism, Roman law attained supremacy as the common
written law of Germany. It was about this same period that a
common literary language grew up and dominated over the different Germanic dialects.[1] To the craving for a common law there
was added, in the time of the humanistic period of the Renascence,
and of the increasing culture of the upper classes of the German
folk, the desire for a scientific law. German law, however, as it
then existed [in a generalized and written form, *post*, §§ 9, 11, 12],
lacked a scientific method of treatment such as the Roman law
had received from the Roman jurists and Italian practitioners
Now this German law itself was just then involved in a transformation which found points of contact, in many fields, in the
" Corpus Juris Civilis ", so that the adoption of the latter appears,
to that extent, as merely the conclusion of a development already
begun in the native law Such an approximation necessarily
facilitated the Reception; whereas the customary laws, just because of their greater unlikeness to the Roman law, had held their
ground against this In England and France, where the partial
adoption of Roman legal ideas had taken place earlier, it acted as
a sort of inoculation, rendering the native law, thus impregnated,
capable of resisting a more extreme doctrinal infection. In Germany the Reception took place at a time when medieval forms
of life were already matured to a degree approaching either dissolution or petrification; a time when the frittering of legal organization and the enfeeblement of the imperial power had already gone

---

[1] The supposed poverty of the German law and superiority of the
Roman law were the real causes of the Reception , this is shown by the
strong resistance to the intrusion of the foreign law offered by precisely
those cities which were economically most important and politically most
independent, such as Lubeck, Bremen, Hamburg, Magdeburg and
Brunswick (*von Below*, "Die Ursachen der Reception des romischen
Rechts in Deutschland," 1905, pp 93 *et seq*. [*Cf* herewith *Stintzing's* views
in § 19 below , the latter being the usual view — Transl]

too far. The Reception worked so intensively, therefore, because it took place so late.

[But a further reason is to be found in the fact that] the German jurists were unmindful of their duties to the native law, and therefore unequal to their task The constitution of the German royal court, as well as of the Germanic purely popular and "Schoffen-courts," had not been favorable to the development of a learned legal profession. It was in the school of the alien law (already a unified system) that such a profession first arose, and perforce it established its own right of existence by battling for the recognition of the foreign law. The manner, however, in which it effected the Reception will always call for criticism and reproach Its small-minded disdain for the native law, the stupid and wholly superficial way in which it grafted Roman principles upon rules of Germanic growth, its unconsciousness of the contrast between the native and the Roman law, making it blind to the truth that no folk can live again in the spirit of another, — these traits were a national catastrophe. When one reflects that the Germans, in consequence of this blunder, have never fully assimilated the Roman law, one can estimate the confusion created in German legal life at the time of the Reception under the lead of an unspeakably illiberal profession

In the following account we shall first consider the Reception on its inward, technical side, and then, in connection with the transformation of legal practice, shall endeavor to make evident its significance for social and political relations.

Topic 1 The Rise of Learning in Roman Law

§ 9. **Eike von Repkow and the "Sachsenspiegel"** — About the same time when the contributions of the Italian Glossators to the Romanesque judicial law were approaching their end in Accursius, and Canon law was receiving fixed form in Gregory IX's collection of decretals (1234), a German knight, from the country of the Hartz Mountains, EIKE VON REPKOW, gathered together the legal principles of his race in the "Sachsenspiegel" (Mirror of the Saxons) This name he gave to his book, following a favored literary usage, because in it the free Saxons might behold their law. He had no predecessors in such a statement of the law, he drew his matter directly from legal practices known to him through many years activity as a lay-judge He describes and lays down the traditional law as then in force, giving to it a felicitous expression and a form which it retained down to much later times.

The German people had then passed the freshness of youth. In its jural evolution, which had been isolated and peculiar, the "Sachsenspiegel" marks the culmination; for no work of later times can be named that rivals it in wealth of original material, — no other so purely popular, so unaffected by foreign influence. This originality distinguishes it in noteworthy manner from the contemporary work of the Englishman, Henry Bracton, " De Legibus et Consuetudinibus Angliæ," in which, under the influence of the method of the Glossarists, the native law is presented in union with the Roman.

In Germany also, however, the power of Roman and ecclesiastical legal learning, cultivated in Italy and patronized by emperors and popes, was beginning to be perceptible   As the downfall of the Hohenstaufen marks a turning-point in the nation's cultural development, so the "Sachsenspiegel" marks the close of the creative period in the national law.   Indeed, we cannot well err if we assume that Eike was impelled to the recording of the Saxon law by the rising authority of the written foreign law, in which he recognized a danger to the native system.   This enables us to understand why his book on Germanic law was composed first in Latin, in order to give it a form equal in dignity to that of the rival foreign law which it confronted

It is significant that the "Sachsenspiegel" (which after all only set forth the law of one racial branch) neither directly stimulated nor was imitated by similar work for other Germanic branches, but itself spread over Germany, being either accepted by others without change or worked over into other law-books and city ordinances.   Wherever we find, in the period immediately following, records of Germanic law in literary form, they rest upon Eike's work   At the same time, the currency and influence of the foreign legal learning becomes more or less plainly visible.[1] A typical complement to the worthy form of Eike, the knightly lay-judge, has been preserved to us, in the satire of the "Occultus Erfordensis" (1282–1283), in the "Carmen Historicum" of Nikolaus von Bibra.[2] It pictures for us the life of one Heinrich von Kirchberg, who returns to Germany, after many years of study in universities abroad, as a " doctor decretorum," and adorned with the halo of foreign legal learning, to take up the exciting and bus-

[1] Stobbe, "Rechtsquellen," I, 609 et seq , Muther, "Rechtswissenschaft," pp 1 et seq   [2] Muther, op. cit., pp 38 et seq.

tling life of an attorney and counselor. The poem shows us that, so early as the middle of the 1200s the doctors of law had assumed a rôle so important in the social life of Germany that the doings of a pedantic pettifogger could be profitably chosen as the subject of satire.

We should err, however, if from such a satire we should form our opinion of the significance and the importance of the doctors. Witnesses are not lacking who present to us men of jurisprudential training as the objects of confidence and profound respect, occupying influential positions From the 1100s onward, German clerics flocked in great numbers toward Paris, Bologna, Padua, and other universities to study foreign law [1] Among the "nations" into which the students at Bologna and Padua were organized, the German "nation" was vested with special privileges Many of them found permanent occupation in Italy, but the majority doubtless returned to Germany, where a learned preparation in the law, and especially a doctoral degree, secured influential positions with lay and ecclesiastical lords, while important cities were at pains to draw learned jurists into their service.

§ 10. **The Clergy and the Canon Law.** — It was the clergy that carried this branch of science — as they carried others — into Germany, in order to utilize it in the Church's law and administration [2] Once the Church had completely assumed (as it had in the 1200s) the character of an establishment outwardly organized in juristic forms, and a purely formal and juristic doctrine had come to dominate the entire life of the Church, so that its law was elaborated to the smallest details, the complicated ecclesiastical administration could be conducted only by clerics thoroughly familiar with the Canon law. An exceptional knowledge of Canon law, the taking of academic degrees, not only insured entry to influential lay positions, but was also a pathway to the higher ecclesiastical dignities and benefices. The range of ecclesiastical jurisdiction was more and more extended over the clergy and the domain of the Church's interests, and the Canon law, far transgressing these limits, had interfered markedly in purely lay concerns Thus the elastic conception of "res ecclesiasticæ" made it possible to draw within the jurisdiction of the clerical courts not only lay cases really involving an interest of the Church, but

---

[1] *Muther, op cit*, pp 399 *et seq*, has compiled a list of German law students in foreign universities down to 1500, *cf* also *Stolzel*, "Richterthum," pp 43, 78, *Ott*, "Beitrage," pp 33 *et seq*
[2] With the following *cf von Schulte*, "Quellen," II, pp 26 *et seq*., pp. 456 *et seq* For Bohemia, *Ott*, "Beitrage," pp. 7–30.

every civil transaction whatever. It was enough to treat the point of law from the standpoint of human sinfulness, and this stamped any case as proper for ecclesiastical cognizance. "One may safely say that there was no legal relation, no aspect of social and public life, which was not subjected under one pretext or another to the jurisdiction of the clergy."

And this extension was generally welcomed by laymen, impelled as they were by the general spirit of the times and by their own interests. Even in cases in which the jurisdiction of an ecclesiastical court was doubtful or was maintainable by neither of the parties, a basis for it was often made by their consent, because the ecclesiastical court promised an orderly procedure and often a more efficient execution of judgment than the civil judge could offer Thus by the beginning of the 1200s the ecclesiastical jurisdiction had acquired an importance in Germany which certainly equalled, if it did not exceed, that of the civil tribunals.

It goes without saying that in the ecclesiastical courts the Canon law was applied, and it thus not only permeated with its consequences the mighty organism of the Church, but also subjected to its regulations the civic life. Attendance at foreign universities was not necessary in order to acquire it, for it was taught in the cloisters; [1] and its execution was insured by the rigorous discipline of the clergy. The superiors of the Church, however, in every way favored the attendance of the clergy at foreign schools for the purpose of acquiring a deeper knowledge and the additional prestige of an academic degree.

Now the Canon law presupposed the legal force of the Roman law. The ecclesiastical judge applied the latter so far as variant doctrines were not prescribed by the former, which in large portions must be regarded as a development and modification of the Roman law under the influence of Germanic and ecclesiastical principles The old maxim, "ecclesia Romana vivit secundum legem Romanam," — thanks to which it was precisely and preeminently within the Church that the Justinian law had been handed down through the dark centuries of the early Middle Ages, — was still true; and the rivalry which now arose between Roman and Canon law ended in the unchallenged dominance of the former's authority. The Roman remained the civil law of the Church; yet only in so far as the Church had not altered it, had decreed no laws of its own.[2] For this reason the decrees of Church councils and the decretals,

---

[1] References in *Ott*, "Beitrage," pp. 32 *et seq*
[2] *Schulte*, "Quellen," I, 98.

which since the 1100s had opposed the study of the Roman law
by the clergy, did indeed avail to promote the study of Canon law
and to raise its authority; but could not effectively discourage
the clergy from busying themselves with the Roman law within
the limits of their calling and of the implications of the Canon law
itself.[1] What is more, those inhibitions were so weakened by
dispensations and licenses that even a scholarly knowledge of
Roman law was by no means a rare exception.[2]

Thus the Canon law drew after it the Roman. Carried by the
clergy, the knowledge and authority of both systems, though
embodied in foreign tongues, made headway among the laity.
Even though the authorities vested with the supreme worldly and
the supreme spiritual power repeatedly combated one another,
still, in medieval theory they blended in a higher unity ordained
by God, and both bodies of law mutually supported each
other's authority, inasmuch as they formed together the "jus
utrumque."

§ 11. **The Conception of the Imperial Law.** — The old idea of
the Holy Roman Empire — the theory that the Roman Empire,
providentially constituted as a permanent institution for the protection of Christendom, continued to live in the imperial dignity
of German kings, the idea that the Empire of the German nation
was simply a continuance of the old Roman Empire — led directly
to the conclusion that the persistent authority of a world law
was immanent in the Justinian books. From the time that Otto
III revived this idea, his successors, whenever political conditions
were favorable and incitement offered, repeatedly insisted upon
the authority of that law and appealed to its particular principles.
The Hohenstaufen only followed the way already marked for them
when they furthered the splendor of the Bologna law school, in
order that it should serve their own political theory of the "dominium mundi" It was, indeed, notably these relations of the
emperor to the great jurists which worked so efficiently for the
dissemination and establishment of the belief and authority of the
Roman law, and this belief attained the status of a political and
constitutional dogma

Under its influence the notion of an imperial law took shape.
This was generally made to include all the written law resting
upon imperial authority It enjoyed, for that very reason, a

---

[1] *Savigny.* "Geschichte" III, 364 *et seq ; Schulte,* "Quellen," I, 105,
Stobbe in K.V J S, XI (1869), 13–14
[2] See proofs in *Stobbe,* "Rechtsquellen," I, 628, K V J S., XI, 13 *et seq.*

general authority throughout the empire; and it was distinguished on the one hand from the papal law, then in rivalry with it for preeminence, and on the other hand from the subordinate law of the different races and territories of the empire   Although the range of the sources that were reputed imperial law was never exactly defined, and the meaning of the word therefore varied, there was, nevertheless, a predominant tendency to include in it the law-books of Justinian as well as the statutes of the German Empire.

§ 12. The "Deutschenspiegel" and the "Schwabenspiegel." — Thus by the 1200 s the theory had made itself at home in Germany that above the laws of the individual races there stood another double legislation, resting on the two supreme authorities of Christendom   Traces of its influence were soon visible, and therewith began its friction with the native law.   Johann von Buch tells us in his gloss (written after 1325) of the "Sachsenspiegel" that this book was contemned in the ecclesiastical courts because it was only "jus unius populi."   It was attempted to sustain it by showing its concord with the two bodies of universal law, and by reviving the legend that the "Sachsenspiegel" rested on a charter of Charles the Great and the Saxon feudal law rested on statutes of Frederick Barbarossa.   Hardly a generation after the composition of the "Sachsenspiegel," we already see the beginning of a literary movement directed to preparing, through expositions fusing the native law with the foreign, law-books that could claim a common authority throughout all Germany.

About the time of the Interregnum, the "Sachsenspiegel" was translated into high German, its unknown translator, from southern Germany, attempted by interpolations to give it the form of a source valid for all the Germanic racial branches   He called his work the Mirror of the German People ("Spiegel deutscher Leute") The author lays claim to scientific training, he does not (he says) content himself with his personal legal experience, but presents the law for Germany as the kings have conferred it and the masters of the law (namely, the Roman jurists) have taught it.   Of Roman law there is, indeed, only little to be found in the work, but it is significant to find here, so early and so clearly expressed, the idea that the Roman law is a part of that which is valid throughout Germany.

This " Deutschenspiegel " seems to have attained but slight currency, and has come down to us in but one manuscript   But the path marked by it was followed, in the early years of the reign of Rudolf I (in 1275 ?), by the unknown author of the Swabian Mirror (" Schwabenspiegel "). He made use of the earlier work, increasing the range of the written sources utilized in it. The application made of the Roman and the Canon laws shows the hand of one who had been more strongly influenced by the doctrine of the Glossarists, the scholarship, and the clerical animus (which leads him to derive the emperor's worldly power from the pope), betray the churchman. He did not, however, like Eike, draw his materials from legal practice, but from written sources, and among them the primitive popular codes and the imperial capitularies had long since fallen into desuetude, and the books of the Roman and Canon law had scarcely begun to be known in Germany, — so that he does not present to us the law as it was, but as, in his opinion, it ought to be His inadequate mastery of his material prevents him from making his work a unity, he succeeds only in making a disorderly compilation full of contradictions and misunderstandings.[1] But in this book we have still only the token and the prelude of a beginning change The popular law still remains in its integrity a possession of the people and of the lay-judges; and when a bold attack upon the " Sachenspiegel " is made in the middle of the following century (1300s) by the churchmen, it broke before the resistance of popular protest that it excited An Augustinian friar, JOHANN KLENKOK,[2] born at Buke (near Hoya) in the beginning of the 1300s and professor of theology at Erfurt, wrote a treatise (" Decadicon ") about the middle of the century at the instance of Walther Kerlinger, a doctor of theology who was invested with the "officium inquisitionis hæreticæ", in this work he impugned ten articles of the " Sachsenspiegel " as unchristian, and repugnant to the Canon law. Irritated by opposition and persecution, he sharpened his attacks in repeated new editions of the " Decadicon," enlarging it finally (about 1365) to include twenty-one articles of the " Sachsenspiegel ", and, as a result, Gregory IX in 1372 condemned fourteen of these in a bull directed to six archbishops and the Emperor Charles V. This attack by the Church, however, aside from provoking a few more tracts upon the " articuli reprobati," remained without important consequences

For a long period after this the " Sachsenspiegel " remained the center and the basis of legal literature. The Latin translations of it (which begin as early as the 1200s); the systematic revisions of it, the Saxon municipal law (" Weichbild ") designed to suit

---

[1] *Stobbe*, " Rechtsquellen," 1, 342.
[2] *Homeyer*, " Johann Klenkok," A B.A., vol. LV.

the needs of the Saxon towns, which appeared in the early 1300 s, and was due to its influence, the "Rechtsbuch nach Distinctionen," which belongs to the second half of the same century; finally, the "Richtsteige" through the territorial and feudal law of JOHANN VON BUCH,—these are the most notable evidences of the national literature that grew out of the "Sachsenspiegel." If we add to these the "Kleines Kaiserrecht" (Little Book of Imperial Law) which appeared in central Germany and belongs to the beginning of the 1300 s, the slightly later law-books of RUPRECHT VON FREYSING, composed under the influence of the "Schwabenspiegel, and finally the systematic collections and compends of the decisions of the lay-judges, we get the impression, as regards the 1300 s, of a flourishing literature, resting directly upon the living law, intended for practical use, and lacking only a scientific method and finish in order to attain an independent maturity.

It was the need of remedying these defects that led German legal scholars to the study of an exotic system. Thus they fell under the influence of the alien school; and the Roman-Canon concepts which they thus artificially borrowed stunted gradually the plastic powers of the decaying native law.

§ 13   **Literature of the Canon and Roman Law down to 1500.** — In the literature thus far described, native law was predominant, while foreign law was drawn upon only as a supplementary aid. But beside this literature there was another which had as its special subject the foreign and particularly the Canon law [1] Its beginnings go back before the time of the "Sachsenspiegel" and reveal the juristic studies among the German clergy which began with Gratian's "Decretum." As the administration of the secular and the ecclesiastical law went on side by side throughout the empire, so for a time there flowed parallel two currents of legal literature, the one teaching of the Germanic customary law, the other of the Canon law and (more incidentally) the Roman law; until finally the first dried up, and the latter, unresisted, broke like undammed waters over Germany.

It was probably as early as the first half of the 1100 s that the celebrated "Ordo Judiciarius" was composed in Germany. Later, under the name of Johannes Andreä it attained extremely wide circulation. [2] This attribution to the celebrated Italian author •

---

[1] *Ott*, "Beitrage," pp 101 *et seq*

[2] *Rockinger*, "Über einen Ordo Judiciarius" (Munich, 1855), *Stintzing*, "Pop Lit," pp. 202 *et seq*, *Bethmann-Hollweg*, "Civil-process," VI, 144 *et seq*; *Muther*, "Rechtswissenschaft," pp. 179 *et seq*.

(a common occurrence) was groundless; the book does not even show the influence of an Italian model. In its Latin form, numerous manuscript versions of its text (some of them with variants and supplements) and many manuscript commentaries attest the wide use made of this little text-book of Roman-Canon procedure; while more than twenty printed editions, down to the beginning of the 1600s, prove that even to a relatively late period it remained one of the most popular of manuals. The Latin original was early recast in German with additions This "Ordnung des Gerichts" was also widely circulated in manuscript and later in printed editions.

The "Speculum Abbreviatum," assigned in a printed edition of 1151 to JOHANNES DE STYNNA [a doctor of theology of Paris, and an abbot, who served his order of the Cistercians in numerous offices and lawsuits], is a work of comprehensive scholarship Thorough investigations [1] have shown that this was written in Germany in the first half of the 1300s Its basis is the "Speculum Juris " of DURANTIS (died 1296), a work which could not well have been known at that time to more than a few in Germany. Since he could not always have with him on his professional excursions this voluminous work and other helps, he prepared (as he himself tells us) for his own use excerpts and compilations, and these he was accustomed to take with him as a "viaticum"; out of them was composed his text-book of the Canon law, a handbook of legal practice In its first part it treats of lawsuits in general, in the second, of pleadings and legal documents; in its third, of the "regulæ iuris," — following Durantis in the first two, and excerpting in the third the commentaries of Dynus and other canonists upon the corresponding title of the sixth book of the "Corpus Juris Canonici." His compilations are discerningly made, and much that is new is added to them out of the special knowledge of the experienced practitioner As formularies he uses largely (besides those found in Durantis) original documents of his own branch of the law. To the "Clementinus sæpe contingit " he devotes a particularly independent commentary.

§ 14. " **Summæ Confessorum** " and **Related Literature.** — Besides this literature designed essentially for actual legal practice, there developed within the circle of the clergy, beginning with the late 1200s, another literature, which originated and had its reason

---

[1] *Stintzing,* "Pop Lit ," pp 229 *et seq* , and (excellent) *Muther,* "Rom - kanon Prozess," pp. 1 *et seq* , *Bethmann-Hollweg,* "Civil-process," VI- 234 *et seq*

in the administration of the sacrament of the confession.[1] As
special cases of conscience ("casus conscientiæ") were often intimately involved with cases of law, occasions were thus offered to
the clergy for forming principles and expressing judgments in such
cases   The more that ethics and dogmatics were developed, under
the influence of the hierarchy, into a system of rules outside men's
consciences and binding upon them, the more the limits that divided
this system from positive law tended to disappear. In a time
when the ecclesiastic alone was regarded as the bearer of culture
the layman quite naturally resorted to him as an adviser; and,
moreover, the endeavor of the hierarchy to assure its influence
upon civil life induced it not only to meet this need of the
confessional, but also to undertake from that basis to secure predominance within the field of law

The Dominican order (to which, along with the Franciscans,
had been conceded the privilege throughout Christendom of administering the sacrament in equal right with the parochial clergy)
was the first to grasp in a practical way the importance of juristic
training to the confessor   While the Cistercians (as seen above)
were writing legal works upon the "jurisdictio contentiosa" and
"voluntaria," there began with the "Summa de Pœnitentia" of
RAIMUNDO DE PEÑAFORT (died 1275) — the celebrated compiler
of the Decretals of Gregory IX and general of the Dominican
order — a literature designed to provide the confessor not only
with all matters worthy of knowledge for the administration of
his office, but particularly to instruct him in the law. The chief
content of the "Summa Raymundi" is a popular presentation, in
easy style, of the legal system of Church and State, including (after
the manner of the scholastics) criminal and private law. Canon
law is of course put in the foreground, but Roman law also has
its place   The Dominican order provided zealously for the circulation of this important work.

Numerous such compendiums, mostly of considerable compass,
appeared in the course of the 1300s and 1400s; the Franciscan
order, in this literature, rivalled the Dominican in authority and
influence; the German clergy, however, had in all this but a scanty
share.

Too great prominence cannot be given to the influence of the
"Summæ" upon the organization of the confessional. And their
significance in the diffusion of the Roman and Canon law through

---

[1] *Stintzing*, "Pop. Lit," ch 10. *Cf von Schulte*, "Quellen," II. 408–
455, 512–526.

Germany was not less; for they equipped with the necessary special-
ized knowledge that class which ruled, from the confessional, the
conscience and the intellective standards of the time.   Among
these the "Summa Angelica"[1] of ANGELUS CARLETUS DE CLAVASIO
(died 1495), a Minorite from Chiavasso, gained in the course of
the 1400s the greatest prestige, by its fulness and its suitable
arrangement.   This book, the chief prop of the Catholic doctrine
of the confessional and of good works, was one of the first objects
of attack in the Reformation.   Luther declared, " it ought not to
be called angelica, but diabolica, for the knavery and sophistry
in it ", and he burned it, with the papal bann and the books of
the Canon law, on December 20, 1520, at Wittenberg

In the course of the Middle Ages, the Church had contrived to
subject to her supreme surveillance the entire legal order of things
The doctrine of usury, with its casuistic elaboration, reprehending
as sinful not only interest on money but all speculative gain whatever, was the prime instrument which gradually drew within the
Church's cognizance all forms of trade.   The sentence of the New
Testament, " Mutuum dati, nihil inde sperantes," uttered merely
as a commandment of charity, was developed (consistently with
the general course of the Church's growth) into a system of coercive
legal principles, by which she controlled men's outward lives.
Only the Jews remained free of this constraint; they could therefore
devote themselves (all the more profitably) to the money dealings
with which men could not dispense[2]   Everywhere the natural
interests of trade struggled painfully against the fetters of the
canonistic doctrine, contriving from time to time new legal forms
that seemed free of its inhibitions, while in the " Summæ " the
Church obstinately pursued each new evasion, seeking to define
the point where mercantile profit passes over into usury.   Toward
the end of the 1300s there appears a parallel literature of casuistic
tracts, which discuss interest, money-changing, commerce, and
indeed all economic transactions[3]

§ 15. **Canon and Roman Law in German Universities.** — The
study of law assumed a secure place in the German Universities

---

[1] *Stintzing*, "Pop Lit ," pp 539 *et seq*

[2] *Endemann*, "Studien in der romanischen-kanonistischen Wirtschafts-
und Rechtslehre bis gegen Ende des 17 Jahrhunderts," vol I (1874), and on
"Die national-okonomischen Grundsatze der kanonistischen Lehre" in
Hildebrand's J N O , I (1863), *Roscher*, "Geschichte," pp 5–12, *Stobbe*,
"Die Juden in Deutschland," p 192

[3] *Stintzing*, "Pop Lit ," pp. 539 *et seq* , *Roscher*, "Geschichte," pp. 18
et seq., *Schulte*, "Quellen," II, 432

at their very foundation, and this law was the same as that which had been cultivated in Italy and France for centuries. The lawbooks of Rome and of the Church constituted therefore, as a matter of course, its only material; the voluminous literature of those countries dominated it German law lay wholly outside the circle of academic interests.

Even if the universities had been dependent in a lesser degree upon academic tradition, insuperable difficulties existed in the way of any university treatment of German law For nowhere was this to be found in unified form; it existed only in local sources; to abstract from them any common principles presumed a power of scientific analysis, a training in juristic thought, and especially a faculty of synthesis, which were not yet even remotely realized. To this add that the native law was regarded (with good reason) as a " jus incertum," a law in constant mutation, whose content was determined by the opinions of the lay-judges in each individual case, and accordingly seemed to defy a scientific formulation. Finally, the prevailing method, which was exclusively exegetic, appeared inapplicable to a law that was uncodified

It would indeed have been possible to subject the records of local law to a glossarial exposition, as Johann von Buch had already done with the " Sachenspiegel." But, for one thing, a commentary upon a lawbook already intelligible to the people seemed superfluous, so that none appeared either worthy or needful of scientific treatment; and, furthermore, the native law did not lie within the interests of that class which controlled the universities. These were founded as clerical establishments, they had remained under clerical influence, and most of the professors were churchmen; the education of the clergy was the paramount purpose; and the preparation for the administration of the Church's polity and of her administration of justice was the preferred end of legal study.[1]

This is why even the Roman law, until toward the end of the 1400 s, took a minor place in German universities Instruction was given mainly in the Canon law, although the faculties of " jus utrumque " counted among their numbers (beside the " doctores decretorum ") many "doctores legum " and " doctores juris utriusque," and conferred degrees in both laws. The papal legislation and discipline were opposed on principle to the study of the Roman law. At the same time, as an auxiliary science it was indispensable to

---

[1] On the following cf Stintzing, " U Zasius," pp 85 et seq , pp. 323–344, Stobbe, " Rechtsquellen," I, 630, II, 12 et seq , Muther, Z R G , IV, 382 et seq , IX, 50 et seq ; Stolzel, " Richterthum," I, 79–124; Muther, " Rechtswissenschaft," p 107, Ott, " Beitrage," pp. 52 et seq

an understanding of the Canon law, moreover, papal charters, granted to individuals and to universities, and a tolerant practice as well, permitted a more particular devotion to its study. On the whole, however, it remained in a subordinate position Only in the second half of the 1400s, when it began to make its way into the civil courts, and the laymen interspersed through the academic body increased in numbers, did the " Leges " (*i.e.* Roman law) attain a secure place in the curriculum, — one equal to that held by the·Canon law. The long-continued predominance of the canonistic studies is reflected in the fact that until the end of the 1400s but few editions of Roman legal sources and their commentaries were prepared in German publishing houses, while different portions of the " Corpus Juris Canonici " and canonistic writings were marketed in considerable numbers

The idea still existed, far more as regarded the Roman than the Canon law, — and it was not an ungrounded prejudice, — that a complete training in that law could be obtained only in foreign universities, and that the calling of foreign doctors lent a special lustre to the German schools. [At Heidelberg (1387), Basel (1460), Ingolstadt (1472), Tubingen (1477), Freiburg (1479), Vienna (1493), and Greifswald (1498) the first chairs in Roman law were filled by Spanish, French, and particularly Italian legists]. These foreign doctors were, however, for the most part but transient ornaments; and the professorships were soon taken possession of by Germans The majority of them received their degrees abroad, and it happened not infrequently that on the first appointment of a professor a condition was made that he should take his doctorate within a certain time at an Italian university. Throughout the entire 1500s a foreign degree was regarded as more respectable than a German, not exactly, perhaps, merely because a prejudice existed in favor of the foreign schools, but principally because the possession of the foreign doctor's cap was evidence that one had not sought one's culture wholly at home, but had acquired a knowledge of other lands. And then, too, though the occupancy of the professorships by native Germans soon became the general rule, there were nevertheless later instances in which foreigners were called

At the end of the 1400s Roman law had won a secure place in the German universities, and it is indicative of its prestige that even outside of the universities men were mindful of its teachings. It was not alone practical legal needs that induced the recourse to Roman sources; for the Humanists also sought them as an element in general culture. [An imperial charter was secured in 1471 to teach Roman Law in an academy at Lüneburg, in 1529, instruction in it was introduced into the schools of Hamburg; in 1532, into the gymnasium of Strassburg In Ulm, Altdorf, Dillingen, Lauingen, Herborn, Brieg, Steinfurt, Rinteln, and Bremen, it was introduced as a humanistic study (in some, as a companion of territorial law) into academies, some of which later became universities.]

But the union in which we find the Roman and the Canon law in the German universities was wholly superficial, notwithstanding that neither one alone covered the whole field of law, and that the " jus commune " was a growth out of the " jus utrumque " For the exegetic method of instruction prevented the jurists of that day from treating their science systematically, and confined them to the topics respectively dealt with in Canon and Roman sources. In Italy the legists (Roman law) and the decretists (Canon law) had formed separate schools In Germany they were united, to be sure, in one faculty, but for a long time formed two separate divisions, each of which bestowed its own degree. We see " doctores legum " and" doctores decretorum." From the early 1500s onward this distinction tends to disappear, the " doctores utriusque juris " becoming ever more numerous, until they are at last the rule; but there was no fusion of the two bodies of law into one subject of university instruction. And this instructional separation was not limited to the two general bodies of law, it extended even to the main subdivisions of their respective sources In Canon law there were separate professorships for the Decretum, the Decretals, the " Liber Sextus," and the " Clementinæ." In Roman law, there were separate chairs for the Institutes, the Code, and the Pandects (Digest); and the old traditional threefold division of the Pandects into a " Digestum vetus," " infortiatum," and " novum," not infrequently gave excuse for a still further subdivision of the professorate. Among these professorships, those of the Decretum and the Code ranked as the most distinguished in academic tradition and ordinances, — the Code because it dealt with the imperial laws (in the narrow sense) and represented (inclusive of the Authenticæ) the latest and conclusive form of the Justinian law. Only gradually did the greater scientific value of the Pandects receive recognition, a recognition which explains the later predominance of the courses upon that branch. The Institutes enjoyed the least degree of esteem.

A systematic distinction based on the nature of the material,

such as to us to-day seems self-evidently necessary, did not yet
exist at the beginning of the 1500s; and only slowly did certain
subjects based upon such separation attain later to independent
treatment. It is true, however, that the legist was primarily concerned with private law and the canonist with ecclesiastical law,
because such was the predominant content of their law-books.
Feudal law fell to the legist, because it rested upon the emperor's
sanction, and accordingly the "Libri Feudorum" were customarily
appended to the Novels as a tenth Collation. So also the criminal
law, which the legist treated in his exposition of the "libri terribilis"
(Dig I, 47–48) On the other hand, procedure — and be it noted
criminal in union with civil procedure — was primarily a subject
for the canonist, which he treated in his exegesis of the second book
("Judicium") of the Decretals; and the importance of this portion
of the Decretals, as the embodiment of the rules of procedure,
made possible its continued authority even at times and places
where the authority of the Canon law was in general combated
(as at Wittenberg and Marburg during the Reformation) The
course was regarded as one in legal procedure, — and thus appears
as the first division of the law according to its subjects. Only after
the middle of the 1500s [1] do we find here and there (as at Tübingen
and Jena) a separate chair in criminal and feudal law, in the
establishment of these the encroaching legislation of the empire
in the domain of criminal law doubtless had particular influence.
Feudal law seems to have been added merely to give a sufficient
task to the professor.

The leading centers of legal science in the 1400s were Cologne,
Erfurt, and Leipzig

TOPIC 2. THE VICTORY OF ROMAN LAW

§ 16. **Basic Conditions making Possible the Authority of Roman
Law** — Though the inveterate belief in the authority of the imperial and papal law was a precondition of its application, yet its
"de facto" naturalization is only to be understood by bearing
in mind the general status of written law in the administration of
justice in Germany.

It was inherent in the nature of the popular courts that the source
of the law, in the last resort, was the personal conviction of the
judgment-giver, who felt bound by no external authority. The

[1] *Wachter*, "Gemeines Recht," pp. 95 *et seq.*

conception of a binding statute, to which personal opinions must unconditionally submit, receives in such a system no recognition. Records of the law, of whatever kind, are not laws that bind the lay-judge, but merely aids to knowledge, instruction which helps him to form his opinion. Even tradition, custom, is to him no formally binding sanction; it is only a motive, a ground of conviction· he judges in accordance with it because he allows himself to be persuaded by it, for he is inclined to hold that to be law which has always been so held, and because it has been so held.[1] Given such an attitude of legal practice toward all law in the objective sense, it was natural that questions regarding the formal basis and extent of validity of traditionary legal records were scarcely raised, still less were closely examined. It was enough that men believed in their essential value, in the wisdom and supereminence of their authors

These authors, to be sure, often supported themselves by legendary traditions of their treatises' origin and outward authority. Between the reverence paid to the law-book and the growth of legends touching its origin there was evidently a mutual reaction. The authority, to all appearances statutory, attained by German law-books of private authorship, as well as their migrations from place to place and people to people, are to be thus explained. Fable had earlier derived the "Sachsenspiegel" from Charlemagne, and fable now taught men that the Emperor Lothar II had commanded by statute the theory and the enforcement of the Roman law, — stories in which the already existent belief in the great importance of those written sources merely found expression, yet also sought support. This nimbus of credent reverence put the Roman law-books into a like position with the German, in any individual case the only question was whether the opinion of the lay-judge would be determined by the one or the other. If the parties or their advocates sought to urge upon him the principles of the alien law, their pretension was not in this less justified than if they had appealed to any principle of the German law that had originated outside the field of jurisdiction of the deciding court; for it was not the law's binding authority that was in question, but the rational force of its doctrine, which shaped the conviction of the "Schoffe."

---

[1] *Martitz,* "Eheliches Guterrecht des Sachsenspiegels,' pp 57 *et seq.;* *Bohlau,* "Aus der Praxis des Magdeburger Schoffenstuhls," Z ¹R G., IX, 24–36; *Planck,* "Das deutsche Gerichtsverfahren im Mittelalter," I, 311 *et seq.*

Here, then, made itself felt another element which promised
victory to the Roman law, — namely, the superior intellectual
power it embodied, the effect of which was bound to increase in the
same measure as the old force of the " Schöffen "-system decayed.

§ 17　**The Superior Technic of the Roman Law** — There was,
certainly, an almost incalculable abundance in Germany of legal
records, for beside the law-books before referred to, the multifari-
ously membered empire possessed, in the statute law of its territories, cities, and other political divisions, written rules in the
fields of constitutional, penal, procedural, property, and family law.
In this abundance of individual legal principles, however, there
lacked coherent statement, unity of principle, technical finish,
and even capability of attaining this

Even the Romans with their special gift of lawmaking could
never have attained to perfection in this respect, if they themselves
had not from the very beginning been subjected to a unitary
organization. Rome was and remained the centre in which the
forces shaping the law were concentrated, every necessity felt
in the wide range of the empire, every opinion that agitated
society, found expression in Rome. Concentrated in this one
focus, the powers of the whole nation worked in unison; whereas
the German spirit frittered itself in party-colored diversity of
effort. And this dispersion of tendency extended down to individuals. For the German lay-judge, the living organ through
which the law continued to develop, gave his judgment, or doom,
for the particular case only, — often shaping it solely according
to his personal convictions, without taking account of reasons, the
interdependence of different legal principles, or of higher and
controlling doctrines He acted as a living source of law, recognizing no higher authority than a science immanent in his own
consciousness. Totally in contrast to this was the generative intellectual process in the Roman administration of justice, a process controlled by the external authority of the "jus" and the
"jurisdictio," and thereby unified This process began with the
" interpretatio " of the law of the XII Tables, and even in the
freer shaping of the prætor's edict it sought in the first instance
at least the formal support of the " verba legis " Wherever we
observe the beginning of a reformation in the law we see an endeavor to fit it into some gap in the reading of the written statute,
be that the " lex " or the edict In this endeavor, juristic technic
and consistent thinking found development; in this subjection to
the written law was rooted the continuity of its evolution, the

maintenance of its inner coherence, and therewith its harmony of principles.

In the difference between the Roman "actio " and the German plaint (" Klage ") we see most palpably the contrast of the two legal systems The latter is only a complaint of some objective wrong, already done and continuing, to remove which the appeal is made to the court; it is left to the lay-judges to " find," in their conscience, what the law may be   But the Roman " actio " is a weapon with which the' citizen comes forward in combat to enforce his right. Two express authorities support him, the " lex " and the edict; upon the basis of these he can demand that the prætor grant him the " actio " Once granted, the question for the judge is no longer one of " finding " the law, but merely of deciding whether the presupposed facts, upon whose existence the validity of the " actio " depends, are actually present in the given case

The legists of the Middle Ages were not conscious of the historical difference that distinguished the Roman " actio " from the German plaint; and just because the specific Roman peculiarities were not recognized, it was possible to " receive " the " actio " It was of course not received in its true Roman character, but in that which remained after stripping off its specifically national qualities. In this altered meaning the " actio " is the subjective right armed for combat, the right of a person formulated as the basis of his legal demand   In this sense the Glossarist Placentinus (died 1192) had already explained the nature of the " actio." [1] In the " actiones," subjective rights are formulated for use before the courts, and the superiority lent to the Roman law by this product of legal technic was bound to strike immediately the German practitioner. For here lay, elaborated in fixed types, what the German law could show only in blurred outline   They embodied legal conceptions in sharp distinction, and at the same time in the form adjusted to the procedure of the court.   A broad path, marked by practical considerations, for the introduction of the Roman law, which had first appeared as a sporadic application of individual principles of law, was thus afforded by the " actio "; which was now transformed into plaint-formulas ("Klagformeln "), forms for legal actions.

§ 18. The " Klagspiegel." — As the Glossators, three centuries earlier, in their endeavor to confirm the practical introduction

---

[1] *Bethmann-Hollweg*, "Civil-process," V, 22 *et seq.*

of the Roman law, had devoted themselves first and foremost to commentaries upon the " actiones," so in Germany there appeared at the beginning of the 1400s a comprehensive work, the first and the most influential lawbook on procedure; it was later given the striking name of " Der richterliche Klagspiegel " (The Mirror of Judicial Plaints).[1] The author (an unknown person, from Hall in Swabia) is thoroughly conversant with civil affairs and a learned practitioner, particularly familiar with city organization and customs, but acquainted also at first hand with the open country. He is deeply impressed by the mischief of the uncertainty and arbitrariness prevalent in the courts   He invokes the application of the written imperial and Canon law, still he does not claim its exclusive authority, but freely grants the force of good customs and of city statutes   His only object, he says, is " to give useful instructions how a party must conduct himself in court, so necessary in the practice of the day, to the end that the darkness of uncertainty may be dissipated, and the common law become clear." His work, a moderate folio, falls into two tractates, of which the first and more important treats of civil law, and the second of criminal law and criminal procedure. He writes for an unlearned public, for whom he seeks to make an easily intelligible handbook for practical use   Accordingly he adds to his pleading forms elementary instruction, partly borrowed from the Institutes, omits the difficult commentaries of the Italian jurist he copies from; and on points of detail and subtle questions refers to the literature or the advice of experts   The author's whole bent is to teach Roman legal procedure, and therefore little account is taken of the German law. Its law-books are not once mentioned, yet place is made for the authority of Germanic custom and statute, and many principles of Roman law are characterized as inapplicable   The limits of its authority are, however, shifting and obscurely stated   Starting from the idea of the binding force of the imperial law, he is prone to find again in Germanic society the Roman institute; and the effacement of their differences is made easier by the trouble he gives himself, in his translations, to find German words to correspond to the Roman principle; for with a likeness of name there seems to be a likeness of thing. He also gives us information of the procedure of his time, especially in criminal law, sometimes accepting it as good, sometimes combating it as unreasonable and irreconcilable with sound justice.

[1] *Bethmann-Hollweg*, "Civil process," V, 18 *et seq.*
[2] Details in *Stintzing*, "Pop Lit ," ch 6

The influence of the "Klagspiegel" upon the introduction of Roman law into the legal practice of the 1400 s cannot be proved with details, but it can in a general way be inferred. For whoever appeared in court with a complaint based on its directions, and could appeal to the authority of the written law, enjoyed through that alone an advantage, — one which the lay-judge could withstand only when the case clearly involved some incontestable principle of the native law. Where there was obscurity and doubt, the lay-judge doubtless conformed to the superior foreign law, taking his lesson from the arguments of the advocates or the learned clerk of the court And if it was a part of the art of counsel to bring him to this state of mental vacillation, still the increasing inadequacy of the popular courts was no mere appearance thus artificially created, but a symptom of their inner decay, ascribable to historical causes.

§ 19 **The Decay of the Popular Courts.** — So long as the system administered by the "Schoffen" (lay-judges) continued in unweakened force, it could repel foreign influences. There were no gaps in the Germanic law, for its matter was in a continual flux; the judgment of the lay-judge in every case sought (really created) the principle adequate to the case But the time came when the vital force of the "Schoffen"-system was exhausted.

The creative impulse generally dies out quickly in all fields so soon as it finds ready-made patterns through imitation of which it can cover its own poverty; and just so the power that was inherent in the "Schoffen"-system slowly wasted The records of Germanic law had attained such importance that some degree of book-learning was necessarily attributed even to the lay-judges; besides these, there were the alien laws ready with counsel Moreover, the increasing complexity of social relations presented problems whose mastery would have been possible only to a "Schoffen"-system of increasing creative power Just here, and in the natural course of events, the institution had reached the limits of efficiency in the task history had assigned it; for it is simply a truth of experience that an advanced civilization involves complicated social relations whose apprehension, thorough investigation, and critical judgment are beyond the knowledge and conception of an unschooled mind Such a civilization develops questions which a subjective sense of justice cannot answer at all, or at best only with biassed narrow-mindedness. Even in the "Schoffen"-guild of Magdeburg, which by tradition was preeminent, there is evident in the 1400s an inability to satisfy the demands of advancing

361

economic development.[1] The literature from the 1300s onward
shows the symptoms of approaching decay and prepares the change.
The works of Johann von Buch, Nickolaus Wurm, Johann von
Brunn, Theodorich von Bocksdorf, are directed to giving consist-
ence to the " Schöffen "-law, and to helping out with supplements
from the Roman law   They evidence the conviction of practitioners that the wisdom of the lay-judges was inadequate; they
encouraged these to form their practice upon the written law, and
this furthered (because presenting the law in finished form) the
paralysis of the creative function

The 1400s is filled with the struggle between the rules of the
Corpus Juris and the oracular dooms of the lay-judges. One
may call this a struggle between the native and the foreign law.
But that misses the essence of the matter. For one reason (as
already remarked), the adoption of foreign legal rules was in large
part spontaneous. But, most of all, the Middle Ages knew not in
the field of law a national German consciousness (in a modern sense)
nor perceived so sharp a contrast as the one assumed. The authorities of the Roman-Canon law were not looked upon as alien;
they were closely bound up in European historical traditions;
they were elements of civilization and of political existence
Germanic law did not stand in contrast with the other as a unified
national product   It rested only in local consciousness, in particularistic practice   What was valid in one locality was foreign in
the next, and not less foreign than the law laid down by those
authorities who stood in acknowledged sovereignty over all society,
secular and spiritual   The lay-judge saw no essential difference;
and as he adapted himself to the conveniences of the imperial law,
so also we see him declining to enforce the local customs and statutes
of other jurisdictions.[2] And finally, it must not be forgotten that
in the Reception there was no question of the pure Roman law,
but only of that form of it which had been shaped in Italian theory
and practice. In fact, the Corpus Juris itself was not received,
but the fruits of the literature of the post-Glossators, in which Justinian's law had been worked over into a law half modern
The sharpest contrasts with Germanic law were therein re-

---

[1] *Martitz*, "Eheliches Guterrecht des Sachsenspiegels," pp. 67, 372;
Bohlau in Z ¹R G , IX, 24–36 , *Stobbe* in K V₁ S , XI, 21 *et seq*   The
general truth of the view here expressed is not affected by the fact that
in some places, as *e g* in Lubeck (*von Duhn*, "Deutsch-rechtliche Arbeiten,"
pt 2), men succeeded in getting along very well with the city law   [*Cf.*
above, § 8, note 6]

[2] *Stobbe*, 'Rechtsquellen," II, 67, and in K.V₁ S , XI, 22; *Bohlau*,
Z ¹R G , IX, 14 *et seq*

moved or masked; the whole appeared as a living system of legal practice.

§ 20. **Transformations in the Administration of Justice.** — Other contrasts issued from the conflict between the foreign and the native law

(1) The historical change that took place lies not merely in the fact that new and alien legal rules were given application in the courts, but also in the fact that the manner of declaring the law was radically transformed   Outwardly this was manifested in the invasion of the courts by legal experts.   A legal profession takes form and replaces the lay-judges.   The inner and essential change lay, however, not in this change of personnel, but in the fact that the decay of the " Schoffen "-system signified the extinction of the principle of the autonomic " finding " of the law   A law "found" in subjective convictions was replaced by the formal authority of a written system [1]   The learned judge is distinguished from the lay-judge not only by the tag of academic training, but also by the fact that the latter proceeds upon a legal principle lying in his own consciousness and experience, while the former applies a law that exists independently of him and has entered into his knowledge.[2]   When the lay-judge declares the law, he at the same time creates it, he shapes the law to his convictions   but the judgment of the learned judge is purely an application of given rules, he shapes his convictions to the law.   Therefore the change signified the victory of a new principle, namely, subordination to a formal, binding, legal authority external to the judge

This principle had long since been carried through in the ecclesiastical jurisdiction   The organic theory and discipline of the Church had early robbed the judge of his free hand in declaring the law, and had bound him by the statement of the canons. Even the field of morals, the " forum conscientiæ " of the confessional, was subjected to extrinsic statutes, following the progress of formal authority.   The extension of this principle into the secular courts had long been prepared for by the ever increasing records of the principles of Germanic law, these became (if not formally, at least in fact) binding norms, especially in the appellate courts   And so, here too, in the transition to the modern form of legal practice there was no break.   But its final

---

[1] On this process, which repeats itself analogously in the legal history of all peoples, everywhere exciting the same complaints, in part justifiable, in part unjustifiable, compare *Ihering,* "Geist des romischen Rechts," II, 34 *et seq*
[2] *Planck,* "Das deutsche Gerichtsverfahren im Mittelalter," I, 315 *et seq.*

stage was reached only when (as a part of larger political changes) radical transformation took place in the organization of the courts. To this we may now proceed

(2) In the old Germanic judicature, the judge-president ("Richter") was not the judgment-finder, but the one who held the court (in his own right or under some lord), the lay-judges ("Schoffen"), and not the judge-president, found the judgment. With the rise in power of the territorial rulers, the officials whom they appointed as judges gradually engrossed the function of judgment-finders, becoming judges in the modern Continental sense of the word, thus the lay-judges were superseded by the body of trained civil officials that was now forming.[1]

In the rural districts of the territories we find generally three classes of officials· a provincial governor or superintendent ("Amtmann," "Landvogt," "Drost"), who, as representative of the territorial ruler, had the general administration within his district, a treasurer ("Rentmeister," "Kastner," "Keller"), who collected taxes, kept accounts, and was deputy of the "Amtmann", and finally, the magistrate ("Schultheiss"), named by the ruler as chairman of the court. The court is indeed still composed of the lay-judges, but these too, by the beginning of the 1500s, are often named by the ruler through his officials. This system of offices was not brought about uniformly, but in a variety of degrees and forms. We find them now united, now separated, here all of them, there only some of them; but everywhere, the fact repeats itself that the judicial function is exercised by civil officials. Ulrich Tengler, a trustworthy witness for the practice of his time, in his "Mirror for Laymen" ("Laienspiegel," ed. 1511), treats the law-judges as assessors of the judge, aiding him in the finding of the judgment, which is pronounced by him after consultation with them, his opinion prevailing in case of differences of opinion. In many territories (e g. Hesse) this participation of the judge-president in the judgment was first developed in the early 1600s

Similar conditions came about in the towns· jurisdiction belongs to the territorial ruler or, in the free cities, to the council, the "Richter" is the magistrate named by the one or the other. The court consists of the lay-judges, who may either be members of the council or constitute a bench distinct from it. In the town

---

[1] *Stolzel.* "Richterthum ," *Isaacsohn,* "Geschichte des preussischen Beamtenthums," vol I (1874), *Stintzing,* in H Z , XXIX (1873), 409 *et seq* , on the history of Roman law in Germany.

courts the same transformation takes place as that attested by the
"Laienspiegel." The decay of the functions of the lay-judges
and the advance of the alien law were reciprocal phenomena.
The more the latter was asserted and enforced in the higher courts,
and therefore demanded by parties and attorneys in the lower
courts, the more uncomfortable must have become the position
of the lay-judge. Help was sought in the employment of clerks
learned in the law, to aid him with their knowledge, that he
might not be sacrificed in uncounselled vacillation to the rabbling
advocates. From the end of the 1300s onward the cities began
taking into their service assessors to their councils,[1] who at the
same time acted as assessors of the municipal courts. From the
end of the 1400s probably no considerable German town was without such a learned clerk, counsellor, or syndic

And in the rural districts also the same help was sought The
lay-judges in their perplexity gladly took this easy way out of
difficulty. But we find also that they sought advice of foreign
jurists or turned for advice to the nearest public authority, the civil
official trained in the law, and so soon as the latter took part in the
determination of the judgment, it was in fact he who "found" it.
And as the function of declaring the law escaped from the hands of
the lay-judges, another and companion phenomenon is observable,
namely, that the litigants turned their backs upon them, the
confidence in the "Schöffen"-courts vanishes. Moreover, their
organization made litigation difficult; for they were not permanent
functionaries, but were only periodically assembled. The litigants
became accustomed to resort to the territorial officials, who were
always ready with a certain and prompt decision; the parties
voluntarily taking them as arbitrators to avoid the "Schöffen"-
court. This arbitral jurisdiction of territorial officials was developed to a great extent [2] and in the most diverse form with the
favor of the territorial rulers. And this custom of arbitration, so
widely usual in the 1400s, was often taken advantage of precisely
for the purpose of making sure the application of the Roman law,
by choosing as arbitrator some learned doctor. As the ordinary
man turned to the territorial official, so the more important litigants
applied for justice to the lord of the jurisdiction — duke, bishop,
city council; who then did not ordinarily render judgment himself,

---

[1] *Stobbe*, "Rechtsquellen," I, 643 *et seq*, II, 59 *et seq.*, and in K.Vj.S.,
XI, 16 *et seq*
[2] *Stölzel*, "Richterthum," I, 238 *et seq.*, *Stintzing*, in H.Z., XXIX,
416 *et seq.*, *Ott*, "Beitrage," pp. 142 *et seq.*

but procured it from some " Schoffen "-bench or university faculty of law [1]

(3) The evolution of a learned judiciary is seen most clearly and sharply in the courts of higher instance, and evolved along with the right of appeal

Of most general importance, in this respect, was the Imperial Chamber of Justice (" Kammergericht "), created by vote of the Diet of Worms, in 1495, and opened on October 16 of the same year at Frankfort o/M. This court was one of first instance for immediate imperial vassals, and appellate court for the subjects of the territories and imperial cities At its head was a judge-president, either prince, earl, or baron, its membership consisted of sixteen " judgment-finders " (assessors or associates), of whom a half must be doctors " worthy for their learning in the law," and the other half at least of some class of the nobility. They were to judge according to " the common laws of the empire ", but also according to " righteous, honorable, and practised ordinances, statutes, and customs of the principalities, seigniories, and courts." The whole position of this court, to which an acquaintance with the various local laws could not be easily accessible, resulted in the Roman-Canon law's predominance in marked degree in its decisions, so that its creation has not unjustly been considered as a decisive influence in the reception of the Roman system In the territories the appellate system replaced the old custom of submitting the law to the superior popular courts (" Oberhofe "). The appellate system also had long since been established in the ecclesiastical courts.

The traditional position of the " Oberhofe," however, and even that of the newly created Imperial Chamber of Justice, were hard to reconcile with the efforts of the princes for territorial partition and independence, which required that every influence of external authorities should be jealously and painfully excluded Accordingly, they sought to secure themselves against the jurisdiction of the Imperial Chamber of Justice by obtaining the " privilegia de non appellando " The submission of law to foreign "Oberhofe," — e.g. from the cities of the electoral principality of Saxony and from the margravate of Brandenburg to the " Schoffen "-guild of Magdeburg — was prohibited by ordinances of the territorial rulers To assure effect to these defensive measures, it was further necessary to offer a substitute To this end, rescripts of

[1] *Bohlau,* Z ¹R G , VIII, 193 *et seq* , IX, 40 *et seq.*, *Ott,* "Beitrage," pp 135 *et seq*

the princes referred lay-judges and litigants to the sovereign, the princely councils, or the law faculty of the territorial university for counsel and judgment. Still more important, the territorial rulers (from the end of the 1400 s onward), in competition with the imperial courts and the " foreign " " Oberhöfe," instituted high courts and superior courts within their territories as courts of higher instance. In part these were only transformations of the old feudal and servitary courts, which were given a membership in half of nobles that they might serve as courts of first instance for the nobility, while their other half was made up of learned assessors, that they might serve as appellate courts for the other estates

Simultaneously there developed in the courts of the principalities the "chancery," or staff of the prince's counsellors, which was attached to the chancellor's office   For as the Emperor had long since had a chancellor, so also the princes found place for this supreme administrative officer.   Administrative growth and the accumulation of business made necessary the organization of boards And here is repeated the same phenomenon observed in the inferior courts: as the civil official competed with the lay-judges, so the chancery competed with the high court, and the litigants chose by preference the arbitration of the former, because a constantly sitting, and so a more accessible, tribunal; and thus the more bureaucratic triumphed over the more loosely organized and only periodically working court

Finally, we must not forget the jurisdiction of the itinerant judges whom the emperor and the territorial rulers were accustomed to name by commission as needed, following the papal model of ' judices delegati." In this way, also, the jurisdiction of the learned officials was strengthened.

§ 21   **Political Significance of the Reception.** — In the decay of the Germanic " Schoffen "-system is seen again the picture offered by the transformation of the Roman judicature under the influence of the principate. From the " magistratus populi Romani," who merely formulated the " judicium " according to which the " judex privatus " had to give judgment, was developed the imperial official, and because the exceptional cases in which the magistrate might decide a controversy by decree " extra ordinem " constantly increased in number, the decay of the old " ordo judiciorum privatorum " in the 200s gave to the official as imperial judge the power of finding the judgment. Just as the contrast in Roman law between " jus dicere " and " judicare " lost its meaning when

the two things coalesced in one function, — which they did after
Hadrian silenced the prætor's " viva vox juris civilis," transforming
his edict into codified law, and attributing binding authority to
the opinion of the imperial jurists, — so in Germany, out of the
atrophy of the old Germanic autonomy, the rising authority of
the written law, and the increasing power of the State, there arose
the union of the judge-president and the judgment-finder into one
person, who was the judge in the present-day Continental sense.

The origin of the modern State is therefore involved as a primary
implication of this historical process, in which the Roman law was
not the cause, although it does appear as an essential contributing
factor. For its increased study provided a trained class of officials;
its increased use in legal practice gave this class its dominance in
the administration of justice, to which the lay-judges had become
unequal and indisposed; its principles of the rights of the princeps
afforded the territorial rulers the desired support and impulse for
the development of the new political order

That the process of State formation in Germany was territorially
particularistic, and was realized at the cost of the imperial authority, had its cause, however, in historical conditions in which
the nature of the Roman law played no part; for, on the contrary,
the authority of this originally rested, in Germany, precisely on
the central and imperial power. Those men who in the 1400s
had in theory justified and demanded its enforcement — Peter
von Andlau, Sebastian Brant, and others — anticipated from it,
as imperial law, the invigoration of the imperial power as the
highest legal authority within the empire, and the origin of the
conception of the common law actually did create a new legal
bond uniting all members of the empire. Had the imperial authority possessed the vigor to form one German state, then the
reception of the Roman law would have rendered primarily to it
the services which the princes and cities now utilized to their
own advantage

Exhortations to the empire to reduce this weapon to mastery
in its own interest were not lacking To the complaints of the
confusion into which the law had been brought by the schoolmen,
there were regularly joined from the beginning of the 1500s
demands that the Emperor should, as a new Justinian, reduce the
common law of the empire to simplicity and clearness by statutory
reforms. But even if there had been available an intellectual
capacity to prepare a codification of the common law, the central
political power would scarcely have been adequate for its practical

establishment.   Only with the painful efforts of many years was
it possible to bring to a successful end the contest over the reformation of the criminal law and criminal procedure, the publication
of a criminal code (the " Constitutio Criminalis Carolina," C.C.C.)
was even attended with the proviso that the " ancient, just, and
lawful usages of the electoral princes, princes, and estates, handed
down by good tradition," should be in no wise infringed on by the
new arrangement [1] With much greater firmness would particularistic jealousy have resisted a definitive codification of the private
law.   On the other hand, the princes and cities themselves undertook reformatory legislation, and made use of it as a welcome
opportunity of strengthening their own legislative authority and
of creating a proper legal constitution, delimiting and binding together their sphere of sovereignty.[2]   And thus originated, at the
end of the 1400 s, the numerous reforms of municipal and territorial
laws, which had as their end the definition of the law, supplementing it with the principles of the Roman law, and more or less radically recasting it.

§ 22   **The Legal Profession· University Professors and Practising Lawyers.** — There has been an inclination to complain —
indeed, it has been made a ground of bitter reproach — against the
Roman law and its adherents that they smoothed a way for
German particularism   But it must not be forgotten that precisely this political particularism involved and insured the intellectual emancipation of Germany.   A movement of political consolidation at that time in Germany, in favor of the Emperor,
could only have been realized at the expense of the Reformation;
while the political organization of the territories, although
it be true that the loosening of the bonds within the empire had
lamentable consequences, nevertheless signified in still higher
degree the emancipation of the State from the supremacy of the
Church.

There arose also now a secular learning; and the legal profession,
which was a part of this, was no longer an instrument of the Church's
power, but the representative of lay authority, the servant and
official of the State, which through its agency becomes a firmly
articulated organism.   The civil service was the institution through
which was realized in the field of politics the emancipation of life

---

[1] *Wachter*, "Gemeines Recht," pp 30 *et seq* ; *Stobbe*, "Rechtsquellen,"
II, 246 *et seq* , *Guterbock*, "Die Entstehungsgeschichte der Carolina"
(1876), pp. 173 *et seq.*
[2] *Stobbe*, "Rechtsquellen," vol II, part 4 , *Stintzing*, "Geschichte," I,
ch. 13, 14.

from the domination of the hierarchy, the division between modern times and the Middle Ages

Under the influence of these fundamental changes legal science was prepared for its historical mission, a lay bar appeared and took from the clergy the leadership. Just as the study of theology and the taking of holy orders had formerly been the only basis for an assured career, so now the study of law opened manifold positions. The theory, developed in Italy, that the doctors in law enjoyed a status of nobility, had found early entry into Germany.[1] Nobody denied that as " milites legalis militiæ " they stood on a level with the most distinguished and privileged class of knightly descent. We find them in the entourage of emperors and princes as chancellors and councillors, they appear as plenipotentiaries in the imperial Diet, they are employed in political missions for negotiations of all kinds. They were courted by the grandees of the Empire. Well-to-do cities eagerly sought the service of the doctors, and great lords and cities, in order to make sure of such, readily furnished talented young men with ample means for study, if they would obligate themselves to enter their service on completion of their education.[2] And in the same way the banking house of Fugger recruited legal counsellors out of the Geizkofler family.[3]

The functions which we find the doctors serving are in part very changeable. The different functions are also variously combined. Besides the councillors proper, who were bound to keep continuous residence at court, princes were accustomed to name in considerable numbers councillors not in residence, who were bound to render service only under special mandates. Many a doctor was non-resident councillor to different princes at the same time, gave his services as needed and demanded, and often kept up besides a continual correspondence in which he advised the prince regarding important political events that came to his knowledge. Political embassies, commissions, and legal practice of all kinds compelled the doctors to lead a restless life in travel. A councillor not in residence was bound to be ready to undertake such at command, and the appointment of municipal syndics generally contained an explicit liability to " travel " and " ride." Doctors, often several of them, accompanied the princes to the imperial Diet, and the representation of the cities therein was

---

[1] *Fitting*, "Das Peculium Castrense," pp 583 *et seq.*
[2] *Schmidt*, "Symbolæ ad Vitam Gr Haloandri" (1866), p 18 , *Flechsig*, "Gregor Haloander" (1872), pp 13 *et seq*
[3] *Wolf*, "Lucas Geizkofler und seine Selbstbiographie " (1873).

wholly intrusted to them. They did not, however, confine their activities within the offices with which they were formally invested, but practised as a livelihood the giving of opinions.[1] From the end of the 1300s judges and litigants resorted for advice to jurists of repute. At first it is in the ecclesiastical courts and courts of arbitration, the counsellors are canonists. A century later the practice of such counsellors began to be more general, the lay courts also sought their aid   In the second half of the 1500s the chamber practice of individual jurists reached its extreme development.

Side by side with it there had gradually grown up the practice of resorting for opinions to university faculties. What usage in this way developed, statutes settled and encouraged. Imperceptibly the change came about that a formulated judgment was embodied in or transmitted with the opinion   This was only a means of lightening the court's business   But more important was the second development, by which there was given to the faculty's memorandum not only the significance of counsel, but that of a decision binding upon the litigants and the court, a state of things which could only have arisen under the influence of the above statutes, whose application the courts were inclined from indolence and perplexity to make the widest possible   The faculties not only displaced the old " Oberhofe," but obtained a much more influential position than these   Only in a few cases, such as in Leipzig and Jena, where they were merged with the faculties, or in the Halle and Koburg, where they were staffed with legal experts, did any " Schöffen "-guilds retain even in name their former prestige.

The cumulation of offices, the union of practical work with pedagogical duties, had the pernicious effect that the university courses could only be given with long interruptions.[2] Of the extent of the chamber practice, tangible measure is given in the great documentary records of the councils of the 1500s and 1600s. On the other hand, the occupation with practical problems, which no professor of law in Germany could avoid, not only had a decisive influence in shaping the administration of justice, an influence in favor of the foreign scientific jurisprudence, but also reacted

[1] *Stobbe*, "Rechtsquellen," II, 75 *et seq.*, *Seeger*, "Die strafrechtlichen Consilia Tubingensia" (1877), pp 20 *et seq*
[2] *Prantl*, "Geschichte der Ludwig-Maximilians-Universität," I, 73, 310 *et seq.*, *Muther*, "Universitätsleben," p 238, *Thomasius*, ed (1717) of *Melchior von Ossa's* "Testament" (1556), pp. 382, 388, *U Zasius*, "Epistolæ" (*Riegger*, ed , 1774), pp 111, 116, 146, 158, 171, 461, 507; *Wesenbeck*, "Prolegomena de Finibus et Ratione Studiorum Librisque Juris" (Leipzig, 1563), and "Oratio de Mudæo" (Wittenberg, 1572)

upon scientific studies, inasmuch as it forced the foremost scholars into predominantly practical lines   Indubitably there lay in this close connection with practice a gain for legal theory; so far as this can be made more fruitful by a knowledge of practical life, and secured against the aberrations of abstraction.   And the practical experience of the teacher was then the more truly indispensable, because it was his duty to prepare the young jurist completely for the practice into which he must enter so soon as he completed his studies   But it was also impossible to escape, in such a union of theory and practice. the inherent danger that theory was burdened and restrained by the inferior necessities of practice. and the latter by the necessities and traditions of the schools   Nor can one fail to see that the excess of practical affairs very generally dulled the love of free research among those who were called primarily to the advancement of knowledge, so that German legal science long bore a certain stamp of banality, and in only a few of its representatives is to be observed a higher impulse.

It was not, however, merely the doctors, in their prominent positions, who were concerned in the growth of a legal profession, but almost more the widely scattered class of legal practitioners who had failed to attain the " summi honores "   The smaller cities, the lower courts, had to content themselves with scribes who made more modest demands of salary and honors, and the personnel of the government and courts even of the principalities was recruited only for the highest places from among the doctors. Finally, in addition to all these official positions, there were the free professions of notaries, advocates, and attorneys   The notary, as distinguished from the ordinary clerk, exercised his art by virtue of a superior license

However unequally legal attainments may have been diffused among these different classes, such knowledge and its professional employment was still a common element that united its possessors into a legal profession, which from the last quarter of the 1400s exercised an increasing power of attraction through the honors and pecuniary gain it promised.   By that time it was already a custom for members of the highest social classes to take their academic training in the juristic faculty, and the formidable concourse of students reported in the first half of the 1500s shows that the attraction of the profession had then extended to the most diverse classes of society [1]

[1] C Hegendorfinus, "Oratio de Artibus Futuro Jurisconsulto necessariis et frugiferis comparandis," etc   (The Hague, 1529); J. Apel, "Isagoge

§ 23 **Complaints against the Lawyers** — Side by side with the reports of the crowding into the profession go bitter complaints against it.[1] Hutten complains of the increasing influence of venal clerks and jurists, mindful only of profit Zasius pictures their servility and pettifoggery. Equally sharp criticism, of almost identical purport, is to be found in Sichard, Melancthon, Hegendorfinus, Apell, and also in the numerous writers who expatiate on legal study in general. The estates of Bavaria and Wurtemberg protested against the intrusion of alien councillors, alien doctors, and alien law. During the disturbances of the Peasants' War the demand made its appearance that the foreign law and the learned jurists be wholly done away with, — a demand which finds expression in the pamphlets of Erberlin von Gunzburg, in the so-called Reformation of Frederick the Third, and in the twelve articles of the peasants (Articles 4 and 6).[2]

From these and similar expressions there has been inferred a national opposition to the intrusion of the foreign law, a resistance which the *people* supposedly offered to the profession of *expert* lawyers. A closer examination of the complaints shows, however, that they were due to different causes and were directed in part toward inconsistent ends

If we take the " people " to mean the totality of social classes, exclusive of the jurists and the official class, any assertion of a general opposition is made impossible by the fact, already noted, that litigants very often resorted to the learned judges of their own free choice, and turned their backs upon the courts of the lay-judges. That the former gave judgment upon a common and written law, everybody knew, and this was in part exactly the reason for resorting to them. We may indeed assert that the application of the written law was felt by the people as a necessity, however little they were conscious of this. For an unwritten law, living only in the consciousness of the judgment-finder, affords a feeling of legal security only so long as it is " found " and administered by compeers. Just so long does the individual recognize his own judgment in that which appears just and right to the other. But when social solidarity had been weakened by an increasing

---

per dialogum in Quatuor Libros Institutionum D Justiniani Imperatoris" (Ladislaw, 1540) in *Nikolaus Reusner,* "Cynosura Juris" (Speier, 1588), I, 180 *et seq*
[1] *Stobbe,* "Rechtsquellen," II, 44 *et seq , Stintzing,* "Pop Lit ," pp xxiii *et seq ; Modderman and Schulz,* "Rezeption des romischen Rechts". (1875), pp 96 *et seq*
[2] [References in *Zopfl,* "Rechtsgeschichte," I, 226, note 6. — TRANSL.].

separation of class interests and professions and lost from men's consciousness, then legal certainty was no longer to be expected except as coming from a law existing as a formal, external, and binding authority above litigants and judge   And it would be — to use the expression of Justus Moser — the most dangerous innovation to give " to the judge who was not a class-equal the same power as the community had formerly held "   Only where a primitive social fellowship was preserved amid simple conditions did the "Schoffen "-law remain sufficient.   Where that had disappeared, the middle classes in Germany could expect legal certainty from the imperial law, as the Roman plebs hoped it from the written code of the Twelve Tables.   It was precisely the popular elements of the nation which were bound to be devoted to a law that knew not the privileges of a turbulent knighthood, which was an equal law for all, and which offered to the aspiring middle trading-class certain and approved rules of commerce.

The opposition of the rebellious peasants (which must be discussed below in another connection) had not at all a national but a socialistic signification   It was not directed against the alien law as such, but against all secular law whatsoever, in place of which the " godly and natural " law should enter.   It was saturated with hatred of authority and the traditional regimen in general.

Precisely opposite is the explanation of the opposition of the provincial estates, which was due to particular class interests, to a fear of seeing their privileges and autonomous powers endangered.

After all is said, the fact remains that discontent with the administration of justice was widely disseminated.   Men were learning that the influence of the common man in the courts had been lost; and they saw themselves compelled, in tribute to the alien law, to make use of a professional advocate or attorney for the conduct of their own cause, intrusting to him their fate, however little his interest in the issue.   And if the procedure was spread out and dragged out, and a decision was finally given that contradicted the traditional views which the lay-judges had upheld as law, it is understandable that men often, in dejection and indignation, cursed the whole innovation and all connected with it.

Of the deeper causes of the evil we are not left in doubt by the discerning writers of the time   The native law was in many ways sacrificed violently and inconsiderately to the Roman; equity was often overcome by facile pettifoggery.   The ambition and greed of the doctors were efficacious allies of the rising demands of the territorial rulers.   And in the under strata of the profession there was an unclean company. The proverb " Juristen bóse Christen " (lawyers' houses are built on the heads of fools) owed its popular diffusion and significance to the accusations of quibbling, chicanery, and thievery, by which legal practice was universally characterized.[1] The moral elevation of those who manipulate the law is the demand placed foremost in the numerous hodegetic writings of this period.

But the moral shortcomings are hardly more denounced than the lack of scientific training.[2] " Thanks to the stupidity of the judges," writes Melancthon, " the most inane rabulists gain access to the courts as attorneys, draw one cause out into another, flay their clients, plunder cities, and hold the ignorant judges up to ridicule. They have not themselves mastered the law, but have drawn their knowledge from the maxims of tricky practitioners, and are therefore naturally infected with the pest of the most depraved form of scribbling." And Melchior von Ossa[3] writes. " A still greater burden upon the land is that so many untaught and shallow-brained attorneys are suffered alike in the country and in the cities; that craftsmen who want to spoil but not to labor, parish clerks and other petty good-for-naughts that run from work, have the audacity to set up as attorneys, — though they have not only no understanding of the law but often cannot read nor write; they set the simple townsmen and peasants by the ears, hinder fair agreements, and have, too, some of them, their fellows who go around in the inns and beer-houses, and after stirring people up to brawl against their lords or others, direct them to their miserable principals These are in truth the frogs of whom Origen says that in them there is nothing but futile croaking and brawling, — and yet such fellows draw much money out of the poor subjects "

Thus the reasons of the existing evils were found as well in the possession of learning as in its lack; the complaints were directed equally against the learned and the untaught And there was basis for both, for if the old state of things could have remained unchanged, and had remained so, an expert legal training would have been both unnecessary and an evil, but in the change that had begun it was indispensable.

§ 24. **Legal Training: Smatterers and Popular Literature** —

[1] [For a further study of the above proverb, see Professor *Courtney Kenny's* article, "Bonus Jurista Malus Christa," Law Quarterly Review, XIX, 326 Ed.]

[2] *Stintzing,* "Pop. Lit ," pp. xxxii *et seq.*

[3] "Testament," p 461 (ed. *Thomasius*). *Cf. von Langenn,* "Doctor Melchior von Ossa " (Leipzig, 1858)

The normal course of legal studies that led to the " summi honores " began at the university with the study of the " artes liberales," particularly dialectic and rhetoric, and only after the baccalaureate and master's honors had been gained did one pass into jurisprudence, " ad studia altiora, difficiliora, et graviora "

For these a period of five years (on the average) was allowed; so that six to eight years of studies, in which was included when possible a fairly long residence at an Italian or a French university, was not uncommon. Such a course of preparation presumed an expenditure of time and money which only a small portion of those who crowded into legal practice could meet Moreover, university conditions placed the greatest difficulties in the way of a legal training These lay not only in the irregularity of the lectures (already noted), but still more in their unwieldly and unsystematic method. Of him who wished to secure a complete legal training such independent exertions were exacted as only few were equal to The majority, who had only moderate strength and limited time to devote to academic study, were not, as to-day, carried by the power of method to a fair average of legal training, but were inevitably provided with far less.[1]

And thus it happened that, from the middle of the 1400s onward, a multitude of half-trained sciolists, untroubled by such restrictions as the State has to-day created through examinations and educational regulations, spread over the land and acquired predominant influence in petty legal practice. With those who left the universities half-educated were joined the self-taught, who had acquired a superficial knowledge of the foreign law, and in some subordinate employment about the courts had learned the formal routine of the law They constituted together a class of the legal profession lying between the learned doctors and the popular lay-judges. We find them in positions for which the high-bred doctor considered himself too good, scribes, advocates, attorneys, notaries, and assessors, everywhere, in the country and the cities, in petty practice. Little as was their personal prestige, great was their actual influence, for it was through them that the alien law was given root in that broad field of civic life to which the doctors remained strangers.

An extensive and peculiar species of literature corresponds to this inferior level of legal culture.[2] Generated by their necessities, it served also to increase the number of the middle class of lawyers

---

[1] *Stintzing,* "Pop. Lit ," pp xvii *et seq , Ott,* "Beitrage," pp 103 *et seq*   [2] *Stintzing,* "Pop Lit ," pp xxxvii *et seq.*

376

And its historical importance is great, for without it the Reception of the Roman law could scarcely have been perfected; since only through it was the gap filled that existed between the cultured legal science brought from Italy and the social life of Germany In concise rules, summaries, and excerpts, with lists of the divisions and title-headings, the effort was made to convey a mechanical mastery of the content of the great law-books. With few exceptions we find but slight traces of any attention to the native law. The end was the application and acquirement of the foreign law, and of the canon law of procedure. In comparison with this popular literature, the circulation in Germany of the great commentaries of the Italian legists, and of the sources of the Roman law, was very slight. Conditions were certainly more favorable as regards the sources and the scholarly literature of the canon law, yet these also could stand no comparison. If one looks at the scientific merits of the majority of these writings, one understands perfectly the laments of Zasius and Melancthon over " the pest of perverted legal scribbling; " and these strictures were the better grounded because such writings were, for the most part, published in corrupted texts whose faultiness and even senselessness appear to us unexampled. Life was pressing, and could not wait upon the school.

Moreover, a drift of the times, parallel to the humanistic movement, stood the popular legal learning in good stead. Through the 1400s there runs significantly a trait of popular uplift The lower classes worked their way upward into influence; the cities conquered a sure position within the Empire; the gilds attained equal political rights with the patriciate in the cities. The poetry of court and chivalry declined, relatively to popular poetry. The desire of education took hold of the lower classes of society. Respectable but sterile learning was pursued with mordant mockery, but at the same time men labored to improve the schools for the education of the people.

With this tendency of the times, which fixed the character of its literature, the necessities of legal practice were intimately allied. As a remarkable representative of this alliance we have SEBASTIAN BRANT, in whom were united humanism, popular didactic poetry, and popular romantic jurisprudence. The law-book named by Brant " Der richterliche Klagspiegel," at once a theoretical compendium and practical handbook, is remarkable as the first extensive undertaking to translate the Roman legal system into German. Other writings reproduced in German the text of well-known Latin manuals in literal translations or in revisions. To

all these were now added the German formularies, which embody
at once the forms of the German chanceries and the conceptions of
the Roman law. Lastly, as the final result of the whole movement,
the Mirror for Laymen ("Laienspiegel") of ULRICH TENGLER[1]
and translations of the Institutes by Thomas Murner, Fuchs-
berger, and Gobler. To all these must finally be added that
peculiar class of works already discussed (§ 14) which owed their
origin to the promotion of the parochial charge, and which we
might call clerical jurisprudence . . . whose jural content bears
a predominantly popular impression Ulrich Tengler was not a
"doctor juris," but a man of scholarly attainments and large
practical experience His aim is to instruct the laity so that they
might know how to bear themselves as "secular judges, mediators,
assessors, judgment-finders, councillors, clerks, plaintiffs, defend-
ants, witnesses, arbitrators, advocates, and other parties in court
or council " He brought together in it what was most important
in the existing scattered popular literature of legal practice, and
to the use of which men had become accustomed. And precisely
to this faithful conformity to the usage and the need of his time,
we must attribute the extraordinary and undisputed credit which
the "Laienspiegel" found among practicians from the very beginning. One found in it a popular encyclopædia of legal science.
Beside the "Laienspiegel," which had absorbed so large a part of
the popular literature of legal practice, the older writings could not
maintain their original importance. Only the most important of
the works of the older popular literature offers here a noteworthy
exception For the "Klagspiegel," a new lease of life began with
the appearance of the "Laienspiegel," . . . and from this time
on the two together form the most usual apparatus requisite in
petty practice.

TOPIC 3. ITALIAN HUMANISM AND THE REFORMATION

§ 25 **Theology and Legal Science in the Middle Ages.** — Legal
science and theology had stood in the closest relation to one another throughout the Middle Ages, — for one reason, certainly,
because the representatives of the former belonged in their majority
to the clergy. But their parallel development was determined
still more by an inner kinship, namely that both are devoted to
determining the meaning of documents handed down from a far
past Of these documents, one class, those of the ecclesiastical

[1] *Stintzing*, "Pop Lit ," ch 7.

law, brings the two sciences into direct contact with each other,
or rather is common to the two. To this influence was added
the fact that the scholastic dialectic shaped equally in both the
form of scientific endeavor. Similar phenomena, therefore, appear
in the course of their development. What patristics had been to
theology, the period of the early Glossators became to legal science;
which handed down to later times, as high authorities, its Four
Doctors, — the "four lilies of the law " — just as theology rev-
erenced its "Quattuor Doctores Ecclesiæ." Irnerius, the Four
Doctors, and their immediate successors, in direct contact with
the sources, separated from them by no pedagogical traditions,
and having their eyes fixed steadfastly on them, were the first to
unlock the riches of the Justinian law-books. Then the creative
force of legal science gradually flagged; the "Glossa Ordinaria "
of Accursius became authoritative, and assumed the position which
the "Libri Sententiarum " of Petrus Lombardus had long since
occupied in theology. Scholastic theology had scarcely reached
its fullest bloom in Albertus Magnus, Thomas Aquinas, and
Duns Scotus, when legal science boasted of the brilliant names of
Bartolus and his pupil Baldus. It was, indeed, not given to these,
as it was to those great schoolmen, to open up, even though only
in form, a new world of thought, nor to erect a grandiose philosophic
system, but their works did attain, through a kindred power of
scholastic dialectic, finished virtuosity of analysis, and versatile
casuistry, a sway that can only be compared with the authority
of those great masters. As Thomas Aquinas and Duns Scotus
became the chief pillars of dogmatics, so Bartolus and Baldus were
enrolled with the Gloss of Accursius as authoritative; and thus
was consummated the last break with the sources. Not what
these contained, but what those authorities had thought and said
of them, was henceforth decisive in the questionaries and " distinctions " spun out with endless prolixity and dialectic subtlety.
In the steady flood of commentaries, the authority of tradition and
the plentitude of opinions had raised an insurmountable wall before
the sources, and to break through it strength and will were alike
lacking.

The renascence of classical studies in the 1400s prepared the
way for regeneration in both sciences, albeit the Humanism which
sprung from it assumed at first toward them an attitude of polite
disdain and even of hostility. The ideas, however, of which Humanism was the vehicle — the emancipation of the individual in
thought and conscience, in faith and moral judgments, from the

constraint of traditional bonds, ideas which involved a break with
the authority of tradition and a reference of men's understanding
to pure and original sources, ideas which asserted themselves in all
domains of thought, — were bound in time to exercise their quickening influence within the fields of those sciences yet torpid in
scholasticism.

§ 26　**Early Humanism.** — Humanism budded and grew hardy
in Italy about the same time as legal science became enervated
and decayed. It used against the latter a contempt and hostility
even greater than it showed toward other scholastic studies
The prestige and influence that the jurists enjoyed and (notwithstanding all the hollowness and tastelessness of their culture)
knew how to maintain, provoked attack.

The German humanists accepted it as a part of the recognized
good tone of their fraternity, to inveigh arrogantly against legal
learning and its representatives. "Accursianum absynthium
bibere" became the favorite designation among German humanists
for legal studies.[1] "With their Commentaries," says Hutten,
"the jurists have involved in mist a subject otherwise intelligible,
and made it obscurer than Cimmerian darkness."[2] Nor was
Hutten the only one among eminent humanists who had busied
himself with legal studies Reuchlin, Mutian, Coban, Hesse,
cultivated legal science.[3] But its aridity and dreariness repelled
them On the other hand, we find among jurists, from the end
of the 1400s onward, many who in their youth had acquired an
excellent training in the humanities, and who had given themselves up with enthusiasm to the new intellectual movement
Not one of these, however, nor of the other humanists who studied
law and (unlike those named above, who abandoned it) made it
their life calling, understood or attempted to make fruitful within
it the culture he had absorbed from the "poets." Where legal
learning began, taste ended The example of Sebastian Brant
shows instructively how hardly the humanistic mixed with the legal
training[4] Born in 1457 in Strassburg, he plunged with his fellow-

---

[1] *Muther,* "Johann Apell,' p 78, and "Universitatsleben," p 469;
Strauss, "Ulrich von Hutten," I, 167, note 1, *Stintzing,* "Ulrich Zasius"
(1857), pp 97, 103
[2] *Hutten,* "Nemo Præfatio" (1518) and "Prædones" (1520) in his
"Opera" (ed *Bocking*), I, 180, IV, 379 *et seq,* respectively
[3] *Strauss,* "Ulrich von Hutten," I, 155; *Muther,* "Universitatsleben,"
p 242, *Stobbe,* "Rechtsquellen," II, 34
[4] *Strobel,* "Das Narrenschiff von Sebastian Brant" (1839), *Zarncke,*
"Sebastian Brant's Narrenschiff" (1854), *Stintzing,* "Pop Lit," pp.
45 *et seq,* 451-462, *Vischer,* "Geschichte der Universität Basel," pp.

student Reuchlin into classical antiquities at Basel (1475–1477)
under the influence of awakening Humanism; was active later as
a favorite teacher, and soon gained for himself an esteemed name
among Humanists by his editions of classical authors, and still
more by his Latin and German poems.   From a man who had
matured in such a cultural environment, one might justifiably
expect that an ennobled taste would be reflected in his legal writings.
But the opposite is true.   In all these publications there is no
trace to be found of the humanistic movement   On the contrary,
there runs throughout the trait of didactic effort, directed to purely
practical ends   Nor is he an innovator. the Empire in its ancient
splendor, the Church in its pristine purity, morality in its primitive
simplicity, are his ideals.   Naturally therefore he felt no call to be
a reformer of the law.

§ 27. **Later Influence of Humanism.** — It was, however, inevitable that the humanistic movement should, in time, exert a
positive influence upon legal science. Inasmuch as Roman law
itself was an inheritance from classical antiquity, it was merely
a question of carrying over into the treatment of legal texts the
principles of Humanism, and utilizing in their interpretation the
results of classical learning. The first person in Germany to treat
seriously the connection between Humanism and legal science was
Ulrich Zasius, who is accordingly and justly regarded along with
Budæus and Alciat as one of the founders of modern legal science
The more Humanism determined general culture, the greater was
bound to be the prestige and attractiveness of legal learning, for
one could reverence it as a treasure handed down from antiquity.
But in equal degree was the prestige of the Canon law and the
inclination to its study bound to lessen; and in the same pace, the
separation between clerics and laymen, within the profession, to
be consummated. Humanism, however, could feel no interest
in the law save from the aspect of its classical origin; the law's
practical importance was to it indifferent. Its influence led
therefore to a schism in legal science, to a contrast of theory and
practice, such as had theretofore not existed in Germany. The
breach did not, indeed, open so widely as it did in France under
the influence of her great scholars; theory did not rise to an equal
height of elegant scholarship; the practical ends remained controlling, and the theorists did not withdraw from practice. Nevertheless the opposition made itself felt between those who held the

188, 238; *Charles Schmidt,* "Histoire littéraire de l'Alsace" (Paris, 1879),
I, 191–333, II, 340–356; Allg d Biog , III, 256 *et seq.*

humanistic innovations to be idle and troublesome pranks of the "poets," which served no end of life and endangered the certainty of the law, and those who, without limiting themselves to practical aims, were devoted to making legal studies into a more discerning instrument of science

§ 28 **The Reformation** — With the inmost thought of the German Reformation, and its first manifestations in the field of faith, legal science had no direct connection. In so far as Humanism had penetrated into law it had created an inner kinship between it and the reformatory movement; since the problem in theology, as in law, was to carry back men's understanding to the purity of the original sources and to break the authority of traditionary errors. But the course of events soon led to a point where the ways parted. For the Reformation was bound, in logic and necessity, to advance from questions of faith to questions of regimen, historically interwoven therewith, from the championing of theses in conflict with Holy Writ to the negation of papal and conciliar authority, and in so doing it entered a domain where it clashed sharply with positive law The Leipzig "Disputation," and still more Luther's repudiation of the validity of the Canon law, roused the opposition of the jurists. Many, like Zasius, turned their backs thenceforth on the Reformation, though without finding contentment within the other party. Others, and in particular the younger generation, followed the movement notwithstanding, and held to Luther, so far as their convictions of the law did not in special questions hinder. The majority of well-known jurists we find on this side A polemic was conducted over the ecclesiastical law as a whole and individual canons. The jurists successfully championed its validity, so far as it did not conflict with the words of the Holy Writ; and where changes were necessary, they fitted the new with cautious hand into the traditional ordinances, guarding against violent innovations.

Though the attitude of the jurists in the first stages of the Reformation be thus indicated as generally conciliatory, — such as was naturally implanted in them by their professional training, — individual modifications are of course to be understood. There were not lacking impetuous characters like Oldendorp, with whom the poising of legal questions gave way to the ardor of religious zeal Others, like H. Goden, remained at heart indifferent to the new ideas that agitated the time, repulsing them alike from science and the Church There were not lacking, also, those who, while attaching themselves in science to the progressive movement, nevertheless, in theological issues, from conviction or impelled by very diverse motives, entered the lists for tradition and the authority of the hierarchy (Zasius, Vigelius von Aytta, Joachim Hopper), or who, *vice versa*, were devoted to the innovation in the Church, while unwilling to leave the old ways of the law (H. Schurpf, Melchior von Ossa)

At the same time there is still another aspect of the contact between the development of legal science and the reformatory movement. We have seen how there was developing, since the 1400s, under the influence of the growing consequence of imperial law and its administration, a legal profession, which appears, in contrast to the clergy, as the representative of the civil legal order, the State   This divorce of the domains of faith and law, of ethical duty and positive statute, this liberation of the civil regimen from its traditionary hierarchic premises, the general state-building tendency of the time, were manifestations of one intellectual tendency, which found its sharpest and most consequent expression in Protestantism. It could not be initiated, much less consummated, without exciting the opposition of the clergy. Not without jealousy the latter saw the immanent decline of the power and importance of the Canon law; and the essential connection between this turn of events and the movement begun within the Church itself did not escape the quick eye of self-interest   From the standpoint of the ancient Church it might be questioned whether an institution and a science released from her control was still to be considered Christian. Ethical scruples against the study of imperial law so ardently pursued were easy enough to find. Legal science, it was argued, must be a science incompatible with Christianity, since it taught men that they might and should defend their rights, notwithstanding Christ commanded that a man should not seek his own, nor quarrel or litigate with his brothers, but should practise forbearance   From such views men deduced an irreconcilable schism between Christianity and law. This clerical opposition gave a new meaning to the proverb, " Juristen böse Christen " [1]   That opposition was directed solely against the imperial law, and contemplated no detraction from the credit of the Canon law. That their arguments overshot the mark and reached Canon as well as Roman law, they could disregard, since professional legal training was based more and more upon the latter.

[1] *Stintzing,* "Das Sprichwort Juristen bose Christen in seinen geschichtlichen Bedeutungen" (1875) [See Professor *Kenny's* essay above cited in § 23 — Ed]

Last of all, the Reformation exercised, in one respect, an immediate influence upon the subject matter of legal studies For inasmuch as it belittled the importance of Canon law and awakened a widespread antipathy against it (though without destroying its validity, even within Protestant countries, or rendering a knowledge of it superfluous), the effect was that the Canon law, though it did not disappear, took a less prominent place as the object of university courses and scientific literature. On the other hand, the reforms within the Church in Protestant countries prepared the ground for, and gave the impulse to, the creation of a Protestant ecclesiastical law as a new subject of instruction.

Topic 4 Methods of Jurists in the 1500s

§ 29. **General Character of Medieval Science** — In the case of a science whose material is handed down in written records it is self-evident that exegesis must be the beginning of its work, and must always remain its foundation. So it was that the scientific revival of the Justinian law by the Glossators began with such work ; indeed, the significance of their labor lies precisely in the fact that they applied for the first time to the Justinian law the exegetic method in its entirety and purity. With all the freshness lent by entry into a newly discovered field of thought, with interest concentrated upon submersion in their sources, and with no literary medium between them and the object of their study that could hamper, distract, or misguide them, they unlocked the content of the Corpus Juris with a rare power of thought, and made its substance an intellectual possession of succeeding times

When, after more than a century, the decay of legal science began, the cause lay less in a general decline of intellectual force than in the natural law that any method, continued without modifications of tools or mode of application, becomes in time a hollow virtuosity, exhausts its creative energy, and reaches a vertex, beyond which it yields no new results, but expends its labor in mere repetition, analysis, and exposition of the material handed down But what is more, the method of medieval science carried within itself the seeds of decay, because it consisted in pure analysis, prosecuted with a closed mind The intellectual life of the Middle Ages was saturated with faith in authority, all deeper observation of things was controlled by the conviction that truth is something given, which it is not necessary first to discover, but only to receive from tradition Within scholasticism, the authority of Holy Writ in

384

theology and of Aristotle in philosophy stood on an equal plane. To recognize and to prove the harmony of the two was the problem in whose solution scholastic philosophy wore itself out. Where, however, the contradiction was not to be removed, there (they believed) the higher authority of revelation prevailed, for that is the supreme test of truth, and therefore the authority of the Church, as its representative and guardian, is ultimately conclusive. The goal of science can therefore only be, on one hand, to demonstrate the agreement between those metaphysical truths which appear as the content of human reason and revelation, and, on the other hand, to reduce the content of both to knowledge by the instrument of analysis, — that is, by a process of investigation which starts with a material ready and complete, and proceeds to dismember it by the method of syllogistic demonstration   The form in which scholasticism practised this consisted in the statement of " questions," sometimes abstractly formulated, sometimes concretely stated in the form of a " casus ", and which are answered by an exposition of pros and cons with constant dragging in of the authorities.   In this procedure the contradictions that may appear are overcome either by the subordination of one authority to another, or by " distinctions " in which each proposition deduced retains an individual, limited validity.   Analysis by questions and distinctions involved therefore an inconceivable frittering into details.

More even than philosophy, legal science was dominated by the assumption of a given truth and of its inherent consistency Still more in it than in philosophy, and with better reason, is judgment constrained by the materials and the aims   Its material is firm and settled; its task . .   not directed to the discovery of new truths, but to ascertaining rules objectively declared, and to understanding them in their basis, purposes, and relations.   The constraint of legal science was bound to become closer and firmer the more the private legislation with which it dealt should be developed in its details into a perfected system   Add to this that instinct of faith which penetrated the whole intellectual life of the Middle Ages, its credulous reverence of tradition, its willing and habitual subordination of judgment to authority, and it is evident that a beginning of historical criticism was quite impossible.   And so, for example, in the study of the Justinian legislation no importance whatsoever was attributed to the fact that between it and its medieval commentators there lay more than a thousand years   With naive credulity the Glossators took in hand its interpretation as though it were a question of the enforcement of a contemporary statute, and uncritically assumed for the author of their sources the surrounding conditions and accepted notions of their own day

Their faith in authority did not, indeed, extend to the *form* of the text, since this was available in different readings. But their criticism here also was very sparsely exercised, and without any method whatever. A particular form of the text became traditionally fixed as "litera communis" or "vulgata," to which one was considered bound in toto. Still more entrammeling for research was the influence of faith as regards the systematic form and order of the Justinian law-books Even those works which themselves approached a systematic form, the "Summæ," merely give orderly synopses of the content of the corresponding divisions of their sources. Under such conditions legal research was necessarily restricted to pure analysis. The work was therefore more extensive than intensive, directed rather to dissolution than to concentration. And if the exegetic method in itself involved the *danger* of not distinguishing the relative value of different passages, of treating all with equal emphasis, thus heaping particularities fortuitously together, that method, when manipulated in purely analytic fashion, was *bound* to lead to such a frittering of its materials, and to a dissolution into enormous masses of details This dismembering tendency made itself felt even where unification was the apparent goal, since contradictions were on principle not merged into higher unities, but so reconciled by distinctions that every proposition and every opinion stood independent within certain limits.

§ 30. **Legal Science: the "Mos Italicus."** — In the course of time, a fixed type of this analytical exegetic method had been developed, which from the 1500s onward was called (in contradistinction to variant methods) instruction "more Italico" or "magistraliter" It was embodied in identical form in legal literature and in academic courses. From the original simplicity and naturalness which we find in the Glossators [1] exegesis had developed into a complicated mechanism. Hieronymus Schurpf gives the following scheme for the "Vulgaris et usitata sive communis interpretandi ratio." (1) continuatio ad præcedentia; (2) textus partitio, (3) summarii relatio; (4) casus fictio; (5) dubitandi ratio, (6) decidendi ratio; (7) rationis dubitandi confutatio;

___
[1] As to this, *cf Savigny,* "Geschichte," III, ch 23–24, *Schulte,* "Quellen," I, 52–53.

(8) notabilium collectio; (9) glossarum diversarum conciliatio;
(10) neotericorum judicium; (11) communis opinionis judicatio;
(12) ad forum explicatio   A celebrated distich of Matthaus
Gribaldus Mopha (which we follow, since it was used from the
middle 1500s onward to characterize the " Mos Italicus " and as
a mnemonic aid) summarized the elements of the process more
briefly. It runs:

> "Præmitto, scindo, summo, casumque figuro,
> Perlego, do causas, connoto, objicio "

The commentator begins with an introduction (" præmitto "),
in which he characterizes and delimits in a general way the matters
treated of in his texts, defines the terms involved, and adds any
other preliminary explanations   On this follows the " partitio,"
— division of the material into its parts, the indication of the
different matters and principles involved in the text, and which
are to be separately expanded (" scindo ")   After this dismemberment of the text, its essential content is again briefly recapitu-
lated (" summo "), in which process the summaries of Bartolus
and others are commented upon   Next follows the statement of
the " casus."   The assumptions of fact underlying the propositions
involved in the passage under discussion are here indicated, being
taken from the text so far as this indicates them, or otherwise
stated by an example theoretically devised or borrowed from
actual practice.   Abundant examples of these existed in collections of " casus " that were early formed, and in the Accursian
gloss.   If the " partitio " has offered opportunity, place has already
been found under it for a heaping up of authorities   The text
itself is now set out, for the first time, and in this connection are
attached critical elucidations of variant readings   The content
of the text having by these processes been fixed and elucidated,
and the fundamental interpretation thus completed, additional
expositions of its content are begun in huge abundance.   First,
the " causæ " are discussed   By these are understood primarily
the rationale of the decision and of its legal principle, with refuta-
tion of all possible doubts and opposing reasons.   This is also the
place for the discussion of the four Aristotelian causes employed by
the schoolmen: [1] the " causa efficiens," " materialis," " formalis,"
" finalis, " which (according to the commentator's type of mind)
might be dispatched in a purely formal and superficial manner,

[1] *Ratjen*, "Vom Einflusse der Philosophie auf die Jurisprudenz" (Programm, Kiel, 1855) ; *Stintzing*, "Ulrich Zasius," pp. 112 *et seq.*

or made the basis for a particular and didactic treatment. (The four causes are, however, treated by many commentators not in this place, but in the introduction ; this is indeed the older practice, to which, for example, Zasius adheres) Under the " connoto," which follows next, was understood a stringing together of remarks of all sorts in arbitrary order and number. Here belong the colligation of the legal principles deduced in the case in hand with other related principles (" cognata et similia "), parallel passages being to this end stated and expounded, comparisons of the same; excursions into other fields of the law, above all, the deduction of certain general maxims, — which had borne since the Glossators the peculiar name of " brocardica," and later came to be known as " regulæ," " loci communes," and " axiomata " If the commentator is, thus far, drawn off into undue discursiveness, the final operation of the " objicere " offers him an excuse for still wider treatment of controverted questions (" contraria et oppositiones "). In addition to apparently or actually contradictory passages of the text, the variant views of the " Gloss "(i e of Accursius) and of the commentators are here gathered together. Their explanation leads to " distinctiones, amplicationes et limitationes," in whose elaboration is displayed the virtuosity of the scholastic dialectic. Doubts, objections, and disputes are introduced and disposed of, by means of "questiones," for whose solution authorities are cited pro and con

§ 31. **Effects of the " Mos Italicus "** — Had this method been applied with simplicity and a sensible moderation, legal science must have profited (though unconsciously) by the benefits of a thorough exegesis. But if one would understand its actual pernicious influence, one must not forget the formalistic tendencies of legal learning Men believed they had understood the matter when they had understood the operations of a complicated interlocking wheelwork, although such operations were often directed to an understanding far less of the matter itself than of the dialectic laws and forms discoverable in it or in its expression It was a fatal confusion of logical forms with positive knowledge And if the method itself, with its complicated instructions, gave excuse for discursiveness, so too the personal inclination to subtility, the general practice of over nice disputation and distinction, and the habit of interweaving continually with one's own argument appeals to authority, were added influences to the same end. Tradition required that he who lived later should take account of the opinions of those who lived earlier, while vanity led him to

endeavor to shine with a rich and learned apparatus, and to sur-
pass his predecessors in propounding finer distinctions or contriving new "questiones "   And thus not only was legal literature
swollen to an incomprehensible body of uncorrelated details, but
the exegetic method lost sight more and more of its own basis.
Instead of busying itself with its texts, it dealt primarily with
opinions concerning them   As Thomas Aquinas and Duns
Scotus became in theology the chief pillars of dogmatics, and were
even declared by papal authority to be in part infallible teachers,
so legal science came to ground itself upon the Gloss of Accursius
and on Bartolus.   Even statutory dispositions were issued to
strengthen the latter's authority, and to create professorial chairs
for instruction in his writings   That legal practice gladly followed
this tendency was in the nature of things.   When theory renounces
independent investigation, practice does the same the more willingly.

In passing judgment upon these results, modern scholarship is
prone to distinguish insufficiently two points of view.   From the
standpoint of scholarship, one is justified in declaring it a lamentable decline that access to direct understanding of the sources
should have been not only shut off but in general no longer sought
But from the more general historical standpoint of the law's development one must judge otherwise.   Consider first the treatment of the Roman law.   We must not overlook the fact that
explanations of the sources which our sharpened eyes recognize
as misunderstandings were prompted by and based upon those
contemporary legal conceptions with which the minds of the
commentators were engrossed   Unconscious of the historical inconsistencies, bent not at all on recognizing them, but on treating the Corpus Juris ingenuously as a binding code for the
present, the Roman law was re-formed, in the hands of the
medieval jurists, into a half modern law, of Roman mixed with
Germanic conceptions.   Objectionable as this may be from the
standpoint of an uncorrupted exegesis, nevertheless the work done
deserves full recognition from the standpoint of legal practice,
whose positive needs were thus instinctively recognized and satisfied [1]   Had men been conscious, to the degree we are to-day, of
the chasm that separates the present from antiquity, they certainly would have lacked the courage to adopt the inheritance of

---

[1] See as to this and the false judgment of similar phenomena of later
times, the apposite remarks of *Ihering,* "Geist des romischen Rechts,"
IV, 464 *et seq*

the ancient world directly as a binding rule of life. And if they had consciously purposed to put into effect the Roman law in its purity (granting that it could have been understood), the conditions of society would have thrown insuperable obstacles in their way.

As regards the treatment of the Canon law,[1] we must add to these considerations the fact that university professors and law-writers were alike subordinated to a living, active legislative power, whose will, expressed in ecclesiastical ordinances, they were bound in duty and impelled by sentiment to enforce.

But whether it be taken that mere misunderstanding or a law-making instinct guided the Commentators, the influence of both elements to such a degree was made possible only through the domi-nance of the analytical method An individual principle, taken in isolation, can be given by reasoning a signification which is conclusive for a special case but cannot possibly be attributed to it when considered as an organic part of the whole, — i.e. as a consequence of a more general legal concept

§ 32. " Loci " and " Topica " — The unity lacking in the scientific treatment of the subject was to be re-created in the student's mind by memory   This is the explanation of the peculiar rôle played in the scholastic method by the " Locus," — a word with which the most various meanings are associated, but which are all included in the notion of a vantage place, outside of the matter under discussion, whence the details can be objectively surveyed. Such " Loci " scholars were at pains to discover and establish, to the end of securing a firm support for the memory and the judgment, and the memorizing of the " Loci " was one of the first rules of methodology.

By " loci ordinarii " the schoolman of the law understood those passages in the " Corpus Juris " to which were attached, by fixed convention, the exhaustive discussion of any given problem of the law   Thus the " locus ordinarius " of the doctrine of " mora " was lex 32, Digesta de usuris, liber 22, titulus 1, later l. 84, D de V O , 45, 1, of the doctrine of the " statuta," l 9, D. de j. et j 1, 1, the doctrine of " culpa," l. 32, D depositi, 16, 3, for the doctrine of the " obligatio naturalis," the " lex damnata," frater a fratre, l 38, de cond ind., 12, 6.

" Loci communes " we find in various meanings and applica-tions.   In the first place they signified the general conceptions serving as dialectic premises for an exposition, also the analytical

---

[1] Cf Thaner, "Die Summa Magistri Rolandi" (1874), preface ; Schulte, "Quellen," I, 215.

points of view that determine the "partitio et divisio" — in other words, the justifications and divisional links of the subject, or the outline scheme of the analysis By "locus communis" is also to be understood an (Aristotelian) "topic", or, as applied to legal science, a general rule of law, so that the expression "locus" supplants the older "brocardica," and later is synonymously used with "regula" and "axioma."   To these meanings and applications of the "locus" is to be added, finally, that borrowed from rhetoric, "loci (τόπος) est sedes argumenti."   These "loci" constitute the object of the "topica," i.e "ars ratiocinandi."   In fact they are not merely, like a "topic," the premises of a demonstration, but the basis of the reasoning in general, being determined by all the relations and circumstances involved in a given object of exposition.

Legal science made copious use of the "loci."   Indeed it was a part of the traditional pedagogic method to start in argumentation from definitely settled "loci" Only that demonstration was reputed certain and conclusive which had as its starting-point a "locus" recognized and approved by the schoolmen In this respect the syllogistic logic of exegesis and the method of establishing proof in legal procedure were much alike.   The "loci" serve at the same time as aids in the formulation of "questiones."   Legal scholars were at pains to amass the most ample apparatus of useful "loci."   Baldus had already brought the number to a hundred Later many more were added whose doctrinal validity was questionable.   At the end of the 1400s, therefore, men began to sift and clarify them.   [The two works, " De Modo Ratiocinandi et Disputandi in Jure " (Bologna, 1514) of Petrus Andreas Gammarus, and " Topicorum seu Locorum Legalium Opus de Inventione et Argumentatione " (Louvain, 1516) of Nikolaus Everardus[1] were the most famous products of such undertakings]

§ 33. **The Period of Unshaken Authority of the " Mos Italicus "** — In Italy, the land of its nativity, the legal art embodied in the " mos Italicus," which afforded such ample play to the racial disposition to rhetoric and dialectic, remained in full bloom notwithstanding the Humanists' arraignments of its corrupted Latin and bad taste.   It was the art of the method which still drew Germans in large numbers to the Italian universities so late as the 1500s. Guido Panzirolus (1599) presents it in detail as the true and the dominant method, though not indeed, without

---

[1] [*Stintzing,* "Geschichte," I, 119–120, criticises the estimate of Everts (Everardus) given by *Savigny* in his "Geschichte," VI, 465. — TRANSL]

criticising its degeneration into a prolix formalism [1] Not less securely did the Bartolists and Accursianists hold sway in France. In Toulouse, Montpellier, Orléans, Avignon, Valence, Grenoble, and Paris, they maintained their ground, despite the quickening of a new spirit by Alciat and Budé, which attained control only in Bourges   Matthaus Gribaldi (of Chieri, in Piedmont) published in 1541 for his students in Toulouse, after his removal to Valence, his " Libri Tres de Methodo ac Ratione Studendi," in which he expounds the " mos legendi Italicus," — highly esteemed, he tells us, in France: though it is true he makes concessions to the Humanists.   Great jurists were unable to root out the old forms of scholasticism, whose practical worth Albericus Gentilis still championed in 1582 in his dialogues " De Juris Interpretibus "   And if, from the middle of the century, the new tendency, represented by Duaren, Donellus (Doneau), Cujas, and others, was what had drawn German students to the French schools, nevertheless we find them still among the auditors of the old method.   Germany borrows the methods with the materials of Italian scholarship; and though at this period there are noticeable in Germany, as in France, radical counter tendencies tending slowly to bring science into other ways, yet the " mos Italicus " is still, notwithstanding, generally regarded as the true juristic method, and is officially maintained   Like Alciat, who reports as much for France and Italy, Zasius complains of the hindrances thrown by the faculties in the way of every deviation from the old path

The statutes and lecture catalogues of the German universities leave no doubt of the sway of this method, even though from the middle of the century there becomes evident in many of them a new tendency, and one not only actually practised, but also recognized by statute (as at Greifswald, 1545, Rostock, 1564). Yet even Bonifacius Amerbach, so late as 1552, finds it an objection to the call extended to Dauren and Balduin to come to Tubingen, that they had " departed from old established methods in profitendo." [2]   A deviation from tradition was construed as a lack of scholarship so late as the end of the century, in Altdorf, in the case of Hugo Donellus (Doneau), the greatest of all representatives of legal synthesis united with complete control of the sources, and we must regard as a concession to the " mos Italicus " the request directed to him by the school inspectors that he might

---

[1] *Panzirolus*, "De Claris Legum Interpretibus," book 2, ch 4, 6, 8
[2] *Mandry*, "Johann Sichardt," pp 12, 35

be pleased, " in addition to the textual application of his own method to take upon himself to expound for some two hours ' textum in jure.'"

Thus the " mos Italicus " maintained itself down into the 1600s, if in the face of opposition and in an enfeebled form, nevertheless as the method prevailing in the officially primary courses   And it was not solely the force of tradition and the halo of ponderous scholarship that supported it, but the advantages it offered as an introduction to legal controversies, received opinions, and casuistics It was on this account reputed the fittest method to make one an expert and securely seated legal jouster.   To the academic instruction was assigned the task of affording both the theoretical and the practical training, for a practical apprenticeship did not then, as to-day, follow as a matter of course the young lawyer's academic studies.   This predominance of the practical tendency, to which the representatives of legal science were led and confined by social necessities and their own continual occupation with practical work, had the effect that neither the systematic nor the antiquarian method as received in Germany, perfected its development or attained undisputed sway.   And, for the same reason, though Germany can show vigorous efforts and excellent beginnings and a few important achievements, it cannot show one representative of legal learning who can be compared with the great French jurists, or who can be still named (as those can be) as unexcelled models of excellence

From still another point of view was this practical tendency a hindrance to a new method.   Because of the fact that the law itself was developed and transformed by the Commentators, though the Justinian law-books were regarded in Germany as authoritative, it was nevertheless indisputable that their content was not received without limitations and modifications;   these consisted of the traditional " opiniones doctorum," and were only to be determined from legal literature   From this viewpoint it was possible to contest the innovation in scientific method as an unjustified apostasy, and to defend the " mos Italicus " successfully, as the only method by which the body of actually existing law could be truly represented as resting jointly upon the " lex " and the " interpretatio."

§ 34. **Opposition and the Beginning of Reform** — Along with the traditional reverence for the old method, there runs throughout the 1500s complaints of the prolixity into which it had degenerated.   Even five or six years' study led only to a fragmentary knowledge of the law [1] Franz Frosch sent his son to Bourges in 1533 because there, under the influence of the Alciatic method, " in one year, at least as many titles of the Pandects would be disposed of as separate leges ' more Italico ' " According to Vigelius two whole years were devoted in Padua, about this time, to the Institutes, and still only a few titles were run through. Alciat, and later Panzirol, report the same, and tell that a whole year was generally devoted to five passages of the civil or the Canon law. [Late in the century, one German professor boasts of interpreting the Institutes concisely for mature students, in four years; another (and no friend of the " mos Italicus ") in three. Various university statutes — as at Greifswald, 1545; Vienna, 1554, [2] Ingolstadt, 1563; Rostock, 1564; Tubingen, 1588 — attempted to lessen the period of study, particularly the time devoted to the Institutes. According to the lecture lists of Ingolstadt for 1571, which boast that the curriculum is established exactly according to the Italian model, the Institutes are given " cum apparatu " in two years, " textualiter " in a shorter time, while four years are devoted to the Code and eight to the Pandects Rostock,[3] in 1564, preceded by more than half a century any other university in prescribing systematic instruction in the law according to subjects, — the law of persons, contracts, inheritance, feudal law, plaints, procedure, regulæ juris]

§ 35 **Unofficial Academic Courses: Seminars and Disputations.** — The reform of pedagogical method is connected with a change in the organization of academic instruction The official " lecturæ " or " lectiones," which were held " publice et gratis," were, in accordance with traditional arrangement, dissertations upon texts; therefore, however much one might digress from these, their method was essentially exegetic and analytical Only in unofficial courses was it possible to abandon the norm thus prescribed. The less adapted the " lecturæ " were to introduce the beginner into legal science, the more they afforded only a fragmentary knowledge of isolated details, so much the more imperatively was the need felt of seeking aid in private instruction. As a consequence, at all the universities we find younger scholars devoted to such activity, and a great number of professors began their academic work in this way.

---

[1] *Cramer*, "Kleine Schriften," pp 148 *et seq* , *Savigny*, "Geschichte," III, 547

[2] *Kink*, "Die Rechtslehre an der Wiener Universität" (1853), pp. 37 *et seq*

[3] *Krabbe*, "Die Universität Rostock," pp. 598 *et seq.*

Thus arose a mode of instruction, which at first seems, to be sure, to have consisted simply in a drill upon the most important matters, so far as suitable for memorizing, — the "summæ," "tituli et regulæ," and "loci communes" being learned by heart. But a systematizing tendency later made itself evident   We soon observe that the "exercitationes," particularly the disputations of the professors, are held "privatim" (*i e.* unofficially); the public ones, everywhere prescribed (for which Saturday was customarily set aside), were indifferently attended to by the professors, not simply from neglect, but through experience that the usefulness of such public exercises, in which only a few auditors could take effective part, was very slight

For the unofficial courses the later hours of the afternoon were left open   These were arranged for by agreement with the student upon a subject and an honorarium, — thus contrasting with the "lecturæ "   This last name, too, was unsuitable for them, because their method of instruction was conversational. Hence their name "collegia," suggested by the limited number of pupils and their fellowship with the teacher for the purposes of instruction. In time, and increasingly, as the "lecturæ publicæ " sank in credit, because their methods were becoming antiquated, the full professors did not disdain to conduct such "collegia privata," particularly if they had had success in them as young instructors.   Only slowly and against strong opposition did this innovation become settled. The danger threatening the "lecturæ publicæ " was not unappreciated, it seemed objectionable, even improper, to permit private gain from teaching in the "collegia privata," when the "lecturæ " must be given without compensation   By a process of development whose stages cannot here be followed, things went so far that the university instructors transferred the emphasis of their work from the "lecturæ publicæ " to the "collegia privata "; and the more the former sank in repute the more their name also fell into oblivion.   And so it has come about that the word "collegium " has acquired the meaning of an academic lecture generally, — only that custom of speech which unites it with the verb "lesen " (to read) reminding one of its relationship with "lecturæ " and "lectio."

From the seminars (" collegia ") there arose a new type of legal literature, which was long cultivated with especial favor: the disputations held therein, edited by the professor, were united and published in collections.   Inasmuch as a systematic arrangement of the material was attempted, more or less complete manuals

395

resulted　And this practice was soon no longer limited to the civil
law, for the study of criminal law, feudal law, and even Canon
law, " collegia " were likewise formed whose labors appeared later
in print　As examples, Wilhelm Valentin Forster's " Justinianeæ
Tractationes ad Institutiones Juris " (1604–1608), and especially
the much-used work of Treutler, " Disputationum Selectarum "
(1592) deserve especial mention　Treutler's work is so complete
and so methodically put together that it could be used as a compendium of the Pandects　Next to Treutler's Disputations,
the greatest esteem was attained by those published by Borcholten's
pupil, Heinrich Bocer, under the title " Disputationes de Universo
Jura quo Utimur."　They constitute a systematically arranged
collection covering the whole field of the law.

　§ 36　**Attitude of Humanism toward the Mos " Italicus " and the
New " Methodus "** — Although, as already explained (§ 27), the
emancipatory and fecundant influence of Humanism upon legal
science was in truth a mighty one, Humanism has not thus far
been mentioned as an opponent of the " mos Italicus," because
it is clear that its positive claims stood in no irreconcilable repugnance to the " mos Italicus."　For they were satisfied if scientific work was done in better taste and in purer Latin, — if independence of judgment was maintained in the face of authority, —
if, finally, antiquarian learning found application and dialectic
subtilties were moderated.　And all this could be reconciled with
exegetic methods and fitted into the purely analytical method
without essentially altering it.　Yet one can understand how those
who, like Zasius, first accomplished it, appeared as regenerators
of legal science, because their commentaries, though in method
not fundamentally different, nevertheless did reveal a freer spirit,
more critical and open directly to the sources, and also — thanks
to a utilization of historical knowledge — a new substance.

　The question, however, essential to further development was
this. whether synthesis could be elevated into an effective element
of legal method; in other words, whether its mass of particularities
could be reduced to principles, united in greater unities.　This
question also was first raised in humanistic circles　Gelhus'
notice (" Noctes Ambrosianæ," 1, 22) of a lost work of Cicero,
" De Jure Civile in Artem Redigendo," the latter's discussion
(" De Orat ," 1, 41) of the problem of legal science " In Artem
Redigere," raised the question, how far this problem had since then
been solved or its solution was feasible　Without consciously
realizing the significance of the question, men recognized neverthe-

less that the " ars juris " was completely lacking in the traditional legal science.   Going further, it was asked whether then the " ars juris " was to be found in the sources; whether Justinian had succeeded in attaining the goal indicated by Cicero.   The arrangement of the titles in the Codex and the Pandects was examined, the succession of the " Fragmenta " and Constitutions; and when it was found that these were not determined upon systematic grounds,[1] the question arose whether it were not justifiable, yea imperative, to present the law in another order   This was the question of the " methodus," as the systematic presentation was customarily called.   How busily this question occupied the younger jurists from the second decade of the 1500s on their letters show us.

In this agitation of methodics in Germany the influence was felt of the French jurists[2]   In contrast to the "mos Italicus " there was developed the "Mos docendi Gallicus,"—distinguished from the former partly by a philological and antiquarian, partly by a synthetic element.   And it was precisely those French jurists, like Duaren and Doneau, cultivating with preference this second element, who exercised particular attraction upon German jurists.   To this influence was joined that of the allied method represented in the Netherlands by Mudaus and carried into Germany by Matthaus Wesenbeck, as well, finally, as the movement inaugurated by Petrus Ramus, whose influence was perceptible in all branches of science.   Toward the close of the 1500s, the synthetic treatment, illustrated in the most varied forms of legal systematization, triumphed, and " methodice," or some similar label, is adopted with partiality in the titles of books as a claim to preference.

§ 37. **The Ramists and their Doctrines**. — The Ramistic method[3] is deserving of a more particular notice, as well for its essential historical importance as because of the incorrect opinions current regarding it.

In order to understand the movement associated in all fields of science with the appearance of PETRUS RAMUS, one must recall in what degree all scientific activity was dominated by the tradi-

[1] *Cf Bluhme*, "Uber die Ordnung der Fragmenta in den Pandekten," Z G R W., IV, 377 *et seq.*
[2] ["Such was the renown of Cujas that in the public schools of Germany, when his name was mentioned, every one took off his hat" (*Hallam*, "Literature of Europe in the 15th–17th Centuries," II, 169). — Ed]
[3] *Tennemann*, "Geschichte der Philosophie," VI, 420–440, *Ritter*, "Geschichte der Philosophie," V, 471 *et seq ; Waddington*, " Ramus" (Paris, 1855).

tionary Aristotelian-scholastic dialectic Ramus declared war
upon this, denied its correctness, and sought to put another and
simpler in its place.   In the contest, however, that thus developed,
there was not involved merely a schoolmen's question whether the
old or the new dialectic was technically more correct and perfect;
nor whether a new, perhaps a less burdensome, domination should
replace the old and severe.   Rather should the deeper significance
of the contest be thus formulated. whether the authority of any
system whatsoever of tutorial rules should dominate the mind's
activity; whether it should not be permitted to men's minds to
move freely according to the laws set them by nature, and obeying
only these   Ramus starts with the premise that dialectics is and
should be only a practical discipline, — the "ars bene disserendi";
its contents should be determined above all by the nature of the
human mind it teaches merely the art of using well man's natural
capacity for thought, its perfection is attained through "usus"
and "exercitium," through practice in the application of its rules,
whereby these become habits   All reflection begins by searching
out, in the mind, the reasons and premises which reside in the mind
and are there to be found, one then proceeds to reduce these to
expression, unite, and methodically present them. Hence, in accord
with this natural process, the "ars bene disserendi" must consist
of two parts, the "inventio" and the "judicium" The former
supplies the rules by which arguments are found; it is therefore
essentially a topic. The latter teaches the correct use of the arguments; and may be either a "judicium axiomaticum," when it
declares that something is or is not judgment, or "dianoeticum,"
when it derives one axiom from another; its logical forms are the
syllogism and the "methodus," — this last being the highest type
of exposition, which brings together into a natural order, advancing
from the general to the specific, all congruent axiomata.

Upon this simple ground plan was built an equally simple dialectic, which to Ramus signified, not an analysis of the thinking
process and of its different functions and forms, but a set of precepts for the use of natural rules of conception, judgment, inference,
and colligation It was therefore, as the definition suggests,
rather rhetoric than true dialectic, and its opponents reproached
it for being neither For this very reason it was tantamount to
the "methodus," i.e. the doctrine and art of clearly presenting
to the understanding and memory accordant judgments and conclusions. It is from this view "dispositio" — collocation, division,
colligation — of that which is conceived through "inventio,"

determined by "axioma," deduced by syllogism; and constitutes therefore the last part and also the highest type of the "ars bene disserendi."

Ramus lays down as the general rule of the "methodus," that in presenting truth one should start from the general and proceed to the particular. Only that method was, accordingly, to him a true one, which began with the definition and attached to this the distribution, which last is partly "partitio" (disintegration into parts), to some extent "divisio" (distinction of species). In each descendent part down to the most particular the same procedure is repeated The different parts are then to be united by "transitiones."

The goal at which Ramus aimed was, accordingly, a natural synthesis. And his significance in the history of legal science lies in the fact that he supplied the synthetic tendency with a technical apparatus and served to give it scientific support The simplicity and naturalness of his doctrine, compared with the complicated schematism of the Aristotelians, assured to him success He strengthened men's courage to follow in science the path of common sense, to trust in one's natural judgment He is therefore of kin with Humanism and Protestantism

If we thus regard Ramism as a tributary of a general current of the time, then we understand, on one hand, the broad range of its visible influence and the embittered opposition to it; and on the other hand, the fact that there appeared beside, and independent of it, other very similar developments in scientific method. We must not derive from Ramism all that is akin to it. In Germany, questions of methodology were current before anybody knew of Petrus Ramus, and they ran their course in large part uninfluenced by him. In France, Connanus evolved his system; and Dauren and Doneau, and in Louvain Mudäus, elaborated their natural "syntheses" without guidance by him. And, finally, we find in legal science, as in the field of philosophy proper, half-hearted Ramists and eclectics Ramus himself dealt with legal science only in passing (a "Cynosura Juris Utriusque" attributed to him is apocryphal) He touched directly the problem of legal science only through the appeal he directed to Cujas and L'Hospital to take upon themselves the task of a systematic digest of the existing law.[1]

One would suppose that Ramism, whose strength lay in the negation of scholastic routinism, should have led to a complete

[1]*Waddington*, "Ramus," pp. 355 *et seq.*, 474.

shelving of schematics; that a pure naturalism should have characterized his genuine followers. But it was not so. The Ramists claimed to be *scientific* dialecticians: they sought to refute the reproach that Ramus undertook to teach his pupils "to learn to fly before they had wings"; *their* doctrine should be as good as the old dialectic art But even if the rules were taken from nature, still the school first brought them into consciousness, and methodical practice first taught their skilful use. And so it fell out that among the enlightened followers of Ramus a *new* formalism was developed, which manifested itself in a forever recurrent utilization of certain methodical instruments and forms, and was all the more unvarying for the fact that Ramus recognized only the one method, namely, the syllogism and the deduction of the particular from the general. For this reason the original historical significance of Ramus has been in later times forgotten, and its character sought in a definite scholastic form What was originally only a means to an end appeared later to be its essence. And by three characteristics, in particular, it was taken to be distinguished dichotomy, the application of the " quattuor causæ," [1] and tabulation. The method operating with these expedients was called the Ramistic. Practised in pedantic fashion, it survived through the 1600s,[2] another illustration of the phenomenon of a doctrine, once intended for the liberation of inquirers' minds, coming to be set in a scholastic formalism and transformed into a new fetter.

TOPIC 5. LEGISLATION

§ 38. **Imperial and Territorial Legislation of the 1500s** [3] — Since Maximilian I, imperial legislation had shown an extraordinary growth, which continued through the religious wars to

---

[1] *Stintzing*, in K Z , III, 625 *et seq*

[2] *Thomasius*, "Cautelæ circa præcognita Jurisprudentiæ" (1710), ch. 10.

[3] *Eichhorn*, "Rechtsgeschichte," III, 308 *et seq.*, IV, 284 *et seq* , *Von Daniels*, "Handbuch," IV, 549 *et seq* , *Lancizolle*, "Übersicht der deutschen Reichstandschafts- und Territorialverhaltnisse" (1830); *Ficker*, "Reichsfurstenstand," pp 264 *et seq* , 371 *et seq* , *Moser*, "Von den teutschen Reichsstanden" (1767), *Friedenburg*, "Reichstag zu Speier" (1887); *Domcke*, "Virilstimmen im Reichsfurstenrat von 1495–1654" (in *Gierke's* "Untersuchungen," XI (1882), *Erdmannsdörfer*, "Deutsche Geschichte von 1648–1740" (2 vols , 1892–1893), I, 160 *et seq* , 377 *et seq.*, "Graf von Waldeck" (1869), pp 95 *et seq* , *Rauch*, "Traktat uber den Reichstag im 16ten Jahrhundert" (1905, *cf Stutz* in Z [2]R.G , XXXIX, 382); *Stobbe*, "Rechtsquellen," II, 183–205

TEXTS, in *Zeumer*, "Quellensammlung," nos 148–181; *Gerstlacher*, "Handbuch der teutschen Reichsgesetze" (11 vols 1786–1794), *Emminghaus*, "Corpus Juris German Academicum" (2 vols , 1844–1856), *Lehmann*, "Quellen," (1891).

1654. The Imperial Diet, which had become permanent, had accomplished nothing more of importance. While the imperial reformative statutes possessed, for the most part, only a transitory importance, one may regard the permanent Public Peace of 1495 [1] and the Augsburg religious Pact of 1555 (which bore also the title of a " General Constitution of the Public Peace ") [2] as, in a way, fundamental laws of the Empire   A true imperial organic statute was the Peace of Westphalia, which was indeed so designated, and commanded the incorporation of its provisions in the next Resolutions of the Diet and imperial electoral Capitulations   This provision was confirmed by the last imperial Resolution of 1654, which embodied in its text the treaties of peace of Osnabruck and Múnster, and solemnly declared them " a fundamental law established for the Holy Empire, an enduring rule of conduct, and perpetual ' norma judicandi.' " [3]   The imperial electoral Capitulations, also, although not imperial statutes if tested by the manner of their creation, actually possessed the importance of organic laws of the Empire

Imperial legislation was very extensive concerning the constitution and procedure of the Imperial Chamber of Justice, coinage, the organization of the imperial circles, and of the army, although no lasting regulation of the last was realized   The imperial ordinances of police of 1530, 1548, and 1577 were extended over certain matters of private law, and this was also true of the notarial ordinance of 1512.[4]   For the rest, imperial legislation within the field of private law was limited to a few provisions establishing a statutory rule of inheritance — and, it may be noted, in a form exclusive of all particularistic variations; [5] whereas in other imperial statutes affecting the substance of the law more latitude was customarily allowed to territorial legislation.[6]   The last, imperial Resolution of 1654,[7] which was momentous in other respects, included also provisions concerning civil procedure, particularly aimed at shortening it.

---

[1] *Altmann and Bernheim*, "Ausgewählte Urkunden zur Erlauterungen der Verfassungsgeschichte Deutschlands im Mittelalter "(3d ed , 1904), p. 254; *Zeumer*, "Quellensammlung," no 148 , "Neue Sammlung," II, 3.

[2] *Zeumer, op. cit*, no. 163, for the imperial resolution of 1555 (of which the religious pact constitutes §§ 7–30), special ed. of the Recess by *Brandi* (1896), "Neue Sammlung," III, 16 *et seq*

[3] *Zeumer, op cit*, p 383, and "Neue Sammlung," III, 642, §§ 4–6

[4] "Neue Sammlung," II, 151 *et seq*

[5] Same, II, 46, § 37 , II, 206, §§ 18–20, II, 299, § 31   *Cf. Stobbe*, "Rechtsquellen," II, 203, and in Z.²R G , 31, 179 *et seq.*

[6] *Stobbe, op cit*, II, 186

[7] "Neue Sammlung," III, 647–660, §§ 34–103, 107.

By far the most important statute of the Empire was the so-called "Carolina" (C.C C , *i e* "Constitutio Carolina Criminalis"), the criminal code (H G O , "Halsgerichtsordnung") of Charles V, of 1532 [1] The reception of the Roman law, in the field of criminal substantive law as in that of legal procedure, had the character, essentially, of a reception of Italian legal science, and at a time when this had already long attained complete ascendancy in Italian practice. The results of the Italian legal science were designated even by Schwarzenberg as "the imperial" law The Italian jurists (of whom Gandinus, Angelus Aretinus, and Bartolus were of primary influence in Germany) borrowed from Roman law its emphasis of the element of fault as essential to liability (an element too little regarded in earlier Germanic criminal law), with its distinction between "dolus" and "culpa," and its special doctrines of self-defense and of attempt [2] They emphasized also the State's interest in criminal law, and demanded that punishment should be independent of the discretion of the person injured Otherwise they left unchanged the Germanic classification of crimes and the Germanic penal system. They regarded statutory rights and "consuetudo generalis" as unexceptionably valid sources of law, along with the Roman, and adopted nothing from the Roman statutes which conflicted with the legal consciousness of their own time.

The Italian theory of criminal law was made a possession of the people in Germany especially by the "Klagspiegel" (*ante*, § 18), and was carried over into the Revised Ordinances of Worms of 1499, and into the two criminal codes provided by Maximilian I for Tyrol (1499) and Radolfzell (1506).[3] The criminal code prepared for Bishop Georg of Bamberg by Johann von Schwarzenberg rested principally upon these as sources. This so-called "Bambergensis," of 1507, possessed the character at once of a

---

[1] Among the numerous editions is to be preferred that of *Zopfl* "Die peinliche Gerichtsordnung Kaiser Karls V nebst der Bamberger und der Brandenburger Halsgerichtsordnung, mit den Projekten der peinlichen Gerichtsordnung Karls V von 1521 und 1529" (Heidelberg, 1842 , based on the "editio princeps" of 1533, the only text used in actual practice) The edition of *Kohler and Scheel,* "Die Carolina und ihre Vorgangerinnen," I (1900), rests upon a Cologne MS *Von Bar,* "Geschichte des deutschen Strafrechts," §§ 40–45, *Stobbe,* "Rechtsquellen," II, 245 *et seq* , *Stintzing,* "Geschichte," I, 621 *et seq* , *Kantorowicz,* "Goblers Karolinen Kommentar" (1904 , *cf Krammer* in Z²R G , XXXIX, 342) On the content of the law, *cf Gunther,* "Idee der Wiedervergeltung," I, 285 *et seq.,* *Guterbock,* "Entstehungsgeschichte der Karolina" (1876).

[2] *Kohler,* "Strafrecht der italienischen Statuten, 12–16 Jahrhunderten," in his "Studien aus dem Strafrecht" (1895–1897).

[3] *Wahlberg* in *Haimerl's* Vj S , IV, 131 *et seq.*

legislative code and an officially prepared text-book of the Italian criminal law.[1] Thanks to its essential worth, in which it far surpassed its predecessors, it was soon received in different courts outside the jurisdiction of Bamberg, was included in the " Laien-spiegel," (*ante*, § 13) and was made the basis of the Brandenburg-Franconian criminal code of 1516   The first draft of the " Caro-lina," prepared in 1521 in accord with a resolution of the Diet of Worms of that year, was also based throughout upon the " Bam-bergensis," and the "Correctorium in der Bamberger Halsge-richtsordnung," a collection of Bamberg decisions and ordinances of the years 1507–1515. Only after the preparation of two more drafts (Nuremberg, 1523, Speyer, 1529) was the fourth submitted to the Augsburg Diet of 1530, and finally adopted by the Diet of Regensburg in 1532. This long delay in legislation was due to the particularistic opposition offered by the estates of the Empire to a centralized criminal legislation until the Emperor consented to add to the statute its so-called saving-clause, according to which "nothing should be thereby taken from ancient, just, and lawful usages "; the effect being that the statute, save in so far as it embodied (Art. 248) express provisions to the contrary, was given an authority merely subsidiary to the existing territorial laws [2]

The " Carolina " was a greatly improved revision of the " Bam-bergensis," and, like that and its older predecessors, was primarily a code of criminal procedure, in which provisions of substantive criminal law (Art. 104–108) were incidentally interpolated.[3] It was the first true code, in criminal law and procedure, by which the dualism of the native and the foreign law was reconciled. It dominated in German law through two centuries.

Territorial Legislation.[4] — The reception of the alien law and

---

[1] *Kohler and Scheel, op cit*, vol II (1902); *Brunnenmeister*, "Quelle der Bambergensis" (1879); *Stintzing*, "Geschichte," I, 608 *et seq*, *Stobbe*, "Rechtsquellen," II, 241 *et seq*, *Seiz* in Z ¹R G, II, 435 *et seq*, *Hermann*, "Johann von Schwarzenberg" (1841)

[2] That the original intent was that later territorial statutes should not take such precedence, *cf Guterbock, op cit*, 197

[3] *Schotensack*, "Strafprozess der Carolina " (1904)

[4] *Eichhorn*, "Rechtsgeschichte," §§ 560, 816, and "Privatrecht," §§ 15–17, *Gierke*, "Privatrecht," I, 66 *et seq* *Stobbe*, "Rechtsquellen," II, 206 *et seq*., 237 *et seq*., 256–278, 336–413, 443–463, 476 *et seq*, *Stintzing*, "Geschichte," I, 537 *et seq*, 551 *et seq*, *Landsberg*, "Geschichte," III, 214 *et seq*, *Siegel*, "Rechtsgeschichte" (3d ed.), p 141 *et seq*., *Kleinfeller*, "Deutsche Partikular-Gesetzgebung uber Zivilprozess" (Munchener Festgabe fur Planck, 1887); *Luschin von Ebengreuth*, "Osterreichischer Reichsgeschichte" (1896), pp 345–364, 374 *et seq*, *Maurenbrecher*, "Rheinprovinz Landrecht" (2 vols, 1830–1831), *A B Schmidt*, "Ge-schichtliche Grundlagen des burgerlichen Rechts im Grossherzogtum Hessen" (1893); *Carlebach*, "Badische Rechtsgeschichte," pp. 71 *et seq*

the development of the power of territorial rulers into true State
sovereignties stimulated in the 1500s an extraordinarily active
legislation, which took precedence of imperial legislation in all cases
where the provisions of the latter were not absolute [1]　The end
sought was, on one hand and principally, to provide for laymen
associated in the administration of justice, through official text-
books as it were, that knowledge which was indispensable for
them, but also, on the other hand, to protect the native law against
excesses of the learned jurists, who were prone to respect only the
written law, and to ignore the customary law unless when proved
by the party relying upon it　Other reasons were the changes in
legal ideas brought about by the Reception, making necessary
a revision of existing statements of the law; the countless controversies among legal scholars, capable of termination only by
means of legislation; and the new-born notion of the police power,
which had opened up a field, before unknown, of public and legislative concern. In some territories the result went no farther
than some few statutes, or a scanty record of a few bodies of
customary law, in others a conscientious activity was developed
in drafting detailed codes of territorial law (" Landesrecht ") or
in their revision　In many cases " foreign " territorial or city
laws were adapted, or were adopted outright.

None of these codes attempted to be complete; only the most
important topics were covered.　The judges were still bound to give
subsidiary force to the common Pandect law, or, if institutes of
native law were involved, to the customary law, so far as the territorial law did not (as was often the case) explicitly forbid　The
chief subject of legislation was the judicature (organization of the
courts and civil procedure) and private law; in criminal law and
procedure less was done after 1532, since the Carolina sufficiently
provided for these

In many territories the ruler alone exercised the right of legislation, without the participation of the Estates, — at least (in
other territories) in the case of laws which imposed no burdens
upon the land　On the other hand, there were territories in which
nothing could be done without the Estates. At times, under the
excuse of their inadequate legal knowledge, the latter voluntarily
renounced participation in the drafting of the territorial law;
the result being generally that the jurists intrusted with the task
gave their work an impress of Roman law, and crowded out
(more or less) the German law. In drafting the Wurtemberg

---

[1] *Eichhorn, op. cit.,* IV, 292 *et seq.*

code (1555) the excellent material that had been brought together by questionaries submitted to the courts was considered unworthy of regard and thrown aside as an indigestible chaos.[1]

The provisions for publication of the statutes were faulty to an extreme. It was considered sufficient to print them, and to provide for their proclamation by a herald, or by reading them from the pulpits, in the city halls, or in the markets. Examples occur later of proclamation by public posting Sometimes (as at the end of the "Landrecht" of Solm) a yearly catechism in the courts was prescribed, after the ancient manner of declaring judicial dooms.

In the 1500s the territorial laws and ordinances ("Landesordnungen") were of greatest importance, the latter were mainly concerned with police, and supplemented or simply reproduced the police ordinances of the empire. There were also issued, however, numerous special laws of the most various concern. Legislative activity was also exercised to some extent in seigniorial jurisdictions within the territories, by ordinances of judicature, village law, and the like. Among the special territorial enactments, those on judicature,[2] crimes, feudal relations, bills of exchange, dikes, mining, and (in the Protestant territories) church affairs,[3] are most notable. The Pact of Tübingen, of 1514, for Würtemberg, and the Bavarian Declaration of Independence of 1553, were codifications of constitutional law.

Of the great number of territorial laws only the most important can here be mentioned. The territorial codes of Julich (1537), Kedingen, Hadeln (1583), Wurst (1611), the Bremen law-of-knights (1577), the New Munster parish customs and customs of the Bordesholm government,[4] are distinguished by the Germanic character of their law. In addition to these, mention may be made of (1) the Revision of the Bavarian territorial codes ("Landrechte") of 1518 and 1616, both based upon the "Landrecht" of 1346, (2) the "true-German" Tyrolean ordinances of 1526, 1532, and 1573,[5] (3) the "Landrecht" (including a code of judicature) of the

---

[1] Notes of the material in *Fischer*, "Versuch uber die Geschichte der deutschen Erbfolge," vol. 2 (1778); *Reyscher*, "Sammlung altwurtembergischer Statutarrechte" (1834) , *Wachter*, "Wurtembergisches Privatrecht "

[2] The Saxon codes of procedure (*Stobbe*, II, 262 *et seq*) are important.

[3] *Richter*, editor, "Die evangelischen Kirchenordnungen des 16ten Jahrhunderts" (2 vols., 1846), New ed. by *Sehling* (1902 *et seq*)

[4] Ed by *Seestern-Pauly* (1824).

[5] Nevertheless the pure Germanic law could not maintain itself in Tyrol; *Luschin, op cit*, pp 353 *et seq* , 382 *et seq*

county of Solm, prepared by the Frankfort syndic Fichard (1571), at once a code and official text-book, which by reason of its excellence was also adopted as law in many other jurisdictions of Franconia,[1] (4) the " Landrecht " of Wurtemberg of 1555 (revised 1567, and for the last time in 1610), which was prepared mainly by Sichard, a professor of Tubingen, who was the editor of various compilations of popular law, but in a thoroughly Romanistic sense, with slight regard for German law, — likewise much used (as *e.g.* for the code of the Palatinate of 1582–1610) as a model,[2] (5) the Baden regulation of the law of inheritance and guardianship, of 1511, drafted by Ulrich Zasius, and almost wholly Roman,[3] (6) the exhaustive territorial code of Baden, and the local codes of Baden-Baden (1588) and Baden-Durlach (1654), these last two derived from the law of Wurtemberg and the Palatinate, (7) the code of judicature of the duchy of Franconia, or Wurzburg " Landrecht," of 1570 (revisions 1580 and 1618), (8) the Revision of 1538 and " Landrecht " of 1663 of the electorate of Cologne, with interpretations of 1767, (9) the " Landrecht " of Julich-Berg (1555–1564), mainly Roman, (10) the East Frisian code of 1515 and the Ditmarsch code of 1567, and finally, (11) the Brandenburg " constitution " of the law of inheritance of Joachim I (hence known as the " Joachimica) of 1527.[4]

[1] *Fuchs* in Z R G , VIII, 270 *et seq* , *A B Schmidt, op. cit* , pp 72 *et seq* , *Stintzing*, "Geschichte," I 586 *et seq*
[2] *Stintzing*, "Geschichte," I, 543 *et seq*
[3] *Stobbe*, "Rechtsquellen," II, 390 *et seq.*
[4] *Heydemann*, "Elemente der Joachimer Konstitution" (1841).

CHAPTER III. THIRD PERIOD: A.D. 1600–1806

NATURAL LAW, LEGAL RATIONALISM, AND
GERMAN NATIONALISM[1]

TOPIC 1. NATURAL LAW AND LEGAL RATIONALISM

§ 39. Rise of the Natural Law | § 40. Grotius, Bacon, Hobbes,
    Jurists. | Puffendorf, and Leibnitz.

TOPIC 2. GERMAN NATIONALISM

§ 41. Rise of the German National | and Realism Conring,
    Jurists. | Carpzov, Mevius, Tho-
§ 42. Exponents of Nationalism | masius, and Beyer.

TOPIC 3. STATE BUILDING AND LEGISLATION

§ 43. Decline and Fall of the | § 44 Imperial and State Legis-
    Empire (to 1806) | lation (to 1811).

TOPIC 1. NATURAL LAW AND LEGAL RATIONALISM

§ 39. **Rise of the Natural Law Jurists.**[2] — Natural law and nationalism served as the two chief weapons to break the bonds by which the Roman law had too long fettered men's minds.

The doctrine of an absolute law, independent, universal, and

[1] [The sources from which the sections of the present chapter have been derived are as follows · §§ 39 and 42 from §§ 53 and 52 respectively (translated in part) of HEINRICH SIEGEL, "Deutsche Rechtsgeschichte" (3d ed., Berlin, 1895), § 40 from ch 1 (in part) of ERNST LANDSBERG, "Geschichte der deutschen Rechtswissenschaft, Dritte Abtheilung" (Munich, Leipzig, 1898); § 41 from §§ 1–2, in part, of ch 16 of RUDOLF VON STINTZING, "Geschichte der deutschen Rechtswissenschaft, Zweite Abtheilung" (Munich, Leipzig, 1884) For § 42, see note 1 thereto § 43 is a portion of § 58 of HEINRICH BRUNNER's "Grundzuge der deutschen Rechtsgeschichte" (4th ed , Leipzig, 1910) § 44 is a combination of portions of §§ 83 and 91 of RICHARD SCHRODER, "Lehrbuch der deutschen Rechtsgeschichte" (5th ed Leipzig, 1910). — TRANSL]
[2] *Hinrichs,* "Geschichte des Natur- und Volkerrechtes" (3 vols , 1848–1882); *von Kaltenborn,* "Die Vorlaufer des Hugo Grotius" (1848) , *Hanel,* "Melancthon als Jurist" (Z.¹R G , 1869, VIII, 249–270), *Stintzing,* "Geschichte" I, 311–328, esp. 325–329 on Oldendorp , *O Gierke,* "Naturrecht und deutsches Recht, Rectoratsrede" (1883), esp 26–32.

idealistic in basis, — the law of nature, at once divine and human, — was by no means new; nor had there been lacking, in a way, definite statements of such a conception   Indeed, in the fermentative times of the Reformation, isolated groups of thinkers had defined by its means their goal and endeavors   It was only in the 1600 s, however, that men attained to a consistent presentation of such a law derived from human nature   The epoch-making work " De Jure Pacis ac Belli " of HUGO GROTIUS, known as the father of natural law, appeared in 1625, when the great war that was to continue thirty years was already in progress. Huig de Groot, who was born in 1583 at Delft, in Holland, and died in 1645, had aimed primarily at a recasting of the law of nations. But in the endeavor to create for this a universal and reasonable basis, and in proceeding from the postulate that there is innate in man, as a reasoning and moral being, an impulse toward an ordered fellowship with his kind, he hit at the same time upon the idea of natural law. On the principle postulated he established all law, even private law, and this application constituted the novelty of his contribution, which had occurred to none of his predecessors, not even Melancthon nor Oldendorp   The doctrine of natural law, long represented by men of commanding talent, exercised down into the 1800 s a dominating influence, especially in legislation

§ 40   Grotius, Bacon, Hobbes, Puffendorf, and Leibnitz. — Grotius' book was the source of a new movement in legal science. Natural Law, abandoning its pure abstraction, became juristic, engendered as an offspring international law, saturated itself with positive law, and attained a general dominance in legal conceptions. Only in this sense, not absolutely, was Grotius " the father of natural law." [1]

Grotius. — (1) The speculative treatment of legal notions had always been assumed as a problem of philosophy, and scholasticism had so intimately associated with philosophy theological norms that it had attained acceptance in extensive philosophical systems, whose results, constantly adopted as something ordained by civilists and canonists, were regarded and applied by them as self-evidently authoritative   The basis laid down is a natural, unchangeable law springing directly from divinity " per se," — existing before

---

[1] Abundant references by *Rivier*, "Geschichts-Übersicht" in *F   V Holtzendorff*, "Handbuch des Volkerrechts," 1, 403.   See especially *Bluntschli*, "Geschichte," pp 63–74, *Hälschner* in Allg d Biog , 9 : 767–784   and perhaps in addition *Caix de Saint-Aymour*, "Notice sur Hugues de Groot" (Paris, 1884)

and independent of the divine will, — the " jus naturæ primarium."
Applied to the economic conditions of a given people and to the
local institutions of a given time, it becomes a "jus naturæ secund-
arium." Supplementary to this is the "jus divinum," explicitly
ordained of God to men, needful because of our inability, with
visions clouded by original sin, to distinguish the natural law
directly. The Ten Commandments serve as chief luminaries
in the darkness These teachings Melancthon had taken from
later scholasticism. They were developed by him, and afterward
successively by Oldendorp, Hemming, Althusius, and Wincler.
The "Principia Juris" of the last, of 1615, brings us down almost to Grotius.[2]

[The most important of these jurists of the mid-1500s was
JOHANN OLDENDORP (1480–1567),[3] one of those men who because
of the varied elements of their education and many-sided contacts
with contemporary interests appear as central figures in an epoch.
He reflects the influence of both the Reformation, of which he was
a zealous and hard-fighting adherent, and Humanism. He was
no learned investigator, but of a practical nature, and hence the
reform of legal instruction, to the end of freeing it from the " mos
Italicus," appealed particularly to him. To this end he reformed
the law courses of the university of Marburg. Among his works
was an "Elementaria Introductio Juris Naturæ Gentium et
Civilis" (1539), in which he developed the outlines of a system
of legal philosophy or natural law, in which respect priority has
therefore been claimed for him over Grotius.

[Among the "systematizers" of the 1500s one of great im-
portance was JOHANNES ALTHUSIUS (or Althaus; 1557–1638).[4]
His most important works were his "Jurisprudentiæ Romanæ
Libri Duo ad Leges Methodi Rameæ Conformati et Tabellis
Illustrati" (Basel, 1586); his "Dicæologicæ Libri Tres Totum et
Universum Jus, quo Utimur Methodice Complectentes," etc
(Herborn, 1617), and a "Politica Methodice Digesta et Exemplis

---

[1] *Hanel* in Z ¹R G., VIII ; 249 *et seq.*
[2] *Kaltenborn*, "Die Vorläufer des Hugo Grotius"
[3] [See *Stintzing*, "Geschichte," vol I, ch 8, who cites among other
sources *Oldendorp's* collected writings, "Variarum Lectionum Libri ad
Juris Interpretationem" (Cologne, 1540). Also *Kaltenborn*, "Die Vorlaufer des Hugo Grotius" (1848), pp 233 *et seq*, *Hinrichs*, "Geschichte
des Natur- und Volkerechts," I, 19 *et seq*, *Harder*, in Zeitschrift des Vereins
fur Hamburgische Geschichte, vol II, 436 *et seq*. And other references in
Stintzing — TRANSL]
[4] [See *Stintzing*, "Geschichte," I, 468–477, and especially *O. Gierke*,
"Johannes Althusius und die Geschichte der naturrechtlichen Staats-
theorien" (Berlin, 2d ed, 1902) — TRANSL.]

Sacris et Profanis Illustrata　cui in Fine Adjuncta est Oratio
Panegyrica de Utilitate Necessitate et Antiquitate Scholarum"
(Herborn, 1603; revised and enlarged, Groningen, 1610; with
supplements, Herborn, 1614)　He is distinguished by extraordinary
keenness, strength, precision, and logic of thought　In the second
work he developed a complete legal system, with special attention
to private law, public and criminal law being introduced under the
categories and in subordination to the point of view of private law.
The third was his most important work, and is remarkable as the
first detailed political system devised in Germany, exceptional
also for the richness of its content and the originality of its thought
Althusius is important in the history of political theory as a representative of the doctrines of popular sovereignty and the social
compact]

In the interval, however, between these men and Grotius stands
FRANCIS BACON,[1] Baron Verulam　How far Grotius drew directly
from him must be left undecided, but unquestionably Grotius
occupies in essentials the same position.　Bacon demanded of
legal science, as the great desideratum, one work, " Idea Justitiæ
Universalis sive de Fontibus Juris "　He would have sought the
sources of justice and of social utility, from which should be formed
ideal drafts for all branches of the law, by these every one might
test and improve the laws of individual States　This fundamental
task, however, should be performed neither by philosophers, who
might produce much that was beautiful but impractical, nor by
jurists, who would not see beyond their national law, but by
a statesman, who should equally consider equity and the common
weal　For private law is grounded in the need of the majority
for protection against every transgression on the part of an individual, to maintain the private law the State exists, and therewith
public law　But the end of all law is the greatest good of all subjects　Thus, natural law with Grotius, as philosophy with
Bacon, escapes from any deductive dependence upon theology,
which dependence was the link that had chained men theretofore
to scholasticism.

Grotius, however, not only in the form, but also in the matter of
his work, remains frequently bound by that chain, herein taking
place inferior to Bacon　Above all, Grotius did not adopt the
Englishman's principle of induction. To the Dutch thinker,
history and experience were of importance merely to furnish him

---

[1] K Fischer, "Franz Baco von Verulam."

with examples and confirmations; the principles which were to be tricked out with these embellishments should be themselves purely deductive, derived by common sense from the maxims of sociality. And in this respect Grotius' attitude proved to be determinant for the whole later development of natural law. This, like continental philosophy later, appropriated from the English critical philosophy only its rationalism, not its empiricism. From the postulate, however, of the common weal, or from any other similar doctrine, rigid principles of law cannot possibly be derived, no more than the means for its realization result directly from any end, — for the simple reason that they are not involved within it They must always be drawn inductively from experience; and are thereby all the more exposed to the danger of incomplete induction the more unconsciously such induction be made, in the belief that one is *deducing* them. And so it was with Grotius. The provisions of Roman law floated in his mind as its only material for inductive reasoning; any other he scarcely knew. From it he therefore borrows, with a few variations of a routinary and denationalizing tendency, the rules of self-defence, of property, its acquisition and loss, of obligations, contracts, oath, construction, partnership, damages; and not only these, but also such institutions of positive law as slavery, prescription, and testamentary forms, all of which he believes he is deriving from his general principle The fact that what he thus deduced coincided with the Roman law Grotius was pleased to consider as a reciprocal voucher of correctness. Nor did this coincidence, however often it might be remarked, suffice to strike with wonder his followers To the very end of the school of natural law this procedure was persisted in, only with the possible addition of German legal matter to the material of induction.

Of course a reliance upon the Roman law was easiest in the field of private law. For this reason Grotius was able in this respect to go far beyond any of his predecessors Where they had stopped with general legal principles, he gives us a " natural " private law elaborated to the smallest details, albeit one not yet systematically ordered. Private law is given seventeen chapters, criminal law is crowded into one. Despite this brevity of treatment, however, so much more readily did the latter subject lend itself to philosophical treatment, that Grotius' ideas gave immediate promise of a peculiarly independent and fecundant development in this field of legal speculation. In particular, the fundamental problem of criminal law, which immediately emerges, finds in the

411

formula of "malum passionis propter malum actionis"[1] a significant solution; to which, since then, so much has been annexed

Public law is only incidentally treated; and so far as treated it stands wholly under the dominance of scholasticism, adopting the latter's traditional divisions and speculations The public law of the Church is not discussed in the "Jus Belli ac Pacis," reference being made for it to another work, "De Imperio Summarum Protestatum circa Sacra" of 1647, which derives from postulates of political particularism Dutch principles of religious tolerance.

Grotius did not seek to derive even his law of nations inductively and empirically from the observance of international customs and relations, — such a law of nations as was vaguely conceived by the Italian ALBERICUS GENTILIS, (Alberico Gentili, 1552–1608) since 1537 professor "regius juris civilis" at Oxford The latter, in his masterly work "De Jure Belli" of 1598,[2] had taken a first and notable step in this direction by a zealous collection and tactful appraisement of contemporary events; whereas Grotius only gives decorative examples from classic authors, and talks indefinitely, in only a general way, of the "consensus gentium" Gentilis' rudiment of a positive law of nations remained unconsidered, precisely because of the dominating influence won by Grotius and his deductions.

There was also a philosophic, deductive law of nations before Grotius, resting upon the same foundations as the natural law of the schoolmen, and cultivated particularly by the Spanish moralists, especially by Francisco de Vitoria[3] and his followers. These writers had, moreover, developed principles far more humane than those of Grotius, notwithstanding his "temperamenta," with which, as equitable reasons, he mitigated the cruelty of war But these principles, being based solely upon theological sources, had validity only among States which recognized each other mutually as of the true faith. The original contribution of Grotius is, therefore, again to be found in the fact that he separated law from theological and moralizing speculations, and

[1] *Gunther*, "Idee der Wiedervergeltung in Geschichte und Philosophie des Rechts," II, 105
[2] *Albericus Gentilis*, "De Iure Belli Libri Tres" (ed *T E Holland*, 1877).
[3] On Vitoria, Suarez, and other Spanish writers *Kaltenborn, op cit*, pp 124 *et seq*, *Rivier*, "Note sur la littérature du droit des gens avant la publication du Jus Bell ac pacis de Grotius" (Brussels, 1883), also in *v Holtzendorff*, "Handbuch des Volkerrechts," vol I, pt 4, § 85. [And see Part VIII of the present volume — TRANSL]

placed it upon a purely worldly basis of utilitarianism   And
this contribution was . . . especially significant and fruitful because, in last analysis, it was the great idea of a natural community of law embracing all men and peoples as such, and because it made its appearance precisely at the moment when the
medieval community of peoples, based upon community of
religion, had collapsed.

Its acceptance in Germany came late and not without resistance
A barbarous war raged in the land and made a dreary waste; in
philosophy and theology the Aristotelian scholasticism held sway,
in jurisprudence, a Carpzov, — all of these being so many powers
hostile to natural law, because an instrument of humanitarianism
and enlightenment.   To them even the fundamental tenet of natural
law was already impious.   Before the middle of the century nobody
in Germany seems to have paid any attention whatever to Grotius
[In the second half of the century] his acceptance as a figure of
the first rank in political and legal science became assured.

As the law of nature was taken over from the Roman law with
denationalizing simplifications, so it reacted, suffering similar
changes, upon positive law.   Compared with the freedom of the
one, the enchainment of the other to sources in many respects
antiquated became even more intolerable.   The need of innovations of all kinds, born of international and economic friction,
secured recognition first in the broad field of natural law, and thence
penetrated across the ill-guarded frontier into the practice and the
theory of the Pandect law.   To this circumstance, to its mediatory
utility, natural law owed its ever growing favor   In fact, all those
new principles which the empiricism of the second half of the 1600 s
established in the field of the civil law [1] were derived from ideas
of the law of nature.   And in the course of the 1700s this attained
such predominance that the other purely positive and empirical
movement [characteristic of German law at the middle of the
1600 s],[2] was completely absorbed or forced back when it had
hardly come into current.   The steadily growing splendor of
Grotius' fame was an exact index of this development.

(2) *Hobbes and Spinoza.*[3] — In the further course of the 1600 s
the law of nature received its next substantial advancement in
England.   Inasmuch, however, as the incentive to its cultivation
came there from the political interests of the times, men were con-

[1] Enumerated in *Stintzing,* "Geschichte," II, 14–16.
[2] *Stintzing,* "Geschichte," II, 1 *et seq ,* 162, and other places.
[3] *Bergbohm,* "Jurisprudenz und Rechtsphilosophie," I, 164, note 18.

tented solely with the political and constitutional aspect of natural law   Particularly in the case of HOBBES—that mightiest champion of monarchy and most formidable opponent of the Church, the most logical though paradoxical of all thinkers, absolute mathematician and revolutionary absolutist — the Leviathan of State swallowed up the interest even in such of its own functions as were not those of public law.   The chapters " de legibus civilibus" (in the "Leviathan") and "de legibus et peccatis" (in the treatise " De Cive ") afford only a few chief maxims   In the following chapters criminal law is somewhat more thoroughly treated, all crime being reduced in essence to an offence against the State[1]   The denial of any "jus gentium voluntarium" whatever (such as was at least given subsidiary value by Grotius), — a denial made in support of a general law of nations abstractly deduced, — was a result in Hobbes' case of English insularity. This denial, as well as his conception of penal punishment, passed from Hobbes to Puffendorf

Among the English followers of Grotius, natural law became ever more separated from strictly juristic concepts.   In SPINOZA[2] there is no longer any reference to these.   In this respect, as otherwise, he was far in advance of his time   His " right " of the big fishes to devour the little is no right within the meaning of natural law (indeed, no right in the ordinary sense of the word), and the same is to be said of the State's right to exist, which he bases, in the "Tractatus Theologico-politicus " upon positive power, quite disregarding and losing sight of Hobbes's social-contract basis of sovereignty.   And with the rejection of this social-compact Spinoza broke down the bridge which served for Hobbes, and the whole school of natural law, to pass from the pre-State conditions postulated by natural law, to the sharply contrasting conditions of a State organization.   For Spinoza the only source of law in a pre-State condition of society is the strength of the individual, the only source under the State is its despotic order; both powers being sovereign, neither dependent upon nor in type influenced by the other.   Under these principles there could be no question of the development of a national legal system *out of* natural law.   It is true that it was one of Spinoza's most profound and grandiose ideas to have expressed in this equivalence of " virtus " and " potentia " the idea that it is the

---

[1] *Hobbes*, "Opera Latina" (ed *Molesworth*), III, 212.
[2] *Spinoza*, "Tractatus Theologico-politicus," ch. 16 (in the "Opera," ed *Gunsberg*, III, 167 *et seq*, especially 171)

supreme duty of every organism to quicken the powers latent within it, and develop thereby its individuality. The application of this idea to law and State, the construction of both upon a principle of unrestricted self-development, was an achievement to which we must to-day do justice. But it sacrificed that ideal of natural law which aimed at finding a higher unwritten law, above the rule promulgated by the State, to which this rule must accommodate itself so far as it aims to be, not a mere command of force, but an ordinance of justice. For such fine dreams Spinoza has no place: in his State the observance of equity in legislation is not the command of a superior authority, but is essentially a rule of political expediency. If Hobbes was abominated, admired, and followed, Spinoza was doubly abhorred, misunderstood, and shunned, as well for these fundamental theories as for the doctrine of tolerance defended in his "Tractatus Theoretico-Politicus" German legal science in particular held itself far aloof from the ways pointed out by Spinoza.

(3) The man who succeeded in turning the philosophical current of natural law into the fields deserted by them since Grotius was SAMUEL PUFFENDORF.[1] His works on natural law are three "Elementorum Jurisprudentiæ Universalis Libri Duo" (The Hague, 1660), "Libri Octo de Jure Naturæ et Gentium" (Lund, 1672), "De Officiis Hominis et Civis Juxta Legem Naturalem Libri Duo" (Lund, 1673). Of these works the first is an outline study which already embodies the author's entire doctrine,[2] but in immature and undeveloped form The second work is not only by far the strongest, but also the most independent, most systematically ordered, and richest in matter and influence

His general system, — which constitutes one of his most important accomplishments, even though he here leans upon Hobbes' "Tractate de Cive," — begins with the assumptions of human nature and capacity, essential for all law, basing upon these the fundamental legal principles, from which in turn all the rest is derived. First therein come naturally the rights of the individual, independent of family and State These rights rest upon the dogmas of self-preservation, of fair conduct toward others, and performance of contract duties under the social compact, upon the same bases rest the law of things and of obligations.

[1] H Bresslau in the Allg d. Biog, XXVI, 701 et seq ; Bluntschli, "Geschichte," pp 108 et seq , Wegele, "Geschichte," pp 500 et seq ; H von Treitschke, in Preus J.B, XXXV, 614 et seq
[2] [See Stintzing-Landsberg, "Geschichte," III, 5-7, for a comparative table of its contents and that of the "Jus Naturæ et Gentium "— TRANSL.]

Within the first of these Puffendorf includes rights of inheritance,
and, finally, he seeks to construct even a sort of legal process for
this pristine state of social disintegration. From consideration
of the individual the system rises in ever ascending range to that
of the household community, the State, and, so far as Puffendorf
recognizes this, the law of nations. Public law is treated with
especial thoroughness, being divided into constitutional law and
the sovereign rights of the State against its citizens, and ending
with doctrines regarding loss of citizenship, and the extinction,
or changes in the form, of the State itself.

This system, which became typical for all time to come, was
a system of rights, not of duties The development of the school
of natural law was determined for a century by the fact that in its
first philosophic system it started from this point of view. An
unruly emphasis of rights, a subordination of corresponding
duties, runs through all the philosophical, political, and polite
literature of the 1700s, and the German period of "storm and
stress" and the French Declaration of the Rights of Man were
nothing more than its culmination. At the same time the condition was thereby fulfilled for an ingressive influence of Puffendorf's ideas within the fields of positive law. His system, its
philosophic basis once disposed of, was thus a system of positive
law. The "jura imperfecta" of Grotius, purely moral liabilities,
he declined to recognize, as not belonging to the law. His systematizing efforts therefore indicate the resumption of similar
endeavors, already indicated, of the late 1500s and early 1600s,
temporarily abandoned since then under a practical-empiric
tendency in legal science. The scope of law has now become
broader; for public law, in consequence of political interests and
literary achievements of the interim,[1] no longer appears, nor is
perforce content to be, a mere supplement, tacked on inorganically
at the end of the civil law and violently forced into its routinary
moulds. On the contrary it has acquired place as a second, co-
ordinate part of the law, indeed, with the accession of the law of
nations, as the crown and consummation of the entire system,
even its details were carefully and independently developed.

Accordingly we have in Puffendorf the basis of a universal legal
science[2] On one hand is the subject of all rights, man. That

---

[1] *Stintzing*, "Geschichte," vol I, ch 11, on systematizing efforts of the
late 1500s and early 1600s
[2] *Cf Zitelmann*, "Die Moglichkeit eines Weltrechts" (lecture before
the Juristische Gesellschaft of Vienna, March 20, 1888).

he has understanding, and can therefore calculate the consequences
of his acts; that he has free will and can therefore choose his
acts; that therefrom results the very possibility of legal precepts,
whose imperatives are directed to man's free will and threaten
him with punishment for disobedience, — all this is deduced in
the clearest way; and the other questions as to the limits of human
intelligence and accountability are connected with it in detail.
On the other side is the objective, legal norm itself. Puffendorf's juristic sense was not here content, like that of Grotius, to
rest with the indication that what is in accord with the precept of
common sense ought to be law, for, that it may be law and not
a mere moral (the "jus imperfectum" of Grotius), a command
is necessary. And again, as regards this command, it is not sufficient that it issue from any holder whatever of relative power;
a despotic command is not law, the power of him who commands
must further rest upon a just ground, that we may feel bound in
conscience to the obedience outwardly imposed. And upon these
two bases, legal science, in its subjective and objective aspects,
has really essentially rested to the present

In civil law Puffendorf shows a thorough and nice knowledge of
the Roman law, to which he adheres in almost all points, although
occasionally citing Germanic legal sources [1] Wherever in Puffendorff's natural law the Germanic sense of right is enforced against
the principles of the Roman law, this is generally justified by an
appeal to greater simplicity, clarity, or naturalness, — criteria which
are constantly resorted to in correction of the Roman law, and
much more skilfully used than by Grotius Especially, certain
Roman rules of equity, charily introduced under sharp limitations,
are immensely expanded in accordance with the "æquitas juris
naturalis" Here and there, too, political and economic considerations are put forward to determine principles of the law of
nature. The result is a motley whole, whose details sometimes
seem, to our modern legal sense, contradictory, — as, for example,
when a family law quite strictly Roman is set forth, whereas the
principles of Roman law are broken with as regards a transfer of
property without delivery, and the rule of the vendor's risk.
Nevertheless, even from the strict standpoint of the civil law,
the whole is a feat that commands respect. Finally, questions of
principle (such as contract, compensation for nominal damage,

---

[1] "Leges Barbarorum" or capitularies are cited, e q., in the "Jus Naturæ
et Gentium," II, 5, §§ 15, 18, III, 1, § 3, III, 3, § 7, III, 7, § 6, IV,
1, § 6.

the consequences of mistake), make their appearance: the search for some test of principle for legal rights begins with truth, honor, altruism, and in this process, conventional rules conflict sharply with the demands of equity against chicanery and formalism.

Puffendorf's chapters on public law rest essentially on Hobbes. But though based wholly upon the absolutistic doctrine of his time, nevertheless, a transition is prepared to those democratic ideas which, a century later, were to lead the law of nature in triumphant conquest   What has often been said of the political practice of the 1700s was also true from its beginning of the law of nature: that in suppressing all powers between ruler and people, all corporations between the individual and the state, it created first a naked despotism of the individual, and, later, one of the masses.   In particular Puffendorf's excessive emphasis of the right of all men to equality[1] points in this direction. This same universalism of the later law of nature is shown when he makes the duties of men to their fatherland equal to those one owes to any State in which one has settled and made one's way in life. —For the rest, in discussing the forms of government, he holds closely to the types traditional since Aristotle; but considers especially the possibility of uniting separate States in State systems of greater or less coherence[2]

The right to punish appears as a part of public power, and therefore criminal law as a chapter of public law   At its basis is laid a unifying concept strikingly similar — as is well known — to the later so-called psychological theory of restraint.   Although this general justification of punishment is also taken bodily from Hobbes, its juristic elaboration remains Puffendorf's contribution The application to criminal law of the subjective doctrines developed as an introduction to the entire system results here in an extremely fruitful doctrine of guilt, whose adoption by positive law could be a question only of time

A positive law of nations of any kind whatever, whether based on treaties or originating tacitly in the practices of civilized nations, Puffendorf rejects far more decidedly than Grotius, all such regulations lack for him a legally binding character, are not precepts of law, but merely matter of agreement   As international law he finds only that valid in a state of nature between individuals; while Grotius, the discoverer of this analogical source of law,

[1] "Jus Naturæ et Gentium," bk 3, ch. 2.
[2] "Jus Naturæ et Gentium," bk 8, ch 9; and *cf.* various essays in his "Dissertationes academicæ Selectiores" (Upsala, 1677)

at least spoke in addition of a second source, "the consensus gentium."

Puffendorf's works on natural law pay little attention to ecclesiastical law. At the same time, he has the merit here, as elsewhere, of having introduced into German legal science Dutch and English ideas, as well those of a political particularism, grounded (not as theretofore, historically, but) in the law of nature, as those of a tendency toward tolerance, — the latter being indeed rather illiberally conceived, but the former with avoidance of Hobbes's most extreme paradoxes.

By far his most original work was in the field of positive German public law. His series of tractates on the condition and constitution of the German Empire constituted an epoch-making work for that and later times. They rivalled in brilliancy and keenness of presentation and excelled in profundity and sobriety of judgment the celebrated pamphlet of Hippolithus a Lapide,[1] with which they were in origin associated   They appeared first under the title: "Severini de Monzambano Veronensis de Statu Imperii Germanici ad Lælium Fratrem Dominium Trezolani Liber Unus," (Geneva, — really Amsterdam, — 1667)[2]   In the preface (in the form of an introductory letter to the brother) there is here explicitly recommended, as the only method for the study of German public law, the observation of realities, in German courts and German chanceries. From a clear conception of actual political relations he drew the definite conclusion that sovereignty really lay in the German territories. Several sovereign States could not, however, within his definition, form one State together. they could only unite in what he called a "Staatensystem," that is, in a confederacy ("Staatenbund"), as the expression is to-day. And since his sight was much too clear to permit of his admitting that conditions in Germany were consistent with the last conception (since he recognizes the prerogatives of the emperor, the powers of the imperial courts, in short the remnants of the old imperial constitution, as being too strong), he was perforce obliged to label the existing constitution of the Empire as one against reason, fitting under no political concept, in short, as "monstrous." In this method of applying to actualities an "a priori" measure we recognize again the traits of one who proceeds upon principles

[1] *Stintzing*, "Geschichte," II, 45 *et seq.*

[2] On this, see *Bresslau*, preface to his German translation of the work (1870), with bibliography; *Brie*, "Geschichte der Lehre vom Bundesstaat (1874), pp. 21 *et seq*, *Jastrow*, in Z Preus G L K, 19 (1882)

of natural law, in the assertion that Germany was a political
monster we see brought together, as in a focus, the writer's em-
piric and philosophical views

It would be an error to say that German legal science of the
1800s lay under the dominance of Puffendorf's ideas of natural
law, the ideas, essentially taken from Dutchmen and Englishmen,
were not original enough to justify the judgment. But one must
in truth say that the ideas of natural law which he borrowed he
worked over independently, judiciously, and with liberal understanding, into a juristic system, and that his system settled the
union, and therefore the development, of legal philosophy and legal
science in the 1700s

(4) *Leibnitz* — Standing on one side from the above movement,
upon an eminence overtopping and commanding it, was LEIBNITZ [1]
He identifies completely the science of justice and the science of
law, so that this becomes again, for him, truly a " rerum divinarum
et humanarum scientia." It comprehends, in his view, not only
positive law and natural law, equity and policy, but even morals
and theology. The depreciatory estimate which Leibnitz placed
upon Puffendorf, both as a jurist and a philosopher, was especially
due to the latter's inclination to exclude theological, and so far as
possible even ethical, elements from natural law. Leibnitz sets
in sharpest contrast with this his own derivation of natural law
from divine wisdom. If Puffendorf's principle of sociality thus
appears to Leibnitz so wholly inadequate, how completely must
the latter have anathematized the later principles of the social
compact ! For Leibnitz recognized no power in the individual
to dispose of himself and his rights beyond the limits of objective
justice, and therefore no absolute binding force of contracts, but
only one limited by their legal and equitable content [2] Similarly,
in criminal law, he held fast to the principle of absolute requital.

---

[1] *Guhrauer*, "Gottfried Wilhelm von Leibnitz" (2 vols, 2d ed, 1846);
Prantl, in Allg d Biog, XVIII, 172 *et seq.* with references *On his re-*
lations to natural law K Fischer, "Geschichte der neueren Philosophie"
(3d ed, 1888), 11, 565 *et seq*, *Bluntschli*, "Geschichte," p 135, *Zeller*, "Geschichte der Philosophie," pp 122 *et seq*, *Trendelenburg*, "Historische
Beitrage zur Philosophie," II, 233 *et seq*, 257 *et seq*, *Mollat*, "Rechts-
philosophisches aus Leibnitzens ungedruckten Schriften" (2d ed, 1885,
under the title "Mittheilungen aus, etc") *On his relations to positive*
law F Hecht, "Leibnitz als Jurist" in Preuss J B, IV (1879), Heft 1,
Zimmermann, "Das Rechtsprinzip bei Leibnitz" (1852), *Baron*, "Franz
Hotmann's Antitribonian" (Berner Festgabe fur Bologna, 1888)   The
latest and most thorough account in *Gustav Hartmann*, "Leibnitz als
Jurist und Rechtsphilosoph" (Tubingen, 1892).
[2] On this and on criminal law, *Hartmann*, as just cited, pp 81 *et seq*.
109 *et seq*.

To his advanced contemporaries such principles, which readily reveal themselves to us as anticipations of a deepening development, must have appeared as relapses into a scholastic mode of thinking.

All the more unmistakable was the progress marked in legal science, in the narrow sense, by the "Nova Methodus Discendæ Docendæque Jurisprudentiæ" (1667) [1] The extreme youth of the author is in many ways evidenced, — in the unconsidered boldness of his proposals, in many contradictions of his later and clarified opinions, and in his dependence upon Bacon's "Novum Organum" But the work develops an abundance of original and reformative ideas. It starts with legal instruction, proposing to shorten the duration of this from five to two years, by means of a rigorous methodization of legal science To this end, and in analogy to theology (which is deemed essentially similar), legal science is divided into four parts: the didactic, historical, exegetic, and polemic. In order perfectly to adapt the Roman law to introductory didactic instruction, for which its material excellence recommends it, it should be subjected to a formal revision, since in the form in which it is preserved in the Justinian compilation it repels study by an orderless mass of details In place of this chaos, and in abandonment of any fixed "legal" order (the system of the Institutes being also, as regards method, absolutely useless), two systematic textbooks (he asserted) should, in particular, be worked out. one elementary, in lapidary terseness reminiscent of the Twelve Tables, containing merely "definitiones et præcepta," proceeding rigorously from the general to the specific, through titles and subtitles; the other a "novum corpus juris," which should include the matter of the Justinian, but newly and systematically arranged. For the historical division special textbooks should be written: a "historia mutationum juris," and a "historia irenica." The history of the classic and of modern States and that of the Church should also be drawn upon. Legal exegesis required a special basis; to this end there was needed a "philologia juris," a "grammatica legalis seu lexicon juridicum," an "ethica et politica legalis," a "logica et metaphysica juris," — in short, an encyclopædia of law. The exegesis itself should then be made according to the "mos Italicus." Knowing thus the words

---

[1] Edition of 1748, with an introduction well deserving reading, by *Christian Wolf*, reprinted in *Dutens*, "Leibnitii opera," IV, 3, pp. 159–230; *Pfleiderer*, "G. W. Leibnitz als Patriot, Staatsmann und Bildungstrager," pp. 473 *et seq.*

and meaning of the statutes, one would come, finally, to the ocean
of polemics. For the mastery of the whole field, yet another
great compilation would here be necessary, and this should afford,
as a basis for secure objective judgment, the support of the firm
structure of natural law   A " syntagma juris universi " should,
like a new pandect, constitute this final statement.   Such, essentially, was the course of the consistent development proposed.   At
the end, a catalogue of desiderata, analogous to that at the close
of Bacon's " Novum Organum," arranges under thirty-one numbers the works that should accordingly be prepared from the new
viewpoints.

By commission of the electoral-prince of Mainz, Leibnitz entered
immediately upon the preparation of at least one number of this
programme, namely a " reconcinnation " [1] of the Justinian books.
The plan miscarried, clearly not alone for lack of persistence, but
also because essentially impracticable in the existing state of legal
science   But is not precisely the same true of Bacon's desiderata
of philosophy?   And has not Bacon's work, nevertheless, been
of the greatest influence?   Such writings, in truth, exert influence
less through their positive content than through the critical spirit
with which they break through the spell of tradition, and through
the impulse they give to new research.   If Thomasius actually
did introduce later a scheme of legal training, encyclopædic in
basis and arranged upon a two-year term, if the " legal " method
was increasingly abandoned, and short systematic text-books (so-
called compendiums) were made the basis of academic study, if
the jurists steadily learned to break the bonds of a purely civilistic
method, and fecundate their science with philosophy, history, and
politics, — the way to all these results was marked by the " Nova
Methodus "

Significant in the history of public law is Leibnitz's great documentary work, the " Codex Juris Gentium " of 1693, with its supplement (" mantissa ") of 1700.   The legal value of these documents, which were assembled primarily for historical purposes, is
emphasized in the title, and the prefaces refer to this explicitly in
several places.   Including German constitutional law as well as
positive public and international law in general, room is here
made again for the first time since Albericus Gentilis, for the
positive precepts of international law, along with the doctrines of
natural law deduced from first principles   In this respect Leibnitz

---

[1] *Dutens*, as cited, IV, 3, p. 230 ; and *Guhrauer*, "Leibnitzens deutsche
Schriften," I, 256 *et seq*

stood, in his time, in complete isolation, opposed to Grotius and, still more, to Puffendorf.   On the other hand, these same documentary labors, in so far as they concerned public law, were in fruitful harmony with the tendencies of the time; and notably with the "realistic" movement [1]

In estimating Leibnitz's influence upon legal science, one cannot confine one's attention to his ideas of natural law and his juristic writings; one must consider the totality of his activity, in books, letters, and personal relations.   Through all of them runs a characteristic endeavor in favor of codification and legal reform. In a letter written the last year of his life, he counsels that there be formed a new Codex, "short, clear, and adequate," under governmental authority, "out of the Roman statutes, records of German law, and actual legal practice, but above all from obvious principles of equity."   And since in Leibnitz's time it appeared quite hopeless to await the issue of such a code by the Empire, he did not disdain to appeal, for the same end, to territorial legislation   It is especially notable that in Prussia [2] the first page of the proceedings preliminary to the Ordinance of the Chamber of Justice, of March 1, 1709, reproduces an essay from his hand, in which he demands, as emphatically as briefly, comprehensive legal reform.   But that ordinance was in fact the serious beginning of such reform; and thus Leibnitz is directly connected with the whole movement of legislation and codification which repeatedly dominated Prussia in the 1700s, until finally it ended in the code of 1794.   He stands in precisely similar relation to Austrian codification.

Further, in all his activities, — far beyond the occasional opportunities in the "Corpus Juris Gentium," — Leibnitz gave expression in the most masterly way to a historical conception of law, herein anticipating by at least a century the development of legal science.   The significance of certain important isolated facts in legal history could no longer be misjudged since Conring (*post*, § 42); but the first, and for a long time the only, person in Germany who grasped in a profound way the meaning of history, and who at least incidentally utilized it in legal science, was Leibnitz. It was from his law of continuity, which penetrates and supports

---

[1] *Stintzing*, "Geschichte," II, 11, and in various later passages
[2] Influence upon   legislation :   in Prussia — *Trendelenburg*, "Kleine Schriften," I, 245 *et seq*, *Stolzel*, "Brandenburg-Preussens Rechtsverwaltung und Rechtsverfassung" (Berlin, 1888), I, 414 *et seq.*, II, 55 *et seq.*, In Austria — *Pfleiderer*, cited above, p. 456   In Russia — *K. Fischer*, cited above, p. 129.

his entire philosophical system, that he deduced the essence of history.[1]   As all monads are united in chains of infinitesimal differentiation into a harmonious universe, so all things and everything appears as shaped by history and intended for a further historical development   And this holds for the growth of law among different peoples   To this idea was due the emphasis of historical instruction in the " Nova Methodus."   Leibnitz applied it, indeed, in legal science only in incidental notes   But though such elements might not immediately penetrate into juristic circles, in the long run an influence was here also inevitable.   It is true that neither the Halle nor even the Hannoverian school (*post*, § 42) attained the full meaning of Leibnitz's conception, Savigny was the first who did, — but he is united (through those schools and their last stragglers, J. S. Putter and G Hugo) in an unbroken chain of tradition, with Leibnitz.

Thus Leibnitz, as jurist, mathematician, historian, and philosopher united, was active and helpful in all parts of legal science: whether in things that lay near to the understanding and interest of his time — as speculations in natural law, the mathematical treatment of methodology or of isolated civilistic problems, or a documentation of public law, or in things beyond the apprehension of his contemporaries, — the sketch of a comprehensive doctrine of justice, the derivation from public documents of a positive law of nature, the making of legal codes in accordance with new ideas, or the revelation of the meaning of history.   A rich sowing! — although indeed many seeds never sprouted, and many others so late that between him and the ripened harvest the connection is hardly longer provable [2]

---

[1] *Wegele*, "Geschichte," pp. 646, 851, with abundant citations ; *Dutens op cit*, IV, 2, p 53, *Guhrauer*, "Leibnitzens deutsche Schriften," I, 31,
[2] [" In Leibnitz' Methodus, the science which of all others had been deemed to require the most protracted labor, the ripest judgment, the most experienced discrimination, was as it were invaded by a boy, but by one who had the genius of an Alexander, and for whom the glories of an Alexander were reserved   This is the first production of Leibnitz, and it is probably in many points of view the most remarkable work that has prematurely invited erudition and solidity.   There was only one man in the world who could have left so noble a science as philosophical jurisprudence for purposes of a still more exalted nature, and for which he was more fitted ; and that man was Leibnitz himself.   He passed onward to reap the golden harvests of other fields   Yet the study of law has owed much to him. .   . In Germany at least, philology, history, and philosophy have more or less since the time of Leibnitz marched together under the robe of law.   'He did but pass over that kingdom,' says Lerminier, 'and he has reformed and enlarged it ' "(*Hallam*, " Literature of Europe in the 15th–17th Centuries," IV, 208). — ED]

Topic 2   German Nationalism

§ 41   **Rise of the German National Jurists** — The historical process, whose course is indicated in the period thus far run through, has been rightly described as that of the naturalization and assimilation of the Roman law in Germany. The legal science of this epoch bears an alien impress; it is an exotic plant in German soil which slowly takes root, and still more slowly is acclimated. Up to this time one might speak only of legal science in Germany ; the 1600s accomplished the task of establishing a German legal science.

Legal science had been alien, not alone in its materials, in which the native element contributed no part, or one scarcely perceptible; it was alien also in its whole tradition and the influences therein grounded. Italian influence dominated casuistics and legal practice; French influence gave form to historical-antiquarian scholarship and the synthetic method. Men taught and wrote " more Italico " or " more Gallico "; nobody spoke of a " mos Germanicus." However, the German mind, after completed schooling, began to bethink itself of these conditions.

We have shown how, in the first half of the 1600s, side by side with the after effects of the traditions theretofore dominant, a new element made itself felt   Attention was turned to national conditions, and efforts were made, by the collection and study of legal sources, to comprehend their extent and historical coherence. The dominance of foreign law had in fact blinded men's sight. It had thrown over the realities of German legal conditions a web of showily specious traditional notions which maintained themselves despite all contradictions with reality   The old belief in the continuity of the Roman imperiality, with all its simulations and consequences, formed the basis of legal theory   The universality of this authority, the " dominium mundi," — long since, to be sure, no more enforced, yet still maintained in thesi, — made it seem self-evident that one and the same imperial law ruled Christendom, and hence that legal science was a unity. And however sharply these notions conflicted with reality, however inadequate they were to explain conditions as they had actually developed, nevertheless they maintained their sway with the power of a hallowed tradition   Legal science had freed itself from the fetters of scholasticism, it had saturated itself with an understanding of antiquity; it had acquired an insight into the essential unity of the law and a mastery over it as a whole; it had, finally,

endeavored more and more to show regard in details for the necessities of national legal conditions.　But the spell of the dream
in which it indulged, under the faith of tradition and the enchain-
ing power of alien authority, remained to be broken　To accomplish this were needed the profound shocks and hard experiences
brought by the 1600 s　Amid the storms of the Thirty Years' War
the generation was born and grew to maturity that was called to
complete the movement whose beginning in the first half of the
century we have pointed out.　The word that broke the ban
under which legal science lay enfettered was spoken by Hermann
Conring

§ 42.[1]　**Exponents of Nationalism and Realism; Conring,
Carpzov, Mevius, Thomasius, Beyer.**[2] — The first effect of the
transformation of legal doctrine and literature involved in the
return to original sources, and the application to these of philological criticism, as begun by Budé in France, Alciat in Italy, and in
Germany by Ulrich Zasius, was in a way (as has been noted in
§ 27) a separation of theory and practice.　Between these, so
long as legal science was exclusively devoted to the foreign law,
there naturally continued a wide chasm　But this was gradually
closed, thanks to the extensive arbitral and counsel practice, in
which the scholars of that time found themselves involved, both
as members of university faculties, through the traditional practice
of rendering faculty opinions on submitted cases, and individually
by the usage of expert consultation[3]　This practical activity was

---

[1] [This section is a mosaic made of the following sources : the portion
of paragraph 1 after the first sentence, also paragraphs 4, 7, are from
Siegel, "Deutsche Rechtsgeschichte" (3d ed , Berlin, 1895), § 52 (in
part), paragraph 2 is from *Stintzing*, "Geschichte," I, 167–168 ; paragraphs
3, 5, 6 are from *Stobbe*, "Rechstquellen," II, 418–424 (in part), and the last
part of paragraph 3 from *Stintzing*, "Geschichte," II, 5–6, paragraphs
8, 9, 10 are from *Stintzing*, "Geschichte," II, 8–10, 23 (in part). —
Transl]

[2] Cited by *Siegel*　*Böhlau* in K Vj S , XXIII (1881) ; *Luden*, "Jakob
Cujas und seine Zeitgenossen" (1822) , *Stintzing*, "Ulrich Zasius" (1857),
cf Neff, "Udalricius Zasius" (Freiburg University "Programm," 1890,
1891) , *Stintzing*, "Hugo Donellus in Altdorf" (1869) , *Schultz*, "Privatrecht und Prozess in ihrer Wechselwirkung," I (1883), 127–215, discussing "Die Actenversendung von der Rechtssprechung der Oberhofe
bis zum Eintritt der Facultaten," *Stolzel*, "Richtertum," I (1872), pp
187–231, discussing the "Aufkommen der Actenversendung an Juristen-
facultaten", *von Wachter*, "Gemeines Recht Deutschlands" (1844), pp.
66–109, on " Die Wissenschaft des gemeinen Strafrechts."

[3] [*Stintzing*, (I, 523) notes for the university of Greifswald alone above
50 consilia of the law faculty in 4 months of 1589 ; and in 1650, 113, and
in 1653, 144, consilia and decisions　Of the collections of consilia of individual jurists, — "which were designed, like modern reports of the decisions of higher courts, to supply legal practice with forms, assistance,
and authorities," — the first German example was that of Zasius (Basel,

not, in the end, without a reactive effect upon literature and doctrine; for the scholarly representatives of the new common Pandect law found themselves compelled, with few exceptions (in reference to whom was coined the hard phrase " meri legisti sunt puri asni ") to give heed to native modern laws and traditional usages.

Ulrich Zasius never declared his attitude, as matter of principle, toward German law. He attempted as little as his contemporaries generally to lay down in theory a division between the fields of validity of the Roman and the native law. Men found themselves caught within the historical process of the Reception, without being able to survey it as a whole, or to prescribe for it metes and moderation. Starting with the principle that the Justinian law was indubitably a " jus commune," the conclusion followed that all other law within the Empire was " jus particulare ", that its validity was therefore to be proved by custom or by ordinance It was, however, regarded at the same time as self-evident that not all portions of the Roman law were applicable; that conditions and customs notoriously existed in Germany which were either incommensurable, or even in direct conflict, with principles of Roman law; and that in such cases the inapplicability of the latter demanded no special proof. The imperial power was, be it remembered, never conceived of as a despotism; the practical force both of it and its law had limits, nowhere formulated, yet tacitly recognized, and discoverable in any particular case. Accordingly, Zasius explicitly declares his task to be to teach only such part of the Roman law " as should be useful, salutary, and in accord with the customs of Germany " He refers ungrudgingly to Germanic usages, and in his discussions of Roman doctrines does not forget to indicate the variation or agreement of native principles, where they seem to be important. Many institutes of Germanic law (such as serfdom, perpetual charges on land, contracts of inheritance) he treats with more detail, analyzing them judiciously, — though from the standpoint, to be sure, of Roman law and with the help of its concepts [1]

1538–1539). About 200 volumes, mainly folios, of such collections by German and foreign scholars, printed in Germany down to about 1650 are listed in *Stintzing*, I, 526 *et seq.* — TRANSL]

[1] [His independence of mere authority is shown in the following passage : "The so-called 'communis opinio doctorum' is of very questionable value Its sole basis is often merely the fact that scholars have become accustomed to follow one another blindly, instead of investigating for themselves If such 'communis opinio' is justified by the sources, it has authority just because it is correct ; but if it conflicts with

A veritable epoch, alike with reference to the history of legal sources and constitutional history, was begun by HERMAN CONRING (1606–1681) [1] His chief work was the " De Origine Juris Germanici Liber Unus " (Helmstadt, 1643) In this he gave a detailed history (even to-day worthy of attention) of German legal sources, and came to the correct conclusion, which unfortunately was not sufficiently well remembered by those who followed him, that the adoption of the Roman law in Germany dated only from the middle of the 1400s. We owe to him also our first knowledge of the important law of Charles the Great (of 812) regarding the economic management of the royal domains, and a considerable number of works on constitutional and public law. He points out emphatically and explicitly that a one-sided knowledge of the Roman law alone could never fit anybody for legal practice.[2] Conring's investigations gave to legal science in Germany a national basis, inasmuch as they proved the existing common law to be founded, as a historical fact, upon the Reception, in the sense that the Justinian law enjoyed authority, not as such, but as a law assimi-

the sources, then it has no authority at all, and men should not submit to it, but avoid it as a seaman avoids a sand-bank " (*Stintzing*, " Geschichte I, 161–162) On Zasius and his relations with the others, see *Stintzing*, "Geschichte," I, ch 5 — TRANSL]

[1] [*Stobbe's* references (1864) may here be in part replaced by later ones given by *Stintzing*, "Geschichte," II, ch 20 *Stobbe*, "H Conring der Begrunder der deutschen Rechtswissenschaft" (Rectoral address, Breslau, October 15, 1869), *Roscher*, "Geschichte der Nationalokonomik in Deutschland (1874), pp 253 *et seq*, *Conring*, "Opera" (6 vols, Braunschweig, 1730), *Jul Schmidt*, "Geschichte des geistigen Lebens in Deutschland von Leibniz bis auf Lessing's Tod," I (182), 164 *et seq*, 219, 240, *Stahl*, "Rechtsphilosophie," I, 127 *et seq*, 183 *et seq* Abundant references in *Stobbe* and *Stintzing* — TRANSL]

[2] Since *Conring's* merits are usually praised in generalities, but his sound judgment and deep insight into the scientific tendency of his time are little known, a passage may be given from a letter of 1656 ("H Conringii Opera," VI, 65) · "Quoniam vero omnes inter popularum Leges prima dudum fama fuerint Romanae et quidem Justinianeae, usque adeo ut hae Civilis juris nomen prae aliis per excellentiam adeptae sint, hinc . . . has Justinianeas novisse, id praesertim, esse Jus civile tenere, existimatur Et tamen multum id abest ad peritia juris illius, quod in civitate quavis hodie obtinet Nec enim Justinianeum illud jus usquam terrarum, nisi aliqua sui parte et quidem exigua, vim legis amplius habet Alicubi nullum illi pretium est Ubivis statuta et consuetudines domesticae prevalent; et rebus publicis libera est potestas jus illud vel de novo acceptandi vel rejiciendi, etsi jam quadantenus receptum Eoque nec ipse Tribonianus hodie quidem sit idoneus in ulla civitate jus dicere secundum leges Perinde atque observare passim est, quamvis peritissimos juris illius, ipsi pares Cujacio, in foris nostris exiguum admodum posse, sive agendae causae fuerint, sive judicandae " And on p 67 he says of the tendency of Roman legal science "Philologica potius quaedam, sive quod perinde est Grammatica aut Historica haec legum est perita, quam Scientia vel Ars vel Prudentia justi et aequi civilis Civilis cum aio intelligo, tantum illud jus, quod in aliqua singulari obtinet civitate."

lated, adapted, and transformed by German thought   Legal science thus became German in its basis, and also in its ends. [Here Conring's influence joined with the " realistic movement " of which Carpzov was the leader, which was developing the materials for a Germanic legal science.   And so Conring is often called the father of German legal history, and Carpzov the founder of German legal science]

Of great and long-continued influence, in securing for German law and custom a recognition of their legal force, were the tireless endeavors of two jurists, — BENEDICT CARPZOV (1595–1666), who drew his knowledge from the practice of the Leipzig " Schöffen-college; [1] and his contemporary DAVID MEVIUS (1609–1670),[2] under whose guidance the authority of the Supreme Court created in 1653 at Wismar for the Swedish territories of the Empire (in accord with the Peace of Westphalia) quickly attained high credit.

Most insistently of all, however, CHRISTIAN THOMASIUS (1655–1728; professor at Halle) urged the teaching of Germanic law, and in the German tongue, and its establishment in practice.   No one, perhaps, has had greater influence in promoting German law in theory and in practice, nor more forcefully protested against the undisputed sway of the Roman law.   For although it is true that his works deal less with German than Roman law, and are characterized more by rationalism and philosophy than by research, his tendency to judge everything in life ingenuously and without preconceptions, his repugnance to authority in intellectual matters, and his free-thinking (sometimes trivial and lacking in taste), were irreconcilable with the assumption that an alien law should rule with absolute decisiveness in Germany.   With the same zeal with which he battled against the witchcraft superstition and torture, he sought to show that many doctrines of Roman law were, or at least ought to be considered, impractical in German life.   His writings are full of complaints against the miserable conditions of the legal science and practice of his time.   He expresses himself with particular energy in his notes to Ossa's " Testament." [3]   All evils in the German legal conditions he

---

[1] *Diztel*, "Beitrage zur alteren Verfassungsgeschichte des Schoppenstuhls zu Leipzig," in Z ²R G , XX (1886), 89–115.

[2] *Barkow*, "De Davide Mevio Narratio" (1856).

[3] "Testament," (cited *ante*, § 22, note 5), pp 45, 48, 207, 389, 409   In his "Delineatio," cited *supra*, § 42, he says (§ 178) ·   "Et tamen hoc juris Romani progressu evidente, ausus sum sæpius asserere, juris Justinianei et Pandectarum imprimis vix decimam vel vigesimam partem esse in usu in foris Germaniæ."   And as to the adoption of Roman law, he says, "inter alia" (§ 198; cf. 191) · :"Quæstio loquitur de foris Germaniæ, non de uno

deduced from the Reception of the foreign law. Before that, the law had existed in easily comprehensible rules, known to every-body, and procedure was simple and expeditious; the native law had, indeed, been capable of betterment in many respects, but such had not been the result of the Reception of the alien law. The learnedness and the scientific form of this had, much rather, been the cause of the tedious and endless procedure, and there existed no hope of improvement so long as this sort of learning should rule. Neither the method of the Glossators nor that of the Humanists had been useful in the law's growth; because in the study of the alien law men had forgotten their own. There-fore men should quicken Germanic legal studies, and teach the German law historically, they should reprint the "Sachsen-spiegel" and the "Schwabenspiegel" without glosses, and institute academic courses upon them. Thomasius and his con-temporaries[1] subjected to searching criticism the question of the significance of the Reception, and expressed doubts whether the Roman law actually possessed in Germany the character of a com-mon law. The notion now appears in German practice — an idea certainly without countenance in earlier legal practice or in the legislation of the territories — that a party relying upon the Roman law did not "ipso facto" possess a "fundatam inten-tionem," he who appealed to the Roman law now, as formerly he who had relied upon customary law, should henceforth be required to prove that the principle of the Corpus Juris which he asserted had acquired actual authority in Germany.

It was a pupil of Thomasius, GEORG BEYER (1665–1714), who first announced university lectures upon German law. His lectures were first published after his death, under the title "Delineatio Juris Germanici ad Fundamenta sua Revocati" (Halle, 1718). Beyer aimed to present Germanic institutes as embodied in the older sources and in the writing of those practitioners who showed re-gard for German law, to deduce them in their historical develop-ment, and take them out of the inferior place which had been assigned them as an appendix of the "Usus modernus juris Romani." Be his attempt however imperfect, it was still he who gave the impulse that procured for German law a systematic treatment,

---

foro, sed quid communiter in Germania usu forensi observetur. Ergo non poterunt gloriari dissentientes, quando exemplum aliquod afferunt juris Romani in uno aliquo foro aliquando observati. sed deberent pro-bare receptionem communem et frequentatam in pluribus foris, eamque continuatim."

[1] *Cf.* the references in *Reyscher*, Z D.R., IX, 345 *et seq.*

separate from the Roman, in books and lectures.   With him began the academic study and independent literature of German private law.

The transformation, thus produced, of the science of the common Pandect law from one of universal into a German doctrine, was manifested in criminal law and criminal procedure, — the first parts of the law to be made independent academic disciplines Men started thenceforth from the criminal code of Charles V (*ante*, § 38), whereas formerly criminal theory had been treated in the exegesis of the so-called " libri terribiles " of the Pandects. Similarly the basis of civil procedure, which had formerly been customarily treated as a part of Canon law, was thenceforward the practice of the Imperial Chamber of Justice, with the modifications later adopted from Saxon procedure   Finally, in the field of private law, the " usus modernus " of the Roman law, *i.e.* its practice " in foro Germanico," received meet recognition.[1]

This transformation of a universal into a Germanic legal science is hardly referable to that impulse of national feeling which made itself felt here and there in belles-lettres   It appears rather a result of that turn toward empiricism and realism which had come about in intellectual tendencies, and which was given validity in science by Francis Bacon and Thomas Hobbes   There are indeed observable in the 1600 s two distinct and parallel movements in legal science.   The one was directed to the discovery and presentation of positive law; the second (*ante*, § 39) to the foundation and development of natural law.   The first alone attained in that century to dominance and completion, while the second was only prepared for the empire it assumed in the following century   The former attained its zenith under the influence of empiricism.   And to Bacon's empiricism is applicable the general historical truth that a genius is but a focus in which are gathered the scattered intellectual rays that light an age   Empiricism and its consequences appear most palpably in the great practicians Carpzov and Mevius.   They observed and collected, as facts of experience, the legal views embodied in the opinions of the courts, gave them juridical form, and established, through combinations of them, higher principles.   The empirical method of these practitioners is the opposite of the casuistic method of the schoolman

---

[1] *Sam Stryk,* "Usus Modernus Pandectarum" (4 vols , 1690) ; *Schilter,* "Praxis Juris Romani in Foro Germanico" (3 vols , 1698 *et seq* , being the 2d ed. of his "Exercitationes ad Pandectarum 50 Libros," of 1675–1683).

And the attitude of the theorists, of whom GEORG STRUVE (1619–1693) and later SAMUEL STRYK (1640–1710) may be considered as the leaders, was similar   They also considered their problem as the presentation, not of a law established and to be laid down merely in thesi, but of a " practical " law, *i e* an actual and living law judicially determined; and the fact of the actual current validity of a legal principle they made the criterion of its adoption in theory.

Nevertheless they did not succeed in penetrating to the genius of Germanic law. They were lacking in one essential requisite: a historical sense. The leaders of that time did not, indeed, deny the value of historical knowledge, but still, this was to serve only as introduction and ornament for that which was really their end. " Vitæ non scholæ discendum " is their ever repeated motto; to which is attached the warning against " insidere quasi sepulchris priscorum Ictorum " and " nimis curiosum esse ut scias antiqua, obsoleta et abrogata " (Mevius). The aims of the time were practical   As little as research in Roman antiquities was consistent with this prevailing tendency, so little was the concern given to the development of Germanic antiquities.

In what sense one may say that in this time a German legal science was established has been shown above   But a science of German law arose only later. The seeds and the beginnings of such existed already, it is true, in this period, but the opening of the next century brought them first to ripeness and full development.

TOPIC 3. STATE–BUILDING AND LEGISLATION

§ 43. **Decline and Fall of the Empire.** — Since the close of the Middle Ages, the Holy Roman Empire of the German Nation had moved toward a gradual dissolution   Its constitution could not assimilate the atrophied forms, which had become unrealities, of feudalism   Projects and attempts at a constitutional reform which had appeared in the 1400s remained essentially without result. Between the power of the Empire and that of the territorial rulers there resulted an equipoise of forces, neither being able to make itself master of the other. Political development centered in the territories. Of these Austria (in union with non-German lands) retained constant possession of the German royal crown and also of the imperial title (now become almost meaningless) for its princely family, the house of Habsburg. The family policy of the

Spanish-Habsburg house, which subordinated the interests of the Empire, had the consequence that Switzerland, the Netherlands, Burgundy, and Italy were in the end lost to the Empire.   When the greater part of Germany had accepted the Reformation, the counter-Reformation led to internal wars and to the interference of foreign powers.   The peace of Westphalia, by which the civil war was ended, left unchanged the religious and political antagonisms which had brought it about.

Following the Thirty Years' War, the Mark of Brandenburg developed into that political nucleus about which later a new Germany was to be formed.   The electoral prince of Brandenburg had acquired the duchy of Clèves, the county of Mark, and Ravensburg in 1614; in 1618 Johann Sigismund entered into the government of Prussia.   The peace of Westphalia guaranteed to the electoral house of Farther Pomerania the bishoprics of Halberstadt, Minden, and Kammin, and the reversion of the archbishopric of Magdeburg.   The peace of Olivia in 1660 confirmed to the electoral prince the sovereignty of Prussia, which he had until then possessed as a Polish fief.   The electoral prince Frederick III assumed the title of a King of Prussia.   By the conquest and retention of Silesia King Frederick II made place for Prussia among the great powers of Europe.   Because there was no strong territorial power fitted to act as a buffer on the sorely endangered western boundary of Germany, the Empire suffered on this side sensible losses of territory   The peace of Ryswick ceded to France the lands she had torn from the Empire in Alsace.   The last of the Habsburgs, Charles VI, confirmed to France in the peace preliminaries of Vienna of October 3, 1785, the succession of Lorraine, into whose possession she entered in 1776.

The French Revolution and its consequences gave the occasion for the final collapse of the Empire, which had long since lost its vitality.   By the peace of Lunéville in 1801 the whole left bank of the Rhine was ceded to France   On August 1, 1806, Napoleon gave notice to the Diet of the foundation of the Confederation of the Rhine, which sixteen German princes had concluded on July 12, 1806, under his protectorate

After he had already, on August 11, 1804, assumed the title and the honors of a heritable emperor of Austria, the Emperor Francis II, following the precedent of the Confederation, proclaimed the separation from the Empire of himself and his family lands.   By patent of August 6, 1806, he renounced the German imperial crown, declaring that he regarded the imperial office and honors as extinguished, and himself and all his German provinces and imperial lands therewith relieved of all duties to the German empire As the history of later times has shown, this step signified for the dynasty of Habsburg-Lorraine an irrevocable renunciation of the political leadership of the German race.

§ 44 **Imperial and State Legislation (to 1811).** — The 1600s and first half of the 1700s were poor in products of general legislation, but special legislation — though indeed wholly lacking in fruitful ideas — was of rank abundance [To the enumeration made above of the more important statutes of the 1500s, there may now be named among those of the 1600s and 1700s, in addition to revisions of the older statutes, the following]: the " Landrecht " of the duchy (kingdom) of Prussia of 1620, revised in 1684 and 1720 (to which add the Prussian admiralty law of 1727), and the re-enacted territorial ordinances of Bohemia and Moravia of 1627–1628 [1] Of exceeding importance for the development of the " common Saxon law " based upon the " Sachsenspiegel " were the " Saxon constitutions " of the Electoral Prince August of 1572, and the " Decisiones Electorales Saxonicæ " of 1661, which attained great prestige throughout the whole of northern Germany [2] The most modern territorial laws of this period were those of Bamberg (1769), Mainz (1755), and Trier (1668–1714), — the last of which rested upon that of Cologne, and, like that of Mainz, declared abrogated all contrary statutory and customary rights.

The idea of a codification, — already so happily realized in one field by the " Carolina " (*ante*, § 38), — which should overcome the dualism of the native and the alien law, occupied from the 1500s onward the greatest legal minds, especially as regards the civil law [3] In the 1700s, also, men recognized the need of reforming legal procedure, and also the criminal law, inasmuch as the " Carolina " no longer satisfied the views of the period of Rationalism (" Aufklarungszeit ") Its barbarous system of punishment was not to be reconciled with the new notion that the end of punishment is not deterrence through fear, but a healing social

---

[1] *Luschin von Ebengreuth*, "Osterreichischer Reichsgeschichte," pp. 357 *et seq* , 386 *et seq.*

[2] *Muther*, "Beitrage zur Geschichte der sachsischen Konstitutionen und des Sachsenspiegels," in Z R G , IV, 168 *et seq* , *Stintzing*, "Geschichte," I, 551 *et seq*

[3] *Schroder* in Z ²R G , XXXIV, 5 *et seq* The most prominent representative of the idea was Leibnitz *Cf Mollat*, "Zur Wurdigung Leibnizens" in Z ²R G , XX, 71 *et seq*, *Taranowsky*, "Leibniz und die aussere Rechtsgeschichte," Z ²R G , XL, 190 *et seq*, *Stintzing*, "Geschichte," I, 28, *Hartmann*, "Leibniz als Jurist und Rechtsphilosoph " (Tubinger Festschrift for Ihering). [And *cf* above, § 39.]

justice. A greater gradation of penalties was called for, and, above all, the elimination of torture from criminal procedure [1]

The work of codification began first in Prussia, immediately following the accession to the throne of Frederick the Great, who himself sketched its plan. The first result was nothing better than the draft of a "Corpus Iuris Fridericianum" (1749–1751), composed by COCCEJI and of little utility [2] Only in the last decade of Frederick's government were the labors renewed under the minister VON CARMER. In the interval Bavaria took the lead. Under the Electoral Prince Maximilian III three comprehensive codes, of which VON KREITTMAYR was the author and expounder, were prepared [3] The "Codex Iuris Bavarici Criminalis" (covering criminal law and procedure) of 1751, and the "Codex Iuris Bavarici Iudiciarii" (civil procedure) of 1753, were true codes, whereas the short Bavarian "Landrecht" ("Codex Maximilianeus Bavaricus Civilis") of 1756 retained the principle of the subsidiary force of the Pandect law. In Prussia [4] nothing more was realized under Frederick the Great than a code of civil procedure (namely the first book of the "Corpus Juris Fridericianum") of 1781 [5] The other labors of codification were completed only after the death of the great king

In Austria [6] changes were limited to the criminal and the private law. A new criminal code, including the substantive law ("Constitutio Criminalis Theresiana"), came into existence in 1769. On the other hand, the draft of a "Codex Theresianus" [7] for private law, was not approved by the empress; only under Joseph II was the first part — or family law — published as a "Josephanisches Gesetzbuch." A general code of judicature was published

---

[1] Cf. Gunther, "Idee der Wiedervergeltung," II, 1 et seq. The rack was abolished in Prussia by Frederick the Great in 1740

[2] Stintzing-Landsberg, "Geschichte," III, 215 et seq, and Notes, pp 138 et seq

[3] Stintzing-Landsberg, "Geschichte," III, 223 et seq and Notes, p. 142 et seq

[4] The same, III, 465 et seq and Notes, pp 297 et seq Cf. Stolzel, "Svarez" (1885).

[5] The law was subjected after a few years to a revision, the result of which (leaving intact its peculiar inquisitorial principle, which supplanted all usual maxims of procedure) was the General Code of Judicature of 1793. On a Prussian code of judicature of 1709, see Hassenpflug, "Die erste Kammergerichtsordnung Kurbrandenburgs" (1895)

[6] Stintzing-Landsberg, op cit, III, pp 519 et seq, and Notes, pp 322 et seq, Luschin von Ebengreuth, op cit, pp 511 et seq, von Domin-Petrushevecz, "Neuere osterreichische Rechtsgeschichte" (1869)

[7] Edition with commentary by Harras von Harrassowsky (5 vols, 1883–1886) Cf Ofner, "Der Urentwurf und die Beratungsprotokolle des osterreichischen allgemeinen Gesetzbuches" (2 vols, 1889); Saxl, in Z.Pr Ö R, XXIV, 425 et seq

in 1781, a code of criminal law in 1787, a new code of civil procedure
in 1788

Frederick the Great had established a commission to codify
the entire substantive law. Its moving spirit was the Councillor
SUAREZ   The draft was published in 1784 and submitted thus
to criticism.   The publication of the code was by proclamation
of March 20, 1791 (in print 1792), under the title of a " General
Code (' Gesetzbuch ') for the Prussian States." Before going
into force, however, it was again withdrawn, and after a superficial
revision was again published in 1794 as the " General Territorial
Code (' Allgemeines Landrecht ') for the Prussian States," with
applicability to all Prussian territory, except the principalities of
Neuenburg and Valengin.   Because of territorial changes, another
publication was made in 1803, in which the supplements of the
interim were inserted in the appropriate places.   After the wars of
independence the Code was introduced into the newly acquired
territories.   New Farther Pomerania and Rugen, however, as
well as the part of the administrative district of Coblenz (a district,
namely, of the Court of Appeal of Ehrenbreitstein) which lay on
the right bank of the Rhine, retained the common law, and the
entire left bank and a part of the Rhine Province on the right
bank retained the French law.   In the Bavarian margravates of
Ansbach and Baireuth, in Hannoverian East Friesland, the
northern county of Lingen, and in Eichfeld, — territories separated from Prussia as a result of the French wars, — and also in a
part of Saxe-Weimar, the " Allgemeines Landrecht " was retained.

The Code is divided into two parts, the parts into titles, the
titles into paragraphs.   Its most important parts are those of
private law (part 1, and titles 1–6 of part 2), the law of the Church
(pt. 2, tit 11), and criminal law (pt. 2, tit. 20)   Titles 7–10 of
part 2 treat of class law. peasants (tit. 7), the middle class (tit.
8), nobility (tit 9), and civil servants (tit. 10).   Under the peasant
class the village communities are treated; under the middle class
the cities (§§ 86–178), gilds and trades (§§ 179–474), commercial
law (§§ 475–712, 1250–1388, 2452–2464), the law of bills of exchange (§§ 713–1249), admiralty (§§ 1389–1933, 2359–2451), and
insurance (§§ 1934–2358)   Part 2, titles 12–19 contain provisions
on public and administrative law, including the regalia and the law
of guardianship, the conception of the last being wholly bureaucratic   The Code supplanted the various sources of the common Pandect and common Saxon laws, and claimed therefore an
authority subsidiary only to the provincial statutes and legal

systems; whose codification, moreover, was borne in mind. To the customary law was left an authority subsidiary to that of the Code   Unlike the Prussian " Allgemeines Landrecht," the other codifications of State law were restricted to private law, they asserted, however, a primary authority, and permitted effect to customary law only in so far as it was explicitly recognized.

In Austria, Joseph's Code remained for a time a fragment.   Not until 1811 was the task completed by the publication of a " General Civil Code for the Empire of Austria " [1]   It is composed of three parts, which in turn are divided into sections, and (in all) 1502 consecutive paragraphs   Its system is similar to the portions of the Prussian Code that deal with private law.   In form and expression the Austrian code is more satisfactory, for its authors were instructed to restrict themselves to principles and resist all temptations to deal with detailed cases, whereas Frederick the Great desired, if possible, a separate provision for every case. This excessive particularity is the greatest fault of the Prussian Code, which is otherwise favorably distinguished from all others by clarity of expression, sound views, and exhaustiveness   Both Codes contain, in addition to the native law directly adopted (at best, forming a much smaller part than the Roman law), much that was unconsciously embodied in them.   For their authors unconsciously *thought* within Germanic legal conceptions, — although in the main they *consciously* departed from the Roman law only when holding (under the influence of the school of natural law) a different notion of a " rule of reason " or of " the nature of things"

The French Civil Code was published in 1804 as a " Code Civil des Français," then (after the Empire was created) revised and published again in 1807 as the " Code Napoléon."   In its drafting, the pure Germanic customary law of northern France was in many cases adopted; [2] and the Code Civil contained more Germanic law than the Prussian and the Austrian codes.   Other codifications of French law were the " Code de procédure civile " of 1806, " Code de commerce " of 1807, " Code d'instruction criminelle " of 1808, and " Code pénal " of 1810.   The " Code Napoléon," in an official German version and with essential additions, was adopted in Baden by edicts of February 3 and December 22, 1809, as

---

[1] This "Allgemeines hurgerliches Gesetzbuch" is to-day in force in the Austrian crown lands, also in Siebenburgen, Croatia, and the one-time military marches , but was repealed as regards Hungary in 1861
[2] *Cf. von Below,* "Ursachen der Rezeption des Romischen Rechts in Deutschland" (1905) pp. 67 *et seq., Zöpfl,* in Z D.R , V, 110 *et seq.*

" Landrecht; " and with an appendix drawn from the " Code de Commerce." The French codes attained wide authority in Germany during the Napoleonic period [At its end they were kept in force, to the east of the Rhine, only in Baden with some little adjacent territory, and in a small region on the lower Rhine, between Duisburg and Linz.]

Chapter IV. Fourth Period. a.d. 1806–1908

NATIONAL UNIFICATION AND CODIFICATION[1]

45 Influences in the late 1700s favoring Native Law and Codification.
46. Thibaut and Savigny; the Controversy over National Codification.
47. State Codes of the 1800s.
48 Progress of Political Unification, 1806–1871
49 National Codification, 1848–1908

§ 45. **Influences in the late 1700s favoring Native Law and Codification.** — [We have already seen (§ 42) that the 1700s had developed a juristic school which opposed the ascendancy of the alien law, and sought to give consistency and authority to the historic native system.] Beside this Germanistic opposition to the Roman law, there soon appeared another, namely, that of the schools of legal philosophy which arose with the awakening of the Kantian Critical Philosophy. The beginning of this movement is indeed to be dated from the appearance of Christian von Wolf (died 1754). It first became of great significance, however, with Emmanuel Kant (died 1804), whose "Metaphysische Anfangsgrunde der Rechtslehre," of 1797, exercised decisive influence upon the statement of fundamental legal conceptions in all parts of the positive law.

If this critical philosophy was long without bearing the fruit it might and should have had, the chief reason lay in the fact that a knowledge of the Roman law in its details was ordinarily lacking (and naturally) to those who as philosophers occupied themselves

[1] [The sources from which the sections of the present chapter have been derived are as follows · § 45, from §§ 57–58 (translated in part) of vol I of Heinrich Zöpfl, "Deutsche Rechtsgeschichte" (4th ed , 3 vols , Braunschweig, 1871–1872) ; § 46, from Otto Stobbe, "Geschichte der deutschen Rechtsquellen" (2 vols , Leipzig, 1860–1864), vol II, pp 435–40 (in full) ; § 47, from § 91 (a portion) of Richard Schroder, "Lehrbuch der deutschen Rechtsgeschichte" (5th ed , Leipzig, 1910) , § 48, from § 58 (in part) of Heinrich Brunner, "Grundzuge der deutschen Rechtsgeschichte " (4th ed , Leipzig, 1910) , § 49, from § 65 (in part) of the last named work ; together with an original contribution by Professor Ernst Freund, of the Editorial Committee of this Series. — Transl].

with the law. The consequence of this was that these attacks
of modern philosophy,—which was satisfied to set up its own
legal systems, independent of any basis of positive law, — were
not aimed with sufficient directness against the Roman law to be
effective   Moreover, in view of their general lack of practical
experience, the opposition of these philosophers hardly possessed
a greater scientific significance than did formerly the popular
opposition of the early 1500s, whose place, moreover, this new
opposition in part really occupied (particularly as regards the
tendency towards communism).

Nevertheless it is noteworthy that whenever a really great
German thinker abandoned himself fully to the creative power
of his genius, breaking with the fetters of an artificial Romanistic
mode of thought, his most original ideas generally reflected those
historically primary ideas which the German people has from
earliest times developed as peculiarly its own   This is notably true
of G W. F HEGEL   In his "Grundlinien der Rechtsphilosophie"
(Berlin, 1821) he builds his system, in complete harmony with the
German mode of thinking, upon the *subjective* conception of law,
i.e. the conception of authority, whereas the Kantian legal philosophy proceeded from the objective (statutory) conception, therein
standing nearer to the fundamental Roman view. The identification by Hegel of possession and right, wherein he unconsciously
approached the old Germanic conception of the nature of seisin,
is also noteworthy

Slowly, but nevertheless gradually, there developed still another
opposition to the Roman law, far more powerful than any purely
scientific opposition. It arose from the same practical need of
legislation that had contributed so materially three centuries
before to the Roman Reception   Precisely because men were
bound to recognize very soon that the Roman law could not be
given an unqualified application in wholly different times and
another nationality, they had resort, to some extent, as early as
the 1400s, to codification, from which alone relief seemed possible
(*ante*, §§ 3, 38). From the very beginning the problem of codification in Germany lay in two things. (1) on the one hand, to establish definite limits to the use of the Roman law, at the same time
helping the principles of Germanic law to a positive, statutory
force beside the other, thus determining by political authority
the mutual relation of the foreign and the native law, since legal
science unaided seemed unequal to the task, and (2) on the other
hand, to make the Roman law more easily understandable by

declaratory legislation, and its application more simple by a statutory settlement of disputed questions. In later times, in which the national self-consciousness had become, in general, more alive than in the 1700s, a demand was added that codification should give the precedence to the Germanic element over the Roman, — at once emancipating it from its previous subjection to alien legal sources, and reëstablishing its unqualified authority. To these influences, moreover, was added, the continual and powerful development of commerce, with its influence upon all social life.

Thus, inevitably, the need for revision of many institutes, indeed whole portions of the German law, as well as many doctrines of the Roman law theretofore regarded as of universal force, came gradually to be recognized. Some branches of law required a thorough overhauling, — as the criminal law, procedure, mortgages, domicile, etc.; while the complete elimination of others — such as fiefs, manorial services, feudal burdens, private jurisdictions, gild monopolies, etc. — appeared an inevitable necessity. Not less imperative, in still later times, was a new law for the new conditions of life and trade, — such as many usages of commercial law, insurance, partnerships and corporations, etc. And the demand for a home-made code was bound to become the louder and more imperative as men came to see that, under existing conditions, the only way and the shortest way to satisfy the claims of modern life was by legislation based on participation of popular representatives

§ 46. **Thibaut and Savigny; the Controversy over National Codification.** — When, in the course of the wars of independence, a national spirit was wakened, and the German people felt its unity, and it became a living question how the nation could prepare for itself a better future, there arose also the idea of a general legal code, for the entire nation. In the year 1814, ANTON F. J. THIBAUT, a professor of Roman law at Heidelberg, stepped forward as champion, and, with a warmth and patriotic enthusiasm grateful to German hearts, demanded a national code In his pamphlet, "On the Necessity of a General Civil Code for Germany,"[1] he painted in dark colors the legal conditions of the past "Our whole native law is a formless chaos of contradictory, mutually destructive, motley-hued provisions, perfectly suited to keep the

---

[1] "Über die Nothwendigkeit eines allgemeinen burgerlichen Rechts für Deutschland" (Heidelberg, 1814); republished with additions in his "Civilistische Abhandlungen" (Heidelberg, 1814), pp 404 et seq And see *Thibaut* on the origin of the pamphlet in "Archiv fur Civilistische Praxis," XXI, 391 et seq

nation divided and to make a thorough knowledge of the law impossible for judges and lawyers. But even a perfect knowledge of such a chaotic hodge-podge would serve little purpose. For the whole native law is so imperfect and poor that of a hundred questions of law, ninety at least　　must always be settled by recourse to the alien codes we have adopted　The chief and ultimate source of law remains for us a Roman code, the product of an alien and dissimilar nation, in the period of its greatest decay, bearing everywhere evident the traces of that decay. One must be wholly captive to passionate prejudices, to praise the Germans for the adoption of this ill-counselled work, and seriously recommend its retention. Complete, infinitely complete, it is, indeed, but perhaps in exactly the sense that Germans can be called rich, because they own all the treasures under their feet to the middle of the earth. If only all could be easily dug out! that is the unfortunate difficulty! And so it is with the Roman law. Unquestionably jurists learned, keen, and unwearied can compile out of the broken fragments of this Code something pertinent on any subject. It is nothing, however, to the point that good ideas are securely locked up in printed books. What is important is that a living law should dwell in the minds of judges and lawyers, and that it be possible for these to acquire a comprehensive knowledge of the law. In the Roman law, however, this will be forever impossible. The whole compilation is too obscure, too hastily put together. Besides, the true key to it we shall always lack　For we do not possess the ideas, inborn in Roman minds, which must have made immensely easier of understanding, to them, what is perhaps to us a riddle " Therefore, he urged, the German people needed one general code, written in the German tongue; and the slight inconveniences involved would be outweighed by the countless advantages of unity

Political conditions, however, after the wars of independence, would have made impossible any such code, even before the idea had taken hold of the people or the first step could be taken toward its realization. The particularism of the federated States under the constitution adopted for Germany prevented any radical legislation　Indeed, such was the degree of particularistic isolation under that system that the thought of a common law could make no further practical progress. But, more than that, CARL FRIEDRICH VON SAVIGNY, the greatest authority in the field of legal science, immediately entered the lists. not only against the proposals of Thibaut, but against all and any plans whatever of codification. His views were embodied in his famous pamphlet "On the Call of our Times for Legislation and Legal Science." [1] Since in his opinion his generation lacked any deep and comprehensive knowledge of the law, he felt compelled to deny it any "call" for codification. He demanded, as preparation for a future codification, a still more profound study of the sources of the alien law.[2]

New investigations and discussions followed upon his writings [3] Out of the continued controversy arose the so-called Historical and Philosophical Schools.[4] In its later stages, however, the dispute was no longer as to the possibility and advisability of legislation, but as to purely theoretical questions. The historical school, whose chief representatives were von Savigny and Eichhorn, held the advantage, we owe to it the most brilliant works and the fullest bloom of German legal science. Nevertheless the division of effort between Romanists and Germanists had, as the result, that in the historical treatment of the law the practical ends of science were commonly disregarded. In contrast to the older uncritical method which united Roman and Canon law and rules of procedure in a motley jumble,[5] the Romanists now set themselves as almost their exclusive problem the cultivation of the pure Roman law and researches in its history from the time of the Roman kingship down to Justinian; [6] while the Germanists chose, in

[1] "Vom Beruf unserer Zeit zur Gesetzgebung und Rechtswissenschaft" (1814, 3d ed, 1840).
[2] As to this judgment, cf. Ihering in Ihering and Gerber's "Jahrbuch," V, 363
[3] A list of the more important publications in Goldschmidt, "Encyklopädie," pp. 144 et seq.
[4] ["Die geschichtliche Rechtsansicht zelbst freilich war älter (than Savigny's book) Sie hatte schon im letzten Drittel des 18 Jahrhunderts sich aus der beginnenden Gegenstromung gegen den naturrechtlichen Radikalismus emporgerungen."—O. Gierke, "Die historische Rechtsschule und die Germanisten" (Berlin, 1903), p. 5 Schroder, "Lehrbuch," p 938, cites the following: Siegel, "Rechtsgeschichte," pp. 158 et seq, Savigny, op. cit, and Z.G.R.W., I, 373 et seq, Achim von Arnim in Z ¹R.G. XXVI, 228 et seq, Thibaut, op cit, Zöpfl in Z D.R., IV, 91 et seq., Bekker, "Uber den Streit der historischen und philosophischen Rechtsschulen" (Heidelberg, rectoral address, 1868); Biener, "Abhandlungen aus dem Gebiet der Rechtsgeschichte" (1848), pp 3 et seq, Rudorff, "Savigny," in Z.¹R G, II, 1 et seq., Bethmann-Hollweg, "Erinnerung an Savigny," Z ¹R G, VI, 42 et seq, Brinz, "Ubersicht uber die 1879 gehaltenen Gedachtnisreden auf Savigny" in K.Vj S, XXI, 473 et seq., XXII, 161 et seq, Landsberg in Allg d Biog, XXX, 425 et seq On the opposition of Germanisten and Romanisten within the historical school, see O. Gierke, "Die historische Rechtsschule und die Germanisten" (Berlin, rectoral address, 1903) — TRANSL.]
[5] Capitally described in Stintzing, "Von Savigny, ein Beitrag zu seiner Wurdigung" (1862, and in Preuss J B, vol. IX)
[6] Against this one-sidedness Romanisten themselves came to protest.

the main, as the object of their researches the intervening period
before the German reception of the Roman law. The later centuries, in which Roman and Germanic law had met in Germany,
were by both neglected for decades; thus the questions, what
became of the former in Germany, and how the latter was modified
under the former's influence, long remained uninvestigated   All
interest in the law of the present seemed to be lacking , respect for
legal principles which were embodied in practice, but lacked basis
in the pure sources of the law, had disappeared   The science of
the common law was now more divorced from practice than in
that earlier period (ante, §§ 16–24) when men had brought together
(to be sure, in merely a superficial and unsatisfying way) the modifications of Roman theory in an "Usus modernus."   For the
teachers of law and representatives of science of that period,
through their extensive activity in arbitral courts and "Schöffen"
guilds, and as private counsellors, had been more intimately
acquainted with procedural law and, also, had possessed more
abundant opportunities to influence it [1]

The differences between the representatives of the historical
and the philosophical schools, and between Romanists and Germanists, gradually lessened   When men perceived that only a
joint application of the different methods and the utilization of
both bodies of legal material could be remunerative, a reconciliation came about   We owe to this result a series of works which,
with special attention to the history of legal dogma, do justice
from a universal standpoint to both the Roman and the German
law, and, serving not only theory but practice, prepared the way
for legislation [2] With time, even genuine representatives of
historical legal science ceased to be afraid of raising their voices
in favor of codification, — which was again being demanded in
different States   But because the whole political situation, the
antagonisms between the individual States and the constitutions
alike of the Federation and of the States, made a common legislation appear a Utopian dream; and because some felt scruples
against wiping out and sacrificing to the cause of legal unity those
local peculiarities of law existing in different parts of Germany,
whose definition was one of the tasks of the science of German law,

Cf e g Ihering in Ihering and Gerber's J B., I, 30 et seq , 37 et seq. , Bruns
in Bekker and Muther, J B , I, 90 et seq   •
   [1] Eichhorn's judgment (to the above effect) of the 1700s is even truer
of many works of the greatest period of the historical school.
   [2] Cf. the weighty remarks of Biener, op cit , II (1848), 3–17.

— for these reasons, the only progress made towards codification was accomplished by the legislation of individual States.

§ 47. **State Codes of the 1800s.** — In 1863 the Code of Civil Law ("Burgerliches Gesetzbuch") of the kingdom of Saxony was issued   Drafts of codes in Hesse-Darmstadt and Bavaria,[1] and later projects of codification in Prussia, remained without result. Among codifications of criminal law the two Bavarian codes of 1813 (prepared by Feuerbach) and 1861, the Prussian of 1851, and the Austrian of 1852–1853 were of special moment   Among statements of civil procedure, first place is taken by those of Bavaria (1869) and Hannover (1850).   While these followed in essentials the French procedure, Prussia was content with a revision of the General Code of Judicature ("Allgemeine Gerichts-ordnung") of 1793 by ordinances of June 1, 1833 and July 21, 1846, the organization of the courts was wholly altered by an ordinance of January 2, 1849.   Finally, an ordinance of January 3, 1849 (together with a law of May 3, 1852), brought a reform in Prussia too of criminal procedure, — inadequately regulated by the criminal code of 1805, — with public and oral proceedings and jury trial, following the French procedure adopted since the Napoleonic period in the South German States.

§ 48. **Progress of Political Unification, 1806–1871** — In the period from the dissolution of the Holy Roman Empire of the German Nation until the foundation of the new German Empire, Germany passed through a series of transitory constitutional regimens.   To begin with there was the Confederation of the Rhine, an attempt to organize Germany, omitting her two great powers. this did not develop beyond a satellary relation to France, which had created it, and it was shattered by the war of Independence   The articles of confederation of June 8, 1815, united the German States, now including the two great powers, into an imperfect confederacy, which in no way fulfilled the expectations it awakened during the campaign of independence; was, further, in its very constitution fundamentally incapable of further development, and represented under the leadership of Austria only a new, albeit veiled, form of alien rule   National unity became possible only after its enemies, Austria and France, had been vanquished in the wars of 1866 and 1870.   By the peace of Prague, August 23, 1866, Austria agreed to the dissolution of the German Confederation.   Thus was completed the long process of dissolution which began far back in the growth of territorial powers within

---

[1] *Cf. Roth*, "Bayrisches Zivilrecht," I (2d ed.), 2 *et seq.*

the old empire. But affairs did not end with this negative result. In the first place the North German federal constitution of April 17, 1867, united the North German States into a federal State under Prussia's hegemony. The war which France provoked in 1870 ended with the reconquest of the old Rhine lands of Alsace and German Lorraine. The constitution of the German Empire of April 16, 1871, brought to an end the period of transition.

§ 49. **National Codification, 1848–1908.** — The demand for national legal unity was not in the long run to be denied It was realized first in the field of commercial law. At the instance of the Tariff Union, a draft was made of a bills-of-exchange law, which by resolution of the National Assembly was published on November 27, 1848, by the Archduke Johann, vice-regent of the Empire, as an imperial law, but came into force in the greater part of Germany as territorial law, by virtue of publication according to local law. To the federal Diet was due the appointment of a commission, which elaborated at Nuremberg and at Hamburg the draft of a code of commercial law. In accord with a resolution of the Federal Assembly of May 31, 1861, this was recommended to the governments of the different States for adoption, which took place by territorial legislation in the years 1861–1865. The Federation was occupied with still other far-reaching plans, notably with the drafting of a general law of obligations; but they were wrecked by the weakness of the federal constitution. While all rights of legislation were lacking to the old German Federation, and its decrees, strictly considered, could take effect only as local law, through their adoption in territorial statutes, the new North German Federation of 1867 received the right of direct legislation, under the principle that the federal laws should constitute an absolute common law. The federal constitution allotted to federal jurisdiction, among other matters, the law of obligations, negotiable paper, criminal law, and legal procedure. This legislative competency in matters of justice passed unaltered into the constitution of the Empire of 1871, and was extended to the entire field of civil law (including criminal law and procedure) by a law of December 20, 1873 Moreover, the laws of the North German Federation were, with the strengthening of the Federation into the Empire, raised in status to imperial law. Aside from numerous special laws, a law of trade relations was issued by the Federation in 1869; the bills-of-exchange law, together with the Nuremberg Supplements and the Commercial Code were transformed by statutes into formal and absolute common law; in 1870 the criminal law and the law of literary copyright were systematized. The law of patents and that of copyrights in the plastic arts were regulated by the Empire in 1876, and in 1877 the law of judicature, civil and criminal procedure, and the law of bankruptcy were codified. The imperial legislation of the first decade continued to be based for the most part upon individualistic and capitalistic economic theories. In the second decade it abandoned these to follow with increasing clarity of consciousness social-political aims, — a change which is particularly noticeable in the numerous amendments to the law of trade regulations.

The most difficult task, the codification of the private law into a Civil Code, was taken in hand in 1874.[1] In undertaking this codification, the government proceeded with a deliberation and thoroughness corresponding to the magnitude of the task A preliminary commission of five superior judges was first appointed to make suggestions as to the method to be pursued in framing a draft code. One of the principal recommendations made and adopted was that the preparation of the code should not be left to the regular staff officials of the German government who usually draft the legal measures submitted to the legislature, but that a commission " ad hoc " should be created — to consist of judges, officials of the Department of Justice, and law teachers in the universities, with power to employ special assistants and to call for information on the authorities of the several States. It was contemplated that the different parts should be drafted by individual members of the commission, the whole then to be revised by the commission sitting together, and that the result should be published for criticism and suggestions to serve as a basis for a second reading.

In July, 1874, the Federal Council appointed a commission of eleven members, of whom nine were practical jurists (judges and high officials) and two were university professors. The chairman of the commission was Dr. Pape, the president of the Imperial Commission Court, the highest federal tribunal at the time. The commission began its sessions in September, 1874, and the next six years were devoted to the work of preparing preliminary drafts

---

[1] [The remainder of this section is a contribution by Professor Ernst Freund, of the Editorial Committee of this Series In *Georg Maas*, "Bibliographie des Burgerlichen Gesetzbuches, 1888–1898" (Berlin, 1899) and *Otto Mühlbrecht*, same title (3 parts, the first in 3d ed , Berlin, 1898–1901), covering materials through 1900, will be found exhaustive references to the new, and to some extent the older literature of cognate interest. — Transl]

of the five main divisions of the code, each of which was assigned to one member. During this time the draftsmen met weekly, but the commission as a whole had only annual sessions of comparatively short duration. The work of the whole commission began in 1881 and ended with the close of the year 1887, when the first draft code was submitted to the imperial chancellor Thirteen years had thus been spent upon its preparation The draft, together with a condensed edition of the explanatory notes, was published in 1888 These notes, called " Motive," fill five volumes of about four thousand pages in the aggregate, while the unpublished original notes are far more voluminous Even the abridged edition contains an enormous mass of material, and forms the most valuable treatise on comparative jurisprudence ever published

The first draft called forth a flood of papers, pamphlets, and books, -- practically every legal writer in Germany contributing to the work of criticism Criticism had been invited by the publication, and was its main object. But the commissioners could hardly have expected, after the painstaking and conscientious labor of many years, to find that the criticism was in the main unfavorable. Professor Gierke of Berlin, a strong believer in the " social " superiority of German over Roman legal ideas, wrote a book entitled " The Draft of a Civil Code and the German Law," which is the clearest and strongest summary of the various objections brought against the proposed code, and gives the most readable account of its leading provisions and principles.

The government regarded the force of adverse criticism as sufficient to recommend an entire recasting of the first draft, and this work was intrusted, in 1890, to another commission of twenty-two members, partly jurists, partly economists, and partly experts in different branches of trade and industry. This commission adopted the plan of keeping the public informed of the progress of its deliberations and of all conclusions reached, thus getting the benefit of criticism and advice as the work was progressing and before its results were presented as a whole. The first draft was used as a basis, but subjected to manifold changes both in form and substance. The second draft's superiority over the first draft was generally acknowledged, and the improvement was generally credited in the main to the work of Professor Planck of Göttingen.

This second draft went to the Federal Council for discussion in October, 1895. A memorial containing brief comments upon its several provisions was published by authority in 1896. On January 17 of that year the code was submitted to the Reichstag and by it referred to a committee of twenty-one members, which reported on June 12. The discussions in the body of the House occupied the month of June, and the act was passed by a large majority on July 1 Its promulgation by the Emperor on August 18, 1896, completed the constitutional requirements of enactment, and the act itself postponed the time of its taking effect to January 1, 1900.

To the greater part of Germany the new Code did not mean a transition from unwritten to written law. In many of the territories composing the Empire, as has been seen (§§ 45, 48), the common Pandect law had previously given way to codification. The official memorial already referred to which accompanied the second draft enumerated, in addition to the principal codes of Prussia, Saxony, and Baden, thirty of the more important other legal systems. Thirty-three per cent of the Germans had their law written in Latin, fourteen per cent in French. It thus appears how much the new Code meant in the way of unification.

The scope of the codification is indicated by its main divisions. These are · (1) a general part treating of national and juristic persons, different kinds of property and appurtenances, acting capacity, void and voidable acts, offer and acceptance, conditions, agency and ratification, time and limitation and prescription, (2) the law of obligations; (3) the law of property, (4) the law of family, or domestic relations, (5) the law of inheritance A separate introductory act contains in its first chapter a concise statement, in thirty-one sections, of the principles of the so-called conflict of laws, one of the few authoritative codifications of this interesting branch of the law of rapidly growing importance.

It is difficult to speak generally of the character of so comprehensive a work of legislation With regard to form, the Code may well be proclaimed a model of scientific draftsmanship. The language is clear and concise, it avoids on the one hand the prolixity of our own statutes, and on the other hand the epigrammatic brevity of the French code. An intelligent layman can, with some effort, inform himself as to elementary rights, obligations, and principles, and the Code may be truly said to have become a popular handbook.

As regards the substance of the Code, the relative share of Roman and German elements was determined by the previous development of the law, the former being predominant in the more ab-

stract parts of the system and in the law of obligations, the latter
in the law of real property and the family law.

To a certain extent the work of codification naturally became
a work of law reform, though on the whole of a conservative type,
and by a series of important provisions, both fundamental and in
special branches (notably in the law of master and servant, and of
landlord and tenant), recognition was given to the modern "social"
spirit as against the extreme individualism of the Roman private
law.[1] For example, the exercise of a right is not allowed where
the only purpose can be to inflict injury upon another, and it is
provided that whoever intentionally injures another in a manner
contrary to the common standards of right conduct shall be liable
in damages. Some other conspicuous features may serve to indicate the character of the codification: the principle of the in-
formality of contract; the doctrine of comparative fault, the
system of land transfer by registration of title, the non-action-
ability of promises to marry, the recognition of the predominant
power of the husband in the marital relation so long as the power
is not abused; the allowance of incurable insanity as a ground of
divorce (this last the most controverted provision of the entire
Code).

Perhaps the highest tribute to the quality of the work may be
found in the fact that in the first decade of its operation only one
important provision (liability for animals) has called for amendment. It is true that a considerable amount of controversial
matter was eliminated, by leaving to local law or to separate
federal statutes nearly all relations of a public or quasi-public
character. The introductory act enumerated a long list of matters
with regard to which local provisions were to remain untouched,
including perpetuities and restraints on alienation, mortmain,
religious societies, the law of mines and of waters, of fish and game,
of insurance, of author and publisher, of domestic service, nearly
all property relation between the individual and the State, and
nearly all public or semipublic property. The amount of separate
federal legislation in matters of property is likewise very large,
the Commercial Code alone covering many of the most important
transactions of business life, while the whole of the labor legislation is found in separate codes or laws.

Since the enactment of the Civil Code the work of systematic

[1] [Cf e g. P Oertmann, "Die volkswirtschaftliche Bedeutung des
bürgerlichen Gesetzbuches" (Frankfort M , 1899), which has a broader
content than its title. — TRANSL]

450

legislation has progressed in the field thus left uncovered by the provisions of the Code   The last decade has brought comprehensive statutes on the law of copyright, of author and publisher, of insurance, the law of checks, and other matters of less importance.   Even where the province of local autonomy had to be respected, the tendency toward unification has been manifest   Thus Prussia established the principle of the liability of the State for the acts and wrongs of its officials; the Empire followed by a similar enactment, and it is understood that other States have adopted like legislation.   The Civil Code by no means represents the sum total of the work of codification and unification that has been accomplished in Germany since the foundation of the Empire.

PART V

NETHERLANDS

PART V [1]

NETHERLANDS [2]

§ 1. Introductory.
§ 2   Primitive Period.
§ 3. Evolution during the Middle Ages.
§ 4   Beginning of the Renascence.
§ 5. Authority of the Roman Law.
§ 6. Influence of the Canon Law
§ 7   The 1600 s and 1700 s , Formation of the Roman-Dutch Law

§ 8. Same ; Specific Branches of Law (Criminal, Commercial, Constitutional, International).
§ 9. National Unification and Codification after 1795
§ 10 Legal Conditions in Modern Times.

§ 1. **Introductory.** — It will be hardly possible to give a comprehensive view, even a summary one, of the development of *the* law and *the* legal sources in the Netherlands, from the earliest times.   Since their first entrance on the scene of History, the characteristic of the people of the Low Countries has been to nourish individualism, particularism, separatism, — alas, even schismatism, in nearly every respect.   These have formed both its strength and its weakness

The domain of law and legal science was no exception to the rule. The early history of legal sources and literature in the Netherlands forms a story of differences and contrasts, of local growths, and of inter-local emulation.   The beginning of the 1800 s finally brought the unification of the law, — but not under national influences   The period of multifariousness belongs now to the past; but it cannot be said that its substitute, the modern codifications, have been successful in keeping the law in real touch with the

---

[1] [A chapter written for this work by Joost Adriaan van Hamel, Professor of Law in the University of Amsterdam ; for this author, see the Editorial Preface. — Ed]

[2] The author has restricted his summary chiefly to the legal history of his own country, the Northern Netherlands ; and has not dealt systematically with the Southern Netherlands, now the Belgian Kingdom However, as far as both countries passed through similar phases of legal evolution, that is, until about the second half of the 1400 s, dates of special importance regarding the Southern Netherlands have been mentioned in footnotes.

popular sense of justice   Only in later years a tendency can be
observed to meet this complaint, which may be heard nowadays,
to be sure, in all parts of the world.

So, if I should have to name a continuous clue, a line of unity,
in the earlier development of the Dutch law, it would be its infinite
variety and differentiation.   And it must not be overlooked that
the law system of the Netherlands, by this very trait of far-
reaching decentralization, which has proved the incomparable
strength of the little, has exercised strong influences in several respects
far beyond its borders   These will be alluded to in their due place.[1]

It should be borne in mind, that in reality the evolution of law
in the Netherlands has kept somewhat apart from the great central
law-forming factors in Western Europe of earlier and later times.
Neither the legislation of the Frankish kings, nor the laws and
constitutions of the medieval German empire (" Landfriedens-
ordnungen," or " Reichstagsabschiede "), nor the great French
" Coutumiers "; nor even the positive reception of the Roman
law, nor the authority of Church law,—succeeded in establishing
in the Dutch provinces a uniform and general law system.   The
spirit of their population as well as their remoteness from the
sources of central power, resulted in leaving to the Netherlands
a legal development of their own   They were, of course, not
absolutely uninfluenced by the different law sources of other
countries, but they drew upon many different origins, and maintained a state of variety which has for a very long time given to
the Dutch law an original and happily a many-sided though sometimes a little too divergent character

§ 2. **Primitive Period.** — The oldest Teutonic inhabitants of
the Netherlands did not form a separate nation. They formed
parts of the larger German tribes, — the Franks (to whom belonged the Batavians), the Saxons, and the Frisians; of which the
latter have doubtlessly formed the most distinct element of the
population of this country The inhabitants were divided into
hundreds (later, villages), of which several together formed a
" pagus " (" gouw "), the practical unit for the administration
and shaping of the law. For this earlier period, written law or
even definite customs are not known. Justice was administered
by the people in its assemblies, — generally the " gouw " assembly,
but among the Frisians by smaller village courts, — under the
presidency of popular magistrates ("magistratus," "tunginus,"
" centenaurius "); and the law that was applied consisted chiefly

---
[1] See §§ 7, 8.

in the general conceptions and traditions of justice living among the people.

Somewhat more definite institutions arose gradually, with the settlement of the Frankish confederation and the increasing power of the Merovingian kings. The presidency of the popular assemblies was assigned to royal officers (" missi dominici "), who also occupied themselves with the compilation of customary law; and the judiciary power passed more or less from the general meetings to a more restricted number of specially chosen men, — " rachimburgi," later the " scabini " (or, " schoffen ").

The first written document that gives an impression of the law of the earlier part of that period (400s) is the Salic Law, which also applied to the inhabitants of the Netherlands, and has even been said to have had its earliest origin in the southwestern part of that country (Brabant).[1] Of the later tribal laws three should be specially mentioned with relation to the territory of the Netherlands: the " Lex Saxonum " (± A.D. 750), " Lex Frisionum "[2] (±A. D. 780), and the "Ewa Chamavorum"[3] (or "Lex ad Amorem," ± A.D. 800; Amersfoort, near Utrecht (?); doubtlessly compiled by " missi dominici ")

§ 3 **Evolution during the Middle Ages** — The Netherlands being, however, a very remote part of the Frankish dominion, the influence of the central administration of the Carolingians could not be a lasting one   It has even been doubted — though wrongly — whether their capitularies had had real force and effect in this country[4] But small was the success of the effort to modernize and remodel the original legal and judiciary institutions   Even the typical jurisdiction of the Franks by courts of aldermen (" schepenbanken," " scabini ") was not until much later (1200s–1500s) generally accepted in the Dutch provinces; and for a long time the general assemblies (" burengerechten "), in which every member of the population could take part,[5] remained

---

[1] *Van der Spieghel*, "Oorsprong en historie der vaderlandsche rechten" (1769), p 52, and lately Professor *Fockema Andreae*, "Nederlandsche Rechtsgeschiedenis" (1901), IV, p 10.   *Brunner* and *Brissaud* are of a different opinion
[2] Ed by *V Richthofen*, "Friesische Rechtsquellen," XXIX.
[3] Ed "Monumenta germanica" (*Sohm*), "Leges," V, p. 103. *Cf. Froideveaux*, "La Lex dicta Francorum Chamavorum," 1891
[4] *Trotz*, "Leges fundamentales," p 8; *Van de Spiegel*, "Oorsprong en historie," p 64 This doubt has not been felt with regard to the Southern provinces
[5] Though sometimes, as in Friesland and Kennemerland, with the assistance of specially designated "proposers of the law" ("asings," "sapientes"). The law created by those "asing-courts" for a long time kept a distinct

in existence in several parts of the country, with all the drawbacks of such an unorganized and anarchistic form of mob jurisdiction [1]

Gradually, the provincial officers ("judices," "comites"), sent by the central government, succeeded in rendering their position independent of their principals; whilst on the other hand, the popular bodies since the 1200s, the representative Provincial Estates as well as the local assemblies, kept their full share of influence After the rise of the government of these provincial rulers, — counts (Holland, Zeeland, Flanders), dukes (Gelderland), bishops (Utrecht, Overyssel, Groningen, Drenthe), and civic communities (Friesland), — important changes were effected (1100s-1500s). It was in this period that the struggle started for an administration by strong personal rulers, assisted by a staff of professional officers, including the judiciary, — instead of the traditional form of separate local communities under self-government Here the name may be recalled of a Dutch author (a precursor of Bodin and Macchiavelli), whose treatise on this subject of constitutional law has been regarded as an influential vindication of strong princely powers PHILIP OF LEYDEN ("Tractatus de rei publicae et sorte principantis," 1355-1375).[2] His chief object is to attack the feudal thesis that governmental functions should be looked upon as inalienable personal or local rights, and to proclaim that all authority is established for the public benefit only. The same tendency is found in an anonymous pamphlet, edited in Flanders (1358): "Consultatio num princeps privilegia civitatibus in perpetua concessa revocare possit."

By two institutions the provincial rulers attempted to strengthen their central power, the authority of central government and central law, against rural particularism and feudal magnates. Both have had a large influence on the evolution of the law · Towns, municipalities, were created, with separate legal and judicial institutions, and secondly, privy councils ("Vorstelyke Raden ") acting also as high courts of justice ("Gerechtshoven "), were instituted in nearly every province. The powerful Burgundian dukes even

character in matter of inheritance ; " Aasdomslaw," as distinguished from "Schependomslaw" (on this subject, *Rollin-Conquerque*, Haag, 1898).
[1] A separate history of the development of the forms of jurisdiction in the Netherlands is given by Professor *S J. Fockema-Andreae* (Leiden,) "Bijdragen tot de Nederlandsche Rechtsgeschiedenis," IV (1900). Also for Belgium see *Raepsaet*, "Histoire des institutions"; *Jonas Daniel Meyer*, "Institutions judiciaires" , *Warnkoenig*, "Flandrische Staats- und Rechtsgeschichte."
[2] Ed by *R. Fruin*, and reviewed in his "Verspreide geschriften," I, p. 110.

established a central Supreme Court at Malines (1446), in imitation of the French "Grand Conseil du Roi." Both these expedients were destined to have a result the opposite of that intended. The towns managed to become famous as the cradles of a municipal autonomy, and even sovereignty. And the courts ended by growing into independent bodies, desirous on their part to protect local privileges and immunities.

The law in this period remained still mostly common law, as it had been developed by the local traditions and the precedents of the local courts In many statutes regulating judicial procedure, the courts are recommended to decide " according to their common sense"; " to their five senses "; " to their sound reason "; and the like. Yet it is to be taken for granted, that the ancient Frankish law-compilations have been of no small influence on the character of the customary as well as the Statutory law of this period.

The range of the customary law remained chiefly restricted to the local districts ("baljuwschappen "), of which each province was composed. In Holland, *e.g.*, were important the customs of Kennemerland; of Rynland (collected 1570 [1]) and of South Holland (collected 1571) In Friesland, the several districts ("gouwen," "deelen ") had their own customary law; and this was also the case in other provinces.[2]

A sort of legislative function was gradually exercised by those rural districts, in collecting, confirming, and reducing to writing parts of their customary law; and in completing their law by means of ordinances and local statutes (" Keuren "). At first this legislation emanated from the provincial rulers, in the form of charters of privileges (" Handvesten "), granted to the inhabitants. But later we find that, by authorization of those privileges, the legislative and law-forming power is exercised by the local courts themselves.

A similar process of lawmaking took place in the towns. Here the common law was destined to take a more secondary character; and gradually each town or township shaped its separate law system in a series of statutes (" Keuren "), — some of which, as we shall see, became valuable sources for the evolution of special legal subjects.[3] The right to make " Keuren " was conceded to

[1] Ed. *Fruin,* 1877.
[2] For Belgium, see "Coutumes de Brabant," ed. 1874; "Hainaut," ed 1883, "Flandres," ed 1874.
[3] The oldest "Stadtrecht" (municipal law) known is of Valenciennes Hainault (1114).

the cities also by charter; but (especially in earlier times), was subject to the control of provincial ruler; he retained the right to cancel the " Keur " or to replace its rules by a general statute. The law and jurisdiction of certain more important towns were often taken as models for smaller ones, so, *e g* , the courts of Naarden, Muiden, Weesp, even Gouda, were told by charter to "fetch their law " from Leyden, in case of doubt, the smaller places of North Holland, from Haarlem; of West Friesland from Medemblik However, a positive "law of mother cities," such as existed in Germany, and for Ghent in Belgium,[1] cannot be traced

No special mention is needed of feudal territories and dependencies which, still in the 1600s and 1700s, exercised legislative powers of their own [2]

Such was the evolution of the medieval law sources.[3]

[1] Ghent, Bruges, and Ypern had a law in common (1372)

[2] Compare the "Dienstrechte" of Flandres (*Warnkoenig's* "Rechtsgeschichte," III, 2)

[3] A systematical list of the sources of medieval Netherland law will be found in *Dr Fockema-Andreae's* "Oud-Nederlandsche Rechtsbronnen". (Haarlem, 1881)

Texts have been and are being edited (Laws of Brielle, Zutphen, Leiden, Amsterdam, Harderwijk, Friesland a o) by the *Society for the edition of sources of ancient national law* (Vereeniging tot uitgaaf der bronnen van het Oude Vaderlandsche Recht) The best older separate edition of a complete local legal system has been given by *P. H. van de Wall*, "Handvesten van Dordrecht" (1770–1790).

For *Belgium*, very important and complete, the official "Recueil des Anciennes Coutumes de la Belgique," still in course of publication (1869 +). A list of the oldest "Keuren" in Belgium will be found in *Brissaud's* "Histoire du droit Français," p 255.

An interesting general survey, though no longer quite up to date, of the ancient legal institutions in the Netherlands (legal forms and formalities, nobility, freemen and serf, marriage, parental authority, law of succession, of property, of contract, criminal law, procedure) is to be found in *Noordewier*, "Ancient Dutch Legal Institutions" (Utrecht. 1853). A selective synopsis of some principal subjects has been composed by *Dr Fockema-Andreae*, "Nederlandsche Rechtsgeschiedenis," I–III, 1888 (majority, emancipation; marriage, serfdom), more complete in his "Ancient Dutch Civil Law" (1906).

It should, however, be borne in mind, that the official law and statutebooks can but give a very incomplete idea of the law as it really functioned For that purpose a study should be made of private legal documents, contracts, wills, charters, comptes, etc , as contained in the archives; of court rolls and different state papers.

Already in the 1700s efforts had been made to reprint all authentic legal documents from the earlier period, in so-called "Charterbooks " They are, however, not complete Of this category should be mentioned the "Great Charterbook of the Counts of Holland and Zeeland" (up to 1430) by *Frans von Mieris* (1753–1756), not very complete A revised and more correct edition was given as "Oorkondenboek van Holland en Zeeland " (up to 1299) by *L Ph C van den Berg* (1868–1873) (Supplement, 1901) See also "Charterbook of the Guelderland and Zutphen " (up to 1286), by *Petrus Bondam* (1783–1809)

§ 4. **Beginning of the Renascence.** — The general tendency to
political centralization, as well as the example of the Justinian
law codes, and the want of a more comprehensive law system, led
at the end of the Middle Ages to a movement for the compilation
of the existing law sources, and the framing of what might be called
in reality a *general common law.*

The first traces of this tendency were private and local. The
larger law-books of the German dominions, *e.g.* the "Sachsenspiegel," were not directly in force in the Netherlands.[1]   The laws
of some of the Southern provinces, especially those of Hainault,
had been digested in JEAN BOUTILLIER's "Somme rural" (1390,
Tournay), being a kind of encyclopædia of law, where Roman and
Canon law were mingled with local and customary laws of the
North of France and the Southern Netherlands   A similar
enterprise was undertaken, for the law of his city, Brielle, by the
town clerk JAN MATTHIJSEN, whose "Rechtsboek van den Briel"
(Lawbook of Brielle),[2] gives a very important and complete speci-
men of medieval law in the Netherlands.   His work is regarded
as the richest and purest source of ancient Dutch law, at a moment
when it was still free from foreign elements and had reached a very
high standard of development.   Again, about a hundred years
later, a Belgian, PHILIP WIELAND of Gent (died 1520) composed
a treatise on Feudal law, which, after having been examined "in
turba" by the "coustumiers," became the authority on Feudal
law in the Southern Netherlands.   Wieland also published "Civil
Praxis," expounding the procedure of the "Grand Conseil" of
Malines, and of the local courts of Flanders.[3]   WINHOFF's law-
book[4] was also one of private authority only.

The more important official efforts to establish a more general
and common law dated from the beginning of the 1500s.   To the
Dutch provinces this period was to be a critical moment, when
their moulding into one State, with a strong central administration,
seemed probable.   The Burgundian as well as the Habsburg princes
took a great interest in their rich provinces in the Low Countries along the sea, and aimed at uniting their inhabitants into one
powerful nation.   This policy might have succeeded.   Charles V,

---

[1] The influence of the "Sachsenspiegel" transpired principally in
Friesland, where several translations were in use (*Lintelo de Geer*, "De
Sachsenspiegel in Nederland")   An abbreviated translation was printed
at Antwerp in 1500   "de Spiegel der Sassen van alle Kaiserlycke Rechten"
[2] Ed by *Fruin* and *Pols* (Vol. I of the publications of the Society for
Ancient National Law).
[3] Ed by *Bonvalot*, 1870. See p 371
[4] See *infra.*

indeed, had almost attained that aim, but the Reformation and Philip II's reaction against it broke the spell, and again revived the forces of local independence and resistance The result was that the Dutch people, in forming their federative republic of the United Provinces, provided no effective central power, and left it to be maintained by the virtual sovereignty of the larger towns, among which Amsterdam gradually ranked as first. This mode of government proved unfit to produce a more uniform system of law.

Nevertheless, efforts in that direction were not wholly lacking. In some of the provinces, special subjects had already at an earlier date been taken up by provincial regulation ("landrechten"). The earlier ones relate mostly to judicial institutions only, and do not go into the substantive law But the great movement for unification and compilation of the customary law, undertaken by the kings of France for that country up to Henry III, found imitation by the government of Charles V[1] In the years 1540 and 1569, the governor-general of Charles V at Brussels ordered the provincial courts of justice to make a collection of the customary law of their provinces, districts, and municipalities Some of them responded to the call, and the results are very interesting; with all their diversity, a certain unity of character, accentuated by traces of Frankish law, is unmistakable In Friesland, where the ancient "Lex Frisionum" had not yet fallen into oblivion, the greater part of the provincial law was put into one book in 1542; in Drenthe in the same period; Zeeland had its principal collection of "landrecht" (with exception of the municipal law) from 1496; even Holland, where the spirit of decentralization has always been the strongest, and where, as in Utrecht, no comprehensive "landrecht" had been formulated, could show some general "ordonnances" ("placaeten") on the subject of land law (landlease, 1452, sale of land, 1529). The most complete law book was composed in Overijssel, "Het Landrecht van Overissel," by MELCHIOR WINHOFF (1559) This is not an official legal source, the composer being a private annotator of the existing laws His book is, however, very valuable for the study of the legal system of that time.[2] It contains public as well as criminal law, procedure, and chapters on civil law (property, wills).

---

[1] *Grandgagnage*, "De l'influence de la législation française sur celle des Pays-Bas pendant le 16me et 17me siècle," Brussels, 1831.
[2] A second edition with commentaries was published in 1782, by *J. A. de Chalmot.*

The proclamation of the independent United Provinces in 1579, by which the sovereignty now fell to the Provincial Estates, led to renewed efforts of provincial and interprovincial codification. At first, some results were obtained, particularly on the subject of matrimonial law, rendered necessary by the rejection of the Roman Catholic institutions. About 1580 most provinces adopted "Ordonnances" on matrimonial law,[1] in accordance with the principles of the Protestant creed. Starts were made in other subjects also. They lasted not without some success (land law, law of succession) during the 1600s and 1700s[2] Friesland had its important compilation. "Statuten, ordonnantien en costumen of 1602" (law of persons, law of sale, real rights, prescription, law of succession, servant and master, maritime law), revised in 1723, in other privinces the codification of the rules of procedure took the foreground. Besides, in the course of time many special subjects were regulated by provincial statutes (called "Placcates"), which have been collected into "Placcate-books" by private undertaking.[3] For the rest, the municipal legislations remained in force. A systematic complex of legislation was obtained nowhere, and at the end of the 1700s the state of legislation in the Netherlands was generally felt to be very capricious and inconsistent; some critics even used the term "absurd,"[4] and it is stated that even at the end of the 1700s the question had to be formally put in court "whether a case of murder should be decided according to the Roman Law, the Mosaic Law, the 'Constitutio Carolina,' or an old statute of 1342."

The difficulties were still more increased by the uncertainty about the validity of some of the principal legal sources This was especially the case with the criminal law, of which two important statutes must be mentioned here. Whether the criminal ordinance ("Carolina") of Charles V (1532) had gone into force in the territory of his Netherland provinces was still disputed. Al-

---

[1] In Holland by the "Politieke ordonnantie" of 1 April, 1580, repeatedly modified and moderated In Gelderland "Echtordening" of 1597.

[2] An interesting historical survey of the incessant demand for more unity in the law of that time has been given by the famous statesman, *Thorbecke*, "Geschiedenis der provinciaal-burgerlijke wetgeving in de republiek der Vereenigde Nederlanden" (1838, "Historische Schetsen," p 38)

[3] "Great Placcaet-boek" of Holland and Zeeland, 1658–1796, Utrecht (for provincial and municipal law) by *Van de Water*, 1729–1810, Gelderland, 1701–1794; Flandres, 1639–1786, Brabant, 1648–1737

[4] Mr. *Willem Schorer* (president of the Court of Dutch-Flanders), "Over de ongerijmdheid van het Samenstel onzer hedendaagsche Rechtsgeleerdheid," 1777.

though the negative may now be accepted as correct, several courts actually accepted the authority of this imperial law.

In 1570 Philip tried to introduce two meritorious ordinances on criminal justice and criminal procedure By these his governor, Alva, aimed to put an end to the many defects of criminal procedure of that time. The best jurisconsults were charged with the drafting, and far from introducing revolutionary novelties, they followed orthodox authorities Damhouder and Winhoff. After their publication, however, the ordinances were at once (of course !) asserted to be in defiance of local privileges and customs, and as a consequence of Philip's abdication, their authority was disclaimed But in many cases this did not prevent the judiciary from following their provisions.[1] In Belgium they remained in force until the end of the 1700s.

Naturally, this uncertainty and lack of uniformity caused other, more general, legal sources to become influential, in particular, the classic Roman Law, and the Civilian Jurists To those two sources we now come

§ 5 **Authority of the Roman Law.** — The authority of the Roman Law has not been equally strong in every province Traces of the application of Roman law are said to be found even from 1227 A positive " reception," however, as in Germany, cannot be said to have taken place in any jurisdiction. It may be stated, that in some of the older ordinances the courts were instructed to decide " according to the imperial (or written) laws, and their customs", so in Holland, by a letter of confirmation of Charles the Bold (Burgundian House) to his Council, 1462, in Friesland by the acknowledgment of Albrecht van Saksen, 1497, and of Charles V (1524), as well as in the law-book of 1602. Yet, even if it should not be doubted (at least for the earlier years), that these terms alluded to the Justinian Law,[2] a formal and practical reception cannot be said to have taken place. The decentralized state of the judicature did not allow that process. Numerous writers have accepted this view.[3]

---

[1] The "ordonnances" have been edited and annotated by *Bavius Voorda*, 1792, *Nypels*, "Les ordonnances criminelles de Philippe II "
[2] It is doubted by Mr *Fockema Andreae*, "Nederlandsche Rechtsbronnen," IV, pp 87, 437, and annot on Grotius's Introduction, p 7
[3] *P Voet*, "De usu juris civilis et canonici in Belgio Unito " (1657), *G. de Vries Azn* , "Historia introducti in provincias quas deinceps respublica Belgii unita comprehendit Juris Romani " (Leiden, 1839), *W Modderman*, "De receptie van het Romeinsche Recht," 1874, Mémoire sur ce sujet couronné par l'académie de Bruxelles, 1782; *Warnkoenig*, "Encycl ," 255

On the other hand, it cannot be denied that just because of this decentralized state of jurisdiction and legislation, the Roman law did become an important *subsidiary* law source Firstly, even the Frankish law, that had doubtlessly influenced the various customary laws of the country, had been itself in contact with the Roman law, by the " Breviarium Aniani." In the 1000s–1200s young Dutchmen visited the Italian law schools, and thence introduced the notions of Roman law into their country It became a matter of practical learning among the town clerks, as well as among the jurists who formed the councils of the provincial rulers, and later among the members of the provincial Courts of Justice.[1] The latter, in the 1600s and 1700s, were the principal promoters of the Roman legal system. The legal faculties of the Universities concentrated their activity on the study of Roman law, and consequently the academic lawyers (who monopolized more and more the places in the higher courts) were inclined to give it a large share in their practice. But as these courts were not general courts of appeal, they could not infiltrate this Roman law into the judicial law of the local jurisdictions It may be even said that during those periods two currents of practical law have been in continuous competition· the one accusing the legists (or Romanists) of neglecting the national laws and of worshipping the formal Roman system, and the other, indulging in Romanism even to an immoderate extent.[2] This process gave birth to the well-known Roman-Dutch Law, which will be described later on.

As a rule, it can be said that Roman law never acquired more than subsidiary authority; not in Holland (as was expressly stated in the "Placcate" of the States of Holland, 25 May, 1735), not in Groningen, not in Utrecht, not in Drenthe, not in Gelderland, and certainly not in Overyssel, where no provincial court had come into existence. As for legal practice, it certainly seems very often to have been easier for bench and bar to quote Roman law formulas, than to trace the principles of native law. But even from the use of Latin expressions it should not too readily be deduced that Roman law is also materially the basis of the decision.

Its exact status may perhaps be best understood from a passage

---

[1] Yet the local law remained for a long time free from Roman influences. In *Mathijsen's* "Law-book of Brielle" (*ante*, § 4), though it mentions some principles of the Roman law, we do not find that they have influenced the native laws.

[2] This was especially the case with *Simon van Leeuwen* in his "Roman-Dutch Law", and a little less with *Groenewegen*. More moderate were *De Groot, Bijnkershoek, Van der Linden, Van der Keesel*

of Grotius (Introduction, I, 2, § 22) · " If on any subject no written law, statute, ordinance, or custom was in existence, the judges have been from of old bound by oath to follow the best reasons in accordance with their knowledge and discretion. But as wise men have found the Roman laws, especially those that were collected in the time of Justinian, to be full of wisdom and justice, the same have been adopted at first as instances of wisdom and justice, afterwards as customary law "

The greatest influence of Roman law was exercised in Friesland, where the strong position of the provincial court was favorable for its adoption   In that province the Roman law has sometimes been regarded as the " common " law, to which exception could be made only by special charter.[1]

The form in which the Roman law was originally used differed largely from its pure and original Justinian character. It was the Roman law, as fashioned by the Glossators, the Post-Glossators, and the Commentators, sometimes we even find haphazard quotations of Italian, Spanish, or Portuguese writers. It was, however, the merit of the jurists of the 1600 s to purify the traditions of the Roman law [2]

§ 6   Influence of the Canon Law — The above-quoted passage of Grotius continues by saying that in the same way " the Church or Canon law was in force in the Netherlands " In its general sense this statement is incorrect. But in several directions the Canon law did have powerful effects. In the medieval period the strong and skilful organization of the Roman Catholic Church, with its learned clerks, gave to this body a large influence also in the domain of legal practice. It is even reported that, for fear of incompetency of the local courts, many litigants in Holland and Zeeland went to the clerical " provisores " for their law.[3] Those acted as well in civil cases (matrimony, tithes) as in special criminal affairs (religious offenses, but also moral offenses — drunkenness, disorderly conduct, vagrancy, rape); and they showed a strong inclination to extend their jurisdiction at the cost of the worldly powers   The provincial rulers succeeded gradually in restraining this tendency, by strong decrees against clerical usurpation;[4] but it cannot be denied that in this period the clergy

[1] *Huber,* "Hedendaagsche Rechtsgeleerdheid," I, 2, p. 47; *Van den Sande,* "Dec Fris.," II, 2, def 2.
[2] See *post,* § 7
[3] *Philippus of Leyden,* p 237 , *Van Mieris,* "Charterbook," II, p 748
[4] The history of this phase of Church law is given in *Trotz,* "Commentarius Legum Fund Fœd Belg ," p. 41.

and the Church law had a large influence in several directions on the development of the law. The well-known treatise on the Canon law of procedure, so greatly influential in several European countries, the "Summula de Processu Judicii" of JOHN ANDREAE, has also been traced to Dutch, especially Frisian, sources.[1]

With the Reformation, the direct influence of Church law came to an end. On certain subjects, such as marriage, the canon rules were taken by the secular powers. Furthermore, the general traditional authority of the Canon law in some matters continued, and was still to be noted in the end of the 1700s.[2] The High Court of Justice in Holland accepted some principles of Canon law on the right of inheritance of bastards, and the right of patronage And of course the rules of Canon law that have been included in the reception of the Roman law were applied with this law, e.g., separation from bed and board, and "sponsalia."

The law of the Reformed Church never covered a wider range than the internal organization of that church.

§ 7. **The 1600s and 1700s; Formation of the Roman-Dutch Law.** — It will be easily understood that for a country in a state of very strong and rapid economical and intellectual evolution, with a dense and multiform population, and a freedom newly purchased by heroic efforts, — a country, in short, such as the Netherlands were in the 1600s, it was inevitable that legal science should rise beyond the mere traditions and rules of local custom and ordinance, or alien enactments The Netherlands had become at this period a rallying-point for international interests, international relations, and international currents of thought. Maritime commerce, colonization, European finance, and free scientific and philosophical research fostered the development of large conceptions and modern ideas The Universities attracted foreign scholars; the political methods interested foreign statesmen, and the commercial interests involved many foreign peoples All this must have led to a school of legal learning, which at the same time would be heartily welcomed by the national demand for a body of law both more individual and more uniform. And so the Dutch school of jurists in the 1600s and 1700s gained a remarkable authority, not only in the legal practice of their own country, but in the development of juristic thought in the civilized world

It also fell to them (and here again the economical and moral

---

[1] Sectievergadering, *Utrechtsch Genootschap*, 1857.
[2] *Van der Keesel*, "Thes" XXV

position of the Netherlands of that period comes in) to proclaim the principles of Natural Law, — natural justice, natural rights, and legal liberty, freedom of thought, freedom of commerce, freedom of settlement And this system was to be based, not on the force of positive statute law (the legal system of the country would contradict that), but on the natural light of reason and learning [1] The Dutch legal scientists of that period were the leaders of the school of Natural Law which was to become so important.

Their most famous representative was HUGO GROTIUS Inasmuch as his general importance for the development of Natural Law is treated in another chapter of this work, no account is here needed of his " Law of War and Peace " (1625), or of his general activity in that field. His work for the elucidation and propagation of the Dutch law was concentrated in his " Introduction to Dutch Legal Science," [2] written while a political prisoner in the castle of Loevesteyne It is the special attraction of this book that it offered (and was so intended, as the preface lets us understand) a synopsis of a general legal system, governed by common juristic principles, and built up from a combination of Roman law and the Germanic customary and local laws.

It has not always been well understood, but we may now speak positively, that the success of the so-called Roman-Dutch law was due to the combination of those two elements. Such a combination was going to have its influence in other countries (Pothier in France), and the Roman-Dutch law was to become a model for the legal system of newly colonized countries (especially South Africa) [3] It was also the tendency of Grotius,[4] and of some of his followers, not to let their system be absolutely dominated by an abstract theory of law, but to keep in touch with the realistic growth of social institutions; for Grotius was not only a philosopher and a lawyer, but an his-

[1] The point has been made by *Warnkoenig* ("Juristische Encyclopaedie." p 318), and in his footsteps by *Brissaud* ("Manuel d'histoire du droit français," p 358), that the Dutch school of jurisconsults of the 1600 s should be considered as a continuation of the French school of Humanists I will not deny that there existed an affinity between the Humanists of the various countries of that time, but I feel sure that the school of Humanists, Philologists, and Jurisconsults that arose in the Netherlands of the 1500 s and 1600 s had its own roots in native soil

[2] "Inleiding tot de Hollandsche Rechtsgeleerdheid "

[3] See *Burge's* "Commentaries on Colonial and Foreign Laws" (New ed , London, 1911, Vol III), where the modern Roman-Dutch law has been expounded with the cooperation of Drs. Fockema-Andreae, Heeres, and Roosegaarde Bischop.

[4] In Dutch, his name is De Groot (pronounced as in "vote").

torian and an active politician at the same time In several instances we find traces of this, *e.g* the law of husband and wife, parents and children, special contracts, real estate [1]

Of other influential law-books, more particularly destined for practice in court, these may be mentioned· SIMON VAN LEEUWEN, a lawyer, wrote his "Roomsch-Hollandsch Recht" (Roman-Dutch Law, 1664), which seasoned that law for the daily court practice, and paid a good deal of attention (more than Grotius had done) to the law of procedure. Van Leeuwen's book, which gained a great practical authority, is preponderantly influenced by Justinian law, and has to a certain degree diverted attention from the traditional Germanic elements, which had been recognized by Grotius. Another book, very lucidly written but somewhat later in date, giving a practical survey of the law in the Netherlands, is the "Rechtsgeleerd Practicaal en Koopmans Handboek·" (Practical and Commercial Law Book), by JOHANNES VAN DER LINDEN (1800) It was composed at a period when the codification movement had already begun, but as it was originally intended to be a revised edition of a book of 1761, and as the writer looks continually back to the traditional law, it forms an excellent source for the knowledge of the later Dutch legal system.[2]

The great influence exercised in that period by the juristic

[1] Grotius' treatise has several times been annotated and enlarged , these works form valuable contributions to the more detailed knowledge of special chapters of the Roman-Dutch law , they are . 1 "Annotations to the Introduction of Hugo de Groot xɪʏ" by *S van Groeneweqen* (1644), who was especially well informed about the practice of the High Court in the Netherlands, 2 "Observations and Questions to elucidate the Introduction of Hugo de Groot," by a group of lawyers (1776) , 3 "Commentaries," by *W Schorer* (1767) , 4 "Selected Theses (in Latin) to be added to the Introduction of Hugo de Groot" (1800), by *Van der Keesel*, this book is of a special importance, as it is very extensive on the chapters of commercial law, in which the Netherlands law has had a large international influence.

[2] Some writers on more special or practical subjects may be mentioned here   An interesting source for the knowledge of the law of procedure in the Netherlands is the Collection of Legal Forms, "The Papagay," by *Van Alphen   Pieter Bort* (died 1680), one of the best known counsellors of his time, published six treatises, that are in our times of great value, as sources for the older laws (on fiefs, testaments, criminal cases, feudal rights, "complaincte" and "arrests")   *Van Zurk*, "Codex Batavus," gives an alphabetic summary of laws, regulations placeates, and resolutions, in force in Holland and Zeeland in 1742

The more important jurisconsults in the Southern Netherlands (now Belgium), forming at that time a province of Austria, though mainly ruled in accordance with their own ancient institutions, may here be noted · *Anselmo d'Anvers*, "Codex belgicus," 1649; *Zypaeus*, "Notitia juris belgici," 1635 (the first dogmatical essay on Belgian law) , *Ch de Méan*, "Observationes," 1652 , *Deghewiet*, "Institutions du droit belge," 1736. *Cf. Britz*, "Code de l'ancien droit belge."

thought of the Netherlands was also due to the international form and popularity of its Universities. Law professors at the Universities of Leyden, Utrecht, Franeker, and the Athenæum Illustre of Amsterdam, Huber, Voet, Noodt, Schulting, attracted their disciples from various countries, and so spread their principles in various directions. As the characteristic feature of their methods of teaching, it may be said that the domain of the Roman law was given in a more encyclopædic place.[1] The study of law was brought into contact with the study of history and of general philosophy. As a consequence of the increasingly exact knowledge of Latin philology and the history of the ancient world, the Roman law was no longer considered as an abstract legal complex, but as a product of a form of human society, to be analyzed as such, and subject to evolution The lectures of Noodt (professor at Franeker, Utrecht, Leyden, died 1725) were famous for what was called his new " methodus Noodti " of legal teaching. It may be that the school of Cujas had already initiated those conceptions; but still I am led to think that they were especially developed by the Dutch law professors. To mark the contrast of their methods with those of the German universities, the Dutch were often called the " jurisconsulti elegantiores." It was the spirit of Grotius' " Introduction " that prevailed in the legal teaching of these academic coryphei, although it is not to be denied that the minor gods, even clever spirits like ANTONIUS SCHULTING (professor at Hardwijk, Franeker, Leyden, died 1734), adhered, more one-sidedly, to the traditional Roman law.

Perhaps the finest instance of the method just described is afforded by JOHANNES VOET's (died 1719) " Commentarius ad Pandectas " (Leyden, 1698), in which a nice analysis of the texts is combined with a strong feeling for the wants of modern life. Voet is remarkable for his tendency to unite the older trend of legal study with the modern one, for example, he insisted on adding to his title of " Professor of law " the words " and of the practice of law." A similar part was taken by GERARD NOODT (died 1725), whose innovating and broad-minded spirit gave him the name of the Cujas of the Netherlands (" Opera Omnia," 1724). He was afterwards taken as a model of legal science, by that most original figure, poet, philosopher, historian, and lawyer, WILLEM BILDERDIJK (died 1831, " Emendationes et Interpretationes," 1806). The third most

---

[1] "Encyclopædia," in the sense now used for Continental law teaching, especially in Germany, signifies a general introduction to the study of law in all its aspects.

remarkable figure in ULRICUS HUBER (professor at Franeker,
Utrecht, Leyden, died 1694), a man of an extraordinarily many-
sided culture, who regularly had among his hearers German,
English, and Scotch students. Like Grotius, he also took a great
interest in public and political law, and has had a great influence
on the study of these matters (" De jure civitatis libri tres," and
" Hedendagsche Rechtsgeleerdheid " [Modern Legal Science])

§ 8. **The Same: Specific Branches of Law (Criminal, Commercial, Constitutional, International).** — The works of the jurists
just mentioned deal for the most part with Civil Law, and to a
certain extent with Public Law. Separate mention should be made
of some other specific departments of the law.

(1) The *Criminal Law* had an evolution of its own. It is well
known that the influence of the Roman law has been smallest in this
part of the legal system [1] Hence criminal law had to be completed,
apart from the special statute law and customs, by the use of
general authorities. We find chapters devoted to criminal law
in the treatises of Grotius, Van Leeuwen, Voet, Van der Linden,[2]
and others, but they do not show the originality observable in the
parts on civil law. The criminal law of the 1600s and 1700s was
a great deal influenced by both the older and newer Italian writers
(Bartolus, Baldus, Gaudinus, Farinacius, Clarus, Gomez, Menochius), and later by the German Carpzovius, of whom a Dutch
summary was made by PIETER BORT in his " Treatise on Criminal
Causes," and a complete translation by DIRK VAN HOGENDORP
(1751).

Yet a few original Dutch writers in this special field have
acquired general authority in Europe. JODOCUS DAMHOUDER'S (of
Bruges, 1507–1581) " Praxis rerum criminalium " (1555)[3] was
edited in Latin, Dutch, and French. In the 1500s to 1700s it was
often quoted even in the courts of other countries.

A strong scientific influence, far beyond the borders of his own
country, was exercised by the treatise " De criminibus " (1644)
of the Harderwijk professor ANTONIUS MATTHAEUS (1601–1654).
It was his intention to purify the Roman criminal law from German
and canon additions, and although by this process he did not
particularly contribute to the evolution of his subject, it is difficult

---

[1] On the unsuccessful effort to introduce general criminal ordinances see
ante, § 4.
[2] Who published special treatises on criminal procedure.
[3] Damhouder seems to have committed plagiarisms from *Philip
Wielant* of Gent (*ante,* § 4), whose Criminal Practice is more original (as has
been pointed out by *Aug. Orts,* Gent, 1872).

to overrate his work as a systematic authority on the criminal law of that time [1] Yet on the whole it cannot be said that the Dutch legal school exercised a leading influence in the domain of criminal law, as it did in that of civil and international law

But a very interesting literature was produced in the Netherlands on the *reform of criminal law,* of criminal procedure, and of penal institutions. On this subject the Netherlands again played a leading part, which it may be interesting to note. Already in the beginning of the 1600s, by local legislation (*e g* in Amsterdam), moderations and mitigations of penal methods were introduced, *e.g.* in the workhouses and penitentiaries,[2] which suggested to William Penn his ideas on penal institutions, and also influenced John Howard. Again, it was in the Netherlands that the reaction, first against the trials for witchcraft, later against the torture of accused persons, found strong and numerous adherents from the very beginning.[3] In the general reform movement at the end of the 1700s the Dutch took a large share.[4]

(2) *Commercial Law* — Turning to the development of commercial law in the Netherlands, it will be understood that the important commercial cities of that country very early felt the necessity for the legal regulation of some special subjects.* Neither the customary law, nor the Roman law, nor the imported law of the Italian towns, could suffice for this rapidly increasing branch of activity. Even the Middle Ages asked for more up-to-date legislation Commercial law, of course, had started as local law, mostly recorded in statutes, and kept this character until the beginning of the 1800s For the law of *companies,* of *bills of exchange,* and of *insurance,* as well as of *maritime commerce* and of *bankruptcy,* we find many local statutes, especially of Amsterdam, Dordrecht, and Rotterdam. There were also, for maritime law, a series of provincial ordinances We further find that in those matters the courts sometimes had recourse to the " turba " or judicial inquiries

---

[1] A fervent and very interesting argument in favor of fair criminal trials is found in *Grotius'* "Apology of the Dutch Government," in which he analyzes his own case of political persecution

[2] *Von Hippel,* "Beitr zur Geschichte der Freiheitstrafe," Zeitschr. f. d. ges. Strafrechtswissenschaft, XVIII, 419, *Rosenfeld,* ibid , XXX.

[3] *Johannes Wier* (Arnheim), "De præstigiis dæmonum" (1563), *Grevius,* "Tribunal reformatum fugata tortura" (1624), *Jonctys,* "Tooverziekte en pijnbank weersproken" (Witchcraft and torture opposed) (1651), *J van Heemskerk,* "Arcadia Batava" (1637) *Pieter Bort* in his treatise also complained of the abuses of torture A history of criminal institutions and procedure will be found in *De Bosch Kemper,* "Het Wetboek van Strafvordering" (Amsterdam, 1838)

[4] *Van Hamel,* "Inleiding tot het Nederlandsche Strafrecht," p. 74.

among a number of notable merchants, as to the state of the law on a certain point.

And finally the decisions of the courts, as well as some of the authoritative writers already referred to, were regarded as legal sources   The importance of this complex of sources is considerable. It cannot be doubted that (with the Customs of Antwerp) the commercial law of the Netherlands influenced the " Ordonnances du Commerce et de la Marine " of Louis XIV, and in this indirect way (as well as directly) the French " Code de Commerce " [1]

(3) *Constitutional Law.* — The constitutional law and political institutions of the Republic of the Seven United Provinces in the 1600s and 1700s were in that period a matter of frequent study by native as well as by foreign scholars.   Doubtless the federative republican form of government grew out of the Union of Utrecht (1579), and became more and more definite, not so much by deliberate purpose as by the natural course of events.   This remarkable political structure has had two aspects.   On the one hand, it has given the fullest opportunity for the development of local interests and energies, of individual enterprise, and of civic devotion.   Especially in the earlier times, when the spirit of government was still more democratic and progressive, these advantages made the country great   On the other hand, the absence of a real central power, and even of a genuine feeling for common interests, resulted in a slow and inefficient mode of dealing with matters of national welfare; and these defects increased, as the ruling class became more and more oligarchic and self-satisfied.   As official sources of the constitutional law we must regard· (1) the Treaty of the Union of Utrecht (1579), by which the Confederation of the Seven Provinces was settled, although without the design of giving it the permanent character it has acquired in the course of time; (2) " placcates " and ordinances of the General and Provincial Estates; (3) instructions for government bodies and officials, (4) ancient privileges and statutes (among which the " Great Privilege," 1477, intended to be a " magna charta "), (5) the custom and practice of the constitution.

Numerous have been the descriptions and commentaries of the constitutional law of the United Provinces, eulogistic as well as critical.   These should be of special interest to Americans, for it

---

[1] It would be impossible to give complete details of the different sources of local commercial law ; some indications only may be found in *De Wal,* "Dutch Commercial Law," II, 11 ; *Goudsmit,* "History of the Sources of Dutch Maritime Law," 1882.

is generally accepted that the first form of the Constitution of
the United States, the Articles of Confederation (1776), was influenced to a certain extent by the law and practice of the Dutch
constitution.[1] In still another respect the constitutional form of
the United Provinces has exercised a larger political influence. Its
system of municipal autonomy and of decentralization by local
government found many admirers in a period which in other
countries was marked by the culmination of central monarchical
authority.   Men like Voltaire, Montesquieu, d'Argenson,[2] introduced from Holland and Belgium the theory of the natural
" pouvoir municipal."   The political philosophers, as well as the
French Constituent Assembly in its organization of communal
government, were inspired by these principles; which afterwards
found their way also into the Prussian as well as the English institutions of local government [3]

The end of the 1700s, with the rise of the Historical School,
brought a new and strong current of *historical* inquiry into the law
of the constitution   From that period date several important
treatises on constitutional history and national legal history in
general. They mostly had their origin in political purposes,
especially in the democratic movement, which aspired to revive
the popular civic institutions of the past, and to prove that the
natural rights of the people had been then fully recognized.[4]
This same movement increased the popularity of the American
Revolution, in which the Dutch democrats claimed to find again
their original frame of government [5]   On the other hand, the powers
of the State were also defended by historical arguments against
the claims for popular government.[6]   It will be found that as a

---

[1] This is stated, e g , by *Pieter Paulus* in his "Explanation of the Union
of Utrecht" (1777), III, 241–252
　[The influence of Dutch ideas, as carried over by the Puritans from
their observations while sojourning in Holland, has been elaborately
studied (somewhat with "parti pris") by *Douglas Campbell*, in his "The
Puritan in England, Holland, and America." — ED]
　[2] "Considérations sur le gouvernement ancien et présent de la France"
(1765)
　[3] *Hatschek*, "Die Selbstverwaltung in politischer Bedeutung," 1901.
　The modern source for the knowledge of the political institutions of
that period is to be found in the "History of the Constitutional Institution
of the Netherlands to the Fall of the Republic," by *R Fruin* (ed by *H T
Colenbrander*, Haag, 1901)
　[4] The academic champion of this theory was Professor *Van der Marck*,
of the University of Groningen, "Outline of the Rights of Man "   He was
removed by the university authorities in 1773, as soon as he also introduced his liberal philosophy in theological matters!
　[5] *E g* Joan Derk van der Capellen tot der Poll, who has been compared
to Lafayette
　[6] The principal works of this movement are as follows . *Van der Spiegel*,

whole this historical school contributed largely to the historical conceptions of the constitutional evolution, and thus offered a counter-poise to the abstract "natural law philosophy" of the period.

(4) *International Law.*—It may be considered as a typical feature of the local multifariousness of the Dutch law that a doctrine of conflict of laws, intermunicipal and international law, became indispensable, — just as in the Middle Ages the school of Bartolus had to provide the Italian towns with a system of rules for statutory conflicts. Grotius wrote on this subject, Voet[1] as well as Huber[2] devoted parts of their work to its complicated matters. An authority famous on those questions, even for a long time afterwards, was CORNELIS VAN BYNKERSHOEK (died 1743), counsel and president of the High Court of Justice of Holland and Zeeland He wrote as well in Dutch as in Latin, and had an international reputation in matters of conflicts of law (Treatise on State Affairs, "Quæstionis juris publici ac privati") The main tendency of the Dutch theory[3] may be stated as follows · if a sovereign recognizes the laws of a foreign country, he does so by pure "comitas gentium" and never by a requirement of justice. This, as we see, is the older, narrower, and conservative theory. Grotius had taken a much larger and broader-minded view of international legal relations. He may indeed again be said to have been the precursor of the most modern school of international law, which has also found others among its first and most ardent adherents in the Netherlands (*ante*, § 7).

§ 9   **National Unification and Codification after 1795.** — In 1795 the great French Revolution was definitely initiated in the Republic of the United Provinces. The existing form of government was overthrown, and a new, uniform, and centralized political system on the Jacobin model was introduced. This new "Batavian Republic" also planned the introduction of general

"Origin and History of the Laws of the Country" (1769), *Pieter Paulus*, "Explanation of the Union of Utrecht" (1775–1777), in defence of the existing form of government, partly drawn from the writings of the Pensionary of Holland; *Slingelandt* (ed 1784), "Constitutional Restoration of the Political Institutions of the Netherlands" ("Grondwettig Herstel," 1784–1786); for the democratic party, "History of the Dutch Government" (1780, 1802), by *Adriaan Kluy*, opposing the former and very complete, *Trotz*, "Commentarius legum fundament. Fœderati Belgii" (1778), expounding the ancient democratic institutions

[1] "Comm. ad Pand," I, 4 (1698)

[2] "Præl. Jur. civ Dig," I, 3

[3] See also   *Paul Voet*, "De Statutis," 1655 ; *Burgundus*, "Tractatus ad cons Flandriæ" (1621); *Rodenburgh*, "Tract. de jure quod . . ." (1653).

law codes, and some efforts were made to realize this plan.   Several
drafts were prepared, mostly founded on the principles of that
Natural Law philosophy which was in vogue at the time.   But
they all died at birth, or shortly after, and are no longer of more
than casual interest.[1]

At first the Wolffian, afterwards the Kantian, philosophy dominated the legislators of the early 1800 s.   But the movement
soon passed, and a peaceful, unoriginal positivism took possession
of the juristic world.   The lawyers of that time hardly realized
the greatness and fecundity of the scientific work of the past.
They saw only its defects, and they expressly aimed at a plain,
written, and comprehensive codification of the law   What they
feared, above all, was a revival of the scrappiness of the ancient
forms of law in custom and legislation.   No customary, no local,
law, no judge-made law, was to be recognized; the official codes
were to provide for everything.   For this ideal, the legislators
were ready to make two great sacrifices.   They would sacrifice
the close contact existing between the law-system and the national
social life of the country; and they would give up the means of
securing a gradual and easy evolution of the law in the future.
The immediate incorporation of all the law into codes was prescribed by the new Constitution of 1815.[2]

Upon the establishment of the kingdom, these law codes had
to be undertaken   It is remarkable, in this codification movement, that the makers of the law obviously did not feel the necessity
of shaping the written law in accordance with the existing practice
and institutions   The first draft code of civil law (1820), though
it showed some efforts to represent the national Dutch law, and
is therefore still an important source for the study of that law,
was rejected, and the subsequent drafts were all modelled on the
theory of the French code   So it must be noted that the codes
that came into operation in 1838 and have remained in force until
the present time — Civil Code, Commercial Code, Codes of Civil

---

[1] A careful history of the draft codes of that period has been given by
Land in his "Introduction to the Dutch Civil Code."
[2] The Kingdom of the United Netherlands, founded in 1814, was finally
based on the Constitution of 1815   By this Act the constitutional representative monarchy was adopted , in the revisions of 1848 and 1887 it has
more and more taken the shape of parliamentary government   A strong
tendency to centralization was at first omnipotent , the partial restoration of
the ancient forms of local self-government, largely restricted by central
control, was not realized before 1848.   A summary view of constitutional
and administrative law in the Netherlands for foreigners can be found in
the present author's "Staats- und Verwaltungsrecht des Königreichs der
Niederlande " (Hannover, Janecke, 1910)

and of Criminal Procedure — are not so much products of Dutch juristic thought and learning, as they are much-modified copies of the Napoleonic law-books. Of course, exception should be made for some chapters (matrimony, successions, maritime commerce), where the national traditions have been recognized. But on the whole the direct stream of the ancient Dutch law sources was cut off.

§ 10 **Legal Conditions in Modern Times.** — For a long time the French legal school, French authors, and French judicial law were to be the guides of practice and legal science in the Netherlands, for civil as well as for criminal law It is not to be denied that in that period able men were active, and able work was done. But the fact is that juristic thought in the Netherlands did not then possess the typical independent and original character of former times. The general state of mind among jurisconsults was marked by a dominant respect for the formal text of the law This period's most important works consist of commentaries and interpretations of the different codes. [1] and in the courts attention was chiefly paid to the art of formal interpretation. Profounder scientific research was for the most part spent on the study of Roman law. This branch of legal science still wielded a great influence, as well in the legal teaching at the Universities, as in the exegesis of the courts [2]

During the latter half of the 1800s, however, some important changes in the character of legal ideas may be noted.

First of all is the revival of historical law studies. Interest was awakened for the ancient Dutch institutions and legislations, as well in public, as in private, law. This taste for historical law studies was chiefly roused by such statesmen as THORBECKE and GROEN VAN PINSTERER and by university professors like VAN HALL,[3] VREEDE, DE WALL,[4] DE BOSCH KEMPER; later by FOCKEMA ANDREAE, COLENBRANDER, FRUIN, POLS, and HAMAKER. It has resulted in many monographs on various subjects, and in new

---

[1] Civil Code Diephuis, "Het Nederlandsche Burgerlijk Recht " , Opzoomer, "Het Burgerlijk Wetboek " Of more recent date: Asser and Van Heusde, "Nederlandsch Burgerlijk Recht", Land, "Verklaring van het Burgerlijk Wetboek."

[2] A periodical publication of the more important judicial decisions of the country is given is the "Weekblad van het Recht "

[3] "Rechtsgeleerde Verhandelingen " (Amsterdam, 1838) , "Gemengde Geschiften betrekkelijk tot de Geschiedenis der Vaderlandsche Rechtsgeleerdheid," 1849

[4] "Orationes Academicæ de Historico Juris Neerlandici studio," 1852 , very interesting, with historical annotations.

editions of numerous ancient law sources [1] And in recent years, another sign of the changing of the current, though the positive and the Roman law form still predominant subjects of law school teaching, is that the various universities have established professorships of ancient Dutch law and its history.

Secondly, it may be noted that the interest in the legal institutions and practice of other countries has turned from the French to the Germanic direction It is undeniable that since 1870 the drafting of the Imperial German Codes, and the achievements of German legal science, have made a strong impression on Dutch legal study and practice. More and more the lawyers have turned their attention to the works of German scholars The following may be cited as a remarkable instance of the preponderance of German influence. When in 1838 the different law codes came into operation, a Criminal Code was still lacking Chiefly because of the divergencies of opinion on prison systems, none of the five different drafts, then and later offered, became law. So the French " Code Pénal " remained in force for the Kingdom of the Netherlands. The new national Criminal Code, the pride of its framers, was adopted only in 1886 [2] Now it is notable that this code, although in large part a quite national piece of work, has followed far more the German than the existing French example.

The same influence of German conceptions may also be observed in other recent legislations or legislative drafts. An exception here should be made for the *commercial law*. In the Netherlands, the practice and study of commercial law necessarily follow the national traditions, they could not be shaped after any foreign model Hence the treatises on commercial law [3] will be found to have original merits, and Acts like the Cooperative Societies Act (1876) and the Bankruptcy Act (1896) are of characteristic interest.

A third and new phase of juristic thought may be said to have begun with the twentieth century. Our country has not lost its zest for international and comparative law studies; and it still has a special interest in profiting by the experience of other countries. The Netherlands may now be said to be once more a point of con-

---

[1] "Repertoria of treatises and monographs on Dutch legal history," 1863, 1866 (ed Dutch Soc. of Literature)

[2] Commentaries on this Code have been written by Professor *G A. van Hamel*, "Inleiding tot de Studie van het Nederlandsche Strafrecht"; Professor *D. Simons*, "Het Nederlandsche Strafrecht," both representatives of the modern criminalistic school ; *Noyon*, "Het Wetboek van Strafrecht "

[3] Principal works· *Molegraaff*, "Het Nederlandsche Handelsrecht," *Kist-Visser*, "Het Nederlandsche Handelsrecht "

centration for the study of *international law* and related studies, as well as for that of the unification of law. One needs only to cite the names of Dr. T. M. C. ASSER, and Dr. D. JOSEPHUS JITTA, and the works of the International Commission at the Hague for the preparation of international treaties of civil and commercial law   But, furthermore, there has appeared in the Netherlands a trend of juristic thought, running parallel with the same phenomenon elsewhere, and evincing a reaction against the formalism, legalism, and positivism of the 1800 s.   It is the school of " freer judicial law," uttering a warning against the academic ways of shaping and applying the laws, and recommending to the courts a stronger feeling for the social and economical purposes of legal rules.

To a certain extent, the same tendency may be observed in some modern legislative measures, by which the Dutch Parliament has altered the principles of the Napoleonic Code, and introduced more social principles : acts that will be found to be products of a genial Dutch art of lawmaking (Children's Acts, 1905 , Contract between Master and Servant, 1907; Bastardy Act, 1909)   This movement,[1] which leaves much more to the social knowledge, discernment, and wisdom of the jurisconsults, and urges them to recognize a natural *sentiment* of justice, puts greater responsibilities than ever before upon bench and bar, upon the universities and the legal scientists.   In a way, it may be said to possess some traits of the illustrious Dutch school of legal thought of the 1600 s, — a school whose leaders succeeded in combining theoretical learning, historical and realistic feeling, and the natural sense of justice.   We have yet to realize the results of its initial phase.

[1] *Dr J A. Levy,* "Rechter en Wet ;" *Dr. Fockema Andreae,* "Moderne Prætuur"; Professor *Hamaker,* "Recht en Maatschappij.".

PART VI

SWITZERLAND

INTRODUCTION

1. THE PRE-CONFEDERATION PERIOD (TO A.D. 1300).

2. THE OLD CONFEDERATION (A D 1300–1800)

3. THE NEW CONFEDERATION (A.D. 1800–1912).

4. THE JURISTS, AND THE MOVEMENTS OF LEGAL THOUGHT.

ABBREVIATIONS USED IN PART VI

Ab Sch. R = Abhandlungen zum schweizerischen Recht.

Ar Sch G = Archiv fur Schweizer Geschichte

Huber, "System" = *Eugen Huber*, "System und Geschichte des schweiz-erischen Privatrechts" (4 vols , 1886–1893).

J B Sch G. = Jahrbuch fur Schweizergeschichte.

M D Suisse Rom = Mémoires et Documents de la Société d' Histoire de la Suisse Romande

Mitt H V. Schwyz = Mitteilungen des historischen Vereins von Schwyz.

Mitt V L G = Mitteilungen zur Vaterlandischen Geschichte.

Sch R Q = Schweizerische Rechtsquellen, published by a commission of the Schweizerischer Juristenverein, since 1894 (8 vols. to 1911)

Z Sch R = Zeitschrift fur schweizeriches Recht, 22 vols. to 1882.

Z Sch. R. (N F) = same, Neue Folge, since 1882, edited by A. Heusler.

PART VI

SWITZERLAND [1]

§ 1. Introduction.

TOPIC 1 THE PRE-CONFEDERATION PERIOD (TO A.D. 1300).

§ 2. Primitive Germanic Local Law.

TOPIC 2. THE OLD CONFEDERATION (A.D. 1300–1800).

A. CONFEDERATE RELATIONS

§ 3 The Thirteen "Places"
§ 4. The Associated "Places."
§ 5. The Common Territories.
§ 6. The Constitution of the Old Confederation.

§ 7 Religious Relations.
§ 8 Relations with the Empire and Other Foreign States.

B. THE CANTONS

§ 9. Development of the Cantons in General
§ 10. The Reception of Alien Law.
§ 11. The City Cantons.

§ 12. The Rural Cantons.
§ 13. The Associated "Places."
§ 14. The Common Territories.

C. LEGAL SOURCES

§ 15. General Traits.

TOPIC 3. THE NEW CONFEDERATION (A.D. 1800–1912).

§ 16 Confederate Relations.
§ 17. The Cantonal Constitutions

§ 18 Legal Sources.

TOPIC 4. THE JURISTS AND THE MOVEMENTS OF LEGAL THOUGHT

§ 19. From the Period of National Independence to the 1700 s

§ 20. In the 1800 s

[1] [Part VI is a translation of an essay written specially for the present volume by Professor DR. EUGEN HUBER, drafter of the Swiss Civil Code, which went into effect with the opening of 1912. For this author, see the Editorial Preface. — TRANSL.]

§ 1. **Introduction.** — The Swiss Confederation grew out of the German Empire, and Swiss law out of medieval German law Swiss independence was attained " de facto " by the end of the 1400s and was recognized in international law by the Peace of Westphalia of 1648. Until about 1500 Swiss legal history constitutes a part of German legal history, and its development is therefore to be found presented in general outline in the history of German law. From that time on Switzerland went an independent way in legal development. Nevertheless its States (Cantons) and its confederacies remained of essentially Germanic character down to the end of the 1700s. Those portions which to-day are Romanic were in part still independent States essentially Germanic, as Freiburg and Valais; in part dependent territories, as Vaud and Ticino, and in part were only loosely allied with the Swiss Confederation, as the principality of Neuenburg (Neuchâtel) and the Republic of Geneva. Since the end of the 1700s Switzerland has been a single State of mixed nationalities, in which the three national languages, German, French, and Italian, exist with equal rights alongside of one another, although represented by very unequal elements of population.[1]

Topic 1. The Pre-Confederation Period (to a d. 1300)

§ 2. **Primitive Germanic Local Law** — The oldest period distinguishable by research in the history of legal growth is that of Helvetia and Rhætia under the Roman dominion [2] The Germanic racial branches wandered into the region of Helvetia from the 200s onward; from the north in repeated irruptions (213, 260, and 400 A.D.), — the Alemanni, from the southwest about the year 437, — the Burgundians; and from the south in only small bodies, — the Ostrogoths at the end of the 400s, and the Lombards about 550

---

[1] General literature for the history of Swiss law Z Sch R , founded by J. Schnell, professor in Basel, a journal which contains, in addition to legal essays, summaries and prints of cantonal legal sources, referred to in detail below, and a general yearly review of Swiss legislation ; "Amtliche Sammlung der altern eidgenossischen Abschiede" (to 1798, 8 in 22 volumes), continued by the "Aktensammlung der Helvetik," edited by J Strickler, and the votes and acts of the Diets from 1815–1848 ; Schlatter, "Schweizerische Rechtskalender" (new ed. 1895), Sch. R Q., cited below under the various cantons , and A. von Orelli, "Rechtschulen und Rechtsliteratur in der Schweiz vom Ende des Mittelalters bis zur Grundung der Universitaten von Zurich und Bern" (Zurich, 1879). Special literature is further indicated below under the appropriate sections The literature of the present-day law need not be referred to

[2] As to this see particularly W Gisi in his "Quellenbuch zur Schweizergeschichte," vol. 1, where he has collected valuable data.

The folklaws of these Germanic branches thus found entrance into the Helvetian country, and constituted the basis of later legal development. Especially important in this respect are the "Leges Alemannorum" (the "Pactus" of about 550 and the "Lex" of about 720); and secondarily the "Lex Burgundionum" ("Lex Gundobada" of about 501), and the "Lex Romana Curiensis" of the middle of the 700s.[1]   Under the Frankish rule — which began for the Alemannian region in 496, for Burgundy in 534, and for Rhætia in 536 — the popular codes continued, generally speaking, to maintain themselves, being merely supplemented by a scanty royal legislation. The description of the law which thus resulted falls under German legal history. It may be merely mentioned here that the Alemannian folklaw remained in force down into the 1000s, and that the Burgundian law-book was likewise still referred to in the 1000s as generally known[2]   The Romanic population, which must still have been present in great numbers during this period, especially in western Switzerland and in Rhætia, lived under Roman law, which, along with the "Lex Romana Burgundionum" and the "Lex Curiensis" above referred to, was compiled in written form for these portions of the country   This is the explanation of the fact that the influence of the Roman law afterwards remained greater in these regions than in the other parts of Switzerland   From the 1000s on there becomes apparent a rapidly increasing growth of smaller communities, each of which has evolved a special law on the basis of the old racial law. The Germanic medieval law, by this development, was thus in many respects preserved in purer form in Switzerland than in the German Empire itself; and for the reason that in the Swiss development the reception of the Roman law, as well as any considerable influence of Roman imperialism, were repudiated.

The Swiss communities began with the middle of the 1200s to join in alliances for the preservation of their imperial "immediacy," and this development of leagues was thus the true beginning of the Confederation, which continued in unbroken growth until 1798 With the end of the 1700s the period of the new Confederation then begins

From the 1200s onward a great number of cities and rural districts attained development as independent States   These were founded upon the particularistic legal growths of the German

[1] Regarding the determination of the time and place of origin of this "lex" see especially the latest proofs in *Mutzner*, in Z. Sch R (N. F.), XXVII, 48 *et seq.*   [2] *Cf. Huber*, "System," IV, 36 *et seq.*

Middle Ages (cities, mark communities, and seigniories) and exhibit accordingly a varied legal character.

As regards the *cities* we may distinguish the following classes.
One group was founded by the king, or at least held such a position
in the Empire that no fief intervened between the royal supremacy
and the city, the imperial rights being exercised through a bailiff.
These were the imperial cities. To this class belong Zurich,
Solothurn, also later Bern, and in addition a number of other
towns which were only temporarily subjected to immediate
imperial authority, as Rheinfelden and Stein a/R. Another class
of cities were the so-called ecclesiastical cities, which were established by ecclesiastical founders or had originated in connection
with a church manor, as Basel, Lucerne, Schaffhausen, St. Gall,
Chur, Lausanne, Geneva, Sitten, and many others that never
attained later any great importance. Finally, and particularly,
we must note such cities as were established by secular lords,
partly upon a feudal and partly upon a manorial basis; or which
had grown up within their domains, — the territorial cities.
Among the most important seigniorial families which were such
founders of towns were those of Zahringen, to whose activity was
due the establishment of the towns of Freiburg i/U, Murten, Bern,
Burgdorf, Diessenhofen, and others, of Neuenburg, which established or protected in their development the cities of Neuenburg,
(Neuchâtel), Neuenstadt, and Valengin; further the house of
Kyburg and its successor the house of Habsburg, to whose activity
as founders the towns of Winterthur, Mellingen, Baden, Bülach,
Aarau, Brugg, Zofingen, Lenzburg, Sursee, Frauenfeld, and others
trace their existence.

Among these cities there is observable a community of law,
which arose through the conferment of the law of one town upon
others, a continuing current of law between the mother and the
filial town being ordinarily the result of such conferments There
thus arose types of town law, as the Zahringen town law and the
Kyburg-Habsburg law. The city founders availed themselves now
of one and now of the other of these types; Habsburg, for example,
also conferred Zahringen law upon its cities (Aarau, Brugg, Sursee,
and others). Among such groups of town law we may particularly
mention the Constance law, — which Constance conferred upon
Zurich in the so-called "Richtebrief" (Charter Guide), Schaffhausen borrowing it then from Zurich, and St Gall also conforming
in important points to the same law, the Zähringen law, which began in Freiburg im Breisgau, receiving then a further development

in the laws of Bern (to which Laupen and Unterseen conformed), Freiburg im Unterseen (with its filial towns Thun, Burgdorf, Erlach, Nidau, Aarberg, Corbières, Payerne, and others), and Murten, which occupied an isolated position.[1] Mention may also be made of the Habsburg town law, which Winterthur, Aarau, Mellingen, Baden, Bremgarten, Brugg, and others received; although some of these had also been endowed with Zähringen law as above noted[2] Finally we may refer to the Basel law, which attained influence in Biel, Delsberg, Laufen, Pruntrut, the Neuenburg law, which was conferred upon the towns of Neuenstadt, Boudry, and Landeron; and lastly the Vaud-Savoy town law, which exhibits a very slight development of city polity, as is to be seen in the laws of Villeneuve, Aubonne, Vevey, Moudon and Aigle.[3] Of these cities Moudon, Nyon, Yverdon, and Morges showed especial merit in their later development, and have been called "Les quatre bonnes villes du pays de Vaud" (the four good towns of Vaud)[4] In the cities of Ticino legal development was controlled by Milan, and particularly by Como, whence Lugano received its law; while a closer dependence upon Milan is probable in the cases of Bellinzona, Locarno, and Brissago.

As regards the *rural districts* ("Landschaften"). There were still visible under the rule of the Carolingians the last traces of the Alemannian duchy, later Swabia, whereas in the Burgundian region independent kingdoms of varied fortune had been already formed During the 1100s it seemed as though the dukes of Zähringen might be able to establish in these regions an independent principality. But the extinction of the house in 1218 made vain all such plans. The land disintegrated into "gaus" (regions), of which the principal ones were Thurgau, from which the Zurichgau later separated, the Churwalchengau (Grison), Aargau, Frickgau, Sundgau, and Waldgau; and, in the southern valleys, into earldoms, — of Bellenz, Misox, Cleven, Bergell, and others. Particularly powerful among the earls of the succeeding period were the lords of Kyburg, endowed with estates and fiefs in Thurgau and Zurichgau as far as the Aare and Saane; those of Lenzburg, as land-

---

[1] A large part of these town laws have been printed in *Gaupp*, "Deutsche Stadtrechte," vols 1, 2.
[2] *Cf Paul Schweizer*, "Habsburgische Stadtrechte und Stadtepolitik" (1898).
[3] These town laws are collected and printed by *Ch. Le Fort* in the M. D Suisse Rom , vol. XXVII
[4] See *Huber*, "System," IV, 64 *et seq.*

graves of Aargau and Zurichgau, whose house died out in 1172;
those of Habsburg, which had great estates in Aargau and Thurgau;
and the lords (later the earls) of Toggenburg. But there were
many others　Besides these there were many ecclesiastical foundations which possessed great seigniories in all parts of the land. Of
these we may mention especially Chur, Disentis, the Frauenmunster of Zurich, Einsiedeln, Engelberg, and finally, and above
all, St. Gall. Out of the hundreds, which from the Alemannian
period onward had constituted the smallest and closest political
units, and at the same time, as mark communities, economic units
of great importance, there grew the free valley communities of
original Switzerland (Uri, Schwyz, Unterwalden), similar beginnings showing themselves in the valleys of the Bernese Highlands
and in the rural districts of Rhætia. Later, manorial communities
showed a similar free development as in Appenzell and in Grau-
bünden [1]

Out of these elements there was formed the Confederation
("Eidgenossenschaft," — Solemn League and Covenant), whose
first beginnings meet us with the middle of the 1200s.

Topic 2. The Old Confederation (a d 1300–1800)

A CONFEDERATE RELATIONS [2]

§ 3. The Thirteen Places — Confederate relations had their beginnings in an alliance of the three rural territories of Uri, Schwyz,

---

[1] See especially, regarding the rural districts, the essays of *Fr von
Wyss*, "Die freien Bauern," etc., in Z Sch R, XVIII, 19 *et seq*, and
"Die schweizerischen Landgemeinden" in Z Sch R, 1 (pt. 1), 20, and
(pt. 2) 3, both studies reprinted in his "Abhandlungen zur Geschichte
des schweizerischen offentlichen Rechts" (1892)

[2] We refer to the following literature regarding CONFEDERATE RELA-
TIONS under the old Confederacy · W. *Oechsli*, "Die Anfange der Eidgenossenschaft" (1891), *Rilliet*, "Les Origines de la Confédération Suisse"
(1868); F M. *Buhler*, "Compendium des eidgenossischen Rechts" (1696),
cf Z Sch R, XVI (pt 2), 43 *et seq*, J R *von Waldkirch*, "Einleitung
zu der eidgenossischen Bundes- und Staatshistorie" (2 pts, Basel, 1723),
G *Fasi*, "Versuch eines Handbuchs der schweizerischen Staatskunde"
(Zurich, 1796), *Leonard Meister*, "Abriss des Eidgenossischen Staatsrechts
uberhaupt, nebst dem besonderen Staatsrecht jedes Kantons oder Ortes"
(St. Gall, 1786); P *Usteri*, "Hadnbuch des schweizerischen Staatsrechts"
(2d ed, 1821), *Ed Henke*, "Offentliches Recht der Schweizerischen
Eidgenossenschaft und der Kantone der Schweiz" (Aarau, 1821), *Ludwig
Snell*, "Handbuch des schweizerischen Staatsrechts" (vol 1, "Staatsrecht des Bundes," vol 2, "Staatsrecht der Kantone," with abundant
references, Zurich, 1837–1845); *Fr Stettler*, "Das Bundesstaatsrecht der
schweizerischen Eidgenossenschaft" (2 parts, 1844), *Simon Kaiser*,
"Schweizer Staatsrecht in drei Buchern" (1858, 1860); *Cherbuliez*, "De
la démocratie en Suisse" (2 parts, 1843), J J. *Blumer*, "Handbuch des
schweizerischen Bundesstaatsrecht" (2 vols., Schaffhausen, 1863–1865;

and Unterwalden, which sought by this league to protect against the political ambitions of the house of Habsburg-Austria the imperial immediacy which Uri had been granted in 1231 and Schwyz in 1240 As early as the mid-1200s they had joined in their first league On August 1, 1291, after the death of King Rudolf, the first league that has come down to us was concluded; and this was then renewed on December 9, 1315, after the victory over Austria at Morgarten. These three " places," later cantons,[1] then concluded on November 27, 1332, another league with the aspiring city of Lucerne, which had been placed under an Austrian bailiff; and on May 1, 1351, — after a temporary alliance made as early

2d and 3d ed by *Morel*); of especial merit, *J C Bluntschli*, "Geschichte des schweizerischen Bundesrechts von den ersten Bunden bis auf die Gegenwart" (2 vols., 1849–1852; the second volume with documents and constitutions); *Johann Meier*, "Geschichte des schweizerischen Bundesrechts" (2 vols , 1875–1878), and finally *Mohl*, "Geschichte der Literatur der Staatswissenschaften," I, 476 *et seq* — For Swiss CHURCH LAW of this older period the following are of importance *Fr von Baltasar*, "De Helvetiorum Juribus circa Sacra, das ist kurzer historischer Entwurf der Freiheiten und Gerichtsbarkeit der Eidgenossen in sogenanten geistlichen Dingen" (Zurich, 1768); *Joh. Winkler*, "Lehrbuch des (katholischen) Kirchensrechts mit besonderer Rucksicht auf die Schweiz" (2d ed enlarged, 1878); *C Gareis and Ph. Zorn*, "Staat und Kirche in der Schweiz" (2 vols , 1877–1878), and *C Finsler*, "Das Kirchenwesen der reformierten Kirche der Schweiz" in *Wirth*, ' Allgemeine Beschreibung und Statistik der Schweiz," II, 666 *et seq*.

[1] [The reading of the text may be facilitated by collecting here certain explanations, which are scattered through the text (or judged unnecessary), of territorial divisions and nomenclature Those territorial divisions which finally became sovereign States, and are known to-day as cantons, appear first in history as disintegrated amorphous communities ("Gemeinwesen"), hundreds, " gaus," mark communities, manorial communities. At the end of the medieval development they appear in the form of "Städte" (cities) and "Länder" (rural territories) As a common designation the name "Orte" ("place" — though possibly the true etymology would require rather the translation to be "part" or "member") early appears, in the 1700s "Stände," and after 1798, especially, "Kantone." About the "Stadt" there was a "Landschaft" (rural district) — some of the cantons to-day preserving this division in their name. Either "Stadt" or "Land" might be under a lord , but the mark community, the manor, rural jurisdictions ("Landgerichte"), valley communities ("Talschaften"), and communes ("Gemeinde") were characteristic divisions of the "Land" Further, the "Stadte" and "Länder," individually and in leagues, held subject domains ("Untertanengebiete," "unterworfene Herrschaften"), which were administered regularly as bailiwicks ("Amter," "Vogteien"), and also protectorates ("Schirmorte," in "Schutzverhaltnis"); and all the "Orte" together held certain common domains ("gemeine Herrschaften") All of these divisions, natural and artificial, had a more or less independent administrative and legal history, which is related in the text, indeed, communities smaller than these divisions had a great variety of subdivided local laws ("Lokalrechte") In view of the great historical changes that have created the present cantons it has seemed best to render the word "Ort" by "Place" (although the two words are rather indifferently used, even in the original text). With the above explanations the other nomenclature of the chapter will be clear — TRANSL.]

as 1291, — a league with Zurich was concluded. Another league with Glarus followed, of June 4, 1352, and one with Zug of July 27, 1352. Finally, Bern was likewise induced to join the league on March 6, 1353, after having already been united with the rural territories of original Switzerland in alliances, particularly at the battle of Laupen. There was thus formed the league of the " Eight Old Places," which was created essentially for the purpose of maintaining the imperial immediacy, but also for mutual support in struggles against the tyrants of Vaud and the House of Savoy. It was a peculiarity of this Confederation of the Eight Places that no general confederate bond existed, Bern in particular being at first leagued merely with the three rural territories and only much later concluding a permanent alliance (1423) with Zürich.

Confederate relations were later so far developed under this Confederation of the Eight Places that on October 7, 1370, a special league of Seven Places (with exclusion of Bern) — the so-called " Pfaffenbrief " or Parson's Charter — was concluded for the enforcement of secular justice and the public peace; and this was followed by a league of the Eight Places, of July 10, 1399, to which Solothurn also became a party as an ally of Bern; and which contained regulations of the public peace and military affairs, — the so-called Sempach Charter. Confederate relations remained within the narrow limits of the Confederation of the Eight Places when the league, after surviving the severe crisis of the so-called Zurich War, of 1438–1449, was forced to engage in a conflict with the Duke of Burgundy, Charles the Bold. After the defeat of the Burgundian ruler, the cities of Solothurn and Freiburg, which had taken part in the struggle, demanded admittance to the League It was, however, only after protracted negotiations that the rural territories consented, in the compact of Stanz of December, 1481, to the accession of the two cities to the Confederation.[1] In the last decade of the 1400s appears a slackening of the bonds with the Empire, which received confirmation in the victory of the Confederation in the so-called Swabian War, and following this it was joined by the city of Basel on June 13, 1501, the city of Schaffhausen on July 20, 1501, and by Rural-Appenzell in a compact of alliance of December 17, 1513 Thus was formed the Confederation of the Thirteen Places. No addition was later made to the number of the fully qualified cantons in the Confederation.

[1] *Cf. von Segesser*, "Das Stanser Verkommnis," in his "Kleine Schriften," vol II (1877).

In confederate relations as established between the Thirteen Places the following, in brief, may be pointed out as the most essential.

The different compacts generally provide that other alliances made by the different Places shall not be prejudicial to the confederation, or shall be concluded only with the consent of the other confederates. They establish rather definite provisions concerning war and peace and contain regulations regarding the maintenance of the public peace, the security of roads, the abolition of distress, and (later) provisions authorizing freedom of trade between the Places.

The regulation of the so-called "monition" ("Mahnung") in these compacts was particularly important. This might be established in any critical situation in any Place by a sworn declaration of its officials; and appears, moreover, not only when a Place feels itself endangered in its independence and solicits help in war from another, but as the sole procedure in all legal relations under the covenants of the league. It was preliminary to legal relations between the Places; it was the form through which the compacts of the league were made effective; its significance was therefore similar to that of a summons or monition in the Frankish judicature, — not, however, merely as a citation before the court or to judicial compact, but also and distinctively to give help in war.

Provision was also made in the compacts for regular arbitral courts, which were organized in great variety, now in one way, now in another, according to varying experience Sometimes each of the litigating Places named a number of arbitrators and these then selected an umpire; or each Place designated from the council of the other certain arbitral judges, and these then selected the umpire; or the umpire was designated by some member of the Confederation not involved in the controversy and the delegates were then chosen in one or another manner by the parties These and similar combinations appear. The result was that arbitral procedure received in these confederate leagues an extraordinarily complete development, thanks to which the differences between the allies, from the middle of the 1400s onward, often in very serious cases, were amicably adjusted. There came thus into being in confederate matters a spirit to which we, in our time, must wish a like effectiveness in a much wider range of influence.

Finally, reference should be made to the regulations for conflict of jurisdiction which are found in these compacts, according to which the rule of the place of origin was gradually given precedence   In later times a recognition of the jurisdiction of the local forum was established in personal actions.

§ 4. **The Associated Places** — In addition to the thirteen full-powered Places there belong to the Confederation the so-called "associated Places"; that is to say, such as were leagued in a subordinate status with one or another of the full-powered members, or with all. This imperfect union with the Confederation was sought by various cities and rulers for the assurance of their independence, in cases in which the Confederation did not judge it expedient to receive them unreservedly into the League. In this way the Rhætian League (1498), the Bishop of Valais (1533), the city of Geneva (1526), and also the German imperial cities of Rottweil (1519) and Mühlhausen (1515) became associated Places. Some cities joined the league for the special purpose of protecting their independence against their lords and of escaping thus from dynastic ambitions, as was particularly true of Biel with reference to the lordship of the Bishop of Basel, and of the city of St Gall as regarded its abbot. *Vice versa*, some lords allied themselves with the Confederation with the aim of securing eventual support against the democratic tendencies of their subjects, as may be said of Neuenburg and Valengin, of the Abbot of St. Gall (1451), and the Bishop of Basel (1579). Gersau and the abbey of Engelberg were independent Places under the protectorate of the Confederation.

In the leagues with such associated Places mutual help was generally covenanted On the one hand the associated Places bound themselves to begin no war without the advice of the confederates, or these were at least relieved of giving aid if war should be begun without their advice. On the other hand the associated Places were bound to give help to the confederates upon a simple "monition," and no discretion was herein allowed them, such as the full members enjoyed, — an evidence of their less free position. Moreover the associated Places had no share in the conquests of the Confederation. And finally they were only imperfectly represented in the assemblies or so-called Diets of the thirteen Places Their inferiority was also shown by the manner in which they swore to their compacts, the thirteen cantons giving their oaths before the envoys of all the others through their council or the popular Assembly, whereas the other cantons sent only one common envoy to the associated Places for this ceremony

§ 5. **The Common Territories** — As a third part of the Confederation we have the common territories. Conquered territory was acquired at first by each of the Places for itself The cities especially, as Bern, and later Zurich, Lucerne, and Freiburg, managed to acquire what were rather extensive seigniorial rights and domains measured by medieval conditions. But we find also from the 1400 s onward that common conquests were made. Such took place particularly in Aargau after the proscription of Frederick of Austria and at the instance of King Sigismund. The confederates made further conquests in common against Austria in the second half of the 1400 s in Thurgau; and finally against the Duke of Milan in the course of the 1400 s and the beginnings of the 1500 s in the Valleys of Ticino.

At the same time these acquisitions did not by any means always take place through conquest, but very often through direct purchase, or resulted from their being pledged for loans which their embarrassed lords thus raised in the well-to-do cities and were unable to repay.

The more important seigniorial domains were as follows for the different Places: Those of Zurich included the bailiwicks of Greifensee, Grüningen, Regensberg, Kyburg, and the city of Winterthur Bern held the cities of Thun, Burgdorf, Aarau, Lenzburg, and Brugg, the rural districts of Oberhasli, the rural jurisdictions on the Aare, the valley of the Simmen, Interlaken, the valley of the Emmen, and lastly and particularly the rural district of Vaud. The territorial expansion of Bern was so rapid that at the end of two hundred years after its foundation it ruled a greater territory than ancient Rome after a like period of time. Lucerne won the seigniories of Rothenburg, Entlebuch, Munster, Sempach, and Sursee. Freiburg also managed to absorb a considerable territory in Vaud. The Bishop of Valais conquered during the Burgundian Wars important parts of Lower Valais.

Along with the extension of authority of the individual Places of which the preceding are examples, there were even more important acquisitions of common domains of which the following instances should be noted : The Confederation exercised a common authority in the six cities of Baden, Bremgarten, Mellingen, Frauenfeld, Diessenhofen, and Rapperswil, with alternate control by the different ruling Places; but with recognition of the internal independence of the cities, which were practically unfree only in matters of external politics. Also in the earldom of Baden, which was conquered in 1415 and administered by a bailiff named in turn by the ruling Places Further, in the free bailiwicks which were conquered by Lucerne, also in 1415, but ceded to the Places

jointly in 1426   Also in Thurgau, dominion over which was gained
by the Confederation in 1460, but the right of jurisdiction or so-called
" Landgericht " only in 1499.   Of the same class we may mention
further the earldom of Sargans, which was conquered by the Seven
Places in 1493 , the valley of the Rhein, which was bought in 1460
by Appenzell and later held with varying fortune by several members of the Confederation; and, finally and above all, the common
bailiwicks in Ticino, among which last we can distinguish.   (1)
the rural district of Livinen, which was subject to Uri alone,
(2) Bellinzona with the Riviera and Bolenz, which belonged to the
Places of Uri, Schwyz, and Nidwalden , and finally (3) the seigniory
of the Twelve Places (the thirteen excepting Appenzell),—namely
Lugano with the surrounding rural territory, Locarno with four
rural districts and the little city of Brissago, the Val Maggia and
Lavizzara, and lastly Mendrisio, with Balerna and other rural
territories.   These domains were administered by a bailiff (" com-
missario "), who was named alternately by the twelve ruling Places.

It has been often regretted that the confederates should not have
placed under an equal law all the territories conquered or otherwise
acquired.   Such a procedure, however, would not have conformed
to the spirit of that time.   Seigniorial rights were regarded as rights
of usufruct, and were treated as such.   They served to increase
the power and the prestige of the individual Places and of their
leagues.   Also, there resulted from them a community of interests
which contributed greatly to hold in check the antagonistic factors
within the Confederation, and to protect the Confederation from
disruption in times of severe crises.

§ 6.   **The Constitution of the Old Confederation.** — The constitution of the Confederation built up on this basis of the Thirteen
Places, the Associated Places, and the common domains, was not
determined by any single instrument, but was deducible from the
alliances and the practice under these.   The following are to be
emphasized as principles.

The Cantons had attained, in fact, by the end of the 1400s a
territorial sovereignty, and were supreme in matters of war and
peace and internal administration.   Of this, indeed, their power
of making alliances was a consequence   The Confederation, consequently, was no unitary and coherent State, but only a league
in the form of a confederacy ·(" Staatenbund ").   The separate
Places were (in general) bound only by resolutions which were
unanimously agreed upon

The organization of this Confederation appeared at first merely

in common consultations from time to time regarding military
operations. Out of these, however, came meetings of deputies,
which gradually became more regular and were known as Diets.
These Diets were either " ordinary " assemblies of deputies of all
the confederated Places, — attended, that is, by the Thirteen
Places and (later) also by the abbot and city of St. Gall, by Biel,
and, down to the Thirty Years' War, by Rottweil and Muhlhausen;
or else meetings of deputies of the ruling Places for the regulation
of the affairs of the common territories, especially for the purpose
of receiving the annual account of the bailiff   Their regularity
made these latter Diets in the course of time more important than
the ordinary Diets, which as a matter of later practice came to
be annexed to the auditorial Diets. Besides these there were so-
called special Diets, — held more particularly after the Reformation
by the Catholic Places with the addition of the Place of Valais and
the Bishop of Basel and prince abbot of St. Gall, and by the evangelical Places, who summoned also to their meetings the cities of
St. Gall, Muhlhausen, and Biel   Baden was regularly chosen as
the place of assembly of the Diet during the 1400s, but from 1715
onward Frauenfeld enjoyed this position. The Catholic Diets
met in Lucerne, the evangelical in Aarau. The convocation of
the Diet was made at first from time to time by any Place which
desired its meeting, but it became later the practice to charge
Zurich with this duty (and for the Catholic assemblies, Lucerne).
Each Place would send one or more deputies, but it became customary that two should appear in representation of the full-powered
Places and only one for each associated Place. Resolutions were
reached by a vote according to cantons, and the deputies gave
their vote under instructions from their respective governments
in their plenipotentiary powers. If such plenipotentiary powers
were lacking, a resolution was taken either provisionally, or on
condition of ratification; or else the matter was embodied "ad
referendum " in the final enactment (or so-called " recess "); the
Places being then bound to give their decision at the next Diet.
The deputies who voted upon any question without full powers
could be severely punished by the cantons.

Resolutions of the Diet were as a general rule binding only on
Places agreeing to them; but certain matters were exceptionally
specified in the treaties of alliance, — as for example in the compact
of Stanz, and more especially later in the administration of the
common territories, — on which a majority could make resolutions
binding on all. Attempts were made at various times to remedy

this weakest point of the old Confederation by the introduction
of the principle of majority rule, but all such attempts (as in 1515,
1546, 1688, and 1699) remained without result. And this rule
of unanimity, or actual agreement, remained in force until the end
of the old Confederation

Among the subjects of negotiation especially prominent under
the old Confederation we find resolutions regarding war and peace
and neutrality, and representation near foreign governments
Foreign envoys were accredited to the Diet, and the Diet sent its
deputies abroad. Other resolutions were taken, as necessity demanded, regarding highway robbery, the treatment of beggars,
usury, epidemics, coinage, forestalling, freedom of trade between
the cantons, etc. But the Diet busied itself especially often with
interventions in cases of troubles between or unrest within the
individual Places, such intervention being practised at first only
in cases of critical need, whether of a conflict within the government or a conflict of the government with the subjects; but later
at the discretion of the league upon any "monition" that might
call for interference

Just as the Diet took form in practice, so also a capital Place
came to be recognized, upon which it was incumbent, between the
sessions of the Diet, to care for the affairs of the Confederation;
especially to receive foreign envoys, distribute notices, and make
known petitions among the allies. This position was by general
agreement intrusted to Zurich.

Finally, mention must be made of the military organization,
which for the most part was fixed independently in the different
Places, but later, after long endeavors, came to receive confederate
regulation. This was accomplished by the so-called confederate
"defensionale" of 1674, after attempts to this end during the
Thirty Years' War had already been made. According to the
"defensionale," each Place was bound to furnish a certain con-
tingent to the confederate troops The army consisted of a first
draft of 13,000 men (with 16 cannon) and a second and third draft
of equal strength. The command was intrusted to a council of
war consisting of the chief persons of the Place, to which, however,
deputies might also be sent A commander-in-chief was not provided, the troops fought under their cantonal banners. Of importance, finally, was the levying of troops for foreign States,
which, especially as regards France, was sometimes on an extraordinary scale, and from first to last was done for the benefit of not
less than forty different potentates and parties. The Diet devoted

itself to the oversight of these enlistments, and sought especially to prevent a use of such troops abroad against Swiss interests, or in conflicts between States which might have led armies of Swiss against another one Hence, for example, the recall of the troop in the French service in 1507, the recall of those in the Papal service in 1521, from the Duke of Würtemberg in 1519 and 1525, and from the French army at the time of its entry into Franche-Comté in 1668.

§ 7. **Religious Relations.**— Of great influence in the shaping of confederate relations was the schism in matters of faith that came in in the 1520s. The leagues of the different Places remained fixed from that time on, no further extension of them taking place. The differences between Protestants and Catholics dominated the inner life of the Confederation from the 1500s down into the 1700s, and the resulting dissensions often threatened the destruction of the Confederation. This discord led more than once to open war. The treaties of peace provided an increasingly strict regulation of intersectarian affairs, so that these "territorial peaces," as they were called, gave expansion to a new part of the confederate public law. The first territorial peace was agreed upon in the year 1529 and avoided a war, then threatening for the first time. It broke out nevertheless in 1531, and was ended by a second territorial peace. The third followed upon a second war in 1656, and the fourth after a third military conflict in 1712 None of these wars ended with the subjection of the conquered party; at the end of each the opposing rights were, in the main, recognized, and there came about thus a compromise which signified for that time something which approached our modern freedom of faith and conscience We may emphasize, as the principles involved in this development, the following·

Above all there was developed the principle that each canton throughout its own territory might establish that faith for which it should decide, according to the maxim " cuius regio, eius religio," which had also found acceptance in the German Empire. Such establishment resulted in a division of the territory of Appenzell and, in part, of the territory of Glarus.

It was mutually recognized within the Confederation that religious relations should not jeopardize the continuance of the old alliances; and though indeed the " Golden League " united the Catholic Places in a special fellowship of interest during the counter-Reformation, nevertheless loyalty to the Confederation was in the long run not threatened even by this.

In the common domains a number of controlling maxims were developed which received more detailed development in the territorial peaces. According to these, neither communion should combat or suppress the other within the common territory, and nobody should be forced to adopt either the one or the other faith. Protestants should remain as they were, and wherever the mass was read no preacher should obtrude It was further decided that a majority should determine in each parish which confession was to be observed; but the minority should retain the liberty to satisfy in other parishes their religious needs. A return to the old faith was also guaranteed as a liberty for every parish What is more, the principle of majority rule was excluded in matters of religion within the common domains; in particular, suits in matrimonial cases should be directed to a judge of the faith of the party charged. Finally, the principle was established that not only in matters of religion, but in all affairs of government within these territories, there should be equality between the two religions, this principle was then given formal embodiment in the rule that offices should be filled half and half from adherents of the two faiths. Further, wrong-doers should be visited by pastors of their own faith ; mutual abuse within and without the churches should be forbidden to laymen and to clericals, and in matters of justice, inheritances, bankruptcies, and fiefs the adherents of both faiths should be treated alike To the same end, wherever it was of proved necessity, a common use of the churches (so-called " Simultankirchen ") was provided. The church estates, however, were divided between the communions according to the number of their adherents, while chimes and church buildings were divided equally between the two. Finally, taxes for religious services should be borne only by members of either faith, and it was forbidden to impose them upon the adherents of the other These principles became more and more a living part of the law of the Confederation, and constituted, as already mentioned, a preliminary stage in that freedom of faith and conscience which has been realized in the 1800s

§ 8. **Relations with the Empire and Other Foreign States —** As regards the relations of the Confederation with the Empire and other more truly foreign States, we see that until the time of the Reformation a warlike policy prevailed, but afterwards a principle of neutrality was followed, united with a sufferance or an encouragement of extensive levying of troops for foreign military service

In the relations with the Empire we may distinguish the follow-

498

ing stages of development. In the first place, the Places struggled to retain imperial immediacy, especially against the claims of sovereignty made by the house of Habsburg-Austria. This contest lasted till towards the last of the 1300s It was followed by a struggle, also directed especially and repeatedly against the same house, for the preservation of the leagues themselves. The end of this struggle was the expulsion of Austria from the territory of of the Confederation, the conquest of Aargau and of Thurgau being particularly important in this regard. A lasting peace with Austria began with the so-called Compact of Succession of 1477. The third stage was constituted by the fight for independence of the Empire, this was attained after the Burgundian wars in the so-called Swabian War This detachment was completed as a practical fact by the peace of December 22, 1499, inasmuch as the confederated cantons were omitted, after this peace, from representation in the Board of Imperial Regulation — in which the peasants had no representation, although the Confederation consisted in great part of rural Places, — and especially from the judiciary provinces (1512, 1521); being thus exempted from the jurisdiction of the Imperial Chamber of Justice, from all imperial taxes, and levies of troops. At the same time the cantons called themselves still in the 1500s " members " of the Empire, and in official documents are sometimes called " associates of the German Empire." The imperial eagle, too, long kept itself upon the Swiss coins, and other reminiscences of the Empire remained down into the 1800s. Confirmation of old imperial privileges was still sought by some of the Places as late as the beginning of the 1600 s from the emperor, until finally in 1607 the Diet resolved that such confirmation should be no longer sought In 1648 there came the legal separation.

Contemporaneously with this process of detachment from the Empire there went an approach to France, with which in 1452 a first alliance was made, with promises of eternal friendship, and free license to travel and trade for merchants, messengers, pilgrims, and tradesmen. This was followed in 1474 by a second alliance, directed mainly against Burgundy; in the following decades we find these alliances confirmed in 1484 by Charles VIII, and in 1516 transformed into a permanent peace. By these and other ensuing treaties there were assured to Switzerland by France various privileges for merchants, and an increasing annual payment was allowed to the different Places, including the associated Places. On the other hand the confederates promised to the King of France free enlistment of troops, and supported such levies of soldiers to such an extent that France was able to raise in the different cantons, and constantly maintain, on the average, as many as sixteen thousand and more men   The relation grew closer under Louis XIV into a sort of protectorate, a return to neutrality being then attained under Louis XVI. The Confederation maintained similar relations with other countries to the extent that isolated levies took place for Holland, England, the German States, and Austria, though never involving with these a close alliance, such as subsisted with France until the end of the old Confederation.

B   THE CANTONS

§ 9   **The Development of the Cantons in General.** — Parallel to the development of confederate relations went a transformation of the cantons, which was intensified from the time of the Reformation onward under the influence of absolutism.   From the 1500s onward we find an advancing organization of the rural territory about each governing Place. At first the old forms of feudalism were maintained in the exercise of sovereign rights. Especially in the subject territories of the cities the conception endured for centuries that seignorial rights were the lord's profitable rights, and accordingly they were so treated in their traditional extent as against the subjects.   Gradually, however, there was felt a need of developing a conception of sovereignty in the sense of public law, something different from a right of usufruct. This new view found expression in the endeavor to establish a simple administration in place of comminuted fruits and rents. The courts of seigniories and bailiwicks were united, courts of appeal appointed, and care taken in other ways for an administration of the rural territory according to general principles, notably by the introduction of police, the regulation of trade, the building of roads, etc   At the same time offices were ordinarily only honorary, though it is true that feudal dues and incidents made some posts remunerative. This transformation within the cantons found expression in a greater legislative activity, especially on the part of the city councils.   The governing cities strove also for a widening of their city law into territorial law, and local laws were blended in larger bailiwick and seignorial laws.   In these ways the cantons took on in the course of the 1500s quite a different character from that of the Middle Ages. They developed into States, small indeed, but becoming with time more thoroughly organized.

§ 10. **The Reception of Alien Law** [1] — This entire development was completed upon a basis so entirely one of custom that there was no room for the reception of foreign law   In the relation of Germanic law to that of Rome we can distinguish four periods. In the first we find an acquaintance with the Roman law, under which the Roman population lived and which was practised also in the Church   In a second period we come across isolated legal principles in town laws and in documents, without observing any enforcement of Roman legal institutes as a whole   In a third stage we find, in elaborations of city laws and other legal sources, a reliance upon the system of the Roman sources, such as appears particularly in Basel, Solothurn, Schaffhausen, and less so in Bern and St. Gall   The fourth stage is that of the reception of the Roman law as a whole.

The last stage was realized in Germany in 1495, after the administration of justice and the mode of selecting judges had long prepared the way for this step.   In Switzerland this last stage was never reached.   It was avoided for political reasons, and especially in an endeavor to retain the old popular courts.   In these courts judgments were given according to the " special customs and usages of the land"; and in the accounts that have come down to us it is often mentioned that it was forbidden to the advocates to plead " jure Romano."   All the same, there resulted a partial reception of the Roman law in some parts of the country; so that, more especially in western Switzerland, in Basel (the city), in Schaffhausen, and in other smaller jurisdictions, particularly in those under ecclesiastical lordships, the Roman law was declared of subsidiary force.   The Canon law was also retained in the Catholic regions down into modern times, in cases of marriage, usury, and unchastity; in some jurisdictions also as regards testamentary dispositions.   The fate of the so-called Carolina, the imperial code of criminal law of 1532, is interesting   It was given " de facto " application in different parts of Switzerland, and in some Places was declared an official law-book; in Freiburg, as late as 1803. This criminal statute was also enforced in the Swiss regiments of the French army, which according to the conditions of their enlistment usually retained their independent judicature.

Passing now to the individual Places, we may add a brief

[1] On the Reception see *Huber,* "System," IV, 114   On the "Carolina" see especially *A Meier,* "Die Geltung der peinlichen Gerichtsordnung Kaiser Karl V im Gebiete der heutigen Schweiz," in Ab Sch R , no 42; also *Matile,* "De l'autorité du droit romain et de la Caroline dans la principauté de Neuchâtel " (1838).

indication of their legal development　There are first to be considered. —

§ 11　**The City Cantons.** — *Zurich* existed as a city under an imperial bailiff, who according to old privileges was named by the "Frauenmunster" until it was again resumed by the Empire in the 1200 s.　A councillor system, with one council of twelve knights and citizens, was replaced in 1336 by a gild system, under which thirteen gilds were formed of the artisans and a gild so-called "Constafel" out of the knights and other citizens, the council consisting now of the thirteen representatives of the "Constafel" and the thirteen masters of gilds　At the head of the city government was the burgomaster　The first covenant-charter by which this constitution was established was followed in 1372 by a second, in 1373 by a third, and in 1498 by a fourth　The changes introduced by these consisted mainly in modifying somewhat the manner by which the council was elected, and in the creation of a Great Council, which according to the covenant of 1498 consisted of 212 members.　A fifth covenant of 1713 altered nothing essential in these provisions　This constitution remained in force to the end of the old Confederation. Of the expansion of city authority over the rural districts we have already spoken.　Mention must still be made, however, of the fact that among the subject domains Winterthur showed an especially individual legal development　The city itself had a councillor system, which developed what was essentially an autonomous administration of the territory.[1]

Zurich's oldest known law-book is the "Richtebrief" of 1304. After this came collections of statutes, in 1553 a court register, in 1715 a town and territorial law, and in 1716 a statute of inheritance for the town.　Following the acceptance of the Reformation, a special law was developed in matrimonial cases, which, though in essential agreement with the law of the other Protestant Places, was further developed.　In 1719 it was issued as a statute of matrimonial law.[2]

---

[1] *Cf Glitsch,* "Beitrage zur altern Winterthurer Verfassungsgeschichte" (1906)

[2] For Zurich see especially *J C Bluntschli,* "Staats und Rechtsgeschichte der Stadt und Landschaft Zurich" (1838–1839, 2d ed　1856), *F von Wyss,* "Geschichte der Entstehung und Verfassung der Stadt Zurich bis zur Einfuhrung des Zunftregimentes," in his "Abhandlungen zur Geschichte des schweizerischen offentlichen Rechts," p　339 *et seq ,* *Max Huber,* "Verfassung der Stadt Zurich" in the "Schweizerisches Geschlechterbuch."　The imperial bailiwick is treated particularly by *F. von Wyss* in his "Abhandlungen," as cited.

Bern was founded in 1191 by Duke Berthold V of Zähringen, and became an imperial city in 1218 after the extinction of that house. It had a councillor constitution, which was retained without essential changes until the end of the old period. The basis of the city government was originally a Popular Assembly, but this gradually fell into subordination. There was a Supreme Council of two hundred, who were chosen by the Lesser Council and the so-called Sixteen, the latter themselves chosen by lot from the first gilds of the town. The smaller council consisted of two "Schultheiss," two pursers, four " Fenner," seventeen councillors (two of them being "heimlicher," — privy), and was chosen by the larger Council in connection with selection by lot. Bern, as already said, had an extraordinary extent of territory. At the end of the Middle Ages we count within the city's domains — besides that strictly municipal — four rural jurisdictions, thirty-eight German bailiwicks, four country towns, and the territory of Vaud. The administration of these domains was carried on for the most part by bailiffs, who were charged with the collection of rents according to old customary law.

The oldest legal source of the town is the so-called covenant ("Handfest") or " golden bull," which is dated as of April 15, 1218, but originated probably about 1270 [1] This covenant was followed by statutes and collections of statutes, and later by a first code of judicature prepared by the town clerk Hans von Rütte in the years 1537–1539; a codification which shows a distinction of system and originality of content remarkable for that time.[2] A new redaction of this statute followed in 1614, — according to tradition prepared by Steck; and a last in 1761, prepared by S L. von Lerber. Besides these there were statutes of the ecclesiastical courts issued as a part of the legislation of all the Protestant cantons; and for the rural districts a great number of land-books and bodies of territorial law and town law.[3] In Vaud we find a Custumal prepared in 1577 by the council of Moudon on the basis of the law of " the four good cities " already named, also an original private work which attained in practice practically

---

[1] It is printed in many places; we may refer to the reprint in the documentary collection "Fontes Rerum Bernensium," vol I, and in an edition of *Zeerleder* (1891), with commentary, also in the Sch R Q, division on Bern, vol. I, with an introduction by *E Welti* which treats succinctly the entire controversy connected with the question of the document's genuineness

[2] Printed in the Z Sch R, XX (pt. 2), 3 *et seq* and Sch R Q, II, 1

[3] *Cf.* the Z. Sch R, vols. VIII to X, also *Schnell and Sturler*, "Übersicht der Berner Rechtsquellen" (1871).

statutory force, the " Coutumier Commentaire " of Pierre Quizard, of 1562 [1] Bern decreed for Vaud in 1616 certain " Lois et Statuts du Pays de Vaud," which were given an authority subsidiary to other legal sources   A commentary upon this Bernese code by François Boyve of 1756 is worthy of mention   In Vaud Lausanne showed a particularly independent legal development.   The town law, after the different quarters of the city had grown together, was fixed in unusual detail in 1613 by a " Plaict Général " [2]

Lucerne gradually developed into a city, out of an estate about the cloister of St. Leodegar; it was at first under a bailiff of the cloister of Murbach, which passed in the 1200 s to the House of Habsburg   The city, while still a bailiwick, possessed a councillor constitution, under which the council gradually acquired greater independence as against the representative of its lord.   We find here also a large council of over two hundred and a small council of thirty-eight members.   The popular assembly here, as in other places, though never formally done away with, diminished more and more in importance.   The oldest constitution is in the form of a covenant of 1252.   We find next a town law of 1480 in the form of a collection of statutes, a new redaction of the same by Rennward Cysat of 1588, and a " municipale " of 1706, which with sundry additions was issued again as late as 1810 as a civil code. In the rural districts there were a number of bodies of administrative and seigniorial laws, which from the 1500 s onward followed in essentials the town law [3]

Freiburg was founded in 1177 by Berthold IV of Zahringen, and possessed a councillor system based upon a Popular Assembly, the same as in Bern   We find here later on a small council of twenty-four members with two magistrates, a " Great-and-Little Council " consisting of the twenty-four together with one hundred and seventy-two councillors, and further a board called the Sixty, which was made up of fifteen members from each of the four quarters of the town   The covenant preserved in Freiburg dates from the year 1256   There followed collections of statutes of the

---

[1] Printed in the Z Sch R , vols XIII–XV (with a glossary).

[2] See for the older legal sources of Lausanne, *Grimm*, "Weistumer," V, 1 *et seq*   On Bern see *Fr Stettler*, "Staats und Rechtsgeschichte des Kantons Bern" (1845), *J Leuenberger*, "Studien uber bernische Rechtsgeschichte" (1873); *Geiser*, "Berner Verfassungsgeschichte, 1191–1471 " (1888), *Secrétan*, "Essai sur la féodalité, introduction au droit féodal du pays de Vaud" (1858)

[3] For the legal history of Lucerne the extensive work of *Ph A von Segesser*, "Rechtsgeschichte der Stadt und Republik Luzern" (4 vols , 1850 *et seq*), should be especially consulted

1400s and 1500s, and in 1611 a " municipale " was issued, which
was in fact a detailed town law.[1] Of the seigniorial domains of the
city twenty-seven communes were associated more closely with it
as the old rural district of the city; the other bailiwicks (Amter
and Vogteien) had their own independent laws. The Custumals
of Moudon and of Quizard retained subsidiary authority in the
territory of Freiburg.[2]

Solothurn was an old imperial city, important under the Burgundian Kings and later in the Empire as an occasional royal
residence. In the 1200s we find the city under a councillor constitution with a small council of twelve members; later the old council fuses with a smaller one into a board of thirty-five members, and
the great council was constituted out of the six-men (" Sechser ")
of the eleven gilds. Legal development took place on the basis of
a covenant of 1280 and in the form of disconnected statutes, which
were replaced in 1604 by a systematic town law whose author was
the town " Fenner," Hans vom Stall. The rural district here
followed in essentials the town law.[3]

Basel grew gradually from an old settlement as a bishop's see
into increasing independence of the bishop's lordship. We find
here, in the first place, in the 1100s and 1200s a council consisting
of administrative officers and citizens, in 1336 a gild system was
introduced, a member from each gild being added to the council.
The city consisted at first only of the settlement on the left bank
of the Rhine. That on the opposite shore, " Little Basel," was
bought in 1392 from the sons of Leopold of Austria. A great
council of the entire city was then formed out of the six-men, each
gild being represented by two, and four members of each of the
four companies of " Kleinbasel," making in all 196 members
As the city had freed itself from the authority of the bishop it
received the position of a so-called free city, of which there were
besides only six others in the Empire, — Regensburg, Cologne,
Mainz, Worms, Speyer, and Strassburg. It was under no imperial
bailiff, had no imperial taxes to pay, and was bound merely to
render the Emperor services " across the mountain (on pilgrimage
to Rome and for the imperial coronation) and against the enemies

---

[1] *Cf.* Z Sch R , vol XXII, and Z Sch R. (N F), vol. XV
[2] Of the literature relating to Freiburg we refer to *Benz*, "Gerichtsver-
fassung der Stadt Freiburg" (1897), *E Welti*, "Beiträge zur Geschichte
des älteren Stadtrechtes von Freiburg i/U" (1908) in Abh. Sch R.,
no 25; and an edition of the Handfeste by *Lehr*
[3] *Cf. Schuppli*, "Geschichte der Staatsverfassung von Solothurn"
(1897).

of the faith " The old constitution remained in force, so far as it
was applicable, even after the acceptance of the Reformation.

Of legal sources we find in Basel first a covenant which was
repeatedly confirmed by the bishop from the year 1260 down to
the time of the Reformation, and next an episcopal and servitary
law with important data regarding the organization of the serfs and
administrative servants of the bishop[1] From the 1300s on a
statute of judicature was published in various editions, the last
is of 1719 Basel had in addition its matrimonial statute; its
town peace (criminal law), compiled first in 1286 and reedited for
the last time in 1637, and also a peculiar ordinance of judicature
for " travelling folk," the so-called " Kohlenbergordnung " of 1465.
The rural district which Basel acquired was left at first to its own
law, and there thus developed particularly a special law for Liestal,
which had its own council, and after 1654 a magistrate with assessors. For the entire seigniorial domain territorial ordinances were
then promulgated, at first for individual parts, and then for all
regions together in the so-called territorial ordinance of 1757
(reedited in 1813).[2]

Schaffhausen grew out of an estate of the cloister of All Souls
and was under a bailiff of the cloister's founders, the lords of Nellen-
burg. In the year 1330 the town was pledged to Austria, and
remained from then until 1415 under an Austrian bailiff. The
council was here taken in part from the nobility and in part from
the commons Besides the small council there was a great council.
In 1411 a gild polity was introduced, based upon the eleven gilds
and the " lords' chamber." The small council now consisted of
the masters of the gilds and of the six-men of the gilds, the large
council of five members of each gild, and three members of the
noble class. The city possessed a " Richtebrief " based upon the
law of Constance, as already mentioned[3] In 1591 a town law,
in 1714 a law of inheritance, and in 1766 a statute of municipal
judicature were published The rural district here, as in the case
of Solothurn, followed in its entirety the city development.[4]

---

[1] Printed in *Grimm*, "Weistümer," IV, 474 *et seq*, and edited with an
accompanying text by *W Wacknernagel* (1852)

[2] The constitutional development has been exhaustively treated by
A Heusler, "Verfassungsgeschichte der Stadt Basel im Mittelalter"
(Basel, 1860) Reference should be made also to an excellent edition of
"Basler Rechtsquellen" (2 vols , 1856 and 1865)

[3] The town statutes of the 1300s and 1400s are printed in the journal
"Alamannia," vols V and VI (1877–1878)

[4] See the work, *Bachthold*, "Geschichte des Kantons Schaffhausen ";
and *Walter*, "Schaffhausen und Allerheiligen" (1901)

Stein a/R, which to-day belongs to the canton of Schaffhausen, stood under the lordship and protection of Zurich until the end of the old Confederation. The city had its own council and can show a " wisdom " of 1385 of great originality [1]

As regards all the cities thus far described, it remains to be said of them that from the 1500s onward a tendency made itself felt toward the restriction of citizenship, and this as well as in those cities under an old councillor constitution (Bern, Lucerne, Freiburg), as in those into which gild constitutions had been introduced (Zürich, Basel, Solothurn, and Schaffhausen). New and fully qualified citizens were admitted as infrequently as possible. The old families maintained their ability to rule, and there was thus developed in different cities to a varying extent a " de facto " patriciate which monopolized the government. There were not lacking tendencies counter to this development, but they triumphed nowhere; neither in the so-called " Basel troubles " of 1691, nor in the Zurich gild disorders of 1713, the Bern "commons tumult " of 1742, nor the insurrections in Freiburg in 1781 This restriction resulted in part as a consequence of the growth of absolutism which, starting from France, dominated at that time the States of western Europe, whereas in the 1500s a democratic movement, marked by a consultation of the people in all more important matters, had been observable within the cities, — as witness the abolition of serfdom within the Basel rural districts in 1525, and the plebiscites in the rural districts of Zürich and Bern in the 1500s The change toward absolutism found its most striking expression in the suppresion of the peasants' rising of 1653, which was effected mainly by Lucerne, with the help of Zurich and the rural Places.

§ 12. **The Rural Cantons.** — The free valley communities developed partly out of communities of freemen, which go back to origins in the hundreds of the Alemanni, but partly also out of manors that gradually attained to greater freedom as against their lords. In Uri, Schwyz, and both Unterwaldens, as well as in Zug, there was an excess of free population, whereas in Glarus and in Appenzell the manorial estates (in the former of the foundation of Sackingen and in the latter of the cloister of St. Gall) were the nucleus of further development. All six cantons have this in common, that a popular assembly, traditional since the earliest times, composed of all the weapon-bearing population, formed the basis of government. It was generally held once yearly, and

---

[1] Edited by *F Vetter*. [For this term, see § 15]

passed upon laws, taxes, alliances, and questions of war and peace.
It included all men from the age of fourteen (later sixteen) years
belonging as compeers to the valley community. The popular
assembly elected the " Landammann " or chief magistrate, and
later also other territorial officers, as the banneret, the purser, the
master-builder, etc. The " Landammann " occupied the chairmanship of the popular assembly and represented the canton as
" regent " in external relations. There existed, further, in all
the cantons a council which was chosen in part by the popular
assembly and in part by the individual communes. It numbered
about sixty members, but in most of the cantons could be increased
on important occasions, each member then taking with him one or
two men; in which way arose the double or the triple cantonal
council The communes possessed, particularly in Appenzell-
Ausserrhoden a considerable autonomy, and the cantonal assembly
was here constituted of deputies of the communes

The Reformation caused in 1597 the division of the canton of
Appenzell into Protestant Ausserrhoden and Catholic Innerrhoden.
In Glarus there resulted merely a division in the administrative
system, with two popular assemblies, a Protestant and a Catholic,
and appointment to offices from both confessions; in other respects
the unity of the territory was maintained. Schwyz acquired dominion over its so-called outer districts, which were dependent upon
the old canton Uri had a bailiff in Livinen, the valley of Usern
was early allied with the canton of Uri, but treated essentially on
terms of equality. Zug maintained its rural constitution down
to the end of the old Confederation, the rural communes being
incorporated upon a basis of equality of rights with the city
The manorial elements were gradually assimilated in these
cantons to the city element, and there arose thus in the 1400 s a
citizenship of uniform rights, even there where in Glarus and
Appenzell a manorial origin was the prevailing one.

As the chief sources of legislation, we find in all the cantons
statutes passed by the popular assembly. These were collected
in the so-called " land-books " (" Landbucher "),[1] of which the
oldest in Uri has been preserved from 1607 and in Ursern from the
1500 s.[2] In Schwyz there existed in the old territory two great
mark-communities which controlled the economic administration

[1] The statute-books of Uri, Obwalden, and Glarus are still called "Landbucher "
[2] Cf Z Sch R , vols. XI and XII, where the land-book of Livinen is
also to be found And with regard to the relations of the Ursern valley
see the study of *Hoppeler* in the J B Sch G., 1907.

of the canton.[1] The first written records of statutes go back here
to the year 1294 and show plain memorials of the " Lex Alemannorum." From 1524 to 1544 there originated a private collection
which later acquired official character as the " Reding land-book."
The individual districts, such as Einsiedeln, March, Kussnacht,
Wollerau, had their own land-books and valley laws.[2] The oldest
land-book of Nidwalden dates from 1456,[3] the oldest of Obwalden
is one handed down to us from the year 1524 [4] Engelberg was an
independent manor until 1798 and was first united with Obwalden
in 1815. Of particular historical importance is an old " wisdom "
(" Offnung ") of Engelberg of the 1300s.[5] From Glarus we possess
a land-book of 1387, from Zug a town and bailiwick statute-book
of 1432.[6] The individual communes of the canton of Zug had their
own special " Offnungen." Finally Appenzell, before its division
into Ausserrhoden and Innerrhoden, had a land-book of 1409,[7]
revised in 1585; after the division of the canton Innerrhoden retained the old land-book, while Ausserrhoden adopted in 1632 [8]
a new one.[9]

§ 13. **The Associated Places.** — The city of *St. Gall* had already
a council in the 1200s, to which, in the 1300s, was added a great
council. The town freed itself by a slow growth from the authority
of the abbot. The complete separation was secured in 1457 at
the cost of an indemnity paid to the abbot In the 1400s the city
of St. Gall possessed a gild government, the great council being
formed of the eleven-men (" Elfer ") of the six gilds and twenty-
four members of the lesser council, wherein the twelve masters of
the gilds sat. The oldest legal source of the town is a covenant
of 1273 which was given it by the abbot.[10] Later followed statutes.[11]
A town inheritance law was adopted in the year 1721, and a town
statute of judicial procedure of 1781. A peculiar position was held

---

[1] *Cf Reichlin*, "Die schwyzerische Oberallmende" in the Mitt. H. V.
Schwyz, no 18 (1907).
[2] *Cf Kothing*, "Das Landbuch von Schwyz" (1850), and "Die Rechtsquellen der Bezirke des Kantons Schwyz" (1853).
[3] *Cf.* "Geschichtsfreund der Funf Orte," vol XI ; and Z. Sch. R.,
vol. VI.
[4] *Cf* Z. Sch. R , vol. VIII
[5] *Cf Grimm*, "Weistumer," I, 1 *et seq* , and Z. Sch. R , vol. VII.
[6] *Cf.* Z Sch R , vol I.
[7] Edited with notes by *Rusch* (1869).
[8] See the "Appenzellische Jahrbucher," volume for 1855.
[9] In supplement to the above see especially *J. J. Blumer*, "Rechtsgeschichte der schweizerischen Demokratien" (2 vols., St. Gall, 1850–
1858, 1859)
[10] *Wartmann*, "Urkundenbuch der Abtei St. Gallen," III, 196.
[11] Published in the Mitt. V. L G , vols. IV and XI.

in St Gall by the society of " Stonewall Friends " (" zum Notfest-stein "), which embraced the noble class and the most conspicuous merchant families   It had no representation in the council, but gave to the court its presidents, and these could then become members of the small council by election.[1]

The authority of the abbot embraced originally the city and the country district of *Appenzell*, both of which finally purchased their independence. The abbot retained, however, as a seignorial domain the so-called principality, the old rural district which was administered through the officials of the abbey   Particularly important in this region was the town of Wil, which had a coun-cillor constitution.[2]   In 1468 the abbot bought the earldom of Toggenburg, which was administered by a bailiff. In Toggen-burg there was a popular assembly, and the rural districts main-tained an alliance (territorial law) with Schwyz and Glarus, and chose a banneret   For the entire valley community there existed a territorial council, which after the Reformation was filled half and half by Catholics and Protestants. The communes had their own courts, which were chosen by them with confirmation of the abbot   In the old rural districts there existed a variety of local laws, as well as an inheritance law for the members of religious houses   Toggenburg exhibited likewise a number of local land-books as well as bodies of law of its rural districts, the latter con-cerned particularly with inheritance.[3]

Graubunden shows a development of individual valley com-munities, then a formation of different alliances and a general league   In local development Chur, which was under the authority of the bishop, stands out most prominently. It freed itself gradu-ally from his supremacy   It had a council which, chosen from the four quarters of the city, sat under the chairmanship of a burgo-master. In 1465 five gilds appear whose eleven-men constituted the great council   The small council consisted of three members from each gild [4]   The valleys were under the bailiffs and manors of various secular and ecclesiastical lords. The rural population conquered, however, from the 1300s onward a status of steadily increasing freedom. Members of religious houses in the valleys under the lordship of the bishop constituted from the beginning

[1] On the older constitutional development see *Gmür*, "Verfassungs-geschichtliche Entwicklung der Stadt St Gallen" (1900)
[2] *Wild*, "Verfassungsgeschichte der Stadt Wil" (1904)
[3] See the Sch R Q , division on St Gall, vols. I and II.
[4] As regards the town law see especially the town register of 1363, Z Sch R (N F), vol VI , and *Mohr*, "Codex Diplomaticus," vol III.

of the 1400 s the "League of the House of God." The lords of
Disentis and the communes of the upper valley of the Rhine gave
adherence in 1424 to the "Gray League" ("Grauer Bund"); and
the ten jurisdictions of the rural district of Davos constituted from
1429 onward the "League of the Ten Jurisdictions." These
three leagues then joined in a general league. We find here the
three so-called "Bundeshaupter" (league chiefs): the territorial-
judge of the Upper or Gray League, the league-president of the
League of the House of God, and the league-"landammann" of
the league of the ten jurisdictions. General annual Diets of the
league were held, with representatives from all the communes.
The league had also a unitary military regulation, according to
which each ally furnished a colonel and each commune a captain.
In the districts administration was under a bailiff, "landammann"
(or "podestà"), and the judges chosen by the commune The
three leagues acquired in the beginning of the 1400 s dominion
over the Val Tellina, Bormio, and Chiavenna In addition they
possessed the jurisdictions of Maienfeld, Malans, and Jenins, from
1509 and 1537 onward. Legal development took place in part
centrally through territorial ordinances predominately public
in character after the 1400 s, and later under the three leagues. In
the Gray League we find statutory laws particularly developed in
the land-books of Flims, Jlanz, Safien, and Thusis Within the ten
jurisdictions common statutes of inheritance were provided.
Especially important were the rural district of Davos and the
settlement of Valaisans, who had probably wandered over from
Upper Valais, and who constituted a privileged class of subjects.
The League of the House of God consisted of different jurisdictions,
of which each had also its own law-book.[1]

In *Valais* the Bishop of Sitten possessed the rights of an earldom
in the Upper German rural districts. Lower Valais, whose population was of French tongue, stood under the influence of Savoy
The former gradually freed itself from the rule of the bishop,
although this was never completely done away with. Lower Valais,
however, especially as a result of the Burgundian wars, fell under
the rule of the bishop Upper Valais was formed into seven
"Zehnden" (tenths), had its own Diet, and also local laws, of which
the town law of Sitten should be particularly mentioned. Lower

---

[1] See especially the account in *Planta*, "Verfassungsgeschichte der
Stadt Chur im Mittelalter" (1879), and "Die currhatischen Herrschaften"
(1881); also the historical account of the sources in Z Sch R (N. F.),
vols III–VI and XI *et seq*

Valais consisted of a number of seigniorial domains which were administered by the bishop through commissioners, but the cities had their own syndics and were rather independent There was developed for the whole territory, from the 1400s on, a unitary law in the form of "consuetudines" or "statuta terræ Valesii." Cardinal Schinner gave the territory in 1511 its own territorial law. The Bishop of Riedmatten revised this in 1571, and it remained the chief legal source until the modern codifications, enjoying in Upper Valais primary, and in Lower Valais subsidiary, authority [1]

The bishopric of *Basel* completely lost authority over the city of Basel as early as the end of the Middle Ages, but the bishop retained his seigniorial domains in the Jura The towns of Biel and Neuenstadt were likewise subject to the bishop, but maintained an independent alliance with the confederates. Independent territorial assemblies for the whole seigniorial domain were held with deputies of the three estates clericals, knights, and peasants. The bishopric, however, did not attain a perfected territorial organization On the contrary, special bodies of statutory law maintained themselves in different parts of its territory, as Ilfingen, Ergel Munster, Pruntrut, Delsberg, etc We find in Biel a councillor constitution at an early day. A small council under an official of the bishopric administered the city; later a large council was formed under the presidency of the bishop's steward or of a burgomaster. With the city of Biel were united the committees of Ergel and Ilfingen and certain villages directly subject. A rather full town law has come from the year 1614. Neuenstadt had such a law of 1614 and another of 1708

Neuenburg, after the extinction of the earldom of that house, fell under the lordship paramount of Châlons, and later, after various temporary suzerainties (Orleans-Longueville and Orange), under that of Prussia, whose king became in 1707 prince of Neuchâtel The constitution rested here upon the three estates of clericals, vassals, and citizens; after the Reformation, — nobles, placemen, and citizens Out of these was formed a council and the city court. The same organization was established also in Valengin, which belonged to the principality. Peculiar both in Neuenburg and (later) in Valengin was the development of law

---

[1] *Cf* the account of the development in Z Sch R (N F.), vols. VII-IX, — legal sources, with introduction by *A. Heusler*, and on the origin and significance of the seven Zehnden the essay of *Hoppeler* in Ar Sch G , vol X

by judgments of the highest court, — so-called "déclarations" or "points de coutûme."[1]

The city of *Geneva* was under the dominion of a bishop, of whom we hear as early as 318. Its bailiff was named by the Count of Genevois From the 1200s onward the counts of Savoy acquired greater influence, and the city then gradually freed itself from the authority of the bishop, although under the danger of exchanging it for that of the then dukes of Savoy. The city had a council, which was chosen by the "Conseil général," that is, the popular assembly of citizens. The city sought to escape from the influence of Savoy by a union with the cities of Bern and Freiburg in 1477; and the opposition of the rule of Savoy was then fixed by the Reformation. From the time of Calvin onward Geneva associated itself closely with Bern and Zurich, with which it formed in 1584 a perpetual league. In imitation of the constitutions of these cities a councillor polity was created, with a small council of twenty-five members and a great council of two hundred. Between these, as in Freiburg, there stood as a special board the council of sixty, which was associated on important occasions with the small council A committee of the small council, the syndics, administered the city. Throughout the whole period, however, the "Conseil général" remained as an assembly of the citizens, and from time to time its resolutions affected fundamentally the administration and politics of the city In the Middle Ages we find in Geneva a town law which was promulgated in 1383 by Bishop Ademar Fabri in systematic form. After the Reformation special ordinances were published, and in 1568 the city received a town law prepared by Colladon which was an imitation of the " Coutûmes " of the French city of Berry. From the 1600s onward certain edicts were published, which, as the " Édits de Genève,"[2] represent a special class of city legal sources On May 17, 1798, came the " réunion " of the city with France, and from that time on the French laws went into force in the city until 1814.

§ 14. **The Common Territories.** — To the constitution of the common seigniorial domains we have already given detailed references above. It need only be mentioned here that for the earldom of Baden and for the common domain of Thurgau a central law was developed in its first stages by the promulgation of a law

[1] Collected in a "Satzungsbuch" of 1529–1829 Information regarding this is found in *Calame*, "Droit privé, d'après la coutûme Neuchâteloise" (1858). The old constitution is described in *Tripet*, "Exposé de la constitution de la principauté de Neuchâtel et Valengin" (1893).
[2] Several times published since 1707

of inheritance in 1542, for the one and for the other domain. This
was followed by some other edicts, as particularly an ordinance of
guardianship for Baden. With reference to the common domains
of Ticino we may mention that a central law was here in no wise developed. Lugano had a councillor constitution, probably devised
in the first place in imitation of Como, with a large and a smaller
council, which was constituted from the different quarters of the
city and the surrounding communes. Locarno shows us three
estates· the nobles, the burghers, and the farmers Out of these
the council was formed, and in addition territorial Diets, with deputies from the city and the communes, were held. Both of these
cities, as well as Bellinzona (which was ruled by Uri. Schwyz, and
Nidwalden), had their own town law and the valley communities
their land-books.[1]

C. LEGAL SOURCES

§ 15 **General Traits.** — The folklaws (" Leges ") of the Germanic racial branches maintained themselves down into the 1000s.
Then (as generally throughout the European Middle Ages) these
were replaced by a variety of fractionized local laws, which,
especially in the cities, but later also in different rural districts,
came to have a widening significance. This development, in
itself local, but still everywhere based upon the idea, or at least
upon traditions, of an original legal unity, found uniform expression in a law-book known under the name of the " Schwabenspiegel," which attained for the Alemannic portion of Germany
a great importance This record of Alemannic law, written about
1270, had authority also in the Swiss country, as is evidenced by
the many copies still preserved.[2]

With the development of local laws a great change took place;
namely, that of the original personal folklaws into territorial laws
(" Landrechte ") of territorial authority. There remained however, notwithstanding, a special law for the free population, which
even down into modern times was administered in the popular
rural courts among their equal members Side by side with this
territorial law there was the feudal law of fiefs; but this received
in Switzerland no independent development outside of Vaud.
Finally there remained for the manors, both for the artisans of the
" halimote " and for the peasant population, a manorial law.

---

[1] On this development see Z Sch. R. (N. F.), vol XII, with introduction by *A Heusler.*
[2] A French translation ("Miroir des Suabes") edited by *Matile* is still
preserved in the city library of Bern

From the 700s onward this law created for the serfs an increasingly free status, so that after the 1300s a fusion became possible of the manorial with the territorial law [1]

Within these three classes of law there are distinguishable in Switzerland the following groups of legal sources   (1) The territorial laws and land-books for freemen in the open rural districts, which appear as a further development of the folklaws   (2) Next, the town laws for the free inhabitants of the cities and also for the serfs, who were gradually united with the burgesses into a common estate.   (3) Next, the laws of the bailiwicks for the suitors of court of the seigniorial jurisdictions, which included free as well as unfree elements.   (4) And finally, the manorial laws, which existed at first only for the unfree population of the manor, but which were later given force over freemen settled within the manors

According to their origin we may distinguish the following: Privileges and compacts, which were agreements between the population and their lord; statutes, which had their origin in the automony of districts which had become independent; " wisdoms " ("Weisthum ") and "Offnungen," which were records of customary law of predominantly official character, and finally law-books, of which the "Schwabenspiegel" alone had any considerable importance for Switzerland.

Upon the development of the different cities and rural district with their seigniorial domains, a gradual change in legal sources becomes apparent.   In the cities, systematic legal compilations appeared , Bern offers the first and most important example in the statute, elaborated by Rutte, of 1539.   We have already mentioned such statutes individually, under the different Places   The tendency was, however, to make the town law over into a territorial law, and this took place in such a manner that in the rural districts comprehensive administrative-seigniorial laws were prepared, and these were so far as possible modelled upon the town laws.   If Bern as well as Zurich and Freiburg showed in this process a tendency to preserve traditional distinctions, we find in Lucerne a stronger influence of rural districts by the town. Basel developed a unitary rural law, but maintained it intentionally distinct from the town law.   That in Solothurn and Schaffhausen the town law became at the same time the rural law

---

[1] On these three classes of law, and especially on the authority of the manorial law, see *Huber*, "System," IV, 39 *et seq*, 219 *et seq*   Useful information is to be found in the Habsburg land register ("Urbar") of the early 1300s, edited by *Pfeiffer* (1850) and by *Maag*, the latter in "Quellen zur Schweizer Geschichte," vol. XIV.

we have mentioned already   The local laws gradually died out under these influences.

The development in later times shows us a continuance of legal growth through isolated statutes, which only exceptionally were worked over into coherent systems   As a rule the same legal sources (town law, territorial law, land-books, etc) contained provisions in all the fields of the law, and principles of private, procedural, and criminal law are not always separated from one another.   An especially rich development of legal sources is found in the topic of distraint.[1]   So too in that of peace ordinances or criminal law, here it appears that down into the 1700s the form of private accusation had not entirely disappeared, a system of prosecution by official inquisition then gradually gaining the upper hand.   For the development of criminal law particularly useful indications are afforded by the various editions of the public peaces of Basel (town) and later of the 1539 statute of procedure of Bern[2]   On the development of private law we possess for this period an extraordinarily important work, namely the " Confederate Town and Rural Law " (" Eidgenossisches Stadt- und Landrecht ") of Hans Jacob Leu, burgomaster of Zurich, published in four volumes in 1724–1744.   Leu collected in this work statutory provisions from all portions of Switzerland within the field of private law, arranging them systematically in imitation of the Institutes.[3]

Topic 3.   The New Confederation (a d 1800–1912)

§ 16.   Confederate Relations — After the collapse of the old Confederation the Helvetian Republic was established on April 12, 1798, as a unitary State.   In the four years of the Republic's existence the constitution was four times altered, being then replaced by the Mediation Act of February 19, 1803

[1] See especially the account of the historical development of bankruptcy proceedings in *Fr von Wyss*, "Geschichte des Konkursprozesses Stadt und Landschaft Zurich" (1845)   Also *F von Wyss*, "Die Schuldbetreibung nach schweizerischem Recht," and *A Heusler*, "Die Bildung des Concursprozesses nach schweizerischen Rechten," both of these studies in Z Sch R , VII, 8 *et seq* , 117 *et seq.*

[2] *Cf Pfenninger*, "Das Strafrecht der Schweiz" (1890), which is mainly a history of the criminal law ; *Osenbruggen*, "Das alemannische Strafrecht im deutschen Mittelalter" (Schaffhausen), 1860

[3] See *Huber*, "System," vol IV, and the special studies therein referred to   On the development in Switzerland of the manorial common lands ("Allmenden") see *A von Miaskowski*, "Die schweizerische Allmend in ihrer geschichtlichen Entwicklung vom 13ⁿ Jahrhundert biz zur Gegenwart" (1879).

Helvetia, as a centralized State, under its varying constitutions, had a central governing body in the form of a Great Council and a Senate, which were differently constituted; the former of deputies of the cantons, the latter of former officers of State and cantonal delegates. The executive power rested in a Directory, and was exercised by four ministers by it designated. The cantons were administrative districts with governors and lieutenant-governors named by the central executive. Each canton had an administrative board for the execution of the laws and the conduct of the local administration

With the constitution of the Mediation Act, and by the supreme will of Napoleon, a Confederation was created in the place of the former unitary State; though this, to be sure, was very different from the old Confederation. The privileges of the Places, of birth, and of family were abolished, all citizens of towns and rural districts were ‖declared equal before the law, universal rights of residence and freedom of trade in viands were established; the monetary standard was made uniform, and separate regulations were established for many forms of intercantonal legal comity, as, for example, regarding the pursuit of criminals. On the other hand, compared with the constitution of the Republic, there lacked, under that of the Mediation Act especially, a common law of Swiss citizenship and a unity of law. The cantons were recognized as sovereign States, and stood only in Confederate relations with one another. For the nineteen cantons (Valais, Neuenburg, and Geneva not belonging to the Confederation, nor the Bernese Jura) definite forms of government were provided. The cantons with popular assemblies maintained those old traditional bodies as their supreme political organ. The old city cantons were given a representative body, which was constituted from town and rural districts according to a certain census. Side by side with the great councils, which consisted of from 45 to 195 members, administration was carried on by small councils of from 9 to 29 members. The newly formed cantons likewise had a large council as a representative body somewhat differently chosen; their small councils were chosen from the larger. Confederate organization was embodied in a Diet in which each canton had one vote, save the cantons of Zurich, Bern, St. Gall, Aargau, Graubunden, and Vaud, which had two each. The principle of majority rule was recognized, but for more important resolutions a three-fourths majority was required. The chairman of the Diet was the "landammann of Switzerland," the "Schultheiss" or burgomaster of the temporary

capital acting as such. Zurich, Bern, Lucerne, Freiburg, Solothurn, and Basel were alternately and annually designated as the
capital. The " landammann of Switzerland " together with the
government of his canton represented the Confederation when
the Diet was not in session. No confederate court as such existed,
but in certain cases there was a special tribunal formed of the presidents of the cantonal criminal courts. What was important,
Switzerland was bound to furnish Napoleon sixteen thousand
soldiers, and its foreign policy was moreover completely determined by that of France.

After the collapse of the Napoleonic power, different cantons
endeavored to reestablish the old Confederation; but these
attempts were frustrated, particularly by the opposition of the
Congress of Vienna; and only after protracted negotiation could
a new constitution be settled upon This, on August 27, 1815,
was sworn by all the twenty-two cantons.

It rested upon the principle that the Confederation should consist
of the nineteen cantons of the Mediation period, with the addition
of the cantons of Valais, Neuenburg, and Geneva. The bishopric
of Basel and the city of Biel were annexed to the canton of Bern.
The Union was a confederation whose chief organ again consisted
in a Diet. In this assembly the power enjoyed under the Republican constitution was indeed not realized, but there was still
an improvement over the old Confederation, in so far as resolutions
binding upon all could be made by a majority, each canton having one vote. Zurich, Bern, and Lucerne were in turn the capital
for two years. A chancery, chancellor, and State secretary
were attached to the capital. The Diet later developed an
organization of the confederate army, which was made up
of cantonal contingents of troops and maintained by cantonal
subsidies The Diet represented the Confederation in foreign
relations

Various projects for the recasting of this constitution appeared
from 1830 onward, which with other influences finally ended,
after an unquiet period of eighteen years, in the transformation
of the Confederation in 1848 into a federal State ("Bundesstaat").
The constitution of the federation as settled in 1848 is the basis
of the public law to-day In a constitutional revision of 1874
the power of the federal government was enlarged, and popular
rights were greatly increased by the introduction of the optional
referendum. Since then, amendments have granted still further
powers to the federal government, laying the basis especially

for a greater centralization of the military organization, and for legal unity in private and criminal law.

§ 17. **The Cantonal Constitutions.** — After the cantons had again become independent States under the constitution of the Mediation period, they adopted their own constitutions of the form which we have above indicated   The detailed development of these was left to each canton.   After the collapse of the Mediation Act, a part of the cantons sought to return to their former systems of government.   But although this movement was successful in a few cases, yet in a majority of the cantons the public law was generally maintained as the Mediation Act had created it.   The cantons with popular assemblies retained these.   Zug alone replaced a purely democratic by a representative constitution.   The new cantons generally retained the constitutions given them in the Mediation Act, while the city cantons, as notably Bern, Basel, and Freiburg, carried through a subordination of the rural district to the town   With 1830 however there began a movement which was essentially a period of regeneration, the tendency of which was a realization of equality among all portions of the country. It resulted in the division of Basel into the half cantons of Basel City and Basel Rural District.   The canton of Schwyz was also temporarily divided into an "old" and an "outer" territory.   The constitutions whose adoption was brought about following 1830 established everywhere representative governments, and likewise guarantees of individual rights in the general sense of modern public law.   At the same time there were thus early realized the first beginnings in the development of direct democratic legislation.   Several cantons introduced the popular veto, following the example of St. Gall (1830–1831).   This was replaced by the referendum in the modern democratic movement. This has been adopted in a number of cantons since the constitutional agitation in Zürich in 1869.   Zurich and its imitators established the obligatory referendum.   The optional referendum was adopted by the cantons of Lucerne, Zug, Baselstadt, Schaffhausen, St. Gall, Vaud, Neuenburg, Geneva, and Ticino; and this example was followed also by the Federation in 1874.   In addition we find the popular initiative developed in the modern cantonal constitutions with an elaborateness which must be ascribed to a general popular appraisement of the existing law.[1]

---

[1] For the literature *cf.* the accounts of federal public law above cited ; also *Rüttimann*, "Das nord-amerikanische Bundesstaatsrecht verglichen mit den politischen Einrichtungen der Schweiz" (2 vols., 1867–1876);

§ 18   **Legal Sources** — In the field of private law there began
with the 1800s a preponderance of legislation, which crowded out
more and more the customary law   In place of the old town,
rural and seigniorial laws, and the land-books, there now appear
special statutes and codifications   The cantons of Uri, Schwyz,
Obwalden, Baselstadt, Basellandschaft, Appenzell (Auserrhoden
and Innerrhoden), and St. Gall remained without codifications of
private law

The cantons in which such codifications were realized fall into
three groups. The first group either retained the French Code
Civil of 1804, which they had received when a constituent part of
France (Geneva, and the Bernese Jura), or they imitated that code
(Vaud in 1808–1819, Freiburg in 1834–1850, Ticino in 1837,
Neuenburg in 1855, Valais in 1855–1856).   Imitations of the
French law of inheritance were adopted by special statute
in St. Gall in 1808 and Thurgau in 1839. A second group
adopted codifications of private law (Bern 1824–1828, Lucerne
1831–1839, Solothurn 1842–1848, and Aargau in 1826 and 1848–
1856, and the law of persons adopted by Nidwalden in 1853) which
were developments of the Austrian Civil Code of 1811.   A third
group of cantons produced original codes based upon the then
current views of legal science   Thus originated the Zurich code
of private law, 1853–1855, under the editorship of J C Bluntschli,
which was followed by Schaffhausen in 1864–1865, Graubunden
in 1862, Glarus in 1869–1874, Zug in 1861–1876, the law of persons
and family in Thurgau in 1860, and the law of inheritance in
Nidwalden in 1859.

The Federation of 1848 was still essentially without powers in
the field of *private law,* and was therefore limited in this respect to
inter-cantonal compacts, so-called " concordats," which were
promulgated, from the Mediation period onward, in increasing
number, and served to make legal diversities more endurable
in intercantonal intercourse   As a result of the constitutional revision of 1874 the Federation received legislative power over the
law of marriage and of obligations; of which it made use in federal
statutes of 1874 and 1881   In 1898 federal power was extended
over the entire field of civil and criminal law. The Swiss Civil

Theodor Curti, "Geschichte der schweizerischen Volksgesetzgebung" (1882) ;
Hilty, "Offentliche Vorlesungen uber die Helvetik" (1878) , *Ullmer,* "Die
staatsrechtliche Praxis der schweizerischen Bundesbehorden" (1862–
1866), continued by *Salis* (1890 *et seq*), *Dubs,* "Das offentliche Recht der
schweizerischen Eidgenossenschaft" (2 vols , 1878)

Code was adopted on December 10, 1907, by the Federal Assembly, and came into force with the opening of 1912.[1]

Within the field of *civil procedure* we find cantonal regulations shaped essentially according to dominant scientific tendencies. These ordinances of procedure are of the period 1849 to 1907　The later ones incline more than the older to oral proceedings. Of particular importance was the creation of courts of trade, which have been established, with a diversities of organization, in Geneva and Vaud, Bern, St. Gall, Lucerne, Neuenburg, Freiburg, Solothurn, Basel City, Basel County, and Zürich.

In *criminal procedure* we find in one group of cantons oral proceedings in special criminal courts; namely, in the six cantons with popular assemblies, in Lucerne, the two Basels, Grabunden, St. Gall, Schaffhausen, Valais, Schwyz, and Zug. The other cantons have introduced jury courts, which had already been established in nucleus under the Helvetian Republic, and have since been developed (particularly, although indeed not exclusively) under French influence.

The *criminal law* was unified in the time of the Republic in a Helvetian Criminal Code of April 1, 1799. It rested upon the principle of vindictive punishment, and was marked by great severity, so that mitigations of its rigor were found necessary even during the period of the Republic. After the Republic's collapse some of the cantons continued to retain the code until towards the middle of the century; but, in general, criminal legislation reflected the successively dominant theories of the criminal law in Germany　Until about 1835 Feuerbach's theory of intimidation ruled. Aargau in 1815, Ticino in 1814, St. Gall in 1809, Basel in 1821 and 1835, and Schaffhausen in 1835 followed this idea These criminal codes have to-day all been abandoned. The last of them was repealed in Ticino in 1873. In the second third of the century the ruling theory was that of retributive justice. This was followed by Zurich in 1836, and then successively by Lucerne in 1836, by Thurgau 1861, Vaud 1863, Baselstadt 1846 and 1872, Freiburg 1850, Graubunden 1851, St. Gall 1857, Aargau 1857, Schaffhausen 1859, and Solothurn in 1859. Of these the

[1] See *Huber*, "System," *passim*　[The distinguished services of the author of this chapter, Professor EUGEN HUBER, in the drafting of the Code, have been noted in the Preface to this volume　On Jan 1, 1912, the Bern Bar Association, to celebrate the date of the New Code's taking effect, dedicated a stained-glass portrait panel, in honor of Professor Huber, bearing over his portrait the legend, "Dem Schopfer des Schweiz. Civilrechts" (To the Creator of Switzerland's Civil Law) — ED]

criminal codes of Thurgau, Vaud, St Gall, Aargau, Schaffhausen, and Graubunden are still in force (with various supplements). Finally, the last period shows the dominance of the reformative (or the eclectic) theory of criminal law.   As early as 1859 Solothurn adopted this in part, and afterwards Lucerne in 1860, Schwyz 1860, Obwalden 1865, Bern 1866, Glarus 1867, Zurich 1871, Baselstadt and Ticino in 1873, Basselland, Freiburg, Geneva, and Solothurn in 1874, Zug 1876, Appenzell-Ausserrhoden 1878, Neuenburg 1879 (revised in 1891), and Nidwalden and Appenzell-Innerrhoden in 1899.   From the 1880s onward the conditional release (Nidwalden treating it in 1878 as conditional pardon) and the indeterminate sentence were increasingly adopted in the cantons. Corporal punishment is forbidden by the Federal constitution. Capital punishment was abolished in 1874 by the Federal constitution for the entire country (for political crimes as early as 1848)   But this interdiction was abrogated in 1879 by a constitutional amendment, and since then the death penalty has been again introduced in the cantons of Uri, Schwyz, Obwalden, Appenzell-Innerrhoden, Zug, St. Gall, Schaffhausen, Valais, Lucerne, Freiburg, and in principle also in Zürich (although the law has in the last case never been promulgated).[1]   A unitary criminal law is now in preparation.

TOPIC 4. THE JURISTS AND THE MOVEMENTS OF LEGAL THOUGHT [2]

§ 19.   From the Period of National Independence to the 1700s. — It has been noted at the beginning of this chapter that Switzerland was a constituent part of the German Empire in the Middle Ages, and that Swiss law developed out of the medieval German law, offering in that period of its legal evolution, generally speaking, no particularities; but that the beginning of the 1500s constituted in this respect a sharply marked turning-point, from which time onward Switzerland and the Empire went separate ways.   The

---

[1] See for the general historical development *Pfenninger*, as above cited. For cantonal criminal law in the 1800s see *Siegwart-Muller*, "Das Strafrecht der Kantonen Uri, Schwyz, Unterwalden, Glarus, Zug, und Appenzell" (1833) ; *Temme*, "Lehrbuch des schweizerischen Strafrechts" (1855) ; *Wirth*, "Allgemeine Beschreibung und Statistik der Schweiz," I, 741 ; *Stoos*, "Die schweizerische Strafgesetzbucher zur Vergleichung zusammengestellt" (1890), and "Grundzuge dis schweizerischen Strafrechts" (2 vols., 1892–1893).

[2] [With the consent of Professor HUBER, and at the instance of the Editorial Committee, §§ 19, 20 have been compiled from the booklet of *Aloys von Orelli* cited above under § 1, by the TRANSL]

Swabian War had already separated Switzerland in fact from the Empire (§ 8, *ante*), and the contrast between the monarchical and republican polities became increasingly marked   In the internal legal development the fact of most radical significance was (§ 2, *ante*) that the Roman law was not " received " in Switzerland.   Nowhere was early popular opposition stronger to " the learned rubbish of the Corpus Juris," Bartolus and Baldus.   Men held fast to the Germanic popular or customary laws, subsidiary authority being given to the Roman law only in the valley of the Rhone; and the old courts also continued more or less as before, especially in the rural districts, with procedure oral and public   No necessity therefore existed for real law schools; and legal science, generally speaking, was in Switzerland for a very long time only very slightly cultivated or not at all.   Those statesmen or scholars who contributed sporadically to legal literature busied themselves therefore almost exclusively with the public law of the Confederation.

The intellectual currents in legal history, already alluded to in passing, may now be examined in somewhat more detail for their influences in legal literature and legislation from about 1500 onward.   Although in this development Switzerland not infrequently was influenced on all sides by European conditions, no true schools of legal thought were developed.   There were, however, some representatives of legal science worthy of mention, — some of them natives, and others foreign scholars who sought refuge abroad from political troubles at home.

The University of Basel was founded in 1460, and until the 1830s was the only university of Switzerland.   In the pre-reformation period its most distinguished students and professors were men whose names are well known in the history of German legal learning — SEBASTIAN BRANDT, BONIFACIUS AMMERBACH, CLAUDIUS CANTIUNCULA (Chansonette, of Metz)   Originally a foundation dependent on the bishop and cathedral chapter, its scientific spirit was early suffocated by scholasticism, and its attendance extraordinarily diminished in the second decade of the 1500s. The place of Basel in the Reformation had an important influence upon it.   After closure from 1529–1532 the University was reopened upon the basis of a municipal charter in place of the former papal charter.   Up to 1529 legists and decretists alike interpreted the Roman and the Canon laws, as in German, French, and Italian universities.   After 1532 chairs were established in the Pandects, Code, Institutes, and Canon and Feudal law.

"Jus Publicum" and "Jus Gentium" were later introduced, doubtless under the influence of Grotius Natural and international law and morals were assigned to a common professorship in 1706 In its general history, also (for example as regards the giving of expert opinions by the faculty),[1] Basel reflected the legal development of Germany. As an intellectual bond with Germany, the University exercised a steady influence, but the sum of its positive contributions to legal literature — characterized, in the opinion of Orelli, by "much pedantry and lack of taste" — hardly exceeded "a few dull works, whose significance did not extend beyond the law of the city and surrounding territory." In general they were sufficiently appreciated by the judgment passed by critics upon one pretending to be a compendium of "the imperial, papal, or common laws," that in it the imperial, papal, and common laws were converged in a perspective upon the Basel horizon.

In Zurich and eastern Switzerland, during the same period, there were but scanty literary beginnings, limited, with one notable exception, to the public law of the Confederation. Toward the end of the 1700s the beginnings of legal education proper appear in the "Collegium Carolinum;" chairs of politics, local history, and natural law having been established early in the century (1713, 1724). Of works deserving mention the earliest is the "De Republica Helvetiorum Libri Duo" of JOSIAS SIMMLER (died 1576), which was widely used, and was translated into German, French, and Dutch, retaining interest to-day as a presentation of the public law of the old Confederation. The "De Helvetiorum Juribus Circa Sacra" (1768; cf § 3, ante) of JOSEF ANTON FELIX BALTASAR (1737–1810) [2] was the earliest work on Swiss ecclesiastical law. In private law there was but a single, but that a most notable, work (the exception above referred to), namely, the "Town and Rural Law" (cf. § 15, ante) of JOHANN JAKOB LEU (1689–1768), which gives an abstract, in the order of the Institutes, of many manuscript and printed bodies of town law, land-books, and German, French, and Latin local statutes.

In Bern, legal growth was predominately national, even local, in character. A so-called Gymnasium had existed here since the 1500s In 1679 a chair of legal science was created.[3] It

---

[1] Four folios of such opinions, of the 1500s and later, are preserved in the University library

[2] His remarkable collection of historical manuscripts is preserved in the city library of Lucerne, the richest in ancient Helvetics in Switzerland

[3] The first occupant was (1679–1686) *Seelmatter*, a Swiss who had been professor in Leyden "juris naturalis, gentium et publici", and among his

was long occupied, from 1748 onwards, by SIGMUND LUDWIG VON LERBER, with whom began practically the effective influence of the university upon legal literature and legislation. Lerber minimized the importance of the Roman law, vindicated the Germanic origins of the law of Bern, and left as a notable monument a code of judicature of 1761 which embodied his ideas, — for example, by adopting from a judicature statute of 1539, in preference to the Roman doctrines of possession and prescription, the simple conceptions of seisin and physical control (" Gewere " and " Gewalt ")." GOTTLIEB WALTHER (1738–1805), professor of history, endeavored to found and expound the native law upon a historical basis. He wrote a " Versuch zur Erläuterung der Geschichte des vaterlandischen Rechtes " (1765), a " Geschichte des bernischen Stadtrechts " (vol. I, 1794), and began a history of Bernese law. He inveighed with biting satire and a holy zeal against the miserable education of the jurists. In 1787 the town government voted the establishment of a Political Institute to train men for public service. Among its disciplines were national, local, and Roman law, as well as national history. The school was under mimical influences, and did not attain much influence. Among the professors (1806–1817) was one, however, who must be counted among the few leading publicists which Switzerland has produced (though indeed one not all imbued with the ideas which shaped the history of his time), KARL LUDWIG VON HALLER (1768–1854), who devoted his life to anticonstitutional propaganda, and is perhaps the leading representative (at least in the 1800s) of patriarchal and legitimist theories of society and government. His greatest work was his " Restauration der Staatswissenchaft " (2d ed. 6 vols , Winterthur, 1820–1834)

It was only in the Latin part of Switzerland that there developed from the 1500s onward a fruitful literary activity devoted both to practical questions of legislation and politics and to philosophical problems of the law. It is a very noteworthy fact that the scientific cultivation of the law, both in legal literature and especially its utilization in legislation, played a far greater part in the French than in the German parts of Switzerland in the 1500s, 1600s, and above all in the 1700s. Lausanne shared in part in the nationalist characteristics of Bern　Geneva was essentially dominated by French influences. Men no longer walked quietly here, as in Basel and Bern in the 1700s, in the old accustomed paths　The

successors, until called to St Petersburg, was *Nikolaus Bernoulli*, son of the celebrated Swiss mathematician

Academy was in the full flow of the intellectual currents of the time, and its philosophical-juristic faculty took a busy part in the political and social questions which stormily agitated the second half of the 1700 s. The ideas of Rousseau, Voltaire, and the Encyclopædists, Montesquieu, Locke, and the English Tories, found in Geneva intelligent comprehension, enthusiastic partisans, and wide dissemination [1]

This stirring intellectual life was greatly advanced by the Academies of Lausanne, founded in 1537, and of Geneva, founded in 1559 Legal instruction began in the former in 1611, and was regularly kept up after 1708, when a professorship was established. Its first occupant was the Frenchman, JEAN BARBEYRAC (1674–1744), distinguished in the history of natural law by his translations of and commentaries upon Grotius and Puffendorff. The position of Geneva as the theatre of Calvin's activity and center of French Protestantism, and its development under the influence of Calvin (who was as much jurist as theologian) into a special type of polity, gave it a still more commanding influence. A " Collegium " that had existed here since before the Reformation was transformed by Calvin into the Academy It enjoyed from the beginning a large attendance The juristic faculty was first created in 1565. FRANÇOIS HOTMAN (1524–1589), one of the most learned and remarkable men of his age, whose works enjoyed immense reputation in the 1500 s, and ENNEMOND BONNEFOI (known commonly as Bonfidius, 1536–1584) were distinguished, but brief, occupants of professorial chairs; as were also, for ten and thirty-three years respectively the two GODEFROYS, DENIS (1549–1621), a Frenchman, who was foremost in the second rank of jurisconsults of his century, and JACQUES (1587–1652), a native of Geneva, and hardly less distinguished. All of these represented in Geneva the reformatory spirit which carried them, as it did most of the great French jurists, into the Huguenot ranks, and impelled them to that spirit of free thought which placed French legal science upon the pinnacle of that time

This was the lustrous period of Geneva. In the 1600 s legal

[1] Thus, for example, F. A Naville (1752–1794), a Genevan, in his work on the "État Civil de Genève" (1790), was evidently influenced by Montesquieu In it he embodied observations made during a long official experience and on his travels, giving us data regarding the amount of litigation in Geneva, its cost, and the number of officials necessary to attend to it, all relatively to the population He was the first in Switzerland to use the inductive method in legal science J. L de Lolme (1740–1806) wrote an intelligent and passionate defence of English government and justice

science sank in importance, but in the 1700s rose again.   Whereas in the 1600s, and to some extent in the following century, the greatest emphasis was placed upon the study of the Roman law, in the 1700s, the age of natural law and political theories, the cultivation of legal philosophy and public law predominated. Among their cultivators was J. J. BURLAMAQUI (1694–1748), a Genevan, a pupil of Puffendorf and Wolf, twenty-five years a professor.   Celebrated in the history of international law are also the works of EMER DE VATTEL (1714–1767), a native of Neuchâtel, and educated in Basel and Geneva.

Very noteworthy is the attention paid in the French cantons to the history and system of the local laws, upon which there is a considerable literature.[1]

§ 20.   **In the 1800s.** — The first third of the 1800s was not very different in character from the three centuries preceding.   In western Switzerland there was considerable scholarly activity, devoted primarily to problems of legislation and penitentiary systems;   while in German Switzerland scholarship (relatively much greater than the early period) was devoted primarily to theory   In the German cantons the English problems of representative government found echo before the Reform Bill; German university influences were of   exceeding importance,   and

---

[1] In 1764–1781 *M. A. Porta* expounded as a professor of the highest rank the customary law of Vaud   *Pierre Quizard* published in 1562 the epoch-making commentary cited *ante*, § 11, which treats systematically and thoroughly public, feudal, civil and criminal law, and procedure   This was the basis of the code of 1616, which together with the commentary (2 vols , Neuchâtel, 1756–1776) upon it by *J F Boyve* (1692–1771) are also referred to in the text, *ante*, § 11   For indications of materials on feudal law of which Boyve was an especial master, see Z. Sch R , XIII, 119, and *Leu*, "Helvetisches Lexikon," article on Boyve.   In addition to these works on Vaud there are various others which record the local law of Valais , among them the "Principes sur la Formalité Civile Judiciaire du Pays de Vaud" (Lausanne, 1777) of *François Samuel Theodor de Porta* (1716–1790), a work upon legal practice based upon thirty-five years' experience, which was the basis in turn of the Valais statute of procedure in 1825   Similarly, the peculiar and noteworthy law of Neuchâtel was systematically presented by *Samuel Osterwald* (1692–1769) in his work "Les loix, us et coutûmes de la souveraineté de Neuchâtel et Valangin" (1785), which duplicated the scope of the Institutes and attained the authority of statutory law , and the "Sommaire des fiefs de l'état de Neuchâtel et de Valangin" (1673) of *Georges de Montmollin* (printed in the Z. Sch R , XIX, (pt. 2), 15 *et seq*).   Also those of Geneva in *J Pierre Sartoris*, "Elements de la procédure criminelle suivant les ordonnances de France, les constitutions de Savoye et les édits de Genève" (1774, 2 vols.).   In the early 1800s there were other works of this same character, including for Bern a "Handbuch des Civilrechts mit besonderer Hinsicht auf die positiven Gesetze des Cantons Bern" by *Samuel Schnell*, and for Vaud the "Remarques sur le droit civil du canton de Vaud" (Lausanne, 1840) of *Charles Sécretan.*

criminal law was particularly cultivated (*ante*, § 18), following the development of German philosophical theory. The ideas of the German historical school also found echo and application in Switzerland.

The University of Basel in these years was in a stage of transition, not to say decay, and exercised little influence. In Bern, early in the 1800s, a short-lived impetus to legal studies was given by a local Academy into which the higher schools of the canton were recast and unified. Its chairs included one in the law of Bern and the history of Switzerland.[1] In the French cantons the Academy of Lausanne remained under predominant clerical influence, and suffered greatly in the period following the French Revolution. In 1806 two chairs of law were established, one of natural and public law, the other of the civil law and civil procedure of Vaud.[2] In 1822 a chair of criminal law was established. The law faculty, however, failed to attain an importance comparable to that of the theological and philosophical faculties. The Academy of Geneva did not suffer in these years in its non-theological faculties. Geneva enjoyed at the end of the 1700s such repute in the scientific world that even political revolutions could not lessen it. After the end of the Napoleonic period and the re-annexation of Geneva to Switzerland, the Academy occupied a place among nationalistic influences similar to that held by the German universities in the same period.[3] Both in Lausanne and Geneva, among other influences, those of Bentham and utilitarianism were evident.[4]

---

[1] Occupied 1806–1842 by *Samuel Schnell*, editor of the Bernese Civil Code of 1825 and Code of Civil Procedure of 1821, as well as of the work above mentioned; not identical with the founder of the Z. Sch. R., Johann Schnell, who first in Switzerland gave university courses in comparative Swiss law

[2] *Charles Sécretan* (1784–1858), appointed to this chair to 1822, was practically the author of the Code of Civil Law of the canton of 1819, as well as of the attractive commentary upon it noted above

[3] Among the professors was (following 1819) *Pellegrino Rossi* (1787–1848), who taught Roman and criminal law and enjoyed a great name as a criminalist in France and Italy. The Genevan *Pierre François Bellot* (1776–1856) was of no less importance. He was the author of the Genevan Code of Civil Procedure of 1819, a recast and (as generally admitted) an improvement of the French code, based on the principles of publicity and oral proceedings, which excellently approved itself in practice. He also introduced in Geneva in 1820–1830, for mortgages, the principles of the German land registers. See the "Exposé des motifs" accompanying Bellot's Code

[4] This was illustrated in Lausanne by *Charles Comte* (1782–1837), a Frenchman, and in Geneva by *Rossi*, who found the justification of punishment in the moral order but its limits in social utility, and by the Genevan *Etienne Dumont* (1759–1828), who was a pupil of Bentham and

In Zürich there was founded, in 1807, with small means and, modest limits, under the name of a Political Institute, a true school of law, through which was established a firm connection with German legal learning. Bern had influenced Zürich, and Zürich in turn influenced all of German Switzerland. Among the occupants of the professorship of private and public law were some half dozen, all trained in German universities, who were authors of cantonal codes (*cf.* § 18, *ante*) or other works of merit, and were active in public life as judge and politicians.[1] More important than any other was Fr. L von Keller (1799-1860), a distinguished pupil of Savigny and later a professor at Berlin, who procured the establishment of a chair of Roman law. He was also the first in Zürich to advance the systematic historical study of the local private law.

The introduction of instruction in the Roman law met at first with strong and widespread jealousy on the part of those who could not reconcile its study by Swiss judges and other public servants with a due fidelity to republican institutions, and who regarded it unnecessary for jurists to obscure practical justice, which ought to be simple and ingenuous, with overmuch learning.[2] While the majority of Zurich judges had formerly had no university training abroad, and at best had enjoyed only a general education, or possibly a smattering of law-office experience, as a preparation for public service, a great change in all this, evidently due to the Institute, came about from 1820-1830. The cantonal court of first instance became the nucleus of the new movement. Whereas formerly in Zurich the judge's subjective sense of justice had really been decisive in litigation, and expert jurists were regarded with rather unfriendly eye as something foreign and abnormal in the popular tribunals, this court ("Amtsgericht") now assumed to break herein wholly with the past, and to base

friend of Brougham and Romilly, and who devoted himself, in addition to the spread of Bentham's ideas through various works, to penitentiary reforms that attracted European attention.

[1] Among them *Ludwig Meyer von Knonau* (1769-1841), author of cantonal codes of matrimonial and criminal law and of a history of the Swiss Confederation ("Handbuch der Geschichte der schweizerischen Eidgenossenschaft," 2 vols, Zurich, 1826-1829) which met with Niebuhr's praise; *Heinrich Escher* (1789-1870), who wrote a noteworthy "Handbuch der praktischen Politik" (2 vols, Leipzig, 1863-1864), and drafted an excellent cantonal criminal code; *Melchior Hirzel* (1796-1843), who developed the Feuerbach theory of criminal law, *Johann Caspar Ulrich* (1796-18—), the author of the first Zurich code of criminal law of 1835; and *Ferdinand Meyer* (1799-1840), who emphasized the importance of the study of political science, then not yet taught in the German universities, as a discipline for Swiss public servants, and the merits of representative government. [2] *Cf* in Orelli, *op. cit.*, 64-68

its decisions on objective principles of law   Its conflict with the
higher courts and the government caused great excitement   Of
this movement Keller was the soul.   The impulse thus given in
Zürich had great effect in German Switzerland upon legal science
and practice   Along with the growth of the idea that the times
required a law with a scientific basis went the codification of the
civil and later of the criminal law, — the necessary application of
Thibaut's ideas being thus practically recognized.   In this Vaud
and Bern preceded Zürich   The political developments in Switzerland of the 1830s everywhere brought about the realization of this
development.   The law thus became a life calling, and there grew
up a special legal profession in close union with public life.

With the establishment of the Universities of Zurich in 1833 and
of Bern in 1834, and the reformation of that of Basel in 1835, a new
epoch began   The first university courses in comparative private
law and Swiss legal history were now introduced at Basel.   In this
later period mention may especially be made of JOHANN CASPAR
BLUNTSCHLI (1808–1881), whose most important work in the field
of Swiss law was his " Public and Legal History of the City and
County of Zurich ";[1] as well as those of J. J. BLUMER, ANDREAS
HEUSLER, CH. LE FORT, F VON WYSS, CH. SÉCRETAN, J. RUTTI-
MANN, and others, who made particularly valuable contributions
to legal literature in the first three quarters of the last century.

[1] "Staats- und Rechtsgeschichte der Stadt und Landschaft Zurich," 2
parts, Zurich, 1838–1839, 2 ed 1856.

PART VII

SCANDINAVIA

FIRST PERIOD (TO A.D. 1200): THE LAW-MEN AND THE
    LAW-TEXTS

SECOND PERIOD (A.D. 1200–1700): THE MEDIEVAL CODES

THIRD PERIOD (A.D. 1700–1900): THE MODERN CODES

Part VII: SCANDINAVIA

Chapter I[1] First Period: to a.d. 1200

THE LAW-MEN AND THE LAW-TEXTS[2]

§ 1. Primitive Usages.
§ 2. Early Modes of Preserving Traditional Law, the Law-Men
§ 3. The Icelandic Law-saga Man
§ 4. The Swedish Law-Man
§ 5. The Norwegian Law-Man
§ 6. The Danish Law-Man.
§ 7. The Authority of the Law-Men

§ 8. Legal Terms.
§ 9. The "Thing."
§ 10. Early Central Legislation
§ 11. Early Law-Texts, the Right-Books
§ 12. Icelandic Law-Texts
§ 13. Norwegian Law-Texts.
§ 14. Danish Law-Texts.
§ 15 Swedish Law-Texts.

§ 1. Primitive Usages. — Among the prehistoric Germanic races of the North, the law existed for ages merely in the form of customary rules of conduct. These were more or less consciously grouped, with economic, moral, and religious elements, into a common factor which intimately reflected and directly determined the daily order of life.

[1] [Chapter I = HERTZBERG, Part I, §§ 5–30, extracted and condensed. For the citation of this work, and an account of the author, see the Editorial Preface. — TRANSL.]

[2] [BRIEF LIST OF AUTHORITIES FOR THE ENSUING CHAPTER·
TREATISES: *Schlyter*, "Juridiska Afhandlingar" (Uppsala, 1836); *Finsen*, "Om de islandske love i Fristatstiden" (Copenhagen, 1873), *K Maurer*, "Die Rechtsrichtung des alter islandischens Rechtes" (Munchen, 1887); *G. Storm*, "Sigurd Ranessons Proces" (Christiania, 1877); *Snorre*, "Olaf den helliges Saga"; *v Amira*, "Altschwedisches Obligationenrecht" (Leipzig, 1882); *Joh. Steenstrup*, "Inledning i Normannertiden" (Copenhagen, 1876), *Stemann*, "Den Danske Retshistorie" (Copenhagen, 1872), *Maurer*, "Nordgerm. Retskilder" (Christiania, 1878), *J. J Nordstrom*, "Svenska Samhållsforfattningens historia", *R Keyser*, "Norges Stats- og Retsforfatning i Middelalderen." (Christiania, 1867), *Ebbe Hertzberg*, "Den ældste Norske Proces" (Christiania, 1874), *Maurer*, "Gragas", *Secher*, "Kongens Rettertingsdomme", *Holberg*, "Dansk Rigslovgivning" (Copenhagen, 1889), *C. J. Schlyter*, "Sveriges Gamla Lagar."
EDITIONS OF TEXTS AND DOCUMENTS. *V Finsen*, "Grágás" (3 vols, Copenhagen, 1852–1883), *J Sigurdson*, "Diplomatarium Islandicum" (1857–1876), *R Keyser and P A Munch*, "Norges gamle Love" (1846–1848); continued by *G Storm* (1885), and *E Hertzberg* (1895), 5 vols, Second Series, continued by *Taranger* (1904), *C J Schlyter and H S Collin*, "Corpus juris SveoGothorum antiqui" (Lund, 1827–1877, 13 vols.)]

While such spontaneous growth is characteristic of the law in primitive communities, it is, however, to be noted that specially enacted and positive law early appears. Expressed and binding regulations were made necessary, in the establishment of agrarian and religious communities, providing for a stable system of defence, the transition to a new faith, the settlement and organization of a conquered territory, or the subjection to foreign suzerainty and taxation. Sudden changes of this nature brought a pressure for suitable agreements and rules for the new conditions. This was particularly evidenced in Iceland, where such conscious and deliberate enactments first entered the history of Scandinavian law. They absorbed in a measure the ancient law of custom, and brought changes, improvements, and developments, hastening the collection of the materials which were to constitute the special science of law in society.

The ancient body of usages was not always the product of an instinctive and unconscious mode of action. Its provisions were often the result of long discussion. This is demonstrated in the history of Norway, where there was a standing struggle for ages before it was finally provided in its criminal code what amount of damages should suffice for the various injuries to the person; and it was also a mooted question whether such reparation was consistent with prevailing principles of honor. The further question as to such damages in cases of manslaughter was even then left undecided. This would show that, as long as opposing views existed and discussion continued as to what a rule of law should be, it did not attain the force of a principle of the common law of custom.

§ 2 **Early Modes of Preserving Traditional Law; the Law-Men.** — With the gradual growth of the conception of law as a distinct factor in the various domains of society, a demand was felt for the systematic preservation from generation to generation of the unwritten law of customs. Man, in his early development, is slow to realize his social needs and to adopt suitable means therefor, only after a long period of progress was it understood that one of the lawmaking functions was to provide for the preservation of the laws in human memory.

Ordinarily, among primitive races, the custodian of any knowledge beyond that of daily observation is the priest The Germanic tribes, however, and especially the Scandinavian races, were an exception to this rule. The priests of the age of mythology not having attained any special influence, such knowledge as was deemed of value was shared among others. The historical and

534

poetical traditions were preserved by scalds and saga-tellers, and could be acquired by any one so inclined. Likewise the knowledge of the law became a common heritage and the particular study of some according to their talents and needs. Prominent men, such as chieftains and their sons, as well as those of humbler birth desirous of exercising personal dominion, devoted themselves to this pursuit, receiving private instruction while dwelling in the homes of their tutors.

As in the case of the sagas, these legal rules of tradition and their interpretation, to aid the memory and facilitate their repetition, were gradually formed into terse, precise, and artistic phrases, proverbs, and verses, which were as easily remembered as difficult to improve, — alliterative rhyming being also frequently resorted to. Those learned in these traditions of the ancient law of custom, and eminent among their fellows in this respect, were given the title of "Law-men" ("Lovmænd," "lagmenn," "lögmaðr"). They were not only instructors, but also private counsellors, and as they were necessarily also consulted at the eyre, assizes, or "Thing," as "jurisconsulti," they were in effect judges in litigated cases. This semiofficial character they retained for about three centuries, in Norway and Iceland, after the emigration and the settlement of the latter country.

§ 3. **The Icelandic Law-saga Man.** — With increase in the public functionaries the important duty of having custody of the law was bound to become official. During or near the year 930, there arose in Iceland such an office, in connection with the first attempt to form a system of jurisprudence, — that of the "Law-saga Man" ("Lögsögumaðr," "Legifer"). On him it was incumbent to recite [1] the existing rules of law before the yearly General Assizes or "Thing" (the "Althing"), completing the entire body of law in the course of every three years. The immediate motive for this practice was the desire to prevent the confusion which might result from variances between the legal system then used and that brought from the native country, Norway. While this official thus in some degree superseded the law-men and became the authority on questions arising in law, he was, nevertheless, in duty bound on certain occasions to consult a number of the latter, — five or more.

§ 4. **The Swedish Law-man.** — Unlike the Law-men of Norway and Iceland, the Swedish Law-man early attained the dignity and power of a duly elected public official and repre-

[1] ["Saga" = to speak tell, recite — TRANSL.]

sentative His district was one of the regions or "Lands" of
the country, and his electors were the owners and tillers of the soil
(" Bonder "). His duties were to enforce the administration of
justice, to preside at the " Thing" of the " Land," and to render
advice as to the provisions of the law applicable to cases as they
arose (" lagh skila "). In addition to thus serving as the supreme
judicial authority, he also attended to other political and administrative functions The chief cause for this system, peculiar to
Sweden, is probably to be found in the natural antagonism existing
between the central rule, in a small kingdom, constantly bent on
extending its sway, and scattered communities of freeholders chiefly
engaged in agriculture, and constantly on guard against royal encroachments This determination to preserve local legal independence is evidenced in the most ancient Swedish law-text still in
existence, it expressly provides· " Yeoman-born shall law-man
be; to this let every yeoman see." In " The Holy Olaf's Saga,"
it is also recorded: " If king or jarl or bishop sally forth through
the land to hold 'Thing' with the yeomen, the law-man responds
in favor of the yeomanry, and all vote with him, so that those
in power dare hardly appear at their 'Things,' unless the yeomanry
and their law-man permit "

In furtherance of their powers, the Swedish Law-men from
various districts combined under Chieftains, — an important
factor in the history of the country, which already in the eleventh
century had attained considerable development This official,
in addition to being the head of his " Land," under a strong organization, also delivered the regular public address (" Lag-saga ")
containing the law of the land As a peculiar characteristic of
Swedish development is its remarkable and inherent continuity,
the motive for its law-saga cannot be found in any sudden transition to a new legal system, but rather in the extension of the law-
man's authority. Being chosen as the presiding officer of the
" Thing " and attaining eminence over his fraternity of private
advisers, the law-man became responsible for the correct announcement of the law in force, having no time for giving private instruction, he concentrated this duty in his public recital,
which thus served as an official, oral code for the gathered
multitude.

Tradition still preserves the names of law-men, who in the pre-
Christian times distinguished themselves in the formulation of
law-sagas Such are the famous Lum, whose system was known
as " the Laws of Lum," and Vig Spa, after whom was named

Viger's" Lag-saga " or " Viger's Flokker "   In the introduction to the ancient Law of Småland, the practice is expressly recorded: " Now the men shall journey to the Thing; hear ye present and tell those at home, but our Law-saga commences thus " [1]

§ 5 **The Norwegian Law-man.** — Up to the beginning of the 1100 s, the Norwegian law-men appeared at the local and general " Things " collectively, and in considerable numbers. They would " say the law," *i.e* declare the rules of law applicable to a given case, and interpret its effects in concrete instances.   As to the question whether they constituted a class with exclusive privileges, there is a difference of opinion   There were also in Norway public law-recitals, chiefly affecting affairs before the " Things," but no special member of those versed in legal affairs seems to have been elected for this or similar purposes   The ancient laws seem to have been adapted to the spirit of Christianity and monarchy by the Holy King Olaf.   On the whole, the general system of legal administration appears to have developed more slowly here than in Sweden, until the time of King Sverre Sigurdssøn (1184–1202), during whose reign great progress was made and an official character bestowed on law-men, whose districts were termed " Law-sagas."

That the people were averse at first to acknowledging the official authority of their law-men and acquiescing in their decrees as real decisions, is shown by the complaint of King Haakon Haakonsøn, far down in the following century, that their decrees were not recognized as binding   In fact, even in the thorough reform of the judicial system in the latter half of the 1200 s, it was not deemed advisable to make the law-man's judgment directly self-executory.

§ 6. **The Danish Law-man.** — If it were possible to prove that general, public recitals of the existing laws were given in Norway as well as in Sweden from the most ancient periods, it would seem probable that the practice also obtained in Denmark. Assuming, however, that Sweden was the original home of the law-saga, and that this was brought from Sweden to Iceland and later to Norway, it is to be noted that there is no certain evidence that the institution has ever existed in Denmark   Likewise are

---

[1] It is possible that the Swedish practice of public recital of the law at the "Thing" was followed as a model in Iceland after its reorganization Communication over the sea was frequent, and such a notable custom could not have remained unknown long,   It may be observed that the historic island of Gotland apparently never has known either law-man or law-saga.

there few traces of any official character having attached to the Danish law-men. Considering that there was as great a need at the Danish "things" for advice from men versed in the law as in the other Northern countries, the most acceptable supposition is that the Danish law-man in his capacity corresponded to the early Norwegian-Icelandic law-man before the latter class had been relegated to the background through the bestowal of official status on the law-saga-man.

§ 7. **The Authority of the Law-men** — It is not quite clear in what degree popular acquiescence was given to the public recitals of law and the decisions rendered in litigated cases by the law-men In Norway, as appears from the Saga of the "Case of Sigurd Ranessòn," the unanimous declaration of the law-men in a judicial proceeding was simply adopted and followed. In Sweden, according to Snorre, in cases of variance between the laws of different "lands" or between the law-men, the laws of Uppland and the law-man representing Tiundaland were recognized as controlling As each district or "land," however, retained judicial power over its local affairs, this rule as to differences between law-men could have applied only to political affairs. Where law-men abused their position and power (as is recorded concerning one in Westergot-land, that "he was of evil disposition and injected into our laws many wrongs and unrighteous conceits"), there seems to have been no appeal or recourse for remedying the situation, other than by electing a more reliable successor, who would restore the just laws and rights infringed upon. In Iceland, the law-saga man was esteemed so emphatically the preserver and custodian of the law that to one of their number is attributed, in the famous "Nialasaga," the utterance that he could not have believed that any one other than he in that generation had known the rule of the law for a certain case. This manuscript also shows that the decisions of this official were viewed as binding. The law, however, expressly directed him, whenever in doubt, to consult five or more law-men, whence it would appear that in the circles of the latter unofficial group there remained a certain traditional power of control over the law-saga man by way of correction. Even after the writing of the law-texts or codes, the law-men exercised a supplementary legal authority, where not inconsistent with the publicly recited and written rules.

In conclusion, it may be noted that it pertained to the law-making assembly of Iceland ("Lagrett") to render its approval of the regular address, and, in cases of dispute as to interpreting and applying the legal principles, to determine and announce its will.

§ 8. **Legal Terms.** — The inhabitants of the ancient North termed their system of justice " Law " (" lagh," " log," " logh "), thereby indicating that which had been brought into established order and which embraced the entire mass of usages and special regulations and enactments. Distinguished from this word, as representing the causes and foundations of the social order, the word " Right " (" réttr," " rétter," " ræt ") was used to designate the social order itself, viewed as a social relationship from an individual standpoint   The " Right " was the collection of existing relations of justice or justness between the members themselves and between them and society, for which they were endeavoring to establish a safeguard — not a source — in the law. This idea of the Law merely confirming the Right was expressed in giving to later enactments, by kings or people, titles such as the Norwegian " Rettarböt " and the Swedish " Stadga," implying confirmation of rights

The different divisions of the body of rules were termed " bolker " (" bálkr," " bolkr "), " mal," and " flokker." These were grouped according to subjects in classes, such as marine mercantile law (" farmanna-log "), war-law (" hermanna-lóg " or " vikinga-lòg "), market law (" birke-ret "), and ecclesiastical law (" kristin-log ").

§ 9. **The " Thing."** — In *Sweden* the smallest organization of communities among the tribes known as the Goths was termed the " Herred," and among the Svears the Hundred (" Hundari "). The public judicial and legislative assemblies in these districts were hence termed the " Herred-thing " and the " Hundred-thing."   A number of these rural communities were combined into a higher administrative and political unit, which was named the " Land." The " Land-thing " possessed the real general lawmaking and judicial powers. In that part of southern Sweden designated as Gotaland, the " Land-thing " of the West Goths (" Westergotland ") early attained superior influence, and was known as " the Thing of all the Goths." This domain later contained six Lands: Westergötland, Ostergotland, Wermland, Småland, and the Isles of Oland and Gotland   In Svea-land, in Central Sweden, the " lands " numbered five Uppland, Sodermannland, Westmannland, Helsingland, and Nerike. Uppland was divided into Tiundaland, Attundaland, and Fiœdrundaland (the " Lands " of the ten, eight, and four Hundreds).

539

In *Denmark* the Danes were also organized into " Herreds "
Its " lands " originally were. Jylland, Fyen, Sjælland, Laaland,
Skaane, Halland, Blekinge, and Bornholm. Here there was also
a court intervening between those of the " herred " and the " land,"
termed the " Syssel-thing "

In *Norway*, owing to the natural difficulties of travel in its
mountainous districts, the " herreds " of the smaller communities,
even after the commencement of the historic period, retained their
administrative functions, independently of each other   Gradually,
however, these minor organizations were consolidated into " Fylks "
(" Fylker," people), corresponding to the Swedish " lands."   Three
of these, Hedemarken, Raumarike, and Hadafylke, gathered at
the south end of the Mjosen in the famous " Eidsiva-thing."
Hørdaland, Sogn, and Firdafylke formed the " Gula-thing," their
meeting-place at the mouth of the Sogne-fjord being accessible
by water routes during a short period in the summer time.   The
inhabitants of the country surrounding the Throndhjemsfjord
convened at the mouth of the river Nidelven on the " Ore-thing,"
wherein eight " fylks " were represented, and which most resembled the Swedish " Land-thing."

These central organizations of the Norwegian " fylks," known
as " Law-things," were first to introduce essential changes in the
ancient law of custom, by making official enactments   Such
legislative, as well as judicial, functions were delegated to a committee of thirty-six members, chosen among those most influential
and versed in the law by the chieftains, — the board being known
as the " Law-Right " (" Lagretten ").   A forcible illustration
of the intimate relationship existing between the office of
the legislator and that of the judge at the time appears in
the saga of the " Case of Sigurd Ranesson," wherein there
arose a question as to the proper interpretation and application of the law to certain facts.   The proceedings of the
judges were abruptly stopped and changed into a legislative
debate as to what the particular rule of law ought to be.   This
being determined, a law was accordingly enacted and the trial of
the cause resumed.

Such was the incomplete system obtaining in Norway when the
country was united under a monarchy.   At the instance of kings,
further development was made, especially by the introduction of
the principle of representation in the establishment of diets (" Diæ-
ter ").   By means of these, the regular convening of the " law-
things " was made possible and assured, independently of the

exigencies and hardships of the long journeys   During the reign of King Haakon Adelstensfostre (933–961), the " coast-fylks " of Nordmore and Ramsdalen were incorporated in the "Frostu-thing," which met in an island in the Fjord of Throndhjem, and, likewise, the Southern " fylks," Rogaland and Agder, in the " Gula-thing." Under the Holy King Olaf (1015–1030) Gudbrandsdalen was added to the " Eidsiva-thing," and the "Borgar-thing " in Sarpsborg was established.

In *Iceland*, upon the organizing of its system of legal administration (930), the general legislative and the highest judicial powers were conferred on the " Althing "   The active head of this assemblage was an inner circle, corresponding to the Norwegian " Law-Right," consisting of the chieftains of the island (" Goder "), the law-saga man, and (after the introduction of Christianity) the two bishops.   For the trial of cases, four courts were instituted for the four separate divisions of the island (" Fiordungsdomar "), and a fifth tribunal for special cases.   Within each of these divisions there were also three local courts (" Thing-lag "), presided over by their respective chiefs.   The people themselves, however, in form adopted the resolutions and proceedings.   A peculiar observation is to be made in that each freeholder (" Bonde ") himself chose to which chieftain's circle he should belong, the " Thing-lag " being more a union than a district, considerations of neighborhood, distances, and the eminence of the respective chiefs entering into his selection.

§ 10. **Early Central Legislation.** — The lawmaking power exercised by the Swedish and Danish " Land-things " and the Norwegian " Law-things " rested solely in the populace.   Kings and persons in authority were considered in duty bound to conform to these proceedings.   In reality, however, this sovereignty of the people was not altogether dominant in Denmark and Norway. It was most effective in *Sweden*, where royalty in its early stages was more a dignity than a power, and where the influence of kings in the first development of law was insignificant.   Furthermore, wherever it is recorded that a king " gave " a certain law, it is to be understood that such a law was adopted by the Assembly.   With respect to military affairs and his own retinue, the monarch could promulgate regulations   Even the Swedish chieftainships, which appear in the statutes entitled "Alsno-stadgan" and " Skeninge-stadgan " of 1285 as an established institution, were not able to deprive the "Land-things" of their ancient prerogative to examine and adopt or reject acts proposed by the king.

541

In *Denmark*, the activities of the Danish " Land-thing " were
limited by the rise of a General Assembly of the kingdom, which
was named " Danehof " (" parlamentum generale Danorum "),
for the management of the political affairs of the country.   This
body in time assumed legislative functions   Its members were
men prominent in state and church, merchants and rural landowners.   Details of its early history are lacking   By the decree of
Erik Glipping in 1284, it was provided that the " Danehof " should
be held annually at Nyborg.   Notwithstanding the encroachments
of this central organization of the kingdom on many of the " Land-
thing " functions (after the beginning of the 1300 s, it became also
the supreme tribunal), proposed statutes continued for a long time
to be laid before the " Land-thing " for adoption.

In *Norway*, with the formation of a single monarchy, the kings
immediately took the lead in originating legislation.   The weaken-
ing of the " Land-thing " is shown by the fact that in 1046 a
gathering of chiefs (" Høvdingemøde ") enacted an important
statute, and that in 1164, at a meeting of temporal and spiritual
dignitaries of the kingdom, a radical change in the law of succession to the throne was made, and other laws were revised.   Similar
conventions were held later, without, however, attaining any independent title or authority.   Under the leadership of the kings,
they proposed statutes, which were later formally enacted by the
" Land-things."

§ 11. **Early Law-Texts; the " Right-Books."** — The urgent need
felt by the people of old for definite written law-texts, not subject
to the uncertainties of oral repetition, is demonstrated by the fact
that the laws were the subject of the earliest writings in the
Northern countries   The momentousness of this undertaking
appears from the fact that a whole century had elapsed, after the
introduction of Christianity and the acquirement of a knowledge of the Latin and Anglo-Saxon alphabets and manuscripts,
before the written form was adopted and the native speech was
adapted thereto.   This explains why the most ancient writings
preserved the forms and characteristics of oral expression, being
simply copies of the spoken law-sagas and instructions.   These
early law-texts, often made on private initiative, were apt to contain assertions, based on tradition, which were incorrect or disputed.
Hence, when the State expressly or by silent acquiescence acknowledged these most ancient texts (" Skraaer," leather-books) as
authorities for official use, it could not be responsible for the
accuracy of all the details.   In this respect, it remained for the

courts of the "things" to decide the law in the last instance. By reason of this difference between the ancient law-texts and the more modern codes, the former are distinguished by the term "Right-books" ("Retsbøger").

§ 12. **Icelandic Law-Texts.** — In the Scandinavian North, Iceland led in the establishment of written codes. The General Assembly, or "Althing," in the year 1117, appointed a committee, whose members were authorities on the traditional laws, with directions to prepare a written collection of the rules in force and to propose desirable changes and amendments While this text was officially adopted and ratified the following year, it is to be considered as embodying the prevailing rules of custom rather than as being in itself an official statutory code. That it was intended to derive its origin and character from the system of justice already in vogue, is evidenced by its forms, which correspond to those of the law-saga man in his public announcements and interpretations of the law. The book still recognized the opinions of the law-men as auxiliary authorities, where consistent with or explanatory of its provisions. Both in the original and in copies made from it, contradictions appear between the various codes. Nevertheless, this code — named "Haflida-skra," after the chairman of the commission, the Chieftain Haflide Maarson — approached the character of an official enactment of laws as closely as was possible without fully taking the step It embraced all the temporal affairs of the island, but precisely to what extent is not known, as the original is not in existence and it cannot be reconstructed from the later collections. During the period between 1122 and 1133, there was also prepared, at the instance of Bishops THORLAK of Skaalholt and KETIL of Hole, an ecclesiastical code, the "Kristenret."

These two collections served as a basis for numerous texts appearing for a century and a half thereafter, portions whereof are preserved. Chief among such ancient manuscripts still extant are the "King-book" ("Konungsbok," "Codex Regius," in the Royal Library at Copenhagen) and the "Stadarholsbok" ("Codex Arnamagnæanus," in the Library of the University of Copenhagen), both written between 1260 and 1270 These law-texts, dating from the period of independence of Iceland, and originating in the ancient oral law-sagas, are now generally referred to under the title of "The Icelandic Grágas"

§ 13. **Norwegian Law-Texts.** — The example of Iceland in 1118 seems to have been followed in Norway; and it is not probable that many decades passed, after the writing of Haflida-skra, before Norwegian laws were reduced to writing. While the tale of the "Case of Sigurd Ranesson" indicates that even in the early part of the 1100s there was no mention of consulting any written texts, and that the law-men alone were authorities, it appears that during the struggles in the latter half of that century between the monarchy (striving for hereditary succession) and the hierarchy (desirous to establish an electoral succession, in furtherance of its own interests), written laws were invoked by both parties. The priesthood especially cited the revised law-texts, which were claimed to be an agreement between the Archbishop Eystein and the king (crowned by him), Magnus Erlingson. In opposition to these, the adherents of the doctrine of succession by birth quoted earlier texts, containing the traditional law of the land, which must have appeared during the first half of that century. Two ecclesiastical Right-Books of the "Eidivathing" and the "Borgarthing" are ascribed, the former to the period between 1152 and 1162, and the latter, between 1140 and 1152, and these had undoubtedly been preceded by others. The earliest written text in Norway, in all probability, was the "Frostathing-lov," which in 1190, was already in existence in Nidaros, under the title of "Graagas," and was then cited by King Sverre. It contained what was generally known as St Olaf's Laws, and its chief provisions are apparently still preserved in the "Frostathings-bog" dating from the following century. Other right-books written during this period were the "Gulathings-lov," "Guldfjæder," and "Bjarko-ret." Among the numerous revisions and fragments still extant may be noted "Codex Ranzovianus" and "Codex Resimanus" in the University Library of Copenhagen.

These written collections of laws were regarded as law-texts, lacking the official authority of codes. Indeed, the ecclesiastical regulations contained in the "Borgarthingslov" conclude as follows "The law of the church ('Christian-Right') is now written and presented such as we remember it; wherein it be lacking, let the bishop amend therein." Even in revising and amending the early manuscripts in later periods, the characteristics of mere text-books were preserved. Chapter 314 of the revised "Gulathingslov" reads. "Now we have written down (the rules for) our country's defence, and know not if it be accurate or inaccurate, but even if this be inaccurate, we shall still have the law for our institutions which has prevailed of old and was spoken before the men at Gula" Here is an express admission that the written text was not infallible. Nor were these conflicting right-books viewed or referred to as official authorities at the convention of the kingdom in 1223 in Bergen, when the law-men were consulted as to the interpretation of St. Olaf's Law as to the succession to the throne.

Gradually, however, these revised texts became generally considered as authoritative, the transition being almost unnoticeable; and it may be assumed that in the agreement of 1244 the " Frostatings-kristenret " was enacted as law in its strict sense

§ 14. **Danish Law-Texts.** — In Denmark, the earliest written forms of law appeared during the 1100s, in the form of private works   Their authors are unknown, and it has not been determined how far public authority was concerned with their production.   One of these later works was written in Danish between 1203 and 1212, and the other in Latin between 1206 and 1215 by the distinguished Archbishop ANDREAS SUNESON of Lund. Both present the Law of Skaane,[1] and appear to have a common source.   There are also preserved to modern times " King Valdemar's Law of Sjælland " and King Eric's Law for the same " land," — both probably having been private texts which were officially authorized during the reigns of Valdemar Seier (ending 1241) and Eric Plogpenning (ending 1250)   In the Arnamagnæan Collection in Copenhagen is preserved a vellum manuscript, of the ancient law of Skaane, written in runes (" Codex Runicus "), probably dating from the 1200 s.

Among the ecclesiastical codes in Denmark, which were left entirely in the control of the priesthood, a " Kirke-ret " for Skaane was prepared by Archbishop ESKILD of Lund (1137–1178), and another for Sjælland by Bishop ABSALON of Roeskilde, both of which were adopted by the people.

§ 15   **Swedish Law-Texts** — The collections of ancient Swedish law manuscripts afford much enlightenment on the legal conditions of society at an age when the influence of the Christian dogmas had only in a mechanical and superficial manner affected the ancient legal conceptions and practices. The oldest among these is the " Vestgöta-lag," from the early 1200s. This is still in existence, as is also a later revision by Lydekin (1300). At the request of the law-men in Tiundaland, King Birger Magnusson directed a committee to write the laws of Uppland; this code was approved by him on January 2, 1296. Similar law-books were prepared for Ostergötland, Öland, Södermanland, Westman-

[1] [The present province of Scania (Skåne) of Sweden. — TRANSL.]

land, and Helsingland (covering Swedish settlements in Finland). In the year 1374, it is recorded, there were in Helsingland at least four copies of the law-book, the most important of which had its regular place in the Silaanger Church at Medelpad, where it was preserved — fastened to chains. Of the Småland code, the greater part has been lost. Some of these codes were expressly entitled "Lag-saga." Even a remnant of the Småland code covering church matters expressly claims this title.

Municipal codes for Stockholm, Jonkoping, and Soderkoping were entitled "Biærkòa rætter" ("jus civile, jus civitatis"), market laws, as distinguished from rural laws (" leges terræ ").

As to the initiative and influence of Swedish kings on early legislation, the introduction of the doctrine of the wife's share in her husband's estate is ascribed to the Holy King Olaf (1150–1160), but this has not been fully established. The virtual regent of the middle of the 1200s, BIRGER JARL, undertook to formulate regulations covering the whole kingdom and to inaugurate an independent and sovereign monarchy. King Magnus Ladeulås (1275–1290) proclaimed: " What we ordain in writing shall be frequently announced to all men, that they may observe our commands and avoid what we forbid " This order, however, on reaching the " Land-things," was received as a proposition which could be adopted or rejected. At this period there appeared a new factor in the struggle of the monarch for unifying the kingdom, the " Riksråd " (the Council of the Kingdom)

The particular aim of Birger Jarl was the establishment of peace and order — the security of the home, the church, the " Thing," and woman. These were brought directly into the king's oath: having sworn to preserve peace and law in the land, he was empowered to issue edicts therefor, breaches of which were punished by outlawry and forfeiture of all personal property. Simultaneously, trial by ordeal and servitude for debt were abolished; daughters, as well as sons, were given right of inheritance; the doctrine of blood for blood ceased; taverns were established to prevent travellers making themselves guests in private homes by force; and provisions were made for service in the cavalry, — the inception of the nobility.

Chapter II.[1] Second Period: A.D. 1200–1700

THE MEDIEVAL CODES

§ 16   Denmark.
§ 17   Same : The Courts.
§ 18   Norway under the Statutes of King Magnus Lagabøter (1267–1688).

§ 19.   Iceland under the Statutes of King Lagabøter (1271–1732).
§ 20.   Sweden under the Statutes of Kings Magnus Eriksson and Kristoffer, 1347–1736.
§ 21.   Same : Growth of the Courts.

§ 16. Denmark. — The actual transition from the law-texts to statutory law-codes occurred first in Denmark. The ecclesiastical codes for Skaane and Sjælland were essentially ordinances with the authority of enactments. These were succeeded in the year 1241 by the oldest civil code ("Lov-bog"), — that of King Waldemar II Seier, with the consent of a National Assembly ("Riksdag"), held in Vordingborg in March, 1241, — known as the "Jydske" Law. The object seems to have been to enact a system of law which should be up to the standard of those in Skaane and Sjælland. These latter also came to be considered as official laws of the monarchy. Other statutes for the country districts and ordinances for cities were thereupon regularly and expressly passed by assemblies and communities and confirmed by royal authority. This period was viewed by later generations as the commence-

[1] [Chapter II = Hertzberg, Part II, §§ 31–66, extracted and condensed — Transl]
Brief List of Authorities for the Ensuing Chapter:
Treatises : *Holberg,* "Kong Valdemars Lov" (Copenhagen, 1886); *Kofod-Ancher,* "Juridiske Skrifter", *Kolderup-Rosenvinge,* "Samling af gamle danske Love"; *Maurer,* "Nordgerm Retskilders Historie"; *Aschehoug,* "Statsforfatningen i Norge og Danmark"; *Au Cert,* "De nordiske Retskilder"; *Schlyter,* "Sveriges gamla Lagar", *Odberg,* "Den svenske Konungens Domsrätt" (Stockholm, 1875)
Editions of Texts and Documents *Kolderup-Rosenvinge,* "Samling af gamle danske Love" (Copenhagen, 1821–1846); *Id ,* "Uddrag af gamle danske Domme" (4 vols , 1842–1848), *P. G Thorsen,* "Danmarks gamle Provindsial love" (Kopenhagen, 1852–1853), *V. A Secher,* "Judicia placiti regis Daniæ justitiarii" (1881+), *Lange, Unger,* and *Huitfeldt-Kaas,* "Diplomatarium Norvegicum" (1848+ ; 14 vols); *Sigurdsson and Stephensen,* "Lovsamling for Island" (1853+); *Sigurdsson,* "Diplomatarium Islandicum" (1857+, 8 vols.+); *Liljegren, Hildebrand, and Silverstolpe,* "Diplomatarium Suecanum" (1826+, first and second series; 9 vols. +); and other collections mentioned in the note to Chapter I.

ment of the new development   " Leges Valdemari regis " were
invoked as the real kernel of the legal system.

The central government consisted of the King, the King's Council,
and the " Danehof," and (in the 1300s) of the King, the Council
of the Kingdom, and the Assembly of Chiefs (" Herredage ")
The entire kingdom having facilities for easy communication,
there was less occasion for preserving the former judicial powers
of the several " Land-things " The authority of the latter, however, continued to be recognized, and even in the 1400s they
exercised their prerogative of approving general and local laws.
After that period, the political gatherings of the various districts
(" Stænderrigsdage ") ceased to partake in legislative functions.
In the degree that the central monarchy desired to extend the
common legislation for the entire kingdom with the least resistance,
it found its readiest means for this purpose in special laws which
were published as general and local regulations (" Forordninger "),
formally issued by the king, but purporting to have been approved
by the particular law-making body

The " Jydske Law," together with an addition, entitled " The
Articles of Thord," containing a gloss composed of explanations,
decisions, customs, and new rules, was ratified by the King and
" Riksdag " in 1326 as official law. A later revision, instituted by
Chancellor Nils Kaas, was made effective in 1590.

§ 17. **Same: The Courts** — A centralization of the judicial
power, corresponding to that of the legislative, naturally resulted.
While the " Land-things " continued to exercise the most important judicial functions for their domains, also declaring the customary law of the district, there was developed during the 1200s
a court of last resort in the " Danehof " and, later, the King's
Court (" Kongens Retterthing," " placitum regis justitiarium ").
In the latter, the monarch and the Council of the Kingdom
(" Rikets Raad ") constituted the supreme tribunal. Its sessions
were held during the general or provincial meetings of the chiefs,
and at other times when the King and Council were present. While
its judgments were supposed to be based on the laws of the various
districts, the natural tendency, however, was to uniformity.

Inferior courts were the "things" of the Land ("Hered, Syssel "),
" By " (village), and " Birke " (market) During the reign of the
Holy King Canute (1080–1086), there had appeared the " forum
exemptum " of the priesthood. The real judicial authority
gradually passed to a royal official, the " Fogde," presiding over
the " hered " and village courts; and after the beginning of the

1300 s the " Land-thing " was presided over by a judge, appointed by the king (" Landsdommer," " rector placiti generalis," " legifer "), and soon the judicial authority was practically exercised solely by that official.

§ 18. **Norway under the Statutes of King Magnus Lagaboter** (1267–1688). — There had developed in Norway in the middle of the 1200s a strong, united, and hereditary monarchy, whose king implicitly believed in his divine authority. One of the most important and useful results of the growth of this doctrine was the legal reform made during the reign of King MAGNUS LAGABOTER (1263–1280), which gave to the people of all districts a common code. His predecessor, King HAAKON HAAKONSSON, after the cessation of the wars over the throne, had undertaken the task of revising the inherited systems, and in the year 1240 had entered into an agreement with the archbishop for introducing a general ecclesiastical code for the whole kingdom These plans were developed, completed, and established by his son, Magnus, who has been named " the Improver of the Laws " — a recognition by his contemporaries and succeeding generations of the personal share which he had in the work. The necessity of making uniform the laws of the four several " lands " had long been realized; this appears in a systematic attempt toward that end in two works on the church law, " The New Gula-thing " and The New Borgar-thing Christian Right," which were generally referred to as the " Church Law of King Magnus." The tendency to eliminate conflict of laws in those branches indicates that there existed a similar desire as to the laws governing temporal affairs. In this latter respect the ruler had a free hand; for there was here no occasion to fear obstructions by the prelates, based on their selfish interests, against proposed changes. In the annals of Iceland it appears that " a Gula-thing-book which King Magnus made in the year 1267 " was made law, and that during the following year two other codes " which King Magnus proclaimed " were also adopted From this it may be concluded that these church codes were parts of a system promulgated by that monarch in 1267–1268, of which the portions covering temporal affairs have not been preserved for modern times Apparently, then, the principal work of the common codification was accomplished in these years, and the completion and putting into actual operation of the unified system throughout the kingdom were merely the later and natural consequence Assuming this to be true, it may be further supposed that the subjects covered by this first consolidation were the law

of personal security, descent, and barter and sale, while the allodium
and land-title laws of the respective "lands" were not included.
This being the case, there is reason to believe that we still possess the
temporal or civil law of the Gula-thing-book of 1267 in the code
enacted by Iceland in 1271, entitled "Jarnsiða" ("Ironside");
and this assumption is verified by the fact that the latter contains
provisions evidently intended for Norway with such changes as
were deemed necessary for different conditions in Iceland

There is in "Jarnsiða" another feature of importance in respect
to the history of law reform. It contains no Church law in its
earlier sense, but, under the title of "An Act in regard to Christianity" ("Kristendomsbolk"), only a series of general provisions
essentially occupied with civil matters This exclusion of ecclesiastical regulations from the general codes is also noted in the later
statutes of King Magnus, entitled "Land and Village Law." It
is explained by the refusal of the papacy to acknowledge the propriety of including the Law of God among the general statutes,
which were to dominate by traditional popular acquiescence.
When the "Frosta-thing" in 1269 authorized King Magnus to
revise its code, in pursuance of the plan followed in the southern
"lands," such authority was limited "to revise the Book of the
Frosta-thing, as he deemed best, in all matters concerning the
temporal 'Right' and the government of the king." This limitation is ascribed to the ambitious Archbishop Jon Raude, who
later undertook to have prepared a "Christian-Right," thereby
seeking to establish the independent authority of the Church to
formulate its rules. The king, notwithstanding, finally preserved
in this work the same provisions as had been included in the codes
of 1267 and 1268, to wit, such as related to civil affairs, even
though resting on religious principles. "Jarnsiða" is the first
instance in which recourse was had to this alternative. The king
appears later to have been averse to yielding to the demands of
the hierarchy and to have insisted on concerning himself with
several questions of a religious nature

Owing partially to delay caused by negotiations with the archbishop and partially to an extension of the reform plan, the work
of preparing the Frosta-thing Law was not completed until
1274 The king himself in the introduction announced that the
Thronder Right Book surpassed that of other districts both in
respect to contents and clearness. It served as the centre for the
further revision of the legal system in compliance with the demands
of the age Among the most important changes were the con-

stitutional hereditary succession of the throne, in accordance with certain principles fixed during the reign of King Haakon Haakonsson in 1260, to wit, legitimate birth, primogeniture, and single kingship; the abolishment of the blood-feud, and of the principle of collecting damages for homicide from others than the actual offender and of distributing them among others than the nearest heir of his victim; and the introduction of the right of inheritance for the daughter, even although her share equalled only half of that of the son. These and other rules were adopted at two Councils of the Kingdom at Bergen in 1271 and 1273, for formal ratification by the "Land-things." This course necessitated a new revision of the king's earlier codes, which was apparently contemplated at the time of the incorporation into the "Frosta-thing Law" of rules for the allodium and tenantry of land, evidently intended for the whole kingdom. In form, however, the earlier system was preserved, in that each of the four great "law-things" preserved their individual laws, the statutes in force being respectively known as the "Laws of the Gula-thing, Frosta-thing, Eidsivathing and Borgar-thing."

The king's ultimate aim of making the Law of the "Frosta-thing" "a law-book which should go over all Norway" was rapidly realized, however; and it may be taken for certain that it was made operative in the "Gula-thing" in 1275 and in the "Eidsiva- and Borgar-things" in 1276. In the caption of a manuscript of the "Gula-things" from the year 1300, which contains a short decree in the nature of a promulgation, it is expressly recorded that King Magnus ordered "to compile that of all the books of the land which appeared to him to suit the best, after consulting the best men, and to put in leather (' skraasætte ') this book, and journeyed himself to the 'law-thing' (to wit in each 'law-land') and had there the book read and gave the book to the men of the 'thing,' and with it the 'right-command' (' Retterbod '), *which is not the least, that this book hereafter shall be in full force and effect over all Norway* for all times, while the honor of the kingdom shall be untarnished."

Concerning the work of preparing this national code, authentic details are lacking. Those have hardly been mistaken, however, who have claimed to find in a saga of the period the names of the two men who were the king's chief co-laborers, viz. the King's Marshal, AUDUN HUGLEIKSSON, of Hegranaes (executed in 1302), and the Chancellor THORE HAAKONSSON, of Leikvang, Smaalenen (died in 1317); both of these later were made barons; the former

was called " the wisest man in the land-law," and the latter " well
versed in the ecclesiastical law "

The National Code of Magnus Lagabøter is essentially a consolidation of the laws of the " Frosta-thing " and the " Gula-
thing," with additions concerning land tenure culled from those of
the other two " things " A considerable number of changes in
the old law were made, mostly by including resolutions of the
councils of the kingdom, and there were added a series of sermon-
like considerations on the kingdom and the purposes of law, while
the dominant aim was to harmonize its details with the basic legal
principles of the kingdom Like the old collections, it contained
ten parts· First came the rules for the " Thing " (" Thingfare-
bolken "); this was viewed as introductory, and was followed
by such Church regulations as were still preserved from the earlier
" Christian-Right." Then followed the " Mandhelgebolk," in
regard to offences against the person, " Arvebolken," the law of
inheritance; the law of land tenure, allodium, and tenantry, the
law merchant; the law of theft and the pursuit of thieves; and,
finally, the proclamations of Kings Haakon and Magnus for establishing and extending the authority of the code, which also contained a prologue and a decree of promulgation. It would not be
fair to compare the text of this work with the earlier law-texts,
which closely followed the concise oral form of expression. Its
style is broad, such as was developed in the Latin court style of
the Middle Ages, and its superfluous verbiage is to be ascribed
to the custom of the age.   Its great merit is that, in a period when
over all Christendom there was a general separation and localizing
of laws, Norway was able to introduce an almost complete and
common system, which embraced its colonies and operated through
a well-combined series of institutions and legal principles   Their
correspondence with the needs of the people is forcibly seen in the
fact that this code, though afterwards much added to, for four
hundred years continued to constitute the formal basic law   Such
deficiencies in contents, order, and expression as appear in the
Land Law of Magnus Lagabøter are a defect which it has
in common with other similar codifications dating from times of
even greater culture; and these defects were the less avoidable by
reason of the short time consumed in its preparation.   On the whole,
these Norsemen, at the time of the extinction of their ancient race
of kings in the year 1319, were presumably the best situated nation
in Europe with respect to legal organization and obedience to
law

§ 19. **Iceland under King Magnus Lagabøter's Statutes (1271–1732).** — The conquest of Iceland by Norway, which had long been meditated, was made in the years 1262–1264, during the reign of King Sted of Norway. In consequence, a treaty was made in 1262 whereby the king guaranteed to the inhabitants of the island " peace and Icelandic law " This pact King Magnus Lagabøter did not consider as a bar to his undertaking a reformation of its legal system with the consent of the people, since that system had not sufficed to secure the reign of law against the oppression of oligarchic powers, nor did it accord with the new principle of monarchy. He naturally also wished to seize the opportunity, as far as possible, to incorporate Iceland under the new general legal system of Norway Accordingly, in 1271, he forwarded and submitted to the " Althing " a new code for the island, which consisted in substance of a compilation of regulations from the earlier laws of the " Gula- and Frosta-things," and was presumably a copy of the " Gula-thing " code adopted in 1267. During long sessions of the " Althing " in 1271, 1272, and 1273, this work was enacted, section by section, and was entitled "Jarnsiða" (" Ironside," probably from its binding). The ancient law of Iceland was thus supplanted; and this radical change involved the disappearance of the old chieftainships, now considered inconsistent with royal power

Being, however, a part of the crude early efforts under King Magnus, the new law served only to bring the legal conditions on the island into still greater confusion and disorder After the new code of Norway had come into force, a similar work was accordingly prepared for Iceland, in whose preparation the authors exhibited a superior ability, gained by experience. The Icelandic representative seems to have been the law-man JON EINARSSON, who brought the new law home and submitted it to the " thing ", after him, the work received for all time the name " Jonsbok." It was ratified in 1281, with certain reservations, which were later settled by a supplementary code, passed in 1294. Among its provisions peculiar to Iceland may be noted, in the law of descent, those regarding support of the destitute; in the law of land-leases, those regarding riparian rights; and provisions in reference to marine law and taxation.

§ 20. **Sweden under the Statutes of Kings Magnus Eriksson and Kristoffer (1347–1736)** — The characteristic independent development and authority of the Swedish " lands " and " things " retarded the centralization and unification of the legal systems and

their machinery, even as their comparative incompleteness in
Norway had hastened that work   When the first king of the
Union, Magnus Eriksson, in 1340–1350 proceeded to this task in
Sweden, his immediate motive was undoubtedly the great difference between the orderly and uniform conditions obtaining in
Norway and the insecurity and lawlessness in Sweden   Like
Kings Haakon Haakonsson and Magnus Lagabøter, he com-
menced the undertaking with a series of ordinances supplementing
or changing the older law, among which were a " stadga " in Skara
of 1335, which finally abolished serfdom, and others in relation to
the peculiar Swedish jury system, the law of evidence, the bride-
groom's morning gift, and the king's peace. Thereupon he
proceeded to the work of the code. The commission for preparing this was made up of three law-men, viz. Ulf Ambjornson
(Sparre), in Ten-härad Lag-saga in Småland, Algot Bengtson
(Grip), in Westergötland, and Thorgeir in Wermland, who were
summoned by the king in February or March, 1347, to Örebro " ad
corrigendum, reformandum, et ad unam concordantiam et con-
venientiam leges singulorum legiferatuum regni Sveciæ redi-
gendum." The work had by that time already progressed so far
that it was then submitted to another and larger revisional committee   It is recorded that the proceedings were held " in præ-
sentia nobilium et aliorum quam plurium discretorum, ad
præsentis negotii expeditionem destinatorum " As none of the
bishops seem to have been present, however, there being only five
representatives of the bishoprics or canons, this gathering apparently was not a Council of the Kingdom (" Herredag," " Day
of the Sires "), but rather a large committee, which laid the finishing touches on the task.   It was concluded about the middle of the
century, as appears from the oldest manuscripts of the work in
existence.

The Land-law of King Magnus Eriksson had as its essential
basis the laws of Uppland and Östgöta, to which wree added later
proclamations of the king   It is divided into fourteen parts
(" Bolker "), and these are formed into chapters (" Flokker ").
The Law of the Church is lacking. As in Norway, the Swedish
prelates resisted the attempt to incorporate their ordinances into
the general statutes; for that would have opened a way for the
king and layman to take part in preparing ecclesiastical law.
At the meeting in " Orebro," in 1347, the five above-mentioned
canons entered a solemn and general protest against every en-
croachment on ecclesiastical jurisdiction in the work then in prog-

ress, whereof those engaged in the work seem to have felt compelled to take notice. The means to which Norway had resorted, viz. incorporating the basic religious principles of the kingdom under the title of " The Law of Christianity " (" Kristendomsbolk ") in the official public law of the kingdom, were not available in Sweden, for the reason that the Codes of Uppland and Sodermanland already contained these under the title of " The King's Laws " (" Konungsbalker "), and the priesthood did not find it plausible or practical to bring forth an ecclesiastical code suiting the hierarchy. The ancient Church regulations were retained by the respective " lands " and made to suffice. Gradually, the Church law of Uppland became through practice operative throughout the kingdom.

The part which in the Norwegian code concerned the security of the person here formed six separate divisions, viz.: Breaches of the king's peace, felonies, homicide with and without intent, and injuries to the person with and without intent   Other titles were: marriage, inheritances, land-titles, buildings, the law merchant and theft. The arrangement and compilation in this Swedish Code of King Magnus Eriksson are superior to that of former works, and the work as a whole may be acknowledged to be an especially excellent achievement. The Code expressly declared that " in the future no laws should be given to the common people without their aye and good will." Nearly half a century elapsed ere it was adopted by all the various " lands," and some, moreover, still persisted in retaining many of their own local laws and in clinging to " the good old customs of the kingdom."

§ 21. **Same: Growth of the Courts** — King Gustavus Adolphus II, on his accession to the throne in 1610, perceived the defective character of the judicial organizations of Sweden   The old " things" of the " harad " and the " land " had been largely displaced by the decree of King Erik of Pomerania (1413), instituting the royal " Räfste-things," holding two annual sessions. These courts consisted of judges appointed by the king, who, in conjunction with the law-man, sat as a king's bench of appeals from the " land-things." The Land-law passed in the reign of King Kristoffer had provided for an annual session of such a court, to be held either by the king himself, or, in his absence, by a law-man, bishop, or some one else appointed by the king. Lower courts for each " harad " had also been established (law-man-thing), with intermediary courts of appeal (" Rättare-thing ")   This system, however, did not come into effective operation, public opinion not seeming to realize that these new courts represented the judicial authority vested in the monarch. Litigants persisted in the custom of bringing their grievances directly to the king, and he delivered his decisions as he deemed best, usually through the Council of the Kingdom, but over his own name and seal. Thus, the "land-thing" failed to function as a royal "rafste-thing," and such "Ràttare-thing" as had been instituted gradually passed out of existence

In addition to this irregularity in prosecuting appeals, another weakness was due to the fact that the law-men, by virtue of their being also chieftains, held seats in the national council and delegated their judicial tasks to subordinates of inferior accomplishments ("Laglasare") A similar abuse prevailed in the 1500s in the lower "harad" courts, in consequence of King Johan III, on July 9, 1569, conferring on their presiding chiefs titles of nobility. The several judicial posts in a district were thus filled by a single occupant, whose chief concern was the income of the office, and who left the work of administration to incompetents To remedy the situation, King Gustavus Adolphus II, on February 16, 1614, organized a court of final appeals entitled " Svea Court-Right " ("Svea Hofratt"), and issued a proclamation ordering lower judges to perform their judicial functions in person at regular sessions of the "Harad-" and "Law-man-things." In this new system, the ancient "land-things" disappeared. Appellate review was made possible by another order of 1615, providing for appeals from the "Hofrätt" to the King and the Council of State ("beneficium revisionis") Two other " Hofratts " were also established, one in Åbo in 1623, and one in Jonkoping in 1634 An intermediary court of chancery for preparing the frequent appeals from these courts to the government was also established ("Revisionskansliet "), and in 1684 the Svea court was ordered to refer doubtful questions to the king

The legislative functions of the old " land-things " were likewise transferred by the new governmental systems of 1617 and 1634 to the National Assembly, with its four " stands," the nobility, the priesthood, the freeholders, and the burghers.

Chapter III. Third Period: a.d. 1700–1900

THE MODERN CODES[1]

§ 22   The Danish Code of King Christian V
§ 23.   The Norwegian Code of King Christian V
§ 24.   The Swedish Code of 1734
§ 25.   Relation between the Codes and Auxiliary Laws.
§ 26.   Later Legislation   Crimes, Procedure; Courts.
§ 27   Same · Private Law.
§ 28   Same Economic Legislation.
§ 29.   Recent Codes.
§ 30   Customary Law, Force of Judicial Decisions.
§ 31   Philosophy of Law.
§ 32   Literature on Northern Legal History.

§ 22. The Danish Code of King Christian V. — It has been advanced, as a generalization from ancient experience, that rulers who have attained absolute power have found it necessary to issue new codes in order the more effectively to dominate the system of law. At the same time, it has also been pointed out that the strength gained by the State through a transition to royal sovereignty is an important prerequisite for the thorough enforcement of such a work. The accuracy of the latter proposition is clearly taught by the legal history of the North. It is the concentrated power of the Norwegian monarch which as early as the 1200s furnishes both Norway and Iceland with complete statute-books. It is likewise the evident lack of such centralization of authority in Sweden which brings about that praiseworthy struggle of the kings for the same end and yet only results in a confusion lasting for centuries, until King Karl IX by a personal assumption of power, akin to autocracy, provides the kingdom with a law that endures. So, in Denmark, it was only after the sovereign had

---

[1] [Chapter III = Hertzberg, Part III, §§ 67–109, extracted and condensed. — Transl]
    Brief list of authorities for the ensuing chapters Fr Krieger, "Grundlag"; Secher, "Kong Kristian V's Danske Lov"; Kolderup-Rosenvinge, "Christian V's Lov", Goos, "Den danske Strafferet" (Copenhagen, 1875), Joh. Steenstrup, "Den danske Bonde og Friheden" (Copenhagen, 1888); Aschehoug, ed, "Nordisk Retsencyklopædi", Larsen, "Samlede skrifter"; Maurer, "Norgerm Retskilder; Schlegel, "Om de gamle Retssædvaner" (Copenhagen, 1828).

become more independent of "things" and councils that he could establish a common system of law for the kingdom.

King Frederik III had already, in 1661, on the initiative of a State council, directed a commission to prepare a code of practice suitable for the age, and to reconcile the legal system of the nation with the new methods of government. A similar order was also given to the bishops. The task proving laborious beyond expectations, other commissions were appointed in 1662 and 1666, which also fell short in achievement. The king thereupon had recourse to a command to each member of the last body to prepare his own synopsis for a book of law. With this order Peder Lassen and Rasmus Vinding complied. The work of the latter, entitled "Codex Fredericius," served as a basis for a succeeding draft by the same author, in accordance with new instructions to codify, amend, and extend the law in force The task was prosecuted by Count Peder Griffenfeld, Chancellor in Chief under Christian V, and resumed by Vinding, until 1674, whereupon there followed revisions in 1672, 1675, 1680, and 1681 On January 3, 1682, it was adopted and ordered printed by the king, and on April 15, 1683, "Kong Kristian V's Danske Lov" was proclaimed as the law of the land and ordered announced at the "things," to go into effect three months thereafter The original edition was supervised by Caspar Schøller and was published in 1683, while a fine manuscript bound in silver was stored among the State archives Like two other texts still preserved, this does not rank, however, as fully authentic.

The author of the law, Rasmus Vinding (1615-1684), Professor in Greek and later in History at the University of Copenhagen, served for a time as a member of the Supreme Court and the Royal Chancery, and was referee (" referendar ") in the Supreme Court from 1670 until 1677. He apparently received no special reward for his noteworthy labor. He compiled the first book (Courts and Practice), the third (City, Rural, and Family Relations), the fifth (Obligations and Inheritances), and the sixth (Penal Code); while the second (Ecclesiastical Regulations) was in substance composed by churchmen, and the fifth (Marine Law) was edited by Peder Scavenius (1623-1685), professor of law at the same university, attorney-general, and a member of the Supreme Court. Peder Lassen (1606-1681), assessor and senior justitiarius in the High Court, had also an important share in the compiling.

The sources were primarily the previous legislation of Denmark of the 1500s and 1600s For the fourth book, governing maritime affairs, the Marine Code of Frederik II and the Swedish Sea-law of 1667, as well as earlier Norwegian statutes, served as originals The court practice of Denmark was an influential factor, and foreign methods were not extensively utilized. While a series of its provisions originated in canonical, Roman, and German influences, these had already entered into the national law. The compilers, furthermore, displayed considerable independence and introduced numerous changes. Especially was this true in respect to the new principle of absolute monarchy, whence the dignitaries of court and church derived their official authority, and in consequence whereof the people either no longer took part in the election of priests and representatives, or else had limitations placed on such prerogatives. The reform was most radical in the judicial system itself, and the law of evidence was entirely changed. As a whole, it is a meritorious work of legislation Considering the age, its provisions are simple, liberal, and humane, and its language is reasonably clear and easily understood Its internal arrangement, distribution of materials, and general editing are its weak features. There are contradictions between the new and the old; the mutual relation between governing principles and various details is not clearly shown; important subjects are omitted and matters of local nature which do not properly pertain to a general code are included.

§ 23. **The Norwegian Code of King Kristian V.** — After the introduction of royal sovereignty in Norway, the man most prominent in the State, U F GYLDENLØVE, in 1666 received a general command from the king to the law-men for the revision of the legal system. No immediate results followed until the new Code of Denmark appeared in 1680, whereupon the Danish Commission, together with some Norwegian law-men, were directed to proceed with the task A new order was given, on March 2, 1682, to a commission of Norwegians to bring about uniformity in the laws of the two kingdoms as far as possible. The Chancellor, CHRISTIAN STOCKFLETH (envoy at Stockholm 1683–1691, and later justitiarius in the Supreme Court, died 1704), the foremost among the judges, submitted a draft the same year This, while a worthy piece of work, departed from the new Danish Code more than had been contemplated, in that not only provisions unsuitable for Norway were eliminated, but a revision of the Danish law was undertaken by inserting changes and improvements. A new body was accordingly commissioned on January 23, 1683, to amend this draft. As its members were exclusively Danes, in-

cluding the chief author of the Danish Code, Vinding, they restored
in substance the original provisions, disregarding many conditions
peculiar to Norway   However, they confessed their unfamiliarity
with these aspects, and a commission of Norwegians was accordingly convened at Christiania on October 11, 1684, for a contemporaneous revision.   By harmonizing these various labors, the
codification desired was finished in July, 1687   As the prologue
was dated April 15, 1687, this was made the date of its promulgation   " Kong Kristian V's Norske Lov " was thereupon, on April
16, 1688, proclaimed as the law of the land, to go into effect on
St Michael's Day, September 29, the same year.   It was printed
in Copenhagen by Caspar Schøller, and a somewhat unauthentic
handwritten copy is preserved in the archives of the Library of
the University of Christiania.   It differs from the Danish statutes
chiefly in respect to rural matters and courts   While in Denmark
the royal appointee entitled " Fogde of the Hered " served both as
judge and executive, these offices were separated in Norway.   As
corresponding to the Danish " land"-judge, Norway retained the
law-man   In towns, the lowest judge was the " by-fogde ";
whence an appeal went to the councillor (" raad ") or burgomaster,
and thence to the law-man (or "lag-thing"), moreover, for Norway
specially an intermediary court of appeals from the latter court
was established (" Overhofret "), whence in turn an appeal
lay to the Supreme Court (" Høieste-ret "); thus making possible
four appeals of a cause.

   § 24   **The Swedish Code of 1734.** — The sovereignty which the
Swedish people in the Parliaments (" Riksdag ") of 1680, 1682,
and 1693 conferred on the monarch was not as absolute and unlimited as that assumed by King Frederik III of Denmark and
Norway by the Act of 1661.   True, King Karl XI (who died in
1697) had been declared by the representatives of the kingdom
" an autocratic, all-supreme, and sovereign king, who had the
power to govern his kingdom at his pleasure ", and both he and
Charles the Great (Karl XII; died in 1718) had accordingly exercised a power which fell little short of being absolute.   The Estates
in 1680 had responded, to the king's inquiry whether or not he was
bound by the governmental regulations, that the King of Sweden
was bound only by the Law of Sweden, and in 1682 had answered
similarly a question whether or not he could enact a law without
consulting the Parliament (" Riksdag " [1]).   Nevertheless, they had
respectfully asserted their right to partake in every change in the

   [1] " Day of the Realm " — TRANSL.

law; and that body continued to meet on occasions   The Swedish people have, therefore, never passed through an entire reign during which the right of the nation's representatives to take part in legislation has been abolished in form or in fact.

The strengthening of the royal prerogative of Karl XI, however, served as warrant for undertaking the task of codification   In compliance with his wishes, the National Parliament in 1686 made an express request therefor, and on December 6 of the same year he immediately appointed a commission of twelve members, whose first chairman, Count ERIK LINDSKOLD, had already carefully prepared a draft in line with the Danish Code. This plan the committee essentially followed   At his death, in 1690, he was succeeded by Count NIELS GYLDENSTOLPE, who died in 1709, and was followed by Count GUSTAV CRONHJELM (died 1737).   The latter finished the work and to him belongs the chief merit   The length of time required was due both to the careful circumspection with which suggestions and opinions were gathered from numerous judges and magistrates, as well as from learned jurists, and to the obstructions caused by the wars of Karl XII. It was laid before the dignitaries and representatives of the kingdom in 1723; and by reason of their various comments a new commission was formed, at the instance of Cronhjelm, whose revised plan was scrutinized and in substance adopted by the Parliaments of 1731 and 1734   A short prologue was written by Count Gustaf Bonde   The final ratification was made by King Frederik I on January 23, 1736, and it became effective September 1 of the same year.   The first edition was printed in Stockholm in 1736, including an index and the ancient Rules for Judges.   " Sveriges Rikes Lag," approved and adopted by " Riksdagen 1734," was its official title.

The code contains nine parts. the law of Marriage, the Law of Inheritance, the Law of Land Tenure, the Law of Buildings, the Law of Commerce and Market Towns, the Law of Crimes, the Law of Punishments, the Law of Executions, and the Law of Court Practice.   In an editorial respect, the work ranks especially high, due to the leadership and aid of Cronhjelm, in that he succeeded in preserving the ingenuous and rich forms of expression of the ancient law language, with a clear method of presentation. For this merit, credit is also deserved by a professor at Uppsala, KARL LUNDIUS (died 1715), who at the age of eighty years prepared for the commission a new draft of the entire code with the exception of two parts, likewise preserving and interpreting the inherited style of tradition.   The national sentiment also entered strongly into the

work, which throughout breathes a deep affection for the home-
grown and characteristic institutions developed in the country of
the authors and preserved by them in this Code.

§ 25. **Relation between the Codes and Auxiliary Laws.** — The
intent in the new Scandinavian codifications was of course that
they should supersede the preceding legislation, either abolishing
or absorbing them. The preambles of the Danish and Norwegian Statutes, therefore, declared " all former laws, ordinances
and rules, as far as the same are not herein included " to be
repealed   All the three codes, however, omitted a mass of provisions of importance in social and political life, impliedly referring these to such special laws as were in force.   The boundary
between the general law and such special laws was as clearly drawn
as could be asked in that age, — the distinction indicated being
their immutability or subjection to changes   " Laws which by
reason of altering circumstances of the times will have to be
changed " are expressly declared by the Codes of Denmark and
Norway to be beyond their scope; the Swedish Code omitted
ordinances which were found to be subject to change according
to circumstances — terming them " economic and political regulations." To this class, it was considered, belong special ordinances governing affairs of trades, commerce, forestry, harbors,
weights and measures, the post, and the practice of medicine,
and also the special privileges of persons, corporations, dignitaries,
and communities   Military affairs, the State administration, and
the revenue system were also excluded. Of the ecclesiastical
regulations, the Norwegian and Danish. codes preserved a considerable number, while in Sweden a general Church system,
adopted in 1686, was included   The test applied to distinguish
the classes to be covered by the general statutes and those still
to be governed by outside regulations was whether or not the
subject was treated in principle or substantially in fact in the code.
As the Swedish authors may be acknowledged to have worked out
the general plan with the greater consistency and precision, a
decision was the more easily arrived at in that country. The whole
question, however, is of less importance in modern times, owing
to the large extent of special legislation formerly in vogue.

§ 26. **Later Legislation· Crimes; Procedure; Courts.** — From
the view-point of history, each code resembles a Janus figure, at
one and the same time confirming the essentials of preceding legislation and serving as a starting-point for a new progress   In fact,
other legislation immediately followed   In Sweden it was aimed

as far as possible to bestow thereon an interpreting character, by entitling such additional statutes Explanations (" Forklaringar "). In Denmark and Norway, where the monarch's power was more absolute, there seems to have been an excess of such new regulations Especially in Denmark were attempts made in 1701 and 1710 to introduce a code governing political affairs, but no result followed Nor did Sweden succeed in establishing a " Codex constitutionum." A Church Ritual for the two former countries appeared in 1685.

Of the principal subjects, the law of *crimes* and their punishment early proved unsatisfactory. Capital punishment for gross and repeated thefts, which had been abolished by the codes, was again provided for in Denmark and Norway on March 4, 1690; and the age remained somewhat barbaric in the penalties inflicted, until 1776, when a more humane administration (led by the famous minister STRUENSEE) mitigated these severities, abolishing the death penalty for theft and also what was termed the " mild torture " This softening of the spirit of the age was also expressed in a remarkable order of December 30, 1771, inspired by King Gustavus III, of Sweden, which greatly reduced the number of capital offences. Scientific investigation of the theory of punishment for crimes thereupon led to a series of modern penal codes, among which may be noted those on the initiative of S. A. Ørsted in 1833, 1840, and 1841, in Denmark; and those in Norway in 1815 and 1848, and those in Sweden in 1855, 1858, and 1861. Criminal codes in accordance with later conceptions were enacted in Norway on August 20, 1842; in Sweden on February 16, 1864, in Denmark on February 10, 1866; and in Iceland on June 25, 1869.

With these changes in the theory of dealing with crime, there naturally also followed a new *criminal procedure*. While in Sweden the accusatory system of the code was retained, inquisitorial process was in some degree provided for. The latter was more effectively established in Denmark on October 13, 1819, and in Norway on July 24, 1827, and on March 17, 1866. By the Constitutions of Denmark of 1849 and 1866, the jury was introduced In Norway, new criminal codes were enacted on July 1, 1887 and June 27, 1889, establishing a quasi-jury system, and providing for reparation for persons punished through mistake. Similar provisions were enacted in Sweden on March 12, 1886, and in Denmark on April 5, 1888 Witness fees likewise were introduced

Changes in the *civil procedure* were also made, especially in

developing the transition from the ancient custom of oral procedure to documentary forms The system of arbitration was introduced in Denmark and Norway, as were also various new
methods of practice The dominant principles of civil practice,
however, contained in the three respective principal codes, have
been retained

A notable feature is seen in the development, in Denmark
and Norway (here variant from Sweden), of a numerous and influential *profession of the bar*, acting under official sanction, and
called the Conductors of Process (" Sagfører ") (Denmark-
Norway, August 29, 1735, Norway, August 12, 1848, and September 28, 1857, and Denmark, May 26, 1868) Sweden, however,
owing to the labors of King Gustavus Adolphus for the promotion
of the legal practice in the 1600s, has ever since that period
had a legal profession, though in Denmark it arose only
after the order of 1732, providing for lectures on law at the University of Copenhagen, and that of 1736, requiring examinations
for judges and attorneys.

The simplification of the *judiciary organization* has also progressed. Several special courts were abolished in Copenhagen,
and the " Hof " and City Court was established, in 1771. By
the act of August 11, 1797, Norway abolished the " Overhofret,"
the law-" things," certain village courts, and the office of law-man,
and inaugurated the "Stiftsoverret " On July 11, 1800, Iceland
abolished not only the law-" things " but also the " Althing,"
replacing them with the "Landsoverret," from which appeal lay
to the Supreme Court of Copenhagen. The ancient " land-things "
and certain town courts in Denmark were ended on January 25,
1805, and intermediary courts of appeal formed in Copenhagen
and Wiborg. Sweden abolished the law-man's court and made
the " Rådstuguratt " the *nisi prius* court of cities and the
" Hofratt " the sole intermediary court In Copenhagen, also,
were formed a Political and Criminal Court on February 28,
1845, and a Court of Marine and Commerce on February 19,
1861 In Christiania a special City Court was established on
March 17, 1866 Appeals from these courts, as well as from the
" Hof " and City Court of Copenhagen, lie to the Supreme Court.
The introduction of the jury system in Norway has resulted
in various changes, among which is the passing away of the old
ecclesiastical criminal courts.

§ 27. **Same Private Law** — In respect to the law of *property*,
there have been comparatively small changes The chief ones

affect the credit system, arrest for debt, bailments, bankruptcy, and bills of exchange A uniform Law of *commercial paper* was enacted by the three kingdoms on May 7, 1880. Sweden enacted a bankruptcy law on September 18, 1862, Norway, June 6, 1863; and Denmark, March 25, 1872. Acts for the regulation of Commerce were passed in Denmark on July 1, 1832 and February 23, 1866; in Sweden, on May 4, 1855 A commission for the three kingdoms prepared a uniform act for trade-registers, partnership, and agency, etc., which was passed in Sweden on July 13, 1887, in Denmark on March 1, 1889, and in Norway on May 17, 1890.

Passing to the law of *inheritance*, Sweden, on May 19, 1845, extended the right of the daughter to share equally with the son in every instance Similar provisions had also been contained in the Danish and Norwegian codes, and not been followed, but they were put in force in Denmark on May 21, 1845, and December 29, 1857, and in Norway on July 31, 1854. These were followed by acts enlarging the powers of unmarried women, in Denmark on December 29, 1857; in Norway on April 11, 1863, and in Sweden on November 16, 1863, and July 5, 1884 In Norway, the age of minority for both males and females was reduced from twenty-five to twenty-one years by act of March 27, 1869, which also became the rule in Sweden by the same act of 1884. Other measures introduced relate to absent and lost persons, right of homestead, rights of children, payment of debts of deceased persons, and administration of estates The control by a married woman of her own earnings was the subject of an act of Denmark on May 7, 1880, and the act of April 20, 1888, related to her support and maintenance Various amendatory statutes in regard to land titles and master and servant have also been enacted, Denmark enacted its first copyright law in 1741, and Sweden in 1766, and these have since been revised.

§ 28. **Same Economic Legislation** — Legislation on economic subjects has passed through many far-reaching stages in recent periods. Even at the time of preparing the codes, attempts were made to improve the condition of the farmers and peasants In *Norway* there appeared on March 4, 1684, and on February 5, 1685, important statutes which provided for a low maximum land rent; and the law of Norway thereupon took the still more difficult step of imposing on proprietors of land who personally used more than one manor (" gaard ") double taxes for such extra holdings This forcible interference with private rights (which, to be sure, brought about the desired and beneficial result of

lessening the number of landlords and increasing that of cultivating
proprietors) was succeeded by the act of May 6, 1754, which
allotted to those who so desired an acreage in the east parts of
the high lands for cultivation and settlement, — not only on public
domains, but also on private estates, on payment of rent. After
a few years of laborious effort in this direction, this act was repealed on November 15, 1760, whereas the former method of double
taxation first came into disuse by an act of August 7, 1827 In
Denmark, on February 21, 1702, there was abolished a system of
personal servitude (" Vornedskab "); this had obtained on
Sjaelland and some other islands, though it did not go to the length
of that prevailing in the southern and eastern parts of the country,
where the proprietor possessed a sort of estate in the laborers on
his manor (" Livegenskab "). When the desire, however, to secure
the largest possible number of soldiers became a consideration of
more importance than the comfort of the commoners, there was
introduced throughout Denmark, under King Christian VI, on
February 4, 1733, a system (" Stavnsbaand ") which prohibited
every enrolled man from leaving the estate to which he belonged
— a new and oppressive bondage, which was repealed on June 20,
1788. A few years after this enlightened repeal, Denmark next
prohibited the importation of negroes to its colonies in the West
Indies (March 16, 1792). In *Sweden* there was less occasion for
radical changes in similar relationships, which here had grown,
through the ages, in a sound and natural development The worst
feature of it was the exemption of the nobility from taxation, on
what was termed " saving ground " (" fralsejord "). The Act of
1789 of King Gustavus III, and a resolution of Parliament in 1810,
changed this privilege of the nobles, in that the exemption attached
to the particular land, even though passing into the possession of
persons who were not members of the nobility. There should
also be noted the ordinances of March 8, 1770, and July 11, 1780,
for the encouragement of cultivation of new lands; and also
that of June 13, 1800, providing for official recording of leases of
land, for the protection of tenants against the ancient rule, " purchase breaks lease." The personal servitude of peasants in Swedish
Pomerania was abolished on July 3, 1806

On the question of trades and livelihoods, there prevailed in
all the three countries during the 1700s a system of monopoly.
The Swedish acts of February 21, 1879, and August 1, 1805, allowed
the owner of forest land more liberty in his utilization of the timber;
whereas a corresponding statute of Denmark imposed still greater

limitations (September 27, 1805); free trade in this regard became possible only far down in the 1800s. After 1850, there also appeared statutes extending individual liberty, relating to trades, occupations, and apprenticeships, sailors, fishermen, forestry, hunting, etc. Statutes on mint and coinage were also enacted, and various regulations on the manufacture and sale of the national alcoholic beverage (" Branvin ").

§ 29. **Recent Codes.** — With the entry of these diverse new rules and elements into legislation, the need for a more timely code was felt.

In *Denmark*, two eminent jurists, ANDREAS HOIER (1690-1739) and HENRIK STAMPE (1713-1789), labored towards compiling such new laws; and PEDER KOFOD-ANCHER, in accordance with an act of October 20, 1758, continued the task until 1772, when the other members of the committee failed to revise his draft. Other men influential in this direction were CHRISTIAN COLBJØRNSON (1749-1814) and ANDERS SANDØE ØRSTED (1778-1860). Through successive stages there thus appeared a new Penal Code in 1866, a new statute on Civil and Criminal procedure was also prepared and laid by the Minister of Justice before the Danish parliament, which, however, took no action in the matter

The State Assembly of *Norway* at Eidsvold in 1814 inserted in the new constitution a provision for a " new general civil and criminal code " The commission appointed was hampered by numerous obstacles. Among members of succeeding commissions the most noted are " Lector Juris " WINTER-HJELM (1784-1862) and JØRGEN HERMAN VOGT (1784-1862). One of the chief points in dispute was the introduction of the jury system in criminal cases, which finally led to the act of 1887, the codification of civil procedure being still left unfinished. The foremost jurist of Norway at the time was Professor ANTON MARTIN SCHWEIGAARD (1808-1870), whose influence was especially marked in the development of legislation on occupations and on credit.

Likewise, in *Iceland*, several proposed codes appeared, — notably that of Law-man PAUL VIDALIN (died 1727); but in spite of repeated efforts the approval of the Danish Government was still withheld, as also for a draft of March 29, 1826. Since the restoration of the " Althing " in 1843 and the publication of the Icelandic Law of 1874, legislative activities have increased on the island.

In *Sweden* the great commission which prepared the code of 1734 continued its labors in developing the system until 1811,

when a new commission undertook to compile another code of civil
law — its foremost member being the eminent " Haradshofding "
Jan Gabriel Richert (1784–1864). The draft was submitted
to the " Riksdag " in 1815, but no action was taken. This body
in 1840 organized a commission to " prepare the law," under the
leadership of Richert, which has since become a standing institution, and has taken an essential part in preparing the principal
changes of the law. It is notable that in Sweden (more than the
other two countries) it is the rule that such branches of the official
and social organizations as are affected by a law under consideration are to be heard on the subject.

Especially noteworthy for modern times is the important legislative collaboration of the three kingdoms, resulting from the conventions of Northern jurists which are held every third year
By this means have been established numerous uniform laws.
The first part of its future programme may be the preparation of
a code of commercial law, mentioned in a resolution of the Swedish
" Riksdag " of 1876, declaring it desirable that harmony in this
respect with Danish and Norwegian systems should be brought
about   Immediate results from this have been a uniform law of
bills of exchange and of trade-marks, and a new proposed maritime
law

§ 30 Customary Law; Force of Judicial Decisions — While
the ancient system of legal usages was largely displaced by the
gradual introduction of written statutory law, it nevertheless continued to fill an important place in the sphere of legal justice
Especially was this true during the legal confusion in Sweden
from the 1300s to the 1500s. It was expressly provided in the
"Rules for Judges" of the code that "in whatsoever matters there
be no written law, the reasonable custom is to be applied as law
in judgments." The Danish and Norwegian Codes occasionally
refer to such customary law, and later legislation recognizes it as
being in force   The common law thus remains a fountain of
justice, constantly replenished   In Iceland, where the work of
codification has not been completed, it prevails to a larger extent.
The tendency in Norway, also, is to assign to it an important place
both in theory and practice. This is less the case in Denmark, and
its influence is least in Sweden. Its particular domain in modern
times is that of business and occupations, where it operates in
the form of customs of merchants and local usages, which are
implied in contracts, even although not contemplated by all the
parties.

To ascribe the authority of the customary common aw to the approval, expressed or tacit, of the statutory legislator (as did jurists of the 1700s), would be to cross the stream to get water. The fact that statutes have gradually drained the greater part of the ancient unwritten law is no justification for denying to the remainder of the original sources their character of rules directly effective. The undertaking of primitive code-makers to abolish the law of custom arose from an exaggerated belief in the possibility of covering all details by positive enactments, and later writers, in this respect, are unanimous in attributing to the law of custom the character of a supplementary source for legal decisions ("præter legem")

There has, however, arisen of late an uncertainty in regard to conflicts between an old statute and a later positive law of custom ("consuetudo abrogatoria"). The statutes of Sweden expressly limit the application of the customary law to cases which are not covered by written law   In Danish and Norwegian judicial law the dominant view is that such a custom is contrary to the law.

On the other hand, it may be objected that a newer mode of action, introduced into practical life and sanctioned by the courts, should have a repealing effect in cases that may arise thereunder. It is, indeed, a historical fact that considerable portions of the Danish-Norwegian codes have been amended by customary law. Finally, it is agreed that the mere lack of observance in practice of a statute ("desuetudo") is under no circumstances a ground for rejecting its validity.   This is, nevertheless, in some measure dependent on the relative importance of the intention of the legislator and the actual conditions prevalent in the legal system. There are, for example, several old laws of Norway which, although never formally repealed, would not now be held valid

Judicial Decisions as Binding. — In the progress of the common law, the influence of men learned in the law is notable, especially in judicial procedure and in the interpretation of laws through court decisions.   It is true that by construing a statute and determining the will of the legislator, a court adds nothing to the law Nevertheless, when a higher court surveys the legal principles involved in a cause and determines their relative effect, there attaches to its decision a direct authority — not binding, but serving as a guide for the future and as information for lower courts. Thus is formed a system of traditional judicial practice, from which there is only a step to a customary law based upon the rulings of the judiciary.   These interpretations of the tribunals being followed by the community, it arranges its affairs accordingly in practical life, whence a legal status accrues to such rules of custom, whether or not originally so contemplated. To what extent these resultant usages may again be changed by the courts is a mooted question in the North. Sweden, in theory and practice, favors the freedom of each court to follow its own understanding of what is law and justice. Denmark and Norway emphasize the desirability of uniformity throughout the country and for long periods A Swedish Act of April 21, 1876, directed the Supreme Court, whenever the majority in either of its two branches should overrule a previous course of decisions, to refer the cause to the entire court, — thus recognizing the great importance of precedents as guiding and authoritative expressions, as well as the propriety of departing therefrom when considerations of experiments and reason demand.

§ 31 **Philosophy of Law** — The medieval conception was that the Mosaic Law and the Biblical Canons, in general, and in particular the ecclesiastical system of rights developed in historic and dogmatic adherence to these religious sources, ought to be acknowledged as directly and universally in force, as being the " Laws of God," and that it was the duty of the legislator to formulate and develop in accordance therewith the principles of the law in the material world. This attitude by no means entirely disappeared in the Scandinavian countries upon the abolition of the Catholic faith and the authority of its hierarchy. King Karl IX of Sweden, on his publication of Kristoffer's National Code, ordered printed therein, as an appendix, an excerpt from the Pentateuch, with an express direction to judges to be guided, in passing sentences for a number of grave offences, " by the law of God, which is put forth in Holy Writ, and which shall hereafter be included herein " References to the Decalogue and the " Law of God " are also made in the Danish and Norwegian Codes of King Christian V. On the other hand, a tendency began, in the Middle Ages, to evoke " the Law of Cæsar," *i.e* the Roman system of legal science, as a source of law, and its importance increased in the degree that the influence of canonical authority on the spirit of the times was forced to yield ground For example, it was made imperative (in 1539) on the professor of law at the University of Copenhagen to lecture on the Institutes of Justinian, whereas it was not until the 1700s that he was required to cover the native system of law in his lectures. At the University of Uppsala, both the Roman and Swedish systems were taught simultaneously, according to JOH.

Loccenius, — the author of the first methodical work on the Civil Law of Sweden ("Synopsis juris privati ad leges Svecanas accommodata," Stockholm, 1653; Gothenburg, 1673). The age failed to realize its mistaken conception in this course. In the regulation for the Danish University, which has been referred to, the express reservation was made, "although we are not following Roman Law in these kingdoms, but have our own laws" Likewise, the chief writers of the time in Sweden, Charles Rålamb ("Observationes juris practicæ," Stockholm, 1679) and David Nehrmann (knighted Ehrenstråhle; "Indledning till then svenska jurisprudentiam civilem," Lund, 1729) vigorously insisted that the law of Sweden exclusively constituted the foundation for their treatises. Nevertheless, Rålamb extols the excellence of the Roman law and its importance for purposes of comparison and enlightenment, as well as for its character as a system of justice, "for it is the most perfect in all the world and has evolved the most exact justice for all contingencies," and he deduced the merit of the law of Sweden, because equalling that of Rome "in all cases involving natural justice." In this last expression is seen a reference, not only to the doctrine of the law of Nature, which spread over Europe in the 1600 s, but also to the allegiance of philosophers to the law of Rome. Nehrmann, in truth, holds this law of Nature to be the principal source of law, at the same time opening a wide door for Roman legal science to aid in formulating general principles. Nevertheless, he is essentially independent of the Roman system in his treatment of the specific subjects, and he thus materially contributed towards preserving the national legal traditions of the Swedish people in the preparation of the Code of 1734.

In *Danish-Norwegian* Literature, these various elements and theories were collated in an especially instructive manner by Ludvig Holberg in his "Introduktion til Natur- og Folkeretten" (Copenhagen, 1716; 1763), wherein he presents a System of Natural Law similar to those of Puffendorf and Thomasius; that portion relating to property rights is essentially founded on Roman Law, while the treatise as a whole is pervaded by the Christian teachings, and the canons are frequently cited. To bring the basic truths of the law of Nature into actual operation in the life of the law was the aim of J. B Dons, in his "Forelæsninger over den danske og norske lov" (Copenhagen, 1781); of L Norregaard in "Natur- og Folkeret" (Copenhagen, 1776), and "Forelæsninger" (Copenhagen, 1797), and of J. F. W. Schlegel in his works

entitled "Naturrettens første Grundsætninger" (1805) and
"Juridisk Retsencyklopædi," etc (Copenhagen, 1825) Norregaard, a disciple of the German advocate of natural law, Chr.
Wolff, not only taught that "the law of Nature is the sole subsidiary law, to which the Danish and Norwegian jurist must turn
for the decision of anything left doubtful in the laws," but also
that "in the event of a conflict of laws, one must turn to these
natural laws, which, moreover, prevail over the laws of society
when the latter are not in harmony therewith." This philosopher
also emphasizes the kinship between the laws of Nature and of
Rome, urging jurists to consult the latter as a guide to the former.

Schlegel, a disciple of Kant's rationalistic philosophy of law,
refrained from counselling the abrogation of a plain positive law
where conflicting with the universal principles of Nature, nevertheless, his exposition tends to claim for Right Reason a status as
the foundation for all positive legislation, and to turn thereto as
an auxiliary system of law ("jus subsidiarium") wherever the
latter is silent or subject to different interpretations. A similar
view is taken by C. F. Lassen in a treatise on the interpretation
of laws ("Nyt Juridisk Arkiv, XVI," 1816). Among systematic
works and essays on the nature of law, are further to be noted
those of Andreas Højer, "Idea jurisconsulti Danici" (1736),
translated by Sommer under the title, "Forestilling paa en dansk
jurist" (1737); P Kofod-Ancher, "Anvisning for en dansk
jurist angaaende Lovkyndigheds adskillige Dele, Nytte og
Hjælpemidler" (Copenhagen, 1776); L. L Kongslev, "Den
danske og norske private Rets første Grunde" (Copenhagen, 1782),
and F T. Hurtigkarl, "Den danske og norske Rets første Grunde"
(Copenhagen, 1820).

The abandonment of natural law as authoritative and basic
law in the development of positive law was effected by A. S
Ørsted　In his youth, he had been an adherent to the rationalistic
theory, but in 1801 he deserted it. His works set forth clearly
and decisively his understanding of the law of Nature as mainly
including merely such general ideas as have arisen from time to
time within the field of law and especially in that of customary
law ("Supplement til Nørregaards Forelæsninger," Copenhagen,
1804–1812, "Handbog over den danske og norske Lovkyndighed,
etc, Copenhagen, 1822–1835; "Juridisk Arkiv," VII and XI;
"Eunomia, Samling af Afhandlinger, henhørende til Moralfiloso-
fien, Statsfilosofien og den dansk-norske Lovkyndighed," Copenhagen, 1815–1822). These general doctrines have since been

supported by F C. Bornemann ("Om Retsordens Natur og Væsen";
" Samlede Skrifter," Copenhagen, 1863-1868), Kolderup-Rosen-
vinge (" Grundrids af den juridiske Encyklopædi til Brug ved
Forelæsninger," Copenhagen, 1849), J E Larsen (" Samlede
Skrifter," Copenhagen, 1857), E. Vedel (" Den slesvige Privatrets
almindelige Del," Copenhagen, 1857), A. W. Scheel (" Privat-
rettens almindelige Del," Copenhagen, 1866); Gram (" Om
Lovenes Fortolkning og Anvendelse," Copenhagen, 1865), and
J. H. Deuntzer (" Kort Fremstilling af Retssystemet," Copenhagen, 1866), other authorities on the law of the State are. C. G.
Holck (" Den danske Statsforfatningsret," Copenhagen, 1869),
and H Matzen (" Den danske Statsforfatningsret," Copenhagen, 1876-1889). A later and independent presentation of the
source and nature of law is given by C. Goos in his " Forelæsninger
over den almindelige Retslaere" (Copenhagen, 1885-1890). This
thinker expounds a general theory of legal development as the
product of historic, national, and external conditions, largely influenced also by the basic ethical principles common to all law,
and these latter he recognizes as directly available wherever the
existing system of positive law is found incomplete.

The Icelandic legal principles are treated by Magnus Stephensen
" Commentatio de legibus quæ jus Islandicum hodiernum effi-
ciunt " (Havniae, 1819).

At the University of Norway, N Treschow, its first professor
of philosophy, allied himself most closely to Wolff's theory of
natural law, which, however, he subjected to a further eclectic
criticism in " Lovgivningsprincipper " (Christiania, 1821-1823).
The transition to the empirical and historical point of view was
made by A. M. Schweigaard (" Betragtninger over Retsviden-
skabens nærværende Tilstand i Tydskland" in " Dansk Juridisk
Tidskrift," 1834; " De la philosophie allemande," in " La
France littéraire," 17th vol, 1835). The subject has in modern
times been systematically treated by T. H Aschehoug in "Inledning til den norske Retsvidenskab " (Christiania, 1845);
" Norges offentlige Ret"; and " Den nuværende Statsforfatning "
(Christiania, 1875-1885) ; and by L M B. Aubert in " De norske
Retskilder og deres Anvendelse " (Christiania, 1877).

In the *Swedish* literature of legal science, the theories of
natural law gained comparatively less prominence, their most
ardent advocate having been Johan Holmbergsson (" De funda-
mentis et adminiculis jurisprudentiæ legislatoriæ," 1788; omitted
from his " Juridiska Skrifter," Kristiansstad, 1845). The

arguments of the rationalists, however, exercised a potent influence on the attempts at codification resumed after 1811 They served also in a perceptible degree to prepare the way for the peculiar and strongly idealistic spirit which gained rapid supremacy among the jurists upon its introduction by that most independent leader of Swedish philosophy — KRISTOFFER JACOB BOSTROM (1799–1866). His works on legal problems, "Satser om Lag och Lagstiftning," "Grundlineer till philosophiska Statslaran," and "Grundlineer till philosophiska Civilrätten," are collected in H. Edfendt's edition of Bostrom's "Skrifter" (Uppsala, 1872) The teaching of Bostrom concerning the ideal personality and sovereign supremacy of the State over its material and subordinate organisms, the individuals, has, however, been opposed by E V Nordling ("Anteckningar efter Forelasningar i Svensk Civilratt," Upsala, 1822), this author, nevertheless, retaining many of the essential propositions of Bostrom. A systematic work is Schrevelius' "Larobok i Sveriges allmanna Civilratt" (Lund, 1872); R. Montgomery's "Handbok i Finlands allmanna Privatratt" (Helsingfors, 1889), H. L. Rydin's "Svenska Rigsdagen" (Stockholm, 1878), and in Th. Rabenius' "Handbok i Sveriges gallande Forvaltningsratt" (Upsala, 1873).

§ 32 **Literature on Northern Legal History.** — The scientific history of law in the North was begun in Sweden, where activities in this direction started with the publication of the earlier laws and the establishment of professorships of law at the University of Uppsala in the 1600s. One of these "lectores juris et politices," appointed by King Gustavus Adolphus, was Johan Olafsson Stiernhóok (1596–1675), whose classical work, "De Jure Sveonum et Gotorum vetusto libri duo" (Holmiae, 1672), deals with the origin and age of the laws. Among his contemporaries were Joh. Messenius and Karl Lundius, of whom the latter in "Zamolxis primus Getarum legislator" (Uppsala, 1687) advanced the theory that the ancient laws of Sweden had come from Zamolxis, the liberated slave of Pythagoras; while others ascribed them to Odin (Wilde, "Sveriges beskrifna lagars grund, etc.").

In *Denmark*, Chr. Ostersen Weylle published in 1652 a Glossary, or short review of its early legal history; and Chr. Stubaeus, who had access to numerous manuscripts (destroyed in the fire of Copenhagen in 1728), preserved much of value in his "De lege et legislatoribus Danorum" (Copenhagen, 1716–1719). A more important work was Holberg's "Dannemarks og Norges geistlige og verldslige stat" (Copenhagen, 1762), which presented a fairly complete account of early legal history, and was translated into Icelandic by Jon Eriksson. The principal work was that of Peder Kofod-Ancher, entitled "Dansk Lovhistorie," (Copenhagen, 1769–1776), — a meritorious collection of materials. This was included in his "Samlede Juridiske Skrifter" (Copenhagen, 1807–1811), edited with the co-operation of J. F. W. Schlegel, who also wrote "Om de gamle Danskes Retssædvaner og Autonomi" (Copenhagen, 1828). The historic school of Germany in the 1800s thereupon exercised a great influence in further development. Already in 1748 Dettharding in Hamburg had called attention to the North by his "Abhandlung von den islandischen Gesetzen." He was followed by Dreyer in "Beitrage zur Litteratur der nordischen Rechtsgelahrsamkeit" (Hamburg, 1794). Eichhorn's "Deutsche Staats- und Rechtsgeschichte" having appeared in 1808, J. L. A. Kolderup-Rosenvinge in 1822–1823 issued his useful compendium "Grundrids af den danske Lovhistorie" (2d ed.: "Retshistorie," 1832; 3d ed, 1860). J E. Larsen made important criticisms in "Forelæsninger over den danske Retshistorie," and "Samlede Skrifter" (Copenhagen, 1857–1861).

Several doubtful questions were left unanswered by P. G. Thorsen, in his prologue to the old Danish laws, as also in Chr. L. E Stemann's "Danske Retshistorie indtil Christian den Femtes Lov" (Copenhagen, 1871); the latter work, however, is meritorious in its broad general scope. H. Matzen wrote "Den danske Panterets Historie " (Copenhagen, 1869), and A. D. Jørgensen published various essays in "Annaler for nord Oldkynd og Historie," (1873, 1872, 1876, 1880). In recent times the extensive researches of V. A. Secher have served to remove many obscurities and doubts. Chr Kjer published "Valdemars Sjællandske Lov" at Aarhus in 1890. M. Pappenheim wrote "Die altdänischen Schutzgilden" (Breslau, 1885) C. Goos is the author of a work entitled "Den danske Strafferet" (Copenhagen, 1875). Other noted writers are L. Holberg, Kr. Erslev, and Johs. Steenstrup.

In *Sweden*, the great work of C J. Schlyter is a monument, which marks the transition to the critical, systematic, and scientific history of law His collected series, "Sveriges Gamla Lagar" — ("Corpus juris Sveo-Gothorum ") and "Juridiska Skrifter," have already been referred to. Other notable works are· Schrevelius, "Lagfarenhetens tillstånd i Sverige under medeltiden" (Juridiskt Arkiv, VII, 1836); J. J. Nordstrom, "Svenska Samhallsförfattningens Historia" (Helsingfors, 1840); S D. R. K Olivecrona, "Anteckningar i Sveriges Rattshistoria" (1860), Hans

Jarta, "Svenska Lagfarenhetens Utbildning" (1838); J A.
Posse, "Svenska Lagstiftningens Historia" Stockholm, 1850);
Chr. Naumann, "Svenska Statsforfattningens historiska Utveck-
ling "(Stockholm, 1856)

What Schlyter accomplished for Sweden by his researches in
its ancient law, Konrad Maurer, professor at München (born
1823), has achieved for *Norway* and *Iceland* in numerous treatises,
including "Die Entstehung des islandischen Staates und seiner
Verfassung" (Munchen, 1874). This subject was also treated
by Vilhjalmr Finsen, Baldvin Einarsson, and Jon Sigurdson   An
important work is that of L. M. B Aubert, "En Udsigt over de
Norske Loves Historie" (Copenhagen, 1875), as is also Fr Brandt's
"Grundrids af den norske Retshistorie" (Christiania, 1835).
Notable are also P. A. Munch's "Det Norske Folks Historie"
(Christiania, 1863), R. Keyser's "Norges Stats- og Retsforfatning"
(Christiania, 1867).

Among general surveys are Konrad Maurer's in von Holtzen-
dorff's "Encyclopaedie der Rechtwissenschaft" (1889), and his
"Udsigt over de nordgermaniske Retskilders Historie" (Chris-
tiania, 1878), Wilda, "Strafrecht der Germanen" (1842); H.
Hjarne, "Skandinavisk Laghistoria" (1876); Karl von Amira,
article on "Recht" (Strassburg, 1889), and his two-volume treatise,
"Nordgermanisches Obligationenrecht," (1882–1895); and T. H.
Aschehoug, "Norges offentlige Ret" (Christiania, 1866).

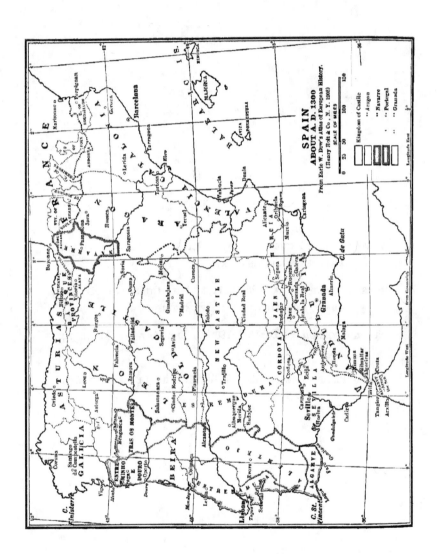

SPAIN
ABOUT A.D. 1300
From Earle W. Dow's Atlas of European History.
(Henry Holt & Co., N. Y. 1905)
SCALE OF MILES
0 25 50   100   150

Kingdom of Castile
"   Aragon
"   Navarre
"   Portugal
"   Granada

PART VIII

SPAIN

———

PRE-NATIONAL PERIOD (TO A.D. 1252). SUCCESSIVE RACIAL
    LAYERS IN SPANISH LAW.

FIRST PERIOD (A.D. 1252–1511)· THE CHRISTIAN RECON-
    QUEST AND POLITICAL UNIFICATION.

SECOND PERIOD (A.D. 1511–1808). THE AGE OF ABSOLUTE
    MONARCHY.

THIRD PERIOD (SINCE A.D. 1808): MODERN LEGAL REFORMS.

Part VIII

SPAIN [1]

Introduction

FACTORS AND PERIODS

§ 1. The Inadequacy of Existing Historical Accounts.

§ 2. General Influences and Traditional Periods in Spanish Legal History.

§ 3. Sketch of Legal Development by Periods from the Origins to the Present Day.

§ 1. **The Inadequacy of Existing Historical Accounts** — That the studies relating to the subject are still for the most part incipient, fragmentary, and full of errors, is the first caution which one undertaking to sketch the history of Spanish law is in duty bound to give. The only contributions made, up to the present

---

[1] [For an account of the author of this Part, Professor Rafael Altamira of Madrid, see the Editorial Preface to this volume   The present chapter is in part a revision of articles published by the author, in the "Revista de Legislación Universal y de Jurisprudencia Española," August, 1908 et seq , on the " Origen y desarrollo del derecho civil español,"— in which the reader will find some points more fully treated than in the present essay. These articles have been, however, wholly recast for the present volume, and much new material has been added.

The translation of the text (the notes less so) has been made as nearly literal as possible.

The works cited frequently in the footnotes under abbreviated titles are as follows

Treatises : R Altamira, "Civilización española" = "Historia de España y de la civilización española" (4 vols., Madrid, 1900–1910) , R. Altamira, "Cuestiones preliminares" = "Historia del derecho español Cuestiones preliminares" (Madrid, 1905); R. Altamira, "Droit Romain" = "Les lacunes de l'histoire du droit Romain en Espagne" (vol. I of the "Mélanges Fitting," Montpelher, 1907), R. Altamira, "Estudios de Historia Jurídica" = "Sobre el estado actual de los estudios de historia jurídica y de la enseñanza de este orden en España " (Memoir presented to the International Congress of Historical Science, Berlin, 1908; printed also in the Bulletin Hispanique, 1909), J. Costa, "Derecho consuetudinario" = D. C. y economía política popular de España" (2 vols., Barcelona, n.d = 1902), J. Costa, "Plan de historia" = "Ensayo de un plan de historia del derecho español en la antiguedad" (in the R G L.J , vols. 68–75, and Madrid, 1889) ; J. Costa, "Colectivismo agrario" = "C a. en España " (Madrid, 1898), E de Hinojosa, "Derecho español" = "Historia general del derecho español," vol I (no more pub. — Madrid, 1887) , E Hinojosa, "Estudios" = "Estudios sobre la historia del derecho español (Madrid, 1903), E Hinojosa, "Discursos leídos" = "D l. en la Real Academia de Ciencias Morales y Políticas en la recepción

time, of a general character (as, for example, by Gutiérrez, Morató, and almost all the historians of the Spanish codes and Spanish legislation) have been histories of the development of certain institutions followed from text to text through the so-called codes, with indication of the mutations which these record, not complete histories of such institutions, utilizing the other sources of the law (custom, the decisions of the courts, the statutes of the Cortes, etc., etc) Such histories, for that matter, must remain impossible until after the completion of an infinity of detailed investigations that are now lacking.[1]

It is clear that the present occasion does not permit the remedy of this deficiency, which it will be impossible to make good until after many years, when innumerable documents, preserved to-day inedited in archives, shall have been printed in critically emendated editions, and the task of synthesis prepared for by a long series of monographs. The writer's pretensions in this essay extend no further — and were he capable of more, the limitations fixed upon the present study permit nothing more — than to present the briefest summary of the actual state of our knowledge of Spanish legal history, without dwelling on details, such a summary as may leave the reader a general impression of the predominant tendencies which the law has apparently followed in the different periods of its development, as well of the frequent gaps which its history presents. To facilitate the amplification of these notions, which each reader can undertake for himself, we shall indicate, in the case of matters of primary importance, the chief sources of information.

§ 2 **General Influences and Traditional Periods in Spanish Legal History.** — Spanish law has taken form gradually under multiple influences and changes These influences, down to the middle of the medieval period, originated in political — or at least in territorial — domination for commercial ends. Phœnicians

---

pública del autor" (Madrid, 1907), *A Marichalar* and *C. Manrique,* "Historia" = "H de la legislación y recitaciones del derecho civil de España" (9 vols , Madrid, 1861–1872), *F Sánchez Roman,* "Derecho civil " = " Estudios de derecho civil   6 historia general de la legislación española," 2d ed. (5 vol in 6, vol 2 = 1889–1890, vol 3–5 and 1 = 1898–1900), *R de Ureña,* "Literatura Jurídica" = "Historia de la literatura jurídica española .   Intento de una historia de las ideas jurídicas en España" (2d ed , Tomo 1 in 2 volumes, Madrid, 1906)

Journals R G L J = Revista General de Legislación y Jurisprudencia, vol .I, 1853+, Bol Ac H = Boletín de la Academia de la Historia , Ann Éc P H Etudes = Annuaire de l'École pratique des hautes études, Section des sciences historiques et philosophiques]

[1] *Altamira,* "Cuestiones preliminares," "Droit romain," and "Estudios de historia jurídica."

(and possibly, before them, other peoples of Asia or Africa), Greeks, Romans, Goths, and Moslems, who came from foreign lands for ends either of conquest or of economic exploitation, brought with them their own systems of law and spread them through the Peninsula, sometimes merely through social contact, sometimes by a deliberate imposition which political circumstances counselled or even rendered indispensable　After the Arabic invasion the influences which operated upon the inhabitants of the Peninsula had another origin.　These were no longer due to invasion, save during the brief period when the Spanish Mark was held by Charlemagne and his successors; but to intercourse and commerce with other peoples, — namely, with the French and the Italians in the northeast, in Catalonia, with the French also at various points in the rest of the Peninsula, where religious communities (for example, the monks of Cluny), or groups of merchants and soldiers (the Dukes of Burgundy were intermarried with Alfonso VI of Castile), either settled permanently or shared for a time in Spanish life.　The same is true of the modern age, beginning with Charles I, in which such influences were broadened and spiritualized in proportion with the growth of international relations — as has been true of all countries It is nevertheless clear that of all influences the most intense were those that resulted from conquests　These also have been the most studied and are the best known, excepting that of the Arabs, which has only begun to be the object of investigation, but is reputed by the majority of authors to have been very feeble in the field of law.　To yet another alien people who lived in the Peninsula in great number and during many centuries — the Jews — it would seem that at most only a very slight influence upon legal institutions is attributable, an influence, however, not as yet accurately defined.　The accession of the Bourbons to the throne of Spain in 1700 has been generally considered in legal history as beginning a new period of foreign domination.　In fact, it does not merit the title　It is indeed true that in the 1700s French intellectual tendencies had great influence in Spain, and French politics greatly influenced Spanish　But if in manners, literature, and science the influence of France caused notable changes, in the field of law these were reduced to certain innovations in administration and political institutions which, in many cases, merely completed an evolution already begun in earlier centuries.　In the other branches of the law there were no important changes that can be attributed to that influence

It is customary, in view of all these factors, to divide the history

of Spanish law into the following nine periods· the primitive
period; Phoenician and Greek colonization; the Roman domination, from the 200 s B C to the 400 s A D ; the Visigothic domination, from the 400 s to the 600 s, the Arabic domination, and early
period of the Reconquest, from the 700 s to the 1200 s; the reigns
of the Christian Kings, and the end of the Reconquest, from the
1200 s to the 1400 s, the absolute monarchy of the Austrian house,
in the 1500 s and 1600 s; the absolute monarchy of the Bourbons,
in the 1700 s; and the constitutional period, the 1800 s. But if
one reflect a moment upon this division (which is the current one),
it will be seen at once that it is not logical, nor are all its divisions
appropriate to legal history. It is not logical, because the criteria
by which the periods are distinguished are unlike; the invasion
of an alien race, for example, is not the same as a change of dynasty,
especially where this, as was the case in the accession of the Habsburgs, did not at all signify a new influence in civilization   Nor
is it proper and congruent to the subject, because the events taken
as divisional lines, though of some import in external politics, did
not always bring them after important modifications in legal
institutions, nor even in legal sources, and consequently cannot
fittingly be used to separate distinct periods.

A succinct résumé of the character of each of the periods named
will make evident the justness of these remarks

§ 3. **Sketch of Legal Development by Periods from the Origins
to the Present Day.** — The primitive period should, in rigorous
accuracy, include the time anterior to all foreign contact, when the
legal institutions of the Iberians and Celts (taking these to be the
indigenous inhabitants of Spain, — although the latter were unquestionably invaders, and almost certainly the former also; one
and the other being new elements superimposed upon and fused
with unknown primitive races) were maintained in purity, free of all
alien influence. Inasmuch, however, as the notices we possess of
Iberian and Celtic law in the Peninsula date from times cotemporaneous with, or even subsequent to, the influence of Phœnicians,
Greeks, and Latins, it is not possible to say, with strict correctness,
how far they indicate original laws or customs, and how far they
present these to us already modified   Although Strabo speaks
of versified laws of the Turdetanians (a tribe of the south of the
Peninsula), it may be safely affirmed that the ordinary type of law
among Iberians and Celts was that of unwritten custom, and its
sources are in consequence lacking. As the Iberian idiom, in which
the earliest inscriptions are written, is imperfectly understood,

we do not know whether or not there may exist among them some utilizable texts of law.

Of the second period as well we have no texts. Saving such knowledge as we may affirm (at times only conjecturally) of the cities and territories where Phœnicians and Greeks, as settlers and rulers, maintained, at least for themselves, their own law, hardly anything can be said of the influence of those races, as factors of legal development, upon the indigenous population.[1]

The third period, that of the Roman rule, is perfectly well marked, and we possess of it numerous legal sources, which will be indicated below, — municipal statutes, imperial constitutions, decrees of Roman governors, treaties, etc. The Roman influence was profound, alike in public and private law, and constitutes an indelible element in history.

The Visigothic rule, without suppressing this element, — and indeed rather affirming it in the beginning, through the recognition of a peculiar law for Spanish-Romans, and the codification of this in the "Lex Romana Visigothorum," — created by the side of the Roman a new Germanic law. This was embodied in two fundamental forms: that of a written law, which is alone apparent in the 400s to 600s, and that of custom; which last, although not outwardly apparent, had great influence in actual legal development. The considerable fusion of the two elements, Roman and German (beginning with the first redaction of the common code, which came to be known later as the "Fuero Juzgo"), although it did not extend to all institutions of the law, marked a new stage in its growth, and incorporated in it definitively Germanic influences.

The Arabic domination had a twofold effect in those territories held by the invaders, — namely, the application as to them and all others who conformed to the Moslem life, of the Moslem law; and as to the Mozarabic population, the continuance, though in a form daily more bastardized, of the Visigothic legislation of the "Fuero Juzgo." Within the Christian kingdoms that gradually took form, very diverse factors were active: the "Fuero Juzgo," whose text suffered interpolations and modifications; the "Lex Romana Visigothorum," which in some districts retained influence as representing the pre-Justinian Roman tradition; a great mass of Germanic customs, which the anarchy of the times and debility of the central powers permitted to appear on the surface, and fre-

---

[1] The most complete picture of these influences (not always determinable with certainty) is to be found in *Costa*, "Plan de historia." And *cf Hinojosa*, "Derecho español," vol. I

quently to be fixed in written precept, the incursive bodies of pre-feudal and true feudal law, which had especial influence in the north and northeast, and, lastly, land allotment-charters, town "fueros," privileges, etc., which constituted the local or cantonal legislation of seigniories and municipalities This multiplicity of factors, — among which three main currents are clearly marked, the Germanic, Roman, and feudal, — in union with new social necessities, peculiar in each kingdom and naturally seeking em-bodiment in new and appropriate legal forms, produced a body of law which can already be called Spanish, inasmuch as it was a product of the idiosyncracies of the country, based upon older sources assimilated and adapted It developed in time a diversity of forms, determined first by the kingdoms formed within the Peninsula (law of Castile, of Aragon, of Catalonia, of Navarre, etc), and secondarily, within each of these, by variations of locality. This was the fermentive period, whence issued (once added the further element of the Justinian law), completely formed, the distinct systems of law that preceded the legal unity of the Peninsula.

This new element appeared in the 1200 s. Its introduction was prepared for by the attendance of many Spaniards in the Romanist schools of France and Italy, and by the coming of Italian jurists to Spain. The Romanism of the Justinian code, which was in essence an influence of pure erudition, but soon dominated legisla-tion and legal practice, was manifested in works of such impor-tance as the so-called "Código de las Siete Partidas" (Code of the Seven Parts). This was written in the time of Alfonso X of Castile (1245) and received a century later (1348) as a supplementary source of Castilian law Concurrently with the doctrines and texts of Justinian, it invaded the customs, legislation, and decisions of the courts of the other Christian kingdoms, although with different intensity of influence The victory of Romanism was nevertheless neither definitive nor complete In Castile, at the same time that the Partidas were circulated as a text and reference book in the universities and in the offices of lawyers, there was digested and promulgated a model "fuero" (the so-called "Fuero Real") that perpetuated the characteristic type of native legis-lation , and other town "fueros" as well were granted or confirmed from the 1200 s to the 1400 s In the other kingdoms, also, the core of the ancient laws persisted. By the side of these there grew up two other species of law, likewise national in origin: the statutes of the Cortes and royal orders (ordinances, pragmatics, letters close and patent, etc), which gradually increase in number, the copious collection formed in the 1400s under the name of "Ordenamiento de Montalvo" containing hardly anything more than these elements.   The legislation of Aragon, Catalonia, Valencia, Navarre, and the Basque provinces was similarly expanded with ordinances of the Cortes and regulations of the crown.

In the opening years of the 1500s the formation of the native law may be said to have ended in all parts of the Peninsula.   The house of Austria went on, indeed, issuing pragmatics and orders, and occasionally a few statutes given with assent of the Cortes, and united these new elements with older ones in the digest known as the "Nueva Recópilación" (1567), but the changes, with the exception of certain matters of public law, were not numerous, and the earlier codes retained in the main their authority.   The greatest novelty, in number and in importance, was represented by the statutes relative to the colonies ("Leyes de Indias," 1680) and by a mass of regulations relative to industry, commerce, the army, and questions of the Church, which had already produced considerable changes in the time of the Catholic Kings.

The house of Bourbon abrogated nothing of the Castilian law. It brought together in successive and enlarged or revised editions of the "Nueva Recopilación" (ten between 1567 and 1777) new royal orders and a new variety of statutes called "autos acordados" (decrees concerted, or accords in Council), which emanated from the Council of Castile.   The Bourbons ended the work of political unification begun by the Austrian house by annulling the "special laws" enjoyed by Catalonia, Majorca, Valencia, and Aragon — in all as regards the public law (with slight exceptions), and in Valencia as regards the civil law as well.   At the same time, and inspired by a liberal spirit (in the social sense of the word), they modified the colonial statutes relative to commerce and administration, modernized *in toto* those relating to industry and public instruction, and in part those that defined the relations of Church and State. For the rest, and particularly as regards the civil law, the legislative diversity, not only as between the different ancient kingdoms of the Peninsula, but also within Castile itself, continued, and the jurisconsults of the 1700s and early 1800s proved unequal to the task of fusing all these elements either into one code or into two (one of public and one of private) that should assemble them organically.   The digest known as the "Novisima Recopilación" (1805) is a chaos of general dispositions for the whole of Spain (but particularly for Castile), in which are mingled provisions of the

Cortes, fueros, kings, and Council of Castile from the medieval period down to the date of publication.

The work of fusion and codification, truly speaking, was the contribution of the 1800s, — in public law through the victory of the constitutional regimen, which accomplished centralization, (above all sacrificing to unity almost all the special regional laws that had remained in force. those of the Basque provinces and Navarre); and in private law, by codifications of the civil and commercial law, the latter for the whole of the Peninsula, but the former for Castile alone, respecting within the field of civil law the peculiar legislation of Catalonia, Aragon, Navarre, and the Basque provinces (save for certain institutions or groups of such, which were made to conform to modern principles and generalized). Political constitutions, organic statutes, and codes were the three-fold expression of this movement, whose details appear in their proper place below. The influences observable in these legal sources are manifold, owing to the variety of foreign relations and the international character of legal science. In political institutions, the dominance of French and English doctrines is particularly marked; in civil law, that of French and Italian thought, but here there is a considerable groundwork purely Spanish. As for the other branches of the law, the origin of the theories and ideas which are to-day, or have been at times, expressed in legislation, could only be indicated by descending to details.

CHAPTER I. PRE-NATIONAL PERIOD: TO A.D. 1252.[1]

SUCCESSIVE RACIAL LAYERS IN SPANISH LAW

TOPIC 1. CELTIC-IBERIAN FOUNDATIONS AND GREEK AND PHŒNICIAN COLONIES (TO B. C. 200)

§ 4. Obscurity of the Celtic-Iberian Origins.
§ 5. Social Organization.
§ 6. Institutions of Civil and Public Law.

TOPIC 2. THE ROMAN RULE (B.C. 200–A.D. 400)

§ 7. The Roman Influence.
§ 8. Institutional Results.

TOPIC 3. THE GERMANIC INVASIONS AND VISIGOTHIC DOMINION (A.D. 400–700)

§ 9. Contrast of the Roman and Visigothic Influences
§ 10. Sources of the Visigothic Law.
§ 11. Legal Institutions of the Visigothic Period.
§ 12. Hybrid Legal Institutions
§ 13. Legislation of Kindasvinth.

TOPIC 4. CHRISTIAN AND MOORISH KINGDOMS (A.D. 700–1300)

§ 14. The Influence of the Church.
§ 15 Roman, Moorish, and other Foreign Influences.

TOPIC 5. THE INDIGENOUS GROUNDWORK OF THE LAW IN THE 1200s

§ 16. Legal Sources in Castile
§ 17. Legal Sources in Aragon, Catalonia, Navarre, and Valencia.
§ 18. General Results and Tendencies

TOPIC 1. CELTIC-IBERIAN FOUNDATIONS AND GREEK AND PHŒNICIAN COLONIES (TO B.C. 200)

§ 4. **Obscurity of the Celtic-Iberian Origins.** — To the historian of Spanish law, it were important to know with accuracy which of

[1] [This Part VIII, on account of the peculiar and complex origins of Spanish law, goes back to the beginning and deals with the first stages in a preliminary Chapter I, "Pre-national Period" Chapter II then takes up the story at the chronological point corresponding roughly to that where Part I of this volume breaks off Thus, the ensuing period is here termed the First Period, in correspondence with the First Periods of Italian, French, and German national law (Parts II, III, and IV of this volume). — ED.]

the customs or laws of the first historic inhabitants of Spain, revealed to us in the writings of Greek and Latin authors or by inscriptions and coins, correspond to the Iberian stock and which
to the Celtic stock, which to the fusion of both, and which to the
pervasion of the colonizing influences already referred to. But
these things cannot to-day be determined (and possibly never can
be), and for various reasons; among them, the uncertainty that still
exists with regard to the origin and peculiarities of the Iberians,
and the imperfection of our knowledge of Celtic law,[1] due to the
universality of certain primitive institutions which may equally
well be Celtic or Iberian The differentiation has nevertheless been
partially attempted, as regards the period supposedly antecedent
to the invasion of the Celts (at the end of the 400s B.C.), and
with limitation to the influences of Phœnician-Carthaginians and
Greeks, by a Spanish historian, Joaquin Costa [2] The conclusions
of the author rest, however, primarily on the hypothesis, not yet
definitely accepted, of a relationship between the Iberians and the
Libyans, and on a further hypothetical attribution to the Iberian
stock (an assumption whose great probability in many cases is not
equivalent in logic to a rigorous exactitude) of legal survivals
much posterior to the primitive period.   The existence of such ten-
dential views in investigations relative to the origins of the civil
law should not be unknown to its students, but it is also necessary
that their doubtful character should be known as well.

§ 5. Social Organization. — Renouncing, then, all attempts to
differentiate institutions in detail, it may be said that the Iberian-
Celtic law known to us to-day, and in which we must assume
Greek and Asiatic influences (some of them concretely determined),
demonstrates. (1) the existence of different legal types, that is,
distinct customs and rules, among the various tribes of the Peninsula , and, (2) legal institutions generally primitive, and proper to
peoples who while conserving very archaic stages of organization
are in a period of transition.   The principal marks of these appear
to be a truncal or gentilitial family; a mixture of monogamy and
polygamy, patriarchy not entirely dominant, inasmuch as there
are visible sporadic survivals of matriarchy, or (more safely
stated) of a law preferential to women, landed property, in places
individual, in other places communal; servitude; commendation,

---

[1] *D'Arbois de Jubainville*, preface to vol 2 of his 'Études sur le droit
celtique" (vol 8, — Paris, 1895, — of the "Cours de littérature celtique,"
12 vol , Paris, 1883–1902)
[2] *J Costa*, "Plan de historia "

or clientship of freemen; and adoption into artificial military brotherhoods [1]

Concretely, nothing more can safely be said as regards institutions of civil law of recognized Celtic type than that (of all which have been up to the present day thoroughly studied) [2] only a single purely civil one — the benefice or fief based upon cattle (" cheptel ") — can, in the opinion of D'Arbois,[3] be referred to with any certainty (on the authority of an inscription of the Roman period) as existing in the Peninsula,[4] for the judicial combat (proved by the narrative of Livy) is not an institution of civil law, but one of legal procedure, and besides is not exclusively Celtic   No others as yet established as existing in Gaul or Ireland appear by reliable testimony to have existed in the Iberian Peninsula, unless exception be made of the communal ownership of land, whose generality among different races in antiquity does not permit its attribution to any one particularly, so that we can only assume its existence, inasmuch as the same race that carried it to Gaul and Ireland settled also in Spain

The division of society into freemen and slaves, apparently universal among all peoples, was doubtless general throughout the Peninsula. As for the slaves, some were privately held, and others by the State, it is a mooted question whether there existed also serfs like the " coloni " of the Roman law or the medieval serfs of the glebe [5] The nobles could boast of the usufruct of the high offices of State under granted franchises, and, by virtue of their social status, of wealth in land or cattle and numerous retinues of clients, — some of whom (" soldurii ") were united to their chiefs by an oath of obedience, and by fidelity which extended to the sacrifice of life (cf. the soldiers of Sertorius). It is possible, also, that the status of nobility involved *ipso facto* in some regions the enjoyment of a larger portion than ordinary of the common

---

[1] J. Costa, "Estudios Ibéricos"(Madrid, 1895), pp lxxv–lxxxi
[2] Cf. the two volumes of D'Arbois cited in § 4 above
[3] D'Arbois, op. cit , vol I, §§ 119–121.   On the relations between the "cheptel" and modern customs of the Basque territories cf W Webster, "Les assurances mutuels du bétail et le cheptel parmi les fermiers et paysans du sud-Ouest de la France et du Nord de l'Espagne " (Bayonne, 1894)
[4] A compact of hospitage and clientage, Corpus inscrip latin , vol. 2, no 2633 , this is the celebrated inscription of the Desonci and Tridiavi, "ex gente Zoelarum," cf Bruns, "Fontes Juris Romani Antiqui," 4th ed , pp 245–246 ; Rodriquez de Berlanga, "El nuevo bronce de Itálica " (Málaga, 1891), pp. 274–278
[5] An excellent résumé of primitive Spanish institutions will be found in Hinojosa, "Derecho Español " Of purely civil "hermandades" (brotherhoods) there are no evidences in this period; cf § 14.

lands which were periodically allotted. Regarding the civil
condition of the ordinary freemen, we possess not a single detail
of evidence.

The truncal family (or "gentilitas," as it is called by the Latin
authors who speak of Spain, and in the Latin inscriptions of this
period) appears to have had the same organization as the primitive
gens of Indo-Germans, Slavs, Indians, Greeks, and other races.
Its basis was supposedly the principle of blood relationship, real or
fictitious. It constituted an association for protection and mutual
defence, whose chief or whose popular assembly exercised penal
power over the members and made resolutions binding upon all.
It is possible that its individuality was recognized as a unit in the
distribution of alloted lands, the labor of the fields being performed
by all the members in common; and that in the localities or regions
where no tribal communities existed there did exist the "gentilitas,"
— as was the case in later centuries and may still be observed to-
day in the "familia labradora" (tiller group) of upper Aragon,
the "sociedad familiar" (family union) of Asturias and Galicia,
etc. The members of each gens bore its name in addition to their
individual and patronymic names [1]

As regards the family in the narrow sense, we know of one form
of marriage among the Lusitanians, analogous to that of the Greeks;
the existence of espousals subject to certain solemnities (and to
civil penalties, in case of transgressions of these) among the Cor-
dovans; the "dot" of the husband, doubtless representing the
purchase price of the woman or of the power of her father over her,
among the Cantabrians (cf. Viriato); the preference enjoyed
by the women of Cantabria over their brothers in inheritance,
and the curious custom of the "couvade" among the Cantabrians,
the explanation and significance of which are still in dispute.[2]

Regarding property law, we possess two classes of data· one
which demonstrates the existence of individual (or family) property
in the soil; the other revealing a tribal communism The latter
has been established with reference to but a single tribe, that of

---

[1] J Costa, "Organización política, civil y religiosa de los celtíberos"
(Madrid, 1881), and "Programa de un curso"

[2] The "couvade" (a peculiar custom for the husband's observance at
the time of a childbirth), whose existence among the Cantabrians is affirmed
by Strabo ("Geography," 3 165), was an institution often found among
primitive peoples of Asia, Europe, and America Cf Cordier, "La famille
chez les Basques" (Revue Historique du droit, vol XIV), Corre, "La mère
et l'enfant dans les races humaines" (Paris, 1887); J. Brissaud, "La
couvade en Béarne et chez les Basques" (Revue des Pyrénées, vol XII,
1900)

the Vacceos in the district of Campos, which apportioned its arable lands annually by lot, the harvest gathered by the members being afterward combined before distribution. It is not known whether this took place according to necessities or social rank.

The compact of hospitage might be, according to the parties making it, either wholly private or semi-public. It was possible, that is to say, to have hospitage between two cities, between two families (clans), and between a city and a foreign individual (and his family), — that is, one belonging to another tribe The existence of compacts of hospitage of the last two kinds in Spain is established.[1] They were made with the intervention of a magistrate, and ordinarily were recorded in a written document ("tessera"). "They created a permanent and reciprocal relation, and, according to the ideas dominant in the peoples of antiquity, not only continued in force during the lives of the contracting parties, but extended likewise to their children and other descendants." The mutual obligations were: lodging and maintenance whenever either party or a representative came within the domicile or the territory of the other; of protection and succor; reciprocal good offices in business; the representation of a contracting city by an individual stranger covenanting with it in the latter's city, and perhaps also the right to participate in the domestic or public cult of the other party. The compact was terminated by express or implied repudiation.[2] It will be seen that there were included in it elements which would be classed under legal notions of the present day as strictly private, and others which would be called public.

Distinct from the compact of hospitage, and likewise consensual, was that of clientship, which might be established between the same classes of persons as the other, except between two cities. We possess evidence of the celebration of this sort of contract between various cities and individuals, between two families and individuals, and between corporations or colleges and one or several individuals [3]

At times compacts of clientship and hospitage occurred in union.

§ 6. **Institutions of Civil and Public Law.** — With respect to the hybrid civil laws, — in general terms, Hispano-Phœnician, Hispano-Greek, and Hispano-Oriental, — the formation of which in various parts of Spain might with probability be assumed (and

---

[1] Five compacts of a city with an individual, one one of a clan with a clan; all of the same tribe See the texts in *Berlanga*, "Nuevo Bronce de Itálica" All are of the Roman epoch

[2] *Hinojosa*, "Derecho español," vol I, pp 85–87.

[3] See the texts in *Berlanga, op cit*, pp. 267–288.

Strabo affirms the fact with reference to the Greek colony of
Emporion), nothing concrete and reliable can be said   The con-
jectures, and very probable ones, which are here permissible can
be found in the " Programa " of Costa already referred to.

In public law, the characteristic fact is the segregation of the
tribes or of groups of these into independent States, which at times,
under necessities of defence against invasion, united in federa-
tions or confederations   Internally, each tribe had a monarchical
or diarchical government, and tribal assemblies

TOPIC 2   THE ROMAN RULE (B C. 200–A.D   400)

§ 7. **The Roman Influence** — In a general way, the measure
of Romanization within the field of law can be fixed to-day without
qualifications ; it was extremely great, but not absolute.   This is
the effect, in the first place, of the evidence, documentary and
official, which we possess of indigenous civil institutions, corresponding to all periods of the Roman domination   It is confirmed, in
the field of legislation, by a constitution of the Emperor Constantine preserved in the Codex of Justinian (VIII, 53), by another
of the Code of Theodosius (V, 22), and by a fragment of the Digest
(De legibus, 1 3); all prove the recognition, down to the latest
times, of the validity of the "mos provintiale."   To what extent,
concretely considered, there existed materials in the 200 s and 300 s
to which this general principle was applicable, especially after the
unitarian prurience of the emperors had broken down those limitations under which the Roman law had originally possessed only
a supplementary and subsidiary character for the alien residents
("peregrini") under provincial laws,[1] cannot be more than very
indefinitely determined. Neither did the Roman legislation
descend to these particulars (which neither its nature nor its interest
led it to consider), nor did the jurisconsults of those times take
sufficient interest to record them   The gradual concession of the
rights of citizenship to the inhabitants of the provinces and of
the territory of Italy itself (" jus Italicum," "jus Latium minus "
and " majus," the decree of Caracalla, etc), and the formation of
the " jus gentium civile," which modified the ancient Roman law,
little by little removed individuals and groups from the action of
the native law, subjecting them in large measure to the authority

---

[1] The order of precedence of the sources of the so-called positive law was,
according to fragment 32 of the Digest, "de legibus " : treaties, the native
law, and the Roman law.

of the new system, although here again the historian cannot determine precisely the results that were thus, and of necessity, produced at any particular time, nor even the definitive conjunct results. Even as regards those institutions which in the end were moulded to the Roman forms, though it were important to know at what moment or by what gradations they lost their original type, we are equally ignorant [1]

In some of the imperial constitutions there occur references to matters of civil law, and especially in private documents that have come down to us in epigraphic form, variants from the pure Roman law, which prove the existence of local legal growths that are extremely interesting.[2] They indicate the influence of the native upon the principles of the Roman law, or testify to the formation of that Roman provincial law, sometimes customary, sometimes enjoying the higher status of regional written law, part of which was revealed in the "Lex Romana Visigothorum," a century after the disappearance of the Western Empire. Detailed studies of these variations have, however, not yet been made; not even the conclusions pertinent to the subject that are to be found in the commentaries of Spanish epigraphists have been utilized in any manual of legal history.

§ 8. **Institutional Results of the Roman Influence.** — Within the schematic form imposed by its conditions, the "Programa" of Sr. Costa, already repeatedly referred to, offers a guide, and the most complete and detailed that we possess, of the institutions of Roman public and civil law that were introduced into the Peninsula (and made *ipso facto* into Spanish law), of the hybrid institutions created by the contact of the two legal types; and of the indigenous variants juxtaposed or fused with the legal forms of the Roman colonies.[3] Of these groups those important for the present purpose are the second and the third. The first represents

---

[1] The single affirmation that we can make at present is a negative one with respect to the end of this period. "There is no evidence whatever which accredits the subsistence of the native law in Spain in the latest period of the Empire" (*Hinojosa*, "Derecho español," p. 142).

[2] Take, for example, the legacy of Fabia Hadriamla, a Sevilian lady, in favor of the illegitimate and free children of the "colonia" Julia Rómula, commented on by *Bachofen*

[3] Among them the betrothal customs of Cordova (paragraph 4), in particular, the statute as to kisses (penalty of lessened inheritance for kissing the bride — before marriage — except in the presence of eight relatives or neighbors), which was adopted as general law by a constitution of Constantine of the year 336, was included in the "Lex Romana Visigothorum" (parag. 9), and was later perpetuated in Castilian codes of the medieval and modern periods. For a general statement of the legal sources of Roman Spain see *Hinojosa*, "Derecho español"

only a phase in the spread of the Roman law, as a part of which it should be studied; on this, it suffices for our purposes to make a single and general remark that the fundamental categories of the Roman law respecting persons, things, and obligations, and those common to the systems of Roman provincial law, governed the law of Spain, constituting a basis in the legal evolution of the national genius which was never to lose its influence.

Taken in the main, this influence made itself felt in a dissolution of the native gentilitial organization, and a development of individualism, as well within the field of family relations (and consequently in heredity) as in the general law of property, in contrast with the communistic modes of enjoyment to whose existence in the Peninsula reference has already been made. That such effects were not uniform in all regions may be safely averred, and also that the process was interrupted by the Germanic invasions when, in all probability, there still existed, in the form of custom, institutions not attested by legal documents and persisting for some time in popular legal practices As regards public law, notwithstanding that the diversity of political status of the primitive native cities (federated, free, tributary, — and, in those assimilated to the Roman classes, the variant types of " jus Latii," " jus Italicum," etc.) apparently persisted down to the latest times of the Roman period, we have no proof whatever of the continuance (and much less in what proportion and extent) of the Iberian and Celtic organization which the Latin writers themselves attest for the earlier period. It is, however, very probable that it disappeared, absorbed in the centralization and reforms of the imperial period.

TOPIC 3   THE GERMANIC INVASIONS AND VISIGOTHIC DOMINION
(A D. 400–700)

§ 9. Contrast of the Roman and Visigothic Influences — The Germans represented in Spain, in the general character of their legal genius, a retrocession to the primitive Iberian-Celtic type, whose customary law, in many essential points, that of the Germans *resembles*[1] Thus, for example, they opposed to the Roman

---

[1] Sources *Tacitus*, "Germania" (or "De Moribus Germanorum"); *Cæsar*, "De Bello Gallico " Two excellent résumés of modern investigations relative to Germanic customs will be found in *Hinojosa*, "Derecho español," and *Dahn*, "Urgeschichte der germanischen und romanischen Volker" (4 vols., Berlin, 1881–1890; Spanish ed , Barcelona, 1890 . "Historia primitiva de los pueblos germánicos y romanos").

individualism, which was destructive of the cohesion of the primitive household, a great respect for ties of blood, and a rigid solidarity which they maintained among all members of the clan ("parentela," "Sippe"), — a solidarity which was influential, not only in civil law (as in tutelage, inheritance, property, etc.), but also in criminal law. They reacted also against the urban life of the Roman epoch, returning in great part to rustic life. This was socially more propitious than that of the cities or urban groups to the maintenance of traditional customs, and, economically, was reflective of the regimen, chiefly agricultural and pastoral, that brought with it these appropriate forms of legal institutions.

It is true, of course, that the importance of both factors appears lessened by the legislation that, before and after Kindasvinth, already appears under the influence of the Roman law But this modification was more apparent than real; and one may to-day aver, upon concrete evidence, that many primitive Germanic customs survived and continued in practice, hidden beneath the external norms of the law, until such time as they could reappear in the 700s and following centuries, after the disappearance of the Visigothic kingdom, with greater indications of purity than those which appear in the documents of the 400s to 600s.[1]

On the other hand, as regards the law of persons, outside of family relations, the Germanic influence was concurrent with that of the Roman of the latest period, excepting only as regards the rights of civil association and the liberty of labor. These the Roman legislation modified in a liberal sense, relaxing the bonds of subjection which had formerly restrained artisans and laborers in the formation of "collegia" and corporations. The characteristics of Visigothic society were therefore an accentuation of the personal dependence of the weak and poor, in relation to the rich and powerful, and an accentuation of agricultural servitude, creating thus a series of numerous social grades between slavery and complete liberty. The practical effect of this, brought about by the transfer

---

[1] This fact, vaguely seen by *P. J. Pidal,* "Historia del gobierno y legislación de España" (Madrid, 1880, pp. 232, 299–300), and by *Muñoz y Romero,* "Discursos leidos ante la Academia de la Historia" on "Instituciónes españolas de la Edad Media" (Madrid, 1860, pp 47–50), has been concretely established by the investigations of *J. Ficker,* "Über die naturliche Verwandtschaft zwischen gotisches und norwegisch-islandisches Recht" (Innsbruck, 1887) See also *Ureña,* "La legislación gótico-hispana" (Madrid, 1905), pp 200–201, and in other places. The most recent and satisfactory monograph on this subject is that of Hinojosa, "Das germanische Element im spanischen Rechte," in Z.²R.G., vol. XXXI, pp 282–359.

of lands, was to merge a majority of the population in one positive status of dependence, which tended toward a constantly increasing transformation of personal into predial servitude   Civil liberty steadily declined in proportion as economic dependence increased, even the "bucelarios" (household servants), freemen by birth, finding it advantageous to maintain their dependence upon a patron, and but rarely breaking it, notwithstanding their right to do so[1] and change their lord.

§ 10   **Statutory Sources of the Visigothic Law.** — A summary of the legal sources of the Visigothic period will aid in understanding the preceding explanations and those that follow.

The first Visigothic law-text known is of the age of Euric (467–485), — notwithstanding a few authors would date it of the preceding reign.   St. Isidore, however, declares explicitly that Euric was the first king who gave laws to the Goths.   These laws, compiled in a code, were in large part only a written record of Germanic custom, although already showing sporadic Roman influences.   It is not certain that we possess to-day the text of this code of Euric; for it is disputed whether a palimpsest in St. Germain des Prés in Paris, containing numerous statutes and fragments of others, manifestly of the Visigothic time, is to be considered a copy of it (if yes, then the only one yet discovered, save for insignificant remnants found in a manuscript of the Vallicellana library at Rome), or a redaction of the time of Reccared.[2]   The only thing certain is that the compilation or code in question was promulgated in the time of Euric, and that as public law it was valid over all inhabitants (with the exceptions discussed below), and as private law in all cases involving parties of different nationality, that is to say, questions between Visigoths and Hispano-Romans   Racial law, or "personal" law, as it was called — respect, that is, for the individual law of subject peoples in all matters not prejudicial to the supremacy of the constituted powers — was a principle of Germanic jural politics   Thanks to this principle, Hispano-Romans continued to live under the Roman law more or less modified by custom, although they also adopted at times the legal principles of their Visigothic conquerors   In the reign of Alaric this condition of things was solemnly ratified, and was regulated in the interest of the natives of the Peninsula themselves, by the

---

[1] Fragment cccx of the Paris palimpsest referred to below in § 10
[2] The question is well set forth, in accord with the most recent studies, in the work of R de Ureña, "La legislación gótico-hispana" (Madrid, 1905, incorporated in his "Literatura Jurídica," vol 2).

compilation of a digest of Roman texts, selected from the codes of Gregory, Hermogenianus, Theodosius, and other imperial sources; a compilation known in history under the name of the Breviary (or Code) of Alaric (506), and among scholars of the present day as the "Lex Romana Visigothorum."[1]   Under this double system of law the two bodies of Spanish population continued to live until the reign of Kindasvinth (642–653)   The only changes were the addition to the common statutes of certain others granted on petition of the Councils of Toledo, and successive editions of the code of Euric, made in the time of Leovigild and his son Reccared (perhaps also one of later date), in which the Roman law seems to have had somewhat more influence than formerly.

With Kindasvinth the situation changed   The double or racial legislation now disappeared, and was supplanted by a law common to all the inhabitants of the Peninsula.   This common law was not one of those formerly existent, but a new one, framed upon the basis of the "Lex Romana Visigothorum," the last editions of the Code of Euric, and the statutes of the Councils, a reconciliation of the interests and ideals of both races being procured through this fusion.   Kindasvinth also abrogated the prohibition of marriages between Romans and Hispano-Romans enforced by the Code of Alaric; by which it is not meant that such unions were not celebrated before the abrogation (witness that of King Theudis), but only that the State did not concede them legal force, unless in exceptional cases.

The son of Kindasvinth, Reccesvinth, improved the work of his father, revising twice the new code and seeking to give it greater uniformity and a systematic character.   The text of Reccesvinth has come down to us in its integrity ("Lex Visigothorum Reccesvindiana," or "Liber Iudiciorum").   It suffered still further modifications or additions in the time of Ervig and of Egica.   Of the revision of Ervig we possess to-day two manuscripts; of that of Egica none whatever.   This code, which covers all fields of the law, but by no means represents all the principles controlling the institutions of that time (as is logically to be concluded from its many gaps and also from the continuance of Germanic customs, not re-

---

[1] In this code one must take account not only of the text of its statutes, but also of the marginal glosses ("interpretatio") that accompany many of them, expressive of the modifications of the statutory precept by custom in the different provinces.   As to this see *Haenel's* preface to his edition of the code; *Fitting* in the Z R G , vol XI , *Lécrivain*, "Remarques sur l'interpretatio de la lex romana visigothorum" (Toulouse, 1909 , reprinted from the Annales du Midi, vol I) , and *Stouff*, "L'interpretatio de la loi romaine des Wisigoths" (in the "Mélanges Fitting").

ferred to in it) is that which later came to be known under the name
of the " Fuero Juzgo."

§ 11. **Legal Institutions of the Visigothic Period.** — It is impossible at this day to trace the history of the institutions of Visigothic Spain before Kindasvinth. It is made so by the scarcity of
documents, the uncertainty in which we still remain (as already
stated) respecting the identification of the fragments of ancient
Visigothic laws as yet discovered, and the like obscurity which involves the question of the greater or less degree to which the
written law (" ley ") was truly positive, that is to say, prevailed
over custom. According as the fragments in the Paris palimpsest
(the most numerous and important) be regarded as of the age of
Euric (end of the 400s) or of Reccared (586–601), the conclusions
one may draw regarding the permeation of Romanism and of the
Canon law into the Visigothic legislation are very different. The
time that elapsed between the two reigns is very considerable (101
year exactly from the death of Euric to that of Leovigild), and
these fragments are the most important documentary source we
possess for determining the legal conditions of Visigothic society
before the first redaction of the common code (" Fuero Jugzo ") in
the time of Kindasvinth (642–649). For these reasons, whatever
averments may be made in detail regarding the civil law of the
Visigoths during the first two centuries of their dominion and the
first half of the third, cannot be more than very fragmentary.[1]

As regards the civil law of the Hispano-Romans, the case is
different. The " Lex Romana Visigothorum " shows us not only
the law in force among them (thanks to the system of " personality "
of laws), but also, what is more important, the modifications introduced by legal practice into the Roman law. These modifications are indicated (as has been remarked) by the "interpretatio"
or gloss which accompanies many laws in the code, either in explanation or in criticism of these. The gloss is anterior to the
date of the code (that is, to the date of the compilation, in 506, of
the Roman texts that compose it), as Lécrivain has shown,[2] and
contributes greatly toward clearing up " the development of the
Roman law in the period between the decline of the classical juris-

---

[1] All that it is possible to say has been said by *Hinojosa* in his "Historia
de España desde la invasión de los pueblos germánicos hasta la ruina de la
monarquía visigoda," vol I (Madrid, 1896)

[2] *Lécrivain,* "Remarques," cited above (§ 10, n 2), pp. 13, 24, 36–37.
The like opinion is expressed by *Kruger,* "Historia, fuentes y literatura del
derecho romano" (Spanish transl.), pp 289–291. *Fitting* believes that
part of the glosses are by the compilers of the code.

prudence and the legislative enterprise of Justinian." [1]   The same is true of the epitome of the Institutes of Gaius ("liber Gaii") which figures in the "Lex Romana Visigothorum."

Not all the matter included in the code relates to the civil law, although — on the strength of the fact that it establishes a divisional line between the legislations of "conquerors" and "conquered" as regards the separation of public and private law, and upon an assumption that the Hispano-Romans enjoyed a peculiar regimen in the latter only — that has been ordinarily believed. On the contrary, the "Lex Romana Visigothorum" treats of subjects of political law (municipal government, public provincial functionaries) and judicature (the judicial hierarchy, competence, and procedure proper).   Matters of civil law do, however, preponderate, and among those which are glossed mention may be made of the appointment of tutors, donations, registry of wills and adoptions, inventories of minors' property, and interracial marriages. [2]

§ 12. **Hybrid Legal Institutions.** — The separation of legal systems between the two races was not, however, so marked as the existence of two different codes might lead one to suppose   The unifying effect produced by the conversion of Reccared, drawing together the Arian and the Catholic classes in society, has been repeadedly extolled.   As regards the approximation thus brought about between the Hispano-Roman "senatores" and the Visigothic "seniores," the process has been partly reconstructed by Pèrez Pujol. [3]   Aside from the indirect influence which religious unity represented (notwithstanding the persistence in Arianism of a considerable Visigothic population), the general contact of the two racial elements, the practical necessities born of common life, and the permeation of the Visigothic statutes by Roman ideas, led to the birth of mixed institutions.   Their expression we find in the texts of the collection of formularies, or models of public documents, known by the name of "Fórmulas Visigóticas," the redaction of which must be placed between 615 and 620.   In these are manifested "in amalgamation the principles of Germanic and of

---

[1] *Hinojosa,* "Derecho español," vol I, p. 357, following *Fitting,* Z.R G., vol. XI
[2] The recent edition of the "Lex Romana Visigothorum," by Professor *Max Conrat* (Cohn), affords a systematic classification by subject matter of the statutes contained in that code which enables one to find readily those of public and those of private law
[3] *Pérez Pujol,* "Historia de las instituciónes sociales de la España goda," vol. IV (Madrid, 1896), pp 193–197, 203.

Roman law, generally   . Although some of them were designed
only for the Roman subjects, many were intended to be common
to the two races " [1]   Thus the formulas were on one hand a
hybrid Hispano-Visigothic law, and on the other hand an embodiment of those provincial modifications of the Roman law which
are represented by the " interpretatio " of the " Lex Romana
Visigothorum "

The civil matters which it covers include. emancipation, the
" peculium " of freedmen, gifts to the Church, the sale of slaves,
bargain and sale, antenuptial gifts, gifts between husband and
wife, dotal property given by the husband to the wife, testaments,
gifts, barter, self-sale into personal serfdom or slavery (a Germanic
principle), partition of inheritances, and leases at will (" precaria ")
Among the amalgamations of Roman and Germanic law the confusion introduced between the " Morgengabe " and the " dos "
(formula xx) may be particularly mentioned. Formula xxxvi
concerning " precaria " is important for the element of personal
submission that figures in it, which connects it with precedents of
the feudal system.[2]

The mere fact of the establishment of the Visigoths in the Roman
provinces of Gaul as allies of the Empire also produced one hybrid
institution (or at least a legal condition that was the source of
numerous and important relations between the two races) in
a matter so essentially one of civil law as the institution of property   We refer to the distribution of lands and other property
which was made in Gaul in conformity to the law of allotments, in
pursuance to which two-thirds of the Roman proprietors became
the property of the Visigoths, a third only remaining to the former
(the " tercia Romanorum ")   It is known positively that in Spain
the Swabians made such a partition, and it cannot be doubted
that the Goths did the same, after the conquests of Euric and in the
regions where they settled, as regards the arable lands and a part
of the woodland. It is probable, also, that a like distribution
would have been made of houses, slaves or serfs used to cultivate
the fields, and of farming utensils   The Visigothic statutes (Paris
fragments), and later the " Fuero Juzgo," necessarily devoted

---

[1] *Hinojosa*, " Derecho español," p 366
[2] *Perez Pujol, op cit*, IV, 216, 220–221   [In translating "precaria
in places as " leases at will," it must of course be understood that the
transition from *true* "precaria" to *true* leases, first by custom (villein
tenure) and then by contract (free tenure), was gradual   But substitution
of leases for years or life as free tenancies for the former servile holdings
is the point indicated — TRANSL]

themselves in detail to this division, which produced a long line of economic-legal relations.[1]

§ 13. **The Legislation of Kindasvinth.** — This hybrid law, as well as that peculiar to each of the two peoples, disappeared, as regards the forms in which they existed prior to Kindasvinth, under the great legislative novelties introduced by that king. The "Lex Romana Visigothorum" was abrogated,[2] the statutes were extended to the Hispano-Romans, and the new code was one which harmonized and fused the two elements. Compared with the texts of the Visigoths statutes that are known to us, it reflects a great influence of Roman legislation, although when compared — as regards its effect upon the Hispano-Romans — with the "Lex Romana Visigothorum" it shows, on the contrary, the imposition of numerous principles of Germanic origin.

The doctrines of civil law which appear in it most different from the Roman law are those relating to marriage, conjugal property, relationship,[3] some principles of property, and much of the law of persons. On the other hand, the preponderance of the Roman law is noted in matters of inheritance (especially testamentary), prescription, and contract, although indeed as regards the form of these last, there prevails a broad and liberal principle very different from the rigid classification of the Roman law

By this legislation the influence of the Germanic spirit was securely affirmed as one of the universal factors in Spanish law, and the work of Romanization, already of so profound effect within the field of law, was (temporarily) shattered[4]

TOPIC 4. CHRISTIAN AND MOORISH KINGDOMS (A D. 700–1300)

§ 14. **The Influence of the Church.** — In the transforming process of this period the Church exercised a partial influence. It is notorious that the actual effect of Christianity upon the laws was not (above all, in the beginning) so ample as its doctrines might be taken to promise. The fact that the Church had accepted the

---

[1] See on this point *Pérez Pujol, op cit*, II, 145–158
[2] This is the prevailing opinion; *Gaudenzi* alone dissents, believing it to have been repealed by Leovigild
[3] As regards the intervention of relatives in tutelage and marriage — wherein one sees the first precedent of the Spanish family council — consult J *Costa*, "Derecho consuetudinario," vol. I, pp. 63–66
[4] See in *Hinojosa*, "Discursos leídos," pp 13–20, the details given regarding certain clan institutions of this epoch, derived from or influenced by Roman or Germanic law.

general conditions of the civil and political organization of the
world in which it had appeared, and had founded and developed
its life in conformity with them, made impossible for the time being
— and this was a canon of its policy — any direct attack, any
action one would to-day call revolutionary, against institutions
which were fundamentally repugnant to the teachings of Jesus.
Thus, for example, the Church did not destroy slavery, nor social
inequalities, nor the institution of individual property; although
it did partially break the cohesion of the pagan households, which,
as we have seen, was later to resurge under the impulse of other
social factors.   The influence of Christianity was for this reason
indirect, and as a rule only moral.[1] Its effects, — apart from the
significance in the law of persons of the mere existence of a juristic person of life so positive and independent of the State as was
the Church itself, — were exercised, essentially, through a constant effort to lessen oppression, the rule of violence of the times,
the inhuman trade in slaves and other classes of dependents, and
to defend the weak by institutions of protection against the despotism of the powerful.   In this sense, the Church was already influential in the Visigothic period   It cooperated with the Roman
law " in the equalizing of the two sexes in matters of inheritance, in
the power of the mother over the children, and in the independence of the widow's status," as well as " in the subordination of
wife to husband, and the establishment of a dowry as a prerequisite of marriage," and of course in safeguarding the rights of in-
feriors.[2] It continued to act in like manner in the period we are
now discussing. This may be seen in the melioration of the
status of the predial serfs through recognizing their family relationships, defining their tributes and services, and rescuing them
thus from the egotistic and capricious will of their lords, in granting the liberty of changing domicile without loss of " peculium "
(resolution of the King of León and the archbishop of Santiago in
1215), and in the establishment of the Truce and the Peace of
God;[3] meliorations in which the economic interest of the landowners powerfully cooperated with religion.[4]

Neither the action of the Church nor that of the Canon law, for
which this was a formative period, could extend much beyond

---

[1] *Hinojosa* summarizes this effect well and weightily, as regards the condition of women, in two paragraphs of his "Discursos leidos," pp 10–11.
[2] The words in quotation marks are from the "Discursos leidos" of
Hinojosa See also the work of *Pérez Pujol* above cited
[3] *Hinojosa*, "Estudios," pp. 39–40
[4] *Ibid*, pp. 40–42.

these effects in the first centuries of the Reconquest   On one hand, the primary contest for the liberation of the Church from the power of the State, which was consummated under Gregory VII at the end of the 1000s, but whose practical influence was not immediately felt in all the fields to which either the autonomy of the Church or its legal influence might extend, largely diverted the application of its energies to other classes of questions.   On the other hand, the fact that the clergy were involved as factors in the existing feudal and seignorial regimen and economic organization was bound to deprive them of any freedom to move in the direction of substantial changes.   Thus, in the territories of León, Castile, and Galicia, we find that the resistance of the ecclesiastical lords to the civil and political emancipation of their serfs and vassals was greater than that of the secular lords, — or at least it provoked more prolonged and bloody struggles;[1] that in Catalonia churches and monasteries constituted great seignories whose efforts continued in the following period to resist the liberation of the peasants; that in Navarre the lot of the monasterial serfs was harder than that of others, etc.[2]

In other fields the influence of the Church began to be used, although the effects upon legislation and customs fall in later centuries, in combating forms of sexual union that differed from the canonic type of marriage — and especially (and logically) the concubinage of the clergy; and also in the law of persons as regards the members of non-Christian religions (canons restrictive of the civil liberties of Jews and Mozarabs) and heretics.

§ 15. **Roman, Moorish, and other Foreign Influences.** — Reference has been already made to other factors influencing Spanish law in this period.

We may begin with the *Roman influence.* This was slight, and hardly visible. It must have continued its action through the Roman portions of the "Fuero Juggo" (*supra*, § 11); but we do not know, in a concrete way, how far and in what regions it was able to overcome the opposing tendencies of the regional law The history of the "Fuero Juzgo" from the 700s to the 1200s remains to be written. Up to the present, writers have confined themselves to the averment that that code continued in practice

---

[1] *Hinojosa*, same work, pp 43–65. The Cluniac influence resulted, in some regions, in an aggravation of the bonds that held the serfs in subjection (Hinojosa, par 16)

[2] *Altamira*, "Civilización española," vol I, pp 322–325, 462–465, 478–480, and vol. II, pp. 127–132 (1st edition) ; *Pella*, "Historia del Ampurdán."

in the different Christian kingdoms and among the Mozarabs, and
to an indication of the scanty evidences, either too indefinite or
too limited (as a citation of some isolated statute, or decision, or
act of Council), upon which the affirmation is based.　We do know
that in the " Usatici Barchinonæ " the code was in part utilized,[1]
as were also two passages of the " Lex Romana Visigothorum," [2]
and others of the " Etymologies " of St. Isidore.　Beyond this we
know nothing definite　No one has thus far undertaken to discover the element of more or less immediate Roman origin, discoverable in the municipal " fueros," in charters, in the acts of
Councils and Cortes, and in the judgments of the courts [3]　The
statement may, however, be ventured *a priori* that it must be
minute　As for the Catalan territories, the generalizations of
writers respecting the persistence of the Romanic element are
(aside from the three concrete facts just mentioned) too vague,
and are usually made in reliance upon documents of relatively
modern date,[4] posterior of course to the influence of the Justinian
revival.

The influence of the *Moslem law* is no better known.　The studies
relating to it are but beginning, and in only very few points have
arrived at trustworthy conclusions.　As for the institutions of
private law, it is said, or is supposed, that the following are of
Arabic introduction·　the Aragonese contract of partnership in
the lease of land on shares (" aparcería "), called " exarica ", [5]

---

[1] *Brocá and Amell,* "Instituciónes del derecho civil catalán vigente"
(Barcelona, 1880, 2d edition, 1886), 2d ed , pp 17–26

[2] In the introductory remarks of *Mommsen's* edition of the Theodosian
Code which are entitled "De uso Breviarii Alariciani forensi et scolastico
per Hispaniam, Italiam, Galliam, etc ," *A. von Wretschko* cites other fragments of the "Lex Romana" in a manuscript of the 1000 s that originated
in Ripoll

[3] An exception is the study of the custom of denying sepulture to debtors
(a custom derived directly from the Roman law, and perpetuated in different parts of Spain) which we owe to *Hinojosa,* "Estudios," pp 145–177.

[4] *Brocá and Amell, op cit ,* tell us that " Roman institutions have been
perpetuated in Catalonia by popular custom and through notarial practices,"
but in support of this they cite only the general statements of Savigny and
a statute of 1337　Equal vagueness in *Durán y Bas,* " Memoria acerca
de las instituciónes del derecho foral de Cataluña" (Barcelona, 1883)
Pella, "Historia del Ampurdán" (Barcelona, 1883), p 575, says: "It is
my opinion that in the counties of Ampurias and Peralada, especially in
the former, the Roman legislation was authority in private or civil law
from a very early date, as the patrimony of the conquered race　Its existence is revealed in the Code of Peralada in the treatment of the Lex Aquilia
of legitimes, and other matters; and in the county of Ampurias in the
preceding decree [one of King Martin], under the name of 'the common law,'
which was that given to the Roman law in the Middle Ages "　But the
Code of Peralada, in the edition known to us, is certainly not of earlier date
than the 1200 s, and the decree of King Martin is of 1402

[5] *Ribera,* "Orígenes del Justicia de Aragón" (Zaragoza, 1897), p 39 ,

the irrigation law of Aragon, Valencia, Murcia, and other regions,[1] a part at least of the primitive market ordinances of certain cities, and the rules therein regulating contracts of sale and barter;[2] the creditor's rights of distress with usufruct (confined to agricultural leases) in the Aragonese law (" Rahu ") ;[3] the plantation partnerships, met with in Toledo, Valencia, Estremadura, Jaén, and Ciudad Rodrigo; and the emphyteutic estates for lives, known as "rabassa-morta" in Catalonia,[4] gifts of unlimited usufruct (" alhob "),[5] partnerships;[6] possibly, the obligation which many "fueros" impose of publicly crying found articles;[7] the general recognition of freedom of contract noticeable in many of the same documents;[8] concubinage and juratory marriage (" á yuras "),[9] the suppression of "mejoras," which had been recognized by the "Fuero Juzgo",[10] the conception of the "patria potestas" as a guardianship in Aragon, Navarre, and in some Castilian "fueros," and its concession to mothers;[11] the dual system of dowry in Aragon, and the "axovar" (paraphernalia);[12] the notion of "hyos manceres" (children of prostitutes);[13] the system of separation of conjugal property, which is found in customs of Cordova and in the law of Valencia and Majorca, as an exception to the general recognition of community;[14] the limitation to one fifth (in cases of sickness) of the property subject

Ureña, "La influencia semita en el derecho medioeval de España" (Madrid, 1898), p 23, reprinted in his "Sumario de las lecciones de historia crítica de la literatura jurídica ospañola" (Madrid, 1897–1898), vol. I, pp. 305–344   On the "exaricos," the two meanings of this word in Aragon and the generality of the contract in other countries, see *Hinojosa*, "Mezquinos y Exaricos"

[1] *Ribera*, pp 37–38   [2] *Ibid* , p. 32.   [3] *Ureña*, p. 21.

[4] *Ibid* , pp 22–33.   [Cf § 18 below, note 3, and § 23, note 2. According to *Sanchez Roman*, "Estudios de derecho civil," vol. I (2d. ed., 1889), p. 462, the "censo enfitéutico casi puede considerarse como originario de toda propiedad en Cataluña" — Transl.]

[5] *Ibid* , pp 24–26   [6] *Ibid* p. 26.   [7] *Ibid.*, p. 9.

[8] *Ibid* , p. 21   [9] *Ibid* , pp 28–29.

[10] *Ibid* , p 39.   ["Mejoras" has two meanings in Spanish law 1st, property added to the estate, fruits and profits, 2d, the excess of beneficial interests under a will given to compulsory heirs above the "legitime," or statutory portion to which they would be entitled   It was in the second sense that "mejoras" (improvements) were recognized by the "Fuero Juzgo"; and it is in the same sense that it appears elsewhere in this essay — Transl]

[11] *Ibid* , pp 30–32.

[12] *Ibid* , pp 10–13, 33–36; and as to the "axovar," *Ribera*, p 38   It may be noted that the dual system is found also in the Celtic law; cf. *D'Arbois de Jubainville*, "Etudes sur le droit celtique" (Paris, 1875), vol I, pp 231–235   See also with reference to these same institutions, *Hinojosa*, "Discursos leidos," pp 26, 29–30   [Paraphernalia is used in the translation in the peculiar sense of the English law, and is not to be confused with "parapherna" — Transl]

[13] *Ibid.*, pp 8–9.   [14] *Ibid* , p 36

to free testamentary disposition, [1] perhaps, the widow's rights of
dower [2] under certain "fueros", and others.   But many of these
ascriptions are still doubtful and disputable. [3]   It is notorious that
in studies of comparative law we fall easily into the danger of im-
agining influences or derivations where there is only a coincidence
of statutes and customs produced among different peoples by identical or analogous circumstances   The universality of not a few
legal institutions practised by nations and tribes of very distinct
origins, and among which there has been no contact known to
history, is good proof of this, and dictates a prudent reserve in
accepting definitive conclusions. [4]

Attention should be called, lastly, to the indubitable but nevertheless vague influence — at one time very greatly exaggerated
— of the *French law*, not only in the Pyrenean regions, but also in
other parts of the Peninsula   That in the former the French influence persisted after the independence of the Spanish Mark,
might be affirmed a priori, considering the multiplicity and continuity of the bonds between Aragon, Catalonia, and the South
of France (Rousillon, the county of Toulouse, etc.), not only in the
political order, but also in religious, literary, and other relations;
but it is also concretely blazoned in the recurrent identity of feudal,
municipal, civil, and other institutions that is observable between
one and the other region.   There is needed, however, a conjunctive
study or series of monographs that shall gather together the scattered data that are at present known, test them, add to them, and
reduce to certain knowledge what as yet cannot be so called. [5]

---

[1] *Ureña*, pp. 38–39.

[2] ["Fuero de viudedad," "viudedad," "derechos de viudedad, "derechos de usufructo," are all translated as in the text.   The only important
difference between the various provincial forms was the extent to which
the rights were consensual or statutory — TRANSL.]

[3] An abundant arsenal of data for the study of these influences and of
their reaction upon the Visigothic law that continued in force among the
Mozarabs, is afforded in the Toledan archives, part of which were made
known by *Pons Boigues* in his "Apuntes sobre las escrituras mozárabes
toledanas" (Madrid, 1897), and which *Ureña* has utilized to some extent.

[4] The one hundred and thirty documents analyzed by Pons are all of
the period with which we are now dealing, from the year 1095 (Era 1133)
to that of 1222, eighty-six of them are of the 1100s and the rest of the
1200s   They comprise contracts of bargain and sale, barter and gift,
wills, etc, and are rich in data relating to civil law

[5] Whenever *Hinojosa* shall publish his promised monograph upon the
"Relaciones entre el derecho español y el de la Francia meridional," the
fruit of extended investigations, the question will be greatly clarified.
Until then the reader should consult   *Bascle de Lagrèze*, "Histoire du droit
dans les Pyrénées" (Paris, 1867), and "La Navarre française" (Paris, 1882) ;
P Dognon, "Les institutions politiques et administratives du pays de
Languedoc" (Toulouse, n d), *H Webster*, "Les loisirs d'un étranger

With regard to León and Castile, although it is certain that the exaggerated conclusions of Helferich and Clermont can no longer be sustained since the criticism to which they were subjected by Muñoz y Romero,[1] it is also indubitable that the French law was influential upon that of those regions, both through the influence of the settlements of the Cluny monks,[2] and through the immigration of groups of French colonists, especially after the Conquest of Toledo. How deeply this influence penetrated, and what legal institutions it eventually modified, are questions which it is desirable that future investigations should determine,[3] but the fact, in a general way, is unquestionable.

TOPIC 5. THE INDIGENOUS GROUNDWORK OF THE LAW IN THE 1200s

§ 16 **Legal Sources in Castile.** — The " external " history (that is, of the sources) of Spanish law in this period is somewhat complicated by the differences it shows in the different kingdoms. For greater clarity we will therefore treat each of these separately; and first, of *Castile*, including all the territories of Northern, Northeastern, and Central Spain that later were united under the Castilian crown.

In the first centuries (600s to 1000s) the " Liber Iudiciorum " or " Iudicum " of the Visigoths continued in force, under varying names, it finally came to be termed the " Forum (or "Fori") Iudicum " — in Castilian, " Fuero Juzgo." Its observance was uninterrupted, being confirmed by ratifications of the kings from Alfonso II onward, and by various decisions of the royal courts, which enforced it. Alfonso III created in Leon a tribunal called that of " the Fuero," or of " the Libro " (book), especially charged

au pays basque" (Châlons-sur-Saône, 1901), *Pella*, "Historia del Ampurdán."

[1] *Muñoz y Romero*, "Fueros francos · Juicio crítico de la obra de Helferich y Clermont" in the R G L J , vol XXXI (1867).

[2] On this important question see the work of *E Sackur*, "Die Cluniacenser in ihrer kirchlichen und allgemeingeschichtlichen Wirksamkeit," vol II (1894), ch. 5, "Die Kluniacenser im Spanien", *U. Robert*, "État des monastères espagnols de l'ordre de Cluny aux 13e et 15e siècles, d'après les actes des visites et des chapitres généraux" (see the Bol Ac. H., 1892); and the reports by *Robin* upon his investigations of the political, military, and monastic influence of France in medieval Spain in the Ann Éc. P. H. Études, 1906–1907 (Paris, 1905–1906) See also an article by *P Fita* in the Bol. Ac. H., vol. XXIV, no 4

[3] It is notorious that the effect of that influence in aggravating the tributes and services of the vassals of certain monasteries (as, *e.g.*, Sahugún), and in modifying the discipline and ritual, has been repeatedly affirmed. See *e.g.*, the "Historia eclesiástica de España" of *V de la Fuente* (Madrid, 1873–1875)

to give judgments conformably to the Visigothic law. As exceptions to its authority, there were delimited little by little the "fueros" of the villages and towns, which in the beginning were apparently not written, but were administered as custom The "fueros," however, did not comprehend all local law, but generally only such regulations as concerned the status of the inhabitants of the foral district, exemption from tributes and services, the local government, and certain details of police and justice Thus there was being created a new political and administrative law that differed from the Visigothic type. In those matters which the local "fuero" did not regulate, men followed either the "Fuero Juzgo" (whose text suffered modifications and received additions that gave rise to a new form of it) or the traditions and customs of the locality These customs were, as already remarked, in large part of Visigothic origin, reintegrated and reëstablished in all their former vigor, thanks to the nature of the age, in which the energy of the central power and the unifying force of the legislation of Toledo had been greatly weakened. The people, returning through the accidents of war to a type of life analogous in certain respects to that of the ancient Germans, returned as well to the ancient customs, ignored by the royal legislation, but preserved in the memory of the masses. In the "fueros" themselves we find reflections of these, and even more in the private "fueros" (liberties) that lie within the field of civil law.[1] It may be, too, that along with these Germanic customs there sprouted also Iberian customs, until then repressed by a Romanistic centralizing legislation

One must also bear in mind the "fueros" conceded by the kings; also those granted by territorial lords and bishops, which form a special body of legislation, although very similar to the royal "fueros", and lastly, the privileges of the nobility, — whose sources were either tradition or special documents by which the kings recognized or granted privileges to individual nobles, — and the privileges similarly conceded to churches and monasteries, whose body of franchises and charters of gift ("cartas de donación"), — respectively immunities from the common law, and licenses to collect tribute, — constitute an important branch of the legislation of the time.

---

[1] With reference to the customary basis of local life declared by the fueros themselves, see *Hinojosa*, "Estudios," pp 21, 29, 30, 34, 36, 47, 67 , *W Webster*, "Influencia de los fueros pirenáicos en la constitución inglesa" ; *J Costa*, "Poesía popular española y mitología y literatura celto-hispanas" (Madrid, 1881)

The king was aided in his legislative functions by the councils. These were continued from the Visigothic period with representation of the palatine nobility and the higher clergy, assembled on the royal initiative, in which it was customary to enact important "fueros" and statutes of a general character. After these councils were transformed into Cortes (1188 would seem the earliest date assignable in Castile), that is to say, when citizens representative of the free municipalities came to form part of the councils, statutes originating in petitions to the king in Cortes and conceded under that authority increased in number and importance   These were designated by the name of "privy" legislation, as a species of statute law which, along with the regulations made by the monarch "motu proprio" (ordinances, pragmatics, "cedulas," letters patent, etc.), signified a unitive and generalizing tendency, in opposition to the diversified and local influence of the "fueros." The latter, however, continued to be granted in great number down to the end of this period.   Besides the "fueros," the particularistic tendency was equally represented by the ordinances issued by municipalities for their interior regimen (subject to the principles of the local "fuero"), whose issue was now beginning; by the sentences of military judges, arbitrators, etc , and even of the judges ordinary.[1] who were creating a new source of law, customary or circumstantial in basis, known in certain cases as "fazañas" (precedents) and "albedrios" (arbitraments).

Even in the foral legislation, however, a unitarian influence (or at least one tending against diversity), made its appearance, — namely, in the creation of so-called type or model "fueros," — "fueros," that is to say. which having originally been given to one municipality were later successively granted without substantial variation to others, which might become (and sometimes were) numerous, by this process the number of different "fueros" was diminished, and groups of homogeneous legislation were gradually formed.

To Alfonso VII has been ascribed the compilation or digest of the "fueros" of the Castilian nobles in an "Ordenamiento" supposedly authorized in the Cortes held at Nájera; although there is no sufficient documentary basis for such averment.   To Ferdinand III is attributed the idea of forming a code or compilation

---

[1] [The "Partidas" recognized three classes of judges · arbitrators, judges legate, and judges ordinary ; the last being permanent district judges of various grades whose jurisdiction was "ex officio," as distinguished from the others, who acted under special commissions. — TRANSL]

of laws that should be of authority throughout the kingdom, and it
is believed that the fragments of a book — called a "Septenario,"
because it was to consist of seven parts — which was begun but
not completed at this time were the fruit of that idea   It is probable, however, that we have to do here with a doctrinal work
analogous to what the "Siete Partidas" represented in a later time.

§ 17 **Legal Sources of Aragon, Catalonia, Navarre, and Valencia.**
— Here, as in the territories of the Castilian crown, the "Fuero
Juzgo" continued at first as the common law, although in its application in the political order it was more corrupted by modifications
of legal practice than in the kingdoms of Asturias and León,
which were the true successors of the Visigothic monarchy. Little
by little, there appeared, as in Castile, various "fueros" and
"leyes especiales" (bodies of special statute law), granted now
to a city or town, now to a social class, some as exceptional privileges, others as confirmations of custom. Of these, supposedly the
most ancient of *Aragon* is that known as the "Fuero de Sobrarbe,"
a supposed collection of purely political dispositions defining the
privileges of the nobility, and long believed to be of the first
years of the Reconquest. Inasmuch, however, as the text of
this "fuero" has not come down to us, and the writers who
first described it are of very much later date (of the 1300s
and later), its existence being moreover unproved by any
authentic document whatsoever, the general opinion of modern
historians considers as purely fabulous this pretended primitive
political charter

As in the kingdoms of Castile there were Councils, so in that of
Aragon there were in these first centuries Assemblies, with the
nobility and the clergy as their constituent elements   The time at
which the Cortes here appeared is uncertain   some authors assign
1163 as the date, others 1274, which would carry the origin down
into the next historical period   The Cortes once established,
legislation originating in them naturally began, while at the same
time the municipal "fueros," — some of them of great fame
throughout all Spain, — were extended, and numerous bodies
of custom, some general and others regional and local, were defined. This varied mixture of sources, which was aggravated by
the corruption of ill-copied texts, gave origin to the idea of a compilation that should order and depurate them. James I, who was
a contemporary of Ferdinand III of Castile and survived the latter
twenty-four years, intrusted with this work Bishop Vidal de
Canellas, who prepared a work known by the name of the "Com-

pilación de Canellas " (or " of Huesca," — 1247). This reflects
the customary law of Aragon, without mixture either of the Canon
or the Roman, although the study of this already claimed many
adherents in that kingdom; but it establishes as supplementary
sources right reason and equity, by which provision, critically
considered, the way was opened for the application of both the alien
systems mentioned. This compilation did not abrogate the special
"fueros" of particular towns and cities; it was considered as
a supplementary law, applicable in cases appealed to the king
It contained originally no provisions whatever of political law.
Those of this class were added later, in 1265, on the occasion of the
confirmation of various privileges of the nobility made by James I
in the Cortes of Egea.

The original law of *Catalonia* embraced the "Fuero Juzgo,"
and the charters and statutes (capitularies) issued by the French
kings during the French domination. When this part of the
Peninsula attained independence, there began to appear municipal
"fueros" (in many of which allusions occur to the "Fuero
Juzgo") and liberties; among which those conceded to Barcelona
from 1025 onward came to constitute, because of the importance
of the city, a notable group. At the same time the customary
law grew and affirmed itself, as in Aragon; an example of this in
its feudal portions being the code of the "Usaticos" granted in
1068 by Ramon Berenguer I, with the advice and assent of the
nobles assembled with the Count of Barcelona. The publication
of this code was due to the necessity of defining, unifying, reducing
to writing, and solemnly promulgating for all the feudal territories
the numerous and varied rules of law that had been developing
under changing circumstances and influences. These "Usaticos"
("Usatici" or "Lex usuaria " · in Catalan, into which idiom it was
later translated, "Usatges") continued provisions of civil, criminal,
political, and procedural nature. In the political order these confirmed the feudal organization, although betraying a certain conception of territorial unity. As regards the social organization,
they recognize the class divisions, affirm the obligations of vassals
under a penal sanction, and accentuate the slavery of the Moorish
prisoners of war. In civil law they establish for the lord, among
other rights, the liberty of testament and the right of succession
to intestate vassals ("intestia ").[1] They prescribe also laws pro-

---

[1] The best edition of the "Usatges" in Latin text is to be found in vol.
I of the "Cortes de Aragon, Cataluña y Valencia" published by the
Academia de la Historia.

tective of the traveller, whatsoever his estate and religion, commanding for him justice more speedy than for the native On the
other hand, they preserve for delicts differences in penalties and
fines based on the social class of the wrong-doer (a common and
characteristic principle of the age); talionic penalties, judicial
combat, the ordeal of boiling water, etc. The " Usatges " attained general observance throughout the ancient Mark, — save
in a few counties in which, apparently, they were never of authority,
— but without prejudice to special " fueros," the " Fuero Juzgo,"
or the customs not included in the " Usatges " itself The primitive text of this has not come down to us   Later this was modified
and added to

In the free municipalities there were formed " cuadernos"
(books) of ordinances or customs, distinct from the " fueros,"
which at times possessed the character of true codes. To this
class belong the Custumal of Lérida, compiled in 1229 by Guillermo Botet, and those of Tortosa, of the end of this period,
which contain political, civil, criminal, and maritime statutes,
and already reflect the influence of the Justinian law. Of
the general customs of Catalonia, aside from those contained
in the "Usatges," a private collection was made at the time of
James I by the canon Pedro Albert. The Cortes date in
Catalonia from 1218.

Navarre. — The legend of the " Fuero of Sobrarbe " is common
to Navarre and Aragon; for both regions were united, until, on the
death of Sancho the Elder (1035), the Aragonese kingdom was
formed, independent of Navarre, but it has already been remarked
that the legend lacks foundation   Down to the middle of the 1200s
— that is to say, until the end of the period we are now discussing
— the Navarrese legislation discloses a character exclusively foral.
Its " fueros " were municipal, and some of them were also of
authority in the Basque territories   The Cortes are of a later
date.

The formation of the general " fuero " of Navarre is attributed
to the time of Theobald I (1237), but it is most probable that the
one known in later time by that name is not so ancient, although
many of its elements, as, for example, the " Fazañas," exhibit an
archaic character, and it is even probable that its first redaction
was a purely private work rather than a statutory expression of
public power.

Valencia, after its conquest by James I of Aragon, was granted
special " fueros," whose history and development will be noted in

the succeeding period.   The same is true of the *Balearic Islands*.

§ 18. **General Results and Tendencies.** — The general phenomenon of this period, and particularly from the beginning of the 1000s onward, was the definition of those original or indigenous particularities that were destined to characterize the genius of the law in the four great divisions of Spain that must, in this respect, be distinguished· the Castilian, with its lesser progeny of the South and East that eventually blended in the general type; the Aragonese; the Catalan, whose sphere of influence included Valencia and the Balearic Islands; and the Navarro-Basque, which was in great measure a mingling of Aragonese and Castilian origins.   From this differentiation (which was itself grounded in multiple causes of an economic and social order, and perhaps, as some believe, in psychological idiosyncracies) there resulted the varying degree to which, in the next period, the Roman law was assimilated and worked results in the four regions indicated   Hence, too, this renascence of Romanism, though it appeared as a unifying solvent, did not operate in that manner, but, on the contrary, brought after it unlike consequences in each region, correspondent to the reaction that each opposed to the new influence.

The general aspect presented at this time by Spanish legal institutions is therefore one correspondent to a society whose personal basis rested in most profound inequalities   Special privileges involved the economic dependence of the greater part of the inhabitants on a few individuals.   The economic basis was agricultural and pastoral, with servile or semiservile labor.   Owing to these two preceding conditions, the dominant forms of property law deal with various fractional interests rather than with absolute titles.   The protection given by the State to personal rights had little force, and was replaced by the protection by magnates in the forms of clientage and the patronage of towns ("benefactoría") — a new source of inequality.   The scantiness of population relatively to territory compelled the protection by all available means of nativity and domicile; hence a great laxity in the matter of sexual unions and blood relationship, and endeavors to consolidate the family also by economic advantages (forms of family and marital and fraternal community, widow's dower, etc).[1]

---

[1] Respecting the antiquity and nature of the contract of continued community and fraternal community ("unidad y hermandad") in León and Castile, see *Hinojosa*, "Discursos leídos," p 25   It occurs also in all the foral regions, as do also the simple "gananciales" (marital community)

This same necessity, with that of territorial exploitation, favored
the cultivation and fallowing of lands, and consequently facilitated
means of appropriation, and the conversion of possession into
ownership wherever there was formed a group of men truly free, or
without lords (" municipios ")   Through the exigencies of agriculture and the cohesion of related social elements for mutual
defence or aid, truncal families were perpetuated or reconstituted
with strong paternalistic power, as in Galicia, the Asturias, the
territory of the Pyrenees, Navarre, Aragon, and Catalonia; the
bonds of kinship were more closely knitted — as witness the
fraternities of artificial brotherhood in the Kingdom of León;
and associations were formed for the needs of social life — communities of serfs, communal property in different forms, gilds,
confraternities, etc [1]

In the same way we must explain the privileges of married persons, particularly those with children; the variety of matrimonial
institutions of equal or very similar legal status (as marriage " by
benediction " — i.e. canonic, "juratory" unions, concubinage);
the facility of conjugal separations, divorces, and the right of
" mañeria " (escheat for defect of heirs); the general prevalence
of communal property between spouses, " a system truly national
. . . whose origins can be referred with cause to the combined influence of Christianity and Germanic customs ", the subjection
of children to paternal and maternal power, and the denial to
them of rights of individual property and of testamentary capacity,
the indivision of the associate property in the family groups of
Aragon, Catalonia, the Asturias, etc., — which was later combined
with a liberty of devise to the eldest (" hereu ") or other son, the
patrimony being thus kept from disintegration; the shortening of
the prescriptive period in acquisition of title, the disappearance
of the "mejoras" (Castilian "fueros"), the equality or approx-

and the widow's dower (Navarrese "fueros" of the 1000s and 1100s,
Catalan documents of this period, etc)   Cf. the work of Hinojosa, pp
26–35 ["Gananciales" were "mejoras" (as defined in the first sense,
§ 15, n 15) of the conjugal estate · i e the fruits of the property contributed by both to the community, property bought by either with money or
labor, acquisitions by common title, whether by gift or for consideration,
and the fruits of all such added property, during cohabitation   The contract of "hermandad" was somewhat more general than that of "unidad."
— Transl]

[1] On the perpetuation of family bonds in the embryonic type of family
council recognized by the "Fuero Juzgo," see Costa, who cites on this point
the "fueros" of Sepúlveda, Cáceres, Salamanca, and Alcalá.   The institution was later adopted for the tutelage of minors by the "Fuero Real"
(par 18).

imation of rights among children of all classes; the right of
kinship ("troncalidad") and the preferential rights of relatives to
purchase of estates;[1] the absolute right of fathers to control the
marriage of daughters, the importance acquired in legislation by
contracts relative to the working of the soil under divided " dominium " (leases at will, emphyteutic and " foro " leases (copyholds) " encomiendas," etc[2]); and the existence in all the Christian kingdom of a social hierarchy of multiple and varied grades,
whose basis was a large population of slaves and serfs (Moors,
predial serfs, vassals " signiservitii," " collazos," " payeses,"
"mezquinos," "exaricos," etc.), or of free clients living on the grace
of others, notwithstanding the noble rank of many of them (" ca-
balleros," "emparats," holders of "encomiendas," etc)[3] Within
these general limits,[1] there persisted a rich variety of local institutional forms, founded upon the observance of custom, in the ample
borderland left to compact, that is to say to the will of the contracting parties.

In the depths, however, of this society, the natural reaction of
repressed elements, the political interest of the crown, and to a
considerable extent changes beyond the will of men, in the economic
conditions of different religions, were already working a profound

---

[1] [The "fuero de troncalidad" was that by which in the law of succession preference was given, among collaterals and descendants, to those in
the line or of the "stirps" of the decedent —On preferential purchase, cf
§ 22, note 3 — As to the leases at will, cf § 12, note 3. — As to emphyteutic leases, cf the author's remark in § 20. "Foro" leases in Asturias
and Galicia, and the "rabassa-morta" leases of Catalonia were temporary,
not perpetual, leases, otherwise emphyteutic in qualities , cf § 23, n 2 —
An "encomienda" was "la merced ò renta vitalicia que se da sobre algun
lugar, heredamiento ò territorio" (Escriche) — The "caballero" was,
strictly speaking, a gentleman ("hidalgo") of *distinguished* nobility The
"collazo" was a predial serf   "Payeses" were serfs of different classes , as
to the "payeses de remensa" cf § 17, n 1 above. — TRANSL]

[2] Besides the customary exposition of the content of each legal source
("fueros," "Usatges") which is given in most histories of law or legislation, the reader will find general accounts, or important details, of the institutions of public and private law in this period in *Martinez Marina,*
"Ensayo histórico-crítico de la antigua legislación" (2 vols , Madrid, 1808) ;
Cárdenas, "Ensayo sobre la historia de la propiedad territorial" (2 vols ,
Madrid, 1873–1875) ; *Muñoz y Romero,* "Del estado de las personas en
los reinos de Asturias y León en los primeros siglos posteriores á la invasión
de los árabes" (Madrid, 1883), and in his "Discursos leidos" cited above,
§ 9, note 2, *Hinojosa,* "Estudios," "El régimen señorial y la cuestion
agraria en Cataluña," "Mezquinos y exàricos," "La servidumbre de la
gleba en Aragon" (in España Moderna, Oct , 1904) and other articles,
Gama Barros, "Historia da administração publica em Portugal" (2 vols ,
Lisbon, 1885–1897) ; *Pella, op cit* above. § 15, n 4, *Costa,* "Colectivismo
agrario", *F. Aznar,* "Los solariegos en León y Castilla" in the Cultura
Española, 1907 ; and the well-known essays of *Durán y Bas, Naval,
Franco y Guillén, Morales,* and others, upon the civil law of the foral
provinces

modification of certain of its bases.   This came to the surface in the
emancipation of servile and dependent classes (a fact substantially
completed in Castile by the end of this period), in the appearance
of a middle class of freemen in the towns, and in the growth of
industry and commerce, which last was bound to raise the economic
status of movable property, depress that of immovables, produce a differentiation of commercial law, and bring after it into
social life new institutions and legal systems.

Chapter II. First Period. a.d. 1252–1511

THE CHRISTIAN RECONQUEST AND THE POLITICAL UNI-
FICATION OF THE PENINSULA

Topic 1. Spread of the Justinian and Canon Law in
Castile and Leon

§ 19. History of the Legal Sources.
§ 20. Roman Elements in the Statutory Law, and particu-
larly in the Partidas.
§ 21. The Status of the Partidas
after the Ordenamiento of
Alcalá (1348).

§ 22. The Leyes de Toro
§ 23. Diffusion of the Canon Law.
§ 24. New Legal Institutions of the
Period.

Topic 2. Spread of the Justinian and Canon Laws in
the Other Kingdoms of the Peninsula

§ 25 History of the Legal Sources.
§ 26. Roman Elements in the Law
of Catalonia.

§ 27 Roman Elements in the Law
of Aragon, Navarre, Va-
lencia, the Balearic Islands
and the Basque Provinces
§ 28. Notable Jurists of the Period

Topic 1. Spread of the Justinian and Canon Law in
Castile and León

§ 19. **History of the Legal Sources** — In order to render understandable the references in the following paragraphs that explain
the fundamental fact in the legal history of this period, namely,
the incurrence of two new influences, alien to the national law, it
is best to sketch briefly the history of legal sources from Alfonso
X to the reign of Joanna the Mad.

One's attention is attracted in the first place to the enormous
legislative activity of these centuries, befitting the transformation
which institutions suffered, and the growing complexity that social
life was rapidly taking on. Of the ordinances of the Cortes alone
a goodly number can be counted Add to these the general statutes
of exclusively royal initiative, the municipal " fueros " granted

without the concurrence of the Cortes, and innumerable charters, letters patent, "cedulas," and king's letters, issued in benefit of private interests, but which often affected matters of a public interest and modified regulations of general character, or filled the gaps in these (above all, at the close of the 1200s and in the 1300s, that is to say in the reigns of Sancho IV, Ferdinand IV, Alfonso XI, and Pedro I), — and one has an idea of the wealth of legal documents which the period has to offer

The predominantly particularistic character of the legislation of the preceding period is apparently not modified in this. The granting of municipal "fueros" — which always signified exceptions and heterogeneity of regimen — continued, in numbers equal or nearly equal to those of preceding centuries[1] Although many of these "fueros" were replicas, with but very slight alterations, of certain models or types, and others were of exceedingly little importance, their swollen numbers attest the persistence of the particularistic spirit. By their side ruled the "Fuero Juzgo" (whose translation into Castilian had been recently begun), albeit greatly wasted in authority, and contradicted in not a few of its statutes. Of its validity and acceptance as a general statute by jurisconsults there are evidences in the 1300s and 1400s. But it is noticeable, in regard to it, that despite its character as a general law, it yielded to the dominant current, assuming at one time or place the character of a municipal "fuero" (in this sense Fernando III conferred it on Cordova), and suffering at another, local alterations of its text such as are observable in comparing the translation supposedly made in the time of Alfonso IX, and is preserved at Santiago, with those that circulated in Castile.

On the other hand, a unitive tendency manifested itself at different times. Even in the field of the "fueros" Alfonso X issued, in 1254, a volume known variously as that of "the Statutes," the "Book of the Councils of Castile," "Fuero Castellano," "Fuero Real," and otherwise — which is nothing else than a model, more complete and systematic than all preceding ones, based upon these and the "Fuero Juzgo" with additions, and conserving with some modifications the general character of Visigothic, Leonese, and Castilian law as elaborated during the first centuries of the Reconquest. It embraces political, procedural, civil, criminal, and commercial law, developed in four books; and its redaction, we are told in the preface, was due to the lack of any true "fuero" in

---

[1] E g more than one hundred and twenty-seven from Alfonso X to 1299, and above ninety-four in the 1300s, most of these of Alfonso XI.

a great part of the kingdom, on which account men were forced to govern themselves under precedents, arbitrations, and customs, which were often pernicious, wherefore the cities themselves demanded that the king give them a new law. This Royal "Fuero" was adopted by the royal court as its authority in appellate cases and for the jurisdiction of the capital. It was also conceded as a municipal "fuero" in 1255, for the first time, to Aguilar de los Campos, and later to other cities, as for example Burgos, Valladolid, Simancas, Tudela, Soría, Ávila, Madrid, Plasencia, and Segovia; being, in short, one of the model "fueros" to which reference has been made, and of these the most widely disseminated. The original text suffered modifications (by Alfonso X himself in 1278–1279, by the Cortes of Valladolid of 1293), and local variants of it also existed, as is evident from the differences between the manuscript copies that remain to us. Its importance is shown, not alone in the modifications just referred to and by the great extent of territory over which its authority extended, but also by the legal problems which its enforcement elicited. These may be seen in a legal manuscript that accompanies some of the copies of the "Fuero Real," entitled "Leyes del Estilo," or interpretations of the foral laws. Although these cannot be designated infallibly as a statute (since it is not established that they were promulgated by King or Cortes), they serve at least to show (and this whether the manuscript be the result of the private initiative of some jurist, or a digest of legal decisions, or of any other nature) the endeavor made to adjust the work of Alfonso X to traditional customs, — in other words the variance between it and the new necessities of the time; and unquestionably, too, gaps and obscurities that blemished it.

More certainty exists regarding another group of statutes called "Nuevas" (new), which are said to have been promulgated by Alfonso X after the "Fuero Real," and which, to judge by the preamble common to many of them, were also issued to settle doubts felt by the judges in the application of the law. In the copies that have come down to us, a chief portion of these laws is duplicated in the different copies along with others that are variable, and which in some respects betray the hand of a private compiler rather than a legislator. At all events these "Leyes Nuevas" embrace only a few legal topics, — the relations between Christians and Jews in the matter of loans, civil procedure, and inheritance.

On this line the unification of the law made, as we have seen, little advance; for the very "Fuero Real" itself, notwithstanding its wide scope (reflected in some of its names), embraced only an exceedingly slight part of the content of the municipal " fueros " in force within the wide territories of the Castilian crown. It has been supposed that Alfonso X and his father devoted no little attention and labor to the aim of accomplishing at a stroke this unification, embodying their efforts in legal works that have made them celebrated, and to which reference must now be made

To Fernando III is attributed, as already seen, not only the conception, but also the partial preparation, of a code which, because it was intended to embrace seven parts, was called the " Septenario," and which was completed by Alfonso X   It is so stated, in fact, in the preface to the work, which, with one book dedicated to the exposition of topics of theology and Canon law, is all of the "Septenario " (or " Setenario ") that has come down to us (in a manuscript of the 1400s).   What is certain is that it was not administered as statute, inasmuch as it was not promulgated; and that the character of the text does not even justify one in considering it a work of true legislation, — but rather only as an encyclopædic and doctrinal work; and finally, that not even the general character of the body of the work, whether characterized like the " Fuero Real " by traditional tendencies or reflecting Romanist influences, can to-day be conjectured.

Of this same period of Alfonso X, and prepared either at his command or on private initiative, we possess a compilation of legal character, analogous to the " Septenario ", namely, the so-called " Espéculo (or " Espejo ") de todos los Derechos," or Mirror of all the Laws, — a name much used at the time throughout Europe to designate doctrinal treatises, — of which there have come down to us fragments preserved in a manuscript of the late 1200s or early 1300s   In the prologue it is stated that the book was composed by selecting from all the " fueros " whatever was best and most valuable, and with the counsel and accord of church authorities, men of wealth, and jurists; and that it was communicated to the cities for their government. The last statement is not, however, established by any historical evidence whatever, and so this new attempt at unification (if it was actually made) remained also fruitless   This " Espéculo " was, however, utilized by lawyers of the time as a text and reference book, as is inferable from manuscripts of the 1300s in which its principles are contrasted with the existing law and with doctrinal treatises.

The " Espéculo " was not the last work of this character produced in the time of Alfonso X   The enterprise of a great legal compilation reappears years later in a new and more ample work, similar in some respects to its predecessors, but of greater scope and of very different fate, — a so-called Statute Book ("Libro de las Leyes"), which, from its division into seven parts, came to be known already in the 1300s as "Las Partidas" or "Leyes de Partidas," names which have prevailed, and which are to-day those used to designate it. Its compilation was begun in 1256 and was completed, it would seem, in 1265. Its sources were the "fueros" and worthy customs of Castile and León (for example, the "Fuero Juzgo," "Fuero Real," and the "fueros" of Cuenca and Córdoba), the accepted Canon law (the Decretals), and the works of the Roman jurisconsults included in the Pandects, together with those of the Italian commentators upon the Justinian law. Of these three elements, the preponderant were the canon and the Roman, and although they were not always accepted with servility, their doctrines being modified as to some points, the general character of the "Partidas" is that of an encyclopædia or systematic compendium of those two legal systems. They signalize a great novelty in the legal history of Castile, as well for the new material which they added as for the modifications they effected of the Visigothic and foral tradition in the field of private and (in part) of public law. The redaction of the "Partidas" was the work of several jurists whose names are not cited in the text, and was done under the supervision, and subject (how much cannot be determined) to the active intervention of Alfonso, who was himself an author of zeal.

What could have been the king's intent in causing the compilation of the "Libro de las Leyes?" Was it to compose a legal encyclopædia, analogous to others which he made in other fields of knowledge, in conformity to the spirit of the time (favorable in both Moslem and Christian countries to this sort of works)? Or did he rather wish to prepare a statute or code expressive of the new influences of the Canon and Roman law, in order to impose it as a common law — and consequently to annul the "Fuero Juzgo," the municipal "fueros," and the very "Fuero Real" itself — upon all his subjects? The latter intent seems inferable from a paragraph of the preface to the "Partidas" in which we read: "We are pleased to command that all persons of our dominion be governed by these statutes and by no other statute or 'fuero,'" and from other similar passages in various statutes of the same collection; and though the same may be read in the "Espéculo," which was never law, the declaration, sufficiently explicit and repeated in other passages, does not on that account the less exist, and appears to justify our inference   Yet if this be trustworthy, it would nevertheless clash with various significant facts in Alfonso's reign: namely, on one hand, with the prohibition against the observance in Castile of the Roman laws embodied in a letter of the king to the alcaldes of Valladolid, August, 1258, and, on the other hand, with the repeated confirmations of the local " fueros " (as of Zamora in 1274, Valladolid, 1255, Segovia, 1256) made by him in different Cortes, the concession of many new ones (the majority of those of the second half of the 1200s being of Don Alfonso), and the promulgation of the "Fuero Real" itself. These were acts preceding, cotemporaneous with, and following the compilation of the " Partidas," and by them the king himself contradicted the ostensible character and purpose of that work.

In whatever way this contradiction may be explained, the fact is that the " Partidas " were not confirmed as a common and inevitably ordained law, either in the reign of that king or of his successors, until Alfonso XI   These went on, as already noted, granting municipal "fueros," sanctioning the "Fuero Juzgo" and " Fuero Real," making alterations in the last, and punishing whatever was contrary to the local liberties, thus denying not only the pretended general authority of the " Partidas," but also the innovations which the doctrine of that work represented.

And yet the compilation of Alfonso X went on gaining ground among men   Among students, notably the lawyers, and in the universities — classes especially influenced by the Roman and the Canon law — the "Partidas" served as a text and reference book. This is indicated by the glosses of the manuscript copies of the 1200s and 1300s, by the fact of its being read and expounded in the university classes (in Portugal and Catalonia as well), and by the publication of isolated fragments as doctrinal texts. This tendency was favored by the strictly didactic character (scientific, ethical, or historical) of not a few of the statutes, — as had been likewise true of the " Fuero Juzgo." Doubtless through the influence of lawyers educated in the universities, who were already devoting much thought to public affairs (Alfonso X states in more than one place in his works that he consulted " men learned in the law "), many portions of the " Partidas " were gaining authority in legal theory, sanctioned by the then new and great prestige of the Roman law, as well as in the practice of the courts, and in the opinions of counsel   One cannot, otherwise understand why, in a number of Cortes (for example those of Segovia in 1347), representations were made to the king against certain details of the Partidas, which, if they had *not* been enforced, could not fittingly have been characterized by the petitioners as infractions of the law. In the Cortes of Alcalá (1348) the ordinance confirmed by Alfonso XI also seems to allude to conflicts provoked by the enforcement of statutes of the Partidas. And indubitably the movement in favor of these had come to be very powerful, for in that same ordinance it was resolved to promulgate the compilation of Alfonso X, making it obligatory in all points not contradictory of the municipal ' fueros," the " Fuero Real," and the privileges of the nobility.

With this the idea of Alfonso the Wise was realized. Thenceforward the Canon and Roman doctrines could influence openly and legally the positive law, in modification of the native law of León and Castile. To Alfonso X was also due a special law relating to the justices of the appellate royal court (" adelantados mayores "), and a regulation of gambling houses

The " Ordenamiento of Alcalá " was not limited to giving the force of law to the " Partidas " (with the limitations mentioned); it also formulated in outline a hierarchy of sources within the positive law. In the first place, it puts the statutes resolved in that Cortes, which concerned various matters of political law, judicature and procedure, civil law, criminal law, and public finance, introducing important changes, to a number of which reference has already been made. After these come the " Fuero Real" (" Fuero de las Leyes ") — " which is observed in our court and which certain cities of our realm keep as their fuero " — and the municipal " fueros," whose authority (except in matters " against God and reason ") Alfonso XI confirmed, though reserving the right to amend and better them   Lastly, and as a supplementary law, come the " Partidas," — " albeit it appears not that they have been thus far published by mandate of the king, nor were ever held for laws "   Similarly it confirmed the " fueros " or privileges of the nobility and their vassals, — the special one of trial by judicial combat (" rieptos "), and the general one of rank (" fijosdalgo "), — which Alfonso XI decreed on the basis of that said to have been granted in the Cortes of Nájera, and which is given at the end of the ordinance   As for the " Partidas," the king notes that he had caused it to be " harmonized, amended, and amplified in certain matters "; that is to say, the text of the " Partidas " in force from this time was not the same as that originally put forth by Alfonso X, which had been revised with regard to the needs of the

623

age It must also be noted that the new statutes of the " Ordenamiento " (whose authority controlled) modified substantially
many important principles of the Alfonsine compilation, for example, in judicial procedure, contracts, the regulation of conjugal
property, and inheritance, while the traditional royal and municipal foral law was in great part affirmed.

Legislative variety continued, as is seen, in the same degree as
that in which Alfonso the Wise left it, and his great-grandson
(Alfonso XI) not only sanctioned it in the " Ordenamiento of
Alcalá," but further confirmed it by concessions of many municipal
" fueros," as has already been pointed out.

The common elements of the positive law, nevertheless, went on
rapidly growing in number and gaining ground   The great legislative activity of the Cortes and the steadily growing absolutism
of the kings — which was manifested in the frequency and abundance with which they legislated " motu proprio " in " cedulas,"
letters patent, king's letters, and ordinances — went on overlaying
the diversities of the " fueros " with a mass of regulations of common observance, which gradually lessened the special province of
the local laws and annulled many of their provisions. And the
unitive process was bound to end thus, even though not through
promulgating any general and common code or expressly abrogating
the " fueros," but instead confirming and even increasing them (as
already seen, and as continued to be done in the statutes of Cortes
and royal acts of the 1300s and 1400s), for these confirmations
and additions had continually less actual meaning, representing
exemptions more apparent than real, increasingly curtailed from
day to day. The ordinances of the Cortes and the dispositions
of the crown had gone on modifying and unifying political and
criminal law, the law of judicature, and that of public finance,
which constituted the very basis of the particularism of the
" fueros ", and the innovations of the private and procedural law
of the " Partidas " passed through these channels from the status
of a supplementary to that of a preferential law. In appearance,
the gradation of sources indicated in the " Ordenamiento of Alcalá"
was not altered   But from Alfonso XI to the Catholic Kings
matters changed greatly in essence, for the power of emending
and bettering the " fueros " which the king had reserved to himself came to be the thing of most importance, through which the
new law was enthroned in supremacy in the greater part of social
relations   In conformity with this tendency Peter I made a new
revision of the text of the " Partidas " in the Cortes of 1351, and

later kings repeatedly confirmed their authority   The fact should be noted that various Cortes of the 1400s (Madrid, 1433 and 1458; Valladolid, 1447; Medina, 1465) petitioned the formation of new compilations of the law and elucidations of those existing; this was yet another proof of the great complexity of the positive law, and of the confusion and doubt that continually resulted in attempting to determine what what really obligatory in any case.

To Peter I has come to be attributed a code comprehensive of the special " fueros " of the nobility, and known under the name of the " Fuero Viejo " of Castile. Its existence was unknown until at the close of the 1700s two Aragonese scholars discovered its text in ancient manuscripts and published it, accepting its authenticity as certain.   But the fact that the preface (in which the history of the " Fuero Viejo " is set forth and the pretension is made that Peter I ordered and republished it in 1356) is full of errors, the circumstance that it contains statutes expressive of legal conditions whose actual existence in Castile is very doubtful, and the clearing up of the royal sources of its text (accomplished in recent times) compel a belief that it was never a legal code, but rather a compilation made in the 1400s on private initiative and for private ends, upon the basis of other private compilations and the " Ordenamiento of Alcalá," although with notable variations. It is true, however, that the compiler does show himself well informed of the actual law, to judge by the concordance of many statutes of this " Fuero " with authentic documents of the time.

The sources of the privileges or " fueros " of the nobility in this period are to be sought mainly in charters, the " Fuero Real," the " Partidas," and the " Ordenamiento de Fijosdalgo " (" Ordinance of Gentlemen ") granted by Alfonso XI.

The reign of the " Catholic Kings," Ferdinand and Isabella, represented in the history of Spain great changes in the political order — the conquest of Granada, the curbing of the nobility of Castile, the annexation of the lands discovered in America and of Navarre, conquests in Italy and in Africa, and the reorganization of the army; as well as in criminal law (the Inquisition), and in society (expulsion of the Jews, conversion of the Andalusian Moors, etc.); and all these changes necessarily produced a great development of legislation.[1]

Despite the importance of certain Cortes of this time, as those

[1] A detailed statement of them will be found in vol. 2 of *Altamira*, "Civilización Española."

of Madrigal, Toledo, and Toro, and others of Aragon, the greater part of the dispositions promulgated were due to the personal initiative of the king, and were in the form of "cedulas," king's letters, provisions, capitulations, instructions, etc. And, notwithstanding all this, the necessity of a new and ordered compilation was profoundly felt, for that of the time of Philip II, incomplete and behind the age, was in many respects deficient. This labor was undertaken by two jurists, by both it would seem by commission of Queen Isabella: Dr. Alfonso (or Alonso) Diaz de Montalvo, and Dr Galindez de Carvajal The publication of only the former's compilation was realized, under the title of "Ordenanzas Reales de Castilla" (1484 ?), it was popularly known as the "Ordenamiento del Doctor Montalvo" The work is divided into eight books and comprises ordinances of the Cortes from that of Alcalá of 1348 onward, and various classes of royal acts from the time of Alfonso X, including some taken from earlier legal source-books: in number, a total of 1163 statutes relative to political, administrative, procedural, civil, and criminal law, of which 230 were of the Catholic Kings. It is doubtful whether Montalvo's collection attained legal authority, or only remained a mere essay which the crown did not come to promulgate as law. At all events it was neither perfect nor complete. There are statutes in it that are duplicated, others of corrupted text, some the ascription of whose origin is not trustworthy; and of course it does not contain all the dispositions of the crown and of the Cortes anterior to the Catholic Kings, nor all those issued in their time down to 1484. There were later promulgated and printed, in casual issues. various instructions and ordinances,[1] and a compilation known by the name of Juan Ramirez, which includes papal bulls and Castilian laws (1503). But the necessity of a good compilation, clear and methodical, continued In her will Queen Isabella recommended its preparation.

An important group among the laws of the time is formed by those relative to the American dominions, which later, in the time of Charles II, came to constitute a part of the "Recopilación de las Leyes de Indias," which will be later referred to.[2]

[1] See their enumeration in the work just cited (2d ed), vol II, p 485. Among them the most important is the group known as the "Leyes de Toro" which are referred to below in § 22
[2] For an enumeration and elaborate analysis of them see generally the book of A Fabié, "Ensayo histórico sobre la legislación de los Estados españoles de Ultramar"(vol I of the "Colección de Documentos Inéditos" in publication by the Academia de la Historia) , and for a systematic exposition of their novelties see especially §§ 574, 575, 587, and 588

§ 20. **Roman Elements in the Statutory Law, and Particularly in the " Partidas "** — Having now described the external history of the sources of the law, it remains to be seen how the Roman law of Justinian and the Canon law made their way into them and into legal practice generally.

The influence of the former found its entry already prepared for by events anterior to the 1200 s, but in that century it was strikingly revealed in legislative measures and didactic works. A formidable struggle was thus begun between it and the legislation and native customs whose distinctive character has been noted above. The renascence of the Justinian law in Europe, thanks to the labors of the Italian and French schools, especially from the end of the 1000 s onward, did not fail to show effects in the Peninsula.[1]

That that law had exercised some influence in Spain before the 1200 s, and even upon legislation, cannot be doubted, although it cannot be affirmed as to all the matters professed by certain writers   Thus, for example, the utilization, albeit inconsiderable, in the " Usatici Barchinonæ " is established by the compilation called " Petri Exceptiones Legum Romanorum " (of uncertain date and authorship) [2]   It is also said that vestiges of the same law are betrayed by a manuscript of Petrus de Ganon of the 1000 s, cited by Nicolas Antonio [3]   That it must have been influential in the Visigothic period is an assumption not indisputable, although it is indeed highly probable that it was introduced into the Spanish territories ruled by the Byzantines, and that the statute of Reccesvinth (or Kindasvinth) prohibiting the application of " remotis alienarum gentium legibus " is a reference to it.[4]   But these Roman

---

[1] It is well known that the classic work of *Savigny* upon this subject, "Geschichte des römischen Rechts im Mittelalter" (1815–1831 and 1834–1835) has been rectified and supplemented in many points by Fitting, Ficker, Schupfer, and many other modern Romanists.   Readers of Spanish will find a good account of the actual state of our knowledge regarding this question in the excellent book of *F. Clemente de Diego*, " Introducción al estudio de las instituciónes de derecho romano" (Madrid 1900)

[2] See *Ficker* on the "Usatici Barchinonæ" and their relations with the "Exceptiones Legum Romanorum" in the "Mitteilungen des Instituts für Osterreichische Geschichtsforschung," vol. VII, suppl vol. II, pt 1.

[3] *N. Antonio*, "Biblioteca Hispana Vetus," vol I, p. 518.   The affirmation is made by *Ureña*, "Sumario "

[4] *Ureña*, who agrees with one or another foreign authority, believes that it is also traceable in the " Fórmulas Visigóticas " (which *Hinojosa* denies) ; as well as in the division into 12 books of the Code of Reccesvinth, and perhaps in a statute (ley 1, tit 3, bk 3) of the "Forum Iudicum."   *Clemente*, *op. cit*, p 192 says   "The legislation of Justinian was introduced into Italy after the conquests of Narses   It attained especial dominance in Romagna, was more or less widely known in the Gallic provinces, and *perhaps also in Spain*."

fragments, even were they to be completely proved to be such,
are of scant importance The Justinian element did not attain
importance in the Peninsula until the 1200 s. In that and the
preceding century the knowledge and cultivation of the Roman
law in Spain is attested by the names of various jurisconsults (some
of them students or professors in foreign Universities, for the most
part at Bologna, others, of Italian origin resident in Spain, as the
" magister " Jacome Ruiz); by the diffusion of Justinian texts in
the original or translations, and by the existence of legal works
inspired by the Justinian system [1]

Of these works, there was in Castile in the 1200 s only one of
a truly legislative character, " The Fuero Real " For it does not
appear that either the " Septenario " of Ferdinand III (whose only
preserved fragment does not permit one either to affirm or deny
that it was Romanist in character, although the affirmative be
probable), or the " Espéculo " was promulgated or enforced as law;
and as for the " Partidas," we have seen that they did not enjoy
the status of an obligatory code in the time of Alfonso the
Wise.

Although the " Fuero Real " was (as already stated) predominantly indigenous in its elements, it offered certain novelties that
indicate the inflow of the Roman law into the field of civil law.
Such are various of the rules of interstate succession; testamentary
executors, adoption — whose regulation is adjusted to the Justinian system; the accession of " insula nata "; and a good part of
the theory of contracts In other matters (such as " mejoras,"
the prescriptive period for gaining title, and marriage), the " Fuero
Real " rectified the earlier municipal " fueros " without adopting
the Roman law, sometimes reviving mandates of the " Fuero
Juzgo " that had fallen into desuetude, at other times establishing rules of distinct form borrowed from the Canon law or other
sources A novelty of importance, and not of Roman origin, is
the testament by agency (" por comisario ").

There was a larger Roman element, as already seen, in the " Partidas " Within the field of civil law the Romanism of this code is
displayed especially in the following topics the theory of the nature
of law and custom, [2] the theory of status; the division of things
and of rights into those real and personal , the doctrine of ownership, modes of acquisition, possession; servitudes, hypothec and

---

[1] Cf Altamira, "Lacunes."
[2] Universidad de Oviedo, "Trabajos de investigación en la cátedra y
seminario de Historia general del Derecho," 1905

pledge; emphyteusis (the principles of which came to be confounded with those of other medieval contracts which were, strictly considered, different, (§ 18 above, n. 3); the classes and formalities of contract; the distinction between pact and contract; extinction of obligations, dowry of the wife (making that derived from the husband ("arras") equivalent to the gift "propter nuptias," and introducing the inalienability of the former and its security by a legal hypothec upon the property of the husband); modification of the rules regulating the ganancial (community) system—which the "Partidas" do not expressly regulate, but, so far as the local custom permits, assume in matrimonial contracts—as respects the property that might constitute them, excluding the fruits of the dowry and the "arras"; the suppression of the widow's dower, —though not of the compact of community (§ 18 above),—and the introduction on the other hand of the rule giving a fourth part of the inheritance to the young widow who brings no dowry; the definition of the legal incapacities of women established by the "Senatus consultum Vellejanum," with the exceptions introduced by the Glossators, and the constitution "Sia qua mulier"; administration of her "parapherna" by a wife when she did not intrust them to the husband for administration by him, the principles of legitimacy and of adoption, and the entire theory of the "patria potestas," with negation of maternal authority; the principles of wills (their classes, formalities, etc.), legitimes (compulsory testamentary shares), which were adjusted to the 118th Novel of Justinian, with some variations; the rules of the division of the inheritance, the repudiation of the right of kinship; and, finally, intestate succession [2]

If the immediate imposition of so considerable a mass of innovations upon the cities of the Castilian crown had been possible, the derangements produced in civil life would have been enormous. Fortunately, impositions of this sort are not reconcilable with the processes of history. When they are attempted, they are futile, since the people will not receive or tolerate them. Nor was this contemplated by Alfonso X, who did not promulgate the "Partidas" (despite the repeated expression in their text of the obligatory character of the laws of that compilation); nor can any such intent be attributed with probability to him, seeing that his

[1] *Hinojosa*, "Discursos leídos," etc
[2] See *Martinez Marina*, "Ensayo histórico-crítico de la antigua legislación," books 8 and 9, *La Serna*, preface to the edition of the "Partidas" published by the editorial house (and known under the name of) La Publicidad, Madrid, 1848 Cf *Altamira*, "Lacunes," pp 10–11.

whole conduct as a legislator contradicts it.[1] As little did his
successors attempt it, until Alfonso XI, who in one of the statutes
passed in the Cortes of Alcalá of 1348 — and inserted, as we have
seen, in the " Ordenamiento " that bears the name of that assembly
— ordered the publication of the " Partidas " (according to them
an authority of the lowest order, as supplementary to the
royal statutes), the " Fuero Real," and, so far as these were of
actual authority, the municipal " fueros." If 1265 be accepted
as the year in which the composition of the " Partidas " was ended,
we have a period of eighty-three years during which the work of
Alfonso X remained, in legal phraseology, suspended.

As we have seen, however, this was so only in appearance. Its
fame, which corresponded to the merits of its execution, rapidly
opened it a way and gave it, among the embodiments of the national
legal genius, a rank as high as any which Alfonso's ambition could
have craved for it. The manner in which its influence was
spread has been indicated above in § 19. But though this process
is known to us in its general features, we know very little of it in
detail. We possess to-day very few data in regard to the actual
enforcement of the Alfonsine compilation in the judgments of the
courts, the resolutions of the Royal Council, and other embodiments of the positive law. Martinez Marina gathered together
all the evidence that on this point is adducible: petitions, passages
in the acts of the Cortes anterior to 1348, some of them of doubtful
meaning; a " ley del Estilo " (§ 19) — likewise questionable as
regards the legal force of the collection to which it belongs, three
statutes of the " Ordenamiento of Alcalá ", and the political question of the succession of the crown of Castile provoked between
the heirs of the eldest son of Alfonso X and his second son Sancho.
A very scanty showing, as is evident; and even of these we must
eliminate, for our purposes, the portions that do not relate to the
private law. In order to arrive at a more precise determination
of the diffusion of the Roman element of the " Partidas " up to
1348 it would be necessary to study the judge-made law of the
preceding eighty-three years (of which it cannot be doubted many
documents will be found in the archives), the diplomatic collections
of the Kings Alfonso X, Sancho IV, Ferdinand IV, and Alfonso XI
(up to 1348); and the papers of the Royal Council,[2] ex-
tracting from them all the concrete references to a preferential en-

---

[1] *Altamira,* "Civilización española," vol II, p 79
[2] On the Council and the influence in it of the legists, see *Conde de
Torreánaz,* "Los consejos del rey en la edad media."

forcement of the Roman doctrines as contrasted with the native. Until this investigation shall have been made (be its results what they may), we cannot rest content with our knowledge of this period, so important in the legal history of Castile.[1]

§ 21. **The Status of the " Partidas " after the " Ordenamiento of Alcalá " (1348).** — The question of the penetration of Roman theory into Spanish civil law was not settled by the statute of the " Ordenamiento of Alcalá " above referred to. The " Ordenamiento " was in this respect evidently the product of compromises. Allusions are made in it to conflicts provoked by the (unlawful) application of the statutes of the " Partidas ", and one need not feel doubts in believing that the solution offered by Alfonso XI proves the strength which the opinions favorable to the Roman element had acquired. In contrast to the satisfaction thus given to these opinions in ranking the " Partidas " as a supplementary law, there appear nevertheless statutes that mark, beyond all uncertainty, a reaction in favor of the native element, and which confirm this, expressly and concretely, in preference to certain principles of the Justinian law. Examples of such statutes are those relative to the dispensation of formalities in contract, the administration of matrimonial property, succession, and the necessity of the appointment of an heir (which they repudiate)

After 1348, however, the question reappears for us in similar terms, — since that which we are interested in knowing is what effective enforcement was enjoyed after that date by the code of Alfonso X (corrected by Alfonso XI when he promulgated it); whether as a law strictly supplementary to, or — in the manner noted before 1348 — as a rule superior to and derogative of the native law, notwithstanding the precedence given these in the " Ordenamiento." Martinez Marina attacked this problem and established in reference to it direct and indirect proofs of the enforcement of the " Partidas " from the 1300s onward.[2] He reaches this general conclusion: That the legists, imbued with the theories of Justinian and the Canon law, and of the Glossators and Commentators of the Renascence, habitually cited all this rubbish in the civil courts, where these doctrines " served as the

---

[1] In the pragmatics and royal orders subsequent to the " Partidas," which we know to-day through the "Compilación del Doctor Montalvo," evidences of Roman influence are not discernible, on the contrary, there are confirmations of statutes of the "Fuero Real," and of native institutions such as the "gananciales" Much still remains to be determined, however, in this field

[2] All are set forth in detail in *Altamira*, "Lacunes," pp 13–15.

norm of judgment, and as interpretations of the national statutes,
particularly the ' Partidas " To this code, because derived from
those sources and especially adjusted to their distortions, they
assigned arbitrarily a chief, or more exactly, a sole authority,
although indeed always maintaining it in a status of dependence
upon Justinian and his interpreters " [1] The author failed however, to develop this averment with the accumulation of concrete
citations that one might desire, and consequently this question
also remains expectant upon scholarly investigations of the documentary source of legal decisions, the acts of the Cortes, and the
pragmatics of the crown.[2]

§ 22   The " Leyes de Toro " — This struggle between Romanism and the native law was prolonged throughout the rest of
the 1300s and all of the 1400s. It was attempted to impose the
former, as has been seen, through two channels the " Partidas,"
on one hand, on the other, the Justinian law and the doctrines of
the Commentators not included in that code, and whose citation
before the courts was prohibited by a pragmatic of John II as early
as 1427. The Catholic Kings followed in this respect a vacillating
and contradictory policy, as is shown by a comparison of the pragmatic of 1499, that of 1502, and that known as of Barcelona.[3]

The result of this struggle was the recurrence at the end of this
period of the same state of doubt, of uncertainty in the application
of the law, and of conflicts between the various sources which, now
statutes and now the servile opinions of the legists, were introducing into practice The " Ordenamiento " of the Cortes of Toledo
of 1502, first promulgated in 1505 in the Cortes of Toro (" Leyes de
Toro ") was an answer to this and an attempt at a new clearing
up of the situation The pragmatic promulgating the " Ordenamiento " expresses with sufficient clearness its motive:

---

[1] *Martinez Marina*, "Ensayo histórico-crítico de la antigua legislación,"
bk 9, par 24   Note the contrasts he establishes between the pure Roman
law and the "Partidas " In this matter he only continues the distinction
which is discernible in all the civilians of the 1700s, who include the
"Partidas" in the Spanish law even when they are protesting against the
Roman and in favor of the native Such inclusion was, for that matter,
traditional, and may be seen in chapter 19 of the instruction for "Corregi-
dores" issued in the time of the Catholic Kings and cited by Martinez
Marina.

[2] As an example of what can be gleaned in these sources, recall the
statute issued by John II at Olmedo on May 15, 1445, declaratory of certain statutes of the 2d "Partida" and of the "Fuero Real," and which
was pointed out by *Asso and De Manuel* in their "Instituciónes del derecho
civil de Castilla" (4th ed , Madrid, 1786,) p lxxxvi

[3] *Altamira*, "Lacunes," pp 14–16

"Be it known that reports of the great hurt and damage done
to my subjects and natives by the great variety and diversities that
prevailed in the understanding of certain statutes of these my
realms, as well of the "Fuero" as of the "Partidas" and of
"Ordenamientos," and of other matters that had need of interpretation though there were no laws concerning them, were reported to the King my lord and father and to the Queen my lady
and mother, whom may God keep: wherefore it came to pass that
in certain parts of these my kingdoms, and even in my own courts
judgments were taken and sentences given in identical cases sometimes one way and other times another, which was the cause of the
great variety and diversity that existed in the understanding of
the said laws among the lawyers of these my realms," etc.

The "Leyes de Toro" resolved some of these cases of "variety
and diversity." Sometimes they inclined toward the native, but
usually to the Roman and Canon law, in certain institutes they
adopted a compromised policy, consisting in the recognition of
both systems at the same time. The familiarity of these laws and
the abundance of extensive and profound commentaries upon them,
some modern,[1] excuses us from tarrying in an exposition of their
principles; but we may indicate their chief novelties and most
important principles. The "Partidas" triumph in them in
the law relative to sealed testaments; various particularities of
succession; the right of preferential purchase by a cotenant;[2]
the dowry brought by the wife, implicitly recognized at the same
time as that derived from the husband, to which was given the
erroneous name of "arras"; prescriptive periods, the validity
of the "Senatus consultum Vellejanum" (relating to a wife's
contracts); and in other details. On the other hand, the principles
of that code were contradicted, or others ignored by it were affirmed,
in the recognition of the testamentary acts of those condemned
to death, and of sons under tutelage; in the ganancial (community) system; in the portion of the inheritance left to free testamentary disposition (only a fifth, as in the "Fuero Real"); in
testament by agency, which was confirmed and perfected; in the
relatives' right of preferential purchase;[2] etc.

[1] By *Antonio Gómez* (1555), by *Llamas y Molina* (1827), by *Pacheco*
(1862); and by *González Serrano* (1867)
[2] [If a tenant in common alienated his share, his fellows had a certain
time to invalidate the sale, taking the share at the same price — "retracto
de comuneros" If a person alienated part of a family estate, his near
relatives had a similar right to invalidate the sale and take the property, —
"retracto de parientes" "Tanteos" differed from "retractos" in this,
that the former were similar rights of bidding in, exercised before the sale
was consummated. — TRANSL]

Other statutes of the " Fuero Real " were also ratified, and the " Ordenamiento " of 1348 was reproduced, as regards the preferential rank of legal sources, the inferior status of the " Partidas " as a supplementary code being thus maintained

An important novelty in the " Leyes de Toro " is the development of estates tail (" mayorazgos ") — already regulated in the " Partidas ", they possessed even a more ancient national lineage, and were rapidly to take root in custom. The entailing of estates began, as is well known, in the time of Alfonso X. under private charters, and went on spreading in like form among the estates of the noble class, both as regards their own estates and of those received by grant from the crown as " heredades " and " villas " in inalienable title and with limitation to primogenital succession. This was the form taken by the greater part of the royal gifts and grants that were so frequent from the time of Henry II onward.[1] The " Leyes de Toro" sanctioned this new institution, providing general rules regulative of it, thus implanting securely one of the peculiarities of Castilian civil law, which persisted until the middle of the 1800 s.[2]

§ 23. **Diffusion of the Canon Law** — At the same time that the Roman influence had been thus penetrating into the legal system of Castile. a like phenomenon was occurring with the Canon law. The renascence which was brought about in the Church from the time of Gregory VII carried with it an extension of the Church's power, a favorable modification of its relations with the State, and the enlargement of the personal and real immunities of the clergy, the latter being reflected in the practices of civil law. At the same time there was operating within the Church's economic administration, and parallel to the development of entails among the nobles, the entailing of immovables, and this process (coincidently again with the development taking place in the municipalities as regards the communal lands and other property) had, by the end of this period, modified the distribution of property to an extent that was of extraordinary importance socially and legally.[3] Again, and

---

[1] [The name "mayorazgo" ("vínculo") — from "major natu" (?) — indicates the original nature of such holdings But at least in the later law a "mayorazgo" was not necessarily primogenital, the "vinculación" (entailment) accomplished merely continuance in a "familia," — i e a truncal family, collaterals not being excluded And they could be temporary as well as perpetual. — TRANSL.]

[2] Sempere y Guarinos, "Historia de los vínculos y mayorazgos" (2d ed , Madrid, 1847), Cambronero, "La institución de los mayorazgos" (Madrid, 1820), Cardenas, op cit above, § 18, n 4

[3] On civil and ecclesiastical amortization, see the book of Cárdenas cited

through the principle of related causes, the Church was at the same time subjecting to its jurisdiction and to the rule of the Canon law many institutions of the civil law, such as marriage, usurious loans, rent-charges,[1] etc.   The slow penetration of that law into the customs and statute-book of Castile is particularly observable in the field of family law, beginning with marriage itself, and in certain classes of contract, — not to mention the modifications it produced in the fields of public, political, and criminal law (concession of the crown by the Pope, absolution of the subjects from oaths of allegiance, changes in criminal procedure).

Among the more remote evidences of the influence of the Church upon family law are the following· the replacement of the direct delivery (" traditio ") of the wife to the husband from the father by the indirect delivery through the priest, which already appears in the Ritual of Cardeña (1200 s)[2]   This was followed by a prohibition in the civil law of all marriages not " solemn " or canonical, a prohibition encountered already in the " Fuero Real," accentuated in the " Partidas," and repeated in the " Leyes de Toro "; the special persecution of the concubinage of the clergy, both directly, through prohibitions and penalties, and indirectly, as for example by disqualifying sacrilegious children from succession to their clerical fathers and other relations (statute 22, tit 3, bk. 1, " Ordenanzas Reales "), or by reducing the sons of the regular clergy to the status of serfs of the Church; the recognition of ecclesiastical jurisdiction in cases of marriage, divorce, etc., — tearing them from the civil jurisdiction, — which appears in the " Fuero Real " and the Alfonsine code; the sanction of the entire lot of canonical impediments to marriage, found in the same two codes; the reduction of the rights of illegitimate children, and even the division of such (common to the Roman and the Canon law) into

above, § 18, n 4, and on the extension of the Church's power see the general picture in *Altamira*, "Civilización española," par 459, 460, 590
[1] ["Censo," — the contract by which one acquired an annuity in exchange for something delivered, or the right to such annuity, or the charge itself   The "censo" was "consignativo" when a charge on the property or labor of the payer, "enfiteútico" when reserved by one who transferred for a long time or forever to the payer the beneficiary title to something, "reservativo" when both the beneficiary title and the legal title were so transferred   "Censos," then, could be owed by the person or the property, but they were most important as rent-charges, notably as quit-rents   The "censo reservativo" was unknown in the Catalan foral law   The "foros" of the North and the "rabassa morta" of Catalonia — cf § 18, n. 3 and § 15, n 9 above — the former most frequently for three lives and the latter of the same or fifty years, were of the emphyteusis type — TRANSL]
[2] *Hinojosa*, "Estudios," pp 105–106.

natural children and those " of corrupt and criminal connection," which the "Leyes de Toro" particularly develop; the continuation of the movement restrictive of the civil rights of Jews and Mudéjars, involved in the negation of capacity to inherit and of capacity to be executors to those who were not Christians (" Fuero Real "); the establishment of the Church's rights to first fruits and tithes (the " Partidas "),[1] the acceptance of canonic doctrines relative to usury, the application of these in the regulation of the " foros,"[2] a contract much used by churches and monasteries; etc

In contrast with these acceptances of the Canon law or of ethico-legal theories of ecclesiastical writers, some restrictions are found that emanated from the crown to check the ecclesiastical intrusions upon the civil order. An example of these is the revocation by the Catholic Kings of the privileges and charters on which the procurators of the Orders of the Trinity and of Saint Olalla founded the right to take legacies bequeathed in their favor by laymen, and the whole inheritance of intestates

§ 24. **New Legal Institutions of the Period.** — Aside from all these innovations, it is important, in an examination of the influx of the Roman and Canon law in this period, to make note of others which (like that of entailed estates already mentioned) either first showed themselves or acquired especially great growth in the 1200s to 1400s because of varied, and frequently complex, causes.

The total property of society had greatly increased, and had continued to accentuate the change of form which it had already begun to show in the preceding period. To speak more exactly, there had been adopted side by side with the primitive forms (agriculture and grazing, as regards the class of industry or the medium exploited; collectivism, concentration in a few hands, and servile cultivation, as regards the subjects of property and of its enjoyment) other new ones, the results of the growth of settlement and of the changes that had intervened in social classes. Urban wealth, movable property from industries, and commerce[3] —

---

[1] Royal tithes (the only ones known in Spain) were, as is well known, anterior to the 1100s. The first certain confirmation to the crown of those which were the share of the Spanish churches is of the time of Alfonso X The "Partidas" contain the entire canonic doctrine of tithes and first fruits (2d "Partida," tit 19 and 20). On the elements of Canon law in the "Partidas" see *Martinez Marina*, "Ensayo histórico-crítico de la antigua legislación ;" which study, however, is not to be supposed complete or definitive

[2] See *J. Villaamil*, "Los foros de Galicia en la Edad Media" (Madrid, 1884)

[3] Which was increasing in progressive ratio, and had developed considerable export relations with France, England, and above all with

were every day growing in importance; while the great mass of seigniorial estates, in earlier times cultivated by servile and semi-servile classes, was disintegrating. This influence, together with the protection of the municipalities, the liberty conceded to the "solariego" and the "forero" (small cultivators) and the conversion of servile holdings into leases, permitted the formation of a class of small proprietors which the regional law protected, throwing obstacles in the way of their being again absorbed by the nobility. The result of this was a great development of the contract of lease (" arrendamiento ") in its various forms, — of which that on shares (" aparcería ") was very frequent, — in place of the ancient contracts of villeinage, copyhold, leases at will, etc.[1]

The old dependence of property upon the social condition of the owner continued nevertheless to show its effects. As a general principle, the land of the noble was free or exempt land; the land of a villein or ordinary freeman was burdened   When a woman of the nobility married a villein her property was converted into tributary property, although on the death of the husband it became again exempt provided the wife repudiated the villein status acquired by her marriage. By analogous reasons every acquisition of lands that a " solariego " might make followed his own status, and was attributed to the noble estate to which he was attached, — unless it should be a royal demesne, in which the rights of the king as regarded taxation were safeguarded. So the law still stood in the " Ordenamiento of Alcalá." It was precisely this great influence of the social condition of the proprietor upon the legal classification of his property to which were due the frequent prohibitions in general and local law of sales to lords and churches   The right of alienation was also limited by other shackles, that reflected the traditions of the clan or quasi-socialistic conceptions of the State, such as the sumptuary regulation of the dowry festivals, and

Flanders See *Altamira*, "Civilización española," vol II, pp 208–219, 487–492, 494–498.
    [1] Reference should here be made to the question of the origin of the "foros" and the historical relation of this contract (the opinion opposed to which as early as the 1400s was already of formidable strength) with other and earlier forms of divided dominium   See as to this the book of *Villaamil* just cited, and that of *R Jove y Bravo*, "Los Foros, Estudio histórico y doctrinal" (Madrid, 1883)   [For the understanding of the text it should be added that the "solariego" was originally one belonging to the ancestral noble estate ("solar "), a villein ; and as the "villanos" or inhabitants of the vill or manor ("villa"), from being serfs came to be the commonalty, so in time a " solariego," as land, came to be a holding in fee simple ; and every building lot became a "solar " The text indicates that the "forero" was once unfree   The "forero" was later the lessee in the contract of "foro." — TRANSL]

apparel, the fixing of market prices and wages, the relatives' preferential right of purchase, etc At the same time, the privileges conceded to the grazing interests, every day greater, limited the rights of owners of the soil Finally, the frequent evidences of arable lands periodically allotted in the cities, and constituting a goodly part of the landed property of the community, indicate the persistence of communal customs, despite the individualistic tendencies of the Roman influence In reference to contracts relating to property, there is noticeable in the "Partidas" the importance which annuities or rent-charges, reserved in perpetual or long leases and in sales ("censo enfiteútico" and "reservativo"), were steadily acquiring; the latter were much used by nobles, churches, and monasteries in substitution of the earlier servile exploitation, and as a secure and convenient source of income.

The growth of industries and commerce gave rise to the creation and greatest development ever reached of collective juristic persons called "cofradías" and "gremios" ("confraternities" and gilds) ; these are important in civil law, not alone for their bearing upon questions of jural capacity or personality, but also with reference to contracts of sale and for services. These corporations of merchants and artisans were generally composed of individuals devoted to the same trade or profession They grew greatly in number from the 1200s onward; but it is evident from the character of their members that there must always have been included in their purposes technical or professional ends, along with that of resistance to external dangers, and it is not always easy to determine surely from such documents as we to-day possess whether the economic end predominates or any other of the social purposes that can be attained through corporate organization. Strictly speaking, the word "gremio," which broadly signifies a professional group, should not be used except with reference to corporations of exclusively or predominately professional character. But as it is not so used, the gilds are confounded with the more general type of "cofraderías" (or "cofradías") and "hermandades" (or brotherhoods, — any body of individuals formed for the better realization of one or more political or social ends, under a religious patronage), and with simple bodies of artisans ("oficiales") In these forms we find the journeymen ("menestrales") grouped from the 1100s onward, and especially and already with perfect clearness (e g. in the "fueros" of Santiago), in the 1200s. Alfonso X, in an ordinance of 1258, alludes to the lawful ends for which the "cofradías" might legitimately be formed, such as providing food for the poor, carrying luminaries, burying the poor, and giving funeral dinners, and prohibits their formation for ends political, immoral, or illegal a prohibition repeated at various times by later kings, and particularly as regards " defensive " or political "cofradías," leagues, and "hermandades." Those attained, however, the greatest development and importance which did not transgress the proper field of trades and industries, much favored by the monarchs of this period , a period marked, if by anything in this field, by an excess of legislation relating to industrial life.

The general ordinances of journeymen and artisans, as well as the special ordinances of each gild, regulated the internal organization of these organizations: the contracts of apprenticeship and of artisanship, liberty of labor; daily tasks, the sale of products, their appraisal, and market qualities; the wage of common laborers, especially agricultural, government pawnshops; and dominical rest (for religious but not for hygienic or other reasons).[1] With reference to the regulation of daily tasks, wages and prices, this legistion had ancient precedents, for many " fueros " since the 1000s declare the right of municipal councils or assemblies to regulate these matters.[2]

Finally, reference should be made to the rights of women in civil life, a matter of singular importance and of very curious manifestations. [3] Those that concern her economic status during marriage and widowhood having already been referred to, we may sum up the general status of the feminine sex by copying the following weighty paragraphs of Hinojosa:

" Until the beginnings of the 1200s (in which century took place the reception of the Roman law) the Germanic law relative to the personal and property relations of married persons predominated in all the kingdoms of Christian Spain. From that century onward, although in degrees very diverse in different States, they begin to be transformed under the influence of the Justinian law, elaborated and modified by the Glossators and post-Glossators: radically in Catalonia, less so but still considerably in León and Castile, and in even less degree in Aragon. Its influence is scarcely

[1] For a book covering the whole matter see Uña, "Las asociaciones obreras en España" (Madrid, 1900) , also Altamira, "Civilización espanola," vol I, pp. 499–500, and vol II, pp 103–105, 492–493, and on "La vida del obrero en España a partir del siglo VIII " in the "Trabajos de Investigación" of the University of Oviedo, 1903–1905 and 1905–1907.
[2] Altamira, "Civilización española," vol. I, §§ 302–303
[3] The only study of the matter is that of Hinojosa, "Discursos leidos "

perceptible in Portugal, Navarre, and the Basque provinces In León and Castile, in contrast with what we observe in the Visigothic period, we find the tutelage of women established, not alone as regards the married woman, but also the spinster, and even widow, in times subsequent to the Arabic invasion.

"If we reflect upon the dangers that constantly threatened women (of which the exceedingly frequent mention of rape in the municipal 'fueros' enables us to form some idea), it will be understood that such tutelage of women was a necessity of the age. The strict subjection of women to domestic authority in the first centuries of the Middle Ages is explainable, in part, by the rude and semi-barbarous manners of the times, and by the absence of a strong and vigorous public power capable of protecting the person and property of the subject Under such circumstances woman could not exercise her rights effectively; she needed the representation and protection of the family head Her personality was absorbed in that of her father, or, in his absence, in that of her nearest male relative, if she were unmarried or a widow; in that of her husband if she were married, and this condition, far from being for her a disadvantage, was a positive good."

This situation was gradually modified in proportion as the medieval period advances until at the end of the period we are examining the change has become of extreme importance

"Various causes " — continues the writer just cited — " were influential in bettering the personal and property rights of women in the Roman-Germanic States and in the modern nations that sprang from them: on one hand, the slow but constant action of Christian ideas; on the other, the modifications suffered by the authority of the family head and by the firm coherence between its members when the State, with full consciousness of its mission, reclaimed for itself the protection and guardianship of the weak, and lastly, the reception of the Roman law, with its principles favorable to the economic independence of women The perpetual tutelage of women disappears completely, or persists only for legal purposes, or was converted into a mere assistance, and ceased completely with respect to widows, from the moment that tutelage came to be based on age, and consequent lack of intellectual development and worldly experience, and not upon inherent incapacity of sex. The movement favorable to the abolition of the tutelage of women went through the same stages in almost all the cultured nations of Europe, as well Latin as Germanic. Its limitation had so far progressed as to have disappeared by the end of the Middle Ages as regarded unmarried women (not minors) and widows, — not, however, without persisting in some parts of Germany and Switzerland; while the authority of the husband over the wife, though reduced to more reasonable limits, still prevails in the majority of the countries of Europe and America Economic transformations, of a character analogous to those which to-day demand transcendent reforms in the civil conditions of the married woman, and like these common to all the civilized nations of Europe, produced in the Middle Ages modifications in this field so important as the recognition, within certain limits, of the civil capacity of women engaged in trade, certain changes favorable to creditors in the administration of conjugal property (which made their appearance in the towns, and were developed in proportion to the progress of industry and commerce), and the admissibility, and frequent practice, of renunciations by the wife of the special privileges granted her by the Roman law, — which were mainly limitations upon her capacity to assume legal obligations (such as the 'Senatus-consultum Vellejanum,' the Authentic 'Si qua mulier,' and the 'Epistola Divi Hadriani')."

Topic 2. Spread of the Justinian and Canon Laws in the Other Kingdoms of the Peninsula

§ 25. History of Legal Sources. — We will now indicate, as has been done in the case of Castile, and before passing to a study of the penetration of the Roman influence in the other portions of the Peninsula, a succinct summary of the history of their legal sources

Aragon. — Upon the basis of the compilation of Huesca (*ante,* § 15), the statutes of general character were collected as additions to that work of Vidal de Canellas. Thus in 1283 the "Privilegio General," of political character, was added; later, in 1300, all the reforms of public and private law made by James II were united in a book that was added as the ninth to the eight earlier ones, and Peter IV (1348) made a tenth out of new texts Finally, in the time of John I and Martin, two more books were added, the eleventh and twelfth. Thus was completed the code or compilation of the "Fueros Generales Aragoneses" , among whose statutes those relating to the political order, the administration of justice, and rights which since the 1800s have been called "individual" predominate. Alongside this code there continued the local legislation of the municipal "fueros" and local customs, relating especially to civil law. Various new "fueros" were granted in this period, as, for example, those of Albarracín (1370), Aran (1313), and Campóodon (1321); and the special "fuero" of the Twenty (a political tribunal) of Saragossa was confirmed (1283).

It is also necessary to note the ordinances of municipalities and communes, and private documents, in which local customs are reflected, in order to form an exact idea of the legal conditions of the country. Custumals, especially, began to be formed in the 1300 s (reign of James II), under the title of "Observancias." The first of such compilers, whose work has been lost, was the justiciar Perez de Salanova. In response to the initiative of Alfonso V, who proposed in the Cortes of Teruel of 1427–1428 the compilation of the customs and practices of the realm, a new collection enlarged by certain "acts of Cortes" was made by Martin Diaz de Aux, who took as a basis for his labors the above-mentioned work and the writings of jurisconsults. These "Observancias," with others known as "New," came later to be united to the twelve books of the "Fueros Generales." And lastly, the resolutions or "fueros" of the Cortes, which were not included in the twelve books and which constitute nine volumes (1413–1467), must be enumerated among the important elements of the Aragonese legislation The subsequent acts of the Cortes were only later included in the general collection

Catalonia. — The same variety of legislation as in the preceding period continues, but with the particularity that the concessions of new municipal "fueros" are now lessening in number, and the constitutions, capitulations, acts of Cortes, pragmatics, and other expressions of the legislative powers of the crown are increasing, — although indeed subject to the condition (at least in theory) that they should not contradict the general statutes of the kingdom, as was repeatedly declared in Cortes of 1289, 1292, 1311, and 1413. In this last year it was resolved to form a compilation of the whole Catalan law, a commission of three jurists (Narciso de San Dionisio, Jaime Callis, and Bonnonatus de San Pedro) being named for that purpose. The commission, taking as their model the "Codex Repetitæ Prælectionis," distributed the material into certain books and titles, translating the "Usatici" and other laws from Latin into Catalan. This collection was printed in the reign of Ferdinand the Catholic. It is to be noted that in the time of King Martin, and by virtue of the annexation to the Aragonese crown of the county of Ampurias, the authority of the "Usatici" and of the Constitutions had been extended over that territory.

Of the 1200 s and 1300 s we possess other compilations made by private individuals or for the use of corporations, such as one of constitutions and customs presented in the cathedral of Lérida. In 1279, in the first years of the reign of Peter III, the customs of

Tortosa were definitely edited and codified in the form in which they have come down to us   This custumal, a sort of settlement between the lord of the city and the inhabitants, is one of the most complete municipal codes of the Middle Ages. Of the following centuries the Constitutions of the "baylia"[1] of Mirabel are interesting in the history of private law   The feudal customs of Gerona were compiled in a custumal of the middle of the 1400s. The "Ordinaciónes de la Casa Real" were promulgated in the time of Peter IV for the government of the court.

Valencia. — In the reign of Alfonso IV the legislation of Valencia suffered a most important modification through the concession made to the nobles that Aragonese legislation (which was called "Alfonsine") should rule in their seigniories, the validity of the "fueros" (there called "furs") being thus limited to the territories of the crown.   The feudal law of Aragon was authority in the territories of Jérica, the baronies of Arenoso, Alzamora, Benaguacil, and Manisa, and in the lieutenancy of Alcalatén, allusions to some twenty-eight municipalities subject solely to these laws appearing in documents much later than this period. The "fueros" of Valencia were of authority in the rest of the land, which was its greater portion; and were continually augmented and modified by the charters granted by different kings (all of which referred to the political and administrative order), and by the resolutions of the Cortes.   It is also to be borne in mind that in the kingdom of Valencia there were cities united to Barcelona by the bond of "carreratge" or patronage, which enjoyed the immunities that went with that relation.   A collection was made of the "fueros" in 1482, comprising those granted from the reign of James I to that of Alfonso V.   Of the charters another collection was made in 1515 with the title "Aureum Opus Regalium Privilegiorum Civitatis et Regni Valentiæ."

Navarre. — The "Fuero General" neither accomplished nor pretended to accomplish legal unification   It was recast with improvements and additions in 1309 by Luis Hutin, in 1330 by Philip III, and in 1418 by Charles III; and Queen Catherine de Foix seems to have contemplated another revision in 1511, shortly before the annexation to Castile.   Although the "Fuero" covered almost all branches of the law, its authority was never more than supplementary to the municipal "fueros" and liberties granted by the crown   It is in these, in the royal ordinances, and in the resolu-

---

[1] [The smallest royal administrative district in Catalonia, — *cf Marichalar and Manrique,* "Historia," vol. VII, p 160. — Transl.]

tions of Cortes that one must seek the elements in the formation of
a common law, which went on steadily limiting the exceptions of
the feudal and regional law   The franchises granted by King
Theobald I were gathered together in a private collection known
by the name of the "Cartulario Magno."   But at the same time
municipal "fueros" continued to be granted or confirmed, as in
Viana, Espronceda, San Juan de Pie de Puerto, Tudela (a confirmation, 1330), Torres, Corcella, Santestéban de Lerin, etc

   Basque (Vascongadas) Provinces —In the first centuries of the
Reconquest, before the annexation to Castile, when *Alava* was constituted of an aggregation of confederated seigniories, which owed
obedience to a common overlord chosen by them in accordance
with the law governing free towns (" behetrías ") the statute law
seems to have consisted of the "Fuero Juzgo" and custumals.

   In proportion as the organization of free municipalities proceeded, under the influence of Castile and Navarre, whose kings
extended to Alavese territories the foral legislation of those States,
the sources mentioned were supplemented by "fueros," — either
original, such as those of Vitoria (1181) and Laguardia (1168), or
mere adoptions of existing ones, — as, for example that of Logroño,
which was granted to many districts.   It is said of Alfonso X that
he gave to Vitoria the "Fuero Real," and of Ferdinand IV that
he granted the "fuero" of Soportilla, applicable particularly to
nobles and seigniorial relations   The compact celebrated with
Alfonso XI ("Privilegio de Contrato") in 1322 provided that
the "Fuero Real" should have authority in private law as a common law of the towns, and at the same time confirmed that of
Soportilla as the special law of the "hidalgos."   The legislation
subsequent to this time was constituted of books of ordinances
issued by the crown (1417, 1458, 1463), of which that of 1417 has
reference to the regulation of the general councils of the provinces.

   Through the confused history of *Biscay* (Vizcaya) in the earliest
centuries one discovers the existence of a feudal nobility who were
the founders of the towns, and of a free popular class dwelling in
the settlements of the plain.   The towns were governed under
seigniorial privileges, which, in proportion with the progress of the
liberation of the original servile classes, were alleviated in their
application to these by the concession of such liberties as "fueros"
like that of Logroño, and by compacts or charters by which rights
were increasingly conceded to the villeins and serfs.   The free
settlements, the nucleus of the middle class, were governed by
custom, and perhaps also under some few "fueros" and privileges

granted by the kings of Navarre and Castile and by the overlords of Biscay. The difference of law between the two parts of the country is confirmed by the diversities of civil law noticeable even nowadays between the cities (of seigniorial origin) and the rural districts. After the consolidation, by inheritance, of the lordship of the province with the Castilian crown (1370), the kings granted some few ordinances of a political and administrative nature, among which are notable those of the licentiate Chinchilla, granted at Bilbao in 1484, for the purpose of repressing and punishing the civil strife between the factions of the country. The customs were first put into written form in 1542, and were confirmed by the Castilian crown

Guipuzcoa's political status was that of a free town until 1200; its lords were sometimes the kings of Navarre and at other times those of Castile, the latter were represented by Counts, the existence of whom in the 1000s and 1100s is established. After the definitive union with the Castilian crown (1200), the territory became a province or administrative-judicial district (" merindad ") of Castile, directly dependent on the crown; except the territory of Oñate with its dependent districts, whose jurisdictional autonomy long prevented its treatment as part of the province. Legislation consisted of the franchises of the lords; the municipal "fueros," whose extension went on little by little, — those of Vitoria and of San Sebastián acquiring the character of model "fueros," which were adopted over a large part of the country; general ordinances issued by the kings; and special ordinances of the hermandades. Deserving of mention among the general ordinances, which were the basis of the " special laws " or " fueros " of Guipuzcoa are those of 1375 and 1377, whose text has been lost; those of the " hermandad " of 1379 prepared by the Junta of Guetaria; those of the " hermandad-general " of the entire province, of 1451 — revised in 1463 and 1472, and the book of statutes granted by Henry IV in 1457, and comprehensive of dispositions relative to the administration of justice and the convocation of the councils (" juntas ").

§ 26. **Roman Elements in the Law of Catalonia.** — We may now proceed to note the chief phenomenon in the legal history of the period: the penetration of the Roman influence into all the regions referred to in this chapter   This penetration was realized in varying extent and result in all of them. The region in which Romanization extended farthest was Catalonia, and this is also the one where the process modificative of civil institutions that resulted

from the double influence of the Roman and the Canon law is best
known to us, — a process which has as yet been but very inadequately investigated as regards Aragon and Navarre [1]

In *Catalonia,* the penetration of the Roman law was primarily
the work of jurists educated in Bologna and in the universities of
Toulouse and Montpellier.[2]   Already in the 1100s there are legislative evidences of the Romanistic influence.   For example a constitution of Alfonso I (1192) which speaks of " Roman laws ";
and a somewhat later pragmatic of the same king (1210) adopts
a certain provision of the Justinian code in the law of emphyteusis.
These are in addition to the curious statement made by a contemporary jurist, Miguel Ferrer, that the Catalan Jews " constantly
use the Roman law as their peculiar law."   The frequent application of the Roman system as a supplementary law at the end
1100s is, in a general way, established.   In the reign of James I
(1213–1276) the Roman influence was so great that the social elements whose privileges and traditional law were threatened by the
innovation, secured in the Cortes of 1243 a prohibition against
the citation of the Roman laws in so far as the customs and the
" Usatges " might suffice   A little later, in 1251, the nobles, carrying still further the reaction against Romanism, secured from the
king its unqualified prohibition, which was extended to the Canon
law   But these measures proved futile.   The Justinian system
and the Canon law continued their progress in custom, in the decisions of the courts, in legal theory, and in legislation, everywhere
imposing themselves.   Evidences of the profundity of this influence
are found in legislative documents of such importance in the 1200s
as the Customary of Lérida, which recognized the Roman as a
supplementary law,[3] and in that of Tortosa (1279). The latter's
plan, as already stated, is copied from the Justinian code, and often
even the rubrics of its titles; whose provisions are also frequently
taken from that source, now directly, now with modifications;
moreover, it accepts the Justinian as a supplementary law [4]

The diffusion of the Roman influence in Catalonia, was not effected, as in Castile, through the increasingly wide enforcement of

---

[1] See *Altamira,* "Lacunes," and especially *Hinojosa,* "La réception du
droit romain en Catalogne" (Mélanges Fitting, vol II).
[2] On the diffusion of Justinian texts, in the original and in translation,
from the 1100s onward, see *Balari,* "Orígenes históricos de Cataluña"
(Barcelona, 1899), pp 470–472 , and *Suchier,* "Die Handschriften der
kastilianischen Ubersetzung des Codi" (Halle, 1900)
[3] *Brocá and Amell,* cited in § 15, n 3 above.
[4] *B Oliver,* "Historia del derecho en Cataluña, Mallorca y Valencia,"
(Madrid, 1876), vol I, ch 9, 13, 14

a largely Romanized general code, — for none such was there produced, but, primarily, through the acceptance and diffusion of the principle that a "natural reason and equity" constitute the suppletory source of national laws and customs. To the jurists imbued with the doctrines of the Digest, Code, and Institutes, a "natural reason and equity" were synonymous with the Roman law. In other words, there was an inevitable bias in favor of that law. In consequence of this mode of diffusion, in localities where the opposition to the change was not over great, the Roman law openly assumed the position of a legal source, the statutes of Justinian being expressly cited. On the other hand, where it met with strong resistance, the jurists adopted the tactics of "vulgarizing the principles of the Digest and of the Code and giving them a national character or color, by translating into the idiom of the country, with slight modifications, the imperial texts"[1] This is what was done in Tortosa, where at times, instead of taking inspiration from the Justinian system, "the Roman law abolished by Justinian was reëstablished."[2]   The penetration of this latter is also noticed in the liberties granted to Barcelona by Peter II in 1283, known by the name of "Recognoverunt Próceres."[3]

To these data of the 1200s others can be added which were the manifestations of the same process in the 1300s and 1400s. It is seen in Barcelona and other parts of Catalonia in legislation on the following points; in the compulsory share of an heir, — respecting which a constitution of Alfonso III (1311) had already extended the application of Roman principles to localities where a custom in accord with the Gothic law had been previously applied,[4] in testaments, in a privilege granted to Barcelona by Peter III;[5] in tutelage, an institution whose regulation evidently tended to follow the Roman law, inasmuch as a constitution of 1350 forbids this, in assignments by insolvent debtors (statute of 1363), in succession (Cortes of Monzón, 1363), in the modification of the Visigothic dowry of a tithe ("Fuero Juzgo"), which we find

[1] Oliver, op. cit

[2] Oliver, op. cit., gives numerous cases of this retrogression, which he is inclined to derive from the "Lex Romana Visigothorum" The importance for the history of the Catalan civil law of this lead in a direction divergent from the Justinian system is evident. Oliver indicates without exhausting it, and it still remains unstudied in other fields of Catalan law.

[3] Brocá and Amell, op. cit

[4] On this extension of the Roman law and its effects, see the article of G M de Brocá, "Sucesión ab intestado de los ascendientes" in the "Revista Jurídica de Cataluña," November, 1896

[5] On the extension of this privilege, see the articles of Joaquin Almela on "La constitución de Don Pedro III de 1399," published in the "Revista Jurídica de Cataluña," vol I (1895), nos. 2 and 5.

subsisting until the 1200s, but which already in the 1100s appears
united with voluntary betrothal gifts ("esponsalicias") of variable
amount, — generally half the value of the paraphernalia; as regards the dowry brought by the wife, which assumes all the features
peculiar to this institution in the Roman law; in the acceptance
of the "Senatus consultum Vellejanum" (as to a wife's contracts)
and the Novel "Si qua muher," conformably to the interpretations
of the Glossators; and in the adoption of the widow's fourth
("cuarta marital," — § 20 above).[1]

This wide pervasion of the Roman system along with that of the
Canon law — which exerted influence in questions of marriage,[2]
the status of children, one form of testament, etc. — was finally
recognized and regularized by a resolution of the Cortes of Barcelona of 1409. This established a hierarchy of sources in the positive law (as the "Ordenamiento of Alcalá" had done in Castile),
admitting the common law ("dret comú"), that is to say, the
Roman and the canonic systems,[3] as a law supplementary to
"usatges," constitutions, capitularies and acts of Cortes, uses,
customs, franchises, immunities, and liberties; but with precedence over equity and natural reason.

Aside from these evidences of the victory of Romanism, —
which nevertheless did not annihilate either the Germanic element or that born of the confluence of the varied factors and
novel circumstances of the time, which may properly be called indigenous, — and aside, also, from others which the character of the
present essay forbids us to detail,[4] we may indicate certain peculiarities of the Catalan civil law that appear, or gain body and development, in the period now under discussion. These include.

[1] On these institutions of family law, beginning with the Visigothic
dowry, see *Hinojosa*, "Discursos leidos," pp 29-37, and on the relation
between dowry and "exovar" or "axovar," the "Datos históricos," published by *Juan de Porciolos* in the Barcelona periodical "La Notaria,"
March, 1901. Many data could be gathered from the decisions of the
courts in these centuries

[2] Nevertheless there persist in the written customs of some localities
principles such as the licit character of the relations of a married man with
an unmarried woman

[3] The "dret comú" on its Roman side, included not only the statutes
but also the "opinions of the doctors," i e to say the doctrines of the
Glossators Of the penetration of these we have already given an example ,
and they were also of influence in Catalonia
  In 1429 a jurisconsult, *Mieres*, compiled the "Usantiæ et consuetudines
civitatis et diócesis Gerundæ," which show an abundant element of
Justinian and pre-Justinian law, — e g in the doctrine of compulsory
shares of heirs. Cf. *J B Torroella*, "Lo dret civil gironí" (Mataró,
1899)

[4] See e g. the studies of *G. Platon*, "La scriptura de terç en droit catalán"
(Paris, 1903), and "Le droit de famille en droit andorrain" (Paris, 1903).

the modification of the amount of the heirs' compulsory share (which according to the customary law constituted eight-fifteenths of the inheritance, and which Peter IV, on the petition of the burgesses of Barcelona, reduced to a fourth part of the corpus, thus favoring the testamentary liberty of the father and the nomination of an heir); the emancipation of sons through marriage, established by a charter of 1351, the widow's rights of dower, of ancient origin, which from the middle of the 1300s lose their obligatory character, "persisting contractually until our days in the designation by the husband of the wife as 'senyora mayora y usufructuaria,'" the family council, provided for cases of gifts, transfers, or renunciations of the property of minors by an "usatge" of Peter III (1351); etc.

In the domain of personal rights, an important innovation was marked by the abolition of "evil practices" that afflicted the peasants "de remensa" (the lowest class of villeins), and affected certain civil rights such as marriage, and the relief of those ancient serfs through the well-known arbitral award of Guadalupe.[1]

The confraternities and gilds developed powerfully in Catalonia owing to the impulse of its great industrial and commercial activity. Their organization and law followed the same lines as in Castile, and their effects upon trade were similar.[2]

§ 27   **Roman Elements in the Law of Aragon, Navarre, Valencia, the Balearic Islands, and the Basque Provinces.** — In *Aragon*, Romanism neither spread so widely as in Catalonia nor had such profound effects upon civil institutions.[3] The Roman law was already cultivated intensively among jurists in the 1200s, and the chronicle of James I testifies to the frequency with which the Roman lawyers figured at the royal court   Against this tendency the Cortes protested (Alcañiz, 1250 and 1251), as in Catalonia, opposing the citation of the Roman and Canon laws in the tribunals of the kingdom.

Among the principal novelties of the period was the establishment of complete liberty of testament, first for the nobles (1307) — who brought it about in the necessity of "conserving their ancestral

---

[1] Fundamental for this is the book of *Hinojosa*, "Régimen señorial," cited in § 18, n. 4
[2] For this the fundamental book is *Capmany's* "Memorias históricas sobre la marina, el comercio y las artes de la antigua ciudad de Barcelona" (Madrid, 1779), and that of Uña cited in § 24, note 3
[3] A well-known expression of protest against the Roman influence is the saying "De consuetudine regni non habemus patriam potestatem" (i e they had not a "patria potestas" of the Roman type, but of the indigenous tutelary type, yes).

estates in good condition," a reason analogous to that which served to give origin to the estates tail of Castile, — and then (1311) for all citizens and inhabitants of the towns, under the single condition that there be left to legitimate sons, if there were such, a compulsory share equal to five "sueldos" of movable and another five of immovable property,[1] — excess gifts ("mejoras") being, with the authorization of the wife, also permissible. By this means, and as a result of Roman theory, there was introduced and given a growing dominance to succession by a single son to the exclusion of the rest, and also the entailed estate. Further we find the creation of a "father of orphans," a sort of guardianship conjectured to date from this period, although it does not appear in legislation until the 1300s By the side of these institutions figure other local ones that trace their origin from earlier times, though suffering indeed some alterations through the Romanist influence: the "axovar" or dowry of the wife; that derived from the husband ("firma de dote "); the community of property between spouses; the "avantajas forales" (foral privileges)[1], the conception of the marital union; the widow's rights of dower; and, very particularly, — at once for its importance and its persistence down to our day, — the type of tillage groups, in which all the sons (as well as persons not related by the tie of blood) live together under the control of the father, or of a family council, or of some member of the family (generally the eldest son), with indivision of the associate property[2] The family council appears to be regulated by a general "fuero" of 1348, also by another in the Huesca collection, and by the first "Observancia de jure dotium." In the law of property there continue the recognition of the right of profits "a prendre" ("adprision") in woods and waste and abandoned lands, and the forms of communal ownership and enjoyment which have persisted down to the present time.[3] The institution of confraternities and gilds was analogous to that already described for Castile and Catalonia, and had likewise a great development.[4]

---

[1] [An exact value cannot be given to the "sueldo" (now "soldo"), but even for that day it was a very slight sum Cf. *Marichalar and Manrique,* "Historia de la legislación de España," vol. II (Madrid, 1861), p 520. — "Pueden los cónyuges antes de proceder á la división de gananciales, reclamar cada uno las aventajas forales," — namely domestic animals, clothing, and other personal effects suited to their respective needs. *Sanchez Roman,* "Estudios de Derecho Civil," vol. I, (2d ed , Madrid, 1899), p 453. — Transl]

[2] *J Costa,* "Alto Aragón Derecho de Familia," in vol I of his "Derecho consuetudinario"

[3] *J Costa,* " Colectivismo agrario en España."

[4] *Uña* as cited in § 24, n 3, and the sources cited by him upon this point

As for the servile classes of society, there is no betterment of their civil rights in Aragon in this period, but rather a retrogression in the direction of tightening and aggravating the civil and economic dependence of the servile cultivators of the soil, over them the courts had no jurisdiction, being consequently unable to protect them [1]

In *Navarre*, very little is known of the spread of Roman law, as indeed generally of the legal history of that region   For this reason it is still impossible to fix the date of origin of most of its institutions, or to define the precise changes that they suffered through the Justinian and Canon law, save in so far as these exerted everywhere an equal influence which has been referred to in treating of Castile   Society, however, resisted longer in Navarre than in other parts of the Peninsula the pressure of the Church against illegitimate unions, such as the simple contractual juratory marriage, without the intervention of the priest, which sufficed for separation and divorce, as well among the nobles as among the working class. Concubinage was so frequent in the 1400s that even the clergy, especially in rural districts, lived in it, as the acts of the Cortes and the narratives of travellers of the time testify   King Charles III (1387–1425) denied the claims of their concubines to enjoy the ecclesiastical immunities of legitimate wives, and ordered that they should pay the taxes to which they were liable, though recognizing at the same time the lawfulness of such unions.   The law and the customs were in general very lenient with illegitimate relations, recognizing those of the noble woman with the villein, those of the widow, and those of the married man, who, though he could not make a contract of concubinage, could live in fact in concubinage. On the other hand, they were severe upon the adulterous wife.   It was permitted to determine the parentage of " natural " children,[2] using the ordeal of boiling water, but differences in rights were early introduced between the various classes of offspring, those of adulterous (singly or doubly), incestuous, and sacrilegious children being very limited.   In the time of John II (1400s) the Cortes

---

[1] *Muñoz y Romero*, "Discurso" cited above in § 9, n 2; *Hinojosa*, "Mezquinos y exaricos," and "La servidumbre de la gleba en Aragón," cited above, § 18, n. 4, *Altamira*, "Civilización española," vol II, pp. 106–108, 408

[2] [In Spanish law "natural" and "illegitimate" children have been regarded differently, and this is still true of the present Civil Code.   Natural children are those that are capable of legitimation — "Heredad" was apparently used, generally, for any cultivated holding; its technical sense, as a definite holding, has not been defined. — Transl]

forbade the custom by which the children of clergy took the inheritance of their fathers

The wife's property right upon widowhood was already recognized in the " fueros " of the 1000s and 1100s. In the " Fuero General " of the 1200 s we find it conceded also to the widower

In the period now in question there continued the dowry derived from the husband (" arras "). fixed at first for nobles (" infanzones ") at three " heredades ",[7] the ganancial community system of marital acquests, the principles governing which were almost identical with those in Castile , compulsory shares of heirs (without excess gifts) for the farming classes, — which were eluded by stipulating in matrimonial contracts the anticipatory nomination of one son as the sole heir with apportionment to the others of unequal shares of the estate, by which means the unity of the family was successfully maintained , the principle of kinship (" troncalidad "), which was evidenced in the reversion to the family of property acquired by junior sons living in the ancestral house, and in the relatives' right of preferential purchase (a condition in the practice of which was that the sales must be made publicly, with ringing of bells); the family council, agrarian communities among the servile classes, and other medieval institutions [1] We find evidence of the existence in this period, among the noble class, of an absolute testamentary liberty whence resulted estates tail; also of the institution of the " father of orphans ", irrigation communities, with ordinances of ancient date , and confraternities for military, religious, and charitable purpose   Of true gilds there are no concrete evidences until the 1500 s.

It was in this same century, in the Cortes of Pamplona, of 1576 (9th statute). that the Roman law received statutory recognition as a supplementary law

The legal history of *Valencia*, as a Christian State, began, as is well known, well on in the 1200 s, and consequently was subjected from the beginning to the influence of the Roman law.   Thus the Valencian foral code follows in the distribution of material that of Justinian, and reproduced in its text many laws of this Code and the Digest, though in others it departs from these to adopt the pre-Justinian Roman law.[2] Apart from the Roman influence, the

---

[1] On certain civil institutions see *W Webster*, cited *ante*, § 15, n 24 ; § 16, n 1

[2] *Oliver*, cited in § 26, above , *R Chabas*, "Génesis del derecho foral de Valencia" (Valencia, 1902); *Danvila*, "Estudios críticos acerca de los orígenes y vicisitudes de la legislación escrita del antiguo reino de Valencia" (Madrid, 1905) The last author merely compares the variations or agree-

law of Valencia shows many others that are Catalan and Aragonese, and possibly a few that are Moslem. It recognizes maternal authority; the systems of double dowry, the reciprocal rights of widowhood, with certain excess amounts in the case of widows who are poor, inheritance by illegitimate children, in default of legitimate descendants, ascendants, and collateral relatives; the "father of orphans ", unlimited community of property between spouses (" agermanament ") — which was of Catalan origin but received rich additions of local variants.[1] The marital community of acquests (ganancial system) is not recognized. The gilds acquired here an extraordinary development, the law relating to them being very similar to the Catalan.[2]

Of the *Balearic Islands* it is true, as of Valencia, that its law was formed of Roman and Catalan elements. We find evidences here of the existence of the Visigothic dowry, along with an " excreix " which by a law of Sancho IV of 1316 was limited to the fourth part of the dowry; an increase of the dowry customary among converted Jews in the 1400s, and which later passed from them to the Christians; the grant of a portion of the "excreix" to the wife, in property up to 1316, and in usufruct from that date onward; the Roman dowry, which was customarily delivered as a part of the marriage ceremony, and might by agreement be reckoned a part of the community property, but not of the acquests; and both the widow's fourth (*ante*, § 26) and the dower authorized by the testament of the husband [3] Of agricultural contracts, singular interest attaches to those of the " forenses," poor farm-hands who acquired the right to cultivate small parcels of land in consideration of obligations and rents complicated by other onerous pecuniary charges; these resulted, when unsatisfied, in liens and sales upon which their city creditors grew rich. Whence resulted the well-known social struggles of the 1400s and 1500s [4]

As for the civil law of the *Basque Provinces*, we have seen that it reflects a mingling of Castilian and Navarrese influences, modified by influences of the Roman and Canon law The only peculiarities are found in the administration of the rural districts of

ments of the Justinian law with the Valencian code in its various manuscripts, and with that of Tortosa.

[1] *Hinojosa*, "Discursos leidos," p. 36
[2] *Tramoyeres*, "Instituciónes gremiales su origen y organización en Valencia" (Valencia, 1889)
[3] "Legislacion foral de España.   Derecho civil vigente en Mallorca" (Madrid, 1888)   Also *Hinojosa*, "Discursos leidos "
[4] *Quadrado*, "Mallorca."

Biscay, whose customs were partially committed to writing along the middle of the 1400s [1]

§ 28. **Notable Jurists of the Period.** — To complete the picture of the legal history of the period, we will indicate briefly the principal jurists and the different tendencies they represented in the various parts of the Peninsula.

Until the 1200s there appears no Spanish jurist of reputation whose works are known to us. In the preceding centuries we come upon the names of a few professors and students in Italy, such as a Juan Español and a Pedro Hispano, but beyond that we know nothing of them. From the 1200s on the situation is quite different.

We do not know who were the authors of the " Partidas "; and in view of our ignorance it is not strange that critics should ascribe that work to the well-known jurisconsults of the time, some of whom are cited in its text. Such are the " magistri, " Jacobo de las Leyes (or Jácome Ruiz), Fernando Martinez, and Roldán. The first was an Italian by birth, naturalized in Spain, where there are traces of him down to 1270. He was tutor to Alfonso X, for whom he wrote a summary, the " Flores de las Leyes," a sort of encyclopædia or anthology in which he compiled various materials relative to civil law, judicial organization, and procedure, from the works of Italian jurists of the time, which he calls " books of the sages " Many of these materials were later incorporated in the " Partidas , " and the " Flores de las Leyes " itself was translated into Catalan and Portuguese. Of the same author are also the two treatises called " Tiempos de las Causas (or Pleitos) " and " Doctrinal de todos los Pleitos," which are both still unpublished. Martinez, a prebendary of Zamora, bishop-elect of Oviedo in 1269, and ambassador of the Italian king near the Pope, was a jurist of celebrity. There are attributed to him two works, both unpublished one entitled " Margarita de los Pleitos " (Pearl of Lawsuits) and the other, in Latin, " De Orden de los Juicios " (" Bullarium sui Ordinis "). Roldán, besides being reputed as a legist, edited the " Ordenamiento de las Tafurerias, " a regulation of gambling houses that were the property of the State and were rented by it to individuals. Mention is made also of a jurisconsult named Oldrado who is believed to have been a contemporary of Fernando IV, but of whom we know nothing, nor of any work

---

[1] *Vicario,* "Derecho consuetudinario de Vizcaya" (Madrid, 1891); *Chalbard,* "La troncalidad en el fuero de Vizcaya" (Bilbao, 1888); *La Plaza,* "El fuero de Vizcaya en lo civil" (Bilbao, 1894–1895), *W. Webster,* above cited

certainly his.   On the other hand, we do know those of Vicente
Airas de Balboa (or Valbuena), bishop of Plasencia, who died in
1414, and who is remembered as a canonist and as the author of
commentaries upon the "Ordenamiento of Alcalá," a gloss upon
the "Fuero Real," and a collection of opinions by contemporary
jurists relative to the succession to the crown of Aragon.

Certainly these were not the only legal writers of the time.
Considering the abundant legislative output that existed from
Alfonso X to Henry IV, and the preeminence enjoyed by lawyers
at the court, one is justified in averring that there must have been
many others   That this was so is evidenced by a fact characteristic
of the 1300s and 1400s, namely, the abundance of private legal
compilations whose materials were distributed in the form of
statutes; an arrangement that has caused modern critics to mistake
for genuine legislation what in fact was the product of some antiquarian's or lawyer's cabinet.   The collections from which, apparently, the "Fuero Viejo" was compiled, that code itself, and
perhaps also the "Leyes del Estilo," the "Leyes Nuevas," the
"Setenario," and the "Espéculo," are all examples of this curious
sort of literature, whose authors are to-day unknown to us   In
the library of the University of Madrid there are preserved various
other unpublished legal treatises of the 1400s.   The questions
chiefly treated in all of these works are those of judicial procedure.
In the libraries and in the loan records of the 1200s and 1300s
the legislative works of Justinian figure repeatedly.

The preceding sketch may be completed by a list of the Spaniards
who appear in foreign universities and at the Papal court as writers
upon and professors of the law.   In the 1200s the earliest one
known to us to-day is one Bernardo of (Santiago de) Compostela,
who was a member of the faculty of Bologna.   Another of like
name, called the younger, was auditor and chaplain of Pope
Innocent IV, and compiler of and commentator upon the third or
Roman collection of decretals.   Likewise of Santiago and contemporary of the latter was a Juan Hispano, a writer upon both
the Roman and the Canon law.   Pedro Hispano, a Dominican and
professor at Paris, was the author of a compendium of Aristotle's
"Logic" entitled "Summula," or briefer summa.   Juan García el
Hispano expounded the civil and Canon law at Bologna, and wrote
notable works.   Similar notoriety was gained as decretalists by
one Lorenzo and one Vicente whose works exist, but of whose life
very little is known   Finally, Cardinal Torquemada lectured at
Paris and wrote certain "Commentaries" upon Gratian's Decretal.

— At the Papal court many Spaniards won distinction as canonists: Juan de Mella, professor of Salamanca and bishop of Zamora, Cardinal Juan de Carvajal, one of the most eminent and talented statesmen that served the Papacy in the 1400 s, a writer, diplomat, and warrior; and the no less celebrated Cardinal Albornóz, a native of Cuenca, contemporary of Alfonso XI and Peter I, a personage of exceeding influence in the Church's policy, the reconqueror of many of the States of the Holy See, and promulgator of the important Italian code entitled " Constituciónes de la Marca de Ancona " In Spain, and especially at the court of Pedro Tenorio (contemporary of John II), archbishop of Toledo and potent politician, there figured a few other prelates as canonists, such as Gonzalo, Bishop of Segovia, and Doctor Juan Alonso of Madrid.

The above data refer to the territories of the Castilian crown. In the same centuries jurisconsults of importance shone with brilliant talent in those of Aragon. Of these the civilians and Romanists included García " el Español " (a Catalan), professor at Bologna in the late 1200 s; Juan Español (an Aragonese), professor of Canon and civil law, Jaime Hospital (Aragonese), collector of and commentator upon the " Observancias ", Jaime Callis (or Calicio), of Vich, commentator upon the " Usatges," and author of various works upon politics and finance Vallseca, Mieres, Socarrat, Marquillas, all (like Callis) expositors and critics of the Catalan law, Micer (Master) Bononat Père, counsellor to the Aragonese crown (1400 s); the celebrated Majorcan, Mateo Malferit, his compatriots Ferrando and Teseo Valenti, especially the latter, who was professor at Bologna, Jaime Pau, called the " gloria juris Cæsaris " because of his notes upon the imperial law; Juan Ramon Ferrer, the author of a legal dictionary, Jerónimo Pau; and others, lawyers or ordinary notaries or court notaries, who lived in the time of Alfonso V, as well in Spain as in Naples.   In the field of Canon law, Catalonia offered as a model the great decretalist Raimundo de Peñafort, a contemporary of James I, professor at Bologna, and compiler, by order of Pope Gregory IX, of a collection of decretals or pontifical constitutions — book V of the " Corpus Juris Canonici." His example and tradition was followed by other writers, among whom mention should be made of Guillermo de Montserrat, the author of a commentary upon the resolutions of the councils of Constance and Basel

The expositors of the science of political theology merit consideration apart.   First place among them is taken by the Catalan Franciscan, Francisco Eximenis (or Jimenez), bishop of Elna,

author of a book that bears the title, " Crestiá " or " Llibre de
regiment de Princeps e de la cosa publica " (1379), — or Book of
Regimen for Princes and the Commonwealth;[1] " not inferior,"
says one critic (Hinojosa) " in its doctrine to the best books of
analogous nature written in other countries, and superior to all
of these in its grandiose plan and copious and select erudition."
Of the same period was Friar Nicolas Eymerich, inquisitor-general
of Aragon, who sets forth the theories and practices of the tribunal
of the Inquisition in his work " Directorium Inquisitorium," which
was probably written in 1376, and was later enlarged by the author
himself

The flowerage of legal science was no less rich in Spain during
the reign of the Catholic Kings. Among civilists, Romanists, or
statesmen there shone then Doctor Montalvo, who, in addition
to the " Ordenanzas Reales " already cited, wrote a " Repertorio de
Derecho " — a sort of dictionary, with a supplement to which
he gave the title " Segunda Compilación," — edited with glosses
and commentary the " Fuero Real " and the " Partidas," and
founded a sort of law school; Juan Lopez de Vivexro, popularly
known as Palacios Rubios (1447–1523), professor at Salamanca
and counsellor to the Catholic Kings, joint editor of the " Leyes de
Toro," upon which he wrote a commentary, compiler of the liberties
of the " mesta " (an association of graziers), author of a treatise
upon gifts between husband and wife, of another and interesting
book in which, on the command of King Ferdinand, who felt scruples
for the conquest of Navarre, he attempted to demonstrate the
legal justification of the annexation of that kingdom, of another
upon the crown advowsons, and several political works; Galindez
de Carvajal (1472–1530?), likewise professor and royal counsellor,
whose compilation of statutes we have already mentioned; Antonio de Nebrija (1444–1522), reviser of the glosses of the Italian
Accursius, author of certain " Observaciones sobre las Pandectas,"
and of a " Lexicon Juris Civilis "; Martin de Azpilcueta, and
Gregorio Lopez, — the former a canonist, the latter a civilian, —
who belong more properly in the succeeding periods; Micer Miguel
del Molino, who wrote a " Repertorium Fororum et Observanti-
arum Regni Aragonum " (1513); and other writers of less importance. As a canonist, Doctor Juan Alfonso de Benavente,

---

[1] For details regarding this "Crestiá," see *Hinojosa*, "Influencia que
tuvieron en el derecho político de su patria y singularmente en el derecho
penal los filósofos y teólogos españoles anteriores á nuestro siglo" (Madrid,
1890), pp. 68 *et seq.*

professor of Salmanca, is cited with especial eulogy by Marineo Sículo; and Alfonso Soto, a native of Ciudad Rodrigo, distinguished himself in Rome, and was the author of a " Glosa " upon the rules of the papal chancery, and of a treatise upon the coming Church Council which he dedicated to Pope Sixtus IV.

Chapter III. Second Period: a.d 1511–1808

THE AGE OF ABSOLUTE MONARCHY

Topic 1. The Austrian Dynasty (1500s and 1600s)

§ 29. Imperfections of Existing His- | § 31. Progress in the Unification of
torical Guides to these Cen- | the Law
turies | § 32 Legal Science and Literature
§ 30. History of the Legal Sources. | in the Habsburg Period.

Topic 2. The Bourbon Dynasty (1700–1808)

§ 33 History of the Legal Sources. | § 34. Legal Science and Literature
| in the Bourbon Period.

§ 29. **Imperfection of Existing Historical Guides to these Centuries.** — By the beginning of the 1500s, Spanish law, in its various regional embodiments, was already substantially formed, equally as regards the essential factors in its general mass, and the character of the different institutions. Its history from that time to the opening years of the 1800s consists, when taken in the large, in an accentuation within the civil law of the Romanist influence This gains ground little by little, to-day supplanting one, to-morrow another, of the Germanic or medieval principles which, up to the end of the 1400s, it had succeeded in withstanding   This substitution is nothing like complete. Romanism advances, it is affirmed in statutes and in scientific theory, but it does not succeed in destroying national institutions that were deeply rooted, such as the husband's dowry in some of the non-Catholic provinces, the ganancial and the community systems, communal organization in the enjoyment of land, etc.[1]

The history of the three centuries mentioned is less complex and abundant in variety than that of those preceding, but it is not for that reason the better known.   The absence in it of great legal

[1] In these institutions there is indeed rather a recrudescence, due possibly to scientific theories that were favorable to them   Cf. *Costa*, "Colectivismo agrario," and *Altamira*, "Civilización española," III, 428–429

events, the occult and peculiar manner in which reforms proceeded, and the mere complement of statutes (mostly ancient) which distinguishes the character of many of the so-called codes that were published in this period in Castile [1] and other provinces, have served to weaken the interest of the historians of these three centuries, who for the most part have studied hardly any other changes than those that were produced in public law.

We may consider first and in a general way the development of the sources.

Topic 1. The Austrian Dynasty (1500s and 1600s)

§ 30. History of the Sources — The regimen of an absolute monarchy, the steadily increasing bureaucracy of the government, and the formalistic and regulative spirit of the lawyers of the age were reflected in the abundance of statutes, in their minute details and casuistic character, and in the increase of those issued directly upon the royal initiative, in consequence of the infrequency of the Cortes, — and especially in Castile, — even before their suppression in the minority of Charles II   The abundance of legislation, along with the pressure of scientific tendencies for its codification in the systematic form that had already been adopted in the "Partidas" and the "Ordenamiento of Alcalá," were the cause of repeated petitions in Castile for new collections, and in the other kingdoms for the continuation of those already realized in the preceding period, — demands which were steadily strengthened by reforms and innovations to which there was no interruption

We have seen that the Ordinances of Montalvo had not by any means removed the difficulty that they were designed to remove. Their deficiencies grew as time passed, and there continued to appear ordinances of the Cortes, pragmatics, "cédulas," royal orders, and resolutions of Council.   It is not to be wondered at, therefore, that at different times in the reign even of Charles I the procurators of the cities petitioned for a codification of statutes, which were scattered and very often contradictory.   In their meeting in 1544 at Valencia they reduced the idea to concrete form, soliciting the publication of the collection of Galindez de Carvajal,

---

[1] The portion of the civil law contained in book 10 of the "Nueva Recopilación" and book 10 of the "Novísima Recopilación," is taken almost wholly from the "Fuero Real," the "Ordenamiento of Alcalá," and the "Leyes de Toro."

this, they said, existed in the possession of the author's sons, — although this can hardly have been the case, since they were told in reply to present that book if they knew where it was to be found, and it does not appear that they did so. Charles I himself had already, before 1523, commanded Doctor Pedro Lopez de Alcocer to make a new collection, and on the death of Alcocer before its termination the commission was intrusted to Doctor Escudero, who failed likewise to conclude it.

The undertaking was prosecuted by Philip II, and was finally realized by the licentiate Bartolomé de Arrieta. A compilation in nine books of "ordenamientos" of Cortes and royal orders — which collection, with reference to that of Montalvo, was named the "Nueva Recopilación" — was published and promulgated, as arranged by him, in 1564   The pragmatic in which Philip II ordained it assigns as reasons for the preparation of the work, not only the number and variety of the existing statutes, but also " the corruption in the text of many statutes, either incorrectly copied or poorly printed, the doubts that many had excited, the unrighteousness of others which, though just enough in their day, had ceased to be so through the change of circumstances; and finally, the disorder with which they were separated and distributed in divers works and volumes, and some of them not even printed, nor incorporated in the others."

It would naturally be expected, in view of so just an understanding of the problem which the Castilian legislation presented, that the various jurists who labored on the " Nueva Recopilación " should have undertaken to reduce to a true doctrinal system the statutory law, defining clearly and concretely the law actually in force; with prime attention to the profound changes slowly brought about in the autonomy and local diversity of the "fueros" by means of the centralization of the monarchy and the establishment of the law of the " Partidas " as an effective factor in the legal practice of Castile. Not such, however, was the view of those jurists, if we may judge by the end which their work embodies. Theoretically, as the promulgatory pragmatic indicates, the elements which it was necessary to reduce to clarity and order were " the many and diverse statutes, pragmatics, ordinances, capitulations of Cortes, and letters in Council." The word " statutes" (" leyes ") might have been given a broad meaning, comprehensive of all that the others did not specify. But in fact they gave it a sense narrow in the extreme, limiting it doubtless to royal orders issued " motu proprio," that is, without petition of the Cortes. Thus the " Nueva Recopilación " turned out to be no more than an elaboration of Montalvo's in its identical elements, enlarged by examples posterior to 1484, it excluded all the other elements which the " Leyes de Toro " had already enumerated, although reduced in the pragmatic here in question (we do not know whether by intention) to the "Partidas" and the " Fuero Real," the only ones it mentions. Even as regards these it must have been necessary to determine clearly what was considered as actually incorporated in the legislative law Neither could the " Fuero Real " be so considered as a whole (since many of its provisions were already abrogated by later statutes, and the best solution would have been to suppress such); nor was it true, as later became evident, that the " Partidas " could be considered as merely a supplementary law, either as a whole or in certain parts, since they had, on the contrary, in *fact* been elevated to the category of primary law.

The result of the failure to clear up the relative status of all these elements, such as the " Fuero Juzgo " (though something of this passed into the " Recopilación ") and the municipal " fueros," was that the previous confusion continued, and the statutory law was one thing in appearance and another in reality.

What made the attempted work the greater abortion was that the " Nueva Recopilación " suffered (even within the limits to which it was reduced) from the defects identical with those of Montalvo's. It neither included all the royal orders and petitions of Cortes that had been granted and were properly to be considered of authority in 1567 (many of both classes, but especially petitions, being omitted), nor eliminated all those fallen into desuetude, nor corrected in all cases corrupted texts. Hence the slight reputation of the " Recopilación," which neither commanded the respect of the legal profession (being simply ignored in legal education), nor was observed in practice, as is evidenced by the representations of the Cortes of 1579, 1586, 1588, and 1602 relative to the observance of the new code. Nevertheless, four editions of it were issued after the original, in 1581, 1592, 1598 and 1640, each including the new statutes that were being continually issued.

In the practice of the courts, and particularly in civil law, more favor was enjoyed by the scientific Roman system. We see this from a resolution of the full Council, which, though issued indeed in 1713, was naturally caused by antecedent facts of the period we are now discussing·

According to this resolution, "Many causes are argued and decided in the courts of these realms, in reliance upon the doctrines of foreign books and authors, . . . and not only this alone, but when there exists a statute clear and determinant, if it be not among those newly collected, many persons are mistakenly persuaded, in ignorance or malicious disregard of what is prescribed (in the national laws), that it is not in force, and need not be respected; and likewise if there be found in the Recopilación some law or other, or pragmatic, that has been suspended or abrogated, then although there be no other explicit statute decisive of the case, and that which is annulled or suspended would elucidate and decide it, no force is given to it; and what is more intolerable, there is a belief that greater weight ought to be given in the royal courts to the civil (that is to say the Roman) and Canon laws than to the laws of these realms, and this though the civil laws are not laws in Spain, nor should be called such, but rather judgments of wise men which may be followed only in the lack of law."

The fact deducible from this is that the "Leyes de Partidas" and the pure Justinian law itself had passed, even to a greater extent than in earlier times, from the status of supplementary to that of predominant factors in the courts, and this augmented the confusion in the positive law.   Instead of recognizing the force of facts, it was zealously endeavored to maintain in legislation the show of an exact obedience to the first of the "Leyes de Toro" relative to the hierarchy of legal sources, a fiction which was thus continued during all the rest of this and in the following period.

At the same time that the effort was made to codify in the "Nueva Recopilación" a part of the general law of Castile (and up to a certain point, as we shall see, of all Spain), a strong impulse was given to the redaction of the municipal ordinances, of which many were published in the 1500 s and 1600 s.   These documents, expressive evidences of the lessened local autonomy that remained in the ancient councils, are interesting for the information they afford of that autonomy, particularly in the field of administration, and for the wealth of legal customs which were in them given fixed form, receiving the sanction of the central government.

The Aragonese, like the Castilians, petitioned repeatedly of their kings the revision and codification of the statutory law, which suffered from defects similar to those of the Castilian legislation. Finally, in 1547, an editorial commission was named, which was composed of representatives of the four "arms" of the Cortes, and completed its labors the same year. The work produced included the twelve books of the "Fueros Generales" and the pamphlet laws of the Cortes issued between 1412 and 1495, — the whole reduced to nine books, and the statutes distributed according to their subject matter, after the model of the Justinian Code, (which was then commonly used in its first nine books only) ; the "Observancias" of Martin Diaz de Aux, "fueros" that had fallen into desuetude, and the resolutions of the Cortes relative to civil law The promulgation of new statutes, some of them so important as those of Tarazona of 1592, necessitated other editions of the collection with variants from the original, the last (in this period) being of 1664–1667. In addition, a few pamphlet-laws of the Cortes were printed, the last one known of these being of 1686–1687.

Catalonia, after various attempts, secured in 1588–1589 (as a result of a resolution of the Cortes of Monzón of 1585) a new compilation, comprehending the "usatges" actually in force, constitutions, capitulations, acts of the Cortes, royal pragmatics, royal judgments, arbitrations, and resolutions, as well as of superfluous, contradictory, or altered statutes, — all of them distributed in books, according to the subject matter. The commission that accomplished the compilations was composed of the regent of the royal chancery, Miguel Cordelles, Doctor Martin Juan Franquesa, a member of the Audiencia, Francisco Puig, a member of the Civil Royal Council; Onofre Pau Celler, a canon of Barcelona; and the "Micer-magnificus" Miguel Pomet, doctor of civil and Canon law and citizen of Barcelona, who was elected by the commonalty. No other compilation was made until the 1700s The customs of Tortosa were printed for the first time in 1539

In *Valencia* various attempts were made to codify the legislative law, but none of them was carried through officially. Private initiative responded better to the aspirations of the time, producing in 1548 an edition of ancient and modern "fueros" down to 1542, arranged according to subject matter, and in 1580 certain "Instituciones de los Fueros y Privilegios del Reino de Valencia." The edition of 1548 was utilized as official, and to it were added in separate issues the "fueros" conceded by the Cortes from 1545 to 1643. ·

The Court of *Majorca* ordered the collection, about the middle of the 1600s, of the legislation of that ancient realm, and this was accomplished in 1663 by the "Ordinacions y Sumari dels Privilegis

Consuetud y Bons Usos del Regne de Mallorca," of the jurist Antonio Moll, — the only compilation known

In *Navarre*, the annexation to Castile disturbed the development of the national legislation, although it is true, as we have seen, that the Castilian kings continued to convoke the separate Cortes of that country with considerable frequency (seventy-three times), and to issue through them statutes and privileges. A reduced edition of the ancient "fuero" was made in 1525 and a complete imprint in 1628-1686; the first enjoying no statutory force, and the second little application in legal practice, notwithstanding that it had been voted in the Cortes   In 1557 a first collection was made of the ordinances and statutes of the Cortes and afterward as many as five others, of these one, made by the syndics Sada and Ollacarizqueta, included the dispositions promulgated up to 1604 and printed in 1614, and was declared the sole official collection; until in 1686 the last was published, the work of a lawyer, Antonio Chavier, this being thenceforward the one officially preferred.

The *Basque Provinces* followed the general tendency. The first result in *Biscay* was a compilation of the custom of the rural district, approved by Charles I in 1527 under the title "Fueros, Privilegios, Franquezas y Libertades, del muy Noble y muy Leal Señorio de Vizcaya." To this were afterwards added various complementary royal statutes, and in 1630 a resolution, as a result of this the traditional differences between the cities and the towns, which affected in certain particulars the autonomic regimen, disappeared   With these additions the collection of 1527 remained in force until the 1800s — *Guipuzcoa,* at the end of the 1600s and upon the basis of a "new book of the Community" (published in 1463 as a revision of its predecessors, and confirmed in 1821 by Charles I), collected all its law then in force in a "Nueva Recopilación de los Fueros, Privilegios, Buenos Usos y Costumbres, Leyes y Ordenes" (1696). — *Alava* formed no such compilation of its statutes, although those collected in the book of 1463 were greatly added to by others, issued by the Castilian crown either "motu proprio" or at the instance of the Junta.

As for the *colonial dominions*, the irregularity and abundance of their legislation necessitated some arrangement of it in codified form. As early as 1543 a "book" was published at Alcalá which contained the statutes and ordinances recently issued by Charles I. In 1563 the Viceroy of New Spain, Luis de Velasco, began a compilation by collecting and printing all the documents that ex-

isted in the audience of that province Shortly afterward the
president of the Council of the Indies, Juan de Ovando, formed a
" Recopilación " in seven books, of which there was published of
the second book a single title, treating of the Council (1571).   A
" Nueva Recopilación," modelled upon this and printed in 1593,
failed to realize the end in view, and after new studies and the
nomination of editorial juntas, there was promulgated in 1680 a
" Recopilación de las leyes de Indias," in nine books, arranged according to subject-matter, which contained all the dispositions
then in force.

§ 31 **Progress in the Unification of the Law.** — What was the
effect of all these collections and codes upon the unification of the
law within the territories of the Spanish monarchy?   If we disregard the " Leyes de Indias " (in view of their special character —
despite the general principle of assimilation to the Peninsular law)
and confine ourselves to the Peninsula, we have already examined
the question in one of its aspects, namely, the political.   On the
part of the State, there could be no interest taken outside of this
field, to the unification of the private law, because unconnected
with the sovereign status and effective absolutism of the crown,
the kings gave no heed   We must remember too, how slight was
the progress of political centralization, notwithstanding the in-
sistance of Olivares, the force of his arguments (given the standpoint which he occupied), and the alluring opportunities offered
by the rebellions of Valencia and Majorca in the times of Charles
I, of Aragon in the time of Philip II, and of Catalonia under Philip
IV.   Nevertheless, if one carefully examines the royal legislation
of the 1500s and 1600s (partly recorded in the " Nueva Recopilación "), one notes the substantial, albeit silent, progress of unification.   It extended to many governmental matters common to all
the subjects of the monarchy, — a unification in harmony with the
aspirations of the kings of that age throughout the world, and
favored in Spain by the circumstance that there was a common
sovereign over all the ancient kingdoms of the Peninsula   Within
the field of the civil law the sole dissolvent was the Roman law;
this, as we have seen, was active not alone in Castile but also in
other regions, and in some, as for example Catalonia, in notable
degree.

This unitive process was more widely and more potently effective
within the different kingdoms taken individually.   It was realized
in a fragmentary manner, affecting to-day one matter and to-
morrow another, varying in its details, and creating new institu-

tions. Without a formal abrogation of the ancient statutes, which it apparently respected, in truth it reduced them, as regards many of their extremes, to mere fleshless skeletons. In this manner, and especially in Castile, there was brought about a tacit and almost absolute annulment of all the ancient charters of municipal legislation within the field of public law, and of many of those which in the medieval period marked the distinctions of social classes, and the dependence in which the members of one regularly stood in relation to those of others   In the other kingdoms and in the same parts of the law like results were realized, although on a lesser scale, as we have seen above in the sections relating to the State and social classes.   Opportunity for these changes was very often found in confirming the municipal "fueros," which were generally profoundly modified and emended upon such occasions.   A salient example of this shrewd method of altering the medieval statute law is found in the treatment of the "fuero" of Teruel in the time of Philip II.

§ 32   **Legal Science in the Habsburg Period.** — The importance of the scientific study of the law was extremely great in the three centuries (1500s to 1700s) of this period.   Legal science was indeed one of the most extensive and most intensely cultivated fields of Spanish learning in the 1500s and 1600s, and one of those in which Spanish writers can present the most indisputable claims of originality and of positive influence upon the culture of other countries   Two leading causes explain the special development of this class of studies.   On one hand, constant incitement must have been offered to thinking men by the many legal problems presented in Spain in consequence of the special orientation of its military and religious policy, and the vast colonization begun at the close of the 1400s   On the other hand, a certain natural tendency is observable in the Spanish mind to busy itself with the practical aspects of questions.   These influences inevitably deflected philosophy towards its applications in morals, law, etc. We can thus understand why two of the greatest philosophers of the age, Vives and Suarez, were, the one a pedagogue and the other a jurist, of unrivalled rank.   Besides, the intrinsic relations of theology (then so much cultivated) and law, and the already traditional philosophical principle of the "connection of causes," naturally led theologians to the study of legal questions, and thus resulted, of course, in a rich flowerage of the Canon law.   And, finally, the extensive participation by the legists (Romanists) in political life, and the frequent consultation by the kings of the

667

learned members of the clergy, were other and powerful influences
in the development of legal studies.

The branches to which Spanish jurists devoted especial
study, and in which they gained the greatest renown, were
those of international, political, criminal, procedural, and civil
law, including in the last both the Roman and the native
systems.

In *international law*, a part of the philosophy of law until then
unknown or barely outlined in incidental studies or in the examination of wholly concrete cases, — such as the conquest of Navarre,
which gave rise to the book of Palacio Rubios, — Spanish writers
laid the basis of what was to be later a special and important
science, and which found already in their works a development of
great significance. The special causes for this are found in the
continual wars between Spanish kings and other European sovereigns, in the grave political questions that were in dispute between
them and the papacy, and in the problems created by the conquest
and colonization of the Indies The chief representatives of this
class of studies were Arias de Valderas, who in his book " De Bello
et Ejus Justitia " (1533) discussed the theory of the persecution of
heretics and the right to make war upon the Pope; Alvarez Guerra,
who undertook to define the doctrines of war, just and unjust
(1543); Soto, the mediator in the dispute between Las Casas and
Sepúlveda, champion of the Indians and enemy of the slave trade;
Vazquez Menchaca, who in his " Libri Tres Controversarium "
(1572) studied the laws of war, Juan de Cartagena, a furious ul-
tramontanist, the champion of the pope in the dispute with Venice,
Covarrubias, who wrote upon the slavery of captives made in war;
Ginés de Sepúlveda, whose ideas regarding the justification of the
conquest of inferior peoples and the slavery of the Indians may be
read in his elegant Latin dialogues entitled " Democrates "; Baltasar de Ayala, Francisco Arias, Juan Lopez, and various others.
All of these were exceeded in genius by Francisco Vitoria, the
master of some of those named, professor at Salamanca, whose
university lectures (which Melchor Cano later published under the
title of " Theologica Relectionis ") treat in a profound manner of
the law of war and of the question of the Indies, in addition to other
theses relative to the ecclesiastical supremacy of the Pope and
Council, the civil power, marriage, etc Hugo Grotius (1583–
1645), who was long considered the founder of the science of international law, owes a great part of his ideas to these Spanish
precursors, whom he cites, and not rarely with especial eulogy (for

example, Vitoria and Vazquez), in his book "De Jure Belli ac Pacis" (1625).

Among the cultivators of *political law*, opinion is almost unvaryingly monarchial, saving only Fox Morcillo, for whom the form of government is indifferent, since it is the substance and manner of administration that are important   The notion of monarchy common to all of them is similar to that of the writers of the Visigothic period and the authors of the "Partidas"   One marks the evident deliberation with which they strive to refute the imperialistic doctrines of the Roman law, so widely spread at that time throughout all Europe, and in Spain itself.   The solicitude with which the king made answer to these ideas led them to defend (Fox Morcillo) the propriety of deposing a monarch who should prove unequal to the discharge of his duties, and to establish, subject to more or less numerous conditions, the people's right of rebellion in the case of tyranny: and even the right of tyrannicide (Molina, Mariana)   In the diffusion of these theories, the fears excited by the example of Protestant kings and princes who had swept their people from their past beliefs were unquestionably influential; to the Catholic writers it seemed that the only way of avoiding the repetition of such occurrences lay in the affirmation of rebellion and tyrannicide as rights inherent in the people whenever the monarch should act against the principles of human and divine law.

More interesting than these doctrines are those that refer directly to factors and actors of the Spanish States at that time, because they reveal to us the character of a portion of the national opinion, and that of the most cultured class.   The defence of the Cortes, of their necessity, of their power in matters of finance, and even of their participation in legislative functions (which is made by a number of writers of such repute as Rivadeneira, Mariana, and Marquez, opposing thus with theory the actual decadence of the institution), is important in this connection.   In speaking of the taxes voted by the Cortes, Rivadeineira says that that which they thus give to the kings is called a service, subsidy, or gift because "it is a voluntary and not an obligatory service."   These doctrines produced, however, no effect whatever upon the policy of the crown.

To the same effect, as regards the internal government of the country, the same writers (Vitoria, Fox, Contreras) pronounced against the sale of public offices, then so commonly resorted to, and with such injury to the nation; and against the perpetuity of

political and administrative charges   They maintain also the
necessity of the king's governing with the counsel of men of experience and culture; and one of those who sustain this thesis
(Sepúlveda) takes much pains to anathematize the institution of
"válidos" or favorites, which he had seen produce disastrous
effects during the reigns of John II and Henry IV, and which was
very soon to be revived in Spain   Perhaps there was no opinion
held more unanimously at that time than this one adverse to royal
favorites, unquestionably because the experience of the harm that
such men produced was not only evident to the view of all but its
effects were felt by all   Finally, the general desire men felt that
the monarch should in fact respond to the directive function in
theory attributed to him, we find demonstrated in the attention
bestowed upon the condition of his political and general education,
a matter that gave rise to a vast literature, which enjoyed as we
shall see, an extraordinary fame throughout the world.

By the side of the leading names already cited — Suarez (who
in his "Tractatus de Legibus et Deo Legislatore," 1612, not only
examines the question of statutes and legislation from the point of
view of practical politics, but from all those it presents to a general
philosopher of the law), Mariana, Vazquez, Fox Morcillo, Molina,
and others — mention must be made of still others, who studied
either general political problems, such as the forms of States and
governments, tyranny, etc., or the special problem of colonial
government, or the theme, then so attractive, of the education of
princes.   Among such writers were Arias Montano, author of an
"Instrucción de Príncipes" and of a book, "Varia Republic";
Rivadaneira, whose "Tratado del Príncipe Cristiano" is a refu-
tation of Machiavelli, Gracian, who in his works, "El Heroe,"
"El Discreto," "El Cortesano," and others, studied the requisites
of a chief of State, and laid down political maxims of an ad-
mirable sagacity; Solorzano Pereira, author of a celebrated work
entitled "Política Indiana," in which he defended the Spanish
colonial system,   Ramos del Manzano, diplomat, and preceptor of
Charles II, for whom he wrote a treatise upon "Reinados de Menor
Edad y de Grandes Reyes" (1674), Castrillo, who showed himself favorable to the pretensions of the Comuneros, though not to
the methods which they, in order to maintain those, were compelled to follow; Sepúlveda, already referred to, Furió y Ceriol,
author of "El Consejo y Consejeros del Príncipe"; Quevedo,
whose works "Marco Bruto" and "Política de Cristo" are two
excellent political studies, Saavedra Fajardo, whose "Empresas

Políticas " attained a great celebrity in all countries; Jerónimo de Blancas and Jerónimo Martel, who expounded and commented upon the parliamentarian law of Aragon, friar Juan de Sta. Maria, who wrote a book " De República y Policía Cristiana ", Antonio Perez, the secretary of Philip II, his homonym, a professor in the University of Louvain from 1619 onward, Jerónimo Mirola, whose curious work " République Original Treta del Cos Humá " (Barcelona, 1587) studies the participation in the government of the different classes of society; Orozco, Torres, Simancas, Osorio, Guevara, — who enjoyed great celebrity abroad; and many others, together a legion, who figured in the literature of court and politics, so popular in those times. The Catalan rebellion of 1640 produced in that country an interesting flowerage of political science, in which Salas and other writers won distinction.

Criminal law was especially cultivated in connection with the controversies over the right to punish heretics and the development given by the persecutions of the Inquisition to the principles and procedure of the criminal law. The chief representatives of this literature were: Alfonso de Castro, whose two books " De Justa Hæreticorum Punitione " and " De Potestate Legis Penalis," aside from their general value as penological studies, are of great importance for an understanding of the prevalent opinions of the age relative to the repression of heresy, Soto, Vitoria, Molina, and others cited above; Antonio Gomez, rated by many as the prince of Spanish criminalists of the 1500 s, besides being a famous civilist, and commentator of the " Leyes de Toro ", the Jesuit Martin del Rio, who in his " Disquisitionum Magicarum " (1593) treated of the magic superstitions of the age, and of their repression, Simancas, author of a work, " De Catholicis Institutionibus " (1552); Cerdán de Tallada, jurisconsult of Valencia of the 1600 s and procedurist, particularly notable for his book entitled " Visita de la Cárcel," which besides giving us a realistic picture of the condition of prisons in the 1500 s, suggests many ideas relative to prison reform; Diego Vallalpando, in the 1400 s in his commentary upon the " Leyes de Partidas," and Bernardino de Sandoval in the 1500 s, had done the like for various questions of criminal law. Of great importance also is a group of Catalan criminalists and procedurists of the 1600 s: Oliba, Ripoll, Xauar, Vilosa, Cancer, and very especially Peguera (a regalianist in issues between Church and State), and Calderó, whose book on criminal jurisprudence (1605) is the most complete of those published in Catalonia.

We may include in the group of *canonists*, with those properly

so called, the writers upon questions of jurisdiction between Church
and State. In the field of Canon law the Spanish clergy had a
glorious tradition to preserve that set them by St. Raimundo de
Peñafort and Cardinal Albornóz. It was followed by Bishop
Antonio Agustin, auditor of the " Rota Romana " (Court of Appeal) and nuncio, a man of the greatest erudition in archæology
and the humanities, emendator of the texts of Gratian (a task in
which, by command of the pope, Torres, Taxaquet, Chacón, and
other Spaniards aided), and founder of the external history of the
Canon law, in which field of study he is to-day considered as notable as Alciat and Cujas in that of the Roman law, Martin Navarro
de Azpilcueta, known as the " master among all the doctors of
Spain," professor of Salamanca and Coimbra, and author of various treatises on " Rentas Eclesiasticas," " Horas Canónicas," etc.;
his disciple Covarrubias, author of the reformatory decree of the
Council of Trent; the Bishop of Calahorra, Diaz de Lugo, author of
a " Práctica Criminal Canónica ", Villalpando, who wrote commentaries upon the councils of Toledo, Loaysa, compiler of the
Spanish councils, Mendoza, compiler of that of Iliberes, Archbishop Carranza, to whom we owe a " Summa " or compendium of
the councils, Bishop Juan Bautista Perez, extremely important
for his historical investigations relative to the same subject, Dr.
Romaguera, of Ampurdán, counsellor to all the monasteries and
ecclesiastical chapters of Catalonia, and author of certain extremely
important " Constitutiones Synodales Diocesis Gerundensis "
(1691); Gouvea, Ruiz de Moros, Retes, Barbosa, Gonzalez Tellez,
Sanchez Simancas, and many others, among whom should be
counted some of the theologians and philosophers already mentioned in other fields   In the second group we must include the
regalianists Salgado de Somoza, Castillo de Sotomayor, Sessé,
Ceballos, Salcido, Pereira, P Enriquez, Ramos del Manzano, and
various of those cited among the cultivators of international law.

Among the *civilians* also there are names that must be repeated
Such are those of Antonio Agustin, editor of an emended text of the
Pandects and a commentator of equal celebrity with Gouvea, a
rival of his contemporary Cujas; Ramos del Manzano, Covarrubias, of whom his contemporaries said that he was the Bartolus
of Spain ; Antonio Vinuesa Pichardo, precursor of Heineccius as a
commentator upon the Institutes, Francisco de Arnaya, whose three
books of " Observationes Juris " (1643) place him in the front rank
among the legists of the 1600s, Loaces, Tomás, Vazquez, Alta-
mirano, Retes, Quintadueñas, and others of great renown.

Although (as already remarked) the national civil (or, private) law, (as distinguished from Roman law and from local customs) was given no chair in the universities, nevertheless, the inevitable necessities of politics, of the administration of justice, and of legal practice caused men to cultivate its study.[1]   This was the desire of Queen Isabella, as shown by the second of the "Leyes de Toro"; and to the same end other statutes must have been issued in the 1500s and 1600s, to which allusion appears to be made in two accords of Council of the early 1700s (1713, 1741) This tendency was manifested in numerous legal works, some designed as commentaries upon, and others as concordances of, the institutes of the national law, some devoted to determining the difference between them and the Roman, and yet others to investigations of their origin and history   The list of commentators is very long; one notes that if many of the Castilian civilians figure in it, almost without exception it includes those of Aragon, Catalonia, Valencia, and the other non-Castilian regions.   It is true that not a few of them write their commentaries from a Romanist point of view, or in their observations make use of an erudition chiefly illustrated by Roman data; but even with these the consideration of the peculiarities of the native law plays a large part, as was inevitable.   Restricting ourselves to names especially eminent, we may refer to Gregorio Lopez, whose text of and commentaries upon the "Partidas" were recognized as official in the courts;[2] Antonio Gomez, commentator upon the "Leyes de Toro" in a work considered as the "vade-mecum" and favorite guide of lawyers and judges, the authority of which is attested by the various editions and summaries that were made of it, Micer Miguel de Molino, author of a famous repertory of the Aragonese "fueros," already cited; and his compatriot Bernardo de Monsoriu, Sessé, commentator on the decisions of the Aragonese courts; Molina, who treated the subject of entailed estates, respecting which he is recognized as the first authority; Micer Pedro Tarazona, author of an "Instituta del Derecho Valenciano"; Acevedo and Gutierrez, commentators upon the "Nuevo Recopilación," and the first also a procedurist, Cristobal de Paz, commentator on the "Leyes del Estilo"; Alfonso de Villadiego, editor of the "Fuero Juzgo; and finally a

---

[1] In this field the professors of Valladolid shone with singular brilliancy
[2] With respect to the great favor which his edition enjoyed in the courts and among jurists, *Martinez Marina* notes that this was a significant mark of the advance of Romanist doctrine, inasmuch as the glosses of Lopez were "adapted to the taste of the schools" and included "all the principles of the [Roman] civil and the canon law, as well as those of the Romanists and glossators."

group of Catalans, — Cancer, Fontanella, Ferrer, and perhaps a
few others of those already mentioned — who collected or wrote
commentaries upon the law of their country. — It is of interest to
note that in this period there were printed various works of jurists
of earlier times, as Marquilles, Vallseca, Callicio, Socarrats, and
others. Among the cultivators of comparative studies we should
not forget Sebastian Jimenez, Juan Martinez de Olano, author of
an " Antinomia Juris Hispanorum et Civile "; and Juan Bautista
de Villalobos. The first showed himself a strong partisan of the
Roman law, but the other two recognize all the value and importance of the native.

Finally, there began in this period the historical study of the
Spanish law, which is represented by the works of certain of the
jurisconsults above mentioned — for example, Villadiego — and
of many of the canonists; by those of Dr. Espinosa, who wrote (in
the 1500 s) upon the origin of the statutes, " fueros," and ordinances
of Spain; those of the chronicler of Charles I, Lorenzo de Padilla,
who provided with historical notes various ancient Castilian statutes, those of certain Catalans and Aragonese, as Oliba, Blancas,
Ustarróz, and — ranking above all others in erudite researches —
Juan Lucas Cortés, author of a " Biblioteca de los Jurisconsultos
Españoles " (the first work of its class), which was appropriated
and published as his own in the first of the 1700 s by a Dane, Ernest
von Franckenau (" Sacra Themidis Hispanae Arcana "). All of
these had predecessors, after whom to follow, in various authors
of the Middle Ages (for example, Socarrats).

Of civilians devoted to pure doctrine (that is, neither commentators nor students of comparative law) there were few, because
legal science was still bound to exegesis and to practical problems,
and was not commonly devoted to pure speculation, much less
had it attained, in its special branches, the systematic construction
characteristic of it centuries later. A similar statement may be
made regarding any pure philosophy of the law, or study of its
general problems. Strictly speaking, of works of this nature one
can only cite that of Suarez; one (to-day lost) upon natural law
written by Vazquez Menchaca; and some of the treatises " De
Justitia et Jure," — among them that of the Jesuit Luis de Molina
(1599–1600), notable for its abundant references to the legal institutions of Spain and Portugal. Lastly, we may cite two of the
rare cultivators of commercial law, which in part was studied by
the civilians and in part by the canonists: Hevia Bolaños, author
of a book entitled " Curia Philípica " (1615) which expounds the

whole mercantile and maritime law, and Diaz Ramon, translator into Castilian of the "Libro del Consulado" of Barcelona.

All this exuberant legal literature was enriched also by numerous translations of classical works upon the philosophy of the law (Aristotle, Plato, Cicero); to this were devoted Hellenists and Latinists like Pedro Simon Abril, Viciano, Sepúlveda, Vergara, and others.[1]

Topic 2. The Bourbon Dynasty (1700–1808)

§ 33 **History of the Legal Sources.** — The 1700s were an age of great reforms in the social and political life of Spain. The causes lay in the influence of France, and in the general spirit of the times, which throughout Europe was propitious to innovations and progress even within the limits of the old régime, — thanks to the dual idealistic currents of philanthropy and enlightened despotism. The reforms carried through by the Bourbon dynasty, only some of which can here be mentioned, gave origin to a great number of statutes, almost all in the form of royal orders (under varying names) and resolutions in council.

(1) As a consequence, the labors of compilation represented by the "Nueva Recopilación" of 1567 not only became insufficient, but were in part confounded and destroyed, the same excess and confusion of statutes again resulting as that of which the Cortes of the 1500s had complained. Nothing more, however, was done during the 1700s than to reedit five times the "Nueva Recopilación," each time adding a part, but not all, of the new legislation. Thus in that of 1723 there was added a volume of acts and resolutions of the Council This could not remedy, however, either the unsystematic division into books, nor the confused assemblage in some titles of statutes belonging in others. The preparation of a supplement, to comprise statutes and resolutions of Council subsequent to 1745, was entrusted to the jurist Lardizabal but was not published. Years later approval was given to the project of another compilation which rearranged that of 1567 and all its

---

[1] Details concerning jurists of the 1500s and 1600s, and of their doctrines considered in relation to public (and especially criminal) law, can be found in the excellent monograph of *Hinojosa,* "Influencia que tuvieron en el derecho publico de su patria, y singularmente en el derecho penal, los filósofos y teólogos españoles anteriores á nuestro siglo" (Madrid, 1890) As the title indicates, it also contains data prior to the 1500s, indeed from the Visigothic period onward Biographical and bibliographical data respecting the chief jurists from the Roman period down to the 1800s will be found in the "Nociónes de bibliografía y literatura jurídicas de España" (Madrid, 1884) of M Torres Campos.

supplements into twelve books, and was printed in 1805 under the title of a " Novísima Recopilación de las Leyes de España." Its author, Juan de la Reguera Valdelomar, claimed to have solved the problem of concentrating the legislative law; but the reality fell far short of the assertion His work suffered from many defects, some of method and others of omission, inasmuch as it did not include all that was actually in force in the classes of royal orders, statutes of Cortes, and resolutions of Council As for the other elements of existing legislation, the " Novísima " left things as they were in 1567: *i e.* it reproduced the statute of the " Ordenamiento of Alcalá," which had been repeated in the " Leyes de Toro " and in the " Nueva Recopilación "; according to which the " Fuero Real," the municipal " fueros " in so far as not repealed, and — with supplementary character — the " Partidas," remained in authority.

Thus the " Novísima " did not satisfy the necessity which it assumed to meet, nor the aspirations of a theoretical nature of the jurists of the day; and Spanish legislation in general, and that of each province as well, continued to lack unity and clarity Every one of the existing bodies of legislative law (wrote a statesman of the time of Charles IV) had been formed by successive aggregations, very often without the complete annulment of the earlier by the later law. Moreover, by the side of the codes of obligatory authority there were supplemental systems of optional character, and resort was frequently taken to the Roman law, to the doctrinal works of jurisconsults of repute, and to the decisions of the courts. The civil judges of the Council, he adds, possess as their sole resource, " a mass of texts more or less well digested, and expect that the king should command them to interpret these to his liking, and that he should give them in recompense the wherewithal to live."

(2) That the Roman law, as in the preceding centuries, continued in great repute is proved among other evidences by the resolution of Council of 1713 (cited above), and by a royal " cedula " of July 15, 1778, in this the king commands his courts to obey, in cases of succession, statue 12, title 2, book 4 of the " Fuero Juzgo " " with less manifestation of adherence to that of the ' Partida,' which is exclusively based upon the Roman Novels and the Canon common law " This " cédula " refers us then, as was to be expected, to the study of the decisions of the courts and the doctrinal works of the time. If to these we should add the statutes issued continually by the crown, and the resolutions of Council

in the "Nueva" and the "Novísima Recopilación," we could determine the concrete advances which not only the "Partidas" (ordinarily cited as primary authority) but also the pure Justinian system and the doctrines of the Glossators continued to make, notwithstanding the unfriendly disposition of the government. For such an investigation great aid is offered by the law manuals published in this period, particularly after the university reforms of the 1700s by which the "royal" (that is, Spanish) law was included in the curriculum of legal studies.   Most of these manuals compare to some extent,[1] and some of them very especially, the native with the Roman law; thus making evident the situation which the institutions of Castile and other provinces had reached, at the dates of their respective publication, as a result of the continued conflict of opposing influences.   Nobody has, however, yet made such a historical study, either with reference to the territories of the Castilian crown or with reference to the other kingdoms.[2]

The law of the Castilian territories suffered great changes in the 1700s as a result of the centralizing and unitarian spirit of the monarchy   An excuse, of unquestionable gravity, for the following of such tendencies was given by the War of Succession, in which a great part of Aragon, Catalonia, and Valencia took a stand against Philip V in aid of the Archduke of Austria   It is true that from the 1400s onward the autonomy and independent administration of the ancient kingdoms, outside of Castile,[3] had continued to suffer certain losses.   But the chief institutions of Aragon, Catalonia, Valencia, Majorca, and the Basque provinces, political, administrative, and of civil law, still subsisted substantially intact at the opening of the 1700s.

Philip V, once the War of Succession was over, radically altered this situation.   By a decree of June 29, 1707, he abolished the "fueros, privileges, practices, and customs until now observed" in *Aragon* and *Valencia*, subjecting them "to the laws of Castile, and to the usages, practice, and form of government that exists

[1] As those of *Torres Velasco, Asso and De Manuel, Maimó, Danvila,* the various ones of *Sala,* and others.

[2] The reception of Roman doctrines in Catalonia in this period (1500s to 1800s) is testified to both by Catalan jurisconsults and foreign glossarists and commentators   But this general affirmation should be developed and made concrete by a study of the works of the Catalan authors, which also contain much information (*Brocá and Amell* advert to this, without detail in their work cited above in § 15, n 1) relative to the judicial law of the period.

[3] See *Altamira*, "Civilización española," vol III, §§ 580 and 681.

and has existed therein and in its tribunals, without variance whatever in any matter." Complementary to this decree were those of September of the same year, in which the king declared his intention not to consider abrogated any "fuero" or custom favorable to the royal prerogative; one of 1708, which maintained in Valencia the seigniorial jurisdictions of the Alfonsine "fuero", and that of August 3, 1711, in which it was ordered that criminal causes should be judged in the tribunal of Saragossa in accord with the "custom and statutes of Castille" and civil cases "under the municipal statutes of this realm of Aragon" In other words, all the peculiar public law of Aragon and of Valencia was abolished, while their special civil law was conserved to Aragon.

In Catalonia and in Majorca the abolition was not accomplished until after the victories of 1714 and 1715. It began in *Catalonia* with the abolition of the special governmental institutions of the Principality (the Council of One Hundred, the Deputation, etc), and was followed by other abolitions or assimilations to the Castilian law. The Cortes were effectually dissolved, the Catalan representation being incorporated in the Cortes of Castile. (It is not true that the Catalan "fueros" were burned, either publicly or privately.) These preliminary reforms were completed by a decree of January 16, 1716, called the "Nueva Planta" (New Plantation), which expressly abolished in toto the ancient forms of government in all the cities, towns, and places of Catalonia, reformed the ancient manners, customs, and practices relative to the political and economic regimen, and offices of supreme and ordinary judicature, establishing also a new system in the institution and conduct of legal causes. Notwithstanding this, the legal peculiarities of Catalonia did not wholly disappear, nor was unification absolute in the field of public law. Not until well after the beginning of the 1800s did Catalonia lose completely her criminal and procedural law, her special coinage, her system of taxation based upon registers of realty, her exemption from military drafts, the office of notary public (though the king assumed the right of nomination), nor other peculiarities, political and administrative, which the decree left in subsistence. And this is explicitly stated by the decree itself as regards "the ordinances that may exist for the political government of the cities, towns, and places in so far as not inconsistent with what is here commanded," — though subject to the reservation of their revision "in matters which may be considered to merit reformation" The civil law and commercial law also remained unaltered in their whole extent including "the liberties and political rights relative to the family, property, and the individual " Commercial contracts continued to be written in Catalan, and primary education continued Catalan as before. In 1768 the king's feudal court of peers, which till then had existed, was abolished, the cognizance of the causes to which its jurisdiction extended being given to the " audiencia."

As for *Majorca*, a decree was issued of November 28, 1715, which modified the government of the city of Palma and established an "audiencia." The civil and criminal law, the "Consulado del Mar" (a court of commercial jurisdiction), and until 1718 the Great and General Council, were all conserved. — Of legislation anterior to these reforms a new compilation was made for Catalonia in 1704, revising that of 1588; and in 1791 the jurist Capmany published a corrected edition of the commercial laws known as the " Consulado del Mar."

In the *Basque Provinces*, although in general its " fueros " were respected, — as was explicitly ordered in the case of Alava by a royal resolution of 1794, — the central government continued to introduce its representatives and delegates who (without apparent violence to the traditional institutions) subjected the provincial government to the oversight or intervention of the ministers or Council. Some modifications also were introduced into the local government.[1]

Navarre preserved intact its Cortes, its permanent Deputation, its Council, its auditorial office, its coinage, its privilege of suffering no other foreign authorities than the viceroy and five others, its exemption from military duties and from the jurisdiction of the treasury, and its civil law In 1735 was published a " Novísima Recopilación " of Navarrese legislation, known as that of Elizondo, approved by the Cortes in 1726, and containing in five books the statutes of the Cortes (till then dispersed) and others.

The mass of *colonial* legislation was continually enlarged by new royal orders and " cédulas." Among them stands out in importance the " Instrucción " of 1786, which established the office of intendants; these were in appearance officers of purely fiscal character, but they supplanted in a goodly part of their functions the viceroys and the judges, inasmuch as they were intrusted with matters of law, police, finance, and war. We note also the " Instrucción " of 1754 to the visitor-general of finance sent to Mexico; the secret instructions to the Viceroy Superunda relative to the administration of justice, the reforms carried through in the matter

[1] *Altamira*, "Civilización española," vol. IV, pp 159–160

of communication (the creation of a naval postal service and the incorporation of the inland service with the crown); in commerce (open commerce between a large number of Spanish ports and others in America, lower tariff duties, abolition of the system of the " flotas," etc.), in agriculture, and other matters; and a multitude of changes made in the political and administrative system, public works, public instruction, etc., by a pleiad of notable viceroys, who, in the time of Charles III and even later, bettered the situation of the colonies [1]

In the law of the Peninsula the chief changes were the following· the modifications of the statute fixing the succession to the crown, made by Philip V in the " Resolution in Council " or Regulation of 1713, and by Charles IV, [2] the increase and alteration of the functions of the ancient secretaryships of the crown, which little by little take on the character of modern ministries, supplanting in many matters the royal Councils; the reform of these last consultative bodies, the reforms of a democratic nature made in municipal government by the " cedula " of May 5, 1766, and others, the great improvements in the financial administration and in the public services of the State, the new ordinances of the army and the navy, the impulse given to education of all grades, and in general to the cultivation of the sciences and arts; the great quantity of dispositions relative to the industries, trades, agriculture, etc., of the Peninsula, and the substantial changes made in the relations of Church and State, manifested in the first Spanish Concordat, signed September 26, 1737, and reformed by that of 1753.[3]

§ 34 **Legal Science and Literature of the Bourbon Period.** — In philosophy, the nature of the questions that were chiefly agitated in Spain under the Bourbon dynasty, and the character of the propaganda carried on throughout the world by the philosophic precursors of the French Revolution and by the publicists who devoted themselves to vulgarizing the principles that inspired that formidable explosion, led men naturally and preferentially to that part of philosophic study that concerns itself with the law. It happens thus that the 1700s constituted in Spain an epoch of flowerage in legal studies; not of a disinterested and speculative character, but

---

[1] Details in *Altamira*, "Civilización española," vol IV, §§ 811–829, 837.
[2] *Altamira*, "Civilización española," vol IV, pp 206–210.
[3] Details as to all these reforms in *Altamira*, "Civilización española," vol. IV The novelties in private law introduced in the time of both the Austrian and Bourbon houses will be found in ch. 8 of *Altamira*, "Origen y desarrollo del derecho civil español," cited above § 1, n. 1.

with the end of examining and defending or combating the most salient facts in the contemporary political life, both of Spain and of foreign countries.

The works of this nature that were then published may be classified in four great groups: one, in which figure all those works directed to the diffusion or discussion of the new juridical ideas, and especially those of the revolutionary authors; another, comprising those books and pamphlets that sustained the struggle for jurisdiction between Church and State, a third, of writings relative to political government and the reforms of which it stood in need; and the fourth, of those manuals necessary for instruction in the law, particularly after the inclusion of new subjects in the university curriculum.

In the first group belong the book of Hervás y Panduro, " Causas de la Revolución de Francia en el Año 1790 " (printed first in 1803 under the title of " Revolución Religiosa y Civil de los Franceses "), that of Joaquin Lorenzo Villanueva, " Catecismo de Estado segun los Princípios de la Religión " (1793), an apology of Cæsarism in the face of revolution, those of Padre Cevallos on the " Causas de la Desigualdad entre los Hombres " and the " Falsa Filosofía, Crimen de Estado," which combat Helvetius, Hobbes, Rousseau, and other authors in the field of politics, while in other writings he reviews Voltaire, Beccaria, etc., the important essay of Professor Campos on the " Desigualdad de las personas en la sociedad civil," against Rousseau; the " Memorias de la Revolución Francesa " of Padre Gustá (in Italian, 1793), and many others, aside from the translations of French revolutionary writers, especially Rousseau, which were numerous.

To the second group belong, among others, the " Información " of Macanáz (1713) relative to questions with the papal court, the " Observaciónes sobre el Concordato de 1753 " of Mayans, the " Tratado de la Regalía de Amortización," the " Memorial Ajustado " (relative to the Bishop of Cuenca), and the " Respuesta " dealing with the Spanish Carthusians, which we owe to the pen of Campomanes; the " Historia Legal de la Bula In Coena Domini," which was compiled by Juan Luis Lopez (1768) of the Royal Council, and is provided with an introduction by Campomanes, the " Juicio Imparcial sobre las Letras en forma de Breve," the " Representación Fiscal sobre el Monitorio de Parma," and other papers of the Conde de Floridablanca.

In the third group belong all the publications made with the intent of modifying the Aragonese, Catalan, and Valencian

" fueros ", the numerous writings of Macanáz, among them the
" Explicación Jurídica é Histórica de la Consulta que hizo el
Consejo de Castilla relativamente a su Autoridad y Atribuciones,"
and the " Auxilios para bien gobernar una Monarquía Católica ";
the " Colección de Memorias y Noticias sobre el Gobierno General
y Político del Consejo " by Antonio Martinez Salazar (1764), the
" Práctica del Consejo en el Despacho de Negocios " by Pedro
Escolano (1796), the " Memorial " of Floridablanca upon administration, the two " Alegaciones Fiscales " of Campomanes in the
question of escheats of the seigniories of nobles to the crown, the
" Respuesta " of Floridablanca, in the like question, relative to the
claim to the seigniory of Montaragut (1768); the " Cartas " of
the Conde de Cabarrús (1792-1795) and the " Cartas Político-
económicas " that are likewise attributed to him; the two works of
Campillo, Minister of State, " Lo que Hay de Mas y de Menos en
España " (which expounds at the same time a political programme
and a sort of national psychology) and " La España Despierta ";
the political writings of Gándara, — " Apuntes sobre el Bien y el
Mal de España " (1762); those of Aranda, Ulloa, Jorge Juan, and
others relative to colonial administration; and others of like character.

Works of the fourth class were numerous, including original
works and translations of Heineccius, Vattel, Van Espen, Berandi,
Filangieri, Bielfeld, and others We may mention, as chief among
the Romanists and Spanish civilians, such authors as Finestres,
Asso and De Manuel, Sala, Berni, Murillo, Maimó, and Marin y
Mendoza To these should be added those whose end was to
modify the plan or methodics of legal studies, — such as the two
" Discursos " of Jovellanos upon the relations between law and
universal history, and upon legal texts and phraseology, as well as
his " Cartas sobre el Modo de Estudiar el Derecho ", and a few
works of other authors.

The study of legal principles was also influenced by the new ideas
presented in several works not directly destined for that purpose
— notably the translation of the " Tratado " of Beccaria upon
Crimes and Penalties, which provoked the excellent " Discurso
sobre las Penas " of Manuel de Lardizábal (1782); the " Observaciónes sobre la perplejidad de la Tortura " of Forner and his ref-
utation of Padre Cevallos (who defended capital punishment),
with whom Alfonso Acebedo likewise carried on a controversy upon
the same subject, the " Biblioteca Española Económica-política "
of Sempere y Guarinos; the " Princípios de la Práctica Criminal "

of Posadilla, the "Noticia de la Cárcel de Filadelfia" (1801) of
Arquellada; the "Tratado Jurídico y Político sobre las Presas de
Mar" of Abreu; and the writings of Mora y Jaraba, Azecevedo,
and others.   Finally, we may note those on the history of Spanish
law, — among which those of Martinez Marina, Burriel, Jovellanos, Sempere, Asso and De Manuel, and Llorente, are most important, — and those of certain economists who treated of the legal
aspects of their respective subjects, — for example, Jovellanos in
his "Informe sobre la Ley Agraria."[1]

It is interesting also to note, as a part of that movement favoring
the study of the genuinely Spanish law, as contrasted with the
Roman to which reference was made in treating of the statutory
sources, the first manifestations of regionalism in the field of law.
As such we must count the allusions to Aragonese law that occur
in the book of Asso and De Manuel; but the same is shown in a
more accentuated character by certain events in Catalonia, and
particularly: by a motion of the secretary of the Academy of Theoretical and Practical Jurisprudence (founded in Barcelona in 1788)
for the study of national Catalan law; by the inedited work of a
jurisconsult of the period (cited by the same secretary) in which
he commented upon the Roman law in union with "the elements
and institutions of our own national legislation", and by the
"Notas de nuestro Derecho Municipal para cada Titulo de las
Instituciónes Romanas," written by Juan Muyal, professor in
the University of Cervera.

[1] On economists and legal historians see *Altamira*, "Civilización española," vol. IV, §§ 41–42.

CHAPTER IV. THIRD PERIOD: SINCE A.D. 1808

MODERN LEGAL REFORMS

§ 35   Reform of the Public Law.   § 39.   General Character and Limi-
§ 36.   Reform of the Private Law   tations of the Código Civil
§ 37   Partial Codifications of the § 40   The Código Civil and the
          Civil Law prior to the   Customary Law
          Código Civil   § 41.   Legal Science and Literature
§ 38   History of the Redaction of   of the Period
          the present Código Civil.

§ 35.   **Reform of the Public Law.** — The last century was in Spain one of great reforms and innovations in the legal order. Its public law suffered a total transformation, legal sources were given unity and regularity; and legal science was opened to influences which, if contrasted with the spirit of preceding centuries, were of exceeding novelty.

These transformations began with public law. The Napoleonic invasion and the exile of the Spanish kings, prisoners in France from 1808–1814, created a peculiar political situation of transcendent consequences. Without a central government that could direct it, and distrustful of the superior authorities left it, who were dominated by the French, the nation took the initiative itself in the War of Independence and in the direction of public affairs. Thus all the political and social aspirations stifled by the absolutism of the antecedent regimen could reveal themselves publicly and unreservedly By a natural tendency the various regions of the Peninsula constituted themselves centres of action under administrative Councils, and aspired to resuscitate the ancient Cortes as a national organ that should be representative of all, and should act in the absence of the king in accord with the necessities and desires of the country. And this was done. An Assembly formed of four classes of deputies — those of the cities which had held votes in earlier Cortes, those of the provincial Juntas recently constituted, those of the people, electing a representative for every 50,000 souls, and those of America (one for every 100,000 whites) — came together at Cadiz (1810–1813) A great number of these deputies, particularly the representatives of the Councils ("Juntas"), brought with them a spirit of reform already manifested in the petitions of those bodies, in which were condensed the philanthropic and liberal ideals of the 1700s and the recent influences of the French Revolution. It is noteworthy that many members of this inspiration were clericals, — for example, Ruiz del Padón and Muñoz Torrero.

The Cortes, once organized as "extraordinary" and supreme in the field of legislation (the first time that they had possessed such character in Spain), and the parliamentary and constitutional system of government being thus inaugurated, they began their task. Its basis was the fourfold oath taken by the members, which bound them to maintain the Catholic religion, the integrity of the national territory, and fidelity to the laws and to Fernando VII, whom they proclaimed as king. In successive laws and resolutions, afterwards condensed in the Constitution of 1812, they developed the new programme of liberalism. Its fundamentals were the sovereignty of the people jointly with the king; constitutional monarchy; separation of governmental powers, inviolability of the deputies to Cortes, the incompatibility of their duties with the occupancy of other public offices, equality of rights between Peninsulars and Americans, abolition of abusive powers over the Indians; political liberty of the press, which should be subject to censorship only in religious questions; submission of Ferdinand to the Cortes in the matter of his marriage, and the same with respect to international treaties which he might make while in captivity, abolition of judicial torture, the formation of a national budget, subjecting even the clergy to taxes necessary for the war; abolition of feudal jurisdictions wherever they still existed, and of rights of lordship and vassalage; initiation of the emancipation of the negro slaves, and abolition of the penalties of the scourge and imprisonment upon Indians rejecting baptism, recognition of intangible individual rights of civil liberty, property, capacity for public offices, equality before the law, etc , amendability of the Constitution, responsibility of the ministers of the crown; municipal governments with elective councils, a national militia and standing army, a great development of public instruction, abolition of the tribunal of the Inquisition, and transfer of the jurisdiction over ecclesiastical offences to the Episcopal tribunals; limitations upon the number of religious communities; distribution of waste and communal lands among the poor and soldiers honorably discharged; suppression of whipping in the schools; establish-

685

ment of a single and direct tax; and still others of a like tendency

Although all these reforms were approved by a great majority of deputies, these did not represent herein other than the opinion of all persons of enlightenment influenced by the reformist spirit of the time. On the other hand, the reforms encountered many enemies, and at their head the King, who with disgust beheld himself thus shorn of the absolutism of his powers. All the social classes and all those organizations whose ancient privileges were threatened by the rise of legal equality, and especially a great part of the clergy, fomented this hostile opinion The masses, passive in indifference, or through ignorance of the new ideals, could more readily be swept away by a movement in line with traditions than by one of reform. Thus it was possible for Ferdinand, on his return to Spain in 1814, to annul entirely the work of the Cortes of Cadiz With this began a bitter struggle between the partisans of absolute and those of constitutional government This filled the greater part of the century, — properly speaking, down to the revolution of 1868. Yet during this time, despite alternative victories for one or the other party, the transformation of the Spanish State was painfully progressing. Legislative landmarks in this progress were the " Letter in Council " or Royal Statute of 1834 (essentially a regulation of the Cortes), the constitutions of 1837, 1845, 1855 (with the supplementary act of 1856), the constitutional project of 1857, and the Constitution of 1869. This was fruit of the Revolution, and reflected the new ideals of liberalism — much more advanced, as was natural, than at the beginning of the century — in combination with those of 1812. The restoration of 1875 annulled the Constitution of 1869, and replaced it with that of 1876, now in force. In this, notwithstanding the vagueness of its phraseology, which leaves ample field for very diverse interpretations, there are recognized in more or less attenuated form some of the principles of liberalism. The action of the Liberal party since 1881, aided by the Republican, has added to the Constitution, in the form of special statutes, other parts of the creed of 1869, such as universal suffrage, trial by jury, liberty of the press, etc.[1]

[1] This exceedingly summary statement can be supplemented by the reading of the "Tratado de derecho político" (3 vols., Madrid, 1893–1894) of *Adolfo Posada*, and the book of *H Gmelin*, "Studien zur spanischen Verfassungsgeschichte des neunzehnten Jahrhunderts" (Stuttgart, 1905) ; and, with special reference to municipal law, — which followed the vicissitudes of political parties, — the book of *A. Posada*, "Evolución legis-

At the same time that liberal principles were thus advancing in legislative law, it was also realizing two ideals which already in the 1700s had received eloquent expression: that of legislative unity within the field of public law, subjecting all Spaniards to identical rules, and that of the equality of all citizens before the law.

To the first of these were opposed the remnants of the political and administrative " fueros " that had persisted in Navarre, in the Basque Provinces, and even in Catalonia (*ante*, § 32), these after successive reductions and abolitions ended by disappearing save in a few details still conserved in Navarre and the Basque Provinces, especially in the economic order. Simultaneously, the organization and procedure of the courts were unified by successive reforms down to the statute of 1870, now in force, with its supplement of 1882. The notarial system was revised by the statute of 1862. Public instruction was centralized by a statute of 1845, and regulated generally by another of 1857; itself modified since then, in almost all its details, by a multitude of decrees, orders, and other statutes. Criminal law was covered by codes of 1810, 1822, 1848 (revised in 1850), and two statutes of procedure of 1872 and 1882. Commercial law was dealt with by codes of 1829 and 1885, the second in force to-day. Military matters were regulated by a penal code of 1882, another of 1884 fixing the organization and attributes of military courts, another of procedure of 1886, and, finally, a code of military law of 1890; aside from many other laws relative to recruitment, organization, etc.

The effect of all these statutes, and of others which in order to avoid details are not enumerated, and which relate to all the fields of public life, has been, as already said, to reform in less than a century the Spanish law; replacing the old régime by that of modern States, and its multiplicity of statutory expressions (which the " Novísima Recopilación " still reflected) by systematic and unitarian statutes applicable throughout the whole of Spain.

The principle of equality before the law had been contradicted, when the century opened, by vestiges of feudal jurisdictions in many regions, and by the existence of special courts for certain classes of society (the clergy, the army, merchants, and others). Even in the enforcement of the criminal law distinctions were made according to the social class of the delinquent, and likewise in the payment of taxes. But the whole spirit of the century, and par-

lativa del régimen local en España," 1812–1909 (Madrid, 1910)   Reference might also be made to chapters 22 to 25 of *Antequera's* "Historia de la legislación española" (4th ed., Madrid, 1895).

ticularly the whole strength of liberalism, were now directed against such exceptions Thanks to those forces, the jurisdictions and " fueros " of special classes have been abolished at different times since 1812, until only those of the army and navy remain.

As regards the relations of Church and State, the Concordat of 1753 was replaced by that of 1851, — following the suppression of the religious orders in 1837, and the mortmain laws of 1837, — and that by one of 1860. But the problem remains unsolved, and has given rise to recent proposals and agitations not yet terminated [1]

The revolution of the continental colonies of America at the beginning of the 1800 s, and the independence which they speedily acquired, put an end in those regions to the authority of the " Leyes de Indias " and their supplements and additions, saving only certain parts taken over into the legislation of the new republics. The problem remained reduced to the Antilles, the Philippines, and other islands. In regard to these, the dominant tendency, and especially as respects Cuba and Puerto Rico, was to consider them not as colonies but as ultramarine provinces, though without adopting on that ground an unlimited policy of administrative assimilation, — in other words, without applying to them, unmodified, all provisions of public law as adopted for the Peninsula. Thus, although in 1878 in making applicable to Cuba the municipal law the island was given again the right to elect deputies to Cortes (which was granted to Puerto Rico in 1869), it was done with considerable restrictions upon the electoral franchise, — greater than in Spain. Similarly there were applied (to both islands), with modifications, the hypothecary legislation of 1880, the Constitution of 1876 in 1881, the code of procedure in 1885, the commercial code in 1886, etc. In 1882 a statute was passed regulating commercial relations between Cuba and Spain, and in 1895 one of political and administrative reforms. For the Philippines the criminal code was promulgated in 1884 (effective beginning with 1886), in 1888 the commercial code, and in 1889 the notarial statute.[2]

§ 36. **Reform of Private Law.** — The same spirit of reform

[1] American readers will find a brief statement of the present status of the question in the article "Church and State in Spain" in the "North American Review" of February, 1911 See also *Luis Morote*, "Los frailes en España" (Madrid, 1904)

[2] Amplifications of this summary, and information regarding other statutes anterior to 1869 can be found in chapter 28 of the book of *Antiquera* cited above

that manifested itself in the public law found expression, albeit with delay and with less disputatiousness and passion, in the private or civil law.   Here too was felt the reformative impulse of the French Revolution and the new currents of idealism that agitated Europe, from the middle of the 1700s onward, within the field of legal speculations.   The effects of this renovation were first made visible, logically enough, in those civil institutions most nearly connected with the public law, or whose public aspect is more striking; and afterwards, as we shall see, the reform spread gradually to other branches more distinctly private, — if indeed such a distinction be strictly permissible.

Taken in the large, the spirit of reform permeated the whole compass of civil law so far as this was regarded in the ideas of that time, as the "positive law" and the "efficient cause" of its changes[1]   It either modified the formative principles that had ruled the past, or introduced novelties totally unconceived of under the old régime   These reforms, nevertheless, do not represent in all their parts a radical change of front significant of the entry into the law of a factor repugnant to those tendencies that had made themselves increasingly evident in civil institutions since the 1200s   Rather may it be said that, on the whole, down to the last third of the 1800s, the reform of the civil law is nothing else than the culmination of the Roman influence, with its characteristic individualism.   This was the consummation on Spanish soil of the victory won by the "Partidas" and the Justinian theories, — excepting only certain points in which the principles of the national law maintained themselves.   A new current in the law peculiar to the present day, and which diverges in many respects from the Romanist tradition, is however observable in the legal ideas of the end of the century, and in the statutes (without precedents in the past) that have widened the field of law under the impulse of new social and economic necessities

The second characteristic of the history of the civil law in this period is that in the reforms of one and the other of these classes there were active influences distinct from those that are noted in earlier centuries   The struggle was no longer merely one between Roman principles and Canon law, on the one hand, and the national

---

[1] [Spanish writers, after treating of the subjects and objects of legal rights, treat the "elemento generador ó causa eficiente" of these , namely such jural *facts* ("hechos") as are not results but causes of legal relations, which special facts they call jural *acts*, "actos jurídicos."   See *e g* *Sánchez Román*, "Estudios de derecho civil," vol. II (2d. ed. 1889–1890), pp 522 *et seq.* — Transl]

medieval law, on the other.   That traditional opposition was now
combined with others, involved in the penetration of ideas derived
from the legislation and legal science of France, England, Germany,
and Italy — from the Code Napoléon, Bentham, Kant, Savigny,
Krause, the Italian Code, and socialist doctrine   All of these give
to the legal history of these years a complexity as yet imperfectly
analyzed and understood, as well as a peculiarly dramatic interest
On one hand is contrasted what is national with what is alien (the
cause of frequent disputes and of declamations very commonly
rhetorical); on the other hand are the various influences just
referred to, each endeavoring to overcome the other, and impose
itself now upon the general course of legal development, now in one
or another institution.   One interesting episode, among others, of
these conflicts was the opposition between the rationalistic spirit of
the jurists educated in the ideas of the 1700 s, and the national and
" customary " spirit (in Spain rather legislative than customary)
of those influenced by the historical school , an episode which, like
all the others, still awaits, in its details, a historian   One result of
it has been a struggle between the partisans of unitarian codification of the civil law and those of regional variants, to which
reference is later made (*post*, §§ 38, 39)

Yet a third characteristic — to whose production the regalianist
traditions of the old régime contributed, on one hand, and on the
other, revolutionary theories — is secularism· the endeavor to
wrest from the jurisdiction and tutelage of the Church and the
Canon law such civil institutions as still remained subjected to
them, — some of which still remain so to-day.

The three characteristics mentioned are supplemented by two
others which we must refer to in more detail· that of the *codification* of the civil law, and that of legislative *unification*, either national, or peculiar to individual regions of the Peninsula, reëlabora-
ating the scattered materials that are the sources of the positive
law, with greater or less additions of elements truly new.

§ 37   **Partial Codifications of the Civil Law prior to the Código
Civil.** — Let us not review summarily the reforms realized prior to
the Civil Code in the different branches of the civil law   They began in the Cortes of Cadiz with a group of provisions which refer
principally to the law of persons and of property.

To the first belong isolated statutes and the articles of the Constitution of 1812 relative to Spaniards and aliens, Americans, the
Indians, and the negro slaves,[1] and reflect as regards the last three

[1] See *R M de Labra*, "La constitución de Cádiz "

classes a spirit of assimilation and liberty, although the emancipation of the negroes was not decreed.

To the second belong five statutes, two of them fundamental in their scope and as expressions of a liberal and individualistic tendency. (1) The decree of August 11, 1811, abolished feudal jurisdictions, and at the same time such services due from the vassals (and this very name itself) as owed their origin to jurisdictional rights; and further the exclusive and prohibitive personal rights of fishing, hearth-wood, mills, and the like, all of which were left to the free enjoyment of the municipalities subject to the common law and to such regulations as should be made in each of these   Therewith the ancient seigniorial and feudal law came to an end, as regards all traces of a legal character.   (2) The decree of June 11, 1813, to the end of "protecting the right of property," declared that all pastures, cultivated estates, or other lands of whatsoever class "held in individual ownership, whether in freehold or in tail" should be forever enclosed or delimited, while other provisions of individualistic and liberal character regulated leases, merchandizing (prohibiting the fixing of prices of provisions), the liberty of sale and commerce in grains, embargo on vegetable products, etc.   Herein was continued and affirmed the spirit of various laws of the 1700 s relating to enclosures (*ante*, § 25) and tending to protect agriculture against the privileges of the grazing interests, or reactive against communistic usages,[1] or embodying ideas hostile to the gilds.   With this decree may be taken (3) the statute of July 19, 1813, abolishing the exclusive and prohibitive property rights of the crown in certain localities of Aragon. — The remaining statutes were (4) the decree of June 10, 1813, for preserving to writers the property of their works during their life and for ten years after death, thus recasting in a broader spirit the regulations of the rights of intellectual property already recognized in the "Novísima Recopilación"; and, finally, (5) the decree of January 4, 1813, which ordered the distribution of waste, crown, and municipal lands, with the exception of enclosed commons.

Of these statutes, the second, third, and last were annulled by the reaction of 1814 (and in part the first); but all three were reestablished by the new constitutional government of 1820.

From that time onward, and very especially after 1833, reforms became every day more numerous and ample.   Thanks to these,

---

[1] See on this *J. Costa*, "Colectivismo agrario," in which the author has also recorded data relative to anti-individualist bills in the Cortes.

the law of property has been profoundly reformed — although
always in the direction indicated and on the basis of Roman conceptions — by the following measures. First, the abolition of
" mayorazgos " and all the species of entailed estates by statute
of October 11, 1820, repealed in 1824, reenacted in 1836 and 1841
Secondly, statutes against mortmain, civil and ecclesiastical,
initiated as early as 1818 by a decree ordering the sale of waste and
crown lands, established more generally in principle in 1820 on the
basis of the decree of 1873, and finally established in full extent by
the statute of May 1, 1855. All of these dispositions, though directed, in legislative intent, only to assuring the alienation of un-
cultivated lands and of the realty of municipalities and religious
corporations, nevertheless in fact reached in their effects the lands
of communal cultivation   This indiscriminate result, though often
due to the heedlessness of the government, was in other cases only
the unconscious expression of the individualistic spirit of the epoch;
which was revealed also in the various dispositions of 1835 and other
years prohibitive of licenses to pasture in stubble (" derrotas ")
and other communal practices.[1] Thirdly, the detailed definition
of the rules regulating expropriation under powers of eminent
domain (statute of July 17, 1836, and others). Fourthly, the
hypothecary system and registry of titles and other real rights.
By this radical change, the old system of implied, general, and judicial hypothecs gave way to one of express and statutory hypothecs, and the registration of claims replaced a system of secrecy
with one of publicity; with other principles of great consequence
in matters of ownership and other rights in realty (statute of 1861,
revised 1870, modified by royal decree of May 20, 1880, and interpreted by various other dispositions). Fifthly, mining legislation,
begun in 1825 and totally renovated in 1868 upon principles which
regulate it to-day. And finally, sundry changes, affecting the use
of inland waters (1880), the acquisition, enjoyment, and encouragement of hunting rights, fixed by a decree of 1835 and later by a
statute of 1879, the disposition of estates unclaimed or in abey-
ance, regulated by a statute of May 16, 1835, industrial property,
which began as a special body of legislation with the decrees of 1826
and 1829, such property being later more amply regulated in a
statute of 1878, the cultivation contracts known as " foros "
(§ 18, *ante*), " sub-foros," grain-rents (" censos frumentarios ")

---

[1] On this see *Altamira*, "Historia de la propiedad comunal" (Madrid,
1890), ch 4, and on the mortmain legislation in general, *Cárdenas* and
Antequera as cited in §§ 18 and 35 above

and annuities " rabassa-morta " (§ 15, *ante*), wherein a change of transcendent influence (already initiated in the 1700s, as already seen) consisted in the redemption of such interests, under a statute enacted in 1873 but suspended in 1874, intellectual property, the principles of 1813–1820 relating to which were modified by various others and finally by the statute of 1879, interest on money loaned, abolished by a law of 1856 and fixed at five per cent as the legal rate by a statute of 1899, appraisement of preferential rights of purchase (§ 22, *ante*, " retractos "), of terminating leases (" desahucios "), and other real rights, modified expressly or implicitly by the code of civil procedure (1881), leases, — law of 1842, and other subjects.

With regard to the law of persons, one may note the statutes relative to religious orders, — those of 1837 suppressing them, modifying them, fixing their rights to hold property, etc., the Concordat of 1851, and others, statutes relative to the abolition of slavery in the colonies (1873, 1880); those relative to liberty of industry and commerce, which put an end to the gilds; those relating to " gracias al sacar," *i.e.* to the concession of emancipation, legitimation, dispensation of age, of capacity, and other matters of ministerial discretion (1838); those of 1852 fixing the civil capacities of aliens, that of 1880 defining civil incapacity; those of 1878 for the protection of children; and various others of civil incapacity relative to the rights of manual workers, — association, strikes, accidents, etc [1] Of capital importance is the statute of 1870, which subjected to civil registry the facts of birth, death, marriage, and naturalization, secularizing them and their documentary proof.

The family law is particularly treated in certain statutes that have not essentially modified the organization or the relations between its members, — such as the royal decree of 1876 fixing the rights of unemancipated children; that of 1862 relative to paternal consent as a precondition of marriage (compare its precedent of the 1700s), various dispositions of the code of civil procedure relative to minors, tutelage, etc , and other statutes of lesser importance. Of great importance was the statute of civil marriage enacted in 1870, which secularized that institution in its legal aspects, respecting the Catholic sacrament but subjecting all citizens to the direct intervention of the State in the celebration of the contract.

---

[1] For legislation in this field of the civil law, to-day of so great and constantly increasing importance, consult the publications of the "Instituto de Reformas Sociales."

This statute, however, was repealed by a decree of 1875, and a modified renewal of it was never realized.

As for the law of succession, a single modification was made respecting intestacy, by a statute of 1836, which, in default of descendants, ascendants, and collateral relatives within four degrees, recognized the successive claims of "natural" children recognized by their father, the decedent's spouse (in the absence of separation between them), and collaterals of the fifth to the tenth degree inclusive. In 1881 a general registry of last wills and testaments was established in the Ministry of Grace and Justice

We may also mention, because of its importance for the establishment and guaranty of titles in many acts of civil character, the statute regulative of "the public faith" (notarial statute of 1862, revised in 1873 and 1874).

And finally, it is to be noted that in the 1800s there was brought about, and that very early, a complete legal differentiation of the civil and commercial law, thanks to the publication of the commercial code of 1829.

§ 38. **History of the Redaction of the Present "Código Civil."** — The movement for codification of the law, which appeared in Spain as in the other countries of Europe, reflecting a tendency general throughout the world, and producing the same struggles as those which in France and Germany are particularly associated with the names of Thibaut and Savigny, represented in Spain two fundamental ideas. One of them, traditional since the 1400s, was the remedy of the confusion resultant from the variety and disorder of legislation, particularly in Castile, — a necessity left unsatisfied, as is well known, by the "Novisima Recopilación." The other and new one was the unification and modernization of the whole law.

As regards unification, strictly considered, without confusing with this the introduction of new principles, — so far, that is to say, as such unification was to be accomplished upon the basis of the actual law and not through its reform, — the question was really, at the opening of the century, rather one of form than of substance; inasmuch as there had been slowly progressing in both the public and the private law (of Castile) a unification which in civil matters was based upon the primacy of the system embodied in the "Partidas" and in the fundamental statutes of the 1500s to 1700s.[1]

---

[1] On this see *Altamira*, "Cuestiones preliminares," ch. 6, and particularly pp 111–116   A writer so little to be suspected of modernism as *Domingo de Morató* has written as follows in his "Estudios de ampliación de historia

The codifiers of the last century aspired, however, to something further. They desired, on one hand, to introduce novelties suggested by the ideas of the period, and above all by the necessities that social and economic changes were creating; and, on the other hand, to fuse in a single mass the diverse civil legislation of Castile, Aragon, Catalona, Navarre, and the Basque Provinces. This made the problem more complex, and gave origin to various important questions to which reference will be made below. As for the manner of its realization, the ideal of many jurists was the redaction of a single code that should embody the whole matter of the civil law; but because of the delays that marked its preparation, and the urgency of necessities, that matter was in fact embodied, in its different branches or subjects, in various groups of statutes, of which only a part have been taken over into the " Código Civil."

The history of the Code is not a simple one. It begins with an article (259) of the Constitution of Cadiz that lays down at once the principles of unification and codification. " a single Civil Code shall be in force in all the dominions of the Spanish monarchy," — an ideal which was repeated in more general form in the Constitutions of 1869 and 1876 Neither the Cortes of Cadiz, nor those of the second constitutional period, succeeded in realizing even the formulation of a draft for a civil code, although in both periods it was attempted. The first work officially accomplished toward that end was that done by the Code Commission of 1843–1846 (namely books 1 and 2, and part of book 3). The Commission that succeeded this one was able to advance farther, delivering to the government in 1851 the draft of a complete code,[1] chiefly based upon the Castilian civil law, with the addition of a number of principles taken from the regional laws and others taken from foreign systems, especially from the French. After the rejection of this draft, the ideal reappeared in 1880, and now with the decided aim of fusing the Castilian civil law with that of the other regions of the Peninsula; to which end there were incorporated in the Code Commission members representing Aragon, Catalonia, Majorca, Navarre, Biscay, and Galicia. The

de los códigos españoles" (3d ed., Valladolid, 1884), p 312 : "But considering the same question from a practical point of view, we may recall what has been pointed out in the introductory essay, namely, that though the legislator has indeed stood still, the procedure and judgments of the courts have reduced legislation in the field of civil law almost to a unitarian system through the preference, little less than exclusive, conceded to the Código de las Siete Partidas over all earlier codes "

[1] Relative to this see the book of *F. Garcia Goyena*, "Concordancias, motivos y comentarios del Código civil español" (Madrid, 1852, 4 vols).

presence of the last, representing a region included in the territory of the Castilian crown, presupposed a recognition, within that, of peculiarities which it was thought necessary to preserve; but at the same time indicates very clearly the illogical attitude of the jurists of that time, inasmuch as Galicia (as is notorious, and as we shall point out below) is not the only region that has peculiar civil institutions, and, there being others, it was unjust to make an exception in favor of one alone

Nevertheless the draft for a uniform Code (or at least one general for the Peninsula) came to nothing The foral territories manifested with the utmost clearness their aspiration to conserve intact their own law, without fusion with the Castilian; and, indeed, even to exclude wholly the influence of this.

In 1881 the Minister of Grace and Justice, Manuel Alonso Martinez, presented to the Cortes, first a statute embodying the principles of a Code (" Ley de Bases "), and afterward the partial text of one, but his labor was rendered fruitless through political changes In 1885 another minister, Sr Silvela, presented in his turn another draft of principles (" bases ") which became law on May 11, 1888. By this the government was authorized to publish a Code that should be prepared by the Section of Civil Law of the General Code Commission, and which should comprise the Castilian law alone; as regards the " provinces and territories in which there exists a foral law " it was declared that this should be respected "for the time being, in all its integrity, without alteration of their present legal system by the publication of the Code, which shall there possess in any of such regions merely an authority supplementary of gaps that may exist in its special law."   The Code was accordingly published by royal decree of October 6, 1888, and after discussion in the Cortes a new and revised edition was prepared in 1889, which is that now in force [1]

§ 39. **General Character and Limitations of the " Código Civil."** — Neither the exposition of the doctrine of the Code (a part of actual legislation), nor even the critical appraisement of its innovations and its tendency,[2] are desirable in this place; but we may

---

[1] For a detailed history of the preparation of the Code see vol I of *Sanchez Roman*, "Estudios de derecho civil" (2d ed., Madrid, 1899), ch 27–29

[2] For this see especially, beside the commentaries on it (*Manresa, Costa*, etc), the book of *Sanchez Roman* just cited , that of *A Comas*, "El proyecto del código civil," (Madrid, 1884), the speeches pronounced in the Cortes in the discussion of the bill — particularly a few, such as those of *Azcárate*, and the articles published in this connection in the press, as e g the anonymous ones that came out in the newspaper "La Justicia "

properly indicate, as historical data, the influences which it principally expresses, and some of the more notable reforms that
it introduced.   The former were very varied, nor were they
united in the Code in subjection to any organic conception.   The
individualist principle naturally predominates, being that which is
dominant with jurists; but with vacillations, — which nevertheless do not do satisfaction to other tendencies in legal thought, nor
even afford them expression, as may be seen, among other details,
in the title improperly styled " Of the community of property,"
and in the deficient regulation of social or juristic persons, and of
contracts which relate to the industrial relations of laborers.   In
this respect the Civil Code presents many less novelties than might
off-hand be expected.   Such as exist refer principally to a few
institutions (tutelage, the family council, preferential rights of
purchase, heirs' compulsory share, etc) which either represent a
national tradition or one borrowed from foreign legislation, especially from the Italian Code; but which do not, we repeat, characterize the work as a whole.   As regards its content, the new statute
does not satisfy the aspirations for codification, not alone because
of its many " lacunæ," which it will be necessary to fill gradually
with special statutes, but also because it left untouched not a few
such anterior to itself, such as the statutes of civil registry, hypothecary law, waters, mines, hunting and fisheries, etc.

Aside from all this, the Code has opened up three interesting
problems, which, because of their historical relations, we should
here consider that of the non-Castilian legislations (a problem
which we have seen was planted with us before the Code), that of
judicial interpretation, and that of the customary law.

As regards the non-Castilian or foral systems, the Civil Code
contains a few general provisions that became obligatory in those
territories, abrogating all law in opposition to them; but in other
matters it is only supplementary, — subordinate to natural reason
and equity in Aragon, to the Canon and Roman law (" dret
comú ") in Catalonia, to the Roman law and the " Partidas " in
Navarre.   There remain in pendency, however, in this connection, two further elements· first, the question of the formulation
of the appendices of " foral institutions which it is desirable to
conserve," forepromised in article 6 of the law-of-bases, and
secondly, the spread of the Castilian law through the decisions of
the Supreme Court, which passes in the last instance upon appeals
from the whole of Spain.

Nothing has been done officially with reference to the appen-

dices of foral law whose preparation is commanded by article 7 of
the statute just mentioned.   That of Aragon is already in writing,
but awaits revision, and of course has not been promulgated.[1]
That of Catalonia, prepared by Sr Trias, following the deliberations and labors of the " Academia de Derecho " of Barcelona, has
been presented to the government, but has likewise not been promulgated [2] The appendices for the other foral territories have not
even been redacted, although the elements for their formulation
are to be found in the books of Morales y Gomez, as respects
Navarre (Pamplona, 1884);   Ripoll y Palou, as respects the
Balearic Islands (Palma, 1885);   Lecanda, as respects Biscay
(Madrid, 1888);   and Lopez de Lago, as respects Galicia (Madrid,
1885).

The question how far the doctrines of the Castilian law may or
do exert influence upon the foral law of the provinces, through the
judgments of the Supreme Court, is one which preoccupies especially the jurists of Catalonia.   Among them it gives rise to obsti-
nate discussions, the importance of which for us lies in the historical
character of the phenomenon which they suggest, — one so often
repeated in former centuries, — and in the consequences which it
may have in the elaboration of a common law of the future if its
action continues.[3]

It should be noted with reference to such judge-made law that
the Code does not include it among the sources of the law; thus it
denies not only a doctrine recognized elsewhere in existing statutes, as e g in the Code of Civil Procedure, but — what is more
grave — a positive fact, which has made itself felt in all periods,
and will continue to do so notwithstanding the Code: the vital
and creative force of the decisions of the courts.   The question

[1] On Aragonese law that must be considered as of actual authority see :
Lapeña, "Fueros y observancias vigentes en Aragón" ;   meetings of the
"Congreso   de   Jurisconsultos   aragoneses, — conclusiones   votadas" ;
Franco López, "Memoria sobre el derecho civil aragonés" (Zaragoza, 1886) ;
Colegio de Abogados de Huesca, "Informe sobre la Memoria," just cited ;
the earlier volumes of Franco Guillén, "Institucíones del derecho civil
aragonés" (Zaragoza, 1841), A. Blas, "Derecho civil aragonés" (Madrid,
1873), and Costa, "La libertad civil y el Congreso de jurisconsultos
aragoneses" (Madrid, 1883)

[2] On the Catalan law see   Durán y Bas, "Memoria," cited above in § 15
n   4 (Barcelona, 1883),   "Exposicion del Instituto agrícola catalán
de San Isidro al Ministro de Gracia y Justicia (1890),   Brocá and
Amell, cited above, § 15, n 1 : and the works cited below in § 40

[3] See Antoni Maria Donell, "El codic civil a Catalunya" (Barcelona,
n.d.— 1904), Q. Marti y Miralles, "La questió de la parcería" (Barcelona,
1904) and "La questió de la parcería y la moral del advocat" (Barcelona, 1905) ; E. Saguer y Olivet, "De la parcería y'l judíci de desahuci"
(Gerona, 1905).

possesses undeniable practical importance, which cannot here be examined; but historical as well (for which reason we point it out), inasmuch as the Code, in overlooking it, ignores an essential factor in the history of the civil law (and of all legal systems), and may give rise to perturbations of a grave nature in future legal developments.[1]

§ 40   **The " Código Civil" and the Customary Law.** — Of even graver import, if that be possible, is the doctrine of the Code relative to customary law, — though indeed it here only repeats, in part, notions current among jurists of the old school, unenlightened by the ideas of the historical school of Savigny, and its derivatives. The Code denies, namely, all value to customs opposed to statutes; and with regard to such as are opposed to no legal precedents because dealing with matters unforeseen by the legislator, it admits the suppletory character of local, but not of general, customs.

Now it is notorious to every one who knows the legal life of the Spanish people (or that of any other), not from books but from the observation of realities, that custom contrary to the statute-book, alike in questions of civil, administrative, political, or other law, is continually produced, frequently prevails in practice, and oftentimes has in its favor not only the assent of the public and the force therefrom derived, but also the principles of justice, — of law that is adjusted to the circumstances, — which the statute does not always possess; and is therefore preferable to the precept of the legislator.

Without discussing the question here under its general aspects (or, as is commonly said, " theoretically "),[2] it must be remarked, as a fact falling within our historical purpose, that the actual civil legislation — the Civil Code, and special statutes; foral codes or compilations, etc. — does not comprise by any means all the positive civil law of Spain; but that this remains to a considerable extent a law of customs, not alone local but general as well, whether contrary or not to the statute-book, and that this in the majority of cases is a continuation of earlier historic conditions, with profound rootage in the spirit of the people, — a spirit which does not merely conserve forms of the past, but continues to modify them,

---

[1] The question was discussed in the Congreso Jurídico of Madrid in 1886 (reports by *Costa, Giner de los Rios, Oliver,* and *Pantoja*) and in that of Barcelona (as the principal thesis) in 1888 (reports by *Gil Robles* and *Plá,* and critiques by various others), See *Altamira,* "Cuestiones preliminares," ch 4, no 9

[2] *Altamira,* "Cuestiones preliminares," ch. 4, nos 1-8.

also by way of custom, following the compass of the times and molding them to new necessities.

However vast the domain of custom may remain to-day, as it has always been,[1] its scope begins at least to be seen, thanks to the investigations of Sr. Costa and of his imitators and disciples, which are revealing the existence of this form of legal life in many regions of Spain   And it is to be noted that its existence is proveable, not only in the regions of foral law, where the statutory law itself has at times assembled it, giving it a written form (as in Aragon, Catalonia, and elsewhere),[2] but in those of Castile as well in spite of the general belief that the statute-book has there imposed itself upon everything and has made everything in life uniform.   It suffices, if one would inform himself of it, to read the essays published [3] upon the customary law of León, Ciudad Real, Galicia, Castilla la Vieja, Mancha, Alicante, Aliste, Salamanca, Asturias, etc., and those upon general agricultural customs, [4] and the very "Memorias " of the registers of property themselves (under the caption of " especialidades," and at times outside of it) refer to numerous living customs in the midst of the Castilian and Valencian territories [5]

The customary law, then, continues to be an essential in the present history of the civil law (and in part of the public), and one must bear in mind its reality in defining the other's contemporary phase, which the uninterrupted succession of events is casting every day into the history of the past; the only history which is vulgarly considered as such, although it is nourished by the present, and is at once creator and offspring of this.

§ 41   **Legal Science and Literature of the Period.** — Spanish legal science in the 1800s does not show a flowerage so abundant as that in the preceding centuries whose history has been outlined; although it can show notable writers, especially in the fields of public, civil (Spanish), and criminal law, and in legal history.

[1] See the same work, ch 5
[2] In Catalonia jurists are at present giving much attention to the customary law, and to the question of the weight it should be given in practice. See e g J D Torroella, "Lo dret civil gironi" (Mataró, 1899), and Borrell, as cited in "Cuestiones preliminares," supra
[3] In the volume by Costa and others, "Derecho consuetudinario"; in the prize essays of the "Academia de Ciencias Morales y Políticas"; in the "Anales" of the University of Oviedo, etc
[4] Espejo, "Memoria" upon customary agricultural contracts in the whole Peninsula
[5] See on this point Altamira, "El método positivo en el derecho civil" in "La Nueva Ciencia Jurídica" of May, August, and September of 1892, where some of these peculiarities are mentioned

The Romanists and Canonists, exceedingly few in number, have not the importance of those of the 1500 s, 1600 s, or even of the 1700 s

Salient facts of the century were· A double influence, French and English in political and administrative law, represented by distinctive groups of liberal refugees at the beginning, and of doctrinaires in the middle of the century;[1] the influence, first of the German Krause, and later of French positivism, upon legal philosophy (thus marking a triple influence of Germany, England, and France), and that of the Italian anthropological school in criminal law, succeeding to that of the German Roder and the reformative school   The influence of the Krausian philosophy has been particularly profound   It sprang from the translation of Ahrens' "Cours de droit naturel" (Paris, 1838) made by Navarro Zamorano in 1841, and from the lectures of Professor Sanz del Rio in his chair of philosophy in the University of Madrid; and went so far as the formation of a school, which — with more or less modification of Krausian principles by the doctrines of the historical and positivist schools, and after exposure to the influence of Ahrens, Roder, and other writers of similar tendency — finally attained a certain character of originality.   The course of the current may still be noted in those jurists who maintain a hostile attitude toward it, or in those who, without going to that extreme, maintain a certain independence of doctrine

Noteworthy jurists of one or the other of these different tendencies (and of others still, such as the Catholic school, so called) have been[2] Pacheco, Alvarez, Vizmanos, Hernandez de la Rua, and Silvela in criminal law, Garcia Goyena, Cortina, Alvarez, Perez Hernandez, Cepeda, Laserna y Montalban, Gutierrez, Vives y Cebriá, Alonso Martinez, Durán y Bas, Perez Pujol, Manresa Galindo de Vera, Escosura, Comas and Costa, in civil law; Arguelles, Florez Estrada, Alcalá Galiano, Pacheco, Donoso, Rios Rosas, Olózaga, Bravo Murillo, Cos Gayon, Colmeiro, Alcubilla, Cánovas Silvela, Martos, Costa, and others in political and administrative law; Ortiz de Zuñiga, Diez de Salcedo, Carromolino,

---

[1] The French influence is the better known and of more abundant literature   The English influence demands a special study, which has not yet been attempted

[2] A bibliography of Spanish legal literature, which although not complete is very abundant, has been published by *Torres Campos*, "Bibliografía española contemporánea del derecho y de la política" (2 vols, Madrid, 1883 and 1898, covering respectively the periods 1800–1880 and 1881–1896).

The text here does not purport to deal with living jurists

Viado, Vicente y Caravantes, Castro y Orozco, Reus, Arrazola, and Manresa, in the law of procedure, Gonzalez Huebra, Marti Eixalá Durán, etc., in commercial law; Aguirre, Inguanzo, Salazar, Aguilar, and La Fuente, in Canon law; Orfila and Mata, in medical jurisprudence. The principal cultivators of the philosophy of law, properly speaking, are still living. As for the historians, they have been numerous throughout the century, from Martinez Marina, who wrote several of his works after 1808, to Joaquin Costa, one of the most versatile and erudite of Spanish writers and a scholar of the most exalted ideals.

PART IX

THE CHURCH

PART IX. THE CHURCH[1]

§ 1   Classification of the Sources   § 4   Later Canon Law.
      of Church Law.   § 5. Judicial Decisions
§ 2   Early Canon Law   § 6. Treatises; the Canonists
§ 3   Medieval Canon Law; Gra-   § 7. Influence of Canon Law on
      tian's Decretum to the   Secular Law.
      "Corpus Juris Canonici "

§ 1. **Classification of the Sources of Church Law.**[2] — Like every society, the Church, or society of the faithful, has its rules, and the Church's are known as Canon Law (" χανών," rule). Canon law, during the Middle Ages, was a " common " law for Europe; it shared in the authority conceded to the Roman law, and, like the latter, played an important part in forming the modern secular systems of law. It had its source in Holy Scripture as well as in the Roman law. From the former were taken many rules, either by the Customs, or by the ecclesiastical authorities legislating or making regulations as Councils or Synods, Popes or Bishops. — From the Sacred Books (as defined by the Church)[3] were drawn such institutions as the tithe and the canonic admonition, such principles as the prohibition of loans on interest, and the maxim " testis unus, testis nullus " (Deuteronomy, xix, 15). The writings of the Fathers of the Church served to round out and interpret the Scriptures.[4] During the period of the for-

---

[1] [This part is translated from pp 126–149 (with a few omissions) of Professor J. Brissaud's "History of French Private Law." For this work and author, see the Editorial Preface — Transl]

[2] Bibliography — *Maassen*, "Geschichte der Quellen und der Literatur des Canon. Rechts im Abendlande," 1870 (up to the time of the False Decretals) , *F. von Schulte*, "Die Geschichte der Quellen u Literatur des Canon Rechts von Gratian bis auf Gregor IX," 1875–1880 , *Phillips*, "Das Kirchenrecht," 3d ed , 1855 *et seq* , French translation by *Crouzet*, "Le droit ecclésiast. dans ses sources," 1852 , *Dodd*, "History of Canon Law," 1884; *Walter*, "Lehrb d Kirchenrechts," 1871 ; *Hinschius* in *Holtzendorff*, "Realencyclopadie d christlichen Alterthumer," published by Krauss, 1882–1886 ; *Tardif*, "Histoire des sources du droit canonique," 1887 (with a detailed bibliography, p. 8 *et seq*) , "Digesto Italiano," *s v.* "Diritto canonico," VI, 1, *Viollet*, "Hist. du dr civ franc ," p. 29 *et seq.*

[3] For the last time by the Council of Trent, session IV.

[4] "Corpus scriptorum ecclesiasticorum,", edited by the Academy of

mation of these laws, the Roman Law was the temporal law of
the Church, and although it was not originally the law of the
clergy, it became so in the end.   Councils and Popes, and Church
practice especially, drew inspiration therefrom, thus, the procedure followed in the ecclesiastical courts is derived from the
Roman procedure of the Later Empire.

   (A) *Canons of the Councils.*[1] — The councils or assemblies of
Bishops were ecumenical, national, or provincial, according as
their resolutions were received by the entire Church, by a national
Church, or by an ecclesiastical province.   The diocesan synods
laid down rules applicable only to a diocese.

   (B) *Decretals of the Popes.*[2] — The letters of the popes are continuations of the Epistles of the Apostles; thus they are called
" litteræ apostolicæ," " epistolæ "; as the pontifical chancery
drew its inspiration from the traditions and usages of the chancery
of the Roman Emperors, they have also been termed, on the example of the Imperial Constitutions, " rescripta," " constitutiones," or " decreta."   Thus is explained the name " Epistolæ
decretales " or Decretals.[3]

Vienna; *Migne*, "Patrologie grecque," 1857–1866 ; "Patrol. latine,"
1844–1855
   [1] Compilations of the Canons of the Councils (non-official) · *Labbe*,
1674 , *Hardouin*, 1715; *Coleti*, 1734 , *Mansi*, 1759; "Collectio Lacensis"
(of the Jesuits of Maria-Laach, containing modern councils), 1870–1890 ,
Bruns, "Canones apostolorum et conciliorum sæculorum IV, V, VI, VII,"
1839, *Maassen*, "Consilia aevi merovingici," M G H.L.S , III, vol I
(1893); *Sirmond*, "Concilia Galliæ," 1629 , Cf *Hefele*, "Concilienge-
schichte," French translation by *Goschler* and *Delarc*, 1869 (2d German
edition, 1873, continued by *Hergenroether*, 1887) , *Mgr Guerin*, "Les
sources théologiques, Les Conciles," new edition, 1896 , "Monum. Concil
gen. s XV," edited by the Academy of Sciences of Vienna, 1857 *et seq.*
   [2] There is no complete collection of the Papal Bulls — *D Coustant*,
"Epist. roman. Pontif ," 1721, and *Thiel*, 1868 (until 523); the "Bullaire
romain de Cocquelines," 1739 to 1857, stops with Gregory XVI   For
enactments of the popes of recent date see the "Acta Sanctæ Sedis," published in Rome since 1865, and Reviews such as the "Analecta juris
pontifici" and the 'Archiv. f. Kathol Kirchenrecht." The inventories
of *Jaffe* (2d ed , 1885) and of *Potthast* (1875), "Regesta pontif roman "
go as far as 1305, *Pflugk-Hartung*, "Acta pont rom." 1880–1886 , "Char-
tarum pont rom. Specimina," 1885–1887 , *Pressuti*, "Regesta Honorii
P ," 1888   The School of Rome has already published "Registers" of
several of the popes (for example Boniface VIII, Nicholas IV) (*Giry*, p.
685)   The "Liber Pontificalis," edited by the Abbé Duchesne, 1886, is
a compilation of the lives of the popes from St Peter to the end of the
800 s, begun about 530 or shortly after 514, and continued until Etienne
VI   On the Pontifical Chancery, see *Giry*, "Diplomatique," p. 664,
682 , *Breslau*, "Hand d Urkundenlehre," I, 67 , *Valois*, "B Ch ," 1881,
257 , *De Mas Latrie*, R des q h , 1886–1887; "Istoria della romana Can-
celleria," 1769
   [3] In the utterances of the popes one may distinguish 1st, legislative
enactments , 2d, judicial decisions ("rescripta ad lites"); 3d, grants of
benefices , 4th, administrative instructions or circulars

In our own time different terms have become current: papal letters, bulls, writs. The *Papal Letters* are addressed to the entire Catholic population. The word *Bull* (an official term) originally designated the hanging seal attached to the Papal Letter; later it was used (1200s) to designate the letter itself (" litteræ bullatæ "), and it was contrasted with the *Writ* (" breve "). Upon the lead seals of the Bulls is found, on one side, the effigy of St. Peter and St. Paul, on the other, the name of the reigning pope. Bulls are written in Latin, with a great wealth of formulæ; the name of the pope is accompanied by the epithet " episcopus servus servorum Dei." For these deeds a script called " littera Sancti Petri," or "bullaticum teutonicum," was used, — so difficult to read that a copy was appended in the current script, this cumbersome usage was abolished by a " motu proprio " of Leo XIII (Dec. 29, 1878), which, however, preserves the leaden seal for documents creating or abolishing Bishoprics All other documents should have the red seal, stamped with the heads of St. Peter and St. Paul and bearing the name of the reigning pope The *Writs* are less solemn documents than the Apostolic Letters, their style is simple, their script has always been the ordinary cursive writing; they bear the stamp in red ink representing St. Peter in his boat (first used under Clement IV, 1268). Bulls and Writs are cited by their opening words, thus, the Bull " Pastor æternus." [1] The *Motu Proprio*, since Innocent VIII (1484–1492), written on parchment, without any seal, with the clause " motu proprio mandamus " (of his own accord and not upon a request), relate especially to the Pontifical Court and to the government of the States of the Holy See.[2]

(C) *Custom.* — " Illa autem quæ non scripta sunt sed tradita custodimus," says St. Augustine.[3] The Church has its traditions and its usages, which are no less respected than its laws. It is especially through custom that the early law of the Church was formed, for the ecclesiastical legislative power could not act freely until the time of the Christian Emperors. Later on, within the Catholic Church, itself, custom strengthened the national and particularist tendencies The need of uniformity which troubles the Roman Church is entirely modern. Until our own day each Diocese had its special usages. The Gallicans were ardent defenders of customs; Fleury seems even to place them above the law, — there is

---

[1] To the Decretals of the popes should be likened the diocesan regulations such as " Capitula episcoporum " Cf Tardif, p 130.
[2] Giry, pp. 708 et seq
[3] Augustine, "Ep." 118; Schwering, "Z. Lehre v d. Kanon. Gewohnheitsrecht" 1888; Baudoin, "De consuetudine in jure canonico," 1888.

no true law, says he, unless it be accepted by custom, and he gives
as an example the abrogation by custom of the prohibition against
eating the blood of strangled animals [1]   Custom is especially
seen in the judicial decisions and the works of the jurists.[2]   The
Decretum of Gratian and the Decretals of Gregory IX require
that the custom shall be ancient, that it shall have been in existence
forty years (the period of prescription against the Church), that
it shall be reasonable and not contrary to the faith or to the fundamental laws of the Church and good morals.   Subject to these
conditions, it may derogate from the positive law or add to it.[3]

§ 2   Early Canon Law — (1) *Greek Compilations falsely attributed
to the Apostles* [4] — The most important are the *Doctrine of the
Twelve Apostles* (end of the first century or beginning of the second),[5] the *Constitutions of the Apostles* (300s) rejected even in the
East by the Council " in Trullo " (692), and the *Canons of the
Apostles* (200s or 300s) looked upon as authentic in the East (692),
but not in the West, moreover the first fifty Canons passed into the
compilation of Denys le Petit and into the " Corpus juris canonici "

(B) *Latin Compilations.* — These were originally private works
like the Greek compilations, of which they were often no more than
translations ("Itala" or "Prisca," " Isidoriana " or " Hispana ").[6]
The ecclesiastical laws are arranged in them in chronological order.
After the 110s official compilations are found, and the texts are
classified according to subjects.

(C) *Compilation of Denys le Petit.* — Denys le Petit (" Diony-
sius Exiguus," as he called himself in humility) was a Scythian
monk who passed the greater portion of his life at Rome; he died
there before 555.   He is credited with having introduced the cus-

---

[1] *Fleury*, "Institution au droit ecclésiastique," I, 2.
[2] The rituals often contain usages bearing upon the law : *D Martene*,
"De antiquis Ecclesiæ ritibus " *Tardif*, p. 238, cites the "ordines romani"
and the Pontificals   *Migne*, "Patrol lat ," vol. 88; *Mabillon*, "Mus.
italic," vol II
[3] Dist XI, c 4, 6, 7, XII, c 4, 6, 7, 8, 11, VIII, c 4, 7, 8; X, I,
4, 11.
[4] *Harnack*, "Texte u Untersuch z Gesch. d altchr. Literatur," II,
1884, *De Lagarde*, "Reliquiæ juris ecclesiastici antiquissimi," 1856;
Achelis, "Die altesten Quellen des orientalischen Kirchenrechts, Canones
Hippolyti," 1891, "Constitutiones Apostolorum," *Lagarde's* edition,
1862, *Bruns*, "Canones Apostolorum," 1839, *Pitra*, "Jus eccles græc.
hist et monum ," 1864
[5] The "Didaché," discovered in 1883, was studied by *Jacquier*, "La
Doctr des 12 Ap ," 1891.   *Cf. Viollet* p. 45, *Tardif*, p 47, B crit.,
1884; B d q hist , 1886
[6] So called because it formed a part of the compilation attributed to
Isidore of Seville   The "Capitula" of *Martin de Braga*, 572, were looked
upon with great favor.

tom of reckoning the calendar from the birth of Christ. Towards the end of the 400 s he translated into Latin (from a Greek compilation which has not come down to us), the canons of the most ancient Councils up to the Council of Carthage in 419. He prefaced this translation with the first fifty canons of the Apostles (whence the name " Codex Canonum"). To this compilation he soon added another which included the Decretals of the popes from Siricius (384) to Anastasius (489) So great was the authority accorded this double collection, that in 774 Pope Hadrian sent a manuscript copy of it ("Codex Hadrianeus") to Charlemagne, who published it as a law of the Empire (802).[1]

(D) *False Decretals or Pseudo-Isidore.*[2] — Toward the middle of the 800 s, there appeared in France a collection of ecclesiastical laws which passed for the work of Isidore of Seville, was cited by the Councils, invoked by the popes, and enjoyed the greatest authority until the 1500 s; when it was found to include many documents not genuine. This collection consisted of three groups of documents: 1st. Following a preface (borrowed from the compilation called " Hispana " or " Isidoriana "), and a few forged documents, came the Canons of the Apostles, the letters of the early popes from Clement to Melchiades (97 to 314), and the famous gift of Constantine to the Pope Sylvester (fifty-eight forged documents). 2d Canons of the Eastern, Greek, African, Gaulish, and Spanish Councils, to the time of the Council of Toledo (694). This part is hardly anything more than a reproduction of the canons contained in the compilation of ecclesiastical laws of the beginning of the 700 s, called the " Hispana " (because made in Spain) or " Isidoriana " (because attributed, without any reason, to Isidore of Seville).[3] 3d. Letters of the popes from the time of Sylvester (335) to Gregory II (731) (thirty-five forged documents).

[1] *Migne,* "Patrol lat," vol. 67; *Voel and Justel,* "Bibhoteca juris canonici," 1661. Bibl. in *Holtzendorff,* p. 166, *Cassiodorus,* "De divin. lect instit," c 23 The "Codex Carolinus," compiled in 791 by Charlemagne's orders, is a collection of the Letters from the popes to Charles Martel, to Pépin le Bref, and to Charlemagne himself· *Migne,* "Patrol. lat," vol. 98

[2] *Hinschius,* "Decretales Pseudo-Isidorianæ," 1863; *Tardif,* p. 140, *Patetta,* "R. ital. p 1 sc giurid," 1890 (two MSS. of the False Decretals), *Maassen,* "Pseudo-Isidore Stud," 1885, *Conrat,* I, 308.

[3] This "Collectio Hispana" or "Isidoriana," must not be confused with the "Versio Hispana" or "Isidoriana," merely a translation of the Greek Councils, made in the 500 s The forged Isidore used the "C. Hispana," not in the form which it had in the 600 s, but in that which it took on in the 700 s, Maassen seems to have proved that this "Hispana" had already been amended in the same way as had the texts of the forged Isidore. Cf. MS. of *Autun,* Vatican, 1341, and *Migne,* "Patrol lat," vol. 84.

The forged documents contained in this compilation were not made out of whole cloth by the author; he made use of elements borrowed from the most varied sources: Scripture, Fathers of the Church, Eusebius, Cassiodorus, the "Liber Pontificalis," and the Breviary of Alaric The documents, thus put together from authentic extracts more or less altered, were falsely placed under the names of the oldest popes, no doubt with the object of giving them a greater weight of authority

The *Date* of the composition of the False Decretals was probably between 847 and 853 They used the False Capitularies (written at the earliest in 847); the first trace of this compilation is to be found in the " narratio " of the clerks irregularly ordained in 841 by the deposed Bishop of Reims, Ebbo, and ousted in 853 by Hincmar, and in 857 they were cited at the " conventus " of Kiersy.[1] As to *Locality*, it used to be thought that Riculf, Archbishop of Mayence (787–814), had received this compilation from Spain. But this was not possible, for the "Hispana " was the only one made use of in Spain until the 1100s; the latter compilation alone could have been brought, and really was brought, into France. And it is in France that the False Decretals must have been written; for the manuscripts are of French origin, and the expressions met with in the apocryphal documents refer to the Frankish Empire ("seniores," " missi," etc.) , moreover, use was made of the False Capitularies, the Breviary of Alaric and its summaries, and the "Codex Hadrianeus,"[2] all of which were official or semiofficial works in France. As this compilation is cited for the first time in 853 in the diocese of Reims, it is probable that it was written at Reims. The disturbances which the deposition of Ebbo gave rise to account for its composition; they were the occasion if not the cause of it, as is proved by the important place given therein to the texts on the deposition of bishops, which obviously had in view the case of Ebbo.[3] Who was their *Author?* Coming from the same place as that in which the False Capitularies were got together, bearing the same date, made in the same way, and written in the same spirit, was their author then the same person? Is he

---

[1] In 852 the False Decretals were also cited in the "Capitula" issued to his clergy by Hincmar *Fournier*, N.R H , 1887, p 92

[2] And of the French compilation called "Quesnelliana" (400 s or 500 s), after its first editor *Quesnel*, "Opp Leon Magni," II, 1675 , it contained about the same subjects as the compilation of Denys, but the latter compilation led to its being forgotten

[3] The False Decretals used formerly to be located at Mainz : but there was nothing in the affairs of the Church of this diocese which could furnish a pretext for a compilation of this nature

that mysterious Benedictus Levita to whom no doubt the "Capitula Angilramni" (850?) should be attributed?[1]　The respected
name of Isidore of Seville is found at the head of the preface,
coupled in certain manuscripts with that of "Mercator," and in
others with the word "Peccator", the latter name the illustrious
Bishop would be supposed to adopt out of humility; the former
was due to a phrase in the preface to a translation of the discourses of Nestorius by Marius Mercator, a contemporary of
St Augustine.

With what *Object* was this bold forgery made? Had the author
the well-defined end of enlarging papal authority over the Church,
and the Church's over the State? Did he wish to create a basis
for these new powers?

In the False Decretals some have seen the source of the preponderance of the Holy See during the Middle Ages. But this is to
attribute a great effect to a slight cause. It is childish to assume
that without this crude compilation the course of history would
have been entirely different. It is not because the False Decretals
existed that the Papacy dominated the Middle Ages; on the contrary, it is because the Papacy prevailed over the other powers
that the False Decretals became the Code of the Church. This
compilation came into existence when the time was ripe for it,
the ideas set forth in it were in the air, and all the author had to do
was to record them

Had this forger, at any rate, the ambition to revolutionize the barbarian world, by merely pillaging a monastic library? No, his object
was a more modest one　His professed aim is to make a compilation more complete than its predecessors; though this is, of course,
no reason why he should forge documents. These forgeries consist
mainly in piecing together citations so chosen as to give conclusive
effect to certain rules; these rules had been vainly invoked by the
Councils of his day. By placing them under the sanction of the
oldest popes, he aimed to assure them more respect. This is the
way much history used formerly to be written, by placing in the
mouths of the great personages of antiquity fine harangues of which
they had not actually spoken a single phrase or even word. This
method shocks us now; but it did not astonish any one in the
Middle Ages.[2]

[1] Ed. *Hinschius,* following the "Pseudo-Isidore"　This name is given
to seventy-one articles dealing especially with accusations against bishops
and clericals; they were invoked by Hincmar, Bishop of Laon, against
Hincmar of Reims.
[1] *Cf.* Councils of 829, 836, 845 and 846 — As to what follows, *cf.*

In the apocryphal passages, the author of the False Decretals seeks especially to establish the independence of the local bishops with respect to the political powers, the metropolitan bishops, and the provincial Council. He undertakes the defence of those bishops who had been ousted from office by violence or expelled from their sees by partisan Councils, and his texts allow them to appeal to Rome And this applied precisely to the then situation. After the civil wars between Louis le Débonnaire and his son, the bishops of the conquered party were treated as enemies; though for a long time the Church had demanded that ecclesiastical persons and property should be judged by its own courts and not by the secular judges, and the False Decretals uphold this same principle. It has been mistakenly maintained that they laid down the celebrated rule that every priest (and even every one whosoever) could in every cause appeal directly to the Pope. This rule is, in fact, not to be found in them, it is even in contradiction to their text. Nevertheless, practice thenceforth accepted it, without regard to the text; which plainly proves that the False Decretals derived their entire authority from their conformity to current ideas. A most important feature of the False Decretals was its texts establishing the superiority of the spiritual over the temporal power; for example, in letters 1 and 3 of Clement I occur phrases like this· " your duty, says St. Peter to the priests, is to teach rulers; the duty of rulers is to obey you as they would God himself." This, to be sure, was common ground for all the ecclesiastical writers of the period. But less commonplace was the principle that popes could depose kings. It is found in a charter to the monastery of Saint-Medard attributed to Pope Gregory the Great (604), and sometimes has been associated with the False Decretals because inspired by the same spirit.[1] In reality, they used less overbearing terms, in one of the papal letters, referring to a law forbidding soldiers to be received into monasteries, the Pope declared to the Emperor of the East that he, compared with himself, was but dust and a miserable worm. One can get an idea, by comparing these texts, of the ground which had been gained by the Church in the space of three centuries [2]

Hinschius, pp. ccxiii et seq. — As to the connection between the False Decretals and the "Liber Pontificalis," see "Anal. jur. pont ," 1881 , "R. des q hist ," 1886, p 377 , Duchesne, "Et sur le Lib. pont ," p 215
  [1] This text, which is perhaps not much later in date than the False Decretals, is reproduced by Blondel Cf Migne, "Patrol lat ," vol 77, no. 1285, and authors cited in the notes. The letter to the Emperor Maurice is of the year 593· M G H Ep , I, 219, and Migne, ibid , I, 3, ep 65
  [2] Fœste, "Die reception d. Pseudo-Isidorus u. Nicolaus I u Hadrian

Discovery of the Forgery. — The forgery was suspected as early as the 1400s by a few learned theologians, such as Nicholas of Cusa, and by the 1500s was acknowledged by scholars like Erasmus and jurists like Dumoulin Since the Jesuit Torrès, whose views David Blondel vigorously refuted in his " Pseudo-Isidorus et Turrianus vapulantes " (1628), the authenticity of the False Decretals had no defenders If one did not know how many errors have been confidently received, one might be astonished that no one had sooner perceived the apocryphal character of this work. Not one contemporary writer cited these pretended letters of the early popes; not one of the letters contained the slightest allusion to the events or topics which disturbed or moved the Church at the time when, if genuine, they must have been composed. To-day, at any rate, with our precise knowledge of the origin of each fragment in this collection, we have (so to speak) a complete demonstration of the forgery

(E) *The Penitentials* (" Libri pœnitentiales ") [1] These are confessors' handbooks enumerating, article by article, the penance proper for each sin. In the 800s and 900s the public penances of the early Church fell into disuse; for these were substituted private penances, fasting, almsgiving, prayers, even these could be bought off, for money to be used in works of charity. This was virtually a compounding with God, like the damage-money paid to men; and the Penitentials therein offered a striking resemblance to the Germanic laws. He who would not fast must pay, in lieu of seven weeks' fasting, if he be rich, twenty sous; if poor, ten sous; [2] instead of a penance of a month's bread and water, recite twelve hundred Psalms, on the knees, if genuflexion is too tiring, then eighteen hundred and sixty Psalms. Pierre Damien (about 1058)

II," 1881. The twenty-seven articles known as "Dictatus Papæ," in which Gregory VII, in 1075, gave the formula of the absolute power of the pope in so trenchant a manner, seem to have been extracts from the False Decretals *Jaffé*, "Monum. Gregoriana," 1865, p. 174, *Rocquain*, "B Ch.," 1872, p 378

[1] EDITIONS: *D'Achery*, "Spicil " I; *Migne*, "Patrol lat.," vols. 89, 99, 105; *Wasserschleben*, "Die Bussordnungen d Ab Kirche," 1851.
    BIBLIOGRAPHY: *Tardif*, p. 123 (and authors cited), *Schmitz*, "D Pœnitentiale romanum," 1875, "Die Bussbucher," 1883; *Viollet*, p 49
    The oldest of the Penitentials date from the 600s The following are cited: the "Penitentiel romain," those of Theodorus (A.D. 690), of Bede (A.D 735), of Hatligar (A D 831), in the 900s, Reginon, "De synodalibus causis" (906 to 915); in the 1000s, Burchard of Worms, author of a "Decretum," book 20, of which, "corrector" or "medicus" (1012 to 1022), is a penitential Beginning with the 1500s, that of St. Charles Borromeus is followed.
    [2] *Réginon*, "De synodal caus.," I, 2, c. 438 *et seq.* To-day, in certain dioceses, one pays five sous per person for the use of meat during Lent.

made the following curious calculation (for flagellation): one thousand self-inflicted blows may be given while reciting ten Psalms, fifteen hundred while reciting the whole book of Psalms; he who recites the book of Psalms twenty times while giving himself three hundred thousand blows performs in six days a penance of a hundred years The *Tariffs of the Apostolic Penitentiary,* established for the first time by Benoit XII (1336), are penitentials for cases reserved for the pope, they were instituted to restrict the emoluments of the officers of the Pontifical Court and to avoid scandalous bargainings [1]

This system of compounding penances led finally to that of indulgences, or the remission of the canonic penalty on condition of the performance of pious works, or even for a money consideration, this money serving to ransom captives, to support the hospitals, and to succor the poor.[2]

§ 3　Medieval Canon Law; Gratian's Decretum to the " Corpus Juris Canonici." — The Canon Law during the feudal period acquires a highly important place.

(A) *Canonic Compilations, A D 900–1100.*[3] — From the time of the False Decretals to that of Gratian (1150), the secular law is neglected, and works upon the ecclesiastical law abound. During this period numerous compilations were being elaborated which later on were to furnish Gratian the materials for his Decretum. Of these too little known sources we need only cite the most important.[4] In the 900s we have · (1) " Collectio Anselmo dicata," dedicated to Anselm II, Archbishop of Milan, from 881 to 897 (unpublished) , [5] (2) "De synodalibus causis," by Reginon, abbot of Prum, near Trèves (between 906 and 915), setting forth the procedure used in the judicial sessions held by the bishops when travelling through the parishes of their Diocese; [6] (3) Abbo, abbot of Fleury (1004), dedicated to Hugh Capet some " Capitula " upon the duties and the property of the clergy.[7] In the 1000s (4) the

[1] *Viollet,* "Rev. histor ," 1880, p 882
[2] Dig X , "de pœnit. et remiss ," 5, 38 , Alexander III, 1159–1181.
[3] BIBLIOGRAPHY *Schulte,* "Gesch d Quellen d. Canon Rechts von Gratian bis auf die Gegenwart," 1875 , *Tardif,* p 173 , *Viollet,* p 60 , *Conrat,* I, 205 *et seq , Wasserschleben,* "Beitr z Gesch d. Vorgratian Kirchenr , ' 1839 , *Schneider,* "Die Lehre s. d Rechtsquellen," 1892
[4] Bibliography in *Tardif,* p 160 (works of *Ballerini, Theiner,* and *Maassen)*
[5] *Conrat,* I, 215 *Patetta,* "Antol giurid.," IV, 3, and "R. ital. p. l. sc. giur ," XI , D *Pitra,* "Anal nov ," I, 140
[6] *Migne,* "Patrol lat ," vols. 132, 139 (?) ; *Wasserschleben,* "Reginonis libri duo," 1840
[7] Migne, " Patrol lat ," vol 131.

Decretum of Burchard, Bishop of Worms ("Decretorum libri XX," written between 1012 and 1023), was generally used, in spite of the slight critical examination which the author displays. (5) IVES DE CHARTRES (117), who studied at Bec under Lanfranc and whose quarrels with Philip I over the repudiation of Queen Bertha are well known, wrote several important letters. Three works have been attributed to him the "Panormie," the "Decretum," and the "Tripartite Collection" (1095). Ives no doubt meant to prepare men's minds for ecclesiastical reform in view of the Councils presided over by Urban II in 1095 and 1096 The majority of the canonic Collections of the early part of the 1100s, for example the "Cæsaraugustana" and the Decretum of Gratian itself, are to a greater or lesser extent derived from the work of Ives de Chartres.[1]

(B) *The Decretum of Gratian*.[2] — The collections of the 900s and 1000s were for the most part no more than compilations; many of them had become out of date; they were all incomplete, including as they did contradictory provisions and superannuated regulations. The Canon law had no classical collection, — a Digest, in which the vast material, the elaborate growth of centuries, should be given orderly form as a concordant whole. A monk of Bologna now supplied this want. At the very height of the juristic revival, in the very town where Irnerius and his disciples had so brilliantly revived the teaching of the Roman law, and at the very moment when theology was taking another advance with Peter Lombard's "Libri sententiarum," GRATIAN achieved his work. Dated between 1141 and 1150 (by the usual opinion) or 1139 and 1141 (by more recent opinion), his collection is generally called the "Decretum" In the older manuscripts, it bears the title "Concordia discordantium canonum." His work is marked off from prior ones of the sort by the compiler's skill in giving a systematic order to the documents and in minimizing the contradictions naturally to be found in documents sometimes separated by several centuries. So well was this done that the Decretum is virtually a treatise on the Canon law with its authorities included. The only defects which critical standards can allege are due to

[1] *Migne*, "Patrol. lat.," vol. 161 The "Collectio trium partium" is unpublished *Tardif*, p. 170; *P Fournier*, "B Ch," 1896 and 1897; *Menu*, "Rech sur . Ives de Chartres," 1880
[2] BIBLIOGRAPHY: *Schulte, op. cit* , "Z. Gesch. d Litterat ub d Decret. Grat.," 1870 , "Die Glosse z. Dec. Grat ," 1872 , "Summa d. Paucapalea," 1889 , *Maassen*, "Paucapalea," 1859; *Friedberg*, "Prolegom " to the "Corpus jur. canon.," I.

Gratian's use of faulty sources, such as the Psuedo-Isidore or Burchard, instead of the originals. The Decretum consists of three parts· 1st, Sources of the law, and ecclesiastical persons; 2d, Ecclesiastical jurisdiction, procedure, and property; marriage; 3d, " De Consecratione ", sacrament and liturgy.[1] In each one of them there are to be distinguished the " Dicta Gratiani," the personal work of Gratian, and the " Paleæ," notes by Paucapalea, a disciple of Gratian's (1100s), and a few others [2] Almost as soon as it appeared the Decretum was treated as an official compilation; it served as the basis for the teaching of Canon law in the Schools, and (like the Roman laws) was furnished with a continuous gloss, by John of Germany (Johannes Teutonicus) before 1215, and by Bartholomew of Brescia about 1236 [3]

(C) The " Quinque Compilationes Antiquæ " [4] — Five compilations were made (before the Decretals of Gregory IX) to complete the Decretum of Gratian, — " Prima," compiled about 1190, by Bernard of Pavia and divided into five books· (1) ecclesiastical hierarchy; (2) procedure, (3) functions and duties of the clergy, (4) marriage; (5) penal law. This order of subjects became thenceforth the accepted one in the compilations of the Canon law. It has been summed up in the well-known verse. " Judex, Judicium, Clerus, Connubia, Crimen " — " Tertia," an official compilation (thus differing from the preceding ones), made in 1210, by Peter of Benevent, by order of Innocent III. — " Secunda," a continuation of " Prima," including the Decretals prior to Innocent III, made by John of Wales between 1210 and 1215. " Quarta," a compilation subsequent to 1216, and including the Decretals issued by Innocent III after 1210 and the canons of the Council of Lateran in 1215. — " Quinta," an official compilation of the Decretals of Honorius III, 1216 to 1226.

(D) Decretals of Gregory IX, or "Extra" (that is, " Decretales

---

[1] *Method of citation.* 1st part · includes 101 Distinctions subdivided into Canons, cited thus. c(anon) 4 · D(istinctio) XI, or c Consuetudinis, D XI, Decree of Gratian, 1st part, is understood — 2d part : is divided into "Causes," the causes into "questions,' the questions into "canons" cited thus c 3 or c Nostrates, C(ausa) XXX, Q(uæstio) 5. Question 3 of cause 33 forms a special treatise " De Pœnitentia," divided into "Distinctions", cited thus c 25 or c Omnis, D(istinctio) I, De Pœn — 3d part Distinctions and canons as in the first part, from which it is distinguished by adding " De cons ," that is to say, " de consecratione "·

[2] The rubrics are by Gratian Tardif, p 176

[3] As to the abridgments, commentaries, etc , of the Decree, cf *Tardif,* p. 183 The "Sommæ" of *Paucapalea, Ruffini,* and *Etienne de Tournay,* have been edited in recent times by *Schulte*

[4] Ed *Friedberg,* 1882, *Friedberg,* "Die canones Sammlungen zw. Gratian u Bern v. Pavia," 1897

extra Decretum vagantes "). — On September 5, 1234, by the Bull
" Rex pacificus," Gregory IX sent to the Universities of Bologna
and Paris (equivalent to an official publication) a compilation of
the Papal Decretals since the Decree of Gratian, most of which
were already contained in the "Quinque Compilationes Antiquæ."
This was thus a continuation of Gratian's work, which, consequently, now became in law what it had been in fact, namely, an
official Code.   At the same time, all authority was taken away from
the Five Compilations.   The author of the new compilation was
the confessor of Gregory IX, RAYMOND OF PENNAFORT.   He
divided it (following the Code of Justinian) into books, titles,
and canons, the method of citation is the same as for the Code,
with this slight difference, that the abbreviation " X " (meaning
" Extra ") takes the place of the abbreviation " C " (meaning
the Code).   The " Extra " consists of five books like the
" Compilatio prima." [1]   It was glossed by Bernard of Parma
(died 1263) [2]

(*E*) *The " Sextus."* — The Decretals subsequent to the Extra
were collected in 1298 by Boniface VIII, and published in the same
manner as the compilation last referred to, that is, by sending them
to the Universities of Bologna and Paris.   The Extra consisted
of five books; the new volume constituted the " Sextus " or " Liber
Sextus Decretalium "; each of its five books (this division following the usage introduced by Bernard of Parma) completed the
corresponding book of the Extra   Thenceforth it was cited in the
same manner, by the abbreviation " in VI " (" in Sexto ").   It
was glossed by Jean André (1348).

(*F*) *The " Clementines "* was another compilation of the same
kind, undertaken by Clement V, and including the Decretals
which he had issued.   It was published by this pope in 1313 and
sent to the Universities on October 25, 1317, by his successor, John
XXII, who had recast it.   It differs from the preceding compilations in not taking away all authority from the Decretals, which it
does not republish

(*G*) *" Extravagantes "* (Decretals left out of the above compila-
tions, " extra-vagantes ").   There are two groups of them.   the
" Extravagantes " of John XXII (twenty constitutions) and the
" Extravagantes communes " (including the Decretals issued by

[1] Compilation of Innocent IV in 1245 accompanied by an order that
its texts be inserted in the Gregorian Compilation under the titles with
which they dealt

[2] As to the editions and commentaries of the Decretals, see *Tardif*,
p. 201.

various popes since the publication of the Sextus). This compilation, differing from the preceding ones, is not official.

(*H*) *The "Corpus Juris Canonici"* — The 1500s did not result in any new compilation, it was deemed enough to bring together the prior compilations, which served as a text for instruction in the Universities and were applied by the courts of the Church. The term " Corpus juris canonici," as the antithesis of the term " Corpus juris civilis " applied to the whole of the Roman law, is found as early as the 1100s; but in the 1500s it acquired a technical meaning, and was used to cover the Decree of Gratian, the Decretals of Gregory IX, the Sextus, the Clementines, and the Extravagantes A commission of Cardinals and scholars, the " correctores romani," worked at Rome from 1563 to 1580 to form a better text than that of the manuscripts or publications then in circulation The edition of this commission made its appearance in 1582 under the pontificate and by the orders of Gregory XIII; it is thus official. The " Corpus juris canonici " thus formed is still the basis of the Canon law in the Catholic Church [1]

§ 4. **Later Canon Law.** — The Canons of the Councils and the Papal Decretals have not been compiled since the " Corpus juris canonici," so as to constitute official or semiofficial Codes of ecclesiastical laws, and are found only in various periodicals or special books

Apart from this general law, there is also local law — the Canons of the national Councils, the diocesan statutes, the episcopal ordinances, and the statutes of chapters and collegiate churches form local laws.

To the sources of Canon law, properly so called, we should also add two classes of sources (*A*) The *Concordats*, — treaties between the Holy See and catholic Powers for the regulation of relations between Church and State Such were the Concordat of Worms in 1122, which put an end to the dispute about investitures; the Concordat between Leo X and Francis I (1515), which was the result of a Papal Bull received and published in France as an official Statute, the Concordat of July 15, 1801 (or 26 Messidor, year IX), between Pius VII and Napoleon, at that time First Consul, the latter united with it the " Articles organiques " of Germinal, year X, which had been enacted without the participation of the Church.[2] (*B*) The sources of *Civil Ecclesiastical Law;* by

---

[1] Other important editions· *Pithou,* 1687 , *Bohmer,* 1747 , *Richter,* 1839 , *Friedberg,* 1879–1881
[2] *Tardif,* p 247 , *Munch,* "Sammlung all. alt und neu Konkordate," 1830–1831

this is understood the laws and regulations enacted by the civil
authorities in ecclesiastical matters without prior agreement with
the Papacy, for example, the Pragmatic Sanction of Bourges
(1437), the Civil Constitution of the Clergy (under the Revolution), and in our own day the Law of Guarantees in Italy (May 13,
1871).   The Codes of Theodosius and of Justinian, the Edicts and
Capitularies of the two first dynasties of French Kings. and the
Ordinances of the third dynasty, contain a great number of provisions concerning the Church [1]

§ 5. **Judicial Decisions** — The most important ecclesiastical
jurisdictions are (at Rome) the Tribunal of the Rota and the Congregations of Cardinals, and (in the various dioceses) the Ecclesiastical Courts (" officialities ")   The special tribunals of the *Inquisition* also left numerous judicial registers and documents [2]

The Decisions of the Tribunal of the *Rota* (or " Auditorium "),
organized at the beginning of the 1300s (1326, 1418, 1422) form
vast collections.[3]   To them should be added, to form some idea of
the judicial law of the superior courts of the Catholic Church, the
decisions of the commissions of Cardinals, or *Congregations*, such
as the Congregation of the Council (of Trent), of Rites, and of the
Index,[4] which after Sixtus V decided cases formerly submitted
to the Consistory or General Assembly of Cardinals [5]   The regulations of the *Apostolic Chancery*, for the granting of benefices or
prebends, date back to 1278; the oldest compilation is that of
John XXIII (1410).[6]

§ 6. **Treatise, The Canonists.** — The Canon law was taught in
the Schools or Universities as a branch of theology, by masters or
doctors of the Decretum.   Their works consisted of Commentaries, " Apparatus," Summaries, " Questiones," and " Consilia,"
like those of the Romanists.   But the method of the latter has
varied, and different schools may be distinguished; whereas the
Canonists are scarcely ever divided into schools, except upon questions of the Papacy's relations to the secular Powers and the

[1] *Tardif*, p 261 (enumeration and bibliography); *G de Champeaux*,
"Le droit civil eccl français," 1849
[2] *Tanon*, "Hist des trib de l'Inquisition," p. 150 (1893)
[3] "Decisiones Rotæ Romanæ," 1754, *Patrizi*, "Decis. 8 Rotæ," 1832.
[4] "Index librorum prohibitorum Leonis XIII jussu," ed Turin, 3d ed.,
1891.
[5] "Resolutiones S. Congreg Concilii," 1741, "Thesaurus resolut. S.
Cong. Conc .," 1739 *et seq* , "Decreta Congr sacr rituum," 3d ed , 1856
(and supplement by *Muhlbauer*).
[6] *Walter*, "Fontes jus eccl ," 1862, p 483 ; *Ottenthal*, "Regulæ cancell
apostol.," 1889, *Dumoulin*, "In reg. Canc. Comment," 1560, *Riganti*,
"Comment in reg Cancell.," 1744

national Churches, in this respect one may contrast the Gallicans
and the Imperialists with the Ultramontanes   Canon procedure
forms a special branch of the literature of the Canon law.   Its
treatises, called " *Ordines Judiciarii* " (Gratian, c II, q 1), are
very numerous, and have as their basis the similar treatises of the
" Legistae " or Romanists.[1]   The " Ordo judiciarius " of TANCRED
(1214–1216) caused all the others to be forgotten.[2]

The best known Canonists were, in the 1100 s, RUFINI and HUGUC-
CIO,[3] in the 1200 s, Tancred, a professor at Bologna, author of the
" Ordo judiciarius," who had the most success; the Cardinal of
Ostia, HOSTIENSIS, to whom we owe the " Summa on the Decretals," called " Somme dorée " because of its merit; WILLIAM
DURAND (G Durandi, that is, " filius Durandi "), born in 1237
at Puimisson near Béziers, Bishop of Mendes in 1285, who wrote
a vast compilation concerned entirely with practice, the " Speculum judiciale " (1271), which had no less than thirty-nine editions;
in the 1300 s, the professor of Bologna, JOHN D' ANDRÉ (Johannes
Andreæ), whose wife Milancia and daughter Novella seem to
have studied law successfully; in the 1400 s, the Spaniard JOHN OF
TORQUEMADA, and the Italian PANORMITANUS, both of whom at the
Council of Constance upheld ultramontane doctrines against such
men as D'Ailly and Gerson.

One of the greatest names of the 1500 s is that of the learned
Archbishop of Tarragona, ANTONIUS AUGUSTINUS.   In France,
P. PITHOU codified the " Libertés de l'Eglise gallicane " (1594),
and P DUPUY developed its proofs, after him, in the 1600 s FEVRET
and VAN ASPEN wrote the same type of books.   Amongst the ultramontanes one should mention HAUTESERRE and REIFFENSTUEL.
The " Ancienne et Nouvelle Discipline de l'Eglise " (1678 and
1688) by the priest of the Oratory, THOMASSIN, is still a useful work
to consult, and there is scarcely any better elementary book than
the " Institution au droit ecclésiastique " by CLÉMENT FLEURY.

[1] Enumeration in *Tardif*, p 299 *et seq* ; "Incerti auctoris ordo jud ,"
(1170–1190), ed *Gross*, 1870, Wien Ak , 1872, p. 235, "Ricardi An-
glici ordo jud ," ed *Witte*, 1853 , "Ord jud ," of *Damase*, ed *Wunderlich*,
" Anecdota "—After Tancred the "Summa de ordine et judicii spiritualis
lis," before 1215 or 1220, altered between 1234 and 1254 , the " Libellus
judicium" of *Jean de Dieu* (1200 s) , the "Ordo jud ," of *Egidius of Fus-
carius* (1260) , the "Processus judicii" (beginning of the 1400s) , the
"Summa de ord. jud.," (id) by *Jean Bely*, Bishop of Lavaur. Also,
Monacelli, "Formular fori ecclesiast ," 1732.
[2] Ed *Bergmann*, 1842 (with the "Ordo" of the Romanist *Pillius*
and that of the canonist *Gratia d'Arezzo*, about 1239).
[3] *Schulte*, "Summa Magistri Rufini," 1892 ; *Tanon*, "Rufin et Huguccio",
(N.R.H., 1888–1889)

The 1700s offer compilations not without their value, such as the
" Lois ecclésiastiques " of Héricourt and the " Dictionnaire de
droit canon " by the member of the Convention, Durand de
Maillane.   In our own day the study of the Canon law has made
great progress in Germany, with the splendid works of such men as
Maassen and Schulte, Philipps and Hinschius, and the remark-
able handbooks of such men as Walter, Richter, Friedberg and
Sohm.

§ 7. Influence of Canon Law on Secular Law.[1] — (A) *Law of
Nations.* — The community of ideas, of morals, and of laws,
created by the Church among the peoples of Europe, contributed
even more than community of interests and of commercial relations towards the formation of the law of nations.   Before they
were ever Frenchmen or Englishmen, men were Christians.   The
law of nations began by being a " jus inter christianos," drawing
its inspiration from Christian morality, lessening the cruelties of
war even when the intervention of the Holy See did not prevent
its outbreaking.   A Decretal as early as Innocent III in a spirit
of humanity forbade the use of certain kinds of arms, — the bal-
lista for example (Extrav. 5, 15, 1), as in our own time it has been
forbidden to use explosive bullets   The " Peace of God " and the
" Truce of God " were both starting-points for important rules of
the law of war.

(B) *Public Law.* — The history of the Middle Ages is to a great
extent made up of quarrels between Church and State.   But the
theocratic conception that the State is at the service of the Church,
just as the body is at the service of the soul, did not prevail.   This,
it would seem, is at least one point gained.   Even during the
periods when the Faith was most deeply sincere, the State found
means to escape from the domination of the clergy.   However,
the ecclesiastical public law carried on the Roman traditions; its
monarchic constitution, with centralized power and hierarchy, has
been the model which modern States have reproduced, — and even
in its most doubtful aspects. the absolute authority of the head
(that is, of the clergy), and the absolute subjection of the members
(that is, of the faithful).   It is in a great measure to the Church

[1] *Hinschius* (in *Holtzendorff*), p 182, and authors cited by him , *D'Espinay*,
"De l'influence du droit canonique sur la législation française," 1857;
Muther, "Röm u. Canon. Recht im Mittelalter," 1871 , *Walter*, "Kirchenr." p. 737 ; *Rocco*, "Jus canonicum ad civilem jurisprud. quid attu-
lerit," 1839 ; *Huc*, "R crit. de lég.," 1856–1858 ; *Padelletti*, "Arch. giur ,"
1874 ; *Brockhaus*, "Ub das canon Recht," 1888 , *Mazeau*, "De l'infl.
du dr canon. sur la législ. fr ," 1889 , *Schupfer*, p. 174.

that we owe the modern conception of the State and its public functions. Where feudalism saw in government only a private property and a right to personal profit, ecclesiastical doctrine has always seen or led up to the idea of the superior interests of all.

(*C*) *Criminal Law.* — Although the Church improved men's morals and has proscribed barbarous customs (such as the right to wreckage), it was inhuman in its repression of heresy and offences purely religious; it was guilty of an economic error (half justified by circumstances) in forbidding the payment of interest as being a form of usury. But, by way of set-off, it always had the modern conception of equality before the law: all are equal before its tribunals, as they are before God Its conception of punishment is the opposite of the Germanic system of private vengeance; in its eyes, the penalty is not the satisfaction of some self-interest of an injured individual, it is a restoration of the supernatural order of things by means of expiation. Moreover it recognized two kinds of penalties. one, an evil inflicted by society, the servant of God, in the name of God, upon the person who violates the divine law ("pœna vindicativa"); the other, a means of bettering the criminal ("censura," "pœna medicinalis"). The Church has a horror of bloodshed, if it did not go so far as to abolish the punishment of death, yet by the right of sanctuary it lessened the atrocious penalties, and its teaching was hostile to corporal mutilation.

(*D*) *Criminal Procedure.* — Still more does criminal procedure owe to the Church. Here the Church accomplished a real revolution. For the accusatory system (private complaint), it substituted the inquisitorial system (public officers with a duty to prosecute). This system was far superior to the other Its evil reputation is chiefly due to the memories left by the tribunal of the Inquisition, with which it has mistakenly been confused. The former and earlier system is based on a formal charge of an offence, made against the real or supposed guilty man by a private person, the victim of the offence or a relative of the victim. People often hesitated before undertaking an act of so serious a nature, carrying with it penalties and reprisals, and exposing the complainant to the greatest dangers in a society like that of the Middle Ages, where the last word lay only too often in the power of the violent and powerful. Under Innocent III (1215), the Church reacted with energy against this crude form of procedure. It held that public rumor ("diffamatio"), or a private complaint, sufficed for the public officer to start inquiry ("inquisitio") as to the offence and to seek out the guilty man; the prosecution was

722

official. Thenceforth, crimes no longer remained unpunished because of the neglect of the accusers, or of the fear with which a too
powerful criminal inspired them. A new instrument made its
appearance in the tribunals, — the Public Prosecutor, whose duty
it was to pursue the charge in the name of all, and who came to the
assistance of the weak As early as the second half of the 1200s,
such an officer is found in the secular courts of Italy.

(E) *Civil Law.* — The Canon law upon marriage was in force
in France until the Revolution, in Germany until 1876; the law of
the Protestant countries felt the influence of the Church in this
field (excepting for divorce) but little less than that of the Catholic
countries. The theory of the " jus ad rem " and the " jus in re "
(as well as that of the " titulus " and the " modus adquirendi
dominii ") comes at least in part from the Canonists. In their
hands the protection of possessors was emphasized; for their benefit the Canonists devised the action and the defence of "spolii";
moved by reasons of equity, they made the possessory actions
apply to rights, and not merely to things, and even allowed them
against third parties, thus changing them into real (petitory) actions. The moral tendency of the Canon law comes to light again
in the importance given to good faith in questions of prescription.
On the subject of contracts, the respect for the religious oath
when joined to an agreement had the effect of accustoming men
to respect the mere agreement, the mere meeting of the minds;
and thus the rule was arrived at, " solus consensus obligat." The
prohibition of loans on interest had a double effect. on the one
hand, it compelled men to devise new combinations so as to make
the prohibition nugatory (for example, the limited partnership,
the rent charge); on the other hand, the desire to repress fraud
led to the idea of contracts of exchange (commutative), in which
each party must give and receive something of equal value, without which each has a right to complain for failure of consideration.
The Canon law also had its share in introducing the principle of
representation of parties by attorney The will, the liberty to
make a will, and testamentary execution are also associated with
the ecclesiastical law.

(F) *Civil Procedure.* — Modern civil procedure is derived from
the canonic procedure, the latter itself being only a recasting
(with alterations) of the procedure of the Lower-Empire It gave
us, as the latter did, a system of reasonable rules, the only criticism
to be made against it is its luxury of formality; but this defect the
Church remedied, as early as the 1300s, by devising a summary

form of procedure for urgent cases. In canon procedure all the proceedings were in writing; whereas in the old Germanic law the proceedings were oral   Its theory of proof also was in contrast with that of the ancient law. the oath with compurgators, the ordeal, and the judicial duel, were in the Church's law replaced by written proofs and witnesses.

APPENDICES

APPENDIX A

COMPARATIVE CHRONOLOGICAL TABLE OF MEDIEVAL LEGAL SOURCES[1]

Explanation :

1 There has been no attempt on the part of the compiler to attain uniformity of spelling or nomenclature.   In each case the source has been indicated by its popular title, which, it need hardly be said, is seldom of official origin.   The dates assigned to the various items are those generally accepted by the leading specialists

2. A title in italics indicates that the source was originally the work of a private composer

3 A title between square brackets, [   ], indicates that the source does not survive in its original form

[1] [This Table was compiled by Professor EDWARD JENKS, Principal and Director of Legal Studies in the Law Society of England, and author of the Introduction to the present Volume.   It was originally published in his "Law and Politics in the Middle Ages" (New York.   Henry Holt & Co), and afterwards reprinted in Vol I of "Select Essays in Anglo-American Legal History" (Boston : Little, Brown, & Co —EDS.).]

FIFTH CENTURY

QUARTER	ENGLAND A.D.	SCOTLAND A.D.	ITALY A.D.	GERMANY A.D.	FRANCE A.D.	SPAIN A.D.	SCANDINAVIA A.D.
4				(Date uncertain) Lex Salica.		(466–485 ?) [Leges Eurici]	

SIXTH CENTURY

QUARTER	ENGLAND A.D.	SCOTLAND A.D.	ITALY A.D.	GERMANY A.D.	FRANCE A.D.	SPAIN A.D.	SCANDINAVIA A.D.
1			512 Edictum Theoderici		517 Lex Gundobada (Burgundians)		
2				Lex Ribuaria (part I)	(bet. 511 and 558) Pactus pro Tenore Pacis Hildeberti (I) et Chlotharii (I)		
3				Lex Ribuaria (part II)	(bet. 561 and 584) Edictum Hilperici (successions and misc.)		
4				596 Hildeberti (II) Decretio (successions)		585–601 Antiqua (Lex Wisigothorum)	

SEVENTH CENTURY

QUARTER	ENGLAND	SCOTLAND	ITALY	GERMANY	FRANCE	SPAIN	SCANDINAVIA
	A.D.	A.D.	A.D.	A.D.	Praeceptio Chlotharii (II) (misc for Neustria)	A.D.	A.D.
1	Æthelbirht's Dooms (Kent)			[Pactus Alamannorum]			
2				614 Edictum Chlotharii (II) Frank Kingdom	(Misc for whole		
			643 Rothari Edictum Renovationis	? Lex Ribuaria (part III)			
3			668 Grimoaldi Correctio.		652–672 Liber Judicum (Fuero Juzgo)		
4	680 Hatfield Decree against heresy (North, Mercia, E. Anglia, Kent)						
	Hlothere's and Eadric's Dooms (Kent).						
	Ine's Ratifications (Wessex)						
	696 Whitred's Dooms (Kent)						

729

EIGHTH CENTURY

ENGLAND	SCOTLAND	ITALY	GERMANY	FRANCE	SPAIN	SCANDINAVIA
A.D.	A.D.	A.D.	A.D.	A.D.	A.D.	A.D.
		718 Liutprandi Leges 785 [Notitia de Actoribus Regis] 781	Lex Ribuaria (part IV) Lex Alamannorum			
		745 Ratchis Edictum et Statuta	743 Statutum Karlmanni (appropriating church lands)	(appropriating		
		750–755 Statuta Ahistulfi	Decretum (Lex) Baiwariorum			
		Capitula A regis (Beneventum)	772 Decretum Tassilonis (Bavaria) 775 Decretum Tassilonis (Bavaria)	785 Capitulare Aquitanicum (Pippin Misc.)		

730

779	Capitulare (v Decretum) Harlstallense of Charles the great (For whole empire Important rules for administration of justice ? Extended to Northern Spain) Im-		
780	Consuetudo et Pactum Aregis (Naples)		
	Notitia Italica (Charles the Great Sales)		
	Capitulare Mantuanum (Pippin *de reng* Misc)	Capitulatio de Partibus Saxonie	
785°		Lex Frisonum	
	Capitulare Pippin (Proceedure Pilgrims)		
787	Capitulare Mantuanum IIm (Pippin Misc)		
787	Capitulare Papiense (Do Misc)		
790	Capitulare Pippini (Misc)		
797		Capitulare Saxoneum	

NINTH CENTURY

ENGLAND	SCOTLAND	ITALY	GERMANY	FRANCE	SPAIN	SCANDINAVIA
A.D.	A.D.	A.D.	A.D.	A.D.	A.D.	A.D.
		800 Statutum Communionum (regulating labor dues of vassals to their lords)				
		Capitulare de Villis (regulating the management of the royal estates, and containing important general rules)				
		801 Capitula legi Lombardicae addita (misc.)				
		803 Capitula (apud Aquisgranum) legibus addita omnioplusions, suretyship, abuse of legal process)	(Murder fines,			
			802 Lex Thuringorum Lex Frisionum (Additio sapientum)			
			803 Constitutio in lege Ribuaria unit tenda Lex Saxonum			
		806 Capitulare Papienal (misc.)				
		809 Capitula Aquisgranensia. (Pardoned criminals, outlaws, attendance at the local courts)				
		810 Capitula Aquisgranensia (containing the important clause limiting jurisdiction of the Hundred courts)				
			810 Capitula ad Legem Baiwariorum addita (The 8 bans)			
		?811 Capitulare de Justiciis Faciendis (Ordinances regulating competence of various courts, and establishing quarterly circuits of the *missi*)				
		812 Capitulare de Latronibus (definitely constituting theft as a "plea of the crown," unless committed between two slaves of same master) [Pactum cum Veneto]		812 Praeceptum pro Hispanis (purprestures of Crown lands).		
				?813 Capitulare Aquis-granense (misc.)		
				815–816 Duae constitutiones de Hispanis profugis.		
		819 Capitula Legibus Addenda (important criminal code, recognizing execution against lands, also power of making wills)				

			844 Praeceptum pro Hispanis.
	?819 Capitula Legi Salicae addita.		
	? Lex Francorum Chamavorum.		
825 Statutum Olonnense (misc.).			
827 Ansegisi Abbatis Capitularium collectio (an imperfect collection of the Capitula of Charles the Great, Ludwig I, and Lothar I).			
829 Capitularia Wormatiensia. (Important rules of imperial administration, authorizing "Inquisitiones.")			
Concordia.			
836 Pactum Sicardi (Naples),			
840 Pactum cum Venetis (prob. founded on earlier of 812, not surviving).			
		853 Capitulare Silvacense (rules for circuit judges).	
		854 Capitulare Attiniacense (rules for circuit judges).	
		861 Edictum Pistense (important general ordinance regulating proceedure, coinage, military service, weights and measures, etc.).	
866 Capitula Adelchis (Beneventum),			
		864 Capitulare Varnense. (Robberies. Regulation of rival jurisdictions.)	
			Ælfred's Code.
2		3	4

TENTH CENTURY

QUARTER	ENGLAND	SCOTLAND	ITALY	GERMANY	FRANCE	SPAIN	SCANDINAVIA
	A.D.	A.D.	A.D.	A.D.	A.D.	A.D.	A.D.
1	901? Eadweard the Elder's (first) Ordinance						
	904 Eadweard the Elder's warnings (C. of Exeter)						
	Æthelstane's ordinance for Tithes						
	Æthelstane's ordinance at Greatanleh						
	Judicia Civitatis Lundoniæ.						
2	940–946 Eadmund's Proclamations and Institutions						
	Eadgar's Counsel of the Hundred	967 Capitulare de duello judicali					
3	Eadgar's Counsel (at Andover?)						
	959–975 Eadgar's (gen¹) Ordinance (at "Withbordesstane")						980 [Eihertsfjord (Iceland)]
4	Æthelred's Counsel at Woodstock.	908 Capitulare de prædiis ecclesiasticis					

QUARTER	ENGLAND	SCOTLAND	ITALY	GERMANY	FRANCE	SPAIN	SCANDINAVIA
	A D	A D	A D	A D	A D	A D	
1	Peace of the English and Danes (Danegelt). *Æthelred's Law of Wantage.* Counsel of the Witan at Enham (? Ensham)		The *Capitulare* (collection of imperial Capitula)				
	1018 Knut's Counsel at Winchester		1019 Capitulare de Successione				
	? *Witherlags Ret* (Knut)		? *Liber Papiensis*				
2			1027? Mandatum de lege Romana				
			1037 Edictum de Beneficiis				
3	? *Rectitudines Singularum Personarum*		1052 Constitutio de Vexellis				
			1070 The *Expositio* (commentary on the Imperial Capitula)				
4	The Ten Statutes of William I. Ordinance excluding spiritual causes from the Hundred Court.		1077 Pax Italica Henrici Quarti				
			? *Lombarda*				

QUARTER	ENGLAND	SCOTLAND	ITALY	GERMANY	FRANCE	SPAIN	SCANDINAVIA
	A.D.	A.D.	A.D.	A.D.	A.D.	A.D.	A.D.
1	1100 Charter of Libertatus (Henry I) 1108? Ordinance for holding courts of County and Hundred Leges Edwardi Confessoris Leis e customes que le roi Will granted al puple de Engleterre Quadripartitus 1118? Leges Henrici Primi	Leges Quatuor Burgorum	1108 Pax Generalis Henrici Quarti 1111 Privilegium (Papæ) de Investituris (reg. mang imperial rights) 1122 Pax Wormatiensis (Surrender of imperial rights on Investitures) 1125 Codex epistolaris Bambergae genas			1127 / 115? El fuero viejo de Castilla	1118 [Hafliðaskra (Iceland)]
2	Constitutio Cnuti Instituta Cnuti aliorumque Regum Angliæ	Assise David Regis	1136 Constitutio de feudorum distractione	1140 Freiburger Stadtrecht Soester Stadtrecht ("Jus tita")			

3				
1164	Record ("Constitutions") of Clarendon.	1152	Constitutio de pace tenenda (Criminal Code of Fredrick I)	
1166	Assise of Novel Disseisin (precedure) [Assise of Clarendon] [Grand Assise]		1154 Concessio Investiturae Episcoporum (Saxony)	1155 Ordonnance de Soissons
		1154	Constitutiones Feudales General Feudal Code)	
			1156 Constitutio Ducatus Austriae	
1176	Assises recorded at Northampton.	1157	Edictum in favorem Judeorum	
1181	Assise of Arms.	1159	Constitutio de jure feudorum (Pax Roncalica)	Établissemens de Rouen.
		1158	Lübecker Stadtrecht	
1184	Assise of Woodstock (Forests)	1165	Constitutio de testamentisfactione clericorum	
		1169	Kölner Stadtrecht	
	Assise Regis Wilhelm	1183	Pacis Placentina (The Lombard League)	
4		1186	Constitutio contra Incendiarios	
			1188 Magdeburger Stadtrecht	
		1191–4	Mandatum de Appellationibus	1196 [Commencements of Exchequer Records (Normandy)]
		1192	Sententia de feodis Ministerialium	
1194	First (?) Plea Roll	1180? 1200	Libri Feudorum vel Usus Feudales	Tres ancien Coutumier de Normandie (part 1)

QUARTER	ENGLAND	SCOTLAND	ITALY	GERMANY	FRANCE	SPAIN	SCANDINAVIA
	A.D.	A.D.	A.D. 1208 Sententia de Teloneis	A.D. ? Treuga Henrici ? Auctor Vetus de Beneficiis 1215? Sachsenspiegel	A.D. 1200 Conventio de feudis regni	A.D.	A.D. 1200–1202 Slesvigs Bærkeret (Denmark) Westgötalag (Sweden) Gulathingslov (Norway)
1	1215 Magna Charta		1216 Cessie juris spolii		? Statuts de Montpellier		Skanelagen (Denmark) Sjællandske Lov (Denmark)
			1218 Sententia de Immunitate Civiatum 1220 Privilegium in favorem principum ecclesiasticorum	1221 Wiener Stadt recht 1223 Renovatio pacis antique Saxonic	1220 Tres ancien Coutumes de Nor mantie (Pt II)	1217 Espejo de todos los derechos	
	1227 The First Register of Writs		1231 Constitutiones Siculae	1231 Edictum contra communia Statutum de constructionibus	1225 Statuts de Marseilles	1229 Fuero Juzge.	
2		Statuta Alexandri II	1232 Constitutio in favorem principum	1234 Kulmisch Handfeste Sententia in favorem ecclesiarum			1241 Jydske Lov (Denmark)
	1236 Statute of Merton		1235 Constitutio Pacis ("Mainzer Landfried")	? Summa prauen tum dictaminis ? Deutschenspiegel ? Schwabenspiegel	1243 Statuts d'Avignon 1245 Statuts d'Arles 1248 Commencement of the Plaide de l'Echevinage (Reims)		1244 Frostathingslov (Norway) Bjarkoret (Norway)

738

England		Scotland / Law books	Germanic / Imperial	France / Spain	Scandinavia
			1251 Constitutio de jure hereditario nepotum		
1267 Statute of Marlborough				1252 Fuero Real	
				1254 Commencement of the "Olim"	1254 Kjöbenhamns Bierkeret (Denmark)
				1256 Ordonnances de villes	1255 Bjärköaretten (Sweden), Grágás (Iceland)
				1260 Ordonnance de batailles (St Louis)	
				1267 Coutumes de Perpignan	
				1268 Commencement of Parlor aux Bourgeois (Paris)	1269 Birger Jarl's Edhsurebrott (Sweden)
				1269 Edictum de Ecclesiis	1269 Ribes Bierkeret (Denmark)
1275 Statute of Westminster 1			1270 Hamburger Stadtrecht ("Ordelbok")	1270 Etablissemens-le Roy (St Louis)	1271 Järnsida (Hákonorbók Norway)
				1275 Ordinatio de possessionibus amortisatis	1274 Magnus Lagabötir's Landslov (Norway)
1279 Statute of Gloucester			1276 Sententia de feodo non requisito		1275-6 Hirdskra (Norway)
1279 Statute of Mortmain			1281 Augsburger Stadtrecht		
1283 Statute of Acton Burnel			1282 Sententia de Parti ("Vihorem condito nem sequi debet")		1280 Jonsbók (Iceland)
1284 Statute of Wales		Lages Inter Scottos et Brettos	1283 Sententia de comitatibus non dividendis	1283 Coutumes de Toulouse	
1285 Statutes of Westminster II. and Winchester; Circumspecte Agatis		Regiam Majestatem		1284 Ordinatio de pace infracta	1285 Ordinances of Alsnö and Skeninge (Sweden).
			1287 Ordinatio de burgesiis		
1290 Quia Emptores			1292 Hamburger Schiffrecht	1291 Ordinatio de Parliamento	1296 Uplandslag (Sweden)
1292 The First Year Book			1298 Oesterreichisches Landrecht		
1297 Confirmatio Cartarum			Goslarer Stadtrecht	Grand Coutumier normand	Gotlandslag (Sweden)
			1299 Sententia Alberti I (excluding women from succession to feudal land)		

QUARTER	ENGLAND	SCOTLAND	ITALY	GERMANY	FRANCE	SPAIN	SCANDINAVIA
	A.D.	A.D.	A.D.	A.D.	A.D.	A.D.	A.D.
1	1307 Statute of Carlisle			1303 Stadtrecht von Brunen	1303 Ordinatio pro gubernatione regni		1303 Westmannalag (Sweden)
				1305? *Sächsisches Wechselbilrecht*	1306 Ordonnance de batailles (Philippe le Bel)		
			1310 Sententia contra Majestatis	*Stemma curia regis*		1312 Ordinance of Justice	
			1313 Constitutio Majestatis		1314 Mandatum de diolis	1314 Ordenamento de las Tafurerias	
					1315 Charte aux Normands		
	1324? Ordinance for Ireland	1320? Artioh ur Itinere Camerarii		1323 Leges Upsala-bomum (Zoelhard) Klaus Kaiser-recht	1320 Ordonnance pour nostre Chasublens de nos Comptes		
2					? *Très ancienne coutume de Bretagne*		1327 Södermannalag (Sweden) Helsingelag (Sweden)
					1330 Ordonnance d'appeals		1334 Magnus Eriksson's Usury Laws (Sweden)
				1342 Reichshofrathsab-schied.	1340 *Style de du Breuil*		1344 Ordinance of Upsala (Sweden).
					1345 Ordonnance de Parlement		1345 Ordinance of Telge (Sweden)

1849	First Statute of Laborers	1834	Use of Merchus *Quoniam Attach- iamenta* *Iter Camerarii*	1846	Bayerisches Land recht	1848	Siete Partidas Ordinance of Al- cala d' Henares	1351	Ordonnance de Police.	1851	*Thord Degn's Artikler* (Den- mark) Göderath (Swe- den), Smålandslag (Sweden), Wisby Stadslag (Sweden), Magnus Eriksson's Stadslag (Swe den) Landherkeret (Denmark).
1851	Statute of Pro- visors.			1847	Münchner Stadt- recht			1355	Ordonnance de l'arrere ban	1847	Magnus Erio- son's Landslag (Sweden).
1352	Statute of Trea- sons.							1361	Serment des bail- lis.		
1353	Statute of Prae- munire, Stat- ute of the Staple			1351	Schlesisches Landrecht			1363	Ordinatio de Par- lamento		
1357	Ordinance for Ireland					1371	Ley de Toru	1372	Ordonnance sur le fait des aides		
1362	Act establish- ing Quarter Sessions			1366	Goldene Bulle			1378	Ordonnance sur l'Amirauté		
1361	Statute of For- cible Entry							1389	Ordonnances sur les Assises *Grand Constum- tar de France*		

FIFTEENTH CENTURY

QUARTER	ENGLAND	SCOTLAND	ITALY	GERMANY	FRANCE	SPAIN	SCANDINAVIA
	A.D.	A.D.	A.D.	A.D.	A.D.	A.D.	A.D.
1	1413 Statute of Forgery	1405 Curia Quattuor Burgorum		1422 Nürnberger Reichs-Heers-Ordnung	1411 [Coutume d'Anjou et Maine]		
	1414 Statute of Heresy	1425 Article of Heresy			1417 Coutume de Poitou		
2		1426 Statute against "particular" and "foreign" laws. Ordinance establishing "Lords Auditors of Complaints"		1437 Arnsberger Reformation (of Westphalian courts)	1438 Sanction pragmatique		1440? Christopher's Landslag (Sweden).
		1428 Ordinances for Commissioners of Shires		1438 Kreis-Ordnung	1450 Stile et Coutume de Berry		
		1440 Ordo Justiciarii (James II)		1442 Frankfurter Reformation			
		1450 Act for Protection of Leaseholders. Act appointing "Lords of the Articles"		1447 Dithmarsches Landrecht			

English	German	French
1455 Statute against hereditary offices		Coutume de Bretagne
Statute establishing borough councils,		
1458 Act of feu-farm		1459 Coutumes de Bourgogne (duché et comté)
		1461 Coutume de Touraine
1462 Statute of Provisors		1462 Ordonnance fondant le Parlement de Bordeaux
		1463 (2nd) Coutume d'Anjou
1469 Act for registration of mortgages,	1471 Kammergerichts Ordnung (Friedrich III)	
Act of Limitation		
Statute of Appeals		1477 Ordonnance fondant le Parlement de Dijon
1482 Decision recognizing alienation of land by a married woman		1484 Coutume de Tours
1483 Statute against Benevolences		
1487 "Star Chamber" Act		
1491 Statute for holding of Session three times a year	1495 Kammergerichts Ordnung (Maximillian)	1495 Ordonnance fondant le Parlement de Rennes
		1491 Mandement sur la publication des coutumes,
1496 Statute for education of heirs of freeholders	1498 Erbfolge Ordnung	
	1500 Reichsregiments Ordnung	1499 Ordonnance fondant le Parlement de Rouen

ENGLAND	SCOTLAND	ITALY	GERMANY	FRANCE	SPAIN	SCANDINAVIA
A.D.	A.D. Statute establishing perpetual court at Edinburgh	A.D.	A.D. 1507 *Bambergensis*	A.D. 1501 Ordonnance fondant le Parlement d'Aix	A.D.	A.D.
	Statute making heirs liable for ancestor's debts			1507 Coutumes de Touraine		
	1504 Statute requiring notice to boroughs when taxation proposed			1508 Coutumes d'Anjou		
	Statute for registration of seisins by sheriffs		1512 Notariats-Ordnung (much about wills)	1509 Coutumes du Maine		
				1510 Coutumes de Troyes		
			1521 ⎫ Erbfolge-Ord-	1511 Coutumes d'Auvergne		
			1529 ⎭ nungen	1514 Coutumes de Paris		
				Coutumes Poitou		
				1520 Coutumes d'Angoumois		
				Coutumes de Bourdeaux		
				1521 Coutumes de Bourbonnois		
	1536 Statute of successions to goods of minors.		1530 Polizei-Ordnung und Reforma- tion	1523 Coutumes de Blois		
1599 Statute of Em- bezzlements	1529 Statute making freeholders responsible for production of their tenants		1532 Peinliche Hals- Gerichts -Ord- nung ("Karo- lina")	1594 Coutumes de Nivernois		
1631? Statutes of fees and enrolments	1532 Ordinance estab- lishing College of Justice					

744

1540	Statute of Wills	1540	Acts for reformation of Courts.			1589	Ordonnance de Villers-Cotterets		
		1535	Statute for notice to quit,			1551	Fors de Béarn. (There had been several earlier collections)		
			Statute against leagues and maintenants						
			Statute for registration of all seisins			1561	Ordonnance d'Orléans		
						1564	Ordonnance de Roussillon		
				1555	Würtemberger Landrecht	1566	Ordonnance de Moulins	1567	Nueva Recopilación
		1567	Statute for seisins to boroughs						
		1578	Act establishing convention of boroughs,			1579	Ordonnance de Blois		
		1579	Statute of prescriptions			1580	(Nouvelle) Coutume du Paris		
		1585	Statute declaring sovereignty of Parliament			1583	(Nouvelle) Coutume de Normandie		
			Statute prohibiting clergy acting as judges or advocates,			1585	Coutumes d'Orléans		
		1587	Constitution Statutes						
			Statutes for furtherance of criminal justice						
		1589	Statute establishing general Land Registry.						

3 4

APPENDIX B

COMPARATIVE CHRONOLOGICAL TABLE OF MODERN CONTINENTAL CODES [1]

By Edward Jenks [2]

Name of Country	Civil Code	Civil Procedure Code	Criminal Code	Criminal Procedure Code	Commercial Code	Constitutional Code
Austria	1812	1895	1852 (1855, military)	1874 (1884, military)	1863	1867
Belgium	1804	1806	1867	1808	1807	1831
Denmark	1683	[in Civil Code]	1866		[in Civil Code]	1849
France	1804	1806	1810	1808	1807	1875
Germany	1900	1879	1872 (1872, military)	1879	1900	1871
Italy	1866	1866	1890 (1869, 1870, military)	1890	1883 (1877, maritime)	1848, 1870
Netherlands	1838	1838	1886 (1903, military)	1838	1838	1887
Norway	1687	[in Civil Code]	1842	1887, 1889	[in Civil Code] (1894, maritime)	1809, 1814, 1905
Portugal	1868	1876	1886	1905	1889 (1905, procedure)	1910
Spain	1889	1881	1870	1882 (1890, military)	1886	1876
Sweden	1734	[in Civil Code]	1864	1866 + [statutes] (1881, military)	[in Civil Code] (1891, maritime)	1809, 1815
Switzerland (Federal)	1912	1850	1853	1851		1874

[1] This Table was originally published in the "Journal of the Society of Comparative Legislation," N. S. 1902, vol. IV, p. 71 (London : John Murray). It is here condensed, omitting the titles of the specific Codes (most of which are mentioned in the text of the present Volume), and omitting the countries of Slavic, etc., law, not represented in the present Volume. It includes only the basic Codes ; omitting the numerous auxiliary or minor ones (on land-title registration, negotiable instruments, etc.). Moreover, it does not note the numerous amending statutes, which are often radical and extensive. A rough line had to be drawn somewhere.

The purpose of the Table is to exhibit the general chronological status of the codified law under which the Continent to-day is living. In several instances (e.g. the Italian and German codes of criminal procedure) new codes have been already drafted and are nearing the point of enactment.

[2] Principal and Director of Legal Studies in the Law Society of England, author of the Introduction to the present Volume.

The Table has been revised to 1910 by John H. Wigmore, of the Editorial Committee.

INDEX

INDEX

[References are to pages]

A.

Accursius, 139, 140
Alamannic Code, 54
Alamannic law, in Switzerland, 485, 574
Alaric, Breviary of, 16, 597
Alcala, Ordinance of, 624, 631.
Aliens, 67.
Altamira, 579
Althusius, 409.
Amalfi, and the Digest, 133, 134.
Aragon, 610, 641, 642, 649–651, 663.
Assizes of Jerusalem, 75.
Austrian Code, 435, 437 ; in Venice and Lombardy, 193, 194.
Authentica, 170
Azo, 138

B.

Bacon, 410
Baldus, 147
Ban, royal, 37
Barbeyrac, 526
Bartolus, 146, 147, theory of statutes, 215
Basel, 505, 512.
Basque Provinces, 644, 645, 653, 665
Baudouin (Balduinus), 257, 258.
Bavarian Code, 56, 435.
Beaumanoir, 228.
Beauvaisis, Custom of, 228.
Beccaria, 187
Benedict Levita, collection of capitularies, 42
Bern, 503
Berytus, law school of, 8
Biology, applied to legal science, 197.
Bluntschli, 530
Bologna, Canon law in, 120 ; law school, 125, 128–131
Brachylogus, 103
Bracton, 226, 227
Breviary of Alaric, 16
Brissaud, 203, 251, 705
Brisson, 264
Brunner, 311
Burgundians and Burgundian law, 7, 18, 49
Byzantine law, 22

C.

Calisse, 9, 87
Cambaceres and plan of French Code, 280.
Canonists, 719–721 ; Spanish, 671, 672
Canon law, 705–724 ; in Italy, 113–117 ; collections and compilations, 114, 115, scope of authority of, 116 ; relation to mercantile interests, 119, and reception of Roman law, 344–346, in German universities, 353–358, in Netherlands, 466, in Spain, 634–636, influence, 708, 719, 721, 724. *See* CHURCH LAW.
Canons, 706
Cantons, Swiss, 489, 494, 500–509, 519
Capitularies, 38, 69, forgeries, 42 ; Italian, 43, 44
Carolina (Criminal Code), 369, 402
Carpzow, 429
Cartularies, French, 239.
Cassation, Court of, of France, 299.
Castile, 607–610.
Catalonia, 611, 642, 645–649, 664.
Chamavian Code, 57.
Charlemagne, 36.
Charters, municipal, in France, 222–224
Chatelet of Paris, Customs of, 237, 258
Christianity and Roman law, 41 ; and Law of Spain, 602, 603
Church, and Roman law, 88
Church law, 92–95, and city statutes, 162, customs in, 707 ; compilations, 708–719. *See* CANON LAW
Cities and city laws, Italian, 159–167, Church law in, 162, adoption and copying, 163, 165, French, 222–224, German, 313, 327–331, Swiss, 486, 487, 502–507
Civil Code, Italian, 195 ; French (*see* CODE NAPOLEON) ; German, 447–457, Swiss, 520, 521, Spanish, 694–700.
Civil Status, Registry of, in Spain, 693

Clergy, and reception of Roman law, 344–346

Chentage, in Spain, 613

Code Napoleon, 190, 191, 279–292, 302–305, 437, in Italy, 191

Code, of Justinian, 4

Codification, 30, 47, 183, 423, 441–443, in Germany (popular customs), 45; maritime law, 167, in Italy, 177, 187, 192–195, Savigny and, 183; in France, 279, 280, 292, in German States, 445; National, 446–451, in Netherlands, 475 476, in Switzerland, 520–522, in Scandinavia, 549–568, in Spain, 690–696

Collections and compilations of law, 41, 74, forgeries, 42; German popular customs, 45; in Canon law, 114, 115, 708–719; private, 177

Commentators in thirteenth and fourteenth century, 142–147.

Commercial law, 168; French, 242, 292; in Netherlands, 472.

Commonplaces, books of, 390.

Compilations See COLLECTIONS.

Concordats, 718

Confederations, Swiss, 488–494, 516–518

Conflict of laws, 66; Bartolus, 215.

Conjugal Property System, Spanish, 614

Conring, 158, 428

Consolato del mare, 167, 243.

Corpus Juris Canonici, 151, 718.

Cortez, Spanish, 609, 685.

Councils, decrees of, in Canon law, 113

Courts, Scandinavian, 548, 555, 556, 564

Coutumes, French, Revisions of, 259–263

Couvade, in Spain, 590

Criminal law and legislation, 68, in Italy, 191, in France (Ordinance of 1670), 265; in Netherlands, 471, in Switzerland, 521, in Scandinavia, 563, in Spain, 671; influence of Canon law on, 722

Cuba, Spanish legislation for, 688

Cujas, 156, 157, 225–257

Custom and customs: in Federal law, 77, requirements and rules regarding 78, 79, 217, German popular, codification of, 45; statutes, 161; in France, 213–222, local and general, 218, proof of, 219, sources of, 221, 222; literature, 224–230; French, revisions of, 259, 263; in Scandinavia, 533, 568, in the law of the Church, 707

Customary and written law, division of France between, 204–206.

Customary law, and the Spanish Code, 699, 700

D.

D'Aguesseau, 269.

Decretals, 115, 706, 709, 716

Decretum Gratiani, 114, 115, 715.

Degrees, university, in law, 210.

Democracy, Swiss, 508

Denmark, 537, 450, 542; law texts, 545, statute law, 547, Courts, 548, Code of 1683, 558.

Dienstrecht, 325, 326.

Diets, Swiss, 495

Digest, Justinian's, 133

Divorce, in French law, 288, 294.

Doctors of law, influence on reception of Roman law, 370, in Germany in fifteenth century, 155

Documents, public and private, 106, 107, German, 331.

Domat, 157, 268.

Donellus, 157

Dumoulin, 267.

Durantis, Speculum Juris, 350.

E.

Ecclesiastical law, territoriality of, 68 See CANON LAW.

Ecclesiastics, influence on legislation, 93.

Economic interpretation of law, 198

Economic legislation in Scandinavia, 565–567

Edict, as form of legislation, 27

Edictum Rotharis and Roman law, 90.

Entails, in Spain, 634

Equity, and German private law, 417.

Euric, laws of, 6, 51, 596

Exceptiones Petri, 103

Extravagants (Canon law decretals), 716, 717.

F.

Family law, differences in, between Northern and Southern France, 205, in Medieval Spain, 614; entails in Spain, 634.

Feudal law and Feudalism, legislation, 71, 72, custom in, 77; Lombard law, 112, in Germany, 312; abolition of feudal jurisdictions in Spain, 691. See LIBRI FEUDORUM.

Filangieri, 187.

Forgeries of collections of laws, 42.

Formularies, 152 ; in Medieval Italy, 104–107, French formularies and documents, 239 ; German, 331.

Fortescue, 246.

France, and French law, 203–305 ; Roman law in, 155–157 ; study of Roman law in, 155–159, 206–213 ; state of law at time of Revolution, 189, 190 ; customary and written law, 204–206 ; municipal charters, 222–224 ; judicial decisions, 229, 231–238 ; formularies and documents, 239, commercial law, 242 ; royal legislation, 246–250, 263–265, revisions of customs, 259–263 ; codification, 279, 280 ; nineteenth-century legislation, 293–299, influence on Spanish legal history, 582.

Franks, 36.

Frederick the Great, legislation, 435.

Freirechtsschule, 479

Freund, 447.

Frisian law, 53, 323, 456, 462.

Fueros, 607–612, 618–628 ; fuero juzgo, 598, 607, 610, 618, fuero real, 618, 623, 628.

G.

Geneva, 513

Gens, family organization in ancient Spain, 590.

Gentilis, Albericus, 152, 180, 412.

Germanic law, 36 ; codification of popular customs, 45, fusion with Roman law, 51

Germany, 307–451 ; doctors of law in fifteenth century, 155 ; law during Middle Ages, 311–314, city laws, 313, 327–331 ; royal legislation, 314–317 ; formularies, 331 ; reformation, 382–384 ; imperial legislation, 400–403 ; territorial, 403, seventeenth- and eighteenth-century legislation, 434–437 ; historical jurisprudence, 443, 444 ; state codes, 445 ; national codification, 446–451 ; influence on Netherlands, 478

Gilds and gild statutes, 165, in France, 223 ; in Spain, 638, 639, 693

Glanvil, 226.

Glossa of Turin, 21.

Glossators, 137–142.

Goths, 9

Græco-Roman law, 22

Grand Coutumier, of Normandy, 225, 230.

Gratianus, Decretum, 718.

Grotius, 158, 180, 408–412, 468.

H.

Haakon, King of Norway, 549.

Hamel, 455.

Hegel, 440.

Hertzberg, 533.

Historical School of Law, 183, 195–197, in Germany, 443, 444.

Hobbes, 414

Hofrecht, 325

Holland. See NETHERLANDS.

Hotman, 258

Huber, 483, 521.

Humanists, 147, 151, 252–254, 380–382, 396.

Husband and wife, 65, 66.

I.

Iberian law, 582, 583, 587–592.

Iceland, 534, 535, 541, law texts, 543

Imperial authority and reception of Roman law in Germany, 368

Imperial legislation, 37 ; its territoriality, 69, for Italy, 169 ; in Germany, 400–403. See ROYAL LEGISLATION.

Inheritance, law of, in France, 205, 277, 278

International law, 412, 413, 418, 422, 475, in Spain, 668.

Irnerius, 130, 138

Italy and Italian law, 87–199 ; Medieval formularies, 104–107 ; Canon law, 113–117, law schools, 125–132, 155, cities, 159–167 ; states, 170, 192, 193 ; imperial legislation for, 169, codification, 177, 187, 192–195, Code Napoleon in, 191, criminal legislation, 191.

J.

Jerusalem, Assizes of, 75.

Jews, and history of Spanish law, 581.

Judges, learned, and the reception of the Roman law, 337, 363, in Netherlands, 458.

Judicial decisions in French law, 231–238, 262, 299, in Scandinavia, 569, in Spanish law, 608, 609.

Jurists and jurisconsults, in Switzerland, 522–530 ; in Scandinavia, 535 ; in Spain, 654–658, 667–675, 630–683.

Justinian, 8, 20.

K.

Kant, 182, 439.

Keuren, Local Dutch statutes, 459.

[References are to pages]

Kindasvinth, Visigothic legislator, 601.
Klagespiegel, 359-361.

L

Labor legislation, French, 297.
Landbuecher, Swiss, 508.
Landfriedensordnung, 315
Landrechte, 405 , Swiss, 514.
Landsberg, 407
Land tenure in Spain, 637, 638 , legislation, 691-693.
Language of law, 27, 47
Latin America See LEYES DE INDIAS
Law Faculties, as advisers of courts, 371
Law-men in Scandinavia, 535-538.
Law-saga, in Scandinavia, 534-538
Law schools and legal studies, 96-101 ; in Berytus, 8 ; in Italy, 125-132 , in Bologna, 125, 128-131 , in Naples, 132 ; influence of Italian, in spreading Roman law, 155 ; in Germany, 176, 394-396 ; in Switzerland, 523-530. See UNIVERSITIES
Lay judges and reception of Roman law, 364, 365
Leagues, Swiss, 509-513
Leases, agricultural, in Spain, 637.
Leeuwen, 469
Legal history, revival of study of, 150, 153
Legal profession, and reception of Roman law, 373-375
Legal science, medieval, 384 ; in modern France, 300 See JURISTS. LAW SCHOOLS, AND LEGAL STUDIES.
Leges barbarorum, 45-59.
Leges Romanæ, 10
Legislation, 10, 26, 29, 36, 38, 46 ; feudal. 71, 72 ; Italian cities and states, 159, 167 ; imperial, for Italy, 169 ; royal, in France, 246-250, 263-265 ; French nineteenth-century, 293-299 , imperial, 400-403 , in Germany, territorial, 403 ; seventeenth- and eighteenth-century, 434-437 ; in Scandinavia, 541, 562-567 , in Spain, 609, 617-626, 660, 666, 691-693
Leibnitz, 420-424 ; and codification, 423
Lettres de cachet, 249
Lex, 38
Leyes de Indias, 666
Leyes de Toro, 632-634
Liber Papiensis, 102.

Libri feudorum, 74 ; reception in Germany, 339.
Liutprand's Lombard legislation, 32.
Lombardy, Lombards and Lombard law, 25, 82 , and Roman law, 91 , influence of Church, 93 ; law schools, 97-99 , after 1100, 110, 111 ; feudal system, 112 , later legislation, 174 , Austrian Code in, 193, 194
Loysel, Institutes Coutumières, 262.

M.

Macchiavelli, 271
Magdeburg law, 313, 328, 329.
Magnus, King of Norway, 549, 550-552.
Mahomedan law, influence in Spain, 605, 606
Maitland, 3
Malbergian glosses, 59
Manorial law, German, 325.
Maritime law and codes, 166, 167 ; French, 242-244
Marriage and marriage law, Canon law, 116 , secularization, 277 , in Spain, 693.
Marsilius of Padua, 245
Medieval law, general features in Germany, 311-314
Mercantile law and law merchant, 166, 168 , relation of Canon law to, 119
Missi, 40
Moors, influence on Spanish legal history, 604-606
Mos Gallicus, 156
Mos Italicus, 146, 386-393, 396
Moslem law. See MAHOMEDAN LAW
Municipal charters in France, 222-224

N

Naples, law school, 132.
Naples and Sicily, legal history, 170, 171.
Napoleon, Code of. See CODE NAPOLEON.
National law, German, 425-432
Natural law and law of nature, 178, 272, 407-424, and codification, 183.
Navarre, 643, 651, 665.
Netherlands, Salic law in, 455-479 ; study of Roman law in, 158 ; Canon law, 466 , criminal law, 471 ; commercial law, 472 , codification, 475, 476 , influence of German Code, 478
Njalssaga (Iceland), 538
Normandy and Norman law : feudal law, 76 , Grand Coutumier, 225 ; judicial records, 231

Norway, 537, 540, 542 ; law texts, 543–545 ; statutes, 549, early Code, 552, Code of 1687, 559, 560
Notaries' registers, 240
Novels, Justinian's, in the law schools, 136.
Novisima Recopilacion, 676.
Nueva Recopilacion, 661, 662.

O.

Oleron, laws of, 244
Olim registers, 235, 237.
Ordinances, royal, in France, 249, 250, 263–265.
Ostrogoth legislation, 10–16.

P.

Pactus, 46, 54, 56, 59.
Padua, law school of, 131.
Papal States, legal history, 172, 193.
Papianus, 18
Paris, Custom of, 262.
Parliament of Paris, Records of, 234–237.
Partidas, 620–632.
Pavia, school of law, 97
Penitentials, 713
People's law, 24, 46.
Personality of laws, principle of, 13, 14, 39, 60, 67 ; in southern Italy, 32
Philosophy, legal, 439, 440, 443, 444 ; in Scandinavia, 579.
Piedmont, legal history, 173.
Planiol, 274.
Pope, Ordinances of, 113, 114 ; charters to universities, 132
Popular customs, 35
Popular law and written law, 373, 374
Popular literature on law in Germany, 376, 377.
Portalis, and French Code, 287.
Porto Rico, Spanish legislation for, 688
Pothier, 157, 262, 269.
Precedents, judicial, 77, in Scandinavia, 569, in Spain, 608, 609.
Private international law, 216
Procedure, 72, influence of Canon law of procedure, 722, 723.
Professiones juris (or legis), 63, 83
Provincial law, in Spain, 64, 99, 697
Prussian Landrecht, 436.
Pseudo-Isidore, 709–713
Public law, study of, 150, science of, 244–246 ; in city statutes, 162 ; in Puffendorf, 415–420
Puffendorf, 415–420

Purchasers, protection of, and French Code, 291.

R

Ramistic method, in study of law, 397–400
Ravenna, school of law, 100, Roman law in, 124–129
Reception See ROMAN LAW
Records, judicial, in France, 231–238.
Reformation, and history of German law, 382–384 ; in Switzerland, 497, 508
Reichskammergericht, 366.
Religion, settlement in Switzerland, 498
Revisions, of city statutes, 163
Revolution, French, effect on law, 274, judiciary reform, 276, law of inheritance, 277, 278
Right books, Scandinavian, 542.
Ripuarian Code, 58.
Roman law, 3, 20, fusion of German law with, 51, as the law of clerics, 65 ; in Medieval Italy, 87–92, influence on feudal law, 90, schools of, 99–101, as common law, 109, recognition by Church, 117 ; rivalry with Canon law, 118–121 ; in Italian duchies and kingdoms, 122, 123, in Ravenna, 124, 129 ; influence of Italian law schools in spreading, 155 ; in France, 155–157, 206–213 ; prohibition of study of, in Paris, 211, 212 ; reception of, in Germany, 334 ; in Netherlands, 464–466, in Switzerland, 501, in Spanish Partidas, 627 ; in Spanish Provinces, 645–654.
Roman-Dutch law, 467–475.
Roman Provinces, law in, 592.
Rome, law school at, 132
Rothar's Edict, 29
Rousseau, 272.
Royal legislation in Germany, 314–317 ; in Spain, 660, 666. See IMPERIAL LEGISLATION.

S

Sachsenspiegel, 318–320, 342–344
Saint Louis, Etablissements de, 228.
Salic Code, 58
Salic law, 6, in Netherlands, 457
Sardinia, legal history, 173, legislation, 194
Savigny, 441–443 ; and codification, 183
Saxon law, 52 ; and reception of Roman law, 340

Saxon Weichbild, 328

Scandinavia, 531–576, custom in, 533, 568, jurisconsulti, 535; courts, 555, 556, 564, criminal law, 563, codification, 549–568

Schœffen, 312, 364, 365, decay of, 361–363

Schroeder, 333, 439.

Schwabenspiegel, 320, 348, 514.

Seal, 332

Secularization of law, in Spain, 690

Seminars in German, 395

Sicily and Naples, legal history, 172; legislation, 192

Siegel, 407

Siete Partidas, 620–632

Spain and Spanish law, 572–702; Jews and, 581, French influence, 582; summary of legal history, 584–586, Roman rule in, 592–594, Christianity and, 602, 603, Mahometan law, 604–606, colonies, 605, 679, judicial precedents, 608, 609, legislation, 609, 617–626, 660, 666; Canon law in, 634–636, 671, 672, gild system, 638, 639, provinces, 641–654, 697, jurists, 654–658, 667–675, 680–683, Austrian dynasty, 660–675, unification, 666, 677–680, 687, 694–700, international law, 668; criminal law, 671; Bourbons, 675–683, law reform, 684–700, codification and code, 690–700, abolition of feudal jurisdictions, 691, land tenures, 691–693, civil marriage, 693

Spinoza, 414

Statutes, imperial, in Germany, 315–317.

Statutes, of Italian cities, 160–167, 121, and local customs, 161

Stintzing, 333, 407.

Stobbe, 439

Study of law   See Law schools and Legal studies

Suarez, Prussian legislator, 436, Spanish jurist, 657, 670

Sweden, 535, law texts, 545, early Code, 554, 555, Code of 1734, 560

Switzerland, 481–530, city laws, 486, 487, 502–507, reformation, 497, 508, leagues, 509–513, landrecht, 514, jurists and law schools, 522–530.

T.

Territoriality, of laws, 38, 40, 60, 80–83, in France, 203, of French customs, 213

Theodoric's Edict, 10–15

Theodosian Code, 5, 21.

Theology, legal science and, 378, 379

Thibaut, and codification, 183, 441.

Thing, in Scandinavia, 535, 539

Thomasius, 429

Thuringian Code, 57.

Toro, leges de, 632–634.

Turba, proof of custom by, 219, 220.

Tuscany, legislation, 188, 193.

U.

Universities and legal studies, in Italy, 127, 128, in France, 209–213, reception of Roman law, 338, 352–356, Canon law, 353–358, in Germany, 371, 376, 392, 394–396, in Holland, 470, in Switzerland, 523, 526, 528–530

Usus modernus Pandectarum, 430, 431

V.

Venice, legal history, 174, Austrian Code in, 193, 194

Vico, 179

Visigoths and Visigoth law, 6, 10–18, 50, in Spain, 594–601

Vœt, 158.

Vulgar law, 20.

W.

Wager of battle, 72.

Weistümer, 221.

Wergeld, 33, 35, 46.

Wolf, 439.

Women, legal status in Spain, 639–641

Writs, 232

Written law, 26; in France, region of, 204–206; and popular law, 373, 374.

Z.

Zasius, 381, 426, 427.

Zoepfl, 439.

Zurich, 502.

www.ingramcontent.com/pod-product-compliance
Lightning Source LLC
LaVergne TN
LVHW012209040326
832903LV00003B/213